WOMEN'S VOICES, FEMINIST VISIONS

Classic and Contemporary Readings

SUSAN M. SHAW   JANET LEE
Oregon State University

Boston   Burr Ridge, IL   Dubuque, IA   Madison, WI   New York   San Francisco   St. Louis
Bangkok   Bogotá   Caracas   Kuala Lumpur   Lisbon   London   Madrid   Mexico City
Milan   Montreal   New Delhi   Santiago   Seoul   Singapore   Sydney   Taipei   Toronto

*Dedicated to all our WS 223 "Women: Self and Society"
students with thanks for all they have taught us.*

WOMEN'S VOICES, FEMINIST VISIONS: CLASSIC AND CONTEMPORARY READINGS
Published by McGraw-Hill, an imprint of The McGraw-Hill Companies, Inc., 1221 Avenue of the Americas,
New York, NY 10020. Copyright © 2007. All rights reserved. No part of this publication may be reproduced
or distributed in any form or by any means, or stored in a database or retrieval system, without the prior
written consent of The McGraw-Hill Companies, Inc., including, but not limited to, in any network or other
electronic storage or transmission, or broadcast for distance learning.

This book is printed on acid-free paper.

3 4 5 6 7 8 9 0 QPF/QPF 0 9 8 7

ISBN 978-0-07-311250-3
MHID 0-07-311250-X

Editor in Chief: *Emily Barrosse*
Publisher: *Phillip Butcher*
Sponsoring Editor: *Sherith Pankratz*
Marketing Manager: *Dan Loch*
Production Service: *Melanie Field/Strawberry Field Publishing*
Manuscript Editor: *Margaret Moore*
Art Director: *Jeanne M. Schreiber*
Cover Designer: *Marianna Kinigakis/Kristin Hull*
Interior Designer: *Marianna Kinigakis/Adrianne Bosworth*
Production Supervisor: *Jason Huls*
Media Supplements Producer: *Stacy Dorgan*
Composition: *10/12 Palatino by Thompson Type*
Printing: *45# New Era Matte, Quebecor World Printing, Fairfield*
Cover image: *Abstract #9* by Diana Ong, 1972. Private collection/Superstock, Inc.

Credits: The credits section for this book begins on page C-0 following the last reading, and is considered
an extension of the copyright page.

Library of Congress Cataloging-in-Publication Data
Women's voices, feminist visions: classic and contemporary readings/[edited by] Susan Shaw and Janet Lee/
    p. cm.
  Includes biographical references and index.
  ISBN: 978-0-07-311250-3; ISBN: 0-07-311250-X
    1. Women's studies 2. Feminism I. Shaw, Susan M. (Susan Maxine) II. Lee, Janet
HQ1180.W689 2006
305.42–dc21   2005045581

The Internet addresses listed in the text were accurate at the time of publication. The inclusion of a Web
site does not indicate an endorsement by the authors or McGraw-Hill, and McGraw-Hill does not guarantee
the accuracy of the information presented at these sites.

www.mhhe.com

About the Authors

SUSAN M. SHAW is associate professor and director of women studies at Oregon State University. Her research interests are in women and rock 'n' roll, women and HIV/AIDS, and women in religion, and she teaches courses in systems of oppression, women and sexuality, feminist theology, and women and pop culture. She is author of *Storytelling in Religious Education* (Religious Education Press, 1999) and coauthor of *Girls Rock! Fifty Years of Women Making Music* (University Press of Kentucky, 2004). She is an avid racquetball player, reader of murder mysteries, and hot tubber.

JANET LEE is professor of women studies at Oregon State University where she teaches a variety of courses on gender and feminism. Research interests include women's history and biography, feminist theories and pedagogy, and issues concerning women and the body. She is author of *War Girls: The First Aid Nursing Yeomanry* (FANY) in the First World War (Manchester University Press, 2005), *Comrades and Partners: The Shared Lives of Grace Hutchins and Anna Rochester* (Rowman and Littlefield, 2000), and coauthor of *Blood Stories: Menarche and the Politics of the Female Body in Contemporary U.S. Society* (Routledge, 1996). She enjoys gardening, riding her horses, and playing tennis.

Contents

11 State, Law, and Social Policy   615

Preface

We decided to create this book after finding our students were increasingly not reading the assigned material in our introductory women's studies course. Our students found the texts to be mostly inaccessible, or alternatively, they enjoyed reading the more testimonial first-person accounts included in some texts but were not getting the theoretical framework necessary to make sense of these more experiential readings. We were tired of creating packets of readings, and students were tired of having to access alternative readings on top of purchasing a textbook. This book was crafted to include a balance of recent contemporary readings with historical and classic pieces as well as both testimonial and more theoretical essays that would speak to the diversity of women's experiences. Each chapter has an introduction that provides an overview of the topic and provides a framework for the readings that follow. Additionally, each chapter provides a variety of learning activities, activist profiles, ideas for activism, and other sidebars that can engage students with the material in various ways.

Although students of women's studies in the early 2000s are in many ways like the students who have preceded them, they are also characterized by certain distinctions from the students of the 1980s and 1990s. Many of today's students come to our classes believing the goals of the women's movement have already been accomplished, and, although most will say they believe in gender equity of some sort, few identify with feminism as a political theory or social movement. Even among students who are supportive of feminist thought, there is a distinct sense of a "third wave" of feminism that reflects the interests of young women who have come of age benefiting from the gains made by their feminist foremothers. Moreover, as women's studies has become institutionalized on college campuses and is fulfilling baccalaureate core requirements, more students are being exposed to women's studies than ever before. Many of these students "choose" women's studies from a menu of options and come to the discipline with varying levels of misunderstanding and resistance. Some of these students have been influenced by the backlash efforts of the 1980s and 1990s and by conservative religious ideologies that seek a return to traditional gender relations. All of these distinctions call for a new, relevant, and accessible introductory women's studies text.

As is typical of contemporary students, students in women's studies today are the kind of visual learners who often prefer reading and interacting in front of a computer screen or watching video clips to reading traditional texts. They are unlikely to wade through long, dense, theoretical readings because they deem them "boring" and "irrelevant." We know from experience that a large percentage of students in introductory women's studies classes only read a fragment of the required readings and that our required readings end up as "fragmented texts."

Our intention in this book is to address these challenges by presenting a student-friendly text that provides short, accessible readings reflecting the diversity of women's experiences and offering a balance of classic/contemporary and theoretical/experiential pieces. The goal is to start where students are rather than where we hope they might be, and to provide a text that enriches their thinking, encourages them to read, and relates to their everyday experiences. We have chosen accessible articles that we hope are readable. They are relatively short, to the point, and interesting in terms of both topics and writing styles. Although most articles are quite contemporary, we have also included several earlier classic articles that are "must-reads." And although the articles we have chosen cover the breadth of issues and eras in women's studies, we hope students will read them and enjoy reading them because of their accessibility, style of presentation, and relevance to their lives. Many are written by young feminists, many are testimonial in format, and, on the whole, they avoid dense, academic theorizing. The cartoons, we hope, bring humor to this scholarship.

We also structure opportunities for students to reflect on their learning throughout the text, and, in this sense, the book is aimed at "teaching itself." It includes not only articles and introductions but also a number of features designed to engage students in active learning around the content. For example, we address students' tendencies to lose interest by creating a format that presents smaller, self-contained, more manageable pieces of knowledge that hold together through related fields and motifs that are woven throughout the larger text as boxes. This multiple positioning of various forms of scholarship creates independent but related pieces that enable students to read each unit in its entirety and make connections between the individual units and the larger text. We see this subtext as a way to address students' familiarity and comfort with contemporary design, multiple windows (as on Web pages), and "sound bytes." By also presenting material in these familiar formats, we intend to create a student-friendly text that will stimulate their interest. We encourage them to actually read the text and then be actively engaged with the material.

Pedagogy is embedded within the text itself. In addition to the textual narrative, we include in each chapter learning activities, questions for discussion that help students explore chapter themes critically, activism ideas that provide students with examples and opportunities for the practical implementation of the content, and suggestions for further reading. Instructors will be able to utilize the various pedagogical procedures suggested in the text (and those in the accompanying instructor's manual) to develop teaching plans for their class sessions. By embedding the pedagogy within the text, we are creating a classroom tool that enables a connection between content and teaching procedure, between assigned readings and classroom experience. Thus, students and instructors should experience the text as both a series of manageable units of information and a holistic exploration of the larger topics.

We hope that this text will address the needs and concerns of students and instructors alike by speaking to students where they are in relation to feminist issues.

Our hope is that the innovations included in this book will invite students into productive dialogue with feminist ideas and encourage personal engagement in feminist work.

Like other women's studies text-readers, this book covers the variety of issues that we know instructors address in the introductory course. We do not isolate race and racism and other issues of difference and power as separate topics, but thoroughly integrate them throughout the text into every issue addressed. We have also chosen not to present groups of chapters in parts or sections but to let the individual chapters stand alone. Pragmatically, this facilitates instructors being able to decide how they want to organize their own courses. At the same time, however, the chapters do build on each other. For example, after introducing students to women's studies, Chapter 2 presents the systems of privilege and inequality that form the context of women's lives and then Chapter 3 explores the social construction of gender, building on the previous chapter by introducing the plurality of sex/gender systems. The following chapters then examine how sex/gender systems are expressed and maintained in social institutions.

For this new edition, we have made changes based on feedback from reviewers, students, and colleagues using the book, as well as our own experiences in our classes. First, we've added a reading about global women's issues in each chapter to help students understand the global context of contemporary social issues. We've also added sidebars that address the roles of technology in women's lives, and we've updated each chapter with the latest statistical and policy information. Finally, we've thoroughly revamped the readings to include the most current, exciting, and diverse writing about the complexities of contemporary women's issues.

ACKNOWLEDGMENTS

Writing a textbook is inevitably a community project, and without the assistance of a number of people this project would have been impossible. We would particularly like to thank our graduate assistant Mehra Shirazi for the many hours of tedious library and Internet research she put into this book. Our office coordinator, Lisa Lawson, also provided invaluable help with the clerical tasks of preparing a manuscript. Additionally, we thank our graduate teaching assistants for their input at various stages throughout the writing and editing process—Janet Armentor, Sriyanthi Gunewardena, Fabiola Sanchez-Sandoval, Susan Wood, Tracy Clow, Rebecca Farrow, Evy Cowan, Michelle Kilkenny, Dawn Cuellar, Kate Atwood, Melanie Love, Melissa Warming, and Amy Leer.

We also would like to acknowledge the work of the many reviewers who provided insights and suggestions that strengthened our work:

Lisa M. Anderson, Arizona State University

Amber Ault, Oakland University

Suzanne Bergeron, University of Michigan, Dearborn

Jill Bystydzienski, Iowa State University

Suzanne Cherrin, University of Delaware

Mary C. Cook, Western Michigan University

Carolyn DiPalma, University of South Florida

Susan Goldstein, Diablo Valley College

Patricia L. Hartman, California University of Pennsylvania

Mazie Hough, University of Maine

John Kellermeier, Plattsburgh State University

Patricia Langley, University of Illinois, Springfield

Amy Lind, Arizona State University

Sujata Moorti, Old Dominion University

Carol O. Perkins, Minnesota State University, Mankato

Dian Ulner, Clark College

Finally, we want to thank Sherith Pankratz, our editor at McGraw-Hill, who has provided invaluable support and encouragement. We'd also like to thank Serina Beauparlant who initiated the first edition of the book with us when she was an editor at Mayfield Publishing.

Women's Studies: Perspectives and Practices

WHAT IS WOMEN'S STUDIES?

Women's studies is the examination of women's experiences that recognizes our achievements and addresses our status in society. Women's studies puts women (in all our diversity) at the center of inquiry and focuses on our reality as subjects of study, informing knowledge through the lens of female experience. This inclusion implies that traditional notions regarding men as "humans" and women as "others" must be challenged and transcended. This confusion of maleness with humanity, putting men at the center and relegating women to outsiders in society, is called *andro-centrism.* By making women the subjects of study, we assume that our opinions and thoughts about our own experiences are central in understanding human society generally. Adrienne Rich's "Claiming an Education" articulates this demand for women as subjects of study. It also encourages you as a student to take seriously your right to be taken seriously.

Women's studies also involves the study of gender as a central aspect of human existence. Gender concerns what it means to be a woman or a man in society. Gender involves the way society creates, patterns, and rewards our understandings of femininity and masculinity. In other words, *gender* can be defined as the way society organizes understandings of sexual difference. Women's studies explores our gendered existence: how we perform femininity and masculinity and how this interacts with other aspects of our identities, such as our race, ethnicity, socioeconomic status, and sexuality.

HOW DID WOMEN'S STUDIES COME ABOUT?

Women's studies emerged as concerned women and men noticed the absence, misrepresentation, and trivialization of women in the higher education curriculum, as well as the ways women were systematically excluded from many positions of power and authority as college faculty and administrators. This was especially true for women of color. In the late 1960s and early 1970s, students and faculty began

Reprinted with permission.

demanding that the knowledge learned and shared in colleges around the country be more inclusive of women's issues, and they asked to see more women in leadership positions on college campuses. It was not unusual, for example, for entire courses in English or American literature to include not one novel written by a woman. <u>Literature was full of men's ideas about women—ideas that often continued to stereotype women and justify their subordination</u>. History courses often taught only about men in wars and as leaders, and sociology courses primarily addressed women in the context of marriage and the family. Similarly, entire departments often consisted exclusively of men with perhaps a small minority of (usually White) women in junior or part-time positions. Although there have been important changes on most college campuses as women's issues are slowly integrated into the curriculum and advances have been made in terms of women in leadership positions, these problems still do, unfortunately, exist in higher education today.

It is important to note that making women subjects of study involves two strategies that together resulted in changes in the production of knowledge and in how colleges do business. First, it rebalanced the curriculum. Women as subjects of study were integrated into existing curricula, and whole courses about women were offered. This shifted the focus on men and men's lives in the traditional academic curriculum and gave some attention to women's lives and concerns. Second, it resulted in a transformation of the existing curriculum. People began questioning the nature of knowledge, how knowledge is produced, and the applications and consequences of knowledge in wider society. Although the first strategy was an "add women and stir" approach, the second involved a serious challenge to traditional knowledge and its claims to truth. In this way, women's studies aimed not only to create programs of study where students might focus on women's issues and concerns, but also <u>to integrate a perspective for looking at things that would challenge previously unquestioned knowledge</u>. This perspective questions how such knowledge reflects women's lives and concerns, how it maintains patterns of male privilege and power, and how the consequences of such knowledge affect women and other marginalized peoples.

Women's studies as a discipline has its origins in the women's movement of the 1960s and 70s (often known as the "second wave" to distinguish it from "first wave" mid-nineteenth-century women's rights and suffrage activity) and is often named as

HISTORICAL MOMENT   **The First Women's Studies Department**

Following the activism of the 1960s, feminists in the academy worked to begin establishing a place for the study of women. In 1970 women faculty at San Diego State University (SDSU) taught five upper-division women's studies classes on a voluntary overload basis. In the fall of that year, the SDSU senate approved a women's studies department, the first in the United States, and a curriculum of 11 courses. The school hired one full-time instructor for the program. Other instructors included students and faculty from several existing departments. Quickly, many other colleges and universities around the nation followed suit, establishing women's studies courses, programs, and departments. In 1977 academic and activist feminists formed the National Women's Studies Association (NWSA) to further the development of the discipline. NWSA held its first convention in 1979. Presently, more than 600 women's studies programs, departments, research centers, and libraries exist in the United States.

its academic wing. The demand to include women as subjects of study in higher education in the late 1960s and early 1970s was facilitated by a broad societal movement in which organizations and individuals (both women and men) focused on such issues as work and employment, family and parenting, sexuality, reproductive rights, and violence against women. The objective was to improve women's status in society and therefore the conditions of women's lives. The women's movement emerged at a moment of widespread social turmoil as various social movements questioned traditional social and sexual values, racism, poverty and other inequities, and U.S. militarism.

The World's Women: Education

- The gender gap in primary and secondary schooling is closing, but women still lag behind men in some countries of Africa and Southern Asia.
- Two thirds of the world's 876 million illiterates are women, and the number of illiterates is not expected to decrease significantly in the next twenty years.
- Women have made significant gains in higher education enrollment in most regions of the world; in some regions, women's enrollment now equals or surpasses that of men.
- More women than men lack the basic literacy and computer skills needed to enter "new media" professions.
- In many countries, women represent a rapidly increasing share of Internet users.

Source: The World's Women 2000: Trends and Statistics. Obtained from *http://unstats.un.org/unsd/ demographic/ww2000/edu2000.htm,* August 2002.

These social movements, including the women's movement and the civil rights movement, struggled for the rights of people of color, women, the poor, gays and lesbians, the aged and the young, and the disabled, and fought to transform society through laws and policies as well as changes in attitudes and consciousness.

Two aspects of the women's movement—a commitment to personal change and to societal transformation—have helped establish women's studies as a discipline. In terms of the personal, the women's movement involved women asking questions about the cultural meanings of being a woman in U.S. society. Intellectual perspectives that became central to women's studies as a discipline were created from the everyday experiences of women both inside and outside the movement. Through consciousness-raising groups and other situations where women came together to talk about their lives, women realized that they were not alone in their experiences. Problems they thought to be personal (like working outside the home all day and then coming home to work another full day taking care of the domestic tasks that are involved with being a wife and mother) were actually part of a much bigger picture of masculine privilege and female subordination. Women began to make connections and coined the notion *the personal is political* to explain how things taken as personal or idiosyncratic have broader social, political, and economic causes and consequences. In other words, situations that we are encouraged to view as personal are actually part of broader cultural patterns and arrangements. Note that the idea that the personal is political has relevance for men's lives as they understand the connections between patterns of gender in societal institutions and personal experiences of gender privilege and entitlement. *Patriarchy* is defined as a system where men dominate because power and authority are in the hands of adult men. It is important to remember that many men are supporters of women's rights and that many of the goals of the women's movement do benefit men as well, although being a supporter of women's rights does not necessarily translate into men understanding how everyday privileges associated with masculinity maintain entitlements in a patriarchal society. Connecting with the personal is political encourages men to potentially function as allies on a deeper, more authentic level.

In terms of societal change, the women's movement continues to be successful in bringing about various legal and political changes that increase women's status in society and in higher education. These legal changes of the second wave include the passage of the <u>Equal Pay Act in 1963</u> that sought equal pay for individuals performing the same work, <u>Title VII of the 1964 Civil Rights Act</u> that forbade workplace discrimination, and the creation of the Equal Employment Opportunity Commission (EEOC) to enforce antidiscrimination laws in the early 1970s. Affirmative action as a legal mechanism to combat discrimination was first utilized in 1961 and was extended to women in 1967, although it has been increasingly under attack in the last few years. In terms of legal changes directly aimed at higher education, <u>Title IX of the Education Amendments Act of 1972</u> supported equal education and forbade gender discrimination in schools. This includes women's access to sports in the context of schooling and most recently covers the right of school officials to sue in cases of retaliation as a result of Title IX school officials' complaints.

Educational Attainment of the Population 25 Years and over by Sex and Age: 2003

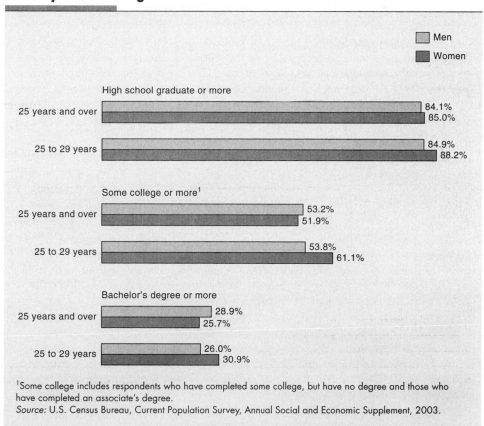

[1]Some college includes respondents who have completed some college, but have no degree and those who have completed an associate's degree.
Source: U.S. Census Bureau, Current Population Survey, Annual Social and Economic Supplement, 2003.

ACTIVIST PROFILE   **Susan B. Anthony**

Born in Massachusetts in 1820, Susan B. Anthony grew up in a Quaker family in which she learned justice and activism. In the 1840s she became involved with the temperance movement, campaigning for stricter liquor laws to address the ill effects of drunkenness on families. In 1853 she was denied the right to speak at the New York Sons of Temperance meeting because she was a woman. That year she joined with Elizabeth Cady Stanton in founding the Women's State Temperance Society. The society gathered 28,000 signatures urging the state legislature to pass a law limiting the sale of liquor, but, because most of the signatures were from women and children, the legislature rejected the petition. As a result of this experience, Anthony realized that women needed the vote in order to have political influence.

From that point on, Anthony campaigned vigorously for women's suffrage. In 1866 she and Stanton founded the American Equal Rights Association and in 1868 began to publish *The Revolution,* with the masthead "Men, their rights, and nothing more; women, their rights, and nothing less." In 1872 Anthony was arrested in Rochester, New York, for voting. At her trial, the judge ordered the jury to find her guilty, and then he fined her $100 plus court fees. Although she refused to pay, he did not imprison her, thereby denying her the opportunity to appeal and force the issue before the Supreme Court.

In 1877 she gathered 10,000 signatures from 26 states, but Congress ignored them. She appeared before every Congress from 1869 to 1906 to ask for passage of a suffrage amendment. Even in her senior years, Anthony remained active in the cause of suffrage, presiding over the National American Women Suffrage Association from 1892 to 1900. Anthony died in 1906, 14 years before American women won the vote with the Nineteenth Amendment, also known as the Susan B. Anthony Amendment.

Legal changes have been accompanied by a small, although significant, increase in women running for political office and taking positions of authority in government, business, education, science, and the arts. Women have become visible and active in all societal institutions. In addition, the gains women have made in U.S. society are being mirrored by women's gains in other Western societies. These societal changes have strengthened the demand for alternative educational models: not only is it the right thing to include women in college life, but it is illegal to prevent their participation. Jennifer Baumgardner and Amy Richards encourage you to think about these second wave gains in the reading "A Day Without Feminism."

WHAT WERE THE ORIGINS OF WOMEN'S RIGHTS ACTIVISM IN THE UNITED STATES?

Although women's studies emerged out of mid- to late-twentieth-century social activism, that activism itself was a part of an ongoing commitment for women's liberation that had its roots in late-eighteenth-century and nineteenth-century struggles for gender equity. Women had few legal, social, and economic rights in nineteenth-century U.S. society. They had no direct relationship to the law outside of their relationships as daughters or wives; in particular, married women lost property rights upon marriage. Women were also mostly barred from higher education until women's colleges started opening later in the nineteenth century.

Most early women's rights activists (then it was referred to as "woman's" rights) in the United States had their first experience with social activism in the abolition movement, the struggle to free slaves. These activists included such figures as Elizabeth Cady Stanton, Lucretia Mott, Susan B. Anthony, Sojourner Truth, Sarah M. and Angelina Grimké, Henry Blackwell, Frederick Douglass, and Harriet Tubman. Many abolitionists became aware of inequities elsewhere in society. Some realized that to improve women's status a separate social movement was required. In this way, for many abolitionists, their experiences with abolition inspired their desire to improve the conditions of women's lives.

English philosopher Mary Wollstonecraft's book *A Vindication of the Rights of Woman* (1792) is seen as the first important expression of the demand for women's equality, although the beginning of the women's movement in the United States is usually dated to the Seneca Falls Convention of 1848. This convention was conceived as a

LEARNING ACTIVITY   **The National Women's Hall of Fame**

How many significant American women can you name? Most students cannot name 20 women from American history. To learn more about some of the women who have made important contributions in the United States, visit the National Women's Hall of Fame at *www.greatwomen.org*. What is the mission of the Hall of Fame? Who are this year's inductees and why were they inducted? What do you think is the significance of having a National Women's Hall of Fame?

Reprinted with permission.

response to the experience of Lucretia Mott and Elizabeth Cady Stanton, who, as delegates to the world Anti-Slavery Convention in London in 1840, were refused seating, made to sit behind a curtain, and not allowed to voice their opinions because they were women. Their experience fueled the need for an independent women's movement in the United States and facilitated the convention at Seneca Falls, New York, in July 1848. An important document, the "Declaration of Sentiments and Resolutions," came out of this convention. Authored primarily by Elizabeth Cady Stanton, it used the language of the U.S. Declaration of Independence and included a variety of demands to improve women's status in the family and in society. Woman's suffrage, the right of women to vote, was included. Other conventions occurred across the country, and national organizations were organized to promote women's rights generally and suffrage in particular. These organizations included the National Woman Suffrage Association (NWSA) formed in 1869 and the National American Woman Suffrage Association (NAWSA) in 1890. NAWSA was formed from the merging of NWSA and the American Woman Suffrage Association and continues today as the League of Women Voters. These organizations fought for women's political personhood—a struggle that continues today. The "Anthony Amendment," the women's suffrage amendment, was introduced into Congress in 1878; it took another 42 years for this amendment to be ratified as the Nineteenth Amendment in 1920, granting women the right to vote.

WHAT IS THE STATUS OF WOMEN'S STUDIES ON COLLEGE CAMPUSES TODAY?

Over the last several decades, women's studies has steadily become institutionalized, or established as a regular custom, on many college campuses. From a scattering of courses (often taught for free by committed faculty when colleges did not want to spend money on these courses) have come whole programs and departments with minors and majors of study and graduate degrees at both the master's and doctoral levels. Although most campuses have adopted women's studies, some have gone with gender studies and others with feminist studies. These different names reflect different perspectives concerning knowledge about and for women.

Professors of women's studies might teach only women's studies, or they might do most of their work in another department like anthropology or history. This illustrates the multidisciplinary nature of women's studies: It can be taught from the point of view of many different disciplines. For the most part, however, women's studies is *interdisciplinary;* that is, it combines knowledge and methodologies from across many academic disciplines. Knowledge integration has occurred at a more rapid rate in the humanities and social sciences than in the biological and physical sciences. This is primarily because these sciences are considered "objective" (free of values) whose topics of study are immune from consideration of issues of gender, race, and class. However, as scholars have pointed out, science is a cultural product and its methodologies are grounded in historical practices and cultural ideas. There are now courses on many campuses examining the history and current practices of science that integrate knowledge about science as a human (gendered and racialized) product.

A list of the goals or objectives of women's studies might look like this:

- To understand the social construction of gender and the intersection of gender with other systems of inequality in women's lives
- To learn about the status of women in society and ways to improve that status through individual and collective action for social change
- To experience how institutions in society affect individual lives and to be able to think critically about the role of patterns of privilege and discrimination in our own lives
- To improve writing and speaking skills, gain new insights, and empower self and others

WHAT DOES WOMEN'S STUDIES HAVE TO DO WITH FEMINISM?

Women's studies is generally associated with feminism as a paradigm for understanding self and society. Although there are many definitions of feminism and some disagreement concerning a specific definition, there is agreement on two core principles underlying any concept of feminism. First, feminism concerns equality and justice for all women, and it seeks to eliminate systems of inequality and injustice in all aspects of women's lives. Because feminism is politics of equality, it anticipates a future that guarantees human dignity and equality for all people, women and men. Second, feminism is inclusive and affirming of women; it celebrates women's achievements and struggles and works to provide a positive and affirming stance toward women and womanhood. Feminism is a personal perspective as well as a political theory and social movement. Put this way, feminism is hardly a radical notion, although many more people (both women and men) believe in equal rights than identify as feminists.

Various kinds of feminisms (while embracing the two core concepts listed above) differ in terms of their specific explanations for understanding the social organization of gender and their ideas for social change. Rosalyn Baxandall and Linda Gordon mention these in their article and make the distinction between the liberal feminism and radical feminism of the women's movement. Liberal feminists believe in the viability of the present system and work within this context for change in such

Thank a Feminist

Thank a feminist if you agree that . . .

- Women should have the right to vote.
- Women should have access to contraceptives.
- Women should have the right to work outside the home.
- Women should receive equal pay for equal work.
- Women should have the right to refuse sex, even with their husbands.
- Women should be able to receive a higher education.
- Women should have access to safe, legal abortion.
- Women should be able to participate in sports.
- Women should be able to hold political office.
- Women should be able to choose any career that interests them.
- Women should be free from sexual harassment in the workplace.
- Women should be able to enter into legal and financial transactions.
- Women should be able to study issues about women's lives and experiences.

One hundred years ago, none of these statements was possible for women in the United States. Only through the hard work and dedication of women in each decade of the twentieth century did these rights become available to women.

Imagine a world without feminism. If you are a woman, you would not be in college. You would not be able to vote. You could not play sports. Contraception is illegal. So is abortion. You're expected to marry and raise a family. If you must work, the only jobs available to you are in cleaning, clerical services, or teaching. And you have no legal protection on the job if your boss pressures you for sex or makes lewd comments. Your husband can force you to have sex, and, if you were sexually abused as a child, most likely no one will believe you if you tell. If you are sexually attracted to women, you are considered mentally ill and may be subjected to an array of treatments for your illness.

Today, young women who claim, "I'm not a feminist, but . . ." benefit from the many gains made by feminists through the twentieth century. So, the next time you go to class or vote or play basketball, thank a feminist!

public areas as education and employment. Liberal feminists attempt to remove obstacles to women's full participation in public life. Strategies include education, federal and state policies, and legal statutes.

Although liberal feminists want a piece of the pie, radical feminists (sometimes known as cultural feminists or difference feminists) want a whole new pie. Radical feminists recognize the oppression of women as a fundamental political oppression wherein women are categorized as inferior based upon their gender. It is not enough to remove obstacles; rather, deeper, more transformational changes need to be made in societal institutions (like the government or media) as well as in people's heads. Patriarchy, radical feminists believe, shapes how women and men think about the world, their place in it, and their relationships with one another as well as the social institutions in which it is embedded. Radical feminists assert that reformist solutions like those liberal feminism would enact are problematic because they work to maintain rather than undermine the system. Not surprisingly, although the focus of liberal feminism is on the public sphere, the focus of this radical approach is the private sphere of everyday individual consciousness and change. Radical feminist offshoots include lesbian feminism, which focuses on how compulsory heterosexuality (the cultural norm that assumes and requires heterosexuality) and heterosexual privilege (the rights and privileges of heterosexuality, such as legal marriage and being intimate in public) function to maintain power in society. It also includes ecofeminism, a perspective that focuses on the association of women with nature and the environment and the simultaneous relationships among patriarchy, global economic expansion, and environmental degradation.

In addition, Baxandall and Gordon write about Marxist feminism, a perspective that uses economic explanations from traditional Marxist theory to understand women's oppression. For Marxist feminists, the socioeconomic inequities of the class system are the major issues. Baxandall and Gordon also mention socialist feminism, a perspective that integrates both Marxist and radical feminism. Socialist feminists use the insights of class analysis alongside radical feminist explanations of gender oppression. Socialist feminists seek to understand the workings of capitalist patriarchal institutions and societies. All these feminist approaches have been critiqued by the perspectives of women of color, who require that these approaches be inclusive of *all* women's lives. Multiracial feminism asserts that gender is constructed by a range of interlocking inequalities that work simultaneously to shape women's experience, and it brings together understandings drawn from the lived experiences of diverse women. The reading by bell hooks fits into this genre. Some feminists have utilized a postmodern perspective to emphasize that truth is a relative concept and that identity is more multifaceted than we often imagine. This approach pays attention to how language constructs reality. It emphasizes that humans actively construct or shape our lives in the context of various social systems, and often in the face of serious constraints.

Many writers now refer to a current "third wave" of feminist activity that is influenced by postmodernism and multiracial feminism and which problematizes the universality and potential inclusivity of the term *woman*. Third wave feminism has its origins in the 1990s and reflects the thinking, writing, and activism of women and men who tended to come of age taking for granted the gains of second wave feminism, as well as the resistance or backlash to it. Third wave perspectives are shaped by the material conditions created by globalization and technoculture, and tend to focus on issues of sexuality and identity. Contemporary third wave activity has been important in fueling feminist activism, especially through musical and art forms, various "rages" or "zines" (consciousness-raising magazines produced locally and usually shared electronically), and the use of electronic information and entertainment technologies generally. The reading by Rebecca Walker (the writer Alice Walker's daughter) titled "We Are Using This Power to Resist" discusses third wave feminism and the founding of the Third Wave Foundation. Despite the advantages of using a "wave" metaphor to characterize the developments in feminism, the metaphor distracts attention from the continuity of feminist activity and runs the risk of setting up distinctions and potential intergenerational divisiveness between a more stodgy, second wave generation, devoid of sexuality and unwilling to share power, and a younger, self-absorbed generation obsessed with popular culture and uncritically sexualized. Neither of these extremes reflects reality; it is enough to say that just as feminism encompasses diversity, so feminists do not all agree on what equality

IDEAS FOR ACTIVISM   **Two-Minute Activist**

Many important legislative issues related to women come before elected officials regularly. You can make your voice to support women heard by contacting your senators and representatives. To become a two-minute activist ("one minute to read, one minute to act"), visit the Web site of the American Association of University Women (AAUW) at *www.aauw.org*. Follow the "Issue Advocacy" link to find the Two-Minute Activist link. There, you'll find links to information about the latest issues before Congress and to prewritten AAUW messages that you can personalize and send to your representatives.

looks like or how to get there. As a social movement, feminism has always thrived on differences of ideology and practice. In "A Day Without Feminsim," third-wavers Jennifer Baumgardner and Amy Richards actively claim feminism as relevant to their lives and underscore the gains of second wave feminist activism.

Finally, feminists recognize both the similarities and differences in women's status worldwide. Women's status in developing and nonindustrialized countries is often very low, especially in societies where strict religious doctrines govern gendered behaviors. Although women in various countries around the world often tend to be in subordinate positions, the form this subordination takes varies. As a result, certain issues, like the ability of women to maintain subsistence agriculture and feed their families—matters of personal survival—take priority over the various claims to autonomy that characterize women's issues in the West. What are considered feminist issues in the United States are not necessarily the most important concerns of women in other parts of the world. It is important to understand this in order to avoid overgeneralizing about feminism's usefulness globally, even though the notion of global feminism is real and useful for political alliances across national borders. It is also important to recognize that any claims for Western feminism are necessarily interpreted internationally in the context of U.S. militarism and the power of U.S.-based corporations and popular culture. Nonetheless, global feminism underscores the similarities women share across the world and seeks strategies that take into account the interdependence of women globally. And, as communication technologies have advanced, the difficulties of organizing women in all parts of the world have lessened. International feminist groups have worked against militarism, global capitalism, and racism, and they have worked for issues identified by local women. Such actions were reflected in the United Nations Fourth World Conference on Women held in Beijing, China, in 1995. More than 30,000 women attended the Beijing conference, and 181 governments signed the "Platform for Action." This platform was a call for concrete action to include the human rights of women and girls as part of universal human rights, thus eradicating poverty of women, removing the obstacles to women's full participation in public life and decision making, eliminating all forms of violence against women, ensuring women's access to educational and health services, and promoting actions for women's economic autonomy. The reading by Estelle B. Freedman titled "The Global Stage and the Politics of Location" focuses on the historical development of the global women's movement.

WHAT ARE THE MYTHS ASSOCIATED WITH FEMINISM?

Feminism suffers from an image problem, one that has grown in proportion to feminist progress, and there has been an institutionalized backlash to the gains feminism has achieved. For example, certain groups who believe they would lose from a redistribution of power have worked hard to discredit and destroy the feminist movement and brand feminists in negative ways. This perspective is known as anti-feminism. Although such anti-feminist activity includes conservative groups and politicians, it also involves women who claim to be feminists yet are resistant to its core principles. These women include such successful female academics as Christina Hoff Summers, Camille Paglia, Daphne Patai, Katie Roiphe, and Rene Denfield. The reading by Deborah L. Rhode, an excerpt from *Speaking of Sex: The Denial of Gender Inequality,* focuses on the backlash that denies the existence of gender inequality despite the concrete realities of women's lives.

One result of this backlash has been the coining of the term *postfeminism* by those who recognize feminism as an important perspective but believe its time has passed, and it is now obsolete. "We're already liberated" is the stance they take. Like other broad

LEARNING ACTIVITY **The Dinner Party**

In *Manifesta: Young Women, Feminism, and the Future,* Jennifer Baumgardner and Amy Richards tell the story of a dinner party they had, reminiscent of the consciousness-raising meetings of the 1970s during which women shared the stories and frustrations of their lives, most of which were directly related to sexism. The point of consciousness raising was to radicalize women, to help them develop the consciousness and motivation needed to make personal and political change in the world. One night in 1999, Jennifer and Amy brought together six of their friends around a dinner table to talk about current issues for women and directions needed for the contemporary women's movement. They found that the conversation wound its way around personal experiences and stories and their political implications and strategies. Their dinner party offered the beginnings of a revolution. They write, "Every time women get together around a table and speak honestly, they are embarking on an education that they aren't getting elsewhere in our patriarchal society. And that's the best reason for a dinner party a feminist could hope for."

Have a dinner party! Invite five or six of your friends over for dinner to discuss issues related to women. What are the experiences of the people around the table in terms of sexuality, work, family, body image, media, religion? What are the political implications of these experiences? What can be done to make the world better around these issues?

After your dinner party, write about what happened. What issues came up? What did various guests have to say about the issues? What strategies for change did the group identify? What plans for action did the group make? What did you learn from the experience?

generalizations, there is some truth to this: Things have improved for some women in some areas. Although generally it is accurate to say that women's status in the United States at the beginning of the twenty-first century is markedly improved, we still have a long way to go to reach equality. In terms of the issues of poverty, violence, pornography, and HIV/AIDS (to name just a few), things are worse for many women than they ever have been. There are still many areas in which women's status might be enhanced, and, for the majority of the world's women, life is very difficult indeed.

The idea that women have achieved equality is reinforced by the capitalist society in which we live. Surrounded by consumer products, we are encouraged to confuse liberation with the freedom to purchase these products or to choose among a relatively narrow range of choices. Often personal style is mistaken for personal freedom as the body becomes a focus for fashion, hair, piercing, exercise, tattoos, and so forth. We are often encouraged to confuse such freedoms of expression with freedom in the sense of equality and social justice. Of course, popular culture and the mass media play a large part in this. We are encouraged to enjoy the freedoms that, in part, feminism has brought, without recognition of this struggle or allegiance to maintaining such freedoms.

Many people, groups, and institutions have attempted to discredit feminism (and therefore women's studies) in other ways. Feminism has been associated with (1) angry, whiny women who have an axe to grind, no sense of humor, and who exaggerate discrimination against women; (2) it is declared that feminists hate men or want to be like men and selfishly want to create new systems of power *over* men; (3) all feminists are said to be lesbians, women who choose romantic relationships with other women; (4) feminists are said to reject motherhood, consider children a burden, and have rejected all things feminine; and (5) feminism is dismissed as a White, middle-class movement that draws energy away from attempts to correct social and economic problems and discourages coalition building.

While several of these myths contain grains of truth, as a whole they can easily be shattered. First, although there are some feminists who respond, some would say rightly, to societal injustices with anger, most feminists work patiently with little resentment. Men as a social group demonstrate much more anger than women,

Yes, I Am

Ashley Judd   Margaret Cho   Camryn Manheim   Whoopi Goldberg

feminists included. Even though male rage comes out in numerous acts of violence, wars, school shootings, and so on, men's anger is seen merely as a human response to circumstance. Note the androcentrism at work here. Because a few angry feminists get much more publicity than the majority of those working productively to change the status quo, a better question might be why women are not more angry, given the levels of injustice against women both in the United States and worldwide. Feminists do not exaggerate this injustice; injustice is a central organizing principle of contemporary society. We should also ask why women's anger provokes such a negative response. The cause of the relatively intense reaction to women's anger is grounded in a societal mandate against female anger that works to keep women from resisting their subordination—that is, it keeps them passive. Anger is seen as destructive and inappropriate, going against what we imagine to be feminine. As a result, organized expressions of anger are interpreted as hostile.

Second, it is often said that feminists hate men. It is accurate to say that, in their affirmation of women and their desire to remove systems of inequality, feminists ask that men understand how gender privilege works in men's lives. Many men are more than willing to do this because the same social constructions of masculinity that privilege men also limit them. Since the demand for the examination of gender privilege is not synonymous with hating men, we might ask why these different concepts are so easily conflated. A more interesting question is why men are not accused more often of hating women. Certainly the world is full of *misogyny,* the hatred of women, and every day we see examples of the ways misogyny influences, and sometimes destroys, the lives of women. The reality, of course, is that most feminists are in relationships with men, and some feminists *are* men. Some men eagerly call themselves pro-feminist because feminism is a perspective on life (even though some feminists would argue that just as people of color are better prepared to understand racial inequality, so women are in a better place to understand how gender works). Nonetheless, the man-hating myth works to prevent many women who want to be in relationships with men from claiming feminism. They are encouraged to avoid a political stance that suggests antagonism toward men.

Feminists often respond to the declaration that they hate men with the observation that the statement illustrates a hypersensitivity about the possibility of exclusion and loss of power on the part of men. Only in a patriarchal society would the inclusion of women be interpreted as a potential threat or loss of men's power. It is a reflection of the fact that we live in a competitive patriarchal society that it is assumed that the feminist agenda is one that seeks to have power over men. And only in an androcentric society where men and their reality is center stage would it be assumed that an inclusion of one group must mean the exclusion of another. In other words, male domination encourages the idea that affirming women means hating men and interprets women's request for power sharing as a form of taking over. This projection of patriarchal mentality equates someone's gain with another's loss.

In response to the assertion that feminists want to be men, it is true to say that feminists might like to share some of the power granted to men in society. However, feminism is not about encouraging women to be like men; it's about valuing women for being women. People opposed to feminism often confuse *sameness* and *equality* and say that women will never be equal to men because they are different (less physically strong, more emotional, etc.) or they say that equality is dangerous because

"I'm really proud of my daughter. She's a thorn in the side of the patriarchy."

women will start being like men. Feminism of course affirms and works to maintain difference; it merely asks that these differences are valued equally.

Third, feminists are accused of being lesbians in an effort to discredit feminism and prevent women both from joining the movement and from taking women's studies classes. The term for this is *lesbian baiting*. Feminism affirms women's choices to be and love whomever they choose. Although some lesbians are feminists, many lesbians are not feminists, and many feminists are heterosexual. Feminists do not interpret an association with lesbianism as an insult. Nonetheless, _homophobia,_ the societal fear or hatred of lesbians and gay men, functions to maintain this as an insult. There is considerable fear associated with being called a lesbian, and this declaration that all feminists are lesbians serves to keep women in line, apart from one another, and suspicious of feminism and women's studies. Note that this myth is related to the above discussion on men-hating because it is assumed that lesbians hate men too. Again, although lesbians love women, this does not necessitate a dislike of men.

Fourth, feminism has never rejected motherhood but instead has attempted to improve the conditions under which women mother. Feminists have rejected some of the constraints associated with femininity such as corsets and hazardous beauty products and practices, although they mostly strive to claim back femininity as a valuable construct that should be respected.

Fifth, feminism has been critiqued as a White, middle-class perspective that has no relevance to the lives of women of color. The corollary of this is that women's studies is only about the lives of White, bourgeois women. This critique is important because throughout the history of the women's movement there have been examples of both blatant and subtle racism, and White women have been the ones to hold most of the positions of power and authority. Similarly, working-class women have been underrepresented. This is also reflected in the discipline of women's studies as faculty and students have often been disproportionately White and economically privileged. Much work has been done to transform the women's movement into an inclusive social movement that has relevance for all people's lives. Women's studies departments and programs today are often among the most diverse units on college campuses, although most still have work to do. It is absolutely crucial that the study of women as subjects both recognizes and celebrates diversity and works to transform all systems of oppression in society. In "Feminist Politics," bell hooks claims back feminism as the movement to do just that. She emphasizes that any call to sisterhood must involve a commitment on the part of White women to examine White privilege and understand the interconnections among gender, race, and class domination. Likewise, Rebecca Walker in "We Are Using This Power to Resist" makes a similar plea for young women. She uses the term *queer* in this essay as a way to affirm and celebrate the diversity of sexual identities. Her hope is for solidarity among all groups.

Although the women's movement has had a profound impact on the lives of women in the United States and great strides have been made toward equality, real problems still remain. Women continue to face discrimination and harassment in the workplace, domestic violence, rape and abuse, inequities in education, poverty, racism, and homophobia. Anna Quindlen responds to this in the short reading "Still Needing the F Word." Women's studies provides a forum for naming the problems women face, analyzing the root causes of these problems, envisioning a just and equitable world, and developing strategies for change. As you read the following articles, keep these questions in mind: What does the author identify as problems women face? What does the author suggest is the root of these problems? What strategies does the author suggest for bringing about change to improve the lives of women?

U.S. Suffrage Movement Timeline

1792   British author Mary Wollstonecraft argues for the equality of the sexes in her book, the *Vindication of the Rights of Woman.*

(continued)

1840	The World's Anti-Slavery Convention is held in London, England. When the women delegates from the United States are not allowed to participate, Lucretia Mott and Elizabeth Cady Stanton determine to have a women's rights convention when they return home.
1845	Margaret Fuller publishes *Woman in the Nineteenth Century,* which has a profound influence on the development of American feminist theory.
1848 July 19:	The first woman's rights convention is called by Mott and Stanton. It is held on July 20 at the Wesleyan Chapel in Seneca Falls, NY.
August 2:	A reconvened session of the woman's rights convention is held at the Unitarian Church in Rochester, NY. Amelia Bush is chosen chair and becomes the first woman to preside over a meeting attended by both men and women. New York State Legislature passes a law which gives women the right to retain possession of property they owned prior to their marriage.
1851	Elizabeth Cady Stanton and Susan B. Anthony meet and begin their fifty-year collaboration to win for women their economic, educational, social, and civil rights.
	Sojourner Truth delivers her "And Ain't I a Woman Speech" at the Woman's Rights Convention in Akron, OH.
1855	Elizabeth Cady Stanton makes an unprecedented appearance before the New York State Legislature to speak in favor of expanding the Married Woman's Property Law.
1863	Stanton and Anthony organize the Women's Loyal National League and gather 300,000 signatures on a petition demanding that the Senate abolish slavery by constitutional amendment.
1866	The American Equal Rights Association is founded with the purpose to secure for all Americans their civil rights irrespective of race, color, or sex. Lucretia Mott is elected president. To test women's constitutional right to hold public office, Stanton runs for Congress receiving 24 of 12,000 votes cast.
1867	Stanton, Anthony, and Lucy Stone address a subcommittee of the New York State Constitutional Convention requesting that the revised constitution include women's suffrage. Their efforts fail.
	Kansas holds a state referendum on whether to enfranchise Blacks and/or women. Lucy Stone, Susan B. Anthony, and Elizabeth Cady Stanton traverse the state speaking in favor of women's suffrage. Both Black and women's suffrage is voted down.
1868	Stanton and Anthony launch their women's rights newspaper, *The Revolution,* in New York City.
	Anthony organizes the Working Women's Association, which encourages women to form unions to win higher wages and shorter hours.

The Fourteenth Amendment to the U.S. Constitution is adopted. The amendment grants suffrage to former male African American slaves, but not to women. Anthony and Stanton bitterly oppose the amendment, which for the first time explicitly restricts voting rights to "males." Many of their former allies in the abolitionist movement, including Lucy Stone, support the amendment.

1869   National Woman Suffrage Association (NWSA) is founded with Elizabeth Cady Stanton as president.

American Woman Suffrage Association (AWSA) is founded with Henry Ward Beecher as president.

Wyoming Territory grants suffrage to women.

1870   Utah Territory grants suffrage to women.

First issue of the *Woman's Journal* is published with Lucy Stone and her husband, Henry Blackwell, as editors.

1871   Victoria Woodhull addresses the Judiciary Committee of the House of Representatives arguing that women have the right to vote under the Fourteenth Amendment. The Committee issues a negative report.

1872   In Rochester, NY, Susan B. Anthony registers and votes contending that the Fourteenth Amendment gives her that right. Several days later she is arrested.

1873   At Anthony's trial the judge does not allow her to testify on her own behalf, dismisses the jury, rules her guilty, and fines her $100. She refuses to pay.

1874   In *Minor v. Happersett,* the Supreme Court decides that citizenship does not give women the right to vote and that women's political rights are under the jurisdiction of each individual state.

1876   Stanton writes a "Declaration and Protest of the Women of the United States" to be read at the centennial celebration in Philadelphia. When the request to present the Declaration is denied, Anthony and four other women charge the speakers' rostrum and thrust the document into the hands of Vice President Thomas W. Ferry.

1880   New York State grants school suffrage to women.

1882   The House of Representatives and the Senate appoint Select Committees on Woman Suffrage.

1887   The first three volumes of the *History of Woman Suffrage,* edited by Susan B. Anthony, Matilda Joslyn Gage, and Elizabeth Cady Stanton, are published.

1890   After several years of negotiations, the NWSA and the AWSA merge to form the National American Woman Suffrage Association (NAWSA) with Elizabeth Cady Stanton, Susan B. Anthony, and Lucy Stone as officers.

(continued)

	Wyoming joins the union as the first state with voting rights for women. By 1900 women also have full suffrage in Utah, Colorado, and Idaho.
	New Zealand is the first nation to give women suffrage.
1892	Susan B. Anthony becomes president of the NAWSA.
1895	Elizabeth Cady Stanton publishes *The Woman's Bible,* a critical examination of the Bible's teaching about women. The NAWSA censures the work.
1900	Anthony resigns as president of the NAWSA and is succeeded by Carrie Chapman Catt.
1902	
October 26:	Elizabeth Cady Stanton dies.
	Women of Australia are enfranchised.
1903	Carrie Chapman Catt resigns as president of the NAWSA and Anna Howard Shaw becomes president.
1906	
March 13:	Susan B. Anthony dies. Women of Finland are enfranchised.
1907	Harriet Stanton Blatch, daughter of Elizabeth Cady Stanton, founds the Equality League of Self-Supporting Women, later called the Women's Political Union.
1910	The Women's Political Union holds its first suffrage parade in New York City.
1911	National Association Opposed to Woman Suffrage is founded.
1912	Suffrage referendums are passed in Arizona, Kansas, and Oregon.
1913	Alice Paul organizes a suffrage parade in Washington, DC, the day of Woodrow Wilson's inauguration.
1914	Montana and Nevada grant voting rights to women.
	Alice Paul and Lucy Burns organize the Congressional Union for Woman Suffrage. It merges in 1917 with the Woman's Party to become the National Woman's Party.
1915	Suffrage referendum in New York State is defeated.
	Carrie Chapman Catt is elected president of the NAWSA.
	Women of Denmark are enfranchised.
1916	Jeannette Rankin, a Republican from Montana, is elected to the House of Representatives and becomes the first woman to serve in Congress.
	President Woodrow Wilson addresses the NAWSA.
1917	Members of the National Woman's Party picket the White House. Alice Paul and ninety-six other suffragists are arrested and jailed for

"obstructing traffic." When they go on a hunger strike to protest their arrest and treatment, they are force-fed.

Women win the right to vote in North Dakota, Ohio, Indiana, Rhode Island, Nebraska, Michigan, New York, and Arkansas.

1918   Women of Austria, Canada, Czechoslovakia, Germany, Hungary, Ireland, Poland, Scotland, and Wales are enfranchised.

House of Representatives passes a resolution in favor of a woman suffrage amendment. The resolution is defeated by the Senate.

1919   Women of Azerbaijan Republic, Belgium, British East Africa, Holland, Iceland, Luxembourg, Rhodesia, and Sweden are enfranchised.

The Nineteenth Amendment to the Constitution granting women the vote is adopted by a joint resolution of Congress and sent to the states for ratification.

New York and twenty-one other states ratify the Nineteenth Amendment.

1920   Henry Burn casts the deciding vote that makes Tennessee the thirty-sixth, and final state, to ratify the Nineteenth Amendment.

August 26:   The Nineteenth Amendment is adopted and the women of the United States are finally enfranchised.

Source: Anthony Center for Women's Leadership: US Suffrage Movement Timeline, prepared by Mary M. Huth, Department of Rare Books and Special Collections, University of Rochester Libraries, February 1995. Obtained from *http://www.rochester.edu/SBA/timeline1.html*, August 2002.

Claiming an Education

Adrienne Rich

For this convocation, I planned to separate my remarks into two parts: some thoughts about you, the women students here, and some thoughts about us who teach in a women's college. But ultimately, those two parts are indivisible. If university education means anything beyond the processing of human beings into expected roles, through credit hours, tests, and grades (and I believe that in a women's college especially it *might* mean much more), it implies an ethical and intellectual contract between teacher and student. This contract must remain intuitive, dynamic, unwritten; but we must turn to it again and again if learning is to be reclaimed from the depersonalizing and cheapening pressures of the present-day academic scene.

The first thing I want to say to you who are students is that you cannot afford to think of being here to *receive* an education; you will do much better to think of yourselves as being here to *claim* one. One of the dictionary definitions of the verb "to claim" is *to take as the rightful owner; to assert in the face of possible contradiction.* "To receive" is *to come into possession of; to act as receptacle or container for; to accept as authoritative or true.* The difference is that between acting and being acted-upon, and for women it can literally mean the difference between life and death.

One of the devastating weaknesses of university learning, of the store of knowledge and opinion that has been handed down through academic training, has been its almost total erasure of women's experience and thought from the curriculum, and its exclusion of women as members of the academic community. Today, with increasing numbers of women students in nearly every branch of higher learning, we still see very few women in the upper levels of faculty and administration in most institutions. Douglass College itself is a women's college in a university administered overwhelmingly by men, who in turn are answerable to the state legislature, again composed predominantly of men. But the most significant fact for you is that what you learn here, the very texts you read, the lectures you hear, the way your studies are divided into categories and fragmented one from the other—all this reflects, to a very large degree, neither objective reality, nor an accurate picture of the past, nor a group of rigorously tested observations about human behavior. What you can learn here (and I mean not only at Douglass but any college in any university) is how *men* have perceived and organized their experience, their history, their ideas of social relationships, good and evil, sickness and health, etc. When you read or hear about "great issues," "major texts," "the mainstream of Western thought," you are hearing about what men, above all white men, in their male subjectivity, have decided is important.

Black and other minority peoples have for some time recognized that their racial and ethnic experience was not accounted for in the studies broadly labeled human; and that even the sciences can be racist. For many reasons, it has been more difficult for women to comprehend our exclusion, and to realize that even the sciences can be sexist. For one thing, it is only within the last hundred years that higher education has grudgingly been opened up to women at all, even to

This talk was given at the Douglass College Convocation, September 6, 1977, and first printed in *The Common Woman,* a feminist literary magazine founded by Rutgers University women in New Brunswick, New Jersey.

white, middle-class women. And many of us have found ourselves poring eagerly over books with titles like *The Descent of Man; Man and His Symbols; Irrational Man; The Phenomenon of Man; The Future of Man; Man and the Machine; From Man to Man; May Man Prevail?; Man, Science and Society;* or *One-Dimensional Man*—books pretending to describe a "human" reality that does not include over one-half the human species.

Less than a decade ago, with the rebirth of a feminist movement in this country, women students and teachers in a number of universities began to demand and set up women's studies courses—to *claim* a woman-directed education. And, despite the inevitable accusations of "unscholarly," "group therapy," "faddism," etc., despite backlash and budget cuts, women's studies are still growing, offering to more and more women a new intellectual grasp on their lives, new understanding of our history, a fresh vision of the human experience, and also a critical basis for evaluating what they hear and read in other courses, and in the society at large.

But my talk is not really about women's studies, much as I believe in their scholarly, scientific, and human necessity. While I think that any Douglass student has everything to gain by investigating and enrolling in women's studies courses, I want to suggest that there is a more essential experience that you owe yourselves, one which courses in women's studies can greatly enrich, but which finally depends on you, in all your interactions with yourself and your world. This is the experience of *taking responsibility toward your selves*. Our upbringing as women has so often told us that this should come second to our relationships and responsibilities to other people. We have been offered ethical models of the self-denying wife and mother; intellectual models of the brilliant but slapdash dilettante who never commits herself to anything the whole way, or the intelligent woman who denies her intelligence in order to seem more "feminine," or who sits in passive silence even when she disagrees inwardly with everything that is being said around her.

Responsibility to yourself means refusing to let others do your thinking, talking, and naming for you; it means learning to respect and use your own brains and instincts; hence, grappling with hard work. It means that you do not treat your body as a commodity with which to purchase superficial intimacy or economic security; for our bodies and minds are inseparable in this life, and when we allow our bodies to be treated as objects, our minds are in mortal danger. It means insisting that those to whom you give your friendship and love are able to respect your mind. It means being able to say, with Charlotte Brontë's *Jane Eyre:* "I have an inward treasure born with me, which can keep me alive if all the extraneous delights should be withheld or offered only at a price I cannot afford to give."

Responsibility to yourself means that you don't fall for shallow and easy solutions—predigested books and ideas, weekend encounters guaranteed to change your life, taking "gut" courses instead of ones you know will challenge you, bluffing at school and life instead of doing solid work, marrying early as an escape from real decisions, getting pregnant as an evasion of already existing problems. It means that you refuse to sell your talents and aspirations short, simply to avoid conflict and confrontation. And this, in turn, means resisting the forces in society which say that women should be nice, play safe, have low professional expectations, drown in love and forget about work, live through others, and stay in the places assigned to us. It means that we insist on a life of meaningful work, insist that work be as meaningful as love and friendship in our lives. It means, therefore, the courage to be "different"; not to be continuously available to others when we need time for ourselves and our work; to be able to demand of others—parents, friends, roommates, teachers, lovers, husbands, children—that they respect our sense of purpose and our integrity as persons. Women everywhere are finding the courage to do this, more and more, and we are finding that courage both in our study of women in the past who possessed it, and in each other as we look to other women for comradeship, community, and challenge. The difference between a life lived actively, and a life of passive drifting and dispersal of energies, is an immense difference. Once we begin to feel committed to our lives, responsible to ourselves, we can never again be satisfied with the old, passive way.

Now comes the second part of the contract. I believe that in a women's college you have the right to expect your faculty to take you seriously. The education of women has been a matter of debate for centuries, and old, negative attitudes about women's role, women's ability to think and take leadership, are still rife both in and outside the university. Many male professors (and I don't mean only at Douglass) still feel that teaching in a women's college is a second-rate career. Many tend to eroticize their women students—to treat them as sexual objects—instead of demanding the best of their minds. (At Yale a legal suit [*Alexander* v. *Yale*] has been brought against the university by a group of women students demanding a stated policy against sexual advances toward female students by male professors.) Many teachers, both men and women, trained in the male-centered tradition, are still handing the ideas and texts of that tradition on to students without teaching them to criticize its antiwoman attitudes, its omission of women as part of the species. Too often, all of us fail to teach the most important thing, which is that clear thinking, active discussion, and excellent writing are all necessary for intellectual freedom, and that these require *hard work*. Sometimes, perhaps in discouragement with a culture which is both antiintellectual and antiwoman, we may resign ourselves to low expectations for our students before we have given them half a chance to become more thoughtful, expressive human beings. We need to take to heart the words of Elizabeth Barrett Browning, a poet, a thinking woman, and a feminist, who wrote in 1845 of her impatience with

studies which cultivate a "passive recipiency" in the mind, and asserted that "women want to be made to *think actively:* their apprehension is quicker than that of men, but their defect lies for the most part in the logical faculty and in the higher mental activities." Note that she implies a defect which can be remedied by intellectual training—*not* an inborn lack of ability.

I have said that the contract on the student's part involves that you demand to be taken seriously so that you can also go on taking yourself seriously. This means seeking out criticism, recognizing that the most affirming thing anyone can do for you is demand that you push yourself further, show you the range of what you *can* do. It means rejecting attitudes of "take-it-easy," "why-be-so-serious," "why-worry-you'll-probably-get-married-anyway." It means assuming your share of responsibility for what happens in the classroom, because that affects the quality of your daily life here. It means that the student sees herself engaged *with* her teachers in an active, ongoing struggle for a real education. But for her to do this, her teachers must be committed to the belief that women's minds and experience are intrinsically valuable and indispensable to any civilization worthy [of] the name; that there is no more exhilarating and intellectually fertile place in the academic world today than a women's college—*if* both students and teachers in large enough numbers are trying to fulfill this contract. The contract is really a pledge of mutual seriousness about women, about language, ideas, methods, and values. It is our shared commitment toward a world in which the inborn potentialities of so many women's minds will no longer be wasted, raveled-away, paralyzed, or denied.

A Day Without Feminism

Jennifer Baumgardner and Amy Richards

We were both born in 1970, the baptismal moment of a decade that would change dramatically the lives of American women. The two of us grew up thousands of miles apart, in entirely different kinds of families, yet we both came of age with the awareness that certain rights had been won by the women's movement. We've never doubted how important feminism is to people's lives—men's and women's. Both of our mothers went to consciousness-raising-type groups. Amy's mother raised Amy on her own, and Jennifer's mother, questioning the politics of housework, staged laundry strikes.

With the dawn of not just a new century but a new millennium, people are looking back and taking stock of feminism. Do we need new strategies? Is feminism dead? Has society changed so much that the idea of a feminist movement is obsolete? For us, the only way to answer these questions is to imagine what our lives would have been if the women's movement had never happened and the conditions for women had remained as they were in the year of our births.

Imagine that for a day it's still 1970, and women have only the rights they had then. Sly and the Family Stone and Dionne Warwick are on the radio, the kitchen appliances are Harvest Gold, and the name of your Whirlpool gas stove is Mrs. America. What is it like to be female?

Babies born on this day are automatically given their father's name. If no father is listed, "illegitimate" is likely to be typed on the birth certificate. There are virtually no child-care centers, so all preschool children are in the hands of their mothers, a baby-sitter, or an expensive nursery school. In elementary school, girls can't play in Little League and almost all of the teachers are female. (The latter is still true.) In a few states, it may be against the law for a male to teach grades lower than the sixth, on the basis that it's unnatural, or that men can't be trusted with young children.

In junior high, girls probably take home ec; boys take shop or small-engine repair. Boys who want to learn how to cook or sew on a button are out of luck, as are girls who want to learn how to fix a car. *Seventeen* magazine doesn't run feminist-influenced current columns like "Sex + Body" and "Trauma-rama." Instead, the magazine encourages girls not to have sex; pleasure isn't part of its vocabulary. Judy Blume's books are just beginning to be published, and *Free to Be . . . You and Me* does not exist. No one reads much about masturbation as a natural activity; nor do they learn that sex is for anything other than procreation. Girls do read mystery stories about Nancy Drew, for whom there is no sex, only her blue roadster and having "luncheon." (The real mystery is how Nancy gets along without a purse and manages to meet only white people.) Boys read about the Hardy Boys, for whom there are no girls.

In high school, the principal is a man. Girls have physical-education class and play half-court basketball, but not soccer, track, or cross country; nor do they have any varsity sports teams. The only prestigious physical activity for girls is cheerleading, or being a drum majorette. Most girls don't take calculus or physics; they plan the dances and decorate the gym. Even when girls get better grades than their male counterparts, they are half as likely to qualify for a National Merit Scholarship because many of the test questions favor boys. Standardized tests refer to males and male experiences much more than to females and their experiences. If a girl "gets herself pregnant," she loses her membership in the National Honor Society (which is still true today) and is expelled.

Girls and young women might have sex while they're unmarried, but they may be ruining their chances of landing a guy full-time, and they're probably getting a bad reputation. If a pregnancy happens, an enterprising gal can get a legal abortion only if she lives in New York or is rich enough to fly there, or to Cuba, London, or Scandinavia. There's also the Chicago-based Jane Collective, an underground abortion-referral service, which can hook you up with an illegal or legal termination. (Any of these options are going to cost you. Illegal abortions average $300 to $500, sometimes as much as $2,000.) To prevent pregnancy, a sexually active woman might go to a doctor to be fitted for a diaphragm, or take the high-dose birth-control pill, but her doctor isn't likely to inform her of the possibility of deadly blood clots. Those who do take the Pill also may have to endure this contraceptive's crappy side effects: migraine headaches, severe weight gain, irregular bleeding, and hair loss (or gain), plus the possibility of an increased risk of breast cancer in the long run. It is unlikely that women or their male partners know much about the clitoris and its role in orgasm unless someone happens to fumble upon it. Instead, the myth that vaginal orgasms from penile penetration are the only "mature" (according to Freud) climaxes prevails.

Lesbians are rarely "out," except in certain bars owned by organized crime (the only businessmen who recognize this untapped market), and if lesbians don't know about the bars, they're less likely to know whether there are any other women like them. Radclyffe Hall's depressing early-twentieth-century novel *The Well of Loneliness* pretty much indicates their fate.

The Miss America Pageant is the biggest source of scholarship money for women. Women can't be students at Dartmouth, Columbia, Harvard, West Point, Boston College, or the Citadel, among other all-male institutions. Women's colleges are referred to as "girls' schools." There are no Take Back the Night marches to protest women's lack of safety after dark, but that's okay because college girls aren't allowed out much after dark anyway. Curfew is likely to be midnight on Saturday and 9 or 10 p.m. the rest of the week. Guys get to stay out as late as they want. Women tend to major in teaching, home economics, English, or maybe a language—a good skill for translating someone else's words. The women's studies major does not exist, although you can take a women's studies course at six universities, including Cornell and San Diego State College. The absence of women's history, black history, Chicano studies, Asian-American history, queer studies, and Native American history from college curricula implies that they are not worth studying. A student is lucky if he or she learns that women were "given" the vote in 1920, just as Columbus "discovered" America in 1492. They might also learn that Sojourner Truth, Mary Church Terrell, and Fannie Lou Hamer were black abolitionists or civil-rights leaders, but not that they were feminists. There are practically no tenured female professors at any school, and campuses are not racially diverse. Women of color are either not there or they're lonely as hell. There is no nationally recognized Women's History Month or Black History Month. Only 14 percent of doctorates are awarded to women. Only 3.5 percent of MBAs are female.

Only 2 percent of everybody in the military is female, and these women are mostly nurses. There are no female generals in the U.S. Air Force, no female naval pilots, and no Marine brigadier generals. On the religious front, there are no female cantors or rabbis, Episcopal canons, or Catholic priests. (This is still true of Catholic priests.)

Only 44 percent of women are employed outside the home. And those women make, on average, fifty-two cents to the dollar earned by males. Want ads are segregated into "Help Wanted Male" and "Help Wanted Female." The female side is preponderantly for secretaries, domestic workers, and other low-wage service jobs, so if you're a female lawyer you must look under "Help Wanted Male." There are female doctors, but twenty states have only five female gynecologists or fewer. Women workers can be fired or demoted for being pregnant, especially if they are teachers, since the kids they teach aren't supposed to think that women have sex. If a boss demands sex, refers to his female employee exclusively as "Baby," or says he won't pay her unless she gives him a blow job, she has to either quit or succumb—no pun intended. Women can't be airline pilots. Flight attendants are "stewardesses"—waitresses in the sky—and necessarily female. Sex appeal is a job requirement, wearing makeup is a rule, and women are fired if they exceed the age or weight deemed sexy. Stewardesses can get married without getting canned, but this is a new development. (In 1968 the Equal Employment Opportunity Commission—EEOC—made it illegal to forcibly retire stewardesses for getting hitched.) Less than 2 percent of dentists are women; 100 percent of dental assistants are women. The "glass ceiling" that keeps women from moving naturally up the ranks, as well as the sticky floor that keeps them unnaturally down in low-wage work, has not been named, much less challenged.

When a woman gets married, she vows to love, honor, and obey her husband, though he gets off doing just the first two to uphold his end of the bargain. A married woman can't obtain credit without her husband's signature. She doesn't have her own credit rating, legal domicile, or even her own name unless she goes to court to get it back. If she gets a loan with her husband—and she has a job—she may have to sign a "baby letter" swearing that she won't have one and have to leave her job.

Women have been voting for up to fifty years, but their turnout rate is lower than that for men, and they tend to vote right along with their husbands, not with their own interests in mind. The divorce rate is about the same as it is in 2000, contrary to popular fiction's blaming the women's movement for divorce. However, divorce required that one person be at fault, therefore if you just want out of your marriage, you have to lie or blame your spouse. Property division and settlements, too, are based on fault. (And at a time when domestic violence isn't a term, much less a crime, women are legally encouraged to remain in abusive marriages.) If fathers ask for custody of the children, they get it in 60 to 80 percent of the cases. (This is still true.) If a husband or a lover hits his

partner, she has no shelter to go to unless she happens to live near the one in northern California or the other in upper Michigan. If a woman is downsized from her role as a housewife (a.k.a. left by her husband), there is no word for being a displaced homemaker. As a divorcée, she may be regarded as a family disgrace or as easy sexual prey. After all, she had sex with one guy, so why not *all* guys?

If a woman is not a Mrs., she's a Miss. A woman without makeup and a hairdo is as suspect as a man with them. Without a male escort she may be refused service in a restaurant or a bar, and a woman alone is hard-pressed to find a landlord who will rent her an apartment. After all, she'll probably be leaving to get married soon, and, if she isn't, the landlord doesn't want to deal with a potential brothel.

Except among the very poor or in very rural areas, babies are born in hospitals. There are no certified midwives, and women are knocked out during birth. Most likely, they are also strapped down and lying down, made to have the baby against gravity for the doctor's convenience. If he has a schedule to keep, the likelihood of a cesarean is also very high. *Our Bodies, Ourselves* doesn't exist, nor does the women's health movement. Women aren't taught how to look at their cervixes, and their bodies are nothing to worry their pretty little heads about; however, they are supposed to worry about keeping their little heads pretty. If a woman goes under the knife to see if she has breast cancer, the surgeon won't wake her up to consult about her options before performing a Halsted mastectomy (a disfiguring radical procedure, in which the breast, the muscle wall, and the nodes under the arm, right down to the bone, are removed). She'll just wake up and find that the choice has been made for her.

Husbands are likely to die eight years earlier than their same-age wives due to the stress of having to support a family and repress an emotional life, and a lot earlier than that if women have followed the custom of marrying older, authoritative, paternal men. The stress of raising kids, managing a household, and being undervalued by society doesn't seem to kill off women at the same rate. Upon a man's death, his beloved gets a portion of his Social Security. Even if she has worked outside the home for her entire adult life, she is probably better off with that portion than with hers in its entirety, because she has earned less and is likely to have taken time out for such unproductive acts as having kids.

Has feminism changed our lives? Was it necessary? After thirty years of feminism, the world we inhabit barely resembles the world we were born into. And there's still a lot left to do.

R E A D I N G   **3**

Dear Sisters

Rosalyn Baxandall and Linda Gordon

SOCIAL ROOTS OF WOMEN'S LIBERATION

Women's liberation was a movement long overdue. By the mid-1950s a majority of American women found themselves expected to function as full economic, social, and political participants in the nation while still burdened with handicaps. As wage-earners, as parents, as students, as citizens, women were denied equal opportunity and, often, even minimal rights and respect. Many women experienced sharp conflict among the expectations placed on them—education, employment, wife- and motherhood. Looking back at the beginning of the twenty-first century, we can see feminism as a necessary modernizing force and, not surprisingly, one which rapidly became global. Within the U.S., the movement gained widespread support so quickly because it met real needs, because the great majority of women stood to benefit from reducing discrimination, harassment, and prejudice against them. A movement that might at first have seemed to promise to rationalize the current political and economic system by integrating women into it quickly took off—as many social movements do—into uncharted territory, exposing the degree to which basic social structures had rested on a traditional gender system. The radical challenge to these fundamental structures can be measured by the virulence of the later worldwide backlash, from the Taliban to the Christian Coalition.

How did an apparently arch-conservative decade like the 1950s produce a movement so radical? To answer that we have to look beneath a veneer that concealed discomforts and discontents. The period between the end of World War II and the birth of women's liberation at the end of the 1960s has usually been described as an era of prosperity, stability, and peace, leading to the conclusion that it was also an era of satisfaction and little change. An intensely controlled and controlling official and commercial culture seemed to provide evidence for that conclusion. The domestic correlate of the cold war and the Korean War was the hysterical anticommunism that stigmatized nonconformity, including that related to family, sex, and gender. Anxiety about the Soviet threat made family stability seem critical and linked women's domestic roles to the nation's security. Just as schoolchildren were drilled in ducking under their desks and covering their heads to protect themselves from atomic bombs, so teenage girls were taught the imperatives of beauty and domesticity. Far from interpreting these women's obligations as constraints, cold war American culture regarded them as freedom. That American middle-class women did not seem to need jobs and enjoyed an expanding array of household appliances demonstrated the superiority of American institutions over Soviet society, where dowdy women grew heavily muscled from their hard labor and could shop only for a narrow array of dreary clothes and consumer goods. In the early 1960s future feminist Betty Friedan was to name this view of women's appropriate destiny the "feminine mystique," a term now used by historians to describe the domestic gendered face of the cold war. Twenty years later historian Elaine Tyler May observed that the concept of containment, first used to characterize the U.S. policy of preventing Soviet expansion, could characterize equally well the stifling of female ambitions, the endorsement of female subordination, and the promotion of domesticity by cold war gender culture. Resistance to these norms was un-American, and that label became a heavy club with which to beat misfits and dissidents.

. . .

Girls grew up in this cold war era barred from wearing blue jeans or sneakers to school, required to sit with their knees together and to set their hair in pin curls. Nothing in the culture encouraged them to become strong or competitive. Girls grew to hate athletics and dread physical education in school, where they were required to wear unfashionable tunics or bloomers. Girls were not encouraged to fantasize about careers, about what they would "become" when they grew up. They were expected to break a date with a girlfriend if a boy asked for a date. They watched movies and TV in which married couples slept in twin beds and mothers were full-time housewives. The people of color on TV were stereotypes, comic or worse: step-and-fetch-it black servants, marauding Apaches, or fat lazy Mexicans. Rape, illegitimacy, abortion—some of women's real problems—were among many tabooed subjects, whispered about but rarely seriously or openly discussed.

But this official feminine-mystique culture obscured an unofficial but probably more widespread reality that was, ironically, designated as deviant. A small band of historians has been uncovering the story of what turns out to be the majority of American women who did not, and often could not, conform. We belonged to that majority. Neither of our families was like *Leave It to Beaver* or *Father Knows Best.* Our mothers "worked,"

which meant, of course, employment for wages, and we thought they were unusual. In fact, in contrast to official norms, women's labor-force participation climbed rapidly throughout the fifties and by 1954 women's employment had equaled that during World War II. Most women displaced from well-paid, industrial jobs at the war's end did not return to domesticity but found work in traditionally female low-paying jobs in the expanding service and clerical sectors. As has long been true in American history, African American women and poor women of all colors had particularly high rates of employment, so that the domesticity myth was in part a racist assumption that elite white norms were universal. Women in "pink collar" employment swelled the membership of unions, such as the Hotel Employees and Restaurant Employees and the National Federation of Telephone Workers. And these working women were not only young and single: By 1960, 30 percent of married women were employed, and 39 percent of mothers with school-age children were in the labor force. By 1955, 3 million women belonged to unions, constituting 17 percent of union members. In unions in which women made up a significant part of the membership, they wielded considerable power, especially at the local level.

The number of married women seeking employment rose fastest in the middle class. Women benefited from an enormous expansion in higher education after World War II. Government investment in universities after the war had multiplied educational opportunity, especially in public institutions. In 1940, 26 percent of American women completed college; in 1970, 55 percent. These relatively privileged American women faced a particular dilemma: educated with men and often achieving, despite discrimination, the same levels of knowledge, discipline, and sophistication as the men of their social class, they were still expected to forego professional or intellectual pursuits after college to become full-time housewives and mothers. Those who resisted this directive and sought employment, through choice or economic necessity, usually found themselves limited to clerical or low-level administrative jobs.

In part as a response to this restriction, many women, like both our mothers, defied the limits of domesticity through community and political activism. Even in the suburbs, where women seemed to be conforming to the "feminine mystique" by staying home with small children, many were active in churches, schools, libraries, and parks. New forms of organizing appeared: In 1956, for example, the first all-female La Leche group met to encourage breast feeding. Other groups, alarmed by Rachel Carson's studies of the dangers of pesticides like DDT, had the audacity to challenge official science. Women Strike for Peace, composed largely of left-wing women, attacked military spending priorities, raised an alarm about strontium-90 fallout in milk, and directly challenged the cold war and American military buildup by contesting U.S. government propaganda about the threat of Soviet expansionism. Even conservative women, while paying official homage to the ideal of women's domesticity, were organizing in the Ku Klux Klan, White Citizen's Councils, John Birch Society, and Republican Party.

. . .

Dissidence in the 1950s was, of course, particularly pronounced in youth culture. Rebellious adolescent voices competed with homogenized "Archie" comic book people and Disney's cute, servile Annette Funicello. Young people identified as "rebels without a cause," the phrase sent reverberating through America by James Dean, Hollywood's symbol of alienated middle-class youth. The idea that they didn't have "a cause" came from their affluence, the fact that they "had everything." But these rebels did have a cause—they just couldn't name it—and the affluence of their parents only heightened their discontent. They rejected the false facades of family, the suburbs, and corporate careers, the measurement of success by large houses and consumer goods. They sought authenticity instead among male outsider figures—cowboys, hoods, oddballs, delinquents, but also blacks and Latinos. As with the beats, women remained followers, but some were choosing geeks or boys on motorcycles instead of jocks. Rebellion among less privileged

groups took different forms, less covered by the mainstream media and less shocking to middle-class whites, who considered the norms of poor people and people of color outside established culture anyway. But the protest was there, among young Chicanos dressing in flashy "zoot suits" and "low-riding" their jazzed-up cars, among the hoods and rockers with their greased ducktail hairdos.

Nowhere was the youth rebellion as intense or as contagious as in music, and the transcendence of race segregation was the proximate cause. The officially dominant 1950s white sound (Peggy Lee, Jo Stafford, Rosemary Clooney, and Pat Boone) combined inane lyrics, like "How Much Is That Doggie in the Window," with soothing melodies, bland orchestration, and ballad rhythms. Yet this is the decade that produced rock and roll, a revolution in popular music. The term was first applied to black rhythm and blues by Alan Freed, the white disk jockey who promoted black music to white audiences. The breakthrough singer was Elvis Presley, the "white boy who could sing black." Not only did whites start to buy records by black artists but they also attended huge concerts where for the first time white and black youth mingled and danced. In Los Angeles, for example, racially mixed rock concerts were busted up by the police. Conservatives considered rock and roll the music of the devil, dangerous, degenerate, mongrel, oversexualized, and in a way they were right: it is difficult to overestimate the impact of rock and roll on the men and women who moved from the inchoate, half-conscious alienation of rebels without a cause to the organized radical movements that began with the civil rights movement.

POLITICAL ROOTS OF WOMEN'S LIBERATION

From the vantage point of the new century, the women's liberation movement appears extravagant, immoderate, impatient, as well as young and naive. It was all those and more, but how one weighs its radicalism, positively or negatively, and how one measures its naivete depend on understanding its historical context. Thirty years later our culture has been so transformed, the expectations of young women so altered, that it is hard to grasp the unique combination of anger and optimism that made second-wave feminism so determined to change so much so fast.

Women coming into adulthood at the end of the 1960s, both middle- and working-class, faced an economy that was producing an ever larger number of jobs for women and for the men they might marry. Even more important, women had unprecedented access to education. But many were disappointed in the jobs they could get. They went from being the equals or even the superiors of men in educational achievement to working as secretaries or "administrative assistants" for the same class of men. Although they faced discrimination in their colleges and universities, they also encountered professors who recognized and challenged their intelligence. Yet their studies, no matter how rigorous, offered them no way to escape the cultural imperative that directed them toward marriage and family as their fundamental and often exclusive source of identity and satisfaction.

If economic and educational abundance opened windows for the women who began women's liberation in 1968, the passionate new social activism of the 1950s and 1960s opened doors and invited women in. But these movements, like the economy as a whole, also sent women a double message. Whenever there have been progressive social change movements in modern history, women's movements have arisen within them, and for similar reasons: in the crucible of activism for civil rights, for peace, for the environment, for free speech, for social welfare, women have been valued participants who gained skills and self-confidence. At the same time, they have been thwarted, treated as subordinates, gophers, even servants, by the men in charge—including men who considered themselves partisans of democracy and equality. Within these movements women learned to think critically about social structures and ideologies, to talk the language of freedom and tyranny, democracy and domination, power and oppression.

Then they applied these concepts to question their own secondary status. It is precisely this combination of raised aspirations and frustration that gives rise to rebellion.

. . .

By the mid-1960s, the more ideologically Left currents within the movement were called the New Left, because they differed fundamentally from the older Lefts: communism, socialism, and New Deal progressivism. At least a decade earlier, the civil rights movement had been the first to break with conventional politics, helped by its high proportion of student activists, ability to stimulate mass participation, decentralized and pluralist organization, and commitment to direct but nonviolent action. Like all mass movements, the civil rights movement had no defined beginning, although the 1955 Montgomery bus boycott announced to the country that something big was happening. Thousands of African Americans were challenging three hundred years of apartheid, demonstrating unprecedented discipline, solidarity, and bravery against brutal retaliation. Their courage forced racist viciousness into the open; journalists and their cameras then brought into living rooms the high-power water hoses turned on peaceful protesters, the grown men who spat on first-graders, the dogs who charged at protesters singing gospel hymns. The news brought a heightened appreciation of the possibility of making change from the bottom up. In contrast to the bitter liberal-versus-conservative national division in the 1980s and 1990s, the civil rights struggles seemed to galvanize, at least among the most articulate citizenry, broad majority approval for social change in the direction of greater democracy and equality. (There may have been a "silent majority" that did not approve.) While any individual battle might be won or lost, it seemed to supporters that their cause was unstoppable, so great was the groundswell of desire for the long-overdue racial equality and respect.

. . .

In the late 1950s, another kind of rebellion was developing, primarily among the more privileged whites: a cultural rebellion. Discovering and inventing unconventional art, music, and poetry; exploring a variety of intoxicants; and signaling defiance in the way they dressed, adherents of this new cultural revolution soon grew visible enough to draw mainstream media attention. The press created popular icons—"flower children" and "hippies"—whose values resembled those of the earlier 1950s beatnik rebels. The influence of this lifestyle dissent can be measured by how quickly it was picked up by commercial interests and sold back to a broader public: the new fashion included beards, long straight hair, psychedelic design, granny dresses, and beads. Handmade, patched, and embroidered clothing and jeans once bought at Sears Roebuck or Goodwill were soon being mass-produced in Hong Kong and sold in department stores. For its most zealous participants, counterculture iconoclasm and adventurousness meant such an extreme rejection of the work ethic, temperance, and discipline that it horrified many observers, including some in the movement. Excessive use of drugs, promiscuous sexuality, and irresponsibility were sometimes destructive to participants, some of whom later rebounded into conventionality. Women suffered particular exploitation, as the counterculture's gender ideology reaffirmed that of the conventional culture, but now with a twist, lauding "free" and "natural" heterosexual relations between women who were sexually open and "giving" and men who could not be tied down. Women were to be earth mothers, seeking fulfillment by looking after men and children, while guys needed freedom from marital or paternal responsibilities in order to find and express themselves.

This cultural rebellion had transformative potential and gave rise to some serious political challenges. When civil rights and the counterculture intersected on campuses, the result was a college students' movement for free speech that would ultimately create the New Left and women's liberation. The first major student revolt, at the University of California at Berkeley in 1964, arose in reaction to the administration's attempt to prevent students from recruiting civil rights volunteers on campus. This protest movement spread to campuses late in the 1960s throughout the U.S., producing a series of protests against *in loco parentis* rules that treated students like children.

Campus protests soon expanded to include national issues and nonstudents. Sensitized to injustice and convinced of the potential of grassroots activism by what they learned from civil rights, more and more Americans began to see the Vietnam War as immoral and undemocratic. In the name of stopping communism, the U.S. was defending a flagrantly corrupt regime that had canceled elections when it seemed likely to lose to a popular, nationalist liberation movement that promised land reform in the interests of the poor peasantry. The most powerful nation in the world was attacking a tiny nation that had demonstrated not the slightest aggression toward Americans. The U.S. employed some of the cruelest weapons and tactics yet developed: shooting down unarmed peasants because of fear that they might be supporting the liberation movement; bulldozing villages; spraying herbicides from planes to deprive the guerrilla fighters of their jungle cover; dropping napalm, a jellied gasoline antipersonnel weapon that stuck to the skin and burned people alive. There was not yet extensive censorship of the press, so Americans routinely witnessed these atrocities on the evening news. American soldiers of color and of the working class were killed and injured in disproportionate numbers. Hundreds of young men began resisting or dodging the draft while scores of soldiers deserted and defied orders. So widespread, vocal, and convincing were the protests at home, including several massive national demonstrations, that by its end the Vietnam War became the only war in U.S. history to be opposed by a majority of the population.

The Vietnamese revolution was part of a wave of nationalist struggles of Third World countries against Western imperial domination, and these also influenced American domestic politics. Many of these emerging nations and movements took socialist forms, as Third World nationalists observed that the introduction of capitalism increased inequality and impoverishment. But many of these newly independent countries fell under Soviet domination as the price of the aid they so desperately needed, and leading parts of the American New Left, already angry at the stultifying domestic culture of the cold war, neglected to subject Soviet control to the same critique. U.S. interventions against communism, both military and covert, had the ironic effect of making the New Left less critical of Soviet and Chinese communism than it might have been otherwise.

. . .

Activism spread throughout the U.S., creating civil rights movements among other racial/ethnic groups, including Chicanos, Asian Americans, Native Americans; movements to protect the environment; a movement for the rights of the disabled; and renewed labor struggles for a fair share of the prosperity. Among whites there soon arose a national student organization that was to become central to the white New Left, Students for a Democratic Society (SDS), established in 1962. With a membership reaching about 100,000 at its peak in the late 1960s, and with many times that number of students—including high school students—who considered themselves a part of the movement, SDS changed the attitudes of a considerable part of a generation. New Leftists and counterculture activists created institutions that spread progressive ideas still further: radical bookstores, a few national magazines, and many local underground newspapers. These were produced by amateurs working in scruffy offices, offering critical perspectives on everything from U.S. foreign policy to the local police to the latest films. Many of these underground newspapers combined words and graphics in innovative ways, inspired in part by the street art of 1968 in France where the *beaux arts* students had considerable influence.

Although the movement (civil rights and the New Left) had no unified ideology—its members included anarchists, social democrats, Marxist-Leninists, black nationalists—it bequeathed identifiable legacies to feminism. Most important among these were anti-authoritarianism and irreverence. Favorite buttons and T-shirts read "Question Authority" and "Never Trust Anyone Over 30." Arrogant and disrespectful, yes, but also understandably rebellious. The movement's message was: look beneath formal legal and political rights to find other kinds of power, the power of wealth, of race, of violence.

Following this instruction, some women began in the mid-1960s to examine power relations in areas that the movement's male leaders had not considered relevant to radical politics. The women's preliminary digging uncovered a buried deposit of grievances about men's power over women within the movement. Women in civil rights and the New Left were on the whole less victimized, more respected, and less romanticized than they were in the mainstream culture or the counterculture. Despite women's passionate and disciplined work for social change, however, they remained far less visible and less powerful than the men who dominated the meetings and the press conferences. Women came into greater prominence wherever there was grassroots organizing, as in voter registration in the South and the SDS community projects in northern cities. Throughout the civil rights and the student movements, women proved themselves typically the better organizers, better able than men to listen, to connect, to reach across class and even race lines, to empower the previously diffident, to persevere despite failure and lack of encouragement. Still, the frustrations and humiliations were galling. In every organization women were responsible for keeping records, producing leaflets, telephoning, cleaning offices, cooking, organizing social events, and catering to the egos of male leaders, while the men wrote manifestos, talked to the press, negotiated with officials, and made speeches. This division of labor did not arise from misogyny or acrimony. It was "natural" and had always been so, until it began to seem not natural at all.

THE RISE OF SECOND-WAVE FEMINISM

Although women's liberation had foremothers, the young feminists of the late 1960s did not usually know about this heritage because so little women's history had been written. Feminist historians have now made us aware that a continuing tradition of activism stretched from "first-wave" feminism, which culminated in winning the right to vote in 1920, to the birth of the "second wave" in 1968. Some women of unusual longevity bridged the two waves. Florence Luscomb, who had traveled the state of Massachusetts speaking for women suffrage during World War I, also spoke for women's liberation in Boston in the early 1970s. Within many progressive social movements, even at the nadir of the conservative 1950s, there were discontented women agitating against sex discrimination and promoting female leadership. Within the Communist and Socialist Parties there had been women's caucuses and demands to revise classic socialist theory to include sex inequality: for example, folksinger Melvina Reynolds, the women of the Jeannette Rankin Brigade. Some women spanned the older progressive causes and the new feminism—Ella Baker, Judy Collins, Ruby Dee, Eleanor Flexner, Fanny Lou Hamer, Flo Kennedy, Coretta Scott King, Gerda Lerner, Amy Swerdlow.

Liberal women had continued to be politically active between feminism's two waves. They were mainly Democrats but there were some Republicans, such as Oveta Culp Hobby, who became the first secretary of the Department of Health, Education and Welfare, established in 1953. In 1961 this women's political network persuaded President Kennedy, as payback for their support in the close election of 1960, to establish a Presidential Commission on the Status of Women. It was chaired by Eleanor Roosevelt, embodying continuity with first-wave feminism and the New Deal, and Women's Bureau head Esther Peterson served as vice-chair. Kennedy may have expected this commission to keep the women diverted and out of his hair. But the commission produced substantive recommendations for a legislative agenda and set in motion a continuing process. Its report, issued in 1963, called for equal pay for *comparable* work (understanding that equal pay for *equal* work would not be adequate because women so rarely did the same work as men), as well as child care services, paid maternity leave,

and many other measures still not achieved. Determined not to let its momentum stall or its message reach only elite circles, the commission built a network among women's organizations, made special efforts to include black women, and got Kennedy to establish two ongoing federal committees. Most consequentially, it stimulated the creation of state women's commissions, created in every state by 1967. The network that formed through these commissions enabled the creation of the National Organization for Women (NOW) in 1966.

NOW's history has been often misinterpreted, especially by the radical women's liberationists, who denounced it, as the radicals of SNCC criticized their elders and the New Left criticized the Old Left, as stodgy and "bourgeois." At first NOW included more working-class and minority leadership than women's liberation did. Many of its leaders identified strongly with civil rights and defined NOW as pursuing civil rights for women. Former Old Leftist Betty Friedan and black lawyer and poet Pauli Murray were centrally involved in the East, while in the Midwest, labor union women like Dorothy Haener of the United Auto Workers and Addie Wyatt of the Amalgamated Meatcutters were prime movers. NOW's first headquarters was provided by the UAW. NOW concentrated heavily on employment issues, reflecting its close ties to the U.S. Women's Bureau and the unions, and NOW's membership was composed largely of employed women. NOW refused to endorse reproductive rights, which the majority considered too controversial, but it rejected the idea that gender was immutable and called for "equitable sharing of responsibilities of home and children and of the economic burdens of their support." This position marked a decisive break with earlier women's rights agitation, which had primarily accepted the traditional division of labor—breadwinner husbands and housewives—as inevitable and desirable. And this position was to give rise to tremendous advances in feminist theory in the next decades.

NOW represented primarily adult professional women and a few male feminists, and at first it did not attempt to build a mass movement open to all women. Although only thirty women had attended its founding conference, and 300 its second conference, NOW demonstrated political savvy in creating the impression that it spoke for a mass power base. It had no central office of its own for three years—networking among a relatively small group did not require one. Its members used their professional and political skills to exert pressure on elected officials.

NOW concentrated on lobbying, using its ties to the few women in influential positions in government; its program focused on governmental action against sex discrimination. Its members met with the attorney general, the secretary of labor, the head of the Civil Service commission. Its board of directors read like entries from a "Who's Who" of professional women and their male supporters. Its initial impetus was anger that the Equal Employment Opportunity Commission (EEOC) was not enforcing the sex-discrimination provisions of the Civil Rights Act of 1965, and it got immediate results: in 1967 President Johnson issued Executive Order 11375, prohibiting sex discrimination by federal contractors. In the same year NOW forced the EEOC to rule that sex-segregated want ads were discriminatory (although newspapers ignored this ruling with impunity for years). NOW's legal committee, composed of four high-powered Washington lawyers, three of them federal employees, brought suits against protective legislation that in the name of protecting women's fragility in fact kept them out of better jobs. (In arguing one case the five-foot, 100-pound lawyer picked up the equipment the company claimed was too heavy for women and carried it around with one hand as she argued to the jury.)

Women's liberation derided NOW's perspective and tactics as "liberal"—not in the 1990s pejorative sense, coined by the Right, of permissive, but in the 1960s sense, used by the Left, as legalistic and compromising. When a mass women's movement arose, it was not liberal but radical in the sense of seeking out the roots of problems and working for structural change at a level more fundamental than law. It wanted not just to redistribute wealth and power in the existing society, but to challenge the sources of male dominance: the

private as well as the public, the psychological as well as the economic, the cultural as well as the legal. Given this radical agenda it was hard for women's liberation to become a player in the political process, and it tended to make purist and moralistic judgments of those who chose to work within the system.

The mass women's movement arose independently of NOW and the government commissions, and its members had a different style: they were younger, typically in their twenties, and less professional. Most importantly, it generated groups consisting of women only. The new women's liberation movement insisted that women needed a woman-only space in which they could explore their grievances and define their own agenda. They observed that women frequently censored not only what they said but even what they thought when men were around. Arriving directly from male-dominated, grassroots social-justice movements, these women longed for a space where they could talk freely with other women. First in Chicago, then in several other cities such as Gainesville, Florida; Chapel Hill, North Carolina; Washington, D.C.; and New York City, women's liberation groups formed in 1967 and 1968. At a 1968 antiwar demonstration in Washington organized by the Jeannette Rankin Brigade, 500 women gathered as a women's liberation counter-conference and then spread the movement to other towns and cities. In August 1968 twenty of them met in Sandy Springs, Maryland, to plan a larger conference. Everyone present was disturbed by the fact that they were all white. But identifying this problem did not mean they could solve it: when over 200 women from thirty-seven states and Canada met in Chicago at Thanksgiving, black women's groups were not represented, because they had not been invited or because they were not interested.

The first women's liberation groups were founded by veteran activists, but soon women with no previous movement experience joined. The decentralization of the movement was so great, despite the few early national conferences and women's frequent travel and relocation, that different geographic locations developed different agendas and organizational structures. In Iowa City, a university town, the movement began with college students and concentrated much of its energies on publishing a newspaper, *Ain't I a Woman?* In Gainesville, Florida, another university town, the movement originated in civil rights networks. In several large cities—Baltimore, Chicago, Boston, Los Angeles—single citywide organizations brought different groups together; in New York City an original group, New York Radical Women, gave birth to several smaller groups with divergent ideologies. Small-town feminists had to hang together despite their differences, while in big cities there was room to elaborate various political positions. Different cities had different ideological personalities: Washington, D.C., was best known for The Furies, a lesbian separatist group, while Chapel Hill, North Carolina, was noted for its socialist-feminist orientation.

The movement developed so widely and quickly that it is impossible to trace a chronology, impossible to say who led, what came first, who influenced whom. This lack of a clear narrative, and the sense that participants across great distances were making some of the same breakthroughs simultaneously, are characteristic of all mass social movements. In this case, though, we can outline some of the major political factions. We are identifying not the various theoretical positions in feminist intellectual debates today, but the theory that informed the practices of women's liberation groups in the early 1970s.

WOMEN'S LIBERATION DEVELOPS

The movement's characteristic form of development was consciousness-raising (CR), a form of structured discussion in which women connected their personal experiences to larger structures of gender.... These discussion groups, usually small, sprung up starting in 1968–70 throughout the country among women of all ages and social positions. They were simultaneously supportive and transformative. Women formed these groups by the hundreds, then by the thousands. In Cambridge/Boston where a core group offered to

help other women form CR groups, a hundred *new* women attended weekly for several months. The mood was exhilarating. Women came to understand that many of their "personal" problems—insecurity about appearance and intelligence, exhaustion, conflicts with husbands and male employers—were not individual failings but a result of discrimination. The mood became even more electric as women began to create collective ways of challenging that discrimination. At first there was agitprop: spreading the word through leaflets, pamphlets, letters to newspapers; pasting stickers onto sexist advertisements; verbally protesting being called "girl" or "baby" or "chick"; hollering at guys who made vulgar proposals on the streets. Soon action groups supplemented and, in some cases, replaced CR groups. Women pressured employers to provide day care centers; publicized job and school discrimination; organized rape crisis hot lines; opened women's centers, schools, and credit unions; built unions for stewardesses and secretaries; agitated for women's studies courses at colleges; published journals and magazines.

Soon different groups formulated different theoretical/political stands. But the clarity and discreteness of these positions should not be exaggerated; there was cross-fertilization, none was sealed off from others, the borderlines and definitions shifted, and there were heated debates *within* tendencies. Liberal feminists were at first associated with NOW and similar groups, although these tended to merge with women's liberation by the end of the 1970s. Those who remained committed to a broad New Left agenda typically called themselves socialist feminists (to be distinguished from Marxist feminists, who remained convinced that Marxist theory could explain women's oppression and were not committed to an autonomous women's movement). Socialist feminists weighed issues of race and class equally with those of gender and tried to develop an integrated, holistic theory of society. Radical feminists, in contrast, prioritized sexual oppression, but by no means ignored other forms of domination. Our research suggests that the radical/socialist opposition was overstated, but small theoretical differences seemed very important at the time because the early feminists were in the process of developing new political theory, not yet making political alliances to achieve concrete objectives. A few separatists, often but not exclusively lesbians, attempted to create self-sustaining female communities and to withdraw as much as possible from contact with men. By the late 1970s, some women had become cultural feminists, celebrating women's specialness and difference from men and retreating from direct challenges to sexist institutions; they believed that change could come about through building new exemplary female communities. But despite this proliferation of ideological groupings, most members of women's liberation did not identify with any of these tendencies and considered themselves simply feminists, unmodified.

Racial/ethnic differences were more significant. Feminists of different racial/ethnic groups established independent organizations from the beginning and within those organizations created different feminisms: black, Chicana, Asian American, Native American. Feminists of color emphasized the problems with universalizing assumptions about women and with identifying gender as a category autonomous from race and class. But here too we found that these *theoretical* differences are sometimes overstated; and feminists of color were not more unanimous than white feminists—there were, for example, black liberal feminists, black socialist feminists, black radical feminists, black cultural feminists. These complexities do not negate the fact that feminists of color experienced racism within the women's movement. The majority of feminists, white women from middle-class backgrounds, were often oblivious to the lives of women from minority and working-class families. Feminists of color faced the additional problems that certain women's issues, such as reproductive rights, had been historically tainted by racism; and that feminist criticisms of men were experienced differently, often as betraying racial solidarity when the men were themselves victims of racism.

Lesbians sometimes created separate feminist groups, but the gay-straight conflict has also been exaggerated. Ironically, while some accused women's liberation of homophobia, others accused it of being a lesbian conspiracy. As lesbians became more open and vocal, they protested the heterosexual assumptions of straight feminists, but they also experienced discrimination from the male-dominated gay movement. For the most part lesbians continued to be active in women's liberation and made important contributions to feminist theory. Lesbians even led campaigns of primary concern to heterosexual women, such as campaigns for reproductive rights.

At the beginning of the movement, feminists tended to create multi-issue organizations, which in turn created committees to focus on single issues, such as day care, rape, or running a women's center. One of the fundamental tenets of early feminist theory was the interconnectedness of all aspects of women's oppression. As political sophistication grew and activists grasped the difficulties of making sweeping changes, feminists settled for piecemeal, fragmented activism. By the mid-1970s feminist politics often occurred in single-issue organizations focused on, for example, reproductive rights, employment discrimination, health, domestic violence, female unions, women's studies. Single-issue politics de-emphasized theory, which reduced divisions; it had the advantage of making coalitions easier but the disadvantage of turning theory construction over to academics, who were usually divorced from activism. The coalitions and compromises necessitated by single-issue politics made the movement less radical and more practical. Single-issue politics also lessened the movement's coherence as its activists became specialized and professionalized.

ORGANIZATIONAL PRINCIPLES OF WOMEN'S LIBERATION

In sharp opposition to its liberal feminist sisters in NOW, women's liberation preferred radical decentralization. In addition to following New Left principles of direct democracy and anti-authoritarianism, these young feminists had their own woman-centered reasons for lack of interest in, even hostility toward, creating a large national organization. Women, whose voices had been silenced and whose actions had been directed by others, were loath to have anyone telling them what to think or do. They understood that central organization would produce principles, programs, and priorities they would be required to follow. They also sensed that a movement growing at such velocity could not be contained by central organizations, which would only inhibit creative growth. Without formal rules of membership, any group of women could declare themselves a women's liberation organization, start a newspaper or a women's center, issue a manifesto. The resulting diversity then made it all the harder to keep track of, let alone unify, the many groups.

Not only was there no formal structure bringing groups together, there was very little structure within groups, and this was, again, by choice. Feminists could dispense with Roberts' Rules of Order because the groups were small and the members usually knew each other well. But they were often also hostile in principle to formal procedures, which they saw as arbitrary and not organic. This attitude was part of the feminist critique of the public/private distinction, and it was a way of making the public sphere accessible to women who were traditionally more experienced with a personal, familial form of conversing. In small meetings, especially in the consciousness-raising groups that were the essence of women's liberation, the informal "rapping" style was nurturant, allowing women to speak intimately and risk self-exposure, and therefore to come up with rich new insights into the workings of male dominance. When there were large meetings and/or sharp disagreements, the sessions often became tediously long, unable to reach decisions, and even chaotic. As a result, small groups of women or strong-minded and charismatic individuals sometimes took charge, and others, exhausted by the long aimless discussions, grudgingly relinquished power to these unelected leaders.

Women's liberation faced a major dilemma with respect to leadership. Its search for direct democracy led the movement to revere the principle of "every woman a leader" and to imagine that collectives could speak with one voice. Consequently the movement empowered thousands of women who had never dreamt they could write a leaflet, speak in public, talk to the press, chair a meeting, assert unpopular points of view, or make risky suggestions. The emphasis on group leadership meant that many important statements were unsigned, written anonymously or collectively, or signed with first names only, indicating the degree to which theory and strategy were being developed democratically. But the bias against leadership hindered action, decision-making, and coherent communication beyond small groups. More problematically, the movement did create leaders, but they were frequently unacknowledged and almost always unaccountable because they were essentially self-appointed rather than chosen by the members. This led to widespread, sometimes intense resentment of leaders. The hostility, usually covert, sometimes escalated to stimulate open attacks, as women publicly criticized or "trashed" leaders in meetings. One result was that individuals who had worked hard and made personal sacrifices felt betrayed and embittered. Another was that women's liberation groups became vulnerable to takeovers by highly organized sectarian groups (mainly the Marxist-Leninist sects) or obstruction by disturbed individuals who could not be silenced. Perhaps the most deleterious result was that many women became reluctant to assert leadership and thus deprived the movement of needed talent. The leadership problem involved the movement's denial of internal inequalities, its refusal to recognize that some women were more articulate and self-confident; had more leisure time, connections, and access to power; or were simply more forceful personalities. These inequalities mainly derived, as the feminists' own analysis showed, from the class and race hierarchy of the larger society. This is an example of utopian hopes becoming wishful thinking: feminists so badly wanted equality that they pretended it was already here.

Despite decentralization and structurelessness, women's liberation created a shared culture, theory, and practice. In an era before e-mail, even before xeroxing, printed publications were vital and feminists spent a significant proportion of their energy, resources, and ingenuity producing them. Mimeographed pages stapled together into pamphlets were the common currency of the early years of the movement, and soon a few feminist publishing houses, such as KNOW in Pittsburgh, Lollipop Inc. in Durham, and the Feminist Press in New York, were printing and selling feminist writings for prices ranging from a nickel to a quarter. These were widely discussed, debated, and answered in further publications. By the mid-1970s over 500 feminist magazines and newspapers appeared throughout the country, such as *Women, A Journal of Liberation* from Baltimore, *It Ain't Me Babe* from the San Francisco Bay Area, *Off Our Backs* from Washington, D.C., *Everywoman* from Los Angeles. The male-dominated New Left underground press, like the New England Free Press in Boston or Liberation News Service, a left-wing news syndicate, also published a great deal of women's liberation news and position papers.

Unlike *Ms.*, a mass-circulation advertisement-supported liberal feminist magazine established in 1972, women's liberation publications struggled along without funds or paid staff, featuring not-quite-aligned layouts, sometimes poorly written pieces, and amateur poetry and drawings. Many articles were signed simply "Susan" or "Randy," or not signed at all, because the movement was hostile to the idea of intellectual private property. The papers sometimes forgot to print dates of publication, addresses, and subscription information. Women worked hard at producing these publications but, unfortunately, less hard at financing and distributing them, so many were irregularly published and short-lived. Nevertheless, it was in these homespun rags that you could find the most creative and cutting-edge theory and commentary.

WHAT WOMEN'S LIBERATION ACCOMPLISHED

. . .

Judicial and legislative victories include the legalization of abortion in 1973, federal guidelines against coercive sterilization, rape shield laws that encourage more women to prosecute their attackers, affirmative action programs that aim to correct past discrimination—but not, however, the Equal Rights Amendment, which failed in 1982, just three states short of the required two-thirds. There are many equally important but less obvious accomplishments: not only legal, economic, and political gains, but also changes in the way people live, dress, dream of their future, and make a living. In fact, there are few areas of contemporary life untouched by feminism. As regards health care, for example, many physicians and hospitals have made major improvements in the treatment of women; about 50 percent of medical students are women; women successfully fought their exclusion from medical research; diseases affecting women, such as breast and ovarian cancer, now receive more funding thanks to women's efforts. Feminists insisted that violence against women, previously a well-kept secret, become a public political issue; made rape, incest, battering, and sexual harassment understood as crimes; and got public funding for shelters for battered women. These gains, realized in the 1980s and 1990s, are the fruits of struggles fought in the 1970s.

Feminist pressure generated substantial changes in education: curricula and textbooks have been rewritten to promote equal opportunity for girls, more women are admitted and funded in universities and professional schools, and a new and rich feminist scholarship in many disciplines has won recognition. Title IX, passed in 1972 to mandate equal access to college programs, has worked a revolution in sports. Consider the many women's records broken in track and field, the expanding number of athletic scholarships for women, professional women's basketball, and the massive popularity of girls' and women's soccer.

Campaigning to support families, feminists organized day care centers, developed standards and curricula for early childhood education, demanded day care funding from government and private employers, fought for parental leave from employers and a decent welfare system. They also struggled for new options for women in employment. They won greater access to traditionally male occupations, from construction to professions and business. They joined unions and fought to democratize them, and they succeeded in organizing previously nonunion workers such as secretaries, waitresses, hospital workers, and flight attendants. As the majority of American women increasingly need to work for wages throughout their lives, the feminist movement tried to educate men to share in house work and child raising. Although women still do the bulk of the housework and child rearing, it is common today to see men in the playgrounds, the supermarkets, and at the PTA meetings.

Feminism changed how women look and what is considered attractive, although the original feminist impulse toward simpler, more comfortable, and less overtly sexual clothing is being challenged by another generation of women at the turn of the century. As women's-liberation influence spread in the 1970s, more and more women refused to wear the constricting, uncomfortable clothes that were required in the 1950s—girdles, garter belts, and stockings; tight, flimsy, pointed, and high-heeled shoes; crinolines and cinch belts; tight short skirts. Women wearing pants, loose jackets, walking shoes, and no makeup began to feel attractive and to be recognized by others as attractive. By the 1980s, however, younger women began to feel that feminist beauty standards were repressive, even prudish, and developed a new, more playful, ornate, and multicultural fashion sensibility that may signal a "third wave" of feminism. Women's newfound passion for athletics has made a look of health and strength fashionable, sometimes to an oppressive degree as women feel coerced to reach a firm muscular, spandex thinness. At the same time, a conservative antifeminist backlash is also influencing fashion, trying to reestablish an allegedly lost femininity. The politics of feminism is being fought out on the fashion front.

Other aspects of the culture also reveal feminism's impact. Finally some older movie actresses, such as Susan Sarandon, Olympia Dukakis, and Meryl Streep, are recognized as desirable, and women entertainers in many media and art forms are rejecting simplistic, demeaning, and passive roles, despite the reemergence of misogynist and hypersexualized entertainments. Soap operas, sitcoms, even cop shows now feature plots in which lesbianism, abortion, rape, incest, and battering are portrayed from women's perspectives. In the fine arts, women's progress has been slower, illustrating the fallacy of assuming that the elite is less sexist than those of lesser privilege. The way we speak has been altered: new words have been coined—"sexist" and "Ms." and "gender"; many Americans are now self-conscious about using "he" to mean a human, and textbooks and even sacred texts are being rewritten in inclusive language. Women now expect to be called "women" instead of "ladies" or "girls."

Some of the biggest transformations are personal and familial, and they have been hotly contested. Indeed, even from a feminist perspective not all of them are positive. Women's relationships with other women are more publicly valued and celebrated and lesbianism is more accepted. People are marrying later and some are choosing not to marry. Most women today enter marriage or other romantic relationships with the expectation of equal partnership; since they don't always get this, they seem more willing to live as single people than to put up with domineering or abusive men. Conservatives argue that the growth of divorce, out-of-wedlock childbirth, and single motherhood is a sign of social deterioration, and certainly the growing economic inequality in the U.S. has rendered many women and especially single mothers and their children impoverished, depressed, and angry. But, feminists retort, is being poor in a destructive marriage really better than being poor on one's own? Even the growth of single motherhood reflects an element of women's choice: in different circumstances both poor and prosperous women are refusing to consider a bad marriage the price of motherhood, and are giving birth to or adopting children without husbands. More women think of marriage as only one possible option, aware that singleness and lesbianism are reasonable alternatives. Even women who do marry increasingly consider marriage only one aspect of life, supplementing motherhood and work. There is a growing sentiment that families come in a variety of forms.

By the mid-1970s an antifeminist backlash was able to command huge funding from right-wing corporate fortunes, fervent support from religious fundamentalists, and considerable media attention. The intensity of the reaction is a measure of how threatened conservatives were by popular backing for women's liberation and the rapid changes it brought about. Even with their billions of dollars, their hundreds of lobbyists and PR men, their foundations and magazines dishing out antifeminist misinformation, as compared to the puny amounts of money and volunteer labor available to women's liberation, the striking fact is <u>that public opinion has not shifted much</u>. Polls show overwhelming support for what feminism stands for: equal rights, respect, opportunity, and access for women.

That there is still a long way to go to reach sexual equality should not prevent us from recognizing what has been achieved. If there is disappointment, it is because women's liberation was so utopian, even apocalyptic, emerging as it did in an era of radical social movements and grand optimism. Unrealistic? Perhaps. But without utopian dreams, without anger, without reaching for the moon and expecting to get there by express, the movement would have achieved far less. In fact, without taking risks, feminists would never have been able to imagine lives of freedom and justice for women.

Feminism is by no means dead. Feminist groups continue to work on specific issues such as reproductive rights, rape, violence against women, sweatshops, sexism in the media, union organizing, and welfare rights. Nevertheless, the mass social movement called women's liberation did dissolve by the end of the 1970s. This is not a sign of failure. All social movements are short-lived because of the intense personal demands they make; few can sustain the level of energy that they require at their peak of activity. Moreover, as people age, most put more energy into family, employment, and personal life. Equally important, women's liberation could not survive outside the context of the other progressive social movements that nurtured hope and optimism about social change. As the Left declined, the right-wing backlash grew stronger. It did not convert many feminists to conservatism but it moved the mainstream far to the right. Given this change in mainstream politics, it is all the more striking that so few feminist gains have been rolled back and many have continued and even increased their momentum. Although the word "feminist" has become a pejorative term to some American women, most women (and most men as well) support a feminist program: equal education, equal pay, child care, freedom from harassment and violence, shared housework and child rearing, women's right to self-determination.

R E A D I N G 4

Feminist Politics
Where We Stand

bell hooks

Simply put, feminism is a movement to end sexism, sexist exploitation, and oppression. This was a definition of feminism I offered in *Feminist Theory: From Margin to Center* more than 10 years ago. It was my hope at the time that it would

become a common definition everyone would use. I liked this definition because it did not imply that men were the enemy. By naming sexism as the problem it went directly to the heart of the matter. Practically, it is a definition which implies that all sexist thinking and action is the problem, whether those who perpetuate it are female or male, child or adult. It is also broad enough to include an understanding of systemic institutionalized sexism. As a definition it is open-ended. To understand feminism it implies one has to necessarily understand sexism.

As all advocates of feminist politics know, most people do not understand sexism, or if they do, they think it is not a problem. Masses of people think that feminism is always and only about women seeking to be equal to men. And a huge majority of these folks think feminism is anti-male. Their misunderstanding of feminist politics reflects the reality that most folks learn about feminism from patriarchal mass media. The feminism they hear about the most is portrayed by women who are primarily committed to gender equality—equal pay for equal work, and sometimes women and men sharing household chores and parenting. They see that these women are usually white and materially privileged. They know from mass media that women's liberation focuses on the freedom to have abortions, to be lesbians, to challenge rape and domestic violence. Among these issues, masses of people agree with the idea of gender equity in the workplace—equal pay for equal work.

Since our society continues to be primarily a "Christian" culture, masses of people continue to believe that god has ordained that women be subordinate to men in the domestic household. Even though masses of women have entered the workforce, even though many families are headed by women who are the sole breadwinners, the vision of domestic life which continues to dominate the nation's imagination is one in which the logic of male domination is intact, whether men are present in the home or not. The wrongminded notion of feminist movement which implied it was anti-male carried with it the wrongminded assumption that all female space would necessarily be an environment where patriarchy and sexist thinking would be absent. Many women, even those involved in feminist politics, chose to believe this as well.

There was indeed a great deal of anti-male sentiment among early feminist activists who were responding to male domination with anger. It was

that anger at injustice that was the impetus for creating a women's liberation movement. Early on most feminist activists (a majority of whom were white) had their consciousness raised about the nature of male domination when they were working in anti-classist and anti-racist settings with men who were telling the world about the importance of freedom while subordinating the women in their ranks. Whether it was white women working on behalf of socialism, black women working on behalf of civil rights and black liberation, or Native American women working for indigenous rights, it was clear that men wanted to lead, and they wanted women to follow. Participating in these radical freedom struggles awakened the spirit of rebellion and resistance in progressive females and led them towards contemporary women's liberation.

As contemporary feminism progressed, as women realized that males were not the only group in our society who supported sexist thinking and behavior—that females could be sexist as well—anti-male sentiment no longer shaped the movement's consciousness. The focus shifted to an all-out effort to create gender justice. But women could not band together to further feminism without confronting our sexist thinking. Sisterhood could not be powerful as long as women were competitively at war with one another. Utopian visions of sisterhood based solely on the awareness of the reality that all women were in some way victimized by male domination were disrupted by discussions of class and race. Discussions of class differences occurred early on in contemporary feminism, preceding discussions of race. Diana Press published revolutionary insights about class divisions between women as early as the mid-'70s in their collection of essays *Class and Feminism*. These discussions did not trivialize the feminist insistence that "sisterhood is powerful," they simply emphasized that we could only become sisters in struggle by confronting the ways women—through sex, class, and race—dominated and exploited other women, and created a political platform that would address these differences.

Even though individual black women were active in contemporary feminist movement from its inception, they were not the individuals who became the "stars" of the movement, who attracted the attention of mass media. Often individual black women active in feminist movement were revolutionary feminists (like many white lesbians). They were already at odds with reformist feminists who resolutely wanted to project a vision of the movement as being solely about women gaining equality with men in the existing system. Even before race became a talked about issue in feminist circles it was clear to black women (and to their revolutionary allies in struggle) that they were never going to have equality within the existing white supremacist capitalist patriarchy.

From its earliest inception feminist movement was polarized. Reformist thinkers chose to emphasize gender equality. Revolutionary thinkers did not want simply to alter the existing system so that women would have more rights. We wanted to transform that system, to bring an end to patriarchy and sexism. Since patriarchal mass media was not interested in the more revolutionary vision, it never received attention in mainstream press. The vision of "women's liberation" which captured and still holds the public imagination was the one representing women as wanting what men had. And this was the vision that was easier to realize. Changes in our nation's economy, economic depression, the loss of jobs, etc., made the climate ripe for our nation's citizens to accept the notion of gender equality in the workforce.

Given the reality of racism, it made sense that white men were more willing to consider women's rights when the granting of those rights could serve the interests of maintaining white supremacy. We can never forget that white women began to assert their need for freedom after civil rights, just at the point when racial discrimination was ending and black people, especially black males, might have attained equality in the workforce with white men. Reformist feminist thinking focusing primarily on equality with men in the workforce overshadowed the original radical foundations of contemporary feminism which called for reform as well as overall restructuring of society so that our nation would be fundamentally anti-sexist.

Most women, especially privileged white women, ceased even to consider revolutionary feminist visions, once they began to gain economic power within the existing social structure. Ironically, revolutionary feminist thinking was most accepted and embraced in academic circles. In those circles the production of revolutionary feminist theory progressed, but more often than not that theory was not made available to the public. It became and remains a privileged discourse available to those among us who are highly literate, well-educated, and usually materially privileged. Works like *Feminist Theory: From Margin to Center* that offer a liberatory vision of feminist transformation never receive mainstream attention. Masses of people have not heard of this book. They have not rejected its message; they do not know what the message is.

While it was in the interest of mainstream white supremacist capitalist patriarchy to suppress visionary feminist thinking which was not anti-male or concerned with getting women the right to be like men, reformist feminists were also eager to silence these forces. Reformist feminism became their route to class mobility. They could break free of male domination in the workforce and be more self-determining in their lifestyles. While sexism did not end, they could maximize their freedom within the existing system. And they could count on there being a lower class of exploited subordinated women to do the dirty work they were refusing to do. By accepting and indeed colluding with the subordination of working-class and poor women, they not only ally themselves with the existing patriarchy and its concomitant sexism, they give themselves the right to lead a double life, one where they are the equals of men in the workforce and at home when they want to be. If they choose lesbianism they have the privilege of being equals with men in the workforce while using class power to create domestic lifestyles where they can choose to have little or no contact with men.

Lifestyle feminism ushered in the notion that there could be as many versions of feminism as there were women. Suddenly the politics was being slowly removed from feminism. And the assumption prevailed that no matter what a woman's politics, be she conservative or liberal, she too could fit feminism into her existing lifestyle. Obviously this way of thinking has made feminism more acceptable because its underlying assumption is that women can be feminists without fundamentally challenging and changing themselves or the culture. For example, let's take the issue of abortion. If feminism is a movement to end sexist oppression, and depriving females of reproductive rights is a form of sexist oppression, then one cannot be anti-choice and be feminist. A woman can insist she would never choose to have an abortion while affirming her support of the right of women to choose and still be an advocate of feminist politics. She cannot be anti-abortion and an advocate of feminism.

Concurrently there can be no such thing as "power feminism" if the vision of power evoked is power gained through the exploitation and oppression of others.

Feminist politics is losing momentum because feminist movement has lost clear definitions. We have those definitions. Let's reclaim them. Let's share them. Let's start over. Let's have T-shirts and bumper stickers and postcards and hip-hop music, television and radio commercials, ads everywhere and billboards, and all manner of printed material that tells the world about feminism. We can share the simple yet powerful message that feminism is a movement to end sexist oppression. Let's start there. Let the movement begin again.

R E A D I N G   **5**

We Are Using This Power to Resist

Rebecca Walker

Life is plurality, death is uniformity.

—*Octavio Paz*

I

Imagine. It's 1992, and I am a graduating senior at Yale University, the school my mother warned me about. I have spent much of my time there protesting: the university's investment in South Africa under apartheid, the paucity of students and faculty of color, the racist-sexist-classist-homophobic characterization and content of my courses. I have attended speak-outs against date rape and sexual harassment and for the creation of a teachers' union, and sat on the founding board of the first paper to bring together voices from the Asian and Asian-American, African

and African-American, Native American, Puerto Rican, and Mexican-American communities under the controversial new term "people of color." For two years I have been directing a documentary on these same "people of color," looking at socioeconomic and ideological diversity among allegedly monolithic communities. When I am not reading queer theorists like Judith Butler (fluidity and performative aspects of gender and sexuality) and cultural critics like Michel Foucault (hegemony and the language of power), or studying with bell hooks (the white supremacist capitalist patriarchy), I am waiting in line to hear the Dalai Lama. When I am not reading Paolo Freire (*Pedagogy of the Oppressed*) and Thich Nhat Hanh (*Peace Is Every Step*), I am being dismissed from lecture halls for asking world-renowned professors why their classes are called The History of Art and not The History of White Western Male Art, and why African women are viciously murdered in so many "postcolonial" texts. When I am not reading Audre Lorde (*Sister Outsider*) and Trinh T. Minh-ha (*Woman, Native, Other*), I am talking with brilliant young black female poets who speak of suicide, and soulful Lebanese philosophers who speak angrily and with great longing of Beirut before the invasion.

Outside my ivory tower, rampant police brutality has been captured on home video (LAPD versus Rodney King), Bush 1 has signed legislation which continues to erode access to reproductive choice to all but the well-heeled and urban (the gag rule, twenty-four-hour notification, and parental consent laws), AIDS deaths mount while the acronym never crosses the administration's lips, and environmental racism perpetuates the dumping of runoff toxins from power plants and factories into poor urban and rural communities around the country. Though it is pre-NAFTA, pre-GATT, and pre-WTO, there are still plenty of international abominations in play—the invasion and interminable bombing of Iraq, for example, and the burgeoning number of women laboring under intolerable conditions at the *maquiladoras,* for another.

Even though almost everyone I know is involved in some form of social change work, from teaching after-school programs for disadvantaged kids to building houses for poor people in inner cities and starting "cheap art" revolutions à la the Guerrilla Girls, the media scream incessantly that ours is the most apathetic and least politicized of any known generation. Feminism is dead, the civil rights movement is not happening, communism is taking its last gasp, and educated twenty-somethings, traditionally the most radical of all demographics, are apparently content to sit back and reap the benefits of our parents' world-changing labor. While some young activists are able to use this distinction to their advantage, incorporating the need to contradict the media into their mission statements, the public hears that the racist, capitalist status quo is acceptable: even the youth have acquiesced.

While my community includes queer-fabulous Chicanos and ACT UP–affiliated lipstick lesbians,

budding black revolutionaries and brilliant baby art stars, neo-utopian Marxist bohemians and well-meaning trust-fund recluses, sensuously defiant womanists and politicized Muslim academics, it seems a rare event to see any of these individuals breaking rank and communicating meaningfully with one another. I certainly never see this happening within the walls of the campus Women's Center, and it's not because I haven't looked. I enter this cramped home of Feminism on the Old Campus once as a freshman and once again as a sophomore, both times looking for resonance and both times finding only the now-too-often cited group of well-off white women, organizing Take Back the Night marches and lectures on eating disorders, neither of which, in the face of all that is going on, manages to capture my imagination.

I am not alone in my assessment that capital *F* Feminism needs an overhaul. By 1992 Feminism has been roundly critiqued by the majority of the world's women, including but not limited to indigenous women, Third World women, American women of color, and working-class women. Even among the privileged and/or converted, there is a resistance to identifying with its rebel yell. Sure, there are those "I am not a feminist but . . . " girls who don't have a clue, but then there are the rest of us, who are feminist but not Feminists. We came to our radical consciousness in the heady postmodern matrix of womanist texts, queer culture, postcolonialist discourse, Buddhism, direct action, sex positivity, and so much more. We are intimate with racist feminists, sexist postcolonialists, and theorists who are so far removed from the street they can't organize their own wallets, let alone a rally. We find that the nexuses of power and identity are constantly shifting, and so are we. We find that labels which seek to categorize and define are historical constructs often used as tools of oppression. We find that many of our potential allies in resistance movements do feminism but do not, intuitively, embrace Feminism.

In the context of all this, to call oneself a Feminist without a major disclaimer seems not only reductive but counterproductive. While this complexity makes for meetings full of fervor and supreme sensitivity to differences of all kinds, it also leaves many of us at the forefront of a movement with no name.

II

Shannon Liss, a young organizer of the Anita Hill conference in New York City, reads an article I have written in *Ms.* magazine titled "Becoming the Third Wave" and telephones me in New Haven to ask if I might be interested in doing something together. In fact, I have been trying to figure out how to organize the two hundred or so young women from around the country who have written me passionate letters echoing my sentiments that "I am not a post-feminism feminist, I am the third wave." To what organization can I refer them? What books can I suggest they read? The book that you are holding in your hands did not exist. There are no articles in *Ms.* magazine about young women doing brave new things. There is not yet a W.E.R.I.S.E., a Black Grrrl Movement, a Shakti, a Third Wave Foundation, an Active Element Foundation. There has not been a "Just do it" Nike campaign for women, an Urban Outfitters chain catering to the earthy, funky DIY young woman, and no WTO protests flying in the face of both. There has been no twenty-something-year-old Julia Butterfly Hill living in a tree for a year to protect it from loggers and then writing a best-selling memoir about the experience. There is no WNBA. Politicians are not trying to win our vote on MTV. There is bell hooks, Queen Latifah, Susie Bright, and the Indigo Girls, but there is no Erykah Badu, no India.Arie, no Ani DiFranco, no asha bandele, no La Bruja on Def Jam Poetry Slam.

In our first of many marathon conversations, Shannon brings her organizing acumen and knowledge of the "Gen X" activism she sees in New York and contextualizes the article and its response within something larger. I bring all of my frustration with identity politics, all of my desires to do social change work that is vibrant and creative and not prone to divisive infighting. Three or four estrogen-packed, burrito-and-margarita-filled meetings later, we decide to found a direct action organization devoted to cultivating young women's leadership and activism in order to bring the power of young women to bear on politics as usual. We want to flex the muscle of young women's might, to make it visible not just to the media and the progressive left but also to the older female activists whose lives have so profoundly shaped our own.

From our first conversation we know that Third Wave Direct Action Corporation will be multiracial, multicultural, and multi-issue. It will consist of people of varying abilities and sexual preferences. It will include men. We hope it will be international. While we have strong opinions about what issues we want to begin to work around, we believe strongly that young women and men will articulate their own concerns, and that it is not our job to decide which are worthy of being included. Our job is to support young activists in whatever ways we can, by connecting them to resources, tools, or most important, one another. The young woman who wants to organize against sweatshop labor or homophobia or toxic dumping in her backyard can call and be connected to other young women with similar foci; groups of young women and men can start chapters (independently acting cells), which can be mobilized for a product boycott, an action, a support group. Because we believe that change is also internal, we plan to initiate projects that bring people of different backgrounds and perspectives together; participants will unite around a common agenda, working interpersonally through issues of difference in the process and learning how to build communities based on mutual respect and understanding.

We pride ourselves on being utopic but also pragmatic. We want to extend the parameters of the "feminist" community and include even those who do not identify with Feminism, and so we make a conscious decision to avoid the use of the word in our mission statement, press releases, and other organizing materials, choosing instead to use "young women's empowerment." We want to be linked with our foremothers and centuries of women's movement, but we also want to make space for young women to create their own, different brand of revolt, and so we choose the name Third Wave. We don't want to be exploited in the name of social change, and so we vow to factor salaries for ourselves into our budgets and call ourselves a corporation. We do not want to be marginalized as we have seen so many activist groups become, and so we vow, too, to be unafraid of both large sums of money and the media, and aggressively seek both out, determined to market our empowerment message.

I speak of marketing social change, and actually feel hopeful when young advertising executives show up at my talks armed with yellow legal pads. They peer at my seemingly incongruous work boots and short dresses, my suit jackets and long dreadlocks, and ask me questions about how young women want to see themselves in the media. I am young and naïve enough to believe that these smart and fresh-faced white women are only on our side, and that by marketing us to ourselves they will help young woman–power of all kinds to grow.

III

What I don't know then is that even though there is no Us and Them, and we need to move beyond binarism and labels and to have compassion for all, including the heads of heinous multinational corporations and the executives at the IMF, the truth is that there is a clear line in the sand. That line is global hypercapitalism, that line is greed, that line is human exploitation, that line is the utter disregard for the delicate balance of the earth. Either you believe that the system that ensures 50 percent of the world's resources for 6 percent of its population by any and all means necessary is leading us to annihilation one cancer case at a time, or you do not. Whether or not you are able to act in opposition to this reality in every instance is beside the point. Do you see it?

What I [didn't] understand in 1992 is that it is this line that separates a system designed to colonize

and homogenize from one that seeks to honor and cultivate the diversity that is our birthright as human beings. Those of us who dare, toil not to force our way upon others but simply to make a space in which all are honored: capitalism and communalism, the patriarch and the matriarch, the exiled settler and the indigenous nomad, and so on. It is this imperative for true pluralism that runs through and connects, however tenuously, all of our different activisms, all of our different feminisms. It is this place where we all may rest that snakes through our dreams. We can barely imagine now what this world fueled by real right to self-determination will look like, and yet we know it must be born. As we belong to it, this planet must belong to all of us.

While I believe that Shannon and I were right about some things—decentralized, multifront, multilingual, and multi-aesthetic movement for one, and working with men and families for another—we were wrong about some other things, like the very real risk of our own complacency, our own tendency to get more cynical and pessimistic with age, more removed from the cultural and political work there is to be done instead of more radical. I think that we were right about pushing our sensibility and ideas into the marketplace of the mainstream but we were shortsighted in that we did not anticipate that young women and men would think buying books or magazines, or supporting films and fashion that reflected their diverse beauty and beliefs, could replace the many important struggles still to be waged against an unjust system. And finally, while we were right to found an organization, we had no idea just how much effort and endurance was necessary to build an institution, let alone a movement.

Third Wave Direct Action had a fairly successful run spearheading projects, building a national network, and raising awareness about the existence of some incredible young women. Ultimately, however, then-Chairwoman of the Board Amy Richards and I decided to reenvision its original scope and, with the cofounders Catherine Gund and Dawn Lundy Martin, to throw ourselves into the Third Wave Foundation, the only national, activist, philanthropic organization serving women aged fifteen to thirty. In other words, we realized we had to get out of the business of direct action and into the business of redistributing wealth, of moving it from one side of the line to the other. We had to get real about what was essential and what we, a group of privileged, educated women born and raised in the United States, could provide.

And yet, I cannot adequately describe here the tremendous pride and gratitude I feel in the knowledge that our dreams for revitalized, multipronged movement are being realized. Whether the work is called third wave, young feminism, hip-hop womanism, humanist global activism, or anything else matters very little. What matters is that this work is being done by women and men from various communities who slowly, step by step, find themselves working alongside those who previously may have been seen only as Other.

There is a fire this time, burning, and it cannot, will not, go out, because that would mean the end of life as we know it. And we, those of us who love this planet and one another, are not yet ready to let that happen.

R E A D I N G **6**

The Global Stage and the Politics of Location

Estelle B. Freedman

To talk feminism to a woman who has no water, no food and no home is to talk nonsense.
—*NGO Forum '80, Denmark, 1980*

Everything is a woman's issue.
—*Charlotte Bunch, United States, 1985*

In her 1984 essay "Notes Toward a Politics of Location," the American poet Adrienne Rich reevaluated her earlier use of the category "woman" in light of the writings of women of color. Acknowledging her own "politics of location" as a North American, white, Jewish lesbian, Rich named "the faceless, raceless classless category of all women as a creation of white, western, self-centered women." Because national and political location affected women throughout the world, Rich reconsidered Virginia Woolf's statement that "as a woman I have no country; as a woman my country is the whole world." One's country, she suggested, deeply influenced one's view of the world and of womanhood.[1]

Other Western feminists, stimulated by women of color and women outside the West, were also recognizing the "politics of location." In 1978, for example, a special issue of the radical feminist journal *Quest* on international feminism asked readers, "Can we talk about the global oppression of women—its causes and lives—in any universal terms?" In an influential 1988 essay, sociologist Chandra Mohanty argued persuasively against the Western feminist assumption of "a commonality of the category of women."[2] Mohanty called on Western feminists to understand how local contexts created gender relations that differed from those in the West. Neither oppression nor liberation looked the same from the perspective of women in Asia, Africa, Latin America, and the Middle East. Just as women of color transformed U.S. feminism, so too exchanges across nations placed Western women's rights movements within the contexts of racial and social justice as well as national sovereignty.

. . .

In addition, international organizations provided a forum for both communication and conflict among diverse women's movements. A key locus of these discussions was the Decade for Women, declared by the United Nations from 1975 to 1985. Subsequent regional and international gatherings, including the UN's Fourth World Conference on Women, held in Beijing in 1995, facilitated transnational feminist organizing across regions. By the end of the twentieth century, women's movements had expanded to all parts of the world—in rural and urban settings, in liberal or conservative states. From a history of colonial encounters to a growing transnational movement, the politics of location have taken both common and diverse paths to gender equality.

. . .

THE ORIGINS OF INTERNATIONAL FEMINISM

Because diverse local contexts forged women's politics, early efforts to create an international movement faced formidable challenges. European and U.S. feminists had corresponded and met since the 1840s. Beginning in the 1880s they built organizations to promote goals ranging from temperance and pacifism to socialism and suffrage. Until World War I, the movement was international in name only. Western European and American women initiated the groups and then encouraged local chapters to form in other parts of the world. As European world domination declined after the war, however, women in Latin America, Asia, and Africa increasingly took part in the International Woman Suffrage Alliance, the International Council of Women, and the Women's International League for Peace and Freedom. The leadership remained dominated by elite, white, Christian women from northern and western Europe. Anti-Semitism placed limits on the roles of European Jewish women, while Huda Sha'arawi from Egypt was the only Muslim among leaders of the suffrage alliance. Significantly, although Sha'arawi aligned with Western feminists on suffrage, she chastised these allies when they supported colonialism. Aware of the

limitations of European women's "universalism," she also fostered pan-Arab women's movements, including the establishment of the regional Arab Feminist Union in 1945.

The earliest efforts to create an international women's movement often reproduced colonial relations. When European women spoke of aiding "primitives," for example, they relied on the same stereotypes of passive, helpless others that characterized missionary and colonialist rhetoric. Just as women of color within the United States challenged white feminists to recognize their racial biases, so too women from Asia, Africa, and the Middle East took issue with what scholars later termed "feminist orientalism," the tendency to view all women outside the West as exotic, sexually oppressed others.[3] In 1920 black women from the United States and Africa responded to comments demeaning to them by forming the International Council of Women of the Darker Races. At an international conference in 1935, Shareefeh Hamid Ali of India spoke for women "of the East" when she explained to "you of the west" that "any arrogant assumption of superiority or of patronage on the part of Europe or America" would alienate "the womanhood of Asia and Africa."[4] These women expected support from Western feminists in their dual struggle for personal and national independence.

Some Western feminists understood that they could learn a great deal from other women, many of whom already enjoyed privileges not available in Europe and North America. In the early 1900s the *Jus Suffragii*, the international suffrage journal, reported on the economic and political rights that women enjoyed as traders in Africa or as municipal voters in Burma. The U.S. suffrage leader Carrie Chapman Catt could be patronizing about the need to "uplift" women outside the West, but she also recognized that millions of these women "have always enjoyed more personal freedom than was accorded to most European women a century ago, and more than is now permitted to thousands of women under our boasted Western civilization."[5] Articles in the suffrage journal also pointed out how European efforts had eroded women's customary authority, and they acknowledged that

Islam was not necessarily oppressive to women. Eventually the international women's movement recognized that women outside the West were perfectly capable of establishing their own women's movements, which could meet on equal terms with European and American organizations.

Most of the European women involved in international feminist organizing espoused liberal goals of educational, property, and voting rights; many shared maternalist sympathies for improving women's family lives through temperance and antiprostitution movements. In addition, socialist women influenced international movements, largely in those countries with strong Marxist politics. The Socialist Women's International organized by Clara Zetkin in 1907 favored woman suffrage for all classes along with social justice. After World War II a Communist Party women's international backed by Moscow raised women's issues but avoided the word *feminist*.

World War II represented a turning point for women's organizing, as it did for international relations generally. Aside from women's cooperative relief efforts, the war gave rise to political institutions, such as the United Nations, that fostered international feminism. In the decades after the war, the rhetoric of democratic rights first articulated two centuries earlier during the European Enlightenment extended far beyond its original geographic boundaries. The remaining colonial empires soon gave way to independent states. This expansion of the ideals of human rights had important implications for both the former colonies and women's movements.

Despite the extension of national self-determination beyond the West, the postcolonial world faced huge economic disparities. Former colonies, termed the "Third World," "developing nations," or the "South," remained dependent on the advanced industrial nations for financial and technological investments. They also became a battleground in the Cold War struggle for alliance with either the "First World" of the West or the "Second World" of the Communist bloc. True independence—for countries or for individuals—required not only national sover-

eignty but also economic stability and international security.

The United Nations provided a potential global forum for discussing human rights, economic justice, and international security. The 1945 UN charter incorporated both Enlightenment ideals and the language of liberal feminism when it reaffirmed "faith in fundamental human rights, in the dignity and worth of the human person, in the equal rights of men and women." The document repeatedly called for rights, freedoms, and respect for all "without distinctions to race, sex, language, or religion."

In 1947, as part of its mechanisms to foster economic and social progress, the UN established the Commission on the Status of Women. Two years later the General Assembly agreed upon the Declaration of Human Rights, which applied the principle of equal rights to thought, opinions, privacy, education, work, leisure, and peace. Significantly, it also incorporated the domestic concerns of maternalist reformers such as Eleanor Roosevelt, who provided the driving force behind its adoption. Along with adult men and women sharing "equal rights as to marriage, during marriage and at its dissolution," the declaration proclaimed that "motherhood and childhood are entitled to special care and assistance," whether a child was born "in or out of wedlock."[6] However idealistic these pronouncements, the UN has had a wide-reaching practical impact on the kinds of health and welfare issues long championed by maternalist reformers. Nongovernmental organizations (NGOs) such as the World Health Organization (WHO) and the United Nations International Children's Emergency Fund (UNICEF) have both channeled aid and nurtured cross-cultural communication among those concerned about the status of women.

These networks expanded after the UN declared 1975 to be International Women's Year, launching the Decade for Women. Three international conferences on women's issues punctuated the decade. Delegates from 133 nations gathered in Mexico City in 1975; in 1980, 145 nations were represented in Copenhagen; and in 1985 representatives from 157 countries met in Nairobi. These conferences provided a critical intersection where Western feminists encountered the political and material realities of women's lives outside the West.

Although a majority of the participants were women, men dominated the speeches and leadership at Mexico City in 1975. The official delegates often represented the interests of their governments, not necessarily those of women's organizations. At Copenhagen, for example, a male delegate from the USSR declared that there was no discrimination against women in the Soviet Union because the law forbade such discrimination, and there was no such thing as sexism in his country because there was no such word in the Russian language. As women at the UN pressed for equality, however, the conferences included more female leadership and the discussions turned to the gaps between male and female opportunities.

Equally important, women from around the world who were not official delegates gathered at parallel meetings held during each of the UN conferences. A tribune outside the Mexico City meeting attracted six thousand activists; the forums at Copenhagen and Nairobi grew from ten thousand in 1980 to fifteen thousand in 1985. Though Western-dominated at first, 65 percent of the participants at Nairobi came from developing countries, and women of color from the West now played leading roles. With no formal governmental agendas, these forums provided opportunities for intense communications, at times quite heated. Representatives of NGOs ran workshops and panels to share their efforts to combat poverty, violence against women, female genital cutting, and illiteracy. Each topic provoked conflict over political strategies. In Copenhagen women spontaneously organized sessions every day, such as one sponsored by Norwegian women called "Sisterhood—A Myth?" A daily free newspaper announced workshops and criticized the politics of the official conference, whose delegates could not avoid the radical ferment around them.

The political tensions that reverberated through each meeting reflected the imbalance of power between advanced industrial and developing nations. When U.S. feminists arrived in Mexico City to talk about equal rights, for example,

they immediately encountered criticism from delegates who did not want to discuss gender outside the context of movements for national self-determination. The U.S. government did not want the politics of apartheid in South Africa or the Israeli-Palestinian conflict on the agenda. Greek delegate Margaret Papandreou called this U.S. position "antifeminist" for trying to separate politics from women's issues.[7]

At the NGO forums women did debate international politics as well as economic development policies. Western feminists arrived with a focus on equal rights to education, property, and political authority. For women from Asia, Africa, and Latin America, however, rural and urban poverty represented the most pressing challenges to human rights. "To talk feminism to a woman who has no water, no food and no home is to talk nonsense," the *NGO Forum* newspaper at Copenhagen explained.[8] Responding to this sentiment, the 1985 NGO Forum in Nairobi convened workshops to discuss the variety of regional contexts that feminism must address.

The exchanges at the official UN conference and the unofficial NGO meetings proved highly educational for Western feminists. Delegates learned about the daily problems that confronted women globally: living under apartheid in South Africa; struggling for self-determination in Palestine; bringing water, sewers, and electricity to poor Brazilian women; trying to feed families throughout the world. The NGO gatherings especially convinced many Western women that world poverty and national liberation were feminist issues because they affected women's lives around the globe. After attending the Copenhagen conference, Charlotte Bunch, a radical lesbian feminist in the United States during the 1970s, began to address international women's issues. In preparing for the 1985 NGO forum in Nairobi, she came to the conclusion that "the beginning point at both conferences must be that *everything* is a woman's issue. That means racism is a woman's issue, just as is anti-Semitism, Palestinian homelessness, rural development, ecology, the persecution of lesbians, and the exploitative practices of global corporations."[9]

Women from developing nations also felt the profound effects of these conferences. Valsa Verghese, who came from India to attend the Copenhagen conference, initially felt "frustration and confusion" at the multitude of choices at the NGO Forum. By the end she found it "heartening to realize that in spite of cultural differences there was so much in common to unite us, to feel the bond of sisterhood, to break the isolation of women and to feel the growing power within us."[10] The meetings also exposed women to the potential of feminism for their own local politics. A Latin American woman who was "not at all interested in feminism" before attending the Copenhagen conference wrote that "after seeing how governments and the UN treat women and what has and has not happened in the Forum, I am now considering the potential of feminism seriously."[11]

. . .

RETHINKING FEMINISM IN THE POSTCOLONIAL WORLD

Creating a transnational women's movement requires that feminists overcome the legacies of colonialism. That challenging task means reaching across cultures without imposing Western notions of superiority and acknowledging the multiple forms that both injustice and emancipation may take. Two international issues embody the tensions inherent in women's global encounters. The first, international development programs, highlights the dilemmas of liberal feminist politics, which founder over the role of gender difference in efforts to achieve gender equality. The second, the notion of "global feminism," highlights the weaknesses of both liberalism and a radical feminism that overlooks class and race distinctions among women. Both serve as reminders that economic and political strategies must take into account the particular strengths of women's local heritage.

During the 1970s and 1980s the United Nations and other international organizations began to rethink the role of women in economic development programs. The international efforts to stim-ulate economic growth in the developing regions begun after World War II had failed to undermine the extensive poverty in these countries. Along with the earlier goal of expanding national productivity, UN agencies turned their attention to the growing inequalities of wealth. The impoverishment of women represented a major obstacle to economic justice, and the UN Decade for Women provided a forum for reviewing development policy through the lens of gender.

In *Woman's Role in Economic Development* (1970) Ester Boserup argued that most development programs had failed to take into account women's productive roles. In the rush to increase productivity in developing nations, planners and lenders such as the World Bank and the International Monetary Fund concentrated on male workers. Foreign aid provided men with land, credit, and tools and expected wives to provide domestic labor. As a result, the gender gap in technology, wealth, and status widened. Describing West Africa in the mid-twentieth century, Boserup observed that "men ride the bicycle and drive the lorry, while women carry head loads, as did their grandmothers. In short, men represent modern farming in the village, women represent the old drudgery."[12] When development programs considered women at all it was usually in their capacity as mothers targeted by family planning efforts to reduce population growth.

In the past, African women had contributed to the economy, especially as producers of food. Boserup and other scholars wanted to integrate rural women into new forms of production though education and training. A school of thought termed Women in Development (WID) made the case that full economic development required a recognition of women's contributions to the economy and their integration into production. Rather than viewing women as dependents in families, WID argued, they should be encouraged to generate income, either as small entrepreneurs or as factory laborers.

WID advocates helped extend modernization policies to women in the developing regions by drawing women into the market economy. As several scholars have noted, WID represented "liberal feminism writ global," for it rested upon liberal values of individualism, self-interest, and private property.[13] To an extent, this approach succeeded in adding gender to the policy debates on international development. In practical terms, WID also laid the groundwork for the influx of young Latin American and Asian women into manufacturing jobs in the free-trade zones where multinational corporations established factories. It also lent support for efforts to educate girls.

Even as international development programs began to integrate women into national productivity goals, criticisms of WID emerged. The South Asian feminist scholar Naila Kabeer summarized the problem: WID recognized women's productive potential at the expense of appreciating their unpaid work in the household. Ignoring reproductive and household labor placed women in a double bind. Women workers could not earn enough money to purchase the household and child care services they needed in order to be able to leave their homes to work for pay. By assuming a similarity between female and male workers, WID overlooked important differences, particularly the realities of motherhood. Without taking into account both women's biological capacity for childbearing and the structural inequalities of race and class, WID could not contribute to solving the problems of women's, and world, poverty.

Moreover, simply mobilizing women as workers did not necessarily empower them, a lesson that women of color in the West long realized. In her study of Malaysian factory workers, anthropologist Aihwa Ong concluded that these women may have exchanged patriarchal control within their families for industrial surveillance and discipline in the factory. As one worker complained of her foremen, "They give this job, that job, and even before my task is done they say do that, do this, and before that is ready, they say do some other work." In the words of another Malaysian factory worker, "It would be nice working here if the foremen, managers, all the staff members and clerks understand that the workers are not under their control."[14]

The flaws of merely drawing women into the labor force became apparent by the end of the UN Decade for Women. During the period when WID

policies dominated, women's economic resources had declined, not improved. In response to the shortcomings of WID, feminists recommended a new approach known as Gender and Development, or GAD. Since the 1980s GAD advocates have attempted to take into account women's customary economic and family responsibilities when they implement development policies. GAD addresses issues such as the relationships of men and women to natural resources and the impact of male migration on women's work and responsibilities. Rather than exclude women from, or integrate them into, a male model, the GAD approach builds upon rural women's practices, such as their traditional knowledge about agriculture. In projects that recognize female expertise in native plant diversity, development agencies turn to local women as authorities for seed selection. As Mona Khalaf, of the Institute for Women's Studies in the Arab World in Beirut, Lebanon, explains, GAD has broadened development analysis to discuss "sustainable human development, a development achieved by people and not for them."[15] The UN has adopted the goal of "stimulating growth with equity" by providing resources to both women and men in sustainable development projects.

[Another] feminist dilemma concerns the controversial notion of a "universal sisterhood" that presumes the relevance of Western politics to the rest of the world, regardless of local conditions. In Amrita Basu's terms, the "challenge of local feminisms" complicates sisterhood.[16] Although patriarchy may subordinate women all over the world, as a group of African women scholars explains, "women are also members of classes and countries that dominate others. . . . Contrary to the best intentions of 'sisterhood,' not all women share identical interests."[17] Just as women of color in the West testified about their racially specific identities, women outside the West have explained why gender cannot be the sole determinant of their politics. Peasant and working-class women in Africa, Asia, and Latin America have been adamant that for them, economic justice, along with cultural and national sovereignty, must become a priority of feminism. In contrast to European and North American drives for individual rights, these local activists often stress women's domestic identities and the needs of family and community. At times they turn to innovative cooperative structures rather than purely individualistic ones, building upon women's mutual support networks.

. . .

Western feminist politics achieved its earliest victories by calling for the extension to women of men's growing political and economic rights. Transnational women's movements recognize as well the political importance of alternative strategies that draw on women's heritage of raising their families, maintaining their cultures, and empowering themselves. Women throughout the world developed these survival skills under patriarchy; before a politics of rights, they often relied on reciprocal family and social obligations to maintain a balance of power between men and women. By insisting on adequate care for women's families, these strategies complement equal rights arguments and broaden the reach of women's movements.

REDEFINING FEMINISM

By the end of the UN Decade for Women, women in the developing world had redefined feminism, rejecting the myth of global sisterhood in favor of a more heterogeneous and flexible framework. As participants at the Nairobi conference explained in 1985, feminism "constitutes the political expression of the concerns and interests of women from different regions, classes, nationalities, and ethnic backgrounds. . . . There is and must be a diversity of feminisms, responsive to the different needs and concerns of different women, and defined by them for themselves."[18] For Western women, the myth of global sisterhood had to give way to the politics of location. The result has been a more realistic notion of transnational feminism. In this model, an understanding of historical and cultural differences among women provides the base for alliances across those differences.

NOTES

1. Adrienne Rich, "Notes Towards a Politics of Location," *Blood, Bread, and Poetry* (New York W. W. Norton, 1986), 210–31.

2. Chandra Mohanty, "Under Western Eyes: Feminist Scholarship and Colonial Discourses," *Feminist Review* 30 (1988), 61–85.

3. Joyce Zonana, "The Sultan and the Slave: Feminist Orientalism and the Structure of *Jane Eyre*," *Signs* 18:3 (1993), 592–617; Leila Rupp, *Worlds of Women: The Making of an International Women's Movement* (Princeton, N.J.: Princeton University Press, 1977), 75ff.

4. Quoted in Rupp, *Worlds of Women,* 80.

5. Ibid., 77.

6. Ibid., 224–25: "Universal Declaration of Human Rights," in *Human Rights Documents* (Washington, D.C.: U.S. Government Printing Office, 1983), 61–67.

7. Quoted in Barry Schlachter, "International News," Associated Press, Nairobi, Kenya, July 15, 1985.

8. NGO *Forum* '80 newsletter (Copenhagen), quoted in Charlotte Bunch, *Passionate Politics: Feminists Theory in Action* (New York: St. Martin's Press, 1987), 299.

9. Charlotte Bunch, "U.N. World Conference in Nairobi: A View from the West," *Ms.* 13:12 (1985), 79–82, reprinted in Bunch, *Passionate Politics.* 325.

10. Quoted in Arvonne S. Fraser, *The U.N. Decade for Women: Documents and Dialogue* (Boulder: Westview Press, 1987), 155.

11. Quoted in Bunch, *Passionate Politics,* 300.

12. Ester Boserup, *Woman's Role in Economic Development* (New York: St. Martin's Press, 1970), 56.

13. Naila Kabeer, *Reserved Realities: Gender Hierarchies in Development Thought* (London: W. W. Norton, 1994), 27.

14. Aihwa Ong, *Spirits of Resistance and Capitalist Discipline* (New York: State University of New York Press, 1999), 163–68.

15. "The 25 Year Life Story of the Institute for Women's Studies in the Arab World," *Al-Raida* 57 (1998). 83–84. See also Helen Zweifel, "The Gendered Nature of Biodiversity Conservation," *National Women's Studies Association Journal* 9:3 (1997), 106–16.

16. The term comes from Amrita Basu, ed., *The Challenge of Local Feminisms: Women's Movements in Global Perspective* (Boulder: Westview Press, 1995).

17. Association of African Women for Research and Development, "A Statement on Genital Mutilation,"

in *Third World, Second Sex: Women's Struggle and National Liberation/Third World Woman Speak Out,* ed. Miranda Device (London: Zed Books, 1983), vol. 2, 217–19.

18. Nilufer Cagatay, Caren Grown, and Aida Santiago, "Nairobi Women's Conference: Toward a Global Feminism?" (1986), quoted in Johnson-Odim, "Common Thomas," 925.

R E A D I N G *7*

Denials of Inequality

Deborah L. Rhode

Americans' most common response to gender inequality is to deny its dimensions. A widespread perception is that once upon a time, women suffered serious discrimination, but those days are over. Barriers have been coming down, women have been moving up, and full equality is just around the corner. If anything, many men believe that women are now getting undeserved advantages. In a series of recent articles with titles like "The Decline and Fall of the White Male," commentators air their view that "merit is out," "special privileges" are in, and the only group that can't claim equal protection under law is white men. "Pale males eat it again," announces a character in Michael Crichton's popular film *Disclosure.* This perspective is widely shared. According to recent polls, close to half of all men think that they are subject to unfair penalties for advantages that others had in the past. Two-thirds of men and three-quarters of male business leaders do not believe that women encounter significant discrimination for top positions in business, professions, or government.

Such views are difficult to square with the facts. White males account for about 40 percent of the population but about 95 percent of senior managers, 90 percent of newspaper editors, 80 percent of the *Forbes* list of richest Americans, and 80 percent of congressional legislators. Significant sex-based disparities in employment salaries and status persist, even when researchers control for objective factors such as education, experience, and hours worked. As *Newsweek's*

article "White Male Paranoia" points out, the pale male certainly appears to be "holding his own (and most of everybody else's) in the world of hard facts"; it's only in the "world of images and ideas . . . [that] he's taking a clobbering."

What explains this gap between popular perceptions and concrete data on gender inequality? Part of the explanation lies with selective perception. Men often deny bias because they fail to recognize it. They usually don't need to, it does not significantly affect their lives. As with race, part of the privilege of dominance is the privilege of accepting without noticing its benefits.

. . .

For obvious reasons, women are more sensitive to gender inequality than men are, but some perceptual blinders persist among both sexes. Not all women encounter all forms of bias, and those who lack personal experience sometimes fail to appreciate collective problems. What sociologists label the "Queen Bee Syndrome" is common among some professionally successful women. Their attitude is "I managed, why can't you?"

Many women also are unable to see patterns of discrimination because important parts of the picture are missing or murky. Salary, hiring, and promotion data that compare similarly qualified men and women are hard to come by, and the most overt sexism has gone underground. As a 1989 Supreme Court case revealed, male employers may still penalize a woman who they think needs courses in "charm school." But that is no longer what they say in mixed company or in personnel records. Moreover, gender is only one of the characteristics, and not always the most important one, that disadvantages women. Race, ethnicity, class, disability, and sexual orientation often overshadow or interact with gender.

. . .

Self-interest complicates the process. For some men, the increasing unacceptability of sexism, coupled with the inconvenience of eliminating it, encourages various strategies of self-deception. These techniques frequently surface on issues of household work. Employed men, who average only half as much time as employed women on family tasks, generally manage not to notice the disparity. In one recent poll, over two-thirds of surveyed husbands reported that they shared childrearing duties equally with their wives, an assessment wildly inconsistent with that of most wives and virtually all reported research.

Moreover, even men who acknowledge disparities often view women's extra tasks as matters of personal choice, not joint responsibility. Rather than accept an equal division of cleaning, cooking, or childcare obligations, some men redefine their share as unnecessary; they don't mind a little mess or a fast-food dinner, and their infants will do just fine with extra time among their "friends" at daycare. Other men seem not to notice when some of their assigned tasks need doing, or else mismanage key parts of the job. Rather than broadcast constant reminders of complaints, many women simply pick up pieces that their partners don't even realize have been dropped. As one wife wearily noted, "I do my half, I do half of [my husband's half], and the rest doesn't get done."

. . .

Part of what keeps men, and often women, from recognizing that gap is their choice of reference groups. Where gender appears to be a relevant characteristic, most individuals compare themselves to members of their own sex. In assessing domestic burdens, husbands look to other husbands or their own fathers rather than to wives. From this perspective, unequal divisions of labor become easy to rationalize because they remain the norm rather than the exception.

Women also tend to compare their family burdens to those of members of their own sex. As a result, many wives deny that their husbands do less than their "fair share" around the home, even when responsibilities are grossly unequal. Cultural attitudes reinforce such perceptions. As Anna Quindlen notes, "When men do the dishes it's called helping. When women do dishes, that's called life." Most women are not fully aware of how much time they or their partners spend on family work and generally believe that their arrangements are far more equal than they truly are.

This is not to imply that women totally fail to notice gender inequalities in household burdens. How much help they receive (or don't receive) from their male partners shows up in opinion surveys as one of the greatest sources of resentment. Yet even women who are most resentful often do not expect an equal division of household work. It is only their partner's refusal to help with particular jobs or his inability to justify refusing, that triggers conflict. And for many women, avoiding conflict is more important than achieving equality. They, like their male counterparts, use selective perception as a form of self-protection.

Similar patterns operate in other contexts. According to workplace surveys, even when women recognize gender discrimination as a problem or where objective evidence points to that conclusion, most individuals still do not believe that they personally have been targets. Although many critics denounce feminism for encouraging women to exaggerate their own victimization, recent research finds that individuals generally are reluctant to see themselves in that light. Acknowledging vulnerability carries a cost: it erodes individuals' sense of control and self-esteem, and involves the unpleasantness of identifying a perpetrator. Many women understandably are unwilling to alienate men whose approval is important personally and professionally.

Although some individuals enjoy nursing grievances and claiming the moral leverage of victim status, most do not. As Hillary Clinton once noted, "Who wants to walk around constantly with clenched fists?" Particularly where women feel powerless to avoid inequality, they are likely to avoid acknowledging it.

Still Needing the F Word

Anna Quindlen

Let's use the F word here. People say it's inappropriate, offensive, that it puts people off. But it seems to me it's the best way to begin, when it's simultaneously devalued and invaluable.

Feminist. Feminist, Feminist, Feminist.

Conventional wisdom has it that we've moved on to a postfeminist era, which is meant to suggest that the issues have been settled, the inequities addressed, and all is right with the world. And then suddenly from out of the South like Hurricane Everywoman, a level '03 storm, comes something like the new study on the status of women at Duke University,* and the notion that we're post-anything seems absurd. Time to use the F word again, no matter how uncomfortable people may find it.

Fem-i-nism *n. 1. Belief in the social, political and economic equality of the sexes.*

That wasn't so hard, was it? Certainly not as hard as being a female undergraduate at Duke, where apparently the operative ruling principle is something described as "effortless perfection," in which young women report expending an enormous amount of effort on clothes, shoes, workout programs and diet. And here's a blast from the past: they're expected "to hide their intelligence in order to succeed with their male peers."

"Being 'cute' trumps being smart for women in the social environment," the report concludes.

That's not postfeminist. That's prefeminist. Betty Friedan wrote *The Feminine Mystique* exactly 40 years ago, and yet segments of the Duke report could have come right out of her book. One

17-year-old girl told Friedan, "I used to write poetry. The guidance office says I have this creative ability and I should be at the top of the class and have a great future. But things like that aren't what you need to be popular. The important thing for a girl is to be popular."

Of course, things have changed. Now young women find themselves facing not one, but two societal, and self-imposed, straitjackets. Once they obsessed about being the perfect homemaker and meeting the standards of their male counterparts. Now they also obsess about being the perfect professional and meeting the standards of their male counterparts. In the decades since Friedan's book became a best seller, women have won the right to do as much as men do. They just haven't won the right to do as little as men do. Hence, effortless perfection.

While young women are given the impression that all doors are open, all boundaries down, empirical evidence is to the contrary. A study from Princeton issued at the same time as the Duke study showed that faculty women in the sciences reported less satisfaction in their jobs and less of a sense of belonging than their male counterparts. Maybe that's because they made up only 14 percent of the faculty in those disciplines, or because one out of four reported their male colleagues occasionally or frequently engaged in unprofessional conduct focusing on gender issues.

Californians were willing to ignore Arnold Schwarzenegger's alleged career as a serial sexual bigot, despite a total of 16 women coming forward to say he thought nothing of reaching up your skirt or into your blouse. (Sure, they're only allegations. But it was Arnold himself who said that where there's smoke, there's fire. In this case,

---

*In the Fall, 2003, Duke University published a comprehensive Women's Initiative Report that documented the full range of women's experiences at the university.

there was a conflagration.) The fact that one of the actor's defenses was that he didn't realize this was objectionable—and that voters were OK with that—speaks volumes about enduring assumptions about women. What if he'd habitually publicly humiliated black men, or Latinos, or Jews? Yet the revelation that the guy often demeaned women with his hands was written off as partisan politics and even personal behavior. Personal behavior is when you have a girlfriend. When you touch someone intimately without her consent, it's sexual battery.

The point is not that the world has not changed for women since Friedan's book lobbed a hand grenade into the homes of pseudohappy housewives who couldn't understand the malaise that accompanied sparkling Formica and good-looking kids. Hundreds of arenas, from government office to the construction trades, have opened to working women. Of course, when it leaks out that the Vatican is proposing to scale back on the use of altar girls, it shows that the forces of reaction are always waiting, whether beneath hard hats or miters.

But the world hasn't changed as much as we like to tell ourselves. Otherwise, *The Feminine Mystique* wouldn't feel so contemporary. Otherwise Duke University wouldn't find itself concentrating on eating disorders and the recruitment of female faculty. Otherwise, the governor-elect of California wouldn't be a guy who thinks it's "playful" to grab and grope, and the voters wouldn't ratify that attitude. Part fair game, part perfection: that's a tough standard for 51 percent of everyone. The first women's-rights activists a century ago set out to prove, in Friedan's words, "that woman was not a passive empty mirror." How dispiriting it would be to those long-ago heroines to read of the women at Duke focused on their "cute" reflections in the eyes of others. The F word is not an expletive, but an ideal—one that still has a way to go.

DISCUSSION QUESTIONS FOR CHAPTER 1

1. Why are you taking a women's studies course?

2. What are your expectations, fears, anxieties, and hopes about taking a women's studies class?

3. Why did women's studies emerge in the academic community?

4. What are negative stereotypes of feminism? Where do they come from? How do these stereotypes serve to perpetuate the dominant social order?

5. Do you think on the whole equality has been achieved? Why or why not? Are there places where you see room for improvement or the need for drastic change?

SUGGESTIONS FOR FURTHER READING

Freedman, Estelle B. *No Turning Back: The History of Feminism and the Future of Women.* New York: Ballantine, 2002.

Henry, Astrid. *Not My Mother's Sister: Generational Conflict and Third-Wave Feminism.* Bloomington: Indiana University Press, 2004.

Hercus, Cheryl. *Stepping Out of Line: Becoming and Being Feminist.* New York: Routledge, 2005.

Hernandez, Daisy, and Bushra Rheman, eds. *Colonize This! Young Women of Color on Today's Feminism*. New York: Avalon, 2002.

hooks, bell. *Feminism Is for Everybody: Passionate Politics*. Boston: South End, 2000.

—. *Teaching to Transgress: Education as the Practice of Freedom*. New York: Routledge, 1994.

MacDonald, Amie, and Susan Sanchez, eds. *Twenty-First Century Feminist Classrooms: Pedagogies of Identity and Difference*. New York: St. Martin's, 2002.

Messer-Davidow, Ellen. *Disciplining Feminism: How Women's Studies Transformed the Academy and Was Transformed by It*. Durham, NC: Duke University Press, 2002.

Rogers, Mary F., and C. D. Garrett. *Who's Afraid of Women's Studies? Feminisms in Everyday Life*. Walnut Creek, CA: Alta Mira Press, 2002.

Rowe-Finkbeiner, Kristin. *The F Word: Feminism in Jeopardy: Women, Politics, and the Future*. Emeryville, CA: Seal, 2004.

CHAPTER 2

Systems of Privilege and Inequality in Women's Lives

Women are as different as we/they are alike. Although sharing some conditions, including having primary responsibility for children and being victims of male violence, women's lives are marked by difference. This is a result of the varying conditions and material practices of women's existence in global communities and the societies in which these communities are embedded. We inhabit different cultures whose norms or cultural expectations prescribe different ways of acting as women and different sanctions if these norms are broken. It is therefore important to recognize difference and, as already discussed in Chapter 1, avoid using "woman" as a universal or homogeneous category that assumes sameness.

In the United States our differences are illustrated by the material conditions of our lives; the values, cultures, behavioral practices, and legal structures of the communities in which we live; and even the geographic region of the country we inhabit. In particular, we are different in terms of race and ethnicity, religion, age, looks, sexual identity, socioeconomic status, and ability. Just as it is important to question the homogenizing notions of sameness in terms of the category "woman" across societies, it is also important to understand that these universalizing tendencies work against our understanding of women in the United States as well. Often we tend to think of women in comparison to a *mythical norm:* White, middle-class, heterosexual, abled, thin, and a young adult, which is normalized or taken for granted such that we often forget that Whites are racialized and men are gendered. Asking the question "Different from what?" reveals how difference gets constructed against what people think of as normal and what is perceived as normal is that which those in power are able to define as normal.

It is important to recognize that the meanings associated with differences are socially constructed. These social constructions would not be problematic were they not created against the notion of the mythical norm. Being a lesbian would not be a "difference" that invoked cultural resistance if it were not for *compulsory heterosexuality,* the notion that everyone should be heterosexual and have relationships with the opposite sex. This concept is illustrated in "The Social Construction of Disability" by Susan Wendell. She makes the case that *ableism,* discrimination against the mentally and physically disabled, is a direct result of social factors that actively create standards of normality against which ability/disability is constructed. In this chapter we focus on differences among women and explore the ways systems of privilege and inequality are created out of these differences.

DIFFERENCE, HIERARCHY, AND SYSTEMS OF OPPRESSION

Society recognizes the ways people are different and assigns group membership based on these differences; at the same time, society also ranks the differences (Figure 2.1). Male is placed above female, thin above fat, economically privileged above poor, and so forth. These rankings of groups and their members create a hierarchy

Figure 2.1
Intersecting Axes of Privilege, Domination, and Oppression

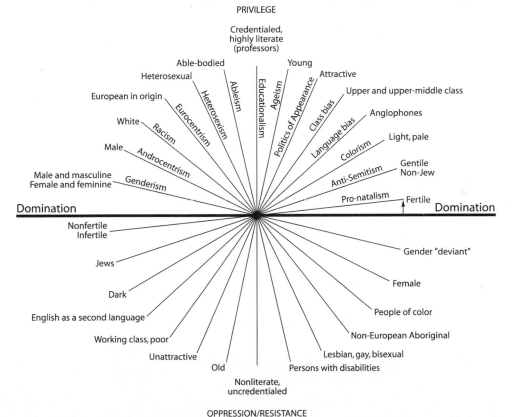

Source: Kathryn Pauly Morgan, "Describing the Emperor's New Clothes: Three Myths of Educational (In)Equality." *The Gender Question in Education: Theory, Pedagogy & Politics,* Ann Diller et al., Boulder, CO: Westview, 1996.

where some ways of being, like being abled or heterosexual, are valued more than others, like being disabled or gay or lesbian. In this way, rankings occur against societal notions of the mythical norm.

The hierarchical ranking of these differences is constructed through social processes such that patterns of difference become systems of inequality and privilege. Inequality for some and privilege for others is the consequence of these processes. *Privilege* can be defined as advantages people have by virtue of their status or position in society. In "White Privilege and Male Privilege," for example, Peggy McIntosh writes that White privilege is the "invisible package of unearned assets" that White people can count on cashing in every day. And, as McIntosh explains, it is easier to grant that others are disadvantaged than to admit being overprivileged. Men might be supportive of women's rights but balk at the suggestion that their personal behavior is in need of modification. Whites might be horrified by the stories of racial injustice but still not realize that taken-for-granted White privilege is part of the problem.

Systems that facilitate privilege and inequality, subordination and domination, include *racism* based upon racial/ethnic group membership (African American, Asian American, Latino/a, Native American—note this also includes anti-Semitism, or discrimination against Jews, as well as discrimination against Arab Americans and/or those who are Muslim [especially a problem after the bombing of the World Trade Center and the consequences of the War in Iraq]); *sexism* based upon gender; *classism* associated with socioeconomic status; *heterosexism,* concerning sexual identity; *ageism* relating to age; *looksism,* concerning body size and looks; and *ableism,* about physical and mental ability. Systems of oppression can be defined as systems that discriminate and privilege based on perceived or real differences among people. Given this, sexism discriminates and privileges on the basis of gender, resulting in gender stratification, racism discriminates and privileges on the basis of racial and ethnic differences, and so forth for classism, heterosexism, ageism, looksism, and ableism.

Every woman is in multiple places vis-à-vis these systems. She might not have access to race and gender privilege because she is African American and a woman; she might have access to heterosexual privilege because she is heterosexual and class privilege because she lives in a family that is financially secure. This is the *confluence,* the flowing together of various identities. As Patricia Hill Collins explains in "Toward a New Vision," it is not as useful to think of these various identities as being stacked or arranged in a cumulative manner. Lives are not experienced as "Here I'm a woman, here I'm abled, here I'm poor," as if all our various statuses are all stacked

LEARNING ACTIVITY   **Unpack Your Knapsack**

Peggy McIntosh lists a number of ways that she experiences White privilege. Based on your various nontarget statuses, make lists of the ways you experience the following categories of privilege:

White	Male	Heterosexual
Middle or upper class	Young	Able-bodied

LEARNING ACTIVITY   **Test for Hidden Bias**

Go to the Southern Poverty Law Center's Teaching Tolerance Web site at *www. tolerance.org*. Click on "Explore your hidden biases" to take a series of tests to uncover unconscious biases you may have. Even though most of us believe we view everyone equally, we still may hold stereotypes and biases of which we are unaware. These tests can check to see if perhaps you hold hidden biases of race, sexual orientation, age, gender, or body image. After you finish the tests, take a few minutes to write about what you learned about yourself. Were there any surprises? Do you hold hidden biases? How do you feel about your test results? Now that you know about your hidden biases, what can you do?

up; we experience ourselves as ordinary people who struggle daily with the inequities in our lives and who usually take the privileges for granted. Various identities concerning these systems of equality and privilege are usually thoroughly blended and potentially shifting depending on subjective orientation and cultural context. Still, it is important to emphasize that people experience race, class, gender, and sexual identity differently depending on their social location in various structures of inequality and privilege. This means that people of the same race or same age, for example, will experience race or age differently depending on their location in gendered structures (whether they are women or men), class structures (such as working class, professional class, or unemployed, etc.), as well as structures associated with sexual identity (whether they identify as heterosexual, bisexual, lesbian, gay, or "queer"), and so on. In "Report from the Bahamas," June Jordan illustrates the multilayered tensions associated with intersecting identities in the context of global inequality, and the shifting limitations/privileges that shift again when a citizen of a "First World" country visits colonized, westernized locations outside the United States.

Systems of inequality like racism, sexism, and classism interconnect and work together to enforce inequality and privilege, each mostly supporting the other. As Baba Copper explains in her article on ageism, age discrimination is very much connected to sexism as well as to looksism. Women learn to "age pass"; that is, we do not want to be mistaken for 40 when we are in our 30s, or mistaken for 70 when only 60. This is part of the pursuit for youth and beauty that encourages women to participate as agents of ageism as we fulfill the expectations of gender. Similarly, Suzanne Pharr writes about the ways homophobia functions as a weapon of sexism. *Homophobia* is the fear and dislike of lesbians and gay men. Pharr emphasizes that homophobia functions as a threat to keep women apart from one another and under male power, thus reinforcing sexism.

INSTITUTIONS

Institutions are social organizations that involve established patterns of behavior organized around particular purposes. They function through social norms and established rules and/or laws. Major institutions in our society include the family,

Challenging Your Assumptions

Read the following sentences and identify the assumptions inherent in each regarding age, ability, appearance, ethnicity, gender, race, religion, sexual identity, and socioeconomic power or status.

Identify the "norm" (a standard of conduct that should or must be followed; a typical or usual way of being or behaving, usually said of a certain group), and discuss how the assumptions reflect this norm.

Discuss how these assumptions operate in your cultural situation. How are you affected by cultural assumptions about the "norm"?

Our founding fathers carved this great state out of the wilderness.

Mrs. Imoto looks remarkably good for her age.

Fashion Tights are available in black, suntan, and flesh color.

Someday I intend to visit the third world.

We need more manpower.

Our facilities all provide handicapped access.

I'm just a person.

The network is down again. We'd better get Kevin in here to do his voodoo on it.

Our boys were having a rough time of it, and the black regiment was, too.

How Neandertal man existed for so long is a mystery. He must have had the ability to adapt to his environment.

I see she forgot to sign her time sheet. She's acting a little blonde today.

Mitochondrial DNA testing should help us determine when our race split off from the lower creatures.

Confined to a wheelchair, Mr. Garcia still manages to live a productive life.

Pat really went on the warpath when the budget figures came out.

I won't be associated with you and your pagan behaviors!

The Academy now admits women and other minorities.

We have a beautiful daycare center where women can leave their children while they work.

See if you can Jew him down to $50.

Personally, I don't think it's right that the foreign students come in here before term and buy up all the insignia bags. Our kids don't get a chance at them.

I completely forgot where I put my car keys. I must be having a senior moment.

Win a fabulous lovers' weekend in Hawaii! Prizes include a day at the spa for her and a relaxing game of golf for him.

That is not a very Christian attitude.

We welcome all guests, their wives, and their children.

May I speak to Mr. or Mrs. Williams?

Source: Janet Lockhart and Susan Shaw, *Writing for Change: Raising Awareness of Issues of Difference, Power, and Discrimination, www.teachingtolerance.org.*

LEARNING ACTIVITY **Combating Hate**

Many Web pages provide valuable information about hate, hate crimes, and hate groups in the United States. Go to the Southern Poverty Law Center's homepage at *www.splcenter.org.* Click on "Intelligence Project" and then on "Hate Incidents." Put in your state to see a list of hate crimes where you live. You may also want to visit these Web sites as well: *www.wiesenthal.com, www.adl.org, www.stopthehate.org, www.hrc.org,* and *www.hatewatch.org.* Using information from these sites, make a list of ways you can help stop hate.

marriage, the economy, government and criminal justice systems, religion, education, science, health and medicine, mass media, the military, and sports. Usually patterns of rules and practices implicit in major societal institutions have a historical component and reflect political, military, legal, and socioeconomic decisions made over decades and centuries. Although institutions are intended to meet the needs of society generally, or people in particular, they meet some people's needs better than others. These social organizations are central in creating systems of inequality and privilege because they pattern and structure differences among women in relatively organized ways. Institutions are important channels for the perpetuation of what Hill Collins calls "structures of domination and subordination." Note also that institutions may resist systems of inequality and privilege through, for example, positive portrayal of women and marginalized people in the media or the activities of some churches for civil rights.

Marilyn Frye focuses on the institutional aspect of systems of inequality and privilege in her article "Oppression." She emphasizes that people who suffer under systems of inequality are oppressed by these systems. Frye goes on to explain the difference between being oppressed and being limited and writes that a fundamental aspect of oppression is the double bind: All potential options have limitations. She uses the metaphor of a birdcage to explain the networks of related barriers that function in systems of oppression. One wire might be like an individual-level prejudice; a bird could just move around it and escape. But a birdcage involves patterns of wires, systematically arranged so that escape is thwarted. The wires of the cage symbolically become institutionalized into a system of oppression.

Institutions encourage the channeling of various systems of gendered inequality to all aspects of women's lives. In terms of the patterning of resources and practices, institutions function to support systems of inequality and privilege. First, institutions assign various roles to women and men and are also places of employment where people perform gendered work. Educational institutions, for example, employ a considerable number of women. However, as the prestige of the teaching position increases, the number of White males in these positions increases, along with higher salaries. Also, it is very difficult for openly lesbian teachers to find employment in schools, and many states are attempting to pass laws preventing lesbians and gay men from teaching in state-funded educational establishments.

LEARNING ACTIVITY **Women in Science and Engineering**

In 2005 Harvard University President Lawrence H. Summers created an uproar when he made the comment at an academic conference that the reasons fewer women than men succeed in science and math may be more related to innate differences than to socialization or discrimination. Many feminists responded by pointing to the wealth of research that indicates that girls and women are just as capable but their performances are often affected by social factors.

Certainly, the numbers do indicate a persistent dearth of women in science and engineering careers, although more women than ever are completing degrees in these areas. A 2000 report by the National Science Foundation found that from 1982 to 2000 the numbers and percentages of women declined in computer science and the numbers and percentages of minorities declined in engineering. Additionally, studies demonstrate that few White women are in tenured and tenure-track faculty positions in science, technology, and engineering, and the numbers are even bleaker for women of color.

Why do you think White women and women and men of color are underrepresented in science, technology, and engineering?

Visit the Web sites of these professional organizations dedicated to increasing the success of White women and women and men of color in various science, technology, and engineering fields. What do these sites suggest about the reasons for underrepresentation? How do they suggest addressing the problem of underrepresentation?

Society of Women Engineers *www.swe.org*

Association for Women in Computing *www.awc-hq.org*

Association for Women in Mathematics *www.asm-math.org*

Association for Women in Science *www.awis.org*

National Action Council for Minorities in Engineering *www.nacme.org*

Second, institutions distribute resources and extend privileges differentially to different groups. Sports are a good example of this. As an institution, athletics has traditionally been male dominated. Men's sports are more highly valued than women's sports and are a major focus for sports entertainment. Compared to men's professional sports, women's are grossly underrepresented. Despite Title IX of the 1972 Educational Amendments Act, which barred discrimination in education, many colleges still are not in compliance and spend considerably more money on men's sports than on women's. Female athletes on some campuses complain that men receive better practice times in shared gymnasiums and more up-to-date equipment. And, within women's sports, some are more "White" than others. Examples that immediately come to mind are gymnastics, ice skating, equestrian sports, tennis, and golf (all relatively expensive sports) as most women's sports—outside of basketball, volleyball, and track—are dominated by White women. In this way, sports and athletics are an example of an institution where resources are inequitably distributed.

HISTORICAL MOMENT **Women of Color Feminism**

Acutely aware of the intersections of gender, race, sexual identity, and social class were women of color who daily experienced the material realities of the confluence of oppressions. From the beginning of the women's movement, women of color participated actively, although their specific concerns were often overlooked by some of the middle-class White women in the movement. In the early 1970s, women of color spoke out about their experiences of racism, sexism, and heterosexism. Barbara Smith co-founded the Combahee River Collective, a Black feminist group that confronted racism and homophobia in the women's, gay, and Black movements. The Collective took its name from a river in South Carolina where Harriet Tubman led a military action that freed hundreds of slaves.

In the late 1970s, Smith joined forces with Cherríe Moraga to found Kitchen Table/Women of Color Press when Moraga and Gloria Anzaldúa could not find a publisher for *This Bridge Called My Back: Writings by Radical Women of Color.* Kitchen Table/Women of Color Press was the first independent press to publish exclusively works by feminists of color. *This Bridge Called My Back* won an American Book Award from the Columbus Foundation.

In 1983 poet and novelist Alice Walker coined the term *womanism* to describe Black feminism in contrast to *feminism,* which has generally been associated with White women. Walker situates womanists in a long line of Black women who have struggled for social change and liberation. Womanists are, in her words, "outrageous, audacious, courageous, and willful, responsible, in charge, serious." They love Black women's culture, Black women's beauty, and themselves.

Another blatant example of inequitable distribution concerns the economic system. Other than inherited wealth, the major way our economic system distributes resources is in terms of remuneration for the work that we do. Women tend to work in jobs that are heavily occupied by women; examples include clerical work, service and retail sales, and professional occupations like teaching and nursing. These jobs are undervalued in our society, contributing to the fact that a woman's average salary generally for all occupations tends to be less than the man's average salary for doing the same work. Some women work under deplorable conditions at minimum wage levels; some work with hazardous chemicals or have to breathe secondhand smoke throughout their workday. Old women and women of color own a tiny percentage of the wealth in this society—another example of the inequitable distribution of resources.

Third, major institutions in society are interconnected and work to support and maintain one another. Often this means that personnel are shared among major institutions; more likely it means that these institutions mutually support one another in terms of the ways they fulfill (or deny) the needs of people in society. For example, close ties to economic institutions include the military (through the military-industrial complex), the government (corporate leaders often have official positions in government and rely on legislative loopholes and taxation systems to maintain corporate profits), health and medicine (with important ties to pharmaceutical companies), the media (whose content is controlled in part by advertising), and sports (through corporate sponsorship).

Stark Intersections: Gender, Race, Class, and HIV/AIDS

"We must address power imbalances in every single policy, strategy, and programme related to prevention, treatment and care if we seriously want to tackle this global challenge. [Gender] equality is not simply a matter of justice or fairness. Gender inequality is fatal."

—*Noeleen Heyzer, UNIFEM*

Gender inequality is fueling the HIV/AIDS epidemic: it deprives women of the ability to say no to risky practices, leads to coerced sex and sexual violence, keeps women uninformed about prevention, puts them last in line for care and life-saving treatment, and imposes an overwhelming burden for the care of the sick and dying. These fundamental threats to women's lives, health, and well-being are critical human rights issues—when women's human rights are not promoted, protected, and fulfilled, gender inequality is the dangerous result. Guaranteeing women's human rights is an indispensable component of the international struggle to combat HIV/AIDS. To combat today's scourge, we must understand the multiple intersections between gender, racial and ethnic discrimination, and the epidemiology of HIV/AIDS.

This intersectional approach derives from the realization that discriminations based on gender, race, ethnicity, caste, and class are not discrete phenomena, but compound one another in almost all socio-economic circumstances.[1] Nine points are critical with regard to HIV/AIDS:

- Economic dependence and social subordination limit the ability of women and members of racial and ethnic minorities to demand safe and responsible sexual practices, including the use of condoms.
- Groups already subject to socioeconomic discrimination—including racial and ethnic minorities, migrant populations, and refugees—rank high among those most vulnerable to HIV infection. In all these groups, women are hardest hit.
- Racial and ethnic identities operate in complicated ways to increase women's vulnerability to sex trafficking, a major factor in women's growing infection rates.
- The culture of silence that surrounds female sexuality in many societies prevents women and girls from accessing information and services for protection or treatment.
- In many countries, especially among racial and ethnic minorities, men receive preferential treatment in anti-retroviral therapies.
- Gender-based violence, both inside and outside the household, increases women's vulnerability to HIV/AIDS. HIV-positive women are frequently shunned by families and communities—and often subjected to further violence.
- This vulnerability mounts because of practices such as polygamy and wife-inheritance, as well as mistaken beliefs, such as that sex with a virgin can cure AIDS.
- Because women are primarily responsible for caregiving, caring for people with HIV/AIDS typically falls to widows and grandmothers or older girl children.

Caregiving responsibilities increase as health and social services decrease and increasingly privatized services require a higher proportion of household income.

- Because women often care for communities as well as families, their illness or absorption in sheer survival activities weakens the vital informal support systems on which poor and marginalized communities depend, deepening and perpetuating poverty.[2]

These intersections are more alarming in light of the gender dimensions of HIV/AIDS:[3]

- Worldwide, of the 17.5 million adults who have died of the disease, 9 million have been women. Approximately 47 percent of all new adult infections aflict women.
- In sub-Saharan Africa, 55 percent of HIV-positive adults are women. In Mozambique, HIV infection is twice as prevalent among girls as boys.[4]
- Of the 1.3 million cases in Eastern Europe and Central Asia reported in 2000, at least half are estimated to be female.
- In parts of Latin America and the Caribbean, the proportion has reached 45 percent, a rapidly rising figure.

Moreover, these statistics represent underestimations due to the personal reluctance to report the disease as well as government reluctance to acknowledge its extent. In addition, medical studies often do not disaggregate data according to race and gender, nor do they examine the specific health issues affecting women from racial and ethnic minorities or indigenous women as a matter of course. Thus, they may fail to uncover medical problems specific to particular groups of women.[5]

[1]For discussion of the concept of intersectionality, see *Gender and Racial Discrimination: Report of the Expert Group Meeting,* November 2000, Zagreb. UN Division for the Advancement of Women, 2001.
[2]Mercedes González de la Rocha and Alejandro Grinspun, "Private Adjustments: Household, Crisis and Work," in Grinspun, ed., *Choices for the Poor: Lessons from National Poverty Strategies.* New York: UNDP, 2001.
[3]Unless otherwise noted, statistics are taken from the UNAIDS *AIDS Epidemic Update,* December 2000, or the UNAIDS *Report on the Global HIV Epidemic,* June 2000.
[4]Dr. Pascoal Macumbi, prime minister of Mozambique, quoted in *Conference News Daily,* UN Special Session on HIV/AIDS, June 25, 2001.
[5]UNIFEM, 2000. "Integrating Gender into the Third World Conference Against Racism, Racial Discrimination, Xenophobia and Related Intolerance." Background Paper prepared for the *Gender and Racial Discrimination: Report of the Expert Group Meeting,* November 2000, Zagreb, Croatia.

Source: www.undp.org/unifem/hrights.htm.

IDEOLOGY AND LANGUAGE

In addition to distributing resources and practices, institutions produce messages that shape our understandings of gender. Importantly, ideas and values (like stereotypes and jokes) or sets of beliefs (often called ideologies) provide the rationale for injustice. Hill Collins calls this the "symbolic dimension" of systems of domination and subordination. For example, the media often reinforce stereotypes about women like dumb blondes, passive Asian Americans, or pushy African Americans. Another example of gendered messages comes from the institution of religion. This institution is especially powerful because it implies the notion of divine sanction. Traditional religious texts tell stories (for example, Eve's behavior that led to the banishment from the Garden of Eden or the chaste role of the Virgin Mary) that convey important messages about moral thought and behavior as well as women's place in society. These messages tend to be strongly gendered and often support different behaviors for women and men. A central code of much religious teaching is that women should be subordinate to men in their spiritual and everyday lives.

An example of an ideology that is supported by various institutions and that affects women's lives is the bootstrap myth concerning economic success. Propagated by the economic system, it paints economic success as a result of hard work and ambition and asserts that people, if properly motivated and willing to work hard, can pull themselves up by their bootstraps. Given this set of ideas, those individuals who are not able to provide for their families must have deficiencies. Perhaps they were unmotivated, did not work hard enough, or were not smart enough. Such ideas encourage blaming the poor for their poverty rather than understanding the wider societal forces that shape people's existence and maintain classism. Notwithstanding the fact that of course hard work and ambition may facilitate some measure of success in the short term, it does not guarantee such success, nor does it tend to transform the bigger picture of structural inequalities. Notice that a particular ideology need not be supported unanimously for it to influence society. Many people would disagree vehemently with the bootstrap myth; yet, still, this is a key part of the ideology of capitalist countries. In this way, institutions perpetuate sets of ideas and practices and use them to justify the institution.

Classism is also addressed in the article by Donna Langston titled "Tired of Playing Monopoly?" Here she explains how class is not just about socioeconomic status, that is, how much wealth you have access to or how much you earn. She writes,

> Class is also culture. As a result of the class you were born into and raised in, class is your understanding of the world and where you fit in; it's composed of ideas, attitudes, values, and language; class is how you think, feel, act, look, dress, talk, move, walk; class is what stores you shop at, restaurants you eat in; class is the schools you attend, the education you attain; class is the jobs you will work at throughout your adult life. Class even determines when we marry and become mothers.

Stereotypes and ideologies that support systems of inequality involve prejudices. *Prejudice* means, literally, to prejudge and involves making premature judgments without adequate information or with inaccurate information. Often these ideas support systems of inequality and privilege because prejudice is often adopted when there is no other basis for understanding. For example, many White people have little contact with people of color, and many young people do not interact on an everyday basis with old people. As a result, there is a lack of accurate information, and stereotypes or images from television or the movies are used instead. This kind of ignorance and misinformation breeds prejudice. In "Something About the Subject Makes It Hard to Name," Gloria Yamato writes about different kinds of prejudice: aware/blatant, aware/covert, unaware/unintentional, and unaware/self-righteous. In this article she emphasizes that much prejudice comes from misinformation and is very often unintentional. She also notes that social norms against racism have pushed some racism underground.

© Copyright Judy Horacek from LIFE ON THE EDGE, 1992.
www.horacek.com.au. Reprinted with permission.

Prejudices are *internalized* (assimilated, integrated, or incorporated into our thoughts and behavior) by all of us, although, of course, since humans have active agency and will, they can be resisted. Generally, however, we can say that individuals negotiate these ideologies, accepting, resisting, and/or modifying them. If we are members of the target group, the group against whom the prejudice is aimed, it can lead to low self-esteem, self-loathing, and shame. Sadly, it can mean individuals are encouraged to believe they are not worthy of social justice and therefore are less likely to seek equality. Although members of target groups may internalize negative messages, members of nontarget groups, groups (often part of the mythical norm) against whom the prejudice is not aimed, also internalize these messages as well as messages about their own privilege. This can encourage or justify hostility against target groups.

Internalizing oppression means that we not only police ourselves but also police one another, encouraging compliance with institutions that may oppress. When individuals direct the resentment and anger they have about their situation onto those who are of equal or of lesser status, this process is called *horizontal hostility*. As a strategy, it is similar to the military notion of "divide and conquer" where groups are encouraged to fight with one another in order to avoid alliances that might collaboratively overpower an enemy. Baba Copper remarks on this horizontal conflict when she writes about woman-to-woman ageism and the ways women compete "for the crumbs of social power."

Language, or the symbolic means by which we communicate, is a central aspect of what makes us human. It is an incredibly sophisticated process of symbols that we learn at an early age and mostly take for granted unless we are confronted with trying to communicate in a language not our own. Because language allows us not only to name the objects of our experience but also to typify them (experience them as similar to something of a similar type), it creates as well as reflects our reality. It shapes as well as expresses thought. And because language helps us sort and anticipate our experiences, it has a primary influence on our lives.

ACTIVIST PROFILE **Fannie Lou Hamer**

She began life in Mississippi in 1917 as the granddaughter of slaves and the daughter of share-croppers, but Fannie Lou Hamer was to become one of the most important leaders of the civil rights movement in the United States. Although Hamer became a share-cropper herself, by 1962 she'd had enough of the second-class life of the segregated South. She joined 17 other African Americans taking a bus to the county seat to register to vote. On the way home, they were stopped by police and arrested. After Hamer returned home, she was visited by the planta-tion owner, who told her that if she insisted on voting, she would have to get off his land, which she did that same day.

The next year, when Hamer joined other civil rights workers in challeng-ing the "Whites only" policy at a bus terminal diner, she was arrested and jailed. The police ordered two other African American prisoners to beat her with a metal-spiked club. Hamer was blinded in one eye from the beating and suffered perma-nent kidney damage.

In 1964 Hamer helped organize the Mississippi Freedom Democratic Party (MFDP) to challenge the all-White Mississippi delegation to the Democratic Convention. Hamer spoke to the credentials committee of the convention, and although her live testimony was preempted by a presidential press conference, it was aired by national networks in its entirety later that evening. The MFDP and the credentials committee reached a compromise, giving voting and speaking rights to two MFDP delegates and seating the others as honored guests. Hamer responded, "We didn't come all this way for two seats when all of us is tired." In 1968 the Mississippi Democratic Party did seat an integrated delegation.

Throughout her life, Hamer continued to work for justice, supporting Head Start for Black schools and jobs for poor African Americans, opposing the Vietnam War, and helping to convene the National Women's Political Caucus in the 1970s.

Hamer died in 1977 and was buried in Mississippi. Her tombstone reads, "I am sick and tired of being sick and tired."

IDEAS FOR ACTIVISM

- Find out how your university ensures access for people with disabilities. If some structures on your campus are inaccessible, advocate with your administration to create accessibility.
- Plan a celebration of Black women during Black History Month.
- Find out what programs your university offers to recruit and retain students and faculty of color. If programs are not in place, advocate with your administration to develop such programs.
- Find out if your university's antidiscrimination policy includes sexual identity as a protected classification, and find out if your university provides benefits for domestic partners. If not, advocate with your administration to include sexual identity in its policy and/or to provide domestic partner benefits.

The English language is structured in such a way that it maintains sexism and racism. Lois Keith's poem "Tomorrow I'm Going to Rewrite the English Language" suggests how the English language helps shape our understandings of gender and limits women's options for self-definition. This poem encourages us to think about the ways that language shapes our reality and helps structure the everyday realities of women's lives. When you grow up knowing 20 different words synonymous with *slut,* you learn something powerful about gender. The English language also maintains racism. For example:

> Some may blackly (angrily) accuse me of trying to blacken (defame) the English language, to give it a black eye (a mark of shame) by writing such black words (hostile). They may denigrate (to cast aspersions; to darken) me by accusing me of being black hearted (malevolent), of having a black outlook (pessimistic, dismal) on life, of being a blackguard (scoundrel)—which will certainly be a black mark (detrimental act) against me. Some may black-brow (scowl) at me and hope that a black cat crosses in front of me because of this black deed. I may become a black sheep (one who causes shame or embarrassment because of deviation from the expected standards), who will be black-balled (ostracized) by being placed on a black list (list of undesirables) in an attempt to blackmail (to force or coerce into a particular action) me to retract my words. . . . The preceding is of course a white lie (not intended to cause harm), meant only to illustrate some examples of racist terminology in the English language.*

In this chapter we focus on the social construction of difference and how systems of inequality and privilege based upon these differences function and are maintained. While we have emphasized that systems of inequality and privilege are maintained through the presence and power of institutions and the interrelated workings of ideologies and language, negotiated by individuals, it is also important to recognize the way hate crimes are central to these power relations. Hate crimes

*Robert B. Moore, "Racism in the English Language." Excerpted in *Experiencing Race, Class, and Gender in the U.S.*, Virginia Cyrus, ed. (Mountain View, CA: Mayfield, 1993), p. 152.

Challenging the Pseudogeneric "Man"

Examine the following phrases that use male nouns as "generic." Describe the mental image created for you by each phrase. Do you see yourself and people like you in the images?

Next, choose a term representing a group of people of a specific age, religion, class, or ethnicity, and substitute that term for the male noun (example: "childkind"). Does use of the new, specific term sound incongruous or unusual? Why?

Describe the mental images created by using the substitute terms. Do you see yourself and people like you in the images?

Finally, suggest a gender-free, inclusive term for each (example: for "mankind," "humanity" or "people").

For the benefit of all mankind

"All men are created equal"

May the best man win

Prehistoric man

Man the pumps!

The first manned mission to Mars

Chairman of the Board

We need more manpower

Not fit for man or beast

The relationship between men and machines

Man's best friend

"To boldly go where no man has gone before"

Man of the Year

"Peace on Earth, goodwill toward men"

The founding fathers

"Crown thy good with brotherhood"

"Friends, Romans, countrymen; lend me your ears"

Source: Janet Lockhart and Susan M. Shaw, Writing for Change: Raising Awareness of Difference, Power, and Discrimination, www.teachingtolerance.org.

include the threat of coercion and violence as well as the actual practice of it, and their motives are hate and bigotry. Evidence shows that most perpetrators of hate crimes are most likely to be heterosexual White males. There has been a substantial increase in hate crimes in the last decade, especially against people of color, lesbians, gay, transgendered, and transsexual (see Chapters 3 and 4) people, although improved reporting systems are also increasing awareness of this social problem. Hate groups include the Ku Klux Klan, racist Skinhead, Christian Identity Movement, Neo-Confederate, and Neo-Nazi (including Aryan Nations). One of the best sources for understanding hate crimes is the Southern Poverty Law Center at *www.splcenter.org*. It is important to emphasize that gender as a category is omitted from most hate-crime statutes despite the fact that women suffer from the crimes of misogyny. Women are often hurt and killed because they are women; if these figures were included, hate-crime statistics would skyrocket. The United Nations now recognizes crimes against women, and the United States is starting to recognize crimes against non-U.S. women as basis for asylum. Hate crimes against women just because they are women, as well as hate against, for example, lesbians or women of color, often involve *sexual terrorism,* the threat of rape and sexual assault that controls a woman's life whether or not she is actually physically or sexually violated.

In concluding this chapter we underscore the need for social change and transformation to improve the conditions of women's lives. Almost all the readings focus on this need. Patricia Hill Collins, for example, writes about awareness and education, the need to build empathy with each other, and the need to work to form coalitions for structural change around common causes. June Jordan also writes of the power of empathy and the possibilities of friendship for alliance building and social transformation. Peggy McIntosh suggests we recognize our privilege and work on our internalized prejudices and privileges. Baba Copper writes about identifying and acknowledging sources of inequality and specifically the ways we have been taught to hate old women and deny them power. She also hopes for alliances across our differences. Suzanne Pharr points out the homophobia of the women's movement and its failure to achieve solidarity when the rights of all women are not recognized. Donna Langston presents ways to challenge classism that involve confronting the behavior in ourselves, making demands on behalf of poor communities, and learning from the skills and strengths of working-class people. Similarly, Gloria Yamato has good ideas for Whites who want to be allies to people of color. The message in all these articles is the need to recognize difference, to understand how the meanings associated with difference get translated into privilege and inequality, and to celebrate those differences through coalitions and other expressions of personal and social concern.

Toward a New Vision

Race, Class, and Gender as Categories of Analysis and Connection

Patricia Hill Collins

The true focus of revolutionary change is never merely the oppressive situations which we seek to escape, but that piece of the oppressor which is planted deep within each of us.

—*Audre Lorde,* Sister Outsider, *123*

Audre Lorde's statement raises a troublesome issue for scholars and activists working for social change. While many of us have little difficulty assessing our own victimization within some major system of oppression, whether it be by race, social class, religion, sexual orientation, ethnicity, age or gender, we typically fail to see how our thoughts and actions uphold someone else's subordination. Thus, White feminists routinely point with confidence to their oppression as women but resist seeing how much their White skin privileges them. African-Americans who possess eloquent analyses of racism often persist in viewing poor White women as symbols of white power. The radical left fares little better. "If only people of color and women could see their true class interests," they argue, "class solidarity would eliminate racism and sexism." In essence, each group identifies the type of oppression with which it feels most comfortable as being fundamental and classifies all other types as being of lesser importance.

Oppression is full of such contradictions. Errors in political judgment that we make concerning how we teach our courses, what we tell our children, and which organizations are worthy of our time, talents and financial support flow smoothly from errors in theoretical analysis about the nature of oppression and activism. Once we realize that there are few pure victims

or oppressors, and that each one of us derives varying amounts of penalty and privilege from the multiple systems of oppression that frame our lives, then we will be in a position to see the need for new ways of thought and action.

. . .

[This discussion] addresses this need for new patterns of thought and action. I focus on two basic questions. First, how can we reconceptualize race, class and gender as categories of analysis? Second, how can we transcend the barriers created by our experiences with race, class and gender oppression in order to build the types of coalitions essential for social exchange? To address these question[s] I contend that we must acquire both new theories of how race, class and gender have shaped the experiences not just of women of color, but of all groups. Moreover, we must see the connections between these categories of analysis and the personal issues in our everyday lives, particularly our scholarship, our teaching and our relationships with our colleagues and students. As Audre Lorde points out, change starts with self, and relationships that we have with those around us must always be the primary site for social change.

HOW CAN WE RECONCEPTUALIZE RACE, CLASS, AND GENDER AS CATEGORIES OF ANALYSIS?

To me, we must shift our discourse away from additive analyses of oppression (Spelman 1982; Collins 1989). Such approaches are typically based on two key premises. First, they depend on either/or, dichotomous thinking. Persons, things and ideas are conceptualized in terms of their opposites. For example, Black/White, man/woman, thought/feeling, and fact/opinion are defined in oppositional terms. Thought and feeling are not seen as two different and interconnected ways of approaching truth that can coexist in scholarship and teaching. Instead, feeling is defined as antithetical to reason, as its opposite. In spite of the fact that we all have "both/and" identities (I am both a college professor and a mother—I don't stop being a mother when I drop my child off at school, or forget everything I learned while scrubbing the toilet), we persist in trying to classify each other in either/or categories. I live each day as an African-American woman—a race/gender specific experience. And I am not alone. Everyone has a race/gender/class specific identity. Either/or, dichotomous thinking is especially troublesome when applied to theories of oppression because every individual must be classified as being either oppressed or not oppressed. The both/and position of simultaneously being oppressed and oppressor becomes conceptually impossible.

A second premise of additive analyses of oppression is that these dichotomous differences must be ranked. One side of the dichotomy is typically labeled dominant and the other subordinate. Thus, Whites rule Blacks, men are deemed superior to women, and reason is seen as being preferable to emotion. Applying this premise to discussions of oppression leads to the assumption that oppression can be quantified, and that some groups are oppressed more than others. I am frequently asked, "Which has been most oppressive to you, your status as a Black person or your status as a woman?" What I am really being asked to do is divide myself into little boxes and rank my various statuses. If I experience oppression as a both/and phenomenon, why should I analyze it any differently?

Additive analyses of oppression rest squarely on the twin pillars of either/or thinking and the necessity to quantify and rank all relationships in order to know where one stands. Such approaches typically see African-American women as being more oppressed than everyone else because the majority of Black women experience

the negative effects of race, class and gender oppression simultaneously. In essence, if you add together separate oppressions, you are left with a grand oppression greater than the sum of its parts.

I am not denying that specific groups experience oppression more harshly than others—lynching is certainly objectively worse than being held up as a sex object. But we must be careful not to confuse this issue of the saliency of one type of oppression in people's lives with a theoretical stance positing the interlocking nature of oppression. Race, class and gender may all structure a situation but may not be equally visible and/or important in people's self-definitions. In certain contexts, such as the antebellum American South and contemporary South America, racial oppression is more visibly salient, while in other contexts, such as Haiti, El Salvador and Nicaragua, social class oppression may be more apparent. For middle class White women, gender may assume experiential primacy unavailable to poor Hispanic women struggling with the ongoing issues of low-paid jobs and the frustrations of the welfare bureaucracy. This recognition that one category may have salience over another for a given time and place does not minimize the theoretical importance of assuming that race, class and gender as categories of analysis structure all relationships.

In order to move toward new visions of what oppression is, I think that we need to ask new questions. How are relationships of domination and subordination structured and maintained in the American political economy? How do race, class and gender function as parallel and interlocking systems that shape this basic relationship of domination and subordination? Questions such as these promise to move us away from futile theoretical struggles concerned with ranking oppressions and towards analyses that assume race, class and gender are all present in any given setting, even if one appears more visible and salient than the others. Our task becomes redefined as one of reconceptualizing oppression by uncovering the connections among race, class and gender as categories of analysis.

1. Institutional Dimension of Oppression

Sandra Harding's contention that gender oppression is structured along three main dimensions— the institutional, the symbolic, and the individual —offers a useful model for a more comprehensive analysis encompassing race, class and gender oppression (Harding 1986). Systemic relationships of domination and subordination structured through social institutions such as schools, businesses, hospitals, the workplace, and government agencies represent the institutional dimension of oppression. Racism, sexism and elitism all have concrete institutional locations. Even though the workings of the institutional dimension of oppression are often obscured with ideologies claiming equality of opportunity, in actuality, race, class and gender place Asian-American women, Native American men, White men, African-American women, and other groups in distinct institutional niches with varying degrees of penalty and privilege.

Even though I realize that many . . . would not share this assumption, let us assume that the institutions of American society discriminate, whether by design or by accident. While many of us are familiar with how race, gender and class operate separately to structure inequality, I want to focus on how these three systems interlock in structuring the institutional dimension of oppression. To get at the interlocking nature of race, class and gender, I want you to think about the antebellum plantation as a guiding metaphor for a variety of American social institutions. Even though slavery is typically analyzed as a racist institution, and occasionally as a class institution, I suggest that slavery was a race, class, gender specific institution. Removing any one piece from our analysis diminishes our understanding of the true nature of relations of domination and subordination under slavery.

. . .

A brief analysis of key American social institutions most controlled by elite White men should convince us of the interlocking nature of race, class and gender in structuring the institutional dimension of oppression. For example, if you are

from an American college or university, is your campus a modern plantation? Who controls your university's political economy? Are elite White men overrepresented among the upper administrators and trustees controlling your university's finances and policies? Are elite White men being joined by growing numbers of elite White women helpmates? What kinds of people are in your classrooms grooming the next generation who will occupy these and other decision-making positions? Who are the support staff that produce the mass mailings, order the supplies, fix the leaky pipes? Do African-Americans, Hispanics or other people of color form the majority of the invisible workers who feed you, wash your dishes, and clean up your offices and libraries after everyone else has gone home?

If your college is anything like mine, you know the answers to these questions. You may be affiliated with an institution that has Hispanic women as vice-presidents for finance, or substantial numbers of Black men among the faculty. If so, you are fortunate. Much more typical are colleges where a modified version of the plantation as a metaphor for the institutional dimension of oppression survives. ← analogy!!

2. The Symbolic Dimension of Oppression

Widespread, societally-sanctioned ideologies used to justify relations of domination and subordination comprise the symbolic dimension of oppression. Central to this process is the use of stereotypical or controlling images of diverse race, class and gender groups. In order to assess the power of this dimension of oppression, I want you to make a list, either on paper or in your head, of "masculine" and "feminine" characteristics. If your list is anything like that compiled by most people, it reflects some variation of the following:

Masculine	*Feminine*
aggressive	passive
leader	follower
rational	emotional
strong	weak
intellectual	physical

Not only does this list reflect either/or, dichotomous thinking and the need to rank both sides of the dichotomy, but ask yourself exactly which men and women you had in mind when compiling these characteristics. This list applies almost exclusively to middle class White men and women. The allegedly "masculine" qualities that you probably listed are only acceptable when exhibited by elite White men, or when used by Black and Hispanic men against each other or against women of color. Aggressive Black and Hispanic men are seen as dangerous, not powerful, and are often penalized when they exhibit any of the allegedly "masculine" characteristics. Working-class and poor White men fare slightly better and are also denied the allegedly "masculine" symbols of leadership, intellectual competence and human rationality. Women of color and working class and poor White women are also not represented on this list, for they have never had the luxury of being "ladies." What appear to be universal categories representing all men and women instead are unmasked as being applicable to only a small group.

It is important to see how the symbolic images applied to different race, class and gender groups interact in maintaining systems of domination and subordination. If I were to ask you to repeat the same assignment, only this time, by making separate lists for Black men, Black women, Hispanic women and Hispanic men, I suspect that your gender symbolism would be quite different. In comparing all of the lists, you might begin to see the interdependence of symbols applied to all groups. For example, the elevated images of White womanhood need devalued images of Black womanhood in order to maintain credibility.

. . .

Assuming that everyone is affected differently by the same interlocking set of symbolic images allows us to move forward toward new analyses. Women of color and White women have different relationships to White male authority, and this difference explains the distinct gender symbolism applied to both groups. Black women encounter controlling images such as the mammy, the matriarch, the mule and the whore, that encourage others to reject us as fully human people. Ironically, the negative nature of these images simultaneously encourages us to reject them. In contrast, White women are offered seductive images, those that promise to reward them for supporting the status quo. And yet seductive images can be equally controlling. Consider, for example, the views of Nancy White, a 73-year-old Black woman, concerning images of rejection and seduction:

> My mother used to say that the black woman is the white man's mule and the white woman is his dog. Now, she said that to say this: we do the heavy work and get beat whether we do it well or not. But the white woman is closer to the master and he pats them on the head and lets them sleep in the house, but he ain't gon' treat neither one like he was dealing with a person. (Gwaltney 1980, 148)

Both sets of images stimulate particular political stances. By broadening the analysis beyond the confines of race, we can see the varying levels of rejection and seduction available to each of us due to our race, class and gender identity. Each of us lives with an allotted portion of institutional privilege and penalty, and with varying levels of rejection and seduction inherent in the symbolic images applied to us. This is the context in which we make our choices. Taken together, the institutional and symbolic dimensions of oppression create a structural backdrop against which all of us live our lives.

3. The Individual Dimension of Oppression

Whether we benefit or not, we all live within institutions that reproduce race, class and gender oppression. Even if we never have any contact with members of other race, class and gender groups, we all encounter images of these groups and are exposed to the symbolic meanings attached to those images. On this dimension of oppression, our individual biographies vary tremendously. As a result of our institutional and symbolic statuses, all of our choices become political acts.

Each of us must come to terms with the multiple ways in which race, class and gender as categories of analysis frame our individual biographies. I have lived my entire life as an African-American woman from a working-class family, and this basic fact has had a profound impact on my personal biography. Imagine how different your life might be if you had been born Black, or White, or poor, or of a different race/class/gender group than the one with which you are most familiar. The institutional treatment you would have received and the symbolic meanings attached to your very existence might differ dramatically from what you now consider to be natural, normal and part of everyday life. You might be the same, but your personal biography might have been quite different.

I believe that each of us carries around the cumulative effect of our lives within multiple structures of oppression. If you want to see how much you have been affected by this whole thing, I ask you one simple question—who are your close friends? Who are the people with whom you can share your hopes, dreams, vulnerabilities, fears and victories? Do they look like you? If they are all the same, circumstance may be the cause. For the first seven years of my life I saw only low-income Black people. My friends from those years reflected the composition of my community. But now that I am an adult, can the defense of circumstance explain the patterns of people that I trust as my friends and colleagues? When given other alternatives, if my friends and colleagues reflect the homogeneity of one race, class and gender group, then these categories of analysis have indeed become barriers to connection.

I am not suggesting that people are doomed to follow the paths laid out for them by race, class and gender as categories of analysis. While these three structures certainly frame my opportunity structure, I as an individual always have the choice of accepting things as they are, or trying to change them. As Nikki Giovanni points out, "we've got to live in the real world. If we don't like the world we're living in, change it. And if we can't change it, we change ourselves. We can do something" (Tate 1983, 68). While a piece of the oppressor may be planted deep within each of us, we each have the choice of accepting that piece or challenging it as part of the "true focus of revolutionary change."

HOW CAN WE TRANSCEND THE BARRIERS CREATED BY OUR EXPERIENCES WITH RACE, CLASS, AND GENDER OPPRESSION IN ORDER TO BUILD THE TYPES OF COALITIONS ESSENTIAL FOR SOCIAL CHANGE?

Reconceptualizing oppression and seeing the barriers created by race, class and gender as interlocking categories of analysis is a vital first step. But we must transcend these barriers by moving toward race, class and gender as categories of connection, by building relationships and coalitions that will bring about social change. What are some of the issues involved in doing this?

1. Differences in Power and Privilege

First, we must recognize that our differing experiences with oppression create problems in the relationships among us. Each of us lives within a system that vests us with varying levels of power and privilege. These differences in power, whether structured along axes of race, class, gender, age or sexual orientation, frame our relationships. African-American writer June Jordan describes her discomfort on a Caribbean vacation with Olive, the Black woman who cleaned her room:

> . . . even though both "Olive" and "I" live inside a conflict neither one of us created, and even though both of us therefore hurt inside that conflict, I may be one of the monsters she needs to eliminate from her universe and, in a sense, she may be one of the monsters in mine. (1985, 47)

Differences in power constrain our ability to connect with one another even when we think we are engaged in dialogue across differences. . . .

In extreme cases, members of privileged groups can erase the very presence of the less privileged. When I first moved to Cincinnati, my family and I went on a picnic at a local park. Picnicking next to us was a family of White Appalachians. When I went to push my daughter on the swings, several of the children came over. They had missing, yellowed and broken teeth, they wore old clothing and their poverty was evident. I was shocked. Growing up in a large eastern city, I had never seen such awful poverty among Whites. The segregated neighborhoods in which I grew up made White poverty all but invisible. More importantly, the privileges attached to my newly acquired social class position allowed me to ignore and minimize the poverty among Whites that I did encounter. My reactions to those children made me realize how confining phrases such as "well, at least they're not Black," had become for me. In learning to grant human subjectivity to the Black victims of poverty, I had simultaneously learned to demand White victims of poverty. By applying categories of race to the objective conditions confronting me, I was quantifying and ranking oppressions and missing the very real suffering which, in fact, is the real issue.

One common pattern of relationships across differences in power is one that I label "voyeurism." From the perspective of the privileged, the lives of people of color, of the poor, and of women are interesting for their entertainment value. The privileged become voyeurs, passive onlookers who do not relate to the less powerful, but who are interested in seeing how the "different" live. Over the years, I have heard numerous African-American students complain about professors who never call on them except when a so-called Black issue is being discussed. The students' interest in discussing race or qualifications for doing so appear unimportant to the professor's efforts to use Black students' experiences as stories to make the material come alive for the White student audience. Asking Black students to perform on cue and provide a Black experience for their White classmates can be seen as voyeurism at its worst.

Members of subordinate groups do not willingly participate in such exchanges but often do so because members of dominant groups control the institutional and symbolic apparatuses of oppression. Racial/ethnic groups, women, and the poor have never had the luxury of being voyeurs of the lives of the privileged. Our ability to survive in hostile settings has hinged on our ability to learn intricate details about the behavior and worldview of the powerful and adjust our behavior accordingly. I need only point to the difference in perception of those men and women in abusive relationships. Where men can view their girlfriends and wives as sex objects, helpmates and a collection of stereotyped categories of voyeurism—women must be attuned to every nuance of their partners' behavior. Are women "naturally" better in relating to people with more power than themselves, or have circumstances mandated that men and women develop different skills? . . .

Coming from a tradition where most relationships across difference are squarely rooted in relations of domination and subordination, we have much less experience relating to people as different but equal. The classroom is potentially one powerful and safe space where dialogues among individuals of unequal power relationships can occur. . . .

2. Coalitions Around Common Causes

A second issue in building relationships and coalitions essential for social change concerns knowing the real reasons for coalition. Just what brings people together? One powerful catalyst fostering group solidarity is the presence of a common enemy. African-American, Hispanic, Asian-American, and women's studies all share the common intellectual heritage of challenging what passes for certified knowledge in the academy. But politically expedient relationships and coalitions like these are fragile because, as June Jordan points out:

> It occurs to me that much organizational grief could be avoided if people understood that partnership in misery does not necessarily provide for partnership for change: When we get the monsters off our backs all of us may want to run in very different directions. (1985, 47)

Sharing a common cause assists individuals and groups in maintaining relationships that transcend their differences. Building effective coalitions involves struggling to hear one another and developing empathy for each other's points of view. The coalitions that I have been involved in that lasted and that worked have been those where commitment to a specific issue mandated collaboration as the best strategy for addressing the issue at hand.

. . .

None of us alone has a comprehensive vision of how race, class and gender operate as categories of analysis or how they might be used as categories of connection. Our personal biographies offer us partial views. Few of us can manage to study race, class and gender simultaneously. Instead, we each know more about some dimensions of this larger story and less about others. . . . Just as the members of the school had special skills to offer to the task of building the school, we have areas of specialization and expertise, whether scholarly, theoretical, pedagogical or within areas of race, class or gender. We do not all have to do the same thing in the same way. Instead, we must support each other's efforts, realizing that they are all part of the larger enterprise of bringing about social change.

3. Building Empathy

A third issue involved in building the types of relationships and coalitions essential for social change concerns the issue of individual accountability. Race, class and gender oppression form the structural backdrop against which we frame our relationship—these are the forces that encourage us to substitute voyeurism . . . for fully human relationships. But while we may not have created this situation, we are each responsible for making individual, personal choices concerning which elements of race, class and gender oppression we will accept and which we will work to change.

One essential component of this accountability involves developing empathy for the experiences of individuals and groups different than ourselves. Empathy begins with taking an interest in

the facts of other people['s] lives, both as individuals and as groups. If you care about me, you should want to know not only the details of my personal biography but a sense of how race, class and gender as categories of analysis created the institutional and symbolic backdrop for my personal biography. How can you hope to assess my character without knowing the details of the circumstances I face?

Moreover, by taking a theoretical stance that we have all been affected by race, class and gender as categories of analysis that have structured our treatment, we open up possibilities for using those same constructs as categories of connection in building empathy. For example, I have a good White woman friend with whom I share common interests and beliefs. But we know that our racial differences have provided us with different experiences. So we talk about them. We do not assume that because I am Black, race has only affected me and not her or that because I am a Black woman, race neutralizes the effect of gender in my life while accenting it in hers. We take those same categories of analysis that have created cleavages in our lives, in this case, categories of race and gender, and use them as categories of connection in building empathy for each other's experiences.

Finding common causes and building empathy is difficult, no matter which side of privilege we inhabit. Building empathy from the dominant side of privilege is difficult, simply because individuals from privileged backgrounds are not encouraged to do so. For example, in order for those of you who are White to develop empathy for the experiences of people of color, you must grapple with how your white skin has privileged you. This is difficult to do, because it not only entails the intellectual process of seeing how whiteness is elevated in institutions and symbols, but it also involves the often painful process of seeing how your whiteness has shaped your personal biography. Intellectual stances against the institutional and symbolic dimensions of racism are generally easier to maintain than sustained self-reflection about how racism has shaped all of our individual biographies. Were and are your fathers, uncles, and grandfathers really more capable than mine, or can their accomplishments be explained in part by the racism members of my family experienced? Did your mothers stand silently by and watch all this happen? More importantly, how have they passed on the benefits of their whiteness to you?

These are difficult questions, and I have tremendous respect for my colleagues and students who are trying to answer them. Since there is no compelling reason to examine the source and meaning of one's own privilege, I know that those who do so have freely chosen this stance. They are making conscious efforts to root out the piece of the oppressor planted within them. To me, they are entitled to the support of people of color in their efforts. Men who declare themselves feminists, members of the middle class who ally themselves with antipoverty struggles, heterosexuals who support gays and lesbians, are all trying to grow, and their efforts place them far ahead of the majority who never think of engaging in such important struggles.

Building empathy from the subordinate side of privilege is also difficult, but for different reasons. Members of subordinate groups are understandably reluctant to abandon a basic mistrust of members of powerful groups because this basic mistrust has traditionally been central to their survival. As a Black woman, it would be foolish for me to assume that White women, or Black men, or White men or any other group with a history of exploiting African-American women have my best interests at heart. These groups enjoy varying amounts of privilege over me and therefore I must carefully watch them and be prepared for a relation of domination and subordination.

Like the privileged, members of subordinate groups must also work toward replacing judgments by category with new ways of thinking and acting. Refusing to do so stifles prospects for effective coalition and social change. Let me use another example from my own experiences. When I was an undergraduate, I had little time or patience for the theorizing of the privileged. My initial years at a private, elite institution were difficult, not because the course work was

challenging (it was, but that wasn't what distracted me) or because I had to work while my classmates lived on family allowances (I was used to work). The adjustment was difficult because I was surrounded by so many people who took their privilege for granted. Most of them felt entitled to their wealth. That astounded me.

I remember one incident of watching a White woman down the hall in my dormitory try to pick out which sweater to wear. The sweaters were piled up on her bed in all the colors of the rainbow, sweater after sweater. She asked my advice in a way that let me know that choosing a sweater was one of the most important decisions she had to make on a daily basis. Standing knee-deep in her sweaters, I realized how different our lives were. She did not have to worry about maintaining a solid academic average so that she could receive financial aid. Because she was in the majority, she was not treated as a representative of her race. She did not have to consider how her classroom comments or basic existence on campus contributed to the treatment her group would receive. Her allowance protected her from having to work, so she was free to spend her time studying, partying, or in her case, worrying about which sweater to wear. The degree of inequality in our lives and her unquestioned sense of entitlement concerning that inequality offended me. For a while, I categorized all affluent White women as being superficial, arrogant, overly concerned with material possessions, and part of my problem. But had I continued to classify people in this way, I would have missed out on making some very good friends whose discomfort with their inherited or acquired social class privileges pushed them to examine their position.

Since I opened with the words of Audre Lorde, it seems appropriate to close with another of her ideas. . . .

Each of us is called upon to take a stand. So in these days ahead, as we examine ourselves and each other, our works, our fears, our differences, our sisterhood and survivals, I urge you to tackle what is most difficult for us all, self-scrutiny of our complacencies, the idea that since each of us believes she is on the side of right, she need not examine her position. (1985)

I urge you to examine your position.

REFERENCES

Collins, Patricia Hill. 1989. "The Social Construction of Black Feminist Thought." *Signs*. Summer 1989.

Gwaltney, John Langston. 1980. *Drylongso: A Self-Portrait of Black America*. New York: Vintage.

Harding, Sandra. 1986. *The Science Question in Feminism*. Ithaca, NY: Cornell University Press.

Jordan, June. 1985. *On Call: Political Essays*. Boston: South End Press.

Lorde, Audre. 1984. *Sister Outsider*. Trumansberg, New York: The Crossing Press.

———. 1985 "Sisterhood and Survival." Keynote address, conference on the Black Woman Writer and the Diaspora, Michigan State University.

Spelman, Elizabeth. 1982. "Theories of Race and Gender: The Erasure of Black Women." *Quest* 5: 36–32.

Tate, Claudia, ed. 1983. *Black Women Writers at Work*. New York: Continuum.

R E A D I N G **10**

Oppression

Marilyn Frye

It is a fundamental claim of feminism that women are oppressed. The word "oppression" is a strong word. It repels and attracts. It is dangerous and dangerously fashionable and endangered. It is much misused, and sometimes not innocently.

The statement that women are oppressed is frequently met with the claim that men are oppressed too. We hear that oppressing is oppressive to those who oppress as well as to those they oppress. Some men cite as evidence of their oppression their much-advertised inability to cry. It is tough, we are told, to be masculine. When the stresses and frustrations of being a man are cited as evidence that oppressors are oppressed by their oppressing; the word "oppression" is being stretched to meaninglessness; it is treated as though its scope includes any and all human experience of limitation or suffering, no matter the cause, degree or consequence. Once such usage has been put over on us, then if ever we deny that any person or group is oppressed, we seem to imply that we think they never suffer and have no feelings. We are accused of insensitivity, even of bigotry. For women, such accusation is particularly intimidating, since sensitivity is one of the few virtues that has been assigned to us. If we are found insensitive, we may fear we have no redeeming traits at all and perhaps are not real women. Thus are we silenced before we begin: the name of our situation drained of meaning and our guilt mechanisms tripped.

But this is nonsense. Human beings can be miserable without being oppressed, and it is perfectly consistent to deny that a person or group is oppressed without denying that they have feelings or that they suffer. . . .

The root of the word "oppression" is the element "press." *The press of the crowd; pressed into military service; to press a pair of pants; printing press; press the button.* Presses are used to mold things or flatten them or reduce them in bulk, sometimes to reduce them by squeezing out the gasses or liquids in them. Something pressed is something caught between or among forces and barriers which are so related to each other that jointly they restrain, restrict or prevent the thing's motion or mobility. Mold. Immobilize. Reduce.

The mundane experience of the oppressed provides another clue. One of the most characteristic and ubiquitous features of the world as experienced by oppressed people is the double bind—situations in which options are reduced to a very few and all of them expose one to penalty, censure or deprivation. For example, it is often a requirement upon oppressed people that we smile and be cheerful. If we comply, we signal our docility and our acquiescence in our situation. We need not, then, be taken note of. We acquiesce in being made invisible, in our occupying no space. We participate in our own erasure. On the other hand, anything but the sunniest countenance exposes us to being perceived as mean, bitter, angry or dangerous. This means, at the least, that we may be found "difficult" or unpleasant to work with, which is enough to cost one one's livelihood; at worst, being seen as mean, bitter, angry or dangerous has been known to result in rape, arrest, beating and murder. One can only choose to risk one's preferred form and rate of annihilation.

Another example: It is common in the United States that women, especially younger women, are in a bind where neither sexual activity nor sexual inactivity is all right. If she is heterosexually active, a woman is open to censure and punishment for being loose, unprincipled or a whore. The "punishment" comes in the form of criticism, snide and embarrassing remarks, being treated as an easy lay by men, scorn from her more restrained female friends. She may have to lie and hide her behavior from her parents. She must juggle the risks of unwanted pregnancy and dangerous contraceptives. On the other hand, if she refrains from heterosexual activity, she is fairly constantly harassed by men who try to persuade her into it and pressure her to "relax" and "let her hair down"; she is threatened with labels like "frigid," "uptight," "man-hater," "bitch" and "cock-tease." The same parents who would be disapproving of her sexual activity may be worried by her inactivity because it suggests she is not or will not be popular, or is not sexually normal. She may be charged with lesbianism. If a woman is raped, then if she has been heterosexually active she is subject to the presumption that she liked it (since her activity is presumed to show that she likes sex), and if she has not been heterosexually active, she is subject to the presumption that she liked it (since she is supposedly "repressed and frustrated"). Both heterosexual activity and heterosexual nonactivity are likely to be taken as proof that you wanted to be raped, and hence, of course, weren't *really* raped at all. You can't win. You are caught in a bind, caught between systematically related pressures.

Women are caught like this, too, by networks of forces and barriers that expose one to penalty, loss or contempt whether one works outside the home or not, is on welfare or not, bears children or not, raises children or not, marries or not, stays married or not, is heterosexual, lesbian, both or neither. Economic necessity; confinement to racial and/or sexual job ghettos; sexual harassment; sex discrimination; pressures of competing expectations and judgments about *women, wives* and *mothers* (in the society at large, in racial and ethnic subcultures and in one's own mind); dependence (full or partial) on husbands, parents or the state; commitment to political ideas; loyalties to racial or ethnic or other "minority" groups; the demands of self-respect and responsibilities to others. Each of these factors exists in complex tension with every other, penalizing or prohibiting all of the apparently available options. And nipping at one's heels, always, is the endless pack of little things. If one dresses one way, one is subject to the assumption that one is advertising one's sexual availability; if one dresses another way, one appears to "not care about oneself" or to be "unfeminine." If one uses "strong language," one invites categorization as a whore or slut; if one does not, one invites categorization as a "lady"—one too delicately constituted to cope with robust speech or the realities to which it presumably refers.

The experience of oppressed people is that the living of one's life is confined and shaped by forces and barriers which are not accidental or occasional and hence avoidable, but are systematically related to each other in such a way as to catch one between and among them and restrict or penalize motion in any direction. It is the experience of being caged in: all avenues, in every direction, are blocked or booby trapped.

Cages. Consider a birdcage. If you look very closely at just one wire in the cage, you cannot see the other wires. If your conception of what is before you is determined by this myopic focus, you could look at that one wire, up and down the length of it, and be unable to see why a bird would not just fly around the wire any time it wanted to go somewhere. Furthermore, even if, one day at a time, you myopically inspected each wire, you still could not see why a bird would have trouble going past the wires to get anywhere. There is no physical property of any one wire, *nothing* that the closest scrutiny could discover, that will reveal how a bird could be inhibited or harmed by it except in the most accidental way. It is only when you step back, stop looking at the wires one by one, microscopically, and take a macroscopic view of the whole cage, that you can see why the bird does not go anywhere; and then you will see it in a moment. It will require no great subtlety of mental powers. It is perfectly *obvious* that the bird is surrounded by a network of systematically related barriers, no one of which would be the least hindrance to its flight, but which, by their relations to each other, are as confining as the solid walls of a dungeon.

It is now possible to grasp one of the reasons why oppression can be hard to see and recognize: one can study the elements of an oppressive structure with great care and some good will without seeing the structure as a whole, and hence without seeing or being able to understand that one is looking at a cage and that there are people there who are caged, whose motion and mobility are restricted, whose lives are shaped and reduced.

. . .

As the cageness of the birdcage is a macroscopic phenomenon, the oppressiveness of the situations in which women live our various and different lives is a macroscopic phenomenon. Neither can be *seen* from a microscopic perspective. But when you look macroscopically you can see it—a network of forces and barriers which are systematically related and which conspire to the immobilization, reduction and molding of women and the lives we live.

R E A D I N G **11**

Tomorrow I'm Going to Rewrite the English Language

Lois Keith

Tomorrow I am going to rewrite the English
   Language.
I will discard all those striving ambulist
   metaphors of power and success
And construct new ways to describe my strength.
My new, different strength.

Then I won't have to feel dependent
Because I can't stand on my own two feet.
And I'll refuse to feel a failure

When I don't stay one step ahead.
I won't feel inadequate if I can't
Stand up for myself
Or illogical when I don't
Take it one step at a time.
I will make them understand that it is a very
   male way
To describe the world.
All this walking tall
And making great strides.

Yes, tomorrow I am going to rewrite the English
  Language
Creating the world in my own image.
Mine will be a gentler, more womanly way

To describe my progress.
I will wheel, cover and encircle.
Somehow I will learn to say it all.

R E A D I N G   **12**

Homophobia
A Weapon of Sexism

Suzanne Pharr

Homophobia—the irrational fear and hatred of those who love and sexually desire those of the same sex. Though I intimately knew its meaning, the word *homophobia* was unknown to me until the late 1970s, and when I first heard it, I was struck by how difficult it is to say, what an ugly word it is, equally as ugly as its meaning. Like racism and anti-Semitism, it is a word that calls up images of loss of freedom, verbal and physical violence, death.

In my life I have experienced the effects of homophobia through rejection by friends, threats of loss of employment, and threats upon my life; and I have witnessed far worse things happening to other lesbian and gay people: loss of children, beatings, rape, death. Its power is great enough to keep ten to twenty percent of the population living lives of fear (if their sexual identity is hidden) or lives of danger (if their sexual identity is visible) or both. And its power is great enough to keep the remaining eighty to ninety percent of the population trapped in their own fears.

. . .

Homophobia works effectively as a weapon of sexism because it is joined with a powerful arm, heterosexism. Heterosexism creates the climate for homophobia with its assumption that the world is and must be heterosexual and its display of power and privilege as the norm. Heterosexism is the systemic display of homophobia in the institutions of society. Heterosexism and homophobia work together to enforce compulsory heterosexuality and that bastion of patriarchal power, the nuclear family. The central focus of the right-wing attack against women's liberation is that women's equality, women's self-determination, women's control of our own bodies and lives will damage what they see as the crucial societal institution, the nuclear family. The attack has been led by fundamentalist ministers across the country. The two areas they have focused on most consistently are abortion and homosexuality, and their passion has led them to bomb women's clinics and to recommend deprogramming for homosexuals and establishing camps to quarantine people with AIDS. To resist marriage and/or heterosexuality is to risk severe punishment and loss.

It is not by chance that when children approach puberty and increased sexual awareness they begin to taunt each other by calling these names: "queer," "faggot," "pervert." It is at puberty that the full force of society's pressure to conform to heterosexuality and prepare for marriage is brought to bear. Children know what we have taught them, and we have given clear messages that those who deviate from standard expectations are to be made to get back in line.

The best controlling tactic at puberty is to be treated as an outsider, to be ostracized at a time when it feels most vital to be accepted. Those who are different must be made to suffer loss. It is also at puberty that misogyny begins to be more apparent, and girls are pressured to conform to societal norms that do not permit them to realize their full potential. It is at this time that their academic achievements begin to decrease as they are coerced into compulsory heterosexuality and trained for dependency upon a man, that is, for economic survival.

There was a time when the two most condemning accusations against a woman meant to ostracize and disempower her were "whore" and "lesbian." The sexual revolution and changing attitudes about heterosexual behavior may have led to some lessening of the power of the word *whore,* though it still has strength as a threat to sexual property and prostitutes are stigmatized and abused. However, the word *lesbian* is still fully charged and carries with it the full threat of loss of power and privilege, the threat of being cut asunder, abandoned, and left outside society's protection.

To be a lesbian is to be *perceived* as someone who has stepped out of line, who has moved out of sexual/economic dependence on a male, who is woman-identified. A lesbian is perceived as someone who can live without a man and who is therefore (however illogically) against men. A lesbian is perceived as being outside the acceptable, routinized order of things. She is seen as someone who has no societal institutions to protect her and who is not privileged to the protection of individual males. Many heterosexual women see her as someone who stands in contradiction to the sacrifices they have made to conform to compulsory heterosexuality. A lesbian is perceived as a threat to the nuclear family, to male dominance and control, to the very heart of sexism.

Gay men are perceived also as a threat to male dominance and control, and the homophobia expressed against them has the same roots in sexism as does homophobia against lesbians. Visible gay men are the objects of extreme hatred and fear by heterosexual men because their breaking ranks with male heterosexual solidarity is seen as a damaging rent in the very fabric of sexism. They are seen as betrayers, as traitors who must be punished and eliminated. In the beating and killing of gay men we see clear evidence of this hatred. When we see the fierce homophobia expressed toward gay men, we can begin to understand the ways sexism also affects males through imposing rigid, dehumanizing gender roles on them. The two circumstances in which it is legitimate for men to be openly physically affectionate with one another are in competitive sports and in the crisis of war. For many men, these two experiences are the highlights of their lives, and they think of them again and again with nostalgia. War and sports offer a cover of all-male safety and dominance to keep away the notion of affectionate openness being identified with homosexuality. When gay men break ranks with male roles through bonding and affection outside the arenas of war and sports, they are perceived as not being "real men," that is, as being identified with women, the weaker sex that must be dominated and that over the centuries has been the object of male hatred and abuse. Misogyny gets transferred to gay men with a vengeance and is increased by the fear that their sexual identity and behavior will bring down the entire system of male dominance and compulsory heterosexuality.

If lesbians are established as threats to the status quo, as outcasts who must be punished, homophobia can wield its power over all women through lesbian baiting. Lesbian baiting is an attempt to control women by labeling us as lesbians because our behavior is not acceptable, that is, when we are being independent, going our own way, living whole lives, fighting for our rights, demanding equal pay, saying no to violence, being self-assertive, bonding with and loving the company of women, assuming the right to our bodies, insisting upon our own authority, making changes that include us in society's decision-making; lesbian baiting occurs when women are called lesbians because we resist male dominance and control. And it has little or nothing to do with one's sexual identity.

To be named as lesbian threatens all women, not just lesbians, with great loss. And any woman who steps out of role risks being called a lesbian. To understand how this is a threat to all women, one must understand that any woman can be called a lesbian and there is no real way she can defend herself: there is no way to credential one's sexuality. ("The Children's Hour," a Lillian Hellman play, makes this point when a student asserts two teachers are lesbians and they have no way to disprove it.) She may be married or divorced, have children, dress in the most feminine manner, have sex with men, be celibate—but there are lesbians who do all those things. *Lesbians look like all women and all women look like lesbians.* There is no guaranteed method of identification, and as we all know, sexual identity can be kept hidden. (The same is true for men. There is no way to prove their sexual identity, though many go to extremes to prove heterosexuality.) Also, women are not necessarily born lesbian. Some seem to be, but others become lesbians later in life after having lived heterosexual lives. Lesbian baiting of heterosexual women would not work if there were a definitive way to identify lesbians (or heterosexuals).

We have yet to understand clearly how sexual identity develops. And this is disturbing to some people, especially those who are determined to discover how lesbian and gay identity is formed so that they will know where to start in eliminating it. (Isn't it odd that there is so little concern about discovering the causes of heterosexuality?) There are many theories: genetic makeup, hormones, socialization, environment, etc. But there is no conclusive evidence that indicates that heterosexuality comes from one process and homosexuality from another.

We do know, however, that sexual identity can be in flux, and we know that sexual identity means more than just the gender of people one is attracted to and has sex with. To be a lesbian has as many ramifications as for a woman to be heterosexual. It is more than sex, more than just the bedroom issue many would like to make it: it is a woman-centered life with all the social interconnections that entails. Some lesbians are in long-term relationships, some in short-term ones, some date, some are celibate, some are married to men, some remain as separate as possible from men, some have children by men, some by alternative insemination, some seem "feminine" by societal standards, some "masculine," some are doctors, lawyers and ministers, some laborers, housewives and writers: what all share in common is a sexual/affectional identity that focuses on women in its attractions and social relationships.

If lesbians are simply women with a particular sexual identity who look and act like all women, then the major difference in living out a lesbian sexual identity as opposed to a heterosexual identity is that as lesbians we live in a homophobic world that threatens and imposes damaging loss on us for being *who we are,* for choosing to live whole lives. Homophobic people often assert that homosexuals have the choice of not being homosexual; that is, we don't have to act out our sexual identity. In that case, I want to hear heterosexuals talk about their willingness not to act out their sexual identity, including not just sexual activity but heterosexual social interconnections and heterosexual privilege. It is a question of wholeness. It is very difficult for one to be denied the life of a sexual being, whether expressed in sex or in physical affection, and to feel complete, whole. For our loving relationships with humans feed the life of the spirit and enable us to overcome our basic isolation and to be interconnected with humankind.

• . . .

What does a woman have to do to get called a lesbian? Almost anything, sometimes nothing at all, but certainly anything that threatens the status quo, anything that steps out of role, anything that asserts the rights of women, anything that doesn't indicate submission and subordination. Assertiveness, standing up for oneself, asking for more pay, better working conditions, training for and accepting a nontraditional (you mean a man's?) job, enjoying the company of women, being financially independent, being in control of one's life, depending first and foremost upon oneself, thinking that one can do whatever needs to be done, but above all, working for the rights and equality of women.

In the backlash to the gains of the women's liberation movement, there has been an increased effort to keep definitions man-centered. Therefore, to work on behalf of women must mean to work against men. To love women must mean that one hates men. A very effective attack has been made against the word *feminist* to make it a derogatory word. In current backlash usage, *feminist* equals *man-hater,* which equals *lesbian.* This formula is created in the hope that women will be frightened away from their work on behalf of women. Consequently, we now have women who believe in the rights of women and work for those rights while from fear deny that they are feminists, or refuse to use the word because it is so "abrasive."

So, what does one do in an effort to keep from being called a lesbian? She steps back into line, into the role that is demanded of her, tries to behave in such a way that doesn't threaten the status of men, and if she works for women's rights, she begins modifying that work. When women's organizations begin doing significant social change work, they inevitably are lesbian baited; that is, funders or institutions or community members tell us that they can't work with us because of our "man-hating attitudes" or the presence of lesbians. We are called too strident, told we are making enemies, not doing good.

The battered women's movement has seen this kind of attack: the pressure has been to provide services only, without analysis of the causes of violence against women and strategies for ending it. To provide only services without political analysis or direct action is to be in an approved "helping" role; to analyze the causes of violence against women is to begin the work toward changing an entire system of power and control. It is when we do the latter that we are threatened with the label of man-hater or lesbian. For my politics, if a women's social change organization has not been labeled lesbian or communist, it is probably not doing significant work; it is only "making nice."

Women in many of these organizations, out of fear of all the losses we are threatened with, begin to modify our work to make it more acceptable and less threatening to the male-dominated society which we originally set out to change. The work can no longer be radical (going to the root cause of the problem) but instead must be reforming, working only on the symptoms and not the cause. Real change for women becomes thwarted and stopped. The word *lesbian* is instilled with the power to halt our work and control our lives. And we give it its power with our fear.

In my view, homophobia has been one of the major causes of the failure of the women's liberation movement to make deep and lasting change. (The other major block has been racism.) We were fierce when we set out, but when threatened with the loss of heterosexual privilege, we began putting on brakes. Our best-known nationally distributed women's magazine was reluctant to print articles about lesbians, began putting a man on the cover several times a year, and writing articles about women who succeeded in a man's world. We worried about our image, our being all right, our being "real women" despite our work. Instead of talking about the elimination of sexual gender roles, we stepped back and talked about "sex role stereotyping" as the issue. Change around the edges for middle-class white women began to be talked about as successes. We accepted tokenism and integration, forgetting that equality for all women, for all people—and not just equality of white middle-class women with white men—was the goal that we could never put behind us.

But despite backlash and retreats, change is growing from within. The women's liberation movement is beginning to gain strength again because there are women who are talking about liberation for all women. We are examining sexism, racism, homophobia, classism, anti-Semitism, ageism, ableism, and imperialism, and we see everything as connected. This change in point of view represents the third wave of the women's liberation movement, a new direction that does not get mass media coverage and recognition. It has been initiated by women of color and lesbians who were marginalized or rendered invisible by the white heterosexual leaders of earlier efforts. The first wave was the 19th and early 20th century campaign for the vote; the second, beginning in the 1960s, focused on the Equal Rights Amendment and abortion rights. Consisting of predominantly white middle-class women, both failed in recognizing issues of equality and empowerment for all women. The third wave of the movement, multi-racial and multi-issued, seeks the transformation of the world for us all. We know that we won't get there until everyone gets there; that we must move forward in a great strong line, hand in hand, not just a few at a time.

We know that the arguments about homophobia originating from mental health, and biblical/religious attitudes can be settled when we look at the sexism that permeates religious and psychiatric history. The women of the third wave of the women's liberation movement know that *without the existence of sexism, there would be no homophobia.*

Finally, we know that as long as the word *lesbian* can strike fear in any woman's heart, then work on behalf of women can be stopped; the only successful work against sexism must include work against homophobia.

R E A D I N G **13**

White Privilege and Male Privilege

Peggy McIntosh

Through work to bring materials and perspectives from Women's Studies into the rest of the curriculum, I have often noticed men's unwillingness to grant that they are overprivileged in the curriculum, even though they may grant that women are disadvantaged. Denials that amount to taboos surround the subject of advantages that men gain from women's disadvantages. These denials protect male privilege from being fully recognized, acknowledged, lessened, or ended.

Thinking through unacknowledged male privilege as a phenomenon with a life of its own, I realized that since hierarchies in our society are interlocking, there was most likely a phenomenon of white privilege that was similarly denied and protected, but alive and real in its effects. As a white person, I realized I had been taught about racism as something that puts others at a disadvantage, but had been taught not to see one of its corollary aspects, white privilege, which puts me at an advantage.

I think whites are carefully taught not to recognize white privilege, as males are taught not to recognize male privilege. So I have begun in an untutored way to ask what it is like to have white privilege. This paper is a partial record of my personal observations and not a scholarly analysis. It is based on my daily experiences within my particular circumstances.

I have come to see white privilege as an invisible package of unearned assets that I can count on cashing in each day, but about which I was "meant" to remain oblivious. White privilege is like an invisible weightless knapsack of special provisions, assurances, tools, maps, guides, codebooks, passports, visas, clothes, compass, emergency gear, and blank checks.

Since I have had trouble facing white privilege, and describing its results in my life, I saw parallels here with men's reluctance to acknowledge male privilege. Only rarely will a man go beyond acknowledging that women are disadvantaged to acknowledging that men have unearned advantage, or that unearned privilege has not been good for men's development as human beings, or for society's development, or that privilege systems might ever be challenged and *changed*.

I will review here several types or layers of denial that I see at work protecting, and preventing awareness about, entrenched male privilege. Then I will draw parallels, from my own experience, with the denials that veil the facts of white privilege. Finally, I will list forty-six ordinary and daily ways in which I experience having white privilege, by contrast with my African American colleagues in the same building. This list is not intended to be generalizable. Others can make their own lists from within their own life circumstances.

Writing this paper has been difficult, despite warm receptions for the talks on which it is based.[1] For describing white privilege makes one newly accountable. As we in Women's Studies work [to] reveal male privilege and ask men to give up some of their power, so one who writes about having white privilege must ask, "Having described it, what will I do to lessen or end it?"

The denial of men's overprivileged state takes many forms in discussions of curriculum change work. Some claim that men must be central in the curriculum because they have done most of what is important or distinctive in life or in civilization. Some recognize sexism in the curriculum but deny that it makes male students seem unduly important in life. Others agree that certain *individual* thinkers are male oriented but deny that there is any *systemic* tendency in disciplinary frameworks or epistemology to overempower men as a group. Those men who do grant that male privilege takes institutionalized and embedded forms are still likely to deny that male hegemony has opened doors for them personally. Virtually all men deny that male overreward alone can explain men's centrality in all the inner sanctums of our most powerful institutions. Moreover, those few who will acknowledge that male privilege systems have overempowered them usually end up doubting that we could dismantle these privilege systems. They may say they will

work to improve women's status, in the society or in the university, but they can't or won't support the idea of lessening men's. In curricular terms, this is the point at which they say that they regret they cannot use any of the interesting new scholarship on women because the syllabus is full. When the talk turns to giving men less cultural room, even the most thoughtful and fair-minded of the men I know will tend to reflect, or fall back on, conservative assumptions about the inevitability of present gender relations and distributions of power, calling on precedent or sociobiology and psychobiology to demonstrate that male domination is natural and follows inevitably from evolutionary pressures. Others resort to arguments from "experience" or religion or social responsibility or wishing and dreaming.

After I realized, through faculty development work in Women's Studies, the extent to which men work from a base of unacknowledged privilege, I understood that much of their oppressiveness was unconscious. Then I remembered the frequent charges from women of color that white women whom they encounter are oppressive. I began to understand why we are justly seen as oppressive, even when we don't see ourselves that way. At the very least, obliviousness of one's privileged state can make a person or group irritating to be with. I began to count the ways in which I enjoy unearned skin privilege and have been conditioned into oblivion about its existence, unable to see that it put me "ahead" in any way, or put my people ahead, overrewarding us and yet also paradoxically damaging us, or that it could or should be changed.

My schooling gave me no training in seeing myself as an oppressor, as an unfairly advantaged person, or as a participant in a damaged culture. I was taught to see myself as an individual whose moral state depended on her individual moral will. At school, we were not taught about slavery in any depth; we were not taught to see slaveholders as damaged people. Slaves were seen as the only group at risk of being dehumanized. My schooling followed the pattern which Elizabeth Minnich has pointed out: whites are taught to think of their lives as morally neutral, normative, and average, and also ideal, so that when we work to benefit others, this is seen as work that will allow "them" to be more like "us." I think many of us know how obnoxious this attitude can be in men.

After frustration with men who would not recognize male privilege, I decided to try to work on myself at least by identifying some of the daily effects of white privilege in my life. It is crude work, at this stage, but I will give here a list of special circumstances and conditions I experience that I did not earn but that I have been made to feel are mine by birth, by citizenship, and by virtue of being a conscientious law-abiding "normal" person of goodwill. I have chosen those conditions that I think in my case *attach somewhat more to skin-color privilege* than to class, religion, ethnic status, or geographical location, though these other privileging factors are intricately intertwined. As far as I can see, my Afro-American co-workers, friends, and acquaintances with whom I come into daily or frequent contact in this particular time, place, and line of work cannot count on most of these conditions.

1. I can, if I wish, arrange to be in the company of people of my race most of the time.
2. I can avoid spending time with people whom I was trained to mistrust and who have learned to mistrust my kind or me.
3. If I should need to move, I can be pretty sure of renting or purchasing housing in an area which I can afford and in which I would want to live.
4. I can be reasonably sure that my neighbors in such a location will be neutral or pleasant to me.
5. I can go shopping alone most of the time, fairly well assured that I will not be followed or harassed by store detectives.
6. I can turn on the television or open to the front page of the paper and see people of my race widely and positively represented.
7. When I am told about our national heritage or about "civilization," I am shown that people of my color made it what it is.
8. I can be sure that my children will be given curricular materials that testify to the existence of their race.
9. If I want to, I can be pretty sure of finding a publisher for this piece on white privilege.
10. I can be fairly sure of having my voice heard in a group in which I am the only member of my race.
11. I can be casual about whether or not to listen to another woman's voice in a group in which she is the only member of her race.
12. I can go into a book shop and count on finding the writing of my race represented, into a supermarket and find the staple foods that fit with my cultural traditions, into a hairdresser's shop and find someone who can deal with my hair.
13. Whether I use checks, credit cards, or cash, I can count on my skin color not to work against the appearance that I am financially reliable.
14. I could arrange to protect our young children most of the time from people who might not like them.
15. I did not have to educate our children to be aware of systemic racism for their own daily physical protection.
16. I can be pretty sure that my children's teachers and employers will tolerate them if they fit school and workplace norms; my chief worries about them do not concern others' attitudes toward their race.
17. I can talk with my mouth full and not have people put this down to my color.
18. I can swear, or dress in secondhand clothes, or not answer letters, without having people attribute these choices to the bad morals, the poverty, or the illiteracy of my race.
19. I can speak in public to a powerful male group without putting my race on trial.
20. I can do well in a challenging situation without being called a credit to my race.
21. I am never asked to speak for all the people of my racial group.
22. I can remain oblivious to the language and customs of persons of color who constitute the world's majority without feeling in my culture any penalty for such oblivion.
23. I can criticize our government and talk about how much I fear its policies and behavior without being seen as a cultural outsider.

24. I can be reasonably sure that if I ask to talk to "the person in charge," I will be facing a person of my race.

25. If a traffic cop pulls me over or if the IRS audits my tax return, I can be sure I haven't been singled out because of my race.

26. I can easily buy posters, postcards, picture books, greeting cards, dolls, toys, and children's magazines featuring people of my race.

27. I can go home from most meetings of organizations I belong to feeling somewhat tied in, rather than isolated, out of place, outnumbered, unheard, held at a distance, or feared.

28. I can be pretty sure that an argument with a colleague of another race is more likely to jeopardize her chances for advancement than to jeopardize mine.

29. I can be fairly sure that if I argue for the promotion of a person of another race, or a program centering on race, this is not likely to cost me heavily within my present setting, even if my colleagues disagree with me.

30. If I declare there is a racial issue at hand, or there isn't a racial issue at hand, my race will lend me more credibility for either position than a person of color will have.

31. I can choose to ignore developments in minority writing and minority activist programs, or disparage them, or learn from them, but in any case, I can find ways to be more or less protected from negative consequences of any of these choices.

32. My culture gives me little fear about ignoring the perspectives and powers of people of other races.

33. I am not made acutely aware that my shape, bearing, or body odor will be taken as a reflection on my race.

34. I can worry about racism without being seen as self-interested or self-seeking.

35. I can take a job with an affirmative action employer without having my co-workers on the job suspect that I got it because of my race.

36. If my day, week, or year is going badly, I need not ask of each negative episode or situation whether it has racial overtones.

37. I can be pretty sure of finding people who would be willing to talk with me and advise me about my next steps, professionally.

38. I can think over many options, social, political, imaginative, or professional, without asking whether a person of my race would be accepted or allowed to do what I want to do.

39. I can be late to a meeting without having the lateness reflect on my race.

40. I can choose public accommodation without fearing that people of my race cannot get in or will be mistreated in the places I have chosen.

41. I can be sure that if I need legal or medical help, my race will not work against me.

42. I can arrange my activities so that I will never have to experience feelings of rejection owing to my race.

43. If I have low credibility as a leader, I can be sure that my race is not the problem.

44. I can easily find academic courses and institutions that give attention only to people of my race.

45. I can expect figurative language and imagery in all of the arts to testify to experiences of my race.

46. I can choose blemish cover or bandages in "flesh" color and have them more or less match my skin.

I repeatedly forgot each of the realizations on this list until I wrote it down. For me, white privilege has turned out to be an elusive and fugitive subject. The pressure to avoid it is great, for in facing it I must give up the myth of meritocracy. If these things are true, this is not such a free country; one's life is not what one makes it; many doors open for certain people through no virtues of their own. These perceptions mean also that my moral condition is not what I had been led to believe. The appearance of being a good citizen rather than a troublemaker comes in large part from having all sorts of doors open automatically because of my color.

A further paralysis of nerve comes from literary silence protecting privilege. My clearest memories of finding such analysis are in Lillian Smith's unparalleled *Killers of the Dream* and

Margaret Andersen's review of Karen and Mamie Fields' *Lemon Swamp*. Smith, for example, wrote about walking toward black children on the street and knowing they would step into the gutter; Andersen contrasted the pleasure that she, as a white child, took on summer driving trips to the south with Karen Fields' memories of driving in a closed car stocked with all necessities lest, in stopping, her black family should suffer "insult, or worse." Adrienne Rich also recognizes and writes about daily experiences of privilege, but in my observation, white women's writing in this area is far more often on systemic racism than on our daily lives as light-skinned women.[2]

In unpacking this invisible knapsack of white privilege, I have listed conditions of daily experience that I once took for granted, as neutral, normal, and universally available to everybody, just as I once thought of a male-focused curriculum as the neutral or accurate account that can speak for all. Nor did I think of any of these perquisites as bad for the holder. I now think that we need a more finely differentiated taxonomy of privilege, for some of these varieties are only what one would want for everyone in a just society, and others give license to be ignorant, oblivious, arrogant, and destructive. Before proposing some more finely tuned categorization, I will make some observations about the general effects of these conditions on my life and expectations.

In this potpourri of examples, some privileges make me feel at home in the world. Others allow me to escape penalties or dangers that others suffer. Through some, I escape fear, anxiety, insult, injury, or a sense of not being welcome, not being real. Some keep me from having to hide, to be in disguise, to feel sick or crazy, to negotiate each transaction from the position of being an outsider or, within my group, a person who is suspected of having too close links with a dominant culture. Most keep me from having to be angry.

I see a pattern running through the matrix of white privilege, a pattern of assumptions that were passed on to me as a white person. There was one main piece of cultural turf; it was my own turf, and I was among those who could control the turf. I could measure up to the cultural standards and take advantage of the many options I saw around me to make what the culture would call a success of my life. *My skin color was an asset for any move I was educated to want to make.* I could think of myself as "belonging" in major ways and of making social systems work for me. I could freely disparage, fear, neglect, or be oblivious to anything outside of the dominant cultural forms. Being of the main culture, I could also criticize it fairly freely. My life was reflected back to me frequently enough so that I felt, with regard to my race, if not to my sex, like one of the real people.

Whether through the curriculum or in the newspaper, the television, the economic system, or the general look of people in the streets, I received daily signals and indications that my people counted and that others *either didn't exist or must be trying, not very successfully, to be like people of my race.* I was given cultural permission not to hear voices of people of other races or a tepid cultural tolerance for hearing or acting on such voices. I was also raised not to suffer seriously from anything that darker-skinned people might say about my group, "protected," though perhaps I should more accurately say *prohibited,* through the habits of my economic class and social group, from living in racially mixed groups or being reflective about interactions between people of differing races.

In proportion as my racial group was being made confident, comfortable, and oblivious, other groups were likely being made unconfident, uncomfortable, and alienated. Whiteness protected me from many kinds of hostility, distress, and violence, which I was being subtly trained to visit in turn upon people of color.

For this reason, the word "privilege" now seems to me misleading. Its connotations are too positive to fit the conditions and behaviors which "privilege systems" produce. We usually think of privilege as being a favored state, whether earned or conferred by birth or luck. School graduates are reminded they are privileged and urged to use their (enviable) assets well. The word "privilege" carries the connotation of being something everyone must want. Yet some of the conditions I have described here work to systemically overempower certain groups. Such privilege simply *confers dominance,* gives permission to control, because of one's race or sex. The kind of privilege that gives license to some people to be, at best, thoughtless and, at worst, murderous should not continue to be referred to as a desirable attribute. Such "privilege" may be widely desired without being in any way beneficial to the whole society.

Moreover, though "privilege" may confer power, it does not confer moral strength. Those who do not depend on conferred dominance have traits and qualities that may never develop in those who do. Just as Women's Studies courses indicate that women survive their political circumstances to lead lives that hold the human race together, so "underprivileged" people of color who are the world's majority have survived their oppression and lived survivors' lives from which the white global minority can and must learn. In some groups, those dominated have actually become strong through *not* having all of these unearned advantages, and this gives them a great deal to teach the others. Members of so-called privileged groups can seem foolish, ridiculous, infantile, or dangerous by contrast.

I want, then, to distinguish between earned strength and unearned power conferred systemically. Power from unearned privilege can look like strength when it is, in fact, permission to escape or to dominate. But not all of the privileges on my list are inevitably damaging. Some, like the expectation that neighbors will be decent to you, or that your race will not count against you in court, should be the norm in a just society and should be considered as the entitlement of everyone. Others, like the privilege not to listen to less powerful people, distort the humanity of the holders as well as the ignored groups. Still others, like finding one's staple foods everywhere, may be a function of being a member of a numerical majority in the population. Others have to do with not having to labor under pervasive negative stereotyping and mythology.

We might at least start by distinguishing between positive advantages that we can work to spread, to the point where they are not advantages at all but simply part of the normal civic and social fabric, and negative types of advantage that unless rejected will always reinforce our present hierarchies. For example, the positive "privilege" of belonging, the feeling that one belongs within the human circle, as Native Americans say, fosters development and should not be seen as privilege for a few. It is, let us say, an entitlement that none of us should have to earn; ideally it is an *unearned entitlement.* At present, since only a few have it, it is an *unearned advantage* for them. The negative "privilege" that gave me cultural permission not to take darker-skinned Others seriously can be seen as arbitrarily conferred dominance and should not be desirable for anyone. This paper results from a process of coming to see that some of the power that I originally saw as attendant on being a human being in the United States consisted in *unearned advantage* and *conferred dominance,* as well as other kinds of special circumstance not universally taken for granted.

In writing this paper I have also realized that white identity and status (as well as class identity and status) give me considerable power to choose whether to broach this subject and its trouble. I can pretty well decide whether to disappear and avoid and not listen and escape the dislike I may engender in other people through this essay, or interrupt, answer, interpret, preach, correct, criticize, and control to some extent what goes on in reaction to it. Being white, I am given considerable power to escape many kinds of danger or penalty as well as to choose which risks I want to take.

There is an analogy here, once again, with Women's Studies. Our male colleagues do not have a great deal to lose in supporting Women's Studies, but they do not have a great deal to lose if they oppose it either. They simply have the power to decide whether to commit themselves to more equitable distributions of power. They will probably feel few penalties whatever choice they make; they do not seem, in any obvious short-term sense, the ones at risk, though they and we are all at risk because of the behaviors that have been rewarded in them.

Through Women's Studies work I have met very few men who are truly distressed about systemic, unearned male advantage and conferred dominance. And so one question for me and others like me is whether we will be like them, or whether we will get truly distressed, even outraged, about unearned race advantage and conferred dominance and if so, what we will do to lessen them. In any case, we need to do more work in identifying how they actually affect our daily lives. We need more down-to-earth writing by people about these taboo subjects. We need more understanding of the ways in which white "privilege" damages white people, for these are not the same ways in which it damages the victimized. Skewed white psyches are an inseparable part of the picture, though I do not want to confuse the kinds of damage done to the holders of special assets and to those who suffer the deficits. Many, perhaps most, of our white students in the United States think that racism doesn't affect them because they are not people of color; they do not see "whiteness" as a racial identity. Many men likewise think that Women's Studies does not bear on their own existences because they are not female; they do not see themselves as having gendered identities. Insisting on the universal "effects" of "privilege" systems, then, becomes one of our chief tasks, and being more explicit about the *particular* effects in particular contexts is another. Men need to join us in this work.

In addition, since race and sex are not the only advantaging systems at work, we need to similarly examine the daily experience of having age advantage, or ethnic advantage, or physical ability, or advantage related to nationality, religion, or sexual orientation. Professor Marnie Evans suggested to me that in many ways the list I made also applies directly to heterosexual privilege. This is a still more taboo subject than race privilege: the daily ways in which heterosexual privilege makes some persons comfortable or powerful, providing supports, assets, approvals, and rewards to those who live or expect to live in heterosexual pairs. Unpacking that content is still more difficult, owing to the deeper embeddedness of heterosexual advantage and dominance and stricter taboos surrounding these.

But to start such an analysis I would put this observation from my own experience: the fact that I live under the same roof with a man triggers all kinds of societal assumptions about my worth, politics, life, and values and triggers a host of unearned advantages and powers. After recasting many elements from the original list I would add further observations like these:

1. My children do not have to answer questions about why I live with my partner (my husband).
2. I have no difficulty finding neighborhoods where people approve of our household.
3. Our children are given texts and classes that implicitly support our kind of family unit and do not turn them against my choice of domestic partnership.
4. I can travel alone or with my husband without expecting embarrassment or hostility in those who deal with us.
5. Most people I meet will see my marital arrangements as an asset to my life or as a favorable comment on my likability, my competence, or my mental health.
6. I can talk about the social events of a weekend without fearing most listeners' reactions.
7. I will feel welcomed and "normal" in the usual walks of public life, institutional and social.
8. In many contexts, I am seen as "all right" in daily work on women because I do not live chiefly with women.

Difficulties and dangers surrounding the task of finding parallels are many. Since racism, sexism, and heterosexism are not the same, the advantages associated with them should not be seen as the same. In addition, it is hard to isolate aspects of unearned advantage that derive chiefly from social class, economic class, race, religion, region, sex, or ethnic identity. The oppressions are both distinct and interlocking, as the Combahee River Collective statement of 1977 continues to remind us eloquently.[3]

One factor seems clear about all of the interlocking oppressions. They take both active forms that we can see and embedded forms that members of the dominant group are taught not to see.

In my class and place, I did not see myself as racist because I was taught to recognize racism only in individual acts of meanness by members of my group, never in invisible systems conferring racial dominance on my group from birth. Likewise, we are taught to think that sexism or heterosexism is carried on only through intentional, individual acts of discrimination, meanness, or cruelty, rather than in invisible systems conferring unsought dominance on certain groups. Disapproving of the systems won't be enough to change them. I was taught to think that racism could end if white individuals changed their attitudes; many men think sexism can be ended by individual changes in daily behavior toward women. But a man's sex provides advantage for him whether or not he approves of the way in which dominance has been conferred on his group. A "white" skin in the United States opens many doors for whites whether or not we approve of the way dominance has been conferred on us. Individual acts can palliate, but cannot end, these problems. To redesign social systems, we need first to acknowledge their colossal unseen dimensions. The silences and denials surrounding privilege are the key political tool here. They keep the thinking about equality or equity incomplete, protecting unearned advantage and conferred dominance by making these subjects taboo. Most talk by whites about equal opportunity seems to me now to be about equal opportunity to try to get into a position of dominance while denying that *systems* of dominance exist.

Obliviousness about white advantage, like obliviousness about male advantage, is kept strongly inculturated in the United States so as to maintain the myth of meritocracy, the myth that democratic choice is equally available to all. Keeping most people unaware that freedom of confident action is there for just a small number of people props up those in power and serves to keep power in the hands of the same groups that have most of it already. Though systemic change takes many decades, there are pressing questions for me and I imagine for some others like me if we raise our daily consciousness on the perquisites of being light-skinned. What will we do with such knowledge? As we know from watching men, it is an open question whether we will choose to use unearned advantage to weaken invisible privilege systems and whether we will use any of our arbitrarily awarded power to try to reconstruct power systems on a broader base.

NOTES

I have appreciated commentary on this paper from the Working Papers Committee of the Wellesley College Center for Research on Women, from members of the Dodge seminar, and from many individuals, including Margaret Andersen, Sorel Berman, Joanne Braxton, Johnnella Butler, Sandra Dickerson, Marnie Evans, Beverly Guy-Sheftall, Sandra Harding, Eleanor Hinton Hoyt, Pauline Houston, Paul Lauter, Joyce Miller, Mary Norris, Gloria Oden, Beverly Smith, and John Walter.

1. This paper was presented at the Virginia Women's Studies Association conference in Richmond in April 1986, and the American Educational Research Association conference in Boston in October 1986, and discussed with two groups of participants in the Dodge seminars for Secondary School Teachers in New York and Boston in the spring of 1987.
2. Andersen, Margaret, "Race and the Social Science Curriculum: A Teaching and Learning Discussion." *Radical Teacher,* November 1984, pp. 17–20. Smith, Lillian, *Killers of the Dream,* New York: W. W. Norton, 1949.
3. "A Black Feminist Statement," The Combahee River Collective, pp. 13–22 in G. Hull, P. Scott, B. Smith, Eds., *All the Women Are White, All the Blacks Are Men, But Some of Us Are Brave: Black Women's Studies,* Old Westbury, NY: The Feminist Press, 1982.

Something About the Subject Makes It Hard to Name

Gloria Yamato

Racism—simple enough in structure, yet difficult to eliminate. Racism—pervasive in the U.S. culture to the point that it deeply affects all the local town folk and spills over, negatively influencing the fortunes of folk around the world. Racism is pervasive to the point that we take many of its manifestations for granted, believing "that's life." Many believe that racism can be dealt with effectively in one hellifying workshop, or one hour-long heated discussion. Many actually believe this monster, racism, that has had at least a few hundred years to take root, grow, invade our space, and develop subtle variations . . . this mind-funk that distorts thought and action, can be merely wished away. I've run into folks who really think that we can beat this devil, kick this habit, be healed of this disease in a snap. In a sincere blink of a well-intentioned eye, presto—poof—racism disappears. "I've dealt with my racism . . . (envision a laying on of hands) . . . Hallelujah! Now I can go to the beach." Well, fine. Go to the beach. In fact, why don't we all go to the beach and continue to work on the sucker over there? Cuz you can't even shave a little piece off this thing called racism in a day, or a weekend, or a workshop.

When I speak of *oppression,* I'm talking about the systematic, institutionalized mistreatment of one group of people by another for whatever reason. The oppressors are purported to have an innate ability to access economic resources, information, respect, etc., while the oppressed are believed to have a corresponding negative innate ability. The flip side of oppression is *internalized oppression.* Members of the target group are emotionally, physically, and spiritually battered to the point that they begin to actually believe that their oppression is deserved, is their lot in life, is natural and right, and that it doesn't even exist. The oppression begins to feel comfortable, familiar enough that when mean ol' Massa lay down de whip, we got's to pick up and whack ourselves and each other. Like a virus, it's hard to beat racism, because by the time you come up with a cure, it's mutated to a "new cure-resistant" form. One shot just won't get it. Racism must be attacked from many angles.

The forms of racism that I pick up on these days are (1) aware/blatant racism, (2) aware/covert racism, (3) unaware/unintentional racism, and (4) unaware/self-righteous racism. I can't say that I prefer any one form of racism over the others, because they all look like an itch needing a scratch. I've heard it said (and understandably so) that the aware/blatant form of racism is preferable if one must suffer it. Outright racists will, without apology or confusion, tell us that because of our color we don't appeal to them. If we so choose, we can attempt to get the hell out of their way before we get the sweat knocked out of us. Growing up, aware/covert racism is what I heard many of my elders bemoaning "up north," after having escaped the overt racism "down south." Apartments were suddenly no longer vacant or rents were outrageously high, when black, brown, red, or yellow persons went to inquire about them. Job vacancies were suddenly filled, or we were fired for very vague reasons. It still happens, though the perpetrators really take care to cover their tracks these days. They don't want to get gummed to death or slobbered on by the toothless laws that supposedly protect us from such inequities.

Unaware/unintentional racism drives usually tranquil white liberals wild when they get called on it, and confirms the suspicions of many people of color who feel that white folks are just plain crazy. It has led white people to believe that it's just fine to ask if they can touch my hair (while reaching). They then exclaim over how soft it is, how it does not scratch their hand. It has led whites to assume that bending over backwards and speaking to me in high-pitched (terrified), condescending tones would make up for all the racist wrongs that distort our lives. This type of racism has led whites right to my doorstep, talking 'bout, "We're sorry/we love you and want to make things right," which is fine, and further, "We're gonna give you the opportunity to fix it while we sleep. Just tell us what you need. 'Bye!!"—which *ain't* fine. With the best of intentions, the best of educations, and the greatest generosity of heart, whites, operating on the misinformation fed to them from day one, will behave in ways that are racist, will perpetuate racism by being "nice" the way we're taught to be nice. You can just "nice" somebody to death with naïveté and lack of awareness of privilege. Then there's guilt and the desire to end racism and how the two get all tangled up to the point that people, morbidly fascinated with their guilt, are immobilized. Rather than deal with ending racism, they sit and ponder their guilt and hope nobody notices how awful they are. Meanwhile, racism picks up momentum and keeps on keepin' on.

Now, the newest form of racism that I'm hip to is unaware/self-righteous racism. The "good white" racist attempts to shame Blacks into being blacker, scorns Japanese-Americans who don't speak Japanese, and knows more about the Chicano/a community than the folks who make up the community. They assign themselves as the "good whites," as opposed to the "bad whites," and are often so busy telling people of color what the issues in the Black, Asian, Indian, Latino/a communities should be that they don't have time to deal with their errant sisters and brothers in the white community. Which means that people of color are still left to deal with what the "good whites" don't want to . . . racism.

Internalized racism is what really gets in my way as a Black woman. It influences the way I see or don't see myself, limits what I expect of myself or others like me. It results in my acceptance of mistreatment, leads me to believe that being treated with less than absolute respect, at least this once, is to be expected because I am Black, because I am not white. "Because I am (*you fill in the color*), you think, "Life is going to be hard." The fact is life may be hard, but the color of your skin is not the cause of the hardship. The color of your skin may be used as an excuse to mistreat you, but there is no reason or logic involved in the mistreatment. If it seems that your color is the reason, if it seems that your ethnic heritage is the cause of the woe, it's because you've been deliberately beaten down by agents of a greedy system until you swallowed the garbage. That is the internalization of racism.

Racism is the systematic, institutionalized mistreatment of one group of people by another based on racial heritage. Like every other oppression, racism can be internalized. People of color come to believe misinformation about their particular ethnic group and thus believe that their mistreatment is justified. With that basic vocabulary, let's take a look at how the whole thing works together. Meet "the Ism Family," racism, classism, ageism, adultism, elitism, sexism, heterosexism, physicalism, etc. All these ism's are systematic, that is, not only are these parasites feeding off our lives, they are also dependent on one another for foundation. Racism is supported and reinforced by classism, which is given a foothold and a boost by adultism, which also feeds sexism, which is validated by heterosexism, and so it goes on. You cannot have the "ism" functioning without first effectively installing its flip side, the internalized version of the ism. Like twins, as one particular form of the ism grows in potency, there is a corresponding increase in its internalized form within the population. Before oppression becomes a specific ism like racism, usually all hell breaks loose. War. People fight attempts to enslave them, or to subvert their will, or to take what they consider theirs, whether that is territory or dignity. It's true that the various elements of racism, while repugnant, would not be able to do very much damage, but for one generally overlooked key piece: power/privilege.

. . .

So, what can we do? Acknowledge racism for a start, even though and especially when we've struggled to be kind and fair, or struggled to rise above it all. It is hard to acknowledge the fact that racism circumscribes and pervades our lives. Racism must be dealt with on two levels, personal and societal, emotional and institutional. It is possible—and most effective—to do both at the same time. We must reclaim whatever delight we have lost in our own ethnic heritage or heritages. This so-called melting pot has only succeeded in turning us into fast-food-gobbling "generics" (as in generic "white folks" who were once Irish, Polish, Russian, English, etc. and "black folks," who were once Ashanti, Bambara, Baule, Yoruba, etc.). Find or create safe places to actually *feel* what we've been forced to repress each time we were a victim of, witness to, or perpetrator of racism, so that we do not continue, like puppets, to act out the past in the present and future. Challenge oppression. Take a stand against it. When you are aware of something oppressive going down, stop the show. At least call it. We become so numbed to racism that we don't even think twice about it, unless it is immediately life-threatening.

Whites who want to be allies to people of color: You can educate yourselves via research and observation rather than rigidly, arrogantly relying solely on interrogating people of color. Do not expect that people of color should teach you how to behave non-oppressively. Do not give into the pull to be lazy. Think, hard. Do not blame people of color for your frustration about racism, but do appreciate the fact that people of color will often help you get in touch with that frustration. Assume that your effort to be a good friend is appreciated, but don't expect or accept gratitude from people of color. Work on racism for your sake, not "their" sake. Assume that you are needed and capable of being a good ally. Know that you'll make mistakes and commit yourself to correcting them and continuing on as an ally, no matter what. Don't give up.

People of color, working through internalized racism: Remember always that you and others like you are completely worthy of respect, completely capable of achieving whatever you take a notion to do. Remember that the term "people of color" refers to a variety of ethnic and cultural backgrounds. These various groups have been oppressed in a variety of ways. Educate yourself about the ways different peoples have been oppressed and how they've resisted that oppression. Expect and insist that whites are capable of being good allies against racism. Don't give up. Resist the pull to give out the "people of color seal of approval" to aspiring white allies. A moment of appreciation is fine, but more than that tends to be less than helpful. Celebrate yourself. Celebrate yourself. Celebrate the inevitable end of racism.

R E A D I N G **15**

Tired of Playing Monopoly?

Donna Langston

I. Magnin, Nordstrom, The Bon, Sears, Penneys, Kmart, Goodwill, Salvation Army. If the order of this list of stores makes any sense to you, then we've begun to deal with the first question which inevitably arises in any discussion of class here in the U.S.—huh? Unlike our European allies, we in the U.S. are reluctant to recognize class differences. This denial of class divisions functions to reinforce ruling class control and domination. America is, after all, the supposed land of equal opportunity where, if you just work hard enough, you can get ahead, pull yourself up by your bootstraps. What the old bootstraps theory overlooks is that some were born with silver shoe horns. Female-headed households, communities of color, the elderly, disabled and children find themselves, disproportionately, living in poverty. If hard work were the sole determinant of your ability to support yourself and your family, surely we'd have a different outcome for many in our society. We also, however, believe in luck and, on closer examination, it certainly is quite a coincidence that the "unlucky" come from certain race, gender and class backgrounds. In order to perpetuate racist, sexist and classist outcomes, we also have to believe that the current economic distribution is unchangeable, has always existed, and probably exists in this form throughout the known universe; i.e., it's "natural." Some people explain or try to account for poverty or class position by focusing on the personal and moral merits of an individual. If people are poor, then it's something they did or didn't do; they were lazy, unlucky, didn't try hard enough, etc. This has the familiar ring of blaming the victims. Alternative explanations focus on the ways in which poverty and class position are due to structural, systematic, institutionalized economic and political power relations. These power relations are based firmly on dynamics such as race, gender and class.

In the myth of the classless society, ambition and intelligence alone are responsible for success. The myth conceals the existence of a class society, which serves many functions. One of the main ways it keeps the working class and poor locked into a class-based system in a position of servitude is by cruelly creating false hope. It perpetuates the false hope among the working class and poor that they can have different opportunities in life. The hope that they can escape the fate that awaits them due to the class position they were born into. Another way the rags-to-riches myth is perpetuated is by creating enough visible tokens so that oppressed persons believe they, too, can get ahead. The creation of hope through tokenism keeps a hierarchical structure in place and lays the blame for not succeeding on those who don't. This keeps us from resisting and changing the class-based system. Instead, we accept it as inevitable, something we just have to live with. If oppressed people believe in equality of opportunity, then they won't develop class consciousness and will internalize the blame for their economic position. If the working class and poor do not recognize the way false hope is used to control them, they won't get a chance to control their lives by acknowledging their class position, by claiming that identity and taking action as a group.

The myth also keeps the middle class and upper class entrenched in the privileges awarded in a class-based system. It reinforces middle- and upper-class beliefs in their own superiority. If we believe that anyone in society really can get ahead, then middle- and upper-class status and privileges must be deserved, due to personal merits, and enjoyed—and defended at all costs. According to this viewpoint, poverty is regrettable but acceptable, just the outcome of a fair game: "There have always been poor people, and there always will be."

Class is more than just the amount of money you have; it's also the presence of economic security. For the working class and poor, working and eating are matters of survival, not taste. However, while one's class status can be defined in important ways in terms of monetary income, class is also a whole lot more—specifically, class is also culture. As a result of the class you are born into and raised in, class is your understanding of the world and where you fit in; it's composed of ideas, behavior, attitudes, values, and language; class is how you think, feel, act, look, dress, talk, move, walk; class is what stores you shop at, restaurants you eat in; class is the schools you attend, the education you attain; class is the very jobs you will work at throughout your adult life. Class even determines when we marry and become mothers. Working-class women become mothers long before middle-class women receive their bachelor's degrees. We experience class at every level of our lives; class is who our friends are, where we live and work even what kind of car we drive, if we own one, and what kind of health care we receive, if any. . . .

Class affects what we perceive as and what we have available to us as choices. Upon graduation from high school, I was awarded a scholarship to attend any college, private or public, in the state of California. Yet it never occurred to me or my family that it made any difference which college you went to. I ended up just going to a small college in my town. It never would have occurred to me to move away from my family for school, because no one ever had and no one would. I was the first person in my family to go to college. I had to figure out from reading college catalogs how to apply—no one in my family could have sat down and said, "Well, you take this test and then you really should think about...." Although tests and high school performance had shown I had the ability to pick up white middle-class lingo, I still had quite an adjustment to make—it was lonely and isolating in college. I lost my friends from high school—they were at the community college, vo-tech school, working, or married. I lasted a year and a half in this foreign environment before I quit college, married a factory worker, had a baby and resumed living in a community I knew....

If class is more than simple economic status but one's cultural background as well, what happens if you're born and raised middle class, but spend some of your adult life with earnings below a middle-class income bracket—are you then working class? Probably not. If your economic position changes, you still have the language, behavior, educational background, etc., of the middle class, which you can bank on. You will always have choices. Men who consciously try to refuse male privilege are still male; whites who want to challenge white privilege are still white. I think those who come from middle-class backgrounds need to recognize that their class privilege does not float out with the rinse water. Middle-class people can exert incredible power just by being nice and polite. The middle-class way of doing things is the standard—they're always right, just by being themselves. Beware of middle-class people who deny their privilege. Many people have times when they struggle to get shoes for the kids, when budgets are tight, etc. This isn't the same as long-term economic conditions without choices....

How about if you're born and raised poor or working class, yet through struggle, usually through education, you manage to achieve a different economic level: do you become middle class? Can you pass? I think some working-class people may successfully assimilate into the middle class by learning to dress, talk, and act middle class—to accept and adopt the middle-class way of doing things. It all depends on how far they're able to go. To succeed in the middle-class world means facing great pressures to abandon working-class friends and ways.

Contrary to our stereotype of the working class—white guys in overalls—the working class is not homogeneous in terms of race or gender. If you are a person of color, if you live in a female-headed household, you are much more likely to be working class or poor. The experience of Black, Latino, American Indian or Asian American working classes will differ significantly from the white working classes, which have traditionally been able to rely on white privilege to provide a more elite position within the working class. Working-class people are often grouped together and stereotyped, but distinctions can be made among the working class, working poor, and poor. Many working-class families are supported by unionized workers who possess marketable skills. Most working-poor families are supported by non-unionized, unskilled men and women. Many poor families are dependent on welfare for their income.

Attacks on the welfare system and those who live on welfare are a good example of classism in action. We have a "dual welfare" system in this country whereby welfare for the rich in the form of tax-free capital gain, guaranteed loans, oil depletion allowances, etc., is not recognized as welfare. Almost everyone in America is on some type of welfare; but, if you're rich, it's in the form of tax deductions for "business" meals and entertainment, and if you're poor, it's in the form of food stamps. The difference is the stigma and humiliation connected to welfare for the poor, as compared to welfare for the rich, which is called "incentives." . . . The "dual welfare" system also assigns a different degree of stigma to programs that benefit women and children, such as AFDC, and programs whose recipients are primarily male, such as veterans' benefits. The implicit assumption is that mothers who raise children do not work and therefore are not deserving of their daily bread crumbs.

Anti-union attitudes are another prime example of classism in action. At best, unions have been a very progressive force for workers, women and people of color. At worst, unions have reflected the same regressive attitudes which are out there in other social structures: classism, racism and sexism. Classism exists within the working class. The aristocracy of the working class—unionized, skilled workers—have mainly been white and male and have viewed themselves as being better than unskilled workers, the unemployed and the poor, who are mostly women and people of color. The white working class must commit itself to a cultural and ideological transformation of racist attitudes. The history of working people, and the ways we've resisted many types of oppressions, are not something we're taught in school. Missing from our education is information about workers and their resistance.

Working-class women's critiques have focused on the following issues:

Education: White middle-class professionals have used academic jargon to rationalize and justify classism. The whole structure of education is a classist system. Schools in every town reflect class divisions: like the store list at the beginning of this article, you can list schools in your town by what classes of kids attend, and in most cities you can also list by race. The classist system is perpetuated in schools with the tracking system, whereby the "dumbs" are tracked into homemaking, shop courses and vocational school futures, while the "smarts" end up in advanced math, science, literature and college-prep courses. If we examine these groups carefully, the coincidence of poor and working-class backgrounds with "dumbs" is rather alarming. The standard measurement of supposed intelligence is white middle-class English. If you're other than white middle class, you have to become bilingual to succeed in the educational system. If you're white middle class, you only need the language and writing skills you were raised with, since they're the standard. To do well in society presupposes middle-class background, experiences and learning for everyone. The tracking system separates those from the working class who can potentially assimilate to the middle class from all our friends and labels us "college bound."

After high school, you go on to vocational school, community college, or college—public or private—according to your class position. Apart from the few who break into middle-class schools, the classist stereotyping of the working class as being dumb and inarticulate tracks most into vocational and low-skilled jobs. A few of us are allowed to slip through to reinforce the idea that equal opportunity exists. But for most, class position is destiny—determining our educational attainment and employment. Since we must overall abide by middle-class rules to succeed, the assumption is that we go to college in order to "better ourselves"—i.e., become more like them. I suppose it's assumed we have "yuppie envy" and desire nothing more than to be upwardly mobile individuals. It's assumed that we want to fit into their world. But many of us remain connected to our communities and families. Becoming college educated doesn't mean we have to, or want to, erase our first and natural language and value system. It's important for many of us to remain in and return to our communities to work, live, and stay sane.

Jobs: Middle-class people have the privilege of choosing careers. They can decide which jobs they want to work, according to their moral or political commitments, needs for challenge or creativity. This is a privilege denied the working class and poor, whose work is a means of survival, not choice. . . . Working-class women have seldom had the luxury of choosing between work in the home or market. We've generally done both, with little ability to purchase services to help with this double burden. Middle- and upper-class women can often hire other women to clean their houses, take care of their children, and cook their meals.

Guess what class and race those "other" women are? Working a double or triple day is common for working-class women. Only middle-class women have an array of choices such as: parents put you through school, then you choose a career, then you choose when and if to have babies, then you choose a support system of working-class women to take care of your kids and house if you choose to resume your career. After the birth of my second child, I was working two part-time jobs—one loading trucks at night—and going to school during the days. While I was quite privileged because I could take my colicky infant with me to classes and the day-time job, I was in a state of continuous semi-consciousness. I had to work to support my family; the only choice I had was between school or sleep: Sleep became a privilege. A white middle-class feminist instructor at the university suggested to me, all sympathetically, that I ought to hire someone to clean my house and watch the baby. Her suggestion was totally out of my reality, both economically and socially. I'd worked for years cleaning other peoples' houses. Hiring a working-class woman to do the shit work is a middle-class woman's solution to any dilemma which her privileges, such as a career, may present her.

Mothering: The feminist critique of families and the oppressive role of mothering has focused on white middle-class nuclear families. This may not be an appropriate model for communities of class and color. Mothering and families may hold a different importance for working-class women. Within this context, the issue of coming out can be a very painful process for working-class lesbians. Due to the homophobia of working-class communities, to be a lesbian is most often to be excommunicated from your family, neighborhood, friends and the people you work with. If you're working class, you don't have such clearly demarcated concepts of yourself as an individual, but instead see yourself as part of a family and community that forms your survival structure. It is not easy to be faced with the risk of giving up ties which are so central to your identity and survival.

. . .

WAYS TO AVOID FACING CLASSISM

Deny Deny Deny: Deny your class position and the privileges connected to it. Deny the existence or experience of the working class and poor. You can even set yourself up (in your own mind) as judge and jury in deciding who qualifies as working class by your white middle-class standards. So if someone went to college, or seems intelligent to you, not at all like your stereotypes, they must be middle class.

Guilt Guilt Guilt: "I feel so bad, I just didn't realize!" is not helpful, but is a way to avoid changing attitudes and behaviors. Passivity—"Well, what can I do about it, anyway?"—and anger—"Well, what do they want?"—aren't too helpful either. Again, with these responses, the focus is on you and absolving the white middle class from responsibility. A more helpful remedy is to take action. Donate your time and money to local foodbanks. Don't cross picket lines. Better yet, go join a picket line.

HOW TO CHALLENGE CLASSISM

If you're middle class, you can begin to challenge classism with the following:

1. Confront classist behavior in yourself, others and society. Use and share the privileges, like time or money, which you do have.

2. Make demands on working-class and poor communities' issues—anti-racism, poverty, unions, public housing, public transportation, literacy and day care.

3. Learn from the skills and strength of working people—study working and poor people's history; take some Labor Studies, Ethnic Studies, Women Studies classes. Challenge elitism. There are many different types of intelligence: white middle-class, academic, professional intellectualism being one of them (reportedly). Finally, educate yourself, take responsibility and take action.

If you're working class, just some general suggestions (it's cheaper than therapy—free, less time-consuming and I won't ask you about what your mother said to you when you were five):

1. Face your racism! Educate yourself and others, your family, community, any organizations you belong to; take responsibility and take action. Face your classism, sexism, heterosexism, ageism, able-bodiness, adultism. . . .

2. Claim your identity. Learn all you can about your history and the history and experience of all working and poor peoples. Raise your children to be anti-racist, anti-sexist and anti-classist. Teach them the language and culture of working peoples. Learn to survive with a fair amount of anger and lots of humor, which can be tough when this stuff isn't even funny.

3. Work on issues which will benefit your community. Consider remaining in or returning to your communities. If you live and work in white middle-class environments, look for working-class allies to help you survive with your humor and wits intact. How do working-class people spot each other? We have antenna.

We need not deny or erase the differences of working-class cultures but can embrace their richness, their variety, their moral and intellectual heritage. We're not at the point yet where we can celebrate differences—not having money for a prescription for your child is nothing to celebrate. It's not time yet to party with the white middle class, because we'd be the entertainment ("Aren't they quaint? Just love their workboots and uniforms and the way they cuss!"). We need to overcome divisions among working people, not by ignoring the multiple oppressions many of us encounter, or by oppressing each other, but by becoming committed allies on all issues which affect working people: racism, sexism, classism, etc. An injury to one is an injury to all. Don't play by ruling-class rules, hoping that maybe you can live on Connecticut Avenue instead of Baltic, or that you as an individual can make it to Park Place and Boardwalk. Tired of Monopoly? Always ending up on Mediterranean Avenue? How about changing the game?

R E A D I N G **16**

Voices
On Becoming Old Women

Baba Copper

When we ask for a chance to live our old age in comfort, creativity and usefulness, we ask it not for ourselves alone, but for you. We are not a special interest group. We are your roots. You are our continuity. What we gain is your inheritance.

—*Irene Pauli,* Some Ironies of Aging

How can old women define the subjects of age and ageism so that false understanding of these issues does not dominate the interactions

between women and keep us forever separate? Aging is a natural and universal personal experience that begins the day we are born. It is a process of challenge—not necessarily growth and development when we are young as opposed to loss and deterioration when we are old—but learning through change. Ageism is the negative social response to different stages in the process of aging and it is a political issue. The ageism that old women experience is firmly embedded in sexism—an extension of the male power to define, control values, erase, disempower, and divide. Woman-to-woman ageism is an aspect of the horizontal conflict that usurps the energies of the colonized—part of the female competition for the crumbs of social power.

How can the same word be used for the experience of teenagers, old women, and the most powerful men in the world? Yet we say that all these are subject to *ageist* attitudes—stereotyping and denigration because of age. But each age group—children, teens, midlife women, old women, old men—have radically different expectations of their due, their rightful social place. For an old woman, ageism is a killer, because her sense of worth has been eroded by a lifelong pursuit of youth/beauty. Age passing—passing for young enough—is part of all female experience. The foundation of lies built into passing and the fear and loathing of female aging are what keep the generations of women—decade by decade—divided from each other.

I believe that age passing is one of the primary learning arenas of female competition, as well as an apprenticeship to hatred of old women. When women pass easily, we gain comfort knowing that we do not have to identify with the woman who, in our view, is not passing. "I am not like her" translates easily into "I am better than her." In our thirties, we do not want to be mistaken for forty. In our forties, we do not want anyone to assume we are fifty. Somewhere in our fifties, the mass of anxieties about age, and the increase of rejection and invisibility we are experiencing, becomes critical. This is often a time when our trained inability to identify with women older than ourselves reaches its climax. Old women cannot rely upon the midlife woman as ally. The midlife woman, in her rage and fear, may unconsciously discharge all kinds of covert aggression against the old woman as the personification of what is threatening her.

Can women afford to ignore issues that surround the aging process? When I have asked younger women what they thought ageism was all about, they talked about the aura of death and decay which permeates age for them, the oppressive power/over of the mythic Mother figure, and the deplorable neglect exhibited by the authorities in making adequate institutional responses to age. None have seen ageism as a problem of prejudice or bigotry on their part. With a righteousness reminiscent of the anchorman on the evening news, most of my young informants have advocated more and better government support for the old. But government subsidies for medicine and institutional care have created a highly profitable industry of geriatric technology, with the elderly aid recipients captive to the modern Grail, longevity. Just staying alive is a false goal. Acceptance of age in women has not kept pace with our increasing life expectancy. It is the quality of that extra time that is important. As long as women allow themselves to be brainwashed into worshiping youth and plasticized beauty, increased life expectancy (and the institutionalized responses to it) will remain a burden for both the young and the old.

How can ageism be defined by women; how can we develop clear vocabulary and theory; can we afford to ignore it? For me these questions are more than rhetorical. I am an old woman living in a highly politicized community of women. I find struggle and change taking place in relation to all the differences between women except age. I need to divert some of that political consciousness toward ageism.

I am an *old* woman. I am sixty-six. Part of the reason I self-identify as *old* is a need to escape the prissy category of "older woman." This label claims descriptive power over women from eighteen to eighty, depending upon the age and consciousness of the user. . . . After lots of internal arguments, I found a rationalization that made me comfortable with the label. Calling myself an old woman was the radical way out of my dilemma. At sixty-six, it may be presumptuous of me to assume a label that is descriptive of women in their nineties, but I have noticed that many of them avoid the term. Like other words that feminists are reclaiming by proud usage, I would take to myself the word everyone seems to fear. My *real* circumstances would not suffer more than they have from the visual impact of my years. Nobody but radical women would stand there beside me, honest and angry about the distortions that surround the time of life all women dread. I would walk through the door-of-no-return and from the other side name the politics of age instead of waltzing around pretending I am just an "older woman." The lies of age passing would not save me from the stigma of age. In fact, it has been my experience that the invention and practice of feminine lies keep women forever in harness, laboring to be someone who fits in, who pleases, who is chosen, who earns (and therefore deserves) love. I have grown sick of the harness.

. . .

Young and midlife women tend to see ageism as a continuing oppression of women throughout their lives. The point of view I tried to voice as an old woman sprang from my new experience, which revealed abrupt changes in the degree or intensity of stigma, when, for whatever reasons, one could no longer pass as middle-aged. I am uncomfortable with the absence of differentiation between the kind of ageism I can remember experiencing as a teenager and what I am experiencing in my sixties.

I felt confused. I did not know how to integrate these concepts into my present circumstances. Was the pain over the ageism I experience intensified by the fact that my youth privilege had been augmented by the privileges of being white, able, thin, blond, tall, middle class? And how did all this relate to age passing, for many women try— and some even succeed by the use of repeated plastic surgery—to appear forever middle-aged? For instance, the small, thin old woman— especially one who plays the "cute" social role— does not receive the same direct hostility that big "motherly" women do. Was the pain of ageism relative also, or was there a pall that settled over an old woman (the year varying for different women) which was similar for all whether or not they had been pretty or middle class?

. . .

Death is an extremely important subject that our culture has mystified, professionalized, sensationalized—and at the same time, made taboo. Everyone needs to make his or her peace with the meaning of death. However, the assumption that death is a preoccupation, or subject of expertise, of midlife or old women is ageist. I understood that we might want to talk about death. But the old should not be seen as standing with death at their elbow. Nor should they be expected to help others on the subject or allow the subject to be age segregated. Repeatedly, younger women make assumptions about my relationship to death. One woman said that she shared identity with me because she had had many losses of people close to her in her life. She assumed that I had too. In reality, other than the death of my mother when she was ninety-three, no one I loved has ever died.

. . .

Here it was, that virulent stereotype—the age/death connection. . . . Apparently only old people die. Death does not hover near the cradle, the motorcycle, the toxic workplace, high bridges, or battlefields. But around old women, everyone is reminded that they have given their own possible mortality insufficient attention. Death is a forbidden subject with all but the old, who are expected to bear the burden of this social suppression. Since my own demise is as distant from my conscious mind as it was when I was twenty, I have come to recognize that it is my looks that evoke the age/death connection in others. Death has become a private buzzword for me, warning me of the shoals of ageism before me.

Talking about choice in relation to dying always makes me very nervous. I reminded the group that we were at the beginning of a worldwide demographic boom of old women. It is easy to predict that our society will soon be subject to all kinds of "new looks" at death and dying. I read a clipping from a futurist magazine suggesting that a demise pill be available to the elderly (but not the young, of course). The old are seen as half dead already. Old women, like everyone else, buy into the prevailing concepts surrounding both worth and death—we are as easy to brainwash as the next. When one believes that one has done everything one wants to do, it may be a way of expressing the feeling that what one has to contribute from a wheelchair, for example, is not valuable.

. . .

How can old women begin to change this? First, we have to name our circumstances more clearly, identifying the root sources of our denigrated place in society. Feminist analysis and the concept of ageism are not used as tools by most old women to explain the increased negative content of our experience. Old women tend to see problems as personal—interpersonal or physical or economic—instead of political. The time of life that should be a final ripening, a meaningful summation, a last chance for all the risks and pleasures of corporeal existence, is all too often deadened by emotional isolation and self-doubts. As the average life expectancy for women keeps creeping upward—almost into the eighties now—the quality of that life-to-be-expected keeps deteriorating.

The "natural alliance" that old women have a right to expect with midlife women will not emerge until all women begin to recognize the pitfalls of age passing. Separating the perspective of the barely-passing older woman from some of my concerns as one-who-no-longer-is-able-to-pass has taken all my confidence and a great deal of hindsight. The midlife woman feels increasing pressure—internal and external—about aging as well as the rejections of ageism. It is natural that she rushes forward to define the problem. In asserting her power over the insights of the old woman—the complaints, the accusations of ageism, the naming of the universal hatred of the Old Woman—she unconsciously silences the inherent radicalism of the only one who can tell her how it really is.

The problem for old women is a problem of power. First, power over the circumstances and directions of our own lives and identity. Second, power as an influence upon the world we live in— the world we have served, in which we have such a large, unrecognized vested interest. This is, of course, the rub. Patriarchal institutions are, without exception, designed to exclude the vision of old women. Most old women have little experience in leadership, influence, or even respect. Mostly, old women know how to serve. The roles reserved and expected of women in old age— grandmothers, self-effacing volunteers to the projects and priorities designed by others, or caretakers of old men—are custom fit to our powerless status.

But there are ways that all women can begin to prepare the way for the empowerment of themselves in the future, when they are old. These changes can first be brought about in the women's community, among lesbians and political women. The first step is for women to recognize that they have been programmed to hate old women and to deny them power. This brainwashing is so subtle that its eradication will take an effort equal to that which we have made and still must expend upon sexism. Further, this brainwashing extends down through our lives, making us fear the processes of our own bodies within time, so that our energies and attention are constantly undermined by ageist competition and self-doubts. These are attitudes and expectations that we can change now, if we decide to. Empowerment of women will come when we identify with women older than we are and not before.

The Social Construction of Disability

Susan Wendell

I maintain that the distinction between the biological reality of a disability and the social construction of a disability cannot be made sharply, because the biological and the social are interactive in creating disability. They are interactive not only in that complex interactions of social factors and our bodies affect health and functioning, but also in that social arrangements can make a biological condition more or less relevant to almost any situation. I call the interaction of the biological and the social to create (or prevent) disability "the social construction of disability."

Disability activists and some scholars of disability have been asserting for at least two decades that disability is socially constructed. Moreover, feminist scholars have already applied feminist analyses of the social construction of the experience of being female to their analyses of disability as socially constructed. Thus I am saying nothing new when I claim that disability, like gender, is socially constructed. Nevertheless, I understand that such an assertion may be new and even puzzling to many readers, and that not everyone who says that disability is socially constructed means the same thing by it. Therefore, I will explain what I mean in some detail.

I see disability as socially constructed in ways ranging from social conditions that straightforwardly create illnesses, injuries, and poor physical functioning, to subtle cultural factors that determine standards of normality and exclude those who do not meet them from full participation in their societies. I could not possibly discuss all the factors that enter into the social construction of disability here, and I feel sure that I am not aware of them all, but I will try to explain and illustrate the social construction of disability by discussing what I hope is a representative sample from a range of factors.

SOCIAL FACTORS THAT CONSTRUCT DISABILITY

First, it is easy to recognize that social conditions affect people's bodies by creating or failing to prevent sickness and injury. Although, since disability is relative to a person's physical, social, and cultural environment, none of the resulting physical conditions is necessarily disabling, many do in fact cause disability given the demands and lack of support in the environments of the people affected. In this direct sense of damaging people's bodies in ways that are disabling in their environments, much disability is created by the violence of invasions, wars, civil wars, and terrorism, which cause disabilities not only through direct injuries to combatants and noncombatants, but also through the spread of disease and the deprivations of basic needs that result from the chaos they create. In addition, although we more often hear about them when they cause death, violent crimes such as shootings, knifings, beatings, and rape all cause disabilities, so that a society's success or failure in protecting its citizens from injurious crimes has a significant effect on its rates of disability.

The availability and distribution of basic resources such as water, food, clothing, and shelter have major effects on disability, since much disabling physical damage results directly from malnutrition and indirectly from diseases that attack and do more lasting harm to the malnourished and those weakened by exposure. Disabling diseases are also contracted from contaminated water when clean water is not available. Here too, we usually learn more about the deaths caused by lack of basic resources than the (often life-long) disabilities of survivors.

Many other social factors can damage people's bodies in ways that are disabling in their environments, including (to mention just a few) tolerance of high-risk working conditions, abuse and neglect of children, low public safety standards, the degradation of the environment by contamination of air, water, and food, and the overwork, stress, and daily grinding deprivations of poverty. The social factors that can damage people's bodies almost always affect some groups in a society more than others because of racism, sexism, heterosexism, ageism, and advantages of class background, wealth, and education.

Medical care and practices, traditional and Western-scientific, play an important role in both preventing and creating disabling physical damage. (They also play a role in defining disability. . . .) Lack of good prenatal care and dangerous or inadequate obstetrical practices cause disabilities in babies and in the women giving birth to them. Inoculations against diseases such as polio and measles prevent quite a lot of disability. Inadequate medical care of those who are already ill or injured results in unnecessary disablement. On the other hand, the rate of disability in a society increases with improved medical capacity to save the lives of people who are dangerously ill or injured in the absence of the capacity to prevent or cure all the physical damage they have incurred. Moreover, public health and sanitation measures that increase the average lifespan also increase the number of old people with disabilities in a society, since more people live long enough to become disabled.

The *pace of life* is a factor in the social construction of disability that particularly interests me, because it is usually taken for granted by non-disabled people, while many people with disabilities are acutely aware of how it marginalizes or threatens to marginalize us. I suspect that increases in the pace of life are important social causes of damage to people's bodies through rates of accident, drug and alcohol abuse, and illnesses

that result from people's neglecting their needs for rest and good nutrition. But the pace of life also affects disability as a second form of social construction, the social construction of disability through expectations of performance.

When the pace of life in a society increases, there is a tendency for more people to become disabled, not only because of physically damaging consequences of efforts to go faster, but also because fewer people can meet expectations of 'normal' performance; the physical (and mental) limitations of those who cannot meet the new pace become conspicuous and disabling, even though the same limitations were inconspicuous and irrelevant to full participation in the slower-paced society. Increases in the pace of life can be counterbalanced for some people by improvements in accessibility, such as better transportation and easier communication, but for those who must move or think slowly, and for those whose energy is severely limited, expectations of pace can make work, recreational, community, and social activities inaccessible.

Let me give a straightforward, personal illustration of the relationship between pace and disability. I am currently just able (by doing very little else) to work as a professor three-quarter time, on one-quarter disability leave. There has been much talk recently about possible increases in the teaching duties of professors at my university, which would not be accompanied by any reduction in expectations for the other two components of our jobs, research and administration. If there were to be such an increase in the pace of professors' work, say by one additional course per term, I would be unable to work more than half-time (by the new standards) and would have to request half-time disability leave, even though there had been no change in my physical condition. Compared to my colleagues, I would be more work-disabled than I am now. Some professors with less physical limitation than I have, who now work full-time, might be unable to work at the new full-time pace and be forced to go on part-time disability leave. This sort of change could contribute to disabling anyone in any job.

Furthermore, even if a person is able to keep up with an increased pace of work, any increase in the pace of work will decrease the energy available for other life activities, which may upset the delicate balance of energy by which a person manages to participate in them and eventually exclude her/him from those activities. The pace of those other activities may also render them inaccessible. For example, the more the life of a society is conducted on the assumption of quick travel, the more disabling are those physical conditions that affect movement and travel, such as needing to use a wheelchair or having a kind of epilepsy that prevents one from driving a car, unless compensating help is provided. These disabling effects extend into people's family, social, and sexual lives and into their participation in recreation, religious life, and politics.

Pace is a major aspect of expectations of performance; non-disabled people often take pace so much for granted that they feel and express impatience with the slower pace at which some people with disabilities need to operate, and accommodations of pace are often crucial to making an activity accessible to people with a wide range of physical and mental abilities. Nevertheless, expectations of pace are not the only expectations of performance that contribute to disability. For example, expectations of individual productivity can eclipse the actual contributions of people who cannot meet them, making people unemployable when they can in fact do valuable work. There are often very definite expectations about *how* tasks will be performed (not the standards of performance, but the methods). For example, many women with disabilities are discouraged from having children because other people can only imagine caring for children in ways that are impossible for women with their disabilities, yet everything necessary could be done in other ways, often with minor accommodations. Furthermore, the expectation that many tasks will be performed by individuals on their own can create or expand the disability of those who can perform the tasks only in cooperative groups or by instructing a helper.

Expectations of performance are reflected, because they are assumed, in the social organization and physical structure of a society, both of which create disability. Societies that are physically constructed and socially organized with the unacknowledged assumption that everyone is healthy, non-disabled, young but adult, shaped according to cultural ideals, and, often, male, create a great deal of disability through sheer neglect of what most people need in order to participate fully in them.

Feminists talk about how the world has been designed for the bodies and activities of men. In many industrialized countries, including Canada and the United States, life and work have been structured as though no one of any importance in the public world, and certainly no one who works outside the home for wages, has to breast-feed a baby or look after a sick child. Common colds can be acknowledged publicly, and allowances are made for them, but menstruation cannot be acknowledged and allowances are not made for it. Much of the public world is also structured as though everyone were physically strong, as though all bodies were shaped the same, as though everyone could walk, hear, and see well, as though everyone could work and play at a pace that is not compatible with any kind of illness or pain, as though no one were ever dizzy or incontinent or simply needed to sit or lie down. (For instance, where could you rest for a few minutes in a supermarket if you needed to?) Not only the architecture, but the entire physical and social organization of life tends to assume that we are either strong and healthy and able to do what the average young, non-disabled man can do or that we are completely unable to participate in public life.

A great deal of disability is caused by this physical structure and social organization of society. For instance, poor architectural planning creates physical obstacles for people who use wheelchairs, but also for people who can walk but cannot walk far or cannot climb stairs, for people who cannot open doors, and for people who can do all of these things but only at the cost of pain or an expenditure of energy they can ill afford.

Some of the same architectural flaws cause problems for pregnant women, parents with strollers, and young children. This is no coincidence. Much architecture has been planned with a young adult, non-disabled male paradigm of humanity in mind. In addition, aspects of social organization that take for granted the social expectations of performance and productivity, such as inadequate public transportation (which I believe assumes that no one who is needed in the public world needs public transportation), communications systems that are inaccessible to people with visual or hearing impairments, and inflexible work arrangements that exclude part-time work or rest periods, create much disability.

When public and private worlds are split, women (and children) have often been relegated to the private, and so have the disabled, the sick, and the old. The public world is the world of strength, the positive (valued) body, performance and production, the non-disabled, and young adults. Weakness, illness, rest and recovery, pain, death, and the negative (devalued) body are private, generally hidden, and often neglected. Coming into the public world with illness, pain, or a devalued body, people encounter resistance to mixing the two worlds; the split is vividly revealed. Much of the experience of disability and illness goes underground, because there is no socially acceptable way of expressing it and having the physical and psychological experience acknowledged. Yet acknowledgement of this experience is exactly what is required for creating accessibility in the public world. The more a society regards disability as a private matter, and people with disabilities as belonging in the private sphere, the more disability it creates by failing to make the public sphere accessible to a wide range of people.

Disability is also socially constructed by the failure to give people the amount and kind of help they need to participate fully in all major aspects of life in the society, including making a significant contribution in the form of work. Two things are important to remember about the help that people with disabilities may need. One is that most industrialized societies give non-disabled people (in different degrees and kinds, depending on class, race, gender, and other factors) a lot of help in the form of education, training, social support, public communication and transportation facilities, public recreation, and other services. The help that non-disabled people receive tends to be taken for granted and not considered help but entitlement, because it is offered to citizens who fit the social paradigms, who by definition are not considered dependent on social help. It is only when people need a different kind or amount of help than that given to 'paradigm' citizens that it is considered help at all, and they are considered socially dependent. Second, much, though not all, of the help that people with disabilities need is required because their bodies were damaged by social conditions, or because they cannot meet social expectations of performance, or because the narrowly-conceived physical structure and social organization of society have placed them at a disadvantage; in other words, it is needed to overcome problems that were created socially.

Thus disability is socially constructed through the failure or unwillingness to create ability among people who do not fit the physical and mental profile of 'paradigm' citizens. Failures of social support for people with disabilities result in inadequate rehabilitation, unemployment, poverty, inadequate personal and medical care, poor communication services, inadequate training and education, poor protection from physical, sexual, and emotional abuse, minimal opportunities for social learning and interaction, and many other disabling situations that hurt people with disabilities and exclude them from participation in major aspects of life in their societies.

. . .

CULTURAL CONSTRUCTION OF DISABILITY

Culture makes major contributions to disability. These contributions include not only the omission of experiences of disability from cultural representations of life in a society, but also the cultural stereotyping of people with disabilities, the selective stigmatization of physical and mental limitations and other differences (selective because not all limitations and differences are stigmatized, and different limitations and differences are stigmatized in different societies), the numerous cultural meanings attached to various kinds of disability and illness, and the exclusion of people with disabilities from the cultural meanings of activities they cannot perform or are expected not to perform.

The lack of realistic cultural representations of experiences of disability not only contributes to the 'Otherness' of people with disabilities by encouraging the assumption that their lives are inconceivable to non-disabled people but also increases non-disabled people's fear of disability by suppressing knowledge of how people live with disabilities. Stereotypes of disabled people as dependent, morally depraved, super-humanly heroic, asexual, and/or pitiful are still the most common cultural portrayals of people with disabilities. Stereotypes repeatedly get in the way of full participation in work and social life. For example, Francine Arsenault, whose leg was damaged by childhood polio and later by gangrene, describes the following incident at her wedding:

> When I got married, one of my best friends came to the wedding with her parents. I had known her parents all the time I was growing up; we visited in each other's homes and I thought that they knew my situation quite well.
>
> But as the father went down the reception line and shook hands with my husband, he said, "You know, I used to think that Francine was intelligent, but to put herself on you as a burden like this shows that I was wrong all along."

Here the stereotype of a woman with a disability as a helpless, dependent burden blots out, in the friend's father's consciousness, both the reality that Francine simply has one damaged leg and the probability that her new husband wants her for her other qualities. Moreover, the man seems to take for granted that the new husband sees Francine in the same stereotyped way (or else he risks incomprehension or rejection), perhaps because he counts on the cultural assumptions about people with disabilities. I think both the stigma of physical 'imperfection' (and possibly the additional stigma of having been damaged by disease) and the cultural meanings attached to the disability contribute to the power of the stereotype in situations like this. Physical 'imperfection' is more likely to be thought to 'spoil' a woman than a man by rendering her unattractive in a culture where her physical appearance is a large component of a woman's value; having a damaged leg probably evokes the metaphorical meanings of being 'crippled,' which include helplessness, dependency, and pitifulness. Stigma, stereotypes, and cultural meanings are all related and interactive in the cultural construction of disability. . . .

SOCIAL DECONSTRUCTION OF DISABILITY

In my view, then, disability is socially constructed by such factors as social conditions that cause or fail to prevent damage to people's bodies; expectations of performance; the physical and social organization of societies on the basis of a young, non-disabled, 'ideally shaped,' healthy adult male paradigm of citizens; the failure or unwillingness to create ability among citizens who do not fit the paradigm; and cultural representations, failures of representation, and expectations. Much, but perhaps not all, of what can be socially constructed can be socially (and not just intellectually) deconstructed, given the means and the will.

A great deal of disability can be prevented with good public health and safety standards and practices, but also by relatively minor changes in the built environment that provide accessibility to people with a wide range of physical characteristics and abilities. Many measures that are usually regarded as helping or accommodating people who are now disabled, such as making buildings and public places wheelchair accessible, creating and respecting parking spaces for people with disabilities, providing American Sign Language translation, captioning, and Telephone Devices for the Deaf, and making tapes and Descriptive

Video services available for people who are visually impaired, should be seen as preventive, since a great deal of disability is created by building and organizing environments, objects, and activities for a too-narrow range of people. Much more could be done along the same lines by putting people with a wide variety of physical abilities and characteristics in charge of deconstructing disability. People with disabilities should be in charge, because people without disabilities are unlikely to see many of the obstacles in their environment. Moreover, they are likely not to see them *as obstacles* even when they are pointed out, but rather as 'normal' features of the built environment that present difficulties for 'abnormal' people.

Disability cannot be deconstructed by consulting a few token disabled representatives. A person with a disability is not likely to see all the obstacles to people with disabilities different from her/his own, although s/he is likely to be more aware of potential inaccessibility. Moreover, people with disabilities are not always aware of the obstacles in our environment *as obstacles,* even when they affect us. The cultural habit of regarding the condition of the person, not the built environment or the social organization of activities, as the source of the problem, runs deep. For example, it took me several years of struggling with the heavy door to my building, sometimes having to wait until someone stronger came along, to realize that the door was an accessibility problem, not only for me, but for others as well. And I did not notice, until one of my students pointed it out, that the lack of signs that could be read from a distance at my university forced people with mobility impairments to expend a lot of energy unnecessarily, searching for rooms and offices. Although I have encountered this difficulty myself on days when walking was exhausting to me, I interpreted it, automatically, as a problem arising from my illness (as I did with the door), rather than as a problem arising from the built environment having been created for too narrow a range of people and situations. One of the most crucial factors in the deconstruction of disability is the change of perspective that causes

us to look in the environment for both the source of the problem and the solutions.

. . .

OBSTACLES TO THE DECONSTRUCTION OF DISABILITY

. . .

Attitudes that disability is a personal or family problem (of biological or accidental origin), rather than a matter of social responsibility, are cultural contributors to disability and powerful factors working against social measures to increase ability. The attitude that disability is a personal problem is manifested when people with disabilities are expected to overcome obstacles to their participation in activities by their own extraordinary efforts. The public adoration of a few disabled heroes who are believed to have 'overcome their handicaps' against great odds both demonstrates and contributes to this expectation. The attitude that disability is a family matter is manifested when the families of people with disabilities are expected to provide whatever they need, even at great personal sacrifice by other family members. Barbara Hillyer describes the strength of expectations that mothers and other caregivers will do whatever is necessary to 'normalize' the lives of family members, especially children, with disabilities—not only providing care, but often doing the work of two people to maintain the illusion that there is nothing 'wrong' in the family.

These attitudes are related to the fact that many modern societies split human concerns into public and private worlds. Typically, those with disabilities and illnesses have been relegated to the private realm, along with women, children, and the old. This worldwide tendency creates particularly intractable problems for women with disabilities; since they fit two 'private' categories, they are often kept at home, isolated and overprotected. In addition, the confinement of people with disabilities in the private realm exploits women's traditional caregiving roles in order to meet the needs of people with disabilities, and it hides the need for measures to make the public realm accessible to everyone.

There also seem to be definite material advantages for some people (people without disabilities who have no disabled friends or relatives for whom they feel responsible) to seeing disability as a biological misfortune, the bad luck of individuals, and a personal or family problem. Accessibility and creating ability cost time, energy, and/or money. Charities for people with disabilities are big businesses that employ a great many non-disabled professionals; these charities depend upon the belief that responding to the difficulties faced by people with disabilities is superogatory for people who are not members of the family—not a social responsibility to be fulfilled through governments, but an act of kindness. Moreover, both the charities and most government bureaucracies (which also employ large numbers of non-disabled professionals) hand out help which would not be needed in a society that was planned and organized to include people with a wide range of physical and mental abilities. The potential resistance created by these vested interests in disability should not be underestimated.

The 'personal misfortune' approach to disability is also part of what I call the 'lottery' approach to life, in which individual good fortune is hoped for as a substitute for social planning that deals realistically with everyone's capabilities, needs and limitations, and the probable distribution of hardship. In Canada and the United States, most people reject the 'lottery' approach to such matters as acute health care for themselves and their families or basic education for their children. We expect it to be there when we need it, and we are (more or less) willing to pay for it to be there. I think the lottery approach persists with respect to disability partly because *fear,* based on ignorance and false beliefs about disability, makes it difficult for most non-disabled people to identify with people with disabilities. If the non-disabled saw the disabled as potentially themselves or as their future selves, they would want their societies to be fully accessible and to invest the resources necessary to create ability wherever

possible. They would feel that 'charity' is as inappropriate a way of thinking about resources for people with disabilities as it is about emergency medical care or basic education.

The philosopher Anita Silvers maintains that it is probably impossible for most non-disabled people to imagine what life is like with a disability, and that their own becoming disabled is unthinkable to them. Certainly many people without disabilities believe that life with a disability would not be worth living. This is reflected in the assumption that potential disability is a sufficient reason for aborting a fetus, as well as in the frequent statements by non-disabled people that they would not want to live if they had to use a wheelchair, lost their eyesight, were dependent on others for care, and so on. The belief that life would not be worth living with a disability would be enough to prevent them from imagining their own disablement. This belief is fed by stereotypes and ignorance of the lives of people with disabilities. For example, the assumption that permanent, global incompetence results from any major disability is still prevalent; there is a strong presumption that competent people either have no major physical or mental limitations or are able to hide them in public and social life.

It seems that the cultural constructions of disability, including the ignorance, stereotyping, and stigmatization that feed fears of disability, have to be at least partly deconstructed before disability can be seen by more people as a set of social problems and social responsibilities. Until that change in perspective happens, people with disabilities and their families will continue to be given too much individual responsibility for 'overcoming' disabilities, expectations for the participation of people with disabilities in public life will be far too low, and social injustices that are recognized now (at least in the abstract), such as discrimination against people with disabilities, will be misunderstood.

To illustrate, let me look briefly at the problem of discrimination. Clearly, when considering whether some action or situation is an instance of discrimination on the basis of ability, the trick is to distinguish ability to do the relevant things from ability to do irrelevant things. But, given that so many places and activities are structured for people with a narrow range of abilities, telling the two apart is not always easy. No one has to walk to be a typist, but if a company is housed in a building that is inaccessible to wheelchairs, and therefore refuses to hire a competent typist who uses a wheelchair because it would be expensive to fix the building, has it discriminated against her on the basis of her disability? Laws may say yes, but people will resist the laws unless they can see that the typist's inability to work in that office is not solely a characteristic of her as an individual. Most people will be ready to recognize refusal to hire her to work in a wheelchair-accessible office, provided she is the most competent typist who applied, as discrimination against her because of her disability; they will regard her disability (like her race) as a personal characteristic irrelevant in the circumstances. But will they be ready to require a company to create wheelchair accessibility so that it can hire her? This is being tested now in the United States by the 1990 Americans with Disabilities Act. Although I expect the Act to have an invaluable educational function, I predict that it will be very difficult to enforce until more people see accessibility as a public responsibility. Only then will they be able to recognize inabilities that are created by faulty planning and organization as irrelevant.

Consider these sentiments expressed in the Burger King case, as described in *The Disability Rag and Resource:*

> When deaf actress Terrylene Sacchetti sued Burger King under the ADA for refusing to serve her when she handed the cashier a written order at the pickup window instead of using the intercom, Stan Kyker, executive vice-president of the California Restaurant Association, said that those "people (with disabilities) are going to have to accept that they are not 100 percent whole and they can't be made 100 percent whole in everything they do in life."

Had a woman been refused service because she used a cane to walk up to the counter, her treatment would, I think, have been recognized at once as discrimination. But since Ms. Sacchetti was refused service because she was unable to perform the activity (ordering food) in the way (orally) that the restaurant required it to be performed, the refusal to serve her was not immediately recognized as discrimination. Indeed, the representative of the restaurant association apparently felt comfortable defending it on the grounds that her individual characteristics were the obstacles to Ms. Sacchetti's being served.

When I imagine a society without disabilities, I do not imagine a society in which every physical and mental 'defect' or 'abnormality' can be cured. On the contrary, I believe the fantasy that someday everything will be 'curable' is a significant obstacle to the social deconstruction of disability. Instead, I imagine a fully accessible society, the most fundamental characteristic of which is universal recognition that all structures have to be built and all activities have to be organized for the widest practical range of human abilities. In such a society, a person who cannot walk would not be disabled, because every major kind of activity that is accessible to someone who can walk would be accessible to someone who cannot, and likewise with seeing, hearing, speaking, moving one's arms, working for long stretches of time without rest, and many other physical and mental functions. I do not mean that everyone would be able to do everything, but rather that, with respect to the major aspects of life in the society, the differences in ability between someone who can walk, or see, or hear, and someone who cannot would be no more significant than the differences in ability among people who can walk, see, or hear. Not everyone who is not disabled now can play basketball or sing in a choir, but everyone who is not disabled now can participate in sports or games and make art, and that sort of general ability should be the goal in deconstructing disability.

I talk about accessibility and ability rather than independence or integration because I think that neither independence nor integration is always an appropriate goal for people with disabilities. Some people cannot live independently because they will always need a great deal of help from caregivers, and some people with disabilities, for example the Deaf, do not want to be integrated into non-disabled society; they prefer their own, separate social life. Everyone should, however, have access to *opportunities* to develop their abilities, to work, and to participate in the full range of public and private activities available to the rest of society.

R E A D I N G   **18**

Report from the Bahamas

June Jordan

I am staying in a hotel that calls itself The Sheraton British Colonial. One of the photographs advertising the place displays a middle-aged Black man in a waiter's tuxedo, smiling. What intrigues me most about the picture is just this: while the Black man bears a tray full of "colorful" drinks above his left shoulder, both of his feet, shoes and trouserlegs, up to ten inches above his ankles, stand in the also "colorful" Caribbean salt water. He is so delighted to serve you he will wade into the water to bring you Banana Daquiris while you float! More precisely, he will wade into the water, fully clothed, oblivious to the ruin of his shoes, his trousers, his health, and he will do it with a smile.

I am in the Bahamas. On the phone in my room, a spinning complement of plastic pages offers handy index clues such as CAR RENTAL and CASINOS. A message from the Ministry of Tourism appears among these travellers tips. Opening with a paragraph of "WELCOME," the message then proceeds to "A PAGE OF HISTORY," which reads as follows:

> New World History begins on the same day that modern Bahamian history begins—October 12, 1492. That's when Columbus stepped ashore—British influence came first with the Eleutherian Adventurers of 1647—After the Revolutions. American Loyalists fled from the newly indepen-

dent states and settled in the Bahamas. Confederate blockade-runners used the island as a haven during the War between the States, and after the War, a number of Southerners moved to the Bahamas.

There it is again. Something proclaims itself a legitimate history and all it does is track white Mr. Columbus to the British Eleutherians through the Confederate Southerners as they barge into New World surf, land on New World turf, and nobody saving one word about the Bahamian people, the Black peoples, to whom the only thing new in their island world was this weird succession of crude intruders and its colonial consequences.

This is my consciousness of race as I unpack my bathing suit in the Sheraton British Colonial. Neither this hotel nor the British nor the long ago Italians nor the white Delta airline pilots belong here, of course. And every time I look at the photograph of that fool standing in the water with his shoes on I'm about to have a West Indian fit, even though I know he's no fool; he's a middle-aged Black man who needs a job and this is his job—pretending himself a servile ancillary to the pleasures of the rich. (Compared to his options in life, I am a rich woman. Compared to most of the Black Americans arriving for this Easter weekend on a three nights four days' deal of bargain rates, the middle-aged waiter is a poor Black man.)

We will jostle along with the other (white) visitors and join them in the tee shirt shops or, laughing together, learn ruthless rules of negotiation as we, Black Americans as well as white, argue down the price of handwoven goods at the nearby straw market while the merchants, frequently toothless Black women seated on the concrete in their only presentable dress, humble themselves to our careless games:

"Yes? You like it? Eight dollar."

"Five."

"I give it to you. Seven."

And so it continues, this weird succession of crude intruders that, now, includes me and my brothers and my sisters from the North.

This is my consciousness of class as I try to decide how much money I can spend on Bahamian gifts for my family back in Brooklyn. No matter that these other Black women incessantly weave words and flowers into the straw hats and bags piled beside them on the burning dusty street. No matter that these other Black women must work their sense of beauty into these things that we will take away as cheaply as we dare, or they will do without food.

We are not white, after all. The budget is limited. And we are harmlessly killing time between the poolside rum punch and "The Native Show on the Patio" that will play tonight outside the hotel restaurant.

This is my consciousness of race and class and gender identity as I notice the fixed relations between these other Black women and myself. They sell and I buy or I don't. They risk not eating. I risk going broke on my first vacation afternoon.

We are not particularly women anymore; we are parties to a transaction designed to set us against each other.

"Olive" is the name of the Black woman who cleans my hotel room. On my way to the beach I am wondering what "Olive" would say if I told her why I chose The Sheraton British Colonial; if I told her I wanted to swim. I wanted to sleep. I did not want to be harassed by the middle-aged waiter, or his nephew. I did not want to be raped by anybody (white or Black) at all and I calculated that my safety as a Black woman alone would best be ensured by a multinational hotel corporation. In my experience, the big guys take customer complaints more seriously than the little ones. I would suppose that's one reason why they're big; they don't like to lose money anymore than I like to be bothered when I'm trying to read a goddamned book underneath a palm tree I paid $264 to get next to. A Black woman seeking refuge in a multinational corporation may seem like a contradiction to some, but there you are. In this case it's a coincidence of entirely different self-interests: Sheraton/cash = June Jordan's short run safety.

Anyway, I'm pretty sure "Olive" would look at me as though I came from someplace as far away as Brooklyn. Then she'd probably allow herself one indignant query before righteously removing her vacuum cleaner from my room; "and why in the first place you come down you without your husband?"

I cannot imagine how I would begin to answer her.

My "rights" and my "freedom" and my "desire" and a slew of other New World values; what would they sound like to this Black woman described on the card atop my hotel bureau as "Olive the Maid"? "Olive" is older than I am and I may smoke a cigarette while she changes the sheets on my bed. Whose rights? Whose freedom? Whose desire?

And why should she give a shit about mine unless I do something, for real, about hers?

It happens that the book that I finished reading under a palm tree earlier today was the novel *The Bread Givers,* by Anzia Yezierska. Definitely autobiographical. Yezierska lays out the difficulties of being both female and "a person" inside a traditional Jewish family at the start of the twentieth century. . . .

. . .

I am thinking about the boy who loaned this novel to me. He's white and he's Jewish and he's pursuing an independent study project with me, at the State University where I teach whether or not I feel like it, where I teach without stint because, like the waiter, I am no fool. It's my job and either I work or I do without everything you need money to buy. The boy loaned me the novel because he thought I'd be interested to know how a Jewish-American writer used English so that the syntax, and therefore the cultural habits of mind expressed by the Yiddish language, could survive translation. He did this because he wanted to create another connection between us on the basis of language, between his knowledge/his love of Yiddish and my knowledge/my love of Black English.

He has been right about the forceful survival of the Yiddish. And I had become excited by this further evidence of the written voice of spoken language protected from the monodrone of "standard" English, and so we had grown closer on this account. But then our talk shifted to student affairs more generally, and I had learned that this student does not care one way or the other about currently jeopardized Federal Student Loan Programs because, as he explained it to me, they do not affect him. He does not need financial help outside his family. My own son, however, is Black. And I am the only family help available to him. . . .

. . .

It's time to pack it up. Catch my plane. I scan the hotel room for things not to forget. There's that white report card on the bureau.

"Dear Guests:" it says, under the name "Olive." "I am your maid for the day. Please rate me: Excellent. Good. Average. Poor. Thank you."

I tuck this momento from the Sheraton British Colonial into my notebook. How would "Olive" rate *me?* What would it mean for us to seem "good" to each other? What would that rating require?

But I am hastening to leave. Neither turtle soup nor kidney pie nor any conch shell delight shall delay my departure. I have rested, here, in the Bahamas, and I'm ready to return to my usual job, my usual work. But the skin on my body has changed and so has my mind. On the Delta flight home I realize I am burning up, indeed.

So far as I can see, the usual race and class concepts of connection, or gender assumptions of unity, do not apply very well. I doubt that they ever did. Otherwise, why would Black folks forever bemoan our lack of solidarity when the deal turns real. And if unity on the basis of sexual

oppression is something natural, then why do we women, the majority people on the planet, still have a problem?

The plane's ready for takeoff. I fasten my seatbelt and let the tumult inside my head run free. Yes: race and class and gender remain as real as the weather. But what they must mean about the contact between two individuals is less obvious and, like the weather, not predictable.

And when these factors of race and class and gender absolutely collapse is whenever you try to use them as automatic concepts of connection. They may serve well as indicators of commonly felt conflict, but as elements of connection they seem about as reliable as precipitation probability for the day after the night before the day.

It occurs to me that much organizational grief could be avoided if people understood that partnership in misery does not necessarily provide for partnership for change: *When we get the monsters off our backs all of us may want to run in very different directions.*

And not only that: even though both "Olive" and "I" live inside a conflict neither one of us created, and even though both of us therefore hurt inside that conflict, I may be one of the monsters she needs to eliminate from her universe and, in a sense, she may be one of the monsters in mine.

I am reaching for the words to describe the difference between a common identity that has been imposed and the individual identity any one of us will choose, once she gains that chance.

That difference is the one that keeps us stupid in the face of new, specific information about somebody else with whom we are supposed to have a connection because a third party, hostile to both of us, has worked it so that the two of us, like it or not, share a common enemy. *What happens beyond the idea of that enemy and beyond the consequences of that enemy?*

I am saying that the ultimate connection cannot be the enemy. The ultimate connection must be the need that we find between us. It is not only who you are, in other words, but what we can do for each other that will determine the connection.

I am flying back to my job. I have been teaching contemporary women's poetry this semester. One quandary I have set myself to explore with my students is the one of taking responsibility without power. We had been wrestling ideas to the floor for several sessions when a young Black woman, a South African, asked me for help, after class.

Sokutu told me she was "in a trance" and that she'd been unable to eat for two weeks.

"What's going on?" I asked her, even as my eyes startled at her trembling and emaciated appearance.

"My husband. He drinks all the time. He beats me up. I go to the hospital. I can't eat. I don't know what/anything."

In my office, she described her situation. I did not dare to let her sense my fear and horror. She was dragging about, hour by hour, in dread. Her husband, a young Black South African, was drinking himself into more and more deadly violence against her.

Sokutu told me how she could keep nothing down. She weighed 90 lbs. at the outside, as she spoke to me. She'd already been hospitalized as a result of her husband's battering rage.

I knew both of them because I had organized a campus group to aid the liberation struggles of Southern Africa.

Nausea rose in my throat. What about this presumable connection: this husband and this wife fled from that homeland of hatred against them, and now what? He was destroying himself. If not stopped, he would certainly murder his wife.

She needed a doctor, right away. It was a medical emergency. She needed protection. It was a security crisis. She needed refuge for battered wives and personal therapy and legal counsel. She needed a friend.

I got on the phone and called every number in the campus directory that I could imagine might prove helpful. Nothing worked. There were no institutional resources designed to meet her enormous, multifaceted, and ordinary woman's need.

I called various students. I asked the Chairperson of the English Department for advice. I asked everyone for help.

Finally, another one of my students, Cathy, a young Irish woman active in campus IRA activi-

ties, responded. She asked for further details. I gave them to her.

"Her husband," Cathy told me, "is an alcoholic. You have to understand about alcoholics. It's not the same as anything else. And it's a disease you can't treat any old way."

I listened, fearfully. Did this mean there was nothing we could do?

"That's not what I'm saying," she said. "But you have to keep the alcoholic part of the thing central in everybody's mind, otherwise her husband will kill her. Or he'll kill himself."

She spoke calmly. I felt there was nothing to do but to assume she knew what she was talking about.

"Will you come with me?" I asked her, after a silence. "Will you come with me and help us figure out what to do next?"

Cathy said she would but that she felt shy: Sokutu comes from South Africa. What would she think about Cathy?

"I don't know," I said. "But let's go."

We left to find a dormitory room for the young battered wife.

It was late, now, and dark outside.

On Cathy's VW that I followed behind with my own car, was the sticker that reads BOBBY SANDS FREE AT LAST. My eyes blurred as I read and reread the words. This was another connection: Bobby Sands and Martin Luther King Jr. and who would believe it? I would not have believed it; I grew up terrorized by Irish kids who introduced me to the word "nigga."

And here I was following an Irish woman to the room of a Black South African. We were going to that room to try to save a life together.

When we reached the little room, we found ourselves awkward and large. Sokutu attempted to treat us with utmost courtesy, as though we were honored guests. She seemed surprised by Cathy, but mostly Sokutu was flushed with relief and joy because we were there, with her.

I did not know how we should ever terminate her heartfelt courtesies and address, directly, the reason for our visit: her starvation and her extreme physical danger.

Finally, Cathy sat on the floor and reached out her hands to Sokutu. "I'm here," she said quietly,

"Because June has told me what has happened to you. And I know what it is. Your husband is an alcoholic. He has a disease. I know what it is. My father was an alcholic. He killed himself. He almost killed my mother. I want to be your friend."

"Oh," was the only small sound that escaped from Sokutu's mouth. And then she embraced the other student. And then everything changed and I watched all of this happen so I know that this happened: this connection.

And after we called the police and exchanged phone numbers and plans were made for the night and for the next morning, the young South African woman walked down the dormitory hallway, saying goodbye and saying thank you to us.

I walked behind them, the young Irish woman and the young South African, and I saw them walking as sisters walk, hugging each other, and whispering and sure of each other and I felt how it was not who they were but what they both know and what they were both preparing to do about what they know that was going to make them both free at last.

And I look out the windows of the plane and I see clouds that will not kill me and I know that someday soon other clouds may erupt to kill us all.

And I tell the stewardess No thanks to the cocktails she offers me. But I look about the cabin at the hundred strangers drinking as they fly and I think even here and even now I must make the connection real between me and these strangers everywhere before those other clouds unify this ragged bunch of us, too late.

DISCUSSION QUESTIONS FOR CHAPTER 2

1. How do different forms of prejudice affect your life?

2. How do ideologies undergird institutions? How do these ideologies show up in the institutions that most affect your life?

3. How do institutions maintain gender inequality? Have you experienced gender inequality in particular institutions?

4. How do institutions work together to support and maintain one another?

5. How do hate crimes help maintain systems of inequality? What images of hate crimes do you recall? What effects do these images have on you?

SUGGESTIONS FOR FURTHER READING

Allison, Dorothy. *Trash*. Ithaca, NY: Firebrand, 1989.

Anzaldúa, Gloria. *Borderlands/La Frontera: The New Mestiza*. San Francisco: Aunt Lute, 1987.

Blee, Kathleen M. *Inside Organized Racism: Women in the Hate Movement*. Berkeley: University of California Press, 2002.

Cole, Johnetta, and Beverly Guy-Sheftall. *Gender Talk: The Struggle for Women's Equality in African American Communities*. New York: One World/Ballantine, 2003.

hooks, bell. *Where We Stand: Class Matters*. New York: Routledge, 2002.

Jones, Charisse, and Kumea Shorter-Gooden. *Shifting: The Double Lives of Black Women in America.* New York: HarperCollins, 2003.

Lorde, Audre. *Sister Outsider.* Freedom, CA: Crossing Press, 1984.

Mihesuah, Devon A. *Indigenous American Women: Decolonization, Empowerment, Activism.* Lincoln, NE: Bison Books, 2003.

Smith, Bonnie G., and Beth Hutchison. *Gendering Disability.* New Brunswick, NJ: Rutgers University Press, 2004.

Stein, Arlene. *The Stranger Next Door: The Story of a Small Community's Battle over Sex, Faith, and Civil Rights.* Boston: Beacon Press, 2002.

Wehbi, Samantha. *Community Organizing Against Homophobia and Heterosexism.* San Francisco: Harrington Park Press, 2004.

CHAPTER 3

Learning Gender in a Diverse Society

Our typical in-class exercise while teaching a unit on the social construction of gender is to ask how many among the large number of women students present identified as tomboys when they were growing up. A sea of hands usually results as women remember their early years as girls resisting traditional notions of femininity. When male students are asked whether they had been called "sissies" when they were young, usually the whole group laughs as one lone male sheepishly raises his hand and remarks that he's always been a sissy. Why is it so easy to say you were a tomboy and so difficult to admit to being a sissy? This has a lot to do with the meanings associated with masculinity and femininity and the ways these are ranked in society. In this chapter we focus specifically on gender and sexism, keeping in mind two important points: first, how gender is constructed in connection to other differences among women like race, ethnicity, and class, and second, how sexism as a system of oppression is related to other systems of inequality and privilege.

BIOLOGY AND CULTURE

In Chapter 1 we explained gender as the way society creates, patterns, and rewards our understandings of femininity and masculinity or the process by which roles and appropriate behaviors are ascribed to women and men. Gender, in other words, can be understood as the social organization of sexual difference. Although biological distinctions create female and male humans, society interprets these differences and gives us "feminine" and "masculine" people. These adjectives are intentionally placed in quotation marks to emphasize that notions of femininity and masculinity are socially constructed—created by social processes that reflect the various workings of power in society. Therefore these notions are culturally and historically changeable. There is nothing essential, intrinsic, or static about femininity or masculinity; rather, they are social categories that might mean different things in different societies and in different historical periods. Society shapes notions of femininity and masculinity through the subtle interactions between nature and nurture.

LEARNING ACTIVITY   **Tomboys and Sissies**

Take an informal poll on your campus. Ask the women if they ever wanted to be a boy when they were growing up. Note their reaction to the question. Then ask why or why not. Also ask the women if they were considered tomboys growing up and how they felt about it if they were. Record responses and observations in a research journal.

Ask men on your campus if they ever wanted to be a girl when they were growing up. Again, note their reaction to the question. Ask why or why not. Then ask if they were considered sissies growing up and, if so, how they felt about it. Record responses and observations.

Once you've completed your poll, compare and contrast the responses you received from women and men. What do you notice? Why do you think responses may have been the way they were? What do responses suggest about gender in American society?

The relationship between biology (female/male) and culture (feminine/masculine), however, is more complicated than the assertion that sex is a biological fact and gender is the societal interpretation of that fact. First, as new scholarship points out, there is much more gender diversity in nature than once thought. As Joan Roughgarden suggests in *Evolution's Rainbow* (2004), many species are not just female or male, but can be both female and male at the same time, or be one or the other at different times. Second, while biology may imply some basic physiological facts, culture gives meaning to these in such a way that we must question whether biology can exist except within the society that gives it meaning in the first place. This implies that sex, in terms of raw male or female, is already gendered by the culture within which these physiological facts of biology exist. In other words, although many people make a distinction between biological sex (female/male) and learned gender (feminine/masculine), it is really impossible to speak of a fixed biological sex category outside of the sense that a culture makes of that category.

An example that highlights how biology is connected to culture concerns the processes by which ambiguous sex characteristics in children are handled. When hermaphrodites or "intersex" children are born without distinct genitalia to characterize them as either girls or boys, health professionals and the family make a sex determination. Hormone therapy and surgeries follow to make such a child fit the constructed binary categories our society has created, and gender is taught in accordance with this decision. This is an example of a breakdown in the taken-for-granted tight connection between natural biology and learned gender. Indeed, anthropologists have questioned this connection and used, for example, the Native American "berdache" status that entailed varying gender identities with behaviors encompassing social and economic roles, religious specialization, and temperament, to demonstrate the range of gender identity on the American continent. Along these lines, Anne Fausto-Sterling questions the tidy organization of human sex into the two categories female and male, emphasizing that sex is not as easy as genetics and

"Why does he always get to be the boy?"

genitalia and arguing for theories that allow for human variation. In the reading "Two Sexes Are Not Enough," Fausto-Sterling comments on an article she wrote in 1993 (published in *The Sciences* [vol. 33, 20–24]) that suggested replacing the two-sex system with a five-sex system to reflect this diversity.

Gender is one of the most important features of a person's identity, shaping social life and informing attitudes, behavior, and the individual's sense of self. Its pervasiveness is also a theme of Judith Lorber's article "The Social Construction of Gender." She explains that gender is a process that involves multiple patterns of interaction and is created and re-created constantly in human interaction. Lorber also makes the important point that because gender is so central in shaping our lives, much of what is gendered we do not even recognize; it's made normal and ordinary and occurs on a subconscious level. In other words, the differences between femininity (passive, dependent, intuitive, emotional) and masculinity (strong, independent, in control, out of touch emotionally) are made to seem natural and inevitable despite the fact that gender is a social script that individuals learn. Importantly, many of the skills and practices associated with gender involve privilege and entitlements. They also involve limitations.

In reality, gender is a practice in which all people engage; it is something we perform over and over in our daily lives. In this sense, gender is something that we "do" rather than "have." Through a process of *gender socialization,* we are taught and learn the appropriate thinking and behaviors associated with being a boy or girl in this culture. We actively learn the skills and practices of gender, and most of us become very accomplished in these various performances. For example, in sports, the way that girls tend naturally to throw a ball is often the object of derision. Throwing the way boys do, however, is actually an act that is learned, then performed again and again until it becomes a skill. Girls can learn to throw like boys if they are taught. As Mariah Burton Nelson contends in her article "Boys Will Be Boys and Girls Will Not," men are not necessarily better athletes than women; rather, sports as an institution has developed to reflect the particular athletic competencies of men. For example, if long-distance swimming or balance beam (activities where women generally outperform men) were popular national sports, then we might think differently about the athletic capabilities of women and men. In addition to sports, there are many other major U.S. institutions that support gendered practices. You only need go to a toy store and cruise the very different girls' and boys' aisles to witness the social construction of gender in contemporary U.S. society. What does it mean to get a child-size ironing board instead of a toy gun, and what kinds of behaviors and future roles do these toys help create and justify?

LEARNING ACTIVITY **Speaking of Women and Men**

Think about the adjectives we typically use to describe women and men and list these words in the columns below. A couple of examples are provided to get you started.

WOMEN	MEN
Passive	Active
Nurturing	Strong

What do you notice about the words we use to describe women and men? How does our language reinforce stereotypical notions about women and men?

Think about the words we use to designate women and list these names in the columns below. Also, try to find parallel names for women and men. And think about the profanities we use as well. Again, a couple of examples are provided.

WOMEN	MEN
Slut	Stud
Chick	

What do you notice here about the terms we use to name women and men? What is the significance of the words for which you could not identify parallels?

How do you think language plays a role in shaping the ways we think about and "do" gender?

This discussion of gender identity and practices does not imply that all men in contemporary North American Society are ambitious and independent and all women domestic and emotional. However, this discussion clarifies the social norms or shared values associated with the two kinds of human beings our society has created. Gender norms provide the standards or parameters through which thoughts and behaviors are molded. If we created a continuum with "feminine" on one end and "masculine" on the other, we would find mostly women on one end and mostly men on the other, and a mixture in between. This means that women and men learn the practices of gender, internalize the norms associated with masculinity and femininity, are rewarded for

appropriate behaviors and sanctioned for inappropriate behaviors, and learn to perform the ones that are expected of them.

It is important to emphasize that gender is embedded in culture and that what it might mean to be "feminine" or "masculine" in one culture is different from meanings in another culture. This means that people growing up in different societies in different parts of the world at different historical moments will learn different notions of gender. As the boxed insert in this chapter on "Rites of Passage" suggests, gender performances vary around the world. In addition, as discussed in the reading "Masculinities and Globalization" by R. W. Connell, contemporary life in the early twenty-first century, which involves global systems of production, consumption, and communication, means that patterns of gender in the United States are exported worldwide and are increasingly linked to patterns of global economic restructuring. This encourages us to consider the ways the social and economic dynamics of globalization (including economic and political expansion, militarism and colonial conquest and settlement, disruption/appropriation of indigenous peoples and resources, exportation of ideas through world markets, etc.) have shaped global gender arrangements and transformed gender relations between people based on these politics.

There are some people who consider themselves *transgendered*. Identifying oneself as transgendered involves resisting the social construction of gender into two distinct categories, masculinity and femininity, and working to break down these

HISTORICAL MOMENT   **Gender Testing**

In 1966 the European Athletics Championships in Budapest required the first sex testing of women athletes. Earlier, charges had been leveled suggesting that some women competitors were really men. In 1966 the first sex test was a visual examination of the naked athletes. Later, this test was replaced by a test that detected the athletes' chromosomal pattern (XX for female and XY for male).

In 1967 Polish sprinter Ewa Klobukowska failed the sex test and was banned from competition. Later, doctors found that she had a condition that once identified would have allowed her to compete.

In 1985 Spanish hurdler Maria Patino expected to compete in the World University Games in Kobe, Japan. Patino had lived her entire life as a woman, and her body type and sex characteristics were typically female. Unfortunately, for Patino, however, her sex test revealed that she did not have two X chromosomes. She was barred from the competition. A few months later, she competed in Spain and won her event. Following her win, however, she was kicked off the Spanish national team, stripped of her titles, and banned from all future competition. Her fight to be reinstated by the International Amateur Athletics Federation took 2½ years.

While our society generally operates under the assumption that people are either male or female, variations from typical biological patterns are common. Some form of intersexuality may occur in as many as 1 in 100 births. Generally, 1 in 400 female athletes will fail the sex test. For many years, women athletes engaged in activism to stop the sex test. Finally, the test was suspended for the 2000 Olympics, although the Olympic Committee reserved the right to reinstate the test at any point in the future.

Notice that sex testing has been used only for female athletes. Why do you suppose this is true? How does the existence of people who do not fit neatly into one or the other of the biological categories of male and female disrupt notions of fixed sexes and fixed genders?

constraining, and polarized, categories. Transgendered people push at the boundaries of gender and help reveal its constructed nature. This constructed aspect of gender is illustrated in the reading by Judy Wajcman titled "Virtual Gender." It encourages us to consider the ways the Internet and other virtual technologies have facilitated transgendered identities through a disruption of the expected relationship between self and body ("feminine" identity/"female" body). These technologies remove physical, bodily cues and allow "gender swapping," or the creation of identities that attempt to avoid the binaries of "femininity" and "masculinity." This supports the postmodern view of gender as performative and identity as multiple and fluid. Wajcman also alludes to the limits of separation between cyborg subject and body as she describes an example of masquerade and betrayal.

The term *transgendered* is often used interchangeably with the term *transsexual* (and simply labeled *"trans"*), although some scholars are more likely to describe transsexuals as transgendered people who believe they are born with the bodies of

Calvin and Hobbes   by Bill Watterson

the wrong sex and who desire chemical or surgical altering. They transition from female to male (FTM) and male to female (MTF). Being transgendered does not imply being gay since transgendered identities are about gender performance and might involve any sexual identity. Similarly, *transvestism* is about wearing the clothes of the opposite gender for sexual pleasure and is not the same as transgendered people wearing "feminine" or "masculine" clothes in order to pass as women or men. T. Eve Greenaway discusses the broader notion of "trans" in the reading "Trans on Campus." Her article raises important questions about identity and entitlement.

As a concept, transgendered is different from androgyny, although in practice, one performance of a transgendered identity might be androgyny. *Androgyny* can be defined as a lack of gender differentiation or a balanced mixture of recognizable feminine and masculine traits. This blurring or balancing is not the only consequence of an attempt to break down or rebel against gender categories. It is interesting to note that contemporary ideas about androgyny tend to privilege the "andro" more than the "gyny," with the presentation of androgyny looking a lot more like a young male than a mature female. The trappings of femininity seem to be the first things that are shed when a body tries to redo itself as androgynous. This is related to androcentrism and the ways masculinity more closely approximates our understanding of "human."

MASCULINITY

In mainstream contemporary North American society, *masculinity* has been constructed from the classical traits of intelligence, courage, and honesty, with the addition of two other key dimensions. One of these dimensions revolves around potent sexuality and an affinity for violence: the machismo element. *Machismo* involves breaking rules, sexual potency contextualized in the blending of sex and violence, and contempt for women (*misogyny*). To be a man is to *not* be a woman. Weakness, softness, and vulnerability are to be avoided at all costs. It is no coincidence that the

Rites of Passage

In almost every culture, adolescents participate in some rite of passage to mark entry into adulthood. Quite often, these rites reinforce gender distinctions. Most rites of passage share four basic elements: (1) separation from society, (2) preparation or instruction from an elder, (3) transition, and (4) welcoming back into society with acknowledgment of changed status.* Notice in the following examples how gender is reinforced through rites of passage:

- Among the Okrika of Africa, girls participate in the Iria, a rite that begins in the "fatting rooms" where the girls are fed rich foods to cause the body to "come out." The girls learn traditional songs from the elderly women, and these songs are used to free the girls from their romantic attachments to water spirits so they can become marriageable and receive mortal suitors. On the final day of their initiation, the water spirits are expected to try to seize the girls, but the Osokolo (a male) strikes the girls with sticks and drives them back to the village, ensuring their safety and future fertility.*
- The Tukuna of the Amazon initiate girls into womanhood at the onset of menstruation through the Festa das Mocas Novas. For several weeks, the girl lives in seclusion in a chamber in her family's home. The Tukuna believe that during this time, the girl is in the underworld and in increasing danger from demons, the Noo. Near the end of the initiation period, the girl is painted with black genipa dye for 2 days to protect her from the Noo, while guests arrive, some wearing masks to become incarnations of the Noo. On the third day, she leaves the chamber to dance with her family until dawn. The shaman gives her a firebrand to throw at the Noo to break the Noo's power and allow her to enter into womanhood.*
- In Ohafia in Nigeria, a father provides his son with a bow and arrows around age 7 or 8. The boy practices shooting at targets until he develops the skill to kill a small bird. When this task is accomplished, the boy ties the dead bird to the end of his bow and marches through his village singing that his peers who have not yet killed their first bird are cowards. His father, then, dresses him in finery and takes him to visit, often for the first time, his maternal family. His new social role distinguishes him from the "cowards" and marks his entrance into manhood.[†]

What are some rites of passage in the United States? How do these rites reinforce gender? How might rites of passage be developed that acknowledge entrance into adulthood without reinforcing gender distinctions?

* Cassandra Halle Delaney, "Rites of Passage in Adolescence," *Adolescence* 30 (1995): 891–987.
[†] *www.siu.edu/~anthro/mccall/children.html*.

LEARNING ACTIVITY   **Performing Gender in the Movies**

Many movies offer gender-bending performances. Choose one or more of the following movies to watch. During the movie, record your observations about how the various characters learn and perform gender. Also note the ways race intersects with gender in these performances. How does sexual identity get expressed in the performance of gender?

- *Victor/Victoria*
- *Tootsie*
- *Mrs. Doubtfire*
- *To Wong Foo, Thanks for Everything! Julie Newmar*
- *The Adventures of Priscilla, Queen of the Desert*
- *Switch*
- *The Birdcage*
- *Orlando*
- *Shakespeare in Love*
- *Boys Don't Cry*
- *Big Momma's House*
- *Sorority Boys*
- *Nutty Professor*
- *Nutty Professor II: The Klumps*
- *Connie and Carla*
- *White Chicks*

symbol of male ♂ represents Mars, the Roman god of war. A second dimension of masculinity is the *provider role,* composed of ambition, confidence, competence, and strength. Research by Deborah David and Robert Brannon characterizes four dictates of masculinity that encompass these key dimensions. The dictates include (1) "no sissy stuff," the rejection of femininity; (2) the "big wheel," ambition and the pursuit of success, fame, and wealth; (3) the "sturdy oak," confidence, competence, stoicism, and toughness; and (4) "give 'em hell," the machismo element.* Although these scripts dictate masculinity in a broad sense, there are societal demands that construct masculinity differently for different kinds of men. Middle-class masculinity puts an emphasis on the big-wheel dimension, the dictates of White masculinity often involve the sturdy oak, and men of color often become associated with the machismo element (with the exception of Asian American men, who are often feminized).

Some changes in the social construction of contemporary masculinity have allowed for a downplaying of the machismo element without a loss of sexual potency or societal control: a few small steps made into the land of the feminine. Although the machismo element is still acted out by countless teenage boys and men, it is also

---

* Deborah S. David and Robert Brannon, eds., *The Forty-Nine Percent Majority: The Male Sex Role* (Reading, MA: Addison-Wesley, 1976), pp. 13–35.

avoided by many men who genuinely do not want to be constrained by its demands. Often these men have realized that moving away from the machismo does not necessarily imply a loss of power. In fact, it seems contemporary women may prefer men who are a little more sensitive and vulnerable. In part, these changes have come about as a result of the focus on gender provided by the women's movement. As feminist writer and activist Gloria Steinem once said, gender is a prison for both women and men. The difference, she said, is that for men it's a prison with wall-to-wall carpeting and someone to bring you coffee. Understanding the limitations associated with masculine social scripts has encouraged many men to transform these scripts into more productive ways of living. Many pro-feminist men and men's organizations have been at the forefront of this work.

Some men have responded to the limitations of masculinity and the advances of women brought about by feminism by focusing on themselves as victims, as demonstrated by the mytho-poetic men's movement, which encourages men to bond and reclaim their power. While this may empower individual men, private solutions to social problems do little to transform patriarchal social structure. Other men more overtly express their desire to take back the power they believe they have lost as a result of changes in contemporary notions of femininity and the gains of the women's movement. These include the Promise Keepers, a group of Christian-affiliated men who want to return men to their rightful place in the family and community through a strong re-assertion of traditional gender roles. They believe that men are to rule and women are to serve within the traditional family system.

FEMININITY

Adjectives associated with traditional notions of femininity in contemporary mainstream North American society include soft, passive, domestic, nurturing, emotional, dependent, sensitive, as well as delicate, intuitive, fastidious, needy, fearful, and so forth. These are the qualities that have kept women in positions of subordination and encouraged them to do the domestic and emotional work of society. Again, no surprise that the symbol of female ♀ represents Venus, the goddess of love. "Doing gender" in terms of femininity involves speaking, walking, looking, and acting in certain ways: in feminine ways. The performative quality involved in being a drag queen (a gay man who is acting out normative femininity) highlights and reveals the taken-for-granted (at least by women) affectations of femininity. Yet, femininity, like masculinity, varies across cultures and groups. For example, due to historical and cultural factors, many African American women have not internalized the association of femininity with passivity and dependence characteristic of White women. Asian American women, on the other hand, often have to deal with societal stereotypes that construct femininity very much in terms of passivity and dependence: the "exotic gardenia" or "oriental chick" described in Nellie Wong's poem "When I Was Growing Up."

A key aspect of femininity is its bifurcation or channeling into two opposite aspects. These aspects involve the chaste, domestic, caring mother or madonna and the sexy, seducing, fun-loving playmate or whore (known in popular mythology as women you marry and women with whom you have sex). These polar opposites cause tension as women navigate the implications of these aspects of femininity in their

ACTIVIST PROFILE **Gloria Steinem**

Gloria Steinem didn't set out to become one of the key spokespersons for feminism. Growing up in poverty and with a mentally ill mother, Steinem often found herself in the role of her mother's caretaker. Despite the difficulties at home, she succeeded at school and was eventually accepted to Smith College, where her interest in women's rights began to take hold. After graduating from Smith, Steinem received a fellowship to do graduate studies at the University of Delhi and University of Calcutta, India. While in India, she did some work as a freelance writer and, upon returning to the United States, began a career in journalism.

As a woman in journalism, Steinem was rarely given serious assignments. Her most famous article resulted from a 1963 undercover assignment as a Playboy Bunny. Steinem saw the article as an opportunity to expose sexual harassment, but following its publication she had a difficult time being taken seriously as a journalist, despite the excellent reviews the article received.

She finally got her chance for key political assignments in 1968 when she came on board *New York Magazine* as a contributing editor. One assignment sent her to cover a radical feminist meeting, and following that meeting she moved to the center of the women's movement, co-founding the National Women's Political Caucus and the Women's Action Alliance.

In 1972 she co-founded *Ms.* magazine. Although Steinem believed there should be a feminist magazine, she had not intended to start it herself. Originally, she had thought she'd turn over the editorship once the magazine got on its feet. But with the success of *Ms.*, Steinem became one of the nation's most visible and important proponents of feminism.

The first issue of *Ms.* featured Wonder Woman on the cover, and its entire first printing of 300,000 copies sold out in 8 days. Steinem remained editor for 15 years and is still involved with the magazine today.

everyday lives. This is an example of the double bind that Marilyn Frye wrote about in her article "Oppression" included in Chapter 2. A woman often discovers that neither sexual activity nor sexual inactivity is quite right. If she is too sexually active, she will be censured for being too loose, the whore; if she refrains from sexual activity, she might similarly be censured for being a prude or frigid. Notice there are many slang words for both kinds of women: those who have too much sex and those who do not have enough. This is the double bind: You're damned if you do and

LEARNING ACTIVITY **Gender Swapping on the Web**

As discussed in the reading by Judy Wajcman, the virtual world of the Internet has provided a fascinating environment in which people often play with gender, although, given the social relations of power in contemporary society, this virtual world can also be a place where individuals use gender as a source of power over, or harassment against, other people. Still, in many text-based virtual environments, Web users are able to take on another gender. Men create "feminine" identities for themselves, and women create "masculine" identities for themselves. As Web users engage in this process of gender swapping, they are able to explore the ways that human interactions are structured by gender and to experience in some ways what life is like as another gender.

Create a virtual identity for yourself as another gender and join a chat room or game on the Web as that person. How does it feel to experience the world as another gender? Do you notice ways you act or are treated differently as this gender? What do your experiences suggest to you about how gender structures the ways humans interact with one another?

Men, by far, gender swap on the Web more than women. Why do you think this is true? Do you think gender swapping on the Web has the potential to challenge gender stereotypes? Or do you think it reinforces them? How might the technology of the Internet be used to challenge the limitations of gender? How might the technology of the Internet be used to reinforce male dominance?

Learn more: The following books offer in-depth exploration of these issues. What do these authors suggest about the nature of gender on the Web?

Cherny, Lynn, and Elizabeth Reba Weise, eds. *Wired Women: Gender and New Realities in Cyberspace.* Seattle, WA: Seal Press, 1996.

Kendall, Lori. *Hanging Out in the Virtual Pub: Masculinities and Relationships Online.* Berkeley: University of California Press, 2002.

Paasonen, Susanna. *Figures of Fantasy: Internet, Women, and Cyberdiscourse.* New York: Peter Lang, 2005.

Spender, Dale. *Nattering on the Net: Women, Power, and Cyberspace.* North Melbourne: Spinifex Press, 1995.

potentially damned if you don't. These contradictions and mixed messages serve to keep women in line.

Unlike contemporary masculinity, which is exhibiting very small steps into the realms of the feminine, femininity has boldly moved into areas that were traditionally off-limits. Today's ideal woman (perhaps from a woman's point of view) is definitely more androgynous than the ideal woman of the past. The contemporary ideal woman might be someone who is smart, competent, and independent, beautiful, thin, and sexy, yet also loving, sensitive, competent domestically, and emotionally healthy. Note how this image has integrated characteristics of masculinity with traditional feminine qualities, at the same time that it has retained much of the feminine social

LEARNING ACTIVITY **Walk Like a Man, Sit Like a Lady**

One of the ways we perform gender is by the way we use our bodies. Very early, children learn to act their gender in the ways they sit, walk, and talk.

Try this observation research:

- Observe a group of schoolchildren playing. Make notes about what you observe concerning how girls and boys act, particularly how they use their bodies in their play and communication.
- Find a place where you can watch people sitting or walking. A public park or mall may offer an excellent vantage point. Record your observations about the ways women and men walk and sit.

Also try this experiment: Ask a friend of the opposite sex to participate in an experiment with you. Take turns teaching each other to sit and to walk like the opposite sex. After practicing your newfound gender behaviors, write your reflections about the experience.

script. The contemporary ideal woman is strong, assertive, active, and independent rather than soft, passive, fearful, delicate, and dependent. The assumption is that she is out in the public world rather than confined to the home. She has not completely shed her domestic, nurturing, and caring dimension, however, or her intuitive, emotional, and sensitive aspects. These attributes are important in her success as a loving and capable partner to a man, as indeed are her physical attributes concerning looks and body size.

To be a modern woman today (we might even say a "liberated woman") is to be able to do *everything*: the superwoman. It is important to ask who is benefiting from this new social script. Women work in the public world (often in jobs that pay less, thus helping employers and the economic system) and yet still are expected to do the domestic and emotional work of home and family as well as stay "beautiful." In many ways, contemporary femininity tends to serve both the capitalist economic system and individual men better than the traditional, dependent, domestic model.

GENDER RANKING

Gender encompasses not only the socially constructed differences prescribed for different kinds of human beings but also the values associated with these differences. Recall the sissy/tomboy exercise at the beginning of this chapter. Those traits assigned as feminine are less valued than those considered masculine, illustrating why men tend to have more problems emulating femininity and trans people moving into femininity are viewed with somewhat more hostility than those transitioning toward masculine identities. It is okay to emulate the masculine and act like a boy, but it is not okay to emulate the feminine. First, gender ranking (the valuing of one gender over another) sets the stage for sexism. Judith Lorber writes, "When genders are ranked, the devalued genders have less power, prestige, and economic rewards than the valued genders." Just as White is valued above Brown or Black, and young (though not too young) above old, and heterosexual above homosexual, masculinity tends to be ranked higher than femininity. To be male is to have privileges vis-à-vis gender systems; to be female means to be a member of a target group. As already discussed, the social system here that discriminates and privileges on the basis of gender is sexism. It works by viewing the differences between women and men as important for determining access to social, economic, and political resources. As defined in Chapter 2, *sexism* is the system that discriminates and privileges on the basis of gender and that results in gender stratification. Given the ranking of gender in our society, sexism works to privilege men and limit women. In other words, men receive entitlements and privilege in a society that ranks masculinity over femininity.

Although all women are limited by sexism as a system of power that privileges men over women, the social category "woman," as you recall from Chapter 2, is hardly homogeneous. Location in different systems of inequality and privilege shapes women's lives in different ways; they are not affected by gender in the same ways. Other systems based on class, race, sexual identity, and so forth interact with gender to produce different experiences for individual women. In other words, the effects of gender and understandings of both femininity and masculinity are mediated by other systems of power. This is the second way that gender ranking occurs: the ranking of additional identities within the same gender. Forms of gender-based oppression and exploitation depend in part on other social characteristics in people's lives, and gender practices often enforce other types of inequalities. This reflects the confluence that occurs as gender categories are informed/constructed through social relations of power associated with other identities and accompanying systems of inequality and privilege (like racial identities and racism, sexual identities and heterosexism, and so forth). These identities cannot be separated, and certainly they are lived and performed through a tangle of multiple (and often shifting) identities. In this way, then, ranking occurs both across gender categories (masculinity is valued over femininity) and within gender categories (for example, as economically privileged women are represented differently than poor women and receive economic and social entitlements, or as abled women live different lives than disabled women, and so forth).

Other examples of this type of gender ranking include the ways African American women are often characterized as promiscuous or matriarchal and African American men are described as hyperathletic and sexually potent. Jewish women are painted as overly materialistic and overbearing, whereas Jewish men are supposedly very ambitious, thrifty, good at business, yet still tied to their mothers' apron strings. Latinas and Chicanas are stereotyped as sexy and fun loving, and, likewise, Latinos and Chicanos are seen as oversexed, romantic, and passionate. Native American women are portrayed as silent and overworked or exotic and romantic, whereas Native American men are stereotyped as aloof mystics, close to nature, or else as savages and drunks. Asian Americans generally are often portrayed as smart and good at science and math while Asian American women have also been typed as exotic, passive, and delicate. All these problematic constructions are created against the norm of Whiteness and work to maintain the privileges of the mythical norm. This concept is illustrated in Nellie Wong's poem. She longed to be White, something she saw as synonymous with being a desirable woman. Although there are ethnic and regional stereotypes for White women (like the dizzy blonde, Southern belle, sexually

IDEAS FOR ACTIVISM

- Be a gender traitor for a day. Act/dress in ways that are not generally considered to be appropriate for your gender.
- Develop and perform on campus a street theater piece about gender performance.
- Plan, create, publish, and distribute a zine challenging traditional gender roles.
- Examine how masculinity is valued above femininity on your campus. Write a letter about your findings to your campus newspaper.

liberated Scandinavian, or hot-tempered Irish), for the most part White women tend not to have discrete stereotypes associated with their race. This reflects the fact that White people are encouraged not to see White as a racial category although it is just as racialized as any other racial group. The fact that being White can be claimed the mythical norm strips Whiteness from the historical and political roots of its construction as a racial category. As discussed in Chapter 2, this ability for nontarget groups to remain relatively invisible is a key to maintaining their dominance in society.

In this way, diverse gendered experiences implies that the expression of femininity, or the parameters of femininity expected and allowed, is related to the confluence of gender with other systems. Historically, certain women (the poor and women of color) were regarded as carrying out appropriate womanhood when they fulfilled the domestic labor needs of strangers. Upper-class femininity meant that there were certain jobs such women could not perform. This demonstrates the interaction of gender with class and race systems. Old women endure a certain brand of femininity that tends to be devoid of the playmate role and is heavy on the mother aspect. Sexually active old women are violating the norms of femininity set up for them: This shows the influence of ageism in terms of shaping gender norms. Other stereotypes that reveal the interaction of gender with societal systems of privilege and inequality include disabled women's supposedly relatively low sexual appetite or lesbians' lack of femininity (they are presumed to want to be like men at the same time that they are said to hate them). In this way the expression of femininity is dependent on other intersecting systems of inequality and privilege and the beliefs, stereotypes, and practices associated with these systems.

Two Sexes Are Not Enough

Anne Fausto-Sterling

In 1843 Levi Suydam, a 23-year-old resident of Salisbury, Connecticut, asked the town's board of selectmen to allow him to vote as a Whig in a hotly contested local election. The request raised a flurry of objections from the opposition party, for a reason that must be rare in the annals of American democracy: It was said that Suydam was "more female than male," and thus (since only men had the right to vote) should not be allowed to cast a ballot. The selectmen brought in a physician, one Dr. William Barry, to examine Suydam and settle the matter. Presumably, upon encountering a phallus and testicles, the good doctor declared the prospective voter male. With Suydam safely in their column, the Whigs won the election by a majority of one.

A few days later, however, Barry discovered that Suydam menstruated regularly and had a vaginal opening. Suydam had the narrow shoulders and broad hips characteristic of a female build, but occasionally "he" felt physical attractions to the "opposite" sex (by which "he" meant women). Furthermore, "his feminine propensities, such as fondness for gay colors, for pieces of calico, comparing and placing them together, and an aversion for bodily labor and an inability to perform the same, were remarked by many." (Note that this 19th-century doctor did not distinguish between "sex" and "gender." Thus he considered a fondness for piecing together swatches of calico just as telling as anatomy and physiology.) No one has yet discovered whether Suydam lost the right to vote. Whatever the outcome, the story conveys both the political weight our culture places on ascertaining a person's correct "sex" and the deep confusion that arises when it can't be easily determined.

European and American culture is deeply devoted to the idea that there are only two sexes. Even our language refuses other possibilities, thus to write about Levi Suydam I have had to invent conventions—s/he and h/er to denote individuals who are clearly neither/both male and female or who are, perhaps, both at once. Nor is the linguistic convenience an idle fancy. Whether one falls into the category of man or woman matters in concrete ways. For Suydam—and still today for women in some parts of the world—it meant the right to vote. It might mean being subject to the military draft and to various laws concerning the family and marriage. In many parts of the United States, for example, two individuals legally registered as men cannot have sexual relations without breaking antisodomy laws.

But if the state and legal system has an interest in maintaining only two sexes, our collective biological bodies do not. While male and female stand on the extreme ends of a biological continuum, there are many other bodies, bodies such as Suydam's, that evidently mix together anatomical components conventionally attributed to both males and females. The implications of my argument for a sexual continuum are profound. If nature really offers us more than two sexes, then it follows that our current notions of masculinity and femininity are cultural conceits. Reconceptualizing the category of "sex" challenges cherished aspects of European and American social organization.

Indeed, we have begun to insist on the male–female dichotomy at increasingly early stages, making the two-sex system more deeply a part of how we imagine human life and giving it the appearance of being both inborn and natural. Nowadays, months before the child leaves the comfort of the womb, amniocentesis and ultrasound identify a fetus's sex. Parents can decorate the baby's room in gender-appropriate style, sports wallpaper—in blue—for the little boy, flowered designs—in pink—for the little girl. Researchers have nearly completed development of technology that can choose the sex of a child at the moment of fertilization. Moreover, modern surgical techniques help maintain the two-sex system. Today children who are born "either/or—neither/both"—a fairly common phenomenon—usually disappear from view because doctors "correct" them right away with surgery. In the past, however, intersexuals (or hermaphrodites, as they were called until recently) were culturally acknowledged.

HERMAPHRODITIC HERESIES

In 1993 I published a modest proposal suggesting that we replace our two-sex system with a five-sex one. In addition to males and females, I argued, we should also accept the categories herms (named after "true" hermaphrodities), merms (named after male "pseudohermaphrodites"), and ferms (named after female "pseudohermaphrodites"). [*Editor's note:* A "true" hermaphrodite bears an ovary and a testis, or a combined gonad called an ovo-testis. A "pseudohermaphrodite" has either an ovary or a testis, along with genitals from the "opposite" sex.] I'd intended to be provocative, but I had also been writing tongue in cheek and so was surprised by the extent of the controversy the article unleashed. Right-wing Christians somehow connected my idea of five sexes to the United Nations–sponsored Fourth World Conference on Women, to be held in Beijing two years later, apparently seeing some sort of global conspiracy at work. "It is maddening," says the text of a *New York Times* advertisement paid for by the Catholic League for Religious and Civil Rights, "to listen to discussions of 'five genders' when every sane person knows there are but two sexes, both of which are rooted in nature."

[Sexologist] John Money was also horrified by my article, although for different reasons. In a new edition of his guide for those who counsel intersexual children and their families, he wrote: "In the 1970s nurturists . . . became . . . 'social constructionists.' They align themselves against biology and medicine. . . . They consider all sex differences as artifacts of social construction. In cases of birth defects of the sex organs, they attack all medical and surgical interventions as unjustified meddling designed to force babies into fixed social molds of male and female. . . . One writer has gone even to the extreme of proposing that there are five sexes . . . (Fausto-Sterling)."

Meanwhile, those battling against the constraints of our sex/gender system were delighted by the article. The science fiction writer Melissa Scott wrote a novel entitled *Shadow Man,* which includes nine types of sexual preference and several genders, including fems (people with testes, XY chromosomes, and some aspects of female genitalia), herms (people with ovaries and testes), and mems (people with XX chromosomes and some aspects of male genitalia). Others used the idea of five sexes as a starting point for their own multi-gendered theories.

Clearly I had struck a nerve. The fact that so many people could get riled up by my proposal to revamp our sex/gender system suggested that change (and resistance to it) might be in the offing. Indeed, a lot *has* changed since 1993, and I like to think that my article was one important stimulus. Intersexuals have materialized before our very eyes, like beings beamed up onto the Starship Enterprise. They have become political organizers lobbying physicians and politicians to change treatment practices. More generally, the debate over our cultural conceptions of gender has escalated, and the boundaries separating masculine and feminine seem harder than ever to define. Some find the changes under way deeply disturbing; others find them liberating.

I, of course, am committed to challenging ideas about the male/female divide. In chorus with a growing organization of adult intersexuals, a small group of scholars, and a small but growing cadre of medical practitioners, I argue that medical management of intersexual births needs to change. *First,* let there be no unnecessary infant surgery (by *necessary* I mean to save the infant's life or significantly improve h/er physical well-being). *Second,* let physicians assign a provisional sex (male or female) to the infant (based on existing knowledge of the probability of a particular gender identity formation—penis size be damned!). *Third,*

let the medical care team provide full information and long-term counseling to the parents and to the child. However well-intentioned, the methods for managing intersexuality, so entrenched since the 1950s, have done serious harm.

R E A D I N G **20**

The Social Construction of Gender

Judith Lorber

Talking about gender for most people is the equivalent of fish talking about water. Gender is so much the routine ground of everyday activities that questioning its taken-for-granted assumptions and presuppositions is like thinking about whether the sun will come up.[1] Gender is so pervasive that in our society we assume it is bred into our genes. Most people find it hard to believe that gender is constantly created and re-created out of human interaction, out of social life, and is the texture and order of that social life. Yet gender, like culture, is a human production that depends on everyone constantly "doing gender" (West and Zimmerman 1987).

And everyone "does gender" without thinking about it. Today, on the subway, I saw a well-dressed man with a year-old child in a stroller. Yesterday, on a bus, I saw a man with a tiny baby in a carrier on his chest. Seeing men taking care of small children in public is increasingly common—at least in New York City. But both men were quite obviously stared at—and smiled at, approvingly. Everyone was doing gender—the men who were changing the role of fathers and the other passengers, who were applauding them silently. But there was more gendering going on that probably fewer people noticed. The baby was wearing a white crocheted cap and white clothes. You couldn't tell if it was a boy or a girl. The child in the stroller was wearing a dark blue T-shirt and dark print pants. As they started to leave the train, the father put a Yankee baseball cap on

the child's head. Ah, a boy, I thought. Then I noticed the gleam of tiny earrings in the child's ears, and as they got off, I saw the little flowered sneakers and lace-trimmed socks. Not a boy after all. Gender done.

. . .

For the individual, gender construction starts with assignment to a sex category on the basis of what the genitalia look like at birth.[2] Then babies are dressed or adorned in a way that displays the category because parents don't want to be constantly asked whether their baby is a girl or a boy. A sex category becomes a gender status through naming, dress, and the use of other gender markers. Once a child's gender is evident, others treat those in one gender differently from those in the other, and the children respond to the different treatment by feeling different and behaving differently. As soon as they can talk, they start to refer to themselves as members of their gender. Sex doesn't come into play again until puberty, but by that time, sexual feelings and desires and practices have been shaped by gendered norms and expectations. Adolescent boys and girls approach and avoid each other in an elaborately scripted and gendered mating dance. Parenting is gendered, with different expectations for mothers and fathers, and people of different genders work at different kinds of jobs. The work adults do as mothers and fathers and as low-level workers and high-level bosses, shapes women's and men's life experiences, and these experiences produce different feelings, consciousness, relationships, skills—ways of being that we call feminine or masculine.[3] All of these processes constitute the social construction of gender.

. . .

To explain why gendering is done from birth, constantly and by everyone, we have to look not only at the way individuals experience gender but at gender as a social institution. As a social institution, gender is one of the major ways that human beings organize their lives. Human society depends on a predictable division of labor, a designated allocation of scarce goods, assigned responsibility for children and others who cannot care for themselves, common values and their systematic transmission to new members, legitimate leadership, music, art, stories, games, and other symbolic productions. One way of choosing people for the different tasks of society is on the basis of their talents, motivations, and competence—their demonstrated achievements. The other way is on the basis of gender, race, ethnicity—ascribed membership in a category of people. Although societies vary in the extent to which they use one or the other of these ways of allocating people to work and to carry out other responsibilities, every society uses gender and age grades. Every society classifies people as "girl and boy children," "girls and boys ready to be married," and "fully adult women and men," constructs similarities among them and differences between them, and assigns them to different roles and responsibilities. Personality characteristics, feelings, motivations, and ambitions flow from these different life experiences so that the members of these different groups become different kinds of people. The process of gendering and its outcome are legitimated by religion, law, science, and the society's entire set of values.

GENDER AS PROCESS, STRATIFICATION, AND STRUCTURE

As a social institution, gender is a process of creating distinguishable social statuses for the assignment of rights and responsibilities. As part of a stratification system that ranks these statuses

unequally, gender is a major building block in the social structures built on these unequal statuses.

As a *process*, gender creates the social differences that define "woman" and "man." In social interaction throughout their lives, individuals learn what is expected, see what is expected, act and react in expected ways, and thus simultaneously construct and maintain the gender order. . . .

Gendered patterns of interaction acquire additional layers of gendered sexuality, parenting, and work behaviors in childhood, adolescence, and adulthood. Gendered norms and expectations are enforced through informal sanctions of gender-inappropriate behavior by peers and by formal punishment or threat of punishment by those in authority should behavior deviate too far from socially imposed standards for women and men.

. . .

As part of a *stratification* system, gender ranks men above women of the same race and class. Women and men could be different but equal. In practice, the process of creating difference depends to a great extent on differential evaluation. . . . The dominant categories are the hegemonic ideals, taken so for granted as the way things should be that white is not ordinarily thought of as a race, middle class as a class, or men as a gender. The characteristics of these categories define the Other as that which lacks the valuable qualities the dominants exhibit.

In a gender-stratified society, what men do is usually valued more highly than what women do because men do it, even when their activities are very similar or the same. In different regions of southern India, for example, harvesting rice is men's work, shared work, or women's work: "Wherever a task is done by women it is considered easy, and where it is done by [men] it is considered difficult" (Mencher 1988, 104). A gathering and hunting society's survival usually depends on the nuts, grubs, and small animals brought in by the women's foraging trips, but when the men's hunt is successful, it is the occasion for a celebration. Conversely, because they are the superior group, white men do not have to do the "dirty work," such as housework; the most inferior group does it, usually poor women of color (Palmer 1989).

. . .

When gender is a major component of structured inequality, the devalued genders have less power, prestige, and economic rewards than the valued genders. In countries that discourage gender discrimination, many major roles are still gendered; women still do most of the domestic labor and child rearing, even while doing full-time paid work; women and men are segregated on the job and each does work considered "appropriate"; women's work is usually paid less than men's work. Men dominate the positions of authority and leadership in government, the military, and the law; cultural productions, religions, and sports reflect men's interests.

In societies that create the greatest gender difference, such as Saudi Arabia, women are kept out of sight behind walls or veils, have no civil rights, and often create a cultural and emotional world of their own (Bernard 1981). But even in societies with less rigid gender boundaries, women and men spend much of their time with people of their own gender because of the way work and family are organized. This spatial separation of women and men reinforces gendered differences, identity, and ways of thinking and behaving (Coser 1986).

Gender inequality—the devaluation of "women" and the social domination of "men"—has social functions and social history. It is not the result of sex, procreation, physiology, anatomy, hormones, or genetic predispositions. It is produced and maintained by identifiable social processes and built into the general social structure and individual identities deliberately and purposefully. The social order as we know it in Western societies is organized around racial, ethnic, class, and gender inequality. I contend, therefore, that the continuing purpose of gender as a modern social institution is to construct women as a group to be the subordinates of men as a group.

THE PARADOX OF HUMAN NATURE

To say that sex, sexuality, and gender are all socially constructed is not to minimize their social power. These categorical imperatives govern our lives in the most profound and pervasive ways, through the social experiences and social practices of what Dorothy Smith calls the "everday/evernight world" (1990, 31–57). The paradox of human nature is that it is *always* a manifestation of cultural meanings, social relationships, and power politics; "not biology, but culture, becomes destiny" (J. Butler 1990, 8). Gendered people emerge not from physiology or sexual orientations but from the exigencies of the social order, mostly, from the need for a reliable division of the work of food production and the social (not physical) reproduction of new members. The moral imperatives of religion and cultural representations guard the boundary lines among genders and ensure that what is demanded, what is permitted, and what is tabooed for the people in each gender is well known and followed by most (C. Davies 1982). Political power, control of scarce resources, and, if necessary, violence uphold the gendered social order in the face of resistance and rebellion. Most people, however, voluntarily go along with their society's prescriptions for those of their gender status, because the norms and expectations get built into their sense of worth and identity as [the way we] think, the way we see and hear and speak, the way we fantasy, and the way we feel.

There is no core or bedrock in human nature below these endlessly looping processes of the social production of sex and gender, self and other, identity and psyche, each of which is a "complex cultural construction" (J. Butler 1990, 36). *For humans, the social is the natural. . . .*

NOTES

1. Gender is, in Erving Goffman's words, an aspect of *Felicity's Condition:* "any arrangement which leads us to judge an individual's . . . acts not to be a manifestation of strangeness. Behind Felicity's Condition is our sense of what it is to be sane" (1983:27). Also see Bem 1993; Frye 1983, 17–40; Goffman 1977.
2. In cases of ambiguity in countries with modern medicine, surgery is usually performed to make the genitalia more clearly male or female.
3. See J. Butler 1990 for an analysis of how doing gender is gender identity.

REFERENCES

Bem, Sandara Lipsitz. 1993. *The Lenses of Gender: Transforming the Debate on Sexual Inequality.* New Haven: Yale University Press.

Bernard, Jessie. 1981. *The Female World.* New York: Free Press.

Butler, Judith. 1990. *Gender Trouble: Feminism and the Subversion of Identity.* New York and London: Routledge.

Coser, Rose Laub. 1986. "Cognitive structure and the use of social space." *Sociological Forum* 1:1–26.

Davies, Christie. 1982. "Sexual taboos and social boundaries." *American Journal of Sociology* 87:1032–63.

Dwyer, Daisy, and Judith Bruce (eds.). 1988. *A Home Divided: Women and Income in the Third World.* Palo Alto, Calif.: Stanford University Press.

Frye, Marilyn. 1983. *The Politics of Reality: Essays in Feminist Theory.* Trumansburg, N.Y.: Crossing Press.

Goffman, Erving, 1977. "The arrangement between the sexes." *Theory and Society* 4:301–33.

Mencher, Joan. 1988. "Women's work and poverty: Women's contribution to household maintenance in South India." In Dwyer and Bruce 1988.

Palmer, Phyllis. 1989. *Domesticity and Dirt: Housewives and Domestic Servants in the United States, 1920–1945.* Philadelphia: Temple University Press.

Smith, Dorothy. 1990. *The Conceptual Practices of Power: A Feminist Sociology of Knowledge.* Toronto: University of Toronto Press.

West, Candace, and Don Zimmerman. 1987. "Doing gender." *Gender & Society* 1:125–51.

R E A D I N G   **21**

Boys Will Be Boys and Girls Will Not

Mariah Burton Nelson

My aunts washed the dishes while the uncles
squirted each other on the lawn with
garden hoses. Why are we in here,
I said, and they are out there?
  that's the way it is,
  said Aunt Hetty, the shriveled-up one.
  —Paulette Jiles, *"Paper Matches"*

Two scientists recently made this forecast: The fastest woman may eventually outrun the fastest man. Their prediction appeared only as a letter to the editor in *Nature* magazine, yet it generated a stampede of interest from the media. *Time,* the *Chicago Tribune, USA Today,* the *New York Times,* the *Washington Post,* and *Sports Illustrated* printed stories. All quoted experts who ridiculed the conjecture as "ludicrous," "sheer ignorance," "a good laugh," "absurd," "asinine," "completely fallacious," and/or "laughable."

In one Associated Press report, the word *ridiculous* was used five times. *Science News* ran the headline "Women on the verge of an athletic showdown." *Runner's World* entitled its article "Battle of the Sexes." Unlike questionable projections that are dismissed without fanfare, this one seems to have struck a nerve.

The researchers, Brian Whipp and Susan Ward of the University of California, Los Angeles, calculated runners' average speeds during record-breaking races over the past seventy years, then compared the rates of increase. Noting that women's average speeds are increasing at a faster rate than are men's, they projected that in the future, the best women may catch up to and even surpass the best men at various distances.

Indisputably, neither women nor men will continue to improve at their current rates forever. Otherwise, humans would one day run the marathon in a matter of minutes. But the very idea that women might someday beat men elicited passionate responses. *Runner's World* writers Amby Burfoot and Marty Post, as if verbally to stop women in their tracks, pointed out that in the past five years, women have made few improvements in world-record times. This is a sure sign, they said, that women "have already stopped" improving.

When I appear on radio and television shows to discuss women's sports or my first book, *Are We Winning Yet? How Women Are Changing Sports and Sports Are Changing Women,* I encounter a similar fury. Female callers are not the problem; they brag about their triceps or gripe about male egos or ask for advice about discrimination. Some male callers tell stories about female martial artists or mountain climbers who taught them, in a way they could understand, about female strength. But at least half of the male callers act as if my views were heretical. Angry and antagonistic, they belittle me, my ideas, my book, and female athletes in general.

What seems to make them angriest is my observation that men are not better athletes than women are. In no sport are all men better than all women, I point out, and in many sports, women routinely defeat men. Although single-sex competitions are often appropriate, and men do have physical advantages in some sports, women should see themselves as men's peers, I suggest, rather than exclusively competing against women.

These men don't want to hear any of that. In voices I can only describe as high-pitched and hysterical, they say, "Yeah, but you're never going to see a woman play pro football!"

It is a taunt and, I think, a genuine fear. I'm not talking about football. I've never met a woman who aspires to play pro football. I'm talking about auto racing, horse racing, dog sled racing, equestrian events, rifle shooting, and marathon swimming, where women and men compete together at the elite levels. I'm talking about tennis, golf, racquetball, bowling, skiing, and other recreational sports, where a wife and husband or a female and male pair of friends are likely to find themselves evenly matched. In sports, as in the rest of life, women do compete with men on a daily basis, and often win.

So it intrigues me that in response to my discussion of women's athletic excellence, men change the subject to football. They try to assert football as the sine qua non of athleticism. Because "women could never play football," they imply, men are physically, naturally, biologically superior.

Most men can't play pro football themselves—but they can take vicarious comfort in the display of male physical competence and aggression.

They take comfort in professional baseball ("Women could never play pro baseball") and in professional basketball ("Women could never play pro basketball") and in boxing ("Women could never box") and in footraces ("Women could never win the marathon").

Here are a few more quotes from men on radio shows, on airplanes, at restaurants:

"Women can't dunk."

"OK, women can play golf, but they can't drive the ball as far as men can."

"OK, female jockeys win, but there's a horse involved."

"Women win at marathon swimming? Who cares? You call that a major sport? I'd like to see a 320-pound female linebacker. That's a laugh."

Most men are not 320-pound linebackers. But, identified with these hulks, average men take great pleasure in the linebackers' exploits (a revealing term). Football, baseball, basketball, boxing, and hockey are important to men in part *because* they seem to be all-male pursuits, because they seem to be activities that *only men can do.* When women demonstrate excellence in sports like running, tennis, and golf, men take great pains to describe that excellence as less important, less worthy, less of an achievement than male excellence.

Psychiatrist Arnold R. Beisser explains the phenomenon this way: "It is small wonder that the American male has a strong affinity for sports. He has learned that this is one area where there is no doubt about sexual differences and where his biology is not obsolete. Athletics help assure his difference from women in a world where his functions have come to resemble theirs."

Sports are about distinction. Who is better? One inch, one point, or one-hundredth of a second can differentiate winner from loser. One pound, one meal, one more set of two-hundred-meter sprints in practice can determine, or seem to determine, whether a person finishes first or last. Athletes may train for the sheer joy of moving their bodies through space, but eventually they grow curious to see how fast they can move, or how well they can perform, compared to others. They want to compare, to contrast, to differentiate. To know where they stand. To win.

It is in this comparative, competitive arena that we are repeatedly told that women and men are different. And men are better. Women may no longer be weak, granted, but they are still weak*er.* Weaker than men. Still the weaker sex.

Still, as de Beauvoir said, the second sex.

Actually, in many ways, men are the weaker sex. Men die on average seven years earlier than women. Women have a better sense of smell, taste, hearing, and sight (colorblindness affects one woman for every sixteen men). Women are more susceptible to migraines, arthritis, and depression, but men commit suicide more and have higher rates of heart attack and stroke. "Women are sick, but men are dead," Edward Dolnick wrote in his *In Health* magazine article on the subject.

Yet men keep pointing to one physical advantage—upper-body strength—to maintain their illusion of supremacy. Sports that depend on such strength—that, indeed, were designed to showcase that strength—bolster the myth.

Those who claim male sports superiority are not thinking of male gymnasts, who lack the flexibility to use some of the apparatus women use. Or male swimmers, who can't keep up with women over long distances. Or male equestrians, who gallop side by side with—or in the dust of—their female peers.

They are not considering how much women and men have in common: the human experience of sport. These same people would never think of comparing Sugar Ray Leonard to Muhammad Ali. One weighed sixty pounds more than the other. Clearly, they deserved to box in different classes. Yet the top female tennis player is often compared to the top

male tennis player ("Yeah but, she could never beat *him*"), who usually outweighs her by sixty pounds.

Those who claim male superiority are not remembering jockstraps. Because men's genitals dangle precariously outside the pelvis, they are vulnerable to speeding baseballs and to angry fists or feet. In addition, "bikes with dropped handlebars bring the rider's legs close to the stomach, and the testicles can get squashed or twisted against the saddle," notes sportswriter Adrianne Blue in *Faster, Higher, Further.* "This can lead to gangrene and amputation." Such cases have been noted in medical journals.

Blue also suggests that men's bigger bodies make more "dangerous missiles" that are more likely than women's bodies to cause injury when they collide. For this reason a case could be made, she says, for banning men from contact sports.

If women and men were to compete together in noncontact sports, a man would currently win at the elite levels of most existing events: running (as long as the race is under 100 miles); swimming (under about 22 miles); throwing shot, discus, or javelin. On average, men can carry and use more oxygen. They tend to be heavier—an advantage in football—and taller: handy in basketball and volleyball. Men have more lean muscle mass, convenient in sports requiring explosive power—which happens to include most of the sports men have invented.

Less muscle-bound, women generally have better flexibility, useful in gymnastics, diving, and skating. Our lower center of gravity can help in hockey, golf, tennis, baseball, and even basketball. We sweat better (less dripping, therefore better evaporation), which is critical since, like car engines, human bodies need to remain cool and well lubricated to function efficiently.

Physiologist Diane Wakat, associate professor of health education at the University of Virginia, tested athletes under various conditions of heat, humidity, exercise, and nutritional intake, and concluded that women are better able to adjust to the environmental changes. "In every case, females were better able to handle the stress," says Wakat.

The longer the race, the better women do. Women's superior insulation (fat) is, believe it or not, prized by some because it offers buoyancy, heat retention, and efficient use of fuel over long distances, whether by land or by sea.

Ann Trason, a California microbiology teacher, became in 1989 the first woman to win a coed national championship—the twenty-four-hour run—by completing 143 miles. The best male finisher completed four fewer miles. Of Ward and Whipp's prediction that women will one day hold the overall world record in the relatively short (26.2-mile) marathon, Trason says: "I'd be there and be really happy to see it, but it seems unlikely. I do think women will get closer."

Helen Klein's world-record distance in a twenty-four-hour race—109.5 miles—exceeds the best distance for an American man in her age group (65–69). She says of the possibility that a woman will one day set the overall marathon record, "I would not say no. There is hope. If I were younger, I might try it myself."

In marathon and long-distance cold-water swims, "women usually out-swim the men," says Bob Duenkel, curator of the International Swimming Hall of Fame. Penny Dean still holds the English Channel record she set in 1978. Diana Nyad is the only athlete to complete the swim from Bimini to Florida. Lynne Cox holds the records for swimming the Bering Strait and the Strait of Magellan. The first person to swim all five Great Lakes, and the first ever to cross Lake Superior (in 1988), was Vicki Keith.

Susan Butcher has been the overall winner of the 1,100-mile Iditarod dog sled race four times. A woman named Seana Hogan recently cycled the four hundred miles from San Francisco to Los Angeles in nineteen hours, forty-nine minutes, breaking the previous men's record by almost an hour.

But women's successes are rarely attributable to gender. In ultra-distance running, swimming, and cycling, as well as in equestrian events, horse racing, auto racing, and dog sled racing, success is determined primarily by physical and mental preparation, competitive spirit, self-discipline, or other non-gender-related factors. Because upper-body strength is not paramount in these sports, women and men become free to compete together as individuals, even at the highest levels of competition.

Men's strength advantage is actually marginal, meaning that there is more variation among individual men than between the average man and the average woman. It only becomes relevant when comparing trained, competitive athletes. On any recreational doubles tennis team, the female player might be stronger.

Age is also important. Men's strength advantage occurs primarily during the reproductive years. Before puberty, girls, who tend to mature faster, have a height and strength advantage which, if not nullified by institutional and cultural discrimination, would actually render the best of them superior to the best boys. In old age, there is little physical difference between female and male strength.

But we've so long been told that men are better athletes. I even catch myself thinking this way, despite daily evidence to the contrary. For instance, in my masters swimming program, the fastest athletes—including college competitors—swim in Lane 1, while the slowest—including fit, fast, white-haired folks in their seventies—swim in Lane 6. There are women and men in all the lanes.

I swim in Lane 3. In Lane 2 is Ken. Because he's about my age and height, I identify with him. We have the same stroke length, so we look at each other sometimes, his breathing to the left, my breathing to the right, as we windmill through the water. But eventually he pulls ahead. He's faster. At first, I attributed his greater speed to the fact that he is male. His shoulders are broader; his muscles are more prominent than mine.

But then I looked over at Lane 4. There swims Bruce. Also about my height and my age, Bruce is slower than I am. He's got those same broad shoulders and big muscles, but there he is anyway, poking along in Lane 4. I'm faster because I've trained longer, or I have better technique, or I'm in better shape, or I'm more competitive, or some combination of those factors—the same reasons Ken is faster than both Bruce and me, and the same reasons Susie, Karen, Diane, Denise, Lynn, and Martha are faster than Ken. It has nothing to do with gender.

. . .

Because "being masculine" has included access to diverse sporting opportunities and "being feminine" has not, it's shortsighted to postulate that current gaps between male and female athletic potential will not close, at least partially, in the future—or that, as Post and Burfoot asserted, women "have already stopped improving." Men prevented women from running marathons until 1967. The Olympics did not offer a women's marathon until 1984, and still doesn't offer a women's swimming event longer than eight hundred meters (the men swim fifteen hundred meters). For every college woman who gets a chance to play college sports, 2.24 men do. For every woman who receives a college scholarship, 2.26 men do. The more women run, the greater the likelihood that some of them will run fast. Increased numbers of female runners—along with female-focused training, coaching, scholarships, equipment, and even clothing—account for the historical improvements in women's times, and greater numbers in the future are likely to improve times further.

If marathon swimming were our national sport, as it is in Egypt—if there were a nationally televised Super Bowl of marathon swimming, and spectators packed college swim meets like sardines—we might think differently about women's and men's athletic capabilities. If men competed against women on the balance beam, or in synchronized swimming or in rhythmic gymnastics, we might rephrase the question about who might catch up to whom.

. . .

One reason male–female athletic comparisons are tempting to make, and hard to argue with, is that they seem natural. What could be more natural than human bodies? Sports seem to offer measurable, inarguable proof of human physical potential. Especially when no machines or animals are involved, sports seem to represent a raw, quintessentially fair contest between individuals or teams. *Ready? Set? Go. May the best man win.*

In fact, few professional athletes have "natural" bodies; otherwise we'd bump into pro football-sized men in the supermarkets. The linebacker has been shaped by many behavioral (nutrition, weight lifting) and often chemical (steroids, growth hormones) factors. Women who play or do not play sports have also been shaped by various factors,

including restricted access to training opportunities, restrictive shoes and clothing, ridicule by peers, and cultural pressure to limit food intake for the sake of creating a thin, rather than strong, body. There's nothing natural about any of that.

But because sports seem natural, and because in the sports media we so often see men who are bigger and stronger than the biggest, strongest women, these men make a convincing subliminal case: not only are men better athletes, men are superior physical specimens. And because the men engaged in sporting events are so often enacting some form of mock combat, we receive the message: Men are inherently, naturally aggressive and, as a gender, dominant.

. . .

As every first-grader knows, there are physical differences between women and men, but these differences would be largely irrelevant except in matters of sex, reproduction, urination, and toupee purchases if it weren't for our culture's insistence on categorizing people first and foremost as "male" or "female." It is from these cultural categories—not from biological realities—that most "masculine" and "feminine" behaviors emerge. Cynthia Fuchs Epstein, author of *Deceptive Distinctions,* writes, "The overwhelming evidence created by the past decade of research on gender supports the theory that gender differentiation—as distinct of course from sexual differentiation—is best explained as a social construction rooted in hierarchy."

Here's where the hierarchy part comes in: we don't just say, boys shouldn't play with dolls and girls shouldn't play with pistols. Through our economic structure and through the media, we say that taking care of children—"women's work"—is less important than war—"men's work." We don't just say that football is for boys and cheerleading is for girls. We say that playing football is more valuable than cheerleading or field hockey or volleyball or Double Dutch jump rope or anything girls do—more important, more interesting, more newsworthy: better.

Thus boys have an incentive to cling religiously to "boy behaviors," and they do. Boys are more likely than girls to insist on sex-typed activities and toys, and with good reason—it cements their place in the dominant class. Boys also have an incentive to keep girls out of their tree forts and clubhouses and sports associations and military elite: like "undesirables" moving into a pricey neighborhood, females lower the property value. Women's participation challenges the entire concept of relevant differences between women and men. "To allow women into sport would be an ultimate threat to one of the last strongholds of male security and supremacy," write Mary A. Boutilier and Lucinda SanGiovanni in *The Sporting Woman*. To put it another way, if women can play sports then "men aren't really men."

Of course, it's too late to keep women out of sports. But they can be kept out of the public eye and kept out of key, visible, highly paid positions like a football or men's basketball coach. Their accomplishments can be ignored or trivialized or sexualized. They can be barred from "masculine" activities—a term having nothing, really, to do with who men are, and everything to do with what men want to claim as their own.

. . .

Female athletes, sweat soaking their muscled chests, aren't half-women, half-men. They aren't Lady Panthers or Lady Rams or Lady Cheetahs, trying in vain to catch up to Gentlemen Bulls. They're people in pursuit of perfection—a quest that human beings, in all their diversity, seem to enjoy.

R E A D I N G **22**

When I Was Growing Up

Nellie Wong

I know now that once I longed to be white.
How? you ask.
Let me tell you the ways.

> when I was growing up, people told me
> I was dark and I believed my own darkness
> in the mirror, in my soul, my own narrow vision

>> when I was growing up, my sisters
>> with fair skin got praised
>> for their beauty, and in the dark
>> I fell further, crushed between high walls

> when I was growing up, I read magazines
> and saw movies, blonde movie stars, white skin,
> sensuous lips and to be elevated, to become
> a woman, a desirable woman, I began to wear
> imaginary pale skin

>> when I was growing up, I was proud
>> of my English, my grammar, my spelling
>> fitting into the group of small children
>> smart Chinese children, fitting in,
>> belonging, getting in line

when I was growing up and went to high school,
I discovered the rich white girls, a few yellow girls,
their imported cotton dresses, their cashmere sweaters,
their curly hair and I thought that I too should have
what these lucky girls had

> when I was growing up, I hungered
> for American food, American styles,
> coded: white and even to me, a child
> born of Chinese parents, being Chinese
> was feeling foreign, as limiting,
> was unAmerican

when I was growing up and a white man wanted
to take me out, I thought I was special,
an exotic gardenia, anxious to fit
the stereotype of an oriental chick

> when I was growing up, I felt ashamed
> of some yellow men, their small bones,
> their frail bodies, their spitting
> on the streets, their coughing,
> their lying in sunless rooms,
> shooting themselves in the arms

when I was growing up, people would ask
if I were Filipino, Polynesian, Portuguese.
They named all colors except white, the shell
of my soul, but not my dark, rough skin

> when I was growing up, I felt
> dirty. I thought that god
> made white people clean
> and no matter how much I bathed,
> I could not change, I could not shed
> my skin in the gray water

when I was growing up, I swore
I would run away to purple mountains,
houses by the sea with nothing over
my head, with space to breathe,
uncongested with yellow people in an area
called Chinatown, in an area I later learned
was a ghetto, one of many hearts
of Asian America

I know now that once I longed to be white.
How many more ways? you ask.
Haven't I told you enough?

Virtual Gender

Judy Wajcman

The idea that the Internet can transform conventional gender roles, altering the relationship between the body and the self via a machine, is a popular theme in recent postmodern feminism. The message is that young women in particular are colonizing cyberspace, where gender inequality, like gravity, is suspended. In cyberspace, all physical, bodily cues are removed from communication. As a result, our interactions are fundamentally different, because they are not subject to judgments based on sex, age, race, voice, accent or appearance, but are based only on textual exchanges. In *Life on the Screen,* Sherry Turkle enthuses about the potential for people "to express multiple and often unexplored aspects of the self, to play with their identity and to try out new ones . . . the obese can be slender, the beautiful plain, the 'nerdy' sophisticated."[1] It is the increasingly interactive and creative nature of computing technology that now enables millions of people to live a significant segment of their lives in virtual reality. Moreover, it is in this computer-mediated world that people experience a new sense of self, which is decentred, multiple and fluid. . . .

Interestingly, the gender of Internet users features mainly in Turkle's chapter about virtual sex. Cyberspace provides a risk-free environment where people can engage in the intimacy they both desire and fear. Turkle argues that people find it easier to establish relationships on-line and then pursue them off-line. Yet, for all the celebration of the interactive world of cyberspace, what emerges from her discussion is that people engaging in Internet relationships really want the full, embodied relationship. Like many other authors, Turkle argues that gender swapping, or

virtual cross-dressing, encourages people to reflect on the social construction of gender, to acquire "a new sense of gender as a continuum."[2] However she does not reflect upon the possibility that gender differences in the constitution of sexual desire and pleasure influence the manner in which cybersex is used.

In a similar vein, Allucquére Rosanne Stone celebrates the myriad ways in which modern technology is challenging traditional notions of gender identity. Complex virtual identities rupture the cultural belief that there is a single self in a single body. Stone's discussion of phone and virtual sex, for example, describes how female sex workers disguise crucial aspects of identity and can play at reinventing themselves. She takes seriously the notion that virtual people or selves can exist in cyberspace, with no necessary link to a physical body. As an illustration of this, Stone recounts the narrative about the cross-dressing psychiatrist that has become an apocryphal cyberfeminist tale. Like many stories that become legends, it is a pastiche of fiction and fact, assembled from diverse sources, including real events.[3]

It is the story of a middle-aged male psychiatrist called Lewin who becomes an active member of a CompuServe chat line, a virtual place where many people can interact simultaneously in real time. One day Lewin found he was conversing with a woman who assumed he was a female psychiatrist. Lewin was stunned by the power and intimacy of the conversation. He found that the woman was more open to him than were his female patients and friends in real life. Lewin wanted more, and soon began regularly logging on as Julie Graham, a severely handicapped and disfigured New York resident. Julie said it was her embarrassment about her disfigurement that made her prefer not to meet her cyberfriends in person.

Over time, Julie successfully projected her personality and had a flourishing social life on the Internet, giving advice to the many women who confided in her. Lewin acquired a devoted following and came to believe that it was as Julie that he could best help these women. His on-line female friends told Julie how central she had become to their lives. Indeed, the elaborate details of Julie's life gave hope particularly to other disabled women as her professional life flourished and, despite her handicaps, she became flamboyantly sexual, encouraging many of her friends to engage in Net sex with her. Her career took her around the world on the conference circuit, and she ended up marrying a young police officer.

Julie's story is generally taken to show that the subject and the body are no longer inseparable; that cyberspace provides us with novel free choices in selecting a gender identity irrespective of our material body. Stone argues that by the time he was exposed, Lewin's responses had ceased to be a masquerade, that he was in the process of *becoming* Julie. However, this story can be read in a radically different manner, one that questions the extent to which the cyborg subject can escape the biological body. Although Julie's electronic manifestation appears at first sight to subvert gender distinctions, it can be just as forcefully argued that it ultimately reinforced and reproduced these differences. For the women seeking Julie's advice, her gender was crucial. They wanted to know that there was a woman behind the name; this is what prompted their intimacies. Julie's gender guided their behaviour and their mode of expression. "It rendered her existence, no matter how intangible and 'unreal' Julie appeared at first, extremely physical and genuine."[4] When Julie was unmasked as a cross-dressing man years later, many women who had sought her advice felt deeply betrayed and violated.

It was the "real" disabled women on-line who first had suspicions about the false identity, indicating that there are limits on creating sustainable new identities in cyberspace. Relationships on the Internet are not as free of corporeality as Stone and Turkle suggest. Although computer-mediated communication alters the nature of interaction by removing bodily cues, this is not the same as creating new identities. Just because all you see is words, it does not mean that becoming a different person requires only different words, or that this is a simple matter. Choosing words for a different identity is problematic.[5] The choice of words is the result of a process of socialization associated with a particular identity. It is therefore very difficult to learn a new identity without being socialized into that role. Although mimicry is possible, it is limited and is not the same as creating a viable new identity.

Research on artificial intelligence and information systems now emphasizes the importance of the body in human cognition and behaviour. Moreover, the sociology of scientific knowledge has taught us that much scientific knowledge is tacit (things people know but cannot explain or specify in formal rules) and cannot be learned explicitly. So it is with becoming a man or a woman. Lewin's false identity was discovered by people who had been socialized in the role that Lewin adopted: namely, that of a disabled woman. Bodies play an important part in what it means to be human and gendered.

That this narrative is about a man posing as a woman is not merely incidental as there is evidence that many more men adopt a female persona than vice versa. The masculine discursive style of much communication on the Web is well recognized. "Flaming" or aggressive on-line behaviour, including sexual harassment, is rife, and has a long lineage all the way back to the original hackers who developed the first networked games such as the notorious Dungeons and Dragons/MUD games. These games were designed by young men for the enjoyment of their peers. This reflected the computer science and engineering "nerd" technoculture that produced the Internet and excluded women from participation.

Cyberspace first appeared as "a disembodied zone wilder than the wildest West, racier than the space race, sexier than sex, even better than walking on the moon" in cyberpunk fiction.[6] It promised to finally rupture the boundaries between hallucination and reality, the organic and the electronic. For cyberpunks, technology is inside the body and the mind itself. Textual and visual representations of gendered bodies and erotic desire, however, proved less imaginative. It was new technology with the same old narratives. Here was a phallocentric fantasy of cyberspace travel infused with clichéd images of adolescent male sex, with console cowboys jacking into cyberspace.

. . .

A popular, contemporary version of these adventure games does feature a female character—notably Lara Croft, in the popular Tomb Raider game, alternatively seen as a fetish object of Barbie proportions created by and for the male gaze or as a female cyberstar. The orthodox feminist view of Lara Croft sees her as a pornographic technopuppet, an eternally young female automaton. By contrast, postmodern gender and queer theorists stress the diverse and subversive readings that Lara Croft is open to.[7] For some she is a tough, capable, sexy adventurous female heroine. For others, Lara as drag queen enables men to experiment with 'wearing' a feminine identity, echoing the phenomenon of gender crossing in Internet chat rooms.

While Lara may offer young women an exciting way into the male domain of computer games, much of the desire projected on to this avatar is prosaic. The game even features a Nude Raider patch that removes Lara's clothing. To cast her as a feminist heroine is therefore a long bow to draw. Perhaps we should let her creator Toby Gard have

the last word: "Lara was designed to be a tough, self-reliant, intelligent woman. She confounds all the sexist clichés apart from the fact that she's got an unbelievable figure. Strong, independent women are the perfect fantasy girls—the untouchable is always the most desirable."[8]

NOTES

1. Sherry Turkle, *Life on the Screen: Identity in the Age of the Internet* (New York: Simon & Schuster, 1995), p. 12.
2. Ibid., p. 314.
3. Allucquére Rosanne Stone, *The War of Desire and Technology at the Close of the Mechanical Age* (Cambridge, Mass.: MIT Press, 1995), ch. 3.
4. Ruth Oldenziel, "Of old and new cyborgs: Feminist narratives of technology," *Letterature D' America,* 14, 55 (1994), p. 103.
5. Edgar A. Whitley, "In cyberspace all they see is your words: A review of the relationship between body, behaviour and identity drawn from the sociology of knowledge," *OCLC Systems and Services,* 13, 4 (1997), pp. 152–63.
6. Sadie Plant, *Zeros and Ones: Digital Women and the New Technoculture* (London: Fourth Estate, 1998), p. 180.
7. Anne-Marie Schleiner, "Does Lara Croft wear fake polygons? Gender and gender-role subversion in computer adventure games," *Leonardo,* 34, 4 (2001), pp. 221–26.
8. Justine Cassell and Henry Jenkins, "Chess for girls? Feminism and computer games," in Justine Cassell and Henry Jenkins (eds), *From Barbie to Mortal Kombat: Gender and Computer Games* (Cambridge, Mass.: MIT Press, 1998), p. 30.

Trans on Campus

T. Eve Greenaway

Graduation, 2001. A crowd at one end of the lawn. Folding chairs in rows across the newly mowed green. Teary faces, fidgeting children. The soon-to-be graduates of a small women's college move slowly through the crowd in white hats and gowns. They ascend a small stage for a certificate marking the end of their undergraduate careers.

The parents of this group in white believe in women's colleges for many of the same reasons they might have 20 years ago. They believe young women have a stronger chance at success, academically and professionally, if they are nurtured in an environment free of gender politics. But many of their daughters are graduating with very different identities—in fact, a whole new kind of gender politics. Some will tell you they are not women at all.

As feminism sees its third wave—and the voices of students identifying themselves as lesbian, bisexual, and transgender grow—women's colleges are witnessing a cultural transformation similar to the '60s. Many of the 74 women's colleges in the U.S. and Canada are now thought to breed the most radical feminists and countercultural types. One of the first questions many students hear when they announce their enrollment in a women's college is "Isn't that a lesbian school?"

And indeed, there is reason for that question. Lesbian and bisexual groups have played a prominent place on many women's campuses since the '70s and queer identity forms the backbone of a large portion of the social activism that goes on there. But as the distinction between gender identity and sexual orientation becomes more of an issue, women's colleges are witnessing a new crop of student groups. Transgender organizing is picking up speed and trans alliances are far more vocal than they were just five years ago.

How many transgender students are there in the U.S.? The numbers are hard to record, and university deans and administrators appear reluctant to comment or speculate on transgender organizing on their campuses. While the term *transgender* applies to anyone who undergoes a shift from female to male (FTM) or male to female (MTF), most associate it with those who don female clothes or traits like Ru Paul.

Until recently, FTM people were relatively invisible. But things are changing fast, especially on America's campuses. Some Americans born between the mid '70s and early '80s are now taking on gender identities as varied as their hair colors. Many will tell you they are simply "trans," but some use words like trannyboy, boydyke, postgenderist, androgyne, and genderqueer.

Korey, for instance, was born female but will tell you he is a straight male. The 19-year-old New Yorker says he questioned his female gender identity for years but didn't find the language to describe himself until he saw author and transgender advocate Leslie Feinberg speak. (Feinberg's novel, *Stone Butch Blues,* is the first step on many trans boys' reading lists. He also has written books about the blurred the lines of gender expression and coined the term "Transgender Warrior.")

Inspired by Feinberg, Korey and his girlfriend began searching the Internet for more clues. Around the same time, he transferred to the women's college at Lesley in Massachusetts and says he didn't think twice about attending a women's college despite his decision to begin "transitioning." Since then, he has taken a gender-neutral name and started testosterone. But he has not had an operation. Like many young "genderqueers," Korey doesn't believe a male physique is necessary to be "male." Nevertheless, Korey ran into some trouble at Lesley University. He was criticized by students and administrators for his gender stance. "The staff reminded me that if I don't identify as female, then I need to reconsider why I am at a women's college," says Korey. "It is frightening that I've become a threat."

Korey is probably still a student at Lesley University because there are no policies there regarding trans students. But Paul Karoff, vice president for Student Affairs at Lesley, is concerned. He speculates: "A situation like this is going to raise practical issues that no one has ever contemplated or dealt with before." As Karloff suggests, the transgender "movement" is difficult to understand. It's based on a language of identity, with which most Americans are unfamiliar. It requires a revision of the use of pronouns, and the inclusion of terms like "hir." Many trans activists seem to spend a great deal of time educating people about this shifting language. Glossaries are popping up right and left. The most comprehensive ones break down the intricacies of "assigned gender," and what it means to be "female-bodied," "pre-op," or "non-op." (The latter refers to the way some trans people position themselves in relation to sex-reassignment surgery.)

But most college administrators are not schooled in these new identity linguistics. In one case, at Moore College of Art and Design, an all-women's art school in Philadelphia, an 18-year-old was questioned in front of a board of administrators. The student claims he was grilled about why he would want to stay in school if he was no longer female, and eventually decided to leave.

Dr. Jadwiga Sebrecht, the president of the Women's College Coalition of the United States and Canada, prefers to see trans identity questions in terms of the law. Asked about policies regarding trans students on women's campuses, she responded: "Women's colleges comply with government regulations, hence they recognize a person's legal sex status. If the person is a female, in the eyes of the law, then any previous sexual identity is irrelevant. If, however, a person is legally male, that status is the one recognized by the women's college. I do not know of any women's college that has a different policy."

Legal identification may seem to solve the problem, but recent incidents on women's campuses tell another story. In an article appearing in *Ms.* magazine last winter, for example, a young student at an unnamed midwestern women's college was told he could stay enrolled as long as he remained a "vagina'd individual." The article did not question how such a thing be regulated, nor did it bring up perhaps the most important point trans activists are raising: that some students see their gender identities as entirely separate from their anatomies.

Colleges like Smith and Mills are at the vanguard of this issue. Trans boys on those campuses are pushing to raise awareness among their faculties and fellow students about alternative gender representation, arguing, "If we are biologically or legally female—regardless of whether or not we identify as women—then we have the same rights to be at Smith as do female students who begin and continue identifying as women."

In a statement produced by the Smith transgender alliance, the answer to the question "Why Are We at Smith?" reads: "We are a single-sex school, which means that every Smith student's sex is labeled as female. But in our single-sex environment we have a multitude of different gender identities and gender expressions. . . . The queer-friendliness of this campus, our affinity with Smith's values, and the connections we have made thus far within the Smith community are aspects many of us appreciate. For these reasons, transgendered students remain at Smith despite the difficulties we face here."

If this sounds more sophisticated than an average college student, there's reason: many trans students are looking at gender in the context of their academic work. Take Ryan. The 22-year-old earned a degree in women's studies and sociology from Smith this May. Like many students, Ryan's academic pursuits lead him to research the history and theory behind the transgender movement. And like many trans boys, Ryan dated a woman who was very supportive of his fluid gender. If pressed, Ryan says he does not identify as transgender, but is comfortable being referred to as both "he" and "she." He rejects the two-gender approach (and refuses to use the word "transition" because it implies a set binary), describing himself instead as "gender variant" or "gender queer." Still, Ryan is unsure how this approach will translate to his life outside the politically charged, academic bubble of Smith. At school, he says his friends were more than accepting. But he fears that some of that comes from a sense that being genderqueer is "the new cool thing." "I've sort of reached a point," he says, "where I'm re-evaluating and trying to figure out, without the queer skew of Smith College and Northampton, what I'm all about."

Women's colleges are not the only place where people are transitioning genders. Tucker, for example, began his transition at age 14. Tucker is a traditional transsexual, meaning he is becoming a man physically as well as emotionally. The 21-year-old junior entered Brown University a "male," has been on testosterone for several years and is fairly open about his identity. "A good portion of the queer community at Brown seems to know that I am a transsexual," he says. "I'm used to avoiding pronouns and pretty skillful at telling stories without them."

Many trans guys say they "pass" for their gender of choice easier than their MTF counterparts. In Tucker's case, he wears his hair long and a pearl necklace sometimes as part of what he describes as his "effeminate" appearance. "I find they help me pass better as a man," he says. "If I wore short hair and no jewelry, I might resemble a butch woman or an obvious FTM. But when I accessorize, people assume 'No butch woman would do that. . . .'" Tucker says cultivating his softer "female" side gives him more options. "I understand something of receptiveness, nonviolence, beauty, cooperation, nurturing. But I construct these as 'gay male' rather than 'female,'" he says. The "male" identity is central to Tucker. To him, it represents autonomy, independence and self motivation. "I need to have that as a starting point," he says. "Otherwise, I would lack the sense of independence to achieve my full potential."

Tucker also believes that more people are identifying as trans than ever before, because of a shift in feminism. "The concept of gender identity and expression, as the transgender movement, defines those terms, is crucial to a healthy feminist movement," he says. Tucker may be on to something. Third wave feminists' fight for equality is no longer just about voting and reproductive rights; it's about the subtler significance of cultural identity and the place of biology in gender roles. Young trans people are looking closer at the parts of our lives that most of us assume are scientifically predetermined.

But some say they may be zooming in a little too closely. Some, like Ryan, say this breeds an element of peer pressure in the transgender phenomenon. "I do think more people are identifying as 'gender queer,'" he says, "and I think there has begun this weird and really troubling competition—at least at Smith—to see who can be the most queer." Ryan points to a growing pattern within the younger lesbian, bisexual, and transgender community that, while sensitive to forms of discrimination, has created yet another power structure. "It's no longer queer enough to be gay or lesbian," he says. "It's a little more queer to be bisexual, and the most queer to be trans. And there is some version of that hierarchy of oppressions that got us into trouble decades ago starting to resurface or manifest itself in this new way," says Ryan.

If what Ryan says is true, why is questioning your gender "the new cool thing"? Are these shifts really happening on a large scale? Patrick Califia, the author of *Sex Changes: The Politics of Transgenderism,* argues the FTM community is reaching a "critical mass." If numbers are hard to come by, it may be largely because FTMs fill a whole spectrum of identities, ranging from those who call themselves butch lesbians to those, like Tucker, who are transsexuals. What seems clear is that by the time some people are in college, they have been living with gender dysphoria for years.

Califia says that the trans community is now "big enough, and visible enough, that people are becoming aware that it's an option, that transsexual doesn't only refer to male-to-females." He also believes that the Brandon Teena story—as told by the 2000 feature film *Boys Don't Cry* and the 1998 documentary about the brutal rape and murder of the same Nebraska boy—was a "quantum leap forward" for the trans community. Some speculate it is only a matter of time before FTMs start showing up on the popular culture radar more frequently.

Because this movement is still young, however, it is almost as politically charged internally as it is on the outside. Within the "old school" lesbian feminist community, there are those who link men with oppression and look to deny trans people a place in their cultural spheres. As Califia puts it, "When people identify as feminist, and are critical of the role that males have played in creating patriarchal culture, they may look for ways to express their masculinity without 'becoming the enemy.' But all this is based on a cultural script that says that women are the solution and men are the problem."

Feminism has always been about rewriting these scripts. And in that way this movement may not be so new. After all, young trans people are questioning, unlearning and creating their own culture. Best of all, they force the rest of us into those awkward, gravity-less moments where nothing is what it seems, and the potential for change is more vast than we may have realized.

R E A D I N G **25**

Masculinities and Globalization

R. W. Connell

[In this article] I offer a framework for thinking about masculinities as a feature of world society and for thinking about men's gender practices in terms of the global structure and dynamics of gender. . . .

THE WORLD GENDER ORDER

Masculinities do not first exist and then come into contact with femininities; they are produced together, in the process that constitutes a gender order. Accordingly, to understand the masculinities on a world scale, we must first have a concept of the globalization of gender.

This is one of the most difficult points in current gender analysis because the very conception is counterintuitive. We are so accustomed to thinking of gender as the attribute of an individual, even as an unusually intimate attribute, that it requires a considerable wrench to think of gender on the vast scale of global society. Most relevant discussions, such as the literature on women and development, fudge the issue. They treat the entities that extend internationally (markets, corporations, intergovernmental programs, etc.) as ungendered in principle—but affecting unequally gendered recipients of aid in practice, because of bad policies. Such conceptions reproduce the familiar liberal-feminist view of the state as in principle gender-neutral, though empirically dominated by men.

But if we recognize that very large scale institutions such as the state are themselves gendered, in quite precise and specifiable ways (Connell 1990), and if we recognize that international relations, international trade, and global markets are inherently an arena of gender formation and gender politics (Enloe 1990), then we can recognize the existence of a world gender order. The term can be defined as the structure of relationships that interconnect the gender regimes of institutions, and the gender orders of local society, on a world scale. That is, however, only a definition. The substantive questions remain: what is the shape of that structure, how tightly are its elements linked, how has it arisen historically, what is its trajectory into the future?

Current business and media talk about globalization pictures a homogenizing process sweeping across the world, driven by new technologies, producing vast unfettered global markets in which all participate on equal terms. This is a misleading image. As Hirst and Thompson (1996) show, the global economy is highly unequal and the current degree of homogenization is often overestimated. Multinational corporations based in the three major economic powers (the United States, European Union, and Japan) are the major economic actors worldwide.

The structure bears the marks of its history. Modern global society was historically produced, as Wallerstein (1974) argued, by the economic and political expansion of European states from the fifteenth century on and by the creation of colonial empires. It is in this process that we find the roots of the modern world gender order. Imperialism was, from the start, a gendered process. Its first phase, colonial conquest and settlement, was carried out by gender-segregated forces, and it resulted in massive disruption of indigenous gender orders. In its second phase, the stabilization of colonial societies, new gender divisions of labor were produced in plantation economies and colonial cities, while gender ideologies were linked with racial hierarchies and the cultural defense of empire. The third phase, marked by political decolonization, economic neocolonialism, and the current growth of world markets and structures of financial control, has seen gender divisions of labor remade on a massive scale in the "global factory" (Fuentes and Ehrenreich 1983), as well as the spread of gendered violence alongside Western military technology.

The result of this history is a partially integrated, highly unequal and turbulent world society, in which gender relations are partly but unevenly linked on a global scale. The unevenness becomes clear when different substructures of gender (Connell 1987; Walby 1990) are examined separately. [These substructures include:]

The Division of Labor. A characteristic feature of colonial and neocolonial economies was the restructuring of local production systems to produce a male wage worker–female domestic worker couple (Mies 1986). This need not produce a "housewife" in the Western suburban sense, for instance, where the wage work involved migration to plantations or mines (Moodie 1994). But it has generally produced the identification of masculinity with the public realm and the money economy and of femininity with domesticity, which is a core feature of the modern European gender system (Holter 1997).

Power Relations. The colonial and postcolonial world has tended to break down purdah systems of patriarchy in the name of modernization, if not of women's emancipation (Kandiyoti 1994). At the same time, the creation of a westernized public realm has seen the growth of large-scale organizations in the form of the state and corporations, which in the great majority of cases are culturally masculinized and controlled by men. In *comprador* capitalism, however, the power of local elites depends on their relations with the metropolitan powers, so the hegemonic masculinities of neocolonial societies are uneasily poised between local and global cultures.

Emotional Relations. Both religious and cultural missionary activity has corroded indigenous homosexual and cross-gender practice, such as the Native American *berdache* and the Chinese "passion of the cut sleeve" (Hinsch 1990). Recently developed Western models of romantic heterosexual love as the basis for marriage and of gay identity as the main alternative have now circulated globally—though as Altman (1996) observes, they do not simply displace indigenous models, but interact with them in extremely complex ways.

Symbolization. Mass media, especially electronic media, in most parts of the world follow North American and European models and relay a great deal of metropolitan content; gender imagery is an important part of what is circulated. A striking example is the reproduction of a North American imagery of femininity by Xuxa, the blonde television superstar in Brazil (Simpson 1993). In counterpoint, exotic gender imagery has been used in the marketing strategies of newly industrializing countries (e.g., airline advertising from Southeast Asia)—a tactic based on the long-standing combination of the exotic and the erotic in the colonial imagination (Jolly 1997).

Clearly, the world gender order is not simply an extension of a traditional European-American gender order. That gender order was changed by colonialism, and elements from other cultures now circulate globally. Yet in no sense do they mix on equal terms, to produce a United Colours of Benetton gender order. The culture and institutions of the North Atlantic countries are hegemonic within the emergent world system. This is crucial for understanding the kinds of masculinities produced within it.

THE REPOSITIONING OF MEN AND THE RECONSTITUTION OF MASCULINITIES

The positioning of men and the constitution of masculinities may be analyzed at any of the levels at which gender practice is configured: in relation to the body, in personal life, and in collective social practice. At each level, we need to consider how the processes of globalization influence configurations of gender.

Men's bodies are positioned in the gender order, and enter the gender process, through body-reflexive practices in which bodies are both objects and agents (Connell 1995)—including sexuality, violence, and labor. The conditions of such practice include where one is and who is available for interaction. So it is a fact of considerable importance for gender relations that the global social order distributes and redistributes bodies, through migration, and through political controls over movement and interaction.

The creation of empire was the original "elite migration," though in certain cases mass migration followed. Through settler colonialism, something close to the gender order of Western Europe was reassembled in North America and in Australia. Labor migration within the colonial systems was a means by which gender practices were spread, but also a means by which they were recon-

structed, since labor migration was itself a gendered process—as we have seen in relation to the gender division of labor. Migration from the colonized world to the metropole became (except for Japan) a mass process in the decades after World War II. There is also migration within the periphery, such as the creation of a very large immigrant labor force, mostly from other Muslim countries, in the oil-producing Gulf states.

These relocations of bodies create the possibility of hybridization in gender imagery, sexuality, and other forms of practice. The movement is not always toward synthesis, however, as the race/ethnic hierarchies of colonialism have been re-created in new contexts, including the politics of the metropole. Ethnic and racial conflict has been growing in importance in recent years, and as Klein (1997) and Tillner (1997) argue, this is a fruitful context for the production of masculinities oriented toward domination and violence. Even without the context of violence, there can be an intimate interweaving of the formation of masculinity with the formation of ethnic identity, as seen in the study by Poynting, Noble, and Tabar (1997) of Lebanese youths in the Anglo-dominant culture of Australia.

At the level of personal life as well as in relation to bodies, the making of masculinities is shaped by global forces. In some cases, the link is indirect, such as the working-class Australian men caught in a situation of structural unemployment (Connell 1995), which arises from Australia's changing position in the global economy. In other cases, the link is obvious, such as the executives of multinational corporations and the financial sector servicing international trade. The requirements of a career in international business set up strong pressures on domestic life: almost all multinational executives are men, and the assumption in business magazines and advertising directed toward them is that they will have dependent wives running their homes and bringing up their children.

At the level of collective practice, masculinities are reconstituted by the remaking of gender meanings and the reshaping of the institutional contexts of practice. Let us consider each in turn.

The growth of global mass media, especially electronic media, is an obvious "vector" for the globalization of gender. Popular entertainment circulates stereotyped gender images, deliberately made attractive for marketing purposes. International news media are also controlled or strongly influenced from the metropole and circulate Western definitions of authoritative masculinity, criminality, desirable femininity, and so on. But there are limits to the power of global mass communications. Some local centers of mass entertainment differ from the Hollywood model, such as the Indian popular film industry centered in Bombay. Further, media research emphasizes that audiences are highly selective in their reception of media messages, and we must allow for popular recognition of the fantasy in mass entertainment. Just as economic globalization can be exaggerated, the creation of a global culture is a more turbulent and uneven process than is often assumed (Featherstone 1995).

More important, I would argue, is a process that began long before electronic media existed, the export of institutions. Gendered institutions not only circulate definitions of masculinity (and femininity), as sex role theory notes. The functioning of gendered institutions, creating specific conditions for social practice, calls into existence specific patterns of practice. Thus, certain patterns of collective violence are embedded in the organization and culture of a Western-style army, which are different from the patterns of precolonial violence. Certain patterns of calculative egocentrism are embedded in the working of a stock market; certain patterns of rule following and domination are embedded in a bureaucracy.

Now, the colonial and postcolonial world saw the installation in the periphery, on a very large scale, of a range of institutions on the North Atlantic model: armies, states, bureaucracies, corporations, capital markets, labor markets, schools, law courts, transport systems. These are gendered institutions and their functioning has directly reconstituted masculinities in the periphery. This has not necessarily meant photocopies of European masculinities. Rather, pressures for change are set up that are inherent in the institutional form.

To the extent that particular institutions become dominant in world society, the patterns of masculinity embedded in them may become global standards. Masculine dress is an interesting indicator: almost every political leader in the world now wears the uniform of the Western business executive. The more common pattern, however, is not the complete displacement of local patterns but the articulation of the local gender order with the gender regime of global-model institutions. Case studies such as Hollway's (1994) account of bureaucracy in Tanzania illustrate the point; there, domestic patriarchy articulated with masculine authority in the state in ways that subverted the government's formal commitment to equal opportunity for women.

We should not expect the overall structure of gender relations on a world scale simply to mirror patterns known on the smaller scale. In the most vital of respects, there is continuity. The world gender order is unquestionably patriarchal, in the sense that it privileges men over women. There is a patriarchal dividend for men arising from unequal wages, unequal labor force participation, and a highly unequal structure of ownership, as well as cultural and sexual privileging. This has been extensively documented by feminist work on women's situation globally (e.g., Taylor 1985), though its implications for masculinity have mostly been ignored. The conditions thus exist for the production of a hegemonic masculinity on a world scale, that is to say, a dominant form of masculinity that embodies, organizes, and legitimates men's domination in the gender order as a whole.

The conditions of globalization, which involve the interaction of many local gender orders, certainly multiply the forms of masculinity in the global gender order. At the same time, the specific shape of globalization, concentrating economic and cultural power on an unprecedented scale, provides new resources for dominance by particular groups of men. This dominance may become institutionalized in a pattern of masculinity that becomes, to some degree, standardized across localities. I will call such patterns *globalizing masculinities,* and it is among them, rather than narrowly within the metropole, that we are likely to find candidates for hegemony in the world gender order.

. . .

MASCULINITIES OF POSTCOLONIALISM AND NEOLIBERALISM

. . .

With the collapse of Soviet communism, the decline of postcolonial socialism, and the ascendancy of the new right in Europe and North America, world politics is more and more organized around the needs of transnational capital and the creation of global markets.

The neoliberal agenda has little to say, explicitly, about gender: it speaks a gender-neutral language of "markets," "individuals," and "choice." But the world in which neoliberalism is ascendant is still a gendered world, and neoliberalism has an implicit gender politics. The "individual" of neoliberal theory has in general the attributes and interests of a male entrepreneur, the attack on the welfare state generally weakens the position of women, while the increasingly unregulated power of transnational corporations places strategic power in the hands of particular groups of men. It is not surprising, then, that the installation of capitalism in Eastern Europe and the former Soviet Union has been accompanied by a reassertion of dominating masculinities and, in some situations, a sharp worsening in the social position of women.

We might propose, then, that the hegemonic form of masculinity in the current world gender order is the masculinity associated with those who control its dominant institutions: the business executives who operate in global markets, and the political executives who interact (and in many contexts, merge) with them. I will call this *transnational business masculinity*. This is not readily available for ethnographic study, but we can get some clues to its character from its reflections in management literature, business journalism, and corporate self-promotion, and from studies of local business elites (e.g., Donaldson 1997).

As a first approximation, I would suggest this is a masculinity marked by increasing egocentrism,

very conditional loyalties (even to the corporation), and a declining sense of responsibility for others (except for purposes of image making). Gee, Hull and Lankshear (1996), studying recent management textbooks, note the peculiar construction of the executive in "fast capitalism" as a person with no permanent commitments, except (in effect) to the idea of accumulation itself. Transnational business masculinity is characterized by a limited technical rationality (management theory), which is increasingly separate from science.

Transnational business masculinity differs from traditional bourgeois masculinity by its increasingly libertarian sexuality, with a growing tendency to commodify relations with women. Hotels catering to businessmen in most parts of the world now routinely offer pornographic videos, and in some parts of the world, there is a well-developed prostitution industry catering for international businessmen. Transnational business masculinity does not require bodily force, since the patriarchal dividend on which it rests is accumulated by impersonal, institutional means. But corporations increasingly use the exemplary bodies of elite sportsmen as a marketing tool (note the phenomenal growth of corporate "sponsorship" of sport in the last generation) and indirectly as a means of legitimation for the whole gender order.

MASCULINITY POLITICS ON A WORLD SCALE

Recognizing global society as an arena of masculinity formation allows us to pose new questions about masculinity politics. What social dynamics in the global arena give rise to masculinity politics, and what shape does global masculinity politics take?

The gradual creation of a world gender order has meant many local instabilities of gender. Gender instability is a familiar theme of poststructuralist theory, but this school of thought takes as a universal condition a situation that is historically specific. Instabilities range from the disruption of men's local cultural dominance as women move into the public realm and higher education, through the disruption of sexual identities that produced "queer" politics in the metropole, to the shifts in the urban intelligentsia that produced "the new sensitive man" and other images of gender change.

One response to such instabilities, on the part of groups whose power is challenged but still dominant, is to reaffirm *local* gender orthodoxies and hierarchies. A masculine fundamentalism is, accordingly, a common response in gender politics at present. A soft version, searching for an essential masculinity among myths and symbols, is offered by the mythopoetic men's movement in the United States and by the religious revivalists of the Promise Keepers (Messner 1997). A much harder version is found, in that country, in the right-wing militia movement brought to world attention by the Oklahoma City bombing (Gibson 1994), and in contemporary Afghanistan, if we can trust Western media reports, in the militant misogyny of the Talibaan. It is no coincidence that in the two latter cases, hardline masculine fundamentalism goes together with a marked anti-internationalism. The world system—rightly enough—is seen as the source of pollution and disruption.

Not that the emerging global order is a hotbed of gender progressivism. Indeed, the neoliberal agenda for the reform of national and international economics involves closing down historic possibilities for gender reform. I have noted how it subverts the gender compromise represented by the metropolitan welfare state. It has also undermined the progressive-liberal agendas of sex role reform represented by affirmative action programs, antidiscrimination provisions, child care services, and the like. Right-wing parties and governments have been persistently cutting such programs, in the name of either individual liberties or global competitiveness. Through these means, the patriarchal dividend to men is defended or restored, without an *explicit* masculinity politics in the form of a mobilization of men.

Within the arenas of international relations, the international state, multinational corporations, and global markets, there is nevertheless a deployment of masculinities and a reasonably clear hegemony. The transnational business masculinity described above has had only one major competitor for hegemony in recent decades, the

rigid, control-oriented masculinity of the military, and the military-style bureaucratic dictatorships of Stalinism. With the collapse of Stalinism and the end of the cold war, Big Brother (Orwell's famous parody of this form of masculinity) is a fading threat, and the more flexible, calculative, egocentric masculinity of the fast capitalist entrepreneur holds the world stage.

We must, however, recall two important conclusions of the ethnographic moment in masculinity research: that different forms of masculinity exist together and that hegemony is constantly subject to challenge. These are possibilities in the global arena too. Transnational business masculinity is not completely homogeneous; variations of it are embedded in differnt parts of the world system, which may not be completely compatible. We may distinguish a Confucian variant, based in East Asia, with a stronger commitment to hierarchy and social consensus, from a secularized Christian variant, based in North America, with more hedonism and individualsim and greater tolerance for social conflict. In certain arenas, there is already conflict between the business and political leaderships embodying these forms of masculinity: initially over human rights versus Asian values, and more recently over the extent of trade and investment liberalization.

If these are contenders for hegemony, there is also the possibility of opposition to hegemony. The global circulation of "gay" identity (Altman 1996) is an important indication that nonhegemonic masculinities may operate in global arenas, and may even find a certain political articulation, in this case around human rights and AIDS prevention.

REFERENCES

Altman, Dennis. 1996. Rupture or continuity? The internationalisation of gay identities. *Social Text* 48 (3): 77–94.

Connell, R. W. 1987. *Gender and power*. Cambridge, MA: Polity.

————. 1990. The state, gender and sexual politics: Theory and appraisal. *Theory and Society* 19:507–44.

————. 1995. *Masculinities*. Cambridge, MA: Polity.

Donaldson, Mike. 1997. Growing up very rich: The masculinity of the hegemonic. Paper presented at the conference Masculinities: Renegotiating Genders, June, University of Wollongong, Australia.

Enloe, Cynthia. 1990. *Bananas, beaches and bases: Making feminist sense of international politics.* Berkeley: University of California Press.

Featherstone, Mike. 1995. *Undoing culture: Globalization, postmodernism and identity.* London: Sage.

Fuentes, Annette, and Barbara Ehrenreich. 1983. *Women in the global factory.* Boston: South End.

Gee, James Paul, Glynda Hall, and Colin Lankshear. 1996. *The new work order: Behind the language of the new capitalism.* Sydney: Allen & Unwin.

Gibson, J. William. 1994. *Warrior dreams: Paramilitary culture in post-Vietnam America.* New York: Hill and Wang.

Hinsch, Bret. 1990. *Passions of the cut sleeve: The male homosexual tradition in China.* Berkeley: University of California Press.

Hirst, Paul, and Grahame Thompson. 1996. *Globalization in question: The international economy and the possibilities of governance.* Cambridge, MA: Polity.

Hollway, Wendy. 1994. Separation, integration and difference: Contradictions in a gender regime. In *Power/gender: Social relations in theory and practice,* edited by H. Lorraine Radtke and Henderikus Stam, 247–69. London: Sage.

Holter, Oystein Gullvag. 1997. Gender, patriarchy and capitalism: A social forms analysis. Ph.D. diss., University of Oslo, Faculty of Social Science.

Jolly, Margaret. 1997. From point Venus to Bali Ha'i: Eroticism and exoticism in representations of the Pacific. In *Sites of desire, economies of pleasure: Sexualities in Asia and the Pacific,* edited by Lenore Manderson and Margaret Jolly, 99–122. Chicago: University of Chicago Press.

Kandiyoti, Deniz. 1994. The paradoxes of masculinity: Some thoughts on segregated societies. In *Dislocating masculinity: Comparative ethnographies,*

edited by Andrea Cornwall and Nancy Lindisfarne, 197–213. London: Routledge.

Klein, Uta. 1997. Our best boys: The making of masculinity in Israeli society. Paper presented at UNESCO expert group meeting on Male Roles and Masculinities in the Perspectives of a Culture of Peace, September, Oslo.

Messner, Michael A. 1997. *The politics of masculinities: Men in movements.* Thousand Oaks, CA: Sage.

Mies, Maria. 1986. *Patriarchy and accumulation on a world scale: Women in the international division of labour.* London: Zed.

Moodie, T. Dunbar. 1994. *Going for gold: Men, mines, and migration.* Johannesburg: Witwatersand University Press.

Poynting, S., G. Noble, and P. Tabar. 1997. "Intersections" of masculinity and ethnicity: A study of male Lebanese immigrant youth in Western Sydney. Paper presented at the conference Masculinities: Renegotiating Genders, June, University of Wollongong, Australia.

Simpson, Amelia. 1993. *Xuxa: The mega-marketing of a gender, race and modernity.* Philadelphia: Temple University Press.

Taylor, Debbie. 1985. Women: An analysis. In *Women: A world report,* 1–98. London: Methuen.

Tillner, Georg. 1997. Masculinity and xenophobia. Paper presented at UNESCO meeting on Male Roles and Masculinities in the Perspective of a Culture of Peace, September, Oslo.

Walby, Sylvia. 1990. *Theorizing patriarchy.* Oxford, U.K.: Blackwell.

Wallerstein, Immanuel. 1974. *The modern world-system: Capitalist agriculture and the origins of the European world-economy in the sixteenth century.* New York: Academic Press.

DISCUSSION QUESTIONS FOR CHAPTER 3

1. How do notions of sex and gender take shape within a cultural context? In what ways has your cultural context shaped your notions of sex and gender?

2. How would you describe the dominant notions of masculinity and femininity in U.S. society? How do these dominant notions help maintain systems of inequality?

3. How do people learn to "do" gender? Can you think of ways you've learned to do gender? From what sources did you learn to do gender?

4. How does gender ranking reinforce sexism?

5. How is the experience of sexism shaped by the confluences of other systems of oppression?

SUGGESTIONS FOR FURTHER READING

Bornstein, Kate. *My Gender Workbook.* New York: Routledge, 1998.

Boylan, Jennifer Finney. *She's Not There: A Life in Two Genders.* New York: Broadway, 2003.

Butler, Judith. *Undoing Gender.* New York: Routledge, 2004.

Fausto-Sterling, Anne. *Sexing the Body: Gender Politics and the Construction of Sexuality.* New York: Basic Books, 2000.

Feinberg, Leslie. *Transgender Warriors.* Boston: Beacon, 1996.

Howey, Noelle. *Dress Codes: Of Three Girlhoods—My Mother's, My Father's, and Mine.* New York: St. Martin's Press, 2002.

Lorber, Judith. *Paradoxes of Gender.* New Haven, CT: Yale University Press, 1994.

Roughgarden, Joan. *Evolution's Rainbow: Diversity, Gender, and Sexuality in Nature and People.* Berkeley: University of California Press, 2004.

West, Candace, and Don H. Zimmerman. "Doing Gender." *Gender and Society* 1 (1987): 125–151.

CHAPTER **4**

Sex, Power, and Intimacy

Sexuality is a topic of great interest to most people. It entertains and intrigues and is a source of both personal happiness and frustration. Over the centuries men have struggled to control women's sexuality through a variety of physical and emotional means; controlling a woman's sexuality has often meant controlling her life. The flip-side of this is that sexuality has the potential to be a liberating force in women's lives. To enjoy and be in control of one's sexuality and to be able to seek a mutually ful-filling sexual relationship can be an empowering experience. This chapter begins with a discussion of the social construction of sexuality and provides definitions for key terms. Following is a focus on two themes associated with sexuality: first, the politics of sexuality, and second, intimacy, romance, and communication.

THE SOCIAL CONSTRUCTION OF SEXUALITY

Human sexuality involves erotic attractions, identity, and practices, and it is constructed by and through societal sexual scripts. *Sexual scripts* reflect social norms, practices, and workings of power, and they provide frameworks and guidelines for sexual feelings and behaviors. There is often embarrassment, shame, and confusion associated with these sexual scripts, and they easily become fraught with potential misunderstandings.

Sexual scripts vary across cultures and through time and are almost always heavily informed by societal understandings of gender and power. As the reading "Women, Sexuality, and Social Change in the Middle East" by Pinar Ilkkaracan sug-gests, in this age of globalization, women's bodies and sexuality are increasingly becoming arenas of intense conflict. The article by Pepper Schwartz and Virginia Rutter, "Sexual Desire and Gender," emphasizes two key points: that sexuality is about society as much as it is about biological urges, and that the most significant dimension of sexuality is gender. For example, as discussed in Chapter 3, feminine sexual scripts have often involved a double bind: To want sex is to risk being labeled promiscuous and to not want sex means potentially being labeled frigid and a prude. For many women, sexuality is shrouded in shame and fear, and, rather than seeing

Rainbow Trivia

1. At what New York bar did the modern gay liberation movement begin?
   a. Studio 54
   b. Stonewall
   c. Club 57
   d. Scandals

2. What were homosexuals required to wear to identify them in concentration camps during World War II?
   a. A yellow star
   b. A lavender H
   c. A pink star
   d. A pink triangle

3. What Greek letter symbolizes queer activism?
   a. Lambda
   b. Alpha
   c. Delta
   d. Sigma

4. What is the name of the religious organization that supports queer Catholics?
   a. Spirit
   b. Celebration
   c. Dignity
   d. Affirmation

5. What is the country's largest political organization working specifically for queer rights?
   a. Human Rights Campaign
   b. ACT-UP
   c. NOW
   d. Christian Coalition

6. What famous athlete came out at the 1993 March on Washington?
   a. Greg Louganis
   b. Reggie White
   c. Tonya Harding
   d. Martina Navratilova

7. What show made television history by having the first gay lead character?
   a. *Soap*
   b. *Roseanne*
   c. *Ellen*
   d. *All in the Family*

8. Who of the following is not a famous lesbian performer?
   a. Sarah McLachlan
   b. Melissa Etheridge
   c. k.d. lang
   d. Indigo Girls

9. Which of the following is a must-read for any good lesbian?
   a. *The Well of Loneliness* by Radclyffe Hall
   b. *Rubyfruit Jungle* by Rita Mae Brown
   c. Anything by Dorothy Allison
   d. All of the above

10. Which of the following movies did *not* have a lesbian character?
    a. *Boys on the Side*
    b. *Personal Best*
    c. *Desert Hearts*
    d. None of the above

Answers: 1. b 2. d 3. a 4. c 5. a 6. d 7. c 8. a 9. d 10. d

themselves as subjects in their own erotic lives, women may understand themselves as objects, seen through the eyes of others. This can be compared to sexual potency, a key aspect of masculinity in contemporary Western societies.

Within the context of sexual scripts, individuals develop their own sexual self-schemas. *Sexual self-schemas* can be defined as identities or cognitive generalizations about sexual aspects of the self that are established from past and present experiences and that guide sexual feelings and behavior. What is desirable or acceptable to one person may be unacceptable or even disgusting to another. Note that sexual scripts are societal-level guidelines for human sexuality, whereas sexual self-schemas are individual-level understandings of the self.

Sexual scripts vary across such differences as race, class, age, and ability. The short story by Emily Oxford, "Prue Shows Her Knickers," tells of the empowerment of an adolescent girl with disabilities as well as the constraints associated with her physical condition. The relentless youth-oriented culture of contemporary U.S. society sees "older" ("older than whom?" you may ask—note how this term encourages a mythical norm associated with young adulthood) people or people with disabilities as less sexual, or interprets their sexuality as humorous or out of place. Much of this is learned from the media and enacted in peer groups, as the reading by Gigi Durham Meengleshi as "Girls, Media, and the Negotiation of Sexuality" suggests.

There have also been strong mandates in U.S. society (such as anti-miscegenation laws) that have maintained racial superiority by outlawing interracial dating and marriage. In addition, there are class and race differences associated with interpersonal relationships that reflect the norms of specific communities. For example, Chicana lesbians have spoken out about intense homophobia that is related to the sexual scripts identifying women as wives and mothers in their communities. In "La Güera," Cherríe Moraga describes how coming out as a lesbian helped her connect with the inequities of race. She is a light-skinned Chicana who had learned to pass as White. She writes, "The joys of looking like a white girl haven't been so great since I realized I could be beaten on the street for being a dyke." Paula Gunn Allen's poem, "Some Like Indians Endure," also makes the connections between racism and heterosexism. Both Indians and lesbians have endured and survived oppression.

World Report 2002: Lesbian, Gay, Bisexual, and Transgender Rights

Although the visibility of lesbian, gay, bisexual, and transgender people throughout the world continued to rise in 2001, their increased visibility was accompanied by attacks based on sexual orientation and gender identity. Human rights activists who sought to use the human rights framework to call to account states that participated in these rights abuses or condoned them also came under attack. In virtually every country in the world people suffered from de jure and de facto discrimination based on their actual or perceived sexual orientation. In some countries, sexual minorities lived with the very real threat of being deprived of their right to life and security of person. A small number of countries continued to impose the death penalty for private sexual acts between consenting adults. In several others, sexual minorities were targeted for extrajudicial executions. In many countries, police or other members of the security forces actively participated in the persecution of lesbians, gay, bisexual, and transgender people, including their arbitrary detention and torture. Pervasive bias within the criminal justice system in many countries effectively precluded members of sexual minorities from seeking redress.

. . .

[The following examples suggest the enormity of discrimination faced by lesbian, gay, bisexual, and transgender people worldwide:]

- In Namibia, President Samuel Nujoma continued to vilify gay men and lesbians, stating, "The Republic of Namibia does not allow homosexuality, lesbianism here. Police are ordered to arrest you, and deport you, and imprison you too." The nationally televised speech came just two weeks after the Namibian Supreme Court overturned a lower court ruling recognizing the right of one member of a same sex couple to confer permanent residency on the other. Soon after the speech, the Rainbow Project, a nongovernmental human rights organization working with sexual minorities, started receiving reports of harassment and beatings by the Special Field Forces, a security unit reporting directly to the president. Nujoma later clarified his statement, "Traditional leaders, governors, see to it that there are no criminals, gays and lesbians in your villages and regions. We . . . have not fought for an independent Namibia that gives rights to botsotsos [criminals], gays and lesbians to do their bad things here."
- In November, Malaysian Prime Minister Mahathir Mohamad also verbally attacked gays, announcing that he would expel any gay British government minister if he came to Malaysia with a partner. Mahathir explained in an interview with BBC radio, "the British people accept homosexual ministers. But if they ever come here bringing their boyfriend along, we will throw them out. We will not accept them."

. . .

- [In Egypt] fifty-three people [were] detained and charged with ["debauchery"-related] offenses after a crackdown in May against men presumed to be gay. . . . There were reports that the men were beaten and subjected to forensic examinations in order to ascertain if they had engaged in anal sex. They were prosecuted before an Emergency State Security Court, which reached a verdict on November 14. Twenty-three were sentenced to between one and five years of hard labor; twenty-nine were acquitted. Because the trial took place before an Emergency State Security Court, those convicted could not appeal their sentences.

. . .

- . . . In April, the National Human Rights Commission of India missed a significant opportunity to address this violation when it announced that it did "not want to take cognizance" of a case brought before the commission objecting to involuntary aversion therapy and other forms of psychiatric abuse aimed at "converting" homosexuals. The commission explained its decision by stating, "sexual minority rights did not fall under the purview of human rights."

- More than a year after the murder of transgender activist Dayana (Jose Luis Nieves), transgender people living in Venezuela continued to face unrelenting police harassment. The Commander of Police in the state of Carabobo announced, "homosexuals and prostitutes are to be ruled by the police code. They cannot move freely in the streets." . . .
- Seven years after the [U.S.] military's "Don't Ask, Don't Tell" policy was codified as law and implemented, the United States military's own surveys and investigations found that training on how to implement the law was deficient and that anti-gay harassment remained pervasive in the military. . . . Although the "Don't Ask, Don't Tell" policy was ostensibly intended to allow gay, lesbian, and bisexual service members to remain in the military, discharges increased significantly after the policy's adoption. From 1994 to 2000, more than 6,500 service members were discharged under the policy, with a record number of 1,231 separations during 2000. Women were discharged at a disproportionately high rate, while the policy provided an additional means for men to harass women service members by threatening to "out" those who refused their advances or threatened to report them, thus ending their careers.

Source: http://www.hrw.org/wr2k2/lgbt.html.

Sexual identity is a person's attraction to, or preference for, people of a given sex. It is an individual's romantic and/or sexual (also called erotic) identity and behavior toward other people. Note that sexual identity does not necessarily require sexual experience. *Heterosexuality* is a sexual identity where romantic and/or sexual attachments are between people of the opposite sex (popularly termed *straight*). *Homosexuality* is a sexual identity where romantic and/or sexual attachments are between people of the same sex. Because the term *homosexual* is stigmatized and because the term seems to emphasize sexual behavior, homosexual communities have preferred the term *gay. Gay* and *homosexual* are terms inclusive of women, although they are used mainly to describe men. The term *lesbian* means the romantic and/or sexual attachment and identification between women, specifically. Bisexuality implies a sexual identification with both women and men. There are derogatory social connotations of bisexuality as hypersexualized: Not only do these people have sex all the time, but they are doing it with both women and with men, simultaneously. Of course, to be bisexual does not imply this at all; it just means the choice of lover can be either a woman or a man. Nonetheless, these connotations reflect the fact that there are many stigmas associated with bisexuality from both the straight and the lesbian and gay communities. Marcia Deihl and Robyn Ochs write about bisexuality and the fears of both heterosexual and homosexual communities toward bisexuality in "Biphobia."

As discussed in Chapter 3, the term *queer* is also used by bisexuals, gays, lesbians, and transsexuals to describe alternative (to heterosexual) sexual identities. Transgendered people of any sexual identity may also claim this term. Originally an insult, the term has become a source of pride and positive identity. You might also hear the terms *dyke, butch,* and *femme. Dyke* is synonymous with *lesbian,* although it connotes a masculine or mannish lesbian. Like *queer, dyke* is a word that is used against lesbians as an insult and has been appropriated or reclaimed by lesbians with pride. This means that if you are not a member of the lesbian, gay, or queer communities, you should use these terms with care. *Butch* and *femme* are roles associated with gender that have been adopted by some lesbians, especially in the past. Butch means acting as the masculine partner, and femme means acting in a feminine role. Although today many lesbians avoid these role types because there is little incentive to mimic traditional heterosexual relationships, others enjoy these identities and appropriate them to suit themselves.

Finally, the term *coming out* refers to someone adopting a gay, lesbian, bisexual, trans, or queer identity. Coming out is a psychological process that tends to involve two aspects: first, recognizing and identifying this to oneself, and second, declaring oneself in a "public" (broadly defined) way. In terms of this second aspect, individuals usually come out to affirming members in their own community before they (if ever) face a general public. Some never come out to families or co-workers for fear of rejection, reprisals, and retaliation. For some, coming out means becoming part of an identifiable political community; for others, it means functioning for the most part as something of an outsider in a straight world. The phrase *in the closet* means not being out at all. In the closet can imply that a person understands her-/himself to be lesbian or gay but is not out to others. It can also imply that a person is in denial about her/his own sexuality and is not comfortable claiming a homosexual identity.

THE POLITICS OF SEXUALITY

The term *politics* used here implies issues associated with the distribution of power in sexual relationships. There are politics in sexual relationships because they occur in the context of a society that assigns power based on gender and other systems of inequality and privilege. As discussed in Chapter 1, the personal is political: Issues and problems taken as personal or idiosyncratic within sexuality or relationships have broader social, political, and economic causes and consequences.

When people get together romantically, what results is more than the mingling of two idiosyncratic individuals. The politics of this relationship implies that people bring the baggage of their gendered lives and other identities into relationships. They have negotiated gender and other systems of inequality and privilege, and these experiences have shaped who they are. Although much of this baggage is so familiar that it is thoroughly normalized and seen as completely natural, the baggage of differently gendered lives implies power. As many feminists have pointed out, heterosexuality is organized in such a way that the power men have in society gets carried into relationships and can encourage women's subservience, sexually and emotionally. Practically, this might mean that a woman sees herself through the eyes of men, or a particular man, and strives to live up to his image of who she should be. It might mean that a woman feels that men, or again, a particular man, owns or has the right to control her body or sexuality, or that she should be the one to ease the emotional transitions of the household or tend to a man's daily needs—preparing his meals, cleaning his home, washing his clothes, raising his children—while still working outside the home. Even though she might choose this life and enjoy the role she has, feminists would argue that this is still an example of male domination in the private sphere where individual men benefit. They have their emotional and domestic needs filled by women and are left free to work or play at what they want.

ACTIVIST PROFILE **Emma Goldman**

According to J. Edgar Hoover, she was one of the most dangerous women in America in the early twentieth century. Emma Goldman came to the United States from Russia as a teenager in 1885, but for a Jewish immigrant, America was not the land of opportunity she had envisioned. Rather, she found herself in slums and sweatshops, eking out a living. Goldman had witnessed the slaughter of idealist political anarchists in Russia, and in 1886 she saw the hangings of four Haymarket anarchists who had opposed Chicago's power elite. As a result of these experiences, Goldman was drawn to anarchism and became a revolutionary.

Goldman moved to New York, where she met anarchist Johann Most, who advocated the overthrow of capitalism. Most encouraged Goldman's public speaking, although she eventually began to distance herself from him, recognizing the need to work for practical and specific improvements such as higher wages and shorter working hours. In 1893 she was arrested and imprisoned for encouraging a crowd of unemployed men to take bread if they were starving.

In New York, Goldman also worked as a practical nurse in New York's ghettos where she witnessed the effects of lack of birth control and no access to abortion. She began a campaign to address this problem, and her views eventually influenced Margaret Sanger and Sanger's work to make contraception accessible. Goldman was even arrested for distributing birth control literature.

Goldman was particularly concerned about sexual politics within anarchism. She recognized that a political solution alone would not rectify the unequal relations between the sexes. Rather, she called for a transformation of values, particularly by women themselves—by asserting themselves as persons and not sex commodities, by refusing to give the right over her body to anyone, by refusing to have children unless she wants them.

Her involvement in no conscription leagues and rallies against World War I led to her imprisonment and subsequent deportation to Russia. There she witnessed the Russian Revolution and then saw the corruption of the Bolsheviks as they amassed power. Her experience led her to reassess her earlier approval of violence as a means to social justice. Instead, she argued that violence begets counterrevolution.

Goldman remained active in Europe and continued to exercise influence in the United States. In 1922 *Nation* magazine named her one of the 12 greatest living women. In 1934 she was allowed to lecture in the United States, and in 1936 she went to Spain to participate in the Spanish Revolution. Goldman died in 1940 and was buried in Chicago near the Haymarket martyrs.

LEARNING ACTIVITY   **As the World Turns**

Tune into your favorite soap opera each day for a week. As you watch, record observations about the depictions, roles, and interactions of women and men. If all anyone knew about heterosexual relationships was what she or he saw on the soaps, what would this person believe?

Work with one or two other people in your class to devise an episode of a feminist soap opera. Who would be the characters? What dilemmas would they face? How would they resolve them? What would you call your soap opera? Is feminist soap opera possible? Would anyone watch?

Of course, their part of the bargain for these services is that they should provide for women economically. This is an arrangement that many women choose rationally in both North America and other parts of the world.

We know that heterosexual relationships are a source of support and strength for many women; it is not heterosexuality that is faulted but the context in which heterosexual coupling takes place. When heterosexual intimacies are grounded in unequal power relationships, it becomes more and more difficult for women and men to love in healthy ways. The politics of sexuality also come into play in lesbian and bisexual relationships. Women come together with the baggage of femininity to work out and often internalized homophobia as well. These relationships also have fewer clear models for successful partnering. An example of this is the "Are we on a date?" syndrome that occurs as two women attempt to deal with the boundaries between being girlfriends and being romantically interested in each other. These relationships also occur in the context of *heteronormativity*, the way heterosexuality is constructed as the norm. A related concept is *compulsory heterosexuality*, as already discussed in previous chapters: that heterosexuality is the expected and desirable sexual identity. For example, various institutions support and encourage heterosexual coupling and dating. Schools offer dances and proms, the entertainment industry generally assumes heterosexual dating, and there is a public holiday (Valentine's Day) that celebrates it. There are billboards, magazine covers, television shows and movies, public displays of heterosexual intimacy in the park, in the cinema, walking on the street, dancing close. And ultimately, there is marriage, an institution that historically has recognized two committed people only if one is a woman and the other a man. Currently, gay marriage is available in Massachusetts and civil unions in Vermont. Other states are struggling with this issue.

Non-heterosexual couples often encounter obstacles when adopting children, raising their biological children (products of previous heterosexual relationships, planned heterosexual encounters with the goal of conception, or artificial insemination), as well as gaining custody of these children. This is because these sexual identities are often constructed by society as an immoral and abnormal "choice" that could have negative consequences on children. It has generally been assumed by the dominant culture that children of homosexual parents will grow up to be homosexual,

LEARNING ACTIVITY   **Heteronormativity: It's Everywhere**

Heterosexism is maintained by the illusion that heterosexuality is the norm. This illusion is partly kept in place by the visibility of heterosexuality and the invisibility of other forms of sexuality. To begin to think about the pervasiveness of heterosexuality, grab a clipboard, pen, and paper and keep a tally.

- Go to a card store and peruse the cards in the "love" and "anniversary" sections. How many depict heterosexual couples? How many depict same-sex couples? What options are there for customers who wish to buy a card for a same-sex partner?
- Look at the advertisements in one of your favorite magazines. How many pictures of heterosexual couples do you find? How many pictures of same-sex couples? If a photo is of a man or woman alone, do you automatically assume the person is heterosexual? Or is that assumption so deep-seated that you don't even think about it at all?
- Watch the commercials during your favorite hour of television. How many images of heterosexual couples do you see? Of same-sex couples?
- Go to the mall or a park and people-watch for an hour. How many heterosexual couples holding hands do you see? How many same-sex couples?

although all the evidence shows that this is indeed not the case. Despite research that suggests that lesbians make fine mothers and lesbian couples fine parents, there are strong social imperatives against lesbian child rearing. A related prejudice is the notion that homosexuals abuse or recruit children. These negative and uninformed stereotypes reinforce homophobia and help maintain heterosexism. Research shows overwhelmingly that it is heterosexual males who are the major predators of children. Nonetheless, because of these societal stigmas, lesbians and "queers" encounter many obstacles concerning voluntary parenting, and, in addition, are often not welcome in occupations involving children.

In this way, sexual self-schemas develop in a social context and are framed by the various workings of power in society. This section has emphasized how politics—the distribution of power—influence and shape every aspect of sexual relationships. On the macro (societal) level these politics are often represented in the forms of public debates about sexuality (like gay marriage, reproductive rights, sex education, interpersonal violence) that are also experienced on the individual level. This micro (individual-level) analysis is the topic of the next section of this chapter.

INTIMACIES

Courtship is that period when two people are attracted to each other, develop intimacy, enjoy each other's company, and identify as a couple. In our society this period usually involves dating. An essential aspect of courtship and dating is the development of romantic love: a mainstay of our culture and one of the most important

LEARNING ACTIVITY   **It's in the Cards**

Go to a local card shop and browse through the cards in the "love" or "romance" sections. What are their messages about heterosexual relationships? How do cards targeted toward women differ from cards targeted toward men?

Now get creative. Design a feminist romance greeting card. How does it differ from the ones you saw at the card shop? How do you think the recipient will feel about this card? Now, if you're really brave, mail it to the one you love.

mythologies of our time. *Romantic love* is about a couple coming together, sharing the excitement of an erotic relationship, and feeling united with the other in such a way that the other is unique and irreplaceable. The clichés of love abound: Love is blind; love is painful; love means never having to say you're sorry; love conquers all; and so forth. bell hooks comments on this phenomenon in the reading "Romance: Sweet Love."

Although cultural constructions of love would have us believe that romantic love as we know it has always been around, it is possible to trace the history of romantic love in U.S. society as a cultural phenomenon. There is a tight relationship between romantic love as an ideology and consumer culture as an industrial development. Prior to the twentieth century, dating as we know it did not exist. As dating developed after the turn of the century, it quickly became associated with consuming products and going places. The emerging movie industry glamorized romance and associated it with luxury products; the automobile industry provided those who could afford it with the allure of travel, get-aways, and private intimacy; and dancehalls allowed close contact between men and women in public. Romance became a commodity that could be purchased, and it made great promises. Women were (and still are) encouraged to purchase certain products with the promise of romantic love. Fashion and makeup industries began revolving around the prospect of romantic love, and the norms associated with feminine beauty became tied to glamorous, romantic images. Romantic love came to be seen as women's special domain; women were encouraged to spend enormous emotional energy, time, and money in the pursuit and maintenance of romantic love.

Romantic love is fun; it can be the spice of life and one of the most entertaining features of women's lives. In particular, it often contrasts starkly with our working lives because romance is associated with leisure, entertainment, and escape. At the same time, however, romantic love and its pursuit have become the means by which women are encouraged to form relationships and the justification for tolerating inequities in interpersonal relationships.

When it comes to sexuality, romantic love plays a large part in feminine sexual scripts. Research suggests that women make sense of sexual encounters in terms of the amount of intimacy experienced; love becomes a rationale for sex. If I am in love, women often reason, sex is okay. Men more easily accept sex for its own sake, with no emotional strings necessarily attached. In this way, sexual scripts for men have involved more of an *instrumental* (sex for its own sake) approach, whereas for

no strings!

women it tends to be more *expressive* (sex involving emotional attachments). There is evidence to suggest that women are moving in the direction of sex as an end in itself without the normative constraints of an emotional relationship. "I Was a *Cosmo Sex Deviant*" by A. E. Berkowitz is a case in point. By and large, however, women are still more likely than men to engage in sex as an act of love. Many scholars suggest that romance is one of the key ways that sexism is maintained in society.

As romantic relationships develop, individuals may become physically intimate and sexually active. These sexual practices can include kissing, hugging, petting, snuggling, caressing, oral sex (oral stimulation of genital area), penis in vagina sex, and anal sex (sexual stimulation of the anus with fingers, penis, or other object). Lesbians do many of the same things as straight couples, although there is no penis-vagina sex. Some women, straight and lesbian, use dildos (penis-shaped objects that can be inserted into a bodily opening) when they are having sex or during masturbation (sexual self-stimulation), and some straight women use dildos to penetrate male partners during sexual intercourse.

In heterosexual relationships, sexual scripts tend to encourage men to be sexual initiators and sexually more dominant. Although this is not always the case, women who do initiate sex often run the risk of being labeled with terms that are synonymous with slut. Having one person in the relationship more sexually assertive and the other more passive is different from sado-masochistic sexual practices (S and M) where one person takes a domineering role and the other becomes dominated. There are both heterosexuals and homosexuals who enjoy sado-masochistic practices. Although usually consensual, S and M can also be coercive, in which case it functions as a form of violence.

Emotional intimacy can be defined as sharing aspects of the self with others with the goal of mutual understanding. Intimacy can sometimes be a source of conflict in heterosexual relationships because women tend to be more skilled at intimacy

LEARNING ACTIVITY **Cybersex**

The growth of technology has created a new form for sexual expression: cybersex. You can create a persona, meet someone online, and have cybersex—with no risk of disease, no commitment, no regrets in the morning. Right? Maybe, but maybe not. On the one hand, cybersex does present an opportunity for a different kind of sexual exploration. On the other, cybersex may raise real problems of isolation, harassment, addiction, and infidelity. Spend a little time surfing the Web for information about cybersex. Then make a list of the pros and cons. How might cybersex be different for women and men? What role does gender play in cybersex? What role does race play? How does sexual identity come into play? How do you think feminists might evaluate cybersex? Would they see it as potentially liberating for women? Or might it reinforce male sexual dominance?

Consider organizing a faculty panel to talk about these issues on your campus. Be sure to include a variety of disciplinary perspectives—women's studies, sociology, psychology, ethnic studies, philosophy, communication, computer science, religion, anthropology, disability studies.

HISTORICAL MOMENT   **The Faked Orgasm**

From 'Venus Observed' by Ruth Davis in *Women: A Journal of Liberation*, 1972, Davis, CA.

In the early days of the second wave of the Women's Movement, women gathered in small consciousness-raising groups to talk about their experiences as women, and, of course, sooner or later, the conversation turned to sex. What surprised most women as they began to talk openly was that they were not the only ones ever to fake orgasm. While the sexual revolution was rolling on for men, opening greater and greater access to sexual exploits with lots of women, women were finding themselves continuing to fall into the role prescribed by their gender—pleasing men sexually even when they themselves were not being satisfied. But as the Women's Movement began to have an impact, women came to expect to be equal partners in the sexual revolution . . . and that meant no longer faking orgasms.

In 1968 Anne Koedt wrote "The Myth of the Vaginal Orgasm," denouncing Freud's construction of the vaginal orgasm as the truly mature sexual response and denigrating the clitoral orgasm as "infantile." She argued that by marginalizing the clitoris, Freud and other doctors and scientists had controlled women's sexuality and had made women feel sexually inadequate for not achieving vaginal orgasm. Soon, the "faked orgasm" became a metaphor for women's sexual exploitation.

And feminists offered a variety of solutions, from sex toys to celibacy. In 1970, Shulamith Firestone argued that sex, not social class, was the root of all oppression. In *The Dialectic of Sex*, she argued that reproductive technologies should be pursued to deliver women from the tyranny of their biology.

Germaine Greer, author of *The Female Eunuch*, contended that all women should become sexually liberated, and she advocated a strike, the withdrawal of women from sexual labor. She said that women should have the same sexual freedom as men and, if need be, should use men for sexual pleasure.

The debate about sexuality swirled among feminists through the 70s, encompassing issues ranging from pornography to rape, abortion to prostitution. And while the question of the dangers and/or pleasures of sex remained an open one, the raising of the question itself had made an important mark on the consciousness of American women.

Source: Ruth Rosen, *The World Split Open* (New York: Viking, 2000).

than men, as the title of John Gray's popular book *Men Are from Mars, Women Are from Venus* suggests. Traditionally, women have been socialized to be emotional and emotionally expressive, and men have been socialized to put their energy into shaping culture and society.

Although scholars have suggested that women are inherently better at connecting with others and that this skill is rooted in early childhood psychosexual development, others have focused on the social context of childhood skill acquisition. They suggest that the interpersonal skills girls learn at an early age are a result of social learning. Certainly these skills are useful for women in terms of intimacy generally, and in terms of their role as keepers of heterosexual relationships in particular. For example, girls are more likely to play games that involve communication: talking and listening, as well as taking the role of the other through imaginary role-playing games. Boys, on the other hand, are more likely to play rule-bound games where the "rights" and "wrongs" of the game are predetermined rather than negotiated. As a result, girls learn to notice: They learn to be sensitive of others' feelings, and they are willing to do emotional work. Boys are often raised to repress and deny their inner thoughts and fears and learn not to notice them. Often they are taught that feelings are feminine or are for sissies. Girls become more comfortable with intimacy, and boys learn to shy away from it because intimacy is often seen as synonymous with weakness. Boys learn to camouflage feelings under a veneer of calm and rationality because fears are not manly. Importantly, as boys grow up they learn to rely on women to take care of their emotional needs, and girls learn that this request is part of being a woman.

Because emotional intimacy is about self-disclosure and revealing oneself to others, when people are intimate with each other, they open themselves to vulnerability. In the process of becoming intimate, one person shares feelings and information about her-/himself, and then the other person (if that person wants to maintain and develop intimacy) responds by sharing too. In turn each gives away little pieces of her-/himself, and, in return, mutual trust, understanding, and friendship develop. Given the baggage of gender, however, what can happen is that one person does more of the giving away, and the other reveals less; one opens up to being vulnerable, and the other maintains personal power. The first person also takes on the role of helping the other share, drawing that person out, translating ordinary messages for their hidden emotional meanings, and investing greater amounts of energy into interpersonal communication. The first person has taken the role prescribed by femininity and the latter the role that masculinity endorses. The important point here is that intimacy is about power. Men tend to be less able to open themselves up because of anxiety associated with being vulnerable and potentially losing personal power.

Central in understanding masculine sexual scripts and issues around emotional intimacy is the mandate against homosexuality. Because boys and men may play rough and work closely together—touching each other physically in sports and other masculine pursuits—there are lots of opportunities for *homoeroticism* (arousal of sexual feelings through contact with people of the same sex). In response to this, strong norms against homosexuality regulate masculine behavior—norms fed by homophobia and enforced by such institutions as education, sports, media, family, the military, and the state. These norms discourage men from showing affection with each other and thus discourage intimacy between men. As an aside, they also encourage male bonding where women may function as objects in order for men to assert

Reprinted with permission from Nicole Hollander

sexual potency. Examples of this include women as entertainment for various kinds of stag parties, women as pinups in places where men live and/or work together, and, in the extreme, gang rape. Homophobia serves to keep women apart too, of course. In particular, women are encouraged to give up the love of other women in order to gain the approval of men.

A key aspect of intimacy, and thus sexuality, is interpersonal communication. Again, the ways we communicate in relationships have a lot to do with gender; these different styles help to maintain gender differences in status and power. Women and men tend to communicate differently in the following ways: First, in terms of speech patterns, women tend to use more polite speech, less profanity, and more standard forms. They use more fillers like "uhm," hedges like "sort of" and "I guess," and intensifiers like "really" and "very." They are more likely to tag questions on statements like "It's hot today, isn't it?" and to turn an imperative into a question: "Would you mind opening the door?" rather than "Open the door!" All these forms of speaking are less authoritative.

Second, women tend to use different intonations than men when they speak. Women have a higher pitch that is recognized as less assertive than a lower pitch. They tend to speak with more emotional affect than men and are more likely to end a sentence with a raised pitch. This sounds like a question and gives a hesitant quality to women's speech.

IDEAS FOR ACTIVISM

- Work with various women's groups on your campus to develop, publish, and distribute a "Check Up on Your Relationship" brochure. This brochure should contain a checklist of signs for emotional/physical/sexual abuse and resources to get help.
- Organize and present a forum on healthy dating practices.
- Organize a clothes drive for your local women's shelter.
- Research gay rights, such as protection against discrimination in employment or housing, domestic partner benefits, or hate crimes legislation in your city or state. If you find that gay, lesbian, bisexual, or transgender people in your area do not enjoy full civil rights, write your government officials to encourage them to enact policies providing civil rights for queer people.
- Organize a National Coming Out Day celebration on your campus.
- Organize an event on your campus in recognition of World AIDS Day, which is December 1.
- Become a member of the Human Rights Campaign. For more information see *www.hrc.org.*

Third, women and men use interruptions differently in speech. Although men and women interrupt at about the same rate in same-sex conversations, in mixed groups men interrupt more than women and are more likely to interrupt women than to interrupt other men. Men are also more likely to change the subject in the process. Although there are cultural differences around interruptions, it is clear that who interrupts and who gets interrupted is about power.

Fourth, women tend to use more confirmations and reinforcements such as "Yes, go on" or "I hear you" or "uh-hums" during conversation than men do. Examples of nonverbal confirmation of the speaker include leaning forward, eye contact, and nodding.

Finally, feminine speech and masculine speech fulfill different functions. Feminine speech tends to work toward maintaining relationships, developing rapport, avoiding conflict, and maintaining cooperation. Masculine speech, on the other hand, is more likely oriented toward attracting and maintaining an audience, asserting power and dominance, and giving information. Given these gendered differences in communication, it is easy to see how problems might arise in interpersonal interaction generally and in sexual relationships in particular, and how these issues are related to the give-and-take of interpersonal power.

In this way, sexual intimacy is as much about society as it is about physiology. Sexuality is wound up with our understandings of gender, and these norms channel our sense of ourselves as sexual persons. These social constructs encourage us to feel desire and enjoy certain sexual practices and relationships, and they guide the meanings we associate with our experiences.

Sexual Desire and Gender

Pepper Schwartz and Virginia Rutter

The gender of the person you desire is a serious matter seemingly fundamental to the whole business of romance. And it isn't simply a matter of whether someone is male or female; how well the person fulfills a lover's expectations of masculinity or femininity is of great consequence. . . .

. . . Although sex is experienced as one of the most basic and biological of activities, in human beings it is profoundly affected by things other than the body's urges. Who we're attracted to and what we find sexually satisfying is not just a matter of the genital equipment we're born with. . . .

Before we delve into the whys and wherefores of sex, we need to come to an understanding about what sex is. This is not as easy a task as it may seem, because sex has a number of dimensions.

On one level, sex can be regarded as having both a biological and a social context. The biological (and physiological) refers to how people use their genital equipment to reproduce. In addition, as simple as it seems, bodies make the experience of sexual pleasure available—whether the pleasure involves other bodies or just one's own body and mind. It should be obvious, however, that people engage in sex even when they do not intend to reproduce. They have sex for fun, as a way to communicate their feelings to each other, as a way to satisfy their ego, and for any number of other reasons relating to the way they see themselves and interact with others.

Another dimension of sex involves both what we do and how we think about it. *Sexual behavior* refers to the sexual acts that people engage in. These acts involve not only petting and intercourse but also seduction and courtship. Sexual behavior also involves the things people do alone for pleasure and stimulation and the things they

do with other people. *Sexual desire,* on the other hand, is the motivation to engage in sexual acts. It relates to what turns people on. A person's *sexuality* consists of both behavior and desire.

The most significant dimension of sexuality is *gender.* Gender relates both to the biological and social contexts of sexual behavior and desire. People tend to believe they know whether someone is a man or a woman not because we do a physical examination and determine that the person is biologically male or biologically female. Instead, we notice whether a person is masculine or feminine. Gender is a social characteristic of individuals in our society that is only sometimes consistent with biological sex. Thus, animals, like people, tend to be identified as male and female in accordance with the reproductive function, but only people are described by their gender, as a man or a woman.

When we say something is *gendered* we mean that social processes have determined what is appropriately masculine and feminine and that gender has thereby become integral to the definition of the phenomenon. For example, marriage is a gendered institution: The definition of marriage involves a masculine part (husband) and a feminine part (wife). Gendered phenomena, like marriage, tend to appear "naturally" so. But as recent debates about same-sex marriage underscore, the role of gender in marriage is the product of social processes and beliefs about men, women, and marriage. In examining how gender influences sexuality, moreover, you will see that gender rarely operates alone: Class, culture, race, and individual differences also combine to influence sexuality.

. . .

DESIRE: ATTRACTION AND AROUSAL

The most salient fact about sex is that nearly everybody is interested in it. Most people like to have sex, and they talk about it, hear about it, and think about it. But some people are obsessed with sex and willing to have sex with anyone or anything. Others are aroused only by particular conditions and hold exacting criteria. For example, some people will have sex only if they are positive that they are in love, that their partner loves them, and that the act is sanctified by marriage. Others view sex as not much different from eating a sandwich. They neither love nor hate the sandwich; they are merely hungry, and they want something to satisfy that hunger. What we are talking about here are differences of desire. As you have undoubtedly noticed, people differ in what they find attractive, and they are also physically aroused by different things.

Many people assume that differences in sexual desire have a lot to do with whether a person is female or male. In large representative surveys about sexual behavior, the men as a group inevitably report more frequent sex, with more partners, and in more diverse ways than the women as a group do. . . . First, we should consider the approaches we might use to interpret it. Many observers argue that when it comes to sex, men and women have fundamentally different biological wiring. Others use the evidence to argue that culture has produced marked sexual differences among men and women. We believe, however, that it is hard to tease apart biological differences and social differences. As soon as a baby enters the world, it receives messages about gender and sexuality. In the United States, for example, disposable diapers come adorned in pink for girls and blue for boys. In case people aren't sure whether to treat the baby as masculine or feminine in its first years of life, the diaper signals them. The assumption is that girl babies really are different from boy babies and the difference ought to be displayed. This different treatment continues throughout life, and therefore a sex difference at birth becomes amplified into gender differences as people mature.

Gendered experiences have a great deal of influence on sexual desire. As a boy enters adolescence, he hears jokes about boys' uncontainable desire. Girls are told the same thing and told that their job is to resist. These gender messages have power not only over attitudes and behavior (such as whether a person grows up to prefer sex with a lover rather than a stranger) but also over physical and biological experience. For example, a girl may be discouraged from vigorous competitive activity, which will subsequently influence how she develops physically, how she feels about her body, and even how she relates to the adrenaline rush associated with physical competition. Hypothetically, a person who is accustomed to adrenaline responses experiences sexual attraction differently from one who is not.

What follows are three "competing" explanations of differences in sexual desire between men and women: a biological explanation, sociobiological and evolutionary psychological explanations, and an explanation that acknowledges the social construction of sexuality. We call these competing approaches because each tends to be presented as a complete explanation in itself, to the exclusion of other explanations. Our goal, however, is to provide a clearer picture of how "nature" and "nurture" are intertwined in the production of sexualities.

THE BIOLOGY OF DESIRE: NATURE'S EXPLANATION

Biology is admittedly a critical factor in sexuality. Few human beings fall in love with fish or sexualize trees. Humans are designed to respond to other humans. And human activity is, to some extent, organized by the physical equipment humans are born with. Imagine if people had fins instead of arms or laid eggs instead of fertilizing them during intercourse. Romance would look quite different.

Although biology seems to be a constant (i.e., a component of sex that is fixed and unchanging), the social world tends to mold biology as much as biology shapes humans' sexuality. Each society has its own rules for sex. Therefore, how people experience their biology varies widely. In some societies, women act intensely aroused and active during sex; in others, they have no concept of orgasm. In fact, women in some settings, when told about orgasm, do not even believe it exists, as anthropologists discovered in some parts of Nepal. Clearly, culture—not biology—is at work, because we know that orgasm is physically possible, barring damage to or destruction of the sex organs. Even ejaculation is culturally dictated. In some countries, it is considered healthy to ejaculate early and often; in others, men are told to conserve semen and ejaculate as rarely as possible. The biological capacity may not be so different, but the way bodies behave during sex varies according to social beliefs.

Sometimes the dictates of culture are so rigid and powerful that the so-called laws of nature can be overridden. Infertility treatment provides an example: For couples who cannot produce children "naturally," a several-billion-dollar industry has provided technology that can, in a small proportion of cases, overcome this biological problem. Recently, in California, a child was born to a 63-year-old woman who had been implanted with fertilized eggs. The cultural emphasis on reproduction and parenthood, in this case, overrode the biological incapacity to produce children. Nevertheless, some researchers have focused on the biological foundations of sexual desire. They have examined the endocrine system and hormones, brain structure, and genetics. Others have observed the mechanisms of arousal. What all biological research on sex has in common is the proposition that many so-called sexual choices are not choices at all but are dictated by the body. A prominent example comes from the study of the biological origins of homosexuality. However, contradictory and debatable findings make conclusions difficult.

The Influence of Hormones

Biological explanations of sexual desire concentrate on the role of hormones. *Testosterone,* sometimes called the male sex hormone, appears to be the most important hormone for sexual function.

Numerous research studies identify testosterone as an enabler for male sexual arousal. But we cannot predict a man's sexual tastes, desires, or behavior by measuring his testosterone. Although a low level of testosterone in men is sometimes associated with lower sexual desire, this is not predictably the case. Furthermore, testosterone level does not always influence sexual performance. Indeed, testosterone is being experimented with as a male contraceptive, thus demonstrating that desire and the biological goal of reproduction need not be linked to sexual desire.

Testosterone has also been implicated in nonsexual behaviors, such as aggression. Furthermore, male aggression sometimes crosses into male sexuality, generating sexual violence. But recent research on testosterone and aggression in men has turned the testosterone-aggression connection on its head: Low levels of testosterone have been associated with aggression, and higher levels have been associated with calmness, happiness, and friendliness.

Testosterone is also found in women, although at levels as little as one-fifth those of men. This discrepancy in levels of testosterone has incorrectly been used as evidence for "natural" gender differences in sex drives. However, women's testosterone receptors are simply more sensitive than men's to smaller amounts of testosterone.

Estrogen, which is associated with the menstrual cycle, is known as the female hormone. Like testosterone, however, estrogen is found in both women and men. Furthermore, estrogen may be the more influential hormone in human aggression. In animal research, male mice whose ability to respond to estrogen had been bred out of them lost much of their natural aggressiveness. Researchers are currently investigating the association between adolescents' moodiness and their levels of estrogen. Of course, many social factors—such as changes in parental behavior toward their teenagers—help explain moodiness among adolescents.

Some biological evidence indicates that a woman's sexual desire may be linked to the impact of hormones as levels change during her reproductive cycle. (No evidence shows men's sexual desire to be cyclical.) Some scientists believe that women's sexual arousal is linked to the fertile portion of their cycle. They believe that sexual interest in women is best explained as the product of thousands of years of natural selection. Natural selection would favor for survival those women who are sexually aroused during ovulation (the time women are most likely to become pregnant). These women would be reproductively successful and therefore pass on to their children the propensity for arousal during ovulation. Neat though this theory is, it doesn't fit all the data. Other research finds no evidence of increased sexual interest among women who are ovulating. Instead, the evidence suggests that women's sexual interest actually tends to peak well before ovulation. Still other evidence finds no variation in sexual desire or sexual activity in connection to the menstrual cycle.

. . . [T]estosterone and estrogen are not clearly linked to either men's desire or women's. Research shows a complicated relationship between hormones and sexuality. Hormonal fluctuations may not be the central cause of sexual behavior or any social acts; instead, social circumstances may be the cause of hormonal fluctuation. A famous series of experiments makes the point. One animal experiment took a dominant rhesus monkey out of his environment and measured [his] testosterone level. It was very high, suggesting that he had reached the top of the monkey heap by being hormonally superior. Then the monkey was placed among even bigger, more dominant monkeys than himself. When his testosterone was remeasured, it was much lower. One interpretation is that social hierarchy had influenced the monkey's biological barometer. His testosterone level had adjusted to his social status. In this case, the social environment shaped physiology.

. . .

SOCIOBIOLOGY AND EVOLUTIONARY PSYCHOLOGY

The past few decades of research on sexuality have produced a new school of human behavior—*sociobiology* and a related discipline, *evolutionary*

psychology—that explains most gender differences as strategies of sexual reproduction. According to evolutionary psychologist David Buss, "evolutionary psychologists predict that the sexes will differ in precisely those domains in which women and men have faced different sorts of adaptive problems." By "those domains," Buss refers to reproduction, which is the only human function that depends on a biological difference between men and women.

The key assumption of sociobiological/evolutionary theory is that humans have an innate, genetically triggered impulse to pass on their genetic material through successful reproduction: This impulse is called *reproductive fitness*. The human species, like other species that sociobiologists study, achieves immortality by having children who live to the age of reproductive maturity and produce children themselves. Sociobiologists and evolutionary psychologists seek to demonstrate that almost all male and female behavior, and especially sexuality, is influenced by this one simple but powerful proposition.

Sociobiologists start at the species level. Species are divided into *r* and *K reproductive categories*. Those with *r* strategies obtain immortality by mass production of eggs and sperm. The *r* species is best illustrated by fish. The female manufactures thousands of eggs, the male squirts millions of sperm over them, and that is the extent of parenting. According to this theory, the male and female fish need not pair up to nurture their offspring. Although thousands of fertilized fish eggs are consumed by predators, only a small proportion of the massive quantity of fertilized eggs must survive for the species to continue. In the *r* species, parents need not stay together for the sake of the kids.

In contrast, humans are a *K*-strategy species, which has a greater investment in each fertilized egg. Human females and most female mammals have very few eggs, especially compared to fish. Moreover, offspring take a long time to mature in the mother's womb and are quite helpless when they are born, with no independent survival ability. Human babies need years of supervision before they are independent. Thus, if a woman wants to pass on her genes (or at least the half her child will inherit from her), she must take good care of her dependent child. The baby is a scarce resource. Even if a woman is pregnant from sexual maturation until menopause, the number of children she can produce is quite limited. This limitation was particularly true thousands of years ago. Before medical advances of the nineteenth and twentieth centuries, women were highly unlikely to live to the age of menopause. Complications from childbirth commonly caused women to die in their 20s or 30s. Where the food supply was scarce, women were less likely to be successful at conceiving, further reducing the possibility of generating offspring.

Sociobiologists and evolutionary psychologists say that men inseminate, women incubate. The human female's reproductive constraints (usually one child at a time, not so many children over a life cycle, and a helpless infant for a long period of time) shape most of women's sexual and emotional approaches to men and mating. According to their theory, women have good reason to be more selective than men about potential mates. They want to find a man who will stick around and continue to provide resources and protection to this child at least until the child has a good chance of survival. Furthermore, because a woman needs to create an incentive for a man to remain with her, females have developed more sophisticated sexual and emotional skills specifically geared toward creating male loyalty and commitment to their mutual offspring.

Sociobiologists and evolutionary psychologists say that differences in reproductive capacity and strategy also shape sexual desire. Buss asserts that reproductive strategies form most of the categories of desire: Older men generally pick younger women because they are more fertile; younger women seek older men who have more status, power, and resources (a cultural practice known as *hypergamy*) because such men can provide for their children. Furthermore, health and reproductive capacity make youth generally sexier, and even certain shapes of women's bodies (such as an "ideal" hip-to-waist ratio epitomized by an hourglass figure, which correlate with ability to readily reproduce), are widely preferred—

despite varying standards of beauty across cultures. Likewise, men who have demonstrated their fertility by producing children are more sought after than men who have not.

According to evolutionary psychologists, men's tastes for recreational sex, unambivalent lust, and a variety of partners are consistent with maximizing their production of children. Men's sexual interest is also more easily aroused because sex involves fewer costs to them than to women, and the ability for rapid ejaculation has a reproductive payoff. On the other hand, women's taste for relationship-based intimacy and greater investment in each sexual act is congruent with women's reproductive strategies.

In a field that tends to emphasize male's "natural" influence over reproductive strategies, evolutionary anthropologist Helen Fisher offers a feminist twist. Her study of hundreds of societies shows that divorce, or its informal equivalent, occurs most typically in the third or fourth year of a marriage and then peaks about every four years after that. Fisher hypothesizes that some of the breakups have to do with a woman's attempt to obtain the best genes and best survival chances for her offspring. In both agrarian and hunter-gatherer societies, Fisher explains, women breast-feed their child for three or four years—a practice that is economical and sometimes helps to prevent further pregnancy. At the end of this period, the woman is ready and able to have another child. She reenters the mating marketplace and assesses her options to see if she can improve on her previous mate. If she can get a better guy, she will leave the previous partner and team up with a new one. In Fisher's vision, unlike the traditional sociobiological view . . . , different male and female reproductive strategies do not necessarily imply female sexual passivity and preference for lifelong monogamy.

Sociobiologists and evolutionary psychologists tell a fascinating story of how male and female reproductive differences might shape sexuality. To accept sociobiological arguments, one must accept the premise that most animal and human behavior is driven by the instinct to reproduce and improve the gene pool. Furthermore, a flaw of sociobiology as a theory is that it does not provide a unique account of sexual behavior with the potential to be tested empirically. Furthermore, other social science explanations for the same phenomena are supported by more immediate, close-range evidence.

Consider hypergamy, the practice of women marrying men slightly older and "higher" on the social status ladder than they are. Sociobiologists would say women marry "up" to ensure the most fit provider for their offspring. But hypergamy makes little sense biologically. Younger men have more years of resources to provide, and they have somewhat more sexual resources. Empirically, however, hypergamy is fact. It is also a fact that men, overall and in nearly every subculture, have access to more rewards and status than women do. Furthermore, reams of imagery—in movies, advertising, novels—promote the appeal of older, more resourceful men. Why not, when older, more resourceful men are generating the images? Social practice, in this case, overrides what sociobiologists consider the biological imperative.

THE SOCIAL ORIGINS OF DESIRE

Your own experience should indicate that biology and genetics alone do not shape human sexuality. From the moment you entered the world, cues from the environment were telling you which desires and behaviors were "normal" and which were not. The result is that people who grow up in different circumstances tend to have different sexualities. Who has not had their sexual behavior influenced by their parents' or guardians' explicit or implicit rules? You may break the rules or follow them, but you can't forget them. . . .

The Social Construction of Sexuality

Social constructionists believe that cues from the environment shape human beings from the moment they enter the world. The sexual customs, values, and expectations of a culture, passed on to the young through teaching and by example, exert a powerful influence over individuals. When Fletcher Christian sailed into Tahiti in Charles

Nordhoff's 1932 account, *Mutiny on the Bounty,* he and the rest of his nineteenth-century English crew were surprised at how sexually available, playful, guilt free, and amorous the Tahitian women were. Free from the Judeo-Christian precepts and straight-laced customs that inhibited English society, the women and girls of Tahiti regarded their sexuality joyfully and without shame. The English men were delighted and, small wonder, refused to leave the island. Such women did not exist in their own society. The women back in England had been socialized within their Victorian culture to be modest, scared of sex, protective of their reputation, and threatened by physical pleasure. As a result, they were unavailable before marriage and did not feel free to indulge in a whole lot of fun after it. The source of the difference was not physiological differences between Tahitian and English women; it was sexual *socialization* or the upbringing that they received within their differing families and cultures.

If we look back at the Victorian, nineteenth-century England that Nordhoff refers to, we can identify *social structures* that influenced the norms of women's and men's sexuality. A burgeoning, new, urban middle class created separate spheres in the division of family labor. Instead of sharing home and farm or small business, the tasks of adults in families became specialized: Men went out to earn money, women stayed home to raise children and take care of the home. Although this division of labor was not the norm in all classes and ethnicities in England at the time, the image of middle-class femininity and masculinity became pervasive. The new division of labor increased women's economic dependence on men, which further curbed women's sexual license but not men's. When gender organizes one aspect of life—such as men's and women's position in the economy—it also organizes other aspects of life, including sex.

In a heterogeneous and individualistic culture like North America, sexual socialization is complex. A society creates an "ideal" sexuality, but different families and subcultures have their own values. For example, even though contemporary society at large may now accept premarital sexuality, a given family may lay down the law: Sex before marriage is against the family's religion and an offense against God's teaching. A teenager who grows up in such a household may suppress feelings of sexual arousal or channel them into outlets that are more acceptable to the family. Or the teenager may react against her or his background, reject parental and community opinion, and search for what she or he perceives to be a more "authentic" self. Variables like birth order or observations of a sibling's social and sexual expression can also influence a person's development.

As important as family and social background are, so are individual differences in response to that background. In the abstract, people raised to celebrate their sexuality must surely have a different approach to enjoying their bodies than those who are taught that their bodies will betray them and are a venal part of human nature. Yet whether or not a person is raised to be at ease with physicality does not always help predict adult sexual behavior. Sexual sybarites and libertines may have grown up in sexually repressive environments, as did pop culture icon and Catholic-raised Madonna. Sometimes individuals whose families promoted sex education and free personal expression are content with minimal sexual expression.

. . .

To summarize, social constructionists believe that a society influences sexual behavior through its norms. Some norms are explicit, such as laws against adult sexual activity with minors. Others are implicit, such as norms of fidelity and parental responsibility. In a stable, homogeneous society, it is relatively easy to understand such rules. But in a changing, complex society like the United States, the rules may be in flux or indistinct. Perhaps this ambiguity is what makes some issues of sexuality so controversial today.

AN INTEGRATIVE PERSPECTIVE ON GENDER AND SEXUALITY

Social constructionist explanations of contemporary sexual patterns are typically pitted against the biology of desire and the evolutionary understanding of biological adaptations. Some social constructionists believe there is no inflexible biological reality; everything we regard as either female or male sexuality is culturally imposed. In contrast, *essentialists*—those who take a biological, sociobiological, or evolutionary point of view—believe people's sexual desires and orientations are innate and hard-wired and that social impact is minimal. Gender differences follow from reproductive differences. Men inseminate, women incubate. People are born with sexual drives, attractions, and natures that simply play themselves out at the appropriate developmental age. Even if social constraints conspire to make men and women more similar to each other (as in the 1990s, when the sensitive and nurturing new man [was] encouraged to get in touch with his so-called feminine, emotional side), people's essential nature is the same: Man is the hunter, warrior, and trailblazer, and woman is the gatherer, nurturer, and reproducer. To an essentialist, social differences, such as the different earning power of men and women, are the consequence of biological difference. In short, essentialists think the innate differences between women and men are the cause of gendered sexuality; social constructionists think the differences between men and women are the result of gendering sexuality through social processes.

Using either the social constructionist or essentialist approach to the exclusion of the other constrains understanding of sexuality. We believe the evidence shows that gender differences are more plausibly an outcome of social processes than the other way around. But a social constructionist view is most powerful when it takes the essentialist view into account. . . . [W]e describe this view of gender differences in sexual desire as *integrative*. Although people tend to think of sex as primarily a biological function—tab B goes into slot A—biology is only one part of the context of desire. Such sociological factors as family relationships and social structure also influence sex. A complex mix of anatomy, hormones, and the brain provides the basic outline for the range of acts and desires possible, but biology is neither where sexuality begins nor where it ends. Social and biological contexts link to define human sexual possibilities.

The integrative approach follows from a great deal that sexuality researchers have observed. Consider the following example: A research project, conducted over three decades ago, advertised for participants stating that its focus was how physical excitement influences a man's preference for one woman over another. The researchers connected college men to a monitor that allowed them to hear their heartbeats as they looked at photographs of women models. The men were told that they would be able to hear their heartbeat when it surged in response to each photograph. A greater surge would suggest greater physical attraction. The participants were then shown a photograph of a dark-haired woman, then a blonde, then a redhead. Afterward, each man was asked to choose the picture that he would prefer to take home. In each case, the man chose the photograph of the woman who, as he believed from listening to his own speeding heartbeat, had most aroused him. Or at least the man thought he was choosing the woman who had aroused him most. In reality, the men had been listening to a faked heartbeat that was speeded up at random. The men thus actually chose the women whom they believed had aroused them most. In this case, the men's invented attraction was more powerful than their gut response. Their mind (a powerful sexual organ) told them their body was responding to a specific picture. The participants' physiological experience of arousal was eclipsed by the social context. When social circumstances influence sexual tastes, are those tastes real or sincere? Absolutely. The social world is as much a fact in people's lives as the biological world.

R E A D I N G   *27*

Romance: Sweet Love

bell hooks

Sweet Love say
Where, how and when
What do you want of me? . . .

Yours I am, for You I was born:
What do you want of me? . . .

—*Saint Teresa of Avila*

To return to love, to get the love we always wanted but never had, to have the love we want but are not prepared to give, we seek romantic relationships. We believe these relationships, more than any other, will rescue and redeem us. True love does have the power to redeem but only if we are ready for redemption. Love saves us only if we want to be saved. So many seekers after love are taught in childhood to feel unworthy, that nobody could love them as they really are, and they construct a false self. In adult life they meet people who fall in love with their false self. But this love does not last. At some point, glimpses of the real self emerge and disappointment comes. Rejected by their chosen love, the message received in childhood is confirmed: Nobody could love them as they really are.

Few of us enter romantic relationships able to receive love. We fall into romantic attachments doomed to replay familiar family dramas. Usually we do not know this will happen precisely because we have grown up in a culture that has told us that no matter what we experienced in our childhoods, no matter the pain, sorrow, alienation, emptiness, no matter the extent of our dehumanization, romantic love will be ours. We believe we will meet the girl of our dreams. We believe "someday our prince will come." They show up just as we imagined they would. We wanted the lover to appear, but most of us were not really clear about what we wanted to do with them—what the love was that we wanted to make and how we would make it. We were not ready to open our hearts fully.

In her first book, *The Bluest Eye,* novelist Toni Morrison identifies the idea of romantic love as one "of the most destructive ideas in the history of human thought." Its destructiveness resides in the notion that we come to love with no will and no capacity to choose. This illusion, perpetuated by so much romantic lore, stands in the way of our learning how to love. To sustain our fantasy we substitute romance for love.

When romance is depicted as a project, or so the mass media, especially movies, would have us believe, women are the architects and the planners. Everyone likes to imagine that women are romantics, sentimental about love, that men follow where women lead. Even in nonheterosexual relationships, the paradigms of leader and follower often prevail, with one person assuming the role deemed feminine and another the designated masculine role. No doubt it was someone playing the role of leader who conjured up the notion that we "fall in love," that we lack choice and decision when choosing a partner because when the chemistry is present, when the click is there, it just happens—it overwhelms—it takes control. This way of thinking about love seems to be especially useful for men who are socialized via patriarchal notions of masculinity to be out of touch with what they feel. In the essay "Love and Need," Thomas Merton contends: "The expression to 'fall in love' reflects a peculiar attitude toward love and life itself—a mixture of fear, awe, fascination, and confusion. It implies suspicion, doubt, hesitation in the presence of something unavoidable, yet not fully reliable." If you do not know what you feel, then it is difficult to choose love; it is better to fall. Then you do not have to be responsible for your actions.

Even though psychoanalysts, from Fromm writing in the fifties to Peck in the present day, critique the idea that we fall in love, we continue to invest in the fantasy of effortless union. We continue to believe we are swept away, caught up in the rapture, that we lack choice and will. In *The Art of Loving,* Fromm repeatedly talks about love as action, "essentially an act of will." He writes: "To love somebody is not just a strong feeling—it is a decision, it is a judgment, it is a promise. If love were only a feeling, there would be no basis for the promise to love each other forever. A feeling comes and it may go." Peck builds upon Fromm's definition when he describes love as the will to nurture one's own or another's spiritual growth, adding: "The desire to love is not itself love. Love is as love does. Love is an act of will—namely, both an intention and action. Will also implies choice. We do not have to love. We choose to love." Despite these brilliant insights and the wise counsel they offer, most people remain reluctant to embrace the idea that it is more genuine, more real, to think of choosing to love rather than falling in love.

Describing our romantic longings in *Life Preservers,* therapist Harriet Lerner shares that most people want a partner "who is mature and intelligent, loyal and trustworthy, loving and attentive, sensitive and open, kind and nurturant, competent and responsible." No matter the intensity of this desire, she concludes: "Few of us evaluate a prospective partner with the same objectivity and clarity that we might use to select a household appliance or a car." To be capable of critically evaluating a partner we would need to be able to stand back and look critically at ourselves, at our needs, desires, and longings. It was difficult for me to really take out a piece of paper and evaluate myself to see if I was able to give the love I wanted to receive. And even more difficult to make a list of the qualities I wanted to find in a mate. I listed ten items. And then when I applied the list to men I had chosen as potential partners, it was painful to face the discrepancy between what I wanted and what I had chosen to accept. We fear that evaluating our needs and then carefully choosing partners will reveal that there is no one for us to love. Most of us prefer to have a partner who is lacking than no partner at all. What becomes apparent is that we may be more interested in finding a partner than in knowing love.

Time and time again when I talk to individuals about approaching love with will and intentionality, I hear the fear expressed that this will bring an end to romance. This is simply not so. Approaching romantic love from a foundation of care, knowledge, and respect actually intensifies romance. By taking the time to communicate with a potential mate we are no longer trapped by the fear and anxiety underlying romantic interactions that take place without discussion or the sharing of intent and desire. I talked with a woman friend who stated that she had always been extremely fearful of sexual encounters, even when she knew someone well and desired them. Her fear was rooted in a shame she felt about the body, sentiments she had learned in childhood. Previously, her encounters with men had only intensified that shame. Usually men made light of her anxiety. I suggested she might try meeting with the new man in her life over lunch with the set agenda of talking to him about sexual pleasure, their likes and dislikes, their hopes and fears. She reported back that the lunch was incredibly erotic; it laid the groundwork for them to be at ease with each other sexually when they finally reached that stage in their relationship.

Erotic attraction often serves as the catalyst for an intimate connection between two people, but it is not a sign of love. Exciting, pleasurable sex can take place between two people who do not even know each other. Yet the vast majority of males in our society are convinced that their erotic longing indicates who they should, and can, love. Led by their penis, seduced by erotic desire, they often end up in relationships with partners with whom they share no common interests or values. The pressure on men in a patriarchal society to "perform" sexually is so great that men are often so gratified to be with someone with whom they find sexual pleasure that they ignore everything else. They cover up these mistakes by working too much, or finding playmates they like

outside their committed marriage or partnership. It usually takes them a long time to name the lovelessness they may feel. And this recognition usually has to be covered up to protect the sexist insistence that men never admit failure.

Women rarely choose men solely on the basis of erotic connection. While most females acknowledge the importance of sexual pleasure, they recognize that it is not the only ingredient needed to build strong relationships. And let's face it, the sexism of stereotyping women as caregivers makes it acceptable for women to articulate emotional needs. So females are socialized to be more concerned about emotional connection. Women who have only named their erotic hunger in the wake of the permission given by the feminist movement and sexual liberation have always been able to speak their hunger for love. This does not mean that we find the love we long for. Like males, we often settle for lovelessness because we are attracted to other aspects of a partner's makeup. Shared sexual passion can be a sustaining and binding force in a troubled relationship, but it is not the proving ground for love.

This is one of the great sadnesses of life. Too often women, and some men, have their most intense erotic pleasure with partners who wound them in other ways. The intensity of sexual intimacy does not serve as a catalyst for respect, care, trust, understanding, and commitment. Couples who rarely or never have sex can know lifelong love. Sexual pleasure enhances the bonds of love, but they can exist and satisfy when sexual desire is absent. Ultimately, most of us would choose great love over sustained sexual passion if we had to. Luckily we do not have to make this choice because we usually have satisfying erotic pleasure with our loved one.

The best sex and the most satisfying sex are not the same. I have had great sex with men who were intimate terrorists, men who seduce and attract by giving you just what you feel your heart needs then gradually or abruptly withholding it once they have gained your trust. And I have been deeply sexually fulfilled in bonds with loving partners who have had less skill and know-how. Because of sexist socialization, women tend to put sexual satisfaction in its appropriate perspective. We acknowledge its value without allowing it to become the absolute measure of intimate connection. Enlightened women want fulfilling erotic encounters as much as men, but we ultimately prefer erotic satisfaction within a context where there is loving, intimate connection. If men were socialized to desire love as much as they are taught to desire sex, we would see a cultural revolution. As it stands, most men tend to be more concerned about sexual performance and sexual satisfaction than whether they are capable of giving and receiving love.

Even though sex matters, most of us are no more able to articulate sexual needs and longings than we are able to speak our desire for love. Ironically, the presence of life-threatening sexually transmitted diseases has become the reason more couples communicate with each other about erotic behavior. The very people (many of them men) who had heretofore claimed that "too much talk" made things less romantic find that talk does not threaten pleasure at all. It merely changes its nature. Where once knowing nothing was the basis for excitement and erotic intensity, knowing more is now the basis. Lots of people who feared a loss of romantic and/or erotic intensity made this radical change in their thinking and were surprised to find that their previous assumptions that talk killed romance were wrong.

Cultural acceptance of this change shows that we are all capable of shifting our paradigms, the foundational ways of thinking and doing things that become habitual. We are all capable of changing our attitudes about "falling in love." We can acknowledge the "click" we feel when we meet someone new as just that—a mysterious sense of connection that may or may not have anything to do with love. However, it could or could not be the primal connection while simultaneously acknowledging that it will lead us to love. How different things might be if, rather than saying "I think I'm in love," we were saying "I've connected with someone in a way that makes me think I'm on the way to knowing love." Or, if instead of saying "I am in love," we said "I am loving" or "I will love." Our patterns around romantic love

are unlikely to change if we do not change our language.

We are all uncomfortable with the conventional expressions we use to talk about romantic love. All of us feel that these expressions and the thinking behind them are one of the reasons we entered relationships that did not work. In retrospect we see that to a grave extent the way we talked about these bonds foreshadowed what happened in the relationship. I certainly changed the way I talk and think about love in response to the emotional lack I felt within myself and in my relationships. Starting with clear definitions of love, of feeling, intention, and will, I no longer enter relationships with the lack of awareness that leads me to make all bonds the site for repeating old patterns.

Although I have experienced many disappointments in my quest to love and be loved, I still believe in the transformative power of love. Disappointment has not led me to close my heart. However, the more I talk with people around me I find disappointment to be widespread and it does lead many folks to feel profoundly cynical about love. A lot of people simply think we make too much of love. Our culture may make much of love as compelling fantasy or myth, but it does not make much of the art of loving. Our disappointment about love is directed at romantic love. We fail at romantic love when we have not learned the art of loving. It's as simple as that. Often we confuse perfect passion with perfect love. A perfect passion happens when we meet someone who appears to have everything we have wanted to find in a partner. I say "appears" because the intensity of our connection usually blinds us. We see what we want to see. In *Soul Mates,* Thomas Moore contends that the enchantment of romantic illusion has its place and that "the soul thrives on ephemeral fantasies." While perfect passion provides us with its own particular pleasure and danger, for those of us seeking perfect love it can only ever be a preliminary stage in the process.

We can only move from perfect passion to perfect love when the illusions pass and we are able to use the energy and intensity generated by intense, overwhelming, erotic bonding to heighten self-discovery. Perfect passions usually end when we awaken from our enchantment and find only that we have been carried away from ourselves. It becomes perfect love when our passion gives us the courage to face reality, to embrace our true selves. Acknowledging this meaningful link between perfect passion and perfect love from the onset of a relationship can be the necessary inspi-

ration that empowers us to choose love. When we love by intention and will, by showing care, respect, knowledge, and responsibility, our love satisfies. Individuals who want to believe that there is no fulfillment in love, that true love does not exist, cling to these assumptions because this despair is actually easier to face than the reality that love is a real fact of life but is absent from their lives.

R E A D I N G **28**

Biphobia

Marcia Deihl and Robyn Ochs

I was in a feminist bookstore. As the woman rang up my purchase, she asked me if a "lesbian discount" was appropriate. I was somewhat taken aback, but I said (half in jest), "Well, I'm bisexual, so how about half?" She didn't smile and I didn't get a discount.

—Marcia

I came out to my brother several years ago and he seems on many levels to accept my bisexual identity. However, about a year ago I was visiting him and he took special care to request that I not discuss being bisexual in front of his roommates.

—Robyn

A friend of ours had been active in her lesbian community for several years. Then she fell in love with a man. When her lesbian "friends" found out, they ostracized her and held a "funeral" for her.

—Robyn and Marcia

I told a heterosexual male friend that I was bisexual. His response was to make repeated attempts to sexualize our relationship. He made the false assumption that since I was bi-SEX-ual, I was attracted to everybody.

—Robyn

STORIES AND STEREOTYPES

These are all stories that happen to bisexuals. Some of these mirror homophobia, others heterophobia, and still others are specifically "biphobic." All of them oppress bisexuals.

Biphobia: What is it? It is fear of the other and fear of the space between categories. Our sexual categories have long been founded on the illusion that there are two separate and mutually exclusive sexual identities: homosexual and heterosexual. The assumption is that you are either one or the other; those who are not like you are very different, and you needn't worry about becoming like them. Biphobia, like homophobia, is prejudice based on negative stereotypes. It is often born of ignorance, but sometimes it is simply bigotry:

Everybody knows about bisexuals—they're *confused* ("just a stage you're going through . . . you'll eventually choose . . . you're not secure in your mature heterosexuality yet . . . you're afraid of the other sex and the same sex is less threatening . . ."): they're *'sex maniacs'* ("They will do it with anyone, anytime"), they're *shallow* ("They can't commit themselves to any one person or even any one sex for a long-term relationship. . . . They're typical swingers . . . they're fickle. . . ."). (Delhi in Blumenfeld and Raymond 1988/1993, 81)

. . .

FEAR FROM HETEROSEXUAL PEOPLE

Homophobic heterosexual men and women alike react to bisexuality as they react to homosexuality. But with bisexuality, there is the added dimension of identification with the "straight half" of a bisexual person. They may be even more threatened, because they see that the "other" is not quite so different as they had believed. It could be a case of fantasy turning into a very real possibility.

Sigmund Freud and Alfred Kinsey agree that there is a spectrum of sexuality from "purely" gay to "purely" straight. (Freud 1938; Kinsey et al. 1948). Scholars working in other disciplines have made similar observations. Margaret Mead, for example, said "I think extreme heterosexuality is a perversion"; W. Somerset Maugham stated, "I tried to persuade myself that I was three-quarters normal and that only a quarter of me was queer . . . whereas it was the other way round" and Richard Aldington, biographer and friend of D. H. Lawrence, wrote, "I should say Lawrence was about eighty-five percent hetero and fifteen percent homo" (all quoted in Rutledge 1988, 20, 46, 142).

If internalized homophobia is keeping some heterosexual people from acting on their gay fantasies, they will probably be biphobic. If they are living a heterosexual life out of negative reasons (e.g., "I don't deserve what I really want"; "It's sick and perverse and sinful to act on these feelings"), then they will probably be threatened by others' bisexuality. If they are truly choosing to respond heterosexually for positive, clear, inner-directed reasons, their chances of being threatened are lessened.

We can't "convert" anyone. We don't have the right to come out for anyone else or to say that someone is "really bisexual." We don't have the right to judge another's reasons for avoiding intimacy with a given sex. We simply want it to be known that there is a third option, encompassing a wide range of variations. Some of our best allies are secure heterosexual people.

Heterosexual men and women will react slightly differently to bisexual men and bisexual women than they might react to gay men and lesbians. A homophobic straight man may respond similarly to a bisexual man as he does to a gay man (e.g., "Sissy!"). This sentiment may mask the outrage that men feel about other men renouncing their patriarchal prerogative of superiority to women. (Matteson 1989, 6). We have seen documentaries in which the Marines refer to recruits in basic training as "ladies" and "girls" in a derogatory sense. These names are considered the worst possible putdown for men who aren't being "masculine" enough. Similarly, taunting gay men with feminine names is a thinly veiled disrespect for all women. Another typical homophobic reaction is, "I just know he's going to make a pass at me." For the first time, a heterosexual man is in the position of potential "prey." Terrified and outraged, he may not be able to say "No!" safely.

Heterosexual women cannot write off bisexual men as "just friends" with no sexual undercurrents the way they might gay men. But, they cannot assume that these men are attracted to them either. Heterosexual women may see bisexual women as better "initiation" experiences than lesbians, or they may assume that bisexual women are after them.

Bisexuality defies old categories and evokes new responses. Bisexuals are relegated to a netherworld by heterosexuals and homosexuals alike. Our sexual minority status is simply one of nonexistence. What fears are expressed about us are largely based on ignorance rooted in our invisibility. (In the mainstream media, gay men and lesbians are becoming more visible.)

Bisexual women who are not middle class or rich, traditionally "beautiful," able-bodied, or white are invisible. Thus, it is hardly surprising that when *Newsweek* finally got around to publishing a feature story on bisexuality in 1995, the principal focus was on the secretive married bisexual men who are passing AIDS along to their wives. The gay community fares little better. We hear in conversation that bisexuals are "really lesbians who want access to heterosexual privilege" and that bisexuals were "really heterosexuals who want access to the support and excitement of the lesbian community."

FEAR FROM GAY AND LESBIAN PEOPLE

The early homophile (1950s and 1960s) and later (1970s) gay liberation movements have fought for the right of gay men and lesbians to exist, to love, and to be treated with dignity. Therefore, any perceived "regression" by gay people "converting" back to heterosexuality is considered a threat. This feeling is understandable. The gay and lesbian communities are under siege, especially in this age of AIDS; people under constant siege band together to form a united front. Thus formerly gay and lesbian people who "turn bi" are often met with feelings of betrayal and anger, but these reactions do not do justice to the truth of the situation.

Why are bisexuals perceived as such a threat to so many gay men and lesbians? We see a combination of society's homophobia and internalized biphobia at work here. A recurring theme in my [Robyn] lesbian relationships is the voiced fear on the part of my lover that I would choose to leave her for a man. After all, so much of our society is structured to encourage and support heterosexual relationships—families, the media, institutions such as marriage and corporations providing health insurance "family plans" are all based on the configuration of the heterosexual couple. Therefore, how could she possibly "compete" with the odds so stacked against us? There is no denying that the encouragement of heterosexuality and the discouragement of homosexuality is a very real fact. However, I also felt that there was a certain amount of internalized homophobia at work here, too: the feeling that whatever she had to offer me and whatever we had together couldn't possibly outweigh the external benefits of being in a heterosexual relationship. There's an underlying assumption there that anyone who has the choice will ultimately choose heterosexuality, that lesbians and gay men choose homosexual relationships because they are unable to be heterosexual. The number of bisexuals who have chosen homosexual relationships shows that this isn't necessarily so.

Some say that bisexuals are only half-oppressed. Yet we are not put on half-time when we are fired by a homophobic boss: we do not lose only half our children when we lose a custody battle; we cannot say to the gay-basher. "Oh! Please only beat me up on one side of my body."

We hear others stating that bisexual women dilute the power of the lesbian community. According to this reasoning, bisexual women should be banned from attending lesbian events despite the fact that bisexual women have greatly contributed to women's music and culture. Ironically, many lesbian organizers and performers downplay the lesbian energy in their own lives and in the history of feminism. For example, many performers who are or have been lesbians never use the "L-word" on stage. The brave ones acknowledge this problem, and address questions of privacy, expectations, and the right to change. Holly Near recently said at a concert, "I know that some of you are uncomfortable because you think I might be a lesbian. And there are others who are upset because I might not be one." Though not explicitly stated. Near seems to be referring to the ongoing and often angry controversy in the women's community over rumors of her involvement with a man.

After I [Marcia] was asked if I warranted the "lesbian discount," I thought seriously about it. I respected the woman's right to run her store the way she wanted. I loved the idea that there was such a thing as a lesbian discount—a rare opportunity for lesbians to be rewarded, not made invisible or degraded. But, then I thought of my ten years of gay marches and my six years of playing in a feminist band that performed 25 to 50 percent lesbian material. I think I *did* deserve at least half of the discount!

Bisexuals should not automatically be categorized along with heterosexuals; bisexuals should not be excluded from the lesbian and gay community. Yet, it is generally only famous bisexual persons—reclassified as "gay" or "lesbian"—(e.g., Virginia Woolf, Sappho, Christopher Isherwood, James Baldwin, Vita Sackville-West, Colette, Kate

Millet) who are embraced by lesbians and gay men; modern-day bisexuals working common jobs and bearing ordinary names are not. For example, if we want to put our name into an organization, we are often called "intruders."

We won't accept it both ways; the lesbian and gay community cannot have it both ways; either bisexuals are in or we're out. The feminist bookstore offering a lesbian discount was a store for *all* women, but, lesbians got a discount; heterosexual and bisexual women did not. It seemed in this instance we were *out* of the lesbian-gay community. We want to be in, but we are called "divisive" when we name ourselves as a third category. Such attitudes often keep us away and only reinforce the impression that we have "deserted the ranks."

Like heterosexual people who may be ignoring their homosexual inner signals, some gay men and lesbians may be repressing their bisexuality. They may fear the loss of their gay identity and their closest friends if they act on these desires. Others are happy. They have chosen positively to be gay or lesbian. These persons tend to be supportive of bisexuality in others; those who are threatened or unsure of themselves are less so.

A clear example of biphobia is the ostracism of some bisexuals from the lesbian and gay community. When women and men come out as bisexuals, their gay and lesbian friends often tell them that they can't really be bisexuals—that they are confused, or that they are waiting to reap the benefits of heterosexism. This is ironic where one considers that the lesbian and gay liberation movement in the United States is united around the right to love whomever we please, and to have our relationships validated and recognized, even when they do not conform to society's norms. Bisexuals are often pushed into a closet *within* a closet.

OUR VISION: THE BISEXUAL ARTIST/CITIZEN TODAY

Can you spot a bisexual when you meet one? Is there any hidden meaning to someone who is wearing one long earring and one short one, very short bangs with long hair in the back, dresses with hightops, or heels with pants (even the women!)? Perhaps. We come in every conceivable outer package—just like all other groups. What is important is what is inside. Our psyches are not split down the middle. We do not get up everyday and think, "Should I be straight or gay today?" We are, every day, in all situations, bisexual. We are like the mint breath freshener, Certs: "TWO . . . TWO . . . TWO sexualities in one." We are like the yin and yang symbol, perhaps emphasizing one aspect but with the seed of the other always present. We are simply a third option.

In sum, we are not defined by our behavior, but by our essence. If we walk down the street holding hands with a woman, people will assume we are lesbians. If we walk down the street holding hands with a man, people will assume we are heterosexual. We aren't shifting; others' perceptions are.

As public television's Mr. Rogers tells very young children, each of us is unique. We are all completely different from anyone else, with our own gifts and limitations. We are all artists; we are all queers; we are all "oddists." And lesbian, gay, bisexual, and transgender people have practically been forced to be creative. We experience a conflict between inner signals and outer demands that requires that we invent ourselves and think on our feet at every moment. Perhaps this is why we have contributed more than our share to the arts. As Fran Lebowitz quipped, "If you removed all of the homosexuals and homosexual influence from what is generally regarded as American culture, you would be pretty much left with *Let's Make a Deal* (quoted in Rutledge 1988, 93). We would do well to join some old Native American Indian cultures in considering differences in sexuality and gender expression as special, honored gifts, not as threatening deviations (Williams 1986).

Being bisexual and naming ourselves makes us special. Yet, we have our cultural work cut out for us. We must invent and create our own lives, music, theater, writing, and art, just as some of us did with women's culture. We need art that reflects, analyzes, reinvents, and inspires our daily lives. We must not simply react to biphobia, we must come together with others like ourselves to name and love ourselves.

Though we are unique, we are also like everyone else: we are citizens of this planet. We need to work in coalitions because we want to help clear up the many problems that face us and our children and grandchildren today. Problems of poverty, pollution, and violence are obvious to us all—female and male, gay, lesbian, bisexual, and straight. In order to solve these problems, action must be taken against heterosexism, sexism, racism, and class privilege. And since we are all minorities, we must work together on common projects in order to be effective. Bisexuals are natural leaders for uniting progressive men and women, and also gays and straights.

Bisexuals are not fence-sitters; there is no fence. Sexuality is a giant field in which mostly lesbian- and gay-identified people are clustered on one side and mostly heterosexual-identified people on the other. We are the middle; sometimes we travel toward one end or the other in a day, in a lifetime. We hereby declare a field day!

REFERENCES

Blumenfeld, W. J., and D. Raymond. (1988/1993). *Looking at Gay and Lesbian Life.* New York: Beacon Press.

Freud, S. (1938). "Infantile Sexuality." In *The Basic Writings of Sigmund Freud,* trans. A. Brel. New York: Modern Library.

Kinsey, A. W. Pomeroy, C. Martin, and R. Gebhard, (1948). *Sexual Behavior in the Human Male.* Philadelphia: Saunders.

Matteson, D. (1989). "Racism, Sexism, and Homophobia." *Empathy 1:* 6.

Rutledge, L. (1988). *Unnatural Quotations.* Boston: Alyson Publications.

Williams, W. (1986). *The Spirit and the Flesh.* Boston: Beacon Press.

R E A D I N G   **29**

I Was a *Cosmo* Sex Deviant

A. E. Berkowitz

Ok, ok, maybe I should've known better; maybe I shouldn't have been there in the first place. But I'm a sucker for those damn quizzes, so there I was on the *Cosmopolitan* Web site letting them ask me, "How sexually liberated are you?" Much to my surprise and chagrin, I found out that I'm so liberated it's sick. Literally. Here's what they had to say about me (my category, by the way, is "Out of control!"): "While you certainly derive some fleeting gratification from your freewheeling sexual style, your lack of inhibition isn't making you happy. Perhaps you're involved in activities that are emotionally or physically harmful, or out of line with your other values. Or unresolved childhood conflicts could be causing you to slip into bed too readily (as a way to gain approval, say)." If that's not bad enough, their expert says that I "can either try to change on [my] own, realizing that route may be difficult and painful, or seek help from a therapist or support group such as Sexual Compulsives Anonymous."

You may be asking yourselves, "What kind of sick answers did this chick give on the test?" Well, here's a sampling: I've had sex with a colleague, and with a close friend; I feel comfortable telling a partner what feels good; I never fake orgasms; I read erotic literature, watch x-rated videos, and play with a vibrator; I don't think alcohol enhances performance; I see myself as a sexual person and I'm perfectly happy taking the lead in bed.

Needless to say, I was a bit confused about why the folks at *Cosmo* were telling me to join a sex addicts support group. After all, my freewheeling sexual style and lack of inhibition are making me happy—when I can find a partner, that is. So after a bit of playing around, answering questions as an "ideal," "healthy" person might, I made some discoveries. The whole quiz pretty much hinges on the following question:

You seek sex in order to . . . (Choose as many as apply.)

✘ Make contact with another human body.

✘ Make a conquest.

✘ Give pleasure.

✘ Satisfy physical or emotional desire.

✘ Prove your attractiveness.

✘ Affirm your sexual identity.

✘ Relieve tension.

✘ Relieve boredom.

✘ Express love.

✘ Feel loved.

Hello. Because my answers reflect the fact that I enjoy sex and indulge in it whenever I can—but without any illusions that I am in love with my partners or vice versa—I need to seek help? Now, being an honest person who's not in a relationship right now, it would've been pretty stupid to choose "express love," since I know damn well that's not what I'm expressing to any of the people I've slept with lately. And it would be even stupider, bordering on self-deluded, to choose "feel loved," 'cause I know very well that if that's what I want I'm barkin' up the wrong pole. So I went ahead and checked all the others, except "give pleasure," which is of course both a goal and a byproduct, but not a motivation. There was nothing in my answers to suggest that my gratification is only fleeting, or that my actions actually make me unhappy. In fact, on the obligatory morning-after question, I checked "Fabulously fulfilled," not "Disappointed, let down," as their diagnosis of me might suggest. But because I checked "Far less often than you'd like" in response to a question about frequency of sex, instead of "Only when your emotions are engaged," or even "Whenever you're attracted and

see an opportunity," I'm a sexual compulsive. Wait, you mean that if I went to more parties and met more people and had sex with them, I'd be fine?

Because, you know, that third choice also applies—but you can only pick one, and the fact that I'm attracted and see opportunities far less often than I'd like really shouldn't be enough to send me running to the shrink.

So not being stupid or self-deluded in any way, I end up labeled a deviant. Thanks so much, *Cosmo*. If I'd chosen only "Give pleasure," "Express love," and "Feel loved," then I'd be a perfectly well-adjusted, even "Exquisitely Experimental" person. As long as you check the "right" boxes on that list of reasons to have sex, you're classed as "Exquisitely Experimental"—even if you also admit that you have sex "Lots of times you shouldn't, frankly." (I shudder to think of the horrifying possibilities there.)

So what all this means is that you can have sex to express love for and feel loved by some partner for whom you have an unrequited emotional desire, realize later that sleeping with that person was a mistake—and you're perfectly healthy. While someone like me who knows why she has sex, never regrets it, and is realistic about what it means to herself and her partners, should get some help.

Ok, I'm not really surprised, 'cause I know what *Cosmo* girls are supposed to be like: dripping sex but pathologically in search of a man. I'm not like that. Oh, well. So what if I'm "Out of Control!"; I'll never let them fix me.

QUIZ: IS POP CULTURE RUINING YOUR SEX LIFE?

Tell us about it:

Part One

1. If you were to describe your attitude towards sex and dating in terms of a prime-time TV show, it would most closely resemble
   a. *Melrose Place*.
   b. *Roseanne*.
   c. *The X-Files*.
   d. *Living Single*.
   e. Please—don't insult me by comparing my values to those of TV characters.

2. You're with your date at the video store. Keeping in mind that you're hoping for some booty later, what do you suggest renting?
   a. *Last Tango in Paris*
   b. *A Room with a View*
   c. *Ace Ventura, Pet Detective*
   d. *Taxi Driver*

3. The most realistic depiction of sex in a Hollywood movie can be found
   a. in any Woody Allen movie.
   b. in any Sharon Stone movie.
   c. in any John Cusak movie.
   d. Nothing in Hollywood ever approaches anything like realism.

4. You're flipping through a glossy mag in the checkout line at Safeway. What article sucks you in first?
   a. Anything involving celebrities and "How They Got That Look."
   b. Anything promising sex tips.
   c. Anything involving clothing or diets.
   d. I read *Newsweek* in the checkout line, thank you very much.
   e. The first one that looks interesting—all that pap is pretty much the same.

5. If held at gunpoint and forced to choose, you would most eagerly jump
   a. good-natured pretty boy Brandon.
   b. lusty, busty Valerie.
   c. avuncular Peach Pit owner Nat.
   d. What are you talking about? Who are these people?
   e. What are you talking about? Claire's the only 90210 character with any sex appeal!

6. What magazine are you most likely to turn to for sex and relationship advice?
   a. *Cosmopolitan*
   b. *Seventeen*
   c. *Hustler*
   d. None, really; I have friends for that.

7. The celluloid sex scene you most wish you'd been in is the one between
   a. Tim Robbins and Greta Scaachi in *The Player.*
   b. Uma Thurman and Maria de Medeiros in *Henry and June.*

   c. Laurel Holloway and Nicole Parker in *The Incredibly True Adventures of Two Girls in Love.*
   d. Geena Davis and Brad Pitt in *Thelma and Louise.*

8. The celluloid sex scene you feel like you have been in is (check all that apply)
   a. Jennifer Jason Leigh's disappointing decoration in *Fast Times at Ridgemont High.*
   b. Winona Ryder's friendship-threatening night with Ethan Hawke in *Reality Bites.*
   c. the kind of lighthearted, sensuous romps— no ice picks involved—usually found only in foreign films like *Belle Epoque.*
   d. Other: _____.
   e. Hey, just because I happen to watch a few movies doesn't mean I see my sexual past reflected in them, okay?

9. When you take a quiz in a magazine, you generally
   a. answer all the questions from the point of view of dotty Aunt Irma.
   b. answer all the questions honestly, insofar as that's possible given how reductive and confining the choices are. Laugh at the outcome.
   c. answer all questions honestly, and worry for the rest of the week about the outcome.
   d. I wouldn't touch one of those idiotic magazine quizzes with a ten-foot pole.

Part Two
How often do you do the following? (Choose often, occasionally, or never.)
   a. Pick up seduction tips from movies, TV, books, or magazines.
   b. Engage in long, involved fantasies about courtships and/or relationships with TV and movie stars.
   c. Feel cheated by the lack of cinema-caliber sex in your own life.
   d. Switch off your television in a fit of disgust and/or boredom.
   e. Spend time with friends avidly debating who would be a better girlfriend for David Duchovny—Angela Bassett or Linda Fiorentino.

f. Feel guilty about and/or conceal your fascination with television and movies.

g. Curl up with a 19th-century novel even on must-see TV nights.

Score Yourself

Part One

1. a - 4, b - 1, c - 1, d - 2, e - 0
2. a - 3, b - 2, c - 2, d - 1
3. a - 3, b - 4, c - 2, d - 0
4. a - 3, b - 4, c - 3, d - 0, e - 2
5. a - 3, d - 4, c - 2, d - 0, e - 2
6. a - 4, b - 3, c - 3, d - 0
7. a - 2, b - 3, c - 2, d - 4
8. a - 1, b - 2, c - 2, d - 1, e - 0
9. a - 1, b - 2, c - 3, d - 0

Part Two

For questions a, b, c, and e: Give yourself 0 points for each never, 1 point for each occasionally, and 2 points for each often.

For questions d, f, and g: Give yourself 0 points for each often, 1 point for each occasionally, and 2 points for each never.

What It All Means

You drama queen, you! (36–52 points)

You, my friend, are scary. You admire characters, you behave like characters, you are a character. While it's fine to see your world reflected in pop culture (after all, we often can't help it . . .), you need to get yourself a real life, and stop worrying about whether Jake and Alison are going to stay together. Keep in mind that TV-style scandals and histrionics do not make for a healthy real-life attitude toward relationships—so knock it off. (Don't feel bad . . . we scored in this category too.)

A shining example (14–35 points)

Congratulations. You're normal. You know that what's up on the screen does not directly translate into anyone's reality, but you're also no stranger to the lure of a little celluloid-induced fantasy. No harm in that, as long as you keep those "reality-based" *Party of Five* plots in perspective.

We smell smoke . . . (3–13 points)

Well well, Ms. Thang, either you spend far too much time reading the *New York Times* and attending the symphony to notice the plebian, trivial world of pop culture, or you're lying—and hey, we know you're reading this magazine [this reading is excerpted from *Bitch* magazine]. Take the quiz again after you've doused those flaming pants.

La Güera

Cherríe Moraga

*It requires something more than personal experi-
ence to gain a philosophy or point of view from any
specific event. It is the quality of our response to
the event and our capacity to enter into the lives of
others that help us to make their lives and experiences our own.*

—*Emma Goldman*[1]

I am the very well-educated daughter of a woman
who, by the standards in this country, would be
considered largely illiterate. My mother was born
in Santa Paula, Southern California, at a time when
much of the central valley there was still farm land.
Nearly thirty-five years later, in 1948, she was the
only daughter of six to marry an Anglo, my father.

I remember all of my mother's stories, probably much better than she realizes. She is a fine
story-teller, recalling every event of her life with
the vividness of the present, noting each detail
right down to the cut and color of her dress. I remember her stories of her being pulled out of
school at the ages of five, seven, nine, and eleven
to work in the fields, along with her brothers and
sisters; stories of her father drinking away whatever small profit she was able to make for the
family; of her going the long way home to avoid
meeting him on the street, staggering toward the
same destination. I remember stories of my mother
lying about her age in order to get a job as a hat-
check girl at Agua Caliente Racetrack in Tijuana.
At fourteen, she was the main support of the family. I can still see her walking home alone at 3 A.M.,
only to turn all of her salary and tips over to her
mother, who was pregnant again.

The stories continue through the war years and
on: walnut-cracking factories, the Voit Rubber factory, and then the computer boom. I remember

my mother doing piecework for the electronics
plant in our neighborhood. In the late evening,
she would sit in front of the TV set, wrapping copper wires into the backs of circuit boards, talking
about "keeping up with the younger girls." By that
time, she was already in her mid-fifties.

Meanwhile, I was college-prep in school. After
classes, I would go with my mother to fill out job
applications for her, or write checks for her at the
supermarket. We would have the scenario all
worked out ahead of time. My mother would sign
the check before we'd get to the store. Then, as
we'd approach the checkstand, she would say—
within earshot of the cashier—"Oh honey, you go
'head and make out the check," as if she couldn't
be bothered with such an insignificant detail. No
one asked any questions.

I was educated, and wore it with a keen sense
of pride and satisfaction, my head propped up
with the knowledge, from my mother, that my life
would be easier than hers. I was educated; but
more than this, I was *la güera:* 'fair-skinned.' Born
with the features of my Chicana mother, but the
skin of my Anglo father, I had it made.

No one ever quite told me this (that light was
right), but I knew that being light was something
valued in my family (who were all Chicano, with the
exception of my father). In fact, everything about
my upbringing (at least what occurred on a conscious level) attempted to bleach me of what color I
did have. Although my mother was fluent in it, I was
never taught much Spanish at home. I picked up
what I did learn from school and from overheard
snatches of conversation among my relatives and
mother. She often called the other lower-income
Mexicans *braceros,* or 'wet-backs,' referring to herself and her family as "a different class of people."

And yet, the real story was that my family, too, had been poor (some still are) and farmworkers. My mother can remember this in her blood as if it were yesterday. But this is something she would like to forget (and rightfully), for to her, on a basic economic level, being Chicana meant being "less." It was through my mother's desire to protect her children from poverty and illiteracy that we became "Anglo-ized"; the more effectively we could pass in the white world, the better guaranteed our future.

From all of this, I experience daily a huge disparity between what I was born into and what I was to grow up to become. Because, as Goldman suggests, these stories my mother told me crept under my *güera* skin. I had no choice but to enter into the life of my mother. *I had no choice.* I took her life into my heart, but managed to keep a lid on it as long as I feigned being the happy, upwardly mobile heterosexual.

When I finally lifted the lid to my lesbianism, a profound connection with my mother was reawakened in me. It wasn't until I acknowledged and confronted my own lesbianism in the flesh that my heartfelt identification with and empathy for my mother's oppression—due to being poor, uneducated, and Chicana—was realized. My lesbianism is the avenue through which I have learned the most about silence and oppression, and it continues to be the most tactile reminder to me that we are not free human beings.

You see, one follows the other. I had known for years that I was a lesbian, had felt it in my bones, had ached with the knowledge, gone crazed with the knowledge, wallowed in the silence of it. Silence *is* like starvation. Don't be fooled. It's nothing short of that, and felt most sharply when one has had a full belly most of her life. When we are not physically starving, we have the luxury to realize psychic and emotional starvation. It is from this starvation that other starvations can be recognized—if one is willing to take the risk of making the connection—if one is willing to be responsible to the result of the connection. For me, the connection is an inevitable one.

What I am saying is that the joys of looking like a white girl haven't been so great since I realized I could be beaten on the street for being a dyke. If my sister's being beaten because she's black, it's pretty much the same principle. We're both getting beaten any way you look at it. The connection is blatant; and in the case of my own family, the differences in the privileges attached to looking white instead of brown are merely a generation apart.

In this country, lesbianism is poverty—as is being brown, as is being a woman, as is being just plain poor. The danger lies in ranking the oppressions. *The danger lies in failing to acknowledge the specificity of the oppression.* The danger lies in attempting to deal with oppression purely from a theoretical base. Without an emotional, heartfelt grappling with the source of our own oppression, without naming the enemy within ourselves and outside of us, no authentic, nonhierarchical connection among oppressed groups can take place.

When the going gets rough, will we abandon our so-called comrades in a flurry of racist/heterosexist/what-have-you panic? To whose camp, then, should the lesbian of color retreat? Her very presence violates the ranking and abstraction of oppression. Do we merely live hand to mouth? Do we merely struggle with the "ism" that's sitting on top of our own heads?

The answer is: yes, I think first we do; and we must do so thoroughly and deeply. But to fail to move out from there will only isolate us in our own oppression—will only insulate, rather than radicalize us.

. . .

Within the women's movement, the connections among women of different backgrounds and sexual orientations have been fragile, at best. I think this phenomenon is indicative of our failure to seriously address ourselves to some very frightening questions: How have I internalized my own oppression? How have I oppressed? Instead, we have let rhetoric do the job of poetry. Even the word *oppression* has lost its power. We need new language, better words that can more closely describe women's fear of and resistance to one another; words that will not always come out sounding like dogma.

I don't really understand first-hand what it feels like being shit on for being brown. I understand much more about the joys of it—being Chicana and having family are synonymous for me. What I know about loving, singing, crying, telling stories, speaking with my heart and hands, even having a sense of my own soul comes from the love of my mother, aunts, cousins. . . .

But at the age of twenty-seven, it is frightening to acknowledge that I have internalized a racism and classism where the object of oppression is not only someone outside of my skin, but the someone inside my skin. In fact, to a large degree, the real battle with such oppression, for all of us, begins under the skin. I have had to confront the fact that much of what I value about being Chicana, about my family, has been subverted by Anglo culture and my own cooperation with it. This realization did not occur to me overnight. For example, it wasn't until long after my graduation from the private college I'd attended in Los Angeles that I realized the major reason for my total alienation from and fear of my classmates was rooted in class and culture. *Click.*

Three years after graduation, in an apple-orchard in Sonoma, a friend of mine (who comes from an Italian working-class family), says to me, "Cherríe, no wonder you felt like such a nut in school. Most of the people there were white and rich." It was true. All along I had felt the difference, but not until I had put the words *class* and *culture* to the experience did my feelings make any sense. For years, I had berated myself for not being as "free" as my classmates. I completely bought that they simply had more guts than I did—to rebel against their parents and run around the country hitchhiking, reading books and studying "art." They had enough privilege to be atheists, for chrissake. There was no one around filling in the disparity for me between their parents, who were Hollywood filmmakers, and my parents, who wouldn't know the name of a filmmaker if their lives depended on it (and precisely because their lives didn't depend on it, they couldn't be bothered). But I knew nothing about "privilege" then. White was right. Period. I could pass. If I got educated enough, there would never be any telling.

Three years after that, another click. In a letter to a friend, I wrote:

> I went to a concert where Ntozake Shange was reading. There, everything exploded for me. She was speaking a language that I knew—in the deepest parts of me—existed, and that I had ignored in my own feminist studies and even in my own writing. What Ntozake caught in me is the realization that in my development as a poet, I have, in many ways, denied the voices of my brown mother—the brown in me. I have acclimated to the sound of a white language which, as my father represents it, does not speak to the emotions in my poems—emotions which stem from the love of my mother.
>
> The reading was agitating. Made me feel uncomfortable. Threw me into a week-long terror of how deeply I was affected. I felt that I had to start all over again. That I had turned only to the perceptions of white middle-class women to speak for me and all women. I am shocked by my own ignorance.

Sitting in that auditorium chair was the first time I had realized to the core of me that for years I had disowned the language I knew best—ignored the words and rhythms that were the closest to me. The sounds of my mother and aunts gossiping—half in English, half in Spanish—while drinking cerveza in the kitchen. And the hands—I had cut off the hands in my poems. But not in conversation; still the hands could not be kept down. Still they insisted on moving.

The reading had forced me to remember that I knew things from my roots. But to remember puts me up against what I don't know. Shange's reading agitated me because she spoke with power about a world that is both alien and common to me: "the capacity to enter into the lives of others." But you can't just take the goods and run. I knew that then, sitting in the Oakland auditorium (as I know in my poetry), that the only thing worth writing about is what seems to be unknown and therefore fearful.

The "unknown" is often depicted in racist literature as the "darkness" within a person. Similarly, sexist writers will refer to fear in the form of the vagina, calling it "the orifice of death." In contrast, it is a pleasure to read works such as Maxine Hong Kingston's *Woman Warrior,* where fear and alienation are described as "the white ghosts." And yet, the bulk of literature in this country reinforces the myth that what is dark and female is evil. Consequently, each of us—whether dark, female, or both—has in some way *internalized* this oppressive imagery. What the oppressor often succeeds in doing is simply *externalizing* his fears, projecting them into the bodies of women, Asians, gays, disabled folks, whoever seems most "other."

> call me
> roach and presumptuous
> nightmare on your white pillow
> your itch to destroy
> the indestructible
> part of yourself
> —*Audre Lorde*[2]

But it is not really difference the oppressor fears so much as similarity. He fears he will discover in himself the same aches, the same longings as those of the people he has shit on. He fears the immobilization threatened by his own incipient guilt. He fears he will have to change his life once he has seen himself in the bodies of the people he has called different. He fears the hatred, anger, and vengeance of those he has hurt.

This is the oppressor's nightmare, but it is not exclusive to him. We women have a similar nightmare, for each of us in some way has been both the oppressed and the oppressor. We are afraid to see how we have taken the values of our oppressor into our hearts and turned them against ourselves and one another. We are afraid to admit how deeply "the man's" words have been ingrained in us.

To assess the damage is a dangerous act. I think of how, even as a feminist lesbian, I have

so wanted to ignore my own homophobia, my own hatred of myself for being queer. I have not wanted to admit that my deepest personal sense of myself has not quite "caught up" with my "woman-identified" politics. I have been afraid to criticize lesbian writers who choose to "skip over" these issues in the name of feminism. In 1979, we talk of "old gay" and "butch and femme" roles as if they were ancient history. We toss them aside as merely patriarchal notions. And yet, the truth of the matter is that I have sometimes taken society's fear and hatred of lesbians to bed with me. I have sometimes hated my lover for loving me. I have sometimes felt "not woman enough" for her. I have sometimes felt "not man enough." For a lesbian trying to survive in a heterosexist society, there is no easy way around these emotions. Similarly, in a white-dominated world, there is little getting around racism and our own internalization of it. It's always there, embodied in someone we least expect to rub up against.

When we do rub up against this person, *there* then is the challenge. *There* then is the opportunity to look at the nightmare within us. But we usually shrink from such a challenge.

. . .

As Lorde suggests in the passage I cited earlier, it is in looking to the nightmare that the dream is found. There, the survivor emerges to insist on a future, a vision, yes, born out of what is dark and female. The feminist movement must be a movement of such survivors, a movement with a future.

NOTES

1. Alix Kates Shulman, ed., "Was My Life Worth Living?" *Red Emma Speaks* (New York: Random House, 1972), p. 388.
2. From "The Brown Menace or Poem to the Survival of Roaches," *The New York Head Shop and Museum* (Detroit: Broadside, 1974), p. 48.

Prue Shows Her Knickers

Emily Oxford

Prue was just a teenager. She was skinny and lean but two budding breasts made faint bumps under her clothes. Boys teased her and Andy kept asking for a flash.

The once-soft face of childhood was harder now, her jaw jutted forward a little, a physical sign of her stubbornness. Circumstance had made her wilful, wary and nervous of the world she lived in, but somewhere the indomitable spirit of her optimism still burned.

She was not normal. She was a cripple, she was handicapped, she was a Special pre-pubescent.

Her legs were unique maps of her illness, stiff and unbending, her knees decorated with tiny craters and variously swelling bumps. She didn't walk on them much and used a wheelchair at times she called simply "agony" days. Her neck, though rarely painful, bent to one side and stayed there. These were her bodily impairments which attracted the labels of doctors, and consequently categorised her neatly for the rest of the world.

The labels attached to her had done their work; her psyche suffered its own impairments as a result, and as she approached adolescence, she found herself nervous about a world which had once seemed a dazzling dance of magic.

She never thought much about her situation, she just accepted that she was these things other people placed on her, and if it kept the peace with her anxious, fretting mother, then she played by the rules that meant she saw lots of white-coats, went to a Special school in a Special bus and didn't expect to do a whole array of things in the hostile, anti-cripple world.

But even these rules had begun to change of late.

Now she was expected to play the Independence game—a game with a particular definition.

Lectures on "Personal Independence" featured in her life these days with growing regularity. She had to go to "Buttons and Bows" classes, where groups of bored teenagers were grilled about how to tie shoe laces; tackle buckles, poppers, buttons, zips; pull this on, pull that off; and sundry other activities. With her twig-like fingers curving at bulbous joints that neither bent very far nor had the strength to stay straight, most of these tasks were to Prue a punishment in ritualised boredom. She knew her own limits, just as she knew what challenges were worth taking on. These activities were pointless and demoralising as she failed at every attempt. The "teachers"—in fact blue-coats serving under the Head's baleful glare—would tut at her and admonish her to try harder.

The enforced ideas about Independence were suffocating shadows closing in on her life. She had to be taught to do everything in her life herself, absolutely, in readiness for adulthood when there would be no kind mum to wait on you, no teachers and Care ladies, oh no. It seemed to Prue it was the sort of Independence you might only need if you were the only person left alive on some fantastic, civilised desert island; and it was the sort of Independence which she knew she could never actually achieve.

What being Independent meant, of course, was being able to present to their real world an approximation of Normality. You wouldn't ever have to bother a nice Normal person with your nasty difficulties, you'd never have to ask for anything. It didn't matter how many hopeless hours of pain and toil were involved.

But who was she to argue? She was just a cripple kid, told every day that she didn't know what was best for herself, in her Special situation. . . .

If you didn't play the game of Independence by their rules, they made fearful threats about putting you in a Home when you reached sixteen. It was up to you, they would shrug, as if they had no say in the decision. If you tried your hardest and were Independent, then you didn't have to worry. You would be allowed into their world.

. . .

Prue had to draw on every ounce of her hard-won reserve of strength today because two traumas were facing her at school. The white-coat prodders had decided to send her away to a new place for "better treatment," so this was her last day for God knows how long. She would be going to another hospital. They all kept insisting that it wasn't hospital—even her mother—but a special residential centre for children and young adults with arthritis; just what she needed. But Prue was not calmed by their explanations. She had grown weary and resigned towards their soothing platitudes and downright lies. With a churning in her stomach, she braced herself for the worst.

But although this imminent event lay in her mind like a heavy, dulling ache, there was a more pressing engagement awaiting her at school.

She had been half dared, half coaxed into promising Andy Easter a look down her knickers—as long as she was allowed a look down his. She and Sally had giggled over the prospect all week, and in high bravado she had announced the forthcoming exploit for days. Now the whole class knew about it, and boys and girls alike laughed and chattered expectantly as she entered the classroom.

Sally was excited and anxious, a great bubbling jitter of worry.

"What if you're caught? What if they tell your mum?"

"Mum won't care, she knows I'm not stupid. I'd say it was just a silly game. Anyway, we won't get caught—he's only getting a few seconds look! That's the dare!"

Sammy Smith, one of their gang, a small compact tomboy of a girl with twisting wiry hair, pulled a face.

"You'll have to watch him, 'e's a bugger! Don't let him touch nothin'! If 'e does I'll whack him for year!"

Sammy was tough, renowned for hurtling down the corridors on her three-wheeled walking frame, scattering unwary younger pupils as she went.

"Oh blimey, no touching, 'course not!" Prue laughed, hiding the lurch in her stomach which reminded her suddenly not only of the present embarrassing scrape she was in, but also of her appointment with new white-coats tomorrow. She could hardly believe that she was leaving all her friends, Miss Tobin, and her mum and brother, for who knew how long. And thoughts of her mum brought back the painful scene at breakfast.

Andy was grinning at her across the classroom, tapping his flies with the palm of his hand, a swanking display for his sniggering mates. She pulled a disgusted face at him before turning back to the gang. At least there was a morning full of lessons before she had to Do It.

No one was allowed to watch, they both insisted on that, meeting inside the stationery cupboard, at the edge of the assembly hall. Their friends waited outside, giggling and hushing each other, keeping a sharp watch for teachers or prowling Snotty Scott.

Prue had worked herself up into a perfect state of arrogant devilry, deciding this was the only way she could get through the ordeal. Anyhow, her mother had taught her not to be ashamed of anything to do with her private parts (although she didn't like Prue to display her bumpy lumpy legs), saying that they were hers and she should be proud to be a woman.

Now here she was, wearing her best pink knickers, facing Andy and staring him in the eye, allowing him no chance to renege on his part of the dare. He looked up at her, sheepish now the door was shut, his grin not so swanky.

"Well?" said Prue, keen to get it over with. Mum might have told her to be proud of her "Miss Mary" but at this instant she felt silly and embarrassed.

"Who's going to go first, then?" he asked uncertainly, playing with the top of his trousers.

"We'll do it together. Let's count to three, then—then show ourselves—only for five seconds—we'll count together."

Her stomach was doing somersaults. A tiny voice somewhere asked her why she was being so childish. It was too late to answer that.

Andy had his hands ready at his zip. Prue hooked her stiff fingers with some difficulty into her knickers. Looking down at him, a pang of pity hit her. What a sorrowful sight he was. He was terrified! But being a boy he couldn't let on, could he? She felt strong and in charge. Why was she afraid? She'd seen a willy, on Rory and in books. His couldn't be any more peculiar or strange. She decided to display herself with a flourish.

"Right then . . . get ready, let's count together . . . one . . . two . . . three!"

A quick extra second of struggle with unwieldy clothes and there they stood.

"One chim-pan-zee, TWO chim-pan-zee . . ." Prue stared hard at the grey-pink length of flesh that lay limp and wrinkled in Andy's hand. She wanted to laugh but managed a less insulting smile instead, noticing that Andy was avidly looking down as she held her dress under her chin. She stepped back slightly, her legs moving apart. His willy looked like a sagging sausage that was going off she decided, and those straggles of hair around it, yuck!

". . . FIVE chim-pan-zee!" they chorused together before hastily covering themselves. Outside the others were growing restless. Andy still looked nervous.

"Er . . . it's not very big, is it? I mean, my brother has got a really huge one."

Prue wanted to laugh out loud. She was going away from all this tomorrow, and she knew how much she would miss it. She would even miss Andy.

"Well, I don't really know. It looked just the same as the others I've seen," Prue remarked airily, amazed at how timid he had become in displaying his prized part to her. 'How did I do?'

She didn't actually care much what he thought but was interested in what he might say.

He looked up at her, taller as she was, and smiled shyly.

"You're great, Prue. I really like you. You're pretty."

Prue was flabbergasted by this response, expecting something rude and smart. But she was in control and she knew it. She also knew now that the great, bragging, flashy bugger Andy Easter had never seen a woman's private part before. She glowed and smiled.

"You're all right too, mate." There was a little devil suddenly inside her. Tomorrow this would all be gone . . . for a long time, she just knew it.

"Give us a kiss, then." The words came out of her mouth, a dancing request half-filled with laughter, half with blank nerve. She bent down to him, put her hand on his shoulder, and pressed her lips against his.

She didn't want him to forget her in a hurry while she was away.

Some Like Indians Endure

Paula Gunn Allen

i have it in my mind that
dykes are indians

they're a lot like indians
they used to live as tribes
they owned tribal land
it was called the earth

they were massacred
lots of times
they always came back
like the grass
like the clouds
they got massacred again

they thought caringsharing
about the earth and each other
was a good thing
they rode horses
and sang to the moon

but i don't know
about what was so longago
and it's now that dykes
make me think i'm with indians
when i'm with dykes

because they bear
witness bitterly
because they reach
and hold
because they live every day
with despair laughing
in cities and country places
because earth hides them
because they know
the moon
because they gather together
enclosing
and spit in the eye of death

indian is an idea
some people have
of themselves
dyke is an idea some women
have of themselves
the place where we live now
is idea
because whiteman took
all the rest
because father
took all the rest
but the idea which
once you have it
you can't be taken
for somebody else
and have nowhere to go
like indians you can be
stubborn

the idea might move you on,
ponydrag behind
taking all your loves and
children maybe downstream

maybe beyond the cliffs
but it hangs in there
an idea
like indians
endures

it might even take your
whole village with it
stone by stone
or leave the stones
and find more
to build another village
someplace else

like indians
dykes have fewer and fewer

someplace elses to go
so it gets important
to know
about ideas and
to remember or uncover
the past
and how the people
traveled
all the while remembering
the idea they had
about who they were
indians, like dykes
do it all the time

dykes know all about dying
and that everything belongs
to the wind
like indians
they do terrible things
to each other
out of sheer cussedness
out of forgetting
out of despair
so dykes
are like indians
because everybody is related
to everybody
in pain
in terror
in guilt
in blood
in shame
in disappearance
that never quite manages

to be disappeared
we never go away
even if we're always
leaving

because the only home
is each other
they've occupied all
the rest
colonized it; an
idea about ourselves is all
we own

and dykes remind me of indians
like indians dykes
are supposed to die out
or forget
or drink all the time
or shatter
go away
to nowhere
to remember what will happen
if they don't

they don't anyway—even
though the worst happens

they remember and they
stay
because the moon remembers
because so does the sun
because the stars
remember
and the persistent stubborn grass
of the earth

Women, Sexuality, and Social Change in the Middle East

Pinar Ilkkaracan

INTRODUCTION

In this age of globalization, women's bodies and sexuality are increasingly becoming arenas of intense conflict. Conservative and religious right political forces are fiercely trying to maintain or reinforce traditional mechanisms of control over women's sexuality and even create new ones. Four UN conferences held in the 1990s—the 1994 International Conference on Population and Development (ICPD) in Cairo, the 1995 Beijing Conference, the 1999 five-year review of the ICPD (ICPD+5), and the 2000 five-year review of the Beijing Conference (Beijing+5)—witnessed the Catholic and Muslim religious right engaging in unprecedented cooperation to oppose and restrict women's right to control their bodies and sexuality.

At the same time, in the last decade, women around the globe have joined forces to counter these moves from the conservative and religious right and have engaged in an international struggle against violations of their sexual and reproductive rights—a struggle transcending national borders as well as real or constructed North–South and East–West dichotomies. A visible sign of the success of this struggle is the significant change in the way international agencies use language. As the global women's movement has become stronger and the "rights" approach has gained credibility, "reproductive rights" discourse has increasingly replaced reproductive "health" and "sexual health" and become a focus of interest and a part of common terminology. The shift from "sexual health" to "sexual rights" constitutes the last link in this chain of global change as introduced by the global women's movement.

In this context, several traditional cultural practices—such as honor crimes, the stoning of women accused of adultery, virginity tests, or female genital cutting—in Muslim societies, including the Middle East, have increasingly drawn the attention of the Western media and public in recent years as human rights abuses. The lack of information on Islam and on the wide diversity of Muslim societies, the parallel rise of the Islamic religious right, which claims such customary practices to be Islamic, and the tendency to "essentialize" Islam are some of the factors that have led to the incorrect portrayal in the West of such practices as Islamic. This depiction is not only misleading, but also stands in sharp contrast to the efforts of women's movements in Muslim societies, which, in their fight against such practices, are campaigning to raise public consciousness that these practices are against Islam. In fact, the incorrect depiction contributes to the Islamic religious right's cause of vigorously trying to create extreme forms of control over women and their sexuality by incorporating and universalizing the worst customary practices in the name of religion.

. . .

SEXUALITY IN THE QUR'AN AND THE EARLY FIQH TEXTS: THE INITIAL ROOTS OF CONTROVERSY

Several researchers have pointed to the contradiction between the notion of gender equality in the Qur'an and the patriarchal misinterpretation of it by male religious authorities in the early and medieval canonical texts traditionally accepted as establishing Islam's normative practices (Mernissi, 1987; Sabbah, 1984; An-Naim, 1990;

Ahmed, 1991, 1992; Hassan, n.d.; Wadud, 1999; Mir-Hosseini, 2001). As in other monotheistic religions, the classical *fiqh* texts—that is, texts of early Islamic legal jurisprudence—ignored gender equality as it was presented in the Qur'an and introduced interpretations in line with the prevailing patriarchal social order. Thus, one can find several logical contradictions in the classical *fiqh* texts since they reflect two dissenting voices: an egalitarian voice inspired by revelation (*wahy*) and a patriarchal voice incorporating the social order and the social, cultural, and political pragmatisms of the time and place where Islam was trying to ensure its survival (Mir-Hosseini, 2001). An analysis of discourses based on the Qur'an and the early literature of Islamic legal jurisprudence leads to contradictory conclusions about the construction of women's sexuality in Islam.

Mir-Hosseini (2001), for example, asserts that this contradiction is most evident in the rules that classical jurists devised for regulating the formation and the termination of the marriage contract—a product of tension in which the voice of the patriarchal social order outweighs the egalitarian voice of the revelation (*wahy*). Her analysis of the classical *fiqh* texts on marriage shows that the model of gender relations in the early texts of Islamic jurisprudence is grounded in the patriarchal ideology of pre-Islamic Arabia, which continued into the Islamic era in a modified form through a set of male-dominated theological, legal, and social theories and assumptions, such as "women are created of and for men."

These theories stood in sharp contradiction to the Qur'an, which holds that the relationship of men and women is one of equality, mutuality, and cordiality. In the Qur'an, Eve is not a delayed product of Adam's rib, as in the Christian and Jewish traditions; instead, the two were born from a single soul: "O mankind! Be careful of your duty to your Lord, who created you from a single soul and from it created its mate and from them twain hath spread abroad a multitude of men and women" (Surah 4:1).[1] It was not just Eve, but both Adam and Eve, who let the Devil convince them to eat the forbidden fruit.[2] Islam has recognized that both women and men have sex drives and the right to sexual fulfillment and has also acknowledged that women, like men, experience orgasms. The Islamic view of love and sexuality—in which pleasure and responsibility are coexistent—removes any guilt from the sexes (Bouhdiba, 1998). Marital intercourse does not need the justification of reproduction and is based on the right to sexual fulfillment; contraception is permitted and abortion tolerated (Musallam, 1989). Women's ejaculation was recognized in the *hadiths,* the traditional body and texts of knowledge and memories about the Prophet's life, his custom and his words, where female sexuality is regarded as active, like male sexuality (Ahmed, 1989).

. . .

Some Qur'anic verses, especially the story of Zuleikha and Yusuf, have laid the foundation for interpretations of women as capable of greater sexual desire and temptation than men—casting women as beguiling seductresses and men as susceptible to seduction but rational and capable of self-control.[3] Yet, several of the customary practices aimed at controlling women's sexuality, like honor crimes, stoning for adultery, or female genital cutting, cannot be justified by appeal to the Qur'an. The Qur'an forbids adultery,[4] like the other two main monotheistic religions, Judaism and Christianity, and foresees heavy punishment (100 lashes) for both women and men guilty of adultery or fornication.[5] It requires, however, four witnesses to the act.[6] Otherwise, if a woman denies the accusation, then it is her word that must be accepted rather than that of her husband.[7] Thus, according to the Qur'an, the punishment for adultery, meant both for women and men, can only be carried out if conviction is based on the testimony of a minimum of four witnesses. In addition, although it foresees a stern punishment of 100 lashes, it is not stoning or execution—contrary to the customary practices of honor crimes or stoning as carried out in some Muslim countries. Stoning as a punishment in cases of adultery has only recently been introduced as an "Islamic" practice by the Islamic religious right in Iran, Pakistan, and Nigeria.

. . .

Islam has set consent of both the woman and the man as a precondition of marriage. In the main classical schools of legal jurisprudence of Islam (*Hanafi* or *Shi'a* law, for example), a girl who has attained majority age is free to contract marriage without the consent of her father or any other relative and cannot be forced into a marriage by her male relatives (Carroll, 2000). Accordingly, the practice of "forced marriages" in Muslim societies constitutes a clear violation of the basic premise of marriage as specified in the Qur'an.

The diversity of Muslim societies shows that Islam does not have a static or monolithic tradition. Islam has absorbed not only the practices and traditions of the two other monotheistic religions—Judaism and Christianity—from the region of its birth, but also other pre-Islamic practices and traditions from the geographic location in which it strove to survive and gain power as a cultural and political system. Thus, it is very difficult to define what is intrinsic to Islam in shaping sexual behavior. The issue becomes even more complicated when we attempt to analyze its interaction with various socioeconomic and political systems. In the following, I will explore some of these factors, which affect the norms governing and practices of women's sexuality in the Middle East and Maghreb.

GENDER INEQUALITY AND SEXUALITY IN THE MIDDLE EAST AND THE MAGHREB

. . .

The Middle East shows a great degree of diversity in the formulation of legal codes and their application to women's everyday lives, which is also the case in the rest of the Muslim world. The extent of the legal reforms redefining gender relations varies greatly between countries. While in Turkey, for example, modernization included the adoption of Western legal codes and aimed at complete secularization,[8] [and] most Gulf countries preserved their interpretation of Islamic legal jurisprudence as the fundamental law in all juridical areas. . . .

Despite the positive impact of all modern legal, educational, and economic reforms on the position of women and the growing strength of feminist movements, the majority of women living in the region have not benefited from the opportunities created, especially in the economic and political spheres. The United Nations Development Program (UNDP) 2002 report, *Arab Human Development,* states that the Arab world shows the fastest improvement in female education of any region, with female literacy expanding threefold since 1970, and primary and secondary enrollment doubling. However, in terms of the Gender Empowerment Measure, which the UNDP introduced in 1995, the Arab region's ranking is lower than any region except sub-Saharan Africa. Arab countries have the lowest rate of women's participation in the workforce and the lowest rate of representation in parliaments. More than half of Arab women are illiterate. The maternal mortality rate is double that of Latin American and the Caribbean and four times that of East Asia (UNDP, 2002). The collective mechanisms aimed at controlling women's bodies and sexuality continue to be one of the most powerful tools of patriarchal management of women's sexuality and a root cause of gender inequality in the region.

THE CONTRADICTORY IMPACT OF MODERNIZATION ON WOMEN'S SEXUAL LIVES

Modernization movements and efforts occupied a central place in the regional political discourses of the nineteenth and early twentieth centuries in the Middle East. Women's status has also occupied a central place in the modernization efforts in the region; for decades, the modernists argued that reforms in the position of women in the economic, educational, and legal spheres would lead to more "modernization," and consequently, to greater gender equality in all spheres. Women were among the first who recognized the complex and contradictory nature of modernity and that modernization projects did not necessarily lead to real gender equality for all or in every sphere.

. . .

Mervat Hatem (1997) illustrates a good example of the contradictory effects of modernization on women's sexual lives in her research on the professionalization of health in nineteenth-century Egypt. The school of *Hakimahs,* which was established in the early nineteenth century and was the first modern state school for women in Egypt, aimed at replacing local midwifery practices with modern female professionals. While the local Egyptian midwives (*daya*s) performed circumcisions on girls, thus implementing patriarchal control of women's sexuality, they also provided women with folk-based means to control their reproductive capacities, such as supplying them with information on fertility and providing quick and effective abortions. Although the establishment of the *Hakimahs* school established an opportunity for middle-class women to become professionals, it also led to a loss of power for traditional midwives, contributed to the extinction of women's indigenous knowledge, and to a state policy of criminalizing abortion. Moreover, the new midwives from the middle class were given the task of policing working class midwives (*daya* s) and their middle and working class clients.

. . .

THE NATIONALIST IDEOLOGIES AND WOMEN'S SEXUALITY

Nationalist movements and ideologies that accompanied the foundation of nation-states in the Middle East have posed contradictory roles for women. On the one hand, they allowed women—especially those from the middle and upper classes—to participate more fully in social and political life, as they disrupted traditional gender roles and relations. On the other hand, they redefined women's roles as mothers and bearers of the nation and its newly constructed legacy (Kandiyoti, 1996; Mehdid, 1996; Pettman, 1996; Saigol, 2000). This led to the emergence of new strategies to control women, and especially their sexuality, which was meant to serve the reproduction and maintenance of the newly constructed "national identity" and "uniqueness" of community.

In Turkey, for example, the foundation of a secular nation-state and the "modern" Turkish Republic set revolutionary changes in gender roles as a priority in order to destroy the links to the Ottoman Empire and to strike at the foundations of religious hegemony. However, nationalist discourses almost competed with Islamic discourses in their zeal to regulate the sexual identity and behavior of Turkish women. The leaders and the ideologues of the Turkish nationalist movement took great pains to establish a new nationalist morality regarding women's sexuality in which the new rights gained by women in the public sphere could be justified as an integral part of so-called Turkish culture (Kandiyoti, 1988). The leading ideologue of the newly constructed Turkish identity, Ziya Gökalp, went so far as to construct the principal virtue of Turkish women as chastity, *iffet.* In fact, this construction has been so powerful that Turkish women are still faced with the human rights violations it causes. The Statute for Awards and Discipline in High School Education, enacted in January 1995, states that "proof of unchastity" is a valid reason for expulsion from the formal educational system. This statute, which served to institutionalize a customary practice, led to suicides of girls whom school authorities sent for so-called virginity tests. Female students were forced to undergo "virginity tests" even in such cases where a girl was merely seen walking with a male classmate on the playground. As a result of the Turkish women's movement's protests and campaigns, the Ministry of Justice banned virginity testing in January 1999.[9] However, in July 2001, the tests were reinstated for student nurses through a decree of the health minister, who is from the far-right National Action Party. The reinstatement of the tests led to extensive protests by the Turkish women's movement and international human rights organizations. Finally, in 2002, the Ministry of Education changed the Statute for Awards and Discipline and deleted the provision that stated "proof of unchastity" as a reason for expulsion from the formal educational system.

. . .

THE RISE OF THE ISLAMIC RELIGIOUS RIGHT AND ITS EFFORTS TO CONTROL WOMEN'S SEXUALITY

In the decades since World War II, several factors have contributed to the creation of a rather difficult and unfavorable atmosphere regarding the extension of liberal reforms, including reforms in the area of sexuality; these factors have also encouraged the growth of religious right-wing movements in the region. The failure of attempted social and economic reforms resulted in an increasing gap between the Westernized elite and the majority, leading to disillusionment with Westernized rulers. The widening gap of economic and political power between Muslim societies and the West, along with urbanization, migration, and increasing poverty, has contributed to the creation of an atmosphere where religious right-wing movements have gained the support of the masses. The founding of Israel and the resulting occupations and war have contributed to an increasingly hostile atmosphere against the West and facilitated the construction by fundamentalist groups of the West and its perceived culture as an "enemy."

The religious and nationalist fundamentalists make utmost use of this perceived threat against "Muslim" identity by constructing a "Muslim" or "national" female identity as a last sphere of control against the "enemy": the West. Thus, pressure on women to become bearers of constructed group identities and the control of women's sexuality are currently at the heart of many fundamentalist agendas. Their strategies are multifold; here I will attempt to outline some of them. The dress code, the most perceptible form of identity creation, has been high on the agenda of the Muslim religious right, which wanted to use the code's visibility as a demonstration of its political power....

Aware of the power of the imagery of *hijab* as a demonstration of its influence and authority, the Islamic religious right has sought to prescribe or violently enforce extreme forms of veiling that were specific to certain communities (for instance, the *chador* or *burqa*); veiling is intended to be a universal uniform for Muslim women, not only in the region but throughout the world, even in places where they were previously unheard of, such as Uzbekistan, Kashmir, or Senegal....

. . .

In the last two decades, the rise of the Islamic religious right has caused women in countries such as Iran, Algeria, and South Yemen to suffer the loss of previously gained legal rights, especially within the family. In 1979, two weeks after the overthrow of the Pahlavi dynasty through the Islamic revolution in Iran, the Family Protection Act of 1967—which restrained men's legal right to polygamous marriage by requiring either the court's or the first wife's permission, enforced a woman's right to divorce with mutual consent, and improved women's chances of retaining the custody of their children or at least visiting rights—was scrapped as un-Islamic (Hoodfar, 1996). Women were dismissed and barred from the judiciary and higher education (Najmabadi, 1998). In Algeria, in July 1984, the government adopted a repressive family law that legalized polygyny and rescinded Algerian women's rights in the family. Algerian women were quick to mobilize wide and fierce opposition but their strong resistance remained ineffective (Mahl, 1995; Moghadam, 1993). In 1990, the unification of North and South Yemen, which had fostered hopes for political openness and democracy in the country, resulted in a major disappointment for Yemeni women, both from the south and the north. Yemeni women in the north had hoped to profit from the egalitarian laws of the socialist regime in the south. These were basically secular in orientation, defining marriage as a contract with equal rights and responsibilities for men and women, including financial responsibility; they also abolished polygyny, made women's consent a basis of engagement for marriage, ended a man's right to unilateral divorce, and set the minimum age of marriage at 15 for girls and 16 for boys. However, because of tribal rebellion, urban terrorism, sharp cuts in Western and Gulf countries aid programs (in response to Yemen's refusal to join the anti-Iraq coalition after Iraq's invasion of Kuwait in

1990), the two factions in Yemen were usurped by open warfare, which contributed to the rise of the Islamic religious right. As is very often the case in war, the losers were women. Upon unification, the progressive family laws of the south were abolished. Not only did the women in southern Yemen lose the legal rights they had enjoyed since 1974, but the women of North Yemen, who had hoped for the incorporation of the greater degree of gender equality enshrined in the southern codes, had to bury their hopes (Boxberger, 1998; al-Basha, 2001).

THE IMPACT OF CHANGING SOCIAL VALUES AND FEMINIST ACTIVISM AROUND WOMEN'S SEXUAL RIGHTS

The violent imposition of practices leading to the Islamic religious right's violations of women's sexual rights presents a contradictory picture of the changing social values regarding sexuality in the region. Although premarital sex is still strongly prohibited in many countries, there is evidence, for example from Morocco, Lebanon, Tunisia, and Turkey, that it increasingly forms part of the experience of young people and that this change has created a social conflict between the patriarchal control of women's sexuality and the socioeconomic changes taking place in the region (Obermeyer, 2000; Khair Badawi, 2001; Belhadj, 2001; Mernissi, 1982; Cindoglu, 1997). Female genital cutting, which clearly has nothing to do with Islam, is now outlawed as a result of the efforts of women's advocacy groups in Egypt (al-Dawla, 2000). In recent years, activism against honor crimes in Palestine, Jordan, Pakistan, Egypt, and Turkey has grown, and women's NGOs have succeeded in putting the issue onto the agenda of national and international bodies (Albadeel Coalition, 2000; Yirmisbesoglu, 2000; Rouhana, 2001; Tadros, 2002; International Women's Health Coalition, 2000; Clarke, 2001). A popular Friday night television program in Lebanon, *Al-Chater Yehki* (*Let the Brave Speak Out*), topped the ratings with its live debates on sexuality, with issues ranging from masturbation to incest or homosexuality (Foster, 2000). . . .

Alongside the legal setbacks in Iran, Algeria, and Yemen must be set the advocacy and lobbying by national women's movements that have led to legal reforms for greater gender equality in the family in Turkey, Egypt, and Jordan. In Turkey, the reform of the civil code in 2001 ended the supremacy of men in marriage by removing a clause defining the man as the head of the family. Through the reform of the its civil code, Turkey has become the only predominantly Muslim country that has legally established the full equality of men and women in the family. The new Turkish civil code raises the legal age for marriage to 18 for both women and men (it was previously 17 for men and 15 for women) and makes the equal division of property acquired during marriage as the default property regime. The concept of "illegitimate children"—that is, children born out of wedlock—has been abolished, and the custody of these children is given to their mothers.[10] In addition, in October 2001, Article 41 of the Turkish constitution was amended, redefining the family as an entity that is based on equality between spouses. . . .

The last two decades have also witnessed the emergence of a reformist discourse that argues for equality in Islam on all fronts. This reformist discourse seeks to analyze "women's sexuality as defined by social circumstances, not by nature and divine will" (Mir-Hosseini, 2001: 12). As such, it removes the issue of sexuality or women's status from the domain of *fiqh* rulings to social practices and norms, which are neither sacred nor immutable but human and changing. This new movement is opening new windows by bridging the gap between the traditional divide of the so-called traditionalists—ranging from conservatives to the religious right—and the so-called progressives, including the feminists, blurring the traditional fixed fronts in Muslim societies as constructed in the last century. In addition, women are increasingly daring to participate and invade the domain of production of religious knowledge, a domain of power traditionally owned by men.

CONCLUSION

The sexual oppression of women in the Middle East and elsewhere in the Muslim world is not the result of an oppressive vision of sexuality based on Islam, but a combination of historical, sociopolitical, and economic factors. Although an analysis of the Qur'an and the literature traditionally accepted as establishing the normative practices of Islam leads to contradictory conclusions about the construction of women's sexuality in early Islam, several customary practices that allow violations of women's human rights in the region—honor crimes, stoning, female genital cutting, or virginity tests—have no Koranic basis, as women researchers and activists in the region point out. Moreover, the prevalence of these practices varies greatly among the countries in the region.

. . .

The changing social values in the region and the increasing activity of women's groups in the last decade have begun to act as powerful agents of change that have led to new attitudes toward sexuality, especially among young people, and to new progressive legal and social reforms. These have established the basis of new rights regarding women's sexuality and their status in the family in, for example, Turkey, Egypt, and Jordan. The last two decades also witnessed the emergence of a reformist discourse that argues for equality in Islam on all fronts. This reformist discourse seeks to analyze "women's sexuality as defined by social circumstances, not by nature and divine will" (Mir-Hosseini, 2001: 12). As such, it removes the issue of sexuality or women's status from the domain of *fiqh* rulings to social practices and norms. This approach builds a bridge between the old fixed fronts in their struggles of power over the construction of women's sexuality as constructed in the last century. Another factor that also promises change in the sexual domain is the increasing participation of women in the traditionally male-dominated production of religious knowledge.

NOTES

1. All references to the Qur'an in this article use the translation by Pickthall (1953).

2. "And We said: O Adam! Dwell thou and thy wife in the Garden and eat ye freely (of the fruits) thereof where ye will; but come not nigh this tree lest ye* become wrongdoers. But Satan caused them to deflect therefrom and expelled them from the (happy) state in which they were; and We said: Fall down**, one of you a foe onto the other! There shall be for you on earth a habitation and provision for a time." (Surah 2:35–36). (*Here, the command is in the dual, as addressed to Adam and his wife; **here, the command is in the plural, as addressed to Adam's race.)

3. For an analysis of the discussion about the story of Zuleikha and Yusuf in the Islamic tradition, and the need for and possibilities of alternative feminist readings of the story, see Merguerian and Najmabadi (1997).

4. "And come not near unto adultery. Lo! It is an abomination and an evil way" (Surah 17:32).

5. "The adulterer and the adulteress, scourge ye each one of them (with) a hundred stripes. And let not pity for the twain withhold you from obedience to Allah, if ye believe in Allah and the Last Day. And let a party of believers witness their punishment." (Surah 24:2)

6. "And those who accuse honourable women but bring not four witnesses, scourge them (with) eighty stripes and never (afterward) accept their testimony—They indeed are evildoers." (Surah 24:4)

7. "As for those who accuse their wives but have no witnesses except themselves; let the testimony of one of them be four testimonies (swearing by Allah that he is of those who speak the truth;

   And yet a fifth, invoking the curse of Allah on him if he is of those who lie.

   And it shall avert the punishment from her if she bear witness before Allah four times that the thing he saith is indeed false,

   And a fifth (time) that the wrath of Allah be upon her if he speaketh truth. . . .

   Why did they not produce four witnesses? Since they produce not witnesses, they verily are liars in the sight of Allah" (Surah 24: 6, 7, 8, 9, 13).

8. The Turkish Civil Code was translated and adapted from the Swiss Civil Code of the time and the Turkish Penal Code was adapted from the Italian Penal Code.

9. For a discussion of the virginity tests in Turkey from a human rights perspective, see Human Rights Watch (1994) and Seral (2000).

10. For a more comprehensive analysis and description of the reform of the Turkish Civil Code, see Women for Women's Human Rights–New Ways (2002).

REFERENCES

Ahmed, Leila. "Arab Culture and Writing Women's Bodies." *Feminist Issues* 9:1 (Spring 1989): 41–55. Rpt. in Ilkkaracan, ed. (2000): 51–65.

————. "Early Islam and the Position of Women: The Problem of Interpretation." *Women in Middle Eastern History: Shifting Boundaries in Sex and Gender.* Eds. Nikki R. Keddie and Beth Baron. New Haven: Yale University Press, 1991: 58–73.

————. *Women and Gender in Islam.* New Haven: Yale University Press, 1992.

Albadeel Coalition. "Albadeel Coalition Against 'Family Honor' Crimes." In Ilkkaracan, ed. (2000): 399–401.

al-Basha, Amal. "Reproductive Health in Yemen: Aspirations and Reality in Applications of Human Rights to Reproductive and Sexual Health." Paper presented at the international meeting on "Women, Sexuality and Social Change in the Middle East and the Mediterranean," organized by Women for Women's Human Rights (WWHR)–New Ways, Istanbul, Sept. 28–30, 2001.

An-Naim, Abdullah. *Toward an Islamic Reformation.* Cairo: American University in Cairo Press, 1990.

Belhadj, Ahlem. "Le Comportement Sexuel des Femmes en Tunisie." Paper presented at the international meeting on "Women, Sexuality and Social Change in the Middle East and the Mediterranean," organized by Women for Women's Human Rights (WWHR)–New Ways, Istanbul, Sept. 28–30, 2001.

Bouhdiba, Abdelwahab. *Sexuality in Islam.* London: Saqi Books, 1998 [1975].

Boxberger, Linda. "From Two Sisters to One: Women's Lives in the Transformation of Yemen." *Women in Muslim Societies: Diversity within Unity.* Boulder: Lynne Riener Publishers, 1998: 119–133.

Carroll, Lucy. "Law, Custom and the Muslim Girl in the U.K." *Dossier 20.* Montpellier: Women Living Under Muslim Laws, n.d.: 68–75. Rpt. in Ilkkaracan, ed. (2000): 245–252.

Cindoglu, Dilek. "Virginity Tests and Artificial Virginity in Modern Turkish Medicine." *Women's Studies International Forum* 20:2 (1997): 253–261. Rpt. in Ilkkaracan, ed. (2000): 215–228.

Clarke, Lisa. "Beijing+5 and Violence against Women." *Holding on to the Promise: Women's Human Rights and the Beijing+5 Review.* Ed. Cynthia Meillon in collaboration with Charlotte Bunch. New Jersey: Center for Women's Global Leadership, 2001: 147–155.

al-Dawla, Aida Seif. "The Story of the FGM Task Force: An Ongoing Campaign against Female Genital Mutilation." In Ilkkaracan, ed. (2000): 427–433.

Foster, Angel M. "Conference Report: Sexuality in the Middle East, Oxford, June 23–25, 2000." Oxford: St. Anthony's College, The Middle East Center, 2000.

Hassan, Riffat. "The Role and Responsibilities of Women in the Legal and Ritual Tradition of Islam (Shari'ah)." *Riffat Hassan: Selected Articles.* Montpellier: Women Living Under Muslim Laws, n.d.

Hatem, Mervat F. "The Professionalization of Health and the Control of Women's Bodies as Modern Governmentalities in Nineteenth-Century Egypt." *Women in the Ottoman Empire: Middle Eastern Women in the Early Modern Era.* Ed. Madeline C. Zilfi. Leiden: Brill, 1997: 66–80. Rpt. in Ilkkaracan, ed. (2000): 67–79.

Hoodfar, Homa. "The Women's Movement in Iran: Women at the Crossroad of Secularization and Islamization." Paper presented at the conference on "Women's Solidarity Beyond All Borders," organized by Women for Women's Human Rights (WWHR), Istanbul, Oct. 11–12, 1996.

Human Rights Watch. *A Matter of Power: State Control of Women's Virginity in Turkey.* New York: Human Rights Watch, 1994.

Ilkkaracan, Pinar. *A Brief Overview of Women's Movements in Turkey: The Influence of Political Discourses.* Instanbul: Women for Women's Human Rights (WWHR), 1996. Rpt. in *Dossier 16.* Montpellier: Women Living Under Muslim Laws, n.d.: 93–103.

————. "Introduction." In Ilkkaracan, ed. (2000): 1–15.

————. "Conference on Women, Sexuality and Social Change in the Middle East and the Mediterranean." *Women's Global Network for Reproductive Rights Newsletter* 75:1 (2002).

Ilkkaracan, Pinar, ed. *Women and Sexuality in Muslim Societies.* Istanbul: Women for Women's Human Rights (WWHR)–New Ways, 2000.

International Women's Health Coalition. "Beijing+5: Analysis of Negotiations and Final 'Further Actions' Document." Comp. Francoise Girard. New York: International Women's Health Coalition, 2000 <www.iwhc.org/uploads/FutherActions%2Epdf>.

Kandiyoti, Deniz. "Contemporary Feminist Scholarship and Middle East Studies." *Gendering the Middle East.* Ed. Deniz Kandiyoti. London: I. B. Tauris, 1996: 1–27.

————. "Slave Girls, Temptresses and Comrades: Images of Women in the Turkish Novel." *Feminist Issues* 8:1 (Spring 1988): 35–50. Rpt. in Ilkkaracan, ed. (2000): 91–106.

Khair Badawi, Marie-Therese. "Le Désir Amputé, Sexual Experience of Lebanese Women." Paper presented at the international meeting on "Women, Sexuality and Social Change in the Middle East and the Mediterranean," organized by Women for Women's Human Rights (WWHR)–New Ways, Istanbul, Sept. 28–30, 2001.

Mahl. "Women on the Edge of Time." *New Internationalist* 270 (August 1995) <www.newint.org/issue270/270edge.html>.

Mehdid, Malika. "En-Gendering the Nation State: Women, Patriarchy and Polities in Algeria." *Women and the State: International Perspectives.* Eds. Shirin M. Rai and Geraldine Lievesley. London: Taylor and Francis, 1996: 78–102.

Merguerian, Gayane Karen, and Afsanah Najmabadi. "Zuleykha and Yusuf: 'Whose Best Story'?" *International Journal of Middle East Studies* 29 (1997): 485–508.

Mernissi, Fatima. "Virginity and Patriarchy." *Women's Studies International Forum* 5:2 (1982): 183–194. Rpt. in Ilkkaracan, ed. (2000): 203–214.

————. *Beyond the Veil: Male-Female Dynamics in a Modern Muslim Society.* Bloomington: Indiana University Press, 1987 [1975].

Mir-Hosseini, Ziba. "The Construction of Gender in Islamic Legal Thought and Strategies for Reform." Paper presented for the workshop on "Islamic Family Law and Justice for Muslim Women," organized by Sisters in Islam, Kuala Lumpur, June 8–10, 2001.

Moghadam, Valentine M. *Modernizing Women: Gender and Social Change in the Middle East.* Boulder: Lynne Riener Publishers, 1993.

Musallam, Basim F. *Sex and Society in Islam.* Cambridge: Cambridge University Press, 1989 [1983].

Najmabadi, Afsaneh. "Feminism in an Islamic Republic." *Islam, Gender and Social Change.* Eds. Yvonne Yazbeck Haddad and John L. Esposito. New York: Oxford University Press, 1998. 59–84.

Obermeyer, Carla Makhlouf. "Sexuality in Morocco: Changing Context and Contested Domain." *Culture, Health and Sexuality* 2:3 (2000): 239–254.

Pettman, Jan Jindy. "Boundary Politics: Women, Nationalism and Danger." *New Frontiers in Women's Studies: Knowledge, Identity and Nationalism.* Eds. Mary Maynard and June Purvis. London: Taylor and Francis, 1996: 187–202.

Pickthall, Mohammed Marmaduke, trans. *The Meaning of the Glorious Koran.* New York: Mentor Books, 1953.

Rouhana, Zoya. "Obedience: A Legalized Social Custom." Paper presented at the international meeting on "Women, Sexuality and Social Change in the Middle East and the Mediterranean," organized by Women for Women's Human Rights (WWHR)–New Ways, Istanbul, Sept. 28–30, 2001.

Sabbah, Fatna A. *Woman in the Muslim Unconscious.* New York: Pergamon Press, 1984.

Saigol, Rubina, "Militarisation, Nation and Gender: Women's Bodies as Arenas of Violent Conflict." In Ilkkaracan, ed. (2000): 107–120.

Seral, Gülsah. "Virginity Testing in Turkey: The Legal Context." Women and Sexuality in Muslim Societies. In Ilkkaracan, ed. (2000): 413–416.

Tadros, Mariz. "Like a Match Stick." *Al-Ahram Weekly Online.* No. 573 (14–20 February 2002) <www.ahram.org.eg/weekly/2002/573/lil.htm>.

United Nations Development Program (UNDP). *The Arab Human Development Report 2002.* New York: UNDP, 2002 <www.undp.org/rbas/ahdr/english.html>.

Wadud, Amina. *Qur'an and Woman: Rereading the Sacred Text from a Woman's Perspective.* Oxford: Oxford University Press, 1999.

Women for Women's Human Rights (WWHR)–New Ways. *The New Legal Status of Women in Turkey.* Istanbul: WWHR–New Ways, 2002.

Yirmisbesoglu, Vildan. "Sevda Gök: Killed for Honor." Rpt. in Ilkkaracan, ed. (2000): 389–391.

Girls, Media, and the Negotiation of Sexuality

Gigi Durham Meengleshi

Adolescence for girls in the United States has been characterized as "a troubled crossing,"[1] a period marked by severe psychological and emotional stresses. Recent research indicates that the passage out of childhood for many girls means that they experience a loss of self-esteem and self-determination as cultural norms of femininity and sexuality are imposed upon them.[2]

Much attention has been paid over the last decade or more to the role of the mass media in this cultural socialization of girls:[3] clearly, the media are crucial symbolic vehicles for the construction of meaning in girls' everyday lives. The existing data paint a disturbing portrait of adolescent girls as well as of the mass media: on the whole, girls appear to be vulnerable targets of detrimental media images of femininity. In general, the literature indicates that media representations of femininity are restrictive, unrealistic, focused on physical beauty of a type that is virtually unattainable as well as questionable in terms of its characteristics, and filled with internal contradictions. At the same time, the audience analysis that has been undertaken with adolescent girls reveals that they struggle with these media representations but are ultimately ill-equipped to critically analyze or effectively resist them.

These studies are linked to the considerable body of research documenting adolescent girls' difficulties with respect to issues such as waning self-esteem,[4] academic troubles,[5] negative body image,[6] conflicts surrounding sexuality,[7] and other issues related to girls' development. Although the majority of these studies were conducted with upper-middle-class White girls, some of them take into account the impact of race, ethnicity, and class on girls' experiences of adolescence. These findings indicate that—contrary to popular belief—girls of color and girls from lower socioeconomic backgrounds are very hard hit by adolescence and have fewer available resources for help with problems like eating disorders, pregnancies, or depression.[8]

Bearing these issues and their implications for girls in mind, this study seeks to broaden and deepen our understanding of the role of the mass media in girls' socialization, with a particular emphasis on the context in which this socialization takes place. New theories of child development contend that socialization is context-specific and that the peer groups of childhood and adolescence are responsible for the transmission of cultural norms as well as the modification of children's personality characteristics.[9] However, most of the research done to date on adolescence and mass media does not take into account the peer group dynamics involved in media use, nor the race and class factors that might influence these processes.

The key question in this study, then, is how peer group activity and social context affect adolescent girls' interactions with mass media, especially in terms of their dealings with issues of gender and sexuality. This study consisted of a long-term participant observation of middle-school girls combined with in-depth interviews with the girls and their teachers. A significant aspect of the study is that the girls were from sharply varying race and class backgrounds, and these factors were crucial components of the analysis.

. . .

METHOD

Background of the Study

In order to gain a deep understanding of the social processes at work in adolescent girls' peer groups, a participant observation was conducted over a five-month period at two middle schools in a midsize city in the southwestern United States. The schools were very dissimilar. The first school, which I will call East Middle School,[10] was located on the "nonwhite" side of the racially segregated metropolis. The segregation is not, of course, officially codified; rather, the informal color line is the interstate highway that runs through the center of town. All areas to the east of the highway are tacitly designated as the African American and Latino[11] sections. The west side is the White side. The west side is also more affluent, more developed, supposedly safer, and more desirable in terms of real-estate values. The second school, West Middle School, was located on the west side of the city, in a different school district from East Middle School.

. . .

While many peer groups existed at both schools, the researcher became closely involved with just a few, and the findings discussed here are based on observations and interviews with the members of these few. The group names came from the girls themselves—terms like "preps" and "gangstas" were used by the students to identify various peer groupings. At East Middle School, the groups studied were:

1. The "preps." These girls were academic achievers, involved in school activities like student government and cheerleading, and relatively affluent in comparison to the rest of the students. They were known as the popular crowd. The group was fairly large, but its core members were Ariana (14, biracial—Latino and African American), Brittany (14, Anglo), Lourdes (14, Latina), Nona (15, African American), Marta (15, biracial—Latino and Native American), Rosa (14, Latina), and Rachel (14, African American). Girls who frequently associated with this group also included Mariah (14, African American), Mariana (14, Latina), Mercedes (15, Latina), and Janina (13, Latina).

2. The "gangstas." These girls were affiliated with the juvenile gangs of East Middle School and were considered to be at risk of academic and social failure by school authorities. Many of them were academic underachievers, and they tended not to be involved in school-sanctioned extracurricular activities. These girls were not economically advantaged, and many of them came from very troubled family backgrounds, with drug-addicted parents, histories of domestic violence, etc. The girls in this group included Nydia (15, Latina), Maria (15, Latina), Vanessa (14, Latina), Amy (14, Latina), and sometimes Mariana and Mercedes, who floated between the prep group and the gangsta group.

At West Middle School, two peer groups were studied:

1. The "preps." These girls were academic achievers, also involved in extracurricular activities like sports and cheerleading. They were considered to be "popular." They came from wealthy families and were trendsetters with regard to fashion, music, and the like, among the other students. The three girls who were central to this group were Jenny (14), Tara (14), and Sydney (14). All three were of Anglo/European ethnicity. The boys who were associated with them were athletes and the "skater" crowd.

2. The "regular girls." These girls were academic achievers but were not considered to be "popular," although they had many friends and were well-regarded by most of the other students. All of them were of Anglo/European ethnicity; one, Judith, was Jewish. The girls in this group were Audrey (14), Emma (15), Jonquil (14), Judith (14), Bobbi (14), and Lila (15). Judith and Bobbi were best friends.

ANALYSIS

While references to mass media abounded in the peer group conversations observed at both schools, it is important to note at the outset that none of the groups made any use of the news media in their day-to-day peer interactions. Discussions of politics and current events did not arise during the five months of observations; rather, popular culture was the common currency among the girls, and the media with the greatest communicatory utility were television, consumer magazines, and movies. These observations corroborate recent findings of declining use of the news media by young people.[12]

Media references cropped up much more frequently in the conversations of the students at West Middle School than at East. Students at East Middle School did use the mass media, but in their peer group discussions they were much more likely to talk about their community and church activities, their friends and relatives, and the incidents in their daily lives—for instance, the *quinceanera* celebrations which many of the Latina girls were planning. At West Middle School, by contrast, media references were almost constant: talk of movies, TV shows, and pop music featured in every conversation.

At both schools, mass media were in evidence. For example, most of the girls at both schools subscribed to *YM* and *Seventeen* magazines and carried them in their backpacks. Girls at both schools watched TV shows like *The X Files, Friends, Seinfeld, Daria, Sabrina the Teenage Witch,* and *Buffy the Vampire Slayer.* Girls at West Middle School were more likely to have seen current movies than the girls at East; they were also more involved with pop music.

The pervasiveness of popular culture at both schools was tied very closely to the single most important theme that emerged from the data: the dominance of the sociocultural norm of heterosexuality in the girls' lives. While this was addressed and negotiated in different ways depending on various contextual factors, compulsory heterosexuality functioned as the core ideology underpinning the girls' interpersonal and intragroup transactions, although it was seldom explicitly acknowledged. What was striking was that this norm of heterosexuality was central to the social worlds of girls at both schools, and it guided the girls'

behaviors and beliefs regardless of their racial, ethnic, and class differences, although it manifested itself in different ways based on these cultural variances.

The girls' efforts to understand and adapt to perceived social norms of heterosexuality played out principally through their ongoing constructions of femininity. The use of the mass media was woven into those constructions and served in various ways to cement the girls' identities within their peer groups as well as to secure their relationships to the broader social world. Themes of heterosexuality criss-crossed the girls' conversations and actions in multiple ways, but certain practices occurred frequently and repeatedly enough to constitute clearly discernible modalities of mass mediated heterosexual expression. These are described and analyzed in detail, below, under the thematic headings of (1) the discipline of the body, (2) brides and mothers, (3) homophobia and sexual confusion, and (4) iconic femininity.

The Discipline of the Body: Cosmetics, Clothes, and Diets

Bartky points out that "femininity is an artifice" and that women engage in "disciplinary practices that produce a body which in gesture and appearance is recognizably feminine."[13] My observations of the schoolgirls at East and West Middle Schools indicate that these disciplinary practices are acquired fairly early in life and are essential to the maintenance of adolescent girls' peer group configurations. At both schools, peer relationships hinged on these techniques for molding the female body in group-sanctioned ways.

Cosmetics and Grooming

At East Middle School, the application of cosmetics was a common group occurrence and one that sometimes transpired with the aid of magazines like *YM, Seventeen,* and *Glamour.* This happened most often among the "gangsta" girls, and it usually occurred in the classroom when students were given unstructured work time. On several occasions I observed them braiding and styling each others' hair, painting each others' fingernails, and applying makeup. During the yearbook class one afternoon, for example, when some students were writing stories or working on layouts, a group of the "gangsta" girls drifted together; one pulled out a makeup bag and began to apply cosmetics to another, while several gathered around to watch and comment. Most of the girls in this gathering belonged to the same friendship group, with a few outsiders joining them. Other girls who belonged to different peer groups kept away from them; one commented that the classroom wasn't a beauty salon.

Mariana, the 14-year-old Latina girl who was doing the make-over, went about it with great concentration, first applying lip-liner, then lipstick, then powder foundation, then eyeshadows of various colors, and finally mascara to her friend Mercedes' face. The girls were quiet and rapt while this was going on, watching the process in almost reverent silence, but after it was over they began to talk.

> LAURA: That looks good. That looks cute.
>
> MARIANA: I saw in *YM* that if you put white eyeshadow on like that, it makes your eyes look bigger.
>
> MERCEDES: (Opening her eyes wide): Does it work?
>
> MARIANA: I don't know. Yeah. A little bit, maybe.
>
> NYDIA: Her hair is pretty. My hair is so ugly.
>
> LAURA: Your hair is pretty.
>
> NYDIA: Naw, it's all dry and damaged. (Much discussion about their hair . . .)
>
> NYDIA: I like long hair. I want long hair. What shampoo do you use?
>
> MERCEDES: Pantene Pro-V.
>
> MARIANA: I use Wella conditioner.
>
> MERCEDES: My hair is all dry and I have split ends.

Nydia pulled a *Seventeen* magazine out of her backpack and flipped though it until she found an ad for Suave conditioner. "I need this," she said. "It's mois . . . tur . . . izing," she read from the ad, stumbling over the pronunciation. "'To replenish moisture in dry or damaged hair.' That's me."

This episode serves as an exemplar of the girls' preoccupation with the tools and techniques required to achieve physical beauty, and their use of mass media for guidance in the acquisition of those commodities. At East Middle School the girls who were more knowledgeable about beautification were also more "popular," which is to say that they were the central figures in their peer groups.

Clothes

Further, at East Middle School, peer groups were defined in part by their costuming. Conversations with the girls confirmed this: the main groups of girls were the "gangstas," students who were gang-identified; the "gangsta wannabes," who dressed and acted like gang affiliates, but who were not included in gang activities; the "preps," who were the honor students and the cheerleaders; and the "dorks," the social outcasts. The "dorks," according to Ariana, a member of the "prep" group, "didn't know how to dress." The Latina girls in the "gangsta" group had thin plucked eyebrows, wore dark lipstick and heavy eye makeup, and had chemically lightened their hair color. The girls in the "prep" group wore minimal makeup, but they plucked their eyebrows and sometimes experimented with hairstyles within a very conservative range of options (ponytails or sometimes curled hair). Their clothes usually reflected current trends in shopping-mall fashions. The "dorks" wore bluejeans and tee-shirts and tended not to draw attention to themselves via their costuming.

At West Middle School the groups, or "cliques" as they were called by the students, were also marked by their appearance and costuming. As Judith, a 14-year-old Jewish girl, explained,

> Some of the cliques have um like certain styles. Like the most popular people are kind of like preps, and they wear like The Gap and J. Crew, and then the other groups that kind of get stuff like that are, the skater group who are like grunge influenced . . . and then um, like there's this one group of girls that are like really into Contempo clothes, and they wear that a lot.

Her friend Bobbi added: "The people at the prep tables wear Nike, and Nike, and Nike . . . then there are the Kickers. You know, like cowboy wear. Like, they wear cowboy boots." Judith: "We don't like that style."

Consumer fashion thus was the principal means by which group identity was demarcated, although pop music was also used in the same way. Fashion traits seemed to be derived from advertising; music was related to clothing, and these connections were made from MTV as well as peer references. The skaters listened to hard rock and heavy metal music; the preps made much of knowing which bands were currently "hot" on the charts. The Kickers listened to country music.

    . . .

Diet and Weight

At East Middle School the girls were extremely critical of those who showed no interest in conforming to media-driven standards of fashion and beauty, and they were also very open about their own interest in those standards.

This was particularly striking during a conversation about food and dieting that occurred at the lunch table among the "popular" girls at East. One of the girls, Ariana, had brought to the table a newspaper article about teenagers' eating habits, which the girls all looked at. The article described teenage girls' poor eating habits, stating that teen girls are "more likely to skip meals, avoid milk, eat away from home, and fret about their weight."

BRITTANY: It's true, this is how we eat. Milk has calcium, doesn't it? I don't drink milk.

RACHEL: I only drink milk on cereal.

BRITTANY: I only drink water and tea.

ROSA: I drink everything except water and milk.

BRITTANY: I'm addicted to tea.

MARTA: I'm addicted to Dr. Pepper.

BRITTANY: I used to starve myself.

ARIANA: I did, too. It's easy after the first day. The first day is hard. But after that it's easy, you don't notice it.

MARTA: We don't eat real food, we'd get food poisoning.

They were eager to reify the connections between themselves and the girls described in the article, and it was important to them to find points of similarity between themselves and the news article's mediated construction of "teenage girls," however negative that construction might be.

Despite this, these girls did not usually discuss their bodies or their weight to any significant degree in their peer group conversations; nor did the girls in the "gangsta" group. At West Middle School, however, there was more open talk about body norms and more criticism of girls whose bodies did not conform to the ideal.

BOBBI: There is a girl who will wear like really really tight pants and like stripes with flowers or something, things that don't go together at all.

JUDITH: Who?

BOBBI: Kathy Smith. [author's note: name changed to protect privacy]

JUDITH: That's a fashion faux pas right there. Not to say any names or anything, but she wears like tank tops with really thin straps but she doesn't really have the body for it. . . .

BOBBI: It isn't her fault!

JUDITH: It isn't her fault or anything but I think she wears the wrong kind of stripes, I think there's certain kinds of stripes that like reveal certain things . . . and then she wore the opposite kind that reveal certain things. . . . She just looks all wrong. She does not have the right body for those kind of clothes.

The girls at West school were sensitized to issues of body image and eating disorders, and these topics cropped up frequently in their conversations. Eating disorders were a serious problem at this school; teachers informed me that a student had recently died of anorexia nervosa. Yet, interestingly, the girls' discussions hovered around resistance to dysfunctional images of body; they used discourse around these issues to find solidarity in critiquing problematic concepts of body.

AUDREY: Like anorexia and all that stuff, I don't understand that. It's just so stupid, I don't get it. How can you not eat?

JONQUIL: I couldn't ever be bulimic and keep throwing up.

EMMA: And there are some people at school, these girls, they'll eat like a carrot, 'cause they're afraid the guys will see them eating. I hate that.

AUDREY: At lunch, I eat like so much, I eat like three pieces of pizza every day. I don't care what guys think. People have to eat. That's just natural. . . .

JONQUIL: Biology.

AUDREY: Yeah. And people, they're afraid they'll think they're pigs or something if they eat too much. So they'll like go to the bathroom and eat. Some people eat lunch in the bathroom.

EMMA: It's so sad. You know Laurel. . . . She kind of copies things off magazines and TV and things . . . she's into like being perfect and skinny and not eating.

AUDREY: But you have to eat! I feel like saying, eat something!

Conversations with one of the teachers revealed that Jonquil in fact had had some problems with eating disorders; how many of the others had suffered from them was not ascertainable, but the issue was clearly on their minds. Here, the peer group served as a means of consolidating ideas about rejecting and resisting damaging ideals for female bodies. Individually, their engagement with their bodies may have been different, more self-critical and less defiant,[14] but the group context appeared to moderate those tendencies in more progressive directions. The conversation reflected the paradoxical nature of eating disorders and the culture of thinness in U.S. society:[15] while the girls understood eating disorders as pathological and abnormal, they would not admit their own involvement with these problems even as they subscribed in their daily lives to mediated norms of slenderness and beauty.

. . .

The girls' conversation kept the smoke-screen up, distancing the girls with obvious eating problems from the sociocultural norms of thinness and beauty that pervaded the group members' everyday lives.

Brides and Mothers

Flipping through magazines in the classroom, Nydia and Maria pause at an advertisement featuring a bride in a formal white wedding dress. They examine the photograph for several minutes.

NYDIA: Oh, that's a pretty dress.

MARIA: She looks so beautiful.

NYDIA: I want to have a long dress like that. I want a big veil and flowers.

At East Middle School mediated images of brides and motherhood were of vital interest to the girls. Again and again, they discussed TV and celebrity weddings with admiration and obsessive attention to detail.

ARIANA: You know what I did? I saw this wedding on TV, and the guys all wore Wranglers and tuxedo shirts . . . and then the bridesmaids were late, and the bride got wet and her hair got all messed up . . .

MARTA: What are you talking about?

ARIANA: A wedding where these guys wore Wrangler jeans and tuxedo shirts and jackets . . .

BRITTANY: That's how you're gonna get married.

MARTA: She's gonna have horses at the reception. (Giggles.)

ROSA: I want a formal wedding. Ariana, what color were the bridesmaids' dresses?

ARIANA: Pink, a really gross pink. I'm having pastel colors for my wedding.

BRITTANY: Did any of you watch the Waltons reunion?

ROSA: I did!

MARTA: I watched "The Brady Girls Get Married." Marcia and Jan were going to have a double wedding, but they kept fighting about what kind of wedding to have. . . .

BRITTANY: What kind did they want?

MARTA: I don't know, one wanted to go all formal, and the other one wanted something modern, I think. One ended up wearing a short gown, I think they call them tea-length? The other one was long.

ROSA: I want a long gown. And lots of brides-maids. Big weddings are nice.

ARIANA: Weddings should be special. It's your day, your special day.

On another occasion, when the girls were working in the computer lab on the Internet, a group of them found Madonna's home page and zeroed in instantly on photographs of her with her baby. They were especially delighted with one image of her when she was pregnant, exclaiming aloud about how "sweet" and "adorable" it was.

This valorization of marriage and maternity appeared to be in line with the trends in their lives. Teenage pregnancy is a significant problem at East Middle School—it is the main reason that girls drop out of that school. During the five months of this observation, on four different occasions, former seventh- and eighth-graders returned for campus visits with their babies in their arms. Their appearances were not greeted with any derision or gossip from their erstwhile classmates; rather, they were feted and embraced, the babies were cooed over, and the girls spoke with some longing of the day when they too would be mothers.

. . .

Homophobia and Sexual Confusion

On April 30, 1997, the TV show *Ellen* aired its notorious "coming-out" episode, in which the main character declared herself a lesbian. The show precipitated a discussion of homosexuality among the girls in the "prep" group at East Middle School; this conversation reiterated the refrain of homophobia that was a constant current in the students' lives at both East and West Middle Schools.

While overt discrimination based on race was rare at both schools, homophobia was an openly declared prejudice in the peer groups that were studied. Words like "fag" and "queer" were used casually as epithets; gossip about students' sexual orientations were a way of marking the social outcasts. At East Middle School the "coming-out" episode of *Ellen* served as a catalyst for a brief,

impassioned exchange about the iniquity of homosexuality.

ROSA: I don't think she should have done that. It's just wrong to go on TV and put that in front of everybody.

ARIANA: She should just keep it to herself.

BRITTANY: I think it's a sin and it shouldn't be on TV.   *Lesbians*

At the time, there was also a festival in town that the local hippies had celebrated for about twenty-five years. Marta asked me if I had ever been to it and whether "funny people" were there.

I asked her what she meant by "funny people" and she said, "You know. Like Ellen." She said she was afraid of those people.

None of the girls in the peer group expressed opinions that differed from these, but later that day, Nona was looking through a *People* magazine in class and came across a photograph of Ellen DeGeneres. At that point she paused and said thoughtfully to her teacher, who was sitting nearby, "It's kind of good that they showed that on TV because it lets people who are gay know that people's lives are like that."

Her comment was unusual in a milieu where gay-bashing was considered high sport. At West Middle School homophobia was similarly open and aggressive. One student, Jenny—one of the most popular girls in the eighth grade—had a notebook covered with pictures cut out of magazines. The right side of the notebook displayed pictures of celebrity figures she disliked, and the left side was adorned with photos of people she admired. Prominent on the right side of the notebook was the band Luscious Jackson, and Jenny had written "Sucks! Dikes, too!" (*sic*) across their image.

The "regular girls" were very aware of the rhetoric of compulsory heterosexuality in teen magazines and talked about it with some anger. As Audrey put it, "They make it seem like if you don't have a boyfriend, you're just nothing, which is really . . . I don't think it's true." Later, she added, "All of the articles are so superficial, they make you think like you have to be pretty to have friends or you have to have a boyfriend to be cool . . . and that's kind of stupid. . . ." Interestingly, in phrasing this resistance, she acknowledged her own susceptibility to the rhetoric. In other conversations these girls expressed aversion to the concept of homosexuality and distress at the idea of other students identifying themselves as gay or lesbian.

. . .

. . . Students were open in their rejection of homosexuality and their need to position themselves in the heterosexual mainstream. In order to bolster this positioning, they chose role models whom they considered to epitomize femininity in terms of the heterosexual ideal.

Iconic Femininity

At both schools, the girls made frequent references to media figures who served as emblems or icons of ideal femininity. At East Middle School these included Whitney Houston, Toni Braxton, Brandy, and Selena. . . .

The East Middle School girls were critical and mocking of many white celebrities, especially the stars of television shows aimed at teenage girls. "I just don't like it that she changes her clothes and she does her hair and her makeup all perfect even though she's fighting monsters," Rosa said of *Buffy the Vampire Slayer*. But they took nonwhite singers and actresses more seriously and were vocal in their admiration of them.

At West Middle School the girls admired Claire Danes, Tyra Banks, Neve Campbell, and, above all, Drew Barrymore. Several of the popular girls cited her as their "hero":

JENNY: She's really pretty, she's an actress. I want to be an actress when I grow up.

TARA: I really like Drew Barrymore. She ditched her mother when she was 15. She's real independent.

They seemed unaware of Barrymore's declared bisexuality, and it can only be speculated how a knowledge of it might have altered their admiration of her or challenged their biases.

The "regular girls" tended to be more critical of the models who appeared in teen magazines and the rhetoric accompanying their images, but they did admire certain film and television actresses, including Melissa Joan Hart and Claire Danes.

All of the women who were chosen by the girls as role models or heroines exemplified media and sociocultural ideals of beauty; and they were admired by the girls specifically for their beauty, although other characteristics were sometimes mentioned as reasons for revering them. But none of the girls professed to admire women who had not been identified in the mass media as being physically beautiful according to dominant standards.

CONCLUSIONS

The girls' overall use of the mass media to reconstruct ideals of heterosexuality with regard to physical appearance, the goals of marriage and maternity, and active homophobia reveal a fairly direct appropriation of the dominant ideology of femininity. Race and class factors impacted the ways in which the parameters of ideal femininity were defined; but in general, the peer context was one in which emergent gender identity was consolidated via constant reference to acceptable sociocultural standards of femininity and sexuality.

This conformity was not seamless; pockets of resistance occurred in peer group discussions, but when they did, their functioning was paradoxical. In the West Middle School girls' dialogue about eating disorders, or the "gangsta" girls' rejection of the prospect of early motherhood, the privileged voices in the discussion shut out some of the participants in such a way that their personal struggles with these issues could not be recognized. Jonquil's history of eating disorders, Maria's sexual activity that culminated in pregnancy a few months later, Lila's sexual ambiguity could not be given full voice. Thus, the peer group served to achieve ideological closure in terms of how issues of gender and power could be addressed.

. . .

In the peer groups in this study, surface levels of resistance cloaked some of the participants' more private and interiorized struggles with dominant codes of femininity. The group discourse provided a text that could be analyzed, but the research cited earlier in this essay, as well as information gathered by this researcher from sources outside of the peer groups, point to the existence of subtexts that tended to be suppressed by the group process. Some evidence of this kind of suppression was provided by the West Middle School girls' insistence that they were individuals when their outward behaviors indicated complete capitulation to the norms of the group. . . .

Eating disorders were not openly discussed at East Middle School, yet the girls' casual references to starving themselves in one conversation indicated that body image issues were of more concern than was openly evidenced. Thompson points out that eating disorders among Latina and African-American women tend to be severe because they are not taken seriously or diagnosed quickly.[16] The girls at East Middle School were uncritical and unreflexive about the norm of thinness to which they subscribed.

Thus, this research indicates that while race and class were differentiators of girls' socialization and concomitant media use, the differences highlighted the ways in which their different cultures functioned to uphold different aspects of dominant ideologies of femininity.

Watkins suggests that minority youth in particular have generated cultural practices of resistance that have grown out of their social marginalization.[17] Such resistance was not obviously manifested among the girls at East and West Middle Schools, yet the potential for resistance was an ever-present subcurrent. At West Middle School, for example, the peer group discourse among the "regular girls" was more resistant than that of the "preps." Because peer acceptance is of paramount importance in girls' culture,[18] a real subversion of dominant norms *could* certainly happen in a peer group where that was part of the group identity. It is possible that the peer group's social standing with respect to other groups would influence the degree of resistance expressed in the group. A larger study in which more, and more diverse, peer groups were observed would be needed to further investigate these phenomena.

It could be argued that the girls' observed tendency to accept dominant norms of femininity was related to the fact that most of the subjects were honors students—academic achievers who conformed to social expectations in every aspect of their lives. Yet an adherence to codes of what might be called "hegemonic femininity" was also evident in the behaviors of the "gangsta" group from East Middle School, who were considered to be at risk of dropping out, delinquency, and other "antisocial" behaviors. In fact, they demonstrated even more interest in costuming, makeup, beautification, and maternity than did the more "prosocial" peer groupings. It can be tentatively concluded from these data, then, that the peer group generally serves to consolidate dominant constructions of gender and sexuality.

However, race and class factors appear to intercede in the process of meaning-making, within as well as around the peer group context. The predominantly white, upper-middle-class students at West Middle School were primary targets of advertising-driven media, and they concomitantly paid significantly more attention to the mass media than did students at East Middle School. Nonetheless, media were used to shore up systems of belief held by students at both schools.

. . . Among the girls in this study, a key strategy for blending into the peer group involved participating in activities that marked the limits of acceptable femininity; however, these were deployed within their racial, cultural, and class environments. Deviance from normative sexuality was a means of identifying the social outcast; conformity was a way of bonding with the group, and mass media were used as instruments in the bonding process.

These findings have multiple implications. First, they establish the centrality of mass media in adolescent society and underscore the links between socialization into dominant norms of sexuality and consumer culture. The teenagers in this study were hyperaware of the need to use the media to find their foothold in the group. Their uses of the media were more than discursive: consumption of the necessary products that openly established their acceptance and understanding of sexual norms was a necessary part of peer interaction. Thus socialization into femininity was linked to the multi-million-dollar fashion, beauty, and diet industries that thrive on women consumers. As McCracken has pointed out, "the material object that advertising tries to sell is never sufficient in itself: it must be validated, often only in fantasy, by additional meanings."[19] The peer group is the context in which these additional meanings are given authority.

Second, perhaps more important, it makes clear that the peer group must be taken into account in the contemplation of interventions or counteractions against the mediated norms that play into girls' gendered behaviors. Such interventions tend to be "top-down," devised and administered by adults; yet the significance of the peer group in girls' social lives indicates that the most effective resistant practices would germinate and take root within the peer group. In this study, the peer group was shown to be a training ground where girls learned to use the mass media to acquire the skills of ideal femininity, but it was also a place where rejection of these norms could sometimes be voiced. This study points to a relationship between peer attitudes toward mediated constructions of female beauty, body type, motherhood, and homosexuality, and teenage girls' real-life experiences of eating disorders, teenage pregnancy, depression related to sexual orientation, and problems with self-esteem. All of these issues engage questions of power, gender, race, and class.

While girls individually have some sense of the social environment that operates to regulate their expressions of gender and sexuality, and while they may try on an individual level to resist damaging normative constructions of femininity, the peer group dynamic tends to mitigate against such resistance. Effective interventions for girls must work within the peer context to try to encourage more nuanced and less univocal conceptualizations of normative femininity. Beyond this, the peer group's relationship to broader levels of society must be taken into account. Interventions such as media literacy efforts will not be effective unless they are sensitive to issues of race, class, and culture; a recognition of institutionalized networks of power that constrain and limit girls' autonomy is necessary before strategies for resistance and emancipation can be devised.

NOTES

1. Lyn Mikel Brown and Carol Gilligan, *Meeting at the Crossroads: Women's Psychology and Girls' Development* (New York: Ballantine Books, 1992).
2. Peggy Orenstein, *Schoolgirls: Young Women, Self-Esteem, and the Confidence Gap* (New York: Doubleday, 1994); Mary Pipher, *Reviving Ophelia: Saving the Selves of Adolescent Girls* (New York: Ballantine, 1994); Lori Stern, "Disavowing the Self in Female Adolescence," in *Women, Girls and Psychotherapy: Reframing Resistance,* ed. Carol Gilligan, Annie G. Rogers, and Deborah L. Tolman (New York: Haworth Press, 1991), 105–17.
3. Margaret Duffy and Micheal Gotcher, "Crucial Advice on How to Get the Guy: The Rhetorical Vision of Power and Seduction in the Teen Magazine *YM*," *Journal of Communication Inquiry* 21 (spring 1996): 32–48; Lisa Duke and Peggy J. Kreshel, "Negotiating Femininity: Girls in Early Adolescence Read Teen Magazines," *Journal of Communication Inquiry* 22 (January 1998): 48–71; Meenakshi Gigi Durham, "Dilemmas of Desire: Representations of Adolescent Sexuality in Two Teen Magazines," *Youth and Society* 29 (March 1998): 369–89; Ellen McCracken, *Decoding Women's Magazines: From Mademoiselle to Ms.* (New York: St. Martin's Press, 1993); Angela McRobbie, "Jackie: An Ideology of Adolescent Femininity," in *Mass Communication Review Yearbook,* vol. 4, ed. Ellen Wartella, D. Charles Whitney, and Sven Windahl (Beverly Hills, CA: Sage, 1983), 251–71; Angela McRobbie, "Shut Up and Dance: Youth Culture and Changing Modes of Femininity," in *Postmodernism and Popular Culture,* ed. Angela McRobbie (London: Routledge, 1994), 155–76; Kate Pierce, "A Feminist Theoretical Perspective on the Socialization of Teenage Girls through *Seventeen* Magazine," *Sex Roles* 23 (1990): 491–500; Kate Pierce, "Socialization of Teenage Girls through Teen-Magazine Fiction: The Making of a New Woman or an Old Lady?" *Sex Roles* 29 (1993): 59–68.
4. Brown and Gilligan, *Meeting at the Crossroads;* Pipher, *Reviving Ophelia.*

5. Orenstein, *Schoolgirls;* American Association of University Women Educational Foundation, *How Schools Shortchange Girls* (Washington, DC: American Association of University Women, 1992).

6. Susan Bordo, *Unbearable Weight: Feminism, Western Culture, and the Body* (Berkeley: University of California Press, 1993); Naomi Wolf, *The Beauty Myth: How Images of Beauty Are Used Against Women* (New York: Anchor, 1991).

7. Sue Lees, *Sugar and Spice: Sexuality and Adolescent Girls* (Harmondsworth, England: Penguin, 1993); Naomi Wolf, *Promiscuities* (New York: Random House, 1997).

8. Jill McLean Taylor, Carol Gilligan, and Amy M. Sullivan, *Between Voice and Silence: Women and Girls, Race and Relationship* (Cambridge, MA: Harvard University Press, 1995); Becky W. Thompson, *A Hunger So Wide and Deep: American Women Speak on Eating Problems* (Minneapolis: University of Minnesota Press, 1994).

9. Judith Rich Harris, "Where Is the Child's Environment? A Group Socialization Theory of Development," *Psychological Review* 102 (1995): 458–89.

10. The names of all schools, students, social workers, teachers, and places have been changed so as to preserve anonymity and confidentiality.

11. The word *Latino* was used to describe the ethnicity of a group of students who were mainly U.S.-born Mexican Americans; the group also included students of Puerto Rican, Cuban, and other Central and South American origin. Some of these students were mixed-race and self-identified in ways other than according to the school's classification system. In this essay the corollary term *Mexicanos* is used to designate first-generation Mexican immigrants to the United States. This term was used by the schoolchildren at East Middle School to distinguish second- and third-generation students from new immigrants.

12. Kevin G. Barnhurst and Ellen Wartella, "Newspapers and Citizenship: Young Adults' Subjective Experience of Newspapers," *Critical Studies in Mass Communication* 8 (June 1991): 195–209; Kevin G. Barnhurst and Ellen Wartella, "Young Citizens, American TV Newscasts, and the Collective Memory," *Critical Studies in Mass Communication* 15 (September 1998): 279–305; Leo Bogart, *Commercial Culture: The Media System and the Public Interest* (New York: Oxford University Press, 1995).

13. Sandra Lee Bartky, "Foucault, Femininity, and the Modernization of Patriarchal Power," in *Feminism and Foucault: Reflections on Resistance,* ed. Irene Diamond and Lee Quinby (Boston: Northeastern University Press, 1988), 64.

14. See Duke and Kreshel, "Negotiating Femininity."

15. Bordo, *Unbearable Weight.*

16. Thompson, *A Hunger So Wide and Deep.*

17. S. Craig Watkins, *Representing: Hip-Hop Culture and the Production of Black Cinema* (Chicago: University of Chicago Press, 1998).

18. Griffiths, *Adolescent Girls and Their Friends;* Brown and Gilligan, *Meeting at the Crossroads.*

19. McCracken, *Decoding Women's Magazines,* 67.

DISCUSSION QUESTIONS FOR CHAPTER 4

1. In what ways is the personal political for you in your relationships?

2. How is the personal political in heterosexual relationships generally?

3. How does socialization into gender affect intimacy in relationships?

4. How does homophobia discourage intimacy? Have there been instances in your life when homophobia has prevented you from developing intimacy with someone?

5. How would you describe women's and men's different ways of communicating? How do women's and men's different ways of communicating affect relationships?

6. How is romantic love related to consumerism? Give some examples.

SUGGESTIONS FOR FURTHER READING

Bright, Susie, ed. *Herotica: A Collection of Women's Erotic Fiction,* 2nd ed. San Francisco: Down There Press, 1998.

Collins, Patricia Hill. *Black Sexual Politics: African Americans, Gender, and the New Racism.* New York: Routledge, 2004.

Hite, Shere. *The Hite Report: A National Study of Female Sexuality.* New York: Seven Stories Press, 2005.

Kamen, Paula. *Her Way: Young Women Remake the Sexual Revolution.* New York: Broadway Books, 2002.

Stoltenberg, John. *Refusing to Be a Man: Essays on Sex and Justice,* revised ed. London: UCL Press, 1999.

White, Emily. *Fast Girls: Teenage Tribes and the Myth of the Slut.* New York: Penguin, 2003.

Wolf, Naomi. *Promiscuities: A Secret History of Female Desire.* London: Random House, 2000.

CHAPTER **5**

Inscribing Gender
on the Body

In contemporary U.S. society we are surrounded by images of beautiful, thin (although increasingly fit and sculpted, large breasted, and, in some communities, full bottomed), young, abled, smiling women. Most of these bodies are White, and when women of color are depicted, they tend to show models with more typically White features or hair. These images set standards for appearance and beauty that are internalized—standards that affect how we feel about our own bodies. As a result, most of us grow up disliking our bodies or some parts of them. We are especially troubled by those parts of our bodies that we see as larger than societal ideals.

It is distressing that women often experience their bodies as sources of despair rather than joy and celebration. This is especially true as we age and measure our bodies against notions of youthful "beauty." These images of perfect bodies are fabricated by a male-dominated culture and are reinforced by multi-billion-dollar industries that serve to maintain both corporate profits and patriarchal social relations. The images we are given are flawless and give the illusion of absolute perfection. In reality these images tend to be airbrushed and computer enhanced, and, increasingly, completely computer generated. These digital representations integrate all the "positive" features associated with contemporary North American "beauty" in one image. Fashion models today weigh more than 20 percent less than the average woman, with only about 5 percent of the female population in our society weighing in at the average fashion model's weight given her height. Obviously, real women come in all shapes and sizes. Our diversity is part of our beauty!

Although the body is an incredibly sophisticated jumble of physiological events, our understanding of the body cannot exist outside of the society that gives it meaning. Even though bodies are biophysical entities, what our bodies mean and how they are experienced is intimately connected to the meanings and practices of the society in which we reside. This is clearly demonstrated in the reading by Amy Bloom on intersexuals and the cultural consequences for children born with "ambiguous genitalia." In "Hemaphroctites with Attitude," Bloom discusses the culturally

LEARNING ACTIVITY **Considering Body Size, Shape, and Movement**

Take a tour examining the public facilities of your school or campus, which may include

Telephone booths or stalls

Drinking fountains

Bleachers

Sinks and stalls in public restrooms

Curbs, ramps, and railings

Chairs and tables

Turnstiles

Elevators and escalators

Stairs and staircases

Vending machines

Doors and doorways

Fire alarm boxes

Answer the following questions:

What assumptions about the size and shape of the users (height, weight, proportionate length of arms and legs, width of hips and shoulders, hand preference, mobility, etc.) are incorporated into the designs?

How do these design assumptions affect the ability of you and people you know to use the facilities satisfactorily?

How would they affect you if you were significantly:

Wider or narrower than you are?

Shorter or taller?

Heavier or lighter?

Rounder or more angular?

More or less mobile/ambulatory?

Identify any access or usage barriers to people with physical disabilities. Answer the following questions:

Are classrooms accessible to people who can't walk up or down stairs?

Are emergency exit routes usable by people with limited mobility?

Are amplification devices or sign language interpreters available for people with hearing impairments?

Are telephones and fire alarms low enough to be reached by people who are seated in wheelchairs or who are below average height?

Are audiovisual aids appropriate for people with hearing or vision impairments?

Describe the experience of a person in your class or school who has a mobility, vision, speech, or hearing impairment.

Variation 1. Identify one assumption incorporated into the design of one of the facilities (drinking fountain, phone booth, etc.). Gather formal or informal data about the number of people on campus that might not be able to use the facility satisfactorily, based on the design assumption. Suggest one or two ways to make the facility more useful to those people.

Variation 2. Choose one of the access or usage barriers you have identified and suggest a way to remove the barrier. Research the cost involved. Identify one or two ways of funding the access strategy you have suggested.

Source: Janet Lockhart and Susan M. Shaw, *Writing for Change: Raising Awareness of Difference, Power, and Discrimination, www.teachingtolerance.org.*

mediated process of gender reassignment. In this way, bodies are like cultural artifacts; culture becomes embodied and is literally inscribed or represented through the body at the same time that the *objectification* of women's bodies (seeing the body as an object and separate from its context) is supported by the media and entertainment industries. Note how these norms about the body rely on a notion of the healthy and/or abled body.

Bodies, however, are not only reflections of social norms and practices but also sites of *identity* and *self-expression*. The current disruption of binary notions of gender have encouraged discussion of the body as a site for identity and of the performative use of the body in gender displays. It has been suggested that as our lives become more complex and we have less power over the way we live them, we are encouraged to focus more on the body as something we *can* control and as something we can use to express our identity. As a result, the body becomes something to be fashioned and controlled; at the same time, this control over body—and the ability to shape, clothe, and express it—becomes synonymous with personal freedom. Scholars discussing backlash (organized resistance) have emphasized that the preoccupation within the body represents the ways society has responded to the gains of marginalized groups through "distractions" that focus energy on the body and its management.

Perhaps the current trend for tattoos and piercing among young women is an example of this trend toward self-expression in the context of mass-market consumerism. Having a tattoo or multiple tattoos—traditionally a masculine or an outlaw, rebellious act—is increasingly a form of self-expression for women. Similarly, the current fad of multiple piercing of many body parts, including erogenous and sexually charged areas of the body, can be seen as a form of rebellion against the constraints of gender. Both tattooing and piercing can also be interpreted as reactionary trends and as examples of the many ways women are encouraged to mutilate and change parts of their bodies. Note that these "rebellious" practices have now been appropriated as relatively ordinary fashion practices. You can buy nose and belly-button rings, for example, that clip on without ever having to pierce anything, just as you can buy fake tattoos. In fact, the self-consciousness involved in the parody of the real thing is now a form of self-expression all its own. This issue of body image and its consequences for women's lives is a central issue for third wave feminism, mobilizing many young feminists.

Although men are taught to be concerned with their bodies and looks (and increasingly so given the advertising industry's desire to create a new market for beauty products), women are particularly vulnerable to the cultural preoccupation with the body. There is a *double standard* of beauty for women and men: Physical appearance is more important in terms of the way women are perceived and treated. This is especially true in terms of the aging body where there is a much stronger mandate for women to keep their bodies looking young.

We want to focus on two issues associated with the cultural preoccupation of women and the body: (1) the close relationship between women and nature and bodily functions, and (2) norms associated with appearance and beauty that help determine women's identity and worth. We examine these two issues next and then discuss eating disorders and methods for resisting the beauty ideal.

BODIES, NATURE, AND WOMEN

Although both women and men have bodies, an obvious aspect of the social construction of the body is that what female and male bodies stand for or signify implies different things in most cultures. Women have been associated with *nature*: the body, earth, and the domestic, whereas men, because of historical and mythological associations with the spirit and sky, have been associated with *culture*: the mind rather than the body and abstract reason rather than earthly mundane matters. Importantly, Western civilizations have incorporated not only a distinction between nature and culture but also a domination of culture and mind over nature and body. In particular, Western societies' notions of progress have involved the taming and conquering of nature in favor of civilization. As a result, the female/nature side of this dichotomy is valued less and often denigrated.

A prime example of this is the way the normal processes of the female body have been seen as smelly, taboo, and distasteful. Menstruation is regarded negatively and described with a multitude of derogatory euphemisms like "the curse" and "on the rag," and girls are still taught to conceal menstrual practices from others (and men in particular). As Gloria Steinem suggests in the reading "If Men Could Menstruate," the experience would be something entirely different if it was men who menstruated. Advertisements abound in magazines and on television about tampons, pads, douches, feminine hygiene sprays, and yeast infection medicines that give the message that women's bodies are constantly in need of hygienic attention. Notice we tend not to get ads for jock itch during prime-time television like we do ads for feminine "ailments." In this way, there is a strange, very public aspect to feminine bodily processes at the same time that they are coded as very private.

These notions about women and the body have helped shape gender ideologies and reinforce *biological determinism*, a tendency that sees women in terms of their reproductive and biological selves. Male bodies are not so marked by these earthly

ACTIVIST PROFILE   **Maggie Kuhn**

Most people are getting ready to retire at 65. Maggie Kuhn began the most important work of her life at that age. In 1970 Kuhn was forced to retire from her career with the Presbyterian Church. In August of that year, she convened a group of five friends, all of whom were retiring, to talk about the problems faced by retirees—loss of income, loss of social role, pension rights, age discrimination. Finding new freedom and strength in their voices, they also concerned themselves with other social issues, such as the Vietnam War.

The group gathered in Philadelphia with college students opposed to the war at the Consultation of Older and Younger Adults for Social Change. A year later, more than 100 people joined the Consultation. As this new group began to meet, a New York television producer nicknamed the group the Gray Panthers, and the name stuck.

In 1972 Kuhn was asked at the last minute to fill in for someone unable to speak during the 181st General Assembly of the United Presbyterian Church. Her stirring speech launched the Gray Panthers into national prominence, and calls began to flood the organization's headquarters. Increased media attention came as the Gray Panthers became activists. They co-sponsored the Black House Conference on Aging to call attention to the lack of African Americans at the first White House Conference on Aging, and they performed street theater at the American Medical Association's 1974 conference, calling for health care as a human right. At the core of Panther activities was the belief that older people should seize control of their lives and actively campaign for causes in which they believe.

The Gray Panthers have been instrumental in bringing about nursing home reform, ending forced retirement provisions, and combating fraud against the elderly in health care. Kuhn, who was active with the Panthers until her death at age 89, offered this advice to other activists: "Leave safety behind. Put your body on the line. Stand before the people you fear and speak your mind—even if your voice shakes. When you least expect it, someone may actually listen to what you have to say. Well-aimed slingshots can topple giants."

Body Art

Across practically all times and cultures, humans have practiced various forms of body modification for such differing reasons as warding off or invoking spirits, attracting sexual partners, indicating social or marital status, identifying with a particular age or gender group, and marking a rite of passage (Lemonick, et al.). People all over the world have pierced, painted, tattooed, reshaped, and adorned their bodies, turning the body itself into an artistic canvas.

The earliest records of tattoos were found in Egypt around the time of the building of the pyramids. Later, the practice was adopted in Crete, Greece, Persia, Arabia, and China. The English word *tattoo* comes from the Polynesian *tatau*, a practice observed by James Cook when he visited Tahiti on his first voyage around the world. In the Marquesas, Cook noted that the men were marked from head to foot, and, while the men had their entire bodies tattooed, women tattooed only their hands, lips, shoulders, ankles, and the area behind the ears.

Today, many of the Maori men of New Zealand are returning to the practice of wearing the elaborate tattoos of their ancestors. In Morocco, henna designs on the hands and feet are an integral part of significant celebrations, such as weddings and religious holidays. In Ethiopia, Hamar men earn raised scars made by cutting with a razor and then rubbing ash into the wounds for killing a dangerous animal or enemy. Surma girls have their earlobes stretched by clay plates and paint their faces during courtship season.

As you may have noted, body art is a gendered practice. Tattooing, piercing, painting, and reshaping the body also serve the purpose of marking gender. What are common body modification practices in the United States? How do these practices express and reinforce gender?

Sources: Monica Desai, "Body Art: A History," *Student BMJ* 10 (2002):196–97. Michael Lemonick et al., "Body Art," *Time South Pacific* (12/13/99), 66–68. Pravina Shukla, "The Human Canvas," *Natural History* 108 (1999): 80.

LEARNING ACTIVITY   **On the Rag**

Collect a wide variety of women's magazines such as *Cosmopolitan, Glamour, Vogue, Elle, Mirabella,* and so on. Identify advertisements for "feminine hygiene products"—tampons, pads, douches, feminine hygiene sprays, yeast infection medicines. What do the visual images in the ads suggest? What do the words tell readers? What messages do these advertisements send about women's bodies? Now collect a variety of men's magazines such as *GQ, Maxim, Men's Journal,* and so on. Identify advertisements for "masculine hygiene products." What do you find? What does the difference imply about women's bodies in contrast to men's bodies? How does this implication reinforce structures of gender subordination?

reminders, and men have been able to imagine their bodies free of such constraints. And, as feminist scholars have reminded us, men as a group have been able to project their fears and anxieties about frailty and mortality onto women's flesh. Although these notions affect all of us in Western societies, women and men, it is important to understand that the body and its expressions have stronger repercussions in women's lives.

THE "BEAUTY" IDEAL

In this section we discuss four points associated with the beauty ideal. First, contemporary images of female beauty are changeable. What was considered beautiful or feminine for an aristocratic Elizabethan woman in Tudor England involved whitening the face, plucking eyelashes, and shaving back the hairline to show a prominent forehead—hardly beauty practices that would help you get a date in contemporary U.S. society. Some societies encourage the insertion of objects into earlobes or jawline or other mechanics to increase neck length or head shape. Other societies consider large women especially attractive and see their fat as evidence of prosperity; again, in most contemporary Western societies, thin is closer to standards of ideal beauty, although there are differences within specific ethnic communities within the United States. In other words, what is considered beautiful is culturally produced and therefore changes across time and across cultures. Importantly, however, Western standards of body appearance are exported along with the exportation of fashion and other makeup products. A poignant example of this is in the reading by Jonathan Watts titled "China's Cosmetic Surgery Craze." He discusses a procedure that aims to bring Chinese women closer to Western ideals of beauty through leg-lengthening operations.

A look at standards of Western female beauty over time reveals that in the nineteenth century White, privileged women were encouraged to adopt a delicate, thin, and fragile appearance and wear bone-crushing (literally) corsets that not only gave them the hourglass figure but also cramped and ruptured vital organs. These practices made women faint, appear frail, delicate, dependent, and passive—responses to nineteenth-century notions of middle-class femininity. Victorian furniture styles accommodated this ideal with special swooning chairs. Standards for weight and body shape changed again in the early twentieth century when a sleek, boyish look was adopted by the flappers of the 1920s. Women bound their breasts to hide their curves. Although more curvaceous and slightly heavier bodies were encouraged through the next decades, body maintenance came to dominate many women's lives. Fueled by an emerging multi-million-dollar fashion industry, the 1960s gave us a return to a more emaciated, long-legged look, but with very short skirts and long hair. At the beginning of this new century, we see a more eclectic look and a focus on health and fitness, but norms associated with ideal female beauty still construct the thin, White (tanned, but not too brown) body as the beautiful body.

A second point concerning the beauty ideal is that the ideal reflects various relations of power in society. Culture is constructed in complex ways, and groups with more power and influence tend to set the trends, create the options, and enforce the standards. Standards tend not to be created by the ordinary women whose lives these

HISTORICAL MOMENT   **Protesting Miss America**

In 1921 a group of hotel owners in Atlantic City came up with the idea to stage a bathing beauty contest to get tourists to stay in town after the Labor Day holiday. Eight finalists were chosen from photo entries in newspapers, and Margaret Gorman, representing Washington D.C., was crowned the first "Miss America" at the age of 16.

Throughout the rest of the twentieth century, the Miss America pageant continued to reinforce norms of the ideal woman. By 1968 the women's movement had begun to challenge beauty ideals and the ways women were judged by their appearance. In the days leading up to the 1968 pageant, members of the New York Radical Women made known their intentions to protest the oppressive image of the beauty queen. On September 7, as the winner paraded onstage, activists in the auditorium unfurled a women's liberation banner and chanted slogans. While people in the hall barely noticed the protest, network TV picked it up and broadcast it to the nation.

Outside the hall, 200 women protested. In a mock mini-pageant, protestors led out a sheep which they crowned as Miss America. Into a "Freedom Trash Can," they threw "instruments of torture"—girdles, curlers, false eyelashes, cosmetics, issues of *Cosmopolitan* and *Playboy*, and bras. While they had originally planned to set a fire in the can, they chose to comply with local fire regulations and did not. When a reporter asked Robin Morgan why, she explained that the mayor had been concerned about fire safety. She added, "We told him we wouldn't do anything dangerous—just a symbolic bra-burning." While the *New York Times* correctly reported no fire had been lit, only a few weeks later the paper referred to "bra-burning" as if it had actually taken place. The image caught on with the media, and, without reference to any reality, the media promoted the myth of the bra-burning feminist.

Source: Ruth Rosen, *The World Split Open: How the Modern Women's Movement Changed America* (New York: Viking, 2000).

beauty ideals affect. In our culture, beauty standards are very much connected to the production and consumption of various products, and, indeed, the beauty product and fashion industries are multi-billion-dollar enterprises. As the reading excerpted from Joan Jacobs Brumberg's *The Body Project* explains, garment industries in the United States helped sexualize women's breasts through their development of the bra. Corporate powers, advertising, and the fashion, cosmetics, and entertainment industries all help create standards for us and reinforce gender relations. Even the "natural look" is sold to us as something to be tried on, when obviously the real natural look is devoid of marketing illusions in the first place. Most of these industries are controlled by White males or by other individuals who have accepted what many scholars call ruling-class politics. The main point is that most of us get offered beauty and fashion options constructed by other people. Although we have choices and can reject them, lots of resources are involved in encouraging us to adopt the standards created by various industries. However, as the reading "Body Ethics and Aesthetics Among African American and Latina Women" by Lisa R. Rubin, Mako L. Fitts, and Anne E. Becker suggests, college-educated African American and Latina women found ways to reject the thin, White body aesthetic and actively created alternative constructions of beauty.

In this way, the beauty ideal offered to us reflects social power in that these standards tend to be White, abled, and middle class. White standards of beauty can humiliate fat or non-White women as well as the poor, the aged, and the disabled. These norms help enforce racism, classism, ableism, ageism, and fat oppression, as well as sexism generally. Many ethnic communities, however, have alternative notions of feminine beauty and actively resist the normalizing standards of Anglo culture. Lisa Miya-Jervis understands the racial politics of appearance and explains in "Hold That Nose" why she avoided surgery to change the shape of her nose.

The third point concerning beauty practices is that standards are enforced in complex ways. Of course, "enforcement" does not mean, as Sandra Bartky has said, that someone marches you off to electrolysis at gunpoint. Instead, we adopt various standards, integrate them as choices we make for ourselves, and police one another in a general sense. Norms are internalized, and we receive various positive and negative responses for complying with or resisting them. This is especially true when it comes to hair. Hair plays significant roles in women's intimate relationships, as the reading "What We Do for Love" by Rose Weitz on women and their hair suggests. It is interesting to think about these everyday behaviors we engage in to maintain the body: the seemingly trivial routines, rules, and practices. Some scholars call these *disciplinary practices*. They are "practices" because they involve such taken-for-granted routinized behaviors as shaving legs, applying makeup, or curling/straightening/coloring hair; and they are "disciplinary" because they involve social control in the sense that we spend time, money, effort, and imbue meaning in these practices. Again, disciplinary practices are connected to the production and consumption of various products. Of particular concern is the connection between practices associated with weight control and smoking. A study from the National Institutes of Health reported that weight concerns and a "drive for thinness" among both Black and White girls at ages 11 to 12 years were the most important factors leading to subsequent daily smoking (*www.nih.gov*).

By Ann Telnaes in Six Chix, May 31, 2001. Reprinted by authors permission.

You can probably think of many disciplinary practices that you or your friends take part in. Men have their practices too, although these tend to be simpler and involve a narrower range of products. Alongside fashion and various forms of cosmetics and body sculpting, women are more likely to get face-lifts, eye tucks, nose jobs, collagen injections to plump up lips, liposuction, tummy tucks, stomach stapling, and, of course, breast implants as well as breast reductions. By the early 1990s, more than 150,000 women a year were paying for breast implants, with about 80 percent for nonmedical reasons. The FDA (Food and Drug Administration) now requires women receiving silicone-gel breast implants to sign a "known risks" (leaking and rupture, loss of sensation in the nipples) and "possible risks" (fibrositis or pain and stiffness of muscles, ligaments, and tendons) clause. There has also been new protocol for saline implants too. Along these same lines, Simone Weil Davis discusses labiaplasty in the reading "Designer Vaginas." She discusses the politics of these surgeries and relates this to the typically non-Western practice of female genital cutting. In considering these practices—from following fashion and buying clothes and accessories to makeup application to breast enhancement and all the other practices in between—it is important to keep in mind how much they cost, how they channel women's energies away from other (perhaps more productive) pursuits, and how they may affect health and well-being.

An interesting development is the popularity of "reality" television shows that take people (especially women) out of communities, isolate them, and then transform their bodies through surgery, cosmetics, and other technologies of body management,

Body Image Quiz

INTRODUCTION

When was the last time you looked in the mirror and liked what you saw? Most women have to think long and hard before answering this question. Whether or not we admit it, women are active players in the beauty game, which requires us to think looks and body weight are the true sources of our happiness. The truth is women are their own worst critics when it comes to their bodies. Yet, experts tell us that self-esteem is closely tied to body image, even more so than our actual physical appearance. Take this quiz to learn more about body image and self-esteem.

1. In a national survey in which 200 women were asked, "If you could change one thing about your body, what would it be?" How many women said they would leave their bodies unchanged?
    a. 50
    b. 25
    c. 10
    d. 0

2. What percentage of American women overestimate their body size?
    a. 20 percent
    b. 35 percent
    c. 50 percent
    d. 95 percent

3. Which of the following do psychologists call "eating disorder breeding grounds" for women?
    a. Sports teams
    b. Dance troupes
    c. High schools and colleges
    d. Commercial weight-loss programs
    e. All of the above

4. In a national survey, women were asked what they thought was the "peak age" for attractiveness. Which was the most frequent age answer from the following choices?
    a. 16
    b. 22
    c. 33
    d. 45

5. How many women in the United States suffer from eating disorders?
    a. 200,000
    b. 2 million
    c. 4 million
    d. 5 million
    e. 12 million

ANSWERS

1. d. 0. In a body image survey, conducted by Rita Freeman, Ph.D., the author of *Bodylove: Learning to Like Our Looks—And Ourselves,* not a single woman out of 200 was willing to leave her body

(continued)

alone. Body areas and/or conditions that women seem most dissatisfied with run from head to toe. Some of the body changes women wish for include wider eyes, freckles, longer legs, smaller feet, better posture, firmer thighs, thinner ankles, longer nails, and bigger breasts. Above all else, American women want to lose weight. Two-thirds of the women surveyed wanted to drop weight, particularly in the area between their waist and knees. Why such an obsession with weight loss? Psychologists say the reasons abound. Obviously American society sets unrealistic, even ridiculous standards by glorifying models who are dangerously thin. Psychologists say there is also a social tendency to associate good looks and thinness with success. It's called "looksism," and it is a form of stereotyping.

2. d. 95 percent. The condition of not being satisfied with one's weight is far more prevalent in women than men, and it includes American women of all races, ethnic groups, religions, professions, and economic classes. Most women who weigh in the normal, healthy range for their age and height still tend to consider themselves overweight. Many remain in a lifelong, futile diet mentality, thinking that life would be bliss if only they could lose 10 pounds. Two-thirds of all American women list fear of getting fat on their list of life's worst fears. Finally, women over age 60 report that gaining weight is their second most serious concern, with losing their memory as first.

Many health care experts believe that women have a poor notion of what a healthy weight should be for themselves. Health care providers say that a healthy weight is based on several factors, including weight history (your weight, age, and activity level over several years), genetic factors, age, activity level, as well as other factors such as hormonal changes, stress, and use of nicotine and/or alcohol.

3. c. High schools and colleges. It is during the teenage years that many women first begin their un-healthy preoccupation with their body and appearance. On the brink of puberty, many girls describe a tremendous pressure to be feminine, which, sadly, often equates to being beautiful like a movie star and having an emaciated look. For this reason, eating disorders, such as anorexia and bulimia, are detected more frequently in high school girls and college women than in any other group.

4. c. 33. The good news in the results of this survey is that most women didn't check off the earliest age. Still, 33 is less than half the age expectancy for most women, and psychologists say that women should strive to accept themselves at every age and to see themselves as continuously attractive in a different, more mature way.

A couple of myths exist on women and aging. Dispelling these myths may help women come to a better acceptance of themselves and their bodies.

Myth 1: As time passes, more women become increasingly unhappy with their bodies. In reality, a survey showed that women in their 20s, 30s, and 40s said they felt no different about their bodies than they had earlier in life.

Myth 2: With age women become even more self-conscious of their looks and minor imperfections. In reality, women become less self-conscious. Again, good news!

5. d. 5 million. Eating disorders are devastating mental illnesses that affect more than 5 million American women. Ninety percent of the people who suffer from anorexia nervosa and bulimia nervosa are women, according to the National Association of Anorexia Nervosa and Associated Disorders. Although they revolve around eating and body weight, eating disorders aren't about food, but about feelings and self-expression. Women with eating disorders use food and dieting as ways of coping with life's stresses. For some, food becomes a source of comfort and nurturing or a way to control or release stress. For others, losing weight is a way to gain the approval of friends and family. Eating disorders are not diets, signs of personal weakness, or problems that will go away without treatment. And although the teenage years are considered a high-risk period for these eating disorders, women of all ages can experience the problem or have a relapse later in life.

Anorexia is a condition of self-induced starvation. The desire to lose weight becomes an obsession because the woman has a distorted body image and cannot see herself as anything but fat. Ten percent of women with anorexia die from it.

Bulimia is an eating disorder that involves bingeing and purging. A bulimic woman will eat a large quantity of food and then take separate measures to purge herself of the food by vomiting, taking laxatives, or heavy exercising.

If you think you may have an eating disorder, you should consult a health care provider. Eating disorders are complex medical and psychological conditions, but with therapy and medical intervention, they can be treated.

Source: www.electra.com/electraquiz/admin/Body_Image_Quiz.html.

before reintroducing them back into their communities as radically transformed people (implying that their lives will now be better, more successful, happier, etc.). Such shows encourage people to pass for a younger age and have normalized cosmetic surgery (especially breast implants) as something ordinary women should seek and want. While these shows are often entertaining and seductive in their voyeuristic appeal, it is important to recognize the role they play in the social construction of "beauty," the advertising of products and body-management technologies, and the social relations of power in society.

The body and the various practices associated with maintaining the female body are probably the most salient aspects of what we understand as femininity and are crucial in social expressions of sexuality. Note how many of these bodily practices that are so wound up with contemporary femininity encourage women to stay small, not take up space, and stay young. Maturity in the form of body hair is unacceptable; we are encouraged to keep our bodies sleek, soft, and hairless—traits that some scholars identify with youth and powerlessness.

The final point regarding the beauty ideal is that while it shapes women's bodies and lives, it is a huge aspect of corporate capitalism and U.S. consumerism. Enormous profits result from fashion, cosmetics, beauty, and entertainment industries yearly. It is important to remember that gendered beauty practices are related to specific products and commodities that women are encouraged to purchase. And, of course, the underlying message is that women are not good enough the way they are but need certain products to improve their looks or their relationships. This is not good for women's self-esteem in most cases. In addition, there is also a huge weight-loss industry in the United States. Millions of dollars are spent every year by people who seek to cram their bodies into smaller sizes. Of course, many individuals want to make their bodies smaller out of a concern for better health and mobility, and the weight and exercise industries help them attain these goals. But many have learned to despise flesh and fat and participate in these industries' profits out of a desire to more closely fit the cultural standard. Again, there is a double standard here whereby fat women have a harder time than fat men in our culture. This is not to say that fat men have an easy time; certainly prejudice against large-size people is one of the last bulwarks of oppression in our society. Many people have no qualms about blatantly expressing their dislike and disgust for fat people even when they might keep sexist or racist attitudes hidden. However, fat women have an especially difficult time because of the interaction between sexism and fat phobia. In this way

LEARNING ACTIVITY **Feminism and Plastic Surgery**

In recent years, technology has made plastic surgery more successful and more accessible for a large number of American women. Women are having nearly every body part resized and reconstructed. Televisions shows such as *The Swan, Extreme Makeover,* and *Nip/Tuck* have popularized the notion of creating a new self through surgery. Beyond nose and breast jobs, however, women are now also having all sorts of plastic surgery to have their labia reduced or their hymen "repaired." Put the word *labiaplasty* or *vaginoplasty* in your Web search engine. Visit the sites of some of the doctors who offer these forms of plastic surgery. What are these surgeries? Why do these sites suggest women might want these surgeries? Why do you think so many women are choosing these surgeries? Read Elizabeth Haiken's *Venus Envy: A History of Cosmetic Surgery* (Baltimore: Johns Hopkins University Press, 1999) for one feminist's take on the issue of plastic surgery.

the beauty ideal supports the weight-loss industry and encourages lookism and fat oppression.

Finally, at the very same time that we are bombarded with messages about being thin, the food industry in the United States (the third largest industry nationally) has considerable clout. Never before have North Americans (and, increasingly, people in developing countries) been bombarded with advertising for cheap and often toxic (high sugar, fat, salt, preservatives) food to such a degree. Children, for example, watch approximately 10,000 food ads per year on television, 90 percent of which are for four types of "food": sugar-coated cereals, soft drinks, fast food, and candy.

Eating Disorder Information

The following organizations provide information about eating disorders. Visit their Web sites to learn more about anorexia, bulimia, and other forms of disordered eating.

Academy for Eating Disorders   Telephone: 703-556-9222   Web site: *www.aedweb.org*

National Association of Anorexia Nervosa and Associated Disorders   Telephone: 847-831-3438   Web site: *www.anad.org*

National Eating Disorder Information Center (Canada)   Toll-free: 866-633-4220   Web site: *www.nedic.ca*

National Eating Disorders Association   Toll-free: 800-931-2237   Web site: *www.NationalEatingDisorders.org*

EATING DISORDERS

Contemporary eating disorders are compulsive disorders that include a variety of behaviors. Among these are *anorexia nervosa* (self-starvation), *bulimia nervosa* (binge eating with self-induced vomiting and/or laxative use), *compulsive eating* (uncontrolled eating), and *muscle dysmorphia* (fear of being inadequately muscled). Alongside these diagnostic categories are general eating-disordered behavior that may include occasional binge eating and fasting, overly compulsive food habits such as eating only certain foods, not being able to eat in public, and general problems associated with compulsive dieting and/or compulsive overexercising (sometimes called *anorexia athletica*, although at this time this is not recognized as a formal diagnosis). The latter catchall category of generalized disordered eating/exercising seems to be widespread among North American women. These disorders are culturally mediated in that they are related to environmental conditions associated with the politics of gender and sexuality. As L. K. G. Hsu (2004) reported in the *Journal of the American Medical Women's Association* (59, 2: 113), the number of eating-disordered women in any given community is proportional to the number of individuals who are dieting to control weight. Dieting seems to trigger the onset of an eating disorder in vulnerable individuals.

Anorexics can become very thin and emaciated: refusing to maintain a healthy body weight, having intense fears of gaining weight, and tending to strive for perfection. Bulimics eat large amounts of food in a short time (binge) and then make themselves vomit, or they purge with laxatives or overexercising, or they may purge through diuretics and/or amphetamines. Bulimics are more likely to be of normal weight than anorexics, although they both share emotions and thoughts associated with self-punishment, or feelings of being overwhelmed because they feel fat, or feelings of frustration and/or anger with other factors in their lives. Compulsive eating (that may involve bingeing) is understood as an addiction to food and often involves using food as comfort and includes eating to fill a void in life, hide emotions, or cope with problems. Compulsive eaters often have low self-esteem and feel shame about their weight. Individuals with muscle dysmorphia believe that their physiques are too small and unmuscular rather than too large. They participate in maladaptive exercise and dietary practices, and often use performance-enhancing substances. Although early studies focused on male bodybuilders, recent scholarship suggests that this symptomatology does appear in the general population and that women are increasingly demonstrating this disorder. Similarly, while boys and men tend to use steroids more than women to increase athletic performance, new scholarship has shown that girls and women are also using steroids. A 2005 study at Oregon Health and Science University found that two-thirds of female steroid use was not by athletes but by women hoping to improve their body image, look more toned, and control their weight.

Eating disorders (with the exception of muscle dysmorphia) affect women primarily; the ratio of women to men among anorexia nervosa and bulimia is 10:1. In Western society, these disorders primarily affect young (aged 15 to 25 years) women. Current statistics suggest about 1 percent of female adolescents have anorexia and 4 percent have bulimia, with about half of the former also developing bulimic patterns.

Accurate numbers associated with compulsive eating and generalized eating problems are unknown, although it is assumed that the number of women who indulge in disordered eating patterns of some kind is quite substantial. While these disorders occur in all populations in the United States, White women and those with higher socioeconomic status are somewhat more likely to suffer these problems, although as the reading by Rubin et al. suggests, African American and Latina women's beauty ethics are more nurturing and self-accepting and do not necessarily protect them from eating disorders. In addition, however, reporting bias occurs as reported statistics reflect in part the ways "incidence" is tied to resource availability for treatment in various communities. We do not know the incidence of unacknowledged or untreated eating disorders that occur in communities where treatment resources are scarce or unavailable. Finally, while eating disorders are a relatively Western phenomenon and tend not to manifest in countries with food scarcity, Asian countries have recently experienced a surge in the incidence of eating disorders as a result of increased westernization and urbanization.

There are often serious physical and emotional complications with these disorders, and up to 20 percent of people with serious eating disorders die from the disorder, usually of complications associated with heart problems and chemical imbalances, as well as suicide. With treatment, mortality rates fall to 2–3 percent; with treatment, about 60 percent recover and maintain healthy weight and social relationships; 20 percent make only partial recoveries and remain compulsively focused on food and weight; and approximately 20 percent do not improve, even with treatment. The latter often live lives controlled by weight- and body-management issues, and they often experience depression, hopelessness, and loneliness. Chronic obesity that may follow compulsive eating also has important consequences for health and illness.

Many students who live in dorms and sororities report a high incidence of eating disorders; perhaps you have struggled with an eating disorder yourself or have had a close friend or sister similarly diagnosed. If the huge number of women who have various issues with food—always on a diet, overly concerned with weight issues, compulsive about what they do or do not eat—are also included in the figures on eating disorders, then the number of women with these problems increases exponentially. Indeed, one study has suggested that 80 percent of fifth-grade girls report being on a diet. Although this does not mean that 80 percent of these girls really *are* on a diet, it does highlight the way the discourses of dieting and bodily control are being internalized even by 10-year-old girls. Food and bodies are central preoccupations in so many women's lives. We need to ask, why women and why food?

First, women have long been associated with food and domestic pursuits; food preparation and focus on food is a socially accepted part of female cultural training. Given that women have been relegated to the private sphere of the home more than the public world, food consumption is easily accessible and unquestioned. Second, food is something that nourishes and gives pleasure. In our culture, food has been associated with comfort and celebration, and it is easy to see how eating can be a way of dealing with the anxieties and unhappiness of life. Put these two together, and we get food as the object of compulsion; when we add the third factor, the "beauty" ideal, with all the anxieties associated with closely monitoring the size and shape of women's bodies, the result can be eating disorders.

IDEAS FOR ACTIVISM

- Organize an eating disorders awareness event. Provide information about eating disorders and resources for help. Invite a therapist who specializes in treating eating disorders to speak. Create awareness posters to hang around your campus.
- Organize a letter-writing campaign to protest the representation of such a small range of women's shapes and sizes in a particular women's magazine.
- Organize a speak-out about beauty ideals.
- Organize a tattoo and piercing panel to discuss the politics of tattooing and piercing. Have a tattoo and piercing fashion show, and discuss the meaning of the various tattoos/piercings.

Scholars also emphasize that eating disorders might reflect the ways that women desire self-control in the context of little power and autonomy. In other words, young women turn to controlling their bodies and attempt to sculpt them to perfection because they are denied power and control in other areas of their lives. Central in understanding eating disorders, however, is the pressure in our society for women to measure up to cultural standards of beauty and attractiveness, what is often called the "culture of thinness." These standards infringe on all our lives whether we choose to comply with them or resist them. Messages abound telling women that they are not good enough or beautiful enough, encouraging us to constantly change ourselves, often through the use of various products. The result is that girls learn early on that they must aspire to some often-unattainable standard of physical perfection. Such a bombardment affects girls' self-esteem and constantly assaults women's psyches as we age. In this way, eating disorders can be read as cultural statements about gender.

RESISTING "BEAUTY" IDEALS

Although many women strive to attain the beauty ideal on an ongoing, daily basis, some actively resist such cultural norms. These women are choosing to not participate in the beauty rituals, not support the industries that produce both images and products, and create other definitions of beauty. Some women are actively appropriating these standards by highlighting and/or exaggerating the very norms and standards themselves. They are carving out their own notions of beauty through their use of fashion and cosmetics. For them, empowerment involves playing with existing cultural standards. Most women comply with some standards associated with the beauty ideal and resist others. We find a place that suits us, criticize some standards and practices and yet conform to others, usually learning to live with the various contradictions that this implies.

A question that might be raised in response to ideas about resisting beauty ideals and practices is: What's wrong with being beautiful? In response, feminists say that it is not beauty that is a problem but, rather, the way that beauty has been constructed by the dominant culture. This construction excludes many beautiful women

Learn to Love Your Body

Do you ever stand in front of the mirror dreaming about where you'd get a few nips and tucks? Or feeling like life would be better if only you had smaller thighs, a flatter tummy, or there was simply less of you? These are all signs of a not-so-hot body image.

It's important that you feel good about who you are. And until you like yourself as is, trying to change your body shape will be a losing proposition. High self-esteem is important for a healthy, balanced lifestyle—and it's a definite must if successful weight loss is one of your goals. So it's time to smile back at that image in the mirror and value all the wonderful characteristics about the person reflected there. Try these techniques:

1. *Recognize your special qualities.* Make a list of all your positive qualities—not including your physical traits. Are you kind? Artistic? Honest? Good in business? Do you make people laugh? Post your list near the mirror or another place where you'll see it every day.

2. *Put your body back together.* Most of us with negative body images have dissected our bodies into good and bad parts. "I hate my thighs and butt." "My butt's okay, but my stomach is fat and my arms are flabby." Reconnect with your body by appreciating how it all works to keep you going. Try stretching or yoga—the fluid movements are great for getting in touch with the wonders of the human body.

3. *Remember the kid inside you.* Give yourself permission not to be perfect. Inside all of us is the kid we used to be—the kid who didn't have to be perfect and worry about everything. Remember that kid, and give yourself a break. Place a photo of yourself as a child in your bedroom or at your desk at work so that you can see it each day and remember to nurture yourself and laugh a little.

4. *Enjoy your food.* Eating is pleasurable. So enjoy it! Food gives us energy and sustains life. Don't deprive yourself or consider eating an evil act. If you allow yourself to enjoy some of the foods you like, you'll be less likely to overeat. In turn, your body won't feel bloated and uncomfortable.

5. *Indulge in body pleasures.* One step toward being kind to your body, and inevitably yourself, is to indulge yourself. Get a massage, take a long, hot bath, use lotions that smell good, or treat yourself to a manicure or pedicure.

6. *Speak positively.* Pay attention to your self-talk. It's amazing how often we put ourselves down throughout the day. Each time you catch yourself making critical comments, fight back by immediately complimenting yourself.

7. *See the world realistically.* It's common to compare ourselves to people in magazines or movies, but this can make you feel self-conscious. If you want to compare yourself to others, look at the real people around you. They come in different shapes and sizes—and none of them are airbrushed or highlighted.

8. *Dress in clothes that fit.* When we feel badly about our bodies, we often dress in shabby clothes, waiting until we lose weight before we buy something we like. But why? Feel good now! Find attractive clothes that fit your current size. Treating yourself will make you feel renewed.

9. *Be active.* Movement and exercise can make you and your body feel terrific. Not only does exercise help boost your mood, it stimulates your muscles, making you feel more alive and connected to your body.

10. *Thrive!* Living well will help you feel better about who you are and how you look. Strive to make your personal and professional life fulfilling. You are a unique, amazing person. A healthy, happy life can be all yours!

Source: www.thriveonline.com/shape/countdown/countdown.feature2.week7.html.

and helps maintain particular (and very restricted) notions of femininity. Maya Angelou's poem "Phenomenal Woman" celebrates female beauty and encourages women to rejoice in themselves and their looks.

Another common question is: Can you wear makeup and enjoy the adornments associated with femininity and still call yourself a feminist? Most feminists (especially those who identify as third wave) answer with a resounding yes. In fact, you can claim back these trappings and go ultra-femme in celebration of your femininity and your right to self-expression. What is important from a feminist perspective is that these practices are *conscious*. In other words, when women take part in various reproductions of femininity, it is important to understand the bigger picture and be aware of the ways the "beauty" ideal works to limit women, encourages competitiveness (Is she better looking than me? Who is the cutest woman here? How do I measure up?), and ultimately tends to lower women's self-esteem. Understand also how many beauty products are tested on animals, how the packaging of cosmetics and other beauty products encourages the use of resources that end up polluting the environment, and how many fashion items are made by child and/or sweatshop global labor. The point is for us to make conscious and informed choices about our relationships to the "beauty" ideal and to love and take care of our bodies.

Hermaphrodites with Attitude

Amy Bloom

Beautiful, the doctor says. Ten fingers, ten toes, and the mother's beautiful blond curls. Baby and parents crying with relief, three weary, joyful travelers. They place the baby on the mother's stomach, clamp the cord, and hand the father a pair of slim scissors to cut it. The parents expect both these things—they've seen it done in the Lamaze video, they've seen it on the Lifetime channel. The OB nurse cleans and swaddles the baby quickly while the aide washes the mother's face and changes the bloody sheet under her for a fresh one. They give the baby the Apgar test, a visual assessment taken minutes after birth—a nice experience in most cases, since a baby will get a gratifyingly high score, 8 or 9 out of 10, just by being his or her healthy baby self. It is a high score in this case too, but the doctor shakes his head, in such a small gesture that the father doesn't even see it. The mother sees it, through the anaesthetic, through the sweat, right past the sight of her beautiful baby held tight in the nurse's arms.

Finally, the baby is in the mother's arms. The doctor is thinking fast and trying to hide it. As Dr. Richard Hurwitz instructs in *Surgical Reconstruction of Ambiguous Genitalia in Female Children,* a 1990 training videotape produced by the American College of Surgeons, "The finding of ambiguous genitalia in the newborn is a medical and social emergency." A hundred years ago, midwives examined babies and assigned gender in doubtful cases, or they brought the babies to priests or doctors and the team consulted and assigned gender, and little was made of it until the occasional married, childless woman went to her doctor for a hernia and discovered she had testes, or the married, childless farmer went to the doctor

and discovered he had ovaries. Today many physicians regard "genital anomaly" as a dire matter. "After stillbirth, genital anomaly is the most serious problem with a baby, as it threatens the whole fabric of the personality and life of the person," one doctor wrote in 1992; only slightly worse to be dead than intersexed.

The baby is taken to the nursery. The next day the doctor comes in and sits down, and speaks softly. "Your baby will be fine," he says. The parents brace themselves: a faulty valve, a hole where there should be none, something invisible but terrible. "Somehow your baby's genitals haven't finished developing, so we don't quite know right now what sex it is. We're going to run a couple of tests and we'll know very soon. Don't worry. It may be that some cosmetic surgery is required, but don't worry," the doctor tells the parents, who are already well past worrying. "This will all be okay. We can solve this in just a few days. The sooner, the better." As the doctor leaves, he is already calling a pediatric urologist for a consult, getting a pediatric endocrinologist to come over and take a look, getting a geneticist to come on board, to help assign sex and then do what is medically necessary to have the baby's genitals resemble the standard form of that sex.

This scene occurs about two thousand times a year in hospitals all over America. Far from being an exceptionally rare problem, babies born with "genitals that are pretty confusing to all the adults in the room," as medical historian and ethicist Alice Dreger puts it, are more common than babies born with cystic fibrosis. Or, to think of it differently, there are probably at least as many intersexed people in the United States as there are members of the American College of Surgeons.[1]

Imagine a baby born with an oddly shaped but functional arm. Would one choose an invasive, traumatizing pediatric surgery that almost inevitably produces scarring and loss of sensation, just to make the arm conform more closely to the standard shape? Yet parents believe there must be tests that will show their baby's true sex, and surgery that will ensure and reinforce their baby's true sex, and parents want it to happen, quickly. A few days, even a few hours, of having Baby X is too long. One cannot raise a nothing; when people say, "What a beautiful baby! Boy or girl?" one cannot say, "We don't know." In a culture that's still getting used to children who are biracial and adults who are bisexual, the idea of a baby who is neither boy nor girl, or both boy and girl, is unbearable. How do you tell the grandparents? How do you deliver the happy news that you have a healthy it?

The parents hold the baby, still beautiful, still raw but shapely, and they peer at what is under the diaper. Let's say that what they see is a tiny—even for a baby—tiny penis, technically, a microphallus, both misshapen and far smaller than the standard (less than about two centimeters when stretched out from the body). The prevailing approach for the last fifty years has been to declare that a baby boy with such a small and inadequate penis is better off as a girl. In the straightforward words of surgeons, "Easier to make a hole than build a pole," and the collective medical wisdom has been that a boy without much of a pole, and even more, a man without much of a pole, is doomed to live ashamed, apart, and alone. In the face of the assumption that suicide is likely and profound depression inevitable, a physician with the best intentions and the support of his peers might well declare the boy a girl, remove the micropenis and the testes, fashion labia and a small vagina, and tell the parents as little as possible so as to spare the entire family further anxiety and troubling questions of gender (parents who don't know that their little girl was born a boy are less likely to wring their hands over persistent play with trucks and a refusal to wear dresses). . . .

Or let's say that what the parents see is a baby girl with a larger than standard clitoris (more than one centimeter in length). You might not think that this is a problem of "doubtful sex" or confusing genitals, but in infants the gap between clitoris and penis is only about half a centimeter, so the large clitoris that doctors fear will worry her parents every time they change the diaper, and will alarm or even dissuade her future husband, also requires the surgical solution, as early as possible. The surgeries include "clitoral reduction," and if necessary, some enlargement of the vaginal cavity by metal dilators inserted by the parents daily for six months, beginning two weeks postoperatively. Monthly dilation of the seven-or eight-year-old continues into adolescence to prevent narrowing or closure of the vaginal cavity. (The standard for a "good" vagina is one that can be penetrated adequately.) And then, perhaps, following the early vaginoplasty, further molding of delicate and cosmetically pleasing labia may be required.

"Ambiguous genitals," "doubtful sex," "intersexed babies," "male and female pseudohermaphroditism," "true hermaphroditism"—these phrases sometimes describe the same conditions, sometimes very different conditions. Some conditions require hormonal treatment or surgery or both; some require no treatment at all except counseling and time. Symptoms range from the physical anomaly—an unusual-looking set of genitals—to symptoms that will not become apparent until adolescence, to symptoms that will never be apparent from the outside. Some anomalies are defects in the plumbing; others are simply unusual fixtures.

There is a range of medical conditions that fall under the umbrella term "congenital anomalies of the reproductive and sexual system." Boys may suffer from hypospadias, meaning in mild cases that the urethral opening (the "pee hole"), which is supposed to be at the tip of the penis, is perhaps in the glans, on the underside of the penis, or in more severe cases is open from mid-shaft out to the glans, or is even entirely absent, with urine exiting the bladder from behind the penis. Hypospadias sometimes results in ambiguity as to sexual organs, as does Klinefelter's syndrome, which is quite common, occurring in one in five hundred to one in a thousand male births. Most men inherit a single X chromosome from their mother and a single Y chromosome from their father. Men with Klinefelter's inherit an extra X chromosome from either father or mother, and their testes often produce smaller than average quantities of testosterone, so that they don't virilize (develop facial and body hair, muscles, deep voice, larger penis and testes) as strongly as other boys at puberty. (Many also develop small breasts, one of Nature's variations that is often found in those with no intersex conditions at all.) Despite an absence of sperm in their generally small, firm testes, many men with Klinefelter's are never diagnosed because their genitals are typical in appearance.

In androgen insensitivity syndrome (AIS), the body of an XY individual lacks a receptor that enables it to decode messages from androgens (virilizing hormones). AIS results in people with male chromosomes and obviously female bodies; although they produce male hormones, their cells are not sensitive to those hormones, and their bodies never masculinize. There is also partial androgen insensitivity syndrome (PAIS), which typically results in "ambiguous genitalia." The clitoris is large or, alternatively, the penis is small and hypospadic (two different ways of labeling the same anatomical structure). PAIS seems to be quite common, and has been suggested as the cause of infertility in many men whose genitals are typically male.

Among the most prevalent causes of intersexuality among XX (usually female) people is congenital adrenal hyperplasia (CAH), in which the adrenal gland produces an excess of androgens but feminizing occurs at puberty because the ovaries function normally. When excess androgens are produced in utero (sometimes not because of CAH but because an unborn XX baby's metabolism converts hormonal drugs such as progestin, which was frequently administered to prevent miscarriage in the 1950s and 1960s, into an androgen), the female baby may be born with an enlarged clitoris and fused labia that look very much like a scrotum. Sometimes the genitals look typically female, with barely perceptible variations. Sometimes the babies appear to be healthy boys

without testes, and it may be that no one in the delivery room thinks anything is amiss. And less often, the babies' genitals are not just misleading but the hallmark of what has historically been called hermaphroditism: truly ambiguous genitals, both male and female, although not a complete set of either.

. . .

In modern America, we have done our own disappearing act on hermaphrodites: we have turned a lot of baby boys into baby girls, and a lot of healthy baby girls into traumatized ones. A number of scientists and academics have written about this in the last ten years (most notably, the gifted researcher Dreger, the eminently readable and imaginative Fausto-Sterling, the less readable, provocative Judith Butler, and the psychologist Suzanne Kessler), but the person who has almost single-handedly changed both the dialogue on the subject and the surgical practice itself is Cheryl Chase, businesswoman turned activist. . . . In a world of megacorporations, tobacco-sponsored rock concerts, and vast, unsavory alliances, Cheryl Chase, perceived as a "true hermaphrodite," first declared a girl, then a boy, then not much of a boy, then operated upon to make her a more suitable girl by removing her "too large" clitoris (what was too large as a clitoris was, of course, terminally too small as a penis), is a modest, relentless, sleepless army of one.

In 1993, she was just an angry woman, distressed and puzzled by the little she knew of her own traumatic history, and anxious to move past it by offering support to people born intersexed (that is, people who have historically been called, with mystery but not much meaning, "hermaphrodites"). She did outreach and information-sharing and complained to anyone who would listen about the unnecessary and usually damaging surgery routinely visited upon babies born with ambiguous genitals—five babies every day, as a conservative estimate, to state the incidence in another way. She picketed; she fired off press releases from her home in the name of her fledgling group, the Intersex Society of North America (ISNA); she organized support meetings and sent out an indignant and well-informed newsletter (now the *ISNA Newsletter,* formerly and more compellingly called *Hermaphrodites with Attitude*). Cheryl Chase and her lieutenants, volunteers all . . . , have changed the terms of discussion about surgery and treatment for intersexed babies. The head of pediatric endocrinology at Oakland Hospital now supports the ISNA point of view, the American Medical Association's *Archives of Pediatrics and Adolescent Medicine* has run articles that mirror ISNA's position, and Chase herself has been invited to give talks at the Albert Einstein College of Medicine in New York City, at Denver Children's Hospital, and at the 2000 meeting of the Lawson Wilkins Pediatric Endocrine Society, as the honored closing speaker.

It may be that if you can tell the right story, at the right moment, even people who don't wish to hear will hear. The story of intersex babies is medically complicated, but ISNA simplified it. . . . Through careful study and the pained honesty of intersexed adults, ISNA has undermined the standard argument of good-hearted people ("Surgery may not be a great solution, but it's the only one we have, and it would be worse to raise those poor children as 'nothings'"), and it has undone the peculiar psychological argument that many pediatricians made (parents would be so upset every time they changed a diaper that they would not be able to love the child, and a child with inadequate genitals, especially a boy, would not be able to survive the scrutiny of other children). As common sense dictates, ISNA supports surgery when a medical condition requires it, and encourages families to consult with endocrinologists, knowledgeable psychotherapists, and, if appropriate, the best surgeons they can find. . . .

    . . .

"No lying," Philip Gruppuso says. "No delusions of grandeur on the part of the doctor."

Gruppuso is both a doctor and a dad. He's a bearded, fatherly middle-aged man with twin daughters, now twenty-one years old. When sexual orientation comes up over drinks or at conferences, he tells his colleagues that he wouldn't care if either or both of his girls were lesbians. The straight men around him eye him dubiously, and he's not sure whether they're wondering why he's saying something that couldn't possibly be true, or whether they're wondering if it *is* true—which makes them wonder what kind of normal middle-aged physician and family man from the Bronx would feel that way.

"Physicians, like everyone else, find it hard to change. Not just because of habit but because, in the history of treating these kids, there is an element of homophobia. It doesn't make my colleagues happy when I say this. If you look back at the standard texts of the fifties and sixties, the underlying concern was that people who were 'really' male but looked female would want to have sex with males, and the same for females who appeared male. Homosexual sex was the underlying fear. Not worrying about sexual orientation allows me to think about what's best for the patient and what's good medical practice."

If this criticism has not endeared Gruppuso to his pediatric colleagues, neither has his straightforward assessment of the most common treatment for intersexed babies, and of why it's still more common than what ISNA recommends: "This isn't complicated, it's simple. There are a million ways to screw this up, and most of them have to do with doctors being too sure of themselves, imagining that they control the outcome for sexual orientation and gender identity, and then doing irreversible surgery."

Ten years ago, Phil Gruppuso, now director of research in pediatrics at Rhode Island Hospital and professor of pediatrics and biochemistry at Brown University, was a doctor just like that.

"I was a pediatric endocrinologist and very much in the mainstream. Anne Fausto-Sterling was a colleague and became a friend. I started thinking: I'm a scientist, look at the evidence, look at the follow-ups. I looked at the evidence, and the evidence that this genital surgery is a good idea is just—junk. There's no such evidence that doing surgery on infant genitals for appearance' sake, surgery without consent and which frequently results in sexual dysfunction—there's no evidence at all that this is a good thing. And I am unwilling to harm patients to protect the reputations of physicians who are fine academicians and thoughtful men, but who were—mistaken."

And his advice to doctors confronting their first intersexed baby? "Get a specialist and don't do anything irreversible. Be willing to say, 'It may take a month for us to have a diagnosis and a determination of gender.' Help the parents, help the grandparents, and always, always—it's the first thing we learn as doctors—do no harm. This surgery, and intersexed babies treated by people who don't know what they're doing, does harm."

At the other end of the debate on the treatment of the intersexed are Drs. Richard Hurwitz and Harry Applebaum, creators of the American College of Surgeons training videotape on ambiguous genitals in female children. The tape begins with Vivaldi and a statement of goals: reduce the size of the clitoris, exteriorize the vagina (making it penetrable), and make the genitals cosmetically normal. There is no mention at all of either function or feeling. Hurwitz looks into the camera and says, with quiet confidence, "The treatment of the clitoris depends on its size and the preference of the surgeon." I'm sure it is so; I'm surprised that he says it. "If the clitoris is very large, however," Hurwitz continues as the camera carefully follows the scalpel and the removal of erectile tissue from the clitoris until it folds back into itself, accordionlike, "it may need to be taken care of for social reasons."

It is hard to imagine what social reasons a baby girl might have. It's harder still to imagine how the odd results, described repeatedly in the videotape as cosmetically pleasing, could be anything other than a source of shame and discomfort. Not only are the results not cosmetically pleasing, they're not even good. The surgically altered vaginas and reduced clitorises are painful to contemplate (and even more painfully, the vaginas will probably close and require dilation in the course of the patients' childhood). And according to U.K. research reported in the *Lancet,* follow-up studies of intersexed children show more sexual and psychological dysfunction among those who have had these pull-through vaginoplasties and clitoral reductions than among those who have had no surgery at all. To watch the surgery is to wonder who in their right mind could think that stripping away and excising nerves protects sexual

function or that this surgery is not only preferable but essential and urgent—far more so than helping parents help their child to live with a large clitoris, or with a tiny penis, or even with other, more puzzling anomalies.

Not monsters, nor marvels, nor battering rams for gender theory, people born intersexed have given the rest of the world an opportunity to think more about the odd significance we give to gender, about the elusive nature of truth, about the understandable, sometimes dangerous human yearning for simplicity—and we might, in return, offer them medical care only when they need it, and a little common sense and civilized embrace when they don't.

NOTE

1. In a 1998 article in *The Hastings Center Report,* Dreger writes, "Most people . . . assume the phenomenon of intersexuality to be exceedingly rare. It is not. But how common is it? The answer depends, of course, on how one defines it. Broadly speaking, intersexuality constitutes a range of anatomical conditions in which an individual's anatomy mixes key masculine anatomy with key feminine anatomy. One quickly runs into a problem, however, when trying to define 'key' or 'essential' feminine and masculine anatomy. In fact, any close study of sexual anatomy results in a loss of faith that there is a simple, 'natural' sex distinction that will not break down. . . . For our purposes, it is simplest to put the question of frequency pragmatically: How often do physicians find themselves unsure which gender to assign at birth? One 1993 gynecology text estimates that 'in approximately 1 in 500 births, the sex is doubtful because of the external genitalia.' I am persuaded by more recent, well-documented literature that estimates the number to be roughly 1 in 1,500 live births." The authors of a peer-reviewed 2000 article in the *American Journal of Human Biology* write, "We surveyed the medical literature from 1955 to the present for studies of the frequency of deviation from the ideal of male or female. We conclude that this frequency may be as high as 2% of live births. The frequency of individuals receiving 'corrective' genital surgery, however, probably runs between one and two per 1,000 live births (0.1 to 0.2%)." The Intersex Society of North America bases its

estimate of one in 2,000 (which, given about four million births a year, yields an annual total of two thousand births) on "statistics of how many newborn babies are referred to 'gender identity teams' in major hospitals." By any of these reckonings, intersexuality is significantly more common than cystic fibrosis, which has an incidence of one in 2,300 live births, according to the Cystic Fibrosis Research website, and affects some forty thousand children and adults in the United States. The number of fellows of the American College of Surgeons fluctuates a bit from year to year but is about fifty thousand.

R E A D I N G   36

Breast Buds and the "Training" Bra

Joan Jacobs Brumberg

In every generation, small swellings around the nipples have announced the arrival of puberty. This development, known clinically as "breast buds," occurs before menarche and almost always provokes wonder and self-scrutiny. "I began to examine myself carefully, to search my armpits for hairs and my breasts for signs of swelling," wrote Kate Simon about coming of age in the Bronx at the time of World War I. Although Simon was "horrified" by the rapidity with which her chest developed, many girls, both in literature and real life, long for this important mark of maturity. In Jamaica Kincaid's fictional memoir of growing up in Antigua, *Annie John,* the main character, regarded her breasts as "treasured shrubs, needing only the proper combination of water and sunlight to make them flourish." In order to get their breasts to grow, Annie and her best friend, Gwen, lay in a pasture exposing their small bosoms to the moonlight.

Breasts are particularly important to girls in cultures or time periods that give powerful meaning or visual significance to that part of the body. Throughout history, different body parts have been eroticized in art, literature, photography, and film. In some eras, the ankle or upper arm was the ultimate statement of female sexuality. But breasts were the particular preoccupation of Americans in the years after World War II, when voluptuous stars, such as Jayne Mansfield, Jane Russell, and Marilyn Monroe, were popular box-office attractions. The mammary fixation of the 1950s extended beyond movie stars and shaped the experience of adolescents of both genders. In that era, boys seemed to prefer girls who were "busty," and American girls began to worry about breast size as well as about weight. This elaboration of the ideal of beauty raised expectations about what adolescent girls should look like. It also required them to put even more energy and resources into their body projects, beginning at an earlier age.

The story of how this happened is intertwined with the history of the bra, an undergarment that came into its own, as separate from the corset, in the early twentieth century. In 1900, a girl of twelve or thirteen typically wore a one-piece "waist" or camisole that had no cups or darts in front. As her breasts developed, she moved into different styles of the same garment, but these had more construction, such as stitching, tucks, and bones, that would accentuate the smallness of her waist and shape the bosom. In those days, before the arrival of the brassiere, there were no "cups." The bosom was worn low; there was absolutely no interest in uplift, and not a hint of cleavage.

The French word *brassière,* which actually means an infant's undergarment or harness, was used in *Vogue* as early as 1907. In the United States, the first boneless bra to leave the midriff bare was developed in 1913 by Mary Phelps Jacobs, a New York City debutante. Under the name Caresse Crosby, Jacobs marketed a bra made of two French lace handkerchiefs suspended from the shoulders. Many young women in the 1920s, such as Yvonne Blue, bought their first bras in order to achieve the kind of slim, boyish figure that the characteristic chemise (or flapper) dress required. The first bras were designed simply to flatten, but they were superseded by others intended to shape and control the breasts. Our current cup sizes (A, B, C, and D), as well as the idea of circular stitching to enhance the roundness of the breast, emerged in the 1930s.

Adult women, not adolescents, were the first market for bras. Sexually maturing girls simply moved into adult-size bras when they were ready—and if their parents had the money. Many women and girls in the early twentieth century still made their own underwear at home, and some read the advertisements for bras with real longing. When she began to develop breasts in the 1930s, Malvis Helmi, a midwestern farm girl, remembered feeling embarrassed whenever she wore an old summer dimity that pulled and gaped across her expanding chest. As a result, she spoke to her mother, considered the brassieres in the Sears, Roebuck catalog, and decided to purchase two for twenty-five cents. However, when her hardworking father saw the order form, he vetoed the idea and declared, "Our kind of people can't afford to spend money on such nonsense." Although her mother made her a makeshift bra, Malvis vowed that someday she would have store-bought brassieres. Home economics teachers in the interwar years tried to get high school girls to make their own underwear because it saved money, but the idea never caught on once mass-produced bras became widely available.

The transition from homemade to mass-produced bras was critical in how adolescent girls thought about their breasts. In general, mass-produced clothing fostered autonomy in girls because it took matters of style and taste outside the dominion of the mother, who had traditionally made and supervised a girl's wardrobe. But in the case of brassieres, buying probably had another effect. So long as clothing was made at home, the dimensions of the garment could be adjusted to the particular body intended to wear it. But with store-bought clothes, the body had to fit instantaneously into standard sizes that were constructed from a pattern representing a norm. When clothing failed to fit the body, particularly a part as intimate as the breasts, young women were apt to perceive that there was something wrong with their bodies. In this way, mass-produced bras in standard cup sizes probably increased, rather than diminished, adolescent self-consciousness about the breasts.

Until the 1950s, the budding breasts of American girls received no special attention from either bra manufacturers, doctors, or parents. Girls generally wore undershirts until they were sufficiently developed to fill an adult-size bra. Mothers and daughters traditionally handled this transformation in private, at home. But in the gyms and locker rooms of postwar junior high schools, girls began to look around to see who did and did not wear a bra. Many of these girls had begun menstruating and developing earlier than their mothers had, and this visual information was very powerful. In some circles, the ability to wear and fill a bra was central to an adolescent girl's status and sense of self. "I have a figure problem," a fourteen-year-old wrote to *Seventeen* in 1952: "All of my friends are tall and shapely while my figure still remains up-and-down. Can you advise me?"

In an era distinguished by its worship of full-breasted women, interest in adolescent breasts came from all quarters: girls who wanted bras at an earlier age than ever before; mothers who believed that they should help a daughter acquire a "good" figure; doctors who valued maternity over all other female roles; and merchandisers who saw profits in convincing girls and their parents that adolescent breasts needed to be tended in special ways. All of this interest coalesced in the 1950s to make the brassiere as critical as the sanitary napkin in making a girl's transition into adulthood both modern and successful.

The old idea that brassieres were frivolous or unnecessary for young girls was replaced by a national discussion about their medical and psychological benefits. "My daughter who is well developed but not yet twelve wants to wear a bra," wrote a mother in Massachusetts to *Today's Health* in 1951. "I want her to wear an undervest instead because I think it is better not to have anything binding. What do you think about a preadolescent girl wearing a bra?" That same year a reader from Wilmington, Delaware, asked *Seventeen:* "Should a girl of fourteen wear a bra? There are some older women who insist we don't need them." The editor's answer was an unequivocal endorsement of early bras: "Just as soon as your breasts begin to show signs of development, you should start wearing a bra." By the early 1950s, "training" or "beginner" bras were available in AAA and AA sizes for girls whose chests were essentially flat but who wanted a bra nonetheless. Along with acne creams, advertisements for these brassieres were standard fare in magazines for girls.

Physicians provided a medical rationale for purchasing bras early. In 1952, in an article in *Parents' Magazine,* physician Frank H. Crowell endorsed bras for young girls and spelled out a theory and program of teenage breast management. "Unlike other organs such as the stomach and intestines which have ligaments that act as guywires or slings to hold them in place," Crowell claimed, the breast was simply "a growth developed from the skin and held up only by the skin." An adolescent girl needed a bra in order to prevent sagging breasts, stretched blood vessels, and poor circulation, all of which would create problems in nursing her future children. In addition, a "dropped" breast was "not so attractive," Crowell said, so it was important to get adolescents into bras early, before their breasts began to sag. The "training" that a training bra was supposed to accomplish was the first step toward motherhood and a sexually alluring figure, as it was defined in the 1950s.

In the interest of both beauty and health, mothers in the 1950s were encouraged to check their daughters' breasts regularly to see if they were developing properly. This was not just a matter of a quick look and a word of reassurance.

Instead, Crowell and others suggested systematic scrutiny as often as every three months to see if the breasts were positioned correctly. One way to chart the geography of the adolescent bustline was to have the girl stand sideways in a darkened room against a wall covered with white paper. By shining a bright light on her and having her throw out her chest at a provocative angle, a mother could trace a silhouette that indicated the actual shape of her daughter's bosom. By placing a pencil under her armpit, and folding the arm that held it across the waist, mothers could also determine if their daughter's nipples were in the right place. On a healthy breast, the nipple was supposed to be at least halfway above the midway point between the location of the pencil and the hollow of the elbow.

Breasts were actually only one part of a larger body project encouraged by the foundation garment industry in postwar America. In this era, both physicians and entrepreneurs promoted a general philosophy of "junior figure control." Companies such as Warners, Maidenform, Formfit, Belle Mode, and Perfect Form (as well as popular magazines like *Good Housekeeping*) all encouraged the idea that young women needed both lightweight girdles and bras to "start the figure off to a beautiful future."

The concept of "support" was aided and abetted by new materials—such as nylon netting and two-way stretch fabrics—developed during the war but applied afterward to women's underwear. By the early 1950s, a reenergized corset and brassiere industry was poised for extraordinary profits. If "junior figure control" became the ideal among the nation's mothers and daughters, it would open up sales of bras and girdles to the largest generation of adolescents in American history, the so-called baby boomers. Once again, as in the case of menstruation and acne, the bodies of adolescent girls had the potential to deliver considerable profit.

There was virtually no resistance to the idea that American girls should wear bras and girdles in adolescence. Regardless of whether a girl was thin or heavy, "junior figure control" was in order, and that phrase became a pervasive sales mantra. "Even slim youthful figures will require foundation assistance," advised *Women's Wear Daily* in 1957. In both *Seventeen* and *Compact,* the two most popular magazines for the age group, high school girls were urged to purchase special foundation garments such as "Bobbie" bras and girdles by Formfit and "Adagio" by Maidenform that were "teen-proportioned" and designed, allegedly, with the help of adolescent consultants. The bras were available in pastel colors in a variety of special sizes, starting with AAA, and they were decorated with lace and ribbon to make them especially feminine. In addition to holding up stockings, girdles were intended to flatten the tummy and also provide light, but firm, control for hips and buttocks. The advertisements for "Bobbie," in particular, suggested good things about girls who controlled their flesh in this way; they were pretty, had lots of friends, and drank Coca-Cola. As adults, they would have good figures and happy futures because they had chosen correct underwear in their youth.

By the mid-1950s, department stores and specialty shops had developed aggressive educational programs designed to spread the gospel of "junior figure control." In order to make young women "foundation conscious," Shillito's, a leading Cincinnati department store, tried to persuade girls and their mothers of the importance of having a professional fitting of the first bra. Through local newspaper advertisements, and also programs in home economics classes, Shillito's buyer, Edith Blincoe, promoted the idea that the purchase of bras and girdles required special expertise, which only department stores could provide. (*Seventeen* echoed her idea and advised a "trained fitter" for girls who wanted a "prettier" bosom and a "smoother" figure.) Blincoe acknowledged that teenage girls were already "100% bra conscious," and she hoped to develop the same level of attention to panty girdles. In order to attract junior customers and get them to try on both items, she had the corset department place advertising cards on the walls of dressing rooms in sections of the store where teenagers and their mothers shopped. Strapless bras were suggested on cards in the dress and formal wear departments; light-weight girdles were suggested in the sportswear and bathing suit sections.

In home economics classes, and also at the local women's club, thousands of American girls saw informational films such as *Figure Forum* and *Facts About Your Figure,* made by the Warner Brassiere Company in the 1950s. Films like these stressed the need for appropriate foundation garments in youth and provided girls with scientific principles for selecting them. They also taught young women how to bend over and lean into their bras, a maneuver that most of us learned early and still do automatically. Most middle-class girls and their mothers embraced the code of "junior figure control" and spent time and money in pursuit of the correct garments. Before a school dance in 1957, Gloria James, a sixteen-year-old African-American girl, wrote in her diary: "Mommy and I rushed to Perth Amboy [New Jersey] to get me some slacks, bras and a girdle. I don't even know how to get it [the girdle] on."

In the postwar world, the budding adolescent body was big business. Trade publications, such as *Women's Wear Daily,* gave special attention to sales strategies and trends in marketing to girls. In their reports from Cincinnati, Atlanta, and Houston, one thing was clear: wherever American girls purchased bras, they wanted to be treated as grown-ups, even if they wore only a AAA or AA cup. In Atlanta, at the Redwood Corset and Lingerie Shop, owner Sally Blye and her staff spoke persuasively to young customers about the importance of "uplift" in order "not to break muscle tissue." And at Houston's popular Teen Age Shop, specially trained salesgirls allowed young customers to look through the brassieres on their own, and then encouraged them to try on items in the dressing room without their mothers. Although many girls were shy at first, by the age of fourteen and fifteen most had lost their initial self-consciousness. "They take the merchandise and go right in [to the dressing room]," Blincoe said about her teenage clientele. Girls who could not be reached by store or school programs could send away to the Belle Mode Brassiere Company for free booklets about "junior figure control" with titles such as "The Modern Miss—Misfit or Miss Fit" and "How to Be Perfectly Charming." In the effort to help girls focus on their figures,

Formfit, maker of the popular "Bobbies," offered a free purse-size booklet on calorie counting.

Given all this attention, it's not surprising that bras and breasts were a source of concern in adolescents' diaries written in the 1950s. Sandra Rubin got her first bra in 1951, when she was a twelve-year-old in Cleveland, but she did not try it on in a department store. Instead, her mother bought her a "braziere" while she was away on a trip and sent it home. "It's very fancy," Sandra wrote. "I almost died! I ran right upstairs to put it on." When she moved to New York City that September and entered Roosevelt Junior High School, Sandra got involved with a clique of seven girls who called themselves the "7Bs." Their name was not about their homeroom; it was about the cup size they wanted to be. "Flat, Flat! The air vibrates with that name as my friends and I walk by," Sandra wrote in a humorous but self-deprecating manner. By the time she was sixteen, Sandra had developed amply, so that her breasts became a source of pride. One night she had an intimate conversation with a male friend about the issue of chests: "We talked about flat-chested women (of which, he pointed out, I certainly am not [one])."

Breasts, not weight, were the primary point of comparison among high school girls in the 1950s. Although Sandra Rubin called herself a "fat hog" after eating too much candy, her diary reportage was principally about the bosoms, rather than the waistlines, she saw at school. Those who had ample bosoms seemed to travel through the hallways in a veritable state of grace, at least from the perspective of girls who considered themselves flat-chested. "Busty" girls made desirable friends because they seemed sophisticated, and they attracted boys. In December 1959, when she planned a Friday-night pajama party, thirteen-year-old Ruth Teischman made a courageous move by inviting the "gorgeous" Roslyn, a girl whom she wrote about frequently but usually only worshiped from afar. After a night of giggling and eating with her junior high school friends, Ruth revealed in her diary the source of Roslyn's power and beauty: "Roslyn is very big. (Bust of course.) I am very flat. I wish I would get

bigger fast." Many girls in the 1950s perused the ads, usually in the back of women's magazines, for exercise programs and creams guaranteed to make their breasts grow, allegedly in short order.

The lament of the flat-chested girl—"I must, I must, I must develop my bust"—was on many private hit parades in the 1950s. There was a special intensity about breasts because of the attitudes of doctors, mothers, and advertisers, all of whom considered breast development critical to adult female identity and success. Although "junior figure control" increased pressure on the entire body, and many girls wore waist cinches as well as girdles, it was anxiety about breasts, more than any other body part, that characterized adolescent experience in these years. As a result, thousands, if not millions, of girls in early adolescence jumped the gun and bought "training bras" at the first sight of breast buds, or they bought padded bras to disguise their perceived inadequacy. In the 1950s, the bra was validated as a rite of passage: regardless of whether a girl was voluptuous or flat, she was likely to purchase her first bra at an earlier age than had her mother. This precocity was due, in part, to biology, but it was also a result of entrepreneurial interests aided and abetted by medical concern. By the 1950s, American society was so consumer-oriented that there were hardly any families, even among the poor, who would expect to make bras for their daughters the way earlier generations had made their own sanitary napkins.

Training bras were a boon to the foundation garment industry, but they also meant that girls' bodies were sexualized earlier. In contemporary America, girls of nine or ten are shepherded from undershirts into little underwear sets that come with tops that are protobrassieres. Although this may seem innocuous and natural, it is not the same as little girls "dressing up" in their mother's clothing. In our culture, traditional distinctions between adult clothing and juvenile clothing have narrowed considerably, so that mature women dress "down," in the garments of kids, just as often as little girls dress "up." While the age homogeneity of the contemporary wardrobe helps adult women feel less matronly, dressing little girls in adult clothing can have an insidious side effect. Because a bra shapes the breasts in accordance with fashion, it acts very much like an interpreter, translating functional anatomy into a sexual or erotic vocabulary. When we dress little girls in brassieres or bikinis, we imply adult behaviors and, unwittingly, we mark them as sexual objects. The training bras of the 1950s loom large in the history of adolescent girls because they foreshadowed the ways in which the nation's entrepreneurs would accommodate, and also encourage, precocious sexuality.

R E A D I N G   **37**

If Men Could Menstruate

Gloria Steinem (1978)

A white minority of the world has spent centuries conning us into thinking that a white skin makes people superior—even though the only thing it really does is make them more subject to ultraviolet rays and to wrinkles. Male human beings have built whole cultures around the idea that penis-envy is "natural" to women—though having such an unprotected organ might be said to make men vulnerable, and the power to give birth makes womb-envy at least as logical.

In short, the characteristics of the powerful, whatever they may be, are thought to be better than the characteristics of the powerless—and logic has nothing to do with it.

What would happen, for instance, if suddenly, magically, men could menstruate and women could not?

The answer is clear—menstruation would become an enviable, boast-worthy, masculine event:

Men would brag about how long and how much.

Boys would mark the onset of menses, the longed-for proof of manhood, with religious ritual and stag parties.

Congress would fund a National Institute of Dysmenorrhea to help stamp out monthly discomforts.

Sanitary supplies would be federally funded and free. (Of course, some men would still pay for the prestige of commercial brands such as John Wayne Tampons, Muhammad Ali's Rope-a-dope Pads, Joe Namath Jock Shields—"For Those Light Bachelor Days," and Robert "Barretta" Blake Maxi-Pads.)

Military men, right-wing politicians, and religious fundamentalists would cite menstruation ("*men*struation") as proof that only men could serve in the Army ("you have to give blood to take blood"), occupy political office ("can women be aggressive without that stead-fast cycle governed by the planet Mars?"), be priests and ministers ("how could a woman give her blood for our sins?"), or rabbis ("without the monthly loss of impurities, women remain unclean").

Male radicals, left-wing politicians, and mystics, however, would insist that women are equal, just different; and that any woman could enter their ranks if only she were willing to self-inflict a major wound every month ("you *must* give blood for the revolution"), recognize the preeminence of menstrual issues, or subordinate her selfness to all men in their Cycle of Enlightenment.

Street guys would brag ("I'm a three-pad man") or answer praise from a buddy ("Man, you lookin' *good!*") by giving fives and saying, "Yeah, man, I'm on the rag!"

TV shows would treat the subject at length. ("Happy Days": Richie and Potsie try to convince

Fonzie that he is still "The Fonz," though he has missed two periods in a row.) So would newspapers. (SHARK SCARE THREATENS MENSTRUATING MEN. JUDGE CITES MONTHLY STRESS IN PARDONING RAPIST.) And movies. (Newman and Redford in "Blood Brothers"!)

Men would convince women that intercourse was *more* pleasurable at "that time of the month." Lesbians would be said to fear blood and therefore life itself—though probably only because they needed a good menstruating man.

Of course, male intellectuals would offer the most moral and logical arguments. How could a woman master any discipline that demanded a sense of time, space, mathematics, or measurement, for instance, without that in-built gift for measuring the cycles of the moon and planets—and thus for measuring anything at all? In the rarefied fields of philosophy and religion, could women compensate for missing the rhythm of the universe? Or for their lack of symbolic death-and-resurrection every month?

Liberal males in every field would try to be kind: the fact that "these people" have no gift for measuring life or connecting to the universe, the liberals would explain, should be punishment enough.

And how would women be trained to react? One can imagine traditional women agreeing to all these arguments with a staunch and smiling masochism. ("The ERA would force housewives to wound themselves every month": Phyllis Schlafly. "Your husband's blood is as sacred as that of Jesus—and so sexy, too!": Marabel Morgan.) Reformers and Queen Bees would try to imitate men, and *pretend* to have a monthly cycle. All feminists would explain endlessly that men, too, needed to be liberated from the false idea of Martian aggressiveness, just as women needed to escape the bonds of menses-envy. Radical feminists would add that the oppression of the non-menstrual was the pattern for all other oppressions. ("Vampires were our first freedom fighters!") Cultural feminists would develop a bloodless imagery in art and literature. Socialist feminists would insist that only under capitalism would men be able to monopolize menstrual blood. . . . In fact, if men could menstruate, the power justifications could probably go on forever.

If we let them.

R E A D I N G **38**

Body Ethics and Aesthetics Among African American and Latina Women

Lisa R. Rubin, Mako L. Fitts, and Anne E. Becker

INTRODUCTION

This paper reports on an investigation of the relationships among ethnicity, self-representation, and body aesthetics among a sample of college-educated black and Latina women. Until recently, there has been a clinical and lay misperception that body image and weight-related concerns predominantly affect white upper- and middle-class girls and women. Because the ideal of thinness for women is viewed as a European American aesthetic preference, women of color—particularly African American and Latina women—have been considered relatively "protected" from the development of body dissatisfaction and disordered eating common among white women. Contemporary research among women of color has challenged the myth that ethnic minority women in the United States are "immune" from body dissatisfaction and disordered eating (Root 1990). However, within this growing body of research are suggestions that the nature and expression of these concerns may in many cases be distinct from symptom patterns described within the established eating disorders literature (Kuba and Harris 2001).

. . . Clinical research on sociocultural contributions to disordered eating and body image has produced a literature with a relatively narrow focus on the relationship between body satisfaction and culturally-promoted aesthetic body ideals. Clinical research has also been dominated by quantitative methods. Moreover, its exclusive use of measures developed and validated among predominantly White, Northern American, and Western European samples has limited the scope of understanding of more diverse experiences of eating and embodiment (Davis and Yager 1992). Indeed, the clinical significance attributed to body aesthetics among other populations may be misguided, and may in fact have obscured other important protective and risk factors for eating disorders in ethnically diverse populations. This provides insight into the clinical paradox that the greater body satisfaction reported among African American women as compared with white or Latina women (Akan and Grilo 1995; Altabe 1998) has not conferred the expected protection from disordered eating. That is, several studies among African American subjects have found equivalent rates of purging behavior and notably higher rates of laxative and diuretic abuse relative to white girls and women (Emmons 1992; Pumariega et al. 1994). Similarly, whereas Latina girls and women have been found to report larger (i.e., less thin) aesthetic body ideals (Winkleby et al. 1996) and less concern about weight than whites (Crago et al. 1996), research suggests that disordered eating among Hispanic youth is equivalent to that among whites (Crago et al. 1996; Smith and Krejci 1991). . . . These data strongly suggest that there is a different relationship among aesthetic ideals, body satisfaction, and disordered eating among women of color than has been found among white women.

. . .

Representation and Resistance

Bordo argues that mainstream Western media imagery tends to homogenize female beauty, removing racial, ethnic, and sexual differences that "disturb Anglo-Saxon, heterosexual expectations and identifications" (1993:25). These beauty ideals become models against which women measure, judge, and discipline their bodies. Whereas these models typically represent an unhealthful ideal for any woman to achieve, they may be particularly oppressive for many women of color, whose body size, shape, and features may differ significantly from mainstream representations of female beauty (see Becker et al. 2002). Their looks are either denigrated or simply erased from mainstream cultural imagery. Although women of color are now more likely to be represented in beauty and fashion magazines, these representations rarely subvert the dominant imagery. Rather, they typically reinscribe prevailing stereotypes by featuring women with lighter skin and "Anglo" features to the exclusion of other women, and by exoticizing and eroticizing racial difference (hooks 1992).

. . .

Black feminist appeals to women of color to resist hegemony echo a growing interest in the examination of how cultural representations oppress individuals and whether and how this oppression can be resisted. Collins argues that "the controlling images applied to black women are so uniformly negative that they almost necessitate resistance" (2000:100). . . .

Culture and Embodiment

. . .

Previous research suggests important differences in the concepts of body and beauty ideals among both African American and white working-class girls and their white middle- and upper-class counterparts. Mimi Nichter (2000) examined culturally-valued forms of self-presentation, as identified by African American girls, and, in particular, the context and motivation in which these forms are exhibited. She found that while white girls in the study maintained a fixed concept of beauty, "a living manifestation of the Barbie doll" (Parker et al. 1995:106), the African American girls defined beauty through attitude, style, personality, and presence rather than through attaining the "perfect" look. This finding parallels statements from Collins (1990), who argues that while Eurocentric beauty is rigid, Afrocentric beauty is "not based solely on physical criteria" (1990:89). Similarly, participants in Lyn Mikel Brown's (1998) study of white working-class adolescent girls recognized the "perfect" look as a culturally constructed fiction, mocking it (even as they admired it), and ultimately identifying qualities such as trust and attitude as valued over physical appearance. Although this work provides a beginning framework for understanding beauty ideals among girls of diverse social backgrounds, further research is needed to explore these concerns among White working-class women and African American women of all classes.

. . .

METHODS

Narrative data generated in focus group discussions were used to investigate relationships among ethnicity, self-representation, and body aesthetic ideals among ethnically diverse women. . . .

A total of 18 women participated in this study, eight who self-identified as black or African American and ten who self-identified as Latina or Chicana. Five of the women participating in the Latina focus groups were born outside of the United States, in Mexico and Central America, and five were born in the United States. Among participants in the black women's focus group, two were born in the Virgin Islands and the rest were born in the United States. All participants had been living in the United States for several years. Participants ranged in age from 18 to 60 years old, with a mean age of 25. All participants had at least some college education, and four were graduate students. Most participants were raised in middle- and working-class family

households and had already exceeded their parents' educational attainment.

. . .

RESULTS

Study participants described embodied experiences that in many ways resonate with familiar theoretical discourse regarding women's bodies, such as encountering bodily objectification or engaging in social comparison processes. However, their ethnic identities—including cultural values regarding the care and presentation of the body, as well as personal and political commitments—provided alternative, often more positive ways of experiencing their bodies and cultural norms and practices. Inasmuch as participants felt that their ethnic identities also problematized body image, they described strategies for identifying affirming images of women of color and fostering positive self-image against the backdrop of powerful dominant cultural ideals. Several themes relating to ethnic identity and self-representation through the body emerged and are presented below.

Body Aesthetic Ideals Versus Body Ethics

Citing research indicating that African American and Latina girls and women are, on average, heavier than their white counterparts, some investigators have questioned whether African American and Latino/a cultures support different aesthetic body ideals from the dominant Euro-American ideal of a "lean, svelte, almost prepubescent body" (Chamorro and Flores-Ortiz 2000:126; see also Parnell et al. 1996). However, focus group participants resisted identifying a uniform African American or Latina body ideal. Throughout the group discussions, study participants expressed acceptance and appreciation of diverse body types. In fact, data from these focus groups suggest that rather than endorsing different particular *body aesthetic ideals* per se, respondents endorsed a set of *body ethics*—values and beliefs regarding care and presentation of the body—different than those documented among

Euro-American White women. Unlike the dominant culture, in which thinness has arguably become a key defining aspect of beauty, participants in both focus groups endorsed a multifaceted beauty ideal that promotes personal style, self-care, and spirituality.

Styling the Body, the Self

African American participants described style as a key aspect of community aesthetic ideals. One African American participant, a graduate student in her mid-twenties, raised in a mostly black urban community, explained,

> I'm gonna have to say for our community, like for us growing up . . . the emphasis was not on your body. Like you can see someone who is huge, but as long as they're dressed, like it's more [a matter] of dress to present yourself. If you're dressed, and you know how to dress, and you know how to wear your clothes, and you know how to comb your hair and present yourself, you're OK.

For this study participant, looking good is defined through a style that communicates respect and care for one's body and appearance. . . .

One African American study participant, a college student in her mid-twenties who was born and had lived most of her life in the U.S. Virgin Islands, described similar acceptable modes of self-presentation in her culture:

> You're attractive, like people are attracted to you because how you [dress]. . . . Over there, ironing is the huge thing. Like you have to have seams in your pants. . . . You sit just to try not to wrinkle your shirt, like you would not lean up sometimes, just so you won't wrinkle your shirt. And it's like, if you don't have that, you're not attractive. . . . I remember, it would be times where the popular girls who got all the guys would like come to school one day wrinkled, and that was it for them. It was like, "Did you see Tiffany today?" "Oh yeah, her shirt was wrinkled huh, I don't know what happened to her." Like it was like a huge thing. . . . So I think in a lot of ways, like for us, it wasn't a big thing in how your body looked,

but it was a big thing with how you presented yourself in terms of clothes and your hair. I don't know, hygiene kind of stuff, it was huge. You can be as ugly as a beast. It didn't matter.

The valuation of style and grooming *over* bodily control and manipulation emerged as a shared theme among these participants, despite their being raised in radically different cultural settings, and resonates with findings from other studies on women in the Caribbean and Latin America (Cohen et al. 1996; Wilk 1996).

Cultural messages about the relative importance of hygiene and grooming were also noted by Latina study participants, such as this early-twenties college student, born in Mexico and raised in the southwestern U.S., who recalls a premium placed on grooming in her household during childhood.

> [My mom] always just took care of her[self]. She was very clean . . . so we grew up—my sisters, my siblings—we grew up with that. Like we had to take a shower every day, you know, just that hygiene type of thing and keep our clothes clean . . . be dressed nice, have our hair clean.

Cherishing God's Temple

In contemporary Western culture, the emphasis on "seeming" (Bourdieu 1984:200) encourages the deliberate reshaping and aesthetic manipulation of the body as a means of projecting qualities of the self (Becker 1995). Women are especially vulnerable to the illusion that the body not only *is* malleable, but that it *should* be cultivated to achieve a particular body size and shape (Becker and Hamburg 1996). By contrast, participants were far less invested in attaining a specific aesthetic ideal through cultivation of their bodies and, instead, espoused an ethic of body acceptance. Religion and spirituality provided a rationale for body acceptance and a rejection of body modification, particularly modifications to accommodate mainstream, dominant aesthetic values. Several participants explained how religion and personal spirituality helped them frame their relationships to their bodies in terms of being the custodian of something precious. One African American participant explained,

> There's a scripture in The Word that talks about [how] you're wonderfully and fearfully made. When I became a Christian and I read that I was like, oh God! It did something for me, you know. I'm fearfully and wonderfully made in the sight of God . . . it empowered me. It really did . . . it really empowered me to know that there's a high being, if you will, that values me the way I am.

In a similar vein, a Latina participant explained,

> I'm real happy with the way God gave me whatever he gave me, you know, and . . . that's okay with me. . . . I don't want to be this way or that way, I'm fine with what I've got.

Whereas the previous two comments demonstrate how spirituality has helped them accept their body, one African American participant describes how spirituality actively influences how she treats her body. She explains,

> Spiritually, I believe that there's a verse in the Bible, in the New Testament, that says your body is a temple, a temple of God. When I think in that way, I'm more careful about what I eat . . . about what I put in my body, I'm careful how I adorn myself. Not to the point of being fanatical, but to the point of treating what I have as something that's precious even when other people don't value it . . . and it's hard sometimes finding [food that's] . . . organic.

Her qualifier, "even when other people don't value it," again suggests that this orientation toward self-nurturance may signal resistance to dominant cultural aesthetic ideals and may comprise a strategic response to negative representations of women of color in the consciousness of white America.

Self-Representation, Dignity, and Self-Respect

In addition to examining the devaluation of black women's beauty, focus group participants discussed troubling cultural representations and stereotypes of African American women's manners and styles of behavior. Similar to participants in Nichter's (2000) study, participants in the present study discussed strategies of self-representation as an important aspect of beauty; in the present study, however, participants explicitly linked these values with the need to counter negative cultural stereotypes, resist hegemonic imagery, and promote self-determination. As one participant explained,

> I think that [looking ghetto] is more, I think that, come on now, you guys know. . . . That's more of an issue [than weight] though, I think. That you don't wanna be ghetto. Unless you're ghetto because you don't know.

Johnson et al. define "ghetto" as "a mode of acting, dressing, or speaking, that comes off as abrasive, and well, ghetto" (2001:205). These comments lend support to the earlier discussion of body ethics: beauty is described here as more than a static image or aesthetic ideal—it is how one carries and cares for oneself. However, in contrast to the girls in Nichter's study, for whom the ideal girl embodied attitude and spontaneity, as adult women negotiating various life roles and cultural contexts, participants in the present study explained how they sometimes monitored their own behavior, reining in some of their spontaneity in particular contexts. The following exchange between two study participants highlights how they have learned to manage self-representation in order to gain respect in the dominant culture and resist cultural stereotypes that portray African American women as loud and abrasive:

> P1: I think too, in the black community, there's a stereotype, that black people are loud.

> P2: Right, so trying to like turn that stereotype around whatever, we're kinda taught not to be loud.

The second participant further explained,

> We were at IHOP and people were turning around because we were laughing. . . . The first thing that you think is, they're looking at us like

that because we're black. And we know that people are gonna think we're gonna be loud anyway, just because we are black. And we know we're not supposed to be loud because we are black. That's another issue that [goes] beyond the health and beauty . . . you're not loud in public places like this, because you're gonna be looked at.

In the paper "Those Loud Black Girls," based on an ethnography of a predominantly African American urban high school, Signithia Fordham argues that, for African American girls, being invisible, "dissociating oneself from the image of 'those loud Black girls'" (1993:22), is a prerequisite for academic (and professional) success, though at the cost of disconnection from one's self and community. As the African American women in this study have all achieved considerable academic success, it is not surprising that struggles regarding management of visibility and representation emerged as an important theme. . . .

Latinas: Achieving Health, Fighting Disease

Whereas among African American participants, self-nurturance was described as the embodiment of self-respect, Latina study participants provided a somewhat different rationale for their self-care practices. Among Latinas in this study, self-care practices were described as being motivated by their desire to be healthy and their concerns about health and disease, rather than a desire to control body size or shape. Data demonstrating that Latino/as have significantly higher body mass index (BMI) and prevalence of overweight than whites (Winkleby et al. 1996) provide a tangible and substantial basis for concern about a healthy body weight. Indeed, several Latina study participants had friends and family with diabetes, hypertension, or other potentially weight-related diseases, or had one of these conditions themselves.

As one Latina participant, a woman in her late thirties who attended the group in her workout clothing, explained,

Mine's become more of a health issue now. Because I have to do it because I have diabetes, and in order to stay alive with all my limbs and stuff,

[maybe] be able to see for the rest of my life, I gotta do it. So yeah, it's just for me now.

For this participant, changing her lifestyle—eating more healthful foods and exercising—was literally a matter of life and limb. . . .

Several group members described their orientation towards eating and exercise as a departure from their families' eating and exercise practices. According to several participants, it was not uncommon for their mothers to complain about their own weight, and several discussed "fad" diets, teas and other strategies their mothers and aunts would use to lose weight. The participant in workout clothes in her late thirties, quoted above, explained,

My mama and my aunt were very vain about their weight. . . . My mom would drink like these laxative teas and stuff, like that's gonna help her lose weight. . . . There was these chocolates they would eat, okay, they were called AYDS, I think, A-Y-D-S, ask your moms, or whoever. . . . They were suppose to suppress the appetite. . . . Now I never saw them exercise a day in their life. I never saw them eating differently, salads and stuff. . . . If it was, it was for a week and that was it.

In contrast to these descriptions of their mothers' quick-fix diets and diet aids, Latina participants in this study did not place a high value on food restriction, as this participant in her late twenties explained,

I just wanna be healthy. I mean I still eat what I want to, and I will, just because if I'm gonna exercise I'm gonna still eat you know, I mean I'll eat sensibly, I won't go and eat tons of junk. Although I do sometimes do that.

. . .

Study participants' emphasis on body ethics over aesthetics—of working with the body instead of trying to fight it, of caring for the body rather than trying to control it—mirrors the results of a study recently completed by Anderson-Fye examining cultural change processes among adolescent girls in Belize. The "central ethnopsychological tenet"

(Anderson-Fye 2002:159) expressed among girls in this study was the importance of staying true to oneself, honestly experiencing and responding to one's thoughts, emotions and bodily needs, summarized by the expression "never leave yourself" (2002:161). Like the girls in Anderson-Fye's study, the African American and Latin women participating in this study expressed values of self-acceptance, self-nurturance, and self-care in the face of, and perhaps as a response to, an onslaught of messages, images, and representations devaluing and discouraging these moral and ethical ideals.

Contesting Cultural Representations

Study respondents' efforts to accept and nurture their bodies are certainly an extraordinary achievement, given the negative representations of women of color in the media and the countless products available to help women alter and reshape their appearances to accommodate mainstream beauty ideals. In fact, a central theme that emerged in every focus group was the perceived devaluation of "ethnic" looks by the dominant culture. Whether addressing overt racism, such as exclusionary practices or the exoticization of women of color in the media, or more subtle forms of othering, such as the commercial co-opting of cultural identities, most respondents were concerned with cultural representations of women of their shared ethnic background. Participants describe a very conscious and deliberate struggle with the mainstream cultural representations and aesthetic ideals, marked by tremendous pressure confronting women of color to accommodate mainstream beauty ideals in order to be accepted within society.

Cultural Representations of Black Women

In the African American women's focus groups, participants expressed their dissatisfaction and frustration with the lack of affirming images of black women in mainstream and black media sources. Participants expressed their opinion that, despite a small degree of tokenism, black women are rarely represented in mainstream iconography. Two participants in the same focus group, both in their early thirties, one a graduate

student and one a nondegree student quoted earlier, described their alienation from mainstream representations, stating,

> Most of the images in this culture are, you gotta be thin, white, what else, young. As a black woman, I look at those images and I don't see me.

And

> That white Caucasian look thing, it's not real to me, and it totally ignores the black woman's experience, and other women of color. . . . Of course they throw a little tokenism in there, but their basic images is still thin, Anglo-Saxon.

. . .

Numerous studies have documented the pernicious effects of exposure to media imagery on indices of disordered eating (e.g., Field et al. 1999; Stice and Shaw 1994), including body dissatisfaction among American women. Similarly, cultural representations of African American women in media imagery powerfully influence self-concept and body image among black women in Western culture. One African American participant, the nondegree student quoted above, describes the insidious and noxious nature of these controlling images and messages as "the new kind of slavery," stating,

> You don't have to shackle a person physically if you already have them convinced they're not anything, that they have no value.

. . . Several women participating in the African American focus groups grew up with familial messages regarding appearance that accommodated or even reproduced the dominant culture's aesthetic values, such as preferences for lighter skin and straighter hair. One subject now in her early sixties, who grew up a generation ahead of the others, explained,

> I come from a family where it was something about being dark-skinned with nappy hair, versus being light with Caucasian features and straight hair. . . . I didn't have straight hair or really kinky hair. . . . My mom, she made me feel like my look, African look, was not acceptable,

and I felt bad for a long time about that. . . . She would always be sure that my hair was straightened . . . and don't get in the sun, you know. So it was a negative experience, and it took me a long time to overcome those things.

. . .

The aesthetics of hairstyle and presentation has considerable sociopolitical relevance among African American women (Banks 2000; Byrd and Tharps 2002; Caldwell 1997). For instance, several of the participants seemed to have chosen to "go natural" or "do locks" while in college as a way to celebrate Afrocentric aesthetic ideals and resist the white aesthetic norms imposed on African American women. Study participants described their personal strategies for resisting, challenging, and overcoming mainstream aesthetic ideals. As the 60-year-old returning student explained,

> It took me a long time to overcome those things . . . to accept my African features, nappy hair . . . like you said it was a struggle. But one day you say, this don't make no sense for me to be worrying about something that I had nothing to do with. . . . I didn't have anything to do with my hair being happy, my nose being big. It must be alright. . . . So then I decided to think to myself, hey I'm beautiful just the way I am. I don't like to sit in the beauty parlor for three hours getting my hair relaxed, scalp burns and all those things. I'm so off that now. It's just over and I feel so free.

The participant mentioned earlier who was growing dreadlocks explained,

> [My mother will] just fall out when she sees my hair now because I did these [dreadlocks] myself . . . I had my hair in braids, and I liked the braids and everything, but it was just time out, it's time for something new and I had been thinking about doing locks for a while, so I said you know what, I'm just gonna do it.

Russell et al. argue that "a certain level of black consciousness would seem to be necessary before a woman dares go natural" (1992, 87).

. . .

For African American study participants, strategies of self-representation were experienced as linked to one's social location (e.g., student versus corporate employee). Study participants negotiated their own self-interests against the backdrop of the interests of their community. Thus, while hair-straightening may be considered to perpetuate racist and classist notions of "good hair" and "bad hair," it may also be critical to attaining a high-paying job after college. One participant, an early-twenties college senior, explained,

> Unless you're trying to achieve something . . . that's when you start [thinking] I have to look this way and I have to act this way, and I can't, you know, if I'm gonna do this certain activity I can't have my typical friends with me because then I'm gonna look bad. But it's only when . . . it's only when black people are really trying to achieve something in their life . . . whether it's going for a job . . . you've gotten a job and you're trying to live that lifestyle . . . then that's when the rest of the world comes into play.

The comments of this participant, herself about to leave college to find a job, suggest that economic success often necessitates accommodating dominant white, middle-class aesthetic and cultural values.

Latinas in the Media: Celebrating and Contesting Imagery

Latina participants expressed fewer concerns regarding the negative messages embedded in cultural representations, but rather were concerned with the lack of representations of Latinas in mainstream iconography. Historically, Latino/as were conspicuously underrepresented in the mainstream media, despite their growing numbers in the United States. . . .

. . .

Participants had somewhat polarized opinions about cultural representations of Latinas. Given the paucity of images, some study participants felt that any representation was positive, as this participant, a student from Central America, explained,

> Like even now, but I remember when I was really young, a teenager, I would see a Latina in a magazine or someone that looked Latina, even though they were probably from Europe or something, I would get excited. I'm like there's a Latina in this magazine! Or even in the movies, I probably would wanna go watch the movie just because there's another Latino in there.

Other participants were concerned that the Latinas that are represented in popular media merely reified mainstream aesthetic values, such as this participant in her mid-twenties who was born in Mexico.

> And even with the models, they still pick the stereotype. They might be colored, but still thin. They still look beautiful. And it's like, what happened to the others? . . . Selena is one of my faves, and she wasn't like very stereotypical thin. She looked more like a real person. I really like her because of that. Then there's Jennifer Lopez, and I'm like okay, she's kinda real, but then at the same time I see that her image has changed to fit some of those rules—the skimpy clothing and dyeing your hair. It's like hmmmm? . . . Because if you don't fit that, the stereotypical, you don't cross over.

Another participant, a theatre major, remarked, "There's one image of being a Latina, and it's Jennifer Lopez," provoking laughter from the group. As these focus group participants suggest, it is difficult for Latino/a actors and musicians to "cross over," or be accepted by the dominant cultural group, without changing their look to be more "Anglo." Like the group member that contrasted the "real" Selena to the "kinda real" Jennifer Lopez, the laughter that follows this remark may point to the discrepancy between "trendy" commercial representations of Latinas and this focus group participant's own personal definitions of Latina identity.

However, some participants, noting the insufficient representation of Latinas in the media, felt that "even just" seeing Jennifer Lopez made them happy, and offered a compassionate reading of the position of this singer/actress. One remarked,

> I get so happy when I see even just Jennifer Lopez on the screen. You know, good. Lopez, Lopez! I mean she's got her music, and then I think she's gonna be taking out a line of clothes too . . . at least she's promoting her own thing. She growing, and it's hard for a person who is a minority to be at the top.

Still, others were pleased with the increasing diversity of Latinas represented in the media, as is suggested in the following remark made by a graduate student in her late twenties:

> I think the good part about the media right now [is] the Latinas that are coming out. . . . The variety of them is unbelievable.

Participants' complex reactions to these images suggest that they are still grappling with their somewhat ambivalent feelings towards current representations of Latinas in popular culture. These participants expressed satisfaction with the increasing social and political power of Latinas but concern regarding the commodification and dilution of their ethnic heritage. . . . Similarly to the black women participating in these focus group discussions, Latina participants are grappling with how to negotiate mainstream and local cultural values and ideals and how to stay true to themselves and their cultural heritage.

CONCLUSION

Ethnically based differences in aesthetic body ideals have previously been suggested as the key underpinning for the reportedly greater body shape satisfaction experienced by women of color. However, contrary to this notion, African American and Latina women participating in these focus groups did *not* endorse specific alternative body aesthetic ideals that could be contrasted with the prevailing aesthetic ideal favoring slimness promoted and disseminated by the commercial media. More notably, study participants' emphasis of body ethics rather than body aesthetic ideals suggests the need for an important reframing of a presumed core orientation toward the body—one that is perhaps recognizable and dominant among Euro-American cultures but is by no means universal. Specifically, narrative data from both black and Latina subjects presented in this study reflect a central concern with body care and nurturance—glossed here as body *ethics,* as contrasted with the central *aesthetic* concerns that have previously been described among women in Euro-American culture.

. . .

Among the women participating in this study, staying "true to oneself," one's own personal values and ideals as well as one's cultural heritage, was itself considered a sign of this well-being (cf. Anderson-Fye 2002). These sentiments are echoed in the lyrics of the African American soul singer/songwriter India.Arie, who sings about learning to "love myself unconditionally," by fashioning herself according to "whatever feels good in my soul" (India.Arie 2001). For black and Latina women, and likely for other women of color negotiating two distinct cultural worlds, embodying an ethic of self-valuation and self-acceptance is a positive and strategic means to resist cultural aesthetic ideals that oppress virtually all women but which can be particularly oppressive to women of color. Hurtado argues, "White women, as a group, are subordinated through seduction, women of color, as a group, through rejection" (1990: 12). For women who maintain an ethic of self-acceptance and nurturance, such rejection necessitates resistance, a cherishing of one's body and self-rooted in both spiritual and political ideologies "even when other people don't value it," perhaps *especially* because other people do not value it.

In addition to comprising a strategic response to ethnically and racially based oppression, we propose that the ethic of self-acceptance exhibited by the participants in this study may also modulate risk for the body dissatisfaction that is associated with disordered eating. We further hypothesize that women of color who are economically and/or socially marginalized and who are disconnected from their cultural roots

may be less able to call upon an ethic of self-acceptance and consequently are at greater risk for the body- and self-disparagement associated with eating disorders. Indeed, this may explain the equivalent or even higher rates of eating disorder symptoms among some women of color compared with white women. Pumariega et al.'s (1994) finding that a strong black identity may play a protective role against eating disorder risk factors supports this hypothesis, as does the association between acculturation and higher prevalence of eating disorders found in numerous studies (Anderson- Fye and Becker in press).

Insofar as this study presents perspectives from African American and Latina women with a critical consciousness of culture, body, and health, it suggests and elaborates new avenues for investigating the nexus of embodiment, ethnicity, and disordered body image and eating. Further research will be important for probing the dimensions of body ethics and aesthetics, identity and self-representation in larger, more representative samples of black and Latina women. Such research will be instrumental in exploring whether the alternative body ethics described in this study may actually confer protection from the development of eating or weight disorders among ethnically diverse populations of women. . . .

REFERENCES

Akan, G., and C. Grilo. 1995. Sociocultural Influences on Eating Attitudes and Behaviors, Body Image, and Psychological Functioning: A Comparison of African-American, Asian-American, and Caucasian College Women. *International Journal of Eating Disorders* 18:181–187.

Altabe, M. 1998. Ethnicity and Body Image: Quantitative and Qualitative Analysis. *International Journal of Eating Disorders* 23:153–159.

Anderson-Fye, E. 2002. Never Leave Yourself: Belizean Schoolgirls' Psychological Development in Cultural Context. Unpublished Dissertation, Harvard University.

Anderson-Fye, E., and A. E. Becker. In press. *Cultural Dimensions of Eating Disorders.* TEN: Trends in Evidence-Based Neuropsychiatry.

Banks, I. 2000. *Hair Matters: Beauty, Power, and Black Women's Consciousness*. New York: New York University Press.

Becker, A. E. 1995. *Body, Self and Society: The View From Fiji*. Philadelphia: University of Pennsylvania Press.

Becker, A. E., R. A. Burwell, S. Gilman, D. B. Herzog, and P. Hamburg. 2002. Eating Behaviours and Attitudes Following Prolonged Television Exposure Among Ethnic Fijian Adolescent Girls. *British Journal of Psychiatry* 180:509–514.

Becker, A. E., and P. Hamburg. 1996. Culture, the Media, and Eating Disorders. *Harvard Review of Psychiatry* 4:163–167.

Bordo, S. 1993. *Unbearable Weight: Feminism, Western Culture, and the Body*. Berkeley, CA: University of California Press.

Bourdieu, P. 1984. *Distinction*. Cambridge, MA: Harvard University Press.

Brown, L. M. 1998. *Raising Their Voices: The Politics of Girls' Anger*. Cambridge, MA: Harvard University Press.

Byrd, A. D., and L. L. Tharps. 2002. *Hair Story: Untangling the Roots of Black Hair in America*. New York: St. Martin's Press.

Caldwell, P. 1997. *A Hair Piece: Perspectives on the Intersection of Race and Gender*. Pp. 297–305 in *Critical Race Feminism: A Reader*. A. K. Wing, ed. New York: New York University Press.

Chamorro, R., and Y. Flores-Ortiz. 2000. Acculturation and Disordered Eating Patterns Among Mexican-American Women. *International Journal of Eating Disorders* 28:125–129.

Cohen, C., R. Wilk, and B. Stoeltje, eds. 1996. *Beauty Queens on a Global Stage: Gender, Contests, and Power*. New York: Routledge.

Collins, P. H. 1990. *Black Feminist Thought: Knowledge, Consciousness, and the Politics of Empowerment*. Boston: Unwin Hyman.

———. 2000. *Black Feminist Thought: Knowledge, Consciousness, and the Politics of Empowerment*. New York: Routledge.

Crago, M., C. M. Shisslak, and L. S. Estes. 1996. Eating Disturbances Among American Minority Groups: A Review. *International Journal of Eating Disorders* 19:239–248.

Davis, C., and J. Yager. 1992. Transcultural Aspects of Eating Disorders: A Critical Literature Review. *Culture, Medicine and Psychiatry* 16:377–394.

Emmons., L. 1992. Dieting and Purging Behavior in Black and White High School Students. *Journal of the American Dietetic Association* 92:306–312.

Field, A. E., L. Cheung, A. M. Wolf, D. B. Herzog, S. L. Gortmaker, and G. A. Colditz. 1999. Exposure to the Mass Media and Weight Concerns Among Girls. *Pediatrics* 103 (3): 36.

Fordham, S. 1993. "Those Loud Black Girls": (Black) Women, Silence, and Gender "Passing" in the Academy. *Anthropology and Education Quarterly* 24:3–32.

hooks, b. 1992. *Black Looks: Race and Representation*. Boston: South End Press.

Hurtado, A. 1990. Relating to Privilege: Seduction and Rejection in the Subordination of White Women and Women of Color. *Signs* 14:833–855.

India.Arie. 2001. Video. *Acoustic Soul*. New York: Motown Record Company.

Johnson, K., T. Lewis, K. Lightfoot, and G. Wilson. 2001. *The BAP Handbook: The Official Guide to the Black American Princess*. New York: Broadway Books.

Kuba, S. A., and D. J. Harris. 2001. Eating Disturbances in Women of Color: An Exploratory Study of Contextual Factors in the Development of Disordered Eating in Mexican-American Women. *Health Care for Women International* 22:281–298.

Nichter, M. 2000. *Fat Talk*. Cambridge, MA: Harvard University Press.

Parker, S., M. Nichter, N. Vukovic, C. Sims, and C. Ritenbaugh. 1995. Body Image and Weight Concerns Among African-American and White Adolescent Females: Differences That Make a Difference. *Human Organization* 54:103–114.

Parnell, K., R. Sargent, S. H. Thompson, S. F. Duhe, R. F. Valois, and R. C. Kemper. 1996. Black and White Adolescent Females' Perceptions of Ideal Body Size. *Journal of School Health* 66:112–118.

Pumariega, A. J., C. R. Gustavson, J. C. Gustavson, P. Motes, and S. Ayres. 1994. Eating Attitudes in African-American Women: The Essence Eating Disorders Survey. *Eating Disorders* 2:5–16.

Root, M. 1990. Disordered Eating in Women of Color. *Sex Roles* 22:525–536.

Russell, K., M. Wilson, and R. Hall. 1992. *The Color Complex*. New York: Anchor Books.

Smith, J. E., and J. Krejci. 1991. Minorities Join the Majority: Eating Disturbances Among Hispanic and Native American Youth. *International Journal of Eating Disorders* 10:179–186.

Stice, E., and H. Shaw. 1994. Adverse Effects of the Media Portrayed Thin-Ideal on Women and Linkages to Bulimic Symptomatology. *Journal of Social and Clinical Psychology* 13:288–308.

Wilk, R. 1996. Connections and Contradictions: From the Crooked Tree Cashew Queen to Miss World Belize. Pp. 217–232 in *Beauty Queens on the Global Stage: Gender, Contests, and Power*. C. Cohen, R. Wilk, and B. Stoeltje, eds. New York: Routledge.

Winkleby, M., C. Gardner, and C. Barr Taylor. 1996. The Influence of Gender and Socioeconomic Factors on Hispanic/White Differences in Body Mass Index. *Preventive Medicine* 25:203–211.

R E A D I N G   **39**

What We Do for Love

Rose Weitz

Rapunzel's life turned around the day a prince climbed up her hair and into her stairless tower. The rest of us sometimes suspect that, as was true for Rapunzel, our hair offers us the key to finding a prince who'll bring us love and happiness. Yet surprisingly often, when we talk about hair and romance, we talk not only about love but also about power—the ability to obtain desired goals through controlling or influencing others. Power exists not only when a politician fixes an election or an army conquers a country, but also when we style our hair to get boyfriends or to keep men away, and when our boyfriends browbeat us into cutting our hair or growing it longer.

CATCHING A MAN

Hair plays a central role in romantic relationships, from start to finish. If we're in the mood for love (or sex), from the moment we meet someone, we begin an internal calculus, reckoning how attractive we find him and how attractive he seems to find us. If he finds us attractive, our power will increase, for in any relationship, whoever wants the relationship most holds the least power.[1]

Attractiveness, of course, means many different things. A man might be attracted to a woman because of her income, interest in sports, or good sense of humor. But when it comes to dating—especially first dates—pretty women, like pretty girls, usually come out ahead. In a recent experiment, researchers placed bogus personal ads for two women, one a "beautiful waitress," the other an "average looking, successful lawyer." The waitress received almost three times more responses than the lawyer. (The reverse was true for men: the "successful lawyer" received four times more responses from women than did the "handsome cabdriver.") Other studies also have found that men choose their dates based more on women's looks than on women's earning potential, personality, or other factors.[2]

In a world where beautiful waitresses get more dates than do successful women lawyers, it makes perfect sense for women to use their looks to catch and keep men. Although some writers imply that women who do so are merely blindly obeying cultural rules for feminine appearance and behavior—acting as "docile bodies," in the words of the French philosopher Michel Foucault—most women are acutely aware of those rules and know exactly what they are doing and why.[3]

The first step in getting a man is catching his eye. A classic way to do so is with the "hair flip." Of course, the flip can be an innocent gesture, intended only to get the hair out of our eyes or move a tickling strand off our cheeks. But often it's consciously used to get men's attention while on dates, in classes, stopped at red lights, and elsewhere. If you want to see it in action, sit at any bar. Sooner or later a woman will look around the room, find a man who interests her, wait until he turns toward her, and then—ever so nonchalantly—flip her hair.

Hair flipping can be an amazingly studied act. In response to an e-mail query on the subject that I sent to students at my university, a white undergraduate female replied,

> I have very long hair and do use the hair flip, both consciously and unconsciously. When I do it [consciously], I check the room to see if anyone is looking in my direction, but never catch a guy's eye first. I just do it in his line of vision. [I] bend over slightly (pretending to get something from a bag or pick something up) so that some of my hair falls in front of my shoulders. Then I lean back and flip my hair out, and then shake my head so my hair sways a little. I make sure that the hair on the opposite side ends up in front of my shoulder. I keep that shoulder a little bit up with my head tilted and lean on the hand that I used to flip my hair.

Similarly, in the film *Legally Blonde,* the lead character, Elle, instructs her dumpy friend Paulette how to "bend and snap"—bending over so her hair will fall forward, then standing up while snapping her head and hair back to catch men's attention.

Other times the hair flip is less studied, but the motivation is the same. A Mexican-American student writes:

> I tend to flip my hair when I see an attractive male, but I do it unconsciously. I don't think, "Okay, here he comes, so now I have to flip my hair," It's more of a nervous, attention-getting thing. When I see a good-looking guy and get that uneasy feeling in my stomach, I run my fingers through my hair and flip it to make it look fuller and to attract his eye as he passes. If there isn't enough room to flip my hair, I'll play with a strand of hair instead.

Whether conscious or unconscious, hair flipping works. In a world that expects women to speak in a low tone, keep eyes down, and sit quietly with legs together and elbows tucked in, the hair flip says, "Look at me." This in itself makes it sexy. It's also inherently sexy: the back of the hand rubbing upward against the neck, then caressing the underside of the hair, drawing it out and away from the body, while the chin first tucks down into the shoulder and then tilts up, arching the neck back.

Even when a man finds neither long hair nor the flip inherently attractive, flipping hair can whet his interest. The gesture itself draws the eyes by taking up space and causing motion. Perhaps more important, men know the flip can be a form of flirtation. As a result, they pay close attention to any woman who flips her hair to see whether she's flirting with them, flirting with someone else, or simply getting the hair out of her eyes.

This use of the hair flip doesn't escape notice by women with short hair. An undergraduate writes:

> In Hispanic culture hair is very important for a woman. It defines our beauty and gives us power over men. Now that I cut my hair short, I miss the feeling of moving my hair around and the power it gave me. . . . It is kind of a challenge [to other women] when a woman flips her hair. [She's] telling me that she has beautiful healthy hair and is moving it to get attention from a male or envy from me.

The hair flip is especially aggravating for those black women whose hair will not grow long. As one black graduate student explains,

> As an African-American woman, I am very aware of non-African-American women "flipping" their hair. . . . I will speak only for myself here (but I think it's a pretty global feeling for many African-American women), but I often look at women who can flip their hair with envy, wishfulness, perhaps regret? . . . With my "natural" hair, if I run my fingers through it, it's going to be a mess [and won't] gracefully fall back into place.

She now wears long braided extensions and, she says, flips her hair "constantly."

In the same way that women use their hair's motion to catch men, they use its style and color.

Cecilia told how she dyed her hair Kool-Aid bright to horrify others in her small Southern town. These days her hair decisions serve very different purposes:

> I can think of an occasion where I changed my hair while I was dating this guy. I had this feeling that he was losing attraction for me and I'd just been feeling the need to do something to my appearance. And my hair is always the easiest way to go. It's too expensive to buy a new wardrobe. There's nothing you can do about your face. So your hair, you can go and have something radically done to it and you'll look like a different person.

With this in mind, Cecilia cut off about seven inches of her hair:

> It was kind of a radical haircut, shaved, kind of asymmetrical, and [dyed] a reddish maroon color. When he saw me, [he] was like, "Whoa! ... Oh, my God, look at it!" He just couldn't stop talking about it. ... He said, "I don't know, there's just something about you. I really want to be with you."

When I ask how she felt about his rekindled interest in her, she replies, "I was pretty pleased with myself."

Few women would cut their hair asymmetrically and dye it maroon to capture a man's interest, but millions try to do so by dyeing their hair blonde. Of the 51 percent of women who dye their hair, about 40 percent dye it blonde.[4] (Most of the rest dye it brunette shades simply to cover any gray.) Several women I've talked to, when asked why they dye their hair blonde, responded by singing the old advertising ditty: "Is it true blondes have more fun?" These women, like many others, have found blonde hair a sure way to spark men's interest.

But being a blonde can be a mixed blessing: Remember Marilyn Monroe. To catch men's attention without being labeled dumb, passive, or "easy" (stereotypes that haunt all blondes, dyed or natural), about 20 percent of women who dye their hair instead choose shades of red. Red hair,

they believe, draws men's interest while calling on a different set of stereotypes, telling men that they are smart, wild, and passionate.[5] Brenda, a quiet, petite twenty-eight-year-old, for many years envied her golden-blonde sister's popularity. A few years ago she began dyeing her hair red to "let people know I'm a competent person, independent, maybe a little hotheaded—or maybe a lot hotheaded, [even] fiery." Dyeing her hair red, she believes,

> *made* people see me. ... Before I dyed my hair, my sister and I would go out and all these guys would ask her to dance and talk to her and ask for her number and I would just be standing there. And after I started dyeing my hair, I started getting noticed a little bit more. I also stopped waiting to be asked.

Brenda credits her marriage in part to her red hair; her husband approached her initially because he "always wanted to date a redhead."

Using our hair to look attractive is particularly important for those of us whose femininity is sometimes questioned. Since Jane Fonda began selling her fitness videos in 1982, women (or at least middle-class women) have been expected to look as though they "work out." Yet those whose broad shoulders and muscular arms and legs announce them as dedicated athletes are still often stigmatized as unfeminine, or denigrated as suspected lesbians. Since most true athletes can't have manicured nails (which can break during sports) or wear makeup (which can smear from sweat), those who want to look attractively feminine often rely on their hair. The tennis-playing Williams sisters and the U.S. women's soccer team won the hearts of Americans not only through their athletic skills but also because their beaded braids and ponytails, respectively, told us they were still feminine and heterosexual (an image bolstered by constant news coverage about the Williamses' fashion sense and the soccer players' boyfriends and husbands). Similarly, most professional female bodybuilders counterbalance their startlingly muscular bodies with long, curled, and dyed blonde hair. Those who don't do so risk losing contests, no matter how large and well-sculpted their muscles.[6]

Similar pressures weigh on black women. Although it is far less true today than in the past, many people—whites and blacks, men and women—still regard black women as less feminine and less attractive than white women. For example, when I asked 270 white undergraduates in 2003 to choose from a list all the adjectives they felt described the "average" white, non-Hispanic woman, 75 percent chose "feminine" and 48 percent chose "attractive." In contrast, when asked to describe the average black woman, only 33 percent chose "feminine" and only 21 percent chose "attractive."

As a result of such attitudes, black women often feel especially obligated to do what they can to increase their attractiveness. Within the black community attractiveness still primarily centers on having light skin and long, straight hair.[7] Since there's little one can do about one's skin color (Michael Jackson notwithstanding), much of black women's attention to their looks focuses on their hair. Norma explains,

> If you are an African-American woman and you have long hair, you are automatically assumed to be pretty, unless your face is just awful! [But if you have short, tightly curled hair like mine,] African-American males [will] say "I'm not going out with her, her head is as bald as mine!" Or they will call [you] "nappy head."

To avoid such treatment without subjecting herself to the difficulties and expense of straightening her hair, Norma now wears a wig with shoulder-length straight hair. Her husband approves. Many other black women do the same, creating a substantial market in the black community for wigs (ads for which appear regularly in the major black magazines), while many others rely on purchased hair extensions.

But each of these options carries a price. In choosing straightened hair, wigs, or extensions over natural hair, black women obtain hair that *looks* good in exchange for hair that *feels* good to the touch. If your lover starts stroking your wig, it might fall off or come askew. If he strokes your extensions, expensive hair that took hours to attach may come out. If you've got a weave, his fingers will hit upon the web of thread holding the hair in. And if he tries to stroke your carefully coiffed straightened hair, not only will it lose its style, but it will feel stiff and oily or, if it hasn't been moisturized in a while, like brittle straw. Or it might just break off. To avoid these problems, black women teach the men and boys around them never to touch a woman's hair. Stephen, a twenty-three-year-old black student, told me:

> The same way you learn as a kid not to touch that cookie in the cookie jar, you learn not to touch that hair. I remember once trying to touch my mother's hair and having her slap my hands away. . . .
>
> You learn at beauty parlors, too. When I was a kid, my mom would go to the beauty parlor every two weeks. And it would take six hours to do her hair sometimes, and we would have to sit around the whole time. So we saw how long it took and how important it was for them. And then you'd hear the stylists tell the little girls not to touch their hair afterwards. And you'd hear all the women talking about their own hair, and how they would have to sleep sitting up to keep from messing it. Or they'd say, "That man better not try to touch my head, I just paid $200 for this hair!"

When black women date either white men or the rare black man who hasn't been properly trained, the women keep the men's hands away by covering their hair before coming to bed, relying on quick maneuvers to keep their hair out of harm's way, saying they need to get their hair done and it's not fit to be touched, or saying they just had their hair done and don't want it ruined.[8]

Like black women, overweight and disabled women also can rely on their hair to make themselves seem more feminine and attractive. Although many famous beauties of the late nineteenth century, such as the actress Lillian Russell, were admired for their voluptuous curves, and still today in some African beauty contests no women under 200 pounds need apply, in contemporary America overweight women are often ridiculed as unattractive and asexual. So, too, are disabled women, leaving them more likely than either disabled men or nondisabled women to remain single, to marry at later ages, and to get divorced.[9]

When I interviewed Debra, who became quadriplegic in a car accident when she was twenty, she was sitting in her kitchen. Her hair was immaculately styled: dyed and frosted shades of blonde, with perfectly placed bangs and neat waves falling below her shoulders.

Although Debra always cared about her appearance, her disability has heightened its importance for her. As she explains,

> When people first see someone in a wheelchair, the image they have [is] like a "bag of bones" or something toting urine. They expect the person to not have a high level of hygiene. . . . People will actually say things to me like "You are so much cleaner than I expected," and will give me shampoo as gifts because they assume I need the help. I'm trying to beat that image.

For Debra, keeping her hair nicely styled is a point of pride. It also offers her the pleasure of feeling more feminine and feeling at least partly in control of her body. Like other disabled and overweight women, this is particularly important for her because in other ways she can't make her body do what she wants. Controlling her hair also takes on special significance because it's difficult for her to find attractive, nicely fitting clothes suitable for someone who spends her days in a wheelchair and who can't dress herself.

At the same time, Debra's hair remains "a point of great frustration" that sometimes causes her a "huge amount of stress." Because she can't lift her arms high enough to style her own hair, she must rely on her personal attendant to do so. But in choosing a personal attendant, her first priority must be selecting someone she feels comfortable trusting with the most intimate details of her life and her body, not selecting someone who both has hairstyling skills and will follow her styling

wishes. In addition, because the work of a personal attendant is poorly paid, emotionally stressful, and physically draining, few attendants stay long. Consequently, Debra frequently must find and train new attendants, ratcheting up her anxiety levels and diminishing her sense of control over her body and her appearance anew each time.

But even able-bodied, slender white women take risks when they rely on their appearance to bolster their self-confidence and their attractiveness. Attractiveness offers only a fragile sort of power, achieved one day at a time through concentrated effort and expenditures of time and money. As a result, the occasional "bad hair day" can seem a catastrophe. From the moment we realize our hair just isn't going to cooperate, things start going badly. We spend extra time trying to style our hair in the morning, then have to run out the door because we're late. By the time we get to work or school, we're feeling both frazzled and self-conscious about our appearance. Throughout the day, a small voice in the back of our head may nag, berating us either for not having our act together or for worrying what others are thinking. As a result, we lose self-confidence and the ability to concentrate, as well as prospects for male approval. In the long run, too, if a man is interested in us only because of our looks, his interest likely won't last. (It may not even survive the morning after, when we awake with bleary eyes, no makeup, and "bed head.") And attractiveness must decline with age, as more than one middle-aged society woman dumped for a younger "trophy wife" has discovered.

HAIR IN RELATIONSHIPS

Once we are in a relationship, hair can bring pleasure to our partners and ourselves. If our hair is long enough, we can drape it over our partner's chest to form a silky curtain, or swing it from side to side to tease and caress him. And whether our hair is long or short, our partner can enjoy the pleasure of brushing it, washing it, smoothing his hands over it, or weaving his fingers through it. In addition, caring for our hair enables the men in our lives to show their love and affection without having to put their feelings into words.

Eva's relationship with her husband, Stanley, epitomizes this dynamic. After more than forty years of marriage, it's clear that he's still smitten. While I am interviewing Eva, Stanley seems unable to stay out of the room. Once in the room, his eyes linger on her. His hand grazes her hair and keeps drifting to her shoulder. Although to me Eva's hair seems ordinary, he makes more than one comment about its beauty.

Ever since he retired, Stanley has dyed Eva's hair for her. They describe this as a way to save time and money, and I'm sure it does. But they're retired and wealthy, so I'm convinced that Stanley cares for Eva's hair primarily as a way of caring for Eva.

Sometimes, though, the pleasures of hair turn to perils if our partners come to view our hair as an object for their own pleasure. Learning to do so begins early, when boys realize they can pull girls' braids in schoolyards and classes and touch girls' hair against their will, with few if any repercussions. Once in relationships, some boys and men will come to think of their girlfriend's or wife's hair as their property or as a reflection on them. When this happens, our hair becomes an object for a man to critique or control. For example, when Debra met her first boyfriend, a couple of years before her accident, her hair was waist-length. The boyfriend had previously dated a hairstylist who taught him how to style hair and gave him his own haircutting equipment. Although Debra wasn't happy about it, he quickly took charge of her hair and began cutting it shorter and shorter with each passing month. "It ended up being a control feature in our relationship," she says. "He always wanted it worn very spiky and short, and I hated that look." He also took control of dyeing her hair. "It ended up being a trust game," she recalls, "where he'd say, 'I'm going to go get a hair color, and you're not going to know what color it is. So you have to trust me that I will not make you ugly'. . . . In retrospect, the relationship really was very controlling."

At the extreme, men's control of women's hair can become violent. In a recent study, the sociologist Kathryn Farr looked at thirty consecutive reported cases of woman-battering that escalated to attempted homicides. In three of those cases, the police noted in the record that the man had cut the woman's hair by force during the attack. (The men may well have done so in additional cases without the police noting it.) The attitude of these men toward their wives and girlfriends comes through clearly in a fourth case that did not quite meet Farr's definition of attempted homicide. After the man in that case finished punching and kicking his girlfriend, he forced her to kneel on the floor and began cutting her hair. When she asked why he was doing this, he replied, "You belong to me and I can do anything I want."[10]

But if men can demonstrate their power over us by controlling our hair, we can demonstrate our own power within a relationship by asserting control over it. Until recently, Stacy, who is twenty-two, wore her hair falling loosely to her waist. She now wears it parted in the middle and just long enough to pull back into a ponytail. Surprisingly, she cut her hair *because* her boyfriend liked it long. Irritated by his frequent remarks about how her hair made her so attractive, she says, "I deliberately cut it off, a little bit spitefully, to say I'm more than my hair." Doing so made her feel "powerful," she explains, "in the sense that I feel that they [men] prefer long hair, that I wasn't ruled by that, and that I could set my own standards." (Their relationship continued anyway.)

. . .

CELEBRATING INDEPENDENCE FROM MEN

In the same way we sometimes use our hair to attract men, we also can use our hair to proclaim our independence from a particular man or from men in general. Darla first met her husband on a blind date in 1949, when she was fifteen. Normally before a date Darla would wash her hair, set it, and leave it to dry in curlers for three hours before combing it out and styling it. This time, though, to show that she "was not the kind of girl who went out on blind dates, [and] was just not impressed with that idea at all," she didn't set her hair until right before he arrived.

When the doorbell rang, Darla went to greet her date with her hair in curlers and wrapped in a bandanna. She immediately realized she'd made a big mistake:

> Here was this young god standing there. Black wavy hair, way better [looking] than James Dean. And not only that, he was all dressed up. He had on a white shirt and tie. And there was nothing I could do about my hair.

To compensate for her hair faux pas, Darla excused herself so she could triple-check her makeup and swap her pedal-pushers for a pretty skirt. Then they went out, as if there were nothing unusual about going on a date wearing curlers:

> He did not say anything [about my hair]. And he didn't seem to be turned off. . . . I think he found me attractive. . . . The fact that I had my hair up in curlers didn't seem to bother him at all, which impressed me.

When he called for a second date, Darla made sure her hair looked great. They've now been married more than fifty years.

Although few of us would, like Darla, use our hair to signal our lack of interest in a man at the beginning of a relationship, many of us do so when a relationship breaks up. After Roxanne got divorced, she dated a man who loved her hair and who took great pleasure in braiding, brushing, and especially washing it. But they had "a very bad breakup," leading Roxanne to decide to cut her hair. When I ask her why, she replies by singing the lyric from *South Pacific:* "I'm gonna wash that man right out of my hair." As she explains, "I had to get rid of everything that he liked, and I started with my hair." She "felt great" afterward.

Dana tells a similar story. Twenty-six years old, she now wears her hair past her waist and favors "vintage" clothing and dramatic makeup. A few years ago she broke up with a long-term boyfriend. Afterward, she recalls, "I wanted to do

something different, . . . to completely shut off that old self and be somebody new. . . . I wanted to appear sexier [and to] regain confidence in myself." Although fear kept her from making any drastic changes, a slight change to her hairstyle allowed her to feel better about herself and to feel like a new person.

Although both Roxanne and Dana used their hair to reject their former partners, neither wanted to reject men in general and both continued to use their hair to attract men's attention. But other women use their hair, at least occasionally, to *reduce* men's interest in them. For example, LaDonna, a black woman who [has] described the attention her hair brought her as a child, usually enjoys the power her naturally long and wavy hair now gives her over black men. Nonetheless, her hair is a mixed blessing, because she can't control who will be attracted to it (her handsome neighbor or her married boss?) or why (because he simply likes long hair or because he thinks hair that looks "white" is superior?). As a result, she says, "It's kind of funny, because I know it [my hair] will get me attention, and I do things to make it look nice that I know will get me attention, but sometimes I don't wear my hair down because I *don't* want the attention. I don't feel like dealing with this."

Susan goes to even greater lengths to avoid male attention. She's probably the prettiest woman I interviewed, with the prettiest hair. Her blue eyes and cascade of naturally curling dark hair contrast attractively with her pale skin, giving her a girl-next-door sort of appeal that matches her outgoing nature. Susan met her husband, who is an Egyptian Muslim, when they were both studying in England. Once she began dating him, the other Arab men in the school seemed to consider her "fair game." So long as her boyfriend was around she felt safe, but her fears grew when he left the school six weeks before she did. During those weeks, she recalled, "The Arab men were all over me, constantly bugging me. . . . I was afraid I would get raped by one of them one night."

After they returned to the United States, Susan and her boyfriend married. As she began to learn more about Islam, her interest in it grew, and she decided to convert. A few months later they went to visit her husband's family home. Expecting the men there to treat her as they would any Muslim woman, she was appalled when they instead treated her as a "loose" American. To convince others that she was a chaste Muslim and to protect herself from sexual harassment or worse when her husband was absent, she began wearing a hijab (a traditional robe) and covering her hair in Muslim fashion. Her husband, aghast, told her that if he'd wanted a traditional Muslim bride, he would have married one. Moreover, in his city only the oldest women still wore head coverings, which were now considered old-fashioned, ugly, and "backward." It's not surprising, then, that, as Susan describes, "He flipped out. He got so upset. He *wants* my hair to show, because . . . he wants to show me off."

Still, feeling that her physical safety was at risk, Susan ignored his wishes and began covering her head. Her strategy succeeded:

If you are not born Muslim and you are American, [and] you're not dressed the way they [Arab men] think is best for a Muslim women, and covering your head, . . . they'll think you're loose [and] treat you disrespectfully. . . . But when I put the hijab on and covered my head, . . . everybody changed how they treated me.

After they got back to the United States, Susan decided to continue veiling. Like other Muslim-American women who veil, she enjoyed the sense of empowerment the veil brought her by reminding her of her religion and her God.[11] And, even though she no longer felt physically at risk, she continued to appreciate the protection from men's eyes that the veil afforded her. Without the veil, she says, "You feel like you're naked. . . . Men would look at me and smile and I'd know that they thought I was beautiful. I don't want that. I just want my husband to think that."

Susan's husband objected even more vociferously to her desire to veil herself once they returned to the United States. After a series of fights, they compromised and agreed that she

could cover most of her hair with a turban if he was with her in public, and could veil more completely if he wasn't.

For Susan, the fights and the eventual compromise were worth it. She recognizes that women gain rewards for displaying attractive hair, but feels that the power she gets from *covering* her hair is greater:

Men open doors for you. Not just Arabic men but, even more, American men. What must be going through their heads is exactly what you are trying to put across: that I am . . . a person of God, someone who is chaste. And they're very helpful, very respectful. And I don't think it's that they think you are submissive, because I don't appear submissive. I talk, I stand tall. I'm by myself. It's not like I'm with my husband and I don't say anything.

Most tellingly, she notes, "It's hard for Americans to think that a woman could be empowered without using her body and beauty to do it. [But] my power comes from within."

At the same time, Susan has paid a price for her choice. Her husband remains unhappy about her veiling, which strains their marriage. She's also sentenced herself to a hot, uncomfortable head covering, given up the pleasure of playing with personal ornamentation, and foresworn the myriad benefits—in addition to those that occur within intimate relationships—that come to those who look attractive to the world in general.

Still, because Susan is married and doesn't work outside the home, she can afford to make this choice. Women who have paid jobs, on the other hand, must style their hair in ways that balance relationship issues with career requirements—or pay the consequences.

. . .

NO MORE BAD HAIR DAYS

There's no getting around it: As it was for Rapunzel, hair is central to our identities and our prospects. Whenever we cut our hair short or grow it long, cover the gray or leave it alone, dye it blonde or dye it turquoise, curl it or straighten it, we decide what image we want to present to the world. And the world responds in kind, deciding who we are and how to treat us based in part on what our hair looks like.

At one level, this is perfectly natural. Whenever we first meet someone, we need to figure out what sort of person he or she is (a threat? a potential friend? a new boss? a new client?), and often need to do so quickly. As a result, we use any clues available to decipher whether that person is wealthy, middle-class, or poor; friendly or aloof; athletic or bookish; and so on. Hair offers one of the most visible clues. This is why people who have no hair typically look less individualistic; although their bald heads are distinctive, their faces often seem vaguely alike.

But for all its naturalness, this process of defining ourselves and others through hair is also a product of culture. As we've seen, girls have to be taught to consider their hair central to their identities and to use their hair to manipulate both their self-identity and the image they project to others. And although it's probably true that humans are innately attracted to beauty, the definition of beautiful hair varies across time and culture—how many beautiful women these days sport six-inch-high beehives?—and so girls must learn how beauty is defined in their particular social world. Once they do, they quickly also learn that a wide variety of rewards accrue to those who most closely meet beauty norms.

In part because our hair plays such a large role in how we view ourselves and are viewed by others, it offers us many opportunities for pleasure. Each day our hair provides us with the means to create ourselves anew—at least until our perm, relaxer, or hair dye grows out. And in comparison to losing weight, affording a better-looking wardrobe, or finding true love, changing our lives by changing our hair seems downright easy. Styling our hair also offers the artistic and, at times, intellectual pleasure of sculpting a highly malleable substance. Often, too, hairstyling is a community affair, involving friends, relatives, or stylists and bringing us the pleasures of laughing, joking, working, talking, and sharing our lives with other women. What's more, the results of our efforts bring sensual and sexual pleasures to us and to our lovers, be they male or female.

But each of these pleasures of hair also carries dangers. As girls learn the importance of attractive hair (and of attractiveness in general); start spending time, energy, and money on their appearance; and come to evaluate both themselves and other girls on their appearance and on their ability to attract the opposite sex, they help perpetuate the idea that only a limited range of female appearance are acceptable. More insidiously, their actions make it seem as if focusing on appearance is something that girls do naturally, rather than something girls must learn to do. This in turn limits the life chances both of girls who succeed at attractiveness and of those who don't, for those who succeed sometimes must struggle to be seen as more than just a pretty image and those who fail are often denigrated not only as unattractive but also as lazy, unintelligent, and incompetent. At the same time, the focus on appearance teaches girls to view each other as competitors and limits the potential for true friendship between them.

By the time we reach adulthood, all of us have, at least to some extent, absorbed these lessons. Yet this does not mean that we docilely internalize them and blindly seek male approval for our appearance, as some writers seem to suggest.[12] Rather, each of us chooses daily how far she will go to meet beauty expectations. As we've seen, some of us choose hairstyles for convenience, some to project a professional image, some to reject notions of proper femininity or to reject male approval altogether. Moreover, those of us whose main goal in styling our hair is to attract men typically know perfectly well what we're doing. Far from meekly and unconsciously following cultural scripts, we actively use our appearance to get what we want: wearing long extensions, dyeing our hair blonde or red, flipping it off our shoulders to catch men's eyes, spiking it with gel to suggest sexy rebelliousness, and so on. In a world that still all too often holds women back and expects them to accept passively whatever life brings, those of us who manipulate our appearance to manipulate men and to create opportunities that might otherwise be denied us—whether getting a promotion or marrying well—can sometimes seem like rebels, resisting the narrow role in which others would place us.

That said, it would be equally wrong to overstate the extent to which, in manipulating our appearance, we manipulate our social position and so resist those who would constrain our lives and options.[13] Whether we wear our hair in blonde curls to attract men's interest or in short, professional styles to move ahead in the corporate world, we're still limited by social stereotypes regarding women's nature and capabilities. Although our hair can help us achieve our personal goals, it cannot change those stereotypes. Rather, such strategies *reinforce* stereotypes by reinforcing the idea that appearance is central to female identity. In the long run, therefore, they limit all girls' and women's opportunities. Even those hair strategies that seem most to embody resistance, like "lesbian power cuts" and voluntary baldness, have limited ability to change women's position since, like Afros, they either stigmatize their wearers and reduce their ability to achieve their goals or evolve into mere fashions that lack political effect.

The truth, then, lies somewhere in between these two positions. In our decisions about hair, we actively and rationally make choices based on a realistic assessment of how we can best obtain our goals, given cultural expectations regarding female appearance and given our personal resources. As this suggests, girls and women are far from free agents. If we ignore cultural expectations for female appearance we pay a price in lost wages, diminished marital prospects, lowered status, and so on. If we attempt to follow cultural expectations, we pay a price in time, money, and energy when we obsess about our hair; in low self-esteem when our hair fails us; and in low esteem from others when we are considered little more than the sum total of our hair and our appearance.

Is this double-bind inevitable? Is there a way to stop setting up ourselves and our daughters for more "bad hair days"?

As we've seen, from birth girls are taught to emphasize their appearance. No parent—or, for that matter, teacher, lover, or friend—can fully counteract all these cultural pressures. But we can make those pressures tolerable, and at least plant the seeds for a better future. For better or worse, all of us serve as role models for the girls and younger women around us. When we allow our lovers or spouses to dictate our hairstyles, we teach our children to value their hair primarily for its effect on others. When we obsess over our hair, we teach them to do the same. Conversely, when we joke about our hair "flaws" and move on with our life or enjoy the pleasures our hair brings us without worrying what others think about it, we help create an environment in which an alternative message can begin to take root. This doesn't mean that we should dismiss our children's concerns about appearance—all children need to feel that they fit in, and having a socially acceptable appearance is part of that—but it does mean we shouldn't reinforce those concerns (through such actions as paying for modeling lessons or arranging birthday parties at hair salons).

As teachers, parents, aunts, scout leaders, and youth group leaders, we also have the opportunity to expose children to alternative ways of thinking about appearance. Several books are now on the market that teach young black girls to take pride in their natural hair, including Carolivia Herron's *Nappy Hair*, bell hooks's *Happy to Be Nappy*, and Natasha Tarpley's *I Love My Hair*. The only equivalent book I've seen for white girls is *This Is My Hair*, by Todd Parr; more such books are definitely needed. We also have the power to begin pressuring the media to change how it portrays girls and women. Write a letter asking why *InStyle* uses so few black models, why *Ebony* uses so few models with natural hair, or why *Ladies' Home Journal* uses almost no models with graying hair. Even better, organize those in your church, synagogue, Girl Scout troop, or women's group to do the same.

None of this means that we should keep girls from playing with their hair, or stop playing with our own hair. Nor do I mean to suggest that there's anything inherently bad or good, sexist or feminist, rebellious or conformist, about blonde, turquoise, gray, dreadlocked, curled, or straightened hair. These styles are only problematic when they are forced "choices," prices we must pay to keep a job, find romance, or be accepted by the in-crowd at our school. We don't want to lose the pleasure of changing our hair color or style any more than we would want to lose the pleasure of changing the color or style of our bedroom. But we *do* want to make sure that hair play is voluntary and fun.

For this to happen, we need to consider not only what we teach girls, but also how we live our own lives. We need to explore honestly how we interact with other women. When do we compliment others on their hair? When do we withhold compliments? Why? What do we say (and think) when a friend decides to let her hair go gray, or decides to dye it hot pink, blonde, or black? In our remarks, are we honoring our friend's individuality? Recognizing the constraints under which she lives? Or reinforcing the pressures on her to use her appearance to bolster her identity, self-esteem, and life chances? Conversely, we need to recognize that a friend who routinely criticizes our appearance is not much of a friend. The same issues apply in the work world. Do we assume that coworkers, employees, and underlings who have long hair aren't professional, or that those with short hair aren't feminine? And do our thoughts and actions limit the potential of other women?

By altering our behavior in response to these questions and issues, we can start to chip away at the prison bars of the beauty culture. But although such actions are crucial for improving the lives of individual girls and women, they can bring only limited change. In the long run, the only way to truly break the hold of the beauty culture is to change girls' and woman's position in society.

For minority girls and women, that change must include improving the social and economic positions of their ethnic communities. We can already see this happening. Although white women with frizzy "Jewish" hair and black women with Afros still raise eyebrows and sometimes lose jobs for leaving their hair in its natural state, their

hair is no longer the mark of shame it once was. And in some circles it's considered downright attractive. In the same fashion, if disparaging stereotypes of overweight and disabled people decline, overweight and disabled girls and women will no longer have to rely on their hair to "prove" their femininity.

More broadly, only when all girls and women are freed from stereotypical expectations about our natures and abilities will we also be freed from the bonds of the beauty culture. Again, we can see those effects already. Girls whose athletic, creative, or academic interests are nurtured, taking into account and valuing all levels of abilities; whose special talents are rewarded with approval from parents and teachers; who attend schools and universities where their particular skills and talents are appreciated; and who believe that their futures hold myriad intriguing possibilities are far less likely than other girls to center their identities on their appearance. In such environments, too, others are more likely to evaluate girls on their personality and achievements and less likely to evaluate them on their looks. By the same token, women whose social and economic positions are based not on their looks but on their intellect, personality, skills, talents, and achievements can afford to regard their hair as a personal pleasure rather than as a tool for pleasing or manipulating others.

Rapunzel had only one way to change her life: attracting a prince through her hair and her beauty. All of us these days have more options than that. Still, as it was for Rapunzel, our hair remains an almost magical substance: both uniquely public, open to others' interpretations, and uniquely personal, growing out of our bodies and molded (if imperfectly) to our individual desires. For this reason, hair will continue to serve as a marker of our individual identity throughout our lives. Yet our hair can also be simply fun: an idle amusement, a sensuous pleasure, an outlet for creativity, a means for bonding with others, and a way of playing with who we are and who we might become. The more control we gain over our lives as girls and women, the more freedom we will have to truly enjoy and celebrate our hair.

NOTES

1. On the social psychology of relationships, see Judith A. Howard, "Social Psychology of Identities," *Annual Review of Sociology* 26 (2000): 367–93.

   Physical appearance also, of course, plays a role in romantic relationships between women. However, existing data on this topic are very mixed. Some studies suggest that lesbians find a broader range of appearance acceptable than do heterosexuals, and other studies indicate that mainstream appearance norms are equally important in the lesbian community. See Dawn Atkins, ed., *Looking Queer: Body Image and Identity in Lesbian, Bisexual, Gay, and Transgender Communities* (New York: Haworth, 1998); and Jeanine C. Cogan, "Lesbians Walk the Tightrope of Beauty: Thin Is In But Femme Is Out," *Journal of Lesbian Studies* 3, no. 4 (1999): 77–89. This topic deserves a fuller treatment than I can give in this [reading], and so I have chosen only to discuss heterosexual relationships here.

2. David M. Buss, Todd K. Shackelford, Lee A. Kirkpatrick, and Randy J. Larsen, "A Half Century of Mate Preferences: The Cultural Evolution of Values," *Journal of Marriage and the Family* 62 (2001): 491–503; Susan Sprecher, "The Importance to Males and Females of Physical Attractiveness, Earning Potential, and Expressiveness in Initial Attraction," *Sex Roles* 21 (1989): 591–607; Erich Goode, "Gender and Courtship Entitlement: Responses to Personal Ads," *Sex Roles* 34 (1996): 141–69.

3. Michel Foucault, *Discipline and Punish: The Birth of the Prison* (New York: Vintage, 1979), and *History of Sexuality* (New York: Pantheon, 1980). For critiques of feminist writings that emphasize women's docility, see Lyn Mikel Brown, *Raising Their Voices: The Politics of Girls' Anger* (Cambridge, Mass.: Harvard University Press, 1998); Kathy Davis, "Remaking the She-Devil: A Critical Look at Feminist Approaches to Beauty," *Hypatia* 6, no. 2 (1991): 21–42; and Lois McNay, "The Foucauldian Body and the Exclusion of Experience," *Hypatia* 6, no. 3 (1991): 125–39.

4. *DSN Retailing Today*, "Salon-Inspired Hair Products Weave Their Way into Mass Market," 40 (5): 17 (2001), and Victoria Wurdinger, "The Haircolor Report," *Drug and Cosmetic Industry* 161 (4): 38–47 (1997). In contrast, about 10 percent of men dye their hair (a sharp increase over previous years), with most doing so to impress other young men with their "coolness." See Dana Butcher, "More than a Shave and a Haircut," *Global Cosmetic Industry* 166, no. 1 (2000): 45–48.

5. For stereotypes of blondes and redheads, see Wendy Cooper, *Hair: Sex, Society, and Symbolism* (New York: Stein and Day, 1971); Saul Feinman and George W. Gill, "Sex Differences in Physical Attractiveness Preferences," *Journal of Social Psychology* 105 (1978): 43–52; Druann Maria Heckert and Amy Best, "Ugly Duckling to Swan: Labeling Theory and the Stigmatization of Red Hair," *Symbolic Interaction* 20 (1997): 365–84; Dennis E. Clayson and Micol R. C. Maughan, "Redheads and Blonds: Stereotypic Images," *Psychological Reports* 59 (1986): 811–16; and Diana J. Kyle and Heike I. M. Mahler, "The Effects of Hair Color and Cosmetic Use on Perceptions of a Female's Ability," *Psychology of Women Quarterly* 20 (1996): 447–55.

6. For further discussion of this process (referred to in the scholarly literature as a "feminine apologetic"), see Dan C. Hilliard, "Media Images of Male and Female Professional Athletes: An Interpretive Analysis of Magazine Articles," *Sociology of Sport Journal* 1 (1984): 251–62; and Maria R. Lowe, *Women of Steel: Female Body Builders and the Struggle for Self-Definition* (New Brunswick, N.J.: Rutgers University Press, 1998). Quote is from Lowe, 123–24.

7. For data on the prevalence and nature of attitudes toward black women, see Rose Weitz and Leonard Gordon, "Images of Black Women among Anglo College Students," *Sex Roles* 28 (1993): 19–45. Numerous books discuss attitudes toward black women's bodies and hair, including Ingrid Banks, *Hair Matters: Beauty, Power, and Black Women's Consciousness* (New York: New York University Press, 2000); Patricia Hill Collins, *Black Feminist Thought: Knowledge, Consciousness, and the Politics of Empowerment* (London: Routledge, 1991), 67–90; Maxine Craig, *Ain't I a Beauty Queen?: Black Women, Beauty, and the Politics of Race* (Berkeley: University of California Press, 2002); Noliwe M. Rooks, *Hair Raising: Beauty, Culture, and African American Women* (New Brunswick, N.J.: Rutgers University Press, 1996); and Ayana D. Byrd and Lori L. Tharps, *Hair Story: Untangling the Roots of Black Hair in America* (New York: St. Martin's Press, 2001).

8. Cherilyn Wright, "If You Let Me Make Love to You, Then Why Can't I Touch Your Hair?" in

Tenderheaded: A Comb-Bending Collection of Hair Stories, edited by Juliette Harris and Pamela Johnson (New York: Pocket Books, 2001), 64–165.

9. Regarding the importance of fatness in African beauty contests, see Norimitsu Onishi, "Maradi Journal: On the Scale of Beauty, Weight Weighs Heavily," *New York Times,* February 12, 2001. Regarding stereotypes and experiences of disabled women, see Michelle Fine and Adrienne Asch, eds., *Women with Disabilities: Essays in Psychology, Culture, and Politics* (Philadelphia: Temple University Press, 1988); Adrienne Asch and Michelle Fine, "Nurturance, Sexuality, and Women with Disabilities: The Example of Women and Literature," in *Disability Studies Reader,* edited by Lennard J. Davis (New York: Routledge, 1997); and William John Hanna and Betsy Rogovsky, "Women with Disabilities: Two Handicaps Plus," in *Perspectives on Disability,* 2nd ed., edited by Mark Nagler (Palo Alto, Calif.: Health Markets Research, 1993).

10. Kathryn Farr, Department of Sociology, Portland State University, personal communication with the author.

11. Jen'nan Ghazal Read and John P. Bartkowski, "To Veil or Not to Veil? A Case Study of Identity Negotiation among Muslim Women in Austin, Texas," *Gender & Society* 14 (2000): 395–417.

12. Writers who have been criticized for emphasizing women's docility include Sandra Lee Bartky, "Foucault, Femininity, and the Modernization of Patriarchal Power," in *Feminism and Foucault,* edited by Irene Diamond and Lee Quinby (Boston: Northeastern University Press, 1988), and Susan R. Bordo, "The Body and the Reproduction of Femininity: A Feminist Appropriation of Foucault," in *Gender/Body/Knowledge,* edited by Alison M. Jaggar and Susan R. Bordo (New Brunswick, N.J.: Rutgers University Press, 1989).

13. Writers who have been criticized for overstating women's resistance include Lyn Mikel Brown, *Raising Their Voices: The Politics of Girls' Anger* (Cambridge, Mass.: Harvard University Press, 1998); Kathy Davis, "Remaking the She-Devil: A Critical Look at Feminist Approaches to Beauty," *Hypatia* 6, no. 2 (1991): 21–42; Kathy Davis, *Reshaping the Female Body: The Dilemma of Cosmetic Surgery* (New York: Routledge, 1995); and Lois McNay, "The Foucauldian Body and the Exclusion of Experience," *Hypatia* 6, no. 3 (1991): 125–39. Among those who have criticized such research are Scott Davies, "Leaps of Faith: Shifting Currents in Critical Sociology of Education," *American Journal of Sociology* 100 (1995): 1448–78; Joan Ringelheim, "Women and the Holocaust," *Signs: A Journal of Women in Society* 10 (1985): 741–61; and Myra Dinnerstein and Rose Weitz, "Jane Fonda, Barbara Bush and Other Aging Bodies: Femininity and the Limits of Resistance," *Feminist Issues* 14 (1994): 3–24.

R E A D I N G   **40**

Hold That Nose

Lisa Miya-Jervis

I'm a Jew. I'm not even slightly religious. Aside from attending friends' bat mitzvahs, I've been to temple maybe twice. I don't know Hebrew; my junior-high self, given the option of religious education, easily chose to sleep in on Sunday mornings. My family skips around the Passover Haggadah to get to the food faster. Before I dated someone from an observant family, I wouldn't have known a mezuzah if it bit me on the butt. I was born assimilated.

But still, I'm a Jew, an ethnic Jew of a very specific variety: a godless, New York City–raised, neurotic middle-class girl from a solidly liberal-Democratic family, who attended largely Jewish, "progressive" schools. When I was growing up, almost everyone around me was Jewish; I was stunned when I found out that Jews make up only 2 percent of the American population. For me, being Jewish meant that on Christmas Day my family went out for Chinese food and took in the new Woody Allen movie. It also meant that I had a big honkin' nose.

And I still do. By virtue of my class and its sociopolitical trappings, I always knew I had the option to have my nose surgically altered. From adolescence on, I've had a standing offer from my mother to pay for a nose job.

"It's not such a big deal."

"Doctors do such individual-looking noses these days, it'll look really natural."

"It's not too late, you know," she would say to me for years after I flat-out refused to let someone break my nose, scrape part of it out, and reposition it into a smaller, less obtrusive shape. "I'll still pay." As if money were the reason I was resisting.

My mother thought a nose job was a good idea. See, she hadn't wanted one either. But when she was 16, her parents demanded that she get that honker "fixed," and they didn't take no for an answer. She insists that she's been glad ever since, although she usually rationalizes that it was good for her social life. (She even briefly dated a guy she met in the surgeon's waiting room, a boxer having his deviated septum corrected.)

Even my father is a believer. He says that without my mother's nose job, my sister and I wouldn't exist, because he never would have gone out with Mom. I take this with an entire salt lick. My father thinks that dressing up means wearing dark sneakers; that pants should be purchased every 20 years—and then only if the old ones are literally falling apart; and that haircuts should cost $10 and take as many minutes. The only thing he says about appearances is, "You have some crud . . ." as he picks a piece of lint off your sleeve. But he cared about the nose? Whatever.

Even though my mother is happy with her tidy little surgically altered nose, she wasn't going to put me through the same thing, and for that I am truly grateful. I'm also unspeakably glad that her comments stayed far from the "you'd be so pretty if you did" angle. I know a few people who weren't so lucky. Not that they were dragged kicking and screaming to the doctor's office; no, they were coerced and shamed into it. Seems it was their family's decision more than their own—usually older female relatives: mothers, grandmothers, aunts.

What's the motivation for that kind of pressure? Can it be that for all the strides made against racism and anti-Semitism, Americans still want to expunge their ethnicity from their looks? Were these mothers and grandmothers trying to fit their offspring into a more white, gentile mode? Possibly. Well, definitely. But on purpose? Probably not. Their lust for the button nose is probably more a desire for a typical femininity than for any specific de-ethnicizing. But given the society in which we live, the proximity of WASPy white features to the ideal of beauty is no coincidence. I think that anyone who opts for a nose job today (or who pressures her daughter to get one) would say that the reason for the surgery is to look "better" or "prettier." But when we scratch the surface of what "prettier" means, we find that we might as well be saying "whiter" or "more gentile" (I would add "bland," but that's my personal opinion).

Or perhaps the reason is to become unobtrusive. The stereotypical Jewish woman is loud and pushy—qualities girls really aren't supposed to have. So is it possible that the nose job is supposed to usher in not only physical femininity but a psychological, traditional femininity as well? Bob your nose, and become feminine in both mind and body. (This certainly seems to be the way it has worked with Courtney Love, although her issue is class more than ethnicity. But it's undeniable that her new nose comes with a Versace-shilling, tamed persona, in stark contrast to her old messy, outspoken self.)

Even though I know plenty of women with their genetically determined schnozzes still intact, sometimes I still feel like an oddity. From what my mother tells me, nose jobs were as compulsory a rite of passage for her peers as multiple ear-piercings were for mine. Once, when I was still in high school, I went with my mother to a Planned Parenthood fund-raiser, a cocktail party in a lovely apartment, with lovely food and drink, and a lovely short speech by Wendy Wasserstein. But I was confused: We were at a lefty charity event in Manhattan, and all the women had little WASP noses. (Most of them were blond, too, but that didn't really register. I guess hair dye is a more universal ritual.)

"Why are there no Jewish women here?" I whispered to my mother. She laughed, but I think she was genuinely shocked. "What do you mean?" she asked. "All of these women are Jewish." And then it hit me: It was wall-to-wall rhinoplasties. And worse, there was no reason to be surprised. These were women my mother's age or older who came of age in the late '50s or before, when anti-Semitism in this country was much more overt than it is today. Surface assimilation was practically the norm back then, and those honkers were way too, ahem, big a liability on the dating and social scenes. Nose jobs have declined since then. They're no longer among the top five plastic surgeries, edged out by liposuction and laser skin resurfacing.

I don't think it's a coincidence that, growing up in New York, I didn't consider my nose an "ethnic" feature. Almost everyone around me had that ethnicity, too. It wasn't until I graduated from college and moved to California that I realized how marked I was. I also realized how much I like being instantly recognizable to anyone who knows how to look. I once met another Jewish woman at a conference in California. In the middle of our

conversation, she randomly asked, "You're Jewish, right?" I replied, "With this nose and this hair, you gotta ask?" We both laughed. The question was just a formality, and we both knew it.

Only once did I feel uneasy about being "identified." At my first job out of college, my boss asked, after I mentioned an upcoming trip to see my family, "So, are your parents just like people in Woody Allen movies?" I wondered if I had a sign on my forehead reading "Big Yid Here." His comment brought up all those insecurities American Jews have that, not coincidentally, Woody Allen loves to emphasize for comic effect: Am I *that* Jewish? I felt conspicuous, exposed. Still, I'm glad I have the sign on my face, even if it's located a tad lower than my forehead.

Judaism is the only identity in which culture and religion are supposedly bound closely: If you're Irish and not a practicing Catholic, you can still be fully Irish; being Buddhist doesn't specify race or ethnicity. To me, being a Jew is cultural, but it's tied only marginally—even hypothetically—to religion, and mostly to geography (New York Jews are different from California Jews, lemme tell ya). So what happens when identity becomes untied from religion? I don't know for sure. And that means I'll grab onto anything I need to keep that identity—including my nose.

R E A D I N G **41**

Dancing Toward Redemption

Meredith McGhan

When I remove my top during the second song, the audience claps and cheers. I look at them now, not really afraid anymore, just a little nervous. I recognize genuine lust in some of the men's eyes. I can hardly believe it—they think I'm sexy, me. These men are strangers—strangers who typify The American Male and what he wants. These

are the men who hide Playboy *under their beds. They're clapping, cheering and coming up to the stage to tuck bills into my thong. Exhilarated, I walk offstage, wanting more of their attention, more of their money. I count the bills in my waistband—ten dollars for a ten-minute routine. I had done it! I had guts. I had nerve. I had power.*

And so began my career as a topless dancer.

When I tell people that I used to strip for a living, they're always surprised. "What? You, a feminist?" There's an immediate, visceral association. Exotic dancers are supposed to be hard, jaded and, well, not exactly bright. Aside from supporting our various drug addictions, we dance because we're so economically oppressed we can't recognize our own exploitation. We're tall, bleached-blond bimbos with breast implants, who occasionally appear on *Jerry Springer* to reveal our "secret" occupations to shocked parents and boyfriends, followed by a gratis studio performance.

I don't fit the expectation. I've never had a guy beg me to "quit the profession" on national TV. I'm also a middle-class white chick with a master's degree in women's studies, a woman who's far shorter and heavier than the buff Demi Moore in *Striptease* or the lean, leggy Elizabeth Berkley of *Showgirls*. And I'm neither blonde nor tan. But I often think that my not being a Demi or an Elizabeth propelled me into the sex industry, where, ironically or not, I pieced together a new self-image.

The women's movement has always faltered when feminist sex workers bring their voices to the discourse. There's a hesitation to support the premise that women can *choose* to do this work, that feminism should advocate for women's rights to use sexual power in a professional way. Many feminists strongly disagree that sex work offers women an element of choice at all—and to an extent that may be true. After all, we live in a system that makes it difficult for women to earn as much money in jobs that don't involve their beauty or their sexuality.

Still, I never got the impression that any of my co-workers felt trapped in their jobs, unable to leave or forced into dancing—at least not anymore than anyone else working in the blue- or white-collar worlds. The dancers I met came from a variety of situations. Some, like me, were artists or students looking for a part-time job that paid a lot and left them with time to pursue their interests. Others were single mothers who needed the free time to look after their children. For the most part, they enjoyed or tolerated their jobs like anyone.

Besides the money, why did I choose the sex industry? To answer that, I have to go back to the stash of soft-core porn magazines I discovered in my father's study when I was nine years old. *Playboy, Penthouse, Oui* and the occasional *Hustler* were my first exposure to what adult women supposedly looked like naked. I didn't know that photographers used tricks to make models look like fantasy women—airbrushing, soft focus, strategic posing (any woman's breasts look perky when her arms are raised and her chest is pushed out like a pigeon's). And it didn't occur to me that I wouldn't resemble those images when I grew up.

Not long after finding the magazines, my breasts started to develop. In fourth grade, my mother was urging me to wear a bra. I was terrified. It was too early. No one else in my class wore one yet, and I felt like a freak—I couldn't even bring myself to say the word *bra*. I wore layers of clothing to hide my chest, but my breasts grew rapidly. By the end of the school year, I was getting different looks from men on the street, and it frightened me. At school, boys would tease me and try to grab my breasts or snap my bra strap, and other girls would remark, "Wow, you have big boobs." By fifth grade, I was wearing a 34B and had reached my full height of five feet nothing. I thought there was something wrong with me. Why did I have to be short and curvy, when it was obvious even to a fifth grader that only the tall and willowy were considered beautiful? And if you weren't beautiful, you weren't anything, right?

I begged my mother to take me to the doctor to find out if, indeed, something was wrong with me. My mother didn't have much time or patience for this. She told me that early development ran in the family and I should just deal with it. The doctor agreed. So I dealt with it. I dealt with it by deciding that my body was a traitor and I hated it. I dealt with it by ignoring most of the other kids at school (who needed friends? I could always read a book instead of play). And I dealt with it by deciding that I had better start overcompensating for being a freak by being perfect in every other way.

So when my father suggested I stop eating desserts and take smaller portions, I began dieting in earnest, turning my precocious reading skills to weight-loss books. The books told me that a five-foot-tall woman should weigh a hundred pounds, and for each inch over five feet, five more pounds were permissible. My overcompensation kicked in, and I decided to beat the hundred-pound standard and try for ninety-five. I drank a lot of diet soda to fill my empty stomach, ignoring the head rushes and tremors. But even as I hovered just below a hundred pounds, my curves were still obvious. By the time I was twelve, my war against my body was firmly entrenched. I was convinced I was a fat, ugly freak, and I was miserable.

Imagine my surprise when I turned eighteen and met a guy who was genuinely attracted to me. Though I still saw a disproportionate dwarf in the mirror, I began to hold male opinion as an article of faith. I told myself that as long as I was attractive to men, the ugliness I saw in the mirror must be a delusion. That was as close as I could get to feeling good about my body.

The topless dancing seed was planted when I noticed that a few women from my hometown were driving across the border to strip in Canada three nights a week—and raking in the money. I was intrigued but disdainful. Why would they want to exploit themselves that way? Wasn't it dangerous and humiliating?

The idea crept closer to home, though, when my friend Jen began dancing at the local Déjà Vu strip club. One night, a couple of guys I knew convinced me to go to a show—just to see what it was like. Jen wasn't working that night, but we stayed for a couple hours anyway. To my surprise, I wasn't really offended. As I watched the dancers grind their hips and gyrate in men's laps, I was captivated. Their bodies were vastly different from what I had expected—and far from perfect. They had sagging breasts, stretch marks, cellulite on their thighs. Some were unabashedly plump. And they were all getting money—and compliments—from men.

I turned to my friend and whispered, "I thought you had to be a super-skinny model type to do this kind of work."

"Some clubs you do, but not here," he answered; then he teasingly nudged my shoulder. "Why—you thinking of doing it?"

"No way," I said. "I'd feel exploited."

"The men are the ones getting exploited," he argued deftly. "The women are in control. I mean, they're making all the money."

I wasn't sure I agreed, but the idea stayed in my mind.

A few years later, I met a woman named Katie at a party. We got to talking, and she told me she danced at a local club that was owned and operated by women. "I make about $300 a week for twenty hours of work," she told me. "The rest of the time I spend writing and going to college. It's great."

What a luxury, I mused, reflecting on the gamut of dull, low-wage temp jobs I'd worked since graduation. After forty hours a week, I was usually too tired to find much inspiration for my writing. I confessed to Katie I was looking for an easy, part-time gig that would pay my bills without draining my creativity.

"Oh, it's a *perfect* job for a writer," Katie gushed. "You should totally try it."

"Yeah, well, there's one problem," I said, waving a dispassionate hand at myself. "I hardly have the body for it."

"Are you kidding?" she laughed, patting my arm. "Just come to my club sometime and see what you think. If you want a job, I'll get you in."

A week later, I gathered up my courage and asked a male friend to drive me to Katie's club. We parked on a rundown street, below a painted sign of a dancing, bikini-clad woman. "I don't know," my friend looked at me. "It looks like a dive." I pulled him through the doorway.

The club made no pretense at classiness. Its squat, shabby tables and chairs were mostly empty that afternoon, and a woman danced on stage to an audience of one disheveled, hooting old man. The place reeked of the cigarette smoke hanging visibly in the air and an undertone of sweat. A sweetness touched the air, too, the scent of the dancers' many mingled perfumes and lotions and shampoos.

My friend, uncomfortable with the scene, averted his eyes. I watched avidly, taking stock of the scene, measuring out a place for myself in this foreign terrain. I spied Katie across the room, doing a table dance. She picked up her breasts, leaned toward a guy and shook them in his face. Another dancer rubbed her small breasts surreptitiously against a man's cheek. "Oh, baby," he groaned, and tucked a twenty-dollar bill into the elastic of her fuschia thong.

Katie finished her table dance and headed my way. I covertly checked out her body as she walked. She was a little taller than I was, with large breasts and a thick waist. We were shaped differently, but neither of us fit my image of topless dancers. A glance around the room showed me that the other dancers didn't either. A few were what some might call fat. Some were bone-thin. Only a couple were, by society's standards, drop-dead gorgeous. And their work didn't look that difficult. Since there were hardly any customers, most of the dancers were sitting at a table near the DJ booth, talking and sipping water. No one had any fancy moves. No one was sweating. The atmosphere was almost comfortable. It certainly wasn't intimidating.

"What do you think?" Katie asked, plopping down next to me.

"It looks pretty easy," I said, trying not to stare at her breasts. "But do I have to touch the customers?"

"You're not supposed to," she answered, twisting her hair into a ponytail. "And they're not supposed to touch you. I've smacked people before for trying stuff."

The small-breasted dancer had obviously been playing against the rules. Katie didn't, though, and she made just as much money.

"So when are you going to audition?" she asked.

"I don't know. I have to think it over," I said. But I already knew I would. I had spent over half my life hating my body. I wanted redemption. I wanted to be someone's fantasy for once. Just long enough to prove that I could be. If it was too hard to reconcile with my feminist principles, I could always quit. But I'd never know unless I tried.

The next morning, I called Katie. "I want to audition," I said. She volunteered to come over and help me practice. In my basement, Katie demonstrated a few moves on the thick, floor-to-ceiling

pipes, showing me how to remove skimpy clothing as part of the dance. I mimicked her, feeling self-conscious as she adjusted my hips and stepped back to appraise my performance. But after a while, she said I had gotten the gist, so we drove to Woolworth's to shop for cheap lingerie. "You're going to need a few thongs," she directed, dumping a handful of them into our shopping basket. "Get some matching bras, too, and a couple of lacy tops."

The next day I went to the club, already dressed and made up "for the stage," as Katie had advised. I introduced myself to the other dancers, who were friendly and encouraging. One even rushed off to get me a shot of liquor. "Drink this," she patted my shoulder. "Then just get up there and dance. Pretend you're all alone in the room. Don't look at anyone. The men don't care, and they're going to hire you anyway."

When the DJ called my name, my walk was surprisingly steady in my three-inch heels. I felt as if someone else was taking over—someone on the brink of tasting a new kind of power. A glance in the mirror behind the *barre* showed me that the heels slowed me down, made me sway my hips, elongated my legs. I held the *barre* for balance, gyrating and bending as I had seen the other dancers do. I didn't dare look at the audience during the first song, but I could hear their primal hoots and inarticulate pleas. As I continued to dance, I grew more comfortable under their gaze. It was all context. I began to relax and enjoy the music and the movement. And when the manager told me that I could start tomorrow, I felt good about my body for the first time in my life.

During my six-month stay at the club, at least two men would tell me I was beautiful every day. I was surrounded by women of different shapes, sizes, ages and ethnicities, all of whom had their particular admirers, as did I. Some men would come into the club, ignore the tall, thin, blond dancers and be all over me. I can't count the compliments I got. "Your legs look so strong," one guy told me. "You must work out." My friend Kitty, considered among the dancers as the most attractive with her waist-length blonde hair and willowy figure, said she envied my legs and wished her own "weren't so damn skinny." Twenty hours a week for six months, I got positive reinforcement for my body—and a paycheck to boot. I had put myself in an environment where I was saturated with praise for my looks, and my old self-image was eroded there, little by little, until I became proud of my appearance. Even my severely distorted perception could not withstand the power of the relentless compliments—and the money I made responding to them.

At the time, I didn't analyze the drastic way my self-confidence rose when I stepped on the platform. I was drunk with the validation, the thrill that I had faced my inner demons and walked away victorious. There were no disparaging "fat" remarks, no eyes scanning me with disapproval. The men there were as delighted by my body as I was with their attention. I made them weak with desire, like the pictures in my father's magazines. The mere sight of me flipped on a primal switch in these men, as though I held some mysterious power.

And all it took was a simple dance number. Reveling in the movements of my body, the sight of my own skin, freed me from a lifetime of self-hatred. Never had I imagined that my body—my despicable body—could grant me so much control. Once I discovered it, I was willing to go to extremes, to put politics aside, to keep that feeling alive.

Yes, there were things I wanted to be other than just a body—a poet, an editor, a student. But more than anything, I wanted to be beautiful. My body hatred had superseded all I wanted for myself spiritually, intellectually and ethically. I had friends in the fat acceptance movement, but my own body obsession drove a wedge between us. I felt terrible about my own hypocrisy, but I felt even worse when I looked in the mirror and didn't see what the men at the club did, a body that could command the power of lust and desire.

When the initial glow of realizing that I was as attractive as anyone else wore off, the men at the club became annoying. I started to feel cheapened and objectified, and I became increasingly aware of the inherent danger tingeing my new position. The fantasy realm began to spill into the safety of my outside reality. Customers began asking me for my phone number and wanting to see me off the job. A couple of the other dancers had stalkers. I was worried; the place was in a rough neighborhood, and I couldn't even walk to my car alone.

I finally quit when the bar made lap dances legitimate. Once the owners relaxed the rules, the dancers who didn't allow a little feel-copping wouldn't get tipped. My earnings fell off, and the customers' out-of-line behavior got worse. Work became a dangerous place.

For the first time in my life, I felt that being attractive could make one vulnerable. When I had believed I was ugly, I imagined that beauty would make me safe—acceptable, not a reject. I hadn't bargained that beauty would make me into an object, an object that some men believed belonged to them. I knew I had truly crossed the line then—when I was so sure that I was attractive that I could afford to wish, sometimes, that I wasn't.

Dancing convinced me that I'm physically attractive to many men. To a degree, that will always matter to me. Feel like your body is unattractive—even unacceptable? Take it all off onstage, and you'll hear a different story.

Yet, I realize the irony of my experience. My original body hatred was the result of our society's appropriation of the female body as an object of consumerism. Had there been no *Playboy* standard with which to compare my developing figure, no father who told me I was gaining weight, there would have been no obsession with looking perfect. I conquered much of that body hatred by proving to myself that my body was an adequate object of consumerism, that it wasn't too much worse than the standard. What if I had not been able to do that? What if, instead of a bad body *image*, I had a body that truly could not, in our society, conform to the norm? I like to think I would have somehow been able to love my body anyway. I like to think I would have found a way.

There are so many contradictions in the sex industry. My sense of empowerment from dancing was bound on all sides by not only the glass ceiling, but the glass floor and walls, which keep women from having easy access to well-paying jobs. And I wonder how my self-image would change if I suddenly no longer fit the norms of attractiveness. My body image, though now fairly good, is still dependent upon outside forces.

I can't deny that I feel better after dancing, but I also can't deny the irony. I haven't become a person who can accept her body unconditionally— not yet. I have become a person who is tremendously relieved to discover that she really does look okay to her oppressors. Thus, I tacitly admit that my oppressors have the right to define who I am, and I tacitly betray my sisters who are crusading for a new standard of beauty. How do I live with this? I want to resolve these contradictions. But perhaps they can never be resolved in our culture. However, by owning my struggle with them, I can begin.

R E A D I N G **42**

Phenomenal Woman

Maya Angelou

Pretty women wonder where my secret lies.
I'm not cute or built to suit a fashion model's
   size
But when I start to tell them,
They think I'm telling lies.
I say,
It's in the reach of my arms,
The span of my hips,
The stride of my step,
The curl of my lips.
I'm a woman
Phenomenally.
Phenomenal woman,
That's me.

I walk into a room
Just as cool as you please,
And to a man,
The fellows stand or
Fall down on their knees.
Then they swarm around me,
A hive of honey bees.
I say,
It's the fire in my eyes,
And the flash of my teeth,
The swing in my waist,

And the joy in my feet.
I'm a woman
Phenomenally.
Phenomenal woman,
That's me.

Men themselves have wondered
What they see in me.
They try so much
But they can't touch
My inner mystery.
When I try to show them
They say they still can't see.
I say,
It's in the arch of my back,
The sun of my smile,
The ride of my breasts,
The grace of my style.
I'm a woman
Phenomenally.
Phenomenal woman,
That's me.

Now you understand
Just why my head's not bowed.
I don't shout or jump about

Or have to talk real loud.
When you see me passing
It ought to make you proud.
I say,
It's in the click of my heels,
The bend of my hair,

The palm of my hand,
The need for my care.
Cause I'm a woman
Phenomenally.
Phenomenal woman,
That's me.

R E A D I N G **43**

China's Cosmetic Surgery Craze

Jonathan Watts

The expression "no pain, no gain" has long been used in association with cosmetic surgery, but it has perhaps never been as appropriate as in today's China, where men and women are increasingly willing to undergo expensive and painful operations to change their appearances.

According to the local media, consultants report a 25% increase in women seeking nips and tucks. The most popular operation puts an extra fold in eyelids. Like nose-lengthening, jaw reshaping, and breast enlargements, the procedure aims to bring women closer to western ideals of beauty.

But the most dramatic—and agonising—operation is leg-lengthening, which involves breaking a patient's legs and stretching them over several months using an external cage.

In part, the popularity of such surgery can be explained by the surge of interest in fashion and beauty as an increasingly affluent urban middle class shakes off a dowdy communist legacy.

Good looks are becoming increasingly important. During the cultural revolution, beauty pageants were banned as the "nonsense" of a decadent west, but late last year, China hosted its first Miss World competition.

With the economy surging forward at the rate of more than 8% per year, more and more people who are dissatisfied with their appearance can afford to change their physical appearance.

For a minimum US$4000 price tag, doctors are offering to make people up to 10 cm taller. The leg-lengthening procedure has three stages. First, the legs are broken and steel pins—27 cm long and 8 mm in diameter—are pushed through the tibiae. These are fixed to an external frame by eight or so screws, each of which is 4 mm in diameter. Next comes the stretching, which is done over several months (depending on how much the customer wants to grow) by turning the screws each day and lengthening the bone at the point where it was broken. When the stretching is complete the external frame is removed. In the final stage, the steel pins are left in place for about a year as a support for the newly regenerated bone. Once it has hardened, the pins are removed.

The complex procedure was initially developed in Russia for people with stunted growth, mismatched legs, or disfigurements. But at one Beijing clinic, which undertakes 150 such operations per year, doctors say customers are increasingly driven by cosmetic motivations.

Height has long been socially important in China. It is often listed among the criteria required on job advertisements. To get a post in the foreign ministry, for instance, male applicants need not bother applying unless they are at least 5 ft 7 in., while women must be at least 5 ft 3 in.

Chinese diplomats are expected to be tall to match the height of their foreign counterparts.

For more glamorous positions the conditions are even tougher: air stewardesses must be over 5 ft 5 in. But height discrimination is evident even at ground level: in some places, people under 5 ft 3 in. are not even eligible to take a driving test. To get into many law schools, women students need to be over 5 ft 1 in. and men over 5 ft 5 in.

The surgery can help people find jobs and marriage partners. But if not done carefully, the dangers are considerable. Bones stretched too rapidly will not grow strong enough to support the body's weight. Legs extended at different speeds can become misshapen and nerves can be damaged. Horror stories about other less capable surgeons appear from time to time in the Chinese media. Young women have reportedly been left with their feet splayed outwards on weirdly twisted legs; others' bones have never properly healed and continue to break at the slightest knock. In one of the worst cases, a 31-year-old woman was left in the frame for a year because her bones proved so brittle that they could not

support her weight after being stretched. Her feet still point in odd directions and she is unable to squat.

But despite the risks involved, surgeons and consultants report an increase in demand for cosmetic procedures among the increasingly affluent urban populations. In Shanghai, there are five large cosmetic surgery outfits and about 100 smaller clinics that offer specialised procedures.

The fascination with such makeovers has created at least two cosmetic surgery celebrities. Last summer, the domestic media was filled with stories about Hao Lulu, a 24-year-old fashion writer who is undergoing a 7-month marathon of face and body altering procedures costing $US24,000 so that she can work as a spokeswoman for the industry.

Soon after, Shanghai newspapers announced the winner of what they dubbed the "grey girl" competition—to select the girl in the city most in need of a makeover. Despite the unflattering moniker, more than 50 women applied for the contest, in which the victor was awarded a prize of $US12,000 worth of cosmetic surgery.

R E A D I N G   **44**

Designer Vaginas

Simone Weil Davis

Perhaps you noticed some of the articles in women's magazines that came out in 1998; *Cosmopolitan, Marie Claire,* and *Harper's Bazaar* each carried one, as did *Salon* on-line, articles with titles like "Labia Envy," "Designer Vaginas," and "The New Sex Surgeries." More recently, *Jane* magazine covered the topic, and Dan Savage's nationally syndicated advice column, "Savage Love," stumbled explosively upon it as well. These pieces all discussed labiaplasty, a relatively recent plastic surgery procedure that involves trimming away labial tissue

and sometimes injecting fat from another part of the body into labia that have been deemed excessively droopy. In contrast to the tightening operation known as "vaginal rejuvenation," labiaplasty is sheerly cosmetic in purpose and purports to have no impact on sensation (unless something were to go terribly awry).[1] Throughout coverage here and in Canada, the aptly named Doctors Alter, Stubbs, and Matlock shared much of the glory and the public relations. In the name of consumer choice, these articles provoke consumer anxiety. The *Los Angeles*

Times quotes Dr. Matlock: "The woman is the designer . . . the doctor is just the instrument. . . . Honestly, if you look at *Playboy,* those women, on the outer vagina area, the vulva is very aesthetically appealing, the vulva is rounded. It's full, not flat. . . . Women are coming in saying, I want something different, I want to change things. They look at *Playboy,* the ideal women per se, for the body and the shape and so on. You don't see women in there with excessively long labia minora."[2]

All the popular articles about the "new sex surgeries" that I've reviewed also include remarks from skeptical colleagues and from polled readers who feel okay about their labia. (In an unfortunate turn of phrase, one plastic surgeon describes Dr. Matlock as a bit too "cutting edge.") Despite this apparently balanced coverage, a brand-new worry is being planted, with the declaration in *Salon* that "many women had been troubled for years about the appearance of their labia minora," and with the use of words like "normal" and "abnormal" to describe nonpathological variations among genitalia. The November 1998 article in *Cosmopolitan* has an eye-catching blurb: "My labia were so long, they'd show through my clothes!" Having taken *that* in, the reader suddenly looks up at the accompanying photo with new eyes: the photograph is of a slim woman in fairly modest underwear; because of the picture's cropping, she is headless, but the posture is distinctive, awkward. She's somewhat hunched forward, her hands are both crotch-bound, and one finger slips beneath the edge of her panties. Having read the caption, you think, "My God, she's tucking in her labia!"[3]

Ellen Frankfort's 1972 book, the women's liberationist *Vaginal Politics,* begins with the following scene.[4] Carol from the Los Angeles Self-Help Clinic "slips out of her dungarees and underpants," hops onto a long table in an old church basement and inserts a speculum into her vagina. The 50 other women present file up and look with a flashlight, and learn, too, how to self-examine with a speculum and a dimestore mirror. This self-exploration of what has been referred to as "the dark continent" or just "down there" seemed the perfect symbol for the early claim of women's

liberation that "the personal is political." How could a woman call for sexual autonomy without self-awareness? To reverse the phrasing of one of Second Wave feminism's most famous byproducts, how could we know "our selves" without knowing "our bodies" first?[5] This image of women using a well-placed mirror to demystify and reclaim their own bodies is rooted dimly in my teen-years memory. I found it eerily resurrected when the *Salon* piece by Lousia Kamps came up on my computer screen. Kamps starts off like this: "'Ladies, get out your hand mirrors,' begins a curious press release I find at my desk one Monday morning. 'Yes, it is true . . . the newest trend in surgically enhanced body beautification: Female Genital Cosmetic Surgery.'" The hand mirror this time is used to alert the would-be vagina shopper to any deficiencies "down below" that she may have been blithely ignoring. From 1970s' consciousness-raising groups and Judy Chicago's dinner plates, through Annie Sprinkle's speculum parties of the 1980s, and on to Eve Ensler's collaborative *Vagina Monologues,*[6] we came at the end of the 1990s to Dr. Alter and Dr. Stubbs. What's the trajectory from Second Wave feminist "self-discovery and celebration" to the current almost-craze for labiaplasty? And does the fact of this trajectory provide us with a warning?

. . .

These days, in part because of the video dissemination and the mainstreaming of pornography, women, regardless of gender preference, can see the vaginas of a lot of different other women. They may desire those vaginas, they may simultaneously identify with them, but if they are rich enough or have great credit, they can definitely have them built.[7] A 1997 article in the Canadian magazine *See* interviews a patient of Dr. Stubbs in Toronto. Deborah "has had her eyes done and had breast implants and some liposuction. She says that she started thinking about her labia when her first husband brought home porn magazines and she started comparing herself. 'I saw some other ones that were cuter than mine' and I thought, 'Hey, I want that one,' she laughs."[8] Of course, the images we relish or bemoan in pornography are almost always tweaked technically. As Deborah did her "catalog shopping," the women she was admiring were perhaps themselves surgically "enhanced," but additionally, they were posed, muted with makeup and lighting, and the resultant photographic images were then edited with an airbrush or the digital modifications of Photoshop.

This is especially true of pornography that presents itself as "upscale," whether soft or hard core. As Laura Kipnis helps us realize, there's a crucial link between *Hustler's* targeting of a working-class market and its being the first of the big three glossy "wank mags" to show what it called "the pink."[9] *Hustler's* aggressive celebration of vulgarity informed its initial rejection of soft-core decorum about genitals; thus, its representations of vaginas were matter-of-fact, and often enough contextualized with very explicit, poorly lit Polaroid shots sent in by readers. When the vagina finally came to the pages of *Penthouse,* by contrast, it was as flaw-free and glossy as the rest of the models' figures. In "The Pussy Shot: An Interview with Andrew Blake," sex writer Susie Bright discusses the classed aesthetics of this pornographer, whose trademarks are his lavish sets (straight out of *Architectural Digest,* Bright remarks) and high-end production values: in this posh setting, it comes as no surprise that the star's labia are small and her "pussy is perfectly composed, with every hair in place."[10]

. . .

In part because of the prevalence of a mainstreamed *Penthouse* and *Playboy* aesthetic, labias in pornography are often literally tucked away (in the most low-tech variant of body modification).[11] If you review enough porn, however, especially lesbian porn or that which is unsqueamishly "déclassé" as in *Hustler,* you will see a wide variety in the female genitalia on display—wide enough to evoke the "snowflake uniqueness" analogy that is bandied around in popular coverage of the new cosmetic enhancement surgeries. And indeed the before-and-after shots available at some of the surgeons' web sites that I've found so far do reveal, unsurprisingly, that the single favored look for these "designer vaginas" is . . . the clean slit. Louisa Kamps of *Salon* magazine agrees: "What strikes me in the 'after'

shots is the eerie similarity between the women . . . their genitalia are carbon copies of each other."

. . .

Bodies do change with the passage of time, of course. If the living body is to approximate sculpture, change itself must be managed, *fixed.* Reading the following quote from Dr. Alter's web site, one is reminded of the Renaissance theory of the wandering womb, whereby female hysteria and misbehavior were deemed the results of a uterus that had dislodged and begun to storm about internally, wreaking havoc. A woman's "womb was like a hungry animal; when not amply fed by sexual intercourse or reproduction, it was likely to wander about her body, overpowering her speech and senses."[12] In Dr. Alter's prose, the older woman, "in dialogue with gravity,"[13] may find her previously pleasing vagina dangerously "on the move": "The aging female may dislike the descent of her pubic hair and labia and desire re-elevation to its previous location," Dr. Alter warns. So, it is woman's work to make sure her genitalia are snug, not wayward.

We are talking about vaginal aesthetics, and aesthetic judgments almost always evidence socially relevant metaphors at work on the material and visual planes. Ideas about feminine beauty are ever-changing: the classic example is a comparison of Rubens's fleshy beauties and the wraithlike super-model Kate Moss (who succeeded Twiggy). But, in a world where many women have never thought about judging the looks of their genitals, even if they care about their appearance more generally, we should ask what criteria make for a good-looking vagina, and who is assigned as arbiter. These (mutating) criteria should tell us something about the value system that generates them. To tease out some answers to these questions, this article goes on to put the labiaplasty phenomenon in a contextual frame with other vaginal modifications.

MODIFYING/CLASSIFYING

What representations of vulvas circulate in our society? And who, beyond Dr. Tight, is modifying the female genitalia, how and why? For one, among alternative youth (and the not-so-alternative, not-so-youthful, too) piercings are being sought to modify and decorate the labia, sometimes to extend them, and, ideally, to add to clitoral stimulation. What sensibilities mark these changes? Among body modifiers on the Web, conversation about body image, self-mutilation, and, contrarily, healing, is common, with an accepted understanding that many turn to piercing as a means of overcoming perceived past abuse. "'Most folks use BodMod to get back in touch with the parts of themselves that were hurt or misused by others. BodMod has helped me undemonize pain. . . . I was able to handle [childbirth] better, knowing that I'd survived . . . two ten-gauge labial piercings. . . .'" Changing one's relationship to one's genitalia by becoming their "modifier" leads here to an aesthetic reassessment: "'You know, I never liked to look at [myself] until I got my rings. I have well-developed inner labia that always show, and I was always envious of those women who seemed to [be neat] with everything tucked inside. So one reason I *know* I wasn't mutilating myself when I got my privates pierced was how much I liked to look at myself after the work was done. You might actually say I'm *glad* my labia are the way they are now.'"[14]

"Glad" is what the cosmetic surgeons do *not* want you to be about prominent labia minora. If you look at the opening paragraph of Ensler's *Vagina Monologues,* you begin to wonder if the unruliness now coming under the governance of the cosmetic surgeon isn't at least as symbolic as it is aesthetic. This is Ensler, introducing her project (interviews with real women, transcribed, performed onstage, and then collected in a book):

> I was worried about vaginas. I was worried about what we think about vaginas, and even more worried that we don't think about them. . . . So I decided to talk to women about their vaginas, to do vagina interviews, which became vagina monologues. I talked with over two hundred women. I talked to old women, young women, married women, single women, lesbians, college professors, actors, corporate professionals, sex workers, African American women, Hispanic women, Asian American women, Native American women, Caucasian women, Jewish women. At first women were reluctant to talk. They were a little shy. But once they got going, you couldn't stop them.[15]

Just as Ensler's own catalog of interviewees seems to burgeon and proliferate, so too the women with whom she spoke were "unstoppable." With a similar metaphoric expansion, in the cosmetic surgeons' promotional material, not only are women's *labia* depicted as in danger of distention, but one woman customer also described her *"hang-up"* about her preoperative labia as "just growing and growing," until the doctor cut it short, that is. Loose lips sink ships.

        . . .

CONFOUNDING THE BOUNDARIES

The U.S. Congress passed a measure criminalizing the circumcision of a minor female in 1996, and nine or ten states have passed anti-FGO acts since 1996 as well. In Illinois, Minnesota, Rhode Island, and Tennessee, this legislation felonizes operations performed on adults as well as on minors. But *which* operations? Anti-FGO laws that now exist in a number of U.S. states describe procedures that would definitely include those practiced by Drs. Alter and Matlock, but they use only language that addresses the "ritual" or custom and belief-based cutting of African immigrant bodies. Meanwhile, this legal language either elides or okays both the "corrective" cutting of the intersexed child and the surgery sought by the unsettled consumer who has been told by plastic surgeons that her labia are unappealing and aberrant. Thus American law marks out relations between the state and its citizen bodies that differ depending on birthplace, cultural context, and skin color.

In fact, however, it is a (prevalent) mistake to imagine a quantum distinction between Euro-American and African reshapings of women's bodies: far too often, they are measured with entirely different yardsticks, rather than on a continuum.

Nahid Toubia, executive director of the advocacy group Rainbo, remarks that "[t]he thinking of an African woman who believes that 'FGM is the fashionable thing to do to become a real woman' is not so different from that of an American woman who has breast implants to appear more feminine."[16] . . .

Soraya Miré, Somali maker of the film *Fire Eyes,* remarks in Inga Muscio's (wo)manifesto, *Cunt: A Declaration of Independence:* "[Western women] come into conversations waving the American flag, forever projecting the idea that they are more intelligent than I am. I've learned that American women look at women like me to hide from their own pain. . . . In America, women pay *the money that is theirs and no one else's* to go to a doctor who cuts them up so they can create or sustain an image men want. Men are the mirror. Western women cut themselves up voluntarily."[17] Significantly, in Miré's construction, consent to genital surgery does *not* okay it so much as it marks the degrading depths of women's oppression. Although consent is at the heart of the issue of genital operations on children, a topic both urgent and not to be downplayed, we must also look at the social and cultural means whereby consent is manufactured, regardless of age, in the West as well as in African and other countries engaging in FGOs. In the North American popular imagination, the public address of advertising is not understood as infringing upon our power of consent. Indeed, the freedom to "pay the money that is [one's] own" is too often inscribed as the quintessential exemplar of life in a democracy. Perhaps due to that presumption, beauty rituals hatched on Madison Avenue or in Beverly Hills do not bear the onus of "barbarism" here, despite the social compulsions, psychological drives, and magical thinking that impel them.

. . .

SURGERY, SISTERLINESS, AND THE "RIGHT TO CHOOSE"

Among the key motivating factors raised by African women who favor female genital surgeries are beautification, transcendence of shame,

and the desire to conform; these clearly matter to American women seeking cosmetic surgery on their labia, as well. Thus, the motivations that impel African-rooted FGOs and American labiaplasties should not be envisioned as radically distinct. Not only does such oversimplification lead to a dangerous reanimation of the un/civilized binary, but it also leaves the feminist with dull tools for analysis of either phenomenon. There are aesthetic parallels between the Western and the African procedures. The enthusiasm for the clean slit voiced so vigorously by the American plastic surgeon I consulted is echoed among a group of Egyptian mothers discussing female genital operations for their daughters in the 1990 documentary *Hidden Faces.* Although several of the women laughingly nudge each other and say they wouldn't want the excisers to interfere much with "the front" (showing a clear zest for clitoral pleasure), one woman voices an aesthetic principle about which she feels strongly. Energetically, she decries the ugliness of dangling labia, and explains to the filmmaker, with appropriate hand gestures, "Do you want her to be like a boy, with this floppy thing hanging down? Now, it should be straight. Shhh. Smooth as silk." This aesthetic judgment is in keeping not only with the views of labiaplasters in the United States but also with the vocabulary of Mauritanian midwives: one such woman, who has argued to her colleagues for a milder version of circumcision in place of vigorous excision, "use[s] two words to refer to female circumcision, 'tizian,' which means to make more beautiful, and 'gaaad,' which means to cut off and make even."[18]

The group of women chatting on a rooftop in *Hidden Faces* invokes another continuum between African and American women's approaches to feminine beauty rituals and vaginal modifications. Simplistic depictions of a global patriarchy, wherein men curb, cow, cut, and dominate "their" women, may drive home the ubiquity of female subjugation, but they leave out an important factor at the same time: although both labiaplasties and African female circumcision should be (and are here) investigated through a feminist lens, that feminism should be informed by an awareness of women's agency. A knee-jerk celebration of that agency misleads, but its disavowal in the name of victimhood leads to dangerous blind sports. Across many different cultural contexts, female genital operations are contemplated and undergone by girls and women in a social and psychological framework shaped *in part* by other women.

The plastic surgeon whose office I visited provided me with two referrals, patients who had had the procedure done by him. As part of what seemed a well-worn sales pitch, he referred often to "self-help groups," a network of supportive, independent women helping each other find the professional care they wanted and deserved, in the face of an unfeeling, disbelieving medical profession. I was interested by what seemed an invocation of rather feminist sensibilities and wondered about this swelling, grassroots support group he seemed to be conjuring up for me. And, indeed, the image of the surgery consumer as a liberated woman and an independent self-fashioner did provide a crucial spin for the doctor, throughout his consultation. The consumer-feminist in support of other women he condoned; by contrast, he expressed an avowed disapproval of the women who came to him solely to please a domineering partner. He brought up this posited bad, weak, man-centric woman three times as we spoke, and each time his face clouded, he frowned, and his brow furrowed: he said that it was only this type of woman who complained of pain after the procedure, for instance, just to get the attention of her partner, whereas for most women, he insisted, the pain was minimal. He seemed to use these diverging models of female behavior to answer in advance any reservations the prospective client might have about a cosmetic operation on the genitalia (such as, "Should I really do something so drastic to my body just to please men?"). By insisting on his antipathy toward women who kowtowed to the male perspective, and celebrating the fearless vision of the pioneer consumer of "cutting edge" surgery, the doctor tried, I suspect, to ward off potential surges of feminist resistance to the procedure.

In the same spirit, one web site advertising the surgery fuels itself on a long-standing feminist call

for a more responsive medical establishment by contrasting the surgeon being advertised with other doctors less sensitive to the needs of women. "Very few physicians are concerned with the appearance of the female external genitalia. A relative complacency exists that frustrates many women."[19] Rachel Bowlby has addressed the theoretical conflations between feminist freedom and the "freedom" to choose as a consumer.[20] The surgeon to whose sales pitch I listened and the creators of the web site noted here certainly understood that the feminist discourse of choice can be appropriated, funneled toward the managed choosing-underduress of the consumer, becoming saturated along the way with commodity culture's directives.

One goal of this article is to raise the question of this ready appropriation. In *States of Injury: Power and Freedom in Late Modernity,* Wendy Brown examines some of the liabilities of the Left's reliance on the rhetoric of identity, injury, and redress, suggesting that it can result in a politics of state domination.[21] From Bakke on, we have certainly seen the language of affirmative action hauled into the arena of "reverse racism." Perhaps by the same token, the language of choice, as central to the feminist project in this country as we could imagine, sprang up in a culture where the glories of consumer "choice" had already been mythologized. Revisiting and perhaps refiguring the conceptual framework behind "choice" in the face of manufactured consent, then, is to enable, not critique, feminism. The hand mirror that allowed feminists of the 1960s and 1970s to get familiar with "our bodies, our selves" is positioned again so that we can see our vaginas. Only, it comes now with the injunction to look critically at what we see and to exert our selfhood through expenditure and remodeling of a body that is not "ourself" any longer but which is "ours," commodified and estranged, to rebuild.

Although the approach of the doctor I visited seemed agenda-driven and rather theatricalized, when I talked with the women to whom he referred me, I was struck by how very friendly and supportive they *did* seem. I had found the doctor likable but showy, like a much rehearsed salesman, but these women were engaged, candid, and genuinely warm. They were generous with their time (and with their permission to be cited anonymously in the present article), and they made it clear that they really did want to help other women with their "experience, strength, and hope." Perhaps these women were "incentivized" to speak well of the doctor (about whose care they raved): maybe they received discounted work in exchange for talking with prospective clients. Even with this possibility in mind they seemed sincerely ready to assume a common perspective, in fact an intimacy, between women discussing their bodies and body image. To overlook their candor, generosity, and *sisterliness* in order to critique the misogynist judgments that may have driven them to surgery would be to mischaracterize the phenomenon of gender display. We typically learn about and develop a gendered bodily performance, not in isolation, but as members of both real and imagined female "communities."[22] And in 2002, one senses the cultural shading that twentieth-century feminism has, ironically, brought to this community building: the rhetoric of choice making and of solidarity developed during the Second Wave ghosts through our conversations. It's a stereotypical joke that women *really* dress for each other— a deeper look at how this female-to-female hodgepodge of peer pressure and peer support really manifests itself is useful. And again, a look at the web of relations among women is helpful in understanding African female genital operations as well.

One online World Health Organization report discusses the impact of female circumcisions on girls' psychological health. Importantly, it mentions not only "experiences of suffering, devaluation and impotence" but also the "desirability of the ceremony for the child, with its social advantage of peer acceptance, personal pride and material gifts." Claire Robertson points out that among the functions of the circumcision ceremony in Central Kenya is the role female initiation plays in maintaining the social strength of organizations of older women.[23] The flip side of approving support, of course, is peer pressure. "When girls of my age were looking after the

lambs, they would talk among themselves about their circumcision experiences and look at each other's genitals to see who had the smallest opening. If there was a girl in the group who was still uninfibulated, she would always feel ashamed since she had nothing to show the others."[24]

A reminiscent bodily shame lurks behind the support for labial modifications that my American patient contacts expressed. One (heterosexual) woman explained to me that although none of her boyfriends had ever remarked on her labia, "ever since I was fourteen, I felt like I had this abnormalcy; I felt uncomfortable changing in front of girlfriends." She went on to say that she felt she had to hide her vagina around other women and could never enjoy skinny-dipping because of her concerns about other women judging her appearance. Another labiaplasty patient reported a "120% shift" in her "mental attitude," and a "night-and-day" improvement in the looks of her genitalia, thanks to the surgery. "As sad as it is, it makes you feel inferior," she commented.[25] Her use of the second person (or the ethical dative, as it's known), so intimate in its extension of subjectivity, meant that her language included me. . . . I too felt sad, I too felt inferior. And for a fee, the kind doctor was there to correct me.

NEW RITES

It is probably obvious from this piece that, even in the age where both informational and medical technology have led to bodies being reshaped, extended, reconfigured, and reconceptualized like never before, I believe that erotic tissue is far better enjoyed than removed.[26] In approaching the politics of female genital operations, however, I would argue that it is imperative that both consent issues and vaginal modifications themselves be considered *on a continuum* that is not determined along hemispheric, national, or racial lines. . . .

In "Arrogant Perception, World-Traveling, and Multicultural Feminism: The Case of Female Genital Surgeries," Isabelle R. Gunning attempts to define and model a responsible approach to thinking about genital operations across cultures. She urges activists "to look at one's own culture anew and identify [. . .] practices that might prove 'culturally challenging' or negative to some other," and "to look in careful detail at the organic social environment of the 'other' which has produced the culturally challenging practice being explored."[27] I have tried, in this article, to meet her first criterion, and I hope that rendering American cosmetic surgery strange through a heedful look at this latest, not-yet-naturalized procedure can aid us in contextualizing and understanding genital surgeries born in other contexts as well.

NOTES

Thanks to former students Jenn Sanders and Wacuka Mungai for their help in developing this article.

1. Things certainly can happen. See Louisa Kamps, "Labia Envy," 16 Mar. 1998, <http://www.salon.com/mwt/feature/1998/03/16feature.html> (9 Dec. 2001).

2. *Los Angeles Times,* 5 Mar. 1998. See, too, the following Internet resources on labiaplasty: Dr. Alter: "Female Cosmetic and Reconstructive Genital Surgery," <http://www.altermd.com/female/index.html> (9 Dec. 2001); Julia Scheeres, "Vaginal Cosmetic Surgery," 16 Apr. 2001, <http://thriveonline.oxygen.com/sex/sexpressions/vaginal-cosmetic-surgery.html> (9 Dec. 2001); Dr. Stubbs, <http://psurg.com>; Laser Rejuvenation Center of LA, <http://www.drmatlock.com>; Dan Savage, "Long in the Labia," 16 Dec. 1999, <http://www.the stranger.com/1999-12-16/savage.html> (13 Dec. 2001); iVillage.com Archive Message Board, "Cosmetic Surgery," 7 Jan. 2000, <http://boards.allhealth.com/messages/get/bhcosmeticsx2.html> (13 Dec. 2001); Patients' chatboard, <http://boards.allhealth.com/messages/get/bhcosmeticsx2.html>.

3. See Kamps. Also, see Carrie Havranek, "The New Sex Surgeries," *Cosmopolitan,* November 1998, 146.

4. Ellen Frankfort, *Vaginal Politics* (New York: Quadrangle, 1972). See, too, Julia Scheeres, "Vulva Goldmine: How Cosmetic Surgeons Snatch Your Money," *Bitch* 11 (January 2000): 70–84.

5. Boston Women's Health Collective, *Our Bodies, Ourselves* (New York: Simon & Schuster, 1973).

Updated editions have continued to be released. See Boston Women's Health Collective, *Our Bodies, Ourselves for the New Century: A Book by and for Women* (New York: Simon & Schuster, 1998).

6. See Amelia Jones, ed., *Sexual Politics: Judy Chicago's Dinner Party in Feminist Art History* (Berkeley: University of California Press, 1996); Shannon Bell, "Prostitute Performances: Sacred Carnival Theorists of the Female Body," from her *Reading, Writing, and Rewriting the Prostitute Body* (Bloomington: Indiana University Press, 1994), 137–84; and Eve Ensler, *The Vagina Monologues* (New York: Villard Press, 1998).

7. On the thin line between identification and desire, between wanting to be like someone and wanting to bed down with them (so exploited in consumer culture), see Diana Fuss, "Fashion and the Homospectatorial Look," in *On Fashion,* ed. Shari Benstock and Suzanne Ferriss (New Brunswick, N.J.: Rutgers University Press, 1994), 211–32; and Judith Butler, *Gender Trouble: Feminism and the Subversion of Identity* (New York: Routledge, 1990), esp. 57–72.

8. Josey Vogels, "My Messy Bedroom," *See,* 10 July 1997, <http://www.greatwest.ca/SEE/Issues/1997/970710/josey.html> (13 Dec. 2001).

9. Laura Kipnis, *Bound and Gagged: Pornography and the Politics of Fantasy in America* (New York: Grove, 1996).

10. Susie Bright, "The Pussy Shot: An Interview with Andrew Blake," *Sexwise* (New York: Cleis Press, 1995), 82.

11. See Nedahl Stelio, "Do You Know What a Vagina Looks Like?" *Cosmopolitan,* August 2001, 126–28, on sex magazines' doctoring of vaginas and the increased prevalence of labiaplasty.

12. Natalie Zemon Davis, "Women on Top," in her *Society and Culture in Early Modern France* (Stanford: Stanford University Press, 1975), 124–31.

13. Denise Stoklos, remark made in Solo Performance Composition, her course offered by the Performance Studies Department, New York University, Spring 2000. "Our primary dialogue is with gravity," Stoklos says.

14. See Ambient, Inc., "Body Modification: Is It Self-Mutilation—Even if Someone Else Does It for You?" 2 Feb. 1998, <http://www.ambient.on.ca/bodmod/mutilate.html> (13 Dec. 2001). Another Web site dealing with body modification is <http://www.perforations.com> (13 Dec. 2001).

15. Ensler, 3–5.

16. Nahid Toubia, *Female Genital Mutilation: A Call for Global Action,* 3d ed. (New York: Women, Ink, 1995), 35.

17. Inga Muscio, *Cunt: A Declaration of Independence* (Toronto: Seal Press, 1998), 134–35.

18. Claire Hunt and Kim Longinotto, with Safaa Fathay, *Hidden Faces,* videorecording (New York: Twentieth Century Vixen Production/Women Make Movies, 1990). And see Elizabeth Oram, introduction to Zainaba's "Lecture on Clitoridectomy to the Midwives of Touil, Mauritania" (1987), in *Opening the Gates: A Century of Arab Feminist Writing,* ed. Margot Badran and Miriam Cooke (Bloomington: Indiana University Press, 1990), 63–71.

19. See <http://www.altermd.com/female/index.html> (13 Dec. 2001).

20. See Rachel Bowlby, in *Shopping with Freud: Items on Consumerism, Feminism, and Psychoanalysis* (New York: Routledge, 1993), on theoretical conflations between feminist freedom and the "freedom" to choose as a consumer.

21. Wendy Brown, *States of Injury: Power and Freedom in Late Modernity* (Princeton: Princeton University Press, 1995).

22. Anonymous telephone interviews with two West Coast labiaplasty patients, August 1999. For an on-line example of this, see the fascinating archived chat between women about cosmetic surgery at iVillage, "Cosmetic Surgery Archive Board," 7 Jan. 2001, <http://boards.allhealth.com/ messages/get/ bhcosmeticsx2.html> (13 Dec. 2001).

23. See Claire Robertson, "Grassroots in Kenya: Women, Genital Mutilation, and Collective Action, 1920–1990," *Signs* 21 (Spring 1996): 615–42.

24. Anab's story, from "Social and Cultural Implications of Infibulation in Somalia," by Amina Wasame, in *Female Circumcision: Strategies to Bring about Change* (Somali Women's Democratic Organization), quoted in Toubia, 41.

25. Anonymous telephone interview with author, August 1999.

26. An important caveat: As the transgendered community has made clear, for some individuals, erotic enjoyment is enhanced via the genital modification that comes along with reassigning gender, even if that surgery has resulted in a reduction in nerve endings or sensation.

27. Isabelle R. Gunning, "Arrogant Perception, World Traveling, and Multicultural Feminism: The Case of Female Genital Surgeries," *Columbia Human Rights Law Review* 23 (Summer 1992): 213.

DISCUSSION QUESTIONS FOR CHAPTER 5

1. How are power relations reflected and reinforced in beauty norms?

2. How do beauty norms affect women and men differently? How have beauty norms affected you?

3. Two of your readings talk about women's connections with particular aspects of their bodies—vaginas, hair, and noses. What aspects of your body reflect key elements of your sense of self?

4. What are some of the connections between beauty standards and women's health?

5. How can women resist the beauty ideal?

SUGGESTIONS FOR FURTHER READING

Bordo, Susan, and Leslie Haywood. *Unbearable Weight: Feminism, Western Culture, and the Body, Tenth Anniversary Edition.* Berkeley: University of California Press, 2004.

Gimlin, Debra L. *Body Work: Beauty and Self-Image in American Culture.* Berkeley: University of California Press, 2002.

Grogan, Sarah. *Body Image: Understanding Body Dissatisfaction in Men, Women, and Children.* New York: Routledge, 1999.

Hesse-Biber, Sharon. *Am I Thin Enough Yet?: The Cult of Thinness and the Commercialization of Identity.* New York: Oxford University Press, 1997.

Holmlund, Chris. *Impossible Bodies: Femininity and Masculinity at the Movies.* New York: Routledge, 2002.

Karp, Michelle. *The Bust Guide to the New Girl Order.* New York: Penguin, 1999.

Solovay, Sondra. *Tipping the Scales of Justice: Fighting Weight-Based Discrimination.* Amherst, NY: Prometheus, 2000.

Weitz, Rose. *Rapunzel's Daughters: What Women's Hair Tells Us About Women's Lives.* New York: Farrar, Straus and Giroux, 2004.

Health and Reproductive Rights

HEALTH AND WELLNESS

Health is a central issue in women's lives. Ask parents what they wish for their newborns and they speak first about hoping the baby is healthy; quiz people about their hopes for the new year and they speak about staying healthy; listen to politicians debate their positions before an election and health care is almost always a key issue. In contemporary U.S. society, good health is generally understood as a requirement for happy and productive living. Because women are prominent as both providers and consumers of health care, health issues and the health care system affect us on many levels. To make sense of the complexities of women's relationships to health care systems, we will discuss five concepts: equity, androcentrism, medicalization, stereotyping, and corporate responsibility.

First, medical institutions in the United States provide different levels of service based on health insurance status and general ability to pay. This is the issue of *equity:* some people have better health care than others because of a two-tier system for those who can pay/have health insurance and those who cannot, and because the United States, unlike most Western industrial societies, does not have a system of nationalized or state-supported health care. This affects all aspects of health care, including access to fertility, contraceptive, and abortion facilities. Low-income women (who are disproportionately women of color), for example, are not as healthy as women at higher socioeconomic levels. More than a quarter of women living at or near poverty are in fair or poor health, twice the level for women with middle-level incomes and three times the level for women with high incomes. This pattern is similar for mental health issues. Access to health insurance is a major concern for poor women; low-income women are five times as likely to be uninsured as high-income women and ten times as likely to rely on public assistance. Having a job, however, does not necessarily help access health resources: while in 2000, two out of three low-income single mothers worked outside the home, only 14 percent of such women received work-based health care insurance. The reading by Jael Silliman and colleagues, "Women of Color and Their Struggle for Reproductive Justice," touches on these issues in the context of reproductive health.

Professional health-related organizations (such as the American Medical Association [AMA]), Health Maintenance Organizations (HMOs), insurance companies, and pharmaceutical companies, and corporations representing other medical products and practices, have enormous influence over health politics. In addition, health is not just about medical services. Health conditions, including incidence and mortality rates, are related to such socioeconomic factors as poverty, interpersonal violence, poor housing, and lack of education. Many of the social issues that affect women on a daily basis and which contribute to increased tobacco use among women, chemical addictions, stress, and poor nutrition, have their consequence in increased rates of heart disease, cancer, chronic obstructive pulmonary disease, and diabetes, to name just a few. Health problems are confounded with an aging population such that by the year 2030, women (who are likely to have fewer economic resources than men) will represent approximately 81 percent of people who are over 85 years old. As suggested in the reading "American Women and Health Disparities" by former U.S. Surgeon General David Satcher, MD, while strides have been made in dealing with many women's health issues, more activism is still needed to ensure equity in health care, especially for women of color. Vivian M. Dickerson, MD, president of the American College of Obstetricians and Gynecologists, describes these forms of activism necessary to ensure equity and justice in the reading "The Tolling of the Bell: Women's Health, Women's Rights."

Globally, women's health access is one of the most important issues determining justice and equity for women. The short reading by Kari Browne on "The Fight Against Fistulas" discusses medical access for women in Ethiopia suffering from the stigmatizing, although preventable and easily treatable, condition of fistulas. The HIV/AIDS epidemic is an important illustration of issues of gender and racial/ethnic equity both nationally and globally. As the boxed insert in this chapter shows, in 2003 the rate of AIDS diagnoses for African American women was approximately 25 times the rate for white women and 4 times the rate for Hispanic women; the rate for newly diagnosed women generally increased 15 percent compared to a 1 percent increase among men. Although men make up a larger proportion of AIDS patients than women, the relative increase is greater for women. This is especially true globally. Risk factors for women, both in the United States and globally, include lack of power in relationships (male decision to wear a condom, visit a prostitute, have multiple sexual partners, etc.), lack of education about body and sexuality, and the biological vulnerability of women during sexual intercourse.

President George W. Bush has announced increased funding for HIV/AIDS prevention, treatment, and care in Africa and the Caribbean. However, the administration also made public its intention to expand the application of the "global gag rule" on the U.S. Agency for International Development (USAID) population-control program. This policy restricts foreign nongovernmental organizations (NGOs) that receive USAID family-planning funds from using their own, non-U.S. funds to provide legal abortion services, lobby their own governments for abortion law reform, or even provide accurate medical counseling or referrals regarding abortion. This policy undermines funding for other, related health issues (as well as health and infant screening, nutritional programs, and health education) and encourages narrow, often religious, and abstinence-based approaches to HIV/AIDS prevention that exclude condom use. It is important to consider the ways anti-choice policies in the United States threaten the quality of women's lives around the world.

The second theme of this chapter is *androcentrism*. Men's bodies are the norm, and much medical research has focused on men (mostly White men) and has been overgeneralized to others. Baseline data for heart monitors, for example, were based on middle-aged, White men, causing serious complications for patients who did not fit this norm.

HIV/AIDS Among Women

Early in the epidemic, HIV infection and AIDS were diagnosed for relatively few women. Today, the HIV/AIDS epidemic represents a growing and persistent health threat to women in the United States, especially young women and women of color. In 2001, HIV infection was the leading cause of death for African American women aged 25–34 years and was among the four leading causes of death for African American women aged 20–24 and 35–44 years, as well as Hispanic women aged 35–44 years.[1] Overall, in the same year, HIV infection was the 6th leading cause of death among all women aged 25–34 years and the 4th leading cause of death among all women aged 35–44 years.

CUMULATIVE EFFECTS OF HIV INFECTION AND AIDS (THROUGH 2003)

- Through 2003, 170,679 women were given a diagnosis of AIDS, a number that represents about one-fifth of the total 929,985 AIDS diagnoses.[2]
- An estimated 81,864 women with AIDS died. These women account for 16 percent of the 524,060 deaths of persons with AIDS.[2]
- Women with AIDS made up an increasing part of the epidemic. In 1992, women accounted for an estimated 14 percent of adults and adolescents living with AIDS.[3] By the end of 2003, this percentage had grown to 22 percent.[2]
- From 1999 through 2003, the annual number of estimated AIDS diagnoses increased 15 percent among women and increased 1 percent among men.[2]
- According to a recent CDC study of more than 19,500 patients in 10 U.S. cities, HIV-infected women were 12 percent less likely than infected men to receive prescriptions for the most effective treatments for HIV infection.[3]

AIDS IN 2003

- An estimated 11,498 women had a diagnosis of AIDS, a number that represents 27 percent of the 43,171 AIDS diagnoses.[2]
- The rate of AIDS diagnoses for African American women (50.2/100,000 women) was approximately 25 times the rate for white women (2.0/100,000) and 4 times the rate for Hispanic women (12.4/100,000).[2]
- African American and Hispanic women together represented about 25 percent of all U.S. women,[4] yet they account for 83 percent of AIDS diagnoses reported in 2003.[2]

(continued)

- An estimated 88,815 women were living with AIDS, representing 22 percent of the estimated 405,926 people living with AIDS.[2]
- An estimated 4,736 women with AIDS died, representing 26 percent of the 18,017 deaths of persons with AIDS.[2]
- Heterosexual contact was the source of almost 80 percent of these HIV infections.[2]
- Women accounted for 27 percent of the estimated 32,048 diagnoses of HIV infection.[2]
- The number of estimated HIV diagnoses for women remained stable during 2000–2003.[2]

For more information on HIV and AIDS, contact

CDC National STD & AIDS Hotlines   1-800-342-AIDS; Spanish: 1-800-344-SIDA; Deaf: 1-800-243-7889

CDC National Prevention Information Network   P.O. Box 6003, Rockville, MD 20849-6003; 1-800-458-5231

Web Resources

NCHSTP: www.cdc.gov/nchstp/od/nchstp.html

DHAP: www.cdc.gov/hiv

NPIN: www.cdcnpin.org

REFERENCES

1. Anderson RN, Smith BL. Deaths: leading causes for 2001. *National Vital Statistics Reports* 2003;52(9):32–33,53–54. Available at http://www.cdc.gov/nchs/data/nvsr/nvsr52/nvsr09.pdf. Accessed November 9, 2004.
2. CDC. *HIV/AIDS Surveillance Report 2003;* (Vol. 15). Atlanta: U.S. Department of Health and Human Services, CDC. In press.
3. McNaghten AD, Hanson DL, Aponte Z, Sullivan P, Wolfe MI. Gender disparity in HIV treatment and AIDS opportunistic illnesses (OI). XV International Conference on AIDS; July 2004; Bangkok, Thailand. Abstract MoOrC1032.
4. U.S. Census Bureau. Census Brief: Women in the United States: a profile. March 2000. Available at http://www.census.gov/prod/2000pubs/cenbr001.pdf. Accessed August 27, 2004.

Source: Centers for Disease Control and Prevention, 2004.

LEARNING ACTIVITY   **Obsessed with Breasts**

Go to the Web page of the Breast Cancer Fund's "Obsessed with Breasts" ad campaign at *www.breastcancerfund.org/campaign.htm*. What are the goals of the campaign? Why is the campaign necessary? Now go to the Fund's "Facts, News, and Opinions" page. Identify five facts about breast cancer that are new to you.

For Better or For Worse®   **by Lynn Johnston**

© Lynn Johnston Productions, Inc./Distributed by United Features Syndicate, Inc.

Women's Top Health Threats: A Surprising List

Do you know what threatens your life the most?

Below are the top causes of death for women in the United States, starting with the most common. Take this opportunity to learn about each health concern and how you can reduce your risks. What you learn may surprise you.

NO. 1 — HEART DISEASE

Surprised? Many women are. It's common to think breast cancer is the No. 1 threat to women's health when, in fact, heart disease is responsible for more deaths in women than all forms of cancer combined. Heart disease is the most significant health concern for women in the United States today, responsible for almost 366,000 deaths each year.

The common belief that heart disease affects mostly men is a dangerous myth. In reality, more women than men die of heart disease in the United States each year. But according to the American Heart Association, only 8 percent of women know that heart disease is a major threat to their health.

The good news is that heart disease is one of the most preventable health conditions. You have the power to reduce some of your risks:

- Avoid smoking and limit alcohol.
- Eat a diet rich in fruits, vegetables, and grain products.
- Exercise regularly.
- Control other health conditions that may put a strain on your heart, such as high blood pressure, diabetes, and high cholesterol.

(continued)

NO. 2 — CANCER

It's easy to believe cancer is a major threat to women's health, but the kinds of cancer women are dying of might surprise you. According to the American Cancer Society (ACS), the most common cause of cancer death in U.S. women is lung cancer. It's estimated that nearly 66,000 women in the United States died of lung cancer in 2002, with 90 percent of these deaths linked to cigarette smoking.

Breast cancer is the second-leading cause of cancer death in U.S. women, and it's estimated that more than 203,000 women were diagnosed with breast cancer in 2002. The ACS estimates that about 40,000 women die each year of breast cancer.

The third-leading cause of cancer death for women in the United States is colorectal cancer. Like heart disease, colorectal cancer is often mistakenly thought of as a man's disease, but more women than men die of colorectal cancer each year. Estimates suggest that it claims the lives of approximately 28,000 women in the United States annually.

At least one-third of all cancer deaths are related to nutrition and other controllable lifestyle factors. Do all you can to reduce your risks:

- Don't smoke or chew tobacco.
- Exercise regularly.
- Eat a healthy diet.
- Avoid excessive sun exposure.
- Limit alcohol.
- Have regular preventive health screenings.
- Know your family medical history and review it with your doctor.

NO. 3 — STROKE

About 167,000 people in the United States die of stroke each year, and almost two-thirds of them are women. Stroke not only is women's No. 3 killer but also is one of the leading causes of disability in America.

Smoking and uncontrolled high blood pressure are important risk factors for stroke. Although stroke is highly preventable, certain risk factors such as family history, age, sex, and race cannot be controlled. Even if you're at increased risk of stroke, you can still take steps to prevent it:

- Don't smoke.
- Control your blood pressure.
- Lower your cholesterol.
- Limit saturated fats.
- Exercise regularly.

NO. 4 — CHRONIC OBSTRUCTIVE PULMONARY DISEASE (COPD)

COPD is an overall term for a group of chronic lung conditions, including bronchitis and emphysema. The main cause of COPD is smoking, and it's strongly associated with lung cancer, the No. 1 cause of cancer death in women.

About 62,000 women in the United States die of COPD each year. The quality of life for a person with COPD diminishes as the disease progresses. Shortness of breath and activity limitations develop, and you may eventually require an oxygen tank or even mechanical respiratory assistance to breathe.

How do you reduce your risks of dying of COPD? This one's easy: Don't smoke, and avoid secondhand smoke.

NO. 5 — DIABETES

Diabetes, a group of diseases that affect the way your body uses blood sugar (glucose), is a serious health condition that affects more than 17 million Americans. In 2000 it claimed the lives of almost 69,000 people in the United States, and more than half of them were women.

It's estimated that 5 million Americans don't know they have diabetes. Many people become aware of it only when they develop one of its life-threatening complications. Advanced diabetes can cause blindness, kidney disease, and severe nerve damage. People with diabetes are also two to four times more likely to have heart disease and suffer from stroke.

The most common type of diabetes is type 2 diabetes (formerly called adult-onset or noninsulin-dependent diabetes). This type of diabetes, generally developing after age 40, can be prevented. Follow these steps to reduce your risk:

• Maintain a healthy weight.
• Eat a healthy diet.
• Exercise regularly.
• Get your fasting blood sugar level checked periodically.

NO. 6 — PNEUMONIA AND INFLUENZA

Pneumonia and influenza combined are the sixth-leading cause of death for women in the United States today. Together they took the lives of more than 36,000 women in 2000.

When associated with other chronic health conditions, pneumonia and influenza can be life-threatening. People with COPD, asthma, heart disease, diabetes, and conditions that suppress the immune system are at high risk. Because both pneumonia and influenza affect the lungs, smoking increases the danger of these two diseases.

The risk of both pneumonia and influenza can be reduced by immunizations. A yearly flu shot can be up to 90 percent effective in preventing influenza in healthy adults. The pneumococcal vaccine can reduce the risk of getting pneumonia by 60 percent to 70 percent. Stay healthy—get those shots.

(continued)

NO. 7 — ALZHEIMER'S DISEASE

Alzheimer's disease—which affects almost 4 million Americans—is a progressive, degenerative brain disease that goes beyond simple forgetfulness. What may start as slight memory loss and confusion may eventually lead to irreversible mental impairment.

More women than men have Alzheimer's. In fact, about 35,000 women die of Alzheimer's disease each year—more than twice the number of men. One reason women may be more affected is that women generally live longer, and the risk of Alzheimer's increases with age.

Current treatments focus on stabilizing the symptoms, improving well-being, and easing caregiver burden.

NO. 8 — ACCIDENTS

Each year, about 34,000 women die from accidents (unintentional injuries). Although the statistics on accidental death are unclear, these top health threats for women may surprise you:

- *Motor vehicle accidents.* Traffic-related accidents were responsible for 40 percent of all accidental deaths for women in 2000. You can reduce your chances of a fatal crash by routinely using your seat belt, keeping your speed down, and not driving while sleepy or under the influence of drugs or alcohol.
- *Falls.* One out of every three people over age 75 falls each year, and about 6,200 women in the United States die from such falls. Most falls—75 percent—occur in the home, so making some commonsense changes can help prevent falls and their potentially debilitating consequences. Getting regular eye exams, exercising regularly, and improving your balance also can help reduce your risk.

Leading a healthy lifestyle, getting regular checkups, and paying attention to your environment can help you reduce your risk factors for many of these conditions.

Source: © 1998–2005 Mayo Foundation for Medical Education and Research. www.mayoclinic.com/ invoke. cfm?id=W000014.

Fortunately, due to new guidelines with the Food and Drug Administration (FDA), now half of all subjects in large-scale drug studies are female. However, less than a quarter of subjects in small-scale safety trials are female and a third of new drug applications do not include separate safety and efficiency data for men and women as required by the FDA. In addition, more money has been spent on diseases that are more likely to afflict men. Related to this is the notion of "anatomy is destiny" whereby female physiology, and especially reproductive anatomy, is seen as central in understanding behavior. Social norms about femininity have come to guide medical and scientific ideas about women's health, and female genital organs have long been seen as sources of special emotional and physical health problems.

LEARNING ACTIVITY **Bad Science**

Should health policy decisions be based on science or philosophical positions? In 2004 a group of more than 60 scientists, including Nobel laureates, criticized the Bush administration for ignoring or suppressing scientific analysis and recommendations in its decision making. They cited as one example the suppression of an FDA study that reported that the Senate's Clear Air bill would be more effective in reducing mercury contamination in fish and preventing more deaths than the Clear Skies Act proposed by the administration. Despite all scientific evidence to the contrary, the administration has continued to increase funding for abstinence-only programs, although they have been demonstrated to be ineffective in preventing sexual activity and disease transmission.

How might political decisions that ignore science affect women's health? Visit the following Web sites and create a list of decisions and policies that have been made in contradiction to the scientific evidence about women's health. Find out what decisions related to women's health are pending in Congress or various government agencies, and write letters to your representatives encouraging them to base decisions on scientific evidence rather than political positions.

Reproductive Health Technologies Project *http://rhtp.org/index.htm*

Coalition to Protect Research *www.cossa.org/CPR/cpr.html*

American Association for the Advancement of Science *www.aaas.org/port_policy.shtml*

American Foundation for AIDS Research *www.amfar.org/cgi-bin/iowa/ programs/publicp/index.html*

Association of Reproductive Health Professionals *www.arhp.org/advocacy/index.cfm*

Society for Women's Health Research *www.womens-health.org/policy/home.htm*

Union of Concerned Scientists *www.ucsusa.org/global_environment/rsi/ index.cfm* .

LEARNING ACTIVITY **Women, Heart Disease, and Cancer in Your State**

- To learn more about the prevalence of heart disease among women in your state, visit the Centers for Disease Control's Web site at *www.cdc.gov/ nccdphp/cvd/womensatlas/factsheets/index.htm* and click on your state's name.
- To learn about the prevalence of cancer in your state, go to *www.cdc.gov/ cancer/dbdata.htm* and select your state.

Alcohol Abuse

Alcohol/substance abuse and alcohol/substance dependence are complicated illnesses that present unique threats to women's health. Medical research is showing that women who abuse alcohol and other drugs may develop addictions and substance-related health problems faster than men.

Recent surveys show that alcohol consumption is most common among

- Women between the ages of 26 and 34
- Women who are divorced or separated

Binge drinking (consumption of four or more drinks at one sitting) is most common among women between the ages of 18 to 25. And drinking is more prevalent among Caucasian women than other ethnic/racial groups, although African American women are more likely to drink heavily. It is binge drinking, as opposed to drinking in general, that causes most of the alcohol-associated harm occurring on our campuses and in students' lives.

Results of a major, eight-year study involving the drinking habits of thousands of college students were reported in the March 2002 edition of the *Journal of American College Health.* The 2001 Harvard School of Public Health College Alcohol Study surveyed students at 119 four-year colleges that participated in the 1993, 1997, and 1999 studies. Responses in the four survey years were compared to determine trends in heavy alcohol use, alcohol-related problems, and encounters with college and community prevention programs.

The findings revealed that, despite efforts to curb binge drinking on our campuses through the implementation of alcohol-prevention programs, services, activities, and policies, we have not yet solved the problem. Here are the key findings:

- In 2001 approximately two in five (44.4 percent) college students reported binge drinking, a rate almost identical to rates in the previous three surveys.
- Very little change in overall binge drinking occurred at the individual college level.
- A sharp rise (from 5.3 percent in 1993 to 11.9 percent in 2001) in frequent binge drinking was noted among women attending all-women's colleges, and a lesser, but still significant, increase of the same behavior for women in coeducational schools.
- The percentages of abstainers and frequent binge drinkers increased, indicating a polarization of drinking behavior first noted in 1997.
- Other significant changes included increases in immoderate drinking and harm among drinkers.
- More students lived in substance-free housing and encountered college educational efforts and sanctions resulting from their alcohol use.
- The prevalence of drinking among underage students is lower (77.4 percent) than that among 21- to 23-year-old students (85.6 percent). In addition, underage students drink less frequently than do their "legal age" peers, and the percentage of underage students who binge drink (43.6 percent) is lower than that of students who are over the age of 21 who do (50.2 percent).
- Half of the underage students who were studied reported obtaining alcohol easily; other students are their primary source. But since 1993, the use of fake identification cards to obtain alcohol illegally has declined, whereas the role of parents as providers of alcohol to underage students has increased.
- Having more laws restricting underage drinking or governing the volume of sales and consumption of alcohol in effect is associated with less drinking among underage students.

All of these statistics aside, the latest word from the National Institute on Alcohol Abuse and Alcoholism is that all women are more vulnerable to alcohol-related organ damage, trauma, and interpersonal difficulties:

- Liver damage: Women develop alcohol-induced liver disease in a shorter time period than men even if they consume less alcohol. And, women are more likely to develop alcohol hepatitis and die from cirrhosis (liver disease).
- Brain damage: Studies of brains, as seen via magnetic resonance imaging (MRIs), show that women may be more vulnerable to brain damage due to alcohol consumption than men.
- Heart disease: Among heavy drinkers, women develop heart disease at the same rate as men, despite the fact that women consume 60 percent less alcohol than men over their lifetimes.
- Breast cancer: Some studies have shown a link between moderate or heavy alcohol consumption and an increased risk for breast cancer.
- Violence: College women who drink are more likely to be the victims of sexual abuse. And high school girls who use alcohol are more likely to be the victims of dating violence.
- Traffic crashes: Although women are less likely than men to drive after drinking, they have a higher risk of dying in a vehicle crash.
- Women are more likely than men to use a combination of alcohol and prescription drugs.
- Women may begin to abuse alcohol and drugs following depression, to relax on dates, to feel more adequate, to lose weight, to decrease stress, or to help them sleep at night.

Poor self-esteem is a major issue for most women who develop problems with drugs and alcohol. The following conditions may also increase their risk for developing substance abuse problems:

- A history of physical or sexual abuse. Physical and sexual violence against women is common when one or both partners have been drinking or using drugs. Women also are more likely to drink or use drugs when their partners use.
- Depression, panic disorder, and post-traumatic stress disorder. Researchers now know that there is a strong family (genetic) component to addiction. If you have a family history of addiction, you should be aware of the risk for developing dependency, especially during stressful periods in your life.

So, why are women more vulnerable to the effects of alcohol?
- Alcohol is absorbed faster in women's bodies than in men's bodies because of stomach enzyme differences. After a woman drinks, alcohol is delivered into her bloodstream more rapidly because a stomach enzyme that works to break down alcohol before it enters the bloodstream is less active in women, especially in alcoholic women, than in men. Women have a smaller ratio of water to fat than men. Alcohol circulates in the water and therefore alcohol is more concentrated. Your blood alcohol level will be higher and you will get drunker faster by drinking the same amount of alcohol as a man your own size.
- Hormonal fluctuations in women may affect how alcohol is metabolized. Some women report feeling the effects of alcohol more quickly or strongly when they drink at certain times during their cycle. Post-menopausal women who take hormone replacement therapy (HRT) have higher blood alcohol levels when they drink.

Source: www.healthywomen.org.

In terms of women as health care providers, androcentrism has supported sexism and encouraged systems where men have more positions of power and influence in the health care system. Although nursing is still overwhelmingly a feminine occupation, increasingly more women are becoming physicians, even though most prestigious specialties are still dominated by men. It remains to be seen whether this increase in female physicians will change the face of medicine as we know it.

Third, *medicalization* is the process whereby normal functions of the body come to be seen as indicative of disease. This tends to be the model by which modern medicine works. This affects women in two ways. One, because women have more episodic changes in their bodies as a result of childbearing (for example, menstruation, pregnancy, childbirth, lactation, and menopause), they are more at risk for medical personnel interpreting these natural processes as problematic. Note how this tends to reinforce the argument that biology is destiny. Two, medicalization supports business and medical technologies. It tends to work against preventive medicine and encourages sophisticated medical technologies to "fix" problems after they occur. Medical services are dominated by drug treatments and surgery, and controlled by pharmaceutical companies, health maintenance organizations, and such professional organizations as the American Medical Association.

Fourth, *stereotyping* encompasses how notions about gender, race/ethnicity, and other identities inform everyday understanding of health care occupations and influence how medical practitioners treat their patients. For example, patients often assume white-coated white male orderlies to be doctors and call women doctors "nurse." Furthermore, as the reading by Patti Lou Watkins and Diane Whaley, "Gender Role Stressors and Women's Health," suggests, women interact differently with the health care system and are treated differently, often to the detriment of women's health. For example, research suggests that physicians generally are more likely to consider emotional factors when diagnosing women's problems, and they are more likely to assume that the cause of illness is psychosomatic when the patient involved is female. It is well known that physicians also prescribe more mood-altering medication for women than they do for men. In addition, physicians attribute stereotypical notions of ethnicity, as well as gender, to patients, expecting Latinas/os, for example, to be more nervous and excitable. Homophobia prevents lesbians from receiving fully informed care as also does accusations of deviance associated with trans individuals that affect their options for health care and their access to these options.

Finally, a focus on women's health must discuss the issue of corporate responsibility and the role of the state in guiding and establishing that responsibility. This relates to the ways the development of national and global corporations with strong profit motives affect our lives in terms of environmental degradation and toxic exposure, food additives, and problematic medical practices, and the ways the decisions at the state and federal level affect these practices. For example, increasing concern associated with greenhouse gases and global warming, use of pesticides and herbicides, genetically modified food, and growth hormones in beef and dairy food products: all these issues are related to the corporatization of life and the global economy, modernization, westernization, and urbanization, and ultimately the quality of life on the planet. While these issues affect everyone, there is differential impact based on where a person lives, the kind of work s/he performs, the food s/he can afford to eat, and so forth. *Environmental racism* reflects the fact that people of color in the United States are disproportionately exposed to toxic environments due to the dumping of chemical and other waste on Native American lands and urban areas where more people of color live. Environmental waste tends not to be dumped in areas populated by people of high socioeconomic status or where property rates are high. The dumping of radioactive waste at Yucca Mountain, Nevada, that ignores the impact on the Western Shoshone tribe who consider the mountain sacred is a case in point. *Environmental justice* is the social movement to remedy this problem. People in developing countries who work in factories and sweatshops within the global economy (especially young women, who are often hired because they are cheap, dispensable, and easily controlled workers) are particularly at risk for occupational disease.

Breast cancer is one important health issue closely tied to environmental problems and therefore corporate responsibility. One in eight women will develop breast cancer in their lifetimes, and approximately 40,000 women and 400 men die annually from the disease. White women are more susceptible than African Americans, although the latter are 2.2 times more likely to die since they tend to have more advanced tumors on detection as a result of poorer screening and reduced access to health care resources. Although breast cancer research works to find a cure, a focus on environmental contributors could work more effectively to prevent breast cancer. This is especially true since less than 10 percent of breast cancer cases are genetically caused and the number of women with breast cancer has doubled in the last 35 years. In particular, the rapidly evolving field of research in synthetic chemicals (found in pesticides, some fuels, plastics, detergents, fire-retardant sprays, and some pharmaceutical drugs) has named "endocrine disrupters" or "xenoestrogens" (hormone mimickers) as key to understanding the environmental link to breast cancer. Exposure to xenoestrogens can cause cells to rapidly grow out of control and form tumors; research at Tufts University Medical School has demonstrated that xenoestrogens make human breast cancer cells grow in the laboratory. A recent *Ms.* magazine article suggested that even if exposure to chemicals in the environment was shown to be associated with only 10–20 percent of breast cancer cases, policy on the part of the U.S. government controlling individual and corporate use of hazardous chemicals could prevent between 9,000 and 36,000 women from contracting the disease each year. The reading "Eyes on the Prize" by Seldon McCurrie shares the story of a breast cancer survivor.

REPRODUCTIVE CHOICE

Reproductive choice involves being able to have safe and affordable birthing and parenting options; reliable, safe, and affordable birth control technologies; freedom from forced sterilization; and the availability of abortion. In other words, a key aspect of reproductive rights is the extent to which women can control their reproduction and therefore shape the quality and character of their lives. This choice is increasingly under attack in contemporary society. For women of color in particular, as the reading "Women of Color and Their Struggle for Reproductive Justice" emphasizes, "Resisting population control while simultaneously claiming their right to bodily self-determination, including the right to contraception and abortion or the right to have children, is at the heart of their struggle for reproductive control" (p. 355).

Sterilization Practices

Female sterilization includes tubal ligation, a surgical procedure where the fallopian tubes are blocked, and hysterectomy, where the uterus is removed. A non-invasive alternative to tubal ligation is a springlike device called *Essure* that

HISTORICAL MOMENT   **The Women's Health Movement**

From the beginnings of the medical industry, women often suffered from the humiliation and degradation of medical practitioners who treated women as hysterical and as hypochondriacs, who medicalized normal female body functions, and who prevented women from controlling their own health. In 1969, as the women's movement heightened consciousness about other issues, women also began to examine the ways they had been treated and the ways women's biology and health had been largely unexplored. In the spring of that year, several women participated in a workshop on "women and their bodies" at a Boston conference. As they vented their anger at the medical establishment, they also began to make plans to take action. Although most of them had no medical training, they spent the summer studying all facets of women's health and the health care system. Then they began giving courses on women's bodies wherever they could find an audience. These women became known as the Boston Women's Health Collective and published their notes and lectures in what would eventually be known as *Our Bodies, Our Selves.*

Their efforts resulted in a national women's health movement. In March 1971, 800 women gathered for the first women's health conference in New York. Women patients began to question doctors' authority and to bring patient advocates to their medical appointments to take notes on their treatment by medical professionals. Feminists questioned established medical practices such as the gendered diagnosis and treatment of depression, the recommendation for radical mastectomies whenever breast cancer was found, and the high incidence of cesarean deliveries and hysterectomies.

While the original members of the women's health movement tended to be well-educated, middle-class, white women, the movement quickly expanded to work with poor women and women of color to address the inequities caused by the intersections of gender with race and social class. Together, these women worked on reproductive rights, recognizing that for many poor women and women of color, the right to abortion was not as paramount as the right to be free from forced sterilization. Their work shaped the agenda of the National Women's Health Network, founded in 1975 and dedicated to advancing the health of women of all races and social classes.

Source: Ruth Rosen, *The World Split Open: How the Modern Women's Movement Changed America* (New York: Viking, 2000).

blocks the fallopian tubes. Although hysterectomies are usually performed for medical reasons not associated with a desire for sterilization, this procedure results in sterilization. Countless women freely choose sterilization as a form of permanent birth control, and it is a useful method of family planning for many. "Freely choose," however, assumes a range of options not available to some women. In other words, "freely choose" is difficult in a racist, class-based, and sexist society that does not provide all women with the same options from which to choose. As a result, women on welfare are more likely to be sterilized than women who are not on welfare, and women of color and Third World women are disproportionately more likely to receive this procedure. Although Medicaid pays for sterilization, it does not pay for some other birth control options. Lingering here is the racist and classist idea that certain groups have more right to reproduce than others, a belief and social practice called *eugenics*. Policies providing support for sterilization that make it free or very accessible obviously do not force women to be sterilized. Rather, policies like these make the option attractive at a time when other options are limited.

One of the unfortunate legacies of reproductive history is that some women have been sterilized against their will, usually articulated as "against their full, informed consent." In the 1970s it was learned that many poor women—especially women of color, and Native American women in particular, as well as women who were mentally retarded or incarcerated—had undergone forced sterilization. Situations varied, but often they included women not giving consent at all, not knowing what was happening, believing they were having a different procedure, being strongly pressured to consent, or being unable to read or understand the options told to them. The latter was especially true for women who did not speak or read English. Forced sterilization is now against the law, although problems still remain. Vasectomy is permanent birth control for men, or male sterilization. It is effective and safe and does not limit male sexual pleasure.

"All I really want is control over my own body!"

Parenting Options

In considering reproductive choice, it is important to think about the motivations for having children as well as the motivations for limiting fertility. Most people, women and men, assume they will have children at some point in their lives, and, for some, reproduction and parenting are less of a choice than something that people just do. Although in many nonindustrial and developing societies children can be economic assets, in contemporary U.S. society, for the most part, children consume much more than they produce. Some women do see children as insurance in their old age, but generally today we have children for emotional reasons such as personal and marital fulfillment, and for social reasons like carrying on the family name and fulfilling religious mandates.

Childbirth is an experience that has been shared by millions of women the world over. Women have historically helped other women at this time, strengthening family and kinship bonds and the ties of friendship. As the medical profession gained power and status and developed various technologies (forceps, for example), women's traditional authority associated with birthing became eclipsed by an increasing medicalization of birthing. Again, the medicalization of childbirth regards birthing as an irregular episode that requires medical procedures, often including invasive forms of "treatment." Women who could afford it started going to hospitals to birth their children instead of being attended at home by relatives, friends, or midwives. Unfortunately,

Exorcizing the Witch, Midwife, and Healer

By Amy Leer

Women have always been healers. They were the unlicensed doctors and anatomists of ancient history. They were abortionists, nurses, and counselors. They were pharmacists, cultivating healing herbs and revealing their clandestine uses. They were midwives, traveling from home to home and village to village. For centuries women were doctors without degrees, barred from books and lectures, learning from each other, and passing on experience from neighbor to neighbor and mother to daughter. They were called wise women by the people, witches or charlatans by the church and authorities. Medicine is part of our heritage as women, our history, our birthright.

Women's position in the health system today is not "natural." Femininity has become a diseased condition which is medically explained and "fixed." The question remains: How did women arrive at their current position of subservience from their former positions of leadership and power in health and healing? The historical antagonist of the female lay healer is the patriarchal medical profession. The rise of androcentric medicine and female medicalization was not the inevitable triumph of right over wrong, fact over myth; it began with a bitter conflict that set Pagan against Christian, woman against man, class against class. The notion of medicine as a profession was in some ways progressive over the unexamined tradition of female healing: a profession requires systematic training and, at least in theory, some formal methods of accountability. But a profession is also defined by its exclusiveness. While the female lay healer operated within a network of information sharing and mutual sustainability, the male professional hoarded up his knowledge as a kind of property, to be dispensed to affluent patrons or sold on the market as a commodity. His goal was not to distribute the proficiency of healing, but to concentrate medicine within the elite interest group that the profession came to represent.

The triumph of the male medical profession is of crucial significance in our story. It involved the destruction of women's sovereignty and authority—leaving women in positions of isolation and dependency. Today, we are living in the aftermath of the social and economic oppression of masculinist medicine. In consciousness-raising groups and women's studies classrooms, women are questioning scientific "facts" about health, refusing to remain on the margins of society, refusing the patriarchal social order, and insisting that the values of women become equal organizing principles of health and medicine once again.

in these early days, hospitals were relatively dangerous places where sanitation was questionable and women in childbirth were attended by doctors who knew far less about birthing than did midwives. As the century progressed and birthing in hospitals became routine, women gave birth lying down in the pelvic exam position with their feet in stirrups, sometimes with their arms strapped down; they were given drugs and episiotomies (an incision from the vagina toward the anus to prevent tearing) and were routinely shaved in the pubic area. More recently, thanks to a strong consumer movement, women give birth under more humane conditions. Birthing centers now predominate in most hospitals, and doctors no longer perform the routine procedures and administer the drugs that they used to. Nonetheless, a large number of pregnant women do not receive any health care at all, and a larger number still receive inadequate health care. Women of color are especially underserved.

Why might women want to control their fertility? The first and obvious answer concerns health. Over a woman's reproductive life, she could potentially birth many children and be in a constant state of pregnancy and lactation. Such a regimen compromises maximum health. Second, birthing unlimited numbers of children might be seen as irresponsible in the context of a society and an earth with finite resources. Third, birthing is expensive and the raising of children even more expensive. Fourth, given that in contemporary Western societies women have primary responsibility for childcare and that the organization of mothering tends to isolate women in their homes, it is important to consider the emotional effects of constant child rearing. And, finally, if women had unlimited children, the constant caretaking of these children would preempt women's ability to be involved in other productive work outside the home. This "indirect cost" concept involves the loss or limitation of financial autonomy, work-related or professional identity, and creative and ego development.

Although today women are as likely to have children as they ever were, three facts stand out. First, the average family size decreased as the twentieth century progressed. Second, women are having children later in life than they did in earlier times in our society. Both of these trends are related to changes in health care technologies that have raised health care standards and encouraged parenting at later ages, the availability of birth control and abortion, and the increase in women's education and participation in paid labor with subsequent postponement of marriage and child rearing. Third, there has been a large increase in the number of children born to single women, especially among non-White populations. About 16 percent of family households are headed by single women compared to 4 percent headed by single men. This increase in households headed by single women can be attributed to lack of knowledge about reproduction and contraception in the context of an increasingly sexually active population, poverty and lack of opportunities for work and employment, failure of family and school systems to keep young people in school, and increased use of alcohol and other drugs. Some girls see motherhood as a rite of passage into adulthood, as a way to escape their families of origin, or as a way to connect with another human being who will love them unconditionally. The rise in the number of babies born to single women also reflects changing norms, at least among middle-class populations, that it is okay to raise a child alone rather than "having to get married."

Birth control technologies have been around for a long time. Many preindustrial societies used suppositories coated in various substances that blocked the cervix or functioned as spermicides; the condom was used originally to prevent the spread of syphilis, although it was discovered that it functioned as a contraceptive; and the concept of the intrauterine device was first used by Bedouins who hoped to prevent camels from conceiving during long treks across the desert by inserting small pebbles into the uterus. Nineteenth-century couples in the United States used "coitus interruptus" (withdrawal before ejaculation), the rhythm method (sexual intercourse only during nonfertile times), condoms, and abstinence. Although technologies of one kind or another have been around for generations, the issue for women has been the control of and access to these technologies. Patriarchal societies have long understood that to control women's lives it is necessary to control women's reproductive options. In this way, information about, access to, and denial of birth control technologies are central aspects of women's role and status in society.

In the 1880s, the Comstock Law (statutes supposed to control pornography) limited contraception because these technologies were considered obscene. At the same time, however, women realized that the denial of contraception kept them in the domestic sphere and, more importantly, exposed them to repetitive and often dangerous pregnancies. In response, a social movement emerged that was organized around reproductive choice. Called "voluntary motherhood," this movement not only involved giving women access to birth control, but also worked to facilitate reproduction and parenting under the most safe, humane, and dignified conditions. Margaret Sanger was a leader of this movement and writes about her decision to become involved in "My Fight for Birth Control."

One unfortunate aspect, however, was the early birth control movement's affiliation with an emerging eugenics movement. Following Charles Darwin's theory of the survival of the fittest, eugenics argued that only the "fit" should be encouraged to reproduce and that birth control was necessary to prevent the "unfit" from unlimited reproduction. The "unfit" included poor and immigrant populations, the "feeble-minded," and criminals. Using a rationale grounded in eugenics, birth control proponents were able to argue their case while receiving the support of those in power in society. Nonetheless, although contraceptive availability varied from state to state, it was not until a Supreme Court decision (*Griswold v. Connecticut*) in 1965 that married couples were allowed rights to birth control. The Court's ruling said that the prohibition of contraceptive use by married people was unconstitutional in that it violated the constitutional right to privacy. This right was extended to single people in 1972 and to minors in 1977.

Today there are a variety of contraceptive methods available. Their accessibility is limited by the availability of information about them, by cost, and by health care providers' sponsorship. As you read about these technologies, consider the following questions: Whose body is being affected? Who gets to deal with the side effects? Who is paying for these methods? Who will pay if these methods fail? Who will be hurt if these side effects become more serious? These questions are framed by gender relations and the context of the U.S. economy and its health organizations. For example, since hitting the market in 1998, prescriptions for Viagra (a male impotence medication) were covered by more than half of health insurance plans whereas most plans did not cover birth control pills. Fury over this has created bills passed in over 20 states to date to require insurers to provide contraceptive coverage. A federal bill is in the works.

Other than tubal ligation where women are surgically sterilized and vasectomy where men are surgically sterilized, birth control methods include, first, the intrauterine device (IUD), a small piece of plastic with copper inside it that is inserted into the uterus. It prevents the implantation of a fertilized egg. One trade name is the ParaGard; the Progestasert or Mirena is another IUD that contains hormones. IUDs generally last up to 10 years, can result in heavier periods, and may increase risk of pelvic inflammatory disease among women with multiple sexual partners. The Dalkon Shield was an IUD that caused infection, infertility, and death among women in the 1970s and was subsequently banned in the United States.

ACTIVIST PROFILE   **Margaret Sanger**

Margaret Sanger completed her nursing training in 1900 at the age of 21. Following her marriage and the birth of three children, Sanger returned to work as a visiting nurse in some of the worst slums in New York City. A great deal of her work involved assisting poor women in giving birth, and she began to see the impact of bearing too many children on the health and welfare of these women. She also saw the suffering and near fatality of many women who obtained unsafe, illegal abortions to avoid having even more children. Often these women would beg Sanger to tell them how to prevent pregnancy, but by law Sanger was forbidden to share this knowledge with them. When at last a young woman who had pleaded with Sanger for this information died from giving birth to yet another baby, Sanger decided to take action.

Convinced that women had a right to know how to prevent pregnancy and that the improvement of women's lives depended on family planning, Sanger began to educate herself about birth control. Armed with her newfound information, Sanger began her real life's work. Her plan was to educate the public about birth control, form a birth control organization to help raise awareness and money, seek to overturn the Comstock Law, which prevented sending birth control information through the U.S. mail, and lobby Congress to allow doctors to prescribe birth control devices, which were illegal even for married couples.

In 1914 Sanger started the *Woman Rebel,* a magazine encouraging women to think for themselves and promoting family planning. Under the Comstock Law, the magazine was banned by the U.S. Postal Service, and Sanger was charged with nine counts of obscenity. She fled to England for 2 years until the charges were dropped. Upon her return to New York, she founded the National Birth Control League, which later became Planned Parenthood. In 1916 she opened a birth control clinic in a poor section of Brooklyn. After only 9 days in operation, the clinic was raided and shut down. Sanger was sentenced to 30 days in a workhouse. Upon her release, Sanger reopened the clinic out of her home.

In 1921 Sanger moved her battle to the national level and started *The Birth Control Review.* During the first 5 years of its publication, she received more than a million letters from women detailing the horrors of poverty and unwanted pregnancy. In 1928 Sanger organized 500 of the letters into a book, *Mothers in Bondage,* which became highly influential in the fight for birth control. Throughout the 1930s Sanger continued her fight, speaking and lobbying. At last, the Supreme Court overturned the Comstock Law in 1936, and the American Medical Association (AMA) reversed its position, giving doctors the right to distribute birth control devices. After her victory, Sanger persisted in her work for affordable and effective contraceptives. Her tireless efforts to secure research funding at last led to the development of the most significant contraceptive of the century—the birth control pill. Only a few months before Sanger died in 1966, the U.S. Supreme Court, in *Griswold v. Connecticut,* made birth control legal for married couples.

(It was then exported for use by women overseas.) It is important to remember that IUDs do not protect against sexually transmitted diseases.

Second are the hormone regulation methods. The pill is an oral contraceptive that contains a combination of two hormones: progestin and estrogen. It became widely available in the United States in the 1960s and quickly became the most popular means of contraception despite such side effects as nausea, weight gain, breast tenderness, and headaches. Combination pills usually work by preventing a woman's ovaries from releasing eggs (ovulation). They also thicken the cervical mucus, which keeps sperm from joining with an egg. The minipill contains no estrogen and a small dose of progestin and has fewer side effects than the regular pill, and it works by thickening cervical mucus and/or preventing ovulation. Taking the pill daily maintains the level of hormone that is needed to prevent pregnancy. Norplant is a contraceptive device that lasts 5 years. Six flexible capsules are inserted beneath the skin on the upper arm where they release progestin to suppress ovulation. Implants such as Norplant are continuous long-lasting birth control without sterilization and can be used by women who cannot take estrogen, and ability to become pregnant returns quickly when use is stopped. However, implants can cause irregular bleeding and the possibility of pain and scarring upon removal. Depo-provera is an injection of synthetic hormones that suppresses ovulation for 11 to 13 months. There are similar side effects as the pill, including depression and heavier, more frequent periods. In addition, the effects are not easily reversible, and it may take up to a year before a woman is fertile again. Some groups have questioned the safety of Norplant and Depo-provera. A device marketed under the name NuvaRing was approved in 2001. It is a flexible, transparent ring about 3 inches in diameter that women insert vaginally once a month. The ring releases a continuous dose of estrogen and progestin.

Sexually Transmitted Diseases

Every year more than 12 million cases of sexually transmitted diseases (STDs) are reported in the United States. These infections result in billions of dollars in preventable health care spending. In addition, the health impact of STDs is particularly severe for women. Because the infections often cause few or no symptoms and may go untreated, women are at risk for complications from STDs, including ectopic (tubal) pregnancy, infertility, chronic pelvic pain, and poor pregnancy outcomes.

CHLAMYDIA

Chlamydia is the most common bacterial sexually transmitted disease in the United States. It causes an estimated 4 million infections annually, primarily among adolescents and young adults. In women, untreated infections can progress to involve the upper reproductive tract and may result in serious complications. About 75 percent of women infected with chlamydia have few or no symptoms, and without testing and treatment the infection may persist for as long as fifteen months. Without treatment, 20–40 percent of women with chlamydia may develop pelvic inflammatory disease (PID). An estimated one in ten adolescent girls and one in twenty women of reproductive age are infected.

PELVIC INFLAMMATORY DISEASE

PID refers to upper reproductive tract infection in women, which often develops when STDs go untreated or are inadequately treated. Each year, PID and its complications affect more than 750,000 women. PID can cause chronic pelvic pain or harm to the reproductive organs. Permanent damage to the fallopian tubes can result from a single episode of PID and is even more common after a second or third episode. Damage to the fallopian tubes is the only preventable cause of infertility. As much as 30 percent of infertility in women may be related to preventable complications of past STDs.

One potentially fatal complication of PID is ectopic pregnancy, an abnormal condition that occurs when a fertilized egg implants in a location other than the uterus, often in a fallopian tube. It is estimated that ectopic pregnancy has increased about fivefold over a twenty-year period. Among African American women, ectopic pregnancy is the leading cause of pregnancy-related deaths. The economic cost of PID and its complications is estimated at $4 billion annually.

GONORRHEA

Gonorrhea is a common bacterial STD that can be treated with antibiotics. Although gonorrhea rates among adults have declined, rates among adolescents have risen or remained unchanged. Adolescent females aged 15–19 have the highest rates of gonorrhea. An estimated 50 percent of women with gonorrhea have no symptoms. Without early screening and treatment, 10–40 percent of women with gonorrhea will develop PID.

HUMAN IMMUNODEFICIENCY VIRUS

Human immunodeficiency virus (HIV) is the virus that causes AIDS. The risk of a woman acquiring or transmitting HIV is increased by the presence of other STDs. In particular, the presence of genital ulcers, such as those produced by syphilis and herpes, or the presence of an inflammatory STD, such as chlamydia or gonorrhea, may make HIV transmission easier.

HERPES SIMPLEX VIRUS (HSV)

Genital herpes is a disease caused by herpes simplex virus (HSV). The disease may recur periodically and has no cure. Scientists have estimated that about 30 million persons in the United States may have genital HSV infection. Most infected persons never recognize the symptoms of genital herpes; some will have symptoms shortly after infection and never again. A minority of those infected will have recurrent episodes of genital sores. Many cases of genital herpes are acquired from people who do not know they are infected or who had no symptoms at the time of the sexual contact. Acyclovir is a drug that can help to control the symptoms of HSV, but it is not a cure. HSV is frequently more severe in people with weakened immune systems, including people with HIV infection.

HUMAN PAPILLOMA VIRUS (HPV)

HPV is a virus that sometimes causes genital warts but in many cases infects people without causing noticeable symptoms. Concern about HPV has increased in recent years after several studies showed that HPV infection is associated with the development of cervical cancer. Approximately twenty-five types of HPV can infect the genital area. These types are divided into high-risk and low-risk groups based on whether they are associated with cancer. Infection with a high-risk type of HPV is one risk factor for cervical cancer, which causes 4,500 deaths among women each year. No cure for HPV infection exists.

SYPHILIS

Syphilis is a bacterial infection that can be cured with antibiotics. Female adolescents are twice as likely to have syphilis as male adolescents. African American women have syphilis rates that are seven times greater than the female population as a whole.

Such infections among infants are largely preventable if women receive appropriate diagnosis and treatment during prenatal care. Death of the fetus or newborn infant occurs in up to 40 percent of pregnant women who have untreated syphilis.

(continued)

CONDOM EFFECTIVENESS AND RELIABILITY

When used consistently and correctly, latex condoms are very effective in preventing a variety of STDs, including HIV infection. Multiple studies have demonstrated a strong protective effect of condom use. Because condoms are regulated as medical devices, they are subject to random testing by the Food and Drug Administration. Every latex condom manufactured in the United States is tested electronically for holes before packaging. Condom breakage rates are low in the United States—no higher than 2 per 100 condoms used. Most cases of condom failure result from incorrect or inconsistent use.

For further information, contact the Office of Women's Health, Centers for Disease Control and Prevention, 1600 Clifton Road, MS: D-51, Atlanta, GA 30033; phone: (404) 639-7230.

Source: www.cdc.gov/od/owh/whstd.htm.

The ring remains in the vagina for 21 days and is then removed and discarded and a new ring inserted. Other hormone regulation methods include hormone patches such as Ortho Evra that must be changed weekly and work by preventing ovulation. None of the hormone methods protect against sexually transmitted diseases.

Next are the barrier methods. The diaphragm, cervical cap, and shield are barrier methods that are inserted into the vagina before sexual intercourse, fit over the cervix, and prevent sperm from entering the uterus. They work in conjunction with spermicidal jelly that is placed along the rim of the device. Some women use them in conjunction with spermicidal foam that is inserted into the vagina with a small plunger. Unlike the other methods, spermicides are available at any drugstore. Also available at drugstores are vaginal sponges that are coated with spermicide, inserted into the vagina, and work to block the cervix and absorb sperm. All these barrier methods work best when used in conjunction with a condom and are much less effective when used alone. The male condom is a latex rubber tube that comes rolled up and is unrolled on the penis. The female condom is a floppy polyurethane tube with an inner ring at the closed end that fits over the cervix and an outer ring at the open end that hangs outside the vagina. Condoms block sperm from entering the vagina and, when used properly in conjunction with other barrier methods, are highly effective in preventing pregnancy. Another very important aspect of condoms is that they are the only form of contraception that offers prevention against sexually transmitted diseases (STDs) generally and HIV/AIDS in particular. All health care providers emphasize that individuals not in a mutually monogamous sexual relationship should always use condoms.

Finally, emergency contraception pills (ECPs) used after unprotected heterosexual intercourse are available. Commonly known as the "morning-after pill," this hormonal contraception was approved by the FDA in 1997. ECPs are effective if taken up to 120 hours after unprotected intercourse, although they are most effective if taken within 12 hours, by providing a high dose of the same hormones in birth control pills to prevent ovulation and fertilization. A *New England Journal of Medicine* study reported that about 1.7 million of the approximately 3 million unintended pregnancies a year might be prevented if emergency contraception was more readily available. In addition, a new study in the *Journal of the American Medical Association* reported that women with easy access to emergency contraception were not more likely to engage in unprotected heterosexual contact or abandon the use of other forms of birth control. In 2004 the FDA rejected access to "Plan B," or emergency, contraception without a prescription. Currently ECPs, while safe and effective, are available only through prescription, although some states do have a collaborative drug therapy agreement that allows women to receive ECPs directly from pharmacists. The copper-T intrauterine device can also be used as an emergency contraceptive. ECPs are different from the drug mifiprex (also known as RU-486) that works by terminating an early pregnancy and is known as a "medical abortion." In very low doses, however, mifiprex can be used as a method of emergency contraception. Emergency contraception does not terminate a pregnancy but prevents one from occurring.

Abortion

Although induced abortion, the removal of the fertilized ovum or fetus from the uterus, is only one aspect of reproductive choice, it has dominated discussion of this topic. This is unfortunate because there is more to reproductive rights than abortion. Nonetheless, this is one topic that generates unease and often heated discussion. *Pro-choice* advocates believe abortion is women's choice, women should not be forced to have children against their will, a fertilized ovum should not have all the legal and moral rights of personhood, and all children should be wanted children. Pro-choice advocates tend to believe in a woman's right to have an abortion even though they might not make that decision for themselves. *Pro-life* advocates believe that human personhood begins at conception and a fertilized ovum or fetus has the right to full moral and legal rights of personhood. These rights about the sanctity of human life outweigh the rights of mothers. Some pro-life advocates see abortion as murder and doctors and other health care workers who assist in providing abortion services as accomplices to a crime.

Although there are exceptions (most notably the Feminists for Life of America organization whose motto is "Pro Woman Pro Life"—they advocate opposition to all forms of violence and characterize abortion as violence), most people who consider themselves feminists are pro-choice. There are several issues raised by this perspective. The first issue is the moral responsibilities associated with requiring the birth of unwanted children, because the forces attempting to deny women safe and legal abortions are the very same ones that call for reductions in the social, medical, educational, and economic support of poor children. Does "pro-life" include being "for life" of these children once they are born? "Pro-life" politicians often tend to vote against increased spending for services for women and families. The second issue raised includes the moral responsibilities involved in requiring women to be mothers against their will. If you do grant full personhood rights to a fertilized ovum or fetus, then at what point do these rights take priority over the rights of another fully established person, the mother? What of fathers' rights? Third, several studies have shown that between two-thirds and three-quarters of all women accessing abortions would have an illegal abortion if abortion were illegal. Illegal abortions have high mortality rates; issues do not go away just by making them illegal.

According to Gallup polls, about 50 percent of registered voters consider themselves "pro-choice" (defined as in favor of women's choice to access abortion facilities), with about 36 percent as "pro-life" (against abortion under varying circumstances) and the rest uncertain. Forty percent believe abortion laws should stay as they are, and 20 percent believe they should be less strict. Seventeen percent want to make abortion illegal in all circumstances. Approximately 1.37 million abortions take place in the United States annually, a slight reduction over the last decade in part due to the availability of emergency contraception. Approximately 1 percent of abortions occur after rape or incest. The Centers for Disease Control report that 58 percent of legal abortions occur in the first 8 weeks of gestation and 88 percent are performed in the first 12 weeks. Only 1.5 percent of abortions occur after 20 weeks. Since the nationwide legalization of abortion in 1973, the proportion of abortions performed after the first trimester has decreased because of access to and knowledge about safe and legal abortion. More than 50 percent of pregnancies among U.S. women are unintended, and about half of these are terminated by abortion. At current rates, about 43 percent of women will have an abortion by the time they are 45 years old. Among women obtaining abortions, approximately half of these are younger than 25 years and 19 percent are teenagers. The abortion rate is highest among women who are 18 to 19 years old. African American women are three times as likely to have an abortion than White women, and Latinas are twice as likely, reflecting in part socio-economic issues associated with raising children and, possibly, reduced adoption opportunities for children of color compared to White children. Approximately two-thirds of all abortions are obtained by never-married women, and the same number (although not necessarily the same women) intend to have children in the future.

In the United States, abortion was not limited by law or even opposed by the church until the nineteenth century. Generally, abortion was allowed before "quickening," understood as that time when the fetus's movements could be felt by the mother (usually between 3 and 4 months). In the 1820s, however, laws in New England declared abortion of an unquickened fetus a misdemeanor and a quickened fetus, second-degree manslaughter. As the century progressed, more restrictive laws were passed in various states, and in 1860 the Catholic Church officially ruled against abortion. Nonetheless, abortion continued. By the early twentieth century, abortion of any kind was illegal in the United States. In the reading "The Way It Was," Eleanor Cooney writes about her attempt to have an abortion in the 1960s, before the procedure was legal.

The major abortion decision came in January 1973 with the Supreme Court ruling of *Roe v. Wade*. Although some states such as California and New York had reformed their abortion laws before this time, the Supreme Court ruling overturned all states' bans on abortion. The ruling used the *Griswold v. Connecticut* decision in arguing that abortion must be considered part of privacy rights in deciding whether to have children. It did not, however, attempt to decide the religious or philosophical decisions about when life begins. The Court did agree that, under the law, a fetus is not treated as a legal person with civil rights. The ruling went on to divide pregnancy into three equal stages, or trimesters, and explained the differential interventions that the state could make during these different periods. The *Roe v. Wade* ruling held

LEARNING ACTIVITY   **Walk in Her Shoes**

Go to the California Abortion Rights Action League (CARAL) homepage at
www.caral.org and follow the links to "Walk in the Shoes" of a woman deciding
about having an abortion in the time before choice was legal. Explore the barriers
women faced in seeking an abortion before *Roe v. Wade.* Now go to the homepage of the International Planned Parenthood Federation (IPPF) at *www.ippf.org.*
Follow the links to resources and then country profiles. Click on a country to find
out the status of women's reproductive rights in that nation. Return to the IPPF homepage and follow the links to resources and then the IPPF Charter on Sexual and
Reproductive Rights to learn what basic rights IPPF is demanding for women. Go
to the homepage for the National Abortion Rights Action League (NARAL) at
www.naral.org and click on "100 Ways to Fight 4 Choice" under "Take Action" to
discover things you can do to help protect freedom to choose. To find out about
your state's abortion and reproductive rights, select "Access to Abortion & Reproductive Rights" under "Get Informed About Reproductive Rights Issues." Then under
"Facts and Information," select "NARAL Report: Who Decides? A State-by-State
Review of Abortion and Reproductive Rights."

that the U.S. Constitution protects a woman's decision to terminate her pregnancy
and allowed first-trimester abortions on demand. It declared that only after the fetus
is viable, capable of sustained survival outside the woman's body with or without
artificial aid, may the states control abortion. Abortions necessary to preserve the
life or health of the mother must be allowed, however, even after fetal viability. Prior
to viability, states can regulate abortion, but only if the regulation does not impose
a "substantial obstacle" in the path of women.

Although there has been a general chipping away of women's rights to abortion
since *Roe v. Wade,* there has been no ruling as of yet that says life begins at conception and therefore no complete overturning of *Roe v. Wade.* However, there has
been legislation that declares a fetus of any gestational age a "person" with legal
rights. In terms of the various attacks on abortion rights, these include, first, the
Hyde Amendment, sponsored by Henry Hyde, a Republican senator from Illinois. It
was an amendment to the 1977 Health, Education, and Welfare Appropriations Act
and gave states the right to prohibit the use of Medicaid funds for abortion, thus
limiting abortion to those women who could afford to pay. Note that this was accompanied by Supreme Court rulings (*Beal v. Doe,* 1977) that said that states could refuse
to use Medicaid funds to pay for abortions and that Congress could forbid states to
use federal funds (including Medicaid) to pay for abortion services (*Harris v. McRae,*
1980). The latter ruling also allowed states to deny funds even for medically necessary abortions.

Second, the 1989 *Webster v. Reproductive Health Services,* sponsored by Missouri
State Attorney William Webster, upheld a state's right to prevent public facilities or
public employees from assisting with abortions, to prevent counseling concerning
abortion if public funds were involved, and to allow parental notification rights.

Facts About Abortion, Choice, and Women's Health

- Between 1973, when abortion was made legal in the United States, and 1990, the number of deaths per 100,000 legal abortion procedures declined tenfold. By 1990, the risk of death from legal abortion had declined to 0.3 death per 100,000. (This rate is half the risk of a tonsillectomy and one-hundredth the risk of an appendectomy.)
- The mortality rate associated with childbirth is ten times higher than for legal abortion.
- Worldwide, 125,000 to 200,000 women die each year from complications related to unsafe and illegal abortions.
- In 84 percent of the counties in the United States, no physicians are willing or able to provide abortions.
- Only 12 percent of ob-gyn residency programs in the United States offer routine training in abortion procedures.
- Eighty-eight percent of abortions are performed before the end of the first trimester of pregnancy.
- Sixty-four percent of states prohibit most government funding for abortion, making access to the procedure impossible for many poor women.
- Thirty-eight states have enacted parental consent or notice requirements for minors seeking abortions.
- Abortion has no overall effect on the risk of breast cancer.
- Abortion does not increase the risk of complications during future pregnancies or deliveries.
- Emergency contraceptives reduce a woman's chance of becoming pregnant by 75 percent when taken within 72 hours of unprotected sex with a second dose 12 hours after the first.
- Emergency contraceptives do not cause abortions; they inhibit ovulation, fertilization, or implantation before a pregnancy occurs.
- Use of emergency contraceptives could reduce the number of unintended pregnancies and abortions by half annually.
- Eighty-nine percent of women aged 18 to 44 have not heard of or do not know the key facts critical to the use of emergency contraceptives.

Sources: NARAL Publications: *www.naral.org;* Reproductive Health and Rights Center: *www.choice.org.*

Third, *Planned Parenthood v. Casey,* although upholding *Roe v. Wade* in 1992, also upheld the state's right to restrict abortion in various ways: parental notification, mandatory counseling and waiting periods, and limitations on public spending for abortion services.

Fourth, in September 2000, the FDA approved mifepristone (mifeprex TM), formerly known as RU-486, an anti-progesterone drug that blocks receptors of progesterone, a key hormone in the establishment and maintenance of human pregnancy. Used in conjunction with a prostaglandin such as misoprostol, mifepristone induces abortion when administered early in a pregnancy, providing women with a medical alternative to aspiration (suction) abortion. Although this drug has proven to be a safe

IDEAS FOR ACTIVISM   **Ten Things You Can Do to Protect Choice**

1. *Volunteer for a pro-choice organization.* Pro-choice organizations need volunteers. There are dozens of organizations working in various ways to help women get the services they need. For pro-choice organizations nationwide, check *www.choice.org*.
2. *Write a letter to a local clinic or abortion provider thanking them for putting themselves on the line for women.* Doctors and clinic workers hear vociferously from those opposed to abortion. Hearing a few words of thanks goes a long way.
3. *Monitor your local paper for articles about abortion.* Write a letter to the editor thanking them for accurate coverage or correcting them if coverage is biased.
4. *Find out how your elected representatives have voted on abortion.* Call and ask for their voting records, not just on bills relating to legality of abortion, but also on related issues such as funding for poor women, restrictions meant to impede a woman's access to services (such as waiting periods and informed consent), and contraceptives funding and/or insurance coverage. Whether or not you agree with the votes of your elected officials, write and let them know that this is an issue on which you make voting decisions. Anti-choice activists don't hesitate to do this; you should do it too.
5. *Talk to your children now about abortion.* Explain why you believe it's a decision only a woman can make for herself.
6. *If you have had an abortion, legal or illegal, consider discussing it with people in your life.* Over 40 percent of American women will have at least one abortion sometime during their lives. More openness about the subject might lead to less judgment, more understanding, and fewer attempts to make it illegal.
7. *Volunteer for a candidate whom you know to be pro-choice.*
8. *Be an escort at a clinic that provides abortions.*
9. *Vote!*
10. *Hold a house meeting to discuss choice with your friends.* You could show one or all of Dorothy Fadiman's excellent documentaries from the trilogy, *From the Back Alleys to the Supreme Court and Beyond. When Abortion Was Illegal* is a good conversation starter. For information on obtaining these videos, contact the CARAL ProChoice Education Fund or *Concentric Media*.

Source: www.choice.org.

and effective option for women seeking an abortion during the first few weeks of a pregnancy since its approval in France in 1988, it has been the target for anti-choice lobbying and activism to block access to the drug. Currently, FDA approval in the United States requires that a doctor administer and supervise the use of the drug for use as an abortifacient. Research in Europe suggests that the availability of this drug has not increased abortion rates generally.

Fifth, in November 2003, the "Partial Birth" Abortion Ban was passed and signed by President George W. Bush. In this ban, "partial birth" is a political term for the medical procedure named intact dilation and extraction (D&X) and describes the "overt act" to "kill a partially delivered fetus." This is a very controversial topic: Proponents of the ban argue that it is a gruesome procedure and not medically necessary.

Opponents of the ban emphasize that it is an infrequently performed procedure, done mostly when the life or health of the mother is at risk or when the baby is so malformed (for example, in severe cases of hydrocephalus where the baby cannot live and a normal delivery would kill the mother), and that anti-choice organizations and politicians have been using this issue to galvanize opposition to abortion and facilitate the banning of all abortions. In addition, opponents of the ban (including the American Medical Association, which recently withdrew support for the ban, the American College of Obstetricians and Gynecologists, the American Medical Women's Association, the American Nurses Association, and others, as well as pro-choice groups like Planned Parenthood and NARAL Pro-Choice America) describe the law as too broad in scope, emphasizing it will dramatically curb the availability of second-trimester abortions that become necessary as a consequence of parental notification and consent laws that delay young women accessing a first-trimester abortion, or as a result of diagnostic tests that can be done only at a certain gestational age. Opponents also believe the law is too punitive in that it results in jail time to medical practitioners assisting in such procedures. Finally, opponents of the federal ban say that it lacks a health exemption for women as set up in *Roe v. Wade*. Indeed, immediately after passing, the law's constitutionality was challenged on this item and three district judges (in New York, Nebraska, and California) had declared the ban unconstitutional. The U.S. Supreme Court had already overturned a Nebraska state "partial birth" abortion law in 2000 because it did not provide a health clause or an exemption to protect a woman in the event that she would suffer serious medical consequences if she were denied an abortion. Despite this, as of this writing, 23 states have passed state laws banning this procedure. The reading by Eleanor Cooney comments on the "partial birth" abortion debate.

Sixth, in April 2004, President George W. Bush signed the Unborn Victims of Violence Act into law, giving the zygote, embryo, or fetus the same legal rights as a person and preparing the groundwork for further restrictions on abortion access. Also known as the Laci Peterson Law, in reference to the murder of a woman and her unborn child, this law creates the notion of double homicide in the case of the murder of a pregnant woman, although the law has jurisdiction only for homicides committed on federal property. This law was somewhat controversial for women's rights supporters since it is written to support survivors of violence at the very same time that by establishing a fetus of any gestational age to have equal personhood with a woman, it jeopardized women's rights to safe and legal abortions.

Finally, in April 2005, a bill passed the House of Representatives making it a crime to take a minor woman (under 18 years of age) residing in a state with parental notification and/or consent laws across state lines to access an abortion. It would also create a national requirement for parental notification for underage women seeking to terminate a pregnancy and require a 24-hour waiting period for a minor's abortion. Doctors could be prosecuted under the legislation. Supporters of the bill say that it is necessary to protect young women because an adult predator could impregnate a girl and then force her to have an abortion to hide the crime. Opponents say the bill is too far-reaching, sets up more roadblocks for women who have the right to safe and legal abortion, and could further isolate young women by making it a crime for a family member or other caring adult to provide assistance.

The situation at present is that abortion is legal at the same time that its availability and accessibility have been limited and all these obstacles and limitations in access disproportionately affect poor women, women of color, and young women. One piece of legislation, however, was passed in 1994 to safeguard women's right to access their legal rights. After the public outcry associated with the public harassment, wounding, and death of abortion services providers, and the vandalism and bombing of various clinics, the Supreme Court ruled in *Madsen et al. v. Women's Health Center, Inc.* to allow a buffer zone around clinics to allow patients and employees access and to control noise around the premises. The same year, the Freedom of Access to Clinic Entrances (FACE) Act made it a federal crime to block access, harass, or incite violence in the context of abortion services.

American Women and Health Disparities

David Satcher, M. D.

In the last century, American women have been given 30 bonus years of life, thanks to such sweeping public health initiatives as sanitation and immunization programs. The America of the next century, however, presents us with new, more complex, and exceedingly interesting public health challenges.

Nearly 40 million of America's 140 million women are now members of racial and ethnic minority groups.[1] These women represent many diverse populations, but encompass 4 major groups: African Americans represent 13% of the total population of US women; Hispanic women, 11%; Asian-American/Pacific Islander women, 4%; and American Indian/Alaska Native women, just under 1%. The remaining 71% of American women are white.[2]

Although these women experience many of the same health problems as white women, as a group, they are in poorer health, use fewer health services, and continue to suffer disproportionately from premature death, disease, and disabilities. Many also face tremendous social, economic, cultural, and other barriers to optimal health.

It is a growing national challenge. The US Census Bureau estimates that by the year 2050, barely 53% of America's women will be classified as non-Hispanic white, and 25% will be Hispanic, 14% non-Hispanic black, 9% Asian and Pacific Islander, and just under 1% American Indian and Alaska Native.[3] Reclassification standards under the new 2000 census have blurred these categories somewhat, but it remains clear that if we are to leave our children and grandchildren a healthier nation, we must address health disparities immediately. The challenge grows more difficult when we consider the aging population. By the year 2050, nearly 1 in 4 adult women will be 65 years old or older, and an astonishing 1 in 17 will be 85 years old or older.[4]

For public health leaders, the mission of eliminating disparities among a diverse, aging population is daunting. Each group of minority women is made up of subgroups, who have diverse languages, cultures, degrees of acculturation, and histories. African-American women have a common African heritage, but they may also have roots in the United States, Great Britain, the Cribbean, or other countries. Hispanic women, or Latinas, have the distinction of being a multiracial ethnic group. Many Hispanic women in the United States are recent immigrants; most are of Mexican, Puerto Rican, Cuban, Central American, or South American descent. Asian-American/Pacific Islander women may be of Chinese, Japanese, Vietnamese, Cambodian, Korean, Filipino, Native Hawaiian, or other ancestry. Nearly 75% of this population group are foreign born, including an increasing number of immigrants and refugees from Southeast Asia.[5] American Indian/Alaska Native women are members of more than 500 federally or state-recognized tribes or unrecognized tribal organizations. Major subgroups of this population are American Indians, Eskimos, and Aleuts.[5]

These seemingly impersonal statistics have faces. A potpourri of cultures, traditions, beliefs, challenges, and family styles has always been America's greatest strength. Our challenge for the next century is to close the disparities gap, without compromising the uniqueness and richness of each culture.

We see disparities among these racial and ethnic groups and subgroups in almost every area of health. In breast cancer, for example, white women have a higher incidence rate (114 per 100,000) than African-American women (100), but black women have a higher mortality rate (31 v 25). This likely reflects lower rates of early detection as well as treatment disparities, but there could also be undiscovered physiological factors. Hispanic women have an incidence rate of 69 and a death rate of 15, compared to 75 and 11 for Asian and Pacific Islander women, and 33 and 12 for American Indian women.[6]

For these statistics to be meaningful, we need to take a closer look at each subgroup. Native Hawaiian women, for example, have an unusually high death rate from breast cancer (25 per 100,000), although the overall rate for Asian-American women is lower than average.[6] American Indian women in New Mexico report the lowest incidence (32 per 100,000) and the lowest death rate (9), but much higher rates are reported in many other Indian Health Service areas. There is no clear explanation for this phenomenon.[5(p74)]

When we look at cervical cancer, we see different trends. The incidence rate of invasive cervical cancer is higher among Asian-American than among white women (10.3 v 8.1 per 100,000). The incidence rate is nearly 5 times higher in Vietnamese women than in white women, yet we cannot explain the causes of this unusually high rate.[6]

If we look at death rates for diseases of the heart, African-American women are clearly at risk, with a staggering 147 deaths per 100,000, compared to 88 for white women, 70 for American Indian/Alaska Native women, and 63 each for Hispanic women and Asian-American/Pacific Islanders. This reflects rates of obesity and the lack of access to preventive health care services, including blood pressure screening and management.[7]

We cannot make assumptions about the health status of any particular racial group. Asian Americans are often viewed as a "model" minority because of their low unemployment and disease rates. Asian-American/Pacific Islander women age 65 and older, however, have the highest death rate from suicide (8 per 100,000) of all women in their age group, 4 times higher than the rate

among elderly black women and twice the rate of white women.[5(p32)]

Disparities are perhaps most striking when we look at the human immunodeficiency virus (HIV) and acquired immune deficiency syndrome (AIDS) rates among women. Twenty percent of Americans currently living with HIV are women, and 77% of those are African American or Hispanic. Many people are shocked to learn that AIDS is the second leading cause of death among African-American women age 25 to 44, their peak childbearing years, which leaves untold numbers of children motherless[8] and affects entire communities.

Not surprisingly, we also see disparities in key risk factors for disease. *The Surgeon General's Report on Women and Smoking,* released March 2001, reported that Alaska Native women have the highest rate of smoking at a discouraging 35%, compared to 24% for white women, 22% for African-American women, 14% for Hispanic women, and 11% for Asian and Pacific Islander women.[9]

In obesity, another major risk factor, we see significant disparities that clearly affect rates of disease. Non-Hispanic black women have the highest rate of obesity, 38%, compared to 35% for Mexican-American women, and 22% for non-Hispanic whites.[7(p247)] We know that cultural and lifestyle factors play a role in these disparities.

We have begun to address these differences through Healthy People 2010, the nation's health agenda for the next decade. Healthy People 2010 has 2 overarching goals: to increase the quality and years of life and to eliminate health disparities. Healthy People 2010 has 220 objectives relevant to women's health, including cancer, heart disease, stroke, diabetes, and access to quality health services. Goals for most ethnic groups are equal, even though some are starting from different baselines. For example, we want to reduce the death rate from breast cancer to 22.3 per 100,000, regardless of baseline disparities.

At the heart of Healthy People 2010 is improved access to such clinical preventive services as mammography and Papanicolaou tests. We also need improved access to high-quality health education and mental health and support services at the community level, so specific ethnic and cultural needs can be addressed. Health providers must use the clinical setting to better educate underserved women about risk factors they can modify, such as smoking and obesity, using culturally and linguistically appropriate approaches.

This cannot be done without change in the structure of the U.S. health care system, including the increasing influence of market forces, changes in payment and delivery systems, and welfare reform. Reinventing health care delivery is nearly useless without evaluating how these systemic changes will affect the most vulnerable and at-risk populations. Federal, state, and local public health agencies must redouble their efforts to address language and other access barriers and reduce disparities for these underserved Americans.

Throughout the federal health agencies, strategies are being developed to address health disparities. One model to watch is the Breast and Cervical Cancer Early Detection Program sponsored by the Centers for Disease Control and Prevention. It has grown from 8 states in 1991 to 50 states, 6 US territories, the District of Columbia, and 12 American Indian/Alaska Native organizations in 2000. More than 2.7 million breast and cervical cancer screening tests have been provided to more than 1.7 million underserved women from inception through March 2000. Federal and state programs now are addressing how to provide appropriate treatment for the women who are screened.

We have also increased our educational efforts. In 1998 the Health and Human Services Office on Women's Health (OWH) launched the National Women's Health Information Center Website and toll-free telephone service (www.4woman.gov or 1-800-994WOMAN, TDD: 1-888-220-5446). Women who cannot use the Internet can call information specialists, including Spanish-speaking experts, to get referrals to public and private organizations that can offer culturally appropriate information about specific health problems. The OWH has also launched an educational campaign that specifically targets women of each racial and ethnic group. *Pick Your Path to Health* offers simple-to-understand, culturally appropriate, weekly action steps to improve health status.[10]

The OWH-sponsored National Centers of Excellence in Women's Health[11] and Community Centers of Excellence in Women's Health[12] have taken a leadership role in developing model minority outreach programs and services.

Another good model is the work being done at the National Cancer Institute (NCI). Last spring the NCI launched a special populations network to address the unequal burden of cancer; 18 grants at 17 institutions will create or implement cancer control programs in minority and underserved populations.[13] The NCI, as well as many other institutes at the National Institutes of Health, have created centers and offices designed specifically to reduce health disparities.[14]

Another innovative program is the Reducing Health Care Disparities National Project at the Centers for Medicare and Medicaid Services (formerly known as the Health Care Financing Administration), which works at the state level to reduce health care disparities.[15] Descriptions and details of many other health disparities programs can be found on the websites of individual health agencies. I also recommend the *Women of Color Health Data Book*[5]; it is rich with information on the health, lives, and backgrounds of many ethnic groups of women.

Of course, when we discuss the elimination of health disparities, it must be emphasized that disparities take many forms: racial, ethnic, gender, geographic, income, educational, cultural, and others. Many of these disparities are interlinked. For example, some of the worst health outcomes are experienced by poor, undereducated, African-American women in the rural southern United States. Looking at data from specific racial and ethnic groups, however, is an important place to start as we develop strategies to encourage state and local health care experts to focus on our Healthy People 2010 objectives. Clearly, the one-size-fits-all approach to public health that was so effective for expanding the lifespan of women in the last century will not meet the challenges of the new century.

REFERENCES

1. U.S. Census Bureau, Population Division, Population Estimates Program. *Resident Population Estimates of the United States by Age and Sex: April 1, 1990 to October 1, 1999.* Available at www.census. gov/ population/estimates/nation/intfile2-1.txt. Internet release date: November 26, 1999.
2. U.S. Census Bureau, Population Division, Population Estimates Program. *Projections of the Population by Age, Sex, Race and Hispanic Origin for the United States: 1990–1999.* Available at www.census.gov/population/www/estimates/nation3.html.
3. U.S. Census Bureau, Population Division, Population Estimates Program. *Projections of the Population by Age, Sex, Race and Hispanic Origin for the United States: 1999–2100 (middle series).* Available at www.census.gov/population/projections/nation/detail/d2041_50.pdf.
4. U.S. Census Bureau, Population Division, Population Estimates Program. *Resident Population Estimates of the United States by Age and Sex: 2035–2050.* Available at www.census.gov/population/projections/nation/detail/d2041_50.pdf.
5. *Women of Color Health Data Book.* Available at www4.od.nih.gov/orwh/WOCEnglish.pdf.
6. *Cancer Facts & Figures 2001.* Atlanta, Ga.: American Cancer Society; 2001:28.
7. *Health, U.S. 2000.* Available at www.cdc.gov/nchs/products/pubs/pubd/hus/hus.htm.
8. Healthy People 2010. Available at www.health.gov/healthypeople.
9. *Women and Smoking: A Report of the US Surgeon General.* Available at www.cdc.gov/tobacco.
10. Pick Your Path to Health Educational Campaign. Available at www.4woman.gov/PYPTH/index.htm.
11. National Centers of Excellence available at www.4woman.gov/COE/index.htm.
12. Community Centers of Excellence available at www.4woman.gov/owh/CCOE/index.htm.
13. Minority Health Initiative formerly available at www1.od. nih.gov/ormh/mhi.html.
14. The NCI Strategic Plan to Eliminate Health Disparities. Available at http://ospr.nci.nih.gov/healthdisprpt.pdf.
15. Reducing Health Care Disparities National Project. Available at www.hcfa.gov/quality/3x.htm.

R E A D I N G   **46**

The Tolling of the Bell: Women's Health, Women's Rights

Vivian M. Dickerson, M. D.

As physicians for women's health, we are inextricably involved in women's lives. We cannot be less than fully engaged. The poet John Donne expressed this most eloquently in his poem "For Whom the Bell Tolls": ". . . And therefore, never send to know for whom the bell tolls; It tolls for thee."

A tenet of leadership is to seek the truth and embrace it. As the third female President of the American College of Obstetricians and Gynecologists (ACOG), the truth is that my years in ACOG have coincided with the coming of age of women in our society, in the workplace, in leadership roles, and in this fellowship.

Over time, I have watched female physicians grow in number, acceptance, and distinction as they achieve fulfillment of their goals. Today, however, the truth is that who we are transcends gender. Our future must be based on active membership and leadership by both male and female colleagues. It is time to embrace our wholeness rather than to dwell on our differences.

The truth is that not only has our membership changed, but so has the world of health care. The provision of health care today requires new definitions, new roles, and a markedly expanded scope. My own awareness was born of a brief sojourn into public health in Togo, West Africa, before I became a physician. Working with women and children in clinics, schools, and communities, it was overwhelming to see the poverty, the treatment of women in society, the ubiquitous illness and suffering, and most of all, the futility. The sense of helplessness was pervasive. For me, it emphasizes the true definition of women's health, namely a coalescence of emotional, social, cultural, spiritual, and physical well-being. Thus, it is determined not only by biology but by the milieu in which women live their lives.[1]

With time and professional growth, the political and social underpinnings for what I had experienced in that little village in Togo have become increasingly clear. That clarity has resulted in my belief that resolution of many women's health problems in our own country mandates our collective involvement as physicians in the social and political arenas that impact change in a democratic society.

ACOG prescribes such an advocacy role in health care by stating: "Fellows should exercise their responsibility to improve the status of women and their offspring both in the traditional patient–physician relationships, and by working within their community, and at the state and national levels to assure access to high-quality programs meeting the health needs of women."[2]

Many physicians may be reluctant to participate in the "policy and politics" arena of health care. In our pluralistic society, socioeconomic and political issues do polarize advocates, create dissension among competing interest, and divide colleagues including physicians such as ourselves. Nonetheless, the truth is that many women are not receiving their fair share of the benefits or the bounty of this great nation. This pertains not just to their reproductive health care but to the care they receive in society, politics, science, research, and the workplace. If we as physicians limit our involvement to our individual clinical practices, we cannot effect the changes that must happen for women in this country.

I therefore propose that we embrace a Women's Health Bill of Rights for the purpose of improving the overall quality of women's lives as well as their health care. I do so in the conviction that the women for whom we care, and those whom we have yet to see, are entitled to these 10 rights.

NUMBER 1: SAFETY AND ACCOUNTABILITY IN HEALTH CARE

Physicians are now acting upon recommendations from academicians, government officials, and health care experts to improve the safety of patients under their care. Ever since the Institute of Medicine published its report "To Err Is Human,"[3] there is a public imperative as well. Unfortunately, much of the response has been that of finger pointing and blame. Physicians, already under severe stress over liability insurance issues, have feared a disconnect, that is, admitting a mistake is tantamount to a lawsuit. The truth of course is that most medical errors are systems errors, not individual ones. The increasingly troubled relationship between the tort system and patient safety makes it apparent that one cannot be resolved without addressing the other.[4] Self-assessment of normative behaviors, assessment of interactive processes and procedures, maintenance of certification, and programs of lifelong learning are assuredly in order. In the name of safety, society must in turn create a protected no-fault environment in which errors may be identified and corrected without threat of litigation and with the sole goal of patient protection. Just as "first do no harm" is our oath as physicians, the right to safety is the first right in the women's health bill of rights.

NUMBER 2: FREEDOM FROM DOMESTIC AND SOCIOPOLITICAL VIOLENCE BOTH HERE AND THROUGHOUT THE WORLD

As specialists, obstetrician–gynecologists have brought the epidemic of violence against women in this country into national focus. The vigilance must continue, making sure that evey patient is asked: "Are you safe?" "Is anyone hurting you?" Physicians cannot truly be vigilant, however, if concerns are limited to clinical practice. We must also look at what we can do in society to reduce the potential for violence.

Social and economic inequalities contribute to increased violence and abuse against women, a fact that has been documented world-round.[5] We must recognize and remember that when we vote, campaign, or espouse any social legislation or candidate, we can and should examine how it may impact the ongoing violence against women in our world.

As an example, data show that women in this country are disproportionately victims of firearm homicides. A recent analysis of 25 high-income nations shows the United States to be an outlier, having the highest level of household gun ownership of any nation studied. And while only 32% of the females studied came from the United States, the United States accounted for 70% of the female homicides and 84% of female homicides by firearms.[6]

Addressing issues that contribute to societal violence throughout the world is part and parcel of health policy. We must look at the price that women in the war-torn countries of the world are now paying and have paid throughout history. The deaths, rapes, undiagnosed and untreated sexually transmitted infections, forced pregnancies, loss of family and home, and injuries have all taken an unacknowledged and often unreported toll on women's lives.

Fellows of the College must voice their concerns and stand up for women who cannot stand up for themselves. Who better to carry the banner than those who have dedicated themselves to the health and well-being of women?

NUMBER 3: APPROPRIATE AND EFFECTIVE INSURANCE COVERAGE

ACOG has worked long and hard to bring about universal health care coverage. Our efforts have been particularly directed toward maternal benefits and will continue to be a high priority in the year to come.

Similarly, seniors must be assured that Medicare will indeed cover the cost of their care and that they will not be marginalized because the government chooses not to provide for them. Reimbursement for services performed on women versus those same or analogous services performed on men are often inequitable. Such discrimination is inexcusable and hurts both women and the physicians who care for them.

We have other opportunities to promote appropriate insurance coverage for the truly disenfranchised: for the undocumented pregnant woman, for the uninsured working poor mother, for the physically and mentally disabled, for the morbidly obese patient whose insurance refuses to recognize obesity as a medical entity, for the elderly who choose palliative services in their final days, and for the chronically ill who require supportive therapies when cures for their extraordinary and life-long morbidities have eluded the medical establishment. Universal health care coverage and access are a woman's right.

NUMBER 4: EQUITY IN GENDER-SPECIFIC RESEARCH

Gender equity in research has always been an ACOG priority. Research protocols have come a long way from the days when female participation was denied, either because women might become pregnant or because they were "inherently biologically unstable." The inclusion of women in clinical trials, a policy of the National Institutes of Health since 1986, has been implemented slowly and incrementally amidst significant political maneuvering.[7]

As physicians continue to advocate for equitable funding and the prioritization of women's health research, we also must be instrumental in defining that research. This includes a multitude of unresolved questions in reproduction, in gynecologic disease, and even the dosing of pharmacological therapies as modified by the metabolism of the aging.[8,9] Equity in the allocation of research is a basic woman's right that all must embrace.

NUMBER 5: FREEDOM FROM DISCRIMINATION BASED ON GENDER, GENDER IDENTITY, SEXUAL ORIENTATION, AGE, RACE, OR ETHNICITY

According to the U.S. Census Bureau, by 2030 women will represent 53% of the population and 81% of the population over the age of 85 will be female. These women will be more likely to live alone and be poorer than older men.[10] Thus, as health problems increase with age, they will occur at a time when many women have fewer resources.

By 2050, 47% of the U.S. female population will be members of racial or ethnic minorities. The racial disparities in health outcomes for these women will likely increase rather than improve. While mortality rates for women are decreasing overall, there is an increasing gap between those rates and the rates for minority women, independent of risk behaviors and health care access. However, the lack of equal opportunities in education and employment for women—particularly women of color—results in discrimination via disproportionate exposures to environmental toxins, dangers, and risks.[11] Advocacy for change demands a clearer understanding of these sociopolitical dynamics. The Institute of Medicine, in a comprehensive treatise on the issues of racial inequity, examined the effects of racism and racial biases on the U.S. health care system.[12] Their recommendations include increased awareness, regulatory and policy interventions, and health system changes. Issues of discrimination based on sexual orientation often stem from lack of knowledge or information and have no place in the care of patients. Increasingly, physicians groups such as ACOG are educating and addressing issues germane to sensitive and appropriate care for all women, regardless of gender identity. Physicians must be increasingly aware of the diversity of patients for whom we care and support progressive changes to guarantee the right of all women to be free from discrimination.

NUMBER 6: SOCIOECONOMIC AND POLITICAL EQUALITY

Socioeconomic status is a predictor of health. This fact is unchallenged in the public health literature. Socioeconomic inequalities for women are well documented. Eight percent of all families living in poverty consist of single women and their children.[13] Many heads of these households are women (with children) on public assistance whose income doesn't cover expenses; only about one-third are ever extricated from poverty under the current welfare system.[14] Women in general have double responsibilities: their jobs in the workplace and their roles in the home.[15] While some women choose this dual role, others have no choice. Dual roles result in working women earning about 30% less than their male counterparts.[16] Indeed, men often earn more than women for similar occupations even when women have higher educational levels. There remain significant disparities between men and women in income and job prestige. Depression, lack of job satisfaction, and inability to support family needs economically and socially are common ramifications with all of their health consequences.[17]

Such facts are important to society in terms of law and public policy, and they are important to us as physicians because low-income status along with subordinate occupations and lack of socioeconomic prestige affects growth and development prenatally, throughout childhood, into young adulthood, and beyond. In short, socioeconomic issues shape health, health habits, and health decision-making.[18] Social equality is a health goal. It won't eliminate disparity, but it will contribute to further understanding of women's health determinants and protection of women's health status. Physicians must face these inequalities and work to empower women to have control of their own lives.

NUMBER 7: ACCESSIBLE, AFFORDABLE, AND SAFE FORMS OF CONTRACEPTION INCLUDING POSTCOITAL CONTRACEPTIVES

The care of the pregnant woman must include taking measures to insure that every pregnancy is a wanted and planned pregnancy. It means addressing the issues of sexual politics, rape, forced conception, and forced abandonment of contraception. It requires recognizing that an unintended or unwanted pregnancy can happen to anyone. The issues surrounding the decision to terminate such a pregnancy are profoundly divisive. Obstetrician–gynecologists cannot be less than engaged and cannot believe that the only entity that resonates in this debate is the embryo or fetus. The woman counts, too.

As intelligent and compassionate individuals, physicians may agree to disagree about abortion. As a profession, the only way not to become mired in an irresolvable debate about when life begins and the moral constructs of abortion is to give women the ability to protect themselves, physically, emotionally, and with appropriate contraceptive measures. The only way to prevent abortions is to prevent the pregnancy in the first place with long-term, carefully constructed family planning programs.

Teaching and advocating abstinence is certainly an important component of the prevention of unintended pregnancy. But it does not serve our young women well to teach abstinence ONLY, without concomitant education about sexually transmitted infections, contraceptive options, sexual assault, and empowerment to take reproductive control.

Accidents and coercion happen, and postcoital contraception must be made available to reduce unintended pregnancy and abortion rates. It is a travesty that the United States has the highest rate of teen pregnancy in the industrialized world. Teens in particular need affordable postcoital contraception. Members of ACOG must continue to support the Executive Board policy to seek over-the-counter status for emergency contraceptives.

NUMBER 8: FREEDOM OF REPRODUCTIVE CHOICE

Reproductive choice, despite the current vernacular, is not limited to the decision to carry a pregnancy or to have an abortion. A woman's right to choose abortion is only one aspect of control over reproductive choice. Reproductive choice is a much broader issue.

There are many reproductive choices that are denied to women. For example, choice may be denied through discrimination against women who are incarcerated, women who are single, or women who choose women as their partners. Women's health care providers must be alert to their own ethical dilemmas. How do obstetrician-gynecologists care for the woman seeking fertility services who is HIV positive, or indigent, or 55 years old?

Other questions remain. Is it fair for a gag rule to have been perpetrated on poor women in the United States during the first Bush administration, or on women internationally in the current administration? Is it fair to pay for Viagra and not for oral contraceptives? Reproductive choice is complex and must rest in the hands of the women herself. It is she, after all, who bears the risk and the ultimate responsibility for the birth of her children. We must speak out and reach out to support women's rights to reproductive choice.

NUMBER 9: CULTURALLY SENSITIVE EDUCATION AND INFORMATION

How to best and most effectively communicate with patients is not addressed simply. This country continues to be a haven for the world's displaced populations. The result is tremendous cultural diversity of the patient population. Patients are diverse not only in genetic predispositions and racially determined risks but also in how they understand and process both disease and cure. This diversity affects their access to physicians and their ability to comprehend the care that is offered when access is available.

Fourteen million Americans are not able to speak English proficiently. In addition, almost 1 in 5 American women cannot read and 1 in 4 are functionally illiterate.[18] Many more women do not understand written instructions either from physicians or in pharmaceutical inserts. They cannot interpret lab tests and do not know what they are signing in terms of Medicare rights or Health Insurance Portability and Accountability Act disclosures, let alone surgical procedure consents.

Our endeavors to address this goal are well served by the Agency for Healthcare Research and Quality as it continues its efforts to develop evidence-based strategies for the improvement of health outcomes across diverse populations.[19]

NUMBER 10: ACCESS TO HEALING ENVIRONMENTS AND INTEGRATIVE APPROACHES TO HEALTH AND HEALTH CARE

The patient whom we treat may or may not be cured, but there must be opportunity for each one to be healed. We may have medical knowledge about her disease, but frequently do not understand her illness. We have modalities for relief of pain, but may not be able to help her cope with nor understand her suffering.

What are the differences between curing and healing, disease and illness, and pain and suffering? Curing, disease, and pain are the traditional concerns of the physician. But the other half of each dyad—healing, illness, and suffering—represent the perspective of the patient and her family. A patient does not come to us and say, "I am diseased." No, she says, "I am ill." Similarly, while physicians focus on pain and pain management, the broader concern of suffering represents the social, emotional, psychological, financial, and spiritual ramifications of illness, both for the patient and for those who care for and about her. Cure has been the dominant focus of our training. But the truth is that sometimes, to do so is not in

our power. We all have patients in whom the surgery or therapy fails. But health and quality of life are about more than cure; they are also very much about caring and healing.[20]

As the population ages and is beset by chronic disease, physicians must begin to look at what heals patients and how an environment can be created that speaks to the harmony and balance between mind, body, and spirit. It is time to commit research into identifying and enhancing the components of an optimal healing environment.[21] Medicine cannot advance if it attends only to pathogenesis as a road to the understanding of treatment and disease. We must seek further understanding of and research in salutogenesis—the process of health and healing.[22] This tenth item in my Women's Health Bill of Rights addresses the very basis for the quality of life that we all pursue.

In conclusion, I am asking a great deal of all of us. I know that we have precious little time to spend with our patients. In the clinical setting, we cannot possibly accomplish all of these things single-handedly. Nevertheless, I am asking you to become political and to be advocates for women in venues that are not traditionally a part of our role as health care providers.

As in Togo, West Africa, health care in the United States will not succeed if physicians maintain the normative biophysical view of medicine and fail to participate in the social and political system. We must face the fact that we are dealing with women who often have limited power, even over their own lives. We must redefine the frontiers, redefine care, and redefine advocacy. By adopting this Women's Health Bill of Rights, we bring together the two most basic tenets of ACOG: that in this world, physicians matter . . . and in this world, women matter.

REFERENCES

1. Women's Health Office–McGill University. Women's health in obstetrics and gynecology: their relationship and suggestions for a practical integration. J Soc Obstet Gynecol Can 1996;18:589–98.

2. Statement of Policy: Access to Women's Health Care. Washington, DC: American College of Obstetricians and Gynecologists. 2003.

3. Institute of Medicine. To err is human. Washington, DC: National Academy Press; 2001.

4. Mello MM, Brennan TA. Deterrence of medical errors: theory and evidence for malpractice reform. Texas Law Review 2002;80:1595–637.

5. Adler N, Boyce T, Chesney M, Cohen S, Folkman S, Kahn RL, et al. Socioeconomic status and health: the challenge of the gradient. Am J Psychol 1994;49:15–24.

6. Hemenway D, Shinoda-Tagawa T, Miller M. Firearm availability and female homicide victimization rates among 25 populous high-income countries. J Am Med Womens Assoc 2002;57:100–4.

7. U.S. General Accounting Office, National Institutes of Health: Problems in implementing policy on women in study populations. Statement of Mark V. Nadel, Associate Director of National and Public Health Issues, Human Resources Division, before the Subcommittee on Health and the Environment, Committee on Energy and Commerce, U.S. House of Representatives (GAO/T-HRD-90-80), June 18, 1990.

8. Lazarou J, Pomeranz H, Corey PN. Incidence of adverse drug reactions in hospitalized patients: a meta-analysis of prospective studies. JAMA 1998;279: 1200–5.

9. Cohen JS. Do standard doses of frequently prescribed drugs cause preventable adverse effects in women? J Am Med Womens Assoc 2002;57:105–10.

10. Rowland Hogue CJ. Gender, Race and Class: From Epidemiologic Association to Etiologic Hypotheses. In: Goldman M, Hatch M, editors. Women and Health. San Diego (CA): Academic Press; 2000.

11. Williams DR. Race and health: basic questions emerging directions. Ann Epidemiol 1997;7:322–2.

12. Institute of Medicine. Unequal treatment-confronting racial and ethnic disparities in healthcare. Smedley BD, Stith AY, Nelson AR, editors; 2003. Available at www.nap.edu/books/030908265X/html/.

13. Williams DR, Collins C. U.S. socioeconomic and racial differences in health: patterns and explanations. Annu Rev Soc 1995;21:349–86.

14. U.S. Bureau of the Census. Populations by age, sex, race and origin: 2000. Washington, DC: The Bureau; 2001.

15. McGuire GM, Reskin B. Authority hierarchies at work: the impacts of race and sex. Gender Soc 1993;7:487–506.

16. Burkhauser R, Duncan GJ. Economic risks of gender roles: income loss and life events over the life course. Soc Sci Q1998;70:3–23.

17. Tennstedt S, Cafferata GL, Sullivan L. Depression among caregivers of impaired elders. J Aging Health 1992;4:58–76.

18. Baker DW, Parker RM, Williams MV, et al. The relationship of patient reading ability to self-reported health and health services. Am J Public Health 1997;87:1027–30.

19. www.ahcpr.gov/research.

20. Lerner M. Choices in healing: integrating the best of conventional and complementary approaches to cancer. Cambridge (MA): MIT Press; 1994.

21. Jonas WB, Chez RA, Duffy B, Strand D. Investigating the impact of optimal healing environments. Altern Ther Health Med 2003;9:58–64.

22. Malterun K, Hollnagel H. Talking with women about personal health resources in general practice: key questions about salutogenesis. Scand J Prim Health Care 1998;16:66–71.

Gender Role Stressors and Women's Health

Patti L. Watkins and Diane Whaley

WOMEN'S HEALTH PROBLEMS

Unarguably, significant gender differences exist in the experience of health problems. For instance, morbidity rates of musculoskeletal and connective tissue diseases such as osteoporosis are much greater for women. Women, more often than men, also experience neurologic disorders, including migraine headaches, as well as psychiatric disorders, particularly affective, anxiety, and eating disorders (Litt, 1993). In the keynote address at the Society of Behavioral Medicine's annual meeting, Chesney (1997) implored those assembled to add domestic violence to the list of women's health problems. The Midcourse Review of the Healthy People 2000 goals (U.S. Department of Health & Human Services [USDHHS], 1995) acknowledged that "[w]omen are frequent targets of both physical and sexual assault often perpetrated by spouses, intimate partners, or others known to them" (p. 60). Unfortunately, this report also states that homicides, weapons-related violent deaths, and assault injuries have increased since 1990. As such, women account for nearly two thirds of the medical visits and are recipients of most medications prescribed (Hoffman, 1995).

Chronic disease risk factors, such as smoking, have increased dramatically among women in recent years (Litt, 1993). Furthermore, the USDHHS (1995) reported that although the general public has made progress toward smoking cessation goals, the inverse is true for pregnant women and women without a high school education. Obesity rates have also increased since health objectives were established in 1990, especially for women. The Surgeon General's Report on Physical Activity and Health (USDHHS, 1996) implicated women's relative lack of exercise in explanation of this trend. Gender differences in mortality rates are fast disappearing as cardiovascular disease (CVD) is now the leading cause of death among women as well as men. Cancer mortality rates are also roughly equivalent, with women's lung cancer death rate rising rapidly over the past 30 years. Finally, women are developing AIDS at a faster pace than men (Litt, 1993).

Given these patterns, it is little wonder that women consistently perceive themselves as having worse health than men (Verbrugge, 1989). Although women currently live approximately 7 years longer than men, the quality of their lives may be vastly diminished. Verbrugge (1989) contended that gender differences in health status transcend biological predispositions, resulting more from sociocultural forces such as well-documented employment inequities (Amott & Matthaie, 1996). Contributing to the problem, women are also less likely than men to have adequate health insurance coverage (Stanton & Gallant, 1995). Indeed, Anson, Paran, Neumann, and Chernichovsky (1993) found that gender differences in health perceptions disappeared when they controlled for risks embedded in the social construction of gender and gender roles, leading the authors to suggest that women's socialization results in less successful coping with the "inevitable stressors faced in human life" (p. 426). A feminist perspective, however, might argue that the stressors for women are not inevitable. Rather, many are socially constructed, and perpetuated through existing power structures.

In summary, contemporary women are suffering and dying from disorders that the lay public, along with the medical profession itself, have long considered diseases of men—and in the case of AIDS, gay men. Additionally, women experience debilitating, although not imminently life-threatening, medical problems more than men. In conjunction with relatively greater psychological distress, deteriorating health habits, and frequent victimization, women's quality of life may be severely compromised as they negotiate their life spans. The next section explores the influence of gender roles on these problems.

Gender Roles: Interpersonal Communication

Women interact with the health-care system differently than men do, with increased visits and different types of complaints. In turn, the health-care system responds to women and men in a different fashion, often to the detriment of women's health. Studies have shown that medical practitioners treat CVD less aggressively in women relative to men. In fact, across conditions, treatment protocols are based on a male model of medicine, with women's health problems viewed as deviations from a male-defined norm (Hoffman, 1995). Lee and Sasser-Cohen (1996) contended that the medical profession has, in fact, pathologized women's normal biological processes and body structure.

In a recent study, Chiaramonte and Friend (1997) asked medical students to review cases of women and men with either only symptoms of heart disease or heart disease symptoms accompanied by anxiety. When presented with unambiguous cases, students were able to detect heart disease in both genders. However, when presented with cases evidencing both cardiac and anxiety symptoms, they correctly detected heart disease among the male cases, referring them to cardiologists. Conversely, they more often misdiagnosed heart disease among the female cases, referring them instead to psychologists. Advanced medical students were more likely to make this error, suggesting that medical school training serves to increase gender biases in diagnostic and treatment decisions. Russo, Denious, Keita, and Koss (1997) asserted that battered women also escape detection when they are in

medical settings. Like women with CVD symptoms, they are likely to receive psychiatric diagnoses along with tranquilizing medication.

Communication of diagnostic information and treatment recommendations by medical practitioners represents another area of concern for the female patient. Smith (1996) saw physicians' failure to interact with patients in a courteous, informative fashion as a breach of ethics, rather than a case of poor "bedside manner." In her view, most medical encounters constitute interviews in which patient-initiated questions are discouraged, thereby establishing the practitioner's position of power. Such interactions prevent patients from taking charge of their health. Smith contrasts this to a model in which practitioners might interact with patients as participants in a shared project, with mutual understanding as the goal. As such, patients should have the right "to speak, to question, to challenge, and to express themselves" (p. 202). Smith contends that women, particularly women of color and those of lower socioeconomic status (SES), receive less information than male patients. In a survey of Black women who had been physically and sexually abused, Russo et al. (1997) found that lower income participants, indeed, perceived physicians as "patronizing and unhelpful" (p. 340). Although the FGRS [Feminine Gender Role Stress] construct suggests that women may be less inclined to assert themselves in such situations, Smith notes that practitioners dub women "difficult patients" when they ask questions during the medical interview. A female patient "may be taken as hostile, uncooperative, and confrontative, whereas a male patient might be viewed as rational and actively involved in his own treatment" (p. 194). Roter and Hall (1992) disagreed, noting that in some studies, female patients received relatively more information from practitioners. In fact, women's communication styles may make them "more savvy users of their time with doctors" (p. 44). These authors admit that exploration of gender differences in patient–practitioner communication is a relatively new endeavor, with many questions remaining unanswered at this point.

Indirect support for Smith's (1996) claims, however, may come from studies of individuals who present to medical settings with symptoms of anxiety and depression. A number of researchers (e.g., Agras, 1993) agree that these patients, predominantly women, leave the medical setting with a limited understanding of their complaints. Watkins, Nock, Champion, and Lidren (1996) found that practitioners typically spent less than 5 minutes explaining diagnostic information to individuals with panic disorder (PD). In only a few cases were patients actually provided with an accurate diagnosis. Rather, they received a variety of vague explanations such as "some strange flu" and "hidden problems" (p. 180). One participant remarked, "First few times he suggested it was 'just' stress, then, later, after a few months, he said it was depression, then later, without much concern, he suggested it was anxiety" (p. 184). This broad array of unclear explanations resulted in low levels of patient understanding and satisfaction, perhaps best summarized by one patient's experience of "resentment" toward the practitioner "for not being as sympathetic and respectful of this being a real and true experience for me" (p. 184). Watkins et al. (1996) found that participants rarely received referrals, although most received pharmacological treatment. Compared to cognitive-behavioral therapy (CBT) for PD, medications have a higher relapse rate (Gould, Otto, & Pollack, 1995). This difference may be due to the superior ability of CBT to enhance self-efficacy, the belief that one can successfully manage a situation, in this case panic attacks (PA) and the circumstances that surround them. Finally, the high cost of medications compared to various forms of CBT (Gould et al., 1995) may present a greater problem for women whose economic resources are generally less than those of their male peers.

Roter and Hall (1992) agreed that physicians often substitute medications for effective communication. In terms of gender differences, [it was] observed that physicians prescribe psychotropic medications to women relatively more often and that these prescriptions extend for longer periods of time than those provided for men. She asserts that medicating women without attempting to impart coping skills, or more importantly, to resolve the inequities that women suffer at home and in the workplace, equates to oppression. This practice prompts women to nurture others at the expense of their own health. When physicians prescribe psychotropic medications, they may be abetting dysfunctional, possibly abusive, social arrangements as well as fostering women's self-blame.

Practitioner communication most assuredly warrants further research. Russo et al. (1997) suggested that such work address diversity issues within, as well as across, gender. Their findings also suggest that various presenting complaints may elicit specific types of problem behavior from practitioners. In their study, women who had been sexually abused reported that physicians had acted in sexually inappropriate ways toward them. Concurrent examination of practitioners' gender might enhance understanding of communication problems in the medical setting. Hall, Irish, Roter, Ehrlich, and Miller (1994) conducted a study in which they found female physicians to be more nurturant, expressive, and interpersonally oriented than males. This, along with Gross's (1992) finding that male physicians encounter more interpersonal difficulties with patients, aligns with the concepts of gender role stressors outlined here. Although organized efforts are under way to improve the communication skills of medical practitioners (e.g., Levinson & Roter, 1993), many Americans, especially women, are turning to treatment strategies that minimize practitioner contact. . . .

REFERENCES

Agras, W. S. (1993). The diagnosis and treatment of panic disorder. *Annual Review of Medicine, 4,* 39–51.

Ammott, T., & Matthaie, J. (1996). *Race, gender, and work: A multicultural economic history of women in the United States.* Boston: South End Press.

Anson, O., Paran, E., Neumann, L., & Chernichovsky, D. (1993). Gender differences in health perceptions and their predictors. *Social Science and Medicine, 36,* 419–427.

Chesney, M. A. (1997, March). *Unanswered challenges to behavioral medicine: Broadening the agenda.*

Paper presented at the Society of Behavioral Medicine annual meeting, San Francisco.

Chiaramonte, G., & Friend, R. (1997, March). *Do medical schools reinforce gender bias in diagnosing CHD?* Paper presented at the annual meeting of the Society of Behavioral Medicine, San Francisco.

Gould, R. A., Otto, M. W., & Pollack, M. H. (1995). A meta-analysis of treatment outcome for panic disorder. *Clinical Psychology Review, 15,* 819–844.

Gross, E. B. (1992). Gender differences in physician stress. *Journal of the American Medical Women's Association, 47,* 107–112.

Hall, J. A., Irish, J. T., Roter, D. L., Ehrlich, C. M., & Miller, L. (1994). Gender in medical encounters: An analysis of physician and patient communication in a primary care setting. *Health Psychology, 13,* 384–392.

Hoffman, E. (1995). *Our health, our lives: A revolutionary approach to health care for women.* New York: Simon & Schuster.

Lee, J., & Sasser-Cohen, J. (1996). *Blood stories: Menarche and the politics of the female body in contemporary U.S. society.* New York: Routledge.

Levinson, W., & Roter, D. (1993). The effects of two continuing medical education programs on communication skills of practicing primary care physicians. *Journal of General Internal Medicine, 8,* 318–324.

Litt, I. (1993). Health issues for women in the 1990s. In S. Matteo (Ed.), *American women in the nineties: Today's critical issues* (pp. 139–157). Boston: Northeastern University Press.

Roter, D. L., & Hall, J. A. (1992). *Doctors talking with patients/patients talking with doctors: Improving communication in medical visits.* Westport, CT: Auburn House.

Russo, N. F., Denious, J. E., Keita, G. P., & Koss, M. P. (1997). Intimate violence and Black women's health. *Women's Health: Research on Gender, Behavior, and Policy, 3,* 335–348.

Smith, J. F. (1996). Communicative ethics in medicine: The physician–patient relationship. In S. M. Wolf (Ed.), *Feminism and bioethics: Beyond reproduction* (pp. 184–215). New York: Oxford University Press.

Stanton, A. L., & Gallant, S. J. (1995). Psychology of women's health: Challenges for the future. In A. L. Stanton & S. J. Gallant (Eds.), *The psychology of women's health: Progress and challenges in research and application* (pp. 567–582). Washington, DC: American Psychological Association.

U.S. Department of Health and Human Services (1995). *Healthy people 2000: Midcourse review and 1995 revisions.* Washington, DC: Public Health Service.

U.S. Department of Health and Human Services (1996). *Physical activity and health: A report of the Surgeon General.* Atlanta, GA. USDHHS, Centers for Disease Prevention and Health Promotion.

Verbrugge, L. (1989). The twain meet: Empirical explanations of sex differences in health and mortality. *Journal of Health and Social Behavior, 30,* 282–304.

Watkins, P. L., & Lee, J. (1997). A feminist perspective on panic disorder and agoraphobia: Etiology and treatment. *Journal of Gender, Culture & Health, 2,* 65–87.

Watkins, P. L., Nock, C., Champion, J., & Lidren, D. M. (1996). Practitioner–patient communication in the presentation of panic symptoms. *Mind/Body Medicine, 4,* 177–189.

R E A D I N G **48**

Eyes on the Prize

Selden McCurrie

On July 29th I was initiated into a vast unwilling sisterhood—I was diagnosed with breast cancer. . . .

. . .

"I'm sorry, Selden." My doctor's husky voice was inordinately gentle. "You have cancer in both breasts. The left breast shows extensive ductal carcinoma in situ [DCIS], almost three centimeters. The right is infiltrating ductal carcinoma, around a centimeter. They're both highly treatable, though I'd like it better if the right wasn't infiltrating. I've taken the liberty of making an appointment with a surgeon for you. I'll fax you the biopsy results."

. . .

[After my diagnosis I tried] to assemble an emotionally charged clinical jigsaw puzzle, but the pieces kept multiplying. Lumpectomies vs. mastectomies. Mastectomies were becoming a very real option. Mastectomies without reconstruction. "Reconstruction" was a term I had come to loathe for signifying that mastectomy was the ultimate de-construction. Implants were out because of my track record of allergies. . . . Reconstruction would always be an option. Nonetheless, I called our health insurance companies. If I wanted reconstruction at a later date, it would be covered but would require a letter of medical necessity from my doctor. I pondered that—letter of medical necessity. Losing your breasts to mastectomies wasn't enough on its own? What would make it a *necessity?* Nervous breakdown? Severe back problems?

For now, my choice was mastectomies without reconstruction vs. lumpectomies [to just remove the tumors]. . . . Statistics, studies, and medical opinions couldn't put a human face on mastectomies, so I wanted to go straight to the source. Early on, I had started going to a breast cancer support group at The Wellness Community. I felt an instant bond of sisterhood when I walked into the room.

These were the human faces behind the statistics. There were five women there that first day and I listened in awe as we went around the circle and told our stories. Theirs were the faces of choices: lumpectomy with radiation, lumpectomy with chemotherapy, mastectomy with reconstruction, and recurrence. Hope. These women were the embodiment of coping and hope. Yet there was no face for the choice of mastectomy *without* reconstruction.

I had put the word out that I was facing this decision and wanted to talk with women who had had double mastectomies—bilateral mastectomy in medical jargon. I discovered that this is the quietest group within this sisterhood to which I had been unwillingly initiated. There were women out there, granted not a lot, who were

unreconstructed, but they were silent. I prayed for help. My prayers were answered.

Alice, a friend of a sister-in-law, called from her family's beach house one Sunday afternoon. Like me, she'd had cancer in both breasts. Unlike me, she had been a DD-cup before her mastectomies. She had forgone reconstruction. What's it like? I had asked.

"It's more comfortable than before and in fact, my back problems have gotten better," she said with a trace of a Boston accent. "I decided that I had to be consistent—either I was going to wear the prostheses all the time or not. So when I leave the house, I have them on. I hated the first prostheses and I loathed the mastectomy bras. I'm happier now that I've found this sports bra. It took some trial and error, so be sure you get measured by a certified fitter.

"I've lost part of my sexuality—my breasts, but my husband has been great. It will take you some time to get used to it."

Susan. I never knew how she found me—she left a message on my voice-mail. She told me she was a tall, athletic woman, and had also had a bilateral mastectomy without reconstruction.

"I was an A-cup before the surgery and now I can choose. For example, today, I wore B-cup prostheses, but tonight I'm going out and I'll wear C-cups. My insurance pays for a pair every year, so I've got several pairs. I like the ones that stick to your skin. They feel like a part of my body. I don't even think about it anymore," she said in a soft voice.

Jan, a geek like me—a computer project manager for a Fortune 500 company—also called one evening.

"I was small," Jan said. "I didn't even wear prostheses for the first two years. Nobody ever noticed. In fact, one day at work I mentioned my mastectomies to a programmer in the next cube who was a lean, tall, marathon runner. We stood side by side and you couldn't tell the difference. She was muscular and flat. I was short and flat.

"Then my husband started telling me my posture was changing. So I told him that for Christmas, I wanted a pair of boobs. I hit a department store that stocked prostheses and bought a pair.

It did make a difference in my posture, and now I even wear them around the house."

. . .

Three surgeons were steering me toward bilateral mastectomy. Only the oncologist had said the survival odds at five years were the same for lumpectomies as mastectomies. A Mayo Clinic paper in Medline had turned up a slightly different outlook at ten years in favor of mastectomies. All four doctors had mentioned the hereditary potential of my cancer. In addition to my mother's breast cancer, my father had colon cancer at age seventy-eight. So had two of his brothers. I had had a colonoscopy in January so I knew I was clean. For now.

Back to assembling my clinical puzzle. My emotions nibbled at the edges of the pieces, making a good fit difficult. Where did my feelings go—in the middle or on the edges of the puzzle? And what were my feelings? Every time I thought about a bilateral mastectomy, I felt a sickening thud in the pit of my stomach. Yet, intellectually, I was leaning in that direction.

Snap. A genetic piece of the puzzle. My Medline queries had turned up papers implicating the hereditary aspects of breast cancer, which all my physicians had discussed with me.

Snap. A surgical piece of the puzzle. The surgeons who looked at my films, when pushed for an opinion on lumpectomies, had said it would be difficult to remove the entire duct. They could take the tumor out, but because of my dense, fibrous breasts could not be certain they would get the entire duct. I worried about what they could not see. The tumor was growing in a duct that had never been biopsied.

Snap. An anatomical piece of the puzzle. Breast cancer, especially DCIS, follows the duct. The oncologist said if I opted for lumpectomies, she would want to irradiate both breasts. Irradiation of my dense, heavy, elongated breasts, even with the best technology, carried a small chance of setting me up for potential heart disease. My mother had died of a heart attack—her seventh. I knew there were advances in radiation treatments, but I recalled a friend who had undergone radiation for his Hodgkin's disease, only to die twenty years later from leukemia. With mastectomies, at least I could duck radiation if the cancer wasn't in the lymph nodes.

Snap. A chemotherapy piece of the puzzle. We went to see the oncologist—a deceptively gentle woman whose businesslike demeanor hid a scientist's analytical mind. I walked away from her convinced she never forgot a single thing you ever told her. Despite multiple drug allergies and my complex medical history of chemical sensitivities, she was certain she could manage chemotherapy if I needed it. This hurdle was still an unknown— my final pathology report would determine whether or not I needed chemotherapy. I was operating under the assumption that I would. If not, then it would be a pleasant surprise.

Snap. A radiological piece of the puzzle. The radiologist who had diagnosed me said that only 40 percent of DCIS showed on mammograms. Who knew what else was cooking in my breast ducts?

Snap. A pathological piece of the puzzle. Most of what I read indicated that the woman most likely to get breast cancer was a woman who *had* breast cancer. If I chose lumpectomies, what were my odds of recurrence with cancer already in both breasts?

So much for medical and scientific opinions. Where did the human factors fit? How could I gauge what it would be like to lose my breasts? How would I know unless I had mastectomies? Would it be comfortable? Would I turn into the Hunchback of Notre Dame? If I had lumpectomies, would the cancer come back? Could I live with the stress of the three-month, six-month interval mammograms and ultrasounds? Could I face additional surgery? Did I want to gamble and take that chance? How would I handle all of this? How was I going to learn how to be a cancer patient?

I sat on the screened-in porch, in total darkness. . . . I now owned my cancer, my enemy, and knew it well, but decided it would not *own* me. . . .

. . .

The painful realization dawned: bilateral mastectomy was my best option, but I wanted to see my radiologist one more time to ask about lumpectomies. I would have to live with my decision a long time. The only way I would have peace was to know all my questions had been answered.

"So what have you decided after your travels?" she said, walking into the examining room.

"I'm thinking about lumpectomies. Tell me how hard detection would be, given the way I scar?" I asked.

She clipped my mammograms on the light box, sighed, and turned to catch my eyes.

"If you want lumpectomies, we're here for you 24/7. We'd do mammograms and ultrasounds every six months for the rest of your life. But I want to tell you about a patient I had like you with cancer in both breasts. She chose lumpectomies and had chemo. She was fine until she developed ovarian cancer a few years later. Once again, she had surgery and did chemo. A few years after that, she developed breast cancer again, and even with careful monitoring, by the time we caught it, it was advanced. She died a few months later. Now I'm not saying that would be you. We can treat this breast cancer, but it's your potential for another breast cancer that I worry about. It's a chance you have to be willing to take."

"Thanks," I said with a sigh because she had crystallized what I had been afraid of. "I'm going to have a bilateral mastectomy."

The decision was made. I was ready to tell the family and friends who had been calling since the news of my diagnosis. I debated about going public with the mastectomies, but I decided if by being open, I could help one woman, even if it was through word of mouth, it would be worth it.

I told my brother-in-law one afternoon when he called. "You've got a great pair, but they ain't worth dying over," was his succinct response.

. . .

All too quickly, the time before surgery passed and suddenly it was the night before. My surgery was scheduled for 2:00 p.m. on September 3—five years and one day to the day my father had died.

By now, my anxiety had channeled into "what ifs?" Ever prepared, I keyed in a one-page list of instructions for my friend Abby, who would wait with Sam [author's husband] during the surgery and then stay with me in the hospital. My cousin Amy was coming from Alabama and would stay until the surgery was over.

The years of experience in information processing showed in my list. It was a decision tree of "if-then" statements. If the surgery goes well, stop here. If the surgery doesn't go well, call Sam's brother—he can be here in three hours, then call my shrink—here's her emergency number, here's the phone number of a friend who is also a shrink if you can't get my shrink, and by the way, here's a bottle of tranquilizers for Sam, if it's real bad.

"Take care of Sam, first. He's got to take care of me. I like to think the doctors will be looking after me," I told Abby as we talked one last time that night. "I left a twenty-dollar bill, so once surgery starts, go feed him. I've packed a kit bag for him—munchies and bottled water, but he'll need to eat. I'm leaving you my cell phone to make calls. Also, promise me you won't tell anybody if I wake up screaming in the recovery room, 'Put 'em back on!'"

There was one more thing left on my list that only my husband and I could do. Although reconstruction was out for the time being, I wanted to document my breasts. That way, down the road, if I wanted reconstruction, a plastic surgeon could see what the originals looked like.

I slipped my shirt off and my husband took pictures. Pictures from all angles—front, side, three-quarter profile. Grabbing a yardstick and standing with my back flat against the bathroom wall, we measured my D-cup breasts, both in a bra and without. From my back to my nipple was exactly twelve inches.

"I love your breasts," Sam said, hugging me when we finished. "But I love *you* so much more."

The next morning, the nurse handed me a pen. I opened my hospital gown and wrote "yes" on both breasts, careful not to come near the mark made earlier that would guide the surgeon to the sentinel lymph node. I remembered writing "no" on my mother's right breast seven years earlier. They couldn't make a mistake with me. I was going to lose both breasts. I was tempted to draw smiley frowns. I said goodbye to my breasts.

A few minutes later, as I climbed on the operating table, I prayed for strength. When the anesthesiologist injected something into my IV line, I closed my eyes. My last conscious thought was: it all does end in the blink of an eye.

They tell me I woke up in the recovery room wailing, "Nodes?" "No nodes," was the response. The wonder drug I'd been given didn't just mask pain but made you forget it. "Nodes?" I couldn't remember from one second to the next. "No nodes?" It finally registered. The sentinel node biopsy had shown my lymph nodes were clean.

. . .

Three days after surgery, I couldn't resist peeling back the edge of a bandage for a peek at where my right breast had been. My breast was replaced by a long row of silver, surgical staples. It looked exactly like a zipper.

I sniffed as I pushed the bandage back in place. No deodorant and I was ripe. I had not had a shower or bath since the morning before my surgery. My hair was so oily even the cats were trying to clean it.

I healed and passed the days. I was so grateful just to be alive that, for the time being, the loss of my breasts seemed insignificant. I had jumped one hurdle in this race—surgery. The next would come with the pathology results.

A week after surgery and it was time for the drains to come out. I felt like a caged animal that had finally been freed. I had not wanted to leave the house until the drains were gone. I threw a shirt on over my T-shirt and drove myself to the doctor's office. Sam followed me there so he could go on to work.

It took just seconds for the surgeon to remove the drains, and I didn't feel a thing. We talked while he was doing it. It would still be a few more days before the final pathology would be in, but he explained the preliminary report.

He told me it was good. The infiltrating tumor in the right breast was only 1.2 centimeters (about the size of a dime) with no sign of vascular or lymphatic involvement, encircled by fibrosis—my body had started to wall it off with scar tissue.

The most frightening part of the pathology was the left breast. One phrase leapt out at me from the report: "A 2.3 centimeter by 1.8 centimeter by 1.8 ill-defined mass. . . . The mass shows finger-like

projections." Finger-like projections—tentacles holding an area about the size of a quarter. I shuddered, thinking DCIS had been reaching out to grasp the entire breast.

Walking out of the doctor's office, I decided to own my flatness. If traffic wasn't bad, I could just make the breast-cancer support group meeting at The Wellness Community. I was interested in seeing what other women thought.

"Am I flat or what?" I said as I walked into the meeting room.

"You look great," said the facilitator.

"How long has it been?" asked one of the women.

"A week," I said proudly.

"Lookin' good," said another.

"Nodes?" one woman questioned.

"No nodes," I said.

"Go, girl!" two women said in unison, as we made high-fives.

"You know, I think this is the first time I've seen the top of my stomach since puberty," I said, looking down and laughing.

They all laughed with me. Then one by one they offered their support and encouragement, knowing I was waiting for the final pathology report. The group was emotionally validating. It was safe. These women were further ahead of me in this race and had clocked many laps. I had only jumped the first hurdle: surgery. The next hurdle would come with the final pathology—the question of chemotherapy.

. . .

A week later, the final pathology report was in, and bleary-eyed at 8:00 a.m., Sam and I sat waiting in the oncologist's office.

"How are you healing?" the oncologist asked as she strode into the room.

"I'm good. So what's the verdict? Do I need chemo?" I took a deep breath.

"No," she said, smiling, looking very pleased. "We caught this early enough. It was a small tumor, slow growing, and highly hormone receptive. I want to put you on tamoxifen for five years."

"I'll do it," I said, thrilled. In my mind I sailed over a major hurdle.

So, what is it like losing your breasts? It was the unspoken question from friends and family. It's not uncomfortable, though it feels like my body's center of gravity has shifted. My posture has changed, but not to the shoulders-hunched-in "protective" posture that I had expected. I keep trying to tuck my pelvis under to compensate for the shift but those muscles won't cooperate. With or without prostheses, weighted or not, I think I stand straighter. I have to, and I make a conscious effort to monitor my posture, taking every opportunity to catch my reflection in a mirror. I refuse to become the Hunchback of Notre Dame.

. . .

Before surgery, I had bought a mastectomy bra and a weighted inexpensive pair of swimmer's B-cup prostheses. The bra's cups were seamed, not smooth like my regular bras, and it was heavily reinforced. A soft fabric was sewn to the back of the cup and would hold the prosthesis in place. It had been the best looking of the lot I had seen that day in the mastectomy boutique.

The first time I put on the bra and prostheses, I pulled on a cotton turtle neck, a staple of my fall wardrobe. Examining myself in the mirror, I decided my bust looked like something out of the 1950s—pointy breasts with bra seams showing through the cotton fabric. So not me. And what's worse, the prostheses I had bought were seamed and pointy, too. Their seams came together in the center of the prostheses to form a totally unnatural looking pseudo-erect nipple. Think June Cleaver with erect nipples wearing a tight sweater. Or today, Madonna in a cone bra. But I had bought the pointy guys so I was stuck with them—no returns on prostheses. I would have to make do until I could get a proper pair. Pointy nipples and all, I headed off to the nearest fabric shop. A little soft padding and a cover would work for the time being.

I had my sewing basket out and was working on a prosthesis when Sam came home that evening.

"Ah, my industrious little wife," he chuckled, bending down to kiss me. "Some women do needlepoint, you make boobs." He eyed the prosthesis and plopped down his laptop.

I wasn't shy about letting Sam see my incision scars; in fact, we made a point of checking them periodically in the beginning. The surgeon had been proud of his work—the scars were perfectly symmetrical. My battle scars. Of course, the scars are numb, just like the area under my right arm where the surgeon removed the sentinel node. Nerves were severed and may not grow back.

There's a long mirror in the foyer at the foot of the stairs in our house. Every time I go up or down the steps, I make a point of glancing in it. I check to see if I am hunched over and then correct my posture. The more time that passes since the surgery, the easier it is to maintain a good posture. There's a mirror in the antique sideboard in the kitchen, and I check my reflection there. Are the prostheses riding "high," up near my shoulders, or at an appropriate height?

The only problem has been the bras. I keep reminding myself that I had to experiment to find comfortable bras before the surgery. It's no different now. Problem is I can't tell if a bra works until I've worn it for a day or two, so returns are impossible. After spending fifty dollars for a "seamless, smooth cup" mastectomy bra that was miserably uncomfortable and rode up, I have forsworn mastectomy bras.

I have made an art of studying bras. I have found some that I like and that go with a new pair of prostheses. Rounder, softer, more natural. I'm comfortable.

It's now been several months since my surgery, and I have no regrets about my choice. It may seem odd, but I'm thankful for everything that has happened and especially for the women I've met. Breast cancer creates a powerful bond. I still tear up when I think of all the women who opened their hearts and their shirts to me, as I made a difficult decision.

I heard from one of my cousins recently who had a blip on her mammogram and was worried. She's scheduled for another mammogram and an ultrasound. I hope her doctor is just being hypervigilant because of my diagnosis. But if this turns out to be breast cancer, I envision myself offering her a hand at the starting line of the race, as so many women did for me. Side by side we'll run her first lap together, keeping our eyes on the prize.

The Fight Against Fistulas

Kari Browne

Imagine this scenario: A pregnant woman labors for days and nights without medical care, knowing her child is likely to be stillborn. As a result of the painfully traumatic labor, part of the mother's vaginal tissue is pressed between her pelvic bone and the baby's head. The blood supply to the tissue is cut off and the tissue dies, leaving a hole, or fistula, between the vagina and either the bladder or the rectum. She becomes incontinent and is banished from her home.

The first fistula hospital opened in New York City in 1850, back when fistulas were common in the United States. By 1895 the hospital had closed its doors because basic medical care and improved technology had made the disorder practically unknown.

But fistulas are still prevalent in the developing world, in part because of female genital mutilation. Although accurate counts are hard to come by in the regions where the problem is common, the United Nations estimates that about 2 million women live with obstetric fistulas, causing lifelong incontinence and terrible health problems. And because of the severe social stigma surrounding the condition—women with fistulas are considered "dirty" because of constant urine and/or stool leakage—their husbands typically abandon them and they have difficulty securing jobs.

Fortunately, fistulas are preventable, and when they occur they're treatable with a simple reconstructive operation that costs between $100 and $400. But most women suffering from fistulas don't have access to reconstructive surgery, or cannot afford it. Leading the fight to treat and end fistulas, Catherine Hamlin, M.D., co-founded the Addis Ababa Fistula Hospital (www.fistulahospital.org) in Ethiopia in 1974. Hamlin and her staff have treated more than 25,000 women.

"In Ethiopia alone, more than 8,500 women will suffer from new fistulas this year," Hamlin told an audience in Los Angeles during a recent visit. "We can help these women all over Africa and the developing world, but we need support."

A sign of growing support came in 2002 when the U.N. Population Fund announced its global "Campaign to End Fistula" in 18 developing countries. But when George W. Bush cut off $34 million earmarked for the population fund because of concern that it was promoting abortion, monies for preventing and treating fistulas also got cut. The "34 Million Friends" campaign (www.34millionfriends.org) was launched by Jane Roberts and Lois Abraham with the aim of getting people to donate $1 each to replace the money Bush cut. It has already funneled some funds to fistula treatment.

My Fight for Birth Control

Margaret Sanger (1931)

Mrs. Sacks was only twenty-eight years old; her husband, an unskilled worker, thirty-two. Three children, aged five, three and one, were none too strong nor sturdy, and it took all the earnings of the father and the ingenuity of the mother to keep them clean, provide them with air and proper food, and give them a chance to grow into decent manhood and womanhood.

Both parents were devoted to these children and to each other. The woman had become pregnant and had taken various drugs and purgatives, as advised by her neighbors. Then, in desperation, she had used some instrument lent to her by a friend. She was found prostrate on the floor amidst the crying children when her husband returned from work. Neighbors advised against the ambulance, and a friendly doctor was called. The husband would not hear of her going to a hospital, and as a little money had been saved in the bank a nurse was called and the battle for that precious life began.

It was in the middle of July. The three-room apartment was turned into a hospital for the dying patient. Never had I worked so fast, never so concentratedly as I did to keep alive that little mother. Neighbor women came and went during the day doing the odds and ends necessary for our comfort. The children were sent to friends and relatives, and the doctor and I settled ourselves to outdo the force and power of an outraged nature.

Never had I known such conditions could exist. July's sultry days and nights were melted into a torpid inferno. Day after day, night after night, I slept only in brief snatches, ever too anxious about the condition of that feeble heart bravely carrying on, to stay long from the bedside of the patient. . . .

At the end of two weeks recovery was in sight, and at the end of three weeks I was preparing to leave the fragile patient to take up the ordinary duties of her life, including those of wifehood and motherhood. Everyone was congratulating her on her recovery. All the kindness of sympathetic and understanding neighbors poured in upon her in the shape of convalescent dishes, soups, custards, and drinks. Still she appeared to be despondent and worried. She seemed to sit apart in her thoughts as if she had no part in these congratulatory messages and endearing welcomes. I thought at first that she still retained some of her unconscious memories and dwelt upon them in her silences.

But as the hour of my departure came nearer, her anxiety increased, and finally with trembling voice she said: "Another baby will finish me, I suppose."

"It's too early to talk about that," I said, and resolved that I would turn the question over to the doctor for his advice. When he came I said: "Mrs. Sacks is worried about having another baby."

"She well might be," replied the doctor, and then he stood before her and said: "Any more such capers, young woman, and there will be no need to call me."

"Yes, yes—I know, Doctor," said the patient with trembling voice, "but," and she hesitated as if it took all of her courage to say it, "*what* can I do to prevent getting that way again?"

"Oh ho!" laughed the doctor good naturedly, "You want your cake while you eat it too, do you? Well, it can't be done." Then, familiarly slapping her on the back and picking up his hat and bag to depart, he said: "I'll tell you the only sure thing to do. Tell Jake to sleep on the roof!"

With those words he closed the door and went down the stairs, leaving us both petrified and stunned.

Tears sprang to my eyes, and a lump came in my throat as I looked at the face before me. It was stamped with sheer horror. I thought for a moment she might have gone insane, but she conquered her feelings, whatever they may have been, and turning to me in desperation said: "He can't understand, can he?—he's a man after all—but you do, don't you? You're a woman and you'll tell me the secret and I'll never tell it to a soul."

She clasped her hands as if in prayer, she leaned over and looked straight into my eyes and beseechingly implored me to tell her something— something *I really did not know*. It was like being on a rack and tortured for a crime one had not committed. To plead guilty would stop the agony; otherwise, the rack kept turning.

I had to turn away from that imploring face. I could not answer her then. I quieted her as best I could. She saw that I was moved by the tears in my eyes. I promised that I would come back in a few days and tell her what she wanted to know. The few simple means of limiting the family like *coitus interruptus* or the condom were laughed at by the neighboring women when told these were the means used by men in the well-to-do families. That was not believed, and I knew such an answer would be swept aside as useless were I to tell her this at such a time.

A little later when she slept I left the house, and made up my mind that I'd keep away from those cases in the future. I felt helpless to do anything at all. I seemed chained hand and foot, and longed for an earthquake or a volcano to shake the world out of its lethargy into facing these monstrous atrocities.

The intelligent reasoning of the young mother— how to *prevent* getting that way again—how sensible, how just she had been—yes, I promised myself I'd go back and have a long talk with her and tell her more, and perhaps she would not laugh but would believe that those methods were all that were really known.

But time flew past, and weeks rolled into months. That wistful, appealing face haunted me day and night. I could not banish from my mind memories of that trembling voice begging so humbly for knowledge she had a right to have. I was about to retire one night three months later when the telephone rang and an agitated man's voice begged me to come at once to help his wife who was sick again. It was the husband of Mrs. Sacks, and I intuitively knew before I left the telephone that it was almost useless to go.

I dreaded to face that woman. I was tempted to send someone else in my place. I longed for an accident on the subway, or on the street—anything to prevent my going into that home. But on I went just the same. I arrived a few minutes after the doctor, the same one who had given her such noble advice. The woman was dying. She was unconscious. She died within ten minutes after my arrival. It was the same result, the same story told a thousand times before—death from abortion. She had become pregnant, had used drugs, had then consulted a five-dollar professional abortionist, and death followed.

The doctor shook his head as he rose from listening for the heart beat. I knew she had already passed on; without a groan, a sigh or recognition of our belated presence she had gone into the Great Beyond as thousands of mothers go every year. I looked at that drawn face now stilled in death. I placed her thin hands across her breast and recalled how hard they had pleaded with me on that last memorable occasion of parting. The gentle woman, the devoted mother, the loving wife had passed on leaving behind her a frantic husband, helpless in his loneliness, bewildered in his helplessness as he paced up and down the room, hands clenching his head, moaning "My God! My God! My God!"

The Revolution came—but not as it has been pictured nor as history relates that revolutions have come. It came in my own life. It began in my very being as I walked home that night after I had closed the eyes and covered with a sheet the body of that little helpless mother whose life had been sacrificed to ignorance.

After I left that desolate house I walked and walked and walked; for hours and hours I kept on, bag in hand, thinking, regretting, dreading to stop;

fearful of my conscience, dreading to face my own accusing soul. At three in the morning I arrived home still clutching a heavy load the weight of which I was quite unconscious.

I entered the house quietly, as was my custom, and looked out the window down upon the dimly lighted, sleeping city. As I stood at the window and looked out, the miseries and problems of that sleeping city arose before me in a clear vision like a panorama: crowded homes, too many children; babies dying in infancy; mothers overworked; baby nurseries; children neglected and hungry—mothers so nervously wrought they would not give the little things the comfort nor care they needed; mothers half sick most of their lives—"always ailing, never failing"; women made into drudges; children working in cellars; children aged six and seven pushed into the labor market to help earn a living; another baby on the way; still another; yet another; a baby born dead—great relief; an older child dies—sorrow, but nevertheless relief—insurance helps; a mother's death—children scattered into institutions; the father, desperate, drunken; he slinks away to become an outcast in a society which has trapped him. . . .

. . . For hours I stood, motionless and tense, expecting something to happen. I watched the lights go out, I saw the darkness gradually give way to the first shimmer of dawn, and then a colorful sky heralded the rise of the sun. I knew a new day had come for me and a new world as well.

It was like an illumination. I could now see clearly the various social strata of our life; all its mass problems seemed to be centered around uncontrolled breeding. There was only one thing to be done: call out, start the alarm, set the heather on fire! Awaken the womanhood of America to free the motherhood of the world! I released from my almost paralyzed hand the nursing bag which unconsciously I had clutched, threw it across the room, tore the uniform from my body, flung it into a corner, and renounced all palliative work forever.

I would never go back again to nurse women's ailing bodies while their miseries were as vast as the stars. I was now finished with superficial cures, with doctors and nurses and social workers who were brought face to face with this overwhelming truth of women's needs and yet turned to pass on the other side. They must be made to see these facts. I resolved that women should have knowledge of contraception. They have every right to know about their own bodies. I would strike out—I would scream from the housetops. I would tell the world what was going on in the lives of these poor women. I *would* be heard. No matter what it should cost. *I would be heard.*

R E A D I N G **51**

Women of Color and Their Struggle for Reproductive Justice

Jael Silliman, Marlene Gerber Fried, Loretta Ross, and Elena R. Gutiérrez

REDEFINING REPRODUCTIVE RIGHTS

Women of color in the U.S. negotiate their reproductive lives in a system that combines various interlocking forms of oppression. As activist, scholar, and co-author Loretta Ross puts it: "Our ability to control what happens to our bodies is constantly challenged by poverty, racism, environmental degradation, sexism, homophobia, and injustice in the United States."[1] . . . It is because of these intersections that women of color advance a definition of reproductive rights beyond abortion. Their critique of "choice" does not deny women of color agency; rather, it shows the constraints within which women of color navigate their reproductive lives and organizing.

Early in the abortion rights struggle, . . . , women of color resisted the coercion that masqueraded as "choice." In a 1973 editorial that was supportive of the *Roe v. Wade* Supreme Court decision legalizing abortion, the National Council of Negro Women sounded this important cautionary note:

> The key words are "if she chooses." Bitter experience has taught the black woman that the administration of justice in this country is not colorblind. Black women on welfare have been forced to accept sterilization in exchange for a continuation of relief benefits and others have been sterilized without their knowledge or consent. A young pregnant woman recently arrested for civil rights activities in North Carolina was convicted and told that her punishment would be to have a forced abortion. We must be ever vigilant that what appears on the surface to be a step forward, does not in fact become yet another fetter or method of enslavement.[2]

Twenty-five years later, in her introduction to *Policing the National Body,* co-author Jael Silliman expands their critique:

> The mainstream movement, largely dominated by white women, is framed around choice: the choice to determine whether or not to have children, the choice to terminate a pregnancy, and the ability to make informed choices about contraceptive and reproductive technologies. This conception of choice is rooted in the neoliberal tradition that locates individual rights at its core, and treats the individual's control over her body as central to liberty and freedom. This emphasis on individual choice, however, obscures the social context in which individuals make choices, and discounts the ways in which the state regulates populations, disciplines individual bodies, and exercises control over sexuality, gender, and reproduction.[3]

"Choice" implies a marketplace of options in which women's right to determine what happens to their bodies is legally protected, ignoring the fact that for women of color, economic and institutional constraints often restrict their "choices." For example, a woman who decides to have an abortion out of economic necessity does not experience her decision as a "choice." Native American activist Justine Smith writes: In the Native context, where women often find the only contraceptives available to them are dangerous, where they live in communities in which unemployment rates can run as high as 80 percent, and where their life expectancy can be as low as 47 years, reproductive "choice" defined so narrowly is a meaningless concept.[4]

. . .

FIGHTING FOR THE RIGHT TO HAVE—OR NOT HAVE—CHILDREN

Women of color have had no trouble distinguishing between population control—externally imposed fertility control policies—and voluntary birth control—women making their own decisions about fertility. For women of color, resisting population control while simultaneously claiming their right to bodily self-determination, including the right to contraception and abortion or the right to have children, is at the heart of their struggle for reproductive control.

Although there has never been an official policy to reduce the growth of the US population, controlling fertility has been a persistent feature of other domestic policies directed at men and women of color, sometimes attempting to increase their fertility, but most often aiming to limit it. For example, during the colonization of the United States, Native American women were intentionally given blankets infected with smallpox. Population control during slavery took the form of brutal and coercive efforts to increase African American women's reproduction, with slave owners using rape and forced marriages to achieve this end. However, since then, population control efforts have been intended to prevent women of color from having children. Eugenics laws, immigration restrictions, sterilization abuses, targeted family planning, and welfare reform have all been vehicles for population control.

Since the 19th century, all of these population control strategies have been employed using racist ideologies as justifications. For example, efforts to maintain white "racial purity" underlie private and publicly funded efforts to control the fertility of those deemed "unfit" and "defective," understood by policy-makers to mean poor or not white. The mid-20th century saw advocates for domestic and international population control promulgating alarmist time bomb theories with strong racist overtones and raising fears among whites of people of color overrunning the Western world. In 1970, President Nixon supported establishing federal family planning services by appealing to whites' fears about population explosions that would make governance of the world in general—and inner cities in particular—difficult. Nixon's policy advisors assembled statistics that pointed to a "bulge" in the number of black Americans between the ages of five and nine, claiming the cohort was 25 percent larger than ten years before.[5] Population alarmists warned that this group of youngsters soon entering their teens was "an age group with problems that can create social turbulence."[6]

Recognizing the relationship between numbers of people and political power,[7] white politicians favored "helping" racial minorities limit their fertility. Determined to lower population growth in African American and Latino communities, many pro-segregation Southern politicians—both Republicans and Democrats—who had formerly opposed family planning, suddenly favored it as a way of regulating the reproduction of these groups. Opposition to welfare and the commitment to reduce welfare rolls by supplying free birth control services to poor women were joined in a race and class direct social policy. In one of the more overt expressions of this position, Leander Perez, a Louisiana judge, revealed in 1965 the link between coercive birth control and racism: "The best way to hate a nigger is to hate him before he is born."[8]

In the 1980s and 90s, fertility control remained a centerpiece of the nation's welfare program and continued to undermine the rights of low-income women and women of color to have children. Federal welfare reform policies such as family caps, institutionalized in President Clinton's 1996 Personal Responsibility and Work Opportunity Reconciliation Act (PRWORA), deny additional benefits to women who have more children while receiving public assistance. Women of color in the economic justice and reproductive rights movements have criticized family caps and other aspects of welfare reform, such as marriage promotion and funding for abstinence-only sexual education. These policies punish women for being poor by attacking their fertility while not offering any substantive relief from structural poverty.[9]

Although rooted in racism, population control programs did at times, at least in part, meet the needs and desires of women of color for birth control, thus creating a complicated political dynamic. This was the case when Nixon's federally funded family planning and contraceptive program was created in 1970s.[10] African American communities provided the majority of family planning clinic clients in the Deep South because, since slavery, controlling one's own fertility had been associated with upward mobility. Despite the racist motivations of some proponents of the family planning–birth control movement, anthropologist Martha Ward, who researched federal population policies, notes: "Family planning became synonymous with the civil rights of poor women to medical care."[11]

Nevertheless, attempts to use family planning clinics to limit the population growth of communities of color were so blatant that they aroused a strong response from Nationalist movements that came to the conclusion that birth control and abortion were genocide. African American and Chicana women supporting birth control and abortion rights as part of their civil rights activism continually faced opposition from Nationalists who felt that the best way to fight racism and xenophobia was to encourage black and Latino communities to expand their population base. Thus, while women of color frequently worked with mainstream and Nationalist civil rights organizations, they had to criticize these organizations when they supported positions hostile to reproductive freedom.[12] In 1970, Frances Beal, coordinator of the Black Women's Liberation Committee of the Student Non-Violent Coordinating Committee (SNCC), made clear her support for both reproductive rights and civil rights:

> We are not saying that black women should not practice birth control. Black women have the right and the responsibility to determine when it is [in] the interest of the struggle to have children or not to have them, and this right must not be relinquished to anyone. It is also her right and responsibility to determine when it is in her own best interests to have children, how many she will have and how far apart. The lack of the availability of safe birth control methods, the forced sterilization practices, and the inability to obtain legal abortions are all symptoms of a decadent society that jeopardizes the health of black women (and thereby the entire black race) in its attempts to control the very life processes of human beings.[13]

Almost 20 years later, in 1989, activist and scholar Dorothy Roberts encountered the same issues when she spoke about threats to abortion rights at a neighborhood meeting, and a man in the audience took her to task: "He said that reproductive rights was a 'white woman's issue,' and advised me to stick to traditional civil rights concerns, such as affirmative action, voting rights, and criminal justice."[14]

However, women of color have refused to divide civil rights from reproductive rights. Rather, they have transformed the fight for both by creating an ever expanding comprehensive reproductive justice agenda. Their agenda includes fighting against two of the methods frequently employed by the racially motivated family planning apparatus that have undermined women of color's right to have children: coercive sterilization and invasive long-term birth control technologies.

In the 20th century, Native American, Mexican American,[15] African American, and Puerto Rican women and other women of color were denied the right to have children through systematic and widespread sterilization abuses[16] practiced by the U.S. government and by private doctors (who were more often than not subsidized by the U.S. government). Women of color responded by taking up the fight against sterilization abuse. Native American, African American, and Latina groups documented and publicized sterilization abuses in their communities in the 1960s and 70s, showing that women had been sterilized without their knowledge or consent. They demonstrated that women who spoke only Spanish were asked to sign consent forms in English, and sometimes pressured to do so during labor and childbirth. Native American women were given hysterectomies by Indian Health Service without their permission.

In the 1970s, a group of women, which included Dr. Helen Rodríguez-Trías, founded the Committee to End Sterilization Abuse (CESA) to stop this racist population control policy begun by the federal government in the 1940s—a policy that had resulted in the sterilization of over one-third of all women of childbearing age in Puerto Rico.[17] CESA helped to create the Advisory Committee on Sterilization, a coalition of groups that developed regulations to protect women using public hospitals in New York City.[18]

Native American and African American women were also active on this issue. Norma Jean Serena, of Creek-Shawnee ancestry, filed the first civil suit of its kind in 1973, addressing sterilization abuse as a civil rights violation.[19] In 1974, another successful lawsuit advanced by the National Welfare Rights Organization and the Southern Poverty Law Center demanded restitution for the involuntary sterilization of the Relf sisters. These 12- and 14-year-old African American sisters were sterilized in Alabama without their parents' knowledge or consent.[20] By 1978, the federal government was forced to establish guidelines regarding sterilization. These included required waiting periods and authorization forms in a language understood by the woman, to prevent women from being sterilized without their knowledge or informed consent.[21]

Despite these efforts, new forms of coercion have arisen. In the 1990s, the Committee on

Women, Population, and the Environment (CWPE) initiated a campaign to raise awareness about and to challenge CRACK (Children Requiring a Caring Kommunity), now called Project Prevention, a privately funded organization that pays women who are addicted to drugs $200 to be sterilized or to use long-acting contraceptives. Although private, CRACK is in fact implementing the same racist agenda manifest in the government policies previously discussed, namely, preventing "undesirable" women, overwhelmingly women of color, from having children.[22] Such continuing reproductive abuses of women of color lead CWPE to argue that a meaningful reproductive health agenda must include explicit opposition to policies that are disproportionately directed at controlling the reproductive capacity of women of color. The rights to bodily and reproductive autonomy are fundamental human rights.

While the resistance of women of color to oppressive reproductive restrictions has been focused on the government and private population control organizations, they have also had to contend with those white pro-choice activists in the mainstream movements for contraception and abortion who have been unable see how what may be reproductive freedom for them is reproductive tyranny for others. The mainstream movements have not linked policies and practices dressed in the benign language of family planning and welfare reform to restrictions on reproductive freedom. Thus, they were not the allies of women of color and sometimes were even at odds with women of color struggling for racial, economic, and reproductive justice.

Activist and philosopher Angela Davis wrote about this failure to confront racism:

> Birth control—individual choice, safe contraceptive methods, as well as abortions when necessary—is a fundamental prerequisite for the emancipation of women. Since the right of birth control is obviously advantageous to women of all classes and races, it would appear that even vastly dissimilar women's groups would have attempted to unite around this issue. In reality, however, the birth control movement has seldom succeeded in uniting

women of different social backgrounds, and rarely have the movement's leaders popularized the genuine concerns of working-class women. Moreover, arguments advanced by birth control advocates have sometimes been based on blatantly racist premises.[23]

The fact that these views generally went unchallenged—and were sometimes embraced or not even recognized as racist—by the mainstream movements meant that women of color who opposed population control could not rely on these movements to counter such policies.

Further, Davis notes that the priorities of women of color are different from those of white women because of their different experiences. Thus, the reproductive rights agendas are shaped by the dynamics of class and race. The failure of white women to address their internalized racism and classism, and to appreciate the power of race and class dynamics to influence activist agendas, has sometimes had disastrous political results—specifically when initiatives promoted by the mainstream movement have actually turned out to limit the reproductive rights of women of color and poor women.[24]

For example, in the 1970s, when the major pro-choice and feminist organizations did not join women of color in demanding sterilization guidelines it was because their experiences with sterilization were radically different. While women of color were targets for coercive sterilization, white middle-class women had trouble persuading doctors to perform voluntary sterilizations, and often had to obtain permission from medical committees to do so.[25] Pro-choice organizations perceived guidelines regulating sterilization as infringing on women's choices, not enhancing them. While the National Organization for Women (NOW) did not take a position on the issue, the National Abortion and Reproductive Rights Action League (NARAL)[26] and other groups that had traditionally supported abortion rights, such as Planned Parenthood, Zero Population Growth, and the Association for Voluntary Surgical Contraception, opposed the sterilization regulations on the grounds that they deprived women of "freedom of choice." In general, mainstream white feminists believed the guidelines were unnecessary and paternalistic and interfered with the doctor-patient relationship.[27]

More recently, we have seen a similar divergence in views regarding hormonal contraception. Population groups and mainstream pro-choice organizations enthusiastically greeted the development of Norplant and Depo-Provera as an expansion of reproductive choice for women. Depo-Provera injections were promoted in their joint campaigns as "highly effective, long-acting . . . and [offering] privacy to the user since the woman has no need to keep contraceptive supplies at home."[28] Their endorsement came despite the risk that Depo-Provera causes menstrual cycle irregularities, principally amenorrhea (the absence of periods), and increases the risk of endometrial and breast cancer.[29]

In contrast, along with progressive women's health groups around the world, women of color have been more skeptical of provider-controlled hormonal methods of contraception whose side effects and risks were unclear.[30] For example, they have criticized Norplant (subdermal implants) and Depo-Provera (injectibles), the two methods most aggressively marketed to young African American, Latina, and Native American women. In 1991, NBWHP [National Black Women's Health Project], NAWHERC [Native American Women's Health Education Resource Center], and NLHO [National Latina Health Organization] issued warnings of the potential for Norplant abuses.[31] Their concerns were validated merely two days after the contraceptive implant was approved by the United States Food and Drug Administration, when the *Philadelphia Inquirer* newspaper published an editorial advocating its use "as a tool in the fight against black poverty."[32] Although the newspaper later apologized for its racist editorial, judges and state legislatures continued to advocate for the use of Norplant among disadvantaged women.

There was a similar although much less publicized division in 1988, when mainstream pro-choice groups developed a campaign to introduce

mifepristone into the United States. Also known as RU 486, mifepristone is taken orally and is a non-surgical option for ending a pregnancy up to 49 days after the beginning of the last menstrual period. These organizations were not concerned that mifepristone had not been sufficiently tested on women of color in the United States, nor was attention given to the fact that women of color were less likely to have access to the follow-up care that is necessary for safe usage. The major pro-choice groups were universally enthusiastic about the campaign. Any criticisms that there might be a problematic side to mifepristone tended to be discouraged or dismissed as playing into the hands of the anti-abortion movement. It seemed that once again, in the drive to expand choice, women of color and their particular concerns were being ignored.

. . .

IDENTITY-BASED ORGANIZING

. . .

Women of color understood that white women and men of color, even with the best of intentions, could not speak to the uniqueness of their issues or represent the authenticity of their experiences. Women of color needed to claim leadership for themselves. By establishing organizations that were racially and ethnically specific and separate from white organizations, women of color created the visions and gained the support necessary to raise the visibility of their reproductive health concerns in their communities and in the broader society. Placing race and class at the center of their reproductive freedom agenda has allowed many of the groups studied to recruit supporters from other social justice movements, such as the civil rights, immigrant rights, economic justice, and environmental justice movements. This has also led to building support bases in communities of color for reproductive health issues. By grounding their organizing in community-identified needs, women of color do not have to isolate or separate themselves from the day-to-day concerns of their communities.

Women of color are subjected to racist and sexist stereotypes which send messages that they should not be in charge of their own reproductive and sexual destinies. When women of color internalize these stereotypes, it is damaging psychologically and a barrier to their activism. Groups based on racial and gender identities help participants overcome important barriers to activism by combating their internalized oppression. Toni Bond, founder and executive director of African American Women Evolving, writes about the toll of internalized oppression:

> Many of us have so internalized [racial] oppression that it has transformed into a self-hatred and seeps into and impedes even our ability to work together collectively, resulting in organizational upheaval and our further disenfranchisement. . . . So emotionally bruised are women of color from racist oppression and our internalization of that oppression that we have trouble letting our guards down to share personal stories about our experiences around health or any other issue.[33]

Eveline Shen, director of Asians and Pacific Islanders for Reproductive Health, echoes Bond's point when she talks about the need to confront stereotypes just to make activism possible. She says, "Asian women are supposed to be docile and obedient. This model is not compatible with fighting for women's rights."[34] For women of color, challenging these myths and stereotypes is part of the process of reclaiming their humanity and redefining their own identities.

Women from all four racial/ethnic groups have faced and challenged racial stereotyping. For African American women, the images of Mammy and Sapphire emphasize maternalism and promiscuity.[35] Asian women are also portrayed in contradictory ways, as concubines, prostitutes, or model minorities, deriving unfair advantage from affirmative action.[36] Racist descriptions represent the Native American woman as a willing squaw, an alcoholic, or "a brown lump of drudge."[37] Reservation Indians are said to "wallow in welfare, food stamps, free housing and medical care, affirmative action programs, and gargantuan

federal cash payments."[38] Latinas are stereotyped as oversexed "hot tamales" or as illegal immigrants wanting to have babies in the United States so they can obtain citizenship and welfare benefits. Some social scientists describe Latinas as "idelly submissive, unworldly, and chaste" or "at the command of the husband who keeps her as he would a coveted thing, free from the contacts of the world, subject to his passions, ignorant of life."[39]

These myths and stereotypes are part of the larger system of oppression and play an important part in perpetuating it. Characterizing women of color as sexually promiscuous and too irresponsible to make their own reproductive decisions and be good mothers serves as the rationale for enacting and legitimizing discriminatory policies, programs, and laws. For example, the 1950s image of the lazy "welfare queen" was rejuvenated during the 1970s and 80s to fuel cutbacks in public assistance. President Reagan referred to a woman on welfare as a "pig at the trough."[40] Images of hyper-fertile Mexican women crossing the border to bear their children on United States soil so that their children could secure social benefits helped to pass restrictive legislation such as Proposition 187 in California, which denied undocumented immigrants educational and health benefits.[41] Continuing the assaults against Latinos, Harvard professor Samuel Huntington's new book, *Who Are We? The Challenges to America's National Identity*,[42] suggests that Hispanic immigrants are undermining the "greatness" of the United States by diluting our national identity as an "Anglo-Protestant" country, a diatribe offered by someone who has been a lifelong Democrat.

Reproductive rights organizing by women of color challenges both the stereotypes and the policies that undermine reproductive autonomy. Through activism, women of color assert the value and dignity of their lives, the lives of their children, and their roles as mothers.

NOTES

1. Loretta Ross et al., "Just Choices: Women of Color, Reproductive Health, and Human Rights," in *Policing the National Body*, ed. Jael Silliman and

Anannya Bhattacharjee (Cambridge, MA: South End Press, 2002), 147.

2. *Black Woman's Voice* 2, no. 2 (Jan/Feb, 1973).

3. Jael Silliman, "Introduction," in *Policing*, x–xi.

4. Justine Smith quoted in Andrea Smith "Better Dead Than Pregnant: The Colonization of Native Women's Reproductive Health," in *Policing*, 141.

5. Thomas B. Littlewood, *The Politics of Population Control* (Notre Dame, IN: University of Notre Dame Press, 1977), 56.

6. Ibid.

7. Ibid., 3.

8. Martha C. Ward, *Poor Women, Powerful Men: America's Great Experiment in Family Planning* (Boulder, CO: Westview Press, 1986), 31.

9. COLOR, *The Impact of Welfare Reform on Latina Reproductive Health,* Policy Position Paper (Denver: COLOR, September 2003).

10. A series of legislative reforms set the stage for federal support for family planning. Under the Economic Opportunity Act of 1964, known as the War on Poverty and launched by President Johnson, federal funds were used to increase the number of people eligible for public assistance. The Office of Economic Opportunity (OEO) was created to provide grants for public and private agencies for social programs to address poverty. When Congress passed the Voting Rights Act of 1965, which made it possible for more African Americans and Latinos to participate in the political process, some elected officials felt it was urgently necessary to minimize the impact and effectiveness of minority voters. The 1965 Immigration Reform Act, which removed the national-origins quotas on immigration, also added to the pressure to limit minority political strength. The first direct OEO grant for family planning services went to Corpus Christi, Texas, in 1964 to target low-income Mexican American families. Despite some congressional opposition, OEO support for family planning grew rapidly under the Johnson administration. Even more importantly, in terms of available funding, the Social Security Act governing Aid for Families with Dependent Children (AFDC) was modified to require that at least 6 percent of all funds available for maternal and infant care be spent on family planning. Moreover, states were authorized to purchase services from nongovernmental providers, such as Planned Parenthood, which created open-ended funding by the federal government for family planning.

11. Ward, *Poor Women, Powerful Men,* xiii.

12. For example, in the late 1980s when leading civil rights organizations wanted to expand support for affirmative action in the Civil Rights Restoration Act legislation, they compromised with Catholic anti-abortion groups who wanted Catholic colleges and universities exempted from the provisions of the legislation that would have made it illegal to discriminate against women faculty and students who supported abortion rights. For more on this see Loretta Ross's article "Blacks and Fertility" in the magazine of the Congressional Black Caucus, *Point of View,* Winter 1988, 12.

13. Frances Beal, "Double Jeopardy: To Be Black and Female," in *The Black Woman,* ed. Toni Cade (New York: Signet, 1970) quoted in Jennifer Nelson, *Women of Color and the Reproductive Rights Movement* (New York: New York University Press, 2003), 80.

14. Dorothy Roberts, *Killing the Black Body* (New York: Pantheon Books, 1997), 5.

15. Elena R. Gutiérrez, "Policing Pregnant Pilgrims: Situating the Sterilization Abuse of Mexican Origin Women in Los Angeles County," in *Women, Health and Nation: Canada and the United States Post–WW II,* ed. Molly Ladd-Taylor et al. (Toronto: McGill-Queens University Press, 2003).

16. See chapter two of *Killing the Black Body* and Angela Davis's chapter "Women Under Attack: Victories, Backlash and the Fight for Reproductive Freedom," in her *Women, Race, and Class* (New York: Vintage Books, 1983).

17. Davis, *Women, Race, and Class,* 14.

18. Nelson, *Women of Color,* 140–143.

19. Sally Torpy, "Endangered Species: Native American Women's Struggle for Their Reproductive Rights and Racial Identity: 1970–1990" (master's thesis, University of Nebraska, 1998), 38.

20. Nelson, *Women of Color,* 66–67.

21. Suzanne Staggenborg, *The Pro-Choice Movement: Organization and Activism in the Abortion Conflict* (New York: Oxford University Press, 1991), 111; Roberts, *Killing the Black Body,* 95; Susan E. Davis and the Committee for Abortion Rights and Against Sterilization Abuse (CARASA), *Women Under Attack: Victories, Backlash and the Fight for Reproduction Freedom* (Boston: South End Press, 1988).

22. Judith A. M. Scully, "Killing the Black Community: A Commentary on the United States War on Drugs," in *Policing,* 55–80.

23. Davis, *Women, Race, and Class,* 204–206.

24. While in this [reading] we focus on race and class, we acknowledge that sexual orientation, disability, and age also play critical roles in determining a woman's reproductive experience. It is important to note that historically the struggle for abortion rights had significant participation and leadership from lesbians who were not "out" in the organizations. Issues of sexual orientation did not become explicitly part of the pro-choice agenda until the late 1980s and still have not been fully incorporated into the pro-choice agenda. Neither the pro-choice nor the disability rights movement has consolidated around a position on "choice" and disability, and young people continue to struggle for recognition of their issues and for leadership in the mainstream movement.

25. Lucinda Cisler, "Unfinished Business: Birth Control and Women's Liberation," in *Sisterhood Is Powerful: An Anthology of Writings from the Women's Liberation Movement*, ed. Robin Morgan (New York: Vintage Books, 1970), 255–256.

26. NARAL has gone through three name incarnations. It was founded in 1969 as the National Association for the Repeal of Abortion Laws. With the legalization of abortion in 1973, it became the National Abortion and Reproductive Rights Action League. In 2003, it became NARAL Pro-Choice America. This book uses all three depending on which time period is referenced.

27. Davis and CARASA, *Women Under Attack*, 29.

28. Robert Hatcher, ed., *Contraceptive Technology: International Edition* (Atlanta, GA: Printed Matter Inc., 1989), 301.

29. Ibid.

30. Women and Pharmaceuticals Project, Women's Health Action Foundation, and WEMOS, *Norplant: Under Her Skin* (Delft, The Netherlands: Eburon Press, 1993), 3.

31. Ibid., 108.

32. Asoka Bandarage, *Women, Population and Global Crisis* (London: Zed Books, 1997), 85.

33. Toni Bond, "Barriers Between Black Women and the Reproductive Rights Movement," *Political Environments* 8 (Winter/Spring 2001): 1–5.

34. Eveline Shen, interview by Marlene Gerber Fried, January 2001, APIRH office, Oakland, CA.

35. Deborah Gray White, *Too Heavy a Load: Black Women in Defense of Themselves, 1894–1994* (New York: W. W. Norton, 1999), 19.

36. Huping Ling, *Surviving on the Gold Mountain: A History of Chinese American Women and Their Lives* (New York: State University of New York Press, 1998), 167.

37. Shirley Hill Witt, "Native Women Today: Sexism and the Indian Woman," *Civil Rights Digest* 6 (Spring 1974): 29.

38. Center for Democratic Renewal, "Indian Issues and Anti-Indian Organizing," in *When Hate Groups Come to Town: A Handbook of Effective Community Responses* (Atlanta: CDR, 1992), 138.

39. Adaljiza Sosa Riddell, "Chicanas and El Movimiento," in *Chicana Feminist Thought: The Basic Historical Writings*, ed. Alma M. Garcia (New York: Routledge, 1997), 93.

40. Found in Solinger, *Beggars and Choosers*, 156; originally quoted in Johnnie Tillmon, "Welfare Is a Woman's Issue," *Liberation News Service*, February 26, 1972, reprinted in *America's Working Women*, ed. Rosalyn Baxandall, Linda Gordon, and Susan Reverby (New York: Random House, 1976), 357.

41. Elena R. Gutiérrez, "Policing Pregnant Pilgrims."

42. Samuel Huntington, *Who Are We? The Challenges to America's National Identity* (New York: Simon & Schuster, 2004).

The Way It Was

Eleanor Cooney

In 1959, when I was a precocious smarty-pants still in grade school, I wrote a fake letter to Doris Blake, the *New York Daily News* advice columnist. I pretended to be a teenage girl "in trouble." I spun a tale of a liquor-soaked prom night and passing out in the back of a car. I included a cast of entirely fictional characters—a worthless boyfriend, a mentally unstable mother, a strict, brutal father. I ended my letter with: "Now I think I am pregnant. Please help me. I am desperate."

I'm not sure what I expected, but my letter was not printed, and no advice was forthcoming. The silence was utter. Possibly Miss Blake, like Nathanael West's Miss Lonelyhearts, had a drawer where such letters were tossed. If so, the other letters in that drawer were no doubt a lot like mine—except that they were not written by wiseass children. They were real. And for the writers of those letters, the silence was real. And I remember thinking: *Gee*, what if I really were that girl I made up? What would I do?

One summer night some years later, when I was not quite 18, I got knocked up. There was nothing exciting or memorable or even interestingly sordid about the sex. I wasn't raped or coerced, nor was I madly in love or drunk or high. The guy was another kid, actually younger than I, just a friend, and it pretty much happened by default. We were horny teenagers with nothing else to do.

Nature, the ultimate unsentimental pragmatist, has its own notions about what constitutes a quality liaison. What nature wants is for sperm and egg to meet, as often as possible, whenever and wherever possible. Whatever it takes to expedite that meeting is fine with nature. If it's two people with a bassinet and a nursery all decorated and waiting a shelf full of baby books, fine. If it's a 12-year-old girl who's been married off to a 70-year-old Afghan chieftain, fine. And if it's a couple of healthy young oafs like my friend and me, who knew perfectly well where babies come from but just got stupid for about 15 minutes, that's fine, too.

In the movies, newly pregnant women trip, fall down the stairs, and "lose the baby." Ah. If only it were that easy. In real life, once that egg is fertilized and has glided on down the fallopian tube, selected its nesting place, and settled in, it's notoriously secure, behaves like visiting royalty. Nature doesn't give a fig about the hostess's feelings of hospitality or lack of them. If the zygote's not defective, and the woman is in good health, almost nothing will shake it loose. Anyone who's been pregnant and didn't want to be knows this is so.

On November 5, 2003, three decades after *Roe v. Wade* established a woman's constitutional right to terminate a pregnancy, President George W. Bush signed the Partial Birth Abortion Ban bill into law. We've all seen the photograph: The president sits at a table with a modest little smile on his lips. Nine guys—senators and congressmen—stand behind him, watching that signature go onto the paper, giddy grins on their faces. They look almost goofy with joy.

Two of these happy fellows are actually Democrats: Jim Oberstar and Bart Stupak. The rest are Republicans to their marrow: the bill's sponsor, Rick Santorum, as well as Steve Chabot, Orrin Hatch, Henry Hyde, Tom DeLay, Mike DeWine, and Dennis Hastert.

Be assured that it's not just "partial-birth" abortion they're so happy about passing a law against. It's all the law heralds. Like some ugly old wall-to-wall carpeting they've been yearning to get rid of, they finally, *finally* loosened a little corner of *Roe*. Now they can start to rip the whole thing up, roll it back completely, and toss it in the dumpster.

For with the PBAB, Bush and Co. have achieved the first federal legal erosion of *Roe v. Wade* since its adoption in 1973. *Roe* states that a woman may terminate a pregnancy up to the point of "viability," approximately 24 weeks. After that, states may prohibit or restrict abortion, but exceptions must be made to preserve "the life or health of the woman." The PBAB has been around the block before—in 1995, 1997, 1999, and 2000. What stopped it before was always the debate over allowances for women's health. President Clinton vetoed it three times because it disallowed exceptions to prevent serious disabling injury to the woman. But when the bill came up again in 2002, allowances for prevention of disabling injury to the mother were left out, as were those for rape and incest. A "partial-birth" abortion would be permitted only as a last resort to save the mother's life, or if the fetus was already dead. In other words, the risk of permanent injury to the woman if she proceeds with the pregnancy is not a good enough reason to perform one—not in Santorum's book. She has to be literally on death's doorstep. A couple of Democrats tried to offer an amendment that brought up that pesky women's health issue again. The bill's authors objected. Women and their doctors will just use the amendment as a loophole! Chabot worried it would create "a phony ban" and Santorum predicted it would be defeated. It was.

One Democratic senator proposed a nonbinding resolution, expressing ". . . the sense of the Senate that . . . *Roe v. Wade* was appropriate and secures an important constitutional right and should not be overturned." This amendment passed in the Senate by a 52-46 vote. The House version of the PBAB lacked any such amendment. In conference, the Republicans quickly took care of that feeble bleat on behalf of *Roe:* They simply deleted it. When the bill landed on Bush's desk, the resolution to reaffirm *Roe* was gone.

What, you might ask, is "partial-birth" abortion? Most of us know that the term is not a medical one. Invented by the pro-life folks in the last decade or so, it's a vague reference to "intact dilation and extraction," or D&X. Introduced in 1992, D&X is a variation on a similar, well-established second- (and sometimes third-) term procedure—"dilation and evacuation," or D&E—used after the fetus has grown too large to be vacuumed or scraped out in a simple D&C, or "dilation and curettage."

In a D&E, the fetus is usually dismembered inside the uterus and extracted in pieces. Old obstetrics books from as far back as the 1700s have disquieting illustrations of the various tools of yore used for fetal dismemberment. Nowadays, powerful gripping forceps are used, making the procedure much less dangerous for the women.

The D&X was developed with the same objective. An inherent hazard of D&E—aside from potential damage by the instruments themselves and the risk of leaving tissue behind, increasing the chances of infection—is that fetal bones begin to calcify at about 13 weeks. As they are broken up, the sharp bone ends can puncture, scrape, and perforate. Hence the "intact" dilation and extraction. The fetus is brought out whole instead of being pulled apart bit by bit. The head is punctured and then collapsed by suction or compression so that it will fit through the partially dilated cervix. The fetus is dead, but in one piece. This, specifically, is the procedure the PBAB has sought to criminalize—when the fetus is killed while its body is outside the uterus, therefore "partially born."

Under the PBAB of 2003, a D&X would be permitted only to save the woman's life or if the fetus is dead. It would require a girl who'd been impregnated by her uncle, father, or brother, and who, out of shame, ignorance, and fear had hidden her condition until it was obvious to the world, to carry the fetus to term and give birth. If a woman discovers, late in her pregnancy, that the fetus has, say, anencephaly—a brain stem but no actual brain—then she must carry it to term, give birth, and let it die on its own.

Since lurid descriptions of partial-birth abortion have been so effective in rallying support for the bill, perhaps some balance is needed. I've read and heard hundreds of accounts of pre-*Roe* abortion, and there was a wide range of danger, squalor, sanitary conditions, provider skill, follow-up care. The well-heeled and well-connected often flew to Puerto Rico or Sweden and checked into clinics. Of the ones who couldn't do that, some were lucky enough to find competent, compassionate doctors. Some were treated kindly and recovered without incident. The other extreme was pain, terror, and death worthy of the Inquisition. A typical picture emerges, though, and it matches up just about perfectly with a story told to me by a woman I know.

After a date rape (by a "poet") during a trip to Paris in 1967 when she was 23, she found herself pregnant. She tried the usual "remedies"—scalding hot baths, violent jumping, having someone walk on her belly. When she got home to Minnesota, she was two months along. A doctor friend there said he couldn't help her himself, but sent her to a local prostitute who did abortions.

The prostitute had her own speculum. The procedure was done on the prostitute's bed: The catheter was inserted through the cervix and left there. After four days of high fever, chills, bleeding, and passing big chunks of tissue, she landed in the hospital. They said her uterus was perforated, that she had acute peritonitis and an "incomplete" abortion. She was given a huge dose of penicillin and treated as if she were some sort of contemptible lower-life form. The emergency-room doctor snarled, "What have you done to yourself?" Later, she realized that the first doctor—her friend—had known all along that she'd probably get desperately ill. Only then could a hospital legally give her a D&C.

She recovered—sterile, violently allergic to penicillin, and so "paralyzed and ashamed" by the experience that she stayed away from men for four years. Who says deterrence doesn't work?

Then there's the famous 1964 police photograph of a woman's corpse on a motel-room floor in Connecticut. She's kneeling naked, facedown as if to Mecca, legs bent to her chest, bloody towels bunched under her. The case had made local headlines, but the picture wasn't seen by the

general public until *Ms. Magazine* ran it in a 1973 article lauding the ruling of *Roe v. Wade*. Details emerged about the woman's life and death: She was 27, married with two young daughters, but estranged from her violent husband. Her lover had performed the abortion, using borrowed instruments and a textbook. When she started hemorrhaging, he panicked, fled the motel, and left her there.

Compared to those two women, I got off easy. By the middle of September, I'd missed two periods and my cigarettes were tasting peculiar. I was bound for freshman year at college in Boston, though, so I just ignored the facts and went off to school. It took a third missed period and almost throwing up in the backseat of a car packed with kids to penetrate my adolescent thickheadedness.

I had a savvy friend in New York, Kat, who only dated rich older men. I figured she'd be the one to call. Soon a long ride on buses and trains took me out to a house in a Boston suburb. The doctor's wife answered the door. There was no waiting room, no magazines, no other patients. The house was completely ordinary, perhaps a touch rundown. She showed me into a room off the front hall and vanished.

Except for a small sink, the office was just a regular room, a parlor, with green walls and venetian blinds and a worn rug on the floor. A tall, battered, glass-doored porcelain cabinet stood in a corner. Through the glass, I could see on the shelves a dusty disorderly jumble of stethoscopes, hypodermics, bottles, little rubber hammers, basins, forceps, clamps, speculums, wads of cotton. There were rust stains in the sink and a tired old examining table.

The doctor, a little nervous man with glasses and a bald head, came in. I explained my problem. I have to examine you, he said. And he said: Everything has to be clean, very clean. He went to the sink and washed and washed his hands.

He finished and stood there without saying anything. His eyes were sort of glittering behind his glasses, and he acted as if I was supposed to know what to do next. I glanced around for a gown, but he was looking impatient, so I just took off my underwear and climbed onto the table.

He didn't bother with a glove. He poked around a while, then told me that I'd waited too long, I was too far gone, it would be too risky for him, and that would be $25.

. And I was back out on the suburban street, the door shut firmly behind me.

Kat told me to come to New York and bring $500. I slept on the couch in her apartment. Kat's roommate, Elaine, gave me the address of a doctor over in Jersey City. I took a train and walked 10 blocks to a street of old brownstones, some of them with their windows boarded up. There had been no calling ahead for an "appointment"; you were supposed to just show up.

This doctor had a waiting room, with dark walls and a very high ceiling, the front room of the brownstone. It was full of people, facing each other along opposite walls, sitting in old, cracked, brown leather parlor chairs with stand-up ash-trays here and there, like in a bus station. A set of tall sliding wooden doors stood closed between that room and the next. Everyone was smoking, including me. The air was blue.

Several Puerto Rican–looking women chat-tered away in Spanish and seemed perfectly cheerful. There were a few men, who looked as if they might be accompanying somebody, and some more women who sat silent and staring.

And there was a couple who stood out like a pair of borzoi among street mutts: a man and woman, tall, slim, expensively dressed WASPS, faces grim, looking like people who'd taken a seri-ously wrong turn off the highway. I remember feeling sorry for them.

The tall wooden doors separated. A potbellied man in shirtsleeves who resembled Harpo Marx minus the fun stood there. His eyes moved around the room. He looked at the Puerto Rican women, the tall WASP woman, then at me, then the WASP woman again, considered for a moment, turned back to me, and pointed.

You, he said.

I got up and went in. He slid the doors shut. We were alone.

The windows in here had been nailed over with plywood, and the floor was ancient linoleum. There was a smell of insecticide. Boxes and bundles of paper were piled high in the dim corners and on a rolltop desk, and along the walls were shelves crammed messily with stethoscopes, hypodermics, speculums. The examining table was the centerpiece of the room, antique and massive, from the last century, dark green leather, steel and ceramic, designed so that the patient did not lie flat but in a semi-reclining position. Instead of stirrups, there were obstetrical leg sup-ports. A tall old-fashioned floor lamp with a rose silk shade and a fringe, the only light in the room, stood next to the table alongside a cylinder of gas. An unlit crystal chandelier dangled in the over-head shadows.

The doctor had a trace of some sort of Euro-pean accent. German, I guessed. He was about a foot shorter than I was, and behaved with obse-quious deference, as if I had dropped in for an afternoon sherry. He gestured toward the exam-ining table with a courtly flourish. I sat between the leg supports while he stood close and asked questions: Last period, how many times had I had sex, was I married, how many men had I had sex with, did they have large or small penises, were they circumcised, what positions, did I like it?

He moved the floor lamp closer. I put my legs in the apparatus and looked up at the chandelier.

He didn't bother with a glove, either. He thrust several fingers in, hard, so I could feel the scrape of his nails.

Ouch! I said politely.

Ouch, he mocked. Never mind your ouch. He pushed his fingers in harder and pressed down on my belly with his other hand.

You are very far along, he said. It will be a very difficult procedure. Come back tomorrow. Be here at seven o'clock in the evening. Give me one hundred dollars now because this will be difficult. You can pay the rest when you come back. Bring cash. Five hundred more.

I borrowed the extra hundred from Kat, and enlisted someone I knew to ride out to Jersey City with me on the train, a guy who was something of an ex-boyfriend. Even though I was enigmatic about why we were going to Jersey City at night, he guessed what was up, and seemed fairly enter-tained at the prospect.

This time, there was no one in the waiting room. The doctor looked very annoyed when he saw that I wasn't alone. My friend stayed out there while I went into the office. The doctor locked the door behind us.

When I was on the table, he stood between my legs and pressed and ground his pelvis against me and then put his fingers in for a while.

Then he said: You are too far gone. I cannot do it.

I put my legs down and sat up. He stood next to me, leaned on me heavily, and rubbed his two hands up my thigh, all the way up, so that his fingertips collided with my crotch. I understood then that he'd known perfectly well on my last visit that he wasn't going to go through with it.

You are a beautiful girl, a beautiful girl, he breathed moistly onto my face as his hands slid up and down, up and down. It is too late. Take my advice. Have the baby. Have the baby.

He unlocked the sliding doors and beckoned my friend in.

Get married, he said. Have the baby.

Hey, I'm not the guy, said my friend.

What about my hundred dollars? I asked.

Get out of here, the doctor said, and turned his back.

When we got to my friend's train stop, he walked off whistling a jaunty tune. Good luck, he said, and was gone.

Today, chat rooms and message boards related to abortion show a disturbing trend among some young people: Not only is disinformation rife ("The only reason abortion is still legal," writes one correspondent, "is becuz the babies organs are prossed and some of that money is forwarded to the libral party."), but many young people haven't the remotest notion of pre-*Roe* reality. Abortion's been legal since before they were born. Some even believe that abortion was invented with *Roe v. Wade*.

Abortion was not always illegal before *Roe*. Into the 19th century, what a woman did with her early pregnancy was considered a purely domestic matter. Until "quickening," when the fetus was perceived to be alive and kicking, it wasn't even considered a pregnancy, but a "blocking" or an "imbalance," and women regularly "restored the menses," if they so chose, through plants and potions. Abortifacients became commercially available by the mid-1700s.

Quality control was not great, and the earliest abortion legislation in the 1820s and '30s appears to have been an effort to curtail poisoning rather than abortion itself. According to several historians of the issue, as abortion—both through drugs and direct procedures—became a bigger and bigger commercial venture, "orthodox" physicians, who were competing with midwives, homeopaths, and self-styled practitioners of all stripes, pushed to make abortion illegal. The nascent American Medical Association established its dominance over lay practitioners through abortion laws, and women were kept in their place. Eugenics played a role, too: With "undesirables" breeding prolifically, motherhood was hailed as a white woman's patriotic duty, abortion a form of treason. By the mid-1800s, most of the "folk" knowledge had been lost and abortion became "infanticide." Between 1860 and 1880, antiabortion laws spread city by city, state by state. Now there was a ruthlessly pragmatic aspect: In the aftermath of the slaughter of half a million men during the Civil War, the births were needed. First the men were conscripted, then the women.

Demand for abortion continued to grow in spite of the laws. Periods of relative tolerance gave way to periods of stricter enforcement, which inevitably corresponded to periods of women's activism. In the late 19th century, it was when they demanded a voice in politics. After World War II and through the 1960s, it was when they demanded sexual freedom. All kinds of change, rebellion, and upheaval were busting out then, and the reflexive reaction of the authorities was to crack down. For women getting illegal abortions, this era was particularly marked by fear, secrecy, ignorance, shame, and danger. This was the era that put the rusty coat hanger into the collective consciousness.

The day after I returned from Jersey City, there was another doctor in a seedy little basement office in

New York who didn't even touch me. He said the only way to do it at this point would be to perform a miniature caesarean, not something he could do in his office.

Kat and Elaine were plainly getting tired of having me and my problem on their couch. They came up with a phone number in Florida. I called. A male voice said I should fly to Miami. They'd meet me and take me to one of the islands, to a clinic. Give us the telephone number of where you're staying now in New York. We'll call you back and confirm the arrangements.

He called back within an hour. It was set: Fly to Miami next Thursday, between the hours of noon and five. Wear something bright red so we'll know you when you get off the plane. And bring eight hundred dollars, in cash.

One last thing, he said. You must not tell anyone where you're going.

They understand that I'm over three months, right? I said.

Yeah, yeah. They know. It's all set.

I hung up. This didn't feel good at all. Florida, the islands, wads of cash, distant voices.

I thought about doing what I should have done in the first place: calling my mother.

Not calling her in the beginning wasn't because my mother was a prude or religious or anything like that. Hardly. It was because I was naturally secretive, had wanted to take care of things on my own. I just wanted it to go away. But there was a limit to even my pigheadedness. I thought about how sad it would make my mother if I just disappeared. My mother, who was right there in the city, swung into action instantly. She made arrangements with a doctor she knew, and borrowed the $1,500 it would cost because of the added risk.

This doctor had a clean, modern office in Midtown. He drew a diagram showing the difference between a first-trimester D&C and what I'd be having. After three months, he said, the placenta and the blood vessels that feed it grow too complex to simply be scraped out. To do so would be to just about guarantee a hemorrhage. In a normal birth or miscarriage, he said, the uterus contracts, shearing off the placenta and pinching off the connecting blood vessels. We induce a miscarriage, he said, by injecting a saline solution into the amniotic sac. The fetus dies. The uterus rejects it by contracting. That way, no hemorrhage. Then we go in and take it out. If it were done any other way, it could easily kill you.

A date was made for the following week. I was off of Kat and Elaine's couch and on my mother's.

One evening, my mother's phone rang. It was the man in Florida. He'd tracked me down through Kat, and he was angry. What the hell had happened? Where was I? They'd waited all day at the airport in Miami, met every plane. I apologized, told him I'd made other arrangements here at home. He said I was a fucking bitch who owed money to him and a lot of other people, told me to go fuck myself, and hung up.

Maybe everything would have been peachy if I'd gone to the islands. Maybe I'd have come back with a tan and heartwarming stories of kindness and caring that I'd remember fondly through the years. A rather different picture always comes to mind, though, and it involves a morgue in a rundown little hospital with heat and flies, and then a dinghy with an outboard, or maybe a fishing boat with a rumbling, smoky diesel engine, heading out into the Caribbean at night bearing a largish canvas bag weighted with cinder blocks. . . .

That year in the 1960s, several thousand American women were treated in emergency rooms for botched abortions, and there were at least 200 known deaths. Comparing my story with others from the pre-*Roe* era, what impresses me is how close I veered to mortal danger in spite of not living under most of the usual terrible strictures. Unlike so many of the women I've read about and talked to, especially the teenagers, I was quite unburdened by shame and guilt. I'd never, ever had the "nice girls don't do it" trip laid on me. I came from a religion-free background. I wasn't worried in the least about "sin," was not at all ambivalent about whether abortion was right or wrong. I wasn't sheltered or ignorant. I didn't face parental disapproval or stigmatization of any kind. I had no angry husband. My mother would have leapt in and helped me at any point. There was no need at all to keep my condition secret and to procrastinate, but

I did it anyway. What does this say about how it was for other young girls and women who didn't have my incredible luck? I was luckier than most in another department, too—being raped by the abortionist was a major hazard of the era. I merely got diddled by a couple of disgusting old men. It was nasty and squalid, but it certainly didn't kill me. As I said, I got off easy.

Ironically, it was the medical profession, which had made abortion illegal in the first place, that started to speak out. Doctors treating the desperately sick women who landed in hospitals with raging peritonitis, hemorrhages, perforated uteruses, and septic shock often had to futilely watch them die, because the women had waited too long to get help—because they were confused and terrified, because what they had done was "illegal" and "immoral."

One doctor's "awakening" is vividly described in *The Worst of Times,* a collection of interviews with women, cops, coroners, and practitioners from the illegal abortion era. In 1948, when this doctor was an intern in a Pittsburgh hospital, a woman was admitted with severe pelvic sepsis after a bad abortion. She was beautiful, married to someone important and wealthy, and already in renal failure. Over the next couple of days, despite heroic efforts to save her, a cascade of systemic catastrophes due to the overwhelming infection culminated with the small blood vessels bursting under her skin, bruises breaking out everywhere as if some invisible fist were punching her over and over, and she died. Being well-to-do didn't always save you.

Her death was so horrible that it made him, he recalls, physically ill. He describes his anger, but says he didn't quite know with whom to be angry. It took him another 20 years to understand that it was not the abortionist who killed her—it was the legal system, the lawmakers who had forced her away from the medical community, who ". . . killed her just as surely as if they had held the catheter or the coat hanger or whatever. I'm still angry. It was all so unnecessary."

All so unnecessary.

In the same book, a man who assisted in autopsies in a big urban hospital, starting in the mid-1950s, describes the many deaths from botched abortions that he saw. "The deaths stopped overnight in 1973." He never saw another in the 18 years before he retired. "That," he says, "ought to tell people something about keeping abortion legal."

In February 2004, seven abortion doctors in four states sued Attorney General John Ashcroft, claiming that D&X was indeed a medically necessary procedure. Ashcroft retaliated by subpoenaing their hospitals for the records of all patients who'd had late-term abortions in the past five years—most long before the PBAB—to determine, ostensibly, if any D&Xs had actually been prompted by health risk. In June, a federal judge in San Francisco declared the PBAB to be unconstitutional—saying it was vague, placed an "undue burden" on abortion rights, and contained no exception for a woman's health—but she did not, in deference to other cases wending their way through the legal system, completely lift the ban.

One doctor, writing about D&X, said something that particularly struck me—that the actual practice of medicine, the stuff that goes on behind closed doors, is often gruesome, gory, and messy. Saws whine, bones crack, blood spatters. We outside of the profession are mostly shielded from this reality. Our model is white sheets, gleaming linoleum, and Dr. Kildare. Face-lift, hip replacement, bypass, liver transplant—many people would faint dead away at a detailed description of any of these. Doctors roll up their sleeves, plunge in, and do tough, nervy, drastic, and risky things with our very meat-bone-and-gristle bodies, under occasionally harrowing circumstances.

The gruesome aspect of D&X has been detailed and emphasized, but as a procedure, it's in line with the purpose of medicine: to get a hard flesh-and-blood job done. What makes it different from other procedures is that it can involve a live fetus. This puts it in a class by itself. But the woman undergoing a D&X knows this. If she's doing it, there will be powerfully compelling reasons, and it's not for anyone else to decide if those reasons are compelling enough.

. . .

Teenagers—especially those who are poor and uneducated—are by far the group having the most elective late-term abortions. If we truly wish to protect the young and vulnerable, promote a "culture of life," as President Bush said so grandly in his signing speech, then we must make teenage girls a top priority. Make sure they don't get pregnant in the first place, and not just by preaching "abstinence only." If they do get pregnant, don't throw a net of fear, confusion, and complication over them that will only cause them to hide their conditions for as long as they can. Because that's exactly what they'll do. You could argue that "partial-birth" abortion is the price a society pays when it calculatedly keeps teenage girls ignorant instead of aggressively arming them with the facts of life and, if necessary, the equipment to protect themselves from pregnancy.

. . . When a woman does not want to be pregnant, the drive to become unpregnant can turn into a force equal to the nature that wants her to stay pregnant. And then she *will* look for an abortion, whether it's legal or illegal, clean or filthy, safe or riddled with danger. This is simply a fact, whatever our opinion of it. And whether we like it or not, humans, married and unmarried, will continue to have sex—wisely, foolishly, violently, nicely, hostilely, pleasantly, dangerously, responsibly, carelessly, sordidly, exaltedly—and there will be pregnancies: wanted, unwanted, partly wanted, partly unwanted.

A society that does not accept the facts is a childish society, and a society that makes abortion illegal—and I believe that the PBAB is a calculated step in exactly that direction—is a cruel and backward society that makes being female a crime. It works in partnership with the illegal abortionist. It puts him in business, sends him his customers, and employs him to dispense crude, dirty, barbaric, savage punishment to those who break the law. And the ones who are punished by the illegal abortionist are always women: mothers, sisters, daughters, wives.

It's no way to treat a lady.

DISCUSSION QUESTIONS FOR CHAPTER 6

1. How do patriarchal norms constitute a threat to women's health?

2. How are women treated differently in the health care system? What is the effect of this differential treatment? How does racism have an impact on the gendered experiences of women of color in the health care system? Have you ever had a negative experience based on gender in the health care system?

3. Why is reproductive choice important for women?

4. What have been the consequences of women's loss of control of their reproductive processes?

5. How does the chipping away of abortion rights threaten the achievements of *Roe v. Wade?*

SUGGESTIONS FOR FURTHER READING

Boston Women's Health Book Collective, *Our Bodies, Our Selves for the New Century.* New York: Simon & Schuster, 1998.

Eisenstein, Zillah. *Manmade Breast Cancers.* Ithaca, NY: Cornell University Press, 2001.

Farmer, Paul, Margaret Connors, and Janie Simmons, eds. *Women, Poverty, and AIDS: Sex, Drugs, and Structural Violence.* Monroe, ME: Common Courage, 1996.

Gorney, Cynthia. *Articles of Faith: A Frontline History of the Abortion Wars.* New York: Touchstone, 2000.

Morgen, Sandra. *Into Our Own Hands: The Women's Health Movement in the United States, 1969–1990.* New Brunswick, NJ: Rutgers University Press, 2002.

Nelson, Jennifer. *Women of Color and the Reproductive Rights Movement.* New York: New York University Press, 2003.

Solinger, Rickie, ed. *Abortion Wars: A Half Century of Struggle, 1950–2000.* Los Angeles: University of California Press, 1998.

Weddington, Sarah. *A Question of Choice.* New York: Penguin, 1993.

CHAPTER **7**

Family Systems, Family Lives

The title of this chapter, "Family Systems, Family Lives," reflects the reality of the family as both a major societal institution and a place where individuals experience intimate relationships. Using the definition of institution as established patterns of social behavior organized around particular purposes, the family is constituted through general patterns of behavior that emerge because of the specific needs and desires of human beings and because of the societal conditions of our lives. At the institutional level, the family maintains patterns of privilege and inequity and is intimately connected to other institutions in society such as the economy, the political system, religion, and education. At the level of experience, the family fulfills basic human needs and provides most of us with our first experiences of love and relationship as well as power and conflict. Scholarship on the family has demonstrated that family forms are historically and culturally constructed and that family is a place for the reproduction of power relations in society. In this way, the family is a primary social unit that maintains other institutions and reinforces existing patterns of domination. At the same time, however, family networks provide support systems that can reduce the indignities and/or challenge the inequities produced by various systems of inequality in society.

DEFINITIONS OF FAMILY

Families are part of what social scientists call kinship systems, or patterns of relationships that define family forms. Kinship systems vary widely around the world, although they tend to pattern such features as the meaning of marriage, the number of marriage partners permitted at one time (monogamy involves one husband and one wife, and polygamy is multiple spouses, the most common form being polygyny, or multiple wives), norms about marriageability, determination of descent, and distribution of property. The family is a central organizing principle among humans around the world and, as a result, the status and role of women in families not only is dependent on women's access to power in society generally, but also is related to

Facts About U.S. Families

- Fifty-two percent of American households are maintained by married couples (54.5 million households).
- The second most common type of American household consists of people living alone (27.2 million households).
- Family households increased from 64.5 million in 1990 to 76.5 million in 2004.
- Nonfamily households increased from 27.4 million to 35.7 million during the same period.
- The highest proportion (63 percent) of married-couple households are in Utah.
- Households headed by women with children under 18 years old increased from 6 million in 1990 to 8.5 million in 2004.
- Multigenerational families (made up of more than two generations) numbered 3.9 million or 3.7 percent of all households.
- Of all families 9.3 percent live below the poverty level.
- Of all households headed by women 27.8 percent are below the poverty level.
- Although children represent only about 26 percent of the population, children under age 18 represent nearly 40 percent of people living in poverty.
- Eighteen percent of all children live in families with incomes below the poverty line.
- Nearly a third of Black and Latino children live in poverty. Ten percent of White children live in poverty.
- Seniors are the fastest growing population group in the United States. There are currently about 35 million people age 65 and older, 13 percent of the population, but that number is expected to double by 2030 and represent 20 percent of the population.

Source: U.S. Census Bureau; Centers for Disease Control.

The World's Women: Women and Families

Some important findings:

- Women are generally marrying later, but more than a quarter of women aged 15 to 19 are married in 22 countries—all in developing regions.
- Informal unions are common in developed regions and in some countries of the developing regions.
- Birthrates continue to decline in all regions of the world.
- Births to unmarried women have increased dramatically in developed regions.
- More people are living alone in the developed regions, and the majority are women.
- In many countries of the developed regions, more than half of mothers with children under age 3 are employed.

Source: http://unstats.un.org/unsd/demographic/ww2000/wm2000.htm.

Myths and Facts About Lesbian Families

MYTH 1: Lesbians don't have lasting relationships.

FACT: Many lesbians are in long-term partnerships. Unfortunately, social supports and civil rights are not accorded to lesbian partnerships as they are to heterosexual marriages. Only Massachusetts recognizes gay marriage, and in 1999 the Vermont Supreme Court ruled that denying lesbian and gay couples the benefits of marriage was unconstitutional and ordered the legislature to develop a form of civil union to allow lesbian and gay partnerships the same rights and responsibilities as married couples in Vermont.

MYTH 2: Lesbians don't have children.

FACT: The American Bar Association estimates that at least 6 million American children have

lesbian or gay parents. Many lesbians have children from previous heterosexual relationships before they came out. Others have children through artificial insemination, and others adopt children. Unfortunately, because the courts may believe stereotypes about lesbians, lesbian mothers often lose custody of their children in a divorce, despite research indicating the fitness of lesbian mothers. In many states, adoption is difficult for lesbians, and rarely can both partners in a lesbian relationship legally adopt a child together.

MYTH 3: Children of lesbian parents develop psychological disorders.

FACT: Research indicates that there is no difference in the development or frequency of pathologies between children of heterosexual or homosexual parents. In fact, study after study suggests that children in lesbian families are more similar to than different from children in heterosexual families. Studies of separation-individuation, behavior problems, self-concept, locus of control, moral judgment, and intelligence have revealed no major differences between children of lesbian mothers and children of heterosexual mothers.

MYTH 4: Children of lesbian parents become gay themselves.

FACT: Research indicates no difference between children raised in lesbian families and children raised in heterosexual families with respect to gender identity, gender role behavior, and sexual orientation. Studies suggest that children in lesbian families develop along the same lines as children in heterosexual families; they are as likely to be happy with their gender, exhibit gender role behaviors, and be heterosexual as children of heterosexual mothers.

LEARNING ACTIVITY   **What Makes a Family?**

Conduct an informal survey of the people on your dorm floor or in an organization to which you belong about the structure of their family of origin. Whom do they consider to be in their family? What relation do these people have to them? Did all of these people live in the same house? Who had primary responsibility for caring for them as children? Who was primarily responsible for the financial well-being of the family? For the emotional well-being of the family? Was the family closely connected to extended family? If so, which extended family members and in what ways?

Compare your findings with those of your classmates. What do your findings lead you to surmise about what makes a family? How closely do the families of your interviewees resemble the dominant notion of the nuclear family—a husband and wife (in their first marriage) and their two or three children? What do you think is the impact of our stereotype of the nuclear family on social policy? How do you think this stereotype affects real families dealing with the real problems of everyday family life?

the status of families within a society—especially their access to economic resources. As the reading "Cheaper than a Cow" by Miranda Kennedy, a journalist based in New Delhi writing for *Ms.* magazine, demonstrates, in countries where many families are in poverty, accompanied by male power over women in these families, women are sold and traded as commodities. In the United States, there is no "normal" family even though it tends to be constructed as the nuclear family of the middle-class, White, married, heterosexual couple with children. Nuclear family implies a married couple residing together with their children, and it can be distinguished from an extended family in which a group of related kin, in addition to parents and children, live together in the same household. The nuclear family arose as a result of Western industrialization that separated the home from productive activities. In pre- and early-industrial times, the family was relatively self-sufficient in producing goods for family consumption and exchange with other families. As industrial capitalism developed, family members increasingly worked outside the home for wages that were spent on goods for family consumption. In this era of global expansion and production/consumption, family labor is both utilized and central to maintaining corporate profits.

Traditional myths about the normative family are rampant in the United States, and they hide the reality of the wide diversity of family life. There has been a significant drop in the number of legally married heterosexual couples in recent years with more cohabitation (living together), delayed marriage, and lesbian partnerships. These changes are related to the increased economic independence of women. Divorce rates have decreased slightly, although remarriage rates are still high. As a result, this diversity of families includes single parents, extended and multigenerational families, lesbian and gay families with and without children, people (single or not and with or without children) living in community with other adults, grandparents raising grandchildren or nieces and nephews, and so forth. And, of course, these families represent all social classes and all sexualities and racial and ethnic groups. Globally, family structure is affected by the consequences of the global economy as well as by militarism and colonial expansion.

Despite such diversity among U.S. families, legislation such as the Defense of Marriage Act (DOMA) passed in 1996 and subsequent state mandates have restricted the legality of unions beyond the male/husband and female/wife relationship. Still, Massachusetts does recognize gay marriage—and Vermont, civil unions—as of this writing. The reading "Partners as Parents: Challenges Faced by Gays Denied Marriage" by Charlene Gomes discusses these issues in the context of parenting, adoption, and custody legislation. The ongoing political debate concerning "family values" illustrates how supporters of the *status quo* (or existing power relations) in society have made the term *family values* synonymous with traditional definitions of the family and its role in society. This includes seeing women defined in terms of their domestic and reproductive roles, men as the rightful sources of power and authority, and married heterosexual families as the only legitimate family. Many people are offended by this narrow construction of family and its association with a repressive political agenda, and they reject these values as *their* family values. Determining what kinds of families get to be counted as "real" families and determining whose "family values" are used as standards for judging others are heated topics of debate in the United States.

The notion of family—with all its connotations of love, security, connectedness, and nurturing—is a prime target for nostalgia in the twenty-first century. As economic forces have transformed the ways that families function, we yearn for a return to the traditional family, with its unconditional love and acceptance, to escape from the complexities and harsh realities of society. Although many families do provide this

"You just wait until your other mother gets home, young man!"

respite, dominant ideologies about the family have idealized and sometimes glorified the family, and women's roles in the family, in ways that hide underlying conflict and violence. In addition, these ideologies present a false dichotomization between public (society) and private (family) spheres. Poor and non-White families have rarely enjoyed the security and privacy assumed in this split between family and society. For example, the state, in terms of both social welfare policies and criminal justice statutes, has stronger impact and more consequences on poor families than middle-class families. This is the topic of the next section: the connections between the family and other social institutions.

INSTITUTIONAL CONNECTIONS

The family interacts with other institutions in society and provides various experiences for family members. For example, economic forces shape women's family roles and help construct the balance between work and family responsibilities. As discussed in Chapter 8, women perform over two-thirds of household labor—labor that is constructed as family work and often not seen as work. In addition, the family work that women do in the home is used to justify the kinds of work women are expected to perform in the labor force. It is no coincidence that women are congregated in a small number of occupations known for their caretaking, educating, and servicing responsibilities. In addition, the boundaries are more fluid between women's paid work and home life than between men's. This is structured into the very kinds of jobs women tend to perform, as well as part of the expectations associated with hiring women. These assumptions can be used against women very easily as women attempt to advance in their careers. At the same time, the more rigid boundaries between work and home for male-dominated jobs mean that men have a more difficult time with parenting responsibilities when they want to be more actively involved in their children's lives.

The economic system impacts families in many ways; in turn, families support and impact economic systems. Women care for and maintain male workers as well as socialize future generations of workers, thus supporting economic institutions that rely on workers to be fed, serviced, and able to fulfill certain work roles. Although in contemporary U.S. society some families are still productive units in that they produce goods directly for family consumption or for exchange on the market, most families are consumptive units in that they participate in the market economy through goods purchased for family consumption. As a result, advertisers target women as family shoppers. The family is a consumptive unit that provides the context for advertising, media, and other forms of entertainment. In these ways family systems are intimately connected to economic forces in society.

The impact of shifting economies and changing technologies on families varies considerably by gender, class, sexuality, and race, such that a family's placement in the larger political economy directly influences diverse patterns of family organization. Economic factors impact single-headed families such that households headed by women have about half the income and less than a third of the wealth (assets) of other U.S. households and are three times as likely to be at or below the poverty level. Most recent census data show that the poverty rate for single mothers

(34 percent) is twice as high as the rate for single fathers (17 percent). Almost half of children living in single-headed households live in poverty. Race impacts this economic situation such that households headed by women of color are the most likely to experience poverty. It is well known that the most effective anti-poverty program for families is one that includes educational opportunities, a living wage with benefits, and good quality child care. In this way families are shaped by their relationship to systems of inequality in society. This means, for example, that working-class women's lack of flexible work scheduling affects how families are able to meet their needs, as does the lower pay of working-class women, making them less able to afford quality daycare. Similarly, higher unemployment among men of color as compared to White men impacts families and pushes women in family relationships with unemployed men to work outside the home full-time while also taking care of young children. Similarly, Charlene Gomes, attorney and women's rights activist, focuses on heterosexism and the challenges facing gay couples in "Partners as Parents." Jobs with different incomes and levels of authority and seniority affect access to such family-friendly benefits as flextime, on-site childcare, and company-sponsored tax breaks for childcare. For example, although parenting leave is a legal right of all U.S. employees, many companies provide better family benefits for their higher level and better paid employees than they do for their lower level employees.

The family experience is also affected by the state and its legal and political systems. The government closely regulates the family and provides certain benefits to legally married couples. Couples need a license from the state to marry, and the government says they may file a joint tax return. Most lesbian and gay couples who jointly own property and share income and expenses do not have the privileges of marriage, joint tax filing, and, in many situations, domestic partner benefits. Benefits accrue to certain family members but not to people who, even though they might see themselves as family, are not recognized as such by the state. In addition, although an advanced industrial society, the United States has no national funding of daycare centers, and this affects the social organization of the family and the experience of parenting. Federal and state policies also impact the family through legal statutes that regulate marriage and divorce legislation, reproductive choice, and violence in families.

Indeed, the family has connections to all societal institutions, and these connections help shape the kind and quality of experiences that we have as family members. Religion and the family are closely tied as social institutions. Religious socialization

LEARNING ACTIVITY   **Families and Poverty**

Go to the Web site of the 2000 U.S. Census at *www.census.gov/main/www/cen2000.html.* Click on the link to the American FactFinder. In the "Basic Facts" box, select "Economic Characteristics: Employment, Income, Poverty, and more." Select your state and town to find out more information about income and families in poverty where you live.

of children occurs in the family through religious and moral teachings, and religious institutions often shape societal understandings of families as well as provide rituals that help symbolize family and kin relations (such as baptisms, weddings, and funerals). Educational institutions rely on the family as a foundation for socialization and care and maintenance of children, and health systems rely on parents (and women in particular) to nurse and care for sick and elderly family members as well as provide adequate nutrition and cleanliness to prevent disease. Military institutions need the family as a foundation for ideologies of combat and for socialization and support of military personnel. Sports and athletics are tied to the family through gender socialization, the purchase of certain equipment and opportunities, and the consumption and viewing of professional sports in the home. Although we might like to think of the family as an "oasis" apart from society, nothing could be further from the truth. *You cannot dissociate family from society*

POWER AND FAMILY RELATIONSHIPS

At the direct level of experience, the family is the social unit where most people are raised, learn systems of belief, experience love, perhaps abuse and neglect, and generally grow to be a part of communities and society. It is in the family where most of us internalize messages about ourselves, about others, and about our place in the world. Some of us learn that love comes with an abuse of power as large people hit little people, all in the name of love. Others learn that love means getting our own way without responsibility—a lesson that may detract from the hopes of a civil society where individuals care about one another and the communities of which they are a part.

Family is where many of us first experience gender because societal understandings of the differences between girls and boys are transferred through early teachings by family members. Parents bring home baby girls and boys, dress them in gender "appropriate" colors, give them different toys, and decorate their bedrooms in different ways. As Chapter 3 emphasized, the family is a primary institution for teaching about gender. Experiences of gender are very much shaped by the gender composition of family members. A girl growing up in a family of brothers and a boy growing up with only women and girls in his family have different experiences of gender. This is illustrated in the reading by writer Sandra Cisneros titled "Only Daughter."

Central in any discussion of family is a focus on power. Power in families is understood as access to resources (tangible or intangible) that allows certain family members to define the reality of others, have their needs met, and experience more resources. In most U.S. families today, power is distributed according to age and gender. Older family members (although not the aged, who often lose power in late life) tend to have more power than children and young people, who are often defined as "dependents." Men have more power in the family than women do if this is measured in resource management and allocation and decision-making authority. Women, however, do have power if this is defined as day-to-day decisions about the running of the household and how certain household chores get done. Sociologists, however, tend to emphasize that this latter sort of "power" is vulnerable to changes in broader family dynamics and subject to decisions by men in positions as major economic providers or heads of household. Sean Elder focuses on issues of power

ACTIVIST PROFILE **Hannah Solomon**

Hannah Greenbaum Solomon believed that "woman's sphere is the whole wide world" and her first responsibility was to her family. Solomon worked tirelessly in turn-of-the-century Chicago for social reform. Laboring alongside Jane Addams at Hull House, Solomon worked to improve child welfare. She reformed the Illinois Industrial School for Girls, established penny lunch stations in the public schools, and led efforts for slum clearance, low-cost housing, child labor laws, mothers' pensions, and public health measures.

In 1876 Solomon became the first Jewish member of the Chicago Woman's Club, where she developed a sense of women's ability to work together for social good. In 1893 she organized the Jewish Women's Congress at the Chicago World's Fair, which led to her founding the National Council of Jewish Women (NCJW) to enhance social welfare and justice. Solomon saw her commitment to justice as a part of her responsibility as a Jew, a woman, and an American.

Under Solomon's leadership, the National Council of Jewish Women sponsored programs for the blind, formed the Port and Dock Department to assist immigrant women in finding housing and jobs, established a permanent immigrant aid station on Ellis Island, supported Margaret Sanger's National Birth Control League, raised relief dollars during World War I, and participated in the presidential effort to create jobs during the Depression.

Solomon's legacy has continued in the NCJW since her death in 1942. Following World War II, the NCJW provided assistance to Holocaust survivors in Europe and Israel. During the McCarthy era, NCJW organized the Freedom Campaign to protect civil liberties. Additionally, the organization was the first national group to sponsor Meals on Wheels, built the Hebrew University High School in Jerusalem, helped establish the Court Appointed Advocate Project (CASA) to protect the rights of children in court cases, and launched a national campaign to try to ensure that children were not harmed by changes in welfare law.

Currently, the National Council of Jewish Women has 90,000 members and continues the work of Hannah Solomon by bringing her vision of justice to bear in the world.

and intimacy and provides suggestions for men who seek or find themselves in relationships with independent women in the reading "The Emperor's New Woes."

The United States has among the highest marriage and the highest divorce rates of any industrialized country despite some recent decline. Although a large number of people get divorced, this does not seem to indicate disillusionment with marriage because large numbers of people go on to remarry. Marriage traditionally has been based on gender relations that prescribe authority of husbands over wives and that entail certain norms and expectations that are sanctioned by the state. The traditional

LEARNING ACTIVITY   **Divorce Law: Who Benefits in My State?**

Research your state's divorce laws. How is property divided in a divorce? How is custody determined? How are alimony and child support determined? How do these laws affect women and children in actuality in your state? What are the poverty rates for divorced women and their children in your state? How many fathers do not pay child support as ordered by the court? How does your state deal with nonpaying fathers? What can you do to challenge the legal system in your state to be more responsive to women and children's needs following divorce?

IDEAS FOR ACTIVISM

- Become a Court Appointed Special Advocate (CASA) for children.
- Offer to baby-sit for free for a single mother one evening a month.
- Lobby your state lawmakers to enact legislation recognizing lesbian and gay unions.
- Organize an educational activity on your campus around alternative family models.

marriage contract assumes the husband will be the head of household with responsibilities to provide a family wage and the wife will take primary responsibility for the home and the raising of children and integrate her personal identity with that of her husband. As in "Mrs. John Smith" and "Dr. and Mrs. John Smith," Mrs. Smith easily can become someone who loses her identity to her husband. The declaration of "man and wife" in the traditional marriage ceremony illustrates how men continue to be men under this contract and women become wives. These norms are increasingly challenged by contemporary couples who have moved from this traditional contract to one whereby women are expected to contribute financially and men are expected to fulfill family roles. Despite these modifications, husbands still tend to hold more power in families and women do the majority of physical and emotional family work. The rituals of marriage ceremonies illustrate these normative gender relations: the father "giving away" his daughter, representing the passage of the woman from one man's house to another; the wearing of white to symbolize purity and virginity; the engagement ring representing a woman already spoken for; and the throwing of rice to symbolize fertility and the woman's obligation to bear and raise children.

It is especially in the family where many girls and women experience gender oppression; in close relationship with men, they often experience gender domination. In other words, it is in the home and family where many girls and women feel the consequences of masculine power and privilege. Writing in 1910, socialist anarchist Emma Goldman saw marriage as an economic transaction that binds women into subservience to men (through love and personal and sexual services) and society

HISTORICAL MOMENT   **The Feminine Mystique**

In 1963 Betty Friedan, a housewife and former labor activist, published the results of a series of interviews she had conducted with women who had been educated at Smith College. Despite their picture-perfect lives, these women reported extreme despair and unhappiness and, unaware that others shared this experience, blamed themselves. To deal with this "problem that has no name," these women turned to a variety of strategies, ranging from using tranquilizers to having affairs to volunteering with church, school, and charitable organizations.

What had happened to these educated women? Following World War II, when women had found a prominent role in the workforce, a national myth emerged that the place for (middle-class, White) women was in the home. To conform to this ideal, women sublimated their dreams and desires and fell in line with "the feminine mystique."

When Friedan's book, *The Feminine Mystique,* appeared in 1963, it spoke loudly to the unspoken misery of millions of American housewives. In its first year, it sold 3 million copies. Unfortunately, during the era just immediately following the repressive, anti-Communist McCarthy years, Friedan feared that were she to push the envelope in her book to include an analysis of race and social class, her work would be discredited. So, rather than choosing to address the more complex problems of working-class women and women of color and likely be dismissed, she chose to be heard and addressed the safer topic of middle-class housewives.

Despite its shortcomings, *The Feminine Mystique* found a readership that needed to know that they were not alone in believing that something was seriously wrong with their lives. Friedan suggested that that something wrong was a conspiracy of social institutions and culture that limited the lives of women. She challenged women to find meaningful and purposeful ways of living, particularly through careers. ✳

While Friedan did not go so far as to question the need for men to move into equitable work in the home as she was encouraging women to move out into the workforce or to examine the social and economic, as well as psychological, forces at work in limiting women's lives, she did bring to national attention the problem of women's circumscribed existence and offered a call for women to begin to examine the limitations imposed on them.

Source: Ruth Rosen, *The World Split Open: How the Modern Women's Movement Changed America* (New York: Viking, 2000).

(through unpaid housework). In the reading "Marriage and Love," she advocated "free love" that is unconstrained by marriage and relations with the state. Goldman believed love found in marriages occurred in spite of the institution of marriage and not because of it.

Sexism in interpersonal relationships among family members reduces female autonomy and lowers women's and girls' self-esteem. Consequences of masculine privilege in families can mean that men dominate women in relationships in subtle or not-so-subtle ways, expecting or taking for granted personal and sexual services,

*"Yes, this is a two career household.
Unfortunately I have both careers."*

Reprinted with permission from Carol Simpson Productions.

making and/or vetoing important family decisions, controlling money and expenditures, and so forth. In addition, power in family and marital relationships may lead to psychological, sexual, and/or physical abuse against women and children. Often the double standard of sexual conduct allows boys more freedom and autonomy compared to girls. Also, girls are very often expected to perform more household duties than boys, duties that may include cleaning up after their brothers or father.

In particular, the balance of power in marriage (or any domestic partnership) depends in part on how couples negotiate paid labor and family work in their relationships. Marriages or domestic partnerships can be structured according to different models that promote various ways that couples live and work together. These models include "head–complement," "junior partner/senior partner," and "equal partners"—relationships that each have different ways of negotiating paid work and family work, and, as a result, provide different balances of power within these relationships.

The "head–complement" model reflects the traditional marriage contract as discussed previously whereby the head/husband has responsibilities to provide a family wage and the complement/wife takes primary responsibility for the home and the raising of children. In addition the complement sees (usually her) role as complementing the head's role by being supportive and encouraging in both emotional and material ways. The balance of power in this family system is definitely tilted in the direction of the "head" of the head–complement couple. Power for the complement is to a large extent based on the goodwill of the head as well as the resources (educational and financial in particular) that the complement brings into the relationship. Although the complement does tend to have control over the day-to-day running of the household, this power may disappear with divorce or other internal family disruption. It is estimated that heterosexual head–complement families make up only about 14 percent of all families in the United States.

The "junior partner/senior partner" model is where, as discussed above, the traditional marriage contract has been modified. Both members of the couple work outside the home, although one member (usually wife or female domestic partner) considers her work to be secondary to the senior partner's job. She also takes primary responsibility for the home and childcare. This means that the junior partner has taken on some of the provider role while still maintaining responsibility for the domestic role. In practice this might mean that if the senior partner is transferred or relocated because of (usually his) work, the junior partner experiences a disruption in her work to follow. If someone is contacted when the children come home from school sick, it is the junior partner. She might enter and leave the labor force based on the needs of the children and family. This model, the most frequently occurring structure for marriage or domestic partnerships today, encourages the double day of work for women where they work both inside and outside the home.

In terms of power, there is a more equitable sharing in this model than in the head–complement model because the junior partner is bringing resources into the family and has control over the day-to-day running of the household. Note in both models described here, the head and senior partner loses out to a greater or lesser degree on the joys associated with household work—especially the raising of children. Junior partners tend to fare better after divorce than the "complements" of the head–complement model. But junior partners do have the emotional stress and physical burdens of working two jobs. These stresses and burdens are affected by how much the senior partner helps out in the home.

The "equal partners" model is one in which the traditional marriage contract is completely disrupted. Neither partner is more likely to perform provider or domestic roles. In practice this might mean both jobs or careers are valued equally such that one does not take priority over the other and domestic responsibilities are shared equally. Alternatively, it might mean an intentional sharing of responsibilities such that one partner agrees to be the economic provider for a period of time and the other agrees to take on domestic responsibilities, although neither is valued more than the other, and this is negotiated rather than implied. In this model financial power is shared, and the burdens and joys of domestic work and childcare are also shared. Although this arrangement gives women the most power in marriage or domestic partnerships, not surprisingly it is a relatively infrequent arrangement among contemporary couples. This is because, first, most men in domestic relationships have been socialized to expect the privileges associated with having women service their everyday needs or raise their children, and most women expect to take on these responsibilities. Both men and women rarely question this taken-for-granted gendered division of labor. Second, men's jobs are more likely to involve a separation of home and work, and it is more difficult for them to integrate these aspects of their lives. Third, men tend to earn more money than women do on the average, and although it might be relatively easy to value women's paid work equally in theory, it is difficult to do so in practice if one job brings in a much higher salary than the other. For example, imagine an equal partner relationship between a dentist and a dental hygienist. These occupations are very gender segregated, with the majority of dentists being men and dental hygienists women. Although the couple may value each other's work equally, it might be difficult for a family to make decisions concerning relocation and so forth in favor of the one partner who works as the dental hygienist because she makes a small percentage of her partner's salary as a dentist.

It is important to emphasize that despite these various arrangements and the differential balance of power in marriage or domestic partnerships, for many women the family is where they feel most empowered. Many women find the responsibilities of maintaining a household or the challenges of child rearing fulfilling and come to see the family as a source of their competency and happiness. Sometimes this involves living in traditional family forms, and sometimes it means devising new ways of living in families. In this way the family is a positive source of connection, community, and/or productive labor. These diverse experiences associated with family life suggest how family relationships are a complex tangle of compliance to and resistance against various forms of inequities. Mothering, in particular, is one experience that often brings women great joy and shapes their experiences of family relations at the very same time that in patriarchal societies it may function as a form of behavioral constraint. This is the topic to which we now turn.

MOTHERING

Although the meaning and practice of motherhood is culturally constructed, it tends to be conflated with notions of innate, biologically programmed behavior and expectations of unconditional love and nurturance. In other words, even though the meanings associated with motherhood vary historically and culturally, women are expected to want to be mothers, and mothers are expected to take primary responsibility for the nurturing of children. Unlike the assumptions associated with "to father," "to mother" implies nurturing, comforting, and caretaking. You might mother a kitten or a friend without the assumption of having given birth to them. To have fathered a kitten implies paternity: you are its parent; you did not cuddle and take care of it. Similarly, to father a friend makes no sense in this context. In contemporary U.S. society, there is a cultural construction of "normal motherhood" that is class and race based, and sees mothers as devoted to and sacrificing for their children. In addition, as global societies have developed and the expectations associated with the role of motherhood have been framed by patterns of consumption in "First World" postindustrial societies, the role of the "perfect" middle-class mother has also been transformed to involve managing a child's life and providing educational opportunities as well as succeeding in a career. Judith Warner addresses the stresses associated with these issues in "The Myth of the Perfect Mother."

This primary association between women and the nurturing aspects of mothering has brought joys and opportunities for empowerment as well as problems and hardship. It has justified the enormous amount of work we do in the home and encouraged girls to set their sights on babies rather than on other forms of productive work. It has justified the type of labor women have traditionally done in the labor force as well as justified lower pay, it has kept women out of specific positions such

Facts About Singles

Singleness

100 million
Number of unmarried and single Americans. This group comprises 44 percent of all U.S. residents age 15 and over.

53 percent
Percentage of unmarried and single Americans who are women.

64 percent
Percentage of unmarried and single Americans who have never been married. Another 22 percent are divorced, and 14 percent are widowed.

14.9 million
Number of unmarried and single Americans age 65 and over. These older Americans comprise 15 percent of all unmarried and single people.

87
Number of unmarried men age 15 and over for every 100 unmarried women in the United States.

49 million
Number of households maintained by unmarried men or women. These households comprise 44 percent of households nationwide.

Parenting

33 percent
Percentage of births in 2002 to unmarried women.

12.4 million
Number of single parents living with their children. Of these, 10.1 million are single mothers.

41 percent
Percentage of opposite-sex, unmarried-partner households that include children.

680,000
Number of unmarried grandparents who are responsible for caring for their grandchildren. These grandparents comprise nearly 3 in 10 grandparents who are responsible for their grandchildren.

Unmarried Couples

4.6 million
Number of unmarried-partner households. These households consist of a householder living with someone of the opposite sex who was identified as their unmarried partner.

Voters

36 percent
Percentage of voters in the 2004 presidential election who were unmarried.

Education

82 percent
Percentage of unmarried people age 25 or older who are high school graduates.

23 percent
Percentage of unmarried people age 25 or older with a bachelor's degree or more education.

Source: U.S. Census Bureau Public Information Office.

as in the military where they might be involved in taking life rather than giving life, and it has encouraged all kinds of explanations for why men are, and should be, in control in society. The close relationship between womanhood and mothering has caused pain for women who are not able to have children as well as for those who have intentionally chosen to not have any. In addition, mothering a disabled child brings its own challenges and joys, as the reading by Eva Feder Kittay aptly demonstrates. This article discusses how ableism and the normatively abled notion of childhood construct institutional responses that affect the experience of mothering.

In this way, contemporary constructions of mothering, like the family, tend to be created around a mythical norm that reflects a White, abled, middle-class, heterosexual, and young adult experience. But, of course, mothers come in all types and reflect the wide diversity of women in the United States. Their understandings of their roles and their position within systems of inequality and privilege are such that mothering is a diverse experience. This is because society has different expectations of mothers depending on class and culture and other differences at the same time that these differences create different attitudes toward the experience of mothering. For example, although society often expects poor mothers to work outside the home rather than accept welfare, middle-class mothers might be made to feel guilty for "abandoning" their babies to daycare centers. Because of class, ethnicity, and/or religious orientation, some women experience more ambivalence than others when it comes to combining work and family roles. A little over one-quarter of all births in the United States are to single mothers, and many more women become single in the process of raising children. Motherhood for single mothers is often constructed through societal notions of stigma.

Interracial or lesbian couples or people who adopt a child of another race are often accused of not taking into account the best interests of their children. Of course, it is society that has these problems and the families are doing their best to cope. Lesbian mothers in particular have to deal with two mutually exclusive categories that have been constructed as contradictory: mother and lesbian. This illustrates the narrow understandings of motherhood as well as the stereotypes associated with being a mother and with being a lesbian. In addition, as discussed in the Gomes reading, in most states lesbian mothers (although often mothering with a female partner who also parents) are legally understood as single mothers: women parenting with an absent father. As a result, they must deal with that stigma too. Audre Lorde goes one step further and focuses on the stigma and difficulties of raising male children in lesbian families. This classic article encourages all acts of mothering to be guided by feminist anti-racist practices.

In this way, American families are increasingly diverse forms of social organization that are intricately connected to other institutions in society. The family is a basic social unit around which much of society is built; it is fundamental to the processes of meeting individual and social needs. The centrality of the family in U.S. society encourages us to think about the way the family reproduces and resists gender relations and what it means to each of us in our everyday lives.

Marriage and Love

Emma Goldman (1910)

The popular notion about marriage and love is that they are synonymous, that they spring from the same motives, and cover the same human needs. Like most popular notions this also rests not on actual facts, but on superstition.

Marriage and love have nothing in common; they are as far apart as the poles; are, in fact, antagonistic to each other. No doubt some marriages have been the result of love. Not, however, because love could assert itself only in marriage; much rather is it because few people can completely outgrow a convention. There are today large numbers of men and women to whom marriage is naught but a farce, but who submit to it for the sake of public opinion. At any rate, while it is true that some marriages are based on love, and while it is equally true that in some cases love continues in married life, I maintain that it does so regardless of marriage, and not because of it.

On the other hand, it is utterly false that love results from marriage. On rare occasions one does hear of a miraculous case of a married couple falling in love after marriage, but on close examination it will be found that it is a mere adjustment to the inevitable. Certainly the growing-used to each other is far away from the spontaneity, the intensity, and beauty of love, without which the intimacy of marriage must prove degrading to both the woman and the man.

Marriage is primarily an economic arrangement, an insurance pact. It differs from the ordinary life insurance agreement only in that it is more binding, more exacting. Its returns are insignificantly small compared with the investments. In taking out an insurance policy one pays for it in dollars and cents, always at liberty to discontinue payments. If, however, woman's premium is a husband, she pays for it with her name, her privacy, her self-respect, her very life, "until death doth part." Moreover, the marriage insurance condemns her to life-long dependency, to parasitism, to complete uselessness, individual as well as social. Man, too, pays his toll, but as his sphere is wider, marriage does not limit him as much as woman. He feels his chains more in an economic sense.

Thus Dante's motto over Inferno applies with equal force to marriage. "Ye who enter here leave all hope behind."

. . .

From infancy, almost, the average girl is told that marriage is her ultimate goal; therefore her training and education must be directed towards that end. Like the mute beast fattened for slaughter, she is prepared for that. Yet, strange to say, she is allowed to know much less about her function as wife and mother than the ordinary artisan of his trade. It is indecent and filthy for a respectable girl to know anything of the marital relation. Oh, for the inconsistency of respectability, that needs the marriage vow to turn something which is filthy into the purest and most sacred arrangement that none dare question or criticize. Yet that is exactly the attitude of the average upholder of marriage. The prospective wife and mother is kept in complete ignorance of her only asset in the competitive field—sex. Thus she enters into life-long relations with a man only to find herself shocked, repelled, outraged beyond measure by the most natural and healthy instinct, sex. It is safe to say that a large percentage of the unhappiness, misery, distress, and physical suffering of matrimony is due to the criminal ignorance in sex matters that is being extolled as a great virtue.

Nor is it at all an exaggeration when I say that more than one home has been broken up because of this deplorable fact.

If, however, woman is free and big enough to learn the mystery of sex without the sanction of State or Church, she will stand condemned as utterly unfit to become the wife of a "good" man, his goodness consisting of an empty brain and plenty of money. Can there be anything more outrageous than the idea that a healthy, grown woman, full of life and passion, must deny nature's demand, must subdue her most intense craving, undermine her health and break her spirit, must stunt her vision, abstain from the depth and glory of sex experience until a "good" man comes along to take her unto himself as a wife? That is precisely what marriage means. How can such an arrangement end except in failure? This is one, though not the least important, factor of marriage, which differentiates it from love.

Ours is a practical age. The time when Romeo and Juliet risked the wrath of their fathers for love, when Gretchen exposed herself to the gossip of her neighbors for love, is no more. If, on rare occasions, young people allow themselves the luxury of romance, they are taken in care by the elders, drilled and pounded until they become "sensible."

The moral lesson instilled in the girl is not whether the man has aroused her love, but rather it is, "How much?" The important and only God of practical American life: Can the man make a living? Can he support a wife? That is the only thing that justifies marriage. Gradually this saturates every thought of the girl; her dreams are not of moonlight and kisses, of laughter and tears; she dreams of shopping tours and bargain counters. This soul poverty and sordidness are the elements inherent in the marriage institution. The State and the Church approve of no other ideal, simply because it is the one that necessitates the State and Church control of men and women.

Doubtless there are people who continue to consider love above dollars and cents. Particularly is this true of that class whom economic necessity has forced to become self-supporting. The tremendous change in woman's position, wrought by that mighty factor, is indeed phenomenal when we reflect that it is but a short time since she has entered the industrial arena. Six million women wage workers; six million women, who have the equal right with men to be exploited, to be robbed, to go on strike; aye, to starve even. Anything more, my lord? Yes, six million wage workers in every walk of life, from the highest brain work to the mines and railroad tracks; yes, even detectives and policemen. Surely the emancipation is complete.

Yet with all that, but a very small number of the vast army of women wage workers look upon work as a permanent issue, in the same light as does man. No matter how decrepit the latter, he has been taught to be independent, self-supporting. Oh, I know that no one is really independent in our economic treadmill; still, the poorest specimen of a man hates to be a parasite; to be known as such, at any rate.

The woman considers her position as worker transitory, to be thrown aside for the first bidder. That is why it is infinitely harder to organize women than men. "Why should I join a union? I am going to get married, to have a home." Has she not been taught from infancy to look upon that as her ultimate calling? She learns soon enough that the home, though not so large a prison as the factory, has more solid doors and bars. It has a keeper so faithful that naught can escape him. The most tragic part, however, is that the home no longer frees her from wage slavery; it only increases her task.

According to the latest statistics submitted before a Committee "on labor and wages, and congestion of population," ten percent of the wage workers in New York City alone are married, yet they must continue to work at the most poorly paid labor in the world. Add to this horrible aspect the drudgery of housework, and what remains of the protection and glory of the home? As a matter of fact, even the middle-class girl in marriage can not speak of her home, since it is the man who creates her sphere. It is not important whether the husband is a brute or a darling. What I wish to prove is that marriage guarantees woman a home only by the grace of her husband.

There she moves about in *his* home, year after year, until her aspect of life and human affairs becomes as flat, narrow, and drab as her surroundings. Small wonder if she becomes a nag, petty, quarrelsome, gossipy, unbearable, thus driving the man from the house. She could not go, if she wanted to; there is no place to go. Besides, a short period of married life, of complete surrender of all faculties, absolutely incapacitates the average woman for the outside world. She becomes reckless in appearance, clumsy in her movements, dependent in her decisions, cowardly in her judgment, a weight and a bore, which most men grow to hate and despise. . . .

The institution of marriage makes a parasite of woman, an absolute dependent. It incapacitates her for life's struggle, annihilates her social consciousness, paralyzes her imagination, and then imposes its gracious protection, which is in reality a snare, a travesty on human character.

R E A D I N G **54**

Cheaper than a Cow

Miranda Kennedy

On a muggy monsoon morning in Kufurpur village, north India, Pornita Das is making tea for the man who owns her.

She is a pretty girl in her late teens, wearing a *choli,* or short blouse, and a long underskirt—the typical underclothes of the region. She had come here believing she would be married, but instead she's become part of a sad demographic: a growing number of girls sold by their families in India's poorest states and bought for as little as $10 by men in prosperous parts of the country.

When young women such as Pornita arrive in their new village, their trafficker often displays them under a tree in the main market, like a slave on an auction block, and takes bids. Those bids can range up to $400, depending on the girl's age and the degree of abuse already inflicted on her by the trafficker. The girls are almost always virgins, and they are usually sold for less than the price of a cow.

In their new home, the girls often become a combination of family sex slave and domestic servant. Some girls are found chained in their owner's house; others are repeatedly raped and tortured. Even those who are better treated are expected to give birth to a son, considered a prize in Indian culture. If they fail to, they are often resold.

India's newest flesh trade is different from the trafficking of girls into brothels, although that still takes place across India. This form of trafficking emerged from the common and perfectly legal practice of finding brides in far-flung areas of the country. But when people realized how cheaply they could get girls from underprivileged West Bengal, Bihar, and the more remote string of northeastern states, they started buying young women for uses besides marriage, such as providing sexual favors to the men in a family. For propriety's sake, the eldest son will call the woman his wife, but rarely bothers with the expense—and official interference—of a wedding. Most Indian marriages are arranged, and after marriage the bride usually goes to live with her husband's family, which makes it difficult to detect girls exploited in this way.

Pappu Singh Ahir, the man Pornita calls her husband, has never married her, probably because she was underage when he bought her and he didn't want to alert the authorities. He is around 40—at least double her age, although it is hard to know for certain because his family is deliberately vague about how old Pornita is. Marriage under the age of 18 is illegal in India, although in rural areas it is still common practice. Buying girls and using them as sex slaves, however, was never common in India—until recently, when villagers became desperate for brides, and for sons.

Like many buyers, Pappu and his family refuse to admit that money exchanged hands. They say the only money they paid was the cost of transporting Pornita from her village in Assam state, in the far east of India. But Pappu Singh is not new to this business: He is accused of previously buying another young girl, Kanika, who mysteriously disappeared soon after he purchased her. As the tea boils, Pappu's mother steps into the room to warn Pornita, Kanika's replacement, not to speak openly.

It takes less than an hour to get to Kufurpur village from New Delhi, India's cosmopolitan political capital. Yet in almost every way, the villages in this region seem centuries behind the capital's world of frappuccinos and brand-name malls. There are few paved roads; during the long monsoon season, the surrounding "highways" are lined with trucks flipped on their sides in thick mud. This isn't a poor area, though: Kufurpur lies in Haryana state, the center of north India's prosperous and fertile "Hindi belt." Many farmers tend their fields with tractors here, rather than with the water buffaloes used in less affluent regions. Yet few men attend school past the age of 16, and women rarely attend at all. The attitudes are deeply feudal, and every other household includes a girl known as a *paro,* or outsider bride.

"Although it is one of the most economically affluent areas of the country, there is basically no social sensitization here," says Ravi Kant, director of Shakti Vahini, an organization fighting for sex workers' rights. "The villagers are not even aware that trafficking is a problem. They think it is their right to purchase girls and bring them back to their homes."

The Kufurpur men, hearing word of visitors, gather in the courtyard of Pappu Singh's house. The haunting sound of a peacock's mating cry echoes through the village as rain pours down.

The men have rough, weathered faces; although it is barely midday, most of them are swaying from the effects of cheap liquor. Like Pappu, they are landowners, and do not have to work much. They are more than happy to gather and give their opinions on Pappu Singh's *paro.* "Pappu had to marry a girl from outside because time had passed. He was too old and no one here wanted him," one explains. "There are no girls here for us to marry," shouts another, who says he is 25 but looks more like a ragged 45. "So we bring girls from outside, what's wrong with that?"

The problem for Indian men, says Vina Mazumdar of the Center for Women's Development Studies in New Delhi, is a shocking gender gap—"an acute shortage of brides for young men. That's the result of the steadily declining proportion of girls being born across India."

In the decade between 1991 and 2001, the number of girls (up to age 6) per 1,000 boys dropped from 945 to 927. In certain Indian regions, the problem is far worse: In one part of Haryana state, for example, the ratio has plummeted to 770 girls per 1,000 boys. Meanwhile, the population of India has ballooned above the 1 billion mark and is expected to surpass China by midcentury.

"A stage may soon come when it would become extremely difficult, if not impossible, to make up for the missing girls," predicts the United Nations Fund for Population Activities.

This dramatic differential has been created by the purposeful abortion of female fetuses, and even girl infanticide. According to the Campaign Against Female Feticide, 90 percent of the estimated 3.5 million abortions done annually in India are for the purpose of preventing the birth of girl children.

"In places like Punjab and Haryana, if you go into the village and ask people how many children they have, they say two, and they mean two sons, not two children," says Mohan Rao, a professor in the social medicine department at Jawaharlal Nehru University in New Delhi. Aborting a fetus because of its sex is illegal (standard abortions are legal in India), and the government recently toughened laws against prenatal gender screening. Nonetheless, an extremely high demand for the screening tests remains, and little can be done to stop doctors from using ultrasound machines for sex determination. "Unqualified doctors are doing ultrasounds," affirms J.B. Babbar, head medical officer at the Family Planning Association of India. "It's an easy way to make money, because we have such a strong preference for the male child in our culture."

Even poor parents often prefer to front the hefty expense of a sex determination test and abortion rather than to raise a girl. Daughters are commonly viewed as a burden in India, even among the educated classes. It's a belief facilitated by the dowry system—the illegal, but still prevalent practice of the bride's family giving money to the groom—and by the Hindu belief that a father's last rites must be carried out by his son. Many parents perceive girls to be more expensive than boys because girls require dowry money, do not support their parents in their old age, and are traditionally not earners.

"The social belief that sons are the only way to continue the family lineage perpetuates the falling sex ratio," says Indian health minister Sushma Swaraj, who insists her ministry is committed to correcting the problem. Swaraj recently proposed that the government begin an advertising campaign warning that there would not be enough women for men to marry if the trend continued.

But the Indian government is largely unwilling to recognize the connection between the ratio of male to female children and the purchasing of girls.

One woman who certainly grasps that connection is Deepa Das, suspected to have trafficked both Pornita and Kanika to Haryana state. Deepa, a 30-something woman who modestly covers her face in the company of men, was herself bought from Assam 10 years ago by her "husband." Now she lives on a large property dotted with cattle and, according to social workers in the Haryana area, runs a flourishing trade in Assamese girls. Deepa regularly travels back to her home state and convinces villagers to let her take their daughters, jangling her gold bangles and boasting about the buffalo she now owns. Then, she allegedly sells them, at a profit, to families who need brides.

Deepa freely acknowledges that she brings girls to be married in Haryana, but denies that money is involved. "I am doing a social good to bring them here," she insists. "I would have died of poverty if I had not come here. My life is so much better now."

Pornita's story begins some 1,300 miles east of Kufurpur, in a lush green village fed by the Brahmaputra, one of India's largest rivers. She grew up in a house made of bamboo and mud plaster, surrounded by waterlogged rice paddies and groves of coconut palms. Rural Assam is desperately poor, devastated by annual floods, economic isolation and a violent separatist insurgency that has ravaged the region for more than 20 years. Discrimination in greater India against the ethnically distinct Assamese is widespread, and most Assamese do not even speak India's national language, Hindi. Pornita is one of six children, so when a strange woman and man came to her village in search of a girl to take back to their rich land, her parents thought they were lucky and were happy to oblige—especially after they were offered a little money.

"Most parents who live below the poverty line believe that getting their girls married into a good family is the best thing they can give them," explains Hasina Kharbhih, a social worker who rehabilitates girls trafficked from the northeast. "What they don't realize is that these marriages are about exploitation more than anything else."

Pornita's parents had never educated their daughter, and they saw few prospects for her in their depressed village. But they had no idea they were sending her off with a man who would never actually marry her. On a bright afternoon in their village, they sat in their mud courtyard, their cows grazing nearby on freshly cut grass in wicker baskets. Pornita's father's bare legs were spattered with mud from working in the fields, and his teeth stained orange from chewing betelnut *paan*. The frames of his thick glasses were twisted. "I know nothing of Pappu Singh marrying another girl," he crowed. "Pornita is his wife now. She told us she lives in a concrete house. She has three meals a day. What else can matter?"

His wife was more emotional. A photo of their young daughter in her new house in Haryana, wearing the strange new Haryani dress, made her weep. The red *bindi* mark on her forehead smeared into a bloody-looking mark as she wiped her tears. Pornita had recently come back to visit them, bringing her new son, but then she had been dressed in Assamese clothes. She didn't complain to her family about her new life—but that's to be expected. Marriage is seen by many as part of a person's preordained destiny, and the wife's position in her in-laws' house is traditionally very low. Pornita did look a little weaker, her mother recalled. She told them she had recently had her kidney removed, although she had no history of kidney trouble. Rishi Kant of Shakti Vahini suspects that Pappu Singh sold Pornita's kidney for the money. Singh had told his neighbors he needed 10,000 rupees (about $200), and that's just about the price of a kidney on the black market.

Nonetheless, back in Kufurpur, Pornita clearly states that she doesn't want to return permanently to Assam. "I have a child and live with a family," she says as if by rote, her mother-in-law watching her carefully.

"In the villages [of Assam], poor means having no clothes to wear, no food to eat, no house to live in," says Arnab Deka, a superintendent of police for a district in Assam. "So these girls are lured, and their parents think this is an offer from god. By the time that they realize they have been cheated, that this girl has been sold, maybe one year has passed. Then, it is not possible for us to do anything."

Three years ago, Deepa Das showed up in Kanika's village in Assam. Kanika's mother, Omari, a widow, had six daughters and no sons. She barely managed to support her children by weaving saris in her dark one-room shack and working as a maid in a nearby village. It didn't take much to convince her to accept 1,000 rupees (about $20) in exchange for her daughter. But now, sitting on a cot made of woven rope outside her bamboo hut, she says that day was cursed.

"Deepa Das told us there is nothing to worry about," chimes in Kanika's 15-year-old sister, who steps out from the crowd of villagers in a ragged pink dress. "When we called her, she said only 'Kanika is not here.' We asked, 'Who has Kanika married?' But she did not say. Then, she told us Kanika died of some stomach problem, and hung up. But she never gave us the death certificate." Without the confirmation of a body or a proper cremation, Kanika's family refuses to believe she is dead. They suspect she has been resold, perhaps after failing to bear Pappu Singh a son. The police have not yet registered Kanika's case, and social workers despair that they will ever be able to trace her.

After pressure from the media and social workers, village elders mounted an investigation into the charge that Deepa Das was trafficking girls from Assam, but police officials stepped in to vouch for her. Some social workers and activists say it's police involvement in the girl trade that allows it to continue unabated, even alleging that police take kickbacks in exchange for their silence. When asked about the trend of trafficking girls into Haryana, Rajender Kumar, the police superintendent for one Haryana district, simply reiterates that it is not illegal to marry girls from outside the state. "You can't call it trafficking if the mediator charges money," he claims.

Recently, though, the Haryana police have begun cracking down. Last summer, they rescued four female minors from families, arrested the trafficker, and put him behind bars. Once rescued, however, the girls are offered few options. Rehana, a 13-year-old Assamese girl freed from a family after being repeatedly raped and beaten, has been languishing in a Haryana government home for months. Lacking a rehabilitation program, the government put her in a halfway house for female criminals, where she received no counseling.

In Meghalaya, the northeastern state that borders Assam, social worker Hasina Kharbhih has set up a working model that offers some hope. Her group, Impulse NGO Network, works closely with the state government and police to rehabilitate girls who have been trafficked out of the northeast and sold into families or brothels. After they receive counseling, they are taught a trade—usually handicraft or beautician skills. Eventually they are given a microcredit loan to start their own small businesses. They are reintegrated with their families, but not before the family and neighbors are educated about trafficking and sexual violation.

"The most important thing is they have to get back into society," says Hasina. She envisions a time when communities will band together to prevent their girls from being sold. In Kanika's village, such an awareness may already be growing, spurred by her unexplained disappearance. Her neighbors say they will never take money from a stranger for one of their daughters. They see Kanika's mother every evening, as dusk falls, waiting outside her bamboo shack for her daughter to come home.

R E A D I N G **55**

The Myth of the Perfect Mother

Judith Warner

Back in the days when I was a Good Mommy, I tried to do everything right. I breast-fed and co-slept, and responded to each and every cry with anxious alacrity. I awoke with my daughter at 6:30 AM and, eschewing TV, curled up on the couch with a stack of books that I could recite in my sleep. I did this, in fact, many times, jerking myself back awake as the clock rounded 6:45 and the words of Curious George started to merge with my dreams.

Was I crazy? No—I was a committed mother, eager to do right by my child and well versed in the child care teachings of the day. I was proud of the fact that I could get in three full hours of high-intensity parenting before I left for work; prouder still that, when I came home in the evening, I could count on at least three more similarly intense hours to follow. It didn't matter that, in my day job as a stringer for this magazine, I was often falling asleep at my desk. Nor that I'd lost the ability to write a coherent sentence. My brain might have been fried, but my baby's was thriving. I'd seen the proof of that everywhere—in the newsweeklies and the *New York Times,* on TV, even in the official statements that issued forth from the White House, where First Lady Hillary Clinton herself had endorsed "singing, playing games, reading, storytelling, just talking and listening" as the best ways to enhance a child's development.

All around me, the expert advice on baby care, whether it came from the *What to Expect* books or the legions of "specialists" hawking videos, computer software, smart baby toys, or audiotapes to advance brain development, was unanimous: *Read! Talk! Sing!* And so I talked and I read and I sang and made up stories and did funny voices and narrated car rides . . . until one day, when my daughter was about four, I realized that I had turned into a human television set, so filled with 24-hour children's programming that I had no thoughts left of my own.

And when I started listening to the sounds of the Mommy chatter all around me in the playgrounds and playgroups of Washington, D.C.— the shouts of "Good job!," the interventions and facilitations ("What that lady is saying is, she would really prefer you not empty your bucket of sand over her little boy's head. Is that okay with you, honey?")—I realized that I was hardly alone.

Once my daughter began school, I was surrounded, it seemed, by women who had surrendered their better selves—and their sanity—to motherhood. Women who pulled all-nighters hand-painting paper plates for a class party. Who obsessed over the most minute details of play-ground politics. Who—like myself—appeared to be sleep-walking through life in a state of quiet panic.

Some of the mothers appeared to have lost nearly all sense of themselves as adult women. They dressed in kids' clothes—overall shorts and go-anywhere sandals. They ate kids' foods. They were so depleted by the affection and care they lavished upon their small children that they had no energy left, not just for sex, but for feeling like a sexual being. "That part of my life is completely dead," a working mother of two told me. "I don't even miss it. It feels like it belongs to another life. Like I was another person."

It all reminded me a lot of Betty Friedan's 1963 classic, *The Feminine Mystique*. The diffuse dis-satisfaction. The angst, hidden behind all the obsession with trivia, and the push to be perfect. The way so many women constantly looked over their shoulders to make sure that no one was out-doing them in the performance of good Mommy-hood. And the tendency—every bit as pronounced among my peers as it had been for the women Friedan interviewed—to blame themselves for their problems. There was something new, too: the tendency many women had to feel threatened by other women and to judge them harshly—nowhere more evident than on Urbanbaby and other, similarly "supportive" Web sites. Can I take my 17-month-old to the Winnie the Pooh movie?, one mom queried recently. "WAY tooooo young," came one response.

I read that 70 percent of American moms say they find motherhood today "incredibly stress-ful." Thirty percent of mothers of young children reportedly suffer from depression. Nine hundred and nine women in Texas recently told researchers they find taking care of their kids about as much fun as cleaning their house, slightly less pleasura-ble than cooking, and a whole lot less enjoyable than watching TV.

And I wondered: Why do so many otherwise competent and self-aware women lose themselves when they become mothers? Why do so many of us feel so out of control? And—the biggest ques-tion of all—why has this generation of mothers, arguably the most liberated and privileged group

of women America has ever seen, driven them-selves crazy in the quest for perfect mommy-dom?

I started speaking with women from all over the country, about 150 in all. And I found that the craziness I saw in my own city was nothing less than a nationwide epidemic. Women from Idaho to Oklahoma City to the suburbs of Boston—in middle and upper middle class enclaves where there was time and money to spend—told me of lives spent shuttling back and forth to more and more absurd-seeming, high-pressured, time-demanding, utterly exhausting kids' activities. I heard of whole towns turning out for a spot in the *right* ballet class; of communities where the compe-tition for the *best* camps, the *best* coaches, and the *best* piano teachers rivaled that for admission to the best private schools and colleges. Women told me of their exhaustion and depression, and of their frustrations with the "uselessness" of their husbands. They said they wished their lives could change. But they had no idea of how to make that happen. I began to record their impres-sions and reflections, and wove them into a book, which I named, in honor of the sentiment that seemed to animate so many of us, *Perfect Madness*.

I think of "us" as the first post–baby boom generation, girls born between 1958 and the early 1970s, who came of age politically in the Carter, Reagan and Bush I years. We are, in many ways, a blessed group. Most of the major battles of the women's movement were fought—and won—in our early childhood. Unlike the baby boomers before us, who protested and marched and shouted their way from college into adulthood, we were a strikingly apolitical group, way more caught up in our own self-perfection as we came of age, than in working to create a more perfect world. Good daughters of the Reagan Revolution, we disdained social activism and cultivated our own gardens with a kind of muscle-bound, tightly wound, über-achieving, all-encompassing, never-failing self-control that passed, in the 1980s, for female empowerment.

We saw ourselves as winners. We'd been bred, from the earliest age, for competition. Our schools had given us co-ed gym and woodworking shop, and had told us never to let the boys drown out our voices in class. Often enough, we'd done better than they had in school. Even in science and math. And our passage into adulthood was marked by growing numbers of women in the professions. We believed that we could climb as high as we wanted to go, and would grow into the adults we dreamed we could be. Other outcomes—like the chance that children wouldn't quite fit into this picture—never even entered our minds.

Why should they have? Back then, when our sense of our potential as women was being formed, there was a general feeling of optimism. Even the most traditional women's magazines throughout the 1980s taught that the future for up-and-coming mothers was bright: The new generation of fathers *would* help. Good babysitting *could* be found. Work and motherhood *could* be balanced. It was all a question of intelligent "juggling." And of not falling prey to the trap of self-sacrifice and perfectionism that had driven so many mothers crazy in the past.

But something happened then, as the 1990s advanced, and the Girls Who Could Have Done Anything grew up into women who found, as the millennium turned, that they couldn't quite . . . get it together, or get beyond the *stuck* feeling that had somehow lodged in their minds.

Life happened. We became mothers. And found, when we set out to "balance" our lives—and in particular to balance some semblance of the girls and women we had been against the mothers we'd become—that there was no way to make this most basic of "balancing acts" work. Life was hard. It was stressful. It was expensive. Jobs—and children—were demanding. And the ambitious form of motherhood most of us wanted to practice was utterly incompatible with any kind of outside work, or friendship, or life, generally.

One woman I interviewed was literally struck dumb as she tried to articulate the quandary she was in. She wasn't a woman who normally lacked for words. She was a newspaper editor, with a husband whose steady income allowed her many choices. In the hope of finding "balance," she'd chosen to work part-time and at night in order to spend as much time as possible with her nine-year-old daughter. But somehow, nothing had worked out as planned. Working nights meant that she was tired all the time, and cranky, and stressed. And forever annoyed with her husband. And now her daughter was after her to get a day job. It seemed that having Mom around most of the time wasn't all it was cracked up to be, particularly if Mom was forever on the edge.

The woman waved her hands in circles, helplessly. "What I'm trying to figure out—" she paused. "What I'm trying to remember . . . Is how I ended up raising this princess . . . How I got into . . . How to get out of . . . this, this, this, *this mess.*"

Most of us in this generation grew up believing that we had fantastic, unlimited, freedom of choice. Yet as mothers many women face "choices" on the order of: You can continue to pursue your professional dreams at the cost of abandoning your children to long hours of inadequate child care. Or: You can stay at home with your baby and live in a state of virtual, crazy-making isolation because you can't afford a nanny, because there is no such thing as part-time day care, and because your husband doesn't come home until 8:30 at night.

These are choices that don't feel like choices at all. They are the harsh realities of family life in a culture that has no structures in place to allow women—and men—to balance work and child rearing. But most women in our generation don't think to look beyond themselves at the constraints that keep them from being able to make *real* choices as mothers. It almost never occurs to them that they can use the muscle of their superb education or their collective voice to change or rearrange their social support system. They simply don't have the political reflex—or the vocabulary—to think of things in this way.

They've been bred to be independent and self-sufficient. To rely on their own initiative and "personal responsibility." To *privatize* their problems. And so, they don't get fired up about our country's lack of affordable, top-quality child care. (In many parts of the country, decent child care costs more than state college tuition, and the quality of the care that most families can afford is abysmal.) Nor about the fact that middle class life is now so damn expensive that in most families both parents must work gruelingly long hours just to make ends meet. (With fathers averaging 51 hours per week and mothers clocking in at an average of 41, the U.S. workweek is now the longest in the world.) Nor about the fact that in many districts the public schools are so bad that you *can't,* if you want your child to be reasonably well educated, sit back and simply let the teachers do their jobs, and must instead supplement the school day with a panoply of expensive and inconvenient "activities" so that your kid will have some exposure to music, art and sports.

Instead of blaming society, moms today tend to blame themselves. They say they've chosen poorly. And so they take on the Herculean task of being absolutely everything to their children, simply because *no one else is doing anything at all to help them.* Because if they don't perform magical acts of perfect Mommy ministrations, their kids might fall through the cracks and end up as losers in our hard-driving winner-take-all society.

This has to change.

We now have a situation where well-off women can choose how to live their lives—either outsourcing child care at a sufficiently high level of quality to permit them to work with relative peace of mind or staying at home. But no one else, really, has anything. Many, many women would like to stay home with their children and can't afford to do so. Many, many others would like to be able to work part-time but can't afford or find the way to do so. Many others would like to be able to maintain their full-time careers without either being devoured by their jobs or losing ground, and they can't do that. And there is no hope at all for any of these women on the horizon.

Some of us may feel empowered by the challenge of taking it all on, being the best, as Téa Leoni's "Spanglish" character did on her uphill morning run, but really, this perfectionism is not empowerment. It's more like what some psychologists call "learned helplessness"—an instinctive giving-up in the face of difficulty that people do when they think they have no real power. At base, it's a kind of despair. A lack of faith that change

can come to the outside world. A lack of belief in our political culture or our institutions.

It *really* needs to change.

For while many women can and do manage to accept (or at least adjust to) this situation for themselves, there's a twinge of real sadness that comes out when they talk about their daughters. As a forty-something mother living and working part-time in Washington, D.C. (and spending a disproportionate amount of her time managing the details of her daughter's—and her husband's—life), mused one evening to me, "I look at my daughter and I just want to know: what happened? Because look at us: it's 2002 and nothing's changed. My mother expected my life to be very different from hers, but now it's a lot more like hers than I expected, and from here I don't see where it will be different for my daughter. I don't want her to carry this crushing burden that's in our heads. . . . [But] what can make things different?"

For real change to happen, we don't need more politicians sounding off about "family values." Neither do we need to pat the backs of working mothers, or "reward" moms who stay at home, or "valorize" motherhood, generally, by acknowledging that it's "the toughest job in the world." We need solutions—politically palatable, economically feasible, home-grown American solutions—that can, collectively, give mothers and families a break.

• We need incentives like tax subsidies to encourage corporations to adopt family-friendly policies.

• We need government-mandated child care standards and quality controls that can remove the fear and dread many working mothers feel when they leave their children with others.

• We need flexible, affordable, locally available, high-quality part-time day care so that stay-at-home moms can get a life of their own. This shouldn't, these days, be such a pipe dream. After all, in his State of the Union message, President Bush reaffirmed his support of (which, one assumes, includes support of funding for) "faith-based and community groups." I lived in France before moving to Washington, and there, my elder daughter attended two wonderful, affordable, top-quality part-time pre-schools, which were essentially meant to give stay-at-home moms a helping hand. One was run by a neighborhood co-op and the other by a Catholic organization. Government subsidies kept tuition rates low. A sliding scale of fees brought some diversity. Government standards meant that the staffers were all trained in the proper care of young children. My then 18-month-old daughter painted and heard stories and ate cookies for the sum total in fees of about $150 a month. (This solution may be French—but do we have to bash it?)

• We need new initiatives to make it possible for mothers to work part-time (something most mothers say they want to do) by creating vouchers or bigger tax credits to make child care more affordable, by making health insurance available and affordable for part-time workers and by generally making life less expensive and stressful for middle-class families so that mothers (and fathers) could work less without risking their children's financial future. Or even, if they felt the need, could stay home with their children for a while.

• In general, we need to alleviate the economic pressures that currently make so many families' lives so high-pressured, through progressive tax policies that would transfer our nation's wealth back to the middle class. So that mothers and fathers could stop running like lunatics, and start spending real quality—and quantity—time with their children. And so that motherhood could stop being the awful burden it is for so many women today and instead become something more like a joy.

Women today mother in the excessive, control-freakish way that they do in part because they are psychologically conditioned to do so. But they also do it because, to a large extent, *they have to.* Because they are unsupported, because their children are not taken care of, in any meaningful way, by society at large. Because there is right now no widespread feeling of social responsibility—for children, for families, for *anyone,* really—and so they must take everything onto themselves. And because they *can't,* humanly, take everything onto themselves, they simply go nuts.

I see this all the time. It never seems to stop. So that, as I write this, I have an image fresh in my mind: the face of a friend, the mother of a first-grader, who I ran into one morning right before Christmas.

She was in the midst of organizing a class party. This meant shopping. Color-coordinating paper goods. Piecework, pre-gluing of arts-and-crafts projects. Uniformity of felt textures. Of buttons and beads. There were the phone calls, too. From other parents. With criticism and "constructive" comments that had her up at night, playing over conversations in her mind. "I can't take it anymore," she said to me. "I hate everyone and everything. I am going insane."

I looked at her face, saw her eyes fill with tears, and in that instant saw the faces of dozens of women I'd met—and, of course, I saw myself.

And I was reminded of the words of a French doctor I'd once seen. I'd come to him about headaches. They were violent. They were constant. And they would prove, over the next few years, to be chronic. He wrote me a prescription for a painkiller. But he looked skeptical as to whether it would really do me much good. *"If you keep banging your head against the wall,"* he said, *"you're going to have headaches."*

I have thought of these words so many times since then. I have seen *so many mothers* banging their heads against a wall. And treating their pain—the chronic headache of their lives—with sleeping pills and antidepressants and anxiety meds and a more and more potent, more and more vicious self-and-other-attacking form of anxious perfectionism.

And I hope that somehow we will all find a way to stop. Because we are not doing ourselves any good. We are not doing our children—particularly our daughters—any good. We're not doing our marriages any good. And we're doing nothing at all for our society.

We are simply beating ourselves black and blue. So let's take a breather. Throw out the schedules, turn off the cell phone, cancel the tutors (fire the OT!). Let's spend some real quality time with our families, just talking, hanging out, not doing anything for once. And let ourselves *be.*

Partners as Parents

Challenges Faced by Gays Denied Marriage

Charlene Gomes

If the right of privacy means anything, it is the right of the individual, married or single, to be free from unwarranted governmental intrusion into matters so fundamentally affecting a person as the decision whether to bear or beget a child.

— Supreme Court Justice William Brennan, Eisenstadt v. Baird, *1972*

I had just read these words in my constitutional law class in 1997 when a coworker of mine shared with me his and his partner's struggles to have a child. They, together with a lesbian couple with whom they were close, had made numerous attempts at pregnancy "the old-fashioned way"— by tracking ovulation and inserting the sperm with a turkey baster—to no avail. They had recently begun to explore artificial insemination and were again frustrated to realize they would have to travel quite far from their Virginia home to get to a state where the procedure was legally available to them. A Virginia statute restricts the procedure to couples who are husband and wife. Numerous other states have similarly restrictive statutes. It seems that these laws aren't constitutional in light of the Supreme Court's 1972 decision in *Eisenstadt v. Baird*. Although the *Eisenstadt* ruling dealt specifically with laws restricting the use of contraceptives to married couples, the language of the decision was broad enough to encompass efforts to have a child as well as to avoid having a child.

In the past several years, issues regarding gay marriage and gay families have become a regular part of the national debate and, to a lesser extent, political debate. In 1996 Congress passed the Defense of Marriage Act (DOMA) in response to a Hawaii law that granted same-sex couples the right to marry (the law was later overturned by the Hawaii state legislature). Since then, thirty-seven states have passed their own DOMAs.

At the same time, it has become progressively easier for gay families to gain custody of biological children, conceive biological children through various fertilization methods and services, and adopt children. Yet President George W. Bush, many religious conservatives, and even some Democratic presidential hopefuls have reaffirmed their belief that marriage by definition applies only to unions between one man and one woman.

Given all the national rhetoric about the sanctity of marriage and the importance of raising children within a legally recognized relationship, one would assume that legislators would take note of the growing numbers of young children being raised by gay parents and get to work passing legislation legitimizing their parents' relationship. Yet nothing could be further from the truth. Despite Canada's recent move toward legalizing same-sex marriages, the United States continues to show every intention of fighting tooth and nail against this broadening of marriage laws, including a recently proposed constitutional amendment barring same-sex marriage. Unfortunately, the opposite mood has prevailed.

Data from the 2000 U.S. census reveal that approximately one in three lesbian/bisexual couples and 22 percent of gay/bisexual couples are raising children. According to the National Gay and Lesbian Task Force (NGLTF), estimates of the total number of children with at least one gay or lesbian parent range from six million to fourteen million. Yet these numbers only track gays who were willing to self-report on the census; many remain unwilling to reveal their sexual orientation to the federal government, as the government offers them no protection from discrimination. Thus, the numbers certainly underestimate the true number of gays raising children. Married heterosexual couples with children comprise only 23 percent of U.S. households.

Gay or straight, not all parents raise children equally. Parenting ability relies on a complex and unquantifiable mix of skills and emotions. Love, patience, empathy, and respect, along with the ability to provide necessities and discipline without being abusive, are a mere sampling of points along the infinite parenting spectrum. It is curious—and telling—that current debate focuses on the legal ability of gays to marry rather than their actual ability to maintain life partnerships and to raise productive, well-adjusted children.

Even so, gay parents face unique barriers in their efforts to care and provide for their children. According to the NGLTF, privileges enjoyed by heterosexual married couples but denied to gay parents include legal recognition of the parent-child relationship for children born during the relationship; recognition of parental status under the Family and Medical Leave Act; access to child support when the parental relationship ends; the right to petition for visitation and custody after the dissolution of a relationship; and (in some states) adoption and foster parenting.

PATHS TO PARENTHOOD

Same-sex couples become parents in a variety of ways. Some have children from previous heterosexual relationships while others are adoptive or foster parents. Lesbians may become pregnant through donor insemination, and gay male couples are turning more and more to surrogacy arrangements.

According to the NGLTF, donor insemination use among lesbian couples has increased since the 1980s. While insemination seems like an ideal

solution, practical and legal barriers make it less so. Insemination is very expensive and results aren't always guaranteed. Insurance rarely covers these services—at least where lesbians are concerned—and clinical infertility hasn't been demonstrated. In addition, the majority of states have yet to address the issue of whether the sperm donor is the legal father of the child. This leaves the child's legal parentage to chance, opening the door for future legal problems. Also, the inability to prove paternity can be a stumbling block later on if one or both of the partners needs to be availed of public benefits.

Likewise, the NGLTF reports that the use of surrogacy among gay men has been on the rise in recent years. Unlike donor insemination, a generally accepted practice across the social and professional landscape, surrogacy is often considered controversial. Many states discourage the practice and two prohibit it outright. Other states prohibit payment to the surrogate mother. As with insemination, the law is unclear as to who are considered the legal parents of the offspring. Some states recognize the surrogate and her spouse while others attribute parentage to the couple contracting with the surrogate.

ADOPTION

Only Florida specifically prohibits individual lesbians and gay men or same-sex couples from adopting children. Mississippi only prohibits same-sex couples from adopting, and some states, such as Utah, prioritize heterosexual married couples as adoptive and foster parents. Other states that don't make it a specific consideration in adoption determinations often take sexual orientation into account if raised in the course of the proceeding. Even so, many states allow gays to adopt as individuals and many—including California, Connecticut, the District of Columbia, Massachusetts, New Jersey, New York, and Vermont—now allow joint adoptions by same-sex couples.

What is truly harmful for children of gay parents is the lack of legal protection arising out of a failure to recognize same-sex marriage or to allow adoption by nonbiological life partners. The situation of nonbiological same-sex partners is most similar to that of stepparents in heterosexual marriages. Generally, if the noncustodial biological parent consents, stepparents may adopt the children. Yet, in the same situation, same-sex life partners usually require rigorous home visits and family studies. Most states have recognized that in some limited circumstances stepparents can adopt even without the noncustodial biological parent's consent, yet this doesn't hold for same-sex life partners.

The child suffers needlessly when the nonbiological partner is unable to establish a legal relationship, especially should the biological parent die or the relationship otherwise dissolve. The child isn't entitled to financial support or inheritance rights if there is no will. Lack of legal protections for the nonbiological partner include custody and visitation privileges, consent to emergency medical treatment, and permission to attend parent-teacher conferences.

Children with an adoptive stepparent enjoy other benefits not available to children living with a same-sex parent who is unable to adopt. Some state worker's compensation programs and the federal Social Security survivor benefit program now permit minor stepchildren living with and dependent upon a stepparent to receive benefits after the stepparent's death. Additionally, the Family and Medical Leave Act allows unpaid leave to care for a stepchild. Extending these benefits and protections to same-sex couples by legitimizing their relationships would ensure that the children of these couples will be treated equally with children of heterosexual married couples. The benefits of according these protections to all children easily outweigh the externalities imposed on third parties disapproving of homosexual relationships.

The landscape is somewhat different in cases of second-parent adoption, where one member of a same-sex couple is a biological parent and the nonbiological partner wishes also to become a legal parent. Stepparents in heterosexual marriages encounter little or no barriers when it comes to adopting the child of the biological parent. The law assumes that such an arrangement is in the child's best interests. Approximately twenty-five states allow same-sex second-parent adoptions, but the adoptions are costly and littered with invasive and time-consuming procedures. Unlike heterosexual couples in the same situation, same-sex couples are subjected to numerous home visits and intensive social work assessments to determine the suitability of the adoption.

Because heterosexual couples are often the preferred placements for adoptive children, many gay and lesbian couples willingly adopt the least "adoptable" children. Most married couples seek to adopt healthy babies. As a result, children with physical or mental disabilities often spend their lives being shuffled around between countless foster homes. By the time they are of school age, finding adoptive parents for them becomes next to impossible. According to Allison Beers' 1997 article "Gay Men and Lesbians, Building Loving Families," published by the Adoption Resource Exchange for Single Parents, many of these children are now placed in stable, loving homes with gay individuals or gay couples. Beers cites the example of Elmy Martinez, who adopted five special-needs children. At the time the article was written, four out of the five children had graduated from high school, two went on to the army, one received vocational training and was holding a steady job, and one had completed two years of community college. As proud as any parent, Martinez states in the article, "These kids have made a big difference in my life. You take them away from me and what am I?"

That gays are more readily allowed to adopt special-needs children raises an interesting question: why are the people who some label as "unfit to parent" often given children needing the most care? Where are the protests from heterosexual couples and conservative groups that proclaim homosexual relationships to be both immoral and illegal? Why aren't they rushing in to rescue these children from adoption by parents who suffer from what the Family Research Council has called a "pathological condition"?

CUSTODY

As challenging as it might sometimes be for same-sex couples to create a family, keeping the family together can be equally challenging. For gay and lesbian parents, custody disputes, by nature emotionally charged and often contentious, pose additional threats not faced by their heterosexual counterparts. Although the laws governing custody vary from state to state, two universal principles govern: that the court should consider the "best interests" of the child when determining custody and that there is a strong preference for placing the child with a natural parent as opposed to a third party. Courts considering custody disputes between two natural parents have generally followed one of three approaches for determining the fitness of gay and lesbian parents: the nexus approach, the nexus approach as a minor factor, and the per se approach.

The nexus approach is used by the majority of states. It asks the court to consider the causal connection between the conduct of the parent and any adverse effect on the child. The court inquires into the abilities of the parent rather than deeming the parent per se unfit based on sexual orientation. Of the three approaches, the nexus test is the most fact based, focusing on actual evidence of the child's best interests as opposed to stereotypes or presumptions about the parent. The parent's sexual orientation is considered only if harmful effects are proven. Currently, the District of Columbia is the only jurisdiction in which sexual orientation in and of itself cannot be a conclusive factor in custody and visitation matters.

Similarly, the nexus as a minor factor approach has led some courts to maintain that the parent's sexual orientation is merely one of many considerations in determining the best interests of the child. It differs from the strict nexus approach in that courts using nexus as a minor factor will automatically consider the parent's homosexuality in determining the best interest of the child.

The per se approach holds that the parent's homosexuality presents a refutable presumption that the parent is unfit. It rests on the notion that

children of homosexual parents cannot possibly thrive because of social stigma, peer harassment, and the threat to their own "normal" heterosexual development. For the most part, even very conservative courts have shifted away from this approach in recent years. The per se rule isn't without support, however. Noted family law scholar Lynn Wardle of Brigham Young University would apply a refutable presumption to all cases involving a homosexual parent. Wardle would allow the heterosexual ex-spouse who has been denied custody to use a gay parent's new relationship as grounds for modifying the custody agreement and thus grant custody to the formerly noncustodial ex-spouse.

Unfortunately, the per se rule ultimately harms the child it seeks to protect by fueling power struggles between parents and undermining the state's (and the child's) interest in the finality and continuity of the custody agreement. The per se approach effectively eradicates the requirement for the party seeking to gain custody to show a change in circumstances that would serve the child's best interests.

In addition, courts often impose restrictions on divorcing parents that typically deny economic support (and sometimes custody) to parents who are cohabiting with a partner to whom they aren't married. These restrictions unfairly burden gay parents because they aren't legally able to marry their partners like heterosexual parents can, forcing them to choose between their children and their partner.

For the most part, gay parents today have a much easier time gaining custody of their children than they have in the recent past. Cases denying gay parents custody on factors other than actual fitness stand out as an area that generally receives little attention. Two cases are worth nothing.

In the 1996 *Ward v. Ward* decision, the First District Court of Appeals for the district of Florida awarded the father's petition for a change in custody based on the mother being a lesbian, despite the fact that the father had been convicted of murdering his first wife. What's more, the father had been less than a model parent in following the original custody agreement: he declined the mother's offer to extend his summer visitation, didn't attend doctors' appointments or parent-teacher conferences, wasn't knowledgeable about the child's attention deficit disorder, and fulfilled his child support obligation only sporadically.

In *Bottoms v. Bottoms,* a Virginia court in 1994 denied the mother custody in favor of the maternal grandmother, finding that a lesbian was per se unfit to parent. Ignoring expert testimony concluding that the child wasn't adversely affected by his mother's relationship with her partner, the judge based his ruling on his personal belief that the mother's conduct was illegal and immoral. At the time the case was tried, a Virginia sodomy statute made oral and anal sex a felony offense. But the statute applied to heterosexuals as well as homosexuals, and while the judge thoroughly probed the nature of the mother's relationship with her lesbian partner in graphic detail, he never questioned the grandmother's sexual practices.

In the *Bottoms* case, both the mother and the grandmother were high school dropouts with no special skills or training. Sharon Bottoms, the child's mother, had been sexually molested by her mother's boyfriend from the age of twelve to seventeen. Up until two weeks before the custody proceedings began, the grandmother continued living with the boyfriend who she knew had molested her daughter. Despite this, she was granted custody of the grandchild because the judge felt that she was a better parent than any homosexual could ever be. The grandmother's history of cohabiting with a man known to be molesting her own child should clearly have reinforced the presumption for the natural parent. Instead, the judge allowed prejudice to subjugate the law and stripped Sharon Bottoms of her parental rights.

Despite legal advancements since the *Bottoms* case, lesbian mothers continue to face unique custody challenges. According to the NGLTF, approximately 30 percent of all lesbian and bisexual female parents have been threatened with a loss of custody. Among those seeking to obtain custody from lesbian mothers are biological fathers, sperm donors, female co-parents, grandparents, and other relatives.

In addition, many gay individuals and families live in poverty. Yet gay families who rely on public benefits often find themselves up against a welfare system that favors married heterosexual couples above all other families. According to the NGLTF, gay couples face challenges in all areas of public benefits—from housing assistance, where they are often unable to register as a family, to Temporary Assistance to Needy Families regulations that assume all children are the products of heterosexual unions. For example, lesbian mothers unable to establish paternity of their children risk losing a large percentage of benefits and may forfeit benefits altogether. Single fathers on the other hand aren't required to disclose the maternity of their children in order to receive benefits.

CHILDREN OF GAY PARENTS

In her 1997 *Family Advocate* article "Debunking Myths About Lesbian and Gay Parents and Their Children," Kathryn Kendall addresses the gender identity and sexual orientation of children raised by gay parents. Kendall points out that numerous studies conducted since 1978 have found that children raised by gay or lesbian parents are "indistinguishable from other children in terms of gender identity, gender role behavior, and general psychological health" and that the incidence of same-sex orientation among children of gay and lesbian parents is the same as for heterosexual parents. Likewise, Kendall found that in terms of self-esteem, divorce does more damage to children than does their parent's sexual orientation.

Another argument frequently made by conservatives is that gay parents will surely raise gender-confused children. However, studies have consistently shown that this isn't the case. Carlos Ball and Janice Farrell Pea surveyed a series of studies from 1978 to 1996 regarding the sexual orientation of children raised by homosexual parents. Their survey concluded that, with the exception of one study, the percentage of children of gays and lesbians who were identified as gay or lesbian ranged from zero to nine.

Perhaps the most widely used argument against allowing gays to marry, adopt, or retain custody of their children is the assumption that being raised by gay parents will cause children to "become" gay. But is this really the case? And if so, is it really harmful? We tend to think of heterosexuality as the norm, but the most conservative estimates allow that approximately 3 percent of the population is gay. Although 3 percent seems next to insignificant, a different picture is presented when translated into raw numbers. For example, if there are 1,674,000 self-identified same-sex couples in the United States, then there are at least 3,348,000 gay individuals in the United States. It is a lot harder to overlook three million than 3 percent. So, besides marginalizing the incidence of homosexuality, the fear that children will turn out to be gay assumes that being gay is in and of itself detrimental to the child.

THE MYTH OF HOMOSEXUALITY AND PEDOPHILIA

It is a common misperception that gays are more likely to molest children than heterosexuals. In fact, the vast majority of child molestation acts are perpetrated by heterosexual men. In her 1994 *Pediatrics* magazine article "Are Children at Risk for Sexual Abuse by Homosexuals?" Carole Jenny found that 94 percent of molested girls and 86 percent of molested boys were abused by men. Of the boys abused by an adult male, 74 percent were abused by someone in a heterosexual relationship with the child's mother, while only 2 percent of perpetrators could "possibly" be identified as homosexual.

Yet these unambiguous statistics on child molestation aren't at issue when heterosexual men seek physical custody of their children. And yet at least one family law scholar, Lynne Wardle, has argued that potential abuse is a factor to be considered when gays and lesbians seek custody. The disparity between stereotype and reality is indicative of the level of harm that can ensue by allowing prejudice to determine custody placements.

CONCLUSION

Issues addressing the rights of homosexuals appear daily in the news. Debates abound about gays' right to marry, raise children, and hold a leadership role in public, private, and religious entities. The fact that these issues have come to the fore and are being publicly discussed says much about current attitudes regarding homosexuals as people. As with previous civil rights struggles, the road to full personhood under the law is long and hard but worth the journey.

Those who continue to oppose the right of homosexuals to marry and otherwise be free from discrimination in employment, housing, inheritance, family matters, and the countless other rights that many heterosexuals take for granted base their objections largely on religious grounds. Hiding behind the facade of morality, they call upon "tradition" as their key witness for refusal to change. But tradition is a red herring attempting to disguise what is fundamentally a religious objection based on—as Bush so eloquently put it—the "sanctity of marriage," meaning a one-man/one-woman relationship for the purpose of creating and raising God's children.

But truth will ultimately trump tradition, and the truth is that God is an optional party to a marriage in the United States. The real foundation of a marriage is having a legally recognized relationship between two people that affords them numerous benefits and protections, along with a handful of duties. While many couples choose to marry in a religious ceremony and plan to raise a family together, neither of these options is required and a couple is just as married if they have a civil ceremony and never have children. So, how relevant is the "sanctity of marriage"? It is relevant only to those who choose to make it so within their own relationship.

Marriage is a wonderful and important societal institution. It signals to the community a dedicated respect, affection, and commitment to one's partner. It fosters a recognizable and familiar family structure that makes it possible to confer and enforce the legal benefits, protections, and responsibilities that go along with it. It provides stability and safety for one's partner and children in the event of tragedy or dissolution of the relationship. As such, it should be available to all people, regardless of their sexual orientation. Conception, adoption, and custody likewise shouldn't be compromised by an unfounded concern that exposure to homosexuality poses a danger to children. Rather, they should be based on the long-standing principle of the best interests of the child and a presumption in favor of the parents who choose to conceive, adopt, or otherwise raise the child.

As popular as ideas about the instability of gay families may be, they are based on fear and not on fact. Nearly all children are teased about something, whether it be the child's physical appearance, speech, ethnicity, race, religion, or economic status. Society will have its prejudices. In the 1984 case of *Palmore v. Sidoti,* the Supreme Court overturned a case refusing custody to a child's mother based on fear of harassment arising out of her interracial marriage, stating, "The Constitution cannot control such prejudices but neither can it tolerate them." Likewise, prejudice against gays' right to adopt is unconstitutional and should no longer be tolerated in the United States.

R E A D I N G   **57**

Man Child
A Black Lesbian Feminist's Response

Audre Lorde

This article is not a theoretical discussion of Lesbian Mothers and their Sons, nor a how-to article. It is an attempt to scrutinize and share some pieces of that common history belonging to my son and to me. I have two children: a fifteen-and-a-half-year-old daughter, Beth, and a fourteen-year-old son, Jonathan. This is the way it was/is with me and Jonathan, and I leave the theory to another time and person. This is one woman's telling.

I have no golden message about the raising of sons for other lesbian mothers, no secret to transpose your questions into certain light. I have my own ways of rewording those same questions, hoping we will all come to speak those questions and pieces of our lives we need to share. We are women making contact within ourselves and with each other across the restrictions of a printed page, bent upon the use of our own/one another's knowledges.

The truest direction comes from inside. I give the most strength to my children by being willing to look within myself, and by being honest with them about what I find there, without expecting a response beyond their years. In this way they begin to learn to look beyond their own fears.

All our children are outriders for a queendom not yet assured.

My adolescent son's growing sexuality is a conscious dynamic between Jonathan and me. It would be presumptuous of me to discuss Jonathan's sexuality here, except to state my belief that whomever he chooses to explore this area with, his choices will be nonoppressive, joyful, and deeply felt from within, places of growth.

One of the difficulties in writing this piece has been temporal; this is the summer when Jonathan is becoming a man, physically. And our sons must become men—such men as we hope our daughters, born and unborn, will be pleased to live among. Our sons will not grow into women. Their way is more difficult than that of our daughters, for they must move away from us, without us. Hopefully, our sons have what they have learned from us, and a howness to forge it into their own image.

Our daughters have us, for measure or rebellion or outline or dream; but the sons of lesbians have to make their own definitions of self as men. This is both power and vulnerability. The sons of lesbians have the advantage of our blueprints for survival, but they must take what we know and transpose it into their own maleness. May the goddess be kind to my son, Jonathan.

Recently I have met young Black men about whom I am pleased to say that their future and their visions, as well as their concerns within the present, intersect more closely with Jonathan's than do my own. I have shared visions with these men as well as temporal strategies for our survivals, and I appreciate the spaces in which we could sit down together. Some of these men I met at the First Annual Conference of Third World Lesbians and Gays held in Washington D.C. in October 1979. I have met others in different places and do not know how they identify themselves sexually. Some of these men are raising families alone. Some have adopted sons. They are Black men who dream and who act and who own their feelings, questioning. It is heartening to know our sons do not step out alone.

When Jonathan makes me angriest, I always say he is bringing out the testosterone in me. What I mean is that he is representing some piece of myself as a woman that I am reluctant to acknowledge or explore. For instance, what does "acting like a man" mean? For me, what I reject? For Jonathan, what he is trying to redefine?

Raising Black children—female and male—in the mouth of a racist, sexist, suicidal dragon is perilous and chancy. If they cannot love and resist at the same time, they will probably not survive. And in order to survive they must let go. This is what mothers teach—love, survival—that is, self-definition and letting go. For each of these, the ability to feel strongly and to recognize those feelings is central: how to feel love, how to neither discount fear nor be overwhelmed by it, how to enjoy feeling deeply.

I wish to raise a Black man who will not be destroyed by, nor settle for, those corruptions called *power* by the white fathers who mean his destruction as surely as they mean mine. I wish to raise a Black man who will recognize that the legitimate objects of his hostility are not women, but the particulars of a structure that programs him to fear and despise women as well as his own Black self.

For me, this task begins with teaching my son that I do not exist to do his feeling for him.

Men who are afraid to feel must keep women around to do their feeling for them while dismissing us for the same supposedly "inferior" capacity to feel deeply. But in this way also, men deny themselves their own essential humanity, becoming trapped in dependency and fear.

As a Black woman committed to a liveable future, and as a mother loving and raising a boy who will become a man, I must examine all my possibilities of being within such a destructive system.

Jonathan was three-and-one-half when Frances, my lover, and I met; he was seven when we all began to live together permanently. From the start, Frances' and my insistence that there be no secrets in our household about the fact that we were lesbians has been the source of problems and strengths for both children. In the beginning, this insistence grew out of the knowledge, on both our parts, that whatever was hidden out of fear could always be used against either the children or ourselves—one imperfect but useful argument for honesty. The knowledge of fear can help make us free.

> for the embattled
> there is no place
> that cannot be
> home
> nor is.*

For survival, Black children in america must be raised to be warriors. For survival, they must also be raised to recognize the enemy's many faces. Black children of lesbian couples have an advantage because they learn, very early, that

---

* From "School Note" in *The Black Unicorn* (W. W. Norton and Company, New York, 1978), p. 55.

oppression comes in many different forms, none of which have anything to do with their own worth.

To help give me perspective, I remember that for years, in the namecalling at school, boys shouted at Jonathan not—"your mother's a lesbian"—but rather—"your mother's a nigger."

When Jonathan was eight years old and in the third grade we moved, and he went to a new school where his life was hellish as a new boy on the block. He did not like to play rough games. He did not like to fight. He did not like to stone dogs. And all this marked him early on as an easy target.

When he came in crying one afternoon, I heard from Beth how the corner bullies were making Johathan wipe their shoes on the way home whenever Beth wasn't there to fight them off. And when I heard that the ringleader was a little boy in Jonathan's class his own size, an interesting and very disturbing thing happened to me.

My fury at my own long-ago impotence, and my present pain at his suffering, made me start to forget all that I knew about violence and fear, and blaming the victim, I started to hiss at the weeping child. "The next time you come in here crying . . . ," and I suddenly caught myself in horror.

This is the way we allow the destruction of our sons to begin—in the name of protection and to ease our own pain. *My* son get beaten up? I was about to demand that he buy that first lesson in the corruption of power, that might makes right. I could hear myself beginning to perpetuate the age-old distortions about what strength and bravery really are.

And no, Jonathan didn't have to fight if he didn't want to, but somehow he did have to feel better about not fighting. An old horror rolled over me of being the fat kid who ran away, terrified of getting her glasses broken.

About that time a very wise woman said to me, "Have you ever told Jonathan that once you used to be afraid, too?"

The idea seemed far-out to me at the time, but the next time he came in crying and sweaty from having run away again, I could see that he felt shamed at having failed me, or some image he and I had created in his head of mother/woman. This image of woman being able to handle it all was bolstered by the fact that he lived in a household with three strong women, his lesbian parents and his forthright older sister. At home, for Jonathan, power was clearly female.

And because our society teaches us to think in an either/or mode—kill or be killed, dominate or be dominated—this meant that he must either surpass or be lacking. I could see the implications of this line of thought. Consider the two western classic myth/models of mother/son relationships: Jocasta/Oedipus, the son who fucks his mother, and Clytemnestra/Orestes, the son who kills his mother.

It all felt connected to me.

I sat down on the hallway steps and took Jonathan on my lap and wiped his tears. "Did I ever tell you about how I used to be afraid when I was your age?"

I will never forget the look on that little boy's face as I told him the tale of my glasses and my after-school fights. It was a look of relief and total disbelief, all rolled into one.

It is as hard for our children to believe that we are not omnipotent as it is for us to know it, as parents. But that knowledge is necessary as the first step in the reassessment of power as something other than might, age, privilege, or the lack of fear. It is an important step for a boy, whose societal destruction begins when he is forced to believe that he can only be strong if he doesn't feel, or if he wins.

I thought about all this one year later when Beth and Jonathan, ten and nine, were asked by an interviewer how they thought they had been affected by being children of a feminist.

Jonathan said that he didn't think there was too much in feminism for boys, although it certainly was good to be able to cry if he felt like it and not to have to play football if he didn't want to. I think of this sometimes now when I see him practising for his Brown Belt in Tae Kwon Do.

The strongest lesson I can teach my son is the same lesson I teach my daughter: how to be who he wishes to be for himself. And the best way I can do this is to be who I am and hope that he will learn from this not how to be me, which is not possible, but how to be himself. And this means how to move to that voice from within himself, rather than to those raucous, persuasive, or threatening voices from outside, pressuring him to be what the world wants him to be.

And that is hard enough.

Jonathan is learning to find within himself some of the different faces of courage and strength, whatever he chooses to call them. Two years ago, when Jonathan was twelve and in the seventh grade, one of his friends at school who had been to the house persisted in calling Frances "the maid." When Jonathan corrected him, the boy then referred to her as "the cleaning woman." Finally Jonathan said, simply, "Frances is not the cleaning woman, she's my mother's lover." Interestingly enough, it is the teachers at this school who still have not recovered from his openness.

Frances and I were considering attending a Lesbian/Feminist conference this summer, when we were notified that no boys over ten were allowed. This presented logistic as well as philosophical problems for us, and we sent the following letter:

Sisters:

Ten years as an interracial lesbian couple has taught us both the dangers of an oversimplified approach to the nature and solutions of any oppression, as well as the danger inherent in an incomplete vision.

Our thirteen-year-old son represents as much hope for our future world as does our fifteen-year-old daughter, and we are not willing to abandon him to the killing streets of New York City while we journey west to help form a Lesbian-Feminist vision of the future world in which we can all survive and flourish. I hope we can continue this dialogue in the near future, as I feel it is important to our vision and our survival.

The question of separatism is by no means simple. I am thankful that one of my children is male, since that helps to keep me honest. Every line I write shrieks there are no easy solutions.

I grew up in largely female environments, and I know how crucial that has been to my own development. I feel the want and need often for the society of women, exclusively. I recognize that our own spaces are essential for developing and recharging.

As a Black woman, I find it necessary to withdraw into all-Black groups at times for exactly the same reasons—differences in stages of development and differences in levels of interaction. Frequently, when speaking with men and white women, I am reminded of how difficult and time-consuming it is to have to reinvent the pencil every time you want to send a message.

But this does not mean that my responsibility for my son's education stops at age ten, any more than it does for my daughter's. However, for each of them, that responsibility does grow less and less as they become more woman and man.

Both Beth and Jonathan need to know what they can share and what they cannot, how they are joined and how they are not. And Frances and I, as grown women and lesbians coming more and more into our power, need to relearn the experience that difference does not have to be threatening.

When I envision the future, I think of the world I crave for my daughters and my sons. It is thinking for survival of the species—thinking for life.

Most likely there will always be women who move with women, women who live with men, men who choose men. I work for a time when women with women, women with men, men with men, all share the work of a world that does not barter bread or self for obedience, nor beauty, nor love. And in that world we will raise our children free to choose how best to fulfill themselves. For we are jointly responsible for the care and raising of the young, since *that* they be raised is a function, ultimately, of the species.

Within that tripartite pattern of relating/existence, the raising of the young will be the joint responsibility of all adults who choose to be associated with children. Obviously, the children raised within each of these three relationships will be different, lending a special savor to that eternal inquiry into how best can we live our lives.

Jonathan was three-and-a-half when Frances and I met. He is now fourteen years old. I feel the living perspective that having lesbian parents has brought to Jonathan is a valuable addition to his human sensitivity.

Jonathan has had the advantage of growing up within a nonsexist relationship, one in which this society's pseudonatural assumptions of ruler/ruled are being challenged. And this is not only because Frances and I are lesbians, for unfortunately there are some lesbians who are still locked into patriarchal patterns of unequal power relationships.

These assumptions of power relationships are being questioned because Frances and I, often painfully and with varying degrees of success, attempt to evaluate and measure over and over again our feelings concerning power, our own and others'. And we explore with care those areas concerning how it is used and expressed between us and between us and the children, openly and otherwise. A good part of our biweekly family meetings are devoted to this exploration.

As parents, Frances and I have given Jonathan our love, our openness, and our dreams to help form his visions. Most importantly, as the son of lesbians, he has had an invaluable model—not only of a relationship—but of relating.

Jonathan is fourteen now. In talking over this paper with him and asking his permission to share some pieces of his life, I asked Jonathan what he felt were the strongest negative and the strongest positive aspects for him in having grown up with lesbian parents.

He said the strongest benefit he felt he had gained was that he knew a lot more about people than most other kids his age that he knew, and that he did not have a lot of the hang-ups that some other boys did about men and women.

And the most negative aspect he felt, Jonathan said, was the ridicule he got from some kids with straight parents.

"You mean, from your peers?" I said.

"Oh no," he answered promptly. "My peers know better. I mean other kids."

R E A D I N G **58**

The Emperor's New Woes

Sean Elder

Last year I was asked by the editor of a men's magazine to write a story about intimacy in relationships. His was one of those publications that advise the American man how to flatten his stomach and increase his chest size—that look, in other words, like a lot of women's magazines. I spoke to the requisite marriage experts: psychologists and sociologists who had stared into the murk of modern male-female relations. Though I tried to steer my sources toward simple declarative sentences and do-it-yourself answers, the editor was not happy.

"Couldn't you just give it to us in bullet points?" he asked. "We want a step-by-step guide on how to be emotionally intimate with your woman."

Therein lies a précis of the principal dilemma in marriage today. Men have come to accept—even celebrate—their wives' careers and paychecks while learning, step-by-step, how to bathe the baby and baste the turkey. But there is no Julia Child–style primer on closeness, no chart with diagrams: Insert A into slot B, and there you go. Intimacy achieved. Let's go have a cold one.

It would be funny if it weren't so painful. "It's probably the real cause of half of all divorces," according to Sam Margulies, a divorce mediator in Greensboro, North Carolina, and author of several books on the subject of marital breakups. The changes in women's lives—their roles, ambitions, opportunities—have been considered from every angle. But men's lives have changed too, in ways that are more confusing, more contradictory, and often less welcome. Men did not ask to have their roles redefined. Now, they're looking for an instruction manual complete with fine print—and a translator's guide as well.

"Very few women could compare their lives to their mothers' and say, 'We look pretty similar,'" says Steven Nock, a professor of sociology at the University of Virginia who has studied what marriage means to men. "Women have so many dramatically different options in their lives. But where are men taking their cues about what it means to be a husband or a father? There is much less discussion in our society about that."

The guidelines for being a good husband used to be simple: provide, protect, maybe trim the hedges now and then. Now wives still want all that in a mate—and more. Today's wife wants a confidante and soul mate as well.

The requirements changed with no warning, and many husbands feel blindsided. Most men were raised with the idea that making it in the outside world is how you score points at home. For many women that also still holds true. It's not as though they want men to be less goal-oriented or less interested in money. They're asking for a breadwinner *and* a best friend.

But the skills needed to be a successful soldier or CEO are literally antithetical to the caring-sharing sort. Success and even heroism are still measured by a man's ability to compartmentalize, desensitize, act decisively, and sacrifice himself. "The essence of masculinity is that what it takes to get love makes us distant from love," says Warren Farrell, San Diego–based author of *Why Men Earn More* and *Why Men Are the Way They Are*. "That is the male dilemma in a nutshell."

"Men are beside themselves," Farrell continues. "There is a fundamental contradiction: If [a man] is successful at work he has really prepared himself to be unsuccessful at home. He's damned if he does and damned if he doesn't."

Marriage changes everything. Most men accept that and even welcome the transition. Men recognize that marriage requires compromise and sacrifice—but their beliefs about what's most important are surprisingly traditional, and not necessarily in line with women's beliefs. In his sociological research, Nock followed more than 6,000 young men for decades, gathering data on their social lives, careers, and habits. His conclusion is that most men undergo a profound personal transformation when they marry. It is a passage into manhood in an era when the very definition of manhood is in flux. "Marriage changes men because it is the venue in which adult masculinity is developed and sustained," he writes in *Marriage in Men's Lives*.

A married man works longer hours, moves up the career ladder faster, and earns more money than his single peers. He spends more time with his relatives. He donates less to charity; he spends less time hanging out with his buddies and more time in formal social organizations like business and civic associations.

A husband even *thinks* differently. "The way men view the world and their place in it changes in the act of marrying," says Nock. "Marriage makes people more conventional. If they are religious, they become more devout. They acquire the trappings of property owners, which makes them more conservative. They're less likely to engage in risky or deviant behaviors. Entering into this traditional arrangement has the effect of making men more traditional." A wedding is more than an expression of love; it's a public declaration that a man plans to abide by a set of social expectations about male adulthood. The seriousness with which men approach marriage and the lengths they are willing to go in order to be better husbands are some of the best evidence we have that men take commitment seriously and are willing to do what is expected of them to make marriage work.

But there's a catch. Nock believes that since he conducted his research in the 1990s, women's expectations have expanded to include greater intimacy. While conducting his research, he says, "I was focused more on ordinary expectations." He believes that emotional expectations may now be the most central part of marriage.

"Even a generation ago, if a man was a good breadwinner and he had no profoundly negative attributes, if every night he came home, had a martini and watched TV all night, then went to bed, he was fine," says marriage and family therapist Terry Real, author of *How Do I Get Through to You? Closing the Intimacy Gap Between Men and Women.* Now the job description has been expanded to include listening and that least measurable of skills, empathizing. Today, simply not cheating on your wife or beating your kids doesn't make you a good husband and father.

Real says he counsels a lot of men who would prefer the bullet-point version of how-to-achieve-intimacy-now. "I say to them, 'She wants you to be more relationship-skilled than you were raised to be. You're a smart guy—this isn't rocket science.'" But for a lot of husbands trying to rise to the demands of their 21st-century wives, the lessons of intimacy are worse than rocket science. They're *poetry.*

When husbands realize what their wives are asking for, the reaction isn't "'I didn't know that you wanted that, too,'" says Margulies. "It's more like 'I don't understand what the hell you're talking about.'" It's not a question of miscommunication, of Mars and Venus. It's a matter of new specifications, of women wanting something more than a traditional husband who, by definition, was removed and even remote. "In a nutshell, women want their husbands to act like girlfriends," Margulies says.

"I wish it were that simple," says Nock. "I don't think we can say, 'Okay, men, here's what you need to do to become better husbands.'" A lot of men would prefer such clear coordinates—even if it meant acting like a girlfriend.

While the conflicted desires of women have created some of this tension, society sends its own mixed signals. Time and feminism have chipped away at the granite facade of traditional masculinity, but old monuments don't fall easily. The last presidential election, after all, was in part a referendum on what kind of father or husband we want for our country. And did not the simple, stubborn, somewhat unintelligible fellow with the apparently traditional marriage best the more nuanced, flexible, loquacious gent with the strong, independent wife? John Kerry was chastised for windsurfing on Nantucket while George Bush was off whacking weeds in the hot Texas sun.

"What's so ludicrous about windsurfing?" asks Real. "It's effete—which is another way of saying it's feminine." Yet guys are forced to contend with such inane stereotypes. (Have you ever tried windsurfing? It's about as easy as riding a shark.)

Worst of all, women are often complicit in the stereotyping. If a single woman goes to a party, says Farrell, her friends don't push her toward the sensitive schoolteacher—they urge her to chat up the banker. "People don't say, 'Look at that man, he's really listening to a woman, asking her questions and drawing her out,'" says Farrell. "You don't get introductions like that, even though you would be introducing the woman to the type of man who would be a wonderful husband and father. Instead, the host will say, 'That fellow is an intern at Mt. Sinai Hospital.'"

So we end up with men wary of the shifting rules of marriage, wondering what's in it for them. The weary white-collar salary-man, having worked his 60-hour week while making time for his daughter's piano recital, may well wonder about the poetry lessons his wife is threatening him with. Suddenly an evening of video games or ESPN doesn't sound so bad, even if it means eating a TV dinner. Hungry-Man meals have gotten a lot better over the years—and they're still nicely compartmentalized, with clear bullet-point instructions on the back of the box.

For the most part, our parents and grandparents did not worry much about the emotional content of marriage. My parents lived through the Great Depression and the Second World War. When their marriage ended in divorce in the 1960s, I doubt either of them thought, "If only we had achieved greater intimacy!" It's not that they were stronger or better than we are today, or that our demands and complaints aren't legitimate. The lack of emotional connection certainly killed many marriages, and the right to personal fulfillment was part of what drove the women's movement—which in turn changed marriage for the better.

But on the communication score, most men are still playing catch-up with women. To care about someone else's feelings you have to be in touch with your own, and getting in touch with your feelings is not something we've been raised to think of as essential, or even admirable.

Collectively, we don't have a lot of positive examples of an open, questioning, emotional hero. Hamlet, who was certainly introspective, was neither husband nor father; he died, quite conveniently, before facing either of those hurdles.

"It's not so much that men can't provide the emotional support that women want as that men and women define emotional support differently," according to Nock. "As marriages become more focused on emotion and happiness, men and women are defining closeness in somewhat different terms." For men, actual physical proximity is often as good as intimacy ("I'm here, aren't I?"), while women want something more demonstrative.

Just look at how men and women communicate with members of their own gender. I have seen my wife sit down knee-to-knee with one of her close friends and unload, with no preamble or pretext of doing anything else besides perhaps drinking a glass of wine or cup of tea. Guys, for the most part, need some distraction in order to talk about feelings.

Two summers ago, while visiting some old friends in France (and how is that for effete?), my wife marveled at how my longtime pal Randy and I reconnected after not seeing each other for years. We sat knee-to-knee as well—with our iBooks linked, swapping music files. But what she did not hear was us comparing notes on aging—his mother had passed away, mine was ailing—or our marriages, topics we would not have easily broached otherwise. It's as though men need something to do with their hands.

Having established that some men are willing to try to meet women halfway, it's safe to ask what women can do for men. Sex is seriously underrated as a passport to that communicative country a lot of wives want to explore. While some women seem to resent the fact that their husbands want them, and want to be wanted back, the very act (as opposed to talk) allows a lot of men to be more emotionally available. And it, too, gives us something to do with our hands.

"The complaints I hear from men are about their spouses not taking their sexual needs seriously enough," says Mark Epstein, a psychiatrist in private practice in New York and author of *Open to Desire: Embracing a Lust for Life.* "Men become vulnerable when they are sexually engaged. Maybe if women didn't feel demeaned or objectified by male sexuality they wouldn't have to push it away so much. They could start to feel it as more of a form of communication." He acknowledges that many women may see it as more work—but isn't that what they're asking of their men? Sex is one area where men and women can explore differences without yielding their individual identities. "One thing that has to happen in a couple is that each one has to make room for the other's desire," says Epstein, "which is different from the way you experience it. You can approach it but never totally understand it."

Women can cut men a bit of slack, and try to empathize with these rough creatures (remember *Beauty and the Beast?*) rather than change them. They can also adjust their expectations. As Farrell says, "If you expect a man to be a killer and be home on time for dinner, you will end up feeling depressed about your partnership."

After all, men have quickly become masters at another kind of intimacy: fatherhood. Many contemporary fathers feel that they are an upgrade from the previous version. Warm, loving, generous fathers are lionized in the culture rather than scorned, points out Terry Real. "The current generation of men is much better as fathers than their fathers were," he says, "but it's not clear to me that we're much better husbands than our fathers were." The difference is that much less risk is involved in being vulnerable or intimate with your child than there is with your mate. The relationship of parent and child is not that of equals, and while we may have a lot of expectations of our children, we generally don't look to them for complete emotional fulfillment.

Truth be known, most men want the same thing from their mates that their wives are looking for in their husbands. They want to be understood by them, even if it means understanding themselves first. There is plenty of evidence that men want and need marriage as much as women do and are willing to learn new dance steps. Just put them in bullet points, and let us lead sometimes.

"Maternal Thinking" in the Raising of a Child with Profound Intellectual Disabilities

Eva Feder Kittay

A CHILD IS BORN, BECOMING A MOTHER

The most important thing that happens when a child with disabilities is born is that a child is born.[1]

When Sesha was born, I, along with Jeffrey, her father and my life-partner, fell madly in love with our baby. It was 1969. I was twenty-three, my husband twenty-five, and we were pioneers in the natural childbirth movement. I was reaping the benefits of being "awake and aware."[2] Exhilarated by the vigorous labor of propelling my baby into the world, and amazed by the success of my own body's heaving, I gazed into the little face emerging from me, a face wearing a pout that slowly became the heralding cry of the newborn infant. The nurses cleaned her off and handed her to me, and my Sesha melted into my arms. With her full head of black hair, her sweet funny infant's face, and her delicious temperament, this baby was the fulfillment of our dreams. We saw in her the perennial "perfect baby": the exquisite miracle of a birth. It was December 23rd, and all the world was poised for Christmas. But we had our own Christmas, our own celebration of birth and the beauty, freshness, and promise of infancy. This birth, and each birth, is unique and universal—common, even ordinary, and yet each time miraculous.

Such were my reflections as I lay in my New York City hospital room watching the snow falling, bathing in the glory of a wanted, welcomed baby. Only the hospital wasn't conforming to my mood or my expectations. The staff was being either bureaucratic or inept. I had anticipated seeing my baby shortly after she had been wheeled out of the delivery room, and I thought she would soon thereafter join me in my room. "Rooming-in" was an innovation, a concession to new women's voices, to women who wanted to breast-feed and to have their infants by their side, not in a nursery down the hall to be fed on a rigid four-hour schedule. I was to have my baby in my room after a twenty-four-hour observation period. But more than twenty-four hours had passed and no one had brought her in. Why? Could something be wrong? The nurses evaded my questions, and the doctors were nowhere to be found. Finally, I ventured down the hall to the nursery and, after encountering still more evasions, eventually found someone with an answer. Sesha had some jaundice ("common, nothing to worry about") and a cyanotic episode of no known origin (that is, she had briefly stopped breathing). She had been examined by a pediatrician, and she seemed fine. I could start nursing her, and we could leave the hospital according to schedule. It was four months before anyone thought again about that episode.

. . .

So the two of us embraced our parenthood and were blissful with our new baby. Sesha didn't cry much, fell asleep at my breast at night, and by day slept and munched (though with less vigor than I had expected). While she slept a great deal, when awake she had a wonderful wide-eyed questioning look that made us feel that she was very alert and taking in everything around her. At four months she was developing into a beautiful little baby, very cooperative and oh so sweet. Only she wasn't doing new "tricks." When friends and relatives would ask us what the little prodigy was up to, we'd have curiously little to report. But then, I wasn't interested in how early my child did such and such. All potential sources of anxiety were water off a duck's back: I was the happy mama, content to be gliding through this new period of my life with duckling and mate in tow. Yet it was precisely at this fourth month that a swell of extraordinary proportions engulfed us and interrupted my blissful journey into motherhood.

At this time, friends with a baby approximately Sesha's age visited us, and we were disturbed by the significant difference in the development of the two infants. A physician friend indicated that I ought to visit a pediatric neurologist. (Our own pediatrician responded to my query of why Sesha, at four months, was still not picking up her head, by saying that she must have a heavier head than the average baby and that such a trait is generally inherited from one of the parents. He advised me to go home and measure my husband's head to see if he too had a large head. Like fools, my husband and I pulled out the tape measure and determined that, yes, my husband's head was somewhat large. What cowardice propelled this pediatrician to evade his responsibility to be forthright and refer us to a specialist?!) The neurologist we visited must have known right away that Sesha was severely impaired, but he broke the news to us gradually, over a period that lasted nearly two years. In contrast to my pediatrician, this physician was being kind, not evasive. He did not try to falsely reassure us. His efforts to gently ease us into the realization of the extensive damage Sesha had sustained were nonetheless thwarted when, on his recommendation, we visited the star pediatric neurologist on the West Coast while on holiday.

Sesha was six months old, still as lovely and sweet and pliant as one might wish any baby to be. The handsome, well-tanned doctor examined our daughter briefly and told us without any hesitation that she was and would always be profoundly retarded—at best severely and not profoundly retarded. His credentials as a physician who can correctly predict an outcome remain secure—but his understanding of how to approach parents with such harsh news, surely

also an important skill for a physician, is quite another matter. The swell that had been threatening to engulf us for two months now crested, and we were smashed onto a rocky shore with all the force that nature could muster against us. Never will I forget how ill I was in that San Francisco hotel room—how my body convulsed against this indigestible information. My husband had to care for Sesha and me, even as he ached. This doctor's brutal, insensitive way of breaking devastating news to parents is a story I have heard recounted again and again. The pain of the prognosis is matched only by the anger at obtuse and insensitive doctors. In our own case, we had a near repeat performance when, just to be certain of his suspicions, our first and humane physician wanted still one more consultation. We thought that we had now visited the Inferno, and we were prepared to begin the arduous climb back up—to find some equilibrium, some way to live with this verdict. But on our encounter with the third pediatric neurologist we were again told outright—after a five-minute exam—that our daughter was severely to profoundly retarded and that we should consider having other children because "one rotten apple doesn't spoil the barrel." As I type these words nearly twenty-seven years later, I still wonder at the utter failure of human empathy in this physician—one whose specialty, no less, was neurological impairment.

Sesha was never to live a normal life. It would be another year before we completed the tests, the evaluations, the questionings that confirmed those first predictions. We couldn't know or fully accept the extent of her impairment, but some things were clear. We knew it wasn't a degenerative disability, and for that we were grateful. But our worst fear was that her handicap involved her intellectual faculties. We, her parents, were intellectuals. I was committed to a life of the mind. Nothing mattered to me as much as to be able to reason, to reflect, to understand. This was the air I breathed. How was I to raise a daughter who would have no part of this? If my life took its meaning from thought, what kind of meaning would her life have? Yet throughout this time, it never even occurred to me to give Sesha up, to institutionalize her, to think of her in any other terms than my own beloved child. She was my daughter. I was her mother. That was fundamental. Her impairment in no way mitigated my love for her. If it had any impact on that love it was only to intensify it. She was so vulnerable, she would need so much of our love and protection to shelter her from the scorn of the world, from its dangers, from its indifference, from its failure to understand her and her humanity. We didn't yet realize how much she would teach us, but we already knew that we had learned something. That which we believed we valued, what we—I—thought was at the center of humanity—the capacity for thought, for reason—was not it, not it at all.

PORTRAIT OF SESHA AT TWENTY-SEVEN

I am awakened and her babbling-brook giggles penetrate my semiconscious state. Hands clapping. Sesha is listening to *The Sound of Music*. Peggy, her caregiver of twenty-three years, has just walked in, and Sesha can hardly contain her desire to throw her arms around Peggy and give Peggy her distinctive kiss—mouth open, top teeth lightly (and sometimes not so lightly) pressing on your cheek, her breath full of excitement and happiness, her arms around your neck (if you're lucky; if not, arms up, hands on hair, which cavemanlike, she uses to pull your face to her mouth). Sesha's kisses are legendary (and if you're not on your toes, somewhat painful).

Sesha was almost twelve before she learned to kiss, learned to hug. These were major achievements. Sesha's chronological age is now that of a young woman. She has the physical characteristics of a teen. She's tall, slender, long-legged, with dark beautiful brown eyes, brown short wavy luxuriant hair, a shy smile that she delivers with a lowered head, and a radiant laugh that will make her throw her head back in delight. Sesha has been beautiful from the day of her birth, through all her girlhood and now into her young adulthood. Her loveliness shines through her somewhat twisted body, the bridge that substitutes for

her natural front teeth (lost in a fall at school), her profound cognitive deficits. The first thing people remark when they meet Sesha, or see her photo, is how beautiful she is. I've always admired (without worshiping) physical beauty and so I delight in Sesha's loveliness. The smoothness of her skin, the brilliant light in her eyes, the softness of her breath, the tenderness of her spirit. Her spirit.

No, Sesha's loveliness is not skin deep. How to speak of it? How to describe it? Joy. The capacity for joy. The babbling-brook laughter at a musical joke. The starry-eyed faraway look as she listens to Elvis crooning "Love me tender," the excitement of her entire soul as the voices blare out "*Alle Menschen warden Brüder*" in the choral ode of Beethoven's Ninth Symphony, and the pleasure of bestowing her kisses and receiving the caresses in turn. All variations and gradations of joy. Spinoza characterized joy as the increase in our power of self-preservation and by that standard, Sesha's is a very well-preserved self. Yet she is so limited. She cannot speak. She cannot even say "Mama"—though sometimes we think she says "Aylu" (our translation, "I love you"). She can only finger-feed herself, despite the many efforts at teaching her to use utensils. She'll sometimes drink from a cup (and sometimes spill it all). She is "time trained" at toileting, which means that she is still in diapers. Although she began to walk at five, she no longer can walk independently—her scoliosis and seizures and we do not know what else have robbed her of this capacity. So she is in a wheelchair. Her cerebral palsy is not severe, but it is there.

She has no measurable I.Q. As she was growing up she was called "developmentally delayed." But delay implies that she will one day develop the capacities that are slow in developing. The jury is no longer out. Most capacities she will not develop at all. Is she then a "vegetable"? The term is ludicrous when applied to her. There is nothing vegetative about her. She is fully a human, not a vegetable. Given the scope and breadth of human possibilities and capacities, she occupies a limited spectrum, but she inhabits it fully because she has the most important faculties of all. The capacities for love and for happiness. These allow those of us who care for her, who love her, who have been entrusted with her well-being to form deep and abiding attachments to her. Sesha's coin and currency is love. That is what she wishes to receive and that is what she reciprocates—in spades.

ON THE VERY POSSIBILITY OF MOTHERING AND THE CHALLENGE OF THE SEVERELY DISABLED CHILD

My mother would help in the early days and months of Sesha's life. My mother, a warm, affectionate woman who miraculously not only survived the Holocaust, but survived it emotionally intact, loves children and especially loves babies. As an only child, I alone could provide her with grandchildren, and Sesha was the first and only grandchild on both sides of the family. All the grandparents were thrilled with Sesha's birth and deeply saddened at the news that there were suspicions of retardation. We thought that we would slowly introduce them to the idea that the prognosis was as dire as we knew it to be. In the meanwhile, my mother would baby-sit Sesha when both Jeffrey and I were busy and would take her for the night when I had a paper to write for graduate school. We had never brought the grandparents to the doctor's visits, hoping to spare them some of the pain we experienced at each visit, but once it could not be helped. It was on that fateful visit that my mother grasped the full extent of the trauma to Sesha's brain. Upon our return, my mother, in her inimitable and insistent fashion, urged me to place Sesha in an institution.

Of all the traumatic encounters in that first year and a half of Sesha's life, none, perhaps not even the realization that Sesha was retarded, was as painful as these words from the woman I loved most in my life: the woman who had taught me what it was to be a mother, to love a child, to anticipate the joys of nursing, of holding and caring for another, of sacrificing for a child. My model of maternal love asking me to discard my child? Would she have banished me to an institution had I been "damaged"? Surely, she couldn't mean this. But, no, she *insisted*, with conviction, with surefooted

rightness that I *had to* put this child out of my life. It made me crazy. I couldn't comprehend it. Only the images and stories of the Holocaust could reclaim for me my mother and her love. Only the knowledge that in those bitter times, a limp was a death warrant. To merely be associated with disability was a death warrant. Of course she was acting like a mother, as someone whose interest was my well-being. I see now that she thought this child would ruin my life, but she was unable to transcend her own maternity and project that quality onto me: to realize that the maternal love and concern she had for me, I had for Sesha. I remained in her eyes a child, a daughter and not a mother with her own daughter. Now I think back and wonder how much of my mother's response was attributable to fear of the unknown (and what was known but in different circumstances), how much was the result of the stigma attached to disability, and how much was resistance to the reality of my maternity? In time, my mother came to understand that we could build a good life with Sesha. She allowed herself to love Sesha with the fullness of a grandmother's love. And in time, I forgave my mother and came to appreciate how her intense, if misdirected, love for me fueled her stubborn insistence that we "put Sesha away."

. . .

It was simply impossible for me to part with my child. This is what I knew of mothering, mothering, at least, that is chosen. A child is born to you. This child is your charge—it is your sacred responsibility to love, nurture, and care for this child throughout your life. Is this "maternal instinct"? I don't know what those words mean. Do all women who become mothers believe thus? Clearly not. Is it then a cultural construct? If so, it is a belief constructed in many cultures, in many historical periods. Perhaps this commitment is rather the condition for the possibility of motherhood— realized differently in different cultures, under different conditions, and differently realized even by women within a single culture, or a single historical period. It may not be inspired by birth, but by adoption, but once a child is "your" child, at that moment you become that child's mother and the duty emerging from that bond is one of the most compelling of all duties. At that point you commit yourself to the well-being of one who is dependent upon you, whose survival, growth, and development as a social being are principally (if never solely) your responsibility. The birth of a child with very significant impairments may test the limit of the commitment that I take to be the very condition for the possibility of mothering. It may do so for some women, under some—adverse—circumstances. In my own understanding this felt conviction is so fundamental that it serves as a benchmark. The extent to which a woman cannot realize it (in the idiom appropriate to her own culture) because of adverse social, political, or economic conditions, to that extent she faces an injustice.[3] I take it, then, that the requirement to be able to mother, that is, to realize the condition for the possibility to mother, constitutes one of the "circumstances of justice."[4]

Mothering Distributed: The Work of Dependency Care

Sesha's expansive, affectionate nature is a gift. In comparison studies with autistic children, researchers have found that "the mother's ability and enthusiasm for functioning in the maternal caretaker role are adversely affected by the developmentally disabled child who is *not* affectionate and *not* demonstrative."[5] But researchers have also found (to no one's surprise, I hope) that the greater the degree of "incapacitation and helplessness," the greater the burden the child poses. Taking care of Sesha, meeting her daily needs, her medical needs, interpreting her needs and desires, not over the span of twenty-seven, months, but twenty-seven years, has posed a substantial challenge.

I never wanted to hire help to care for my child. I believed that with shared parenting it should be possible to care for a child and still pursue an additional life's work. I soon found that I was wrong. All families where each parent takes on work additional to child care and domestic duties require help with child care. Had Sesha been a normal toddler, I would have tried to hunt out the few day care programs that were being established

in the 1970s for women like me who, while not driven by economic necessity, were nonetheless committed to *both* motherhood and some other life's work. But Sesha could not play in the easy way other young children could play. She needed intense stimulation. Her attention faded quickly; if left to her own devices, she'd simply stare off into space. Keeping Sesha stimulated was, and remains, hard work.

For a while Sesha was enrolled in one of the pilot projects in early intervention for the developmentally delayed. She made wonderful progress in the first five months of the program. But Sesha's story, unlike so many I have read about, was not one of continuing development.[6] After several years in that same program the improvements became more and more minimal. While needing child care was something I shared with other mothers, because of my daughter's profound disability I was dependent on housebound help.

Certainly someone could give Sesha perfunctory custodial "care," that is, attend to her bodily needs but without ever seeing the person whose body it is, without tapping into her desires, without engaging her potential, without responding to and returning her affection—her affection that is her most effective means of connecting with others, in the absence of speech and most other capacities required for interpersonal activities. To commit to care for Sesha required an ability to give your heart to a child, who because she would never outgrow the need for your continual care, would not release you from an abiding bond and obligation. While we found a number of talented caretakers, few were willing to yield to the demands of caring for Sesha for an extended time. Caring for Sesha, when done well, is intensive labor, and the relationship enabling such care must also already be intensive.

Sesha was four when a woman walked into our lives who came and stayed. How and where we acquired the instincts I don't know, but we knew immediately that Peggy was right. She was scarcely interested in us. Her interview was with Sesha. But she wouldn't take the job. Peggy feared the intensity of the involvement she knew was inevitable. We pleaded and increased the salary. She told me later that she would never have taken the job if her agency hadn't urged her to do a trial week. At the end of the week, it was already nearly too late to quit. Sesha had worked her way into Peggy's heart. Twenty-three years later, Peggy told me the following story:

> I had been with Sesha in Central Park and I was working on some walking exercises that the folks at Rusk [Sesha's early intervention program] had assigned. I was working terribly hard trying to get Sesha to cooperate and do what I was supposed to get her to do. I sat her down in her stroller and sat down on a park bench. I realized that I was simply exhausted from the effort. I thought, How am I going to do this? How can I possibly do this job? When I looked down at Sesha and saw her little head pushed back against her stroller moving first to one side and then to another. I couldn't figure out what she was doing. Until I traced what her eyes were fixed on. She had spotted a leaf falling, and she was following its descent. I said, "Thank you for being my teacher, Sesha. I see now. Not *my* way, *your* way, slowly." After that, I fully gave myself over to Sesha. That forged the bond.

Sara Ruddick, writing about the relationship between care as labor and care as relationship, remarks: "The work [of caring] is constituted in and through the relation of those who give and receive care." Nowhere is this better illustrated than in this story. And nowhere is the notion that the work of mothering and caring requires thought, understanding—again in Ruddick's words, "maternal thinking"—better illustrated than in this story. Forging the relationship, through this insight into who Sesha is, how she sees the world, made possible the caring labor itself. And a caring labor so infused with the relationship has enhanced the relationship, made it as solid as the bonds of motherhood. . . . We have moved to a model, which for want of any other adequate term, I'll call "distributed mothering." I am Sesha's one mother, but in truth her mothering has been distributed across a number of individuals: father, various caretakers, and Peggy.

In the literature on the care of the disabled child, little attention is given to the team of persons doing the hands-on care of the disabled, whom I have called "dependency workers": those who attend to the very basic needs of a dependent, needs the dependent is incapable of fulfilling on her own behalf. Like the stagehands who serve as Marilyn Frye's (1983) metaphor for the role of women on the stage of world history and culture, the dependency worker is the invisible stagehand in the saga of disability. I hope that the discussion in this set of reflections will open the way to investigating the relationship between dependency work and mothering a disabled child; between dependency work and disability; between the dependency worker and the disabled person.

PEGGY AND I

Peggy and I are like two metals, of not very dissimilar composition, but tempered under very different circumstances. Ten years and one month my senior, Peggy was born before the war and lived her youth in war-torn Ireland and Britain. I was born after the war and grew to maturity in the booming economies of Sweden and the United States. We are both immigrants—though she traveled here, willingly, as a young woman, accompanied only by her sister; I came as a young girl, reluctantly, brought by my parents. She was one of thirteen children raised lovingly but in poverty and wartime, with a father off to fight. I was an only child, the precious projection of hope by two survivors of Hitler's murderous rage against the Jews. She was raised to be fiercely independent; I was overprotected. She was raised to be self-reliant and hardy; I was looked over as a fragile flower. She had to make her own way early. I never *had* to make my own way at all. She is always punctual; I am always late. She is a doer; I am a thinker. She insists on routine; I'm incapable of following routine. We are not easily compatible, Peggy and I, but we come together on politics, on compassion, on a love of books, and most important of all, on our passion for Sesha.

. . .

Sometimes I feel that my relationship to Peggy vis-à-vis Sesha is like the patriarchal relation of husband to wife vis-à-vis their children. Peggy accompanies me to doctor's visits with Sesha. Actually, it is more as if I accompany her and Sesha. I deal with the authorities (much as the father does), she undresses Sesha (much as the mother does), although since it is distasteful to me to stand idly by, I "help" (much as an involved father might). I pay the bills, she wheels Sesha out. Some roles we can reverse, others we can't— they are set in the larger practices in which we participate. Whenever and each time I see the analogies, it makes my feminist and egalitarian flesh creep. And yet, I can't see my way out of this. I cannot function without this privilege, and yet I despise it. I cannot see how to live my convictions. Of course, even this dilemma is a great luxury. So many other mothers with children like Sesha have to make much more difficult choices.

In the literature by and about parents of disabled children, the theme of difference and sameness is persistent. In this [article], *sameness* resonates in the quotation that introduces the personal narrative; *difference* occupies the title. The tension emerges in opposing claims: Parents of disabled children cope as well as parents of normal children; parents of disabled children experience more stress than parents of normal children. There is a sense in which both statements are true. Most mothers and many fathers find the strength to cope with the special burdens of a disabled child—and doubtless more would do so and many would do so better if better resources were available. But read even the cheeriest account, and you will find the enormous cost and pain involved in coming to the point of coping. Nonetheless, every day with even a profoundly disabled child is not a test and it does not require virtual sainthood to be a more-than-adequate parent to such a child.

What I have learned from the experience of mothering Sesha, and what the many accounts of parenting such a child reveal, is that the differences we encounter redefine sameness. Raising a child with a severe disability is not just like parenting a normal child—but more so. It is often very different. Yet in that difference, we come to see features of raising any child that otherwise escape attention or that assume a new valence. One notices aspects of maternal practice that are not highlighted when we begin our theorizing from the perspective of the mother of the normal child.

Ruddick, considering maternal practice as exercised when children are intact,[7] has identified as the three requirements of maternal work preserving the life of a child, socializing her for acceptance, and fostering her development. And in many important regards these requirements hold for the task of mothering the child with a disability. Nevertheless, the scope and meaning of these practices are altered. In the remainder of this [article], I want to discuss how thinking about caring for dependent persons by thinking of mothering the child with severe disabilities reorients our thinking about the meaning of maternal practices in our social life.

PRESERVATIVE LOVE

Preservative love seems to be the most fundamental of all maternal requirements. Disability, however, especially if it is severe and manifests itself early, is too often the occasion for *denying* a child preservative love. This is especially so where resources are too meager to keep even a well child functioning.[8] However, even when material conditions are adequate, the stigma of disability can be sufficient to allow parents of such a child to let the child languish.[9]

Where the commitment to the child has been made, preservative love comes to occupy an often overridingly central place in one's maternal practice. In the case of Sesha, safety and attention to medical needs are the first commandments of her care. Attention to them by her caregivers is paramount. Her fragility elevates this feature of maternal practice and sometimes threatens to overshadow all other aspects of maternal thinking with respect to her.

Preservative love propels parent and child into a medicalized world: corrective procedures for the disability will often involve surgical fixes, and even routine illness can go wrong all too easily. Dealings with medical authorities are among the most frequent complaints one hears when listening to mothers of disabled children. One researcher cites one pediatrician as saying, "'I don't enjoy it . . . I don't really enjoy a really handicapped child who comes in drooling, can't walk and so forth. . . . Medicine is geared to the perfect human body. Something you can't do anything about [what] challenges the doctor and reminds him of his own inabilities.'"[10] In the same study, Rosalyn Darling speaks of the mother of a child with cerebral palsy who says, "[Our pediatrician] didn't take my complaints seriously. . . . I feel that Brian's sore throat is just as important as [my normal daughter's] sore throat."[11]

In my own dealings with physicians, it never occurred to me that any physician wouldn't take my daughter's ailments as seriously as those of a normal child. On the contrary, I have always assumed that a disability gives her a priority because of her fragility and vulnerability. It has never occurred to me that a physician might value her life and well-being less, even though I have had enough negative experiences with the medical profession to make me think otherwise. Perhaps I have needed to refuse to acknowledge such devaluation in sustaining my own preservative love.

. . .

In the struggle to watch over Sesha, to preserve her, to avoid the catastrophe of her death, it is not just the hard wall of medicine I encounter, but her protracted dependency. Preservative love, when directed at the "normally" functioning child, has its most intense period in the early years of the child's life. The individual with severe disabilities does not outgrow her profound vulnerability, nor can she assume the task of her own self-preservation. The effort of preserving a severely disabled child's life is often accompanied by a *lifelong* commitment to *day-to-day physical care* for the child. Dependence is often socially constructed—*all* dependence is not. If you have a fever of 105, the dependence you have is not socially constructed. Sesha's dependence is not socially constructed. Neither "labeling" nor environmental impediments create her dependence—although environment modifications are *crucial* for her to have a decent life.

. . .

SOCIALIZATION FOR ACCEPTANCE

Raising children includes more than caring for and protecting them.[12] It means preparing them for a world larger than the family. Mothers who are wary of the social institutions and practices of the society in which they live, and who understand the oppressive nature of these institutions, are reluctant to socialize their children to be acceptable in situations that they themselves view as unacceptable. Yet the most rebellious mother understands that each human is a social being and that some degree of social acceptance is crucial to their own child's well-being.

The task of socializing the child with disabilities also calls upon a notion of "acceptance." But acceptance is now understood against the background of "normalization." Those who are "different" or those who have, to use Helen Featherstone's (1980) term, a "difference in the family" very much want acceptance: acceptance of who they are, if they are disabled; acceptance of the child they love and the family they have created, if they are parents. *Normalization* is often an avenue to acceptance, but by virtue of the disability, it cannot be the exclusive avenue.

Socializing a disabled child for acceptance may, for instance, encourage a mother to have the child present herself in such a way that the disability is less noticeable—or that the "normal" characteristics of the child are underscored. I often find myself far more concerned with the clothes Sesha wears than I would be with my able child, with making sure her clothes or wheelchair are not in any way soiled, with being certain, that is, that Sesha presents a face to the world that is as attractive as possible so that the first response to her is as positive as I can make it be.

There is something very sad about this need—but I believe it is a realistic response to the repugnance (as harsh as that word is) of so many people toward disability. The sadness comes from the recognition of that repulsion, the need to do what I can to counteract it, and the knowledge that a pretty dress is such a superficial way to address the fear and ignorance that the response bespeaks. And yet I do it and feel I must do it, for Sesha, for myself, for our whole family. For Sesha, because I know that she understands when she is approached with a smile, with delight; that she is tickled when people make a fuss over how pretty she looks; that she feels pain at people's indifference to her. For myself, because it is one thing I can do to integrate Sesha into the community of which she is a part, even if her interactions with it are minimal. For my family, because we all feel the pain of the stigma attached to disability. Dressing Sesha nicely, making sure that she goes into the world looking clean and fresh and well cared for, is my way and our family's way of telling the world that this person is loved and cared for, and hoping that the message that she is worth being cared for will be absorbed by others.[13]

...

Helen Featherstone cites an instance that brings to the fore the way in which the family normalizes the disabled child, and the outer edge of consciousness that is always alert to the stigma and the nonnormality of the situation. She writes of her response to the experience of starting her son Jody, a profoundly retarded boy with cerebral palsy and partial blindness, in a new school:

> On the first day I took him myself, intending to spend the morning. As soon as he was comfortably settled in the classroom I withdrew to the observation booth. The program pleased me, but after a few moments I realized that I felt depressed. . . . I looked at my son as a new teacher might. I saw a little boy with severe cerebral palsy and no useful vision.
>
> Familiarity and routine blunt our awareness of disability after a while. Without meaning to, a stranger can upset this internal balance.[14]

I realized as I read that passage that this is why it is so difficult to take Sesha out in public. I don't want to upset that balance. I don't want to see

Sesha as others see her. I want them to see her as I see her. The blunting of awareness of disability is part and parcel of a socialization that I, as a mother, have had to undergo—one that is a prerequisite to my socializing my child.

This socialization has two parts. First I refuse to see my child as not "normal"—for what she does is *normal for Sesha*. This is a redefining of normalcy that accepts Sesha in her individuality. Without such acceptance, I would not be able to present to the world a child *I* find acceptable. At the same time, I have to see the child as others see her so that I mediate between her and the others— to negotiate acceptability. Where we cannot mold the child, we may work to shape attitudes and the environment in which she moves. Socializing for acceptance can mean altering what the child gets socialized into and what will count as, or form the grounds of, acceptance.

The parental task involves, then, both socializing the child for the acceptance, such as it might be, of the world and socializing the world, as best one can, so that it can accept your child. Yet a precondition for both requires socializing oneself for the acceptance of the child with her disability and establishing a sense of normalcy, for oneself and for the face you present to the world.

FOSTERING DEVELOPMENT

Most "normal" children are remarkably adaptable, and their development will take place in many different circumstances. The aim of maternal practice will be to provide, wherever possible, those conditions that are best suited to foster that development. For a child with disabilities, by contrast, development is never a given. It is not only fostering development but *enabling development* that a mother of a disabled child puts her heart and mind to. Enabling the development of a disabled child involves navigating complex straits.

First, finding appropriate facilities and teachers is integral to the task. This is at once an individual and a collective effort. If it were not for the activism of other parents, Sesha's schooling would not have been funded. Although Sesha was never a candidate for mainstreaming, the mainstreaming of less involved children means that Sesha receives a better reception in public. As other disabled children and adults move into their communities, they open vistas for all disabled persons and facilitate enabling development for even the most profoundly impaired individual.

Second, parents of children with disabilities are dependent upon professional help available for their children—help that was hardly imaginable as little as twenty-five years ago. . . . The difficulty of negotiating professional and personal knowledges is compounded by the different virtues that guide professional care and maternal care. As Darling remarks, "While professional responses to disabled children are generally characterized by affective neutrality, universalism, and function specificity, parental responses are affective, particularistic, and functionally diffuse."[15] No doubt parents generally worry that a professional's "affective neutrality" too often translates as indifference to the particular needs of their particular child. But such "neutrality" can be especially difficult to tolerate when the needs are urgent and when social stigma continues to attach itself to disability, perhaps most of all to cognitive deficits. Affective involvement may be too much to demand of professionals, and without a doubt, an involvement as intense as that of mothering persons should not be expected. Yet parents and professionals need a mutual respect and partnership in order to enable the disabled child to grow and flourish to whatever extent the physical impairment permits. And there is no question in the minds of the many mothers and fathers of disabled children that professionals of all sorts are inadequately trained in the affective requirements of meeting needs of those who are ill or disabled.

The rift between professionals and mothering persons is further aggravated by that aspect of professionalism that assigns the professional a task that is "functionally specific." This means that the professional "focuses exclusively on a part [of the child], indeed a disabled part."[16] To the parent, however, the child's roles as son or daughter, sibling, grandchild, student, playmate, or church member usually supersede his or her disability. This difference is perhaps the source of the greatest dissonance between the mothering person and the professional as they each attempt to ensure a child's thriving.

. . .

A failure in preservative love can result in death or injury. A failure in enabling and fostering development is less visible—but its threat is persistent. It is the continual concern: Am I doing the right thing? Am I pushing too hard? Not hard enough? Are there better, more appropriate programs? How do I balance her needs and those of my other child(ren)? How do I balance the demands of caring for this child and all the other aspects of my life, my life with my partner, my obligations to others? Some of these concerns are common to raising any child. But many of these concerns take on special poignancy when the very possibility of your child developing some fundamental skills to stay alive depends on your making the right decisions. The guilt that you may not be doing enough fuels resentment at those who should understand but never seem to understand well enough.

. . .

As the disability community is anxious to remind us, handicapping conditions are not simply given by the impairment itself but by socially constructed environments and notions of ability. In reflecting on this point I note an irony: it is a source of great inspiration and insight in the disability community that independent living, as well as inclusion within one's community, should be the goals of education and habilitation of the disabled. But this ideal can also disempower and be a source of great distress if applied with too broad a brush. Even as the disability community, including parent advocates, works toward inclusion and the maximum attainable independence, some of its efforts get congealed in concepts and behaviors that have less desirable consequences. Chief among these are the notions that with concentrated parental effort the child will improve, that providing teams of professionals will "fix" things, and that an appreciable degree of independence is the end result of all the appropriate efforts.

Independence, acceptance, and normalcy are generally the goals of parents of disabled children—not very different from the goals of most parents raising most children. But for parents with a severely or profoundly retarded child, development may no longer have as a goal independent living: lifelong dependence may be clearly an inevitability. So it is in Sesha's case. As we try to feed her soul as well as her body, we look for activities that give her joy, that tap into the diverse pleasures she can enjoy and that will make her function as well as possible. She loves the water, and so we arrange for her to "go swimming." "Swimming" in Sesha's case means walking in lap lanes—the only time she can walk independently without support. Back and forth, giving her pleasure and exercise simultaneously. Music is a perpetual treat, so she has headphones and a walkman that, incidentally, connect her to her teen contemporaries. When we can find the appropriate persons, we supply her with music therapy. We have fought on many occasions for funding for her swim therapy and music therapy. But unlike physical therapy and speech therapy, neither of which are especially applicable to her needs, swim and music therapies are considered luxuries, and not offered to her. They are not seen as necessities because, in part at least, they do not appear to be geared to "independent living."

. . .

I believe that a focus on independence, and perhaps even the goal of inclusion, when inclusion is understood as the incorporation of the disabled into the "normal" life of the community, yields too much to a conception of the citizen as "independent and fully functioning." The disability community has achieved enviable recognition of the needs of the disabled by stressing that it is the combination of inherent traits and environmental enablings that results in capabilities, not inherent traits alone. Without sufficient light, the sighted would all be as incapable of seeing as are the blind—and the sighted would be handicapped because those who have lived a life without sight have developed other capacities by which to maneuver

around in their environment. The stress on environmental modification to enhance capabilities is crucial in Sesha's life. Without a wheelchair, she would have only a bed from which to view the world. But no modifications of the environment will be sufficient to make Sesha independent.

I fear that the stress on independence reinstates Sesha as less than fully human. With every embrace, I know her humanity. And it has no more to do with independence than it has to do with being able to read Spinoza. So when we think of mothering a disabled child as enabling and fostering development, we must also reconceive development, not only toward independence, but development in whatever capacities are there to be developed. Development for Sesha means the enhancement of her capacities to experience joy.

A Summation

To conclude, I can only say that, in truth, this essay has no conclusion. The process of mothering will not end, just as marriages are not supposed to end: "till death do us part." Until then I will continue to learn from my daughter, from those who share her mothering with me, and from the unique, but perhaps at times, also generalizable, aspects of this remarkable relationship with an exquisite person we call Sesha.

NOTES

There are many people to thank—first of all Sesha and Peggy and Jeffrey and Leo—for, well, everything. Next, the many individuals who have helped in fashioning this maternal thinking in the care they have provided Sesha. I want to thank my own mother for the model of maternal thinking she provided and my in-laws for their unwavering support in helping us meet Sesha's needs. I want to thank Sara Ruddick and Julia Hanigsberg for providing me with the inspiration and opportunity to write about my experiences, and Sara Ruddick for her extraordinary editing job. A longer version of this article appears as chapters 6 and 7 of my book *Love's Labor: Essays on Women, Equality and Dependency* (New York: Routledge, 1999).

1. Philip M. Ferguson and Adrienne Asch, "Lessons from Life: Personal and Parental Perspectives on School, Childhood, and Disability," in *Schooling and Disability—Eighty-Eighth Yearbook of the National Society for the Study of Education, Part II,* ed. Kenneth J. Behage (Chicago: University of Chicago Press, 1989), 108.

2. This phrase comes from Ferdinand Lamaze, *Painless Childbirth: Psychoprophylactic Method* (Chicago: H. Regnery, 1956).

3. An example of such circumstance is vividly portrayed in Nancy Scheper-Hughes, *Death without Weeping: The Violence of Everyday Life in Brazil* (Berkeley and Los Angeles: University of California Press, 1992). A gripping study of the shantytown dwelling of the sugarcane workers of northeastern Brazil. Their situation of abject poverty, of harsh physical conditions, made a hardiness tested in the first months of life a requirement. These mothers allowed their impaired or weakest offspring to die and buried them "without weeping." These women did not see themselves as abandoning the children in a denial of love—the loving gesture was to allow these unfortunate babes to return to Jesus—so these women believed, or so they rationalized. The conviction which I call the condition for the possibility of mothering, and which is embodied in the notion of *preservative* love, reaches a limiting case with these infants who, because they do not thrive, are "allowed to return to the angels."

4. I have in mind Rawls's use of Hume. See John Rawls, *A Theory of Justice* (Cambridge, MA: Harvard University Press, 1971), 126; see also Eva Kittay, "Human Dependency and Rawlsian Equality," in *Feminists Rethink the Self,* ed. D. T. Meyers (Boulder, CO: Westview Press, 1996).

5. L. Wikler, "Family Stress Theory and Research on Families of Children with Mental Retardation," in *Families of Handicapped Persons: Research, Programs, and Policy Issues* (Baltimore, MD: Paul H. Brookes, 1986), 184 (author's emphasis).

6. See, for example, Martha Moraghan Jablow, *Cara: Growing with a Mentally Retarded Child* (Philadelphia: Temple University Press, 1982); Michael Bérubé, *Life as We Know It: A Father, a Family, and an Exceptional Child* (New York: Random House, 1996).

7. Some readers will note that I am using the categories of Sara Ruddick, *Maternal Thinking:*

Toward a Politics of Peace (Boston: Beacon Press, 1989). I am also challenging them since, as Jane McDonnell ("Mothering an Autistic Child: Reclaiming the Voice of the Mother," in *Narrating Mothers: Theorizing Maternal Subjectivities,* ed. B. O. Daly and M. T. Reddy, Knoxville: University of Tennessee Press, 1991) has noted, in formulating these categories Ruddick seemed to assume that all children are "intact."

8. Scheper-Hughes, *Death without Weeping.*

9. For instance, a U.S. physician participating in the Hastings Center Prenatal Testing Project recently reported a case of an infant in his Neonatal Intensive Care Unit with Down's syndrome and an imperforate anus who had a colostomy created which he will need for a year, if not a lifetime. According to this physician, the social worker—who relates that the parents no longer visit the child and have placed him for adoption—believes that the Down's syndrome and associated medical problems are entirely "unacceptable" for the parents because "of a strong cultural bias." Apparently the parents plan to tell family and friends that the child died.

10. Rosalyn Benjamin Darling, "Parental Entrepreneurship: A Consumerist Response to Professional Dominance," *Journal of Social Issues* 44, no. 1 (1988): 149, cites Darling, 1979, 152.

11. Parents of the disabled have decried the excessive medicalization of disability and the pathologizing of parental responses. See, for example, Ferguson and Asch, "Lessons from Life," and Dorothy Kerner Lipsky, "A Parental Perspective on Stress and Coping," *American Journal of Orthopsychiatry* 55 (October 1985): 614–17. Yet parents are also grateful for medical procedures that are now available. For an eloquent statement of the improvements in medical care and habilitation for Down's syndrome children, see Bérubé, *Life as We Know It,* especially chapter 2.

12. See William Ruddick, "Parenthood: Three Concepts and a Principle," in *Family Values: Issues in Ethics, Society and the Family,* ed. Laurence D. Houlgate (Belmont, CA: Wadsworth, 1998), for a discussion of this distinction.

13. To be sure, dressing her nicely and keeping her in unsoiled clothes is not *the same as* loving and caring for her—but it is sending a message loudly and clearly.

14. Helen Featherstone, *A Difference in the Family* (New York: Basic Books, 1980), 41.
15. Rosalyn Benjamin Darling, "Parent-Professional Interaction: The Roots of Misunderstanding," in *The Family with a Handicapped Child: Understanding and Treatment,* ed. M. Seligman (New York: Grune and Stratton, 1983), 148.
16. Ibid.

REFERENCES

Darling, Rosalyn Benjamin. 1979. *Families Against Society: A Study of Reactions to Children with Birth Defects*. Beverly Hills, CA: Sage Publications.

Featherstone, Helen. 1980. *A Difference in the Family*. New York: Basic Books.

Frye, Marilyn. 1983. *The Politics of Reality: Essays in Feminist Theory*. Trumansburg, NY: Crossing Press.

R E A D I N G   **60**

Only Daughter

Sandra Cisneros

Once, several years ago, when I was just starting out my writing career, I was asked to write my own contributor's note for an anthology I was part of. I wrote: "I am the only daughter in a family of six sons. *That* explains everything."

Well, I've thought about that ever since, and yes, it explains a lot to me, but for the reader's sake I should have written: "I am the only daughter in a *Mexican* family of six sons." Or even: "I am the only daughter of a Mexican father and a Mexican-American mother." Or: "I am the only daughter of a working-class family of nine." All of these had everything to do with who I am today.

I was/am the only daughter and *only* a daughter. Being an only daughter in a family of six sons forced me by circumstance to spend a lot of time by myself because my brothers felt it beneath them to play with a *girl* in public. But that aloneness, that loneliness, was good for a would-be writer—it allowed me time to think and think, to imagine, to read and prepare myself.

Being only a daughter for my father meant my destiny would lead me to become someone's wife. That's what he believed. But when I was in the fifth grade and shared my plans for college with him, I was sure he understood. I remember my father saying, "*Que bueno, mi'ja,* that's good."

That meant a lot to me, especially since my brothers thought the idea hilarious. What I didn't realize was that my father thought college was good for girls—good for finding a husband. After four years in college and two more in graduate school, and still no husband, my father shakes his head even now and says I wasted all that education.

In retrospect, I'm lucky my father believed daughters were meant for husbands. It meant it didn't matter if I majored in something silly like English. After all, I'd find a nice professional eventually, right? This allowed me the liberty to putter about embroidering my little poems and stories without my father interrupting with so much as a "What's that you're writing?"

But the truth is, I wanted him to interrupt. I wanted my father to understand what it was I was scribbling, to introduce me as "My only daughter, the writer." Not as "This is only my daughter. She teaches." *Es maestra*—teacher. Not even *profesora.*

In a sense, everything I have ever written has been for him, to win his approval even though I know my father can't read English words, even though my father's only reading includes the brown-ink *Esto* sports magazines from Mexico City and the bloody *!Alarma!* magazines that feature yet another sighting of *La Virgen de*

Guadalupe on a tortilla or a wife's revenge on her philandering husband by bashing his skull in with a *molcajete* (a kitchen mortar made of volcanic rock). Or the *fotonovelas,* the little picture paperbacks with tragedy and trauma erupting from the characters' mouths in bubbles.

My father represents, then, the public majority. A public who is disinterested in reading, and yet one whom I am writing about and for, and privately trying to woo.

When we were growing up in Chicago, we moved a lot because of my father. He suffered bouts of nostalgia. Then we'd have to let go of our flat, store the furniture with mother's relatives, load the station wagon with baggage and bologna sandwiches and head south. To Mexico City.

We came back, of course. To yet another Chicago flat, another Chicago neighborhood, another Catholic school. Each time, my father would seek out the parish priest in order to get a tuition break, and complain or boast: "I have seven sons."

He meant *siete hijos,* seven children, but he translated it as "sons." "I have seven sons." To anyone who would listen. The Sears Roebuck employee who sold us the washing machine. The short-order cook where my father ate his ham-and-eggs breakfasts. "I have seven sons." As if he deserved a medal from the state.

My papa. He didn't mean anything by that mistranslation, I'm sure. But somehow I could feel myself being erased. I'd tug my father's sleeve and whisper: "Not seven sons. Six! and *one daughter.*"

When my oldest brother graduated from medical school, he fulfilled my father's dream that we study hard and use this—our heads, instead of this—our hands. Even now my father's hands are thick and yellow, stubbed by a history of hammer and nails and twine and coils and springs. "Use this," my father said, tapping his head, "and not this," showing us those hands. He always looked tired when he said it.

Wasn't college an investment? And hadn't I spent all those years in college? And if I didn't marry, what was it all for? Why would anyone go to college and then choose to be poor? Especially someone who had always been poor?

Last year, after ten years of writing professionally, the financial rewards started to trickle in. My second National Endowment for the Arts Fellowship. A guest professorship at the University of California, Berkeley. My book, which sold to a major New York publishing house.

At Christmas, I flew home to Chicago. The house was throbbing, same as always: hot tamales and sweet tamales hissing in my mother's pressure cooker, and everybody—my mother, six brothers, wives, babies, aunts, cousins—talking too loud and at the same time. Like in a Fellini film, because that's just how we are.

I went upstairs to my father's room. One of my stories had just been translated into Spanish and published in an anthology of Chicano writing and I wanted to show it to him. Ever since he recovered from a stroke two years ago, my father likes to spend his leisure hours horizontally. And that's how I found him, watching a Pedro Infante movie on Galavisión and eating rice pudding.

There was a glass filled with milk on the bedside table. There were several vials of pills and balled Kleenex. And on the floor, one black sock and a plastic urinal that I didn't want to look at but looked at anyway. Pedro Infante was about to burst into song, and my father was laughing.

I'm not sure if it was because my story was translated into Spanish, or because it was published in Mexico, or perhaps because the story dealt with Tepeyac, the *colonia* my father was raised in and the house he grew up in, but at any rate, my father punched the mute button on his remote control and read my story.

I sat on the bed next to my father and waited. He read it very slowly. As if he were reading each line over and over. He laughed at the right places and read lines he liked out loud. He pointed and asked questions: "Is this So-and-so?" "Yes," I said. He kept reading.

When he was finally finished, after what seemed like hours, my father looked up and asked: "Where can we get more copies of this for the relatives?"

Of all the wonderful things that happened to me last year, that was the most wonderful.

DISCUSSION QUESTIONS FOR CHAPTER 7

1. What are some myths about the normative U.S. family? To what degree does your family reflect this norm? Has your family experienced discrimination in any ways based on deviation from this norm? What are some of the realities of the diversity of U.S. families?

2. How are families both places of comfort, security, and nurture and at the same time places of domination, conflict, and violence?

3. How do social institutions reinforce power relations in the family? How does the family often reflect power relations of the dominant social order? How do power relations operate in your family?

4. How does the difference between mothering and fathering reflect dominant social norms for women and men?

5. What tasks do various members of your family do within the home? Do these tasks reflect typical social norms?

SUGGESTIONS FOR FURTHER READING

Bem, Sandra Lipsitz. *An Unconventional Family.* New Haven, CT: Yale University Press, 2001.

Coontz, Stephanie. *The Way We Really Are: Coming to Terms with America's Changing Families.* Austin, TX: Basic, 1998.

————. *The Way We Never Were: American Families and the Nostalgia Trap,* reprint. Austin, TX: Basic, 2000.

————. *Marriage, a History: From Obedience to Intimacy, or How Love Conquered Marriage.* New York: Viking, 2005.

Lehr, Valerie. *Queer Family Values: Debunking the Myth of the Nuclear Family (Queer Politics, Queer Theories).* Philadelphia: Temple University Press, 1999.

Mason, Mary Ann, Arlene Skolnick, and Stephen D. Sugarman, eds. *All Our Families: New Policies for a New Century.* 2nd ed. New York: Oxford University Press, 2002.

O' Reilly, Andrea. *Mother Outlaws: Theories and Practices of Empowered Mothering.* Toronto: University of Toronto Press, 2004.

Stacey, Judith. *In the Name of the Family: Rethinking Family Values in the Postmodern Age.* Boston: Beacon, 1997.

Wolf, Naomi. *Misconceptions: Truth, Lies, and the Unexpected Journey to Motherhood.* New York: Anchor, 2003.

CHAPTER 8

Women's Work Inside and Outside the Home

There is an important truth in the saying "women's work is never done." In the United States and around the world, women work long hours because work for them often involves unpaid domestic labor and care of dependent family members as well as paid labor. In addition, when they do get paid for their work, women tend to earn lower wages compared to men and are less likely to have control over the things they produce and the wages they receive. When the United Nations World Conference on Women met in Beijing, China, in 1995, the Platform for Action prioritized strategies to promote economic autonomy for women, ensure their access to productive resources, and encourage equitable sharing of family responsibilities. This commitment was reiterated in the "Beijing Plus 10" meeting held in New York in 2005. In this chapter we examine both women's domestic unpaid labor and their employment in the labor force. In the latter the focus is on the global economy and the changing nature and patterns of women's labor force participation, the dual economy, and the gender gap in wages.

UNPAID LABOR IN THE HOME

The work women do in the home is often not considered work at all: It is something women do for love, or because they are women, and it is the natural thing for women to do. The humorist Dave Barry, for example, declares that 85 percent of men in the United States are "cleaning impaired," satirizing the supposed ineptitude or lack of participation in domestic activities on the part of men as normalized or natural. The point, though, is that there is nothing natural about the fact that women on the average do over two-thirds of all household work. The fact that they may be better at it is only because of years of practice. Gender norms that associate women, the home, and domesticity reinforce the assumption that housework and childcare are women's work.

The reading by Barbara Ehrenreich, "Maid to Order," explains the politics of housework in contemporary U.S. society. She emphasizes that housework is not

LEARNING ACTIVITY   **Housework and Technology**

The conventional wisdom would suggest that modern household inventions have saved time and energy for homemakers. But is that the case? Have technological innovations freed women from household chores? Or have they created more work for women in the home?

Take a look at Susan Strasser's *Never Done: A History of American Housework* and Ruth Schwartz Cowan's *More Work for Mother: The Ironies of Household Technologies from the Open Hearth to the Microwave*. What do they suggest about the role of household inventions?

Use these books and a search engine on the Web to research the following household appliances. Have they saved time and energy for women?

- Vacuum cleaner
- Stove
- Washing machine
- Dryer
- Refrigerator
- Microwave

Watch a couple of hours of daytime television and take note of the advertisements. What sorts of household products are advertised? What do the ads suggest about how these products can make women more efficient homemakers? Do you think these items really improve women's lives? What do these ads imply about women's responsibilities in the home? Do the ads suggest that men are equally responsible for housework? Do they suggest household technologies can help men become more efficient homemakers?

degrading because it involves manual labor but, instead, because it is embedded in degrading relationships that have the potential to reproduce male domination from one generation to the next. She suggests that a contemporary solution to the housework problem among those who can afford it is to hire someone else to do the work. That "someone" is most likely a woman and very often a woman of color. Domestic work is one occupation traditionally held by women of color; it is also an occupation that is usually nonunionized and has low pay, little power, and few or no benefits. In addition, individuals who used to contract services directly with employers are now being replaced by corporate cleaning services that control a good portion of the housecleaning business. Because this new relationship between cleaners and those who can afford to employ them abolishes the traditional "mistress-maid" relationship, it allows middle-class people who are sensitive to the political issues involved with hiring servants to avoid confronting these issues.

Most researchers who study household labor define it as all tasks involved in household maintenance, purchasing and preparing food, taking care of children, garden and yard work, and routine care and maintenance of vehicles. Several findings emerge in this area. Currently women in the United States average about 27 hours of household work per week, a decline by about 2 hours a week over the last 30 years.

Women and Agriculture

- Women make up 51 percent of the agricultural labor force worldwide.
- A study of the household division of labor in Bangladeshi villages found that women worked almost 12 hours a day—compared with the 8 to 10 hours a day worked by men in the same villages.
- In many regions, women spend up to 5 hours a day collecting fuelwood and water and up to 4 hours preparing food.
- In Africa and Asia, women work about 13 hours more than men each week.
- In Southeast Asia, women provide up to 90 percent of the labor for rice cultivation.
- In Africa, 90 percent of the work of gathering water and wood, for the household and for food preparation, is done by women.
- In Pakistan, 50 percent of rural women cultivate and harvest wheat.
- In the world's least developed countries, 23 percent of rural households are headed by women.
- In sub-Saharan Africa, women produce up to 80 percent of basic foodstuffs both for household consumption and for sale.
- Women perform from 25 to 45 percent of agricultural field tasks in Colombia and Peru.
- Women constitute 53 percent of the agricultural labor in Egypt.
- Fewer than 10 percent of women farmers in India, Nepal, and Thailand own land.
- An analysis of credit schemes in five African countries found that women received less than 10 percent of the credit awarded to males who own small farms.
- Only 15 percent of the world's agricultural extension agents are women.

Sources: www.fao.org/gender/en/labb2-e.htm and www.fao.org/gender/en/agrib4-e.htm.

Men average about 16 hours of household work per week, up from 12 hours over the same period. As a proportion of the amount of household labor completed, women perform about two-thirds. In her 2005 reissue of *The Second Shift*, sociologist Arlie Russell Hochschild writes of the "70-30" gender split associated with household work that occurs regardless of women's paid labor status. A study by sociologist Chloe Bird suggests that once married, women do about twice the amount of work in the home as their spouses, increasing their stress and anxiety. When women marry, unfortunately most gain an average of 14 hours a week of domestic labor, compared to men, who gain an additional average of 90 minutes. Husbands tend to create more work for wives than they perform. This can cause stress-related problems and mental and physical exhaustion for women trying to juggle family responsibilities and paid employment. As evidence, studies find that couples who are most contented have the most flexibility regarding work and commitment to sharing responsibilities. According to Julie Shields in *How to Avoid the Mommy Trap: A Roadmap for Sharing Parenting and Making It Work*, men who do more housework and childcare report a better sex life with their wives. Supposedly, the latter have more energy for sexual intimacy when they have fewer dishes to wash and lunches to make.

Cross-national comparisons of the gender gap in housework drawing on data in Japan, North America, Scandinavia, Russia, and Hungary by the Institute for Social Research (ISR) indicate that North American men are less egalitarian (meaning equally sharing power) than Scandinavians (Swedish men do an average of 24 hours of housework a week), but more egalitarian than Japanese men. Russian women do the least amount of housework, although they work the most total hours (employed plus domestic work), and Hungarian women do the most housework and have the least amount of leisure time. An Australian study at the University of Queensland confirms North American data that couples who live together are more egalitarian than married couples, a behavior that does seem to carry over into marriages when cohabitation is a precursor to marriage. This is most likely because cohabiting couples are more likely to have liberal attitudes that are also important determinants of the gender division of labor in any family. All these comparative data must be interpreted with caution as questions are raised in terms of how household labor is defined, whether methods for reporting are standardized, and whether a discussion of "women doing less housework" means overall hours or as a proportion of total hours performed by women and men. Finally, however, Time Use surveys in postindustrial societies show that although total work (paid and domestic) has increased for women and men, these numbers are still less than might be expected given contemporary attitudes that people have less free time now than they used to have. Researchers suggest that differences are explained by the fact that much leisure activity today involves scheduled activities that encourage people to feel busy but not necessarily relaxed. This has importance for women, who are the ones who tend to plan and organize leisure activities (although they may not be the ones to make decisions about them in the first place, especially if the decision involves considerable financial resources). It is well known that family vacations can provide inordinate amounts of emotional work for mothers.

LEARNING ACTIVITY   **Who Does the Work at Your School and in Your Home?**

Use the following charts to discover who does various kinds of work at your school and in your home. Discuss your findings with your classmates. What patterns do you notice? What do your findings suggest about how systems of inequality function in the institution of work, both inside and outside the home?

WHO DOES THE WORK AT YOUR SCHOOL?

Job Description	White Men	White Women	Men of Color	Women of Color
Top administration				
Teaching				
Secretarial				
Groundskeeping				
Electrical/carpentry				
Janitorial				
Food preparation				
Security				
Intercollegiate coaching				

WHO DOES THE WORK IN YOUR HOME?

Job Description	Person in the Family Who Generally Does This Job	Sex of Person Who Generally Does This Job	Hours Per Week Spent in Doing This Job
Laundry			
Mowing the lawn			
Maintaining the car			
Buying the groceries			
Cooking			
Vacuuming			
Washing dishes			
Making beds			
Cleaning bathroom			

The second major finding is that women and men do different kinds of work in the home. Women tend to do the repetitive, ongoing, daily kinds of tasks, and men are more likely to perform the less repetitive or seasonal tasks, especially if these tasks involve the use of tools or machines. This is called the gender division of household work. Some tasks are seen as more masculine and some as more feminine. Note

HISTORICAL MOMENT   **Wages for Housework**

Women do two-thirds of the world's work but receive only 5 percent of the world's income. Worldwide, women's unpaid labor is estimated at $11 trillion. Early in the women's movement, feminists made the connection between women's unpaid labor and the profits accumulated by the businesses that relied on women's household and child-rearing work to support the waged laborers that produced goods and capital. They argued, then, that women should be compensated for the domestic labor that is taken for granted and yet depended on to maintain capitalist economies.

Several groups agitated for wages for housework, and in 1972 the International Wages for Housework (WFH) Campaign was organized by women in developing and industrialized countries to agitate for compensation for the unpaid work women do. They argued that this goal could best be reached by dismantling the military-industrial complex. In 1975 the International Black Women for Wages for Housework (IBWWFH) Campaign, an international network of women of color, formed to work for compensation for unwaged and low-waged work and to ensure that challenging racism was not separated from challenging sexism and other forms of discrimination.

Few American feminists advocated this position, although it constituted a significant position for feminists in Europe. Some feminists opposed the campaign, arguing that to pay women for housework would reinforce women's role in the home and strengthen the existing gendered division of labor.

Both the WFH and IBWWFH campaigns are still active, advocating change in the ways women's work is valued and rewarded. They have been involved in a campaign for pay equity and a global women's strike. For more information, check out these Web sites:

www.ourworld.compuserve.com/homepages/crossroadswomenscentre/WFH.html

www.payequity.net/WFHCampaign/wfhcpgn.htm

www.crossroadswomen.net/BWWFH/BWWHF.html

that if household labor were defined solely as housework, the amount of male participation would decrease. Because the definition generally includes fixing things and yard and garage work, men's contributions tend to increase. These tasks are often (though not always) more interesting, require more skills, and have a higher status than the repetitive household cleaning tasks that women are more likely to perform. In addition, it seems that when women and men perform various tasks they tend to do so in different ways. Women are much more likely to "multitask," or perform a series of tasks simultaneously. This means, for example, that they might be folding laundry at the same time they are feeding the baby, or are cooking dinner at the same time they are vacuuming. Finally, in terms of the gender division of labor, it is important not to forget the emotional and behind-the-scenes kind of work that women do that is so crucial to family functioning. These include such activities as calling the baby-sitter, remembering somebody needs his or her math book or school lunch, and organizing holidays and vacations. These activities are difficult to measure in a quantitative sense. For example, while a recent Cornell University study found men doing approximately 27 percent of housework, the bulk of women's work was increased by emotional coordination and behind-the-scenes work. Women also perform "kin keeping" work: staying in touch with relatives, sending cards, and so on. Women spend approximately three times as many hours a week on kin keeping than men do.

Many readers are probably remembering their father doing the housework or have a partner who shares equally in domestic labor. Although there have been changes over the past decades with some men taking on greater household responsibilities and some assuming an equal share, unfortunately, for every 10 men who do little to no housework, there is a large group who "help" to a greater or lesser extent and a very small percentage who take equal responsibility. Note how the term *helping* assumes that it is someone else's responsibility. Nonetheless, it is important to state that housework, although often dreary and repetitive, can also be creative and more interesting than some paid labor. And, although raising children is among the hardest work of all, it is also full of rewards. Men who do not participate in household work and childcare miss the joys associated with this work even while they have the privilege of being free to do other things.

PAID LABOR

Trends and Legalities

The reading "A Brief History of Working Women" by sociologists Sharlene Hesse-Biber and Gregg Lee Carter overviews the changes in women's labor force participation over the past centuries for different groups of women. Briefly, as U.S. society became industrialized in the nineteenth century, the traditional subsistence economies of producing what families needed to survive from the home, taking in work (like spinning or washing), or working in others' homes or on their land were changed in favor of a more distinct separation between work and home. Factories were established, employees were congregated under one roof (and thus more easily controlled), and emerging technologies started mass-producing goods. Instead of making products in the home for family consumption, people were working outside the home and spending their earnings on these mass-produced goods. Urban centers grew up around these sites of production, and ordinary people tended to work long hours in often very poor conditions. In *Women and Economics*, written in 1898, Charlotte Perkins Gilman explains that the harsh conditions associated with women's wage labor coincided with continuing domestic servitude in the home. This double day of work was recognized by scholars such as Gilman over a hundred years ago and is still a central aspect of women's lives today.

At the same time that working-class women and children were working in factories, mines, and sweatshops, the middle-class home came to be seen as a haven from the cruel world, and middle-class women were increasingly associated with this sphere. From this developed the "cult of true womanhood"—prescriptions for femininity that included piety, purity, and domesticity. Although these notions of femininity could be achieved only by privileged White women, these norms came to influence women generally. At the same time, some women were starting to enter higher education. With the founding of Oberlin Collegial Institute in 1833, other women's colleges like Mount Holyoke, Bryn Mawr, and Wellesley were established as the century progressed. In addition, state universities (beginning with Utah in 1850) started admitting women. By the turn of the century, there were cohorts of (mostly privileged White) women who were educated to be full political persons and who helped shape the Progressive Era with a focus on reform and civic leadership. These women entered the labor force in relatively large numbers, and many chose a career over marriage and the family.

As the twentieth century progressed, more women entered the public sphere. The years of the Great Depression slowed women's advancement, and it was not until World War II that women were seen working in traditionally male roles in unprecedented numbers. The government encouraged this transition, and many women were, for the first time, enjoying decent wages. All this would end after the war as women were encouraged or forced to return to the home so that men could claim their jobs in the labor force. Childcare centers were dismantled, and the conservative messages of the 1950s encouraged women to stay home and partake in the rapidly emerging consumer society. The social and cultural upheavals of the 1960s and the civil rights and women's movements fought for legislation to help women gain more power in the workplace.

The most important legislative gains included, first, the Equal Pay Act of 1963 that made it illegal to pay women and men different salaries for the same job. Next came Title VII of the 1964 Civil Rights Act (which went into effect in 1965) banning discrimination in employment. It made it illegal to discriminate in hiring, firing, compensation, terms, conditions, or privileges of employment. Title VII said that gender could not be used as a criterion in employment except where there is a "bona fide occupational qualification," meaning it is illegal unless an employer can prove that gender is crucial to job performance. For the most part, the law had little influence until the establishment of the Equal Employment Opportunity Commission in the early 1970s to enforce the law. The courts have fine-tuned Title VII over the years, and it remains the most important legislation that protects working women and people of color.

In 1976 the Supreme Court expanded the interpretation of Title VII to include discrimination on the basis of pregnancy as sex discrimination, and 10 years later it declared that sexual harassment is also a form of sex discrimination. In 1993 the Supreme Court then broadened this ruling by stating that women suing on the basis of sexual harassment did not have to prove that they had suffered "concrete psychological harm." Sexual harassment legislation made a distinction between "quid pro quo" (sexual favors are required in return for various conditions of employment) and "hostile work environment" (no explicit demand for an exchange of sexual acts for work-related conditions but being subjected to a pattern of harassment as part of the work environment). In a 2005 poll conducted by the *Wall Street Journal* and NBC, 44 percent of working women said they had been discriminated against because of their gender and a third said they had experienced sexual harassment. In "Hey, Why Don't You Wear a Shorter Skirt?" social scientists Jackie Krasas Rogers and

African American Women in the Workplace: Common Barriers for Advancement

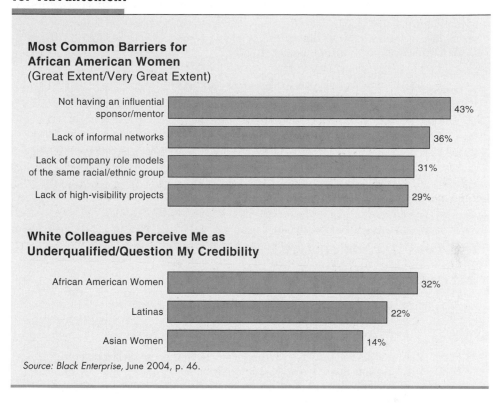

Most Common Barriers for African American Women
(Great Extent/Very Great Extent)

- Not having an influential sponsor/mentor — 43%
- Lack of informal networks — 36%
- Lack of company role models of the same racial/ethnic group — 31%
- Lack of high-visibility projects — 29%

White Colleagues Perceive Me as Underqualified/Question My Credibility

- African American Women — 32%
- Latinas — 22%
- Asian Women — 14%

Source: Black Enterprise, June 2004, p. 46.

Kevin D. Henson focus on the gendered and racialized work settings of temporary clerical workers and their vulnerability in terms of sexual harassment.

Affirmative action policies that encouraged employers to take gender and race into account in terms of hiring were first initiated by President Kennedy in the 1960s. Since that time, affirmative action has helped diversify the workplace and encouraged the hiring of women and people of color. However, there is a lot of misunderstanding as well as serious hostility associated with affirmative action, as evidenced by the dismantling of affirmative action guidelines in many states. Basically, affirmative action creates positive steps to increase the representation of women and people of color in areas of employment, education, and government from which they may have been historically excluded. Affirmative action encourages the diversification of the job pool, but it does not encourage the hiring of unqualified women or people of color. It is a misunderstanding of these policies to think that White males now have a hard time getting jobs because they are being undercut by unqualified women or people of color. Sociologist Michael Kimmel responds to this and other aspects of gender and race inequality in "A Black Woman Took My Job."

What Is Sexual Harassment?

Sexual harassment is legally defined as unwelcome sexual advances or requests for sexual favors. It also includes any verbal or physical conduct of a sexual nature when the following criteria are met:

- Submission is made explicitly or implicitly a term or condition of an individual's employment.
- Submission to or rejection of such conduct by an individual is used as the basis for employment decisions affecting such individual.
- Such conduct has the purpose or effect of substantially interfering with an individual's work performance or creating an intimidating, hostile, or offensive working environment.

Sexual harassment may include physical conduct, verbal conduct, or nonverbal conduct such as sexual gestures or pornographic pictures.

TWO TYPES OF SEXUAL HARASSMENT

Quid Pro Quo

Unwelcome sexual advances, requests for sexual favors, and other verbal or physical conduct of a sexual nature constitute quid pro quo sexual harassment when:

> Submission to such conduct is made either explicitly or implicitly a term or condition of an individual's employment or submission to or rejection of such conduct by an individual is used as the basis for employment decisions affecting such individual.

Hostile Work Environment

In determining whether or not an environment is hostile, it must be determined whether or not the conduct unreasonably interfered with an individual's work performance or created an intimidating, hostile, or offensive work environment.

The Equal Employment Opportunity Commission (EEOC) suggests that the courts look at the following criteria:

- Whether the conduct was verbal, physical, or both
- How frequently the conduct was repeated
- Whether the conduct was hostile or patently offensive
- Whether the alleged harasser was a coworker or a supervisor
- Whether others joined in perpetrating the harassment
- Whether the harassment was directed at more than one individual
- Whether the remarks were hostile and derogatory
- Whether the harasser singled out the charging party
- Whether the charging party participated in the exchange
- The relationship between the charging party and alleged harasser

The Supreme Court established a two-pronged test for determining a hostile environment:

1. The conduct must "be severe or pervasive enough to create an objectively hostile or abusive environment that a reasonable person would find hostile or abusive."
2. The victim must "subjectively perceive the environment to be abusive."

Bernice Sandler of the National Association of Women in Education reports that surveys indicate that up to 30 percent of female college students and 70 percent of women in the workplace have been sexually harassed.

IDEAS FOR ACTIVISM

- Advocate with your elected representatives for an increase in the minimum wage.
- Encourage your school to analyze pay equity and to make corrections where needed.
- Write your elected representatives to encourage legislation and funding for childcare.
- Investigate exploitative employment practices of major national and multinational corporations and launch boycotts to demand improved conditions for workers.
- Encourage your elected representatives to support affirmative action.

The Dual Labor Market and the Changing Economy

At the beginning of the twenty-first century it is important to understand the changing nature of the workplace in the United States and the connections between U.S. corporate capitalism and the global economy. Capitalism is an economic system based on the pursuit of profit and the principle of private ownership. Such a system creates inequality because this profit comes in part from surplus value created from the labor of workers. In other words, workers produce more value than they receive in wages, this difference or surplus being reinvested into capital accumulation and corporate profit. The U.S. economy is able to maintain profit accumulation through the perpetuation of a "dual labor market" that provides a "primary" market, with relatively high wages and employee benefits and protections for workers, and a "secondary" market, where workers (disproportionately women and people of color) receive lower wages, fewer benefits, and less opportunity for advancement. The dual labor market also maintains profit through globalization strategies, discussed below.

In terms of the changing nature of the U.S. economy, three features stand out. First, new technologies (especially electronic communications) have revolutionized work and, in some cases, replaced workers and made some jobs obsolete. In cases where technology cannot replace workers, jobs have been exported overseas to take advantage of

Global Employment Trends for Women

No agreed-upon single indicator exists for assessing the conditions of employment. However, some insights can be gained by analyzing three indicators: status of employment, employment by sector and wages/earnings. An initial assessment of these indicators reveals that although progress has been made in terms of female labour force participation, this has not necessarily been paralleled with progress in the creation of decent work opportunities for women. . . .

INDICATOR 1: EMPLOYMENT BY STATUS OF WOMEN

Family responsibilities are still very much assigned to women. When they have to combine child-raising activities with work activities, women are required to find a solution for balancing these two roles. Role incompatibility is likely to be a greater problem for women in wage employment, less for those in self-employment, and least for contributing family workers who are unpaid (but still count as employed people according to the standard definition of employment). Unfortunately, many developing economies do not have consistent data on employment status broken down by sex. Where available, this information suggests that in the poorest regions of the world the share of female contributing family workers in total employment is much higher than men's and that women are less likely to be wage and salaried workers.

This trend is expected to continue in most parts of the developing world. Especially at times of economic crises or downturns, women are the first to withdraw from wage and salaried work. They may then be forced to enter the informal economy as own-account or unpaid family workers.

Even among wage and salaried workers, more and more women are likely to be in nonregular or atypical employment. Whereas men are more likely to be hired in core or regular and better-paid positions, women are increasingly being hired in peripheral, insecure, less-valued jobs including home-based, casual, or temporary work. These jobs are normally characterized by very low pay, irregular income, little or no job or income security, and lack of social protection.

INDICATOR 2: EMPLOYMENT BY SECTOR OF WOMEN

An analysis of the sectoral data gives an additional indication that women's work is not likely to be status-enhancing or empowering for them. Women have a higher share in agricultural employment in Asia, sub-Saharan Africa, and the Middle East and North Africa and some economies in Latin America and the Caribbean, especially in economies with low per capita income. In all developing regions, women's share in industry is lower than men's. This is despite the fact that export-led industrialization has been strongly female-intensive, particularly in the export-processing zones (EPZs) of developing economies. EPZs have created an important avenue for women to enter the formal economy at better wages than in agriculture and domestic service. However, there is evidence that as the nature of employment in EPZs evolves, with higher technology inputs, the gender profile of the workforce changes.[1]

Within the services sector, women are still concentrated in sectors that are traditionally associated with their gender roles, particularly in community, social, and personal services, whereas men dominate the better-paid sector jobs in financial and business services and real estate.

The sex segregation of occupations is changing, but only slowly. Female stereotypes, such as caring, docile care-giver and home-based worker, are still being reinforced and may be perpetuated into the next generation if restricted and inferior labour market opportunities for women continue to lead to underinvestment in women's education, training, and experience.

INDICATOR 3: WAGES AND EARNINGS

Can wage equality be achieved? The evidence is not favourable in the short term. Women everywhere typically receive less pay than men. This is in part because women often hold low-level, low-paying positions in female-dominated occupations. A review of data available for six diverse occupation groups shows that in most economies, women still earn 90 percent or less of what their male co-workers earn.[2] In a typically male-dominated occupation such as welding in metal manufacturing, the wage disparities are even greater. Female welders in the industrialized economies earned, on average, 79 percent of what male welders earned, and in developing economies even less at 75 percent. Even in "typically female" occupations such as nursing and teaching, gender wage equality is still lacking. In Singapore, for example, male first-level education teachers earned approximately 6 percent more than female teachers, and male nurses 21 percent more.

Traditionally there has been greater wage equality in the transition economies than in industrialized or developing economies. This is still the case today. For example, the wages of female welders and female teachers in transition economies are nearly equitable to those of males (98 percent of the male rate), and female nurses earned even more than their male counterparts in the same occupations (2 percentage points more than the male rate).

One might expect to find near wage equality in high-skill occupations where the education and training level of applicants would presumably be comparable (accountant in the banking sector or computer programmer in the insurance sector, for example).

---

[1] For more information on the employment and social implications of export-processing zones, see ILO, Governing Body Report "Employment and social policy in respect of export-processing zones (EPZs)," GB.286/ESP/3, March 2003; available at Web site http://www.ilo.org/public/english/standards/relm/gb/does/gb286/pdf/esp-3.pdf.

[2] In this section, "wages" refers first to wages defined as the "rates paid for normal time of work, comprising: basic wages and salaries, cost-of-living allowances, and other guaranteed and regularly paid allowances." Earnings are used in countries where only data on earnings and not wages are available. Earnings extend beyond wage rates to include as well "remuneration for time not worked, such as for annual vacation or other paid leave or holidays, and including those elements of earnings which are usually received regularly, before any deductions are made by the employer in respect of taxes, contributions of employees to social security and pension schemes, life insurance premiums, union dues, and any other obligations of employees." See ILO, *Statistics on occupational wages and hours of work and on food prices: October Inquiry results, 2000 and 2001* (Geneva, 2002).

(continued)

This is not the case. Even in these occupations the average female wage is still only 88 percent of the male wage. One of the reasons identified for the wage differential is women's lack of negotiating capability as well as bargaining power.[3]

. . .

WOMEN HAVE A HIGH LIKELIHOOD OF BEING WORKING POOR

The assumption that, in the process of socioeconomic development, women increasingly enter the modern sector, permanent, full-time wage employment does not hold—at least not for the time being. Increases in labour force participation rates have so far not been matched by improvements in job quality, and the working conditions of women have not led to their true socioeconomic empowerment.

As a result, the share of women that are employed but still are unable to lift themselves and their family above the US $1 a day poverty line—the so-called working-poor share—is higher for women than it is for men. Out of the total number of 550 million estimated working poor, around 60 percent, or 330 million, are women.[4]

Only if future creation of decent jobs extends even more to women than to men can this share be reduced.

There is mounting evidence that women's ability to fully enjoy human rights—indeed, even to demand such rights—is integrally linked to their economic empowerment. The ability to make decisions—on marriage, on childbearing, and on contraception, among others—requires a sense of personal autonomy, which develops in tandem with the self-knowledge that women can provide for themselves and their children. Their sense of personhood is sparked by motherhood and nurtured by participation in organized groups, but fundamentally depends on having their own decent income. Whether women work out of need or choice, the focus should be on giving them decent jobs, so that in the long run they can work themselves and their families out of poverty. At the same time, childcare facilities are a necessary precondition for women to be able to go to work and use their productive potential effectively.

[3] For a study on the gender difference in negotiating capacity, see Linda Babcock et al., "Nice girls don't ask," in *Harvard Business Review*, October 2003, p. 14.
[4] The calculation of the number of people that are working poor is based on the poverty figures given by the World Bank. Unfortunately these figures don't exist disaggregated by region. But many experts assume a female poverty rate of 60–70 percent. This is the rate used for the calculation of female working poor in the world for this publication. For details on the calculation of working poor, see Kapsos, S., "Estimating growth requirements for reducing working poverty: Can the world halve working poverty by 2015?," Employment Paper (Geneva, ILO, forthcoming).

Source: Global Employment Trends for Women 2004, March 2004, www.ilo.org/public/english/employment/ strat/global.htm.

lower wages. Second, there has been a huge increase in the service sector and a shift from manufacturing to service-sector work. This has brought a change in the kinds of skills workers need in order to compete in this sector, reflecting the dual labor market and its distinctions between high-skilled service work (e.g., financial consultants, public relations) and low-paid and low-skilled service work (food service, child and elderly care). Women and people of color are more likely found in the latter part of the service sector, illustrating the ways the economy is a conduit for the maintenance of systems of inequality and privilege. Consequences of the dual labor market are discussed in the sections below on women's labor force participation and issues of pay equity.

Third, economies around the world are increasingly connected to, and positioned differently within, a global economy that operates in conjunction with such transnational organizations as the World Bank and the World Trade Organization. Critics emphasize how the latter organizations tend to function to maintain the power of "first world" nations like the United States. Multinational corporations have grown in size and influence, and mergers have resulted in a smaller number of corporations controlling a larger part of the market. They have immense power and influence and often no longer correspond to national borders, functioning outside the jurisdiction of nation states. Because many U.S.-based corporations rely on the cheaper, nonunionized labor force and looser environmental restrictions outside the United States, much manufacturing and increasingly service work is done overseas. Evelyn Hu-DeHart writes about the realities and consequences of these strategies in the reading "Globalization and Its Discontents." As discussed in Chapter 11, the military has close ties to the economy, creating what scholars call the military-industrial complex. Military operations and the presence of international military forces in developing countries serve in part to "stabilize" these nations and protect foreign business interests, often in the name of forging "peace" or "democracy." The current crisis in the Middle East is a case in point.

The effects of the global economy often include profound inequalities between rich and poor nations as well as between rich and poor citizens within individual countries. Often these inequalities are based on older inequities resulting from nineteenth- and early-twentieth-century colonization and imperialism. For individual women, although multinational corporations do give women a wage, they often upset subsistence economies and cause migration and cultural dislocation, which encourages increasing consumerism, sex trading, and the pollution of fragile environments. Women often work in poor and unhealthy conditions for little pay. In addition, many thousands of U.S. workers have lost their jobs as corporations have moved productive processes overseas. These events are not random but part of a broader pattern of global capitalist expansion.

Women's Labor Force Participation

The major change in terms of trends in women's workforce participation has been the increase in the number of women who are in paid employment as the last century progressed. The U.S. Bureau of Labor Statistics reports that this number grew from 5.3 million in 1900 to 18.4 million in 1950 and 68 million in 2005. Women made up 18 percent of the labor force in 1900, almost 30 percent in 1950, and 46 percent in 2005.

Given the large number of women working in the labor force, what kinds of work are they doing? The answer is everything. Women are doing all kinds of work and can be found in all segments of the labor force. At the same time, however, women are much more likely to be found in some sectors than others and are crowded into a small number of fields, many of which are characterized as secondary sector jobs in the dual labor market. This phenomenon of segregating women and men into different jobs

20 Leading Occupations of Employed Women

Full-Time Wage and Salary Workers, 2004 Annual Averages (employment in thousands)

Occupation	Percent Women	Women's Median Weekly Earnings
Secretaries and administrative assistants	96.7	550
Elementary and middle school teachers	96.7	550
Registered nurses	91.8	895
Nursing, psychiatric, and home health aides	88.3	383
Cashiers	75.0	313
First-line supervisors/managers of office and administrative support	69.5	636
First-line supervisors/managers of retail sales workers	43.9	505
Customer service representatives	70.1	504
Bookkeeping, accounting, and auditing clerks	91.2	542
Accountants and auditors	60.8	757
Receptionists and information clerks	93.9	463
Retail salespersons	41.1	386
Maid and housekeeping cleaners	89.7	324
Office clerks, general	83.8	499
Secondary school teachers	54.8	824
Waiters and waitresses	67.3	327
Financial managers	55.7	839
Teacher assistants	91.7	373
Preschool and kindergarten teachers	97.7	515
Social workers	76.1	689

Source: U.S. Department of Labor, Bureau of Labor Statistics, Annual Averages 2004.

is termed *occupational segregation by gender* or *horizontal segregation* (meaning segregation *across* jobs). Not only are women crowded into certain fields, but these types of horizontal segregation have been relatively continuous throughout the twentieth century. These jobs are often called pink-collar jobs and can be understood as an extension of women's work in the home.

As reported in the box on leading occupations of employed women by the Women's Bureau of the U.S. Department of Labor, almost 97 percent of secretaries and administrative assistants, 92 percent of registered nurses, and almost 97 percent of presecondary school teachers are women. Women congregate in clerical, retail, sales, and various service-sector jobs. In comparison, only about 2 percent of working women are employed in precision production, craft, and repair (down slightly from 1990), and 7 percent of working women are employed as operators, fabricators, and laborers (with a more significant decline from 8.5 percent on 1990). Despite these

ACTIVIST PROFILE **Dolores Huerta**

Dolores Huerta is one of the most powerful and influential labor leaders in the United States. Born in Dawson, New Mexico, in 1930, Huerta grew up in Stockton, California, and eventually earned a teaching certificate from Stockton College. After one year of teaching, however, she quit to work with Community Service Organization (CSO) because she thought she could do more to help the hungry children she saw at school by helping organize their farm-worker parents.

While with CSO, she met César Chavez, and in 1962 they founded the United Farm Workers of America (UFW). Although Chavez was more comfortable in the fields organizing workers, Huerta became the voice of the union, becoming the first woman and first Chicana negotiator in labor history. The UFW met with great success in the 1965 Delano Grape Strike, which won the first collective bargaining agreement for farmworkers, and Huerta was instrumental in the negotiations. She also became consciously involved with the feminist movement when she met Gloria Steinem in 1968, although she had always focused on issues specific to women farmworkers.

In 1972 she co-chaired the California delegation to the Democratic Convention, and she led the struggle for unemployment insurance, collective bargaining rights, and immigration rights for farmworkers under the 1985 amnesty legalization program. She was the first Latina inducted into the National Women's Hall of Fame, and she received the National Organization for Women's Woman of Courage Award and the American Civil Liberties Union's Bill of Rights Award. She continues to struggle for farmworkers through the UFW and serve as a role model for Chicanas in their fight against discrimination.

traditional patterns, women's presence in certain once-male-dominated professions has increased. In 1970, 9 percent of physicians were female, compared to almost 30 percent in 2005. Numbers have also increased for women dentists (19 percent) and attorneys (28 percent), and for all these professions, figures increase for women currently in professional schools working toward these degrees. One of the most female-segregated jobs is sex work such as prostitution, where women workers have often struggled to control the conditions of their work against the demoralization and abuse by customers, pimps, and police. Kimberly Klinger's article, "Prostitution, Humanism, and a Woman's Choice," discusses prostitution, the legalities surrounding it, and the necessity of finding a common ground to support women's choice.

The term *blue collar* implies working class or involved with industrial, production, and factory work and can be contrasted with *white collar*, which means office or professional work and is often characterized as middle-class occupations. Note the slippage between industrial work and male-segregated work such that blue collar means working class but also implies male-segregated work with its use of the word *blue* as opposed to *pink*. The Bureau of Labor Statistics reports the following occupations as the most

Selected Nontraditional Occupations for Women*

Occupation	Employed, Both Sexes	Employed, Female	Percent Female
Police and detectives (supervisors)	111,000	11,000	9.9
Dentists	170,000	34,000	20
Architects	214,000	50,000	23.4
Forestry and logging	90,000	7,000	7.8
Truck drivers	3,156,000	167,000	5.3
Airplane pilots and navigators	136,000	5,000	3.7
Firefighters	250,000	7,000	2.8
Automobile mechanics	837,000	12,000	1.4
Garbage collectors	56,000	3,000	5.4
Construction trades	6,253,000	153,000	2.4
Taxicab drivers and chauffeurs	305,000	38,000	12.5
Air traffic controllers	28,000	2,000	7.1

*Nontraditional occupations are any that women constitute 25 percent or less of the total employed.
Source: U.S. Department of Labor.

LEARNING ACTIVITY **Working Women and Unions**

Visit the Web page of the AFL-CIO at *www.aflcio.org* to learn more about women in the workforce. What are some of the key issues for working women identified by the AFL-CIO? What legislative issues does the AFL-CIO identify that would be beneficial to working women? What is a union? What benefits do unions provide? Why are unions important for working women? What steps would people take to form a union at their workplace?

male segregated: engineers, mechanics and drivers, carpenters and construction trades, firefighters, airline pilots and navigators, and forestry and logging work. You will note the obvious ways feminine jobs involve working with people, children, cleaning, and administrative support, whereas masculine employment tends to involve working with machines and inanimate objects. There are other differences too, such as the wages for the heavily male-segregated jobs tend to be higher than wages for the female-segregated, pink-collar work. That is because these jobs are valued more, and they are more likely to be unionized, which tends to pay more. In 2002, two in five union members were female and unionized women workers earned 31 percent more than nonunion members and received better health and pension benefits.

An important aspect of occupational segregation by gender is that there is gender segregation even within the same job classification. This is termed *vertical segregation* (segregation *within* jobs), and, like horizontal segregation, it functions as a result of sexism and racism and other systems of inequality and privilege.

"Whatever happened to a good cry in the Ladies Room?"

Reprinted with permission from Carol Simpson Productions.

For example, although the number of women physicians is increasing, women are still overwhelmingly found in certain specialties as pediatrics, dermatology, and public health work, and less likely to be found in surgical specialties, orthopedics, and more entrepreneurial positions. For example, women's presence has increased dramatically in some specialties (in 1970 only 5 percent of doctors in obstetrics and gynecology were female; in 2005 this number has risen to about 70 percent) and more slowly in other specialties (in 2001 less than 9 percent of orthopedic surgeons and 10 percent of neurosurgeons were women). Observers note that the growing proportion of U.S. physicians who are female is improving the quality of medical care through more emotionally focused and patient-centered practice, although as discussed in the following section, it is lowering physicians' average salaries overall. (As an aside, new research at Harvard Medical School has shown that female physicians have a higher rate of suicide than any other women professionals.) Female physicians on the average earn less than 70 percent of what male physicians make.

Similarly, female lawyers are less likely to be in criminal law and are more likely to practice family law and make about 70 percent of male lawyers' salaries. Male teachers are more likely to teach sciences and are more likely to be with older children; female professors are more typically in the humanities and the social sciences and found in smaller number in the physical and applied sciences and technical fields. Usually specialties and fields that men occupy are more prestigious and the salaries are higher. In this way, women and men do not just tend to perform different jobs, but the jobs that they do are valued differently and have different levels of status and power and bring different problems associated with integration and advancement. This differential is related to sexism in society generally as well as to other systems of inequality and privilege.

Barriers to advancement in the labor force (what is often called the *glass ceiling*) have been challenged by women, by the courts, and by the women's movement. And, although these barriers are beginning to come down, they are still holding strong in many areas as the reading by Ellen Hawkes on Wal-Mart illustrates. Women tend not to be promoted at the same rate as men and they also continue to face obstacles when trying to enter the most prestigious and best-paid occupations. While women are increasingly moving into middle management positions, 2005 data show their relative absence in top leadership positions. Only 9 Fortune 500 companies have women CEOs or presidents (just under 2 percent) and another 10 women CEOs are in the Fortune 1000. Finally, although women make up more than 60 percent of the nonprofit workplace, they still lack access to top management positions, share of foundation dollars, and board positions. Women of color are relatively absent in the higher echelons of corporate power in all sectors. The reading "Power Plays" by Martha Burk explains the six ways the corporate elite keeps women down, emphasizing the power dynamics of the corporate world that continue to maintain the status quo.

Alongside consideration of the problems associated with the glass ceiling, it is important to recognize what researchers have called the *glass escalator* and the *glass precipice*. The glass escalator refers to the practices whereby men who go into traditionally female-dominated professions like teaching, nursing, and social work are disproportionately advanced into management and administrative positions where they receive more prestige, pay, and power than women. The glass precipice is the process whereby women are encouraged into leadership positions in failing organizations and companies and are disproportionately set up to fail professionally.

Finally, it is interesting to look at how the development of certain occupations as female segregated has affected the status and conditions of work. For example, clerical work, although low prestige, was definitely a man's job until the turn of the twentieth century when women quickly became associated with this work. This was due to the following factors: there was a large pool of women with few other opportunities; clerical work's low status made it easier for women to be accepted; typewriter manufacturers began promoting the typewriter as something women used; and the personal service aspect of the work fit gender norms about the feminine aspect of secretarial work. As more women entered this profession, the gap between clerical wages and blue-collar wages generally increased, and the status of the clerical profession fell. A more recent example is the field of pharmacy. Two trends—the increasing number of pharmacies attached to chain drugstores and the increasing number of female pharmacists—have been seen as the reasons why the status of pharmacy has fallen as a profession. It remains to be seen whether the increase of women in human and animal medicine, and in the sciences generally, will decrease the status of these professions.

Reprinted with permission from Nicole Hollander.

Wages and Comparable Worth

In 2005 the median wages for women who work full-time, year-round, were 76 percent of those earned by men. This means that analyzing median wages, for every dollar men earn, women earn approximately 76 cents, down from 77 cents in 2002 (Bureau of Labor Statistics). A 2004 analysis of a subsection of U.S. Census Bureau data revealed women earning 74 cents. For women of color, this figure drops to 64 cents, with African American women at 65 cents and Chicanas/Latinas at 54 cents. The wage gap is largest in sales (where women generally earn only 60 percent of male wages) and highest in farming occupations (where women earned 89 percent of male wages). About 10 percent of women workers are employed in sales and one-half of 1 percent in farming. The starkest inequality is among women aged 35 to 54 years with a bachelor's or advanced degree who overall earn just 55 percent of comparable male earnings (U.S. Census Bureau, 2002). Men of color earn less than White men with African American men at 78 cents and Chicanos/Latinos at 63 cents. Despite such gloomy figures, overall these have risen significantly in the last couple of decades. In 1982, for example, women earned 59 percent of male earnings. The Institute for Policy Research reports that over a lifetime of work, the average 25-year-old woman who works full-time, year-round, until she retires at age 65 years will earn on the average almost a half million dollars less than the average working man. Currently 13 percent of men and 4 percent of women earn over $75,000 a year, while a little more than 19 percent of men and 9 percent of women earn between $50,000 and $75,000 a year.

As you might imagine, there are many more women in the United States living in poverty (at about $19,350 a year for a family of four in 2005) than there are men. While almost 12 percent of the population is below the poverty level, rates are highest for families headed by single women, particularly women of color. As life earnings are calculated, the number of women over 65 years of age in poverty is more than double that of men (U.S. Census, 2002). Women are nearly 60 percent of all social security beneficiaries generally and 72 percent of beneficiaries over 85 years old. For many elderly women, Social Security is all they have; the future direction of Social Security will disproportionately affect women.

Statistics on the wage gap do not include part-time or seasonal workers and compare only year-round, full-time male and female workers. Because a larger number of women work part-time jobs, the inclusion of part-time workers in this statistic would most likely result in a lowering of the above figures because part-time work is often lower status and less stable and has fewer job-related benefits like health insurance.

So, why do women earn less money than men on the average? The answer includes consideration of both horizontal and vertical segregation as well as general discrimination. In terms of horizontal segregation, women tend to be crowded into different jobs than men, and these jobs are more likely to be paid less. Recall that although the Equal Pay Act of 1963 said that men and women working in the *same* job could not receive different compensation, this does not help women who are in *different,* less-valued jobs. In terms of vertical segregation, even within the same fields there are forces to keep women in positions that are less prestigious and poorer paid. The equal pay legislation tends not to apply to distinctions within the same field where women and men are in different subspecialties and receive different levels of pay. Traditional norms about gender, race, social class, and age work to create patterns of institutionalized inequalities that reinforce ideas concerning women's and men's worth and the kind of work various people can do. Finally, researchers emphasize that there are gender disparities in wages that occur when such factors as hours worked, specialty, work settings, and other characteristics are taken into account and are unexplained by factors associated with either horizontal or vertical segregation.

Comparable worth, also known as pay equity, is one means to pay women and men in different occupations comparably. Basically, comparable worth works to compare different jobs on experience, skill, training, and job conditions and assigns relative points on these indices in order to determine their worth. There is no federal-level comparable worth legislation, although many states have enacted laws demanding comparable worth comparisons in determining pay for state workers. In addition, the courts have ruled both for and against workers who have brought comparable worth suits against various corporations. When the courts have ruled in favor of plaintiffs, it has often meant a considerable amount of money in back pay to compensate female workers for years of financial inequities.

In this way inequality in women's work lives has important consequences for inequality in other spheres of life. Because most women work both inside and outside the home and spend a considerable part of their lives working, it is of central importance to understand the conditions under which women work as well as to strive for equality in the workplace.

Women and Economics

Charlotte Perkins Gilman (1898)

... Because of her maternal duties, the human female is said to be unable to get her own living. As the maternal duties of other females do not unfit them for getting their own living and also the livings of their young, it would seem that the human maternal duties require the segregation of the entire energies of the mother to the service of the child during her entire adult life, or so large a proportion of them that not enough remains to devote to the individual interests of the mother....

Is this the condition of human motherhood? Does the human mother, by her motherhood, thereby lose control of brain and body, lose power and skill and desire for any other work? Do we see before us the human race, with all its females segregated entirely to the uses of motherhood, consecrated, set apart, specially developed, spending every power of their nature on the service of their children?

We do not. We see the human mother worked far harder than a mare, laboring her life long in the service, not of her children only, but of men; husbands, brothers, fathers, whatever male relatives she has; for mother and sister also; for the church a little, if she is allowed; for society, if she is able; for charity and education and reform—working in many ways that are not the ways of motherhood.

It is not motherhood that keeps the housewife on her feet from dawn till dark; it is house service, not child service. Women work longer and harder than most men, and not solely in maternal duties.... Many mothers, even now, are wage-earners for the family, as well as bearers and rearers of it. And the women who are not so occupied, the women who belong to rich men—here perhaps is the exhaustive devotion to maternity which is supposed to justify an admitted economic dependence. But we do not find it even among these. Women of ease and wealth provide for their children better care than the poor woman can; but they do not spend more time upon it themselves, nor more care and effort. They have other occupation.

In spite of her supposed segregation to maternal duties, the human female, the world over, works at extra-maternal duties for hours enough to provide her with an independent living, and then is denied independence on the ground that motherhood prevents her working!

A Brief History of Working Women

Sharlene Hesse-Biber and Gregg Lee Carter

WOMEN WORKERS IN PRE-INDUSTRIAL AMERICA

Seven hundred and fifty thousand Europeans came to America between 1600 and 1700. The bulk of them were from Britain, but the colonies also saw significant numbers from Holland, France, and Germany. Many came as indentured servants, exchanging their labor for the cost of passage to the American colonies. Indentured servants often worked from five to ten years to pay back their creditors. As early as the 1600s, prior to the slave trade, some Africans also came to the colonies as indentured servants; they often worked side by side with white indentured servants. Women's lives in this country differed drastically, depending on their race, class, and marital status.

White Women

European women usually arrived in the New World with their families, as daughters and wives, under the auspices of fathers or husbands. In the pre-industrial economy of the American colonial period (from the seventeenth century to the early eighteenth century), work was closely identified with home and family life. The family was the primary economic unit, and family members were dependent on one another for basic sustenance. Men performed the agricultural work, while women's work was done chiefly in the home, which was a center of production in colonial America. In addition to cooking, cleaning, and caring for children, women did spinning and weaving, and made lace, soap, candles, and shoes. Indeed, they manufactured nearly all articles used in daily life. This work was highly valued, and the colonies relied on the production of these "cottage industries."

Single women remained within the domestic sphere, living with relatives, often as "assistant homemakers." For married women, the nature of their work depended on the economic circumstances of their husbands:

> In cash-poor homes and among frontier families, women bore the burden of filling most of the family's basic needs. They worked to reduce cash expenditures by growing vegetables in the kitchen garden and making the family's clothes, candles, soap and household furnishings. If a husband were a craftsman or the proprietor of a shop or tavern, his wife and children might also work in the business, in addition to all the other tasks. In contrast, the wife of a successful farmer, plantation owner, or merchant did little actual work; instead, she supervised household servants and slaves who purchased or made the goods the family needed, cooked the meals, and maintained the house.

The social codes of colonial America did not exclude a woman from working outside the home, and many did so. Colonial women engaged in a great range of occupations, and as old documents are discovered and new histories of women's work are written, that range appears greater still. Women were innkeepers, shopkeepers, crafts workers, nurses, printers, teachers, and landholders. In the city of Boston during 1690, for example, women ran approximately 40 percent of all taverns. During that year, city officials also granted more than thirty women the right to saw lumber and manufacture potash. Women acted as physicians and midwives in all the early settlements, producing medicines, salves, and ointments. Many of the women who worked outside their homes were widows with dependent children, who took their husbands' places in family enterprises. It seems that at one time or another, colonial women engaged in many of the occupations practiced by men. Indeed, most models of the "patriarchal family economy" ill fit the historical evidence; for example, eighteenth-century diaries describe "a world in which wives as well as husbands traded with their neighbors" and "young women felt themselves responsible for their own support." Not surprisingly, however, women's wages in this period were significantly lower than those of men.

For poor women, there were special incentives to work outside the home. Local poor laws encouraged single poor women to work rather than become recipients of relief. The choice of jobs was much more limited, and many poor women became laundresses, house servants, or cooks. Again, however, female laborers were paid approximately 30 percent less than the lowest-paid unskilled, free, white male workers and 20 percent less than hired-out male slaves.

The fact that some women worked in so-called "masculine fields"—that they were merchants, tavern owners, shopkeepers, and so on—has sometimes been interpreted to mean that the colonial period was a "golden age of equality" for women. Contemporary historians argue instead, however, that these jobs were exceptions to the rule, and that in fact "colonial times were characterized by a strict and simple division of labor between men and women, which assigned them to fields and house, or to the public and private spheres, respectively." The dominant ideology was still that a woman's place was at home, raising children. . . .

Women of Color

Historically, the experiences of women of color have differed dramatically from those of white women. If we consider only the present time period, it may appear that women of color and white women have certain experiences in common—relatively low economic position, being the target of discriminatory practices in education and in work, and overall marginality in the power structure. But women of color and white women have reached their present circumstances through very different histories. Although white women's status was clearly inferior to that of white men, they were treated with deference, and they shared in the status privileges of their husbands. African American women almost never had the option of choosing between work and leisure, as did some white women. They were not included in the image of the "colonial housewife." African American women were not considered "weak" females, but were treated more like beasts of burden. Thus these women of color suffered a double oppression of sexism and racism.

Nowhere is this double oppression more clearly demonstrated than within the institution of slavery, which became established in late seventeenth- and early eighteenth-century colonial society—largely as a result of the demand for cheap agricultural labor, especially within the Southern plantation economy. Historians estimate the slave population in the United States, Caribbean, and Brazil consisted of 9.5 million blacks. More than double that number are estimated to have died in transit to the New World. Slave women in the Southern colonies were without doubt the most exploited of all women. They were exploited not only as workers but as breeders of slaves. The following advertisement was typical of the time:

> **Negroes for Sale:** A girl about twenty years of age (raised in Virginia) and her two female children, four and the other two years old—remarkably strong and healthy. Never having had a day's sickness with the exception of the smallpox in her life. She is prolific in her generating qualities and affords a rare opportunity to any person who wishes to raise a family of strong and healthy servants for their own use.

Slave women were also sometimes exploited as sex objects for white men. Like male slaves, they were considered intrinsically inferior. Slaves were property, not people. They faced severe cultural and legal restrictions: their family lives were controlled by their owners, their children were not their own, and their educational opportunities were almost nonexistent.

Sojourner Truth, formerly a slave and an activist in the abolitionist and women's rights movements, eloquently expressed the differences in treatment, under slavery, of black and white women: "That man over there says that women need to be helped into carriages and lifted over ditches, and to have the best place everywhere. Nobody ever helped me into carriages, or over mud puddles, or gives me any best place . . . and ain't I a woman?"

Before the Civil War, a black woman in one of the "cotton states," working on one of the larger plantations, would have been either a house servant or one of several million field hands who produced major cash crops. In the Southern plantation economy, we thus find a "bifurcated" concept of woman. The European woman became "the guardian of civilization," while the African American woman was "spared neither harsh labor nor harsh punishment," though the experience of slaves differed depending on the economic status and individual personality of the slave owner. Even pregnancy did not deter some slavemasters from cruel treatment: "One particular method of whipping pregnant slaves was used throughout the South; they were made to lie face down in a specially dug depression in the ground, a practice that provided simultaneously for the protection of the fetus and the abuse of its mother."

Some white women benefited from such slave labor and shared with their husbands the role of oppressor, although the slave-mistress relationship was psychologically complex: "In their role as labor managers, mistresses lashed out at slave women not only to punish them, but also to vent their anger on victims even more wronged than themselves. We may speculate that, in the female slave, the white woman saw the source of her own misery, but she also saw herself—a woman without rights or recourse, subject to the whims of an egotistical man." Conflict between white

and African American women often resulted in violence, in which "mistresses were likely to attack with any weapon available—knitting needles, tongs, a fork, butcher knife, ironing board, or pan of boiling water." Yet, while the relationship was often filled with strife, white and African American women "also shared a world of physical and emotional intimacy that is uncommon among women of antagonistic classes and different races."

Slavery was justified by notions of race involving the "biological superiority" of the colonists. It was assumed that Europeans in the colonies made up an easily identifiable and discrete biological and social entity—a "natural" community of class interests, racial attributes, political and social affinities, and superior culture. This was of course not exactly true, but given that the differences between white skin and black skin were more noticeable than many of the differences among Europeans themselves, and given that whites were in dominant positions politically and socially, it could easily *seem* to be true.

Slave families often resisted the oppressive workloads by banding together to help one another in the fields and to lessen the workloads of older, weaker, or sicker workers. The extended family was of vital importance under the slave system. African American mothers labored most of the day, some of them caring for white women's families, while their own children were left under the care of grandmothers and old or disabled slaves. While the two-parent, nuclear family may have been the most typical form of slave cohabitation, close relatives were often very much involved in family life. Stevenson's study suggests that in colonial and antebellum Virginia, the slave family was a "malleable extended family that, when possible, provided its members with nurture, education, socialization, material support, and recreation in the face of the potential social chaos that the slaveholder imposed."

Even though African American men were unable to own property, to provide protection and support for their children, or to work within the public sphere, there was a sexual division within the slave household. Men collected the firewood and made furniture—beds, tables, chairs—and other articles of wood, such as animal traps, butter paddles, and ax handles. They also wove baskets and made shoes. African American women grew, prepared, and preserved foods; spun thread, wove and dyed cloth, and sewed clothes; and made soap and candles.

In the North, while slavery was an accepted practice, it was not nearly as widespread. Many African American women worked as free laborers as domestic servants; others worked as spinners, weavers, and printers.

Native American Women

The work and family life experience of Native American women prior to European colonization differed depending on the region of the country and the type of tribal society. But in every Native American nation, women played very important roles in the economic life of their communities:

> They had to be resourceful in utilizing every aspect of the environment to sustain life and engaging in cultural exchanges to incorporate new productive techniques. They gathered wild plants for food, herbs for medicines and dyes, clay for pottery, bark and reeds for weaving cloth. In many nations, they also tilled the soil and sowed the seeds, cultivated and harvested, made cloth and clothing, dried vegetables, and ground grains for breads. In hunting societies, they cured the meats and dried the skins. They also assisted in the hunt in some cultures.

As a general rule, men hunted and women engaged in agricultural work. The more important hunting was to a community's survival, the more extensive the male power within the community; the greater the dependence on agriculture, the greater the power and independence of women. Women had the responsibility for raising children and maintaining hearth and home. Men engaged in hunting, fishing, and warfare.

In the East especially, many Indian communities were predominantly agricultural. Women constituted the agricultural labor force within these communities. An English woman who was held captive by a Seneca tribe observed that

> Household duties were simple and Seneca women, unlike English wives and daughters, were not slaves to the spinning wheel or the needle. In the summer, the women went out each morning to the fields, accompanied by their children, to work cooperatively and in the company of friends and relatives, planting and tending the corn, beans, and squash at a pace to their individual rhythms and skills rather than to the demands of an overseer. They moved from field to field, completing the same tasks in each before returning to the first.

Women within agricultural communities would often maintain control over tools and land—as well as any surplus foods they gathered from the land. This often enabled them (especially elderly women who were heads of households) to garner some political clout within their tribal communities. For instance, if Iroquois women opposed war on certain occasions, they might refuse to let the men have the cornmeal they would have needed to feed their raiding parties or armies. These communities often had a matrilineal family structure (inheritance and family name were through the female line, with family connections through the mother) and matrilocal residence (upon marriage a man lived with his mother-in-law's relatives).

Through the lens of the white colonist, the work roles and family structure of Native American society appeared deviant and, in some cases, perverse. After all, English society was characterized by a patriarchal family structure with patrilocal residence:

> To Europeans, Indian family patterns raised the specter of promiscuous women, freed from accountability to their fathers and husbands for the offspring they produced. . . . Equally incomprehensible—and thus perverse—to many Europeans were the work roles accepted by Indian men and women. In the world the English knew, farming was labor and farmers were male. Masculinity was linked, inexorably, to agriculture: household

production and family reproduction defined femininity. That Indian men hunted was not a sufficient counterpoise, for, in the England of the seventeenth century, hunting was a sport, not an occupation. Many concluded that Indian men were effeminate, lazy; Indian women were beasts of burden, slaves to unmanly men.

European colonization and conquest pushed Native Americans off their land, depriving them of food and livelihood, culture and traditions. Disease or warfare demolished whole societies. Others were radically transformed, especially with regard to the traditional gender and work roles. Having used military force to remove Native Americans from their lands onto reservations, the U.S. government "began a systematic effort to destroy their cultures and replace them with the values and practices of middle-class whites."

Confined to relatively small reservations, Native American men could no longer hunt as extensively as before (nor, defeated by U.S. forces, could they any longer carry on warfare). They therefore needed to redefine their social roles and to find new economic activities. In many a Native American tribe, the men took over agriculture, traditionally the women's work. Family structure also changed, at the prompting of missionaries and others including government officials, to become more like that of the Europeans, with less emphasis on the matrilineal extended family and more on the nuclear family and the husband-wife relationship.

THE ARRIVAL OF INDUSTRIALIZATION

The transformation from an agrarian rural economy to an urban industrial society ushered in a new era in women's work. With the advent of industrialization, many of the products women made at home—clothes, shoes, candles—gradually came to be made instead in factories. For a while, women still performed the work at home, using the new machines. Merchants would contract for work to be done, supplying women with the machines and the raw materials to be made into finished articles. The most common of these

manufacturing trades for women was sewing for the newly emerging clothing industry. Since women had always sewn for their families, this work was considered an extension of women's traditional role, and therefore a respectable activity. As the demand for goods increased, however, home production declined and gave way to the factory system, which was more efficient in meeting emerging needs.

The rise of factory production truly separated the home from the workplace. With the decline of the household unit as the center of industrial and economy activity, the importance of women's economic role also declined. Male and female spheres of activity became more separated, as did the definitions of men's and women's roles. Man's role continued to be primarily that of worker and provider; woman's role became primarily supportive. She was to maintain a smooth and orderly household, to be cheerful and warm, and thus to provide the husband with the support and services he needed to continue his work life. The industrial revolution created a set of social and economic conditions in which the basic lifestyle of white middle-class women more nearly approached society's expectations concerning woman's role. More and more middle-class women could now aspire to the status formerly reserved for the upper classes—that of "lady." The nineteenth-century concept of a lady was that of a fragile, idle, pure creature, submissive and subservient to her husband and to domestic needs. Her worth was based on her decorative value, a quality that embraced her beauty, her virtuous character, and her temperament. She was certainly not a paid employee. This ideal was later referred to as the "cult of true womanhood" because of its rigid, almost religious standards.

Biological and social arguments were also often used to justify women's exclusion from the labor force. Women were seen as too weak and delicate to participate in the rough work world of men. It was believed they lacked strength and stamina, that their brains were small, that the feminine perspective and sensitivity were liabilities in the marketplace. Such arguments rationalized women's accepting the roles of homemaker and mother almost exclusively, as the industrial revolution spread across the country.

During the early years of industrialization, however, because many men were still primarily occupied with agricultural work and were unavailable or unwilling to enter the early factories, male laborers were in short supply. American industry depended, then, on a steady supply of women workers. Yet how could society tolerate women's working in the factories, given the dominant ideology of the times, which dictated that a woman's place was at home? Single white women provided one answer. Their employment was viewed as a fulfillment of their family responsibilities, during an interlude before marriage.

The employment of young, single women in the early Lowell (Massachusetts) mills is a prime example of the reconciliation of ideology with the needs of industry. Francis Cabot Lowell devised a respectable route into employment for such women. Recruiting the daughters of farm families to work in his mill, which opened in 1821 in Lowell, he provided supervised boardinghouses, salaries sufficient to allow the young women to offer financial aid to their families or to save for their own trousseaux, and assurances to their families that the hard work and discipline of the mill would help prepare them for marriage and motherhood.

In the early industrial era, working conditions were arduous and hours were long. By the late 1830s, immigration began to supply a strongly competitive, permanent workforce willing to be employed for low wages in the factories, under increasingly mechanized and hazardous conditions. By the late 1850s, most of the better-educated, single, native-born women had left the mills, leaving newly immigrated women (both single and married) and men to fill these positions.

While women thus played a crucial role in the development of the textile industry, the first important manufacturing industry in America, women also found employment in many other occupations during the process of industrialization. As railroads and other business enterprises expanded and consolidated, women went to work in these areas as well. In fact, the U.S. Labor Commissioner reported that by 1890 only 9 out of 360 general groups to which the country's industries had been assigned did not employ women.

By 1900, more than five million women or girls, or about one in every five of those 10 years old and over, had become a paid employee. The largest proportion (40%) remained close to home in domestic and personal service, but domestic service was on the decline for white working-class women at the turn of the century. About 25 percent (1.3 million) of employed women worked in the manufacturing industries: in cotton mills, in the manufacture of woolen and worsted goods, silk goods, hosiery, and knit wear. The third largest group of employed women (over 18%) were working on farms. Women in the trade and transportation industries (about 10%) worked as saleswomen, telegraph and telephone operators, stenographers, clerks, copyists, accountants, and bookkeepers. Women in the professions (about 9 percent, and typically young, educated, and single, of native-born parentage) were employed primarily in elementary and secondary teaching or nursing. Other professions—law, medicine, business, college teaching—tended to exclude women. The fastest growing of these occupational groups were manufacturing, trade, and transportation. In the last thirty years of the nineteenth century, the number of women working in trade and transportation rose from 19,000 to over half a million. These women also tended to be young, single, native-born Americans; immigrants and minority women were excluded from these white-collar positions.

. . .

By the turn of the century, the labor market had become clearly divided according to gender, race, and class. Fewer manufacturing jobs were being defined as suitable for white women, especially with the rising dominance of heavy industry employment for which female workers were considered too delicate. Working-class women were increasingly devalued by their continued participation in activities men had primarily taken over (such as factory work), because these activities were regarded as lacking in the Victorian virtue and purity called for by the "cult of true womanhood." As the economy expanded and prosperity came to more and more white middle-class families, middle-class women could "become ladies." A "woman's place" was still defined as at home. If these women did work outside the home, the appropriate occupation was a white-collar job (sales, clerical, and professional occupations). White women's occupations shifted from primarily domestic service—which became increasingly identified as "black women's work"—and from light manufacturing to the rapidly growing opportunities in office and sales work. These jobs were also considered more appropriate for feminine roles as defined by the cult of true womanhood. Women of color did not share in this occupational transformation. In 1910, for example, 90.5 percent of African American women worked as agricultural laborers or domestics, compared with 29.3 percent of white women.

The Legacy of Slavery

African American women were not part of the "cult of true womanhood." They were not sheltered or protected from the harsh realities, and "while many white daughters were raised in genteel refined circumstances, most black daughters were forced to deal with poverty, violence and a hostile outside world from childhood on." After emancipation, their employment and economic opportunities were limited, in part because the skills they had learned on the plantation transferred to relatively few jobs, and those only of low pay and status.

African American women's concentration in service work—especially domestic work—was largely a result of limited opportunities available to them following the Civil War. The only factory employment open to them was in the Southern tobacco and textile industries, and until World War I most African American working women were farm laborers, domestics, or laundresses. . . .

Despite the limited range of job opportunities, a relatively large proportion of African American women were employed. The legacy of slavery may partly account for the relatively high labor-force participation rate of African American women. Although women's labor-force participation rate is generally lower than men's, African American women's participation rate was historically much higher than that of white women. Thus, for example, white women's labor-force participation in 1890 was 16.3 percent, while African American women's rate was 39.7 percent.

WORLD WAR I AND THE DEPRESSION

World War I accelerated the entry of white women into new fields of industry. The pressure of war production and the shortage of male industrial workers necessitated the hiring of women for what had been male-dominated occupations. Women replaced men at jobs in factories and business offices, and, in general, they kept the nation going, fed, and clothed. The mechanization and routinization of industry during this period enabled women to quickly master the various new skills. For the most part, this wartime pattern involved a reshuffling of the existing female workforce, rather than an increase in the numbers of women employed. Although the popular myth is that homemakers abandoned their kitchens for machine shops or airplane hangars, only about 5 percent of women workers were new to the labor force during the war years. . . .

Thus the wartime labor shortage temporarily created new job opportunities for women workers, and at higher wages than they had previously earned. This was not necessarily the case for African American women, however. Although World War I opened up some factory jobs to them, these were typically limited to the most menial, least desirable, and often the most dangerous jobs—jobs already rejected by white women. These jobs included some of the most dangerous tasks in industry, such as carrying glass to hot ovens in glass factories and dyeing furs in the furrier industry.

World War I produced no substantial or lasting change in women's participation in the labor force. The employment rate of women in 1920 was actually a bit lower (20.4%) than in 1910 (20.9%). The labor unions, the government, and the society at large were not ready to accept a permanent shift in women's economic role. Instead, women filled an urgent need during the wartime years and were relegated to their former positions as soon as peace returned. As the reformer Mary Von Kleeck wrote, "When the immediate dangers . . . were passed, the prejudices came to life once more."

When the men returned from the war, they were given priority in hiring, and although a number of women left the labor force voluntarily, many were forced out by layoffs. Those remaining were employed in the low-paying, low-prestige positions women had always occupied and in those occupations that had become accepted as women's domain. . . .

The Great Depression of the 1930s threw millions out of work. The severe employment problems during this period intensified the general attitude that a woman with a job was taking that job away from a male breadwinner. Yet during the 1930s, an increasing number of women went to work for the first time. The increase was most marked among younger, married women, who worked at least until the first child, and among older, married women, who reentered the marketplace because of dire economic need or in response to changing patterns of consumer demand. Most jobs held by women were part-time, seasonal, and marginal. Women's labor-force participation increased slowly throughout this period and into the early 1940s . . . , except in the professions (including feminized professions such as elementary teaching, nursing, librarianship, and social work). The proportion of women in all professions declined from 14.2 percent to 12.3 percent during the Depression decade.

WORLD WAR II

The ordeal of World War II brought about tremendous change in the numbers and occupational distribution of working women. As during World War I, the shortage of male workers, who had gone off to fight, coupled with the mounting pressures of war production brought women into the workforce. A corresponding shift in attitudes

about women's aptitudes and proper roles resulted. Women entered the munitions factories and other heavy industries to support the war effort. The War Manpower Commission instituted a massive advertising campaign to attract women to the war industries. Patriotic appeals were common.

. . .

Equal work did not mean equal pay for the women in these varied wartime occupations. Although the National War Labor Board issued a directive to industries that stipulated equal pay for equal work, most employers continued to pay women at a lower rate. Furthermore, women had little opportunity to advance in their new occupations.

World War II marked an important turning point in women's participation in the paid labor force. The social prohibition concerning married women working gave way under wartime pressure, and women wartime workers demonstrated that it was possible for women to maintain their households while also assuming the role of breadwinner with outside employment. More women than ever before learned to accommodate the simultaneous demands of family and work. The experience "pointed the way to a greater degree of choice for American women."

However, at the war's end, with the return of men to civilian life, there was a tremendous pressure on women to return to their former positions in the home. During this time, a new social ideology began to emerge; Betty Friedan later called it "the feminine mystique." This ideology drew in social workers, educators, journalists, and psychologists, all of whom tried to convince women that their place was again in the home. It was not until the "cult of true womanhood" advanced in the late 1800s to differentiate middle-class women from working-class women. As Friedan notes, in the fifteen years following World War II, the image of "women at home" rather than "at work" became a cherished and self-perpetuating core of contemporary American culture. A generation of young people were brought up to extol the values of home and family, and woman's role was defined as the domestic center around which all else revolved. Women were supposed to live like those in Norman Rockwell *Saturday Evening Post* illustrations. The idealized image was of smiling mothers baking cookies for their wholesome children, driving their station wagons loaded with freckled youngsters to an endless round of lessons and activities, returning with groceries and other consumer goods to the ranch houses they cared for with such pride. Women were supposed to revel in these roles and gladly leave the running of the world to men.

. . .

Yet, unlike the post–World War I period, after World War II women did not go back to the kitchens. Instead, women's labor-force participation continued to increase throughout the post–World War II decades, so that by the late 1960s, 40 percent of American women were in the labor force, and by the late 1990s, 60 percent were. Who were the women most likely to be part of this "new majority" of women at work?

AFTER WORLD WAR II: THE RISE OF THE MARRIED WOMAN WORKER

Between 1890 and the beginning of World War II, single women comprised at least half the female labor force. The others were mostly married African American, immigrant, or working-class women.

The decade of the 1940s saw a change in the type of woman worker, as increasing numbers of married women left their homes to enter the world of paid work. . . . Although single women continued to have the highest labor-force participation rates among women, during the 1940s the percentage of married women in the workforce grew more rapidly than any other category. Between 1940 and 1950, single women workers were in short supply because of low birthrates in the 1930s. Furthermore, those single women available for work were marrying at younger ages and leaving the labor market to raise their families. On the other hand, ample numbers of older, married women were available, and these women (who had married younger, had had fewer

children, and were living longer) were eager for paid employment.

In 1940, about 15 percent of married women were employed; by 1950, 24 percent. This increase has continued: by 1960, 32 percent of married women; in 1970, over 41 percent; in 1980, 50 percent; and by 1995, 61 percent. Indeed, as the twentieth century comes to a close, we can see that labor-force participation rates of single and married women have become almost identical. . . .

During the 1940s, 1950s, and 1960s, it was mainly older, married women entering the workforce. In 1957, for example, the labor-force participation rate among women aged forty-five to forty-nine years exceeded the rate for twenty- to twenty-four-year-old women. During the 1960s, young married mothers with preschool- or school-age children began to enter the workforce. This trend continued for the next three decades; by 1995, more than three-quarters of married women with children between six and seventeen years of age were employed, and, most significantly, almost two-thirds of those women with children under the age of six were in the labor force. . . . In short, whereas before 1970 the overwhelming majority of married women stopped working after they had children, today the overwhelming majority of married women do not.

WOMEN OF COLOR

Denied entrance to the factories during the rise of industrialization and, for much of the twentieth century, facing discriminatory hiring practices that closed off opportunities in the newly expanded office and sales jobs, many women of color entered domestic service. From 1910 to 1940, the proportion of white women employed in clerical and sales positions almost doubled, and there was a decline in the numbers of white women in domestic work. Private household work then became the province of African American women: the percentage of African American household workers increased from 38.5 percent in 1910 to 59.9 percent in 1940. . . . For the next three decades, African American women remained the single largest group in domestic service.

African American women's economic status improved dramatically from 1940 through the 1960s, as a result of an increase in light manufacturing jobs, as well as changes in technology. African American women moved from private household work into manufacturing and clerical work, and made significant gains in the professions. Whereas in 1940, 60 percent of employed African American females worked in private households, by the late 1960s only 20 percent did. Their job prospects continued to improve, and by the 1980s, almost half of all working African American women were doing so in "white-collar" jobs—clerical and sales positions, as well as professional jobs in business, health care, and education. Through the 1990s, the historic, job-prestige gap between African American and white working women continued to close. Almost two-thirds of working African American women had jobs in the white-collar world by 1996, compared with nearly three-quarters of working white women. . . .

Other Women of Color at Work

Each minority group has had a different experience in American society and has faced different opportunities and obstacles. Women in each group share with African American women the concerns of all minority women; they share with the men of their ethnic groups the problems of discrimination against that particular ethnic minority.

Native American Women

As we noted earlier, gender roles in Native American communities were disrupted during the conquest and oppression by whites. For example, Navajo society was traditionally matrilineal, with extended families the norm; Navajo women owned property and played an important role in family decisions. But beginning in the 1930s, government policy disrupted this system by giving land only to males. As they could no longer make a sufficient living off the land, more and more Navajo men had to seek employment off the reservations. Nuclear families became the norm.

Navajo women became dependent on male providers. With the men away much of the time, these women are often isolated and powerless. They often face divorce or desertion and thus economic difficulties, because the community frowns on women seeking work off the reservation.

Such disruption of the traditional Native American society left Native American women in very grim economic circumstances. But in recent decades, more and more of them have gotten jobs. Native American women's labor-force participation rate in 1970 was 35 percent (compared to 43% for all women). This rate rose sharply to 55 percent by the early 1990s and is now within a few percentage points of the rate for all women.

Like their African American counterparts over the past half century, Native American women have gradually moved out of low-skill farm and nonfarm work and domestic jobs into clerical, sales, professional, technical, and other "white-collar" jobs. In 1960, one in six working Native American women was employed as a domestic household worker; by the early 1990s only one in a hundred was. During the same period, the proportion of Native American women involved in agricultural work also went from ten to one in a hundred. Manufacturing work was increasingly replaced by white-collar work, reflecting the overall trends in the occupational structure; more specifically, while the percentage involved in factory work (much of it in textiles and traditional crafts) fell from 18.1 to 14.2, the percentage doing white-collar work soared from 28.9 to 61.3. Although many of these white-collar jobs are classified as "professional" (15.7% of all working Native American women) or "managerial" (9.4%), two-thirds of Native American women are still concentrated in the "secondary" sector of the labor market—which is characterized by low wages, few or no benefits, low mobility, and high instability. They are kept there because of the "stagnation of the reservation economy," discrimination, and their relatively low level of educational attainment. A significant number do not have a high school diploma (in 1990, more than one-third of all those over the age of 25, compared to one-fifth of white women).

Latina [Chicana] Women

. . . Large numbers of Chicanas migrated, usually with husband and children, from Mexico to the United States during the 1916–1920 labor shortage created by World War I. They found work in the sprawling "factory farms" of the Southwest, harvesting fruits, vegetables, and cotton in the Imperial and San Joaquin valleys of California, the Salt River valley of Arizona, and the Rio Grande valley of Texas. They also went to the Midwest, for instance to Michigan and Minnesota, to harvest sugar beets. Such migrant workers typically were exploited, spending long, tedious, and physically demanding hours in the fields for very low pay. Some became tenant farmers, which might seem a step up, except too often this system "created debt peonage; unable to pay the rent, tenants were unable to leave the land and remained virtually permanently indebted to their landlords."

During the 1920s, with a shortage of European immigration, new job opportunities opened up for Mexican Americans, and they began to migrate from rural, farm country to the urban, industrial centers, where they found work as domestics and factory workers. By 1930, one-third of working Chicanas were domestics and a quarter worked in manufacturing; at the time, the share employed in agriculture, forestry, and mining had fallen to 21 percent. Wage scales varied according to ethnicity, however. It was not uncommon to pay Chicana workers lower wages than "Anglo" (whites of European descent) women for doing the same job, whether as domestics, laundresses, or workers in the food-processing industries of the West and Southwest. Then the Depression years of the 1930s, with the general shortage of jobs, brought a backlash against Mexican American labor, and thousands of Mexicans were deported or pressured to leave.

World War II once again opened up the American labor market for Mexican migrants, as their labor was needed to offset wartime labor shortages. However, their treatment was deplorable by modern standards. In short, Mexican workers comprised a "reserve army" of exploited labor. Through the government-sponsored Bracero or "Manual Workers" program, Mexican workers were granted temporary work visas so that they could be employed on large corporate farms and elsewhere, but too often they were treated like slaves or prisoners.

World War II and the years following saw a massive shift in the occupational and geographical distribution of Chicana workers:

> Many left Texas for California, and the population became increasingly more urban. Women continued their move from the fields into garment factories throughout the Southwest. . . . [A] comparison of the 1930 and 1950 [census] data shows the magnitude of these shifts. For instance, the share of employed southwestern Chicanas working on farms dropped from 21 percent in 1930 to 6 percent in 1950, while the percentage in white-collar work doubled.

By the 1960s, the largest occupational category for Chicana workers was operatives, followed by clerical and service work. Chicanas became concentrated in particular industries—food processing, electronics (including telecommunications), and garments. Like their Native American counterparts, Chicana women have made some progress in entering professional and managerial occupations (primarily noncollege teaching, nursing, librarianship, and social work). In 1960, 8.6 percent were in these occupations; by 1980, 12.6 percent, and by the early 1990s 17.5 percent. However, like the Native Americans, Chicana women are still overwhelmingly found in the secondary labor market (75%)—much more so than women (60%) and men (32%) of white European heritage.

The dominant reasons behind the low occupational prestige of all minority groups are the same: discrimination and low educational attainment. In the case of Chicana women, over 15 percent "are illiterate by the standard measure (completion of less than five years of schooling)," but studies of functional illiteracy during the 1970s and 1980s suggest "much higher rates—perhaps as high as 56 percent." At the other end of the educational attainment spectrum, only 8.4 percent of Latina women have completed four or more years of college—compared with 21.0 percent of white women and 12.9 percent of blacks. However, education is only part of the formula for success in the U.S. occupational system: for when education is held constant, Latina women make only between 84 and 90 percent of what white women do.

Beyond lack of education, Chicana women face other important obstacles in the labor market. They have high rates of unemployment and underemployment. Many of the jobs they hold are seasonal and often nonunionized. This lack of advancement translates into higher poverty rates (23 percent for Chicana/os in the early 1990s). The median income for full-time Chicana workers is lower than that of any other U.S. racial-ethnic group. For Latina women (in general) with children and no husband present, the poverty rate is even worse: 49.4 percent compared with 26.6 percent of white women in this situation.

Increasingly, Chicana women, like many female workers of color around the globe, are doing service or assembly work for multi-national corporations, especially in the apparel, food-processing, and electronics industries. These women have often displaced men in assembly work because they can be paid less and many do not receive job benefits. The work hours are long, and women are often assigned monotonous tasks that are dangerous to their health.

. . .

Asian-American Women

. . . Asian Americans are considered to be the "model minority." . . . However, this is as much myth as fact. While many among both the native-born and the recent arrivals have high levels of education and professional skills and can readily fit into the labor market, others lack such advantages, often finding work only as undocumented laborers in low-paying jobs with long work days, little or no job mobility, and no benefits.

> We are told we have overcome our oppression, and that therefore we are the model minority. Model refers to the cherished dictum of capitalism that "pulling hard on your bootstraps" brings due rewards. . . . Asian American success stories . . . do

little to illuminate the actual conditions of the majority of Asian Americans. Such examples conceal the more typical Asian American experience of unemployment, underemployment and struggle to survive. The model minority myth thus classically scapegoats Asian Americans. It labels us in a way that dismisses the real problems that many do face, while at the same time pitting Asians against other oppressed people of color.

In 1996, 37.3 percent of Asian women who were 25 years and over had at least a bachelor's degree, compared with 23.2 percent of non-Latina whites. Filipina American women secured the highest college graduation rate of all women, a rate 50 percent greater than that of white males. Following closely behind are Chinese American and Japanese American women, who exceed both the white male and female college graduation rates. Yet, these educational achievements bring lower returns for Asian women than for whites. Census data reveal a gap between achievement and economic reward for Asian American women, who suffer from both race and sex discrimination within the labor market. . . .

And it would be wrong to equate "Asian" with "well educated," because the majority of Asian women immigrating to the United States since 1980 have low levels of education. Though, as just noted, Asian women are much more likely to be college-educated than non-Latina white women, they are also much more likely—two and a half times more likely—to be grade-school dropouts: in 1996, 12.5 percent of Asian women had not gone beyond the eighth grade, compared to only 5.2 percent of their non-Latina white counterparts. This fact is linked to the other most obvious difference between Asian and white women . . . — the proportions working as "operators, fabricators, and laborers," where we find significantly more Asian women.

These women are most commonly employed as sewing machine operators at home or in small sweatshops in the Chinatowns of New York and San Francisco. Asian immigrant women are also heavily employed in the microelectronics industry. Women in general comprise 80 to 90 percent of assembly workers in this industry, and approximately "half of these assembly workers are recent immigrants from the Philippines, Vietnam, Korea, and South Asia." Within the microelectronics industry jobs are often "structured along racial and gender lines, with men and white workers earning higher wages and being much more likely to be promoted than women and workers of color." Karen Hossfeld's research on relationships between Third World immigrant women production workers and their white male managers in the high-tech Silicon Valley of California relates how immigrant women of color negotiate and often employ resistance to primarily white, middle-class management demands. One Filipina circuit board assembler in Silicon Valley puts it this way:

> The bosses here have this type of reasoning like a seesaw. One day it's "you're paid less because women are different than men," or "immigrants need less to get by." The next day it's "you're all just workers here—no special treatment just because you're female or foreigners."
>
> Well, they think they're pretty clever with their doubletalk, and that we're just a bunch of dumb aliens. But it takes two to use a seesaw. What we are gradually figuring out here is how to use their own logic against them.

As clerical or administrative support workers, Asian American women are disproportionately represented as cashiers, file clerks, office machine operators, and typists. They are less likely to obtain employment as secretaries or receptionists. Noting that there is an "overrepresentation of college-educated women in clerical work," Woo suggests that education functions less as a path toward mobility into higher occupational categories, and more as "a hedge against jobs as service workers and as machine operatives or assembly workers."

Asian American women with a college education who obtain professional employment are often restricted to the less prestigious jobs within this category. Asian American women "are more likely to remain marginalized in their work organization, to encounter a 'glass ceiling,' and to earn less than white men, Asian American men, and white women with comparable educational backgrounds." They are least represented in those male-dominated positions of physician, lawyer, and judge, and are heavily concentrated in the more female-dominated occupations of nursing and teaching.

Asian women have been subjected to a range of stereotypes. The "Lotus Blossom" stereotype depicts them as submissive and demure sex objects: "good, faithful, uncomplaining, totally compliant, self-effacing, gracious servants who will do anything and everything to please, entertain, and make them feel comfortable and carefree." At the opposite extreme, the Dragon Lady stereotype portrays Asian women as "promiscuous and untrustworthy,"

> as the castrating Dragon Lady who, while puffing on her foot-long cigarette holder, could poison a man as easily as she could seduce him. "With her talon-like six-inch fingernails, her skin-tight satin dress slit to the thigh," the Dragon Lady is desirable, deceitful and dangerous.

Asian American feminist Germaine Wong notes how stereotypes concerning Asian women operate in the workplace, serving to deter their advancement into leadership roles and to increase their vulnerability to sexual harassment. Additionally, these stereotypes have fostered a demand for "X-rated films and pornographic materials featuring Asian women in bondage, for 'Oriental' bathhouse workers in U.S. cities, and for Asian mail-order brides."

In sum, the notion of Asian Americans as the "model minority" deviates considerably from sociological reality. While Asian American women as a group have achieved some "success" in terms of high educational attainment, they receive lower returns on this investment compared to the white population. They have not "escaped the stigmatization of being minority and recent immigrants in a discriminatory job market."

A Black Woman Took My Job

Michael Kimmel

Over the past three generations, women's lives have been utterly and completely transformed—in politics, the military, the workplace, professions, and education. But during that time, the ideology of masculinity has remained relatively intact. The notions we have about what it means to be a man remain locked in a pattern set decades ago, when the world looked very different. The single greatest obstacle to women's equality today remains the behaviour and attitudes of men.

In the mid-1970s, [scholars] offered what [they] called the four basic rules of masculinity:

1. No Sissy Stuff. Masculinity is based on the relentless repudiation of the feminine.
2. Be a Big Wheel. Masculinity is measured by the size of your paycheck, and marked by wealth, power and status. As a US bumper sticker put it: "He who has the most toys when he dies, wins."
3. Be a Sturdy Oak. What makes a man a man is that he is reliable in a crisis. And what makes him reliable in a crisis is that he resembles an inanimate object. A rock, a pillar, a tree.
2. Give 'em Hell. Exude an aura of daring and aggression. Take risks; live life on the edge.

The past decade has found men bumping up against the limitations of these traditional definitions, but without much of a sense of direction about where they might look for alternatives. We chafe against the edges of traditional masculinity but seem unable or unwilling to break out of the constraints of those four rules. Hence the defensiveness, the anger, the confusion that is everywhere in evidence.

Let me pair up those four rules of manhood with the four areas of change in women's lives—gender identity, the workplace, the balance of work and family life, the sexual landscape—and suggest some of the issues I believe we are facing around the world today.

First, women made gender visible, but most men do not know they are gendered beings. Courses on gender are still populated mostly by women. Most men don't see that gender is as central to their lives as it is to women's. The privilege of privilege is that its terms are rendered invisible. It is a luxury not to have to think about race, or class, or gender. Only those marginalized by some category understand how powerful that category is when deployed against them. I was reminded of this recently when I went to give a guest lecture for a female colleague at my university. (We teach the same course on alternate semesters, so she always gives a guest lecture for me, and I do one for her.) As I walked into the auditorium, one student looked up at me and said: "Oh, finally, an objective opinion!"

The second area in which women's lives have changed is the workplace. Recall the second rule of manhood: Be a Big Wheel. Most men derive their identity as breadwinners, as family providers. Often, though, the invisibility of masculinity makes it hard to see how gender equality will actually benefit us as men. For example, while we speak of the "feminization of poverty" we rarely "see" its other side—the "masculinization of wealth." Instead of saying that US women, on average, earn [a percentage] of what US men earn, what happens if we say that men are earning $1.30 for every dollar women earn? Now suddenly privilege is visible!

Recently I appeared on a television talk show opposite three "angry white males" who felt they had been the victims of workplace discrimination. The show's title was "A Black Woman Took My Job." In my comments to these men, I invited them to consider what the word "my" meant in that title: that they felt that the jobs were originally "theirs." But by what right is that "his" job? Only by his sense of entitlement, which he now perceives as threatened by the movement towards workplace gender equality.

The economic landscape has changed dramatically and those changes have not necessarily been kind to most men. The great global expansion of the 1990s affected the top 20 percent of the labor force. There are fewer and fewer "big wheels." European countries have traded growth for high unemployment, which will mean that more and more men will feel as though they haven't made the grade, will feel damaged, injured, powerless. These are men who will need to demonstrate their masculinity all over again. And here come women into the workplace in unprecedented numbers. Just when men's economic breadwinner status is threatened, women appear on the scene as easy targets for men's anger—or versions of anger. Sexual harassment, for example, is a way to remind women that they are not yet equals in the workplace, that they really don't belong there.

It is also in our interests as men to begin to find a better balance of work and family life. There's a saying that "no man on his deathbed ever wished he had spent more time at the office." But remember the third rule of manhood: Be a Sturdy Oak. What has traditionally made men reliable in a crisis is also what makes us unavailable emotionally to others. We are increasingly finding that the very things that we thought would make us real men impoverish our relationships with other men and with our children. Fatherhood, friendship, partnership all require emotional resources that have been, traditionally, in short supply among men, resources such as patience, compassion, tenderness, attention to process.

In the US, men become more active fathers by "helping out" or by "pitching in"; they spend "quality time" with their children. But it is not "quality time" that will provide the deep intimate relationships that we say we want, either with our partners or with our children. It's quantity time— putting in those long, hard hours of thankless, unnoticed drudge—that creates the foundation of intimacy. Nurture is doing the unheralded tasks, like holding someone when they are sick, doing the laundry, the ironing, washing the dishes. After all, men are capable of being surgeons and chefs, so we must be able to learn how to sew and to cook.

Finally, let's examine the last rule of manhood: Give 'em Hell. What this says to men is: take risks, live dangerously. And this, of course, impacts most dramatically on our bodies, sex, health, and violence. Masculinity is the chief reason why men do not seek healthcare as often as women. Women perform self-exams, seek preventive screenings, and pay attention to diet, substance abuse, far more often than men. Why? As health researcher Will Courtenay writes: "A man who does gender correctly would be relatively unconcerned about his health and well-being in general. He would see himself as stronger, both physically and emotionally, than most women. He would think of himself as independent, not needing to be nurtured by others."[1] Or, as one Zimbabwean man put it, "real men don't get sick."[2]

Indeed. The ideas that we thought would make us "real men" are the very things that endanger our health. One researcher suggested slapping a warning label on us: Caution: Masculinity May Be Hazardous to Your Health. A study of adolescent males in the US [in the 1990s] found that adherence to traditional masculinity ideology was associated with being suspended from school, drinking, use of street drugs, having a high number of sexual partners, not using condoms, being picked up by the police, forcing someone to have sex.[3]

These gender-conforming behaviors increase boys' risk for HIV, STDs, early death by accident, injury, or homicide. It's no exaggeration to say that the spread of HIV is driven by masculinity. HIV risk reduction requires men to take responsibility by wearing condoms. But in many cultures ignoring the health risks to one's partner, eschewing birth control, and fathering many children are signs of masculine control and power.

Finally, let me turn to what may be the single greatest public health issue of all: violence. In the US, men and boys are responsible for 95 percent of all violent crimes. Every day 12 boys and young men commit suicide—7 times the number of girls. Every day, 18 boys and young men die from homicide—10 times the number of girls. From an early age, boys learn that violence is not only an acceptable form of conflict resolution but one that is admired. Four times more teenage boys than girls think fighting is appropriate when someone cuts into the front of a line. Half of all teenage boys get into a physical fight each year.

Violence has been part of the meaning of manhood, part of the way men have traditionally tested, demonstrated, and proved their manhood. Without another cultural mechanism by which young boys can come to think of themselves as men, they've eagerly embraced violence as a way to become men. It would be a major undertaking to enumerate all the health consequences that result from the equation of violence and masculinity.

And just as women are saying "yes" to their own sexual desires, there's an increased awareness of the problem of rape all over the world, especially of date and acquaintance rape. In one recent US study, 45 percent of all college women said that they had had some form of sexual contact against their will, and a full 25 percent had been pressed or forced to have sexual intercourse against their will. When one psychologist asked male undergraduates if they would commit rape if they were certain they could get away with it, almost 50 percent said they would. Nearly 20 years ago, anthropologist Peggy Reeves Sanday proposed a continuum of propensity to commit rape upon which all societies could be plotted—from "rape-prone" to "rape-free." (The US was ranked as a highly rape-prone society, far more than any country in Europe; Norway and Sweden were among the most rape-free.) Sanday found that the single best predictors of rape-proneness were

1. Whether the woman continued to own property in her own name after marriage, a measure of women's autonomy.

2. Father's involvement in child rearing, a measure of how valued parenting is and how valued women's work is.

So women's economic autonomy is a good predictor of their safety—as is men's participation in child rearing. If men act at home the way we say we want to act, women will be safer.

And the news gets better. A 1996 study of Swedish couples found positive health outcomes for wives, husbands, and children when the married couple adopted a partnership model in work-family balance issues. A recent study in the US found that men who shared housework and child care had better health, were happier in their marriages, reported fewer psychological distress symptoms, and—perhaps most important to them—had more sex! That's right, men who share housework have more sex. What could possibly be more in men's "interests" than that?

Another change that is beginning to erode some of those traditional "masculine" traits is the gradual mainstreaming of gay male culture. One of the surprise hit TV shows of the past year has been "Queer Eye for the Straight Guy." Imagine if, 10 years ago, there'd been a TV show in which five flamboyantly gay men showed up at a straight guy's house to go through his clothing, redo his house, and tell him, basically, that he hasn't a clue about how to be socially acceptable. The success of "Queer Eye" has been the partial collapse of homophobia among straight men. And the cause of that erosion is simple: straight women, who have begun to ask straight men: "Why can't you guys be more like gay guys?"

Rather than resisting the transformation of our lives that gender equality offers, I believe that we should embrace these changes, both because they offer us the possibilities of social and economic equality and because they also offer us the possibilities of richer, fuller, happier lives with our friends, with our lovers, with our partners, and with our children. We, as men, should support gender equality, both at work and at home. Not because it's right and just—although it is those things. But because of what it will do for us, as men.

The feminist transformation of society is a revolution-in-progress. For nearly two centuries, we men have met insecurity by frantically shoring up our privilege or by running away. These strategies have never brought us the security and the peace we have sought. Perhaps now, as men, we can stand with women and embrace the rest of this revolution—embrace it because of our sense of justice and fairness, embrace it for our children, our wives, our partners, and ourselves. Ninety years ago, the American writer Floyd Dell wrote an essay called "Feminism for Men." It's first line was this: "Feminism will make it possible for the first time for men to be free."

NOTES

1. W. H. Courtenay, "College Men's Health: An Overview and a Call to Action," *Journal of American College Health* 46, no. 6 (1998).
2. M. Foreman, ed., *AIDS and Men: Taking Risks or Taking Responsibility* (Zed Books, 1999).
3. J. H. Pleck, F. L. Sonenstein, and L. C. Ku, "Masculinity Ideology: Its Impact on Adolescent Males' Heterosexual Relationships," *Journal of Social Issues* 49, no. 3 (1993): 11–29.

R E A D I N G **64**

Maid to Order
The Politics of Other Women's Work

Barbara Ehrenreich

In line with growing class polarization, the classic posture of submission is making a stealthy comeback. "We scrub your floors the old-fashioned way," boasts the brochure from Merry Maids, the largest of the residential-cleaning services that have sprung up in the last two decades, "on our hands and knees." This is not a posture that independent "cleaning ladies" willingly assume—preferring, like most people who clean their own homes, the sponge mop wielded from a standing position. In her comprehensive 1999 guide to homemaking, *Home Comforts*, Cheryl Mendelson warns: "Never ask hired housecleaners to clean your floors on their hands and knees; the request is likely to be regarded as degrading." But in a society in which 40 percent of the wealth is owned by 1 percent of households while the bottom 20 percent reports negative assets, the degradation of others is readily purchased. Kneepads entered American political discourse as a tool of the sexually subservient, but employees of Merry Maids, The Maids International, and other corporate cleaning services spend hours every day on these kinky devices, wiping up the drippings of the affluent.

I spent three weeks in September 1999 as an employee of The Maids International in Portland, Maine, cleaning, along with my fellow team members, approximately sixty houses containing a total of about 250 scrubbable floors—bathrooms, kitchens, and entryways requiring the hands-and-knees treatment. It's a different world down there below knee level, one that few adults voluntarily enter. Here you find elaborate dust structures held together by a scaffolding of dog hair; dried bits of pasta glued to the floor by their sauce; the congealed remains of gravies, jellies, contraceptive creams, vomit, and urine. Sometimes, too, you encounter some fragment of a human being: a child's legs, stamping by in disgust because the maids are still present when he gets home from school; more commonly, the

Joan & David–clad feet and electrolyzed calves of the female homeowner. Look up and you may find this person staring at you, arms folded, in anticipation of an overlooked stain. In rare instances she may try to help in some vague, symbolic way, by moving the cockatoo's cage, for example, or apologizing for the leaves shed by a miniature indoor tree. Mostly, though, she will not see you at all and may even sit down with her mail at a table in the very room you are cleaning, where she would remain completely unaware of your existence unless you were to crawl under that table and start gnawing away at her ankles.

Housework, as you may recall from the feminist theories of the Sixties and Seventies, was supposed to be the great equalizer of women. Whatever else women did—jobs, school, child care—we also did housework, and if there were some women who hired others to do it for them, they seemed too privileged and rare to include in the theoretical calculus. All women were workers, and the home was their workplace—unpaid and unsupervised, to be sure, but a workplace no less than the offices and factories men repaired to every morning. If men thought of the home as a site of leisure and recreation—a "haven in a heartless world"—this was to ignore the invisible female proletariat that kept it cozy and humming. We were on the march now, or so we imagined, united against a society that devalued our labor even as it waxed mawkish over "the family" and "the home." Shoulder to shoulder and arm in arm, women were finally getting up off the floor.

In the most eye-catching elaboration of the home-as-workplace theme, Marxist feminists Maria Rosa Dallacosta and Selma James proposed in 1972 that the home was in fact an economically productive and significant workplace, an extension of the actual factory, since housework served to "reproduce the labor power" of others, particularly men. The male worker would hardly be in shape to punch in for his shift, after all, if some woman had not fed him, laundered his clothes, and cared for the children who were his contribu-

tion to the next generation of workers. If the home was a quasi-industrial workplace staffed by women for the ultimate benefit of the capitalists, then it followed that "wages for housework" was the obvious demand.

But when most American feminists, Marxist or otherwise, asked the Marxist question *cui bono?* they tended to come up with a far simpler answer—men. If women were the domestic proletariat, then men made up the class of domestic exploiters, free to lounge while their mates scrubbed. In consciousness-raising groups, we railed against husbands and boyfriends who refused to pick up after themselves, who were unaware of housework at all, unless of course it hadn't been done. The "dropped socks," left by a man for a woman to gather up and launder, joined lipstick and spike heels as emblems of gender oppression. And if, somewhere, a man had actually dropped a sock in the calm expectation that his wife would retrieve it, it was a sock heard round the world. Wherever second-wave feminism took root, battles broke out between lovers and spouses over sticky countertops, piled-up laundry, and whose turn it was to do the dishes.

The radical new idea was that housework was not only a relationship between a woman and a dust bunny or an unmade bed; it also defined a relationship between human beings, typically husbands and wives. This represented a marked departure from the more conservative Betty Friedan, who, in *The Feminine Mystique*, had never thought to enter the male sex into the equation, as either part of the housework problem or part of an eventual solution. She raged against a society that consigned its educated women to what she saw as essentially janitorial chores, beneath "the abilities of a woman of average or normal human intelligence," and, according to unidentified studies she cited, "peculiarly suited to the capacities of feeble-minded girls." But men are virtually exempt from housework in *The Feminine Mystique*—why drag them down too? At one point she even disparages a "Mrs. G.," who "somehow couldn't get her housework done before her husband came home at night and was so tired then that he had to do it." Educated women would just have to become more efficient so that housework could no longer "expand to fill the time available."

Or they could hire other women to do it—an option approved by Friedan in *The Feminine Mystique* as well as by the National Organization for Women [NOW], which she had helped launch. At the 1973 congressional hearings on whether to extend the Fair Labor Standards Act to household workers, NOW testified on the affirmative side, arguing that improved wages and working conditions would attract more women to the field, and offering the seemingly self-contradictory prediction that "the demand for household help inside the home will continue to increase as more women seek occupations outside the home." One NOW member added, on a personal note: "Like many young women today, I am in school in order to develop a rewarding career for myself. I also have a home to run and can fully conceive of the need for household help as my free time at home becomes more and more restricted. Women know [that] housework is dirty, tedious work, and they are willing to pay to have it done. . . ." On the aspirations of the women paid to do it, assuming that at least some of them were bright enough to entertain a few, neither Friedan nor these members of NOW had, at the time, a word to say.

So the insight that distinguished the more radical, post-Friedan cohort of feminists was that when we talk about housework, we are really talking, yet again, about power. Housework was not degrading because it was manual labor, as Friedan thought, but because it was embedded in degrading relationships and inevitably served to reinforce them. To make a mess that another person will have to deal with—the dropped socks, the toothpaste sprayed on the bathroom mirror, the dirty dishes left from a late-night snack—is to exert domination in one of its more silent and intimate forms. One person's arrogance—or indifference, or hurry—becomes another person's occasion for toil. And when the person who is cleaned up after is consistently male, while the person who cleans up is consistently female, you

have a formula for reproducing male domination from one generation to the next.

Hence the feminist perception of housework as one more way by which men exploit women or, more neutrally stated, as "a symbolic enactment of gender relations." An early German women's liberation cartoon depicted a woman scrubbing on her hands and knees while her husband, apparently excited by this pose, approaches from behind, unzipping his fly. Hence, too, the second-wave feminists' revulsion at the hiring of maids, especially when they were women of color: At a feminist conference I attended in 1980, poet Audre Lorde chose to insult the all-too-white audience by accusing them of being present only because they had black housekeepers to look after their children at home. She had the wrong crowd; most of the assembled radical feminists would no sooner have employed a black maid than they would have attached Confederate flag stickers to the rear windows of their cars. But accusations like hers, repeated in countless conferences and meetings, reinforced our rejection of the servant option. There already were at least two able-bodied adults in the average home—a man and a woman—and the hope was that, after a few initial skirmishes, they would learn to share the housework graciously.

A couple of decades later, however, the average household still falls far short of that goal. True, women do less housework than they did before the feminist revolution and the rise of the two-income family: down from an average of 30 hours per week in 1965 to 17.5 hours in 1995, according to a July 1999 study by the University of Maryland. Some of that decline reflects a relaxation of standards rather than a redistribution of chores; women still do two thirds of whatever housework—including bill paying, pet care, tidying, and lawn care—gets done. The inequity is sharpest for the most despised of household chores, cleaning: in the thirty years between 1965 and 1995, men increased the time they spent scrubbing, vacuuming, and sweeping by 240 percent—all the way up to 1.7 hours per week—while women decreased their cleaning time by only 7 percent, to 6.7 hours per week. The averages conceal a variety of arrangements, of course, from minutely negotiated sharing to the most clichéd division of labor, as described by one woman to the *Washington Post:* "I take care of the inside, he takes care of the outside." But perhaps the most disturbing finding is that almost the entire increase in male participation took place between the 1970s and the mid-1980s. Fifteen years after the apparent cessation of hostilities, it is probably not too soon to announce the score: in the "chore wars" of the Seventies and Eighties, women gained a little ground, but overall, and after a few strategic concessions, men won.

Enter then, the cleaning lady as *dea ex machina,* restoring tranquillity as well as order to the home. Marriage counselors recommend her as an alternative to squabbling, as do many within the cleaning industry itself. A Chicago cleaning woman quotes one of her clients as saying that if she gives up the service, "my husband and I will be divorced in six months." When the trend toward hiring out was just beginning to take off, in 1988, the owner of a Merry Maids franchise in Arlington, Massachusetts, told the *Christian Science Monitor,* "I kid some women. I say, 'We even save marriages. In this new eighties period you expect more from the male partner, but very often you don't get the cooperation you would like to have. The alternative is to pay somebody to come in. . . .' " Another Merry Maids franchise owner has learned to capitalize more directly on housework-related spats; he closes between 30 and 35 percent of his sales by making follow-up calls Saturday mornings, which is "prime time for arguing over the fact that the house is a mess." The micro-defeat of feminism in the household opened a new door for women, only this time it was the servants' entrance.

In 1999, somewhere between 14 and 18 percent of households employed an outsider to do the cleaning, and the numbers have been rising dramatically. Mediamark Research reports a 53 percent increase, between 1995 and 1999, in the number of households using a hired cleaner or service once a month or more, and Maritz Marketing finds that 30 percent of the people who hired help in 1999 did so for the first time that

year. Among my middle-class, professional women friends and acquaintances, including some who made important contributions to the early feminist analysis of housework, the employment of a maid is now nearly universal. This sudden emergence of a servant class is consistent with what some economists have called the "Brazilianization" of the American economy: We are dividing along the lines of traditional Latin American societies—into a tiny overclass and a huge underclass, with the latter available to perform intimate household services for the former. Or, to put it another way, the home, or at least the affluent home, is finally becoming what radical feminists in the Seventies only imagined it was—a true "workplace" for women and a tiny, though increasingly visible, part of the capitalist economy. And the question is: As the home becomes a workplace for someone else, is it still a place where you would want to live?

. . .

The trend toward outsourcing the work of the home seems, at the moment, unstoppable. Two hundred years ago women often manufactured soap, candles, cloth, and clothing in their own homes, and the complaints of some women at the turn of the twentieth century that they had been "robbed by the removal of creative work" from the home sound pointlessly reactionary today. Not only have the skilled crafts, like sewing and cooking from scratch, left the home but many of the "white collar" tasks are on their way out, too. For a fee, new firms such as the San Francisco–based Les Concierges and Cross It Off Your List in Manhattan will pick up dry cleaning, baby-sit pets, buy groceries, deliver dinner, even do the Christmas shopping. With other firms and individuals offering to buy your clothes, organize your financial files, straighten out your closets, and wait around in your home for the plumber to show up, why would anyone want to hold on to the toilet cleaning?

Absent a major souring of the economy, there is every reason to think that Americans will become increasingly reliant on paid housekeepers and that this reliance will extend ever further down into the middle class. For one thing, the "time bind" on working parents shows no sign of loosening; people are willing to work longer hours at the office to pay for the people—housecleaners and baby-sitters—who are filling in for them at home. Children, once a handy source of household help, are now off at soccer practice or SAT prep classes; grandmother has relocated to a warmer climate or taken up a second career. Furthermore, despite the fact that people spend less time at home than ever, the square footage of new homes swelled by 33 percent between 1975 and 1998, to include "family rooms," home entertainment rooms, home offices, bedrooms, and often bathrooms for each family member. By the third quarter of 1999, 17 percent of new homes were larger than 3,000 square feet, which is usually considered the size threshold for household help, or the point at which a house becomes unmanageable to the people who live in it.

One more trend impels people to hire outside help, according to cleaning experts such as Aslett and Mendelson: fewer Americans know how to clean or even to "straighten up." I hear this from professional women defending their decision to hire a maid: "I'm just not very good at it myself" or "I wouldn't really know where to begin." Since most of us learn to clean from our parents (usually our mothers), any diminution of cleaning skills is transmitted from one generation to another, like a gene that can, in the appropriate environment, turn out to be disabling or lethal. Upper-middle-class children raised in the servant economy of the Nineties are bound to grow up as domestically incompetent as their parents and no less dependent on people to clean up after them. Mendelson sees this as a metaphysical loss, a "matter of no longer being physically centered in your environment." Having cleaned the rooms of many overly privileged teenagers in my stint with The Maids, I think the problem is a little more urgent than that. The American overclass is raising a generation of young people who will, without constant assistance, suffocate in their own detritus.

If there are moral losses, too, as Americans increasingly rely on paid household help, no one has been tactless enough to raise them. Almost everything we buy, after all, is the product of some other person's suffering and miserably underpaid labor. I clean my own house (though—full disclosure—I recently hired someone else to ready it for a short-term tenant), but I can hardly claim purity in any other area of consumption. I buy my jeans at The Gap, which is reputed to subcontract to sweatshops. I tend to favor decorative objects no doubt ripped off, by their purveyors, from scantily paid Third World craftspersons. Like everyone else, I eat salad greens just picked by migrant farm workers, some of them possibly children. And so on. We can try to minimize the pain that goes into feeding, clothing, and otherwise provisioning ourselves—by observing boycotts, checking for a union label, etc.—but there is no way to avoid it altogether without living in the wilderness on berries. Why should housework, among all the goods and services we consume, arouse any special angst?

And it does, as I have found in conversations with liberal-minded employers of maids, perhaps because we all sense that there are ways in which housework is different from other products and services. First, in its inevitable proximity to the activities that compose "private" life. The home that becomes a workplace for other people remains a home, even when that workplace has been minutely regulated by the corporate cleaning chains. Someone who has no qualms about purchasing rugs woven by child slaves in India or coffee picked by impoverished peasants in Guatemala might still hesitate to tell dinner guests that, surprisingly enough, his or her lovely home doubles as a sweatshop during the day. You can eschew the chain cleaning services of course, hire an independent cleaner at a generous hourly wage, and even encourage, at least in spirit, the unionization of the housecleaning industry. But this does not change the fact that someone is working in your home at a job she would almost certainly never have chosen for herself—if she'd had a college education, for example, or a little better luck along the way—and the place where she works, however enthusiastically or resentfully, is the same as the place where you sleep.

It is also the place where your children are raised, and what they learn pretty quickly is that some people are less worthy than others. Even better wages and working conditions won't erase the hierarchy between an employer and his or her domestic help, because the help is usually there only because the employer has "something better" to do with her time, as one report on the growth of cleaning services puts it, not noticing the obvious implication that the cleaning person herself has nothing better to do with her time. In a merely middle-class home, the message may be reinforced by a warning to the children that that's what they'll end up doing if they don't try harder in school. Housework, as radical feminists once proposed, defines a human relationship and, when unequally divided among social groups, reinforces preexisting inequalities. Dirt, in other words, tends to attach to the people who remove it—"garbagemen" and "cleaning ladies." Or, as cleaning entrepreneur Don Aslett told me with some bitterness—and this is a successful man, chairman of the board of an industrial cleaning service and frequent television guest—"The whole mentality out there is that if you clean, you're a scumball."

One of the "better" things employers of maids often want to do with their time is, of course, spend it with their children. But an underlying problem with post-nineteenth-century child-raising, as Deirdre English and I argued in our book *For Her Own Good* years ago, is precisely that it is unmoored in any kind of purposeful pursuit. Once "parenting" meant instructing the children in necessary chores; today it's more likely to center on one-sided conversations beginning with "So how was school today?" No one wants to put the kids to work again weeding and stitching; but in the void that is the modern home, relationships with children are often strained. A little "low-quality time" spent washing dishes or folding clothes together can provide a comfortable space for confidences—and give a child the dignity of knowing that he or she is a participant in, and not just the product of, the work of the home.

There is another lesson the servant economy teaches its beneficiaries and, most troubling, the

children among them. To be cleaned up after is to achieve a certain magical weightlessness and immateriality. Almost everyone complains about violent video games, but paid housecleaning has the same consequence-abolishing effect: you blast the villain into a mist of blood droplets and move right along; you drop the socks knowing they will eventually levitate, laundered and folded, back to their normal dwelling place. The result is a kind of virtual existence, in which the trail of litter that follows you seems to evaporate all by itself. Spill syrup on the floor and the cleaning person will scrub it off when she comes on Wednesday. Leave *The Wall Street Journal* scattered around your airplane seat and the flight attendants will deal with it after you've deplaned. Spray toxins into the atmosphere from your factory's smokestacks and they will be filtered out eventually by the lungs of the breathing public. A servant economy breeds callousness and solipsism in the served, and it does so all the more effectively when the service is performed close up and routinely in the place where they live and reproduce.

Individual situations vary, of course, in ways that elude blanket judgment. Some people—the elderly and disabled, parents of new babies, asthmatics who require an allergen-free environment—may well need help performing what nursing-home staff call the "ADLs," or activities of daily living, and no shame should be attached to their dependency. In a more generous social order, housekeeping services would be subsidized for those who have health-related reasons to need them—a measure that would generate a surfeit of new jobs for the low-skilled people who now clean the homes of the affluent. And in a less-gender-divided social order, husbands and boyfriends would more readily do their share of the chores.

However we resolve the issue in our individual homes, the moral challenge is, put simply, to make work visible again: not only the scrubbing and vacuuming but all the hoeing, stacking, hammering, drilling, bending, and lifting that goes into creating and maintaining a livable habitat. In an ever more economically unequal culture, where so many of the affluent devote their lives to such ghostly pursuits as stock-trading, image-making, and opinion-polling, real work—in the old-fashioned sense of labor that engages hand as well as eye, that tires the body and directly alters the physical world—tends to vanish from sight. The feminists of my generation tried to bring some of it into the light of day, but, like busy professional women fleeing the house in the morning, they left the project unfinished, the debate broken off in midsentence, the noble intentions unfulfilled. Sooner or later, someone else will have to finish the job.

R E A D I N G **65**

Globalization and Its Discontents

Evelyn Hu-DeHart

. . .

Nothing illustrates the relationship between the transnational U.S. corporation and Asian capital and labor better than Phil Knight's Nike, Inc. The very establishment newspaper *The Washington Post* charges that "no other company symbolizes the mobilization of American companies overseas more than Nike, Inc. Its thirty-year history in Asia is as close as any one company's story can be to the history of globalization, to the spread of dollars—and marks, and yen—into the poor corners of the earth."[1] Simply put, during the 1970s and 1980s Knight discovered that new computer and fax technology enabled him to export and control the production of his brand-name athletic shoes in Asian countries, where cheap, largely female, labor abounded. By the time he closed down his last U.S. sneaker plants in New Hampshire and Maine, he had discovered the virtues of out-sourcing production. He subcontracted with Asian entrepreneurs from the more affluent Asian countries, such as Taiwan, South Korea, and Hong Kong, to set up assembly plants to manufacture Nike shoes in poorer, and thus labor-cheap, Asian countries such as China, Indonesia, and Vietnam. The subcontractors did all the work of recruiting, training, and disciplining workers, monitoring production, setting wages, and paying workers—in short, handling all aspects of management-labor relations. These Asian subcontractors also took care of dealing with Asian host governments and local officials, greasing palms when necessary. One of Asia's most successful subcontractors was the Tsai family of Hong Kong, whose ninety-seven production lines employing fifty-four thousand workers in China's Pearl River Delta produced forty-five million sneakers in 1995 for Reebok and Adidas, as well as Nike.[2] For a long period of time, the subcontracting system allowed Nike to argue that it had no direct supervision over Asian plants, thus should be absolved from dealing with any problems arising from labor or government relations.

In this global production system, profits are good for the subcontractors, but they are really phenomenal for Nike owner Phil Knight. To expand the worldwide demand for Nike sneakers, he enlisted the alliance of National Basketball Association (NBA) Commissioner David Stern, global media mogul Rupert Murdoch, and most importantly, basketball superstar Michael Jordan. With $20 million in yearly endorsement fees from Knight, Jordan spread his impressive American game to the rest of the world while simultaneously selling the Nike shoes that seemingly propelled him to unparalleled heights. Knight became the sixth wealthiest man in the United States, and Jordan became the most successful global pitchman, but their profits and fame were founded on the labor of legions of faceless, nameless Asian girls and women.

. . .

When this global production system first evolved, Knight was rather guileless in explaining his huge profits: "We were . . . good at keeping our manufacturing costs down," he said.[3] How low? In 1992, four Indonesian plants owned by South Korean subcontractors paid young girls as little as $.15 an hour for an eleven-hour day. A pair of shoes that cost less than $5 to make in Asia sold for $150 in the United States.[4] By the late 1990s, Indonesian factories made 70 million pairs of Nike shoes with twenty-five thousand workers, each of them receiving daily wages of $2.23, which covered only 90 percent of basic subsistence needs for one person. Their combined yearly wages did not equal Jordan's endorsement fee.[5] Wages in Vietnam were even lower, at $1.60 for an eight-hour day in 1997.[6]

The Nike shoe captures the essence of the new global consumer product: A particular model can be designed in Nike headquarters in Oregon, and cooperatively developed by technicians in Oregon, South Korea, and Indonesia by putting together fifty-two separate parts made in five countries. It is manufactured by young women hunched over machines and hand tools and glue, working in factories located in Vietnam, Indonesia, or China and owned by someone from Taiwan or Hongkong.[7] Then it is sold all over the world.

In sum, globalization in late capitalism changes relations of production, marked by a labor strategy that stresses minimizing cost and maximizing flexibility. . . . Somewhat amazingly, global capital and production in continuous and relentless search for cheap labor, manufacturing flexibility, and spatial mobility have come full circle: The global assembly plant employing low-skilled, low-cost female labor can now be found in abundance in the global core—the United States itself—in the form of hundreds of garment sweatshops scattered throughout southern California, the San Francisco–Oakland area, and in and around New York's garment district and Chinatown.[8] Although clothing manufacturing has

constituted a mainstay of the Mexican *maquiladoras* and fly-by-night assembly plants set up in export-processing zones by Asian subcontractors in the Caribbean, Central America, and all over Asia, the fast-changing designs and fluctuating market demands of the garment business has dictated the need to produce certain styles and quantities of garments close to the retailers, manufacturers, and consumers in the United States. New Asian and Latino immigrants (legal and undocumented) quickly meet the needs both for subcontractors and for workers, doing the same work they would in their home countries had they not migrated to the United States. Nike and other American manufacturers are reluctant to claim responsibility for labor problems in their Asian production, and they have a similar policy at home, arguing they have no control over their subcontractors who own and operate the sweatshops.[9]

While hidden for years from the American consuming public and the media, the revived American sweatshop is no longer a secret, and its exposure is helping to fuel the antiglobalization movement. The raid on the El Monte, California, underground sweatshop in August 1995 freed sixty-seven women and five men, Thai workers smuggled into the country by the Thai-Chinese owners who contracted with several well-known U.S. brand-name manufacturers. Paid only $1.60 per hour, these workers were kept in a modern version of indentured servitude, denied their freedom to leave the barbed-wire compound, forced to pay off their passage, and threatened with retribution against family members back home and rape if they disobeyed their captors.[10] In January 1999, the media exposed another shameful sweatshop situation that resembled El Monte. Hundreds of sweatshops owned by Asians and Asian American subcontractors were found in the U.S. Pacific territory of Saipan, where workers—predominantly young women from the Philippines, China, Thailand, and Bangladesh—worked twelve hours daily, seven days weekly, living seven to a room in "dreary barracks surrounded by inward-facing barbed wire."[11]

At the base of this system are the legions of immigrant women workers, Asian and Latina, who have seldom complained because they believe they have no other job options. In converting themselves into an available and flexible labor force almost immediately upon their arrival in the United States, they have enabled the garment industry to keep a critical part of garment production within the United States, right in the manufacturing and retail centers of New York and Los Angeles, where most of these immigrants settle. Those immigrant women absorbed into garment work likely have little formal education and little or no English-language skills, and are deemed to be low-skilled in other areas as well. Research has shown that deficiencies in education and English-language skills are also the most critical factors in determining immigrant job options in the United States.[12] Many women are compelled to work to supplement family incomes because their equally low-skilled, English-deficient spouses also work in low-paying, often dead-end jobs. It would be wrong to dismiss their contribution to family income as merely "supplementary," for many women earn as much as, if not more than, their equally trapped partners.[13] Furthermore, with both partners stuck in these low-wage, dead-end, often seasonal jobs, poverty for many such immigrant families has become a permanent fact of life.[14]

In addition to manufacturing, immigrant women workers from Asia and Latin America are desired in the global core for what might be termed "social reproductive labor."[15] Whether working in domestic, cleaning, janitorial, or food service, or in nursing home or child care, or as prostitutes, sex workers, or mail- or internet-order brides, Third World immigrant women are not just making a living in low-paying, low-status, often demeaning niches that require little English or other skills. In a very crucial way, they, too, are part of the new transnational division of labor, albeit in a less visible and certainly far less acknowledged way. Their paid labor now replaces the previously unremunerated responsibilities of First World women in the social reproduction of daily and family life, both on a daily and intergenerational basis, by relieving professional First World women of much of the burden of the "second

shift." Such social reproductive labor has always been associated with women's work and continues to be debased and devalued when "industrialized," that is, performed for payment by Third World women for their largely white and affluent First World "sisters" in a racial division of labor.[16] In sum, "Most white middle class women could hire another woman—a recent immigrant, a working class woman, a woman of color, or all these—to perform much of the hard labor of household tasks," as they fulfill themselves in careers outside the home.[17] To put it bluntly, the "private sphere" responsibilities of class-privileged women are thereby transferred to racially and socially subordinate women.[18]

Although sex work across national boundaries is not new in the world, sex industries have greatly expanded under late capitalist globalization.[19] Preference for Asian women as sex partners—paid or even unpaid, as in the case of military and mail- or internet-order brides—by many American men dates back to the days of America's serial military involvement in Asia, from WW II, through the Korean War, and on to the Vietnam War. "Militarized prostitution" developed around all army bases in Asia while American soldiers on furlough for "rest and relaxation" stimulated the development and growth of sex tourism to countries far beyond the battlegrounds, such as in Thailand.[20] Just as American transnational capital has constructed Third World women as particularly adept at garment assembly work—both "over there" and after migration to the United States—so have American men fetishized these same women as particularly seductive as girlfriends and attentive and submissive as wives, uncorrupted by Western feminist ideas and values. As in Asia, sex work has greatly expanded in the Caribbean as an extension of the lucrative tourist industry, feeding off the familiar, unequal relationships between First and Third World nations.[21]

. . . Is globalization only about property rights, or should it also be concerned about human rights?[22] Obviously, there are real winners, or else wealthy corporations and individuals backed up by their powerful governments would not be pushing so aggressively and relentlessly for global policies and regulatory bodies such as the WTO and MAI, but do there have to be legions of permanent losers? These are some of the compelling questions that have galvanized protesters from Chiapas to Seattle to Washington, D.C., who have forced onto the world stage the dark side of globalization.[23] The following are some of the issues and contradictions raised by globalization and its discontents, illustrated by the scenarios described above:

1. Corporate-led globalization depends on intense exploitation of labor, especially *female labor*, exacerbated by the subcontracting system that answers to the logic of a race to the bottom of the wage scale.

To win a contract, the subcontractor must submit the lowest bid, then squeezes the workers to make his profit. Thus, Vietnamese workers in factories under contract to Nike and similar U.S. transnational corporations do not even make a living wage, defined as enough to buy three meals a day, let alone pay rent, health care, and support for a family.[24] Subcontracting works in a particularly oppressive way in the garment industry worldwide, whether in Asia, Mexico, Central America, the Caribbean, or the United States itself. Thus, the antisweatshop movement on college campuses correctly focuses its pressure on the manufacturers and not primarily on the Asian subcontractors, because they understand that U.S. manufacturers pocket the lion's share of profits and call the shots.[25]

The biggest losers in this global assembly line are women—Latina and Asian women—characterized as inherently, innately, and naturally suited for the kind of low-skill labor in light manufacturing, whether in Third World export-processing factories or U.S. electronic assembly plants and sweatshops. This "myth of nimble fingers"—a purely ideological construct—is nothing less than rationalization for low wages, not to mention justification for the perpetuation of the notion of Third World women's intellectual inferiority. It is not just the gendered quality of the international division of labor that is so problematic, but that the gendered division is inferred

and inscribed as a permanent hierarchy that is further reinforced by race, class, and nationality differences, as well as denial of immigration and citizenship rights in the case of the smuggled and undocumented.[26]

We are compelled to conclude that Third World women in their home countries and after migration to the United States comprise one continuum in the same gendered, transnational workforce that lies at the base of the extremely exploitative and oppressive global subcontracting system of production.[27] Whether she works in a Nike plant subcontracted to a Taiwanese factory owner in Indonesia or Vietnam, or as a contract worker in an Asian-owned Saipan factory, or in an unregistered, unlicensed underground sweatshop in Los Angeles operated by a Korean immigrant, or in a union shop in New York's Chinatown owned by a newly naturalized Chinese American, she may well be sewing the same style of garment for the same manufacturer, affixing the same name-brand label on the same finished product. How ironic it is that with all its "supposed modernity and wondrous technologies," the "manic logic of capitalism" has reproduced all the old barbarisms associated with early twentieth-century capitalism.[28]

2. Increased trade spurred on by decreased regulation and removal of all barriers does not necessarily produce better jobs.

If anything, removal of regulations only serves to increase the power of the wealthier nations of the North over the poorer nations of the South, which often feel they have little choice but to go along with the dictates of the IMF, the World Bank, the WTO, and, in our hemisphere, NAFTA, and the powerful governments that stand behind these global organizations and policies. Thus, if unregulated, global free trade as we now know it will disproportionately benefit the already wealthy nations to the great disadvantage of the poor nations, enabling a few corporations and individuals to become obscenely rich while furthering the misery of the world's multitudinous poor. Many new studies have demonstrated the growing gap *between* and *within* nations, with the United States providing a notable example of both kinds of inequalities.[29] As some critics point out, contrary to the World Bank's bald assertion that accelerated globalization has produced greater world equality, far from lifting all boats, the rising tide of globalization is "only lifting yachts"![30] Today, the world's richest two hundred people have more wealth than 41 percent of the world's humanity.[31] Increasing the world's productive capacities may be a good thing for all, but it must be accompanied by a broader distribution of wealth.[32]

3. Thus, it cannot be argued that globalization is natural and inevitable, and produces general progress for all.

Rather, it should be made clear that globalization and the global finance system is a "man-made artifact," in the inimitable words of critic William Greider, one of the most trenchant and lucid critics of corporate globalization. It is defined as, "a political regime devised over many years by interested parties to serve their ends," and if man made it, Greider concludes, then man can very well undo it, "because nothing in nature or, for that matter, in economics requires the rest of us to accept a system that is so unjust and mindlessly destructive."[33] In short, globalization is not an inevitable force of history, "but rather the consequence of public policy choices."[34] This is precisely what protesters . . . are demanding of their governments and international organizations behind globalization, and of their university administrators: Make *different* public policy choices. Societies and citizens must act to counter the "destructive social convulsions" sown by the unregulated or deregulated market forces of finance capital through so-called free trade, irresponsible investment, speculative lending, and environmental degradation.[35]

4. Immigrants are not only *not* a drain on the U.S. economy, but an absolute necessity.

Why, then, has nativism or anti-immigrant hysteria accompanied globalization in the United States and in other parts of the global core, such as Australia and Japan? Immigrant labor is indispensable for the labor-intensive, service-dependent economy of the United States, as well as the resurgent sweatshops of the light-manufacturing sector.[36] Lately, well-educated and professionally-trained immigrant labor is also in great demand in the computer programming sector of the American Silicon Valley.[37] The primary role of the INS is not to stop the flow of immigration to the United States but to regulate the level of that flow and to control the type of immigrants who come in at any given time. In other words, rather than unregulate and deregulate immigration, as is the case with finance capital and trade in manufactured goods, the United States wants to regulate and control the free trade of labor in order to keep wages down and unions out, and thereby protect their high corporate profits, although higher wages and strong unions would ensure a broader distribution of wealth in an expanding world economy.

. . .

Greider argues passionately that a productive world economy need not produce widespread misery that results from persistent and gross injustices.[38] While public pressure coming from demonstrations across the nation can succeed in uncovering the veil of secrecy surrounding the instruments of corporate globalization and imposing some measure of corporate responsibility on sweatshops, these tactics can only reduce a few of the worst abuses. Ultimately, these protests and their proposed remedies illustrate the conventional liberal argument that globalization is good, just curb its excesses; moreover, it's inevitable, so mend it, don't end it. Former Clinton Labor Secretary Robert Reich expands on this liberal perspective: "The challenge for those of us who believe that free trade and global capital are essentially good things if managed correctly is to avoid the backlash by developing progressive strategies to overcome the widening inequalities and the environmental depredations."[39]

Finally, some protesters and critics of globalization urge us to question the fundamental class relationship between this globalized working class and global capital, interrogate the supposed logic and rationality of the global assembly line, and resist accepting the inevitability of corporate-driven globalization or the permanency of the grossly unequal North-South divide. Our protests and critiques must seek answers to these more fundamental and vexing questions, not just negotiate remedies for abuses and excesses in the existing relationship between workers and capital in the global economy.[40]

NOTES

1. Quoted by Walter LaFeber in *Michael Jordan and the New Global Capitalism* (New York: W. W. Norton, 1999), 102.
2. LaFeber, *Michael Jordan,* 106.
3. LaFeber, *Michael Jordan,* 104.
4. Thuyen Nguyen, "Nike in Asia: This Is Prosperity?" letter, *Wall Street Journal,* June 4, 1997, A19; and LaFeber, *Michael Jordan,* 105.
5. Nguyen, "Nike in Asia"; and LaFeber, *Michael Jordan,* 147.
6. Bob Herbert, "The Sweatshop Lives," *New York Times,* December 28, 1994, A13, "Brutality in Vietnam: Grim Conditions in Nike's Factories," *New York Times,* March 28, 1997, A19, and "Nike's Boot Camps," *New York Times,* March 31, 1994, A11; LaFeber, *Michael Jordan,* 148; and Julie Schmit, "Nike's Image Problem," *USA Today,* October 4, 1999, B1.
7. LaFeber, *Michael Jordan,* 147.
8. Xiaolan Bao, *Holding Up More than Half the Sky: Chinese Women Garment Workers in New York City, 1948–92* (Urbana: University of Illinois Press, 2001); Center for Economic and Social Rights (CESR), "Treated Like Slaves: Donna Karan, Inc. Violates Women Workers' Human Rights" (Brooklyn, N.Y.: CESR, 1999); Evelyn Hu-Dehart, "Women, Work, and Globalization in Late 20th Century Capitalism: Asian Women Immigrants in the U.S.," Working Papers Series (Pullman: Department of Comparative American Cultures, Washington State University, 1999); and Miriam Ching Yoon Louie, *Sweatshop Warriors: Immigrant Women Workers Take on the Global Factory* (Cambridge, Mass.: South End Press, 2001).
9. Bao, *Holding Up More than Half the Sky;* and Louie, *Sweatshop Warriors.*
10. Julie Su, "El Monte Thai Garment Workers: Slave Sweatshop," in *No Sweat: Fashion, Free Trade, and the Rights of Garment Workers,* ed. Andrew Ross (New York: Verso, 1997), 143–50.
11. *Sweatshop Watch Newsletter* (http://sweatshopwatch.org) 1:1 (1995), 4:1 (1998), and 5:1 (1999); and Steven Greenhouse, "18 Mayan Retailers and Apparel Makers Are Accused of Using Sweatshops," *New York Times,* January 14, 1999, A9.
12. International Ladies Garment Workers' Union (ILGWU), *The Chinatown Garment Industry Study* (New York: ILGWU, 1983), 116; and Fung-Yea Huang, *Asian and Hispanic Immigrant Women in the Work Force: Implications of the United States Immigration Policies Since 1965* (New York: Garland, 1965), 28.
13. Morrison G. Won, "Chinese Sweatshops in the United States: A Look at the Garment Industry," in *Peripheral Workers,* ed. Ida Harper Simpson and Richard L. Simpson. *Research in the Sociology of Work* 2 (1983): 267–79.
14. Dean S. Toji and James H. Johnson, "The Working Poor and the Jobless Poor: Asians and Pacific Islander American Poverty," *Amerasia Journal* 18:1 (1992): 83–91.
15. Grace Chang, *Disposable Domestic: Immigrant Women Workers in the Global Economy* (Cambridge, Mass.: South End Press, 2000); Evelyn Nakana Glenn, "From Servitude to Service Work: Historical Continuities in the Racial Division of Paid Reproductive Labor," *Signs: Journal of Women in Culture and Society* 18:1 (1992): 1–43; Pierrette Hondagneu-Sotelo, *Doméstica: Immigrant Workers Cleaning and Caring in the Shadows of Affluence* (Berkeley: University of California Press, 2001); and Rhacel Salazar Parreñas, *Servants of Globalization: Women, Migration and Domestic Work* (Stanford, Calif.: Stanford University Press, 2001).
16. Milyoung Cho, "Overcoming Our Legacy as Cheap Labor, Scabs, and Model Minorities: Asian Activists Fight for Community Empowerment," in *The State of Asian America: Activism and Resistance in the 1990s,* ed. Karin Aguilar-San Juan (Boston, Mass.: South End Press, 1994), 253–73; Glenn, "From Servitude to Service Work"; Saski Sassen-Koob, "Notes on the Incorporation of Third World Women into Wage Labor Through Immigration and Off-Shore Production," *International Migration Review* 18:4 (1984): 1144–67; and Thanh-Dam Truong, "Gender, International Migration and Social Reproduction: Implications for Theory, Policy, Research and Networking," *Asian and Pacific Migration Journal* 5:1 (1996): 27–52.
17. Phyllis Palmer, quoted in Glenn, "From Servitude to Service Work," 7.
18. Parreñas, *Servants of Globalization.*

19. Kamala Kempadoo and Jo Doezema, eds., *Global Sex Workers: Rights, Resistance, and Redefinition* (New York: Routledge, 1998).

20. Alexandra Suh, "Military Prostitution in Asia and the U.S.," in *States of Confinement: Policing, Detention, and Prisons,* ed. Joy James (New York: St. Martin's Press, 2000), 144–58.

21. Kamala Kempadoo, ed., *Sun, Sex, and Gold: Tourism and Sex Work in the Caribbean* (Lanham, Maryland: Rowman and Littlefield, 1999).

22. Robert Kuttner, "The Seattle Protesters Got It Right," *Business Week,* December 20, 1999, 25.

23. Sarah Anderson and John Cavanagh, "Ten Myths About Globalization," *The Nation,* December 6, 1999, 26–27.

24. Nguyen, "Nike in Asia."

25. Richard Appelbaum and Edna Bonacich, "Choosing Sides in the Campaign Against Sweatshops: The Key Is Enhancing the Power of Workers," *The Chronicle of Higher Education,* April 7, 2000, B4; Mary Beth Marklein, "Making Them Sweat: Students Step Up Pressure to Hold Colleges Acountable for Apparel," *USA Today,* April 13, 2000, 19; David Moberg, "Getting Schooled: Students Are Making Manufacturers Sweat," *In These Times,* December 12, 1999, 20–21; and Martin Van der Werf, "Sweatshop Protests Raise Ethical and Practical Issues," *The Chronicle of Higher Education,* March 5, 1999, 38.

26. Laura Hyun Yi Kang, "Si(gh)ting Asian/American Women as Transnational Labor," *Positions* 5:2 (1997): 403–37.

27. Center for Economic and Social Rights, "Treated Like Slaves"; and Peter Passell, "Unskilled Workers' Short End of the Stick Getting Shorter," *New York Times,* June 14, 1998, A8, reprinted from the *San Francisco Examiner.*

28. William Greider, *One World, Ready or Not: The Manic Logic of Global Capitalism* (New York: Simon & Schuster, 1997), 337–41.

29. William Macklin, "Wealth Distribution Concerns Analysts: Rise of Billionaires in U.S. Frustrates Some Working-Class Citizens," *Sunday Camera* [Boulder], April 30, 2000, 11A; and Mary Williams Walsh, "Latinos Get Left Out of Economic Boom," *Daily Camera* [Boulder], March 25, 2000, 14A, reprinted from the *Los Angeles Times.*

30. "Global Monoculture," paid advertisement, *New York Times,* November 15, 1999, A7.

31. Robert L. Borosage, "The Battle in Seattle," *The Nation,* December 6, 1999, 20.

32. William Greider, "Global Warning. Curbing the Free-Trade Free Fall," *The Nation,* January 13/20, 1997, 11–17.

33. William Greider, "Time to Rein In Global Finance," *The Nation,* December 6, 1999, 11–17.

34. Ethan B. Kapstein, *Sharing the Wealth: Workers and the World Economy* (New York: W. W. Norton, 1999), 8.

35. Greider, "Time to Rein In Global Finance," 12; and Nicholas Kristof and David E. Sanger, "How U.S. Wooed Asia to Let Cash Flow In," *New York Times,* February 16, 1999, A1.

36. Harold Meyerson, "Liberalism with a New Accent: Immigrants Are Helping to Create a Dynamic, Globally Focused Movement," *The Nation,* October 11, 1999, 15–20.

37. William Branigan, "Visa Program, High-Tech Workers Exploited," *The Washington Post,* July 26, 1998, A1; and Marc Cooper, "Class War at Silicon Valley," *The Nation,* May 27, 1996, 11–16.

38. Greider, "Time to Rein In Global Finance."

39. As quoted in Doug Henwood, "Whose Trade?" *The Nation,* December 6, 1999, 17.

40. Walden Bello, "The End of the Asian Miracle," *The Nation,* January 12/19, 1998, 16–21; William Greider, "Saving the Global Economy," *The Nation,* December 15, 1997, 11–16, "The Global Crisis Deepens: Now What?" *The Nation,* October 19, 1998, 11–16, and "AFL-CIO Goes Global"; Kapstein, *Sharing the Wealth;* and E. San Juan Jr., *Beyond Postcolonial Theory* (New York: St. Martin's Press, 1998).

What Wal-Mart Women Want

Ellen Hawkes

The yellow smiley-face logo of Wal-Mart Stores Inc. isn't looking happy these days, not with the huge gender discrimination lawsuit now pending in federal court against the world's largest retail company. Consider some of the allegations that have been filed by current and former female employees (and, no, this is not one of *Ms.* magazine's "No Comment" columns):

- A former district manager was called "our little Mexican princess."
- A male supervisor explained lower pay for women by stating, "Men are here to make a career and women aren't. . . . [H]ousewives just need to earn extra money."
- A woman seeking advancement was told, "You aren't part of the boy's club, and you should raise a family and stay in the kitchen."
- Female employees were subjected to comments like: Women "should be barefoot and pregnant"; they "should be at home with a bun in the oven"; "God made Adam first so women would always be second to men."
- Executives assert that men are "more aggressive" in working for advancement and that to do more to promote women would lead to "lowering standards."
- One former employee claimed that she was forced to attend lunch meetings at Hooters. (Wal-Mart's executive vice-president for people defended this practice by noting that the restaurant was "one of the best places to meet and eat" in town.) Another woman reported that she had to accompany male managers to strip clubs during business trips. (Some Wal-Mart managers confirmed that they "regularly go to strip clubs while attending annual sales meetings.") Also,

women complained that a stripper performed at a store meeting to celebrate a store manager's birthday.

These are only a sampling of complaints from the more than 110 declarations submitted as evidence in the lawsuit against the company that employs more women than any other U.S. firm. First filed in June 2001 on behalf of six plaintiffs in the U.S. District Court in San Francisco, *Dukes v. Wal-Mart Stores Inc.* could become the most extensive discrimination litigation in history—if federal judge Martin Jenkins grants it "class action" status, thereby allowing every former and current female employee of Wal-Mart from December 1998 through the date of the case's resolution to join the suit. If certified, the class action would include an estimated 1.5 million women. (By contrast, Home Depot's $104 million settlement of its gender discrimination suit, while denying any wrongdoing, covered 25,000 women.)

While the experiences recounted in these declarations are startling, the basis of the plaintiffs' case is their experts' statistical, economic, and sociological analyses of the personnel data that the court ordered disclosed during discovery—an unprecedented release of Wal-Mart's Bentonville, Ark., "Home Office" records that minutely track its 3,400 U.S. stores as part of the successful and much-admired organizational structure the late Sam Walton established to create the "Wal-Mart Way."

According to statistician Richard Drogin's study of these records, in 2001 women constituted 65 percent of Wal-Mart's hourly employees but made up only 34.5 percent of its managers and 15 percent of its executive ranks. (Economist Marc Bendick determined that in 20 comparable retail companies, 57 percent of store managers are women; Wal-Mart's 2001 percentage of female managers, he found, was even lower than the 38 percent average of comparable retailers in 1975.) Drogin also concluded that the hourly pay rate of Wal-Mart women employees was on average $1.16 lower than that of male counterparts, and in 2001 women were paid an average of $1,150 less per year than men. Even the pay of those women promoted to management, he asserted, was about $16,400 less per year than men's. (For further details on these employment statistics, see www.walmartclass.com.)

Although Wal-Mart brags that it promotes "from within," Drogin found that before the lawsuit was filed, over 80 percent of promotion opportunities were not posted, and women received 2,891 fewer promotions than would be expected statistically from the general pool of hourly employees. He also noted that despite a lower rate of turnover and higher performance evaluations, women waited an average of 4.38 years to be promoted, compared to 2.86 years for men.

San Francisco attorney Steve Stemerman, of Davis, Cowell & Bowe (one of the six law firms, three private and three nonprofit, representing the plaintiffs), explained that until 2003, Wal-Mart had provided no system by which hourly employees could apply to the management-training program, the required first step to enter management ranks. "Instead, supervisors chose employees arbitrarily, essentially by a 'tap on the shoulder,'" he said. "Because district and regional managers are left to their own discretion and apply their subjective views, the system is vulnerable to the sexist attitudes that seem pervasive in the organization."

Jocelyn Larkin, a co-counsel from the Impact Fund, the Berkeley, Calif., public-interest legal foundation that is coordinating the case, agreed that Wal-Mart's own insistence on its corporate culture combined with managers' discretionary decisions created the disparities throughout the system. "During our yearlong investigation, we found that Wal-Mart has the kind of employment practices that allow and encourage the use of negative gender stereotypes," she said. "Our statistical evidence overwhelmingly shows a systemic pattern

of discrimination, and that is the major criterion for being certified as a class-action case."

It was reading excerpts from the women's stories in a magazine last year that prompted Carolyn Sapp, Miss America 1992 and the founder of Safe Places for Abused Women and Children, a nonprofit organization dealing with issues of domestic violence, to become a spokesperson for the plaintiffs and to launch her Web site (WalmartVersusWomen.com) to bring more attention to the case. "I saw the connection to my own work on domestic abuse immediately," she said. "What Wal-Mart has been doing to its female employees may not be physical, but it's certainly economic abuse. The company is holding women down and making them feel they're not good enough." Sapp is now organizing rallies of support across the country and has filmed a television commercial to urge more Wal-Mart women to come forward.

Wal-Mart has vigorously denied the allegations and is mounting an aggressive campaign in its defense. When asked about the allegations made by the plaintiffs, Mona Williams, vice president of communications for Wal-Mart, conceded that there may have been some random incidents involving men she has described as "knuckleheads." Nevertheless, she defends some of the executives' behavior. "To understand it, you have to understand the Wal-Mart culture. Still, I can see that to the outside world it might look otherwise," she says.

While Wal-Mart filed positive declarations from a number of its female employees (its "success stories"), the crux of its Opposition Brief is the statistical analysis of personnel records done by its expert, Dr. Joan Haworth, whose findings directly contradict those of the plaintiffs' experts. For example, she concluded that while only 10 percent of Wal-Mart stores showed statistically significant disparities in pay and promotion, males were favored only in some stores, while females were favored in others. She also found that after the company began posting openings for assistant manager trainees in 2003, the percentage of female applicants rose only 2 percent, from 41 to 43 percent.

In its brief, Wal-Mart explains that female hourly employees are less likely to apply for management trainee positions than their male counterparts because of the longer hours, night and weekend shifts without overtime compensation, and relocations that are often required. But it also could be argued that such corporate demands disadvantage women as well.

Williams insists: "Wal-Mart selects, even over-selects, women for promotion to management. Still, I admit, while we'd already begun rolling out systems for posting promotions, this lawsuit probably did speed the process up."

As part of its defense, Wal-Mart not surprisingly disparages the women who have brought the lawsuit (its Opposition Brief refers to the "Plaintiffs' histrionics") and claims that several were denied promotions for "legitimate reasons," such as "rule infractions" and "poor attitudes." But the company's main attack is two-pronged: First, the brief argues that the plaintiffs do not meet the criterion of "typicality" or "communality"

required for a class-action case. Second, it asserts that even if the plaintiffs were deemed to represent a class, the sheer size of the estimated 1.5 million women and the potential monetary settlement does not satisfy the federal court's requirement of "manageability" to proceed as a class action.

Indeed, the case could involve billions of dollars, since the plaintiffs are seeking substantial injunctive relief, back pay for the class as a whole, and punitive damages.

Yet the plaintiffs and their attorneys often reiterate that this case is not about money but about changing the Wal-Mart culture and the way it treats women. Indeed, if the plaintiffs are allowed to proceed as a class-action suit . . . and are then able to convince a jury that the company systematically discriminates against women, you may eventually hear the sound of glass ceilings shattering at Wal-Mart stores across the country.

R E A D I N G **67**

Power Plays
Six Ways the Male Corporate Elite Keeps Women Out

Martha Burk

Males, much more so than females, are conditioned almost from birth to view the world in terms of hierarchies, power relationships, and being winners.

In the business world, many symbols of power are built into the system, like merit badges in the Boy Scouts. In the early days of a career, power could get you an office with a window, later the corner office or the reserved parking space. As the career progresses, the badges change; they're now the high-priced car, the $2,000 suit, the right club membership, fatter cigars, better brandy, the bigger expense account, and blonder, younger, thinner women. At the CEO level, corporate jets,

unlimited expense accounts, a phalanx of "yes men," and obscenely high salaries and stock options are the norm.

So how can your average billionaire CEO deal-maker wring one more shred of superiority and one-upmanship out of this situation? He gets something money can't buy—such as belonging to a golf club that is so exclusive you can't apply for membership. And once you've got this thing, boy, are you reluctant to give it up.

When groups achieve a certain level of power and influence, sometimes their original purpose is subverted in favor of holding on to the status and the exclusivity that the group has achieved.

Within that particular sphere, they are a *power elite*. And if the power sphere happens to be business related and male dominated, that's where the problem comes in for working women.

The power dynamic manifests itself in a number of ways:

Power re-creates itself in its own image. Psychologists have long known that we're most comfortable with people who are like us, both in appearance and ways of thinking. It has been well documented that managers like to hire people who look like themselves. In most of corporate America, that still means white and male. That's why laws against employment discrimination were passed in the first place—women and minority men just weren't on the radar screens of the folks doing the hiring and promoting. The so-called neutral processes in corporations were firmly enforcing a white-male quota system. That is still true—most companies have "diversity" in management only to the extent that it does not threaten the traditional balance.

Despite claims by some that women and minority men have taken all the jobs, the results of this recreation process are fairly easy to see, even from casual observation. The numbers speak for themselves—and the higher you go in the hierarchy, the greater the enforcement of traditional quotas in favor of the dominant group. In most companies, there will be a fair number of women and minority men in the rank and file, fewer at lower management, and still fewer at middle management. At the very top level of the Fortune 500, there are only nine female CEOs. Even in companies like Citigroup, where *women* are a 56 percent majority overall, *men* hold 56 percent of the "officials and managers" jobs. There is only one female top executive. She is paid 50 percent of the average for men at her level.

Power elites enforce norms and systems that guarantee continued power. At the highest levels of business, the board of directors is a major enforcer of the status quo—in both its own makeup and that of the top management of the company.

Consider what happens when an individual is chosen to be on a corporate board for the first time. He (or in rare cases, she) is usually nominated by the CEO or someone already on the board, and brought into a new environment with its own culture and skill set. The nominator has an interest in seeing this individual succeed, as it will reflect well on his judgment and business acumen. The newcomer, at the same time, wants to belong, wants to overcome any notion that he is unworthy or an impostor. So the new member is "trained" through mentoring and role modeling, quickly picking up on the board culture and the behavior and knowledge necessary to succeed.

It is not hard for the new individual to figure out what is expected. Boat rockers don't last as board members. So for a person in the minority (a woman or a man of color) there is actually a disincentive to advocate bringing others like herself into the circle, as she is likely to be accused of "pushing an agenda" and not behaving like a "team player."

Power creates a sense of entitlement. Most men at some level know that maleness is valued over femaleness in the culture, and we are all taught in subtle ways that males have first claim on jobs, sports, and opportunities. (Women of color are the first to admit their brothers are sexist, too.) But for the ordinary man, the cultural valuation of all things male does not translate into the sense of super-entitlement that corporate power elites exhibit. That comes from a corporate system where value is placed on its leaders that is far out of proportion to their actual worth.

Consider CEO pay. In 2003 the average CEO pay in large companies was more than 300 times that of the average worker (up from 42-to-1 in 1982). The rise in compensation for the top dogs outstripped rises in inflation, profits, and the S&P 500. Conservative journalist Robert Samuelson had this to say: "The scandal of CEO pay is not that it ascended to stratospheric levels . . . [but that] so few CEOs have publicly raised their voices in criticism or rebuke. . . . [T]here's a widespread self-serving silence. If they can't defend what they're doing, then maybe what they're doing is indefensible."

These words could as easily have applied to the controversy over membership in Augusta National Golf Club. CEOs did not raise their voices against the club's exclusion of women; there was a conspiracy of self-serving silence. It was obvious they believed themselves exempt from society's standards against discrimination, immune to criticism from the public or discipline from their companies, even in the face of employee unrest and questions at stockholder meetings.

Power creates invulnerability, leading to a flaunting of society's standards. As individuals become more powerful, they are increasingly surrounded by others whose job they control and who tell them how clever, smart, and right they are. Power elites are also increasingly insulated from the sanctions that ordinary people are subject to when they misbehave. In fact, breaking the rules to get where you are is excused as nothing more than hard-nosed business, shrewd politics, or the result of occupational pressure.

We've seen this again and again as sports and entertainment figures get a pass on cocaine possession or beating up their girlfriends, politicians get a pass on dallying with interns or taking "contributions" that result in big government contracts, and executives who lose billions and squander the retirements of thousands of workers get a slap on the wrist as they jump out of harm's way with the aid of their "golden parachutes."

Loyalty to power overshadows other loyalties, including gender and race. Statistics show that when it comes to income, black men gain more from being male than they lose from being black, particularly at high levels. It is also well known in business that after women reach a certain level, they are less likely to want to help other women advance. Two dynamics are likely at work here. As association with a certain group conveys more power, individuals begin to identify more with that group and less with other groups to which they belong. They also seek personal validation by the power group (almost everyone feels like an impostor at some level—women more so than men). In the business world this means behaving

like the others. Holding on to the power—and gaining more of it—inevitably becomes more important than loyalty to what is now a less important group. Since the power group in corporate America is still overwhelmingly male and white, the less important group in the woman executive's case is other women.

In the majority male's case, however, the power group aligns perfectly with his race and gender group. So these loyalties, far from being lessened, are actually reinforced. He doesn't have to make a choice between his race and/or gender group and the power elite—he doesn't even have to think about it. When he promotes a member of his group up the executive ranks, or proposes a new board member who is not only like him but like the majority, he is never accused of "pushing an agenda." His candidate's credentials are never questioned because the nomination may be the result of a "special interest" mentality. In fact, it's the opposite; his nomination is seen as merely "normal." So not only is his choice reinforced, but also *his entitlement to make that particular choice.*

Group loyalty combined with power can trump good judgment and override individual moral codes. All Americans, male and female, are inculcated with a strong value for loyalty to one's group. In the great majority of cases, group loyalty is a good thing. It fosters team spirit for athletics, cohesiveness in military units, productivity in business, and dedication to the public good in community service organizations. But most of us know "loyalty" is perverted when it serves a purpose counter to society's values. While we might stay in a group even if it occasionally took a stand we disagreed with, we wouldn't remain if the group stood for something society condemns (like discrimination) or if it conspired to break the law.

At the extremes, group loyalty can go terribly wrong. It can facilitate lawlessness under the cover of secrecy and lead to group actions and cover-ups of those actions that group members would never consider as individuals. Examples can range from illegal accounting schemes to harmful and sometimes fatal hazing by fraternity brothers, to gang rapes (too often by athletic team members), military atrocities, and terrorism. It is probably no accident that most of the excesses occur in male-dominated or exclusively male groups.

Obviously the average man does not participate in illegal, immoral, or harmful group actions. But the average man (much more so than the average woman) has been exposed, again and again, to the code of loyalty to a group that can lead to actions that are not in his best interests, nor in the best interests of society. It's about living in a culture that links masculinity to power, dominance and control. In everyday life it might never affect most, because they're not faced with the stark choice of taking a stand and doing what's right versus betraying an unspoken loyalty oath to the "brotherhood of men."

Women encounter these situations, too—it's just that they have not been conditioned to group allegiance in the same way, or to the same degree, that men have. It is also very rare that we hear of group actions by women that are comparable to fraternity hazings or gang rapes. But not necessarily because women are genetically predisposed to being kinder and gentler human beings, as many would argue. If women had had the same power, status, and conditioning that men have had over the centuries, we might see parallels in female group behavior. But these "antecedent conditions" have not existed historically, and they still don't exist, even in the most advanced societies. So we'll have to leave the genetic arguments to another planet or to another 10 millenia in the future.

R E A D I N G   **68**

"Hey, Why Don't You Wear a Shorter Skirt?"
Structural Vulnerability and the Organization of Sexual Harassment in Temporary Clerical Employment

Jackie Krasas Rogers and Kevin D. Henson

SEXUAL HARASSMENT IN THE WORKPLACE

A large portion of the social research devoted to sexual harassment has focused on documenting the extent of sexual harassment: what percentage of women are sexually harassed (MacKinnon 1979); which women are sexually harassed and in what jobs (Carothers and Crull 1984); and who are the harassers (Gruber and Bjorn 1982; Gutek 1985). Other research categorizes types of sexual harassment (Fitzgerald 1990; MacKinnon 1979), delineates responses to sexual harassment (Gruber 1989; Maypole 1986), determines who labels which experiences as sexual harassment (Giuffre and Williams 1994; Schneider 1982), and asks the question "What factors contribute to sexual

harassment?" Answers to this question have included sex-role spillover (Gutek 1985; Ragins and Scandura 1995), patriarchy (MacKinnon 1979), and compulsory heterosexuality (Giuffre and Williams 1994; Schneider 1982, 1985).

Gutek (1985) describes sexual harassment as a result of the inappropriate spillover of gender roles to the work environment. Sex-role spillover theory, while still widely employed in some fields such as social psychology, assumes that organizations are gender-neutral, asexual environments; gender and sexuality are "smuggled" into organizations by gendered workers. Women workers, in this light, are seen as women first, workers second. In female-dominated jobs, feminine role attributes such as nurturance and (hetero)sexuality spill over into the workplace. When combined with a workplace that emphasizes sexuality, men who interact with women in female-dominated jobs take on the sexual aggressor role, and the result is often sexual harassment.

There are several problems with spillover theory, most of which derive from critiques of sex-role theory in general (Connell 1987; Segal 1990). A sex role is conceptualized as something that exists outside work, a characteristic of individuals, and spills over inappropriately to the workplace. Therefore, sexual harassment is a matter of unprofessional or inappropriate behavior of individuals in the workplace. Organizational responsibility for sexual harassment, then, extends only to punishing the occasional harasser. Consequently, sex-role spillover theory identifies the sex ratio of an occupation as a key contributing factor; jobs that are highly sex segregated are fertile ground for sexual harassment.

However, gender and sexuality construct and are constructed by work relations (see, for example, Acker 1990; Hall 1993; Hochschild 1983; Lorber 1994; Pierce 1995). . . . Schneider (1982, 1985) notes how workers are obligated to enact female receptivity to heterosexual advances, which, in conjunction with their relative lack of power in the work context, creates sexual harassment. . . . A fruitful analysis would use a labor process theory approach to gendered organizations (see West 1990) including a systematic analysis of power and control in the employment relationship as it derives from and results in gender inequality.

In this light, sexual harassment is about the control of women workers, of women as workers and workers as women. Sexual harassment is about particular constructions of gender, especially organizational imperatives to "do gender" in a particular manner (Lorber 1994; West and Zimmerman 1987). Many have implicitly if not explicitly recognized the role of asymmetrical power relations in creating sexual harassment (Fiske and Glicke 1995; Gutek 1985; MacKinnon 1979).

This research explores a form of employment that ties together these themes. Temporary work-

ers are a growing, highly feminized, and relatively powerless group in today's workplace. In the office, temporary workers are often treated as nonpersons, as passive recipients of orders (Henson 1996; Rogers 1995b), much like wait persons or even children. They find themselves interactionally invisible as they do inconspicuous work in conspicuous places, such as filing for hours in a busy hallway (Rogers 1995b). In addition, temporary workers are generally considered to hold the lowest rank in the office, as they are given work and orders by supervisors and coworkers alike. In fact, it is not unusual for permanent coworkers to participate in "dumping" undesirable work on temporary employees (Henson 1996; Rogers forthcoming).

While their low status leaves temporary workers open for many types of workplace abuse, the transitory nature of much temporary work further intensifies this vulnerability. Temporary workers report that people seldom remember their names (referring to them simply as "the temp"), isolate them from office sociability, and often treat them as a piece of furniture (Henson 1996; Rogers 1995b). Thus, temporary workers are objectified and stripped of their personhood, paving the way for poor treatment, including sexual harassment.

Understanding the interplay of gender, sexuality, and power as it relates to the organization of temporary work will enable us to gain a better understanding of some of the shortcomings in theories of sexual harassment. We address the sexual harassment of these workers and attempt to locate structural influences that affect their workplace experience as well as their opportunities for resistance. . . .

It is our contention that temporary work arrangements create an environment that both fosters and tolerates sexual harassment, frequently punishing the harassed rather than the harasser even to a greater extent than in traditional employment relationships. . . . [I]f we consider that temporaries are likely to have the lowest status in an office (virtually everyone is superior to a temporary worker) and to work in a largely female occupation (63 percent of all temporary workers are clerical), it is conceivable that they would be even more likely to be harassed than permanent workers.

METHOD

This research is based on in-depth interviews and extensive participant observation from two broader studies on temporary clerical work. One of the studies was conducted in Chicago in 1990–91, while the other was conducted in Los Angeles in 1993–94. In these studies, the subject of sexual harassment was not initially included in the interview guides; both researchers, however, found it to be of concern to the interview subjects. As a research focus, sexual harassment was emergent from the data and gained in importance throughout the course of the research process. In both studies, the researcher questioned the interview subjects about their relationships with coworkers. For example, general questions such as "Who did you work with and what were those relationships like?" elicited stories of sexual harassment. . . . [A]pproximately 40 percent of the respondents found it troublesome enough to mention without being prompted to do so. It is likely that more direct questioning would have uncovered even more sexual harassment.

Together, these two studies yielded 68 in-depth interviews (35 in Chicago and 33 in Los Angeles) ranging from one to three hours in length. Interview subjects included temporary agency personnel and client company representatives, but the majority were temporary clerical workers. All interviews were tape-recorded, transcribed, coded, and analyzed. All names indicated in the body of this article are pseudonyms.

. . . Collectively, the interview subjects had worked in over 40 temporary agencies, with individual tenure in temporary employment ranging from a few months to over 10 years. The data represent a diverse group of African American, Latino, Asian American, and white men and women ranging in age from 20 to 60 years old. . . .

GENDERED WORKER IN A GENDERED JOB

The clerical sector of temporary employment, like the general full-time clerical sector, is predominantly composed of women (Bureau of Labor Statistics [BLS] 1995; Howe 1986). Historically, this association of temporary work with women's work was reflected in the common inclusion of the infantilizing term *girl* in the names of the earliest temporary agencies (e.g., Kelly Girl, Western Girl, Right Girl). While temporary agencies have formally modernized their names (i.e., Kelly Girl became Kelly Services), the continued popular usage of the outdated names accurately reflects the gendered composition of the temporary workforce. Although more men have been seeking employment through temporary agencies, particularly as industrial temporary workers (Parker 1994), they still make up a relatively small proportion of the clerical temporary workforce. Indeed, a recent survey by the National Association of Temporary Services (1992) estimated that 80 percent of member agency temporaries were women; Belous (1989) estimated that more than 64 percent of the entire temporary workforce are women, and more than 20 percent of the temporary workforce is Black. Furthermore, a recent government survey concluded that "workers paid by temporary agencies were more likely than workers in traditional arrangements to be women, young, and black" (BLS 1995, 4).

In fact, the gender composition of the temporary workforce leads to the expectation, often the assumption, that temporary workers (as secretaries) are women; the job, in other words, is gendered. . . . Furthermore, the feminized nature of the work is particularly highlighted when others fail to even recognize a male temporary as the secretary, mistaking him for someone with higher organizational status. . . .

The feminized nature of the job, shaped in part by sexualized cultural images of temporary workers, actually requires temporary workers to enact a particular construction of femaleness as part of the job. In addition, temporary agencies' demands for particular physical presentations and requirements for doing deference further highlight the gendered, racialized, and sexualized nature of temporary work.

DOING DIFFERENCE

West and Fenstermaker (1995) invoke the concept of *doing difference* to explain the production of social inequalities; some of their critics argue that the notion of doing difference, with its emphasis on interaction, obfuscates power relations and relegates structures of inequality to the realm of performance (Collins 1995). . . . We attempt here to forge some of these links through an empirical examination of the structures of inequality in temporary employment and the ways in which temporary workers' interactions are shaped by the gendered expectations of their clients, their agencies, and even themselves.

Although temporary agencies are legally required to operate under equal opportunity employer legislation (i.e., to hire workers without regard to race, sex, or age), temporaries are nevertheless often hired or placed for personal characteristics other than their jobs skills. Even some of the more specific and egregious requests (e.g., for a young, blond woman with great legs) are often honored. One temporary worker overheard the following exchange:

> One guy had gone through like five secretaries in that year and he had temps, different temps, every couple of weeks. And the office manager asked him if he wanted that temp back the following week because she had to contact the agency to arrange it. And I remember he looked out of his office and kind of looked at her legs and [said], "No, she's kind of on the heavy side." So that was it. (Ludy Martinez, 36-year-old Filipina American)

The temporary industry reinforces this emphasis on physical appearance. A 1986 study of the temporary industry reported a disproportionate emphasis on temporaries' physical appearance or "femininity"; a receptionist at one temporary agency reported filing "evaluation cards of temporary worker applicants that had comments like 'homely' and 'stunning' written on them with virtually no mention of office skills" (National Association of Working Women 1986, 28). Occasionally, . . . clients assert their right to control a temporary's personal appearance by filing a formal complaint with the agency. The agency then "counsels" the errant temporary about her or his appearance (or removes her or him from the job):

> And you're expected to dress like Christie Brinkley! Oh, it's ridiculous. I wear nice clean clothes. I'm clean. My body is clean. I have good breath. I mean, I try to look as good as I possibly can. So I get a call from the temp agency at home at seven thirty at night. . . . I was just mortified. Like, "What is it?!" I felt like I was on death row for temps! So she says, "Well, it seems that you're not dressing professionally enough. Laura gave me a call." And of course I feel horrible. (Helen Weinberg, 24-year-old white woman)

The demands for a particular gendered (even sexy) physical presentation are not freely chosen based on the personal tastes of the temporary worker; rather, they are recognized as a right of the employer (see also Hall 1993; Paules 1991).

The depoliticized managerial prerogative to control the appearance of temporary workers can also be used to justify racial bias in placing temporary workers.

> Nine out of ten times it's a little blond girl with colored eyes. Or somebody with an English accent. Nobody overweight. And if it's a person of color, she's gotta be drop-dead gorgeous. Not just pretty—drop-dead gorgeous. (Regina Mason, 44-year-old Latina)

"Gorgeous" women of color (those beautiful enough to be receptionists) must conform to white notions of female beauty.

Clients and temporary help service personnel also employ racialized notions about workers' capabilities: "articulate" workers are white. This racial logic (Hossfeld 1990) reproduces and naturalizes racial inequality.

I think "articulate" is a code word [for racial preference] that you can't ever really get called on. You can't say, "Oh you were discriminating." You were just telling them what you need. It's kind of a fine line. There's a lot of clients who are like that. Especially a lot for reception people. (Sonja Griffin, 31-year-old white woman)

Closely related is the tendency to assign back-office temporary assignments to women of color. This arrangement shapes interaction and then uses those very interactions to justify the view that people of color cannot "do" front-office work (i.e., white, middle-class sociability).

But there was one Black woman in our group. And she was sent to like way in the back room on some top floor. Which was not like the corporate floor or whatever. She was put in the back. And she said she gets a lot of crappy . . . gets asked to do things that she doesn't think other people would be asked to do. I was put up front. . . . And then there was a very large white woman who was there. And she, too, was sort of hidden in the back so people wouldn't see her. I'm no beauty queen. But they put me in front, I guess, because I was the white woman. (Helen Weinberg, 24-year-old white woman)

It quickly becomes apparent that the type of femininity one must do in temporary work is white, middle-class, heterosexual femininity. While certain exceptions are made, it is nearly impossible to do this brand of femininity if you are a woman of color. The consequences of the gendered/raced/classed organization of temporary work are a lower paid, back-office job or no job.

Men pose an especially interesting case concerning the gendered nature of temporary work. Their presence in female-dominated work has the potential to disrupt gender categories because men who are temporaries fail to live up to normative conceptions of masculinity by not having a "real job." Therefore, they risk gender assessment. One accommodation that underscores the gendered nature of temporary work is the popular construction of male temporaries as gay, which neither disrupts the essential nature of gender for the observer nor challenges the dominant/subordinate statuses of male/female. Male temporary workers, heterosexual and gay, were very aware of this construction. . . . As with other men who cross over into women's work (see also Pringle 1988; Williams 1989, 1995), male temporaries risk their status as "real" (or at least heterosexual) men. In everyday practice, these gender crossings are assumed to say more about the essential nature of the individual men than the gendered organization of the work.

Male temporary workers' individual failings, when faced with the gender assessment of others, do not stop with questioning their sexual orientation. In addition, their drive, motivation, and competence for (male) career success may be questioned—that is, these are dead-end jobs that no "self-respecting" man would accept. Ironically, the dead-end nature of these jobs is rarely seen as problematic for women.

I think men get a little less respect if they're temping. There's that expectation that they should be like career oriented and like moving up in the world and being a businessman and moving himself forward in business. Where women can do that but it's not an expectation. And so I think that, I think that's where that Kelly Girl image, that temporaries are women, is. I have noticed that there is a certain amount, looking down upon. I think that's true of temps in general. They're somewhat looked down upon. I think the men maybe more. (Albert Baxter, 31-year-old white man)

The discussions of male temporaries' masculinity highlight the gendered nature of the work as they struggle with maintaining masculinity in an organizational environment that requires doing femininity.

DOING DEFERENCE

Doing deference is a special case of doing gender that demonstrates how organizational imperatives shape interaction that becomes essentialized.

Temporaries, like many women workers, . . . are also expected to enact a submissive, deferential, even solicitous stance toward management, coworkers, and clients (Henson 1996). Indeed, temporary agencies demanded that their workers adopt a pleasing demeanor while on the client company's premises. Thus, the proper enactment of gender (even an institutionalized *job flirt* [see Hall 1993]) was conflated with proper job performance and monitored by the temporary agency.

Temporaries, like many service workers, were expected to smile whether or not they were particularly happy. . . . Indeed, temporary workers at an agency that one of the researchers worked through were instructed to think of themselves as guests rather than laborers engaged in a primarily economic transaction. . . . Drawing on their personal knowledge of behavior appropriate to a well-behaved guest, temporaries were reminded that a polite guest neither challenges nor otherwise risks offending his or her host.

This guest metaphor, however, also enforces passivity by rendering any complaining or self-assertion by temporary workers on assignment as inappropriate: "Please do . . . observe the hours, procedures, and work methods of the customers without criticism" (Right Temporaries, Inc. 1989). As the commercial nature of the relationship is obscured by the personal relations fiction, criticisms of the work, including those about abusive or disrespectful treatment, are defined as illegitimate. . . .

Being on one's best behavior, or doing good work, may be interpreted as responding to flirtatious behavior on the job, to perform a kind of job flirt (Hall 1993; MacKinnon 1979). . . . Mary LeMoine described putting up with the "flirtatious" (even harassing) behavior of a client on the job to be gracious:

> And then on the phone I've had men ask me out after talking to me. I'm a temporary. And they start talking to me. They start these entire conversations. I had one man at the bank offer to fly me to San Diego to spend the weekend with him. . . . I felt very bad about that because in my normal

situation . . . if someone called me at school and did that, if someone called me at home and did that . . . I wouldn't talk to you. You know, you have no place doing this to me. [*So why didn't you say that there?*] Because it was a bank. Because it was my job. And when I got home I felt very bad about it. I should have just said that anyway. I just kind of ignored it. And I don't think I handled it as well as I should have. (Mary LeMoine, 27-year-old white woman; emphasis added)

Temporary workers, in an effort to conform to the requirements of doing deference, may accept treatment on the job that they would not tolerate in another context.

The extent to which deference was conflated with proper job performance is highlighted by the negative reactions of male temporaries to these demands for subservience and its implicit threat to their sense of masculinity.

> It's a manly thing to be in charge. And men should want to be, supposedly in charge and delegating things. If you're a man and you're being delegated to, it somehow makes you less manly. You know what I'm saying? Whereas it seems to be okay for the person delegating to women. They seem to be okay with that relationship. And the women, maybe they're just projecting that to get by. It seems that they're more okay with that than men are. I guess I'm saying that it makes me feel less of the manly kind of qualities, like I'm in charge, you know. And men should be like takin' meetings and barking orders instead of just being subservient. (Harold Koenig, 29-year-old heterosexual white man)

. . .

Reviewing how the organization of temporary work operates in the daily work lives of temporaries provides us with the opportunity to evaluate the usefulness of sex-role spillover theories. In these examples, gendered (or sexualized) work behavior is not something temporaries freely choose to enact based on their own tastes and preferences. Rather, the low status of temporaries (as secretaries, but lower than secretaries) and the expectations of temporary agencies and clients (which quickly become job requirements) help shape temporary workers' interactions in such a way that their gender (and sexuality) is prominently featured as an aspect of the work. The emphasis placed on temporary workers' physical presentation as well as requirements for doing deference coincides with a particular construction of gender, including heterosexuality and whiteness.

. . . The organization of temporary work, in other words, helps create the gendered workplace. This theoretical stance resonates closely with the gendered organization perspective holding that gender is not something that comes from outside organizations but is constructed and reproduced within them (Acker 1990; Ferguson 1984; Lorber 1994; Williams 1995). Therefore, gendered work behavior (even that which results in sexual harassment) should be understood as constructed within and by gendered workplaces rather than the result of inappropriate sexrole spillover.

. . . We now turn to an analysis of the factors that constrain temporary workers in reporting sexual harassment and the range of temporary workers' responses to sexual harassment.

FACTORS THAT CONSTRAIN REPORTING: THE ORGANIZATION OF VULNERABILITY

The organization of temporary work has a tremendous impact on the extent to which temporary workers find opportunities for resistance. Chief among the organizational constraints are the institutionalization and magnification of asymmetrical power relationships between the agency, client, and temporary worker. These asymmetrical power relationships are exacerbated for temporary workers by the fear of downtime (i.e., inadequate income) and uncertainty about the actual scheduling practices of their agencies.

As employers, most temporary agencies tell their workers to report any kind of problem (such as sexual harassment) to the agency rather than handle it at the work site. At first glance this

would seem to benefit the temporary workers, and indeed there is that potential. However, temporary agencies are also supposed to represent the interests of their (paying) clients. One Los Angeles agency counselor, in fact, portrayed these relationships as completely "equal" and "fair": "You have an . . . allegiance not only to the person who's paying you, but you have an allegiance [and] a responsibility for the applicant that you're sending out" (Sandy Mathers, 28-year-old African American woman).

However, even the agencies themselves recognize that their "natural" alignment is with the client rather than the worker. . . . [A] temporary agency counselor who reported "going to bat" for his temporary felt constrained by the need to maintain client relationships: "But you have to be very careful. This one [incident], I didn't lose a client, but there's been others where you do lose a client" (Manny Avila, 28-year-old Latino). It is almost always easier to replace a complaining temporary worker than an offended client. Therefore, in almost all conflictual circumstances, the client company is favored. . . . Temporary workers are often very much aware of where their agency's interests lie and their own ultimate dispensability: "You don't have an alliance. If you're a temp you don't have an alliance. And I'm afraid if I complain [to my agency], they'll just throw me off the assignment" (Cindy Carson, 38-year-old white woman).

The agency and the client have tremendous power to determine the terms of work, and the relationship ranges from asymmetrical to unilateral. For example, while client companies enjoy staffing flexibility, terminating the assignment at will and often without notice, individual workers are often at the mercy of both their agency and client assignment supervisors (Henson 1996; Rogers 1995a). Neither the company nor the agency need justify these work schedule changes to temporary workers. In some cases, temporaries are replaced rather than just having the assignment cut short. They are seldom advised of the reason for such decisions and may, in fact, not even know that they were replaced.

Temporaries, then, willing and eager to work, often find themselves with time off instead, time off that can be financially catastrophic. This uncertain environment led temporaries to believe that any transgression they committed against their agency, including complaining about abusive treatment, would result in punishment—primarily work deprivation.

> I should have vocalized that [displeasure] more, but I didn't feel like I was really in a position to even say that. Because underneath it all is, if they get pissed at you, they can just not give you work and say, "Oh there's no jobs." (Don Birch, 24-year-old white man)

Temporary workers' fears regarding loss of access to work assignments were not mere paranoia. As we discovered, some temporary agencies do keep records of temporaries who declined assignments to better "direct" work flow. Indeed, one agency counselor said that she gave her temporary workers only "one strike" before they were no longer considered for assignments. The definition of a strike was considerably broad including lateness, asking for higher wages, or complaining about an assignment. More than one agency counselor said that they would not send out any "prima donnas," and this was defined as people who had complaints about any aspect of the job. . . .

. . . It was not uncommon for temporaries to report tolerating offensive jokes and patently hostile environments to maintain their "steady" assignments:

> I didn't walk out on it and I wish I would have. I was really strapped for money. And that was the office where everybody smoked. And everybody was like, I don't know how to put it . . . constantly making like racial jokes, sexist jokes. There was this guy who was like just this really sleazy sales guy. Like a stereotype. He wore like a plaid suit and slicked-back hair. He smoked a cigar. Hairbrush mustache. And he would come over and he'd just be so rude and so sexist. . . . And I was like, "Oh this is horrible! This is so humiliating! I can't take it anymore." But I stayed . . . I had to. Two weeks. It was a drag. (Pamela O'Connor, 26-year-old white woman)

Regardless of how unpleasant, any work is often better than no work at all to a temporary worker at the limits of his or her budget and without access to traditional social safety nets (e.g., unemployment benefits). As marginal workers with an unsteady flow of income from one week to the next, temporary workers feel financial constraints keenly and make decisions regarding their reactions to harassment in light of those constraints. Any behavior that has the real or perceived potential to displease the agency, including reporting legitimate problems with the assignment, is seen as putting the temporary's future prospects for work in jeopardy.

In this context, it is evident that the reporting of any difficulties, like sexual harassment, can work against a temporary worker's economic interests. . . .

DILEMMAS OF RESISTANCE

Not surprisingly, most women do not report incidents of sexual harassment. . . . This research draws on an institutional understanding of women's responses to sexual harassment, but more specifically, it examines how a particular organization of work configures power relations to the detriment of sexual harassment victims. Thus, we view the range of responses to sexual harassment as they are shaped by organizational constraints rather than as individual strategies or coping behaviors.

COMPLAIN TO THE AGENCY

Temporaries are instructed to bring any work-related problems, including sexual harassment, to the attention of their agency rather than the client company. The position of the agency, however, makes bringing complaints directly to the temporary counselors a risky move. Agencies' responses can range from support to passive complicity and even overt complicity:

> They flirt with the applicant . . . oh . . . sexual harassment. I've had applicants call me in tears

saying, "This man won't leave me alone. I don't know what to do. He's lookin' down my blouse. He wants to sit next to me and show me how to use the phone. I don't know what to do." Yeah, and it's difficult to say, "Well, grab your purse and leave." Because then your client's calling you and saying, "How dare you." [*What do you tell them?*] It all depends. It all depends. (Sandy Mathers, 28-year-old African American woman)

Agency representatives often infantilize the workers (Rogers 1995a), diminishing the significance of their complaints, their capability to read situations correctly, and their ability to take constructive action. They are seen as hysterical, overreacting, or oversensitive women....

Most temporary workers are keenly aware (or suspect) that their complaints will not be successfully mediated or dealt with by temporary agencies. Even if they have not experienced it directly, many temporaries are able to relay stories about those they know who were not supported by their agency.

With the allegiance of the agency more closely aligned with the client than the temporary worker, ... [w]hen they recast sexual harassment as flirting or a minor nuisance, they are clearly acting in the interests of their clients. The organization of the relationship among temporaries, clients, and agencies provides the impetus to downplay sexual harassment.

CONFRONT THE HARASSER

The most direct, but least used, avenue of recourse that the women we interviewed followed was to confront the harasser. Although only one woman reported this type of resistance, it is important to note because she was able to use her position as a higher paying executive temporary secretary as well as her personal connections to the temporary agency to her benefit:

I know one instance I had to tell the guy, "If you do that to me again, not only will your wife and human resources know, but I think I will have to

tell the chairman." ... I told the guy I was gonna tell his wife because she and I had become quite chatty friends on the phone. (Ludy Martinez, 36-year-old Filipina American)

In this case, the harassment stopped before the assignment ended.... Ludy was partly successful because this was a longer term executive secretarial assignment in which she had the opportunity to get to know her supervisor's wife and was able to use that relationship as a threat. Such opportunities for resistance are less likely to occur in the lower paying filing or data entry positions in which temporaries are more isolated. Even more important, at this assignment, Ludy was working through an agency managed and owned by a personal friend. This personal connection gave her more assurance that if she were to make a complaint, she would not be risking her job and the complaint would be taken seriously. However, Ludy's situation is unique, and as the exception, her experience further demonstrates the unequal alignment of power in temporary employment.

IGNORE THE HARASSER

The most common response of temporaries to sexual harassment, like other women workers, was to ignore the harasser, take no action at all, and put up with it (Gruber 1989; Schneider 1991). For example, Kara Wallace and Pamela O'Connor described experiencing patently offensive workplace behavior that many would define as hostile environment sexual harassment, yet they chose to reframe it as "nothing major":

Well, nobody actually physically ... sexual harassment like that. But I would always bump into, "Honey, Baby, Sweetheart." And that place that the sleazy sales guy was ... he would like come over and tell me dirty jokes and stuff. And I was like, "My life sucks" at that point. (Pamela O'Connor, 26-year-old white woman)

Particularly with verbal or hostile environment harassment, temporary workers were likely to ignore the harassment or fail to label it as sexual harassment at all.

Temporary workers who ignored the sexual harassment frequently explained their response (or lack thereof) in terms of the transitory nature of the work. In other words, while they noted that their temporary status may have contributed to or fostered the harassment, they also ignored it because "it's only temporary." The time required to file a complaint and procedurally follow through on it would exceed the time of the assignment:

> He'd say, "Hey, why don't you wear a shorter skirt and that would make it more interesting for us." And then later he offered me breakfast . . . and some other things. And I thought, you know, I just don't think this is the way I want to go. And it's because you're a temp. (Cheryl Hansen, 23-year-old white woman)
>
> There has been the usual harassment type stuff that they figure it's a temp. She'll be gone next week. And I didn't make the typical woman-type fuss . . . and that was due to temping more than anything else. . . . It wasn't worth my time filing a complaint anymore because I was a temp and I was gonna be out of there and could refuse to work for that man and everything. (Ludy Martinez, 36-year-old Filipina American)

By focusing on the short duration of the assignment, temporary workers downplay the meaning of sexual harassment. The result is that none of the women we interviewed filed a formal complaint about the sexual harassment they experienced on their assignments. These women's status as temporary seemed to work against filing a formal complaint. They felt that people would see them as making a big deal out of nothing or making the "typical woman-type fuss"; after all, it's only temporary.

While this strategy may help individual temporaries in individual situations, when we consider that several of our interview subjects were sexually harassed on a number of assignments, this strategy seldom works in the long run. . . . Being sexually harassed seems to be a routine part of being a temporary worker. Furthermore, chronic harassers have easy access to a supply of potential victims in the event the person they are harassing decides to leave the assignment.

ABANDON THE ASSIGNMENT OR AGENCY

One way that temporaries have resisted abusive treatment, including sexual harassment, is by finding an "acceptable" reason to leave or not renew a particular assignment. For instance, several of our subjects acknowledged that once they had a difficult assignment, they turned down further assignments at that company. . . . A second acceptable reason for refusing work was that they had something else to do other than work that week. Here, temporary workers play on the misconception that most temporaries are seeking flexible hours to combine either work and family or work and some other interest. . . . These strategies, however, can have serious financial repercussions for temporary workers who, contrary to industry propaganda, are unlikely to be working for pin money (Henson 1996; Martella 1991; Parker 1994). Furthermore, an unfortunate side effect of co-opting the flexibility myth is that it perpetuates the misconception.

Another avenue of recourse is for the temporary worker to move to another agency. . . . This strategy seems to be reserved for extreme circumstances because leaving one agency may require developing relationships with new agencies (Henson 1996; Rogers 1995a). . . . Once the switch is made, there is no guarantee that problems will not arise with the new agency since the structure of the relationships between temporary worker, agency, and client favors the link between the agency and the client.

CONCLUSIONS AND SUGGESTIONS

Temporary clerical work is a highly feminized and disempowering form of employment. The low status, depersonalization, and objectification of temporary workers fosters an environment in which poor treatment including sexual harassment is likely. The gendered (raced, classed, and even heterosexualized) organization of the work is highlighted in numerous ways. . . . Therefore, the metaphor of doing gender (or race or class) can speak to oppression and exploitation when combined with a gendered organizations approach. Similarly, sexual harassment can now be seen as an outgrowth of the organization of work rather than merely the result of individual actions or even sex-role spillover in the workplace.

Possibilities for resistance to sexual harassment are severely constrained (although not eliminated) as temporary clerical work shifts more power to the employers. Judith Lorber (1994) notes that economically marginal women and men cannot be the ones to solve the problem of constant sexual harassment. The temporary employment relationship creates marginal workers as it aligns the agencies' interests with the clients' interests while pushing the demands and rights of the worker into the background. In this environment, proving harassment, damages, or even that the agency had knowledge of the harassment becomes quite difficult. Many workers tolerate harassment or other abuses rather than risk losing access to future assignments and income through the agency.

. . . Temporaries must be provided with more power, through either industry regulation or worker-owned agencies, to address sexual harassment problems without fearing economic reprisals. Yet, this would not eliminate sexual harassment from temporaries' workplaces. Organizational imperatives to do gender contribute to the problems of sexual harassment, and at the same time, they naturalize and solidify inequalities.

REFERENCES

Acker, Joan. 1990. Hierarchies, jobs, bodies: A theory of gendered organizations. *Gender & Society* 4:139–58.

Belous, Richard S. 1989. *The contingent economy: The growth of the temporary, part-time and subcontracted workforce.* Washington, DC: National Planning Association.

Bureau of Labor Statistics (BLS). 1995. *Handbook of labor statistics.* Washington, DC: U.S. Government Printing Office.

Carothers, Suzanne C., and Peggy Crull. 1984. Contrasting sexual harassment in female- and male-dominated occupations. In *My troubles are going to have trouble with me,* edited by Karen Brodkin Sacks and Dorothy Remy. New Brunswick, NJ: Rutgers University Press.

Collins, Patricia Hill. 1995. Symposium on West and Fenstermaker's "Doing Difference." *Gender & Society* 4: 491–94.

Connell, R. W. 1987. *Gender and power.* Stanford, CA: Stanford University Press.

Ferguson, Kathy E. 1984. *The feminist case against bureaucracy.* Philadelphia: Temple University Press.

Fiske, Susan T., and Peter Glicke. 1995. Ambivalence and stereotypes cause sexual harassment: A theory with implications for organizational change. *Journal of Social Issues* 1: 97–115.

Fitzgerald, L. F. 1990. Sexual harassment: The definition and measurement of a construct. In *Ivory power: Sexual harassment on campus,* edited by M. A. Paludi. Albany: State University of New York Press.

Giuffre, Patti A., and Christine Williams. 1994. Boundary lines: Labeling sexual harassment in restaurants. *Gender & Society* 8: 378–401.

Gruber, James E. 1989. How women handle sexual harassment: A literature review. *Sociology and Social Research* 74 (October): 3–7.

Gruber, James E., and Lars Bjorn. 1982. Blue collar blues: The sexual harassment of women autoworkers. *Work and Occupations* 9: 271–98.

Gutek, Barbara. 1985. *Sex and the workplace: The impact of sexual behavior and harassment on women, men, and organizations.* San Francisco: Jossey-Bass.

Hall, Elaine J. 1993. Smiling, deferring, and flirting: Doing gender by giving "good service." *Work and Occupations* 20: 452–71.

Henson, Kevin D. 1996. *Just a temp.* Philadelphia: Temple University Press.

Hochschild, Arlie Russell. 1983. *The managed heart: Commercialization of human feeling.* Berkeley: University of California Press.

Hossfeld, Karen. 1990. Their logic against them: Contradictions in sex, race, and class in Silicon Valley. In *Women workers and global restructuring,* edited by Kathryn Ward. Ithaca, NY: ILR.

Howe, Wayne J. 1986. Temporary help workers: Who they are, what jobs they hold. *Monthly Labor Review* 109 (November): 45–47.

Lorber, Judith. 1994. *Paradoxes of gender.* New Haven, CT: Yale University Press.

MacKinnon, Catharine A. 1979. *Sexual harassment of working women: A case of sex discrimination.* New Haven and London: Yale University Press.

Martella, Maureen. 1991. *Just a temp: Expectations and experiences of women clerical temporary workers.* Washington, DC: U.S. Department of Labor Women's Bureau.

Maypole, D. 1986. Sexual harassment of social workers at work: Injustice within? *Social Work* 31 (1): 29–34.

National Association of Temporary Services. 1992. *Report on the temporary help services industry.* Alexandria, VA: DRI/McGraw Hill.

National Association of Working Women. 1986. *Working at the margins: Part-time and temporary workers in the United States.* Cleveland, OH: National Association of Working Women.

Parker, Robert E. 1994. *Flesh peddlers and warm bodies: The temporary help industry and its workers.* New Brunswick, NJ: Rutgers University Press.

Paules, Greta Foff. 1991. *Dishing it out: Power and resistance among waitresses in a New Jersey restaurant.* Philadelphia: Temple University Press.

Pierce, Jennifer. 1995. *Gender trials: Emotional lives in contemporary law firms.* Berkeley: University of California Press.

Pringle, Rosemary. 1988. *Secretaries talk: Sexuality, power, and work.* New York: Verso.

Ragins, Belle Rose, and Teri A. Scandura. 1995. Antecedents and work-related correlates of reported sexual harassment: An empirical investigation of competing hypotheses. *Sex Roles* 7/8: 429–55.

Right Temporaries, Inc. 1989. *Welcome to Right Temporaries, Inc.* Organizational brochure. Chicago.

Rogers, Jackie Krasas. 1995a. It's only temporary? The reproduction of race and gender inequality in temporary clerical employment. Ph.D. diss., University of Southern California, Los Angeles.

———. 1995b. Just a temp: Experience and structure of alienation in temporary clerical employment. *Work and Occupations* 2: 137–66.

———. Forthcoming. Deskilled and devalued: Changes in the labor process in temporary clerical work. In *Rethinking the labor process,* edited by M. Wardell, P. Meiksins, and T. Steiger. Albany: State University of New York Press.

Schneider, Beth E. 1982. Consciousness about sexual harassment among heterosexual and lesbian women workers. *Journal of Social Issues* 38 (4): 75–98.

———. 1985. Approaches, assaults, attractions, affairs: Policy implications of the sexualization of the workplace. *Population Research and Policy Review* 4:93–113.

———. 1991. Put up and shut up: Workplace sexual assaults. *Gender & Society* 5:533–48.

Segal, Lynne. 1990. *Slow motion: Changing men, changing masculinities.* New Brunswick, NJ: Rutgers University Press.

West, Candace, and Sarah Fenstermaker. 1995. Doing difference. *Gender & Society* 1:8–37.

West, Candace, and Don H. Zimmerman. 1987. Doing gender. *Gender & Society* 1:125–51.

West, Jackie. 1990. Gender and the labor process. In *Labor process theory,* edited by D. Knights and H. Willmott. London: Macmillan.

Williams, Christine. 1989. *Gender differences at work: Women and men in nontraditional occupations.* Berkeley: University of California Press.

———. 1995. *Still a man's world: Men who do women's work.* Berkeley: University of California Press.

Prostitution, Humanism, and a Woman's Choice

Kimberly Klinger

Driving home in the early morning hours after a night out in Washington, D.C., I turn from 14th to L Street near downtown. I'm only on the street for a block before I hit the clogged artery of Massachusetts Avenue, and this particular area seems devoid of important business or commerce. Except for the prostitutes.

Almost every weekend night I can spot women walking up and down the street—sometimes between the cars and quite near to my own. They're stereotypically wearing the tiniest slivers of fabric masquerading as dresses, swishing their hips as they teeter on high heels. I don't recall ever seeing any possible pimps nearby and wonder if these women operate independently. I wonder about a lot of things, actually. Are they happy? Are they safe? Are they making good money? Are they feminists?

That last question may seem incongruous, but to me it's relevant. As a third wave feminist, I find sex and sex work to be important issues—ones which are being addressed in ways unheard of by our foremothers. We third wavers are, in many cases, the lip-gloss wearing, *BUST* magazine reading, pro-sex women of the new millennium. We have taken the liberties of the second wave and run with them, demanding even more freedom as we struggle to find our new identities in the ever-dominating patriarchy. We don't hold consciousness-raising sessions; we hold safe-sex fairs. We still march on Washington, but we have punk rock bands helping us to raise the funds to get there. We're more multicultural and diverse, yet we continue to fight the white face—the opinion that feminism is a white women's movement—put upon us by the media.

We've also had to fight the awful stereotype that feminists are frigid, man-hating, anti-sex zealots. The second wave made incredible changes in how the United States deals with rape and domestic violence, and while we still have a long way to go, these issues are at least taken much more seriously. However, in the process, feminists have been labeled and demonized, thus creating a huge chasm between sexuality and feminism. Women are still the same sexual beings they always were, but to outsiders they have been considered strictly buzz-kills (no fun) or—gasp—lesbians. In 1983 Andrea Dworkin and Catharine A. MacKinnon wrote major antipornography bills that negatively labeled feminists as anti-sex instead of pro–human rights.

In the third wave, pornography, sex, and prostitution aren't presented as black and white issues. For instance, pornography isn't simply seen as degrading sexual imagery made by men, for men. There are female filmmakers and feminist porn stars who want to reclaim their right to enjoy sexual images without violence and negativity. Sex is more widely discussed than ever and taboos are being broken every day. The third wave hopes to expand definitions of sexuality. For women to be liberated sexually, they must be able to live as they choose, to break out of narrow ideas of sexuality, to be sexual and still be respected, and essentially to be whole. Feminism and sex work aren't therefore mutually exclusive. Choice is key here—women need to have the right and freedom to choose how to live their lives as sexual beings. This includes prostitution.

Prostitution. The word normally calls to mind women down on their luck, pitied cases who walk the streets at night with little protection or rights—essentially women who have no other choice. And unfortunately this often isn't far from the truth. In the United States and worldwide, many women turn to or are forced into sexual prostitution because they have limited options. But there are other situations, even in the United States, where women turn to this profession and other sex work because they want to. They are fortunate to have real choices and select this path because it suits them, while practicing prostitution safely and respectfully.

In the United States it is possible to find a number of organizations of sex workers who defend each other, work alongside international groups to decriminalize prostitution and protect prostitutes, and share the common experiences of choosing and enjoying this form of labor. There are advocacy and rights organizations, international conferences, and famous porn stars who all regard prostitution and other sex work as just that: a job and a way to earn a living. They argue that it should be treated as such—protected under the law with safety guidelines, unions, networks, and all the rest. Furthermore, taking a third wave feminist view, they maintain that women need to have the right and freedom to choose how to live their lives as sexual beings, including taking up "the world's oldest profession."

No matter what wave of feminism is applied, all feminists agree that forced, coerced, poverty-based, trafficked, and unprotected prostitution should be opposed. In countries where prostitution is illegal, such as in forty-nine of fifty states in the United States, women have no protection, socially or legally. The situation is messy at best and, at worst, violent, dangerous, and all but devoid of human rights. For example, most American prostitutes have to work for pimps or out of brothels, never seeing much of the money they have earned. If they are streetwalkers they live in fear of criminal assault or arrest—and in some cases, sexual abuse by police. They may be forced to deal with customers they are afraid of or who harm them. If they are raped, police will generally disregard their suffering, not even considering

what in any other profession would be recognized as criminal assault and the forced rendering of service without pay. Beyond that, the victimized woman may even be arrested for practicing prostitution. The situation is even worse in poor countries where it is all too common for young girls to be forced into prostitution and where men from wealthier nations travel specifically to have sex with them.

Second wave feminist author MacKinnon has essentially deemed prostitution sexual slavery, arguing that the relevant laws immensely harm women, classifying them as criminals and denying them their basic civil rights. MacKinnon admits in an essay, "Prostitution and Civil Rights," published in the *Michigan Journal of Gender and Law* (1993, 13:1) that she isn't sure about what to do legally concerning prostitution but that international initiatives and policy responses can help to put the power back in women's hands where it belongs. Does this mean all prostitution would disappear if women had their say? Not if the numerous prostitute rights groups and their sympathizers are any indication.

For many who have thought about this question, dismissing the entire sex industry as abusive and immoral only exacerbates existing problems and tosses the concerns of sex workers aside. Therefore many feminists, civil rights workers, and human rights activists argue for the decriminalization—not necessarily the legalization—of prostitution. Internationally, conferences are held that address decriminalization. The World Charter for Prostitutes Rights is one outcome. Created in 1985 this document is a template used by human rights groups all over the world—it makes certain basic demands abundantly clear:

1. Decriminalize all aspects of adult prostitution resulting from individual decision. This includes regulation of third parties (business managers) according to standard business codes.
2. Strongly enforce all laws against fraud, coercion, violence, child sexual abuse, child labor, rape, and racism everywhere and across

national boundaries, whether or not in the context of prostitution.

3. Guarantee prostitutes all human rights and civil liberties, including the freedom of speech, travel, immigration, work, marriage, and motherhood and the right to unemployment insurance, health insurance, and housing.
4. Ensure that prostitutes' rights are protected.
5. Allow prostitutes to unionize.

Decriminalization essentially means the removal of laws against this and other forms of sex work. The Prostitutes Education Network clarifies that decriminalization is usually used to refer to total decriminalization—that is, the repeal of all laws against consensual adult sexual activity in both commercial and non-commercial contexts. This allows the individual prostitute to choose whether or not she is managed and protects her from fraud, abuse, and coercion.

By contrast the term *legalization* usually refers to a system of governmental regulation of prostitutes wherein prostitutes are licensed and required to work in specific ways. When Jesse Ventura was running for the Minnesota governorship in 1998, he proposed that Minnesotans should consider legalizing prostitution in order to have governmental control and keep it out of residential areas. This is the practice in Nevada, the only state in the United States where brothels are legal. Although legalization can also imply a decriminalized, autonomous system of prostitution, the reality is that in most "legalized" systems the police control prostitution with criminal codes. Laws regulate prostitutes' businesses and lives, prescribing health checks and registration of health status. According to the International Union of Sex Workers, legalized systems often include special taxes, the restriction of prostitutes to working in brothels or in certain zones, licenses, registration of prostitutes and the consequent keeping of records of each individual in the profession, and health checks which often result in punitive quarantine. This is why the World Charter for Prostitutes Rights doesn't support mandatory health checks. This may be

controversial but it fits with the general idea that prostitutes' lives should be protected but not regulated. Easier and more affordable access to health clinics where prostitutes don't feel stigmatized is of greater concern to these human rights groups because compulsory checks can frighten some prostitutes and actually prevent those who are most at risk from getting necessary medical checkups. Many groups that support sex workers have sexual health and disease control as their top priorities and provide education, contraception, and health care referrals.

A well-known example of legalized prostitution is that which has been practiced in the Netherlands since the 1800s; however, brothels were illegal until 2000. When the ban was lifted, forced prostitution came under harsher punishment. Brothels are now required to be licensed, and it is legal to organize the prostitution of another party, provided the prostitution isn't forced. According to the A. De Graaf Foundation, laws in the Netherlands now will control and regulate the exploitation of prostitution, improve the prosecution of involuntary exploitation, protect minors, protect the position of prostitutes, combat the criminal affairs related to prostitution, and combat the presence of illegal aliens in prostitution.

Designated streetwalking zones have also been established. While these aren't without their problems, they have essentially functioned as a safe community for women to work. The zones also offer the benefit of a shelter which affords prostitutes a place to meet with their colleagues, talk to health care professionals, and generally relax. This was a good solution for an occupation that had led both police and prostitutes to feel that frequent raids were only making matters worse. Women felt scared and were always on the run, and police thought they weren't succeeding at making the streets any safer. This system of legalization seems to have worked well because in the Netherlands social attitudes about sex and sex work are more liberal than in other parts of the world. There is a genuine effort to protect and respect the rights of Dutch sex workers.

But this sort of arrangement isn't found all over the world. Nor can one say that the Netherlands example should become a model for every other country. Some societies may benefit more from decriminalization while others are decades away from any regulation whatsoever. The latter seems to be the case in the United States, where puritanical attitudes about sex in general would make it nearly impossible to treat prostitution as just another business.

What, then, is the best choice for women? Put simply, the best choice for women is the choice that the individual woman makes for herself. Furthermore, a humanist perspective would naturally back up the right of women to choose how to live their lives as sexual beings. *Humanist Manifesto II* says:

> In the area of sexuality, we believe that intolerant attitudes, often cultivated by orthodox religions and puritanical cultures, unduly repress sexual conduct. The right to birth control, abortion, and divorce should be recognized. While we do not approve of exploitive, denigrating forms of sexual expression, neither do we wish to prohibit, by law or social sanction, sexual behavior between consenting adults. The many varieties of sexual exploration should not in themselves be considered "evil." Without countenancing mindless permissiveness or unbridled promiscuity, a civilized society should be a tolerant one. Short of harming others or compelling them to do likewise, individuals should be permitted to express their sexual proclivities and pursue their lifestyles as they desire. We wish to cultivate the development of a responsible attitude toward sexuality, in which humans are not exploited as sexual objects, and in which intimacy, sensitivity, respect, and honesty in interpersonal relations are encouraged. Moral education for children and adults is an important way of developing awareness and sexual maturity.

As stated above, any variety of sexual exploration—as long as it isn't exploitative or harmful—can't be considered evil, yet that is exactly how prostitution is regarded. If a woman or man chooses to exchange sex for money and does it in a way that causes no harm to either party, then they should be free to do so.

In this new social environment, many of the prostitutes' rights groups build from the pro-sex ideals of the third wave. Groups such as COYOTE (Call Off Your Old Tired Ethics), the Blackstockings, and PONY (Prostitutes of New York) advocate for women who have chosen to be sex workers. Their Web sites are full of resources—from legal and medical referrals to commonsense safety tips—and they advocate tirelessly for the decriminalization of prostitution.

It would seem that decriminalization should be a key point in any humanistic feminist perspective on prostitution. Every woman's choices should be legally and socially respected whether a given woman chooses to be a wife, a CEO, or a prostitute.

And what is good for women in these instances becomes good for other sex workers, such as male prostitutes, exotic dancers of both sexes, and so on—this applies to both the gay and straight communities. Furthermore, what liberates those who make sex a profession also liberates everyone else who enjoys sex recreationally. General sexiness, for example, can take on more varied and open forms—so much so that no woman would need to fear that frank sexuality in manner or dress would any longer stigmatize her as a "slut" (or if it did, the word would have lost its sting).

Feminism has always advocated for women to enjoy freedom of choice. Women have made great strides in the courtrooms, the boardrooms, and the bedrooms. But there remains a long way to go. Negative attitudes toward sexuality, in particular, have made it hard for women to be fully liberated. But thanks to feminists, prostitute activists, and their supporters, things are slowly changing. Only when women have their sexual and personal choices protected and respected can they truly be free.

DISCUSSION QUESTIONS FOR CHAPTER 8

1. How are systems of inequality evident in women's work inside the home?

2. How do women experience sexism in the paid labor force? How does racism shape the ways women experience sexism in the paid labor force? Have you had experiences of discrimination in the workplace?

3. Why has legislation requiring equal pay and prohibiting discrimination failed to bring about equality for women in the workforce?

4. How has the perception of certain work as feminine affected women's work, both inside and outside the home?

5. What changes do you think need to occur to create equitable systems of work for all women?

SUGGESTIONS FOR FURTHER READING

Burk, Martha. *Cult of Power: Sex Discrimination in Corporate America and What Can Be Done About It.* New York: Scribner, 2005.

Cowan, Ruth Schwartz. *More Work for Mother: The Ironics of Household Technologies from the Open Hearth to the Microwave.* New York: Basic Books, 1983.

Fletcher, Joyce K. *Disappearing Acts: Gender, Power, and Relational Practice at Work.* Cambridge, MA: MIT Press, 1999.

Hertz, Rosanna, and Nancy L. Marshall, eds. *Working Families: The Transformation of the American Home.* Berkeley: University of California Press, 2001.

Hochschild, Arlic, and Barbara Ehrenreich, eds. *Global Women: Nannies, Maids, and Sex Workers in the New Economy.* New York: WI, 2004.

Meyer, Madonna Harrington. *Care Work: Gender, Labor, and the Welfare State.* New York: Routledge, 2000.

Neville, Kathleen. *Internal Affairs: The Abuse of Power, Sexual Harassment, and Hypocrisy in the Workplace.* New York: McGraw-Hill, 1999.

Shields, Julie. *How to Avoid the Mommy Trap: A Roadmap for Sharing Parenting and Making It Work.* Sterling, VA: Capital Books, 2002.

Strasser, Susan. *Never Done: A History of American Housework.* New York: Pantheon Books, 1982.

Williams, Joan. *Unbending Gender: Why Family and Work Conflict and What to Do About It.* New York: Oxford University Press, 1999.

Women Confronting and Creating Culture

Although literature and the arts remain important cultural forms, various forms of popular culture—television, movies, rock music, magazines, the Internet (including blogs, video blogs, and podcasting)—also play a significant role in reflecting, reinforcing, and sometimes subverting the dominant systems and ideologies that help shape gender. Popular cultural forms in particular are very seductive; they reflect and create societal needs, desires, anxieties, and hopes through consumption and participation. As emphasized in Chapter 5, popular culture plays a huge role in setting standards of beauty and encouraging certain bodily disciplinary practices. Popular culture *is* culture for many people; the various forms pop culture takes help shape identity and guide people's understandings of themselves and one another.

Popular culture provides stories and narratives that shape our lives and identities. They give us pleasure at the end of a long day and enable us to take our minds off work or other anxieties. In this regard, some scholars have suggested that popular culture regulates society by "soothing the masses," meaning that energy and opposition to the status quo is redirected in pursuit of the latest in athletic shoes or tickets to an award-winning movie. Of course, popular culture creates huge multi-million-dollar industries that themselves regulate society by providing markets for consumption, consolidating power and status among certain groups and individuals. For example, in 1999 the world's largest media company, Time Warner, was acquired by the largest online company, America Online (AOL), for $162 billion in stock. Time Warner owns CNN, HBO, *Time, People,* and *Sports Illustrated* magazines, and the Warner Bros. movie, television, and music properties. This came after another merger of CBS Corporation and Viacom Inc. These mergers consolidate resources across various technologies and help form powerful conglomerates that control the flow of information to the public. In 2005, National Public Radio (NPR) reported that one film studio even managed to manipulate a scientific discovery to coincide with the release of a film.

The Internet is also transforming society, making personal computers a necessity for communication, entertainment, and advertising. Also increasing at a tremendous rate is the amount of pornography available on the Internet. Although providing new opportunities for making money and helping people connect across wide geographical expanses, the Internet has also encouraged a further widening of the gap between the "haves" (those with the wealth to acquire the necessary computer, modem, Internet service provider, high-speed or wireless connection, DVD player, rewritable CD-ROM, and the list goes on) and the "have-nots" (those who, due to lack of access to the technology, are further disadvantaged). When it comes to new electronic technologies, we find that, again, it is a field overwhelmingly dominated by men, illustrating how the tangle of various privileges works to encourage and maintain power in society. Although there are exceptions, women generally have been less interested in those technologies and fields of expertise that have been coded as masculine. With the increased number of computers in the school and in the home, however, many girls are growing up expecting to use computers and these technologies in their environments. There will most likely be very interesting developments in this area as the century progresses.

Technology is a contested site in which girls and women may experience marginalization, discrimination, or abuse and empowerment. Many young women have fought to make a place for themselves in the technological world, developing their own activist Web sites, blogs, and computer games. Still, by far, technology remains a male domain. The computer-game-character-turned-movie-icon Lara Croft has often been held up as an example of empowered womanhood. But, in many ways, the character actually embodies male fantasies about women's bodies and violence.

TELEVISION

Television is one of the most influential forms of media because it is so pervasive and its presence is taken for granted in most households in the United States. Television has changed family life because it encourages passive interaction, replacing alternative family interaction. In addition, television is a visual medium that broadcasts multiple images on a continual basis. These images come to be seen as representing the real world and influence people's understanding of others and the world around them. This is especially significant for children because it is estimated that most children, on the average, watch far more television than is good for them. Of course, the range and quality of television shows vary, and a case can be made for the benefits of educational television. Unfortunately, educational programming is only a small percentage of television viewing. The explosion of cable and satellite availability means that viewers may have more than 200 channels from which to choose. Such choice, however, has not meant greater access to a wide range of alternative images of women. In fact, in "Pop Culture Is Us," Susan J. Douglas and Catherine Orenstein argue that reality shows, makeover shows in particular, simply reinforce dominant notions of women and standards of beauty.

Advertising sponsors control the content of most commercial television. During male sporting events, for example, there are commercials for beer, cars, electronic products, Internet commerce, and other products targeted at a male audience. During daytime soap operas or evening family sitcoms, on the other hand, commercials are aimed at women and focus on beauty and household

LEARNING ACTIVITY **Talking About Talk Shows**

Watch several television talk shows. Keep a journal describing the topic of the show, the guests, and the commercial sponsors. How would you characterize the host? What do you notice about the interactions among host, guests, and audience? In what ways does gender operate in the shows? Do you think the shows are in any way empowering for the guests, audience members, or television viewers? How do you think these shows reflect either dominant or subordinate American cultures? How do you think these shows contribute to public discourse?

products. As a result, commercial sponsors have enormous influence over the content of television programming. If they want to sell a certain product, they are unlikely to air the commercial during a feature that could be interpreted as criticizing such products or consumerism generally. In this way, commercial sponsors shape television (and increasingly, Internet) content.

Television messages about gender tend to be very traditional. In fact, the assumed differences between the genders very often drive the plot of television programming. The format of shows is also gendered. For example, daytime soap operas focus on relationships and family and employ rather fragmented narratives with plots weaving around without closure or resolution, enabling women to tune in and out as they go about multiple tasks. Scholars have pointed out that these shows reconcile women to the fragmented nature of their everyday lives and to male-dominated interpersonal relationships generally. In other words, soap operas, produced with a female viewing audience in mind, help enforce gendered social relations. Other scholars argue that these shows enable women viewers to actively critique blatant male-dominated situations in ways that help them reflect on their own lives.

A similar analysis can be made of evening family sitcoms. These shows are funny and entertaining because they are relatively predictable. The family or work group is made up of characters with distinct personalities and recognizable habits; each week this family is thrown into some kind of crisis, and the plot of the show is to resolve that crisis back to situation as usual. For the most part, the messages are typical in terms of gender, race, class, and other differences, and they often involve humor that denigrates certain groups of people and ultimately maintains the status quo. Some sitcoms, however, do revolve around conflict between groups. These include social classes in *The King of Queens*, between women and men in *Sex and the City*, and between children and adults in *Malcolm in the Middle*. Although these shows model the status quo, they also offer opportunities for modeling critique and resistance. When Ellen DeGeneres's character came out on her sitcom in 1997 (at the same time DeGeneres herself came out in real life), a national debate ensued. A number of advertisers canceled their ads but received a great deal of criticism for their homophobic reaction. Following *Ellen,* however, a number of gay-themed shows hit the airwaves with little resistance—*Will & Grace, Queer Eye for the Straight Guy, Queer as Folk,* and *L-Word.* The results of these shows are mixed. On the one hand, they have helped normalize gay life for the broader society. But on the other, they have often relied on and reinforced stereotypical representations of gay men and lesbians.

Increasingly, we are seeing shows and advertisements that resist the usual gendered representations, or at least show them with a new twist. Changes in society's views of gender have made sponsors realize that they have a new marketing niche. Often, unfortunately, these new representations involve the same old package tied up in new ways; typically they involve women and men resisting some of the old norms while keeping most intact. For example, although women are starting to be shown as competent, strong, athletic, and in control of their lives rather than ditsy housewives or sex symbols, they still are very physically attractive and are often highly sexualized. Examples abound in the recent popularity of crime dramas such as *Law and Order, CSI, Law and Order: SVU, CSI: Miami,* and *Third Watch.* These shows provide strong, intelligent women as primary characters, but at the same time these women fulfill the stereotypical standards of beauty. They can track down criminals using forensic science and look gorgeous while doing it. An increased visibility of larger-sized women in some advertising and in catalogs (although often "large" is size 12 or 14: a very "normal" size for U.S. women) has come about as a result of the capitalist-driven need to create a new marketing niche and sell clothing to large women as well as from pressures from fat women and the women's movement. In addition, there are performers such as Roseanne Barr and Camryn Manheim who actively resist gendered expectations and cultural constructions of "appropriate" body size in their work. The hit series *Desperate Housewives* provides an interesting case study of the conflicted presentation of women on TV. The "debate" between Jennifer L. Pozner and Jessica Seigel in "Desperately Debating *Housewives*" suggests various feminist readings of the show.

THE MOVIES

In her groundbreaking work on cinema, Laura Mulvey identifies the "male gaze" as a primary motif for understanding gender in filmmaking. Mulvey argues that movies are essentially made through and for the male gaze and fulfill a voyeuristic desire for men to look at women as objects. Viewers are encouraged to "see" the movie through the eyes of the male protagonist who carries the plot forward. Some feminist scholars have suggested the possibility for "subversive gazing" by viewers who refuse to gaze the way filmmakers expect and by making different kinds of movies.

Probably the best genre of film in which to observe gender is the romantic comedy or romantic drama. These films are packed with subtle and not-so-subtle notions of gender, and they are very seductive in the way that they offer fun entertainment. For example, *Pretty Woman* is a contemporary retelling of the Cinderella story, in which a young woman waits for her Prince Charming to rescue her from her undesirable situation. In this case, the prostitute-with-a-heart-of-gold is swept away in a white limousine by the older rich man who procured her services and then fell in love with her. Other types of films are also revealing in terms of norms

Janet and Susan's Chick Flick Picks

One of the results of the feminist movement has been the growing number of films about women that do not follow the same old scripts about women either falling in love (as do the usual and popular romantic comedy "chick flicks") or being killed. These films explore women's lives and relationships more realistically or at least posit resourceful women who do not need to be rescued by a man. Very often these films are made by independent producers, and rarely do they achieve the commercial success of standard-script movies. Here we've listed some of our favorite "chick flicks" that you may not have seen. In these movies, women are strong, smart, and independent, and, if they do "get a man," it's on their own terms. Watch at least one of these movies and compare its representation of women to the representation of women in the recent blockbusters you've seen.

- *I've Heard the Mermaids Singing* (1987) A klutzy "person-Friday" gets a part-time job as a clerical worker in an art gallery run by a lesbian, on whom she develops a crush. Through her misadventures, she and the gallery director gain entry into each other's worlds.
- *Women on the Verge of a Nervous Breakdown* (1988) This comedy of errors follows the intersecting lives of a film dubber, her ex-lover, his crazed ex-mistress, his new lover, his son, and his son's girlfriend, who find the importance of love in the midst of misadventure.
- *Shirley Valentine* (1989) A middle-aged English housewife travels to Greece without her husband and finds a new lease on life and on her relationship.
- *Bagdad Café* (1990) A German businesswoman finds herself stranded in the Mojave Desert after her husband leaves her beside the road. She stumbles upon a run-down café, where she becomes involved with its offbeat patrons.
- *Strangers in Good Company* (1990) A busload of elderly women get stranded in the Canadian wilderness. As they work out their own rescue, they get to know one another as complex, fascinating individuals.
- *Thelma & Louise* (1991) The first of the "feminist-buddy" films, *Thelma & Louise* follows the journey of two friends who start out for a fun weekend vacation and end up dealing with the ugly consequences of unexpected violence.
- *Bhaji on the Beach* (1993) A group of ethnic Indian women living in England take a bus outing to the seaside resort of Blackpool. Their differences and their bonding are focal as they spend their day at the beach.
- *Antonia's Line* (1995) On the day she decides to die, 90-year-old Antonia recalls her unconventional life and the wide variety of relationships between women that have characterized it.
- *The Incredibly True Adventures of Two Girls in Love* (1995) Two high school girls come together across social classes to experience first love. This funny, gentle movie very effectively normalizes relationships between women.
- *Chocolat* (2000) A single mother and her young daughter move to a small French village and open a chocolate shop that changes the lives of many of the town's dour inhabitants.
- *Bend It Like Beckham* (2002) Two girls pursue their dream of playing professional soccer, despite family pressure toward more traditional aspirations.
- *Whale Rider* (2002) A young girl challenges the Whangara tradition of naming only males as chiefs of this New Zealand people.
- *Calendar Girls* (2003) A group of British women produce a nude calendar to raise funds for leukemia research.

LEARNING ACTIVITY   **Women Make Movies**

> Very often the subjects that are important to women are ignored in popular filmmaking or are distorted by stereotypes or the male gaze. Despite lack of funding and major studio backing, independent women filmmakers worldwide persist in documenting the wide range of women's lives and experiences.
>
> Visit the Web site of Women Make Movies at *www.wmm.com*. Browse the catalog and identify movies made by filmmakers outside the United States. What themes do they pursue? Are these themes also common in American women filmmakers' movies? In what ways do they also express cultural distinctions? How do these films differ from mainstream box office releases? Why is an organization like Women Make Movies important?

about gender. Slasher films and horror movies are often spectacular in terms of their victimization of women. The killers in these movies, such as Norman Bates in the classic *Psycho,* are often sexually disturbed and hound and kill women who arouse them. In Norman Bates's case, it was his dysfunctional, demanding mother who pushed him into such psychosis. This is also the subtext of other films like *The Texas Chainsaw Massacre* movies and *Motel Hell.* Often it is sexually active couples who are killed, either after sex or in anticipation of it. The killer usually watches, as in *Halloween II,* as he impersonates the male lover before he then kills the female partner. Although both women and men claim to be entertained by these films, it is important to talk about the messages they portray about men, about women, and about the normalization of violence.

Pornography is an extreme example of the male gaze and the normalization of violence against women (discussed in Chapter 10). With its print media counterpart, pornography extends the sexualization and objectification of women's bodies for entertainment. In pornographic representations, women are often reduced to body parts and are shown deriving pleasure from being violated and dominated. Additionally, racism intersects with sexism in pornography, and African American women in particular are often portrayed in especially demeaning and animalistic ways. Although many feminists, ourselves included, oppose pornography, others, especially those described as "sex radicals," feel that pornography can be a form of sexual self-expression for women. They argue that women who participate in the production of pornography are taking control of their own sexuality and are profiting from control of their own bodies. In "Strip Till You Drop," Alison Pollet and Page Hurwitz point out how advertisers have targeted young girls with stripper and porn-inspired merchandise that creates a very narrow definition of what constitutes sexiness for women.

Some of the more pervasive and lasting gender images in American culture derive from Walt Disney feature films such as *Cinderella, Sleeping Beauty,* and *The Little Mermaid.* Disney heroines live, however, not only on the big screen but also as dolls in little girls' rooms, on their sheets and curtains, on their lunchboxes, and even on their t-shirts. On the whole, Disney characters reflect White, heterosexual, middle-class, patriarchal norms. Later representations, such as Pocahontas, still rely on these norms, even as they attempt to be more inclusive of diversity.

As women have made societal gains, Hollywood filmmaking has also changed and become more inclusive of new norms about gender. In some instances, as in *Terminator 2: Judgment Day* and *Aliens,* women are shown to be powerful, although in both movies the heroines are beautiful, fit, and often scantily clad. In other instances, especially when women have more control over the film as in a number of independent movies, films become more reflective of women's actual lives and concerns.

CONTEMPORARY MUSIC AND MUSIC VIDEOS

Popular music like rock, grunge, punk, heavy metal, techno, and rap are contemporary cultural forms targeted at youth. Often this music offers resistance to traditional cultural forms and contains a lot of teenage angst attractive to young people who are figuring out who they are in relation to their parents and other adults in positions of authority in their lives. In this way, such music serves as contemporary resistance and can work to mobilize people politically. Certainly music functions to help youth shape notions of identity. The various musical forms offer different kinds of identities from which young people can pick and choose to sculpt their own sense of self. In this way, music has, and continues to play, a key role in the consolidation of youth cultures in society. There is a huge music industry in the United States, and it works in tandem with television, film, video, radio, and of course, advertising.

Just as rock music was an essential part of mobilizing the youth of the 1960s to rebel against traditional norms, oppose the war, and work for civil rights, rap music (and hip-hop culture generally) has been influential in recent decades as a critique of racial cultural politics. Originating in African American urban street culture of the late 1970s, rap was influenced by rhythm and blues and rock and quickly spread beyond its roots into television, fashion, film, and, in particular, music videos. At the same time that the rap music industry has been able to raise the issue of racism, poverty, and social violence in the context of its endorsement of Black nationalism, rap has also perpetuated misogyny and violence against women in its orientation and musical lyrics. Although there are Black women performers in hip-hop and new female rappers are receiving much more attention, their status in the industry is far below the male bands. In "From Fly-Girls to Bitches and Hos," Joan Morgan argues that although feminists rightly critique the misogyny of much rap music, they must also address the racist contexts that give rise to the music and create such anger in young Black men. The appeal of pop music is not just an American phenomenon, however, and in "Pop Goes the Arab World," the authors discuss the debates about gender, identity, and politics that are being carried out in popular music.

About 30 years after the advent of rock music, the combination of music with visual images gave rise to the music video genre, which gained immense popularity with the prominence of MTV, a 24-hour music video station. Music videos are unique in blending television programming with commercials such that while the viewer is actually watching a commercial, the illusion is of programmatic entertainment. Music videos are essentially advertisements for record company products and focus on standard rock music, although different musical genres like country-western also

Rock 'n' Roll Camp for Girls

It all started as a women's studies senior project at Portland State University, but it grew into a feminist nonprofit agency that provides a summer camp and an after-school program for girls and a spring camp for women—who want to rock. Women's studies student Misty McElroy originally intended for her rock camp to be a one-time event in the summer of 2000, but the response was so overwhelming that she continued the project.

Why rock? Rock lets girls be loud—something they're not supposed to be. It lets them express themselves and try out their voices. And it's something that's tradition-ally male dominated. Rock camp teaches girls to play rock music. They spend a week with women musicians who teach them guitar, bass, drum, or vocals. They learn to create zines, write lyrics, and run sound. And they learn about feminist issues such as body image and self-defense. At the end of the week, they perform in a local Portland club to the cheers of family and friends. Because the camp has been so successful, McElroy has also launched an institute that provides training after school. Her hope is that local girls can use this option, freeing space for more national and international participants in the summer camp. The Ladies Rock Camp is a fundraiser for scholarships for the girls camp. This camp allows women the chance to try their hands at playing rock 'n' roll. Check out the camp's Web site at *www.girlsrockcamp.org.*

The empowerment envisioned by Rock 'n' Roll Camp for Girls works hand in hand with a recent technological possibility for musicians—DIY (do-it-yourself). Because of increasing access to computers and other musical technological innovations, aspiring artists can create and distribute their own CDs. DIY allows musicians to retain com-plete control over their music, and the advice many veterans of the recording scene offer to newcomers is to do-it-themselves. Perhaps the most famous do-it-yourselfer is Ani DiFranco, whose Righteous Babe Records has demonstrated the possibility of commercial success for music and musicians who don't follow the mainstream pop formula. Indigo Girl Amy Ray, who herself has achieved success on a large label, used her assets and know-how to found Daemon Records, a small label that gives new artists the opportunity to produce a recording. What's most astounding about Daemon is that it is a nonprofit—something unique in the recording industry. And when Amy Ray recorded a solo album on the Daemon label, she limited her expenses to what the label spends on any other artist.

Check out Righteous Babe and Daemon at *www.righteousbabe.com* and *www. daemonrecords.com.*

have their 24-hour video formatting. Most music videos are fairly predictable in the ways they sexualize women, sometimes in violent ways. As in movies, women are generally present in music videos to be looked at. In fact, music videos featuring male musicians are aired in greater numbers than those featuring female musicians.

Nonetheless, we could also argue that the music video industry has allowed women performers to find their voice (literally) and to script music videos from their perspective. This opportunity has given women audience recognition and industry backing. Music videos have also helped produce a feminine voice that has the potential to disrupt the traditional gendered perspective. At its peak in the mid-1980s, MTV helped such women as Tina Turner, Cyndi Lauper, and Madonna find success. Madonna is especially interesting because she has been cast simultaneously as both a feminist nightmare perpetuating gendered stereotypes about sexualized women and an important role model for women who want to be active agents in their lives. On the latter, she has been regarded as someone who returns the male gaze by staring right back at the patriarchy.

New technologies have also provided more ways for women to express themselves. Performing rock music has generally been seen as a male activity, despite the presence of women rockers from the genre's beginnings in the 1950s. The male-dominated record industry has tended to exclude women rockers and to try to force women musicians into stereotypical roles as singers and sex objects. But the advent of new, accessible technologies has allowed women greater control of their own music. Now, instead of needing a recording contract with one of the big labels, an aspiring rocker can write, record, produce, and distribute her own music (see the box "Rock 'n' Roll Camp for Girls"). For years, independent artists sold most of their music out of the back of a van, but now the Internet has made global distribution possible for just about every musician—without a large budget, agent, manager, or record label. For women, this has meant an ability to break out of the expected norms for women in rock and to make more money for themselves than they would with a record company. Now they are able to make music in their own voices rather than following the "hit" formula and to control their music and their image.

PRINT MEDIA

No discussion of popular culture is complete without a discussion of the print media. These mass media forms include magazines, newspapers, comic books, and other periodicals. Like other media, they are a mix of entertainment, education, and advertising. Fashion magazines are heavy on advertising, whereas comic books tend to be geared toward entertainment and rely more on product sales of the comic books themselves. Newspapers fall somewhere in between.

Women's magazines are an especially fruitful subject of study for examining how gender works in contemporary U.S. society. As discussed in Chapter 5, women's magazines are a central part of the multi-billion-dollar industries that produce cosmetics and fashion and help shape the social construction of "beauty." Alongside these advertising campaigns are bodily standards against which women are encouraged to measure themselves. Because almost no one measures up to these artificially created and often computer-generated standards, the message is to buy these products and your life will improve.

Generally, women's magazines can be divided into three distinct types. First are the fashion magazines that focus on beauty, attracting and satisfying men, self-improvement, and (occasionally) work and politics. Examples of these are *Vogue* (emphasizing fashion and makeup), *Cosmopolitan* (emphasizing sexuality and relationships with men), and *Self* (emphasizing self-improvement and employment), although the latter two are also heavy on beauty and fashion and the former is

IDEAS FOR ACTIVISM

- Write letters to encourage networks to air television shows that depict the broad diversity of women.
- Write letters to sponsors to complain about programs that degrade or stereotype women.
- Form a reading group to study novels by female authors.
- Sponsor a media awareness event on campus to encourage other students to be aware of media portrayals of women.

also preoccupied with sex. Most of these magazines have a White audience in mind; *Ebony* is one similar kind of magazine aimed at African American women. Note that there are a whole series of junior magazines in this genre, such as *Seventeen,* aimed at teenage women. However, although its title suggests the magazine might be oriented toward 17-year-olds, it is mostly read by younger teenagers and even preadolescent girls. Given the focus of teen magazines on dating, fashion, and makeup, the effects of such copy and advertisements on young girls are significant.

The second genre of women's magazines includes those oriented toward the family, cooking, household maintenance and decoration, and keeping the man you already have. Examples include *Good Housekeeping, Redbook,* and *Better Homes and Gardens.* These magazines (especially those like *Good Housekeeping*) also include articles and advertising on fashion and cosmetics, although the representations of these products are different. Instead of the seductive model dressed in a shiny, revealing garment (as is usually featured on the cover of *Cosmo*), *Redbook,* for example, features a more natural-looking woman (although still very beautiful) in more conservative clothes, surrounded by other graphics or captions featuring various desserts, crafts, and so forth. The focus is off sex and onto the home.

The third genre of women's magazines is the issue periodical that focuses on some issue or hobby that appeals to many women. *Parents* magazine is an example of an issue periodical aimed at women (although not exclusively). *Ms.* magazine is one aimed at feminists. Examples of hobby-type periodicals include craft magazines on needlework or crochet and fitness magazines. There are many specialized issue periodicals aimed at men (such as hunting and fishing and outdoor activities periodicals, computer and other electronic-focused magazines, car and motorcycle magazines, and various sports periodicals). The best known of the latter is *Sports Illustrated,* famous also for its swimsuit edition, which always produces record sales. This magazine has been described as ultra-soft pornography because of its sexualization of female athletes' bodies. That there are more issue periodicals for men reflects the fact that men are assumed to work and have specialized interests and that women are assumed to be preoccupied with looking beautiful, working on relationships, and keeping a beautiful home.

Again, as in music, technology has also provided a way for women to express their voices through publishing. Zines are quick, cheap, cut-and-paste publications that have sprung up both in print form and on the World Wide Web in recent years. These

LEARNING ACTIVITY **Looking Good, Feeling Sexy, Getting a Man**

Collect a number of women's magazines, such as *Cosmopolitan, Vogue, Elle, Mirabella, Redbook,* and *Woman's Day.* Read through the magazines and fill in the chart listing the number of articles you find about each topic. What do you observe from your analysis? What messages about gender are these magazines presenting?

Magazine Title	Makeup	Clothes	Hair	Sex/ Dating	Dieting	Food/ Recipes	Home Decoration	Work	Politics

publications, which range in quality, often provide a forum for alternative views on a wide variety of subjects, especially pop culture. As Jennifer Bleyer notes in "Cut-and-Paste Revolution," zines have provided an opportunity for young feminists to resist the ideas in mainstream publications that sustain women's subordination.

LITERATURE AND THE ARTS

In "Thinking About Shakespeare's Sister," Virginia Woolf responds to the question "Why has there been no female Shakespeare?" Similarly, in the early 1970s, Linda Nochlin wrote a feminist critique of art history that sought to answer the question "Why have there been no great women artists?" Woolf and Nochlin reached very similar conclusions. According to Nochlin, the reason there had been no great women artists was not that no woman had been capable of producing great art but that the social conditions of women's lives prevented such artistic endeavors.

Woolf wrote her essay in the late 1920s, but still today many critics and professors of literature raise the same questions about women's abilities to create great literature. Rarely, for example, does a seventeenth- or eighteenth-century British literature course give more than a passing nod to women authors of the periods. Quite often, literature majors graduate having read perhaps only Virginia Woolf, George Eliot, Jane Austen, or Emily Dickinson. The usual justification is that women simply have not written the great literature that men have or that to include women would mean leaving out the truly important works of the literary canon (those written by White men).

In her essay, Woolf argues that it would have been impossible due to social constraints for a woman to write the works of Shakespeare in the age of Shakespeare. Although women did write, even in the time of Shakespeare, their works were often neglected by the arbiters of the literary canon because they fell outside the narrowly constructed definitions of great literature. For example, women's novels often dealt with the subjects of women's lives—family, home, love—subjects not deemed lofty

© 2000 T.O. Sylvester. T.O. Sylvester is the pseudonym for Sylvia Mollick (artist) and Terry Ryan (writer). They live in San Francisco.

enough for the canon of literature. Additionally, women often did not follow accepted forms, writing in fragments rather than unified texts. As the canon was defined according to White male norms, women's writing and much of the writing of both women and men of color were omitted.

Yet, toward the end of the twentieth century, more women began to publish novels and poetry, and these have been slowly introduced into the canon. These works have dealt with the realities of women's lives and have received wide acclaim. For example, writers such as Toni Morrison (who received the Nobel Prize for literature), Alice Walker, and Maya Angelou have written about the dilemmas and triumphs faced by Black women in a White, male-dominated culture. Annie Dillard won a Pulitzer Prize at the age of 29 for her nature essays about a year spent living by Tinker Creek. Rita Mae Brown, May Sarton, Gloria Anzaldúa, Dorothy Allison, and Audre Lorde write about lesbian lives and the confluences of sexism, heterosexism, racism, and classism. These writers have been joined by feminist playwrights such as Wendy Wasserstein, feminist performance artists such as Lily Tomlin and Lori Anderson, and feminist comedians such as Suzanne Westenhoffer, Tracey Ullman, and Margaret Cho. In the readings, Audre Lorde and Gloria Anzaldúa write about the importance of literature for women.

Just as female writers have been ignored, misrepresented, and trivialized, so too female artists and musicians have faced similar struggles. Women's art has often

ACTIVIST PROFILE   **Maxine Hong Kingston**

As a young girl, Maxine Hong Kingston could not find herself in the images in the books she read. The public library in her hometown of Stockton, California, had no stories of Chinese Americans and very few that featured girls. For Kingston, this meant a significant need and open space for the telling of her stories.

Kingston was born in Stockton in 1940 to Chinese immigrant parents. Her mother was trained as a midwife in China, and her father was a scholar and teacher. Arriving in the United States, Tom Hong could not find work and eventually ended up working in a gambling business. Maxine was named after a successful blonde gambler who frequented her father's establishment.

Growing up in a Chinese American community, Kingston heard the stories of her culture that would later influence her own storytelling. By earning 11 scholarships, she was able to attend the University of California at Berkeley, where she earned a B.A. in literature. She married in 1962, and she and her new husband moved to Hawaii, where they both taught for the next 10 years.

In 1976 Kingston published her first book, *The Woman Warrior: Memoirs of a Girlhood Among Ghosts*. This story of a young Chinese American girl who finds her own voice won the National Book Critic's Circle Award. Kingston's portrayal of the girl's struggle with silence was met with a great deal of criticism from many Chinese men who attacked Kingston's exploration of critical gender and race issues among Chinese Americans.

Kingston followed *Woman Warrior* with *China Men* in 1980, which also won the National Book Critic's Circle Award. This book explored the lives of the men in Kingston's family who came to the United States, celebrating their achievements and documenting the prejudices and exploitation they faced. Her 1989 novel, *Tripmaster Monkey: His Fake Book,* continued her explorations of racism and oppression of Chinese Americans. Although some critics have accused Kingston of selling out because her stories have not reflected traditional notions of Chinese culture, she has maintained her right to tell her story in her own words with her own voice.

The Fifth Book of Peace, published in 2003, uses her personal tragedy of losing her house, possessions, and an unfinished novel in the Oakland-Berkeley fire of 1991 as a metaphor for war. She asks repeatedly the questions "Why war? Why not peace?"

been labeled "crafts" rather than art. This is because women, who were often barred from entering the artistic establishment, have tended to create works of art that were useful and were excluded from the category of art. Often, female artists, like their sisters who were writing novels and poetry, used a male pen name and disguised their identity in order to have their work published or shown. With the influence of

Janet and Susan's Must-Read Novels

A lot of great literature has been produced by women, especially in the last 30 years. Here are some of our favorites. We recommend that you add these to your summer reading list! You may also want to consider subscribing to the *Women's Review of Books*.

- Isabel Allende, *House of the Spirits* and *Eva Luna*
- Dorothy Allison, *Bastard Out of Carolina*
- Maya Angelou, *I Know Why the Caged Bird Sings*
- Margaret Atwood, *The Handmaid's Tale*
- Rita Mae Brown, *Rubyfruit Jungle*
- Sandra Cisneros, *The House on Mango Street*
- Annie Dillard, *Pilgrim at Tinker Creek*
- Marilyn French, *The Women's Room*
- Mary Gordon, *The Company of Women*
- Kaye Gibbons, *Ellen Foster*
- Ursula Hegi, *Stones from the River* and *Floating in My Mother's Palm*
- Zora Neale Hurston, *Their Eyes Were Watching God*
- Sue Monk Kidd, *The Secret Lives of Bees*
- Barbara Kingsolver, *The Bean Trees*
- Toni Morrison, *Sula* and *The Bluest Eye*
- Sena Jeter Naslund, *Four Spirits*
- Gloria Naylor, *The Women of Brewster Place*
- Marge Piercy, *The Longings of Women* and *Gone to Soldiers*
- May Sarton, *The Education of Harriet Hatfield*
- Amy Tan, *The Joy Luck Club*, *The Hundred Secret Senses*, and *The Bonesetter's Daughter*
- Alice Walker, *The Color Purple* and *The Temple of My Familiar*
- Rebecca Wells, *The Divine Secrets of the Ya-Ya Sisterhood*

HISTORICAL MOMENT   **The NEA Four**

Chartered by the U.S. Congress in 1965, the National Endowment for the Arts (NEA) provides funding for artists to develop their work. In 1990 Congress passed legislation that forced the NEA to consider "standards of decency" in awarding grants. Four performance artists—Karen Finley, Holly Hughes, John Fleck, and Tim Miller—had been selected to receive NEA grants, but following charges by conservatives, particularly Senator Jesse Helms (R–North Carolina), that the artists' works were obscene, the NEA denied their grants. All but Finley are gay, and Finley herself is an outspoken feminist.

Finley's work deals with raw themes of women's lives. She gained notoriety for a performance in which she smeared herself with chocolate to represent the abuse of women. Latching onto this image, conservatives referred to Finley as "the chocolate-smeared woman." Her work is shocking, but she uses the shocking images to explore women's horrific experiences of misogyny, and she uses her body in her performances in ways that reflect how society uses her body against her will.

Hughes' work explores lesbian sexuality, and, in revoking her NEA grant, then-NEA chairman John Frohnmeyer specifically referenced Hughes's lesbianism as one of the reasons she had lost her grant. Some of her performances have included "Well of Horniness," "Lady Dick," and "Dress Suits to Hire."

Following the revocation of their grant, the four sued the U.S. government, and in 1992 a lower court ruled in favor of the plaintiffs, reinstating the grants. The government appealed in 1994 and lost again. Then, in a surprise move, the Clinton administration appealed the decision to the U.S. Supreme Court. In 1998 the Supreme Court overturned the lower court rulings and held that the "standards of decency" clause is constitutional. Since the ruling, the budget and staff of the NEA have been slashed, and, artists like Finley and Hughes must seek funding from other sources to continue their performances.

If you're interested in finding out more about feminism and censorship, visit the Web site of Feminists for Free Expression at *www.ffeusa.org.*

the women's movement, women's art is being reclaimed and introduced into the art history curriculum, although it is often taught in the context of "women's art." This emphasizes the ways the academy remains androcentric with the contributions of "others" in separate courses. Female artists such as Georgia O'Keeffe and Judy Chicago have revitalized the art world by creating women-centered art and feminist critiques of masculine art forms.

The works of female composers and musicians have also been ignored, and very few women have been given the opportunity to conduct orchestras until recently. In fact, through the nineteenth century, only certain instruments such as the keyboard and harp were considered appropriate for women to play, and, even today, women are still directed away from some instruments and toward others. Women continue to produce literature and art and to redefine the canon. As in other male-dominated arenas, women have had to struggle to create a place for themselves. But, as a keen observer once quipped, "Ginger Rogers did everything Fred Astaire did, only backwards and in heels."

Thinking About Shakespeare's Sister

Virginia Woolf (1929)

. . . [I]t is a perennial puzzle why no woman wrote a word of extraordinary literature when every other man, it seemed, was capable of song or sonnet. What were the conditions in which women lived, I asked myself; for fiction, imaginative work that is, is not dropped like a pebble upon the ground, as science may be; fiction is like a spider's web, attached ever so lightly perhaps, but still attached to life at all four corners. Often the attachment is scarcely perceptible; Shakespeare's plays, for instance, seem to hang there complete by themselves. But when the web is pulled askew, hooked up at the edge, torn in the middle, one remembers that these webs are not spun in midair by incorporeal creatures, but are the work of suffering human beings, and are attached to grossly material things, like health and money and the houses we live in.

I went therefore, to the shelf where the stories stand and took down one of the latest, Professor Trevelyan's *History of England*. Once more I looked up Women, found "position of," and turned to the pages indicated. "Wifebeating," I read "was a recognized right of man, and was practiced without shame by high as well as low. . . . Similarly," this historian goes on, "the daughter who refused to marry the gentleman of her parents' choice was liable to be locked up, beaten and flung about the room, without any shock being inflicted on public opinion. Marriage was not an affair of personal affection, but of family avarice, particularly in the 'chivalrous' upper classes. . . . Betrothal often took place while one or both of the parties was in the cradle, and marriage when they were scarcely out of the nurses' charge." That was about 1470, soon after Chaucer's time. The next reference to the position

of women is some two hundred years later, in the time of the Stuarts. "It was still the exception for women of the upper and middle class to choose their own husbands, and when the husband had been assigned, he was lord and master, so far at least as law and custom could make him. Yet even so," Professor Trevelyan concludes, "neither Shakespeare's women nor those of authentic seventeenth-century memoirs, like the Vemeys and the Hutchinsons, seem wanting in personality and character." Certainly, if we consider it, Cleopatra must have had a way with her; Lady Macbeth, one would suppose, had a will of her own; Rosalind, one might conclude, was an attractive girl. Professor Trevelyan is speaking no more than the truth when he remarks that Shakespeare's women do not seem wanting in personality and character. Not being a historian, one might go even further and say that women have burnt like beacons in all the works of all the poets from the beginning of time—Clytemnestra, Antigone, Cleopatra, Lady Macbeth, Phèdre, Cressida, Rosalind, Desdemona, the Duchess of Malfi, among the dramatists; then among the prose writers: Millamant, Clarissa, Becky Sharp, Anna Karenine, Emma Bovary, Madame de Guermantes—the names flock to mind, nor do they recall women "lacking in personality and character." Indeed, if woman had no existence save in fiction written by men, one would imagine her a person of the utmost importance, very various; heroic and mean; splendid and sordid; infinitely beautiful and hideous in the extreme; as great as a man, some think even greater. But this is woman in fiction. In fact, as Professor Trevelyan points out, she was locked up, beaten and flung about the room.

A very queer, composite being thus emerges. Imaginatively she is of the highest importance; practically she is completely insignificant. She pervades poetry from cover to cover; she is all but absent from history. She dominates the lives of kings and conquerors in fiction; in fact she was the slave of any boy whose parents forced a ring upon her finger. Some of the most inspired words, some of the most profound thoughts in literature fall from her lips; in real life she could hardly read, could scarcely spell, and was the property of her husband.

. . .

Be that as it may, I could not help thinking, as I looked at the works of Shakespeare on the shelf . . . it would have been impossible, completely and entirely, for any woman to have written the plays of Shakespeare in the age of Shakespeare. Let me imagine, since facts are so hard to come by, what would have happened had Shakespeare had a wonderfully gifted sister, called Judith, let us say. Shakespeare himself went, very probably—his mother was an heiress—to the grammar school, where he may have learnt Latin—Ovid, Virgil and Horace—and the elements of grammar and logic. He was, it is well known, a wild boy who poached rabbits, perhaps shot a deer, and had, rather sooner than he should have done, to marry a woman in the neighbourhood, who bore him a child rather quicker than was right. That escapade sent him to seek his fortune in London. He had, it seemed, a taste for the theatre; he began by holding horses at the stage door. Very soon he got work in the theatre, became a successful actor, and lived at the hub of the universe, meeting everybody, knowing everybody, practising his art on the boards, exercising his wits in the streets, and even getting access to the palace of the queen. Meanwhile his extraordinarily gifted sister, let us suppose, remained at home. She was as adventurous, as imaginative, as agog to see the world as he was. But she was not sent to school. She had no chance of learning grammar and logic, let alone of reading Horace and Virgil. She picked up a book now and then, one of her brother's perhaps, and read a few pages. But then her parents came in and told her to mend the stockings or mind the stew and not moon about with books and papers. They would have spoken sharply but kindly, for they were substantial people who knew the conditions of life for a woman and loved their daughter—indeed, more likely than not she was the apple of her father's eye. Perhaps she scribbled some pages up in an apple loft on the sly, but was careful to hide them or set fire to them. Soon, however, before she was out of her teens, she was to be betrothed to the son of a neighbouring wool-stapler. She cried out that marriage was hateful to her, and for that she was severely beaten by her father. Then he ceased to scold her. He begged her instead not to hurt him, not to shame him in this matter of her marriage. He would give her a chain of beads or a fine petticoat, he said; and there were tears in his eyes. How could she disobey him? How could she break his heart? The force of her own gift alone drove her to it. She made up a small parcel of her belongings, let herself down by a rope one summer's night and took the road to London. She was not seventeen. The birds that sang in the hedge were not more musical than she was. She had the quickest fancy, a gift like her brother's, for the tune of words. Like him, she had a taste for the theatre. She stood at the stage door; she wanted to act, she said. Men laughed in her face. The manager—a fat, loose-lipped man—guffawed. He bellowed something about poodles dancing and women acting—no woman, he said, could possibly be an actress. He hinted—you can imagine what. She could get no training in her craft. Could she even seek her dinner in a tavern or roam the streets at midnight? Yet her genius was for fiction and lusted to feed abundantly upon the lives of men and women and the study of their ways. At last—for she was very young, oddly like Shakespeare the poet in her face, with the same grey eyes and rounded brows—at last Nick Greene the actor-manager took pity on her; she found herself with child by that gentleman and so—who shall measure the heat and violence of the poet's heart when caught and tangled in a woman's body?—killed herself one winter's night and lies buried at some cross-roads where the omnibuses now stop outside the Elephant and Castle.

That, more or less, is how the story would run, I think, if a woman in Shakespeare's day had had Shakespeare's genius. . . .

This may be true or it may be false—who can say?—but what is true in it, so it seemed to me, reviewing the story of Shakespeare's sister as I had made it, is that any woman born with a great gift in the sixteenth century would certainly have gone crazed, shot herself, or ended her days in some lonely cottage outside the village, half witch, half wizard, feared and mocked at. For it needs little skill in psychology to be sure that a highly gifted girl who had tried to use her gift for poetry would have been so thwarted and hindered by other people, so tortured and pulled asunder by her own contrary instincts, that she must have lost her health and sanity to a certainty. No girl could have walked to London and stood at a stage door and forced her way into the presence of actor-managers without doing herself a violence and suffering an anguish which may have been irrational—for chastity may be a fetish invented by certain societies for unknown reasons—but were none the less inevitable. . . .

But for women, I thought, looking at the empty shelves, these difficulties were infinitely more formidable. In the first place, to have a room of her own, let alone a quiet room or a sound-proof room, was out of the question, unless her parents were exceptionally rich or very noble, even up to the beginning of the nineteenth century. Since her pin money, which depended on the good will of her father, was only enough to keep her clothed, she was debarred from such alleviations as came even to Keats or Tennyson or Carlyle, all poor men, from a walking tour, a little journey to France, from the separate lodging which, even if it were miserable enough, sheltered them from the claims and tyrannies of their families. Such material difficulties were formidable; but much worse were the immaterial. The indifference of the world which Keats and Flaubert and other men of genius have found so hard to bear was in her case not indifference but hostility. The world did not say to her as it said to them, Write if you choose; it makes no difference to me. The world said with a guffaw, Write? What's the good of your writing? . . .

R E A D I N G   **71**

Poetry Is Not a Luxury

Audre Lorde

The quality of light by which we scrutinize our lives has direct bearing upon the product which we live, and upon the changes which we hope to bring about through those lives. It is within this light that we form those ideas by which we pursue our magic and make it realized. This is poetry as illumination, for it is through poetry that we give name to those ideas which are—until the poem—nameless and formless, about to be birthed, but already felt. That distillation of experience from which true poetry springs births thought as dream births concept, as feeling births idea, as knowledge births (precedes) understanding.

As we learn to bear the intimacy of scrutiny and to flourish within it, as we learn to use the products of that scrutiny for power within our living, those fears which rule our lives and form our silences begin to lose their control over us.

For each of us as women, there is a dark place within, where hidden and growing our true spirit rises, "beautiful/and tough as chestnut/stanchions against (y)our nightmare of weakness/"[1] and of impotence.

These places of possibility within ourselves are dark because they are ancient and hidden; they have survived and grown strong through that darkness. Within these deep places, each one of us holds an incredible reserve of creativity and power, of unexamined and unrecorded emotion and feeling. The woman's place of power within each of us is neither white nor surface; it is dark, it is ancient, and it is deep.

When we view living in the european mode only as a problem to be solved, we rely solely upon our ideas to make us free, for these were what the white fathers told us were precious.

But as we come more into touch with our own ancient, noneuropean consciousness of living as a situation to be experienced and interacted with, we learn more and more to cherish our feelings, and to respect those hidden sources of our power from where true knowledge and, therefore, lasting action comes.

At this point in time, I believe that women carry within ourselves the possibility for fusion of these two approaches so necessary for survival, and we come closest to this combination in our poetry. I speak here of poetry as a revelatory distillation of experience, not the sterile word play that, too often, the white fathers distorted the word *poetry* to mean—in order to cover a desperate wish for imagination without insight.

For women, then, poetry is not a luxury. It is a vital necessity of our existence. It forms the quality of the light within which we predicate our hopes and dreams toward survival and change, first made into language, then into idea, then into more tangible action. Poetry is the way we help give name to the nameless so it can be thought. The farthest horizons of our hopes and fears are cobbled by our poems, carved from the rock experiences of our daily lives.

As they become known to and accepted by us, our feelings and the honest exploration of them become sanctuaries and spawning grounds for the most radical and daring of ideas. They become a safe-house for that difference so necessary to change and the conceptualization of any meaning-ful action. Right now, I could name at least ten ideas I would have found intolerable or incomprehensible and frightening, except as they came after dreams and poems. This is not idle fantasy, but a disciplined attention to the true meaning of "it feels right to me." We can train ourselves to respect our feelings and to transpose them into a language so they can be shared. And where that language does not yet exist, it is our poetry which helps to fashion it. Poetry is not only dream and vision; it is the skeleton architecture of our lives. It lays the foundations for a future of change, a bridge across our fears of what has never been before.

Possibility is neither forever nor instant. It is not easy to sustain belief in its efficacy. We can sometimes work long and hard to establish one beachhead of real resistance to the deaths we are expected to live, only to have that beachhead assaulted or threatened by those canards we have been socialized to fear, or by the withdrawal of those approvals that we have been warned to seek for safety. Women see ourselves diminished or softened by the falsely benign accusations of childishness, of nonuniversality, of changeability, of sensuality. And who asks the question: Am I altering your aura, your ideas, your dreams, or am I merely moving you to temporary and reactive action? And even though the latter is no mean task, it is one that must be seen within the context of a need for true alteration of the very foundations of our lives.

The white fathers told us: I think, therefore I am. The Black mother within each of us—the poet—whispers in our dreams: I feel, therefore I can be free. Poetry coins the language to express and charter this revolutionary demand, the implementation of that freedom.

However, experience has taught us that action in the now is also necessary, always. Our children cannot dream unless they live, they cannot live unless they are nourished, and who else will feed them the real food without which their dreams will be no different from ours? "If you want us to change the world someday, we at least have to live long enough to grow up!" shouts the child.

Sometimes we drug ourselves with dreams of new ideas. The head will save us. The brain alone will set us free. But there are no new ideas still waiting in the wings to save us as women, as human. There are only old and forgotten ones, new combinations, extrapolations and recognitions from within ourselves—along with the renewed courage to try them out. And we must constantly encourage ourselves and each other to attempt the heretical actions that our dreams imply, and so many of our old ideas disparage. In the forefront of our move toward change, there is only poetry to hint at possibility made real. Our poems formulate the implications of ourselves, what we feel within and dare make real (or bring action into accordance with), our fears, our hopes, our most cherished terrors.

For within living structures defined by profit, by linear power, by institutional dehumanization, our feelings were not meant to survive. Kept around as unavoidable adjuncts or pleasant pastimes, feelings were expected to kneel to thought as women were expected to kneel to men. But women have survived. As poets. And there are no new pains. We have felt them all already. We have hidden that fact in the same place where we have hidden our power. They surface in our dreams,

and it is our dreams that point the way to freedom. Those dreams are made realizable through our poems that give us the strength and courage to see, to feel, to speak, and to dare.

If what we need to dream, to move our spirits most deeply and directly toward and through promise, is discounted as a luxury, then we give up the core—the fountain—of our power, our womanness; we give up the future of our worlds.

For there are no new ideas. There are only new ways of making them felt—of examining what those ideas feel like being lived on Sunday morning at 7 A.M., after brunch, during wild love, making war, giving birth, mourning our dead—while we suffer the old longings, battle the old warnings and fears of being silent and impotent and alone, while we taste new possibilities and strengths.

NOTE

1. From "Black Mother Woman," first published in *From A Land Where Other People Live* (Broadside Press, Detroit, 1973), and collected in *Chosen Poems: Old and New* (W. W. Norton and Company, New York, 1982), p. 53.

R E A D I N G *72*

The Path of the Red and Black Ink

Gloria Anzaldúa

Out of poverty, poetry;
out of suffering, song.

—*a Mexican saying*

When I was seven, eight, nine, fifteen, sixteen years old, I would read in bed with a flashlight under the covers, hiding my self-imposed insomnia from my mother. I preferred the world of the imagination to the death of sleep. My sister, Hilda, who slept in the same bed with me, would threaten to tell my mother unless I told her a story.

I was familiar with *cuentos*—my grandmother told stories like the one about her getting on top of the roof while down below rabid coyotes were ravaging the place and wanting to get at her. My father told stories about a phantom giant dog that appeared out of nowhere and sped along the side of the pickup no matter how fast he was driving.

Nudge a Mexican and she or he will break out with a story. So, huddling under the covers, I made up stories for my sister night after night. After a while she wanted two stories per night.

I learned to give her installments, building up the suspense with convoluted complications until the story climaxed several nights later. It must have been then that I decided to put stories on paper. It must have been then that working with images and writing became connected to night.

INVOKING ART

In the ethno-poetics and performance of the shaman, my people, the Indians, did not split the artistic from the functional, the sacred from the secular, art from everyday life. The religious, social and aesthetic purposes of art were all intertwined. Before the Conquest, poets gathered to play music, dance, sing and read poetry in open-air places around the *Xochicuahuitl, el Árbol Florido,* Tree-in-Flower. (The *Coaxihuitl* or morning glory is called the snake plant and its seeds, known as *ololiuhqui,* are hallucinogenic.) The ability of story (prose and poetry) to transform the storyteller and the listener into something or someone else is shamanistic. The writer, as shape-changer, is a *nahual,* a shaman.

In looking at this book that I'm almost finished writing, I see a mosaic pattern (Aztec-like) emerging, a weaving pattern, thin here, thick there. I see a preoccupation with the deep structure, the underlying structure, with the gesso underpainting that is red earth, black earth. I can see the deep structure, the scaffolding. If I can get the bone structure right, then putting flesh on it proceeds without too many hitches. The problem is that the bones often do not exist prior to the flesh, but are shaped after a vague and broad shadow of its form is discerned or uncovered during beginning, middle and final stages of the writing. Numerous overlays of paint, rough surfaces, smooth surfaces make me realize I am preoccupied with texture as well. Too, I see the barely contained color threatening to spill over the boundaries of the object it represents and into other "objects" and over the borders of the frame. I see a hybridization of metaphor, different species of ideas popping up here, popping up there, full of variations and seeming contradictions, though I believe in an ordered structured universe where all phenomena are interrelated and imbued with spirit. This almost finished product seems an assemblage, a montage, a beaded work with several leitmotifs and with a central core, now appearing, now disappearing in a crazy dance. The whole thing has had a mind of its own, escaping me and insisting on putting together the pieces of its own puzzle with minimal direction from my will. It is a rebellious, willful entity, a precocious girl-child forced to grow up too quickly, rough, unyielding, with pieces of feather sticking out here and there, fur, twigs, clay. My child, but not for much longer. This female being is angry, sad, joyful, is *Coatlicue,* dove, horse, serpent, cactus. Though it is a flawed thing—a clumsy, complex, groping blind thing—for me it is alive, infused with spirit. I talk to it; it talks to me.

I make my offerings of incense and cracked corn, light my candle. In my head I sometimes will say a prayer—an affirmation and a voicing of intent. Then I run water, wash the dishes or my underthings, take a bath, or mop the kitchen floor. This "induction" period sometimes takes a few minutes, sometimes hours. But always I go against a resistance. Something in me does not want to do this writing. Yet once I'm immersed in it, I can go fifteen to seventeen hours in one sitting and I don't want to leave it.

My "stories" are acts encapsulated in time, "enacted" every time they are spoken aloud or read silently. I like to think of them as performances and not as inert and "dead" objects (as the aesthetics of Western culture think of art works). Instead, the work has an identity; it is a "who" or a "what" and contains the presences of persons, that is, incarnations of gods or ancestors or natural and cosmic powers. The work manifests the same needs as a person, it needs to be "fed," *la tengo que bañar y vestir.*

When invoked in rite, the object\event is "present;" that is, "enacted," it is both a physical thing and the power that infuses it. It is metaphysical in that it "spins its energies between gods and humans" and its task is to move the gods. This type of work dedicates itself to managing the universe and its energies. I'm not sure what it is when it is at rest (not in performance). It may or may not be a "work" then. A mask may only have the power of presence during a ritual dance and the rest of the time it may merely be a "thing." Some works exist forever invoked, always in performance. I'm thinking of totem poles, cave paintings. Invoked art is communal and speaks of everyday life. It is dedicated to the validation of humans; that is, it makes people hopeful, happy, secure, and it can have negative effects as well, which propel one towards a search for validation.

The aesthetic of virtuosity, art typical of Western European cultures, attempts to manage the energies of its own internal system such as conflicts, harmonies, resolutions and balances. It bears the presences of qualities and internal meanings. It is dedicated to the validation of itself. Its task is to move humans by means of achieving mastery in content, technique, feeling. Western art is always whole and always "in power." It is individual (not communal). It is "psychological" in that it spins its energies between itself and its witness.

Western cultures behave differently toward works of art than do tribal cultures. The "sacrifices" Western cultures make are in housing their art works in the best structures designed by the best architects; and in servicing them with insurance, guards to protect them, conservators to maintain them, specialists to mount and display them, and the educated and upper classes to "view" them. Tribal cultures keep art works in honored and sacred places in the home and elsewhere. They attend them by making sacrifices of blood (goat or chicken), libations of wine. They bathe, feed, and clothe them. The works are treated not just as objects, but also as persons. The "witness" is a participant in the enactment of the work in a ritual, and not a member of the privileged classes.

Ethnocentrism is the tyranny of Western aesthetics. An Indian mask in an American museum is transposed into an alien aesthetic system where what is missing is the presence of power invoked through performance ritual. It has become a conquered thing, a dead "thing" separated from nature and, therefore, its power.

Modern Western painters have "borrowed," copied, or otherwise extrapolated the art of tribal cultures and called it cubism, surrealism, symbolism. The music, the beat of the drum, the Blacks' jive talk. All taken over. Whites, along with a good number of our own people, have cut themselves off from their spiritual roots, and they take our spiritual art objects in an unconscious attempt to get them back. If they're going to do it, I'd like them to be aware of what they are doing and to go about doing it the right way. Let's all stop importing Greek myths and the Western Cartesian split point of view and root ourselves in the mythological soil and soul of this continent. White America has only attended to the body of the earth in order to exploit it, never to succor it or to be nurtured in it. Instead of surreptitiously ripping off the vital energy of people of color and putting it to commercial use, whites could allow themselves to share and exchange and learn from us in a respectful way. By taking up *curanderismo*, Santeria, shamanism, Taoism, Zen and otherwise delving into the spiritual life and ceremonies of multi-colored people, Anglos would perhaps lose the white sterility they have in their kitchens, bathrooms, hospitals, mortuaries and missile bases. Though in the conscious mind, black and dark may be associated with death, evil and destruction, in the subconscious mind and in our dreams, white is associated with disease, death and hopelessness. Let us hope that the left hand, that of darkness, of femaleness, of "primitiveness," can divert the indifferent, right-handed, "rational" suicidal drive that, unchecked, could blow us into acid rain in a fraction of a millisecond.

Pop Culture Is Us: Two Essays on a Theme

Susan J. Douglas and Catherine Orenstein

WE ARE WHAT WE WATCH

Susan J. Douglas

A few weeks ago, Fox-TV offered up the finale of *The Swan*—the mutant offspring of the Miss America pageant, *Cinderella,* and *Extreme Makeover.* Women held up as "dogs"—whose supposedly oversized noses, flabby thighs, and saggy breasts were scrutinized and pitied, even ridiculed—subjected themselves to multiple invasive procedures, including as many as 14 surgeries and psychological counseling, before a national viewing audience. The finalists then vied in a beauty contest complete with lingerie competition, and one was chosen winner, the Swan.

As *The Swan* and a swarm of reality shows colonized prime time, the news media was consumed by repugnant images coming out of Abu Ghraib. All were appalling, but possibly the most disturbing were those of young women like Pfc. Lynndie England pointing and laughing at an Iraqi man's genitals and in another shot, seeming to drag a naked Iraqi man by a leash.

How do these seemingly different images of women work together? To understand, we need to consider the synergy between the coarsening of our culture and post-feminism, between TV's sadomasochism-lite and its escalating objectification of women.

Because we often dismiss popular culture as banal and inconsequential, we don't stand back and think about the connections between what we see in the news and what we see in entertainment programming. But we should appreciate that reality TV, particularly, traffics in and relies upon voyeurism, one-upsmanship, humiliation, and often soft-core pornography. This is hardly to say reality TV "caused" Abu Ghraib; the soldier-torturers, including the women, were socialized into highly macho military institutions predicated on conquering and killing those deemed the enemy. But the "few bad apples" argument Rumsfeld and Bush used in their efforts to distance torture from "the true nature and heart of America" fails to acknowledge how common humiliation has become in what passes for daily entertainment.

Perpetuating degradation and terror is the premise of such shows as *Fear Factor* and *The Apprentice.* Near nudity and ridicule of people's bodies, too, is *de rigeur* in reality TV. In *Are You Hot?* "judges" like Lorenzo Lamas used a laser pointer to identify which parts of a contestant's barely clad body were shameful. In the early episodes of "American Idol," when hundreds competed to get to the final phase, we were invited to laugh at those pathetic tone-deaf pop star wannabes.

Others have noted how various cultural practices, from fraternity hazing to torture in U.S. prisons, are of a piece with the sadism at Abu Ghraib. But what's chilling about reality TV is that it exhorts us to be a voyeur of others' humiliation and to see their degradation as harmless, even character-building fun. It is not surprising that, as Susan Sontag wrote in dismay, Abu Ghraib torturers "apparently had no sense that there was anything wrong in what the pictures show."

The other highly disturbing resonance between Abu Ghraib and reality TV is the central role both play in advancing anti-feminism. Right-wing pundits like Linda Chavez suggested that the presence of women in the military "encouraged more misbehavior" in the prison. George Neumayr of the

American Spectator summed it up this way: "The image of that female guard, smoking away as she joins gleefully in the disgraceful melee like one of the guys, is a cultural outgrowth of a feminist culture which encourages female barbarianism. . . . This is Eleanor Smeal's vision come to life."

In other words, not only are women *not* morally superior to men, when they get too much power they are worse than men, so they should be expunged from public life and get back in the kitchen.

Reality TV's obsession with women's appearance, sexuality, ability to please men, desperate need to compete with each other over men, redecorate, have breast implants and liposuction—reinforces and celebrates pre-feminist gender roles. From *The Bachelor* to *Joe Millionaire* to *Trading Spaces,* reality TV keeps women in their place and encourages a retreat from citizenship and world affairs into consumerism and the domestic sphere. With *The Apprentice,* it was clear that no woman could win the top spot—women were cast as too emotional or too bitchy or too reliant on their sexuality to handle a top job with The Donald.

In these shows, the inevitability of female narcissism is rendered utterly natural, almost genetically determined. But so is a culture of surveillance, of voyeurism and of demeaning exposure. The promised prizes are meant to be worth the initial shame, rejection. Post-feminism—the insistence that deep in their hearts women really want a return to 1957—is thus deployed in the service of a culture of humiliation. Others may dismiss reality TV shows like *The Swan* and *Are You Hot?* as mindless drivel. But when they simultaneously naturalize misogyny at home and shamelessness abroad, we need to take a pretty hard look at what our society finds entertaining—and why.

STEPFORD IS US

Catherine Orenstein

Paramount's remake of *The Stepford Wives* is billed as a comedy, but the continuing relevance of this cult classic's dark themes ought to make us all think twice. The original 1975 film, in which suburban husbands killed and replaced their partners with blonder, bustier robotic look-alikes, dramatized the feminist argument that marriage transformed women into ever-smiling, floor-mopping automatons. In those days, the vast majority of new American houses were built in suburbs, and women—who in midcentury began marrying younger, having children earlier, and doing more hours of housework than in previous decades—were complaining of a malaise brought on by what Betty Friedan had dubbed "the feminine mystique." The remake, in contrast, stars Nicole Kidman as a high-powered TV executive who, previews suggest, is more than a match for her husband—or anyone else's.

While the wives of Stepford have advanced since 1975, along with the rest of us, not everything has panned out the way feminists envisioned. American women today tend to delay marriage; we have careers; we demand that men do their share of the housework; we expect to be equal partners. At the same time, we have internalized a piece of Stepford, becoming, metaphorically speaking, our own Stepford husbands—imposing a conformist definition of beauty and femininity. Girls' and women's magazines incessantly promote perfect thighs, abs, and hair, and achieving the perfect look has moved beyond diet and exercise. More and more, we place ourselves willingly under the knife, happily embracing the plastic.

The remake opens at a peak in our Stepfordian obsession with cosmetic surgery. No longer reserved for the rich and the old, reaching for the knife begins these days with the first wrinkle. Along with collagen implants and Botox, summer beauty treatments now include toe-shortening and even pinky-toe removal—the better to fit into pointy shoes.

Television reality shows like *Extreme Makeover* and *The Swan,* in which contestants undergo extensive surgery, reinforce our relentless pursuit of physical perfection. On MTV's *I Want a Famous Face,* men and women endured radical reconstructions to look like their favorite movie stars. On Fox's series *The Swan,* surgically altered women competed against one another for a chance to be part of the beauty pageant in the final episode. Because they undergo many of the same cosmetic procedures—breast and chin implants, nose and teeth straightening, liposuction, and hair lightening—executed by the same surgeons and beauticians, the contestants on these shows ended up looking eerily alike. And, not incidentally, like the two blondes who vied for the Bachelor's hand in marriage, who in turn looked like Britney Spears. All could be knockoffs of the blond Nicole Kidman in the *Stepford* movie posters.

Why do we wish to reinvent ourselves so badly—and so blandly? Our desire taps a powerful myth of self-transformation in which we magically become—and are recognized for—our most ideal selves. The Cinderella Cycle, as folklorists call that fairy tale and its multitude of global variants, is ubiquitous, appearing in ancient texts (the earliest written version is from ninth-century China) as well as in the modern mythic genre of cinema. In movies like *Sabrina, Pretty Woman, Moonstruck, Maid in Manhattan,* or *The Princess Diaries,* the heroine's transformation from Plain Jane to Queen Bee is represented by a montage in which she shops for clothes and gets her hair and makeup overhauled.

Scholars have debated the meaning of this narrative path, some calling it a seasonal or fertility myth, perhaps derived from ancient ritual. In the eyes of Bruno Bettelheim, the popular Freudian psychologist, the Cinderella tale embodies sibling rivalry and Oedipal conflicts. In its modern incarnations, as in our real-life fixations with rehabbing ourselves through diet, cosmeceuticals, and surgery, the fairy tale lends itself to a literal interpretation, as a mere physical makeover. But it also has metaphoric power.

Narratives of physical transformation can be read as symbolic of our desire to be seen, and loved, for who we really are—and to find love, recognition, and acceptance that transcends stereotype, class, age, poverty, and physical imperfection. The truly climactic moment of Charles Perrault's famous 1697 version of *Cinderella* is not the moment soot stains disappear from the heroine's cheeks; rather, it is the moment when she is recognized, while still in rags, by the prince—thanks to her ability to fit her foot into a tiny slipper (a detail that, incidentally, most likely derives from China, where foot-binding produced a standard of beauty and womanhood).

We could say, then, that the myth of self-transformation is really about recognition of the inner person, perhaps explaining why so many "improved" contestants on *The Swan* and *Extreme Makeover* say they feel for the first time that they look like their true selves. At what point, though, does a myth about recognition, acceptance, and truth become just the opposite—a tale of artifice and disguise? Myths often contain the seeds of their own inversion, and so it is in this case. In our quest to be Cinderellas, we are risking becoming her impostor stepsisters—eagerly slicing off toe and heel (as they do in the Grimms' version of the fairy tale) to fit into a false shoe.

It is not men (or at least, not men alone) who do this to us. Indeed, Paramount's Web site for *The Stepford Wives* hardly mentions husbands. Instead, it addresses the female viewer, showcasing "before" and "after" photos of the character played by Bette Midler much like those belonging to *Swan* contestants, and inviting us to upload our own photos for a personalized "Stepford Makeover."

It's a funny but frightening parody of our aspirations, given the original movie's dark ending. As Sylvia Plath warned us, not long before her suicide in 1963: "The woman is perfected—Her dead—Body wears the smile of accomplishment."

Desperately Debating *Housewives*

Jennifer L. Pozner and Jessica Seigel

Dear Jessica,

Say it ain't so! I hear you love *Desperate House-wives,* ABC's hit series that cynically reinforces sexual, racial, and class stereotypes. If that's true, you're in some questionable company.

On the episode of CNN's *Crossfire* during which he mocked "grouchy feminists with mustaches," Tucker Carlson praised *Housewives* as "good entertainment." *Washington Times* columnist Suzanne Fields described it as "sophisticated, edgy television for the era of the values voters who kept George W. on Pennsylvania Avenue."

It's no wonder right-wing culture warriors such as Carlson and Fields love a show whose worldview harks back to a time when two-parent, middle-class families could comfortably thrive on single incomes, women's identities were primarily determined by the men they married and the children they raised, and husbands were not expected to trouble themselves with such pesky matters as child care and housework. *House-wives'* Wisteria Lane is even set on the same Hollywood back lot where *Leave It to Beaver* was filmed.

Hyped as a cunning parody, *Housewives* is light on actual satire and heavy on the sorts of cultural clichés that play well at red-state country clubs. Of the four main characters, three are white, all are wealthy, and only one has a job—divorced mom Susan (Teri Hatcher), supposedly a children's-book illustrator. The only nonwhite wife, Gabrielle (Eva Longoria), plays into every tired cliché about oversexed, "spicy" Latina gold diggers. On Wisteria Lane, female friendships are shallow and only superficially supportive, and the rare woman who doesn't conform to an ultrathin, waxed ideal of beauty gets strangled in her kitchen (literally, as happened to a plump, nosy neighbor).

Jessica, when you find yourself enjoying a show that the *Chicago Tribune* encouraged readers to watch by saying, "Women viewers may find it offensive to wives, mothers, suburbanites, and feminists alike. Definitely stay tuned," it may be time to reevaluate your analysis. Is there something I'm missing?

Desperately Hating Housewives,
Jenn

Dear Desperately Hating,

Yup, you're missing plenty, Jenn, like the delicious Sunday evenings I spend coffee-klatching with my best friend over this madcap send-up of the *Leave It to Beaver* American dream. This show doesn't "hark back" to the past—it skewers the myth of motherhood and suburban bliss with *Feminine Mystique*–inspired irony so sly that conservatives are as divided as liberals over whether to love it or hate it.

Its stealth feminism has not been lost on the "values" crowd, including Rev. Donald Wildmon's American Family Association (AFA), which predictably denounced the show as immoral. Not surprisingly, Wildmon's group condemned its adulterous antics but not the murderous ones, singling out Gabrielle's affair with a hunky teenaged gardener. Disgusting, isn't it? Adult women finally get to ogle hottie jailbait without feeling like Mrs. Robinson—a visual droit du seigneur long enjoyed by men.

Yeah, adultery is bad. I'm against it. But *girl talk?* The AFA condemns that, too, as spokesman Randy Sharp told the *Chicago Tribune:* "Our objection to *Desperate Housewives* is that . . . discussion of intimate details between individuals is open for 'girl talk,' for lack of a better phrase."

Real ladies, we know, shut up and suffer in silence. Girl talk, in fact—formalized as consciousness-raising groups—helped fuel the women's movement. The personal was political, then and now. *Desperate Housewives* dramatizes the "Second Shift" realities of an America in which even full-time working women do most of the housework and only 5 percent of men take primary responsibility for child care. Girl talk is subversive, and it's the emotional heart of *Housewives,* as our four heroines lean on each other to navigate troubled marriages, divorce, children, and romance. Male characters are peripheral on the show, which has resurrected the careers of three fine actresses over age 40—a rarity on sweet-young-thing-obsessed prime-time television.

I think you confuse the starring quartet's long-time, sometimes ambivalent friendships—as in real life—with their spicy conflicts with secondary characters such as the neighborhood biddy (true, the only fatty). Still, when men fight we call it politics; when women fight, it's derided as backbiting or catfighting—words that denigrate females jockeying for position and power.

This show exposes a *Diary of a Mad Housewife* reality *and* the power of sisterhood. For example, when former corporate honcho Lynette's (Felicity Huffman) four unruly children make her suicidal, she confesses to her buddies that motherhood is driving her crazy. "Why don't they tell us this stuff?" she whines. "Why don't we talk about this?"

So they talk. When we finally get to a prime-time hit about women's domestic struggles—previously relegated to sappy daytime soaps—why is it a lightning rod for everything *wrong* with TV and America, including racism, classism, and lookism? Jenn, come on, join our coffee klatch—but no talking except during commercials. Can't you see the winking subversion beneath the impossibly thin, nouveau-riche facade? Or are you lining up with family-values conservatives on this one, like some feminists did in the 1980s antipornography movement?

Desperately Loving Housewives,
Jess

Hey Jess,

If you want "family-values conservatives," don't look to me—look to *Desperate Housewives'* creator Marc Cherry, a gay Republican who believes the real problem facing today's post-feminist women is too much freedom. As he told the *Contra Costa Times,* "We've reached the point where we realize that no, you really can't have it all. . . . Long ago, it used to be easier: Society laid down the rules for you. Now, there are a lot of choices, but sometimes choices can lead to chaos."

Where, exactly, does the "skewering" come in? Certainly not from the show's majority-male writers, or from its creator, who says *Housewives* is darkly comic but not *satirical.* "Satire sounds like you're making fun of something. And the truth is, I'm not making fun of the suburbs," Cherry told The Associated Press, adding to *Entertainment Weekly,* "I love the values the suburbs represent. Family, community, God." But since "stuff happens," the "fun" comes from watching women "making bad choices" and suffering the repercussions.

That's not "stealth feminism," it's just vindictive. Nor is it new—the Right loves punishing female sinners. Sadly, you're buying into regressive stereotyping gussied up as female empowerment. It's fabulous that it illuminates the frustrations accompanying stay-at-home motherhood. But while writer Ellen Goodman points to Lynette as a "signpost of a slowly changing society" and the *Pittsburgh Post-Gazette* branded her a "Generation's Truthsayer," they (and you) are ignoring the show's fundamental premise that child care is solely women's responsibility. Doesn't it bother you that Lynette is the very model of silent suffering? In a key flashback, she nods in queasy acquiescence when her husband tells her to quit her career to stay home with her babies. And no matter how low she sinks under the pressure of raising four kids—popping their ADD pills, self-medicating with red wine—she never asks her husband to share the burden.

As the former hostess of weekly *Xena, Warrior Princess* and *Buffy the Vampire Slayer* parties,

I'd happily join a coffee klatch centered around subversive, kitschy girl power. Friendships between intelligent, fleshed-out female characters were powerful enough to save the world on those shows; in contrast, the *Housewives* keep secrets from—rather than lean on—each other.

Look, I appreciate a good comedy as much as the next gal, but this show is more dangerous than a simple guilty pleasure—it's backlash humor hawking conservative ideology. For example, biological determinism explains a PTA mom's back-stabbing behavior: "It hasn't really changed since Girl Scouts. Girls smile at you to your face, but then behind your back they make fun of you," Susan complains.

"That never would have happened in Boy Scouts," answers Lynette. "A guy takes his opponent on face-to-face, and once he's won, he's top dog. It's primitive but fair."

"Isn't it sexist of us to generalize like this?" Gabrielle asks.

"It's science, Gabrielle," says Lynette. "Sociologists have documented this stuff."

"Well, who am I to argue with sociologists," Gabrielle shrugs.

This is what passes for "girl talk" on Wisteria Lane—too bad it sounds so much like the Best of Dr. Laura.

Desperately Missing Roseanne,
Jenn

Dear Jenn,

At least we agree that *Desperate Housewives* is "darkly comic." Webster's says comedy is "the representation of human error and weakness as provocative of amusement." That means screwups and bad choices—which you seem to see as "vindictive" to women. Does that mean Jerry Lewis, the Marx Brothers, and Three Stooges are "vindictive" to men? But I won't suggest you "lighten up," because "Can't you take a joke?" is often used to undermine legitimate social critique.

Instead, I will deconstruct the joke. On *Desperate,* we're in the land of camp, that often gay, exaggerated aesthetic the late Susan Sontag so brilliantly pegged in "Notes on 'Camp'" (1964). *Housewives* is a textbook case, beginning with the "double sense in which some things can be taken"—a "private zany experience" for insiders. Sontag's characteristics of camp also include exaggerated sex roles, shallow characters, overweening passion, heightened glamour, even pleasure in the "psychopathology of affluence."

That's exactly life on Wisteria Lane: murder, suicide, pedophilia, adultery, prostitution and drug abuse, all on one fabulously landscaped suburban street. *Desperate* creator Marc Cherry—who began his career writing for another woman-centered camp classic, *The Golden Girls*—claims to be a gay Republican (what could be campier?) while creating a show that's cul-de-sac Sodom.

You "got" the tongue-in-cheek aesthetic of *Xena* and *Buffy* because you liked the subject of superheroes fighting evil. I loved them too. But you're so offended by stay-at-home moms that *Housewives'* camp style doesn't register. Yet it's crucial. The show is not making policy recommendations about child care any more than it is recommending fornication and a multitude of sins yet to come (stay tuned!).

But enough critical theory—let's get to the burrito sex scene, my favorite. To win back her husband, domestic diva Bree (Marcia Cross) arrives at his hotel room wearing only red lingerie under an overcoat. At that very moment, however, he is chowing down on a giant burrito. The husband takes the bait, but, no surprise, the burrito topples from the table and distracts her. His wife's concern with a teetering bean wrap symbolizes how she makes him feel stifled.

The camera steps in as feminist, zooming in on the cheesy mess about to hit the floor. Who could think of sex at a time like this? Not us. As Infuriated Husband escorts her out, Bree quips: "Obviously you've never had to clean a cheese stain off a carpet."

"You bet, honey," I tell the TV. I've also urged Lynette to go back to work part-time, even while I identify with her pleasure in feminine arts I love, like sewing. These are women's concerns in a fortysomething woman's world, so rarely seen on prime-time television. That's my "zany private" experience as a feminist who believes women are good enough to be bad.

Still Loving Housewives,
Jessica

Hey Jessica,

What's with your accusation that I'm "offended by stay-at-home moms," rather than by a show which treats them so shabbily? I'm surprised you'd dust off the tired, misguided media chestnut painting feminists as anti-mother. I never implied that mothers shouldn't stay home if they want to (and if they *can*—that choice is a luxury in today's economy).

Jess, I don't need you to deconstruct the joke for me—I just don't buy it. When Roseanne Barr wrestled Meryl Streep in the film *She Devil,* that was camp. But when a bunch of conservative guys create a show in which every female character is portrayed as self-indulgent and incompetent, that's just good old-fashioned Hollywood crap. Can you really be so elitist as to think that burrito stains and arts and crafts are the "woman's world" concerns that most deserve celluloid attention? As for Lynette's "pleasure" in sewing school-play costumes, *please*—that "feminine art" drove her to drugs!

The Golden Girls played by their own rules, letting no societal code (and no man) dictate their behavior. Twenty years later, Lynette lives her husband's choices, Gabrielle trades sex for jewelry, "good girl" Susan is pitted against the "town slut," and Bree would rather keep a cheap motel's carpet clean than have an orgasm.

Yet that's why corporate media finds Wisteria's women so appealing. Remember when *Time* cited neurotic, micro-miniskirted *Ally McBeal* as the poster girl for the supposed death of feminism in 1998? Seven years later, it's the same old story: Reviewers from *The Washington Post* to *The Jerusalem Post* insist *Housewives* represents "reality" in a "typical" American neighborhood, and proves

feminism has "failed" or been "killed." By the time Oprah Winfrey and Dr. Phil paraded around "Real-Life Desperate Housewives," I was ready to throw up. This show and its '50s politics are being used against us; don't confuse that with feminism.

At least Buffy's *on DVD,*
Jenn

Dear Jenn—

You have tried to indict *Desperate Housewives* and its fans with charges of male oppression and elitism. I beg to differ.

Hardly a male cabal, the *Desperate* writing staff is one-third female—slightly exceeding the percentage of women in the Writer's Guild of America, and much higher than that of, say, the popular sitcom *Everybody Loves Raymond* (only one of 10 writers is a woman this season). As to elitism, in today's economy, stay-at-home parenting is no "luxury," as you claim, but a savings for many families, considering child-care costs, income taxes and commuting expenses. So much for housewives = haute bourgeoisie.

You also imply that sewing is elitist. Careerism and girl-power fantasy blind you to women's real experience and history. I learned sewing from my grandmother, who learned from her mother, a seamstress. Making my own clothes is a proud working-class legacy.

Yes, the backlash scolds women. But so do you. You cherry-pick grievances, first faulting a character's "silent suffering," then branding the *Housewives* as "self-indulgent." Which is it? Neither. They're cartoon characters. This is high camp, which Sontag calls a multilayered "mode of enjoyment, of appreciation—not judgment."

You're still welcome to come over for *Desperate* night—I'll teach you to sew (during commercials). We'll start simple: maybe an apron.

Yours in stitches—
Jessica

From Fly-Girls to Bitches and Hos

Joan Morgan

Any feminism that fails to acknowledge that black folks in America are living and trying to love in a war zone is useless to our struggle against sexism. Though it's often portrayed as part of the problem, rap music is essential to that struggle because it takes us straight to the battlefield.

My decision to expose myself to the sexism of Dr. Dre, Ice Cube, Snoop Dogg, or the Notorious B.I.G. is really my plea to my brothers to tell me who they are. I need to know why they are so angry at me. Why is disrespecting me one of the few things that make them feel like men? What's the haps, what are you going through on the daily that's got you acting so foul?

As a black woman and a feminist, I listen to the music with a willingness to see past the machismo in order to be clear about what I'm *really* dealing with. What I hear frightens me. On booming track after booming track, I hear brothers talking about spending each day high as hell on malt liquor and Chronic. Don't sleep. What passes for "40 and a blunt" good times in most of hip-hop is really alcoholism, substance abuse, and chemical dependency. When brothers can talk so cavalierly about killing each other and then reveal that they have no expectation to see their twenty-first birthday, that is straight-up depression *masquerading* as machismo.

Anyone curious about the process and pathologies that form the psyche of the young, black, and criminal-minded needs to revisit our dearly departed Notorious B.I.G.'s first album, *Ready to Die.* Chronicling the life and times of the urban "soldier," the album is a blues-laden soul train that took us on a hustler's life journey. We boarded with the story of his birth, strategically stopped to view his dysfunctional, warring family,

his first robbery, his first stint in jail, murder, drug-dealing, getting paid, partying, sexin', rappin', mayhem, and death. Biggie's player persona might have momentarily convinced the listener that he was livin' phat without a care in the world but other moments divulged his inner hell. The chorus of "Everyday Struggle": *I don't wanna live no more / Sometimes I see death knockin' at my front door* revealed that "Big Poppa" was also plagued with guilt, regret, and depression. The album ultimately ended with his suicide.

The seemingly impenetrable wall of sexism in rap music is really the complex mask African-Americans often wear both to hide and express the pain. At the close of this millennium, hip-hop is still one of the few forums in which young black men, even surreptitiously, are allowed to express their pain.

When it comes to the struggle against sexism and our intimate relationships with black men, some of the most on-point feminist advice I've received comes from sistas like my mother, who wouldn't dream of using the term. During our battle to resolve our complicated relationships with my equally wonderful and errant father, my mother presented me with the following gems of wisdom, "One of the most important lessons you will ever learn in life and love, is that you've got to love people for what they are—not for who you would like them to be."

This is crystal clear to me when I'm listening to hip-hop. Yeah, sistas are hurt when we hear brothers calling us bitches and hos. But the real crime isn't the name-calling, it's their failure to love us—to be our brothers in the way that we commit ourselves to being their sistas. But recognize: Any man who doesn't truly love himself is incapable of loving us in the healthy way we need to be loved. It's extremely telling that men who can only see us as "bitches" and "hos" refer to themselves only as "niggas."

In the interest of our emotional health and overall sanity, black women have got to learn to love brothers realistically, and that means differentiating between who they are and who we'd like them to be. Black men are engaged in a war where the real enemies—racism and the white power structure—are masters of camouflage. They've conditioned our men to believe the enemy is brown. The effects of this have been as wicked as they've been debilitating. Being in battle with an enemy that looks just like you makes it hard to believe in the basics every human being needs. For too many black men there is no trust, no community, no family. Just self.

Since hip-hop is the mirror in which so many brothers see themselves, it's significant that one of the music's most prevalent mythologies is that black boys rarely grow into men. Instead, they remain perpetually post-adolescent or die. For all the machismo and testosterone in the music, it's frighteningly clear that many brothers see themselves as powerless when it comes to facing the evils of the larger society, accepting responsibility for their lives or the lives of their children.

So, sista friends, we gotta do what any rational, survivalist-minded person would do after finding herself in a relationship with someone whose pain makes him abusive. We've gotta continue to give up the love but *from a distance that's safe.* Emotional distance is a great enabler of unconditional love and support because it allows us to recognize that the attack, the "bitch, ho" bullshit—isn't personal but part of the illness.

And the focus of black feminists has got to change. We can't afford to keep expending energy on banal discussions of sexism in rap when sexism is only part of a huge set of problems. Continuing on our previous path is akin to demanding that a fiending, broke crackhead not rob you blind because it's *wrong* to do so.

If feminism intends to have any relevance in the lives of the majority of black women, if it intends to move past theory and become functional it has to rescue itself from the ivory towers of academia. Like it or not, hip-hop is not only the dominion of the young, black, and male, it is also the world in which young black women live and survive. A functional game plan for us, one that is going to be as helpful to Shequanna on 142nd as it is to Samantha at Sarah Lawrence, has to recognize hip-hop's ability to articulate the pain our *community* is in and use that knowledge to create a redemptive, healing space.

Notice the emphasis on "community." Hip-hop isn't only instrumental in exposing black men's pain, it brings the healing sistas need right to the surface. Sad as it may be, it's time to stop ignoring the fact that rappers meet "bitches" and "hos" daily—women who reaffirm their depiction of us on vinyl. Backstage, the road, and the 'hood are populated with women who would do anything to be with a rapper sexually for an hour if not a night. It's time to stop fronting like we don't know who rapper Jeru the Damaja was talking about when he said:

Now a queen's a queen but a stunt's a stunt
You can tell who's who by the things they want

Sex has long been the bartering chip that women use to gain protection, material wealth, and the vicarious benefits of power. In the black community, where women are given less access to all of the above, "trickin'" becomes a means of leveling the playing field. Denying the justifiable anger of rappers—men who couldn't get the time of day from these women before a few dollars and a record deal—isn't empowering or strategic. Turning a blind eye and scampering for moral high ground diverts our attention away from the young women who are being denied access to power and are suffering for it.

It might've been more convenient to direct our sista-fied rage attention to "the sexist representation of women" in those now infamous Sir Mix-A-Lot videos, to fuss over *one* sexist rapper, but wouldn't it have been more productive to address the failing self-esteem of the 150 or so half-naked young women who were willing, unpaid participants? And what about how flip we are when it comes to using the b-word to describe each other? At some point we've all been the recipients of competitive, unsisterly, "bitchiness," particularly when vying for male attention.

Since being black and a woman makes me fluent in both isms, I sometimes use racism as an illuminating analogy. Black folks have finally gotten to the point where we recognize that we sometimes engage in oppressive behaviors that white folks have little to do with. Complexion prejudices and classism are illnesses which have their *roots* in white racism, but the perpetrators are certainly black.

Similarly, sistas have to confront the ways we're complicit in our own oppression. Sad to say it, but many of the ways in which men exploit our images and sexuality in hip-hop is done with our permission and cooperation. We need to be as accountable to each other as we believe "race traitors" (i.e., 100 or so brothers in blackface cooning in a skinhead's music video) should be to our community. To acknowledge this doesn't deny our victimization, but it does raise the critical issue of whose responsibility it is to end our oppression. As a feminist, I believe it is too great a responsibility to leave to men.

A few years ago, on an airplane making its way to Montego Bay, I received another gem of girlfriend wisdom from a sixty-year-old self-declared nonfeminist. She was meeting her husband to celebrate her thirty-fifth wedding anniversary. After telling her I was twenty-seven and very much single, she looked at me and shook her head sadly. "I feel sorry for your generation. You don't know how to have relationships, especially the women." Curious, I asked her why she thought this was. "The women of your generation, you want to be right. The women of my generation, we didn't care about being right. We just wanted to win."

Too much of the discussion regarding sexism and the music focuses on being right. We feel we're *right* and the rappers are wrong. The rappers feel it's their *right* to describe their "reality" in any way they see fit. The store owners feel it's

their *right* to sell whatever the consumer wants to buy. The consumer feels it's his *right* to be able to decide what he wants to listen to. We may be the "rightest" of the bunch, but we sure as hell ain't doing the winning.

I believe hip-hop can help us win. Let's start by recognizing that its illuminating, informative narration and its incredible ability to articulate our collective pain is an invaluable tool when examining gender relations. The information we amass can help create a redemptive, healing space for brothers and sistas.

We're all winners when a space exists for brothers to honestly state and explore the roots of their pain and subsequently their misogyny, sans judgment. It is criminal that the only space our society provided for the late Tupac Shakur to examine the pain, confusion, drug addiction, and fear that led to his arrest and his eventual assassination was in a prison cell. How can we win if a prison cell is the only space an immensely talented but troubled young black man could dare utter these words: "Even though I'm not guilty of the charges they gave me, I'm not innocent in terms of the way I was acting. I'm just as guilty for not doing things. Not with this case but with my life. I had a job to do and I never showed up. I was so scared of this responsibility that I was running away from it." We have to do better than this for our men.

And we have to do better for ourselves. We desperately need a space to lovingly address the uncomfortable issues of our failing self-esteem, the ways we sexualize and objectify ourselves, our confusion about sex and love and the unhealthy, unloving, unsisterly ways we treat each other. Commitment to developing these spaces gives our community the potential for remedies based on honest, clear diagnoses.

As I'm a black woman, I am aware that this doubles my workload—that I am definitely going to have to listen to a lot of shit I won't like—but without these candid discussions, there is little to no hope of exorcising the illness that hurts and sometimes kills us.

Pop Goes the Arab World

Popular Music, Gender, Politics, and Transnationalism in the Arab World

Shereen Abdel-Nabi, Jehan Agha, Julia Choucair, and Maya Mikdashi

Assumptions are often made by scholars and commentators regarding the static nature of contemporary Arab politics and societies. They frequently look for socio-political dynamism in the arenas they are used to—newspapers, television, and parliament/congress, to name a few. When they do not see or hear these debates taking place in the formal institutions that they are familiar with, they are quick to assume that these reassessments are simply not occurring. Nothing could be further from the truth. The Arab world is debating with itself and reassessing such subjects as politics, identity, and gender roles. The space that is being utilized for debate, however, is easily unnoticeable to those who are not adept at finding these forums and are instead used to being *presented* with them. When public space is limited, any opening will be used to the utmost, giving rise to new forums for debate. . . . This paper seeks to examine the political, identity, and gender debates that are currently occurring within the realm of popular music.

Popular music is readily accessible for consumption, easy to understand, and addresses important themes that speak to a collective audience, creating a sense of community. While poetry arguably rivals pop music in this capacity, the appeal of Arabic poetry—both contemporary and classical—is limited by illiteracy rates, censorship, and a gap between the evolution of the Arabic language into the often confusingly separate spheres of written and spoken Arabic. . . . Television, another sphere of debate, is more expensive to own and consume, as well as more easily controlled, by states making it less accessible than popular music. It is within this context

of mass production and consumption that the significant and often overlooked role of popular music must be examined.

THE NEW MEDIA IN THE ARAB WORLD

The notion of globalization forging associations between different people, cultures and nations, resulting in an exchange of ideas and information is not novel. New media, particularly the Internet and satellite television, has emerged as a central agent facilitating this trend. These new technologies have burgeoned the channels through which the exchange of ideas and information can take place even across borders, eroding former barriers that impeded the flow of information.[1] The introduction of these technologies has had tremendous ramifications on the Arab world, particularly concerning culture and identity, and one can look to the changing nature of the region's popular music industry as an example.

Before the advent of these new technologies, communication in the Arab world was structured around the authoritarian regimes characteristic of the region. Communication mediums were used as vehicles through which the regimes reinforced their ideologies and needs for maintaining social cohesion, leaving little room for creativity and diversity.[2] People did not have easy access to information from other Arab countries because two types of boundaries existed: physical borders and government censorship. People from a particular Arab country, for example, had difficulty understanding other Arabic dialects—with the exception of the Egyptian dialect because of the country's leading role in movie and music production—because they were not exposed to them. Access to different information was limited to those who had the means to travel and interact with others. The state censors, then, were seen as a way to help promote national identity, making each individual Arab country's culture homogenous. As a result, Arab audiences had few choices in terms of programming and knowing this, broadcasters were not concerned with excelling or being innovative because they were guaranteed an audience.

Free from censorship and spatial considerations, new media is changing this controlling communications environment by enabling access to foreign as well as regional sources of information, thereby empowering the Arab public with choices. New media's ability to transcend borders has led to an all-encompassing Arab media market, targeting a broader Arab audience. Messages relayed to this broader Arab audience, therefore, have become of primary importance, making the location of where the satellite television programs are produced and where the Web sites are being created of secondary importance. The result is new media's unification of the larger regional market instead of each individual market within each Arab country.[3]

Like other markets, the Arab media market is subject to the laws of supply and demand. Programming then is no longer a reflection of each individual Arab government's propaganda but, rather, a reflection of the viewers' demands. With the introduction of satellite television, the Arab public not only has access to local and regional programming, but also to international programming. As a result, the Arab audience's taste is increasingly becoming more sophisticated and diverse. They expect more because they have choices. Therefore, Arab satellite channels are not only competing with their regional counterparts, but with their international ones as well. Satellite channels are constantly trying to gain advantage over their competition by innovating and providing higher quality programming. Furthermore, because many of the Arab satellite stations first began broadcasting from abroad, foreign standards have been applied to their formatting and presentation. The consequence then is an empowerment of the audience and an improvement in their satisfaction.[4]

This phenomenon is affecting the Arab popular music industry in several ways. It has given greater importance to the visual aspects of popular music because of the mushrooming Arab satellite music television stations, modeled after their foreign competitors such as MTV. Viewers can now vote for their favorite videos by sending e-mails or text messages from their cellular phones to the channels, resulting in a more defined measure of singers' popularity. Not only does the Arab audience take the artist's voice and lyrics into consideration, but they now also consider their image to be of equal importance. Furthermore, they no longer have the attention span for singers to perform two-hour songs as Umm Kulthoum did while standing still on stage. Instead, they expect the experience to be one of participation, stimulating all of their senses. New media has therefore increased competition between Arab singers by rendering conformity and uniformity as obsolete. In order to be successful, Arab artists in turn have to keep up with what has become a fast-paced, cut-throat industry.

This urgency for innovation has caused many Arab singers, such as Amr Diab and Elissa, to revisit the technique of hybridizing Arabic pop music by incorporating foreign elements, such as techno and Spanish flamenco music, into their songs and performances.[5] This has caused the debate surrounding hybridized music to resurface. Its critics deem it to be unauthentic and accuse the artists of polluting the naturally rich Arabic music, while others argue that the fact that the songs are performed in Arabic by Arab artists in and of itself makes them authentic.[6] Critics have also contested the trend among producers to reintroduce classic songs such as those of Umm Kulthoum and Abdel Halim Hafez by remixing them with techno music. Despite their objections, these songs continue to gain popularity and attention both in the region and abroad.

Arab pop music, mainly through music videos, is witnessing an explosion of overt female sexuality as a result of the quest to innovate. Nancy Ajram and Haifa Wehbe are forcibly pushing the boundaries and paving the way for other female singers to capitalize on their femininity in order to secure a bigger following. It is too premature to provide a comprehensive and conclusive evaluation of this movement's influence on Arab society as a whole, however it has unquestionably allowed for important discourse to take place regarding female sexuality and gender roles.

. . .

Western audiences, both those who normally listen to the "world music" genre as well as those who prefer mainstream music, have been extremely receptive to the Arab singers who have reached out to them. It has become commonplace to see trendsetters dancing to the vibrant tunes of Arabic music blaring in the fashionable dance clubs of New York, London and Paris. New media has helped bring Arab music into the international pop music scene. The Internet and digital sampling are factors that facilitated this by making it easier to locate and sample Arabic music.[7] Several mainstream American artists, such as Jay Z, Beyoncé Knowles, and Mandy Moore, have successfully done so; others are sure to jump on the bandwagon.

New media as a facilitating agent for globalization thereby affecting culture and identity is not exclusive to the Arab region. What makes the situation in the Arab world unique is that before the introduction of the Internet and satellite TV, the governments heavily controlled the media environment and censorship was the custom. New media offers the Arab public an alternative, more open media environment. As a result of the symbiotic relationship which exists between technology and communication, the Arab world will continue to witness an evolving popular music industry with the introduction of every new medium and technology. With the onset of each evolution, Arab artists will attempt to adapt and reinvent themselves. Those who do so successfully will emerge in the limelight both at home and abroad, ensuring that Arab pop music continues to garner international attention.

POPULAR MUSIC AND POLITICS

The "new media" phenomenon in the Arab world has found recent expression through the show *Superstar*, the Arab world's version of the program *American Idol*. Arab *Superstar* is a joint venture between TV 19 (UK-based creator of the *Pop Idol* concept), Warner Music International, and its Middle Eastern licensee, Music Master International. The program was broadcast regionally by Lebanese satellite channel Future TV. It was Future Television's idea to negotiate the contract with Fremantle Media for the entire Arab world, as opposed to a single-nation package. Although probably guided by a desire to increase viewership, the result of the decision to make it a regional show transcended its financial effects.

The 10,000 entrants from across the Arab world who originally applied to appear on the show were narrowed down to 12 finalists from seven different countries. Over 21 weeks, viewers got to vote by fax, Internet, or cell phone for their favorite singers, who covered a variety of musical styles from Arabic pop to traditional dance and classical music; there was no Western pop. Viewer response to the program surpassed all expectations. Jordan, Lebanon, and Syria witnessed lavish campaigns including large television screens, posters and e-mail messages urging fans to vote for each national representative. The organizers of Arab *Superstar* claim that more than 30 million people watched the show's 18 August finale, won by 19-year-old Jordanian Diana Karazon. According to Nadim Munla, Future Television's chairman of the board of directors: "No one in his right state of mind would have anticipated 4,800,000 votes in the final round."

. . .

Carl Abu Malham, director at Beirut-based Music Master International, describes the regional impact of the show as, "an earthquake, on a social level. It was the first time the Arab world had voted and participated in the creation of a TV program." Similarly, Marwan Bishara, a politics lecturer at the American University of Paris, asserted: "In the Arab world, where few can speak freely, let alone vote, satellite television channels are becoming a virtual Democracy Wall. They're the only opening, so people try to push as much through them as they can."

Rami Khouri, editor of *The Daily Star,* highlighted this episode as "a fascinating example of how the power of technology—in this case satellite television, Internet, and cell phones—can tap sentiments and prompt people to action." But what was even more striking, Khouri said, was the Jordanian singer Diana Karazon's victory margin:

> She won by only 52 to 48 percent in a region where presidents always win by 99 percent. I do not recall in my happy adult life a national vote that resulted in a 52 to 48 percent victory. . . . Most of the "referenda" or "elections" that take place in our region usually result in fantastic pre-fixed victories. So this outcome—even for just a song contest—is a breath of fresh air. Thank you for allowing ordinary Arabs to show that they are not always willing participants in the political freak shows that are the "official elections" for president and other forms of Great Leader.

From this point of view, the show generated an enclave of autonomy through the creation and maintenance of an alternative psychological reality that becomes a different kind of public space, a new little world within the old—an alternative public realm. . . .

Is this role of popular music as a venue for political expression a mere reflection or summary of public mood, or can it become a communicative forum through which some people engage in political action? In other words, is popular music a tool or resource that increases political capacity, especially for people who have traditionally been blocked from participation in more traditional and institutionalized political arenas?

While some see popular music as empowering, enriching, and "subversive" in the sense of being counter-hegemonic and progressive, others argue that the "empowering potential" of music is based on a limited conception that does not consider power beyond perception and feeling.

Thus, popular music is limited to articulating and altering our perceptions of the world, perhaps even giving a glimpse of other, better, worlds, but is ultimately unable to change the world. Proponents of this view argue that popular music's interplay between everyday common sense and imagination makes it a wholly inappropriate vehicle for inspiring political collective action. . . . In fact, this denial of the empowering potential of popular music can be taken even further through the argument that popular music serves as a "safety-valve," making people feel empowered without them needing to do other things. In this context, music is seen as reinforcing the "hegemony" of the existing social order. . . .

These varying responses reflect a wider debate about the nature of popular music culture and demonstrate that popular culture cannot be conceived as either pure domination or as resistance. Rather, the value of studying these spaces lies in exploring them as sites of contestation where contradictory tendencies are symbolically negotiated and mediated. . . .

. . .

Communities need tools to imagine, reinvent, and reinforce themselves. The Arab nation uses popular music as one of these tools, from Umm Kulthoum singing in praise of pan-Arabism to Yuri Mrakadi adamantly singing "*arabiyyon ana*" in MSA [Modern Standard Arabic], Arabic music has served as perhaps the most important artistic identifier of an Arab community. . . . As discussed earlier in this paper, the retreat of Arab politics into art is strongly manifested in popular music. The politics of identity, a universally controversial debate, often finds its Arab platform in quartertones. There are four significant uses of popular music, all of which speak to its role in the Arab world.

1. Creation of identity: Popular music can answer questions of identity; we use popular music to create for ourselves a particular sort of self-definition, a particular place in society. Popular music reinforces the identification—with the music we like, with the performers of that music, with other people who like it.

The production of identity is also the production of non-identity. It is a process of inclusion and exclusion.

2. Management of feeling: Music serves the social function of management between our public and private emotional lives.

3. Organization of time: Popular music shapes popular memory and organizes our sense of time.

4. Possession of music: The final function of popular music is that it is something possessed. In possessing popular music, we make it part of our own identity and build it into our sense of "self."[8]

. . .

POPULAR MUSIC AND FEMALE SEXUALITY

There exists a fluid yet complex relationship between music, culture, and identity, as it oscillates between reflection of prevailing norms and attitudes, rebellion against these, or a site of contestation and transformation. . . .

. . .

With the rise of the music video and its increased accessibility to Arab populations through satellite TV channels, the visual images of Arab pop singers seem to speak as loud as, if not louder than, the music itself. In an explosion of the visual medium, satellite stations, mostly based in Beirut and Egypt, are home to numerous "top 20 countdowns" as well as stations dedicated solely to music videos, even those which many state-owned and run television stations refuse to air. Among the upsurge are a new crop of racy and at times scandalous female performers who are becoming famous and even infamous, for their choice of music video images. Though notions of gender and sexuality are not novel within the Arab video clip, and can be discussed in a variety of contexts that include the representations of men and women, of homosexuality, and of females within Arab male artists' videos, it is the relatively recent trend of risqué female performers who garner attention here. Singers like Nancy Ajram and Haifa Wehbe, both of Lebanese origin,

have stunned audiences and generated discussion among government, entertainment, and religious officials, with their "sexy" videos and blatant sex appeal. Accordingly, the blitz of dewy looks, pouting lips, and suggestive dance on Arab satellite channels is outraging some critics who have dubbed the performers "weapons of singing destruction."[9] With charges against them ranging from "turning a woman's body and its superior qualities into a commodity," to being "part of an American policy to strip Arab cultures of their values," almost everyone has an opinion on the singers. Though obviously not without their detractors, Ajram and Wehbe have consequently enjoyed tremendous success across the Arab world, with skyrocketing sales and an abundance of performances across the region. Hence lies the contradictory role of popular music, whereby many have noted the paradox of Ajram's and Wehbe's success in societies characterized by both insiders and outsiders as predominantly conservative.

What, then, does the burgeoning phenomenon mean for popular music, its performers, and its active consumers? Nancy Ajram, Haifa Wehbe, and others should be seen not as the product of, but as part of, the process and negotiation of identity and transformation of consciousness. In light of the enormous amount of negative feedback they have received, as well as realities on the ground that include a relative inability to appear on the streets of the countries as the pop singers appear in their video clips, social constraints that limit female mobility, and norms that continue to dictate female sexuality, the images of the singers cannot simply be considered a reflection of larger trends and changes within society. The opening up of the music video does not necessarily denote an opening up of contemporary Arab society. Similarly, they cannot merely be written off as a rebellious fad operating in a market with no buyers. Given that their images have produced such a massive response, both negative and positive, they have obviously touched upon something significant and relevant to the societies within which they operate. Like any social discourse, music and its performance is meaningful precisely insofar as at least some people believe that it is because communities of people invest in it and agree collectively that it serves as some sort of valid currency. In short, music is always dependent on the conferring of social meaning. Ajram and Wehbe are not operating in a vacuum, but rather in societies that have voiced their approval, indifference, or disapproval through consumerism. Some may attack the singers, but others are walking into shops and asking for contact lenses "the color of Elissa's eyes," another of the risqué performers. Though a somewhat naïve and understated view of her own sexuality, Ajram has noted that, while her "clip is bold," looks are not the only factor that have made her and the song a success, for if she did not possess a talent for singing, album sales would not be so high. Her logic, however, can be extended to include the realization that if she did not strike a cord with her audience, an audience that is at once embracing and disowning of her image, her success would be either non-existent or merely quietly achieved.

Not only is the meteoric rise of Ajram and Wehbe notable, but also the reasons behind the response they have provoked. They have spoken to something and have been consumed for something that most have attributed to pure sex appeal. Critics have noted that Ajram's performances witness a large crowd for the mere fact that she is a symbol of feminine seduction and not for her talent to sing.[10] If pure sexuality is in fact the driving force behind their success, is there reason to worry? Sex sells and these artists have realized it and taken the lead. Rather, what should be of concern is the agency of the women involved. In depicting a certain image and profile, are these women choosing their own representations, or are they being chosen for them? It used to be the case that those who were writing the songs and music and producing and directing the music videos were male, but this is presently not entirely the case. There is a new and growing group of female directors, one of whom has directed both Nancy Ajram's and Elissa's videos, as well as increased artistic interpretation and involvement of the female artists in the creative process. Moreover, when approached about their videos and prevalent perceptions of them, most of the female singers appear comfortable with

themselves and their position in the spotlight. Their videos portray women who appear empowered and in control of their sexuality.

The stipulation of reasons behind why it sells in the Arab world has taken some interesting forms. According to one Lebanese sociologist living in Cairo, who has blamed male-dominated societies for making women cover up, "when the condition of women on the street is unnatural, the demand for vulgarity and nudity increases. That's what viewers want and television stations have to cater to that demand."[11] This sentiment, falling somewhere in between the connection between music and inter-gender relations as performance that protests yet maintains the order, and performance that challenges the order, though interesting, does not adequately capture the role of music as a site of contestation and transformation. It does, however, offer testimony to the vital role that musicians often play as cultural guardians. Perhaps these female singers, as part of larger Arab societies, have somehow been entrusted with its preservation, though what is to be preserved is a question that continues to plague the societies. Controversy within these societies has spilled over into the realm of popular music and vice versa, attesting to the reciprocal relationship between the social discourse of music and those that produce it, as well as to the position of pop music as a medium within which the evolution of culture, values and norms can take place. Within this context, popular music, and particularly the music video in the Arab world, continues to be of real significance, and as music video clips continue to sell music, image will play an even greater role within the musical discourse and its potential as a site, target and promoter of social transformation and contestation.

As a realm of music with a larger collective audience than any art form in previous history, popular music occupies a significant, if not entirely clear, role within the society that consumes it. As with any social discourse, music's relationship with the society from which it is produced is one of reciprocity, as it influences the society that in turn confers meaning upon it. Popular music in the Arab world is no exception. Within the context of the proliferation of new media and its consequences, the significant and evolving role of popular music within the Arab world must be understood. In the face of truly limited and limiting public space, popular music has utilized the scarce space available and increasingly continues to do so as a result of new media trends and transformations. Some of the various ways in which popular music has manifested itself, alongside the themes and issues continuously being addressed, debated, contested, and confirmed through the medium have previously been highlighted. The interaction of politics, identity, sexuality, and music have received an introductory treatment as the discussion of any one of these relationships can take vast and varied forms.

NOTES

1. Larry Strelitz, "Where the Global Meets the Local: Media Studies and the Myth of Cultural Homogenization," 2001, at www.tbsjournal.com/archives/spring01/strelitz.htm.
2. Jon W. Anderson, "Technology, Media, and the Next Generation in the Middle East," September 1999, at http://nmit/georgetown.edu/papers/jwanderson.
3. Jon B. Alterman, "Transnational Media and Social Change in the Arab World," 1998, at www.tbsjournal.com/archives/spring1999/articles/alterman.
4. Ibid.
5. Louis Werner, "Arab Pop on the World Stage," *Aramco World,* March/April 2000, at www.cafearabica.com/culture/culturels/culmusic15.
6. Jim Bessman, "Arabic Music Moves West," *Billboard,* 11 August 2001 [online], Academic Search Premier.
7. Georgina Born and David Hesmondhalgh, eds., *Western Music and Its Others: Difference, Representation, and Appropriation in Music* (Berkeley: University of California Press, 2000).
8. Richard Leppert and Susan McClary, *Music and Society: The Politics of Composition, Performance, and Reception* (Cambridge: Cambridge University Press, 1987), pp. 142–143.
9. "Arab Pop Video: 'Weapon of Singing Destruction': Sultry Singers Gain Following Despite Government Censorship," Agence Press, 23 October 2003.
10. "Rotana Furious Over Nancy Ajram's Participation in Jarash."
11. "Arab Pop Video: 'Weapon of Singing Destruction.'"

R E A D I N G *77*

Cut-and-Paste Revolution
Notes from the Girl Zine Explosion

Jennifer Bleyer

When they started publishing *Cupsize* in 1994, most of the other zines that Sasha Cagen and Tara Emelye Needham had seen were "creepy things by boys who hung out in the East Village." The two friends had clicked with each other as disgruntled first-years at Amherst College in Massachusetts, and when circumstances and school transfers found them reunited in New York City a few years later, they knew that making a zine as sassy and smart as themselves was exactly the way to cement their friendship. Cagen was working, ironically, at a major women's glossy—the kind of magazine that runs stories like "Drop Twenty Pounds in Two Weeks!" and "Moves That Will Make Him Beg for Mercy!"—and thus had unlimited access to office equipment and supplies. Late at night Needham would come to Cagen's midtown office building, and the two would ride to the twenty-first floor and take over the corporate suite. Writing, cutting, gluing, and drawing, they would laugh riotously into the wee hours, looking out over the twinkling Manhattan skyline.

Cupsize was the conduit through which their inner censors were silenced and their deepest voices unearthed. They wrote weighty personal tomes about bisexuality and analyzed the virtues of public and private education. At the same time, they wrote jokey stories about excessive eyebrow tweezing and memoirs of their first visit to a porn shop. On the cover, they would photocopy a swatch from a favorite article of clothing that one of them owned, a final wink to this very personal collage. Cagen would surreptitiously make hundreds of copies of the zine at her office over the course of a month. People—especially teenage women, who ordered copies in droves—loved *Cupsize,* and Cagen and Needham loved making it. "I think one of our impulses was political, but on the deepest level it was creative," Cagen recalls, almost five years after the final issue came out. "Tara and I had a fabulous chemistry between us that was really unique. It was just this absolute freedom that we believed in each other and could put whatever we wanted on the page. It was such a unique time in our lives, not having to worry about meeting professional obligations or standards." Cagen, who is now thirty and publishes the magazine *To-Do List* in San Francisco, wistfully remembers the zine heyday as a sort of literary Wild West, in which the utter lack of rules could yield extraordinary results. "You wound up with some really sloppy stuff," she says, "but you also ended up with these beautiful unpolished gems like *Cupsize* that would never make it in a commercial context."

Cagen and Needham were not alone. From the late eighties to the mid-nineties, thousands of zines sprouted up like resilient weeds inside the cracks of the mainstream media's concrete. Like those of most underground phenomena, their origin is fuzzy and debatable. Some trace it to the political broadsheets of the anti–Vietnam War movement; others link it to the raunchy, edgy comix of the seventies and eighties. One thing is certain, however: after Xerox machines became widely accessible and before the explosion of the Internet, there was a brief moment during which people realized that they could make their own rudimentary publications on copy paper, fasten them with staples, and send them out along the zine distribution thoroughfares that coursed across the country, without any permission or guidance whatsoever. There were gay zines, travel zines, country music zines, and film noir zines. There were socialist zines, stripper zines, bicycle zines, and radical environmental zines. As Sasha Cagen explains it, the homemade publications were not bound by any particular standards of quality—sophomoric writing, lunatic ravings, and bizarre obsessions were more common than not—yet there was something beautifully democratic about letting readers sift through it all on their own, instead of having an armada of elite publishers, editors, and critics do it for them. In many ways zines predicted what would soon happen on the Web, and although the comparison is akin to that between a firecracker pop and a nuclear bomb, they helped pave the way for a culture that would allow anyone with anything to say, to say it. Zines demonstrated what by the end of the twentieth century became a credo: Free speech on demand and without apology.

The zine world, as it turned out, was as susceptible to sexism as the larger society from which its niche was carved. Sarah Dyer was the only woman in a collective of male friends working on a music zine in the late eighties, and she was constantly aggravated that people calling about the zine would instinctually ask to speak with someone else when she answered the phone. Even when she branched off to start her own zine, *Mad Planet,* Dyer realized that many people couldn't quite accept that a woman could be doing this on her own. "It got really frustrating," she recalls. "A guy who wrote one review of one comic would somehow get credited with editing my whole zine." During a trip to London, she met another girl zinester who told her about some girl zines in the United States that she had never heard of, and the need for a networking device became obvious. In 1992 Dyer started the *Action Girl* newsletter. It was one of the first resources for girl zines—a single photocopied page with the names and addresses of the few other zines made by young women at the time, folded in thirds, addressed, and mailed off with a single stamp to girls voraciously looking for their own zine community. Coincidentally, Riot Grrrl was born a few months later in Olympia, Washington, and what resulted, given the climate of free expression already engendered by the larger zine community, was a media revolution of unprecedented proportion.

Riot Grrrl, of course, was that anarchic web of punk girls who were outcasts a couple of seasons before "outcast" was "in," who decided that slumber parties and hand-holding were revolutionary activities, and who were rightfully delirious from their collective peeling away of the pretenses of American teenage girlhood. It was a grassroots movement of young women who decided that mosh pits, bands, fanzines, and revolution were not just for boys. They used the same organizational tools that feminists had wielded for decades—a cool name, a manifesto, a tattered phone list, meetings in crowded living rooms—to confront not only myriad problems in their punk scenes, high schools, and dysfunctional families but also the dogma of mainstream feminism and society.

Zines were the perfect outlet for expressing discontent and new beliefs, and thousands of them materialized alongside the Riot Grrrl juggernaut. . . .

. . . Alice Marwick found out about zines through *Sassy* magazine in 1992, when the edgy teen magazine started running a regular feature on zines. Marwick, now twenty-four, went to high school in upstate New York, where she and her friends would order the zines in *Sassy* for the cost of copying and stamps, and devour them as soon as they arrived. "Zines connected me to a lot of things I couldn't find in my hometown, to a larger like-minded community," she says. "It definitely fostered my own feminist consciousness by proving that feminism wasn't something for people my mother's age only, or a dead movement altogether. That was the feeling you got growing up where I did—as if feminism didn't have anything to offer anyone young, that it was something that had happened and was done. But finding out about girl bands and underground feminist filmmaking through zines made it something that was still going on. It was a huge inspiration to me."

Integral to reading zines was the implicit challenge to turn around and write them. Zines made clear that they were not just another product to be consumed but were unique contributions to a vast conversation which everyone was expected to join. Girls who wrote zines did so because it was activism, it was therapy, and it was fun. They did so, as Sasha Cagen and Tara Emelye Needham of *Cupsize* did, to make emblems of their friendship and beliefs. They did it to respond to other girls' zines and to engage in the larger discussion about what exactly constituted "Revolution Girl Style." . . .

. . .

Like Alice Marwick, I found out about zines through *Sassy,* and hunted relentlessly for the Riot Grrrl community that was generating these magical creations. I recall with extraordinary fondness staying up all night in high school making zines with others from my local Riot Grrrl collective. Our backpacks and Glue Stics and stolen copy cards strewn all over the floor of Kinko's, we would scour books picked up from yard sales—housewife manuals, Girl Scout guides, Barbie coloring books, anatomical diagrams—for the most ironic graphics. We were dizzying crucibles of emotion, creating ourselves as well as creating our zines—the two seemed interchangeable. Between the ages of seventeen and nineteen, I published my own zine called *Gogglebox:* a rather candid and often explicit record of my travels back and forth across the country. *Gogglebox* achieved a respectable stature in the zine community, having been named editor's choice by the now-defunct zine bible *Factsheet 5.* It generated tons of mail from girls all around the country, who poured their hearts out to me and who bought three thousand copies of the last issue. For a young writer and feminist, it was an exhilarating experience. Zines basically represented pure freedom; there were no ideological police to say that women's liberation couldn't be alternately sexy, angry, emotional, feminine, combative, childish—and unapologetically contradictory.

Revolution Girl Style was touted with an almost religious fervor. It seemed that if we only churned out enough zines and screamed loud enough, people would listen and society would quake. I do think this happened, in the way that small revolutions happen whenever people challenge the status quo and demonstrate alternative models of living in the world. But there are ways in which zines were not revolutionary, ways that are instructive for those of us committed to writing and publishing as a positive force for social change. One major detraction was how the mainstream media, with its interminable fetish for the salient and absurd, quickly pounced on zines. "Get ready for Riot Grrrl magazines," warned *USA Today.* "Hundreds of small, photocopied pamphlets now circulate, offering gut-wrenching confessional poetry and angry honest prose on topics such as rape, feeling ugly, boys, sex, and masturbation."[1] *The Dallas Morning News* leveled that "girlzines have their downside—bad spelling and layout, an excess of concert reviews, and a tendency toward self-indulgence."[2] Indeed, it was only a matter of time before Riot Grrrl was effectively subsumed by the cultural zeitgeist, and the girl zines it helped inspire became little more than social curios and collectors' items. Of course, they continued to be produced, but the much portended Revolution Girl Style that had seemed so imminent when girl zines, bands, and collectives first exploded soon seemed like little more than a blip on the radar of feminist history, a mere footnote to social trends of the nineties.

Besides the impact of being sensationalized, there was the weakening effect of capitalization. The entire zine movement was effectively over, one could say, almost as soon as it began, having been swallowed up by the great maw of popular culture with dollar signs flashing in its eyes. Like hip-hop, grunge, and punk rock, the language and style of Riot Grrrl were absorbed, repackaged, and marketed back to us in the most superficial form of its origin. Whereas Riot Grrrl's "grrrl power" was about doing it yourself and questioning authority, pop culture appropriated the message to sell a sanitized version of "girl power" that was essentially capitalism dressed up in baby doll dresses, blue nail polish, and mall-bought nose rings. Indeed, the values—fearlessness, independence, daring, and a solid

middle finger to the patriarchy—on which many girls zines were built, and for which their writers were denigrated as "angry" and "self-indulgent," were flipped on their heads and used to sell everything from cars and cigarettes to athletic shoes. The selling of girl power illustrated, as Naomi Klein wrote in *No Logo,* how "the cool hunters reduce vibrant cultural ideas to the status of archeological artifacts, and drain away whatever meaning they once held for the people who lived with them."[3]

Girl power, harnessed for its market potential and translated into consumer culture, had something for everyone. For the little girls, there were the Spice Girls and their endless records, collectibles, and concert tickets. For the bigger girls, there was *Sex and the City* and a bevy of books, movies, and magazines affirming, as Michelle Goldberg wrote, that "shopping-and-fucking feminism jibes precisely with the message of consumer society, [saying] that freedom means more—hotter sex, better food, ever-multiplying pairs of Manolo Blahnik shoes, drawers full of Betsey Johnson skirts, Kate Spade bags, and MAC lipsticks."[4] . . .

Both the denigration and the appropriation of zine style certainly did something to preempt the movement. Both were attacks from the outside in which zinesters essentially became caricatures of their own vision. A deeper blemish, however, was one that actually grew from within: the movement's virtual homogeneity. Despite pools of copier ink spilled in earnest discussions of race and class, girl zines were largely a hobby of white, middle-class young women. Riding on the heels of a feminist movement that had long stood rightly accused of excluding women of color and poor women, Riot Grrrl and its attendant zinesters was still a young version of a ladies' lunch society—except that the ladies have blue hair and weird clothes. Participating in girl zine culture requires that one have the leisure time to create zines, a life generally uncluttered with the rudiments of survival, access to copy machines and other equipment, money for stamps and supplies, and enough self-esteem and encouragement to believe that one's thoughts are worth putting down for public consumption—all marks of a certain level of privilege.

Although they were the exception to the rule, zines by young women of color or working-class backgrounds still found their way to fruition, and they were excellent. *Bamboo Girl,* which is still in print, features sassy, smart indictments of the exoticization of Asian-American women, interviews with Filipina authors on queerness, and analyses of "superwomen of color" in Japanese comix. The writer of *Discharge* zine recounts coming from a working-class, alcoholic, gambling family in Detroit to the D.C. Riot Grrrl community, where the most pressing concern often seemed the achievement of an equal opportunity mosh pit. Claudia von Vacano, a Latina Riot Grrrl in New York, wrote scathing indictments in her zines of Riot Grrrl's failure to confront its own internalized racism—which was for many the first time they had ever heard the phrase. *HUES* (Hear Us Emerging Sisters) was one of the most successful and respected girl zines (though more of a regular magazine than a zine) made by, for, and about young women of every color and shape. However, its content made it seem less a peripheral element of the white-dominated zine scene than a literary element of the growing multicultural scene.

Many of my fellow zinesters never saw or spoke of excellent zines like *Bamboo Girl* and *HUES,* suggesting that even within the self-proclaimed "underground," there is both a mainstream underground and an underground underground. To be fair, the girls in the former category were often writing zines about genuinely difficult things in their lives. But even so, it is difficult to feel completely vested in a slogan like "Revolution Girl Style Now" when the girls shouting it almost all look the same.

I might be giving the impression that zines are a phenomenon that came and went, that their effects were briefly felt, and that they no longer exist, or that Riot Grrrl and the motivations behind the "girl zine explosion" have also petered out. None of these statements is true. Riot Grrrl chapters still exist all over the country, in third- or fourth-generation incarnations, many churning

out zines as they always have. Do-It-Yourself (DIY) zine distributions are still operated out of bedrooms and living rooms, selling zines that reflect the distributors' personal favorites. Anarchist infoshops, independent record stores, and many small bookstores still carry racks of new zine titles. Bigger magazines (some of which have their roots as zines) like *Giant Robot* and *Bust* review new zines and tell people where to send their concealed dollar or two for a copy. . . .

Still, zines are not quite what they used to be, and the most compelling explanation of what happened to them can be told in one word: Internet. Since the Net blew up to unpredictable proportions in the mid-nineties, the essence of zines—namely, that anyone with anything to say can say it to the world—was codified and implemented en masse online. Everyone got a homepage, and e-zines became the electronic equivalents of their paper predecessors. Alice Marwick, who had already been involved with the zine community for several years, started *I Reclaim Wack* online in 1995 and loved the worldwide distribution, instant responses from readers, ability to change and update content, and absolutely free production. Like so many others, she taught herself HTML and learned the rudiments of Web design as an outlet for her creative energy and personal expression, and she has relished watching so many others do the same. "I think it's really good that there are so many e-zines," she says. "And actually, even though there are a lot of feminist girls online, I don't find that most of the e-zines by young women have a feminist slant at all. Yes, some are explicitly feminist, but many of them are just personal zines about girls' lives. If I was fourteen years old and growing up now, I would be so excited to find that community online."

Marwick's view is an important commentary not just on the status of girl e-zines but on the status of feminism as well. She's right that most e-zines for young women—even of the fierce, seemingly feminist variety—don't mention the F word outright. But a quick perusal of content shows that they are largely smart, challenging, socially aware, and independent—in short, feminist in every sense. . . .

It would seem, then, that the Internet and the advent of e-zines have been nothing short of a miracle for girls who previously had to scrounge around indie record stores and punk shows for a portal into the zine underground. Positive things have clearly come from the proliferation of online zines, not least, as Marwick mentions, the ease with which isolated young women pining for like-minded peers can now find them. And although some zine aficionados may lament having lost the exciting sense of tree-house-club secrecy that once shrouded the zine culture, there is something equally exciting about their enormous visibility online. How vindicating is it that e-zines like *My Boot Against the World* and *BratGirl* can be located as easily as the webpage for, say, Amazon? The blank URL bar of an Internet window has proven itself in many ways to be the great cultural equalizer. A Google search for "girl zine" turns up thousands of results; "pro-choice zine" hundreds. The question nowadays is not where to find a good girl zine but rather how to begin sloshing through the glut of them.

And the girls and women making e-zines? Their motivations vary as much online as they do in print. Deanna Zandt never made a print zine and didn't even know they existed until she was in college. As the publisher of *GenerationGrrl,* however, she values helping younger girls foster a sense of themselves by offering an alternative to what she calls the "bullshit of glossy magazines." She says, "I remember reading those and thinking anything from 'I will never have skin that smooth!' to 'I will never have the money to spend two hundred dollars on a pair of jeans!' and also thinking that those things were really inherent to my self-worth as a person. Not to mention the zero-lesbian-visibility factor. Please! We are real girls and women producing these things, telling our life stories—we give life to our words through our designs and pictures. In a very broad sense, it's like being the big sister who shows you how to navigate the world, not just what lipstick to buy." Others see their e-zines more as conduits through which to connect with peers. After producing *Bunnies on Strike* as a paper zine in Holland for several years, Tanja put it online with the help of a Web designer friend.[5]

Since then she has been able to connect with Riot Grrrls and like-minded young feminists all over Europe and North America, and in some parts of Asia and Africa. "E-zines themselves are just a step further in the already existing revolution of paper zines," Tanja explains. "Being online just makes your zine available to more people. It can be revolutionary once you meet other girls through the Internet and decide to take action."

Revolutionary is a powerful term, however, and one that just doesn't apply to what many girls are doing online. Homepages, for example, are pretty closely related to zines—rants, raves, diary entries, some photographs, perhaps some poetry, yet often nothing politicized. In this light, not everyone agrees that the realization of a soapbox for every young woman is the pinnacle of feminist achievement. The website gURL.com hosts around half a million homepages, and its co-founder Esther Drill suggests that while they may be an important rite of self-expression for teenage girls, they may also have gone overboard. "It's great if these girls are smart and have something to say, but if they're talking about stupid things, then it's just one more extraneous voice added to everything," she says. "Girls put up their diaries all the time, and after a while, I wonder if that's a good development. There are other important things for people to talk about besides themselves, and in general, the homepages are really self-focused. For all the good things, I also want to say, 'Guess what, girls, you're not the most important people in the world.'"

More troubling even than the possible over-abundance of homepages and e-zines is the complete absence of them for those without access. The technological landscape reflects the homogeneity of zine makers. The 2000 U.S. census reported that among families with incomes of $25,000 or less, only 19 percent had access to the Internet, compared with 75 percent among families with incomes of $75,000 or higher. Only 33 percent of black homes and 34 percent of Latinos had Internet access, while 53 percent of white non-Hispanics had access, as did 65 percent of Asians and Pacific Islanders.[6] More recent reports, however, show that both the racial and class gaps are closing. By 2001 there were reports that Internet use among blacks had grown at an annual rate of 31 percent, while use among whites grew by 19 percent. During the same period that home access to the Internet increased among blacks, it increased as well for poor people of all races.[7]

Young women of color who do have Internet access are using the information superhighway to build community, express themselves, discover its infinite possibilities, and connect with people both similar to and different from themselves. The resources are certainly not anywhere as abundant as they should be, but they seem to be increasingly present, ranging from *Colorlines* magazine's information on the rampant incarceration of urban youth to Black Grrrl Revolution's *Problackgrrrlfesto,* which states that "still being ingrained in society's consciousness by academia [is] that black only equates African-American and male, and that woman only equates white"[8]—both hopeful signs that when the numbers of young women of color online increase, there will be something there for them beyond Backstreet Boys fanpages and Caucasian beauty tips.

As technology activists continue working to narrow the digital divide, the critical imperative to do so shows no signs of letting up. Beyond zines and e-zines, young women are making films, producing music, publishing books, and otherwise carving space for the DIY ethic in the feminist sphere. Kara Herold interviewed forty-five girl zinesters for her film *Grrlyshow,* a documentary about girl zines and their relationship to contemporary feminism, and found that many identified as strongly as media activists as they did as feminists. "Since just a few corporations essentially own all the magazines, the whole point is getting your writing out there into the culture, even if it's just to ten other people," Herold explains. "If you have something different to say than the mainstream, it's feminist just by virtue of believing that what you have to say is important. That's why I think girl zines and e-zines will continue, because, really, you have to create your own venues. Nobody else is going to do it for you."

NOTES

1. Elizabeth Snead, "Feminist Riot Girls Don't Just Wanna Have Fun," *USA Today,* 7 August 1992, 5D.
2. Margot Mifflin, "Girlzines Attract New Feminist Breed," *Dallas Morning News,* 26 November 1995, 5F.
3. Naomi Klein, *No Logo* (New York: Picador, 1999), 72–73.
4. Michelle Goldberg, "Feminism for Sale," *Alternet,* 8 January 2001, http://www.alternet.org/story.html?StoryID=10306.
5. Tanja's last name was unavailable.
6. U.S. Department of Commerce, *Falling Through the Net: Toward Digital Inclusion* (Washington, D.C., 2000).
7. National Telecommunications and Information Administration, *A Nation Online: How Americans Are Expanding Their Use of the Internet,* 5 February 2002 (Washington, D.C.), http://www.ntia.doc.gov/ntiahome/dn/html/toc.htm.
8. See http://www.thirdwavefoundation.org/programs/summer00.pdf for more information about Black Grrrl Revolution.

Strip Till You Drop

Alison Pollet and Page Hurwitz

Dear Santa,

All I want for Xmas this year is a new bicycle, my very own pony and a stripper pole for the rec room. Thanks, Santa!

> *Luv,*
> *Amber Anykid U.S.A.*

P.S. Strawberry Shortcake thongs make rad stocking stuffers!

Postal workers should not have been shocked this year to receive scores of Christmas wish lists just like little Amber's. Why? Well, in case you haven't tuned in to teen or tween media lately, stripping has gone mainstream. Teenagers of the new millennium have grown up watching college students give lap dances on MTV's *The Real World;* they've listened to Christina Aguilera's album *Stripped;* they've taken cardio strip class at the gym, perused the mall for thongs and flavored body glitter, played video games that feature strippers on their Xboxes and GameCubes, and watched endless music videos for which strip clubs and the denizens thereof provide the *mise-en-scène.* TV shows and movies from *Stripperella* to *Charlie's Angels: Full Throttle* regularly feature voluptuous heroines flashing the flesh. Indeed, a questionnaire for college-age participants in *The Real Cancun,* the 2003 "reality movie" depicting spring-break mayhem, posed the question "What's the wildest thing you've ever done?" Responses included "Stripped at a bar," "Gone on top of a bar and flashed," and "Stripped in a club." Somebody ought to break it to these co-eds: Stripping isn't so wild anymore—it's kid stuff.

Of course, for many girls who buy it, stripper-inspired fare isn't actually about disrobing in public or even having sex but about cultivating what writer and sexpert Susie Bright calls "the essence of titillation," a coy yet brazen, look-but-don't-touch sexual persona. "This is very appealing to the young crowd, the virgins, the pre-orgasmic, who want to flaunt and test their sexuality without actually having to *do* the deed," says Bright. Along with marketing executives promoting their goods, many adolescents embrace these products as a harmless and fun way to wield sexual power, defending their right to express themselves through "Porn Star" T-shirts and "Hot Buns" hot pants, and dismissing those who object as dour, repressed.

Still, critics like Jean Kilbourne, best known for her documentary series *Killing Us Softly,* about gender representation in advertising, warn that the trend is more constraining than liberating, invoking a "very narrow, clichéd version of what's sexy as opposed to any kind of authentic sexuality." It's a debate whose terms are familiar, from the feminist sex wars of the 1980s to the 1990s rise of "girl power" in pop culture to the explosion of feminist cultural criticism that snubbed the old-school women's movement for its perceived lack of an ironic sensibility. But the discussion has acquired a new dimension now that a mass-marketed ideal of female sexiness derived from stripper culture is being sold to an ever younger set. The stripper-infused products aimed at young girls are a creepy synthesis of cute and tawdry—seemingly designed to appeal to a 12-year-old's tastes while gently easing her into the adult arena.

The most ubiquitous stripper-inspired purchase a girl can make is a thong, a product with a heritage in exotic dancing—in 1939 New York Mayor Fiorello La Guardia decreed that the city's nude dancers cover their private parts for the World's Fair. Thongs marketed directly to kids and teens often don't resemble standard lingerie—they're usually cotton, not silk or satin, they've got a colored elastic band, and they're not overloaded with lace or frills. Designwise, they tend toward the self-consciously cute, bearing the visage of a recognizable cartoon character, adorned with a saucy saying and/or cheekily girlish iconography—cherries, gingham checks, teddy bears. The thong's ostensible purpose is to hide panty lines, but what ultimately drives the sale is the nice but naughty message its design implies—and sometimes not so subtly. "Feeling lucky?" begs the Smarty thong by David & Goliath. It's white with a green four-leaf clover stamped on the front, and available at teen-girl fashion emporium Delia's. According to market research firm NPD Group, from August 2002 to July 2003 thong sales in the United States climbed to $610 million—up from the previous year's $570 million. *Time* reported that last year girls between the ages of 13 and 17 spent $152 million on them. Thongs average about $6 apiece, and you pay more for a brand name. (A Simpsons thong goes for $8, a simple glitter one for half that.) It's no wonder, then, that licensers are eager to dole out their characters' likenesses for front-and-center crotch placement; in the age of branding, it's all the better if your Hello Kitty thong matches your Hello Kitty lunch box.

Click the About Us/Investor Relations link on the home page for mall-based teenage chain store Hot Topic, which in fiscal year 2002 produced earnings of $34.6 million, and you'll learn that, founded in 1989, "the Company believes teenagers throughout the U.S. have similar fashion preferences, largely as a result of the nationwide influence of MTV, music distribution, movies and television programs." Under Intimate Apparel/Panties, recent purchase items included a Dr. Seuss Cat in the Hat thong, a Cookie Monster bikini panty, [and] a Hello Kitty Goth Girl thong. Borrowing from underwear for little kids, some of these products—retro Mighty Mouse lingerie by Nick and Nora, for one—no doubt appeal to the older

consumer who's consciously infantilizing herself to look sexy. But they also seem calculated to attract younger girls who might still harbor some genuine affection for cartoon cuddlies. The Muppet thong is the adolescent equivalent of a toddler's pull-up: somewhere between Underoos and lingerie.

The film *Thirteen* depicts the hypersexualized teen-girl consumer marketplace as inextricably linked to its central character's accelerated downward spiral. It's naïve junior high schooler Tracy's demand for a hipper new wardrobe that sets the plot in motion; Tracy first steals to shop at a risqué boutique and clashes with her mother over a puppy-dog thong emblazoned with the words "Wanna Bone?"

The film clearly resonated with many girls' experiences. Emily and Caroline, 13-year-olds at a Los Angeles private school, use "sexy" to describe the eighth grade's most popular girl, who buys her school uniform in diminutive kiddy sizes so as to reveal more skin. Emily says lots of girls at her theater camp wore thongs and that the kids in her class think thongs are cool, though she bristles: "Who would want to see a 13-year-old's butt?" She and Caroline recently attended a barmitzvah where a tattoo artist was hired to airbrush designs onto partygoers' body parts. A popular request, the girls reveal, was Playboy's bunny-head emblem, the allure of which leaves the two momentarily divided. "Kids want it because it's a cute little bunny," says Emily. Caroline begs to differ. "It's Playboy, which makes them sexy or something."

Either way, the Playboy bunny has hopped back into fashion, swishing its cottontail into the teen market. At Hot Topic you can buy bunny trucker hats, pajamas, blankets and pillows. Dr. Jay's carries Playboy bunny rhinestone thongs and camis, sporty shorts and sexy briefs. If for children of the 1970s and '80s the bunny's image is tarnished by connotations of dirty centerfolds and exploitation, Playboy Enterprises is making sure that's not the case for girls of the next millennium. The bunny's getting an extreme makeover; the company's amping up its playful, mildly risqué qualities and de-emphasizing its pornographic ones. Playboy Enterprises still produces X-rated fare, but it relegates it to its adult-only outfit, Spice. "It's rather like Viacom having Nickelodeon [for children] and Showtime [for adults]," company CEO Christie Hefner told *Business Week Online* this past August. Playboy's licensing department targets 18–25-year-olds; they say a crossover into a younger market is unintentional. Yet founder Hugh Hefner—when asked by the *Washington Post* about kids donning Playboy togs—proclaimed, "I don't care if a baby holds up a Playboy bunny rattle."

Retail sales for the Playboy brand's licensed fashion and consumer products have been estimated at more than $350 million for 2003, and the company celebrated its fifty-year anniversary with a November retail launch of limited-edition specialty products. They are in cahoots with rapper P. Diddy's clothing label, Sean John, which is producing bunny-adorned velour tracksuits. There is a Playboy skateboard, a Playboy snowboard and, from M.A.C. Cosmetics, "Playmate Pink" glitter cream and "Bunny Pink" lipstick with a "laser-embossed bunny on the tip." According to the press release, M.A.C. Cosmetics—a company whose progressive advertising tactics have included using openly gay celebrities Elton John and Rupaul as spokesmodels—was inspired by the "sheer fabulousness of the original Playboy Bunnies."

Revamped as cuddly and camp, the bunny is poised to enter the world of family-friendly entertainment with *Hef's Superbunnies,* a cartoon series about Playboy playmates who fight the enemies of democracy. Playboy's entertainment division, Alta Loma, is developing the series with Stan Lee's POW! Entertainment, and the press announcement mentions they're aiming for a mainstream audience, so the superbunnies won't bare it all. Stan Lee, creator of Spiderman and the Incredible Hulk, already has an animated series about strippers on the air. It's the adult cartoon series *Stripperella;* Pamela Anderson lends her voice and image to the superhero Erotica Jones, "a stripper by night and superhero by later night," whose power source resides in her enhanced breasts. On TNN's Web site you can play Strip-pole-rella, the point of which is to avoid falling objects and pole grease and collect as many dollar bills as you can.

Few have surfed the stripper wave with more success than Joe Francis, whose brainchild, *Girls Gone Wild,* is a four-year-old, $100 million entertainment empire solely based on amateur videotapes of college students flashing their breasts. On Amazon.com you can purchase (at about $17 a pop) DVD titles that include *Girls Gone Wild Extreme, Black Girls Gone Wild: Funkin' at Freaknik,* and *Girls Gone Wild Doggy Style,* Francis's creation with Calvin Broadus (*a k a* rap star Snoop Doggy Dogg). Unless Francis goes to jail—charges of filming underage girls for a spring break tape are pending in Panama City, Florida—his next venture, *Newsweek* reports, is a chain of Hooters-style restaurants. Francis, who once compared girls' flashing Mardi Gras–style for his videos to feminists burning bras, doesn't hide the fact that he is taking advantage of the opportunity to offer titillation in the guise of liberation. The fact that there are so many willing participants one can attribute partially to the desire for a quick fix of fame and the culture of reality television that engenders that desire, and partially to Jell-O shots. But perhaps this is, to some degree, what 1990s pop culture wrought.

The spring breakers Joe Francis convinces to "go wild," at least the ones of appropriate age, would have also been the target audience when, in 1996, the Spice Girls shimmied onto the pop landscape, singing about how girls should tell guys "what I want, what I really really want," and pumping up their fans with "girl power," a philosophy that ran as deep as "You're a girl, therefore you're powerful," and that could be easily construed as "Look sexy like this and you will be powerful."

On MTV there were more lessons to be learned about girls and power. The 1995 Aerosmith video for the song "Crazy" features actresses Liv Tyler and Alicia Silverstone playing high school students who break out of school one afternoon and hit the road; they fund their joy ride with a trip to a strip club, where Tyler performs a mocking pole dance and Silverstone, dressed in a man's suit, watches gleefully from below. Thanks in part to the video's homoerotic overtones, the striptease seemed rebellious, transformative and empowering, a paradigm replicated in many a girl-centric coming-of-age flick in its wake, among them *Coyote Ugly* (2000), a movie about bartending table dancers (the film's tagline: "Tonight, they're calling the shots").

This generation also grew up concurrently with hip-hop, a genre whose videos have always pushed the envelope in terms of stripper content. Videos are limited in their storytelling capabilities, certainly, and popular early 1990s videos like WreckX'N' Effect's "Rumpshaker" conceded to this limitation, opting for *Lifestyles of the Rich and Famous*–style locales and high-heeled bikini-clad babes, visual cues that would inform hip-hop videos for the decade to come. Female rappers of the early 1990s adapted what Alondra Nelson, assistant professor of sociology and African-American studies at Yale, calls "masculinist models of rap virtuosity and power as a way to gain respect in hip hop." But eventually, when hip-hop "embraced the pimp archetype," female rappers were forced to "fight back on the same terms, taking up hyper-feminine personas." That means trading the showmanship that comes with skill for the kind of empowerment that comes with stripping. Today's female hip-hop stars, like Lil' Kim and Foxy Brown, are taking their fashion cues from the table-dancing backup dancers and extras who populate male hip-hop stars' videos.

Of course, Madonna's influence on the stripper trend cannot be discounted. While college kids and professors populating cultural studies departments in the early 1990s were eager to endow her pornography-inspired videos and *Sex* book with layered ironic sensibilities, it's possible that irony wasn't translating to those who were children at the time. For example, in the opening to the film *Crossroads,* starring Britney Spears, the character she plays, an uptight good girl on the eve of high school graduation, wears men's underwear and writhes around on her bed to Madonna, who—we're meant to understand—was the soundtrack of the character's early youth. By Act II, Spears's character is on the road to both Los Angeles and girl power, stopping in at a bar for a liberating and lucrative stint of karaoke and pole dancing.

The "Porn Star" tee is this generation's answer to the "I'm With Stupid" shirt; the words were stamped on baby tees, tanks and camisoles and sold at malls across the country. When asked about the shirt, Michelle, 22, a recent graduate of Barnard College, is quick to renounce it as "so five years ago." But she recalls that back in high school, its intention was obvious: to be a calling card, one that says insta-sex. This is helpful for a girl whose look doesn't automatically conjure up sexiness. Wear a Porn Star shirt and as Michelle says, "you're telling people to see you as sexy, as feminine." Talk to girls about stripper culture, and you notice an interesting phenomenon: Stripping equals sexy and sexy equals feminine. Coupled with the adolescent's age-old desires to look good and be looked at, you've got an odd mix of feminine/sexy bravado.

As Susie Bright observes, a stripper's costume says "Long for me, try to win me, throw money at me, but you will never really get very far," a message that holds obvious appeal for the junior high school girl who "want[s] to be mirrored, told [she's] beautiful and desirable and sought-after." A girl can easily meet these competing needs with an outfit that features a body-hugging Porn Star shirt and a thong embossed with a padlock design (made by David and Goliath, available at Delia's). These garments may be a far cry from the confining pinafores and protective bloomers of yesterday, but they introduce a new set of problems. Some, like Jean Kilbourne, argue that they promote a brand of sexuality that "has to do with attracting men, and has nothing to do with a girl being the agent of her own sexual desire." If adolescent girls of the 1950s had only two options, virgin and whore, these clothes seem to blur the line between the two. It's a strange day when Hot Topic's "Pay up, sucker!" thong (the words, in bubble letters, encircle a dollar sign) seems a better option for girls than the padlock one, because it smacks less of sexual puritanism. What's most ironic, Kilbourne argues, is that "this is happening in a culture that's not allowing sex ed in class."

Raising these issues with teens without alienating them is a tricky business. Says Michelle: "We all want to be the girl who's comfortable going with her boyfriend to a strip club, who's all 'What up?' with the stripper. You want to be the girl who isn't fazed by going to Hooters. Boys like big boobs, big deal. No one wants to look repressed." No doubt, that's music to the makers of *Girls Gone Wild*, a moniker that itself seems to proclaim innocence, as in: "Hey, don't blame me! I happened upon these girls, and, dang, they gone wild!" It's a sure thing, in this climate, that lectures about the hazards of thongs will, if anything, make them more appealing. Look what happened at a Long Island high school when, last spring, teachers chaperoning a senior-class field trip to Florida confiscated string bikinis from students' luggage.

The girls argued that they'd been violated, and the community found itself polarized. The melee was even written up in the *New York Times,* which quoted a letter from Catherine Pearce, 18, sent to her local paper, the *Suffolk Times:* "I'm not such a naïve little girl that I'm unaware of my own body, my own sexuality. . . . What exactly was it that they were protecting me from?"

It's a fair question—one that critics of stripper chic have to be prepared to answer in a way that meets girls where they are. Jean Kilbourne advocates educating teenagers in media literacy and fighting for progressive sex ed in schools. But there may be a more expedient way to deflate the trend. This past November Oprah Winfrey devoted an hour to "releasing your inner sexpot"; overworked moms got stripper makeovers complete with pole-dancing lessons and new lingerie. Moms Gone Wild? Now it's *really* over.

DISCUSSION QUESTIONS FOR CHAPTER 9

1. How do you think cultural forms shape gender? How might cultural forms function subversively to challenge traditional gender norms?

2. How do some television shows reflect changing gender norms while at the same time keeping most other norms intact? Can you name some examples?

3. What are some recent movies you've seen? How are women depicted in these movies? How is the gaze constructed in these movies?

4. How does pornography as a cultural form influence gender norms in U.S. society?

5. Why do you think some critics suggest there has never been a female Shakespeare or a female da Vinci? Do you agree with this assessment? Why or why not?

SUGGESTIONS FOR FURTHER READING

Brunsdon, Charlotte. *The Feminist, the Housewife, and the Soap Opera.* New York: Oxford University Press, 2000.

Carson, Mina, Tisa Lewis, and Susan M. Shaw. *Girls Rock! Fifty Years of Women Making Music.* Lexington: University Press of Kentucky, 2004.

Hollows, Joanne. *Feminism, Femininity, and Popular Culture.* Manchester, England: Manchester University Press, 2000.

Kord, Susanne. *Hollywood Divas, Indice Queens, and TV Heroines: Contemporary Screen Images of Women.* Lanham, MD: Rowman & Littlefield, 2004.

Meyers, Marian, ed. *Mediated Women: Representations in Popular Culture:* Bridgehampton, NY: Hampton Press, 1999.

Pohl-Weary, Emily. *Girls Who Bite Back: Witches, Mutants, Slayers, and Freaks.* Toronto: Sumach, 2004.

Pollock, Griselda. *Differencing the Canon: Feminist Desire and the Writing of Art's Histories.* New York: Routledge, 1999.

Valdivia, Angharad N. *A Latina in the Land of Hollywood and Other Essays on Media Culture.* Tucson: University of Arizona Press, 2000.

CHAPTER 10

Resisting Violence Against Women

Gendered violence in the United States and around the world is an important public health and human rights issue. Violence, an assault on a person's control over her/his body and life, can take many forms and has varying consequences depending on the type of assault, its context and interpretation, the chronicity of violence, and the availability of support. *Gendered violence* implies that harm evolves from the imbalance in power between people; in most societies around the world, gendered violence usually occurs when masculine entitlements produce power that manifests itself in harm and injury (physical, sexual, emotional/psychological) toward women. Women are especially vulnerable in interpersonal relationships; most violence against them occurs in their own homes. However, since violence is about the exercise of power over another person, both men and women can perpetrate violence and it occurs in both heterosexual and homosexual relationships.

The range of gendered violence includes acts of intimidation and harassment (stalking, voyeurism, online/chat room, street, school, and workplace harassment, road rage, and obscene phone calls), forcing someone to watch or participate in pornography, forced prostitution and other sex work, emotional/psychological, physical, and sexual abuse (that includes rape and attempted rape), and any other coercive act that harms and violates another person. Despite the fact that anyone can perpetrate violence, women are much more likely to be victims of violence by men since violence is a consequence of power relationships. Men, however, are very likely to suffer physical violence at the hands of other men. In childhood and adolescence, males are also especially at risk for suffering physical abuse by female and male caretakers and sexual abuse by other males. Given the norms about masculine invulnerability, it is often hard for boys and men to talk about sexual abuse and seek help. As a result, men are more likely than women to be in denial about such experiences, and some men who have been abused try to "master" the abuse by identifying with the source of their victimization and avoiding the weaknesses associated with being a "victim."

The rates of violence against women in the United States are quite alarming, and, since intimate violence is so underreported, accurate statistics are difficult to collect.

Nonetheless, the U.S. Bureau of Justice Statistics (2003) reports that a sexual assault (including rape) occurs about every 2 minutes, and approximately 56 women are victimized in some way by an intimate partner every hour. Recent statistics for teen violence are especially disturbing, although different studies ask about victimization in different ways and get different results. Some studies ask about current abuse and some survey past histories; some ask only about physical abuse, while others include questions about emotional or psychological abuse and sexual abuse. It is important to consider whether consent for sexual intimacy can occur in a relationship where physical violence and intimidation is present. According to national statistics published by the National Center for Victims of Crime (2004), one in five high school girls in the United States reported being abused physically and/or sexually by a boyfriend, and 50 to 80 percent of teenagers reported knowing others in violent relationships. Estimates of physical and sexual dating violence among high school students typically range from one in ten to one in four.

Although girls are more likely to be sexually abused than boys and the latter are more likely to be sexually abused by other males, both male and female adolescents report being victims of physical violence in relationships. Some relationships involve mutual abuse, with both partners using violence against each other. However, it is clear that male and female adolescents use force for different reasons and with different results. Researchers have found that girls suffer more from relationship violence, emotionally and physically. They are more likely than males to have serious injuries and report being terrified. In contrast, male victims seldom fear violence by their girlfriends and often say the attacks did not hurt or that they found the violence amusing (National Youth Violence Prevention Resource Center, 2005). Rape victims are 4 times more likely to contemplate suicide and 13 times more likely to actually make a suicide attempt. Helpful links for fact sheets on intimate partner violence, "warning signs" for abusive relationships, and other information can be found at *www.cdc.gov/ncipc/factsheets/ipvfacts.htm; www.ojp.usdoj.gov/vawo;* and *www.ojp.usdoj.gov/bjs/abstract/ipv.htm.*

Another disturbing trend is the increase in stalking behavior directed at women (see also the box in this chapter on "cyberstalking"). The National College Women Sexual Victimization (NCWSV) survey published in 2000 found that 13 percent of female college students had been stalked since school began that year and that four in five women knew their stalkers. Of these stalkers known, most were boyfriends or ex-boyfriends, classmates, acquaintances, or coworkers. Stalking incidents lasted an average of 2 months and included unwanted repeated telephoning (78 percent), having an offender wait outside or inside places (48 percent), being watched from afar (44 percent), being followed (42 percent), being sent letters (30 percent), and unwanted, repeated e-mails (25 percent). Ten percent of women stalked reported that the offender forced or attempted sexual contact; the most common consequence for women was fear and emotional and psychological trauma.

Violence against girls and women is a persistent problem all over the world and is increasingly understood as a human rights issue. The wars of the twentieth century and the new conflicts of the twenty-first, the increase in globalization and scope of global commerce and communications, have all facilitated an increase in global violence against women and children. The 2005 Population Report indicates that around the world, one in three women are beaten, coerced into sex, and otherwise abused. As the reading "War Crimes" by Helen Clarkson reports, sexual violence is a weapon of war all over the world. These issues are addressed by the recent "Beijing Plus" meetings, 5 years and a decade after violence against women was declared a central tenet of the "Platform for Action" of the 1995 conference. Some countries condone or legalize such crimes, and others accept violence against women as a consequence of war and/or civil unrest and ethnic cleansing. The increasing militarism in such postindustrial societies as the United States has important consequences for the safety of women and children in target societies and facilitates prostitution and the international sex traffic in girls and women. Alice Leuchtag in "Human Rights: Sex Trafficking and Prostitution" writes about "sex slavery" and "sex tourism" and discusses global responses to this global problem. She addresses the UN General Assembly's adoption of a convention and protocol on sex trafficking, as well as the U.S. Victims of Trafficking and Violence Act, both passed in 2005.

Similarly, Mariana Katzarova's short piece, "Letter from Juárez," discusses the rape/murders of young women in Ciudad Juárez, Mexico, who worked in the maquiladoras where U.S. and European companies hire cheap female labor. In this way the history of colonialism reveals the complex interactions of race and nation and the ways this is gendered and implicated in the politics of globalization. In addition, the status of women, for example, has often been used as a marker of the level of "civilization" of a society, just as cultural interventions have been justified in part in the name of improving the status of women (as was most recently shown with the U.S. attacks on Afghanistan as "liberating" women from the Taliban, discussed briefly in the reading by Andrea Smith, "Beyond the Politics of Inclusion," and with other discussions on the status of Muslim women associated with the war in Iraq). This creates complexity for feminist activism in these countries as women and men seeking to address nationalist, patriarchal problems can be interpreted as "traitors"; similarly, it causes problems for feminists in North America and Europe whose activism can be interpreted as ethnocentric meddling or support for militarist strategies of their societies.

What do you think would be the societal response if men and boys routinely were victimized in these ways by women and girls? As discussed in Chapter 2, because these crimes are against a whole group of people whose only connection is that they are female, it is appropriate to consider these abuses crimes of hate and misogyny. Although violence against women is not generally understood as a hate crime, there are various laws that have helped in this struggle. These include rape shield laws, which prevent a victim's sexual history from being used by defense attorneys, and various state rape reform laws. Mandatory arrest procedures in cases of domestic violence and the creation of protective or temporary restraining orders have helped survivors of domestic abuse. In addition, the 1994 Violence Against Women Act provides some legal protections for women. This act was reauthorized in 2005.

Any discussion attempting to address the issue of violence against women must involve several key points. First, violence against women must be understood in the context of socially constructed notions of gender. If boys are raised to hide emotion, see sensitivity as a weakness, and view sexual potency as wound up with interpersonal power, and girls are raised to be dependent and support masculine entitlement, then interpersonal violence should be no surprise. As Debra Anne Davis

HISTORICAL MOMENT   **The Violence Against Women Act of 1994**

For decades feminist activists had worked to gain recognition of the extent and severity of violence against women in the United States. On the whole, violence against women had not been fully recognized as a serious crime within the criminal justice system.

Often reports of sexual assault were greeted with skepticism or victim-blaming. Prior to feminist activism in the 1970s, women had to present evidence of resistance to sexual assault; rules of evidence allowed consideration of a victim's entire sexual history; and husbands were exempt from charges of raping their wives. Following the opening of the first rape crisis centers in 1972, grassroots advocacy managed not only to provide care and services to victims, but also to change these laws.

Generally, domestic violence was considered by law enforcement to be a "family matter," and so police, prosecutors, and judges were often reluctant to "interfere." The first domestic violence shelters opened in the mid-1970s, but not until the 1980s did this problem receive widespread attention. Thanks to activists, laws did change in the 1980s to codify domestic violence as criminal conduct, to provide increased penalties, to create civil protection orders, and to mandate training about domestic violence for law enforcement.

Following a Washington, D.C., meeting of representatives from various groups advocating for victims of sexual assault and domestic violence in the 1980s, activists turned their attention to ensuring federal legislation to protect women through interstate enforcement of protection orders, to provide funding for shelters and other programs for victims, and to provide prevention efforts. By demonstrating the need for these protections and programs, grassroots advocates and the National Organization for Women (NOW) Legal Defense Fund were able to develop bipartisan support in Congress and to pass the Violence Against Women Act (VAWA) in 1994. The four subtitles of the Act describe the target areas of concern: Safe Streets, Safe Homes for Women, Civil Rights for Women and Equal Justice for Women in the Courts, and Protections of Battered Immigrant Women and Children. VAWA changed rules of evidence, police procedures, penalties, and court procedures. It also authorized funding for prevention, education, and training.

Since 1994, VAWA has been reauthorized and modified several times. The Act was most recently reauthorized in 2005, although at the time of this writing, the Senate and House have not yet worked out the details of their differing versions. To find out more about VAWA, visit the Web site of the U.S. Department of Justice's Violence Against Women Office at *www.ojp.usdoj.gov/vawo*.

explains in the reading "Betrayed by the Angel," women are raised in ways that may encourage victimization. Second, violence by men is a power issue and must be seen as related to masculine dominance in society generally as represented in interpersonal relationships and in the control of political systems that address crime and create policy. Indeed, entitlements associated with masculinity produce a range that

Cyberstalking

- A U.S. Department of Justice report estimates that there may be tens or even hundreds of thousands of cyberstalking victims in the United States (Report on Cyberstalking, 1999).
- A 1997 nationwide survey conducted by the University of Cincinnati found that almost 25 percent of stalking incidents among college-age women involved cyberstalking (Report on Cyberstalking, 1999).

DEFINITION

Cyberstalking can be defined as threatening behavior or unwanted advances directed at another using the Internet and other forms of online and computer communications.

OVERVIEW

Cyberstalking is a relatively new phenomenon. With the decreasing expense and thereby increased availability of computers and online services, more individuals are purchasing computers and "logging onto" the Internet, making another form of communication vulnerable to abuse by stalkers.

Cyberstalkers target their victims through chat rooms, message boards, discussion forums, and e-mail. Cyberstalking takes many forms such as threatening or obscene e-mail; spamming (in which a stalker sends a victim a multitude of junk e-mail); live chat harassment or flaming (online verbal abuse); leaving improper messages on message boards or in guest books; sending electronic viruses; sending unsolicited e-mail; tracing another person's computer and Internet activity; and electronic identity theft.

Similar to stalking off-line, online stalking can be a terrifying experience for victims, placing them at risk of psychological trauma and possible physical harm. Many cyberstalking situations do evolve into off-line stalking, and a victim may experience abusive and excessive phone calls, vandalism, threatening or obscene mail, trespassing, and physical assault.

CYBERSTALKING AND THE LAW

With personal information becoming readily available to an increasing number of people through the Internet and other advanced technology, state legislators are addressing the problem of stalkers who harass and threaten their victims over the World Wide Web. Stalking laws and other statutes criminalizing harassment behavior currently in effect in many states may already address this issue by making it a crime to communicate by any means with the intent to harass or alarm the victim.

States have begun to address the use of computer equipment for stalking purposes by including provisions prohibiting such activity in both harassment and anti-stalking legislation (Riveira, 1,2). A handful of states, such as Alabama, Arizona, Connecticut, Hawaii, Illinois, New Hampshire, and New York, have specifically included prohibitions against harassing electronic, computer, or e-mail communications in their harassment legislation. Alaska, Oklahoma, Wyoming, and more recently, California have incorporated electronically communicated statements as conduct constituting stalking in their anti-stalking laws. A few states have both stalking and harassment statutes that criminalize threatening and unwanted electronic communications. Other states have laws other than harassment or anti-stalking statutes that prohibit misuse of computer communications and e-mail, while others have passed laws containing broad language that can be interpreted to include cyberstalking behaviors (Gregorie).

Recent federal law has addressed cyberstalking as well. The Violence Against Women Act, reauthorized in 2000, made cyberstalking a part of the federal interstate stalking statute. Other federal legislation that addresses cyberstalking has been introduced recently, but no such measures have yet been enacted. Consequently, there remains a lack of legislation at the federal level to specifically address cyberstalking, leaving the majority of legislative prohibitions against cyberstalking at the state level (Wiredpatrol.org).

IF YOU ARE A VICTIM OF CYBERSTALKING

- Experts suggest that in cases where the offender is known, victims should send the stalker a clear written warning. Specifically, victims should communicate that the contact is unwanted and ask the perpetrator to cease sending communications of any kind. Victims should do this only once. Then, no matter the response, victims should under no circumstances ever communicate with the stalker again. Victims should save copies of this communication in both electronic and hard-copy form.
- If the harassment continues, the victim may wish to file a complaint with the stalker's Internet service provider, as well as with their own service provider. Many Internet service providers offer tools that filter or block communications from specific individuals.
- As soon as individuals suspect they are victims of online harassment or cyberstalking, they should start collecting all evidence and document all contact made by the stalker. Save all e-mail, postings, or other communications in both electronic and hard-copy form. If possible, save all of the header information from e-mails and newsgroup postings. Record the dates and times of any contact with the stalker.
- Victims may also want to start a log of each communication explaining the situation in more detail. Victims may want to document how the harassment is affecting their lives and what steps they have taken to stop the harassment.
- Victims may want to file a report with local law enforcement or contact their local prosecutor's office to see what charges, if any, can be pursued. Victims should save copies of police reports and record all contact with law enforcement officials and the prosecutor's office.
- Victims who are being continually harassed may want to consider changing their e-mail address, Internet service provider, and home phone number, and should examine the possibility of using encryption software or privacy protection programs. Any local computer store can offer a variety of protective software,

(continued)

options, and suggestions. Victims may also want to learn how to use the filtering capabilities of e-mail programs to block e-mails from certain addresses.

- Furthermore, victims should contact online directory listings such as *www.four11. com*, *www.switchboard.com*, and *www.whowhere.com* to request removal from their directory.
- Finally, under no circumstances should victims agree to meet with the perpetrator face to face to "work it out" or "talk." No contact should ever be made with the stalker. Meeting a stalker in person can be very dangerous.

. . .

REFERENCES

U.S. Department of Justice. (August 1999). *Cyberstalking: A New Challenge for Law Enforcement and Industry—A Report from the Attorney General to the Vice President.* Washington, DC: U.S. Department of Justice, pp. 2, 6.

Gregorie, Trudy. *Cyberstalking: Dangers on the Information Superhighway.* The Stalking Resource Center, The National Center for Victims of Crime. Online.

Riveira, Diane. (September/October 2000). "Internet Crimes Against Women," *Sexual Assault Report,* 4 (1).

Wired Patrol. "US Federal Laws—Cyberstalking." Accessed 15 April 2003. *http:// www.wiredpatrol.org/stalking/federal.html.*

some scholars term the *rape spectrum*. This means that all sexist behaviors are arranged along a continuum from unexamined feelings of superiority over women, for example, on one end to rape on the other. In this sense, all these behaviors, even though they are so very different in degree, are connected at some level. In addition, scholars emphasize that these behaviors are also connected to the "backlash" or resistance to the gains made by women and other marginalized peoples. While many men today support these gains and are working on ways to address interpersonal power and violence, hoping to enjoy egalitarian relationships with women, some men have not responded well to these gains. They have responded with anger and feelings of powerlessness and insecurity. Interpersonal violence occurs as men attempt to reestablish power that they believe they have lost as a direct result of the gains of women.

Third, male sexual violence is related to the ways violence is eroticized and sexuality is connected to violence. Although pornography is the best example of this problem, women's magazines and advertising generally are rampant with these themes. Finally, we must understand violence against women in terms of the normalization of violence in society. We live in a society where violence is used to solve problems every day and militarism is a national policy.

Consider the following story told to us. The woman, a White professional in her early 30s, had been having a drink with her colleagues one early evening after work.

A well-dressed man struck up a conversation with her, and they chatted a while. When she was leaving with her colleagues, the man asked if he could call her some-time, and she gave him her business card that listed only work information. He called her at work within the next week and asked her to have dinner with him, and, see-ing no reason not to, she agreed to meet him at such-and-such a restaurant after work. She was careful to explain to us that both times she saw this man she was dressed in her professional work clothes and it was early evening in a public space. There was nothing provocative, she emphasized, about her clothes or her demeanor. At some point during the meal she started feeling uncomfortable. The man was very pushy; he chose and ordered her food for her and started telling her that if she wanted to date him, he had certain requirements about how his girlfriends dressed and acted. She panicked and felt a strong need to get away from him, so, at some point she quietly excused herself saying she needed to visit the ladies' room. She then did a quick exit and did not return to the table. Unfortunately, this was not the end of the story. The man found out where her home was and started to stalk her. One evening he forced his way into her apartment and beat her very badly. Fortu-nately, he did not rape her. Although she took out a restraining order on him, he managed to gain entrance into her apartment building again and beat her senseless one more time in the hallway outside her apartment.

This story is a tragic illustration of misogyny and masculine entitlement. The man felt he had the right to define the reality of women in his life and expected them to be subordinate. He believed it was his entitlement. He was so full of rage that when a woman snubbed him, he would have to subdue her. In addition, the woman's telling of the story is illustrative of societal norms that blame women for their own victimization. When tearfully sharing her story, she had felt the shame and humiliation that comes with such an experience; she wanted it to be known that she had not been "asking for it." He had given no indication that he was anything but clean-cut and upstanding, she was dressed appropriately, she took no risks other than accepting a date, she gave him only her work numbers, and she agreed to meet him in a public place. What more could she have done except be wary of all men she might meet?

It is important to remember that alongside the sheer physical and emotional costs of violence against women, the Centers for Disease Control and Prevention estimated in 2003 that the health-related financial costs exceeded $4 billion a year in direct medical and mental health care. This figure does not include lost wages and productivity. In this chapter we discuss sexual assault and rape, physical abuse, and incest and end with a discussion of pornography as a form of violence against women. Because many forms of pornography are legal, some people object to thinking about pornography in the context of sexual violence and claim instead that it is a legitimate type of entertainment. Despite these concerns, we have decided to discuss it in the context of sexual violence because pornography eroticizes unequal power relations between women and men and often involves representations of coercive sex. Men are the major consumers of pornography, and women's bodies tend to be the ones on display. Pornography thus represents a particular aspect of gender relations that reflects the issue of male sexual violence against women.

RAPE

Although rape can be broadly defined as sex without consent, it is understood as a crime of aggression because the focus is on hurting and dominating. More specifically, it is the penetration of any bodily orifice by a penis or object without consent. Someone who is asleep, passed out, or incapacitated by alcohol or drugs cannot give consent. Silence, or lack of continued resistance, does not mean consent. Likewise, consent is not the same as giving in to pressure and intimidation. Women are often victims of altruistic sex (motivation for consent involves feeling sorry for the other person, or feeling guilty about resisting sexual advances) and compliant sex (where the consequences of not doing it are worse than doing it). Neither of these forms of sexual intimacy involve complete consent. Consent is a freely made choice that is clearly communicated. Consensual sex is negotiated through communication where individuals express their feelings and desires and are able to listen to and respect others' feelings and desires. Rape can happen to anyone—babies who are months old to women in their 90s, people of all races, ethnicities, and socioeconomic status. Both women and men are raped, and, as already discussed, overwhelmingly it is a problem of men raping women and other men. Rape occurs relatively frequently in prisons where dominant men rape men they perceive as inferior. Often dominant inmates refer to these men as "women." In this way, rape is about power, domination, and humiliation and must be understood in the context of male dominance and power in gender relations.

Individuals may be sexually assaulted without being raped. Sexual assault can be defined as any sexual contact without consent and/or that involves the use of force. Like rape, sexual assault is an act of power, control, and domination. The terms can get confusing because sexual assault, sexual abuse, and rape are often used interchangeably. Basically, rape is a form of sexual assault and sexual abuse, but sexual assault and abuse do not necessarily imply rape. The sexual abuse of children is often termed *molestation,* which may or may not involve rape. When children are molested or raped by family members, it is termed *incest.* Although the rates of rape are very high, sexual assault rates generally (which include but are not limited to rape) are even higher.

Current statistics suggest that 95 percent of reported sexual assaults are against females, half of all females raped are under the age of 18 years, and about a fifth are under 12 years old; 1 in 3 women will experience sexual assault (including rape) in her lifetime, and 1 in 4 college women experience sexual violence. Among college women in the NCWSV survey that was sponsored by the U.S. Department of Justice, it was reported that women at a university with 10,000 female students could experience about 350 rapes a year "with serious policy implications for college administrators." More than a third of these college women said they had unwanted or uninvited sexual contacts, and 10 percent said they had experienced rape. In this study, 9 in 10 offenders were known to women. Survivors are more likely to report a rape or sexual assault when the assailant is someone they do not know, and indeed, among the college women in the NCWSV sample, less than 5 percent of completed or attempted rapes were reported to law enforcement officials and about a third of victims

LEARNING ACTIVITY   **How Safe Is Your Campus?**

Investigate the safety and security of your campus by asking these questions:

- How many acts of violence were reported on your campus last year?
- Does your campus have a security escort service?
- What resources does your campus provide to ensure safety?
- What training and educational opportunities about safety does your college provide?
- What specialized training about violence is offered to fraternities and sports teams on your campus?
- How does your school encourage the reporting of violence?
- What support services does your school offer to victims of violence?
- What is your school administration's official protocol for dealing with complaints of violence?
- How does your school's code of conduct address violence?
- Are there dark areas of your campus that need additional lighting?
- Are emergency phones available around your campus?

did not tell anyone. The U.S. Bureau of Justice Statistics (2005) adds that about 7 in 10 female rape or sexual assault victims stated that the offender was an intimate, relative, friend, or acquaintance, and other studies have estimated that about 75 percent of sexual assaults are committed by a friend, acquaintance, husband, or family member. In this way, acquaintance rape (often called date rape), where each person is known to the other, is the most frequent form of rape, and is the most underreported. As social psychologist Arnold S. Kahn explains in "What College Women Do and Do Not Experience as Rape," a large percentage of women (in studies ranging from almost 50 to over 70 percent) who respond to questions indicating they have been raped do not identify as rape victims or survivors. He writes about the conditions under which women do or do not identify their experience as rape.

High rates of rape on college campuses (especially gang rapes) tend to occur by fraternity members, often part of male bonding rituals. This does not mean, of course, that all fraternities are dangerous places for women, only that the conditions for the abuse of women can occur in these male-only living spaces, especially when alcohol is present. About 70 to 80 percent of campus rapes generally involve alcohol or other drugs (with alcohol most pervasive among all drugs). The most common "date rape" or predatory drugs are rohypnol (commonly known as "roofies"), ketamine (commonly known as "special k"), and GHB (gamma hydroxybutyrate). These drugs are odorless when dissolved and are indiscernible when put in beverages. They metabolize quickly and make a person incapable of resisting sexual advances. Memory impairment is associated with these drugs, and a survivor may not be aware of such an attack until 8 to 12 hours after it has occurred. In addition, there may be little evidence to support the claim that drugs were used to facilitate the attack because of the speed at which these predatory drugs metabolize. It is imperative to be vigilant at social occasions where such attacks might happen; do not leave a drink unattended, get your own drinks from an unopened container, and watch out for your friends. A buddy system that includes a designated driver is essential!

In 1990 Congress passed the Campus Security Act, which mandated colleges and universities participating in federal student aid programs to complete and distribute security reports on campus practices and crime statistics. This was amended in 1992 to include the Campus Sexual Assault Victim's Bill of Rights to provide policies and statistics and to ensure basic rights to survivors of sexual assault. This act was amended again in 1998 to provide for more extensive security-related provisions, and, since then, the U.S. Department of Justice has given substantial grants to colleges and universities to address sexual and physical assault, harassment, and stalking on campus.

One specific form of "acquaintance rape" is marital rape. A recent national study reported that 10 percent of all sexual assault cases involve a husband or ex-husband, and the National Resource Center on Domestic Violence suggests that taking into account the underreporting that occurs as women are less likely to label such actions as rape, 10 to 14 percent of married women in the United States have been raped by their husbands. Historically, rape has been understood as a property crime against men as women were considered the property of husbands and fathers. As a result, it was considered impossible to violate something that was legally considered your property, and rape laws defined rape as forced intercourse with a woman who was not your wife. In 1993 marital rape became a crime in all 50 states, under at least one section of the sexual offense codes. In 17 states and the District of Columbia, there are no exemptions from rape prosecution granted to husbands (and 5 states have extended this to cohabiting relationships). However, in 33 states, there are still some exemptions given to husbands from rape prosecution. When his wife is most vulnerable (e.g., she is mentally or physically impaired, unconscious, asleep, etc.) and is unable to consent, a husband is exempt from prosecution in many of these states. Women who are raped by their husbands are likely to be raped many times. They experience not only vaginal rape, but also oral and anal rape. Researchers generally categorize marital rape into three types: force-only rape, where a husband uses only enough force to enact the rape; battering rape, where rape occurs in the context of an ongoing physically abusive relationship; and sadistic/obsessive rape, where husbands use torture or perverse acts to humiliate and harm their wives. Pornography is often involved in the latter case. Women are at particularly high risk for being raped by their partners when they are married to domineering men who view them as "property," when they are pregnant, ill physically or mentally, or recovering from surgery, and when they are separated or divorced.

As will be discussed in Chapter 11, political institutions in the United States have historically supported men's access to women as sexual property, and the history of racism and the lynching of Black men for fabricated rapes of White women have influenced how our society and the courts deal with the interaction of race and sexual violence. Although most rapes are intra-racial (they occur within racial groups), women of color are especially vulnerable as victims of sexual violence because of their marginalized status. They also have less credibility in the courtroom in cases where rape has gone to trail. Men of color accused of rape are more likely to get media attention, are more likely to get convicted, and receive longer sentences. While these differences result from the racism of society that sees Black men in particular as more violent or dangerous, they also are related to class differences whereby men of color are generally less able to provide superior legal counsel. As Andrea Smith explains in the reading "Beyond the Politics of Inclusion," gender violence functions as a tool of racism and colonialism for women of color. She emphasizes the need to make the needs of marginalized women central in the anti-violence movement and implores writers and activists to understand the intersectionality of racism and sexism in social movements for ending violence and supporting racial justice.

Very often, as the reading by Kahn emphasizes, women realize that a past sexual encounter was actually a rape, and, as a result, they begin to think about the experience differently. They may have left the encounter hurt, confused, or angry but without being able to articulate what happened. Survivors need to talk about what occurred and get support. It is never too late to get support from people who care. Feeling ashamed, dirty, or stupid is a typical reaction for those who have experienced sexual assault. It is not their/your/our fault.

Social myths about rape include the following:

- *Rape happens less frequently in our society than women believe. Feminists in particular blow this out of proportion by focusing on women's victimization, and women make up rape charges as a way to get attention.* This is false; rape happens at an alarming rate and is underreported. Rape is considered a crime against the state and rape survivors are witnesses to the crime. As a result, the credibility of the "witness" is challenged in rape cases, and women are often retraumatized as a

Intimate Partner Violence: Fact Sheet

OCCURRENCE

- Nearly 5.3 million intimate partner victimizations occur each year among U.S. women aged 18 and older. This violence results in nearly 2 million injuries and nearly 1,300 deaths.
- Estimates indicate more than 1 million women and 371,000 men are stalked by intimate partners each year.
- Intimate partner violence (IPV) occurs across all populations, irrespective of social, economic, religious, or cultural group. However, young women and those below the poverty line are disproportionately affected.
- Nearly 25 percent of women have been raped and/or physically assaulted by an intimate partner at some point in their lives, and more than 40 percent of the women who experience partner rapes and physical assaults sustain a physical injury.
- As many as 324,000 women each year experience IPV during their pregnancy.
- Intimate partner violence accounted for 20 percent of all nonfatal violent crime experienced by women in 2001.
- Forty-four percent of women murdered by their intimate partner had visited an emergency department within 2 years of the homicide, 93 percent of whom had at least one injury visit.
- Firearms were the major weapon type used in intimate partner homicides from 1981 to 1998.

CONSEQUENCES

Physical

- Women with a history of IPV report 60 percent higher rates of all health problems than do women with no history of abuse.
- IPV victims report lasting negative health problems, such as chronic pain, gastrointestinal disorders, and irritable bowel syndrome, which can interfere with or limit daily functioning.
- The more severe the abuse, the greater its impact on a woman's physical and mental health, resulting in a cumulative effect over time.
- Intimate partner violence also affects reproductive health and can lead to gynecological disorders, unwanted pregnancy, premature labor and birth, and sexually transmitted diseases including HIV/AIDS.
- IPV victims have a higher prevalence of sexually transmitted diseases, hysterectomy, and heart or circulatory conditions.

Psychological

- Adolescents involved with an abusive partner report increased levels of depressed mood, substance use, antisocial behavior, and, in females, suicidal behavior.
- Abused girls and women often experience adverse mental health conditions, such as depression, anxiety, and low self-esteem.

- Women with a history of IPV are more likely to display behaviors that present further health risks, such as substance abuse, alcoholism, and increased risk of suicide attempts.

Social

- Researchers report that children who witness IPV are at greater risk of developing psychiatric disorders, developmental problems, school failure, violence against others, and low self-esteem.
- Women in violent relationships have been found to be restricted in the way they gain access to services, take part in public life, and receive emotional support from friends and relatives.

Economic

- The costs of IPV against women exceed an estimated $5.8 billion [per year]. These costs include nearly $4.1 billion in the direct costs of medical and mental health care and nearly $1.8 billion in the indirect costs of lost productivity.
- Victims of IPV lose a total of nearly 8 million days of paid work—the equivalent of more than 32,000 full-time jobs—and nearly 5.6 million days of household productivity each year as a result of the violence.

  Women who experienced male-perpetrated IPV were more likely to experience spells of unemployment, have health problems, and be welfare recipients.

GROUPS VULNERABLE TO VICTIMIZATION

- Both men and women experience IPV. However, women are 2 to 3 times more likely to report an intimate partner pushed, grabbed, or shoved them and 7 to 14 times more likely to report an intimate partner beat them up, choked them, or tied them down.
- American Indian/Alaska Native women and men report more violent victimization than do women and men of other racial backgrounds.
- In the United States, researchers estimate that 40 to 70 percent of female murder victims were killed by their husbands or boyfriends, frequently in the context of an ongoing abusive relationship.
- In a survey of boys and girls aged 8 to 12 years, girls cited concerns about IPV while boys did not consider IPV an issue.
- Hispanic women are more likely than non-Hispanic women to report instances of intimate partner rape.

Source: www.cdc.gov/ncipc/factsheets/ipvfacts.htm (2005).

result of rape trials. This is among the many reasons why rape is underreported, and, as a proportion of total rapes committed, charges are rarely pressed and assailants rarely convicted. The FBI reports that the rate of false reporting for rape and sexual assault is the same as for other violent crimes: less than 3 percent. Although feminists care about the victimization of women, we focus on surviving, becoming empowered, and making changes to stop rapes from happening.

- *Women are at least partly responsible for their victimization in terms of their appearance and behavior (encouraging women to feel guilty when they are raped).* This is false; rape is the only violent crime in which the victim is not de facto perceived as innocent. Consider the suggestion that a man who has just been robbed was asking to have his wallet stolen.
- *Men are not totally responsible for their actions. If a woman comes on to a man sexually, it is impossible for him to stop.* This is false; men are not driven by uncontrollable biological urges, and it is insulting to men to assume that this is how men behave. Note how this myth is related to the previous one that blames the victim.

These myths not only support masculine privilege concerning sexuality and access to women and therefore support some men's tendency to sexually abuse women, but are also important means for controlling women's lives. Recall again the discussion of sexual terrorism in Chapter 2. Such terrorism limits women's activities and keeps us in line by the threat of potential sexual assault. Research on rapists in the early 1980s revealed that, although there are few psychological differences between men who have raped and those who have not, the former group were more likely to believe in the rape myths, were more misogynous and tolerant of the interpersonal domination of women generally, showed higher levels of sexual arousal around depictions of rape, and were more prone to violence.

BATTERING AND PHYSICAL ABUSE

Although women are less likely than men to be victims of violent crimes overall, women are five to eight times more likely to be victimized by an intimate partner. Intimate partner violence is primarily a crime against women and all races are equally vulnerable. As Nancy Nason-Clark explains in the reading "When Terror Strikes at Home: The Interface Between Religion and Domestic Violence," such terror "knows no boundaries of class, color, or religious persuasion. . . . Violence knows no religious boundaries: it is global and it is gendered." In this reading she writes about abuse and healing in families of strong faith, emphasizing that justice, accountability, and change are all important elements in intervention services. In 2001, women accounted for 85 percent of the victims of intimate partner violence, and approximately 324,000 women experienced such violence during their pregnancy. These incidents may or may not have also included sexual abuse. A 2002 study in the *Journal of the American Medical Women's Association* found homicide to be the leading cause of death for pregnant women, followed by cancer, acute and chronic respiratory problems, motor vehicle collisions and drug overdose, peripartum and postpartum heart problems, and suicide. In terms of injury, male violence against women does more damage than female violence against men, and women are more likely to be injured such that women are 7 to 14 times more likely to suffer severe physical injury. More than three women die daily in the United States from intimate partner violence; in 2000 the yearly figure was 1,247, accounting for over a third of all murders of women. Only 4 percent of homicides caused by intimate partner violence involved male victims.

More than half of all female victims of intimate partner violence live in households with children under 12 years, and studies indicate between 3 and 10 million children witness some form of domestic violence every year. Approximately half of men who abuse domestic partners also abuse the children in those homes. Finally, as already indicated at the beginning of this chapter, violence between teenagers is another huge area of concern among clinicians, educators, and advocates for ending abuse against women and children.

Women who are physically abused are also always emotionally abused because they experience emotional abuse by virtue of being physically terrorized. Emotional abuse, however, does not always involve physical abuse. A man, for example, who constantly tells his partner that she is worthless, stupid, or ugly can emotionally abuse without being physically abusive. Sometimes the scars of emotional abuse take longer to heal than physical abuse and help explain why women might stay with abusive partners.

Why do some men physically abuse women or abuse other men? They abuse because they have internalized sexism and the right to dominate women (or others they perceive as subordinate) in their lives, have learned to use violence as a way to deal with conflict, and have repressed anger. Given this, how is it possible to explain why some women abuse men or abuse other women? Abusive behavior is an act of domination. Women too can internalize domination and can see men in their interpersonal relationships as subordinate to them, even though there is little support for that in society generally. Women in romantic relationships with other women can likewise negotiate dominance and subordination in their relationships and act this out. Battering is a problem in the lesbian community.

Why do women so often stay in abusive relationships? The research on this question suggests that when women leave abusive relationships they return about five to seven times before actually leaving for good. There are several complicated and interconnected reasons that women stay. First, emotional abuse often involves feelings of shame, guilt, and low self-esteem. Women in these situations (like rape survivors generally) often believe that the abuse is their fault. They may see themselves as worthless and have a difficult time believing that they deserve better. Low self-esteem encourages women to stay and to return to abusive men. Second, some women who are repeatedly abused become desensitized to the violence; they may see it as a relatively normal aspect of gender relationships and therefore something to tolerate.

IDEAS FOR ACTIVISM

- Volunteer at a local domestic violence shelter.
- Organize a food, clothing, and toiletries drive to benefit your local domestic violence shelter.
- Interrupt jokes about violence against women.
- Organize Domestic Violence Awareness Month (October) activities on your campus.
- Create and distribute materials about violence against women on your campus.

Check Up on Your Relationship

DOES YOUR PARTNER

Constantly put you down?

Call you several times a night or show up to make sure you are where you said you would be?

Embarrass or make fun of you in front of your friends or family?

Make you feel like you are nothing without him/her?

Intimidate or threaten you? "If you do that again, I'll . . ."

Always say that it's your fault?

Pressure you to have sex when you don't want to?

Glare at you, give you the silent treatment, grab, shove, kick, or hit you?

DO YOU

Always do what your partner wants instead of what you want?

Fear how your partner will act in public?

Constantly make excuses to other people for your partner's behavior?

Feel like you walk on eggshells to avoid your partner's anger?

Believe if you just tried harder, submitted more, that everything would be okay?

Stay with your partner because you fear what your partner would do if you broke up?

These indicators suggest potential abuse in your relationship. If you've answered yes to any of these questions, talk to a counselor about your relationship. Remember, when one person scares, hurts, or continually puts down the other person, it's abuse.

Created by the President's Commission on the Status of Women, Oregon State University.

A third reason women stay in abusive relationships is that men who abuse women tend to physically isolate them from others. This often involves a pattern where women are prevented from visiting or talking to family and friends, are left without transportation, and/or have no access to a telephone. Notice how, when women are abused, the shame associated with this situation can encourage women to isolate themselves. An outcome of this isolation is that women do not get the reality check they need about their situation. Isolation thus helps keep self-esteem low, prevents support, and minimizes women's options in terms of leaving the abusive situation.

A fourth reason women stay is that they worry about what people will think, and this worry keeps them in abusive situations as a consequence of the shame they feel.

Most women in abusive relationships worry about this to some extent, although middle-class women probably feel it the most. The myth that this is a lower-class problem and that it does not happen to "nice" families who appear to have everything going for them is part of the problem. And, indeed, the question about what people will think is a relevant one: Some churches tell abused women to submit to their husbands and hide the abuse, neighbors often look the other way, mothers worry about their children being stigmatized at school, and certainly there is embarrassment associated with admitting your husband or boyfriend hits you. For men this issue is even more pertinent, and the shame and embarrassment may be even greater for abused men.

A fifth reason women stay is that they cannot afford to leave. Women in this situation fear for the economic welfare of themselves and their children should they leave the abusive situation. These women tend to have less education and to have dependent children. They understand that the kind of paid work they could get would not be enough to support the family. Reason six is that some survivors believe that children need a father—and that even a bad father might be better than no father. Although this belief is erroneous in our view, it does keep women in abusive situations "for the sake of the children." Interestingly, the primary reason women do permanently leave an abusive relationship is also the children: When women see that their children are being hurt, this is the moment when they are most likely to leave for good.

The Cycle of Violence

Domestic violence may seem unpredictable, but it actually follows a typical pattern no matter when it occurs or who is involved. Understanding the cycle of violence and the thinking of the abuser helps survivors recognize they are not to blame for the violence they have suffered—and that *the abuser is the one responsible.*

1. *Tension building* The abuser might set up the victim so that she is bound to anger him. The victim, knowing her abuser is likely to erupt, is apologetic. She may even defend his actions.
2. *The abuse* The batterer behaves violently, inflicting pain and abuse on the victim.
3. *Guilt and fear of reprisal* After the violence, the abuser may have feelings of "guilt"—not normal guilt, in which he'd feel sorry for hurting another person, but actually a fear of getting caught. He might blame alcohol for his outburst.
4. *Blaming the victim* The abuser can't stand any kind of guilt feeling for long, so he quickly rationalizes his actions and blames the victim for causing him to hurt her. He might tell her that her behavior "asked for it."
5. *"Normalcy"* At this point, the batterer exhibits kind and loving behavior. Welcomed by both parties, an unusual calm will surround the relationship. He may bring gifts and promise the violence will never happen again.
6. *Fantasy/set-up* Batterers and abusers fantasize about their past and future abuses. These fantasies feed the abuser's anger. He begins to plan another attack by placing his victim in situations that he knows will anger him.

Reprinted from *Take Care: A Guide for Violence-Free Living*, a publication of Raphael House of Portland.

ACTIVIST PROFILE   **Del Martin**

In the 1950s, few lesbians were able to be out about their sexual identity. In fact, in most places homosexual sex was illegal, and lesbians and gay men were easy targets for violence, even by police. Nonetheless, in 1955 Del Martin (left), her partner Phyllis Lyon, and six other women co-founded the Daughters of Bilitis. The group started as a social club for lesbians seeking to meet and socialize with other lesbians, but before long it expanded its mission to include social reform, and chapters of the organization were launched around the country. Martin was president of the national organization from 1957 to 1960.

Martin became involved in the feminist movement in the early 1970s and in 1976 wrote *Battered Wives*, a revolutionary examination of the experiences of victims of domestic violence. One of the most significant contributions of the book was identifying the origins of domestic violence in the patriarchal structure of the nuclear family. She wrote, "The nuclear family is the building block of American society, and the social, religious, educational and economic institutions of society are designed to maintain, support and strengthen family ties even if the people involved can't stand the sight of one another." Martin advocated collective thinking among members of government, social agencies, religious institutions, and political action groups. Her vision led to the creation of a movement addressing the problem of battered women.

In 1975 she helped found the Coalition for Justice for Battered Women. She also co-founded *La Casa de las Madres,* a refuge for battered women in San Francisco. She helped write the protocol for the San Francisco criminal justice system and served 3 years on the California Commission on Crime Control and Violence Prevention.

Partners since 1953, in the late 1990s, Martin and Lyons continued to work for issues of justice, particularly those related to aging. In 1995 they were appointed delegates to the White House Conference on Aging. For nearly 50 years they have worked tirelessly on behalf of marginalized people in order to bring about a more just world.

Another reason women stay is that there is often nowhere to go. Although the increase in the numbers of crisis lines and emergency housing shelters is staggering given their absence only a few decades ago, some women still have a difficult time imagining an alternative to the abusive situation. This is especially true of women who live in rural areas and who are isolated from friends and family. Reason eight is that battered women often believe their partner will change. Part of the cycle of violence noted by scholars in this area is the "honeymoon phase" after the violent episode. First comes the buildup of tension when violence is brewing, second is the violent episode, and third is the honeymoon phase when men tend to be especially remorseful—even horrified that they could have done such a thing—and ask for forgiveness. Given that the profile of many batterers is charm and manipulation, such behavior during this phase can be especially persuasive. Women are not making it up when they think their partner will change.

Finally, women stay because they believe their partner might kill them—or hurt or kill the children—should they leave. Again, his past violence is often enough to make women realize this is no idle threat. Men do kill in these situations and often after wives and girlfriends have fled and brought restraining orders against them.

INCEST

This topic is especially poignant as the poem by Grace Caroline Bridges, "Lisa's Ritual, Age 10," demonstrates. Incest is the sexual abuse (molestation, inappropriate touching, rape, being forced to watch or perform sexual acts on others) of children by a family member or someone with a kinship role in a child's life. There is now an evolving definition of incest that takes into account betrayals of trust and power imbalances, expanding the definition to include sexual abuse by anyone who has power or authority over the child. Perpetration might include baby-sitters, schoolteachers, Boy Scout leaders, priests/ministers, family friends, as well as immediate and extended family members. It is estimated that in 90 percent of cases where children are raped it is by someone they know. Studies suggest that one in every three to five girls have experienced some kind of childhood sexual abuse by the time they are 16 years old. For boys this number is one in six to ten, although this may be underestimated because boys are less likely to admit that they are survivors. Again, like other forms of abuse, incest crosses all ethnic, class, and religious lines. Power is always involved in incest, and, because children are the least powerful group in society, the effects on them can be devastating. Approximately a third of all juvenile victims of sexual abuse are younger than 6 years old. Children who are abused often have low self-esteem and may find it difficult to trust.

Incest can be both direct and indirect. Direct forms include vaginal, oral, and rectal penetration; sexual rubbing; excessive, inappropriate hugging; body and mouth kissing; bouncing a child on a lap against an erection; and sexual bathing. Direct incest also includes forcing children to watch or perform these acts on others. Indirect incest includes sexualizing statements or joking, speaking to the child as a surrogate spouse, inappropriate references to a child's body, or staring at the child's body. Other examples involve intentionally invading children's privacy in the bathroom or acting inappropriately jealous when adolescents start dating.

Violence Against Women: Selected Human Rights Documents

International human rights documents encompass formal written documents, such as conventions, declarations, conference statements, guidelines, resolutions and recommendations. Treaties are legally binding to those States which have ratified or acceded to them, and their implementation is observed by monitoring bodies, such as the Committee on the Elimination of Discrimination Against Women (CEDAW).

GLOBAL DOCUMENTS

The Universal Declaration of Human Rights (1948) has formed the basis for the development of international human rights conventions. Article 3 states that everyone has the right of life, liberty and security of the person. According to article 5, no one shall be subjected to torture or to cruel, inhuman or degrading treatment or punishment. Therefore, any form of violence against women which is a threat to her life, liberty or security of person or which can be interpreted as torture or cruel, inhuman or degrading treatment violates the principles of this Declaration.

The International Covenant on Economic, Social and Cultural Rights (1966), together with the *International Covenant on Civil and Political Rights,* prohibits discrimination on the basis of sex. Violence detrimentally affects women's health; therefore, it violates the right to the enjoyment of the highest attainable standard of physical and mental health (article 12). In addition, article 7 provides the right to the enjoyment of just and favourable conditions of work which ensure safe and healthy working conditions. This provision encompasses the prohibition of violence and harassment of women in the workplace.

The International Covenant on Civil and Political Rights (1966) prohibits all forms of violence. Article 6.1 protects the right to life. Article 7 prohibits torture and inhuman or degrading treatment or punishment. Article 9 guarantees the right to liberty and security of person.

The Convention Against Torture and Other Cruel, Inhuman or Degrading Treatment or Punishment (1984) provides protection for all persons, regardless of their sex, in a more detailed manner than the International Covenant on Civil and Political Rights. States should take effective measures to prevent acts of torture (article 2).

The Convention on the Elimination of All Forms of Discrimination Against Women (1979) is the most extensive international instrument dealing with the rights of women. Although violence against women is not specifically addressed in the Convention, except in relation to trafficking and prostitution (article 6), many of the anti-discrimination clauses protect women from violence. States Parties have agreed to a policy of eliminating discrimination against women, and to adopt legislative and other measures prohibiting all discrimination against women (article 2). In 1992, the Committee on the Elimination of Discrimination Against Women (CEDAW), which monitors the implementation of this Convention, formally included gender-based violence under gender-based discrimination. General Recommendation No. 19, adopted at the 11th session (June 1992), deals entirely with violence against women and the measures taken to eliminate such violence. As for health issues, it recommends that States should provide support services for all victims of gender-based violence, including refuges, specially trained health workers, and rehabilitation and counselling services.

The International Convention on the Elimination of All Forms of Racial Discrimination (1965) declares that States Parties undertake to prohibit and to eliminate racial discrimination in all its forms and to guarantee the enjoyment of the right to security of the person and protection by the State against violence or bodily harm, whether inflicted by government officials or by any individual group or institution (article 5).

The four *1949 Geneva Conventions* and two additional Protocols form the cornerstone of international humanitarian law. The Geneva Conventions require that all persons taking no active part in hostilities shall be treated humanely, without adverse distinction on any of the usual grounds, including sex (article 3). They offer protection to all civilians against sexual violence, forced prostitution, sexual abuse and rape.

Regarding international armed conflict, *Additional Protocol I* to the 1949 Geneva Conventions creates obligations for parties to a conflict to treat humanely persons under their control. It requires that women shall be protected against rape, forced prostitution and indecent assault. *Additional Protocol II,* applicable during internal conflicts, also prohibits rape, enforced prostitution and indecent assault.

The Convention on the Rights of the Child (1989) declares that States Parties take appropriate legislative, administrative, social and educational measures to protect the child from physical or mental violence, abuse, maltreatment or exploitation (article 19). States shall act accordingly to prevent the exploitative use of children in prostitution or other unlawful sexual practices, and the exploitative use of children in pornographic performances and materials (article 34).

The International Convention on the Protection of the Rights of All Migrant Workers and Members of Their Families (adopted by the General Assembly in 1990 and went into force in 2003) contains the right of migrant workers and their family members to liberty and security of person as proclaimed in other international instruments. They shall be entitled to effective protection by the State against violence, physical injury, threats and intimidation, whether by public officials or by private individuals, groups or institutions (article 16).

These indirect forms of incest involve sexualizing children and violating their boundaries.

Often siblings indulge in relatively normal uncoerced sexual play with each other that disappears over time. When this involves a child who is several years older or one who uses threats or intimidation, however, then the behavior can be characterized as incestuous. Indicators of abuse in childhood include excessive crying, anxiety, night fears and sleep disturbances, depression and withdrawal, clinging behaviors, and physical problems like urinary tract infections and trauma to the perineal area. Adolescent symptoms often include eating disorders, psychosomatic complaints, suicidal thoughts, and depression. Survivors of childhood sexual violence may get involved in self-destructive behaviors like alcohol and drug abuse or cutting on their bodies as they turn their anger inward, or they may express their anger through acting out or promiscuous behavior. In particular, girls internalize their worthlessness and their role as sexual objects used by others; boys often have more anger because they were dominated, an anger that is sometimes projected onto their future sexual partners as well as onto themselves. Although it takes time, we can heal from being sexually violated.

PORNOGRAPHY

Pornography involves the sexualization and objectification of women's bodies and parts of bodies for entertainment value. According to feminist legal scholar Catharine MacKinnon, who has written on and debated the issue of pornography at length, pornography can be defined as the graphic, sexually explicit subordination of women through pictures and/or words. She says pornography includes one or more of the following: women presented as dehumanized sexual objects, things, or commodities; shown as enjoying humiliation, pain, or sexual assault; tied up, mutilated, or physically hurt; depicted in postures or positions of sexual submission or servility; shown with body parts—including though not limited to vagina, breasts, or buttocks—exhibited such that women are reduced to those parts; women penetrated by animals or objects; and women presented in scenarios of degradation, humiliation, torture, shown as filthy or inferior, bleeding, bruised, or hurt in a context that makes these conditions sexual. MacKinnon adds that the use of men, children, or transsexuals in the place of women is also pornography. Note the definition includes the caveat that because a person has consented to being harmed, abused, or subjected to coercion does not alter the degrading character of the behavior.

Just as there are degrees of objectification and normalization of violence in pop culture forms, so too in pornography there is a continuum from the soft porn of *Playboy* to the hard-core *Hustler* and along to illegal forms of representation like child pornography and snuff films. Snuff films are illegal because women are actually murdered in the making of these films. The Internet is one of the largest sites for pornography. There are thousands of pornography sites on the Web, including those of "fantasy rape" that depict women being raped, and "sex" is still the top search word. In addition to Internet pornography there is the problem of Internet prostitution since this technology is utilized for the global trafficking and the sexual exploitation of women and children.

Many people do not oppose pornography because they feel that it represents free speech, or because they feel that the women have chosen to be part of it, or because they like the articles in these magazines. This is especially true of soft porn like *Playboy*. Some see pornography as a mark of sexual freedom and characterize those who would like to limit pornography as prudish. In the reading "Pornography and Freedom," John Stoltenberg explains how sexual freedom requires sexual justice and suggests that pornography is a violation of this justice rather than an expression of it. He writes about pornography in the context of gender and male domination in society.

Some people make a distinction between hard core and soft porn and feel that the former is harmful and the latter relatively harmless. Others oppose pornography entirely as a violation of women's rights against objectification and sexualization for male pleasure and believe that people's rights to consume such materials are no longer rights when they violate the rights of others. This is an important debate that has brought some interesting coalitions that normally do not work together, such as feminists and conservative religious groups.

In this way, acts of violence and the threat of violence have profound and lasting effects on all women's lives. We tend to refer to those who have survived violence as "survivors" rather than "victims" to emphasize that it is possible to go on with our lives after such experiences, difficult though that might be. Understanding and preventing violence against women has become a worldwide effort, bringing women and men together to make this a safer place for everyone.

Beyond the Politics of Inclusion
Violence Against Women of Color and Human Rights

Andrea Smith

What was disturbing to so many U.S. citizens about the September 11, 2001, attacks on the World Trade Center is that these attacks disrupted their sense of safety at "home." Terrorism is something that happens in other countries; our "home," the U.S.A., is supposed to be a place of safety. Similarly, mainstream U.S. society believes that violence against women only occurs "out there" and is perpetrated by a few crazed men whom we simply need to lock up. However, the anti-violence movement has always contested this notion of safety at home. The notion that violence only happens "out there," inflicted by the stranger in the dark alley makes it difficult to recognize that the home is in fact the place of greatest danger for women. In response to this important piece of analysis, the anti-violence movement has, ironically, based its strategies on the premise that the criminal legal system is the primary tool with which to address violence against women. However, when one-half of women will be battered in their lifetimes and nearly one-half of women will be sexually assaulted in their lifetimes, it is clear that we live in a rape culture that prisons, themselves a site of violence and control, cannot change.

Similarly, the notion that terrorism happens in other countries makes it difficult to grasp that the United States is built on a history of genocide, slavery, and racism. Our "home" has never been a safe place for people of color. Because many mainstream feminist organizations are white-dominated, they often do not see themselves as potential victims in Bush's war in the U.S. and abroad. However, those considered "alien" in the United States and hence deserving of repressive policies and overt attack are not only people of color. Since 9/11, many organizations in LGBT communities have reported sharp increases in attacks, demonstrating the extent to which gays and lesbians are often seen as "alien" because their sexuality seems to threaten the white nuclear family thought to be the building block of U.S. society.

Furthermore, many mainstream feminist organizations, particularly anti-violence organizations, have applauded the U.S. attacks on Afghanistan for "liberating" Arab women from the repressive policies of the Taliban. Apparently, bombing women in Afghanistan somehow elevates their status. However, the Revolutionary Association of the Women from Afghanistan (RAWA), the organization comprised of members most affected by the policies of the Taliban, has condemned U.S. intervention and has argued that women cannot expect an improvement in their status under the regime of the Northern Alliance with which the United States has allied itself. This support rests entirely on the problematic assumption that state violence can secure safety and liberation for women and other oppressed groups. Clearly, alternative approaches to provide true safety and security for women must be developed, both at "home" and abroad.

BEYOND INCLUSION: CENTERING WOMEN OF COLOR IN THE ANTI-VIOLENCE MOVEMENT

The central problem is that as the anti-violence movement has attempted to become more "inclusive" these attempts at multicultural interventions have unwittingly strengthened the white supremacy within the anti-violence movement. That is, inclusivity has come to mean taking on a domestic violence model that was developed largely with the interests of white, middle class women in mind, and simply adding to it a multicultural component. However, if we look at the histories of women of color in the United States, as I have done in other work, it is clear that gender violence functions as a tool for racism and colonialism for women of color in general (Smith 2002). The racial element of gender violence points to the necessity of an alternative approach that goes beyond mere inclusion to actually centering women of color in the organizing and analysis. That is, if we do not make any assumptions about what a domestic violence program should look like but, instead, ask what would it take to end violence against women of color, then what would this movement look like?

In fact, Beth Richie suggests we go beyond just centering women of color, to centering those most marginalized within the category of "women of color." She writes:

> We have to understand that the goal of our antiviolence work is not for diversity, and not inclusion. It is for liberation. If we're truly committed to ending violence against women, then we must start in the hardest places, the places like jails and prisons and other correctional facilities. The places where our work has not had an impact yet. . . . [W]e have to stop being the friendly colored girls as some of our anti-violence programs require us to be. We must not deny the part of ourselves and the part of our work that is least acceptable to the mainstream public. We must not let those who really object to all of us and our work co-opt some of us and the work we're trying to do. As if this anti-violence movement could ever really be legitimate in a patriarchal, racist society. . . . Ultimately the movement needs to be accountable not to those in power, but to the powerless. (Richie 2000)

When we center women of color in the analysis, it becomes clear that we must develop approaches that address interpersonal and state violence simultaneously. In addition, we find that by centering women of color in the analysis, we may actually build a movement that more effectively ends violence not just for women of color, but for all peoples.

HUMAN RIGHTS FRAMEWORK FOR ADDRESSING VIOLENCE

Developing strategies to address state violence, then, suggests the importance of developing a human rights approach toward ending violence. By human rights I mean those rights seen under international law to be inalienable and not dependent on any particular government structure. When we limit our struggles around changes in domestic legislation within the United States, we forget that the United States government itself perpetrates more violence against women than any other actor in the world. While we may use a variety of rhetorical and organizing tools, our overall strategy should not be premised on the notion that the United States should or will always continue to exist—to do so is to fundamentally sanction the continuing genocide of indigenous peoples on which this government is based.

One organization that avoids this problem is the American Indian Boarding School Healing Project, which organizes against gender violence from a human rights perspective. During the nineteenth century and into the twentieth century, American Indian children were abducted from their homes to attend Christian boarding schools as a matter of state policy that again demonstrates the links between sexual violence and state violence. This system was later imported to Canada in the form of the residential school system. Because the worst of the abuses happened to an older generation, there is simply not sufficient documentation or vocal outcry against boarding school abuses.

Responding to this need, the International Human Rights Association of American Minorities issued a report documenting the involvement of mainline churches and the federal government in the murder of over 50,000 Native children through the Canadian residential school system (Annet 2001). The list of offenses committed by church officials includes murder by beating, poisoning, hanging, starvation, strangulation, and medical experimentation. In addition, the report found that church, police, business, and government officials maintained pedophile rings using children from residential schools. Several schools are also charged with concealing on their grounds the unmarked graves of children who were murdered, particularly children killed after being born as a result of rapes of Native girls by priests and other church officials. While some churches in Canada have taken some minimal steps towards addressing their involvement in this genocidal policy, churches in the United States have not.

As a result of boarding school policies, an epidemic of child sexual abuse now exists in Native communities. The shame attached to abuse has allowed no space in which to address this problem. Consequently, child abuse passes from one generation to the next. The American Indian Boarding School Healing Project provides an entryway to addressing this history of child sexual abuse by framing it not primarily as an example of individual and community dysfunction, but instead as the continuing effect of human rights abuses perpetrated by state policy. This project seeks to take the shame away from talking about abuse and provide the space for communities to address the problem and heal.

A human rights approach can even be of assistance to traditional service providers for survivors of violence. The human rights approach provides an organizing strategy to protest John Ashcroft's dramatic cuts in funding for anti-violence programs, particularly indigenous programs. Adequate funding for indigenous-controlled programs and services is not a privilege for States to curtail in times of economic crises. Rather, as international human rights law dictates, states are mandated to address the continuing effects of human rights

violations. Hence, the United States violates international human rights law when it de-funds anti-violence programs. For indigenous women and women of color in general, sexual and domestic violence are clearly the continuing effects of human rights violations perpetrated by U.S. state policy.

CONCLUSION

For too long, women of color have been forced to choose between racial justice and gender justice. Yet, it is precisely through sexism and gender violence that colonialism and white supremacy have been successful. This failure to see the intersectionality of racism and sexism in racial justice movements was evident at the UN World Conference Against Racism, where the types of racism that women of color face in reproductive rights policies, for example, failed to even register on the UN radar screen. Women of color are often suspicious of human rights strategies because white-dominated human rights organizations often pursue the imperialist agenda of organizing around the human rights violations of women in other countries while ignoring the human rights violations of women of color in the United States. Nonetheless, an anti-colonial human rights strategy can be helpful in highlighting the violence perpetrated by U.S. state policy and combating U.S. exceptionalism on the global scale—as well as right here at home.

REFERENCES

Annett, Kevin. 2001. "The Truth Commission into the Genocide in Canada." Accessed August 31, 2003 (http://annett55.freewebsites.com/genocide.pdf).

Richie, Beth. 2000. Plenary Address, "Color of Violence: Violence Against Women of Color" Conference, Santa Cruz, CA.

Smith, Andrea. 2002. "Better Dead than Pregnant: The Colonization of Native Women's Reproductive Health." In *Policing the National Body: Race, Gender, and Criminalization,* ed. Jael Silliman and Anannya Bhattacharjee. Cambridge: South End Press.

Human Rights: Sex Trafficking and Prostitution

Alice Leuchtag

Despite laws against slavery in practically every country, an estimated twenty-seven million people live as slaves. Kevin Bales, in his book *Disposable People: New Slavery in the Global Economy* (University of California Press, Berkeley, 1999), describes those who endure modern forms of slavery. These include indentured servants, persons held in hereditary bondage, child slaves who pick plantation crops, child soldiers, and adults and children trafficked and sold into sex slavery.

A LIFE NARRATIVE

Of all forms of slavery, sex slavery is one of the most exploitative and lucrative with some 200,000 sex slaves worldwide bringing their slaveholders an annual profit of $10.5 billion. Although the great preponderance of sex slaves are women and girls, a smaller but significant number of males—both adult and children—are enslaved for homosexual prostitution.

The life narrative of a Thai girl named Siri, as told to Bales, illustrates how sex slavery happens to vulnerable girls and women. Siri is born in northeastern Thailand to a poor family that farms a small plot of land, barely eking out a living. Economic policies of structural adjustment pursued by the Thai government under the aegis of the World Bank and the International Monetary Fund have taken former government subsidies away from rice farmers, leaving them to compete against imported, subsidized rice that keeps the market price artificially depressed.

Siri attends four years of school, then is kept at home to help care for her three younger siblings.

When Siri is fourteen, a well-dressed woman visits her village. She offers to find Siri a "good job," advancing her parents $2,000 against future earnings. This represents at least a year's income for the family. In a town in another province the woman, a trafficker, "sells" Siri to a brothel for $4,000. Owned by an "investment club" whose members are business and professional men—government bureaucrats and local politicians—the brothel is extremely profitable. In a typical thirty-day period it nets its investors $88,000.

To maintain the appearance that their hands are clean, members of the club's board of directors leave the management of the brothel to a pimp and a bookkeeper. Siri is initiated into prostitution by the pimp who rapes her. After being abused by her first "customer," Siri escapes, but a policeman—who gets a percentage of the brothel profits—brings her back, whereupon the pimp beats her up. As further punishment, her "debt" is doubled from $4,000 to $8,000. She must now repay this, along with her monthly rent and food, all from her earnings of $4 per customer. She will have to have sex with three hundred men a month just to pay her rent. Realizing she will never be able to get out of debt, Siri tries to build a relationship with the pimp simply in order to survive.

The pimp uses culture and religion to reinforce his control over Siri. He tells her she must have committed terrible sins in a past life to have been born a female; she must have accumulated a karmic debt to deserve the enslavement and abuse to which she must reconcile herself. Gradually Siri begins to see herself from the point of view of the slaveholder—as someone unworthy and deserving of punishment. By age fifteen she no longer protests or runs away. Her physical enslavement has become psychological as well, a common occurrence in chronic abuse.

Siri is administered regular injections of the contraceptive drug Depo-Provera for which she is charged. As the same needle is used for all the girls, there is a high risk of HIV and other sexual diseases from the injections. Siri knows that a serious illness threatens her and she prays to Buddha at the little shrine in her room, hoping to earn merit so he will protect her from the dreaded disease. Once a month she and the others, at their own expense, are tested for HIV. So far Siri's tests have been negative. When Siri tries to get the male customers to wear condoms—distributed free to brothels by the Thai Ministry of Health—some resist wearing them and she can't make them do so.

As one of an estimated 35,000 women working as brothel slaves in Thailand—a country where 500,000 to one million prostituted women and girls work in conditions of degradation and exploitation short of brothel slavery—Siri faces at least a 40 percent chance of contracting the HIV virus. If she is lucky, she can look forward to five more years before she becomes too ill to work and is pushed out into the street.

THAILAND'S SEX TOURISM

Though the Thai government denies it, the World Health Organization finds that HIV is epidemic in Thailand, with the largest segment of new cases among wives and girlfriends of men who buy prostitute sex. Viewing its women as a cash crop to be exploited, and depending on sex tourism for foreign exchange dollars to help pay interest on the foreign debt, the Thai government can't acknowledge the epidemic without contradicting the continued promotion of sex tourism and prostitution.

By encouraging investment in the sex industry, sex tourism creates a business climate conducive to the trafficking and enslavement of vulnerable girls such as Siri. In 1996 nearly five million sex tourists from the United States, Western Europe,

Australia, and Japan visited Thailand. These transactions brought in about $26.2 billion—thirteen times more than Thailand earned by building and exporting computers.

In her 1999 report *Pimps and Predators on the Internet: Globalizing the Sexual Exploitation of Women and Children,* published by the Coalition Against Trafficking in Women (CATW), Donna Hughes quotes from postings on an Internet site where sex tourists share experiences and advise one another. The following is one man's description of having sex with a fourteen-year-old prostituted girl in Bangkok:

> Even though I've had a lot of better massages . . . after fifteen minutes, I was much more relaxed. . . . Then I asked for a condom and I fucked her for another thirty minutes. Her face looked like she was feeling a lot of pain. . . . She blocked my way when I wanted to leave the room and she asked for a tip. I gave her 600 bath. Altogether, not a good experience.

Hughes says, "To the men who buy sex, a 'bad experience' evidently means not getting their money's worth, or that the prostituted woman or girl didn't keep up the act of enjoying what she had to do. . . . [O]ne glimpses the humiliation and physical pain most girls and women in prostitution endure."

Nor are the men oblivious to the existence of sexual slavery. One customer states, "Girls in Bangkok virtually get sold by their families into the industry; they work against their will." His knowledge of their sexual slavery and lack of sensitivity thereof is evident in that he then names the hotels in which girls are kept and describes how much they cost!

As Hughes observes, sex tourists apparently feel they have a right to prostitute sex, perceiving prostitution only from a self-interested perspective in which they commodify and objectify women of other cultures, nationalities, and ethnic groups. Their awareness of racism, colonialism, global economic inequalities, and sexism seems limited to the way these realities benefit them as sex consumers.

SEX TRAFFICKERS CAST THEIR NETS

According to the *Guide to the New UN Trafficking Protocol* by Janice Raymond, published by the CATW in 2001, the United Nations estimates that sex trafficking in human beings is a $5 billion to $7 billion operation annually. Four million persons are moved illegally from one country to another and within countries each year, a large proportion of them women and girls being trafficked into prostitution. The United Nations International Children's Emergency Fund (UNICEF) estimates that some 30 percent of women being trafficked are minors, many under age thirteen. The International Organization on Migration estimates that some 500,000 women per year are trafficked into Western Europe from poorer regions of the world. According to *Sex Trafficking of Women in the United States: International and Domestic Trends,* also published by the CATW in 2001, some 50,000 women and children are trafficked into the United States each year, mainly from Asia and Latin America.

Because prostitution as a system of organized sexual exploitation depends on a continuous supply of new "recruits" trafficking is essential to its continued existence. When the pool of available women and girls dries up, new women must be procured. Traffickers cast their nets ever wider and become ever more sophisticated. The Italian Camorra, Chinese Triads, Russian Mafia, and Japanese Yakuza are powerful criminal syndicates consisting of traffickers, pimps, brothel keepers, forced labor lords, and gangs which operate globally.

After the breakdown of the Soviet Union, an estimated five thousand criminal groups formed the Russian Mafia, which operates in thirty countries. The Russian Mafia traffics women from African countries, the Ukraine, the Russian Federation, and Eastern Europe into Western Europe, the United States, and Israel. The Triads traffick women from China, Korea, Thailand, and other Southeast Asian countries into the United States and Europe. The Camorra traffics women from Latin America into Europe. The Yakuza traffics women from the Phillipines, Thailand, Burma, Cambodia, Korea, Nepal, and Laos into Japan.

A GLOBAL PROBLEM MEETS A GLOBAL RESPONSE

Despite these appalling facts, until recently no generally agreed upon definition of trafficking in human beings was written into international law. In Vienna, Austria, during 1999 and 2000, 120 countries participated in debates over a definition of trafficking. A few nongovernmental organizations (NGOs) and a minority of governments—including Australia, Canada, Denmark, Germany, Ireland, Japan, the Netherlands, Spain, Switzerland, Thailand, and the United Kingdom—wanted to separate issues of trafficking from issues of prostitution. They argued that persons being trafficked should be divided into those who are forced and those who give their consent, with the burden of proof being placed on persons being trafficked. They also urged that the less explicit means of control over trafficked persons—such as abuse of a victim's vulnerability—not be included in the definition of trafficking and that the word *exploitation* not be used. Generally supporters of this position were wealthier countries where large numbers of women were being trafficked and countries in which prostitution was legalized or sex tourism encouraged.

The CATW—140 other NGOs that make up the International Human Rights Network plus many governments (including those of Algeria, Bangladesh, Belgium, China, Colombia, Cuba, Egypt, Finland, France, India, Mexico, Norway, Pakistan, the Philippines, Sweden, Syria, Venezuela, and Vietnam)—maintains that trafficking can't be separated from prostitution. Persons being trafficked shouldn't be divided into those who are forced and those who give their consent because trafficked persons are in no position to give meaningful consent. The subtler methods used by traffickers, such as abuse of a victim's vulnerability, should be included in the definition of trafficking and the word *exploitation* be an essential part of the definition. Generally supporters of this majority view were poorer countries from which large numbers of women were being trafficked or countries in which strong feminist, anti-colonialist, or socialist influences existed. The United States, though initially critical of the majority position, agreed to support a definition of trafficking that would be agreed upon by consensus.

The struggle—led by the CATW to create a definition of trafficking that would penalize traffickers while ensuring that all victims of trafficking would be protected—succeeded when a compromise proposal by Sweden was agreed to. A strongly worded and inclusive *UN Protocol to Prevent, Suppress, and Punish Trafficking in Persons*—especially women and children—was drafted by an ad hoc committee of the UN as a supplement to the Convention Against Transnational Organized Crime. The UN protocol specifically addresses the trade in human beings for purposes of prostitution and other forms of sexual exploitation, forced labor or services, slavery or practices similar to slavery, servitude, and the removal of organs. The protocol defines trafficking as

> The recruitment, transportation, transfer, harboring or receipt of persons, by means of the threat or use of force or other forms of coercion, of abduction, of fraud, of deception, of the abuse of power or of a position of vulnerability or of the giving or receiving of payments or benefits to achieve the consent of a person having control over another person, for the purpose of exploitation.

While recognizing that the largest amount of trafficking involves women and children, the wording of the UN protocol clearly is gender and age neutral, inclusive of trafficking in both males and females, adults and children.

In 2000 the UN General Assembly adopted this convention and its supplementary protocol; 121 countries signed the convention and eighty countries signed the protocol. For the convention and protocol to become international law, forty countries must ratify them.

HIGHLIGHTS

Some highlights of the new convention and protocol are:

For the first time there is an accepted international definition of trafficking and an agreed upon set of prosecution, protection, and prevention mechanisms on which countries can base their national legislation.

- The various criminal means by which trafficking takes place, including indirect and subtle forms of coercion, are covered.
- Trafficked persons, especially women in prostitution and child laborers, are no longer viewed as illegal migrants but as victims of a crime.
- The convention doesn't limit its scope to criminal syndicates but defines an organized criminal group as "any structured group of three or more persons which engages in criminal activities such as trafficking and pimping."
- All victims of trafficking in persons are protected, not just those who can prove that force was used against them.
- The consent of a victim of trafficking is meaningless and irrelevant.
- Victims of trafficking won't have to bear the burden of proof.
- Trafficking and sexual exploitation are intrinsically connected and not to be separated.
- Because women trafficked domestically into local sex industries suffer harmful effects similar to those experienced by women trafficked transnationally, these women also come under the protections of the protocol.
- The key element in trafficking is the exploitative purpose rather than the movement across a border.

The protocol is the first UN instrument to address the demand for prostitution sex, a demand that results in the human rights abuses of women and children being trafficked. The protocol recognizes an urgent need for governments to put the buyers of prostitution sex on their policy and legislative agendas, and it calls upon countries to take or strengthen legislative or other measures to discourage demand, which fosters all the forms of sexual exploitation of women and children.

As Raymond says in the *Guide to the New UN Trafficking Protocol*:

> The least discussed part of the prostitution and trafficking chain has been the men who buy women for sexual exploitation in prostitution. . . . If we are to find a permanent path to ending these human rights abuses, then we cannot just shrug our shoulders and say, "men are like this," or "boys will be boys," or "prostitution has always been around." Or tell women and girls in prostitution that they must continue to do what they do because prostitution is inevitable. Rather, our responsibility is to make men change their behavior, by all means available—educational, cultural and legal.

Two U.S. feminist human rights organizations—Captive Daughters and Equality Now—have been working toward that goal. Surita Sandosham of Equality Now says that when her organization asked women's groups in Thailand and the Philippines how it could assist them, the answer came back, "Do something about the demand." Since then the two organizations have legally challenged sex tours originating in the United States and have succeeded in closing down at least one operation.

REFUGEES, NOT ILLEGAL ALIENS

In October 2000 the U.S. Congress passed a bill, the Victims of Trafficking and Violence Protection Act of 2000, introduced by New Jersey republican representative Chris Smith. Under this law penalties for traffickers are raised and protections for victims increased. Reasoning that desperate women are unable to give meaningful consent to their own sexual exploitation, the law adopts a broad definition of sex trafficking so as not to exclude so-called consensual prostitution or trafficking that occurs solely within the United States. In these respects the new federal law conforms to the UN protocol.

Two features of the law are particularly noteworthy:

- In order to pressure other countries to end sex trafficking, the U.S. State Department is to make a yearly assessment of other countries' anti-trafficking efforts and to rank them according to how well they discourage trafficking. After two years of failing to meet even minimal standards, countries are subject to sanctions, although not sanctions on humanitarian aid. "Tier 3" countries—those failing to meet even minimal standards—include Greece, Indonesia, Israel, Pakistan, Russia, Saudi Arabia, South Korea, and Thailand.

- Among persons being trafficked into the United States, special T-visas will be provided to those who meet the criteria for having suffered the most serious trafficking abuses. These visas will protect them from deportation so they can testify against their traffickers. T-1 non-immigrant status allows eligible aliens to remain in the United States temporarily and grants specific non-immigrant benefits. Those acquiring T-1 non-immigrant status will be able to remain for a period of three years and will be eligible to receive certain kinds of public assistance—to the same extent as refugees. They will also be issued employment authorization to "assist them in finding safe, legal employment while they attempt to retake control of their lives."

A DEBATE RAGES

A worldwide debate rages about legalization of prostitution fueled by a 1998 International Labor Organization (ILO) report entitled *The Sex Sector: The Economic and Social Bases of Prostitution in Southeast Asia*. The report follows years of lobbying by the sex industry for recognition of prostitution as "sex work." Citing the sex industry's unrecognized contribution to the gross domestic product of four countries in Southeast Asia, the ILO urges governments to officially recognize the "sex sector" and "extend taxation nets to cover many of the lucrative activities connected with it." Though the ILO report says it stops short of calling for legalization of prostitution, official recognition of the sex industry would be impossible without it.

Raymond points out that the ILO's push to redefine prostitution as sex work ignores legislation demonstrating that countries can reduce organized sexual exploitation rather than capitulate to it. For example, Sweden prohibits the purchase of sexual services with punishments of stiff fines or imprisonment, thus declaring that prostitution isn't a desirable economic and labor sector. The government also helps women getting out of prostitution to rebuild their lives. Venezuela's Ministry of Labor has ruled that prostitution can't be considered work because it lacks the basic elements of dignity and social justice. The Socialist Republic of Vietnam punishes pimps, traffickers, brothel owners, and buyers—sometimes publishing buyer's names in the mass media. For women in prostitution, the government finances medical, educational, and economic rehabilitation.

Raymond suggests that instead of transforming the male buyer into a legitimate customer, the ILO should give thought to innovative programs that make the buyer accountable for his sexual exploitation. She cites the Sage Project, Inc. (SAGE) program in San Francisco, California, which educates men arrested for soliciting women in prostitution about the risks and impacts of their behavior.

Legalization advocates argue that the violence, exploitation, and health effects suffered by women in prostitution aren't inherent to prostitution but simply result from the random behaviors of bad pimps or buyers, and that if prostitution were regulated by the state these harms would diminish. But examples show these arguments to be false.

In the pamphlet entitled *Legalizing Prostitution Is Not the Answer: The Example of Victoria, Australia,* published by the CATW in 2001, Mary Sullivan and Sheila Jeffreys describe the way legalization in Australia has perpetuated and strengthened the culture of violence and exploitation inherent in prostitution. Under legalization, legal and illegal brothels have proliferated, and trafficking in women has accelerated to meet the increased demand. Pimps, having even more power, continue threatening and brutalizing the women they control. Buyers continue to abuse women, refuse to wear condoms, and spread the HIV virus—and other sexually transmitted diseases—to their wives and girlfriends. Stigmatized by identity cards and medical inspections, prostituted women are even more marginalized and tightly locked into the system of organized sexual exploitation while the state, now an official party to the exploitation, has become the biggest pimp of all.

The government of the Netherlands has legalized prostitution, doesn't enforce laws against pimping, and virtually lives off taxes from the earnings of prostituted women. In the book *Making the Harm Visible* (published by the CATW in 1999), Marie-Victoire Louis describes the effects on prostituted women of municipal regulation of brothels in Amsterdam and other Dutch cities. Her article entitled "Legalizing Pimping, Dutch Style" explains the way immigration policies in the Netherlands are shaped to fit the needs of the prostitution industry so that traffickers are seldom prosecuted and a continuous supply of women is guaranteed. In Amsterdam's 250 officially listed brothels, 80 percent of the prostitutes have been trafficked in from other countries and 70 percent possess no legal papers. Without money, papers, or contact with the outside world, these immigrant women live in terror. Instead of being protected by the regulations governing brothels, prostituted women are frequently beaten up and raped by pimps. These "prostitution managers" have practically been given a free hand by the state and by buyers who, as "consumers of prostitution," feel themselves entitled to abuse the women they buy. Sadly and ironically the "Amsterdam model" of legalization and regulation is touted by the Netherlands and Germany as "self-determination and empowerment for women." In reality it simply legitimizes the "right" to buy, sexually use, and profit from the sexual exploitation of someone else's body.

A HUMAN RIGHTS APPROACH

As part of a system of organized sexual exploitation, prostitution can be visualized along a continuum of abuse with brothel slavery at the furthest extreme. All along the continuum, fine lines divide the degrees of harm done to those caught up in the system. At the core lies a great social injustice no cosmetic reforms can right: the setting aside of a segment of people whose bodies can be purchased for sexual use by others. When this basic injustice is legitimized and regulated by the state and when the state profits from it, that injustice is compounded.

In her book *The Prostitution of Sexuality* (New York University Press, 1995), Kathleen Barry details a feminist human rights approach to prostitution that points the way to the future. Ethically it recognizes prostitution, sex trafficking, and the globalized industrialization of sex as massive violations of women's human rights. Sociologically it considers how and to what extent prostitution promotes sex discrimination against individual women, against different racial categories of women, and against women as a group. Politically it calls for decriminalizing prostitutes while penalizing pimps, traffickers, brothel owners, and buyers.

Understanding that human rights and restorative justice go hand in hand, the feminist human rights approach to prostitution addresses the harm and the need to repair the damage. As Barry says:

> Legal proposals to criminalize customers, based on the recognition that prostitution violates and harms women, must … include social-service, health and counseling and job retraining programs. Where states would be closing down brothels if customers were criminalized, the economic resources poured into the former prostitution areas could be turned toward producing gainful employment for women.

With the help of women's projects in many countries—such as Buklod in the Philippines and the Council for Prostitution Alternatives in the United States—some women have begun to confront their condition by leaving prostitution, speaking out against it, revealing their experiences, and helping other women leave the sex industry.

Ending the sexual exploitation of trafficking and prostitution will mean the beginning of a new chapter in building a humanist future—a more peaceful and just future in which men and women can join together in love and respect, recognizing one another's essential dignity and humanity. Humanity's sexuality then will no longer be hijacked and distorted.

R E A D I N G **81**

Letter from Juárez

Mariana Katzarova

Esther Chavez holds the weeping girl in her arms and chants the words, as if to convince herself that they are true: "It's really wonderful, my dear girl. You are alive. You could've been one of them." Esther looks over the girl's shoulder toward the row of pink crosses placed on the edge of a ditch, where eight raped and mutilated bodies of young girls, the same age as Rosaisela, the girl in Esther's arms, were dumped by their killers in 2001.

Rosaisela Lascano is only 16. She was attacked and raped on December 30 by a man who left her for dead in the desert. But she survived. Now she is pregnant with the baby from the rape. There, in the middle of a rubbish dump, once a cotton field, where the last windowless boxes of the maquiladoras meet open desert, Rosaisela whispers her story. Like thousands of others, she came from the poverty of the south to look for a better life in Ciudad Juárez with its 380 maquilas (US- and European-owned plants, using Mexico's cheap labor and paying young women less than $5 a day) built along the US border. Ciudad Juárez, a city of 1.3 million, lies just across the Rio Grande from El Paso, Texas.

The man dragged Rosaisela by her hair, while hitting her all over her body. Then he raped her and left her for dead among the old tires and broken bottles. She crawled home many hours later, fearful for her life, avoiding people and houses. Her parents took her to the police the next day. The police were barely interested. The only one who offered to help Rosaisela was Esther Chavez—a beautiful, ever energetic and always elegant 70-year-old woman who established Casa Amiga about ten years ago as the first and only crisis center in Juárez to provide help to the victims of sexual abuse and domestic violence.

According to the authorities, some 370 young women have been found murdered since 1993, and a further seventy are still missing, although Mexican women's groups say the figure is over 400. Many victims were sexually assaulted, their bodies mutilated, strangled, and dumped in the desert near Juárez. And not a single perpetrator has been brought to justice for these murders.

Three federal police agents wearing dark sunglasses and looking uncomfortable are standing near the eight crosses. They say their bosses ordered them to guard the ditch because they're afraid the same killers may come back and dump another body there.

It is Valentine's Day and a big protest march, organized by Eve Ensler and the V-Day movement and supported by Amnesty International, has brought between 5,000 and 7,000 people from Ciudad Juárez and El Paso to march through the streets of Juárez. They are demanding an end to the murders of women and girls. We all meet on the Lerdo Bridge, which connects the two cities, chanting *"Ni Una Más"* (not one more), *"No Están Solas"* (you are not alone) and screaming *"Justicia"* (justice), while carrying black balloons and makeshift placards. For the past several years Ensler has called Valentine's Day "V-Day" and used her award-winning play *The Vagina Monologues* to organize actions, raise funds, and create awareness of antiviolence causes around the world. Ensler believes that one person with a vision and the conviction to stop violence in her community is enough. "We need to realize that the Earth is one body," she says, "and if we don't start seeing it as one body, we are all going to die. Because we are dependent on each part of this body to live. So when a woman in the south is beaten, I can't walk—my feet are being crushed. And when a woman in the north is raped, I can't think—my brain is being attacked."

So who is killing the poor young women and girls of Juárez? And why, after more than ten years, do the killings continue? Some of the murders are believed to be the work of serial killers or drug gangs, linked to the powerful Juárez drug cartel. Others link the murders to an organ-trafficking network. Still others say that the perpetrators come from among some 700 sex offenders who live in El Paso and often visit Juárez. Another theory is that a number of the mutilated bodies found in the desert bear the signs of snuff films, the type of violent porn films in which someone is really killed at the end. The inability of the local authorities to stop the murders has convinced many of possible police complicity in the crimes.

Oscar Maynez, a former chief of forensics for the Chihuahua state police, told me he quit two years ago when he found police planting evidence in one of the cases. In recent years, under increased public pressure, the authorities have been eager to show that the murders in Juárez have been solved. A series of arrests were made, but the murders continue. All the suspects detained by the police claim they were tortured to confess to the murders. "We all know that the state police work for the traffickers," said Maynez. "None of the people detained for the murders are responsible, in my opinion. The real murderers are people with no limits. I think they are a highly organized group with political connections and some connection to the police."

Juárez looks to me like the war zones I know—like Chechnya, Kosovo, Bosnia. There is the same casualization of violence, the same sense of despair, the same blurred line between right and wrong, the same wild packs of hungry street dogs roaming the city, the same sense of doom.

The maquilas are now moving out of Juárez, looking forward to even cheaper labor in China. In the meantime, under increased international pressure, President Vicente Fox has appointed two women to deal with the investigations and prosecutions in Juárez but has not yet given them funds, resources, or trained staff. Mexican feminist Marcela Lagarde has invented a word for the situation in Juárez: femicide.

Somebody with resources, power, and impunity continues to kill young poor girls in Juárez. "But now they know—the world is watching them," says Ensler, "and we will keep coming back."

R E A D I N G **82**

Betrayed by the Angel
What Happens When Violence Knocks and Politeness Answers?

Debra Anne Davis

Mrs. W. arranged us alphabetically, so I spent my entire third-grade year sitting next to a sadist named Hank C. Every day, several times a day, whenever the teacher wasn't looking, Hank would jab his pencil into my arm. He was shorter than me, and I'd look down on his straight brown hair and he'd glance up at me with a crooked smile and then he'd do it: jab jab jab.

He'd get up from his seat often to sharpen the point; I'd sit in my seat in dread, listening to the churn of the pencil sharpener in the back of the room, knowing the pencil tip would be dulled not by paper but by my skin. I'd go home with little gray circles, some with dots of red in the center, Hank's own bull's-eye, all up and down my left arm. I remember it was my left arm because I can see myself sitting next to him, wearing one of the outfits, not just a dress, but an *outfit*—matching socks, hair ribbon, even underwear—that my mother would put me in each morning. I look at him and hope *maybe not this time, please no more,* and he glances at me (or doesn't—he got so good at it that after a while he could find my arm without looking)

and: jab jab jab. Each time I hope he won't and each time he does.

Mostly I'd just endure. *This is what is happening; there's nothing I can do about it.* One day after school I decided that I couldn't take it anymore. I decided that I would tell the teacher the very next time he did it. Of course I'd have to wait for him to do it again first. I felt relief.

When I went to school the next day, we had a substitute teacher instead of Mrs. W. I lost some of my resolve, but not all of it. Hank seemed in better spirits than usual. He started in soon after the bell rang while we were doing workbooks. Jab jab jab. I stood and walked to the front of the room, my lime green dress brushing against the gray metal of the teacher's desk. "Hank always pokes me with the pencil," I told the stranger. My voice was much smaller than I'd hoped. I'd said it like a whisper; I'd meant to sound mad.

"You go back to your seat and tell me if he does it again," she said. And that was it. I never could work up the nerve again to walk the 15 feet to the big desk and blurt out the nature of the boy's crime: Always, he pokes me. I continued going home each day with pencil wounds.

The problem, I think, was that I simply wasn't mad at him. When I went to tell the teacher, my voice wasn't loud in a burst of righteous anger; it was demure. I didn't want to bother her. Maybe I didn't want to see Hank punished. Maybe I didn't think I deserved not to be hurt. Maybe it just didn't seem that big an aberration. Even though no one else was being poked at every day, maybe this was just my lot in life.

I'm 25 years old. I'm alone in my apartment. I hear a knock. I open the door and see a face I don't know. The man scares me, I don't know why. My first impulse is to shut the door. But I stop myself: You can't do something like that. It's rude.

I don't invite him in, but suddenly he is pushing the door and stepping inside. I don't want him to come in; he hasn't waited to be invited. I push the door to close it, but I don't push very hard; I keep remembering that it's not polite to slam a door in someone's face.

He is inside. He slams the door shut himself and pushes me against the wall. My judgment: He is *very* rude. I make this conscious decision: Since he is being rude, it is okay for me to be rude back. I reach for the doorknob; I want to open the door and shove him outside and then slam the door in his face, rude or not, I don't care now. But frankly, I don't push him aside with much determination. I've made the mental choice to be rude, but I haven't been able to muster the physical bluntness the act requires.

Or maybe I realize the game is lost already. He is stronger than I am, I assume, as men have always been stronger. I have no real chance of pushing him aside. No real chance of it unless I am *very* angry. And I'm not very angry. I'm a little bit angry.

But, despite the fact that I didn't shove with much force, *he* is angry with *me*. I know why: It's because I've been rude to him. He is insulted. I am a bit ashamed.

We fall into our roles quite easily, two people who have never met each other, two people raised in the same culture, a man and a woman. As it turns out, a rapist and his victim.

I asked my students, college freshmen, these two questions once: What did your parents teach you that you will teach your own kids? What did they teach you that you won't teach your kids?

One young woman said, "My parents always told me to be kind to everyone. I won't teach my children that. It's not always good to be kind to everyone."

She was so young, but she knew this. Why did it take me so long to learn?

Working on this stuff makes me a little crazy. Sitting at my computer typing for hours about being raped and how it made me feel and makes me feel makes me distracted, jittery—both because I drink too much strong coffee and because writing goes beyond imagining into reliving.

I decided I needed to reread Virginia Woolf. I'd been making notes to myself for a while—"angel" or just "Woolf" scribbled on scraps of paper on my desk and in the front pocket of my backpack, to go buy the book, the book with the angel in it. (I could feel her hovering as I typed; I know the exact color and texture of her flowing gown.)

What could be easier than to write articles and to buy Persian cats with the profits? But wait a moment. Articles have to be about something. Mine, I seem to remember, was about a novel by a famous man. And while I was writing this review, I discovered that if I were going to review books I should need to do battle with a certain phantom. And the phantom was a woman, and when I came to know her better I called her after the heroine of a famous poem. "The Angel in the House." It was she who used to come between me and my paper when I was writing reviews. It was she who bothered me and wasted my time and so tormented me that at last I killed her.

—*"Professions for Women"*
Virginia Woolf (1931)

There was TV. Reruns of reruns of *I Love Lucy* and *The Flintstones. I Dream of Jeannie. Bewitched.* I can't even think of a show from my youth that had a single female character who was smart, self-confident, and respected by others. My sister and

I would lie on our stomachs, heads propped on fuzzy cotton pillows with leopard-skin covers, watching, indiscriminate, mildly entertained, for hours.

Samantha was smarter than Darrin, it was obvious, but she hid her intelligence just as she hid her magical powers, powers Darrin didn't have, powers that made him angry. Samantha's mother, Endora, used her powers with confidence and even flair, but she cackled and wore flowing bright green dresses and too much makeup; she was a mother-in-law. I was supposed to learn how to be like Samantha, not like Endora, and I did.

None of this is news, of course; we can all see those sexist stereotypes quite easily now. But just because I can see, understand, and believe that something is false, that it's not right, now, doesn't mean it won't continue to be a part of me, always.

(Barbara Eden calling Larry Hagman "Master." How many times did I hear *that*?)

"It's big," I say. I turn my head up. I smile. Why do I say this? I ask myself, even then. Well it is big. . . . And I want to flatter him, so he won't hurt me any more than he already plans to. I, yes, I am trying to flirt with him. I've learned about flirting and how it works and what it can do. (It can get people to like you, to do things for you, to treat you well.) It's a skill I have honed. And I'm using it now. To save my life. (And, hey, it worked! Unless of course he hadn't planned to kill me in the first place.)

He smiles down at me (I'm on my knees, naked, leaning against my own bed, my hands tied behind me, my head in his crotch) proudly.

You who come of a younger and happier generation may not have heard of her—you may not know what I mean by the Angel in the House. I will describe her as shortly as I can. She was intensely sympathetic. She was immensely charming. She was utterly unselfish. She excelled in the difficult arts of family life. She sacrificed herself daily. If there was chicken, she took the leg; if there was a draught she sat in it—in short she was so constituted that she never had a mind or a wish of her own, but preferred to sympathize always with the minds and wishes of others.

Back when he was pulling my jeans off, this is what happened: He kneeled behind me, reached around the waistband to the fly, and pulled until all the buttons popped open. Then he crawled back a few feet and began to pull the jeans off from the ankles—a stupid way to try to take someone else's pants off, but I didn't say anything.

He was having a little trouble because the pants weren't slipping off as, obviously, he'd envisioned they would. He tugged and then began yanking. "Stop fighting!" he growled at me. Ooh, *that* pissed me off! "I'm *not fighting!*" I sassed back at him. And I wasn't. How dare he! Accuse me, I mean. Of fighting.

Above all—I need not say it—she was pure. Her purity was supposed to be her chief beauty—her blushes, her great grace. In those days—the last of Queen Victoria—every house had its Angel. And when I came to write I encountered her with the very first words. The shadow of her wings fell on my page; I heard the rustling of her skirts in the room. Directly, that is to say, I took my pen in hand to review that novel by a famous man, she slipped behind me and whispered: "My dear, you are a young woman. You are writing about a book that has been written by a man. Be sympathetic; be tender; flatter; deceive; use all the arts and wiles of our sex. Never let anybody guess that you have a mind of your own. Above all, be pure."

One thing being raped did to me: It caused me to be sometimes rude to strangers. Not out of anger, though, but out of fear.

I was 25 when I was raped. I'm 35 now. This happened last week.

I was in a coffee shop, reading a textbook for a class I'm teaching. After a while, I took a little break and brought my now-empty cup back to the counter. There was a guy at the counter waiting for his drink. "What are you reading?" he asked. He had a big smile on his face, a friendly smile. He wasn't creepy; he was being friendly. I sensed these things. "It's a textbook," I answered. I was looking at the floor now, not at his face any longer.

"Oh! What class are you studying for?" he asked.

"It's a class I'm teaching," I said. Oh no.

"Where do you teach? At _____ College?"

"No," I said flatly and tried to smile a little. I felt nervous, pinned. I knew the conversation wasn't over, but I simply turned and went back to my little table. He stood there at the counter, probably watching me walk away and wondering why I wouldn't answer his question, why, against the unspoken code of our culture, I hadn't at least finished the exchange with a friendly word or a wave. But there was no way I would tell him (or *you*, notice) where I taught or what I taught or anything else about me. And there was no way I could explain this to him courteously; the whole exchange made me too nervous. I certainly wasn't angry at him, but I was a bit afraid. And right there in the coffee shop, I felt the presence of my angel, the rustling of her skirts: "Be sympathetic," I heard her reprimand me, sweetly. "Be tender. And pure." I couldn't be polite, but I did feel guilty.

Though I wasn't finished with my reading, when I got back to the table, I gathered up my things and left.

I turned upon her and caught her by the throat. I did my best to kill her. My excuse, if I were to be had up in a court of law, would be that I acted in self-defense. Had I not killed her she would have killed me.

He bent down to gently arrange the towel over my bare and oozing body, after it was all over with. "You were so good-looking, I just couldn't resist," he told me.

And for the first time in my life, I didn't enjoy being complimented on my physical appearance. Why, I wondered at that moment, had I ever wanted to be considered pretty—or kind, or good? Compliments mean nothing. Or worse, compliments mean this. What good does such a compliment do *me*?

Thus, whenever I felt the shadow of her wing or the radiance of her halo upon my page, I took up the inkpot and flung it at her. She died hard. Her fictitious nature was of great assistance to her. It is far harder to kill a phantom than a reality.

I haven't killed her. Yet. Maybe I need to go out and get an inkpot to fling at her. Hmm, I wonder how she'd hold up against a flying laptop. I can imagine hurling this 10-pound black plastic box at her (she's up in the corner, to my right). It easily tears through the soft blue, rough cotton of her ankle-length gown (she has a long, thin white lace apron tied around her waist). The computer crashes into the space where the walls and ceiling meet; she falls to the carpet. And then what? She's dead. And how do I feel about that? Guilty? Relieved? Well, I don't think I'd want to stuff my pockets with rocks and wade into a river. (Did Woolf ever really kill her angel? Or is it the angel that killed her?)

What I want to know is this: If I'm every physically attacked again, will I fight to save myself? And will I be fighting out of righteous anger or out of unstrung fear?

What I need to know is this: Is the angel really the one who needs to die?

"I guess I'll get twenty years in the penitentiary for this," he says and waves his hand across the room at me.

Twenty years? Just for this? Just for doing this to me? Twenty years is a really long time.

In fact, he got 35 years. On a plea bargain. The police, the lawyers, the judge—the state, the legal system—even he, the criminal, the rapist, thought he deserved decades in jail for what he'd done to me. Why didn't I?

What College Women Do and Do Not Experience as Rape

Arnold S. Kahn

Since 1989, together with my colleagues and students, I have conducted research on rape and sexual assault. One particular stream of this research has focused on what determines whether or not a woman labels her sexual assault experience as rape. In this paper I briefly summarize what we know about labeling one's experience as rape and then focus on a very recent study that provides some new data regarding this process.

Researchers who study rape typically use a form of the Sexual Experience Survey (SES) (Koss & Gidycz, 1985) in which women respond *yes* or *no* to a series of questions concerning sexual behaviors. If a woman answers yes to one or more critical questions about her sexual experiences she has likely experienced rape. Research shows that a large percentage of women who answer yes to one or more of the critical SES questions, suggesting they had been raped, respond no when asked the direct question, "Have you ever been raped by a man?" That is, these women had an experience that appears to have been one of rape, but they did not label their experience as one of rape. Koss (1985) referred to these women as "hidden rape victims," women who experienced acts that seemed to fit the legal definition of rape, but who did not conceive of themselves as victims or survivors of rape. In our past research we have referred to these women as "unacknowledged rape victims" (Kahn, Mathie, & Torgler, 1994; Kahn & Mathie, 2000). This terminology, however, has problems. It assumes that these women did in fact experience rape, something we do not know for sure, and it favors the scientist's definition of rape over the definition of the research participant herself. Thus, I will refer to these women as "women who do not call their experience rape," rather than "hidden victims" or "unacknowledged victims."

Past research has shown that a large percentage of women, ranging from 48% (Kahn et al., 1994) to 73% (Koss, Dinero, Seibel, & Cox, 1988), who respond yes to one or more of the SES items, suggesting they had an experience that might legally be rape, respond no to the question "Have you ever been raped by a man?" In most studies the percentage is over 50% of the sample of possible rape victims.

Why Women Do Not Label Their Sexual Assault as Rape

What leads a woman to call or not call her experience rape? A number of researchers have searched for differences in women's personalities or attitudes, or in women's experiences, that would differentiate those who called their experience rape from those who did not. This research has uncovered a number of predictors that appear to distinguish between these two groups. Compared with women who called their experience rape, women who did not label their experience as rape were more likely to have been assaulted by someone they knew well, often a romantic partner (Kahn, Jackson, Kully, Badger, & Halvorsen, 2003; Koss, 1985). These women were also more likely to have a rape script of a very violent stranger rape rather than one of an acquaintance rape (Bondurant, 2001; Kahn et al., 1994). They also experienced less assailant force than women who called their experience rape (Bondurant, 2001; Emmers-Sommer & Allen, 1999; Kahn et al., 1994; Kahn et al., 2003; Layman, Gidycz, & Lynn, 1996; Schwartz & Leggett, 1999).

Finally, although women who did not label their experience as rape had negative emotional reactions during and after the incident, these negative emotional reactions were not as strong as those of women who called their experience rape (Kahn et al., 1994; Kahn & Mathie, 2000; Kahn et al., 2003). Inconsistent results have been found for alcohol use and victim self-blame (Bondurant, 2001; Frazier & Seales, 1997; Kahn & Mathie, 2000; Kahn et al., 2003; Layman et al., 1996; Pitts & Schwartz, 1993; Schwartz & Leggett, 1999). Interestingly, no personality, attitude, or demographic difference has differentiated women who do and do not label their assault experience as rape (Bondurant, 2001; Kahn et al., 1994; Koss, 1985; Levine-MacCombie & Koss, 1986). In short, women who do not call their experience rape tend to see rape as a violent act committed by a stranger, but were themselves assaulted by someone they knew well, often a romantic partner, who did not use a great deal of force. These women experienced strong, negative emotional reactions to their assault, but their reactions were not as strong as women who called their experience rape.

What Actually Happened?

Past research trying to differentiate women who did and did not label their sexual assault experiences as rape has not directly examined what actually happened when the assault occurred. That is, did women who called their assault rape encounter a different set of events than those who did not call their assault rape? In a recent study (Kahn et al., 2003) my students and I did just that: we asked women to tell us what happened to them before, during, and after their assault experience. The details of the method and quantitative findings have been published elsewhere (Kahn et al., 2003). Here I will first summarize the quantitative findings from this study and then focus on some of the qualitative findings (Study One). Then I will include some new data that have not yet been published (Study Two). Because in this research we were interested in what women would and would not label as rape, we created a version of the SES that included a variety of assault behaviors

(see Kahn et al., 2003, for a complete description), some of which would not meet a strict legal definition of rape in some locations.

STUDY ONE

Method

We distributed questionnaires to 504 female college students, 90% of whom were Caucasian and 51% of whom were first-year students. We told participants, in groups of 4–25 that we were studying how people perceive stressful events. The women first completed a questionnaire in which they indicated yes, uncertain or maybe, or no to 16 questions regarding criminal or aggressive acts or attitudes, including the crucial question, "Have you ever been raped by a man?" Next they completed a version of the SES. If a participant answered yes to at least one of seven critical questions, they were considered a possible rape victim. We then asked these women to turn to the next page where they found the following instructions:

> Please take a few moments to describe in detail the circumstances of this experiences. If there was more than one experience, respond about the one you remember best. How did this experience come about? What occurred during the experience? What did he do? What did you do? Remember that this survey is anonymous, and there is no way to match your survey or this description with you. Therefore, be as candid as you feel comfortable. Please write your response on the two sheets of blank paper provided and then continue on the next printed page.[1]

We considered a woman to have labeled her experience as rape if she answered yes to the question about having been raped and yes to one or more of the critical SES questions. We considered a woman not to have labeled her experience as rape if she answered no to the question about having been raped and yes to one or more of the critical SES questions. We considered a woman uncertain as to whether she had been raped if she answered yes to one of the critical SES questions and maybe/uncertain to the question about having been raped.

Of the 504 participants, 13 chose not to complete the survey. Of the 491 remaining women, 33 (6.5%) called an experience they had rape, 56 (11.4%) did not label an experience they had as rape, 8 (1.6%) were uncertain whether an experience they had was rape or not, and 394 (80.2%) indicated they had not been the victim of a sexual assault. . . .

. . .

Results

The quantitative results, reported in Kahn et al. (2003) revealed that women who labeled their situation as rape were (a) more likely to have been assaulted by a nonromantic partner, (b) more likely to have experienced extremely high negative affect after the experience, (c) less likely to be assaulted by an assailant who was intoxicated, and (d) more likely to have experienced forceful male aggression in other sexual encounters with men. Here I wish to further explore the qualitative findings from the participants' descriptions of their assault experiences. The following constitute the eight different assault situations.

Submit to boyfriend involved, after repeated no's, giving in to a boyfriend's continued begging, whining, or arguing for sex. The woman did not want to have sex, but wanted to please him, keep peace, or feared he might become violent.

> My boyfriend of a year and I were home alone together. In prior weeks he had been very agitated at my lack of interest in intimacy and my lack of patience with his temper. His recent outbursts had caused me to distrust him. His manner towards me was angry, but he didn't actually threaten me at this time. In an attempt to appease his anger and prevent another outburst of anger, I consented to his repeated advances and requests for sex. It was so degrading.

Childhood included sexual acts performed by older cousins, a babysitter, or a close family member when the woman was in middle school or younger.

Forced sex acts occurred when a man, regardless of her relationship with him, used force to obtain or perform oral or digital sex.

> I was drunk. He forced me into the bathroom with him. He was drunk, too. He pushed me down so that I was on my knees and undid his pants, basically forcing his penis in my mouth and moving my head. I said stop a lot of times.

Emotionally needy involved situations in which the woman was emotionally unstable and needy, often following the breakup of a relationship. She did not want to have intercourse and told the man so, but eventually gave in to the man because he seemed to care for her.

> I genuinely didn't want to have sex, told him so. However, I was going through a rough time, just broken up with a serious boyfriend and felt insecure, hurt, lonely, etc., etc. This guy made me feel better about myself, told me I had no reason to be lonely, he wanted me, he wanted to help with the pain, etc. I ended up having sex with him because I believed he cared about me even though I didn't think it was right because I wanted the pain of the former breakup to quit.

Dominating boyfriend involved an older, larger boyfriend who used threats or force to obtain sexual intercourse. The woman tried to resist but could not.

> At my senior beach week I had been dating my boyfriend for about a month. . . . We got into bed, unclothed, and started "messing around." After a few minutes I wanted to stop, but obviously he didn't. He held my arms down and I was on my stomach and he tried to perform anal intercourse, but I squirmed and screamed at him until he stopped. . . . P.S. It hurt like hell and I left him the next day.

Forceful acquaintance involved an acquaintance who would not yield to a woman's pleas to stop and used force, threats, or coercion to obtain sexual intercourse. The following occurred during her senior year in high school when the woman turned down a schoolmate's request for a date:

> He got angry and told me that I was a tease and he slapped me across the face. So I pulled open the door to my car and tried to get away, but he grabbed my arm and forced me into the back seat. All I remember after that was crying and trying to push him off me. When he had finished he left me in the back seat of my car bleeding and barely conscious.

Asleep or tricked involved either a woman awaking to find a man performing sexual acts on her, or the man had promised no penile penetration yet did so anyway, but the woman was not immediately aware of it, unfamiliar with the "feel" of penetration.

> He promised me that he would sleep on the couch and I could have his bed. I woke up later that night with him on top of me. I told him to stop but he wouldn't. He continued and managed to take my clothes off. After raping me he rolled over and went to sleep.

Severe impairment occurred when the woman was severely impaired by alcohol or drugs and had neither the presence of mind nor the ability to resist the man, who had intercourse with her.

> We were drunk. I didn't have control over myself and I didn't have the cognitive ability to say NO. I can't remember everything, but I know we had sex and if I were sober it would not have happened. I just could not control myself at all.

Table 1 displays the number of women who called their experience rape and those who did not for each assault situation. Three situations, asleep or tricked, forceful acquaintance, and childhood, accounted for over three-fourths (76.67%) of the descriptions provided by women who called their situation rape. Only four women who did not call their experience rape wrote descriptions that fell into one of these categories. Five situations, severe impairment, submit, forced sex acts, dominating boyfriend, and emotionally needy, accounted for

TABLE 1 Frequencies of Each Assault Situation as a Function of Whether the Woman Labeled Her Experience as Rape or Not Rape

Situation	Labeled Rape	Not Labeled Rape
Submit	3	13
Childhood	3	0
Forced Sex Acts	0	7
Emotionally Needy	1	2
Dominating Boyfriend	0	4
Forceful Acquaintance	8	0
Asleep or Tricked	12	4
Severe Impairment	3	14
Other	0	5
Total	30	49

85.1% of the descriptions provided by women who did not call their experience rape. Only seven women who called their experience rape wrote descriptions that fit into one of these five categories.

Discussion

The main finding from these qualitative results suggest that those women who labeled their experience as rape, for the most part, encountered very different assault situations from those who did not call their experience rape. Women were more likely to label their situation as rape when the assailant was someone other than their boyfriend, who either used force to obtain intercourse or started to perform sexual acts while they were asleep, waking them up. Women also labeled as rape sexual acts which had occurred in childhood. Women were more likely to label their experience as something other than rape when the experience occurred with a boyfriend, whether submitting to his repeated pleas or giving in to his threats and force, when the woman was too impaired by alcohol or drugs to effectively resist the man, when the sexual act was something other than penile/vaginal intercourse, and when the woman gave in to intercourse because she was emotionally needy.

. . .

STUDY TWO

In her interviews with women who had experienced rape, Phillips (2000) discussed situations in which a woman did not view her experience as rape, but when asked how she would describe the identical experience if it had happened to a friend, she gave a very different interpretation.

> If my roommate came home and told me the exact same story had happened to her, I'd tell her, "You call the hotline, you call the police! You're a victim! That guy raped you and you should report it!" Wow! But I don't know. For her it would be rape. For me it was just so complicated. (p. 154)

We were interested in whether naïve observers, like some of Phillips' participants, would be more likely than the women who wrote about their experience to label the situation as one of rape. Phillips found that her participants denied their victimization, in part, to preserve their view of themselves as mature adults who can handle situations, and in part because their experiences were complicated and did not match the "true victim" discourse that rape occurs when a stranger brutally attacks a woman who does everything possible to escape.

Method

I gave the written descriptions of the sexual assaults to four additional female undergraduate students previously unfamiliar with this research. I instructed each rater, working individually, to "Please label each situation as either 'rape,' 'not rape,' or 'not enough information provided.' Avoid using the 'not enough information provided' category; if you lean however slightly to either 'rape' or 'not rape' use one of them instead." I provided no definition of rape to the categorizers.

I then looked at the categorizations of these four naïve raters. If three or four of them categorized the description as rape, I labeled the situation one of rape. Likewise, if three or four of the raters categorized the situation as not rape, I labeled the situation as not rape. Those descriptions for which there was no agreement or for which the raters agreed that there was not sufficient information, I categorized as unclear.

Results

The raters classified 28 descriptions as rape, 32 descriptions as not rape, and were unclear or could not agree about 19 descriptions. When I compared whether or not a woman called her own experience rape with how observers labeled the same situation, I found a very strong relationship, $\chi^2 (2) = 36.87$, $p < .001$, which is shown in Table 2. Those situations that participants labeled as rape were also highly likely to be labeled as rape by naïve raters. Likewise, situations that participants labeled as something other than rape were also highly likely to be called not rape by naïve raters. If we remove the 24% of the situations where the observers who classified the descriptions were uncertain or could not agree and look at percentages, the situation becomes even clearer. Nearly all, 95.6%, of the descriptions for which the victim labeled her situation as rape, the observers also called it rape. Likewise, in 83.4% of the descriptions in which the victim did not call her experience rape, the observers agreed that the situation was not rape.

TABLE 2 Relationship Between Participants' Label of Their Assault Situation and Observers' Label of the Same Situation

	Raters' Label of Situation		
Victims' Label of Situation	Rape	Not Rape	Not Clear
Rape	22	1	6
Not Rape	6	31	13
Total	28	32	19

These results support the hypothesis that observers would be more likely to label a situation as rape than would participants. Only once did a victim label her experience as rape (3.4%) when the raters agreed rape did not occur; however, six of the descriptions that the victims themselves labeled as not rape were clearly labeled rape by the observers (12%). That is, the raters were more likely to label a description as rape than were the victims themselves.

. . .

Discussion

For years we have been trying to understand what determines whether a woman will label her assault situation as rape or as something other than rape. From our latest research I think it is safe to say that a major contributor to a woman's decision to label a situation as rape is the nature of the situation itself. Both the victims and those who read the victims' descriptions of their experience agreed that some situations constituted rape and other situations did not.

Women, both victims and those who read victim descriptions, were most likely to label a situation as rape if sexual intercourse occurred in childhood, was forced by an acquaintance, or occurred while the woman was asleep. Three factors seem to be involved here. First, the woman had sexual intercourse when she had no control—she either was a child, asleep, or forced. Second, the assailant was someone other than her boyfriend. Third, from our quantitative data (Kahn et al., 2003) the woman experienced a very high level of trauma as a result.

Three situations—submitting to the begging, whining, or arguing by a boyfriend; having intercourse because she was emotionally needy; and being too impaired to resist intercourse with an acquaintance—all lead the majority of both victims and those who read victim accounts to believe rape had not occurred.

Although submitting to a whiny boyfriend or being emotionally needy in most cases probably does not constitute rape under most state laws, the inability to stop a man because of impairment

by alcohol or drugs is considered rape in most jurisdictions. The written descriptions provided by these women can help us understand why they, and those who read their descriptions, did not label their experience as rape. The intoxicated women did not seem to believe they were personally at risk, and they attributed their undesired intercourse not to the man's pressure or force but to their own lack of ability to think clearly or resist—the alcohol rather than the assailant took away their options to act otherwise. These women seem to have presumed that a man will have sex with a woman unless the woman forcefully resists, and her inability to resist seemed to mean, to her and to observers as well, that what happened was not rape. Below are some additional extracts of descriptions provided by women who said they were too intoxicated to resist but did not call their experiences rape:

> I was having a bad day and I wanted to get trashed. . . . So I went to my friend's apartment. . . . So I got really drunk and he basically totally took advantage of my weakness. Before I could get the strength to protest, he had quickly um, penetrated me. I know that if I hadn't been so drunk I would have had the strength and I definitely would NOT have wanted to do that with him, and I would have strongly told him no and he knew that too, which is why he waited till I was hammered to do it. So I guess it doesn't really count as rape, since I was the one who wanted to get drunk.

> A man who I trusted very much made me and some friends a few drinks. We played drinking games and we were all pretty drunk. After everyone was asleep, this man and I were up talking and practically begged me to let him give me oral sex. I was drunk, told him I didn't want to, but he kept at it and finally I was just like, fine. The oral sex turned into intercourse. I hadn't wanted to do anything with him at all. I was too drunk to really consider the consequences though.

In reading these descriptions, as well as the descriptions by women who submitted to their boyfriends and those who were emotionally needy, it appears these women felt they could not call what happened to them rape because they didn't resist, even if they couldn't resist because of impairment. It also appears that these women did not experience the trauma found in the descriptions by women who labeled their experience as rape (see Kahn et al., 2003). As Gavey (1999) has suggested, although rape is frequently traumatic, "not all women are traumatized by rape" (p. 70). It may be that the women who were too intoxicated to resist labeled their experience as something other than rape because they were not as traumatized as women who tried to resist and they were adapting the best they could to an unpleasant experience, attempting to "get over it," gain control for similar situations in the future, and escape the label of "victim" (see Phillips, 2000).

Finally, in two situations the victims did not label their experience as rape, but observers could not agree whether or not rape had taken place: forced sexual acts that did not involve penile/vaginal intercourse—digital or oral intercourse—and forced sexual intercourse committed by a boyfriend. Both of these situations would likely be considered rape under most state laws. With regard to digital and oral sex, research by Sanders and Reinisch (1999) suggested that only about one-third of college women consider oral sex as "having sex" and only about 10% consider manual stimulation of genitals as "having sex." To the extent women believe that the act of rape must involve penile/vaginal intercourse, one can understand how the victims of forced oral or digital sex might call their experience something other than rape. Yet it is curious that those who read the descriptions were less clear on the matter. In two descriptions the raters agreed that rape had occurred, for one description they were sure rape had not occurred, and on four descriptions they did not agree among themselves or not enough information was provided to decide whether or not rape had occurred. Clearly this is an area in need of further research and education.

Being forced to have sexual intercourse by one's boyfriend also seems to be an ambiguous situation for those who read the descriptions but not for those who wrote them. In all four cases the victims themselves did not call their experience rape, but those who read the descriptions were unable to agree with one another on any of the four scenarios. The rape by a boyfriend appears an unanticipated situation, one for which women have no script. In our earlier research on rape scripts (Kahn et al., 1994), none of our 174 participants, when asked to write their script for a typical rape, wrote a script involving a boyfriend. Women love and trust their boyfriends, and rape by a boyfriend appears incomprehensible and difficult to categorize as rape.

CONCLUSION

My major goal in conducting this research was to determine what types of assaultive sexual experiences college women consider to be rape and what types of assaultive sexual experiences they consider to be something other than rape. To do this we included several SES items that were likely sexual assault but not rape. We found three situations that were almost always labeled as rape and five situations that were nearly always not labeled as rape. I think this research should be viewed as a first step in this regard. We were able to obtain only a limited number of retrospective descriptions of sexual assaults from predominantly White, middle-class college students. Older, less privileged women from different ethnic backgrounds may label their experiences differently. Furthermore, we developed a crude and imperfect classification system on the basis of written descriptions of sexual assaults, some of which were quite brief. In addition, an occasional written description could have fit into more than one assault situation (e.g., a woman forced by her boyfriend to perform oral sex on him while she was severely impaired by alcohol). Conducting in-depth interviews with samples of women about their assault experiences and the conditions under which they occurred appears to be necessary to further our understanding of what leads a woman to call their sexual assault rape.

I will end this article with the same words I used previously (Kahn et al., 2003). Is it important for a woman to label her experience as rape if it occurs? At the individual level it would appear that each woman is attempting, as best she can, to cope with what had happened to her. Under some conditions, such as awaking to a man performing sexual acts on her or being forced into intercourse by an acquaintance, most women appear to cope best by calling their situation one of rape. Under other conditions, such as being unable to resist because of severe intoxication or because a boyfriend forced them to have sex, most women appear to cope best by labeling what happened to them as something other than rape. Furthermore, their peers, for the most part, agree with this classification system. Should efforts be made to teach women to label their experience as rape if they have had an experience that would legally qualify as rape? Women as a group, and likely women in the future, would certainly be better off if all women who experienced legal rape labeled it as such. Such widespread acknowledgment of rape would highlight the tremendous problem of rape in our society, hold perpetrators responsible for their behavior, and likely lead to greater enforcement of rape statues, greater prosecution of rapists, and ultimately reduce the frequency of rape. But at what cost to individual women who can better cope with what happened to them by not calling their experience rape? Are these women better off by having someone else define their experience for them? This is not a dilemma easily resolved. Perhaps the best perspective has been provided by Gavey (1999), who said of women who do not label their experience as rape:

> Feminist accounts of rape need to be able to take account of such women's experiences without, in effect, dismissing them as the result of false consciousness. Carefully listening to and theorizing such ambivalent and confusing experiences may illuminate the complex relationship between heterosexuality and rape. Moreover, it may produce feminist analyses of rape that are sympathetic to all women who are raped, no matter how they experience it. (pp. 66–70)

NOTE

1. It was possible that participants may have had a rape experience, but chose to describe a less distressing, nonrape situation. We had no way of determining if this occurred.

REFERENCES

Bondurant, B. (2001). University women's acknowledgement of rape: Individual, situational, and social factors. *Violence Against Women, 7*, 294–314.

Emmers-Sommer, T. M., & Allen, M. (1999). Variables related to sexual coercion: A path model. *Journal of Social and Personal Relationships, 16*, 659–678.

Frazier, P. A., & Seales, L. M. (1997). Acquaintance rape is real rape. In M. D. Schwartz (Ed.), *Researching sexual violence against women: Methodological and personal perspectives* (pp. 54–64). Thousand Oaks, CA: Sage.

Gavey, N. (1999). "I wasn't raped, but . . .": Revisiting definitional problems in sexual victimization. In S. Lamb (Ed.), *New versions of victims: Feminists struggle with the concept* (pp. 57–81). New York: New York University Press.

Kahn, A. S., Jackson, J., Kully, C., Badger, K., & Halvorsen, J. (2003). Calling it rape: Differences in experiences of women who do or do not label their sexual assault as rape. *Psychology of Women Quarterly, 27*, 233–242.

Kahn, A. S., & Mathie, V. A. (2000). Understanding the unacknowledged rape victim. In C. B. Travis and J. W. White (Eds.) *Sexuality, society, and feminism: Psychological perspectives on women* (pp. 377–403). Washington, D.C.: American Psychological Association.

Kahn, A. S., Mathie, V. A., & Torgler, C. (1994). Rape scripts and rape acknowledgment. *Psychology of Women Quarterly, 18*, 53–66.

Koss, M. P. (1985). The hidden rape victim: Personality, attitudinal, and situational characteristics. *Psychology of Women Quarterly, 9*, 193–212.

Koss, M. P., Dinero, T. E., Seibel, C., & Cox, S. (1988). Stranger, acquaintance, and date rape: Is there a difference in the victim's experience? *Psychology of Women Quarterly, 12*, 1–24.

Koss, M. P., & Gidycz, C. A. (1985). Sexual Experiences Survey: Reliability and validity. *Journal of Consulting and Clinical Psychology, 53*, 422–423.

Layman, M. J., Gidycz, C. A., & Lynn, S. J. (1996). Unacknowledged versus acknowledged rape victims: Situational factors and posttraumatic stress. *Journal of Abnormal Psychology, 105,* 124–131.

Levine-MacCombie, J., & Koss, M. P. (1986). Acquaintance rape: Effective avoidance strategies. *Psychology of Women Quarterly, 10,* 311–320.

Phillips, L. M. (2000). *Flirting with danger: Young women's reflections on sexuality and domination.* New York: New York University Press.

Pitts, V. L., & Schwartz, M. D. (1993). Promoting self-blame in hidden rape cases. *Humanity & Society, 17,* 383–398.

Sanders, S. A., & Reinisch, J. M. (1999). Would you say you "had sex" if . . . ? *Journal of the American Medical Association, 281,* 275–277.

Schwartz, M. D., & Leggett, M. S. (1999). Bad dates or emotional trauma? The aftermath of campus sexual assault. *Violence Against Women 5,* 251–271.

READING 84

When Terror Strikes at Home
The Interface Between Religion and Domestic Violence

Nancy Nason-Clark

In this short essay, I raise two particular questions concerning the interface between religion and domestic violence: the first focuses on religious victims, the second on religious perpetrators. For almost 15 years, I have been intrigued by the story of what happens when religious people look to their faith communities for help in the aftermath of violence in the family context. For many religious victims, their faith sustains them through long periods of domestic crisis: it empowers them to ultimately flee their abuser and to seek refuge and safety where they begin a new life free of abuse (Nason-Clark and Kroeger 2004). There are others who are not so fortunate: they are consumed by the "sacred silence" on the issue, never finding spiritual or practical support that would enable them to leave the fear or the reality of violence behind (Nason-Clark 1997). As a result, there are many layers we need to unravel as we seek to understand the complex relationship between faith, violence, and family ties. I begin with a brief look at the prevalence of violence against women in families of faith and conclude my essay with several theoretical questions requiring further analysis.

VIOLENCE AGAINST WOMEN IN FAMILIES OF FAITH

Domestic violence knows no boundaries of class, color, or religious persuasion (Stirling et al. 2004; Timmins 1995). Despite the fact that religious rhetoric is replete with references to happy families (Edgell 2003), many religious women are victimized by husbands who promised before God to love and cherish them for life (Nason-Clark 1997). Although religious families may be considered sacred, they are sometimes unsafe. In 1989, the Christian Reformed Church in North America conducted a survey among a small random sample of adult church members: 28 percent had experienced at least one form of abuse (Annis and Rice 2001), a figure close to those of national U.S. samples not specifically targeting churchgoing families. Whether particular religious theologies exacerbate violence in the family is something on which there has been some speculation but very little data. Bartkowski and Anderson (1996), using U.S. data from the National Survey of Families and Households, argue that they found no clear evidence that men or women affiliated with conservative churches were especially prone toward violence. Similarly, Brinkerhoff, Grandin, and Lupri (1992) reported that conservative Christian men in Canada were not significantly more violent than those of other persuasions. Although many religious groups have been slow to acknowledge the prevalence of violence in their midst (Horton and Williamson 1988), psychologist Andrew Weaver (1993) claims that "domestic violence is probably the number one pastoral mental health emergency."

There are specific religious contours both to the abuse that is suffered and to the healing journey. As a result, many in the secular therapeutic community do not like to work with clients who are particularly religious (Whipple 1987). Without spiritual credentials, these workers find it difficult to challenge the religious ideation that is believed by the victim or perpetrator to give license to abuse. Sometimes, secular shelter workers and others believe that it is in fact the religious ideology that gives rise to the violence and undergirds victims' reluctance to seek refuge or assistance in its aftermath. Consequently, they encourage the victim to leave behind both the abuse and their community of faith. In a similar vein, there are religious professionals who are slow to refer their parishioners who have been abused to outside sources of help, believing that a secular shelter is an unsafe place to claim faith. There can be suspicion on both sides and sometimes the voices of the caregivers drown out the voices of the victims (Timmins 1995). For collaborative ventures between the steeple and the shelter to be successful, personnel operating from a secular or sacred paradigm must be willing to see that the condemnation of domestic violence requires both the language of contemporary culture and the language of the spirit (Nason-Clark 2001). A cultural language that is devoid of religious symbols, meanings, and legitimacy is relatively powerless to alter a religious victim's resolve to stay in the marriage no matter what the cost. Correspondingly, the language of the spirit, if devoid of the practical resources of contemporary culture, compromises a victim's need for safety, security, and financial resources to care for herself and her children.

HOW DO NOTIONS OF RECONCILIATION AND FORGIVENESS PLACE WOMEN AT GREATER RISK?

In families of strong faith, many of the patterns that are observed within mainstream culture are intensified: the fear, the vulnerability, the isolation, the promise before God to stay together until *death do us part*. Although there is no compelling evidence that violence is more frequent or more severe in families of faith, religious women are more vulnerable *when abused*. They are less likely to leave, are more likely to believe the abuser's promise to change his violent ways, frequently espouse reservations about seeking community-based resources or shelters for battered women, and commonly express guilt—that they have failed their families and God in not being able to make the marriage work. To be sure, most women victims are reluctant to see their marriage end, experience financial vulnerability, and fear for their own lives (and the abuser's reprisal). Some cling to a fantasy of change and others harbor notions of working harder to ensure the marriage lasts. However, for religious women, these beliefs are commonly and strongly reinforced by a religious ideology that sees women's roles as wife and homemaker as pivotal to her sense of self-worth, believes that happy families build strong nations, and condemns divorce. Moreover, there are explicit religious notions that make it especially difficult for religious victims to see the full extent of their suffering or to sound out the call for help. Paramount among these are Christian notions of forgiveness and women's identity with Jesus the sacrificial lamb. Could battering be a religious woman's *cross to bear*? Are religious batterers' abilities to manipulate their victims dependent on specific features of their religious belief system?

Any discussion of the healing journey of victims of abuse eventually comes to the issue of forgiveness. Writing about forgiveness from a religious standpoint, Hudson argues that the cry of Jesus from the cross, "Father, forgive them; for they do not know what they are doing"[1] is often touted as the model by which victims ought to approach their aggressors. Yet, forgiveness does not erase the pain of the past, nor does it deny its implications. Rather, when forgiveness is placed within a broader context of the journey from victim to survivor, it is achieved when the pain of the past no longer controls the future and the victim is no longer entrapped in a complicated web of anger and despair (Nason-Clark and Kroeger 2004). But the line is a fine one. Marie Fortune claims that forgiveness is the last step on the healing journey, the last rung on the ladder of a woman's struggle to overcome the brokenness of her past. As such, it cannot come before justice or the offender's accountability. In this way, premature forgiveness actually damages the possibility of healing and growth for both perpetrator and victim. Religious pressure on the victim to quickly "forgive and forget" prevents the abuser from being fully accountable for his actions and can be life threatening for the victim. Forgiveness might be the most charitable and compassionate gift religious groups can offer victims in their fold (Fortune 1988), but it cannot be timetabled by someone other than the victim and should never be regarded as a guarantee for safety or protection. Religious language must not pretend that everything is now okay and life for the family should return to normal, as if the abuse never happened.

HOW MIGHT RELIGION IMPROVE MANDATED INTERVENTION?

Justice, accountability, and change are all central ingredients in the intervention services offered to men who have abused their wives. Although some come voluntarily, other men are mandated by the courts or referred by their wives, therapists, or clergy to participate in an intervention program for abusers. Although abused *religious* women want the battery to stop, they may not wish to terminate their relationship with the abuser, either temporarily or forever. Consequently, the resources these women seek in the aftermath of violence in part differentiate them from their more secular counterparts. As a result, religious women in particular place a lot of trust in programs that

purport to help men to stop the abuse and to alter their ways of coping with anger and frustration. Simply put, the stakes to keep the marriage together (and perhaps to accept the battery) are much higher for religious women (Horton and Williamson 1988; Kroeger and Nason-Clark 2001).

Woven through the narratives of abusive men who are travelling toward justice and accountability are the roles of religious congregations and their leaders in supporting the men as they seek help. A pastor or priest is a key player in ensuring accountability in the life of a religious man who is, or has been, abusive. Consequently, houses of worship and religious leaders are unique resources in any community-based efforts to create safe and peaceful homes.

However, there is little agreement about the efficacy of batterer intervention groups (Daly and Pelowski 2000; Hanson and Wallace-Capretta 2002; Scott and Wolfe 2000). Although completion and recidivism rates vary amongst programs (Dalton 2001; Gondolf 2002), it is clear that intervention must be integrated into the overall social context of these men's lives (deHart et al. 1999). Researchers have recognized the critical role played by the courts and other parts of the judicial system, but none has acknowledged any role for religious organizations. Yet, for many abusive men, a key component of their social context is their religious belief system (Dobash and Dobash 1979; Ptacek 1988; DeKeseredy and MacLeod 1998).

In one faith-based batterer intervention program, a case file analysis of over 1,000 closed files of abusive men revealed that men in such a program differ on many personal and family characteristics from men who enter secular programs for batterers (Nason-Clark et al. in press). The men in the faith-based program are more likely to be older, married, and white; to have attained postsecondary education or a university or graduate degree; to be employed and in a white-collar occupation; and to have witnessed or experienced violence in their childhood home. On the other hand, men in this program had similar rates of alcohol abuse and criminal history as men in secular programs. Another finding to emerge from this data is the role of clergy and other religious leaders in encouraging or "mandating" men who seek their spiritual help to attend a faith-based intervention program. In fact, men who were clergy referred were more likely to complete (and graduate from) the program than those whose attendance was mandated by a judge. When the clergy and the courts both referred such men, their rates of program completion were very high indeed.

Attempting to understand exactly why this might be so is important. Past research has shown that religious men and women stay longer in a relationship, even an unhealthy one (Horton and Williamson 1988). Clergy, then, may be especially prone to assist abused women and their partners who are still married and to use the language of reconciliation as motivation for the men to seek help in a faith-based agency (Nason-Clark 1999). Since the men themselves have more life stability factors (currently married, employed, higher education, etc.), this may reinforce their willingness to complete the program and to alter their abusive ways. Sharing a religious worldview with the other men in the program may actually provide a *safe place* for these abusive men to challenge themselves and each other and look toward a day when their abusive past will no longer control their present reality.

Nonetheless, too often forgotten in the growing research literature on batterers is the role of religion in either supporting or challenging men's abusive ways. Achieving accountability is paramount to successful intervention. On this issue, there may be a difference between the sheep and the goats: for religious men, having their violence condemned by not only the language of contemporary culture but also by the language of the spirit may be central. It may well be that accountability factors are more easily set in place in the life of a religious man. A key player in ensuring such accountability is the man's pastor, priest, or other religious leader. But powerful, too, is a religious community—that is, the congregation—when perceived by the abuser or the family as supportive of his journey toward change and wholeness. For

violence to be overcome, the personal struggle will need to acquire public dimensions. In families of faith, the religious community becomes that important ingredient, with the capacity to either augment or thwart the process of recovery. The question then becomes: How can a person's religious ideology be employed by sacred and secular intervention services in a way that will nurture, monitor, and reinforce a violent-free future?

SUGGESTIONS FOR EXPANDING THE RESEARCH AGENDA

Outlined below are several questions that I consider essential in our efforts to unravel the nuanced relationship between religious faith and violence within families. Each of these queries could be addressed at an individual or community level. Each has political or social action implications that permeate beyond the boundaries of any specific groups. However, from my vantage point, it is inconceivable to separate theoretical gains from the direct impact on the lives of hurting people.

1. What are some of the central features of various religious traditions that negate community-wide efforts to raise awareness about violence against women and to suggest strategies that would empower women to reduce the risk of endangering their physical or emotional health in the aftermath of abuse?

I wish to highlight two "central features" of various religious traditions that work against raising awareness about domestic violence and empowering victims: discourse on the salience of *family* for women's lives and thus the undesirability of family dissolution, and the tendency to "spiritualize" social problems by religious ideologies and leaders. A third feature, gender segregation both within and beyond the religious group, contributes to the way the issue of abuse may be marginalized within the discourse of a specific group, but these same single-sex social contexts also offer the practical and emotional support on which many women victims depend. Notions about family values including, but not limited to, an anti-divorce sentiment reinforce a victimized woman's sense of failure and vulnerability. Moreover, when the abuse is conceptualized as a spiritual issue, this exacerbates her dependence on the religious group for guidance concerning the decisions she needs to make to ensure safety.

For fundamentalists of varied world religions, divorce is regarded as a dangerous trend (Hawley 1994), evidence of narcissism at a personal level, and a conduit to later problems for affected children and adolescents. Some conservative Christian traditions argue that divorce is the result of female economic independence augmented by married women's introduction into the paid labor force (Bartkowski 2001). Clearly, any religious tradition that regards women's primary raison d'etre to be child bearing and home making resists societal advances to ensure female participation in all sectors of society (Balmer 1994). Sacred texts and their religious elite interpreters play a critical role in how the issue of abuse is framed. When it is highlighted in the weekly routine of church life—through sermons or informational material available to congregants—victims feel safe to come forward; when it is absent from religious discourse, victims keep silent, seeing the issue as their own personal struggle. Working out one's salvation has never been easy, but it has almost always been gendered. Thus, family failure is interpreted by many religious women as a sign that they have failed God. When women's abuse is at the hands of their religious leaders, their vulnerability is especially high (Jacobs 1989); sometimes, they suffer as secondary victims when priests or other religious leaders of congregations are convicted of sexual misconduct (Nason-Clark 1998).

2. What are the intersections of race and class in any discussion concerning the abuse of women in the family context, especially women of faith?

Social theorists such as Patricia Hill-Collins (1997) remind researcher and activist alike of the "constructs of multiplicity" through which inequalities of race, gender, and class are repro-duced. The problems, as well as the solutions, have multiple layers. In the Caribbean, a Pentecostal woman may ask her prayer group to beseech God that the violence would stop, even as she takes his shirt to the shaman.[2] There is ample evidence that religious women support each other, both when things are going well and at times of great personal trial; often this occurs under the umbrella of women's ministry within congregational life.

Cheryl Townsend Gilkes (2000) recently asked us to consider what would have happened to African-American religious organizations and communities if it weren't for the women. Emilie Townes (1997) provides rich example of womanist perspectives on evil and suffering. Milagros Peña has considered this issue from the perspective of Anglos and Latinas working together on both sides of the Mexican/U.S. border and it may be that the same degree of collaboration might be evident when violence erupts at home (Peña and Frehill 1998). Ebaugh and Chafetz (2000) briefly mention congregational support for women in crisis within immigrant congregations; Timmins (1995) notes assistance within Aboriginal communities. The degree to which sisterly support for abuse victims is enhanced by social factors of heightened marginalization—through race, class, or ethnicity—has yet to be examined in full.

3. To what degree do faith-based initiatives have an added advantage in working with clients for whom a religious worldview is a salient feature of their lives?

Recent years have witnessed growing scholarly debates concerning faith-based initiatives to meet a variety of the social and practical needs of the American population, but little attention has been drawn to the role of faith-based services for perpetrators of domestic violence. Yet as mentioned above, there is evidence that clients in a faith-based batterer intervention program may be more likely to complete the requirements of that program than men enrolled in secular equivalents, and that abusive men in the faith-based program who were encouraged by their priests or pastors to attend had higher completion rates than those whose attendance was mandated by the courts. Although faith-based initiatives cross the spectrum from no religious content in their programming to a high visibility of religious language and ritual, it is clear that there is an important interplay between the religious beliefs of workers, religious beliefs of clients, program content, and the nature of the problems for which the program has been established. Teasing apart these interconnections is as interesting as it is timely.

4. As we consider the prevalence and severity of violence in families around the globe, what are some of the features of the interface between faith, fear, and pressures to keep the family intact in various regions of the world?

Violence against women occurs in every corner of the world, taking a variety of different forms and affecting women's lives differently depending on the social context in which it occurs. A man in Bangladesh may throw acid on a woman's face, a Kenyan man hit his wife with her own market stool, or an American may use his gun, but the result is the same: women learn to fear the men who claim to love them. Whether we consult data compiled by the United Nations Secretariat, the World Health Organization, or the departments of censuses and surveys of individual countries, the prevalence rates are startling: at least one in five women around the globe have been victims (see Kroeger and Nason-Clark 2001).

Recent fieldwork experiences in the Caribbean[3] and eastern Europe[4] offer some interesting clues in the relationship between faith and families in crisis in different parts of the world. In the Jamaican capital of Kingston, a city known for its high rates of violence and prevalence of Christian churches, there is evidence of strong resignation about both the incidence and severity of abuse within the general culture and within families. In this context, individuals and institutions alike develop a strategy that refuses to ignore the problem (rather, it is widely acknowledged) but remain reluctant to conceptualize abuse in such a way as to demand a social-action response from either secular or sacred sources of help. Although

there is little resistance to the principle of churches and community agencies collaborating, without framing the problem in ways that might lead to solutions, the result is impotence to act.

In postcommunist Croatia, on the other hand, clergy and other religious leaders are slow to see the pervasive violence in church families and reveal great hesitation in accepting social-scientific explanations for why abuse is prevalent in families of faith. Perceiving the problem to be primarily of spiritual origins, faith leaders are resistant to making referral suggestions to community-based resources. Social service delivery personnel and other victim advocates, on the other hand, are more likely to recognize the influence of posttraumatic stress disorder in this war-torn region of the world and to see religious ideology as silencing women who are suffering. Despite the high levels of violence experienced in both of these cultural contexts, the reaction to abuse in the family and collaborative ventures between the state and the church differ. In Jamaica, the absent father is considered a fact of life; fatherless families in Croatia are perceived in very negative terms. Religious professionals are regarded in Jamaica as instrumental in any effort for social change and clergy themselves reveal no resistance to working with others in community-based agencies; in Croatia, community-based activists and clergy alike appear very cynical about collaboration.

There are many more questions. What is the interface between religion and violence in same-sex relationships? What are the longer-term implications for children in devoutly religious homes who witness violence against their mother or are victims of parental rage themselves? What are the contours of the healing journey when it is an adult man who has been victimized by his religious partner? How is violence toward the elderly conceptualized in faith-based nursing homes?

Violence knows no religious boundaries: it is a global issue and it is gendered. The journey toward healing and wholeness for religious victims is replete with both secular and sacred overtones—as are its causes and the factors that reinforce it. Breaking the cycle of violence in the family requires both the language of secular culture and the language of the spirit. Researchers and activists alike must unravel the many layers involved in the interface of faith, family, and fear for victimized women and their children.

NOTES

1. Biblical reference is Luke 23:34.
2. Fieldnotes, Jamaican focus group, September 2003.
3. With the assistance of Lanette Ruff, a graduate student at the University of New Brunswick, I conducted personal interviews and focus groups in Kingston, Jamaica in the fall of 2003, and offered training and violence sensitivity workshops to a wide range of religious and secular professionals as well as to students.
4. Together with colleagues at the University of Zagreb (Sinisa Zrinscak and Marina Ajdukovic), the Evangelical Theological Seminary in Osijek (Ela Balog), and within the social-science delivery sector (Suzanna and Zoran Vargovic), I have been considering religion and family violence in a post-communist context. After three fieldwork visits, we have collected both quantitative and qualitative indicators of the resistance and openness to discussion of family violence connected with churches in Croatia; here, too, I have been involved in training workshops.

REFERENCES

Annis, A. W., and R. R. Rice. 2001. A survey of abuse prevalence in the Christian Reformed Church. *Journal of Religion and Abuse* 3(3/4): 7–40.

Balmer, R. 1994. American fundamentalism: The ideal of femininity. In *Fundamentalism and gender,* edited by J. S. Hawley, pp. 47–62. New York: Oxford University Press.

Bartkowski, J. P. 2001. *Remaking the godly marriage: Gender negotiation in evangelical families.* New Brunswick, NJ: Rutgers University Press.

Bartkowski, J. P., and K. L. Anderson. 1996. Are there religious variations in spousal violence? Paper presented at the annual meetings of the Association for the Sociology of Religion. New York.

Brinkerhoff, M., E. Grandin, and E. Lupri. 1992. Religious involvement and spousal violence: The Canadian case. *Journal for the Scientific Study of Religion* 31:12–31.

Collins, P. H. 1997. Comment on Hekman's "Truth and method: Feminist standpoint theory revisited": Where's the power. *Signs* 22:375–81.

Dalton, B. 2001. Batterer characteristics and treatment completion. *Journal of Interpersonal Violence* 16(1):971–91.

Daly, J., and S. Pelowski. 2000. Predictors of dropout among men who batter: A review of studies with implications for research and practice. *Violence and Victims* 15(2):137–60.

deHart, D., R. Kennerly, L. Burke, and D. Follingstad. 1999. Predictors of attrition in a treatment program for battering men. *Journal of Family Violence* 14(1):19–34.

Dekeseredy, W., and L. MacLeod. 1997. *Woman abuse: A sociological story.* Toronto: Harcourt Brace.

Dobash, R. P., and R. E. Dobash. 1979. *Violence against wives: A case against the partriarchy.* New York: Free Press.

Ebaugh, H. R., and J. Chafetz. 2000. *Religion and the new immigrants: Continuities and adaptations in immigrant congregations.* Walnut Creek, CA: AltaMira Press.

Edgell, P. 2003. In rhetoric and practice: Defining "the good family" in local congregations. In *Handbook of the sociology of religion,* edited by M. Dillon, pp. 164–78. Cambridge: Cambridge University Press.

Fortune, M. 1988. Forgiveness the last step. In *Abuse and religion: When praying isn't enough,* edited by A. Horton and J. Williamson, pp. 215–20. Lexington, MA: Lexington.

Gilkes, C. T. 2000. *If it wasn't for the women . . . Black women's experience and womanist culture in church and community.* Maryknoll, NY: Orbis Books.

Gondolf, E. W. 2002. *Batterer intervention systems: Issues, outcomes and recommendations.* Thousand Oaks, CA: Sage Publications.

Hanson, R. K., and S. Wallace-Capretta. 2002. *Predicting recidivism among male batterers 2000–06.* Ottawa: Public Works and Government Services Canada.

Hawley, J., editor. 1994. *Fundamentalism and gender.* New York: Oxford.

Horton, A., and J. Williamson, editors. 1988. *Abuse and religion: When praying isn't enough.* New York: D. C. Health and Company.

Jacobs, J. L. 1989. *Divine disenchantment: Deconverting from new religious movements.* Bloomington, IN: Indiana University Press.

Kroeger, C. C., and N. Nason-Clark. 2001. *No place for abuse: Biblical and practical resources to counteract domestic violence.* Downers Grove, IL: InterVarsity Press.

Nason-Clark, N. 1997. *The battered wife: How Christians confront family violence.* Louisville, KY: Westminister/John Knox Press.

———. 1998. Abuses of clergy trust: Exploring the impact on female congregants' faith and practice. In *Wolves among the fold,* edited by A. Shupe, pp. 85–100. New York: Rutgers University Press.

———. 1999. Shattered silence or holy hush: Emerging definitions of violence against women. *Journal of Family Ministry* 13(1):39–56.

———. 2001. Woman abuse and faith communities: Religion, violence and provision of social welfare. In *Religion and social policy,* edited by P. Nesbitt, pp. 128–45. Walnut Creek, CA: AltaMira Press.

Nason-Clark, N., and C. C. Kroeger. 2004. *Refuge from abuse: Hope and healing for abused Christian women.* Downers Grove, IL: InterVarsity Press.

Nason-Clark, N., N. Murphy, B. Fisher-Townsend, and L. Ruff. In press. An overview of the characteristics of the clients at a faith-based batterers' intervention program. *Journal of Religion and Abuse* 5(4).

Peña, M., & L. M. Frehill. 1998. Latina religious practice: Analyzing cultural dimensions in measures of religiosity. *Journal for the Scientific Study of Religion* 37:620–35.

Ptacek, J. 1988. How men who batter rationalize their behavior. In *Abuse and religion: When praying isn't enough,* edited by A. Horton and J. Williamson, pp. 247–58. New York: DC Health and Company.

Scott, K., and D. Wolfe. 2000. Change among batterers: Examining men's success stories. *Journal of Interpersonal Violence* 15(8):827–42.

Stirling, M. L., C. A. Cameron, N. Nason-Clark, and B. Miedema, editors. 2004. *Understanding abuse: Partnering for change.* Toronto: University of Toronto Press.

Timmins, L., editor. 1995. *Listening to the thunder: Advocates talk about the battered women's movement.* Vancouver: Women's Research Centre.

Townes, E., editor. 1997. *Embracing the spirit: Womanist perspectives on hope, salvation and transformation.* Maryknoll, NY: Orbis Books.

Weaver, A. 1993. Psychological trauma: What clergy need to know. *Pastoral Psychology* 41:385–408.

Whipple, V. 1987. Counselling battered women from fundamentalist churches. *Journal for Marital and Family Therapy* 13(3):251–58.

R E A D I N G **85**

Lisa's Ritual, Age 10

Grace Caroline Bridges

Afterwards when he has finished
lots of mouthwash helps
to get rid of her father's cigarette taste.
She runs a hot bath
  to soak away the pain
    like red dye leaking from her
      school dress in the washtub.

She doesn't cry
When the bathwater cools she adds more hot.
She brushes her teeth for a long time.

Then she finds the corner of her room,
curls against it. There the wall is

hard and smooth
as teacher's new chalk, white
as a clean bedsheet. Smells
fresh. Isn't sweaty, hairy, doesn't stick
to skin. Doesn't hurt much
when she presses her small backbone
into it. The wall is steady
while she falls   away:
  first the hands   lost
arms dissolving   feet gone
    the legs   dis-   jointed
      body cracking down
        the center like a fault

<pre>
        she falls inside
            slides down like
dust   like kitchen dirt
            slips off
    the dustpan into
                noplace
    a place where
nothing happens,
nothing ever happened.
</pre>

<pre>
When she feels the cool
wall against her cheek
she doesn't want to
come back. Doesn't want to
think about it.
The wall is quiet, waiting.
It is tall like a promise
only better.
</pre>

R E A D I N G   **86**

Pornography and Freedom

John Stoltenberg

There is a widespread belief that sexual freedom is an idea whose time has come. Many people believe that in the last few decades we have gotten more and more of it—that sexual freedom is something you can carve out against the forces of sexual repressiveness, and that significant gains have been won, gains we dare not give up lest we backslide into the sexual dark ages, when there wasn't sexual freedom, there was only repression.

Indeed, many things seem to have changed. But if you look closely at what is supposed to be sexual freedom, you can become very confused. Let's say, for instance, you understand that a basic principle of sexual freedom is that people should be free to be sexual and that one way to guarantee that freedom is to make sure that sex be free from imposed restraint. That's not a bad idea, but if you happen to look at a magazine photograph in which a woman is bound and gagged and lashed down on a plank with her genital area open to the camera, you might well wonder: Where is the freedom from restraint? where's the sexual freedom?

Let's say you understand that people should be free to be sexual and that one way to guarantee that freedom is to make sure people can feel good about themselves and each other sexually. That's not a bad idea. But if you happen to read random passages from books such as the following, you could be quite perplexed:

> Baby, you're gonna get fucked tonight like you ain't never been fucked before, he hissed evilly down at her as she struggled fruitlessly against her bonds. The man wanted only to abuse and ravish her till she was totally broken and subservient to him. He knelt between her widespread legs and gloated over the cringing little pussy he was about to ram his cock into.

. . .

After reading that, you might well ask: Where's the freedom from hatred? where's the freedom from degradation? where's the sexual freedom?

Let's say you understand people should be free to be sexual and that one way to guarantee that freedom is to make sure people are not punished for the individuality of their sexuality. And then you find a magazine showing page after page of bodies with their genitals garroted in baling wire and leather thongs, with their genitals tied up and tortured, with heavy weights suspended from rings that pierce their genitals, and the surrounding text makes clear that this mutilation and punishment are experienced as sex acts. And you might wonder in your mind: Why must this person suffer punishment in order to experience sexual feelings? why must this person be humiliated and disciplined and whipped and beaten until he bleeds in order to have access to his homoerotic passion? why have the Grand Inquisitor's most repressive and sadistic torture techniques become what people do to each other and call sex? where's the sexual freedom?

If you look back at the books and magazines and movies that have been produced in this country in the name of sexual freedom over the past decade, you've got to wonder: *Why has sexual freedom come to look so much like sexual repression? why has sexual freedom come to look so much like unfreedom?* The answer, I believe, has to do with the relationship between freedom and justice, and specifically the relationship between *sexual* freedom and *sexual* justice. When we think of freedom in any other sense, we think of freedom as *the result* of justice. We know that there can't truly *be* any freedom until justice has happened, until justice exists. For any people in history who have struggled for freedom, those people have understood that their freedom exists on the future side of justice. The notion of freedom *prior to* justice is understood to be meaningless. Whenever people do not have freedom, they have understood freedom to be that which you arrive at by achieving justice. If you told them they should try to have their freedom without there being justice, they would laugh in your face. Freedom *always* exists on the far side of justice. That's perfectly understood—except when it comes to sex.

The popular concept of sexual freedom in this country has never meant sexual justice. Sexual-freedom advocates have cast the issue only in terms of having sex that is free from suppression and restraint. Practically speaking, that has meant advocacy of sex that is free from institutional interference; sex that is free from being constrained by legal, religious, and medical ideologies; sex that is free from any outside intervention. Sexual freedom on a more personal level has meant sex that is free from fear, guilt, and shame—which in practical terms has meant advocacy of sex

that is free from value judgments, sex that is free from responsibility, sex that is free from consequences, sex that is free from ethical distinctions, sex that is essentially free from any obligation to take into account in one's consciousness that the other person is a *person*. In order to free sex from fear, guilt, and shame, it was thought that institutional restrictions on sex needed to be overthrown, but in fact what needed to be overthrown was any vestige of an interpersonal ethic in which people would be real to one another; for once people are real to one another, the consequences of one's acts matter deeply and personally; and particularly in the case of sex, one risks perceiving the consequences of one's acts in ways that feel *bad* because they do not feel *right*. This entire moral-feeling level of sexuality, therefore, needed to be undone. And it was undone, in the guise of an assault on institutional suppression.

Sexual freedom has never really meant that individuals should have sexual self-determination, that individuals should be free to experience the integrity of their own bodies and be free to act out of that integrity in a way that is totally within their own right to choose. Sexual freedom has never really meant that people should have absolute sovereignty over their own erotic being. And the reason for this is simple: Sexual freedom has never really been about *sexual justice between men and women*. It has been about maintaining men's superior status, men's power over women; and it has been about sexualizing women's inferior status, men's subordination of women. Essentially, sexual freedom has been about preserving a sexuality that preserves male supremacy.

. . .

PORNOGRAPHY AND MALE SUPREMACY

Male-supremacist sexuality is important to pornography, and pornography is important to male supremacy. Pornography *institutionalizes* the sexuality that both embodies and enacts male supremacy. Pornography says about that sexuality, "Here's how": Here's how to act out male supremacy in sex. Here's how the action should go. Here are the acts that impose power over and against another body. And pornography says about that sexuality, "Here's who": Here's who you should do it to and here's who she is: your whore, your piece of ass, yours. Your penis is a weapon, her body is your target. And pornography says about that sexuality, "Here's why": Because men are masters, women are slaves; men are superior, women are subordinate; men are real, women are objects; men are sex machines, women are sluts.

Pornography institutionalizes male supremacy the way segregation institutionalizes white supremacy. It is a practice embodying an ideology of biological superiority; it is an institution that both expresses that ideology and enacts that ideology—makes it the reality that people believe is true, keeps it that way, keeps people from knowing any other possibility, keeps certain people powerful by keeping certain people *down*.

Pornography also *eroticizes* male supremacy. It makes dominance and subordination feel like sex; it makes hierarchy feel like sex; it makes force and violence feel like sex; it makes hate and terrorism feel like sex; it makes inequality feel like sex. Pornography keeps sexism sexy. It keeps sexism *necessary* for some people to have sexual feelings. It makes reciprocity make you go limp. It makes mutuality leave you cold. It makes tenderness and intimacy and caring make you feel like you're going to disappear into a void. It makes justice the opposite of erotic; it makes injustice a sexual thrill.

Pornography exploits every experience in people's lives that *imprisons* sexual feelings— pain, terrorism, punishment, dread, shame, powerlessness, self-hate—and would have you believe that it *frees* sexual feelings. In fact, the sexual freedom represented by pornography is the freedom of men to act sexually in ways that keep sex a basis for inequality.

You can't have authentic sexual freedom without sexual justice. It is only freedom for those in power; the powerless cannot be free. Their experience of sexual freedom becomes but a delusion borne of complying with the demands of the powerful. Increased sexual freedom under male supremacy has had to mean an increased tolerance for sexual practices that are predicated on eroticized injustice between men and women: treating women's bodies or body parts as merely sexual objects or things; treating women as utterly submissive masochists who enjoy pain and humiliation and who, if they are raped, enjoy it; treating women's bodies to sexualized beating, mutilation, bondage, dismemberment. . . . Once you have sexualized inequality, once it is a learned and internalized prerequisite for sexual arousal and sexual gratification, then anything goes. And that's what sexual freedom means on this side of sexual justice.

PORNOGRAPHY AND HOMOPHOBIA

Homophobia is absolutely integral to the system of sexualized male supremacy. Cultural homophobia expresses a whole range of antifemale revulsion: It expresses contempt for men who are sexual with men because they are believed to be "treated like a woman" in sex. It expresses contempt for women who are sexual with women just *because* they are women and also because they are perceived to be a rebuke to the primacy of the penis.

But cultural homophobia is not merely an expression of woman hating; it also works to protect men from the sexual aggression of other men. Homophobia keeps men doing to women what they would not want done to themselves. There's not the same sexual harassment of men that there is of women on the street or in the workplace or in the university; there's not nearly the same extent of rape; there's not the same demeaned social caste that is sexualized, as it is for women. And that's thanks to homophobia: Cultural homophobia keeps men's sexual aggression directed toward women. Homophobia keeps men acting in concert as male supremacists so that they won't be perceived as an appropriate target for male-supremacist sexual treatment. Male supremacy *requires* homophobia in order to keep men safe from the sexual aggression of men. Imagine this country *without* homophobia: A woman raped every three minutes *and a man* raped every three minutes. Homophobia keeps that statistic at a "manageable" level. The system is not foolproof, of course. There are boys who have been sexually molested by men. There are men who have been brutalized in sexual relationships with their male lovers, and they too have a memory of men's sexual violence. And there are many men in prison who are subject to the same sexual terrorism that women live with almost all the time. But for the most part—happily—homophobia serves male supremacy by protecting "real men" from sexual assault by other real men.

Pornography is one of the major enforcers of cultural homophobia. Pornography is rife with gay-baiting and effemiphobia. Portrayals of allegedly lesbian "scenes" are a staple of heterosexual pornography: The women with each other are there for the male viewer, the male voyeur; there is not the scantest evidence that they are there for each other. Through so-called men's-sophisticate magazines—the "skin" magazines—pornographers outdo one another in their attacks against feminists, who are typically derided as lesbians—"sapphic" at best, "bulldykes" at worst. The innuendo that a man is a "fairy" or a "faggot" is, in pornography, a kind of dare or a challenge to prove his cocksmanship. And throughout pornography, the male who is perceived to be the passive orifice in sex is tainted with the disdain that "normally" belongs to women.

. . .

PORNOGRAPHY AND MEN

Now this is the situation of men within male supremacy: Whether we are straight or gay, we have been looking for a sexual freedom that is utterly specious, and we have been looking for it through pornography, which perpetuates the very domination and subordination that stand in the way of sexual justice. Whether we are straight or gay, we have been looking for a notion of freedom that leaves out women; we have been looking for a sexuality that preserves men's power over women. So long as that is what we strive for, we cannot possibly feel freely, and no one can be free. Whatever sexual freedom might be, it must be after justice.

I want to speak directly to those of us who live in male supremacy as men, and I want to speak specifically to those of us who have come to understand that pornography does make sexism sexy; that pornography does make male supremacy sexy; and that pornography does define what is sexy in terms of domination and subordination, in terms that serve *us as men*—whether we buy it or not, whether we buy into it or not—because it serves male supremacy, which is exactly what it is for.

I want to speak to those of us who live in this setup as men and who recognize—in the world and in our very own selves—the power pornography can have over our lives: It can make men believe that our penises are like weapons. It can make men believe—for some moments of orgasm—that we are just like the men in pornography: virile, strong, tough, maybe cruel. It can make men believe that if you take it away from us, we won't have sexual feelings.

. . .

We've got to be telling our sons that if a man gets off by putting women down, *it's not okay.*

We've got to be telling merchants that if they peddle women's bodies and lives for men's consumption and entertainment, *it's not okay.*

We've got to be telling other men that if you let the pornographers lead you by the nose (or any other body part) into believing that women exist to be tied up and hung up and beaten and raped, *it's not okay.*

We've got to be telling the pornographers—Larry Flynt and Bob Guccione and Hugh Hefner and Al Goldstein and all the rest—that whatever they think they're doing in our names as men, as entertainment for men, for the sake of some delusion of so-called manhood . . . well, it's not okay. It's not okay with *us.*

War Crimes

Helen Clarkson

The town of Baraka sits on the shores of Lake Tanganyika in the South Kivu province of eastern Democratic Republic of Congo. It ought to be a prosperous town. The lake is full of fish, the land between the edge of the lake and the nearby mountains is arable, and the mountains hold gold and minerals that could be mined. Clearly this was once the case and buildings show the signs of the commerce they once supported—a photo shop, grocery stores, a smart tailor. But after years of civil war the buildings are crumbling, the roads are hidden beneath mud and grass, and the petrol station sign, riddled with bullet holes, swings in the breeze next to a forecourt that has long since disappeared.

Baraka is at the crossroads of armed groups—from Congo, Rwanda, and Burundi—who have used the area to support themselves economically. They have spread terror through the population by looting and burning villages and raping and murdering their inhabitants. Throughout the fighting many people fled into the bush, where they hid, afraid to come out.

In the Médecins Sans Frontières (MSF) hospital here, we see between 30 and 50 victims of sexual violence each week. Most are women but there are also men and children.

More than half the rapes took place in the fields, as one woman told us in October 2003: "One week ago I was working in the fields with my husband and two other women. Suddenly we saw a group of armed men approaching us. My husband managed to flee but two men caught me. They raped me and at the same time they hit me on the back."

Other rapes took place as part of a wider attack on the village, as another woman who was raped in March 2003 explained: "There was an attack on our village, five armed men entered our house . . . they caught me and took me to the bush . . . [W]hen they had done with me, they carried me back to the village. As it turned out my house had been burnt in the attack and my children had fled. My husband was not there any more either; later we found his body in the bush." Over 80 per cent of the women seen by MSF have been raped by between two and five attackers.

The medical consequences of these rapes are both pathological and psychological. The risk of catching sexually transmitted diseases including HIV/AIDS is high. And the trauma runs very deep. At the clinic the counsellors hear the psychological aftermath of rape: fear, anxiety, and intrusive memories. One young woman spoke of the sound of her sister being raped and killed: "I can still hear my young sister screaming beside me. I did not know what they were doing to her and I could not help her."

There are social consequences too. The stigma of rape leads some men to abandon their wives. As one man explained: "Rape or not rape, having sexual intercourse outside the conjugal house makes her husband ridiculous and for the woman, it means being definitely rejected outside of the house." Others report deteroriated relations between them and their husbands: "Whenever my husband and I have an argument he calls me the wife of the militia men who raped me." says one woman.

Furthermore, because the rapes often take place in the fields, the women are scared to go back to cultivate. "I would rather never go there again, because I felt so close to death," said one. Yet this is not a viable option for most women—they have many children and few other sources of income. Food is scarce in the area and malnutrition is high. Victims also report that after the rape the soldiers stole the food they were growing, and in some cases took control of the fields entirely.

As a weapon of war, sexual violence is highly effective. The outcome is a traumatized, improverised population. The military groups achieve both power and material gain, particularly useful when their pay is erratic. The violence is conducted seemingly with impunity. Despite the truce, many attacks reported took place after the ceasefire commenced, suggesting that it is one weapon demobilized soldiers refuse to surrender.

The question for Baraka now is, with a peace accord in place and a ceasefire being followed, whether it can prosper again. It will depend on a lot of factors: it will need the peace process to last and the military groups to be kept under control; it will need international aid to restore essential services and provide economic assistance. And given the psychological trauma of the population, it will need a lot of time.

DISCUSSION QUESTIONS FOR CHAPTER 10

1. How do violence and the threat of violence exert social control on women? Do you ever fear gender-based violence? How do you think your gender affects your answer to this question?

2. Why do you think many feminists suggest that acts of violence against women are actually hate crimes? Do you think these acts should be classified as hate crimes?

3. Why do you think violence against women is so prevalent in society? Why do you think violence against women is primarily perpetrated by men?

4. How do myths about violence against women silence women and perpetuate sexist systems of oppression?

5. What steps do you believe need to be taken in order to address the problem of violence against women?

SUGGESTIONS FOR FURTHER READING

Bass, Ellen, and Laura Davis. *The Courage to Heal: A Guide for Women Survivors of Child Sexual Abuse.* Rev. ed. New York: Harperperennial, 1994.

Buchwald, Emilie, Pamela R. Fletcher, and Martha Roth, eds. *Transforming a Rape Culture.* Rev. ed. Minneapolis: Milkweed, 2005.

Evans, Patricia. *The Verbally Abusive Relationship: How to Recognize It and How to Respond.* Holbrook, MA: Adams Media Corp., 1996.

Giles, Wenona, and Jennifer Hyndman, eds. *Sites of Violence: Gender and Conflict Zones.* Berkeley: University of California Press, 2004.

Jones, Ann. *Next Time, She'll Be Dead: Battering & How to Stop It.* Rev. ed. Boston: Beacon, 2000.

Ristock, Janice L. *No More Secrets: Violence in Lesbian Relationships.* New York: Routledge, 2002.

Smith, Merril D. *Sex Without Consent: Rape and Sexual Coercion in America.* New York: New York University Press, 2002.

CHAPTER 11

State, Law, and Social Policy

As we have noted in earlier chapters, societal institutions are established patterns of social behavior organized around particular needs and purposes. Gender, race, class, and other systems of inequality structure social institutions, creating different effects on different people. The state, the institution explored in this chapter, is a major social institution organized to maintain systems of legitimized power and authority in society. The state plays an important role in both teaching and enforcing social values. It is a very powerful institution that has profound implications for women's everyday lives.

The *state* is an abstract concept that refers to all forms of social organization representing official power in society: the government, law and social policy, the courts and the criminal justice system, the military, and the police. The state determines how people are selected to govern others and controls the systems of governance they must use. With considerable authority in maintaining social order, the state influences how power is exercised within society. The definition of *state* here is different from state as a geographic region, such as California or Ohio.

Because the state is a conduit for various patterns of social inequity, it does not always fairly regulate and control social order. Historically, White women and women and men of color have been treated poorly by the state, and there are still many problems and challenges at all levels of the political system. However, the state has also been a tool for addressing historical forms of social, political, and economic inequalities through laws and social policy (as evidenced by civil rights and affirmative action legislation). In this way, the state works to both maintain sources of inequality and as an avenue for social justice. A key focus of this chapter is the interaction between the state and gender relations in society.

As already discussed in Chapter 2, the state works with other institutions and assigns roles and distributes resources. In particular, it regulates other institutions and provides guidelines for expected behaviors (roles) and channels resources and power. For example, it regulates the family (such as the Family Leave Act or considering some families to be illegitimate and thus ineligible for state benefits), education (such as Title IX), the economic system (such as antitrust laws that prevent monopolies), and religion (such as state rules for the separation of church and state). The state as nation-state also participates in international policy-making that has important implications for global stability and development. When the United States refuses to ratify international treaties such as CEDAW (the Convention on the Elimination of All Forms of Discrimination Against Women) or the Kyoto Treaty on environmental quality because it seeks to protect U.S. statutes and corporations, it has significant impact globally. The United States is seen as a powerful symbol of urban, secular decadence, with the emancipation of women a central feature. This highlights the importance of gender-sensitive conceptions of development.

Beyond national levels of state policy in the United States is the United Nations (UN), which has tremendous influence on global politics. Although the right to gender equality has been affirmed in international law, still many nations explicitly discriminate against women (including the United States). The reading "Unequal: A Global Perspective on Women Under the Law" by Jessica Neuwirth affirms the necessity of UN regulations beyond the nation-state level in order to establish gender equality worldwide. In "The Postwar Moment: Lessons from Bosnia Herzegovina," Cynthia Cockburn discusses how new thinking about gender has been integrated into UN Resolution 1325 and uses the Bosnian War as an example of a gendered dispute that reflects the need for a clear gender policy at the United Nations.

GOVERNMENT AND REPRESENTATION

Although the terms *government* and *state* tend to be used interchangeably, the government is actually one of the institutions that make up the state. The government creates laws and procedures that govern society and is often referred to as the political system. Although the U.S. government or political system is purported to be a democracy based on the principle of equal representation, the government is not representative of all people, and those who participate as elected officials do not necessarily represent all interests equitably.

LEARNING ACTIVITY **Women and the United Nations**

Visit the Web site of United Nations Division for the Advancement of Women at http://www.un.org/womenwatch/daw/index.html. Follow the link to CEDAW—the Convention on the Elimination of All Forms of Discrimination Against Women, and then follow the link to Country Reports to read about various nations' implementation of the plan. Then visit the UN's WomenWatch site at http://www.un.org/womenwatch to learn more about the UN's promotion of gender equality and empowerment of women. Follow the link to Women of the World for region specific information. Follow the link for Statistics and Indicators for reports, databases and archives relating to gender equality and women's human rights. What do you notice are the pressing issues facing women worldwide? What is the United Nations doing to address these issues?

Women have had a complicated relationship to the Constitution. The liberal doctrine of representation first included women as rights-bearing citizens and represented them as members of the body politic. They came to be excluded for a variety of political reasons, justified in part because the dominant culture assumed that politics and citizenship were purely masculine domains. The founding fathers believed that women's political identity should be restricted because their presence in politics was immoral, corruptive, and potentially disruptive, and that women should be represented by fathers, husbands, or brothers. It was believed that women should be confined to the private sphere of the home where they would be dependent on men, and, as a result, they had no separate legal identity and were legal beings only through their relationship to a man. They had no claims to citizenship rights as women until into the nineteenth century.

As you know from Chapter 1, the Seneca Falls convention in 1848 produced the Declaration of Sentiments and Resolutions that aimed to ensure citizenship rights for women. Women would have to wait until 1920 with the passage of the Nineteenth Amendment to the U.S. Constitution to receive the vote. In 1868, however, the Fourteenth Amendment was ratified, asserting that no state shall "make or enforce any law which will abridge the privileges or immunities of citizens of the United States, nor . . . deprive any person of life, liberty, or property without due process of law, nor deny to any person within its jurisdiction the equal protection of laws." This "person" was assumed to be male, and, as a result, women still could not vote, and the government did not (and, many people would argue, still does not) extend the same protection of the law to women as it does to men. Susan B. Anthony, one of the first feminists who helped write the Declaration of Sentiments and Resolutions, wanted to test her belief that the Fourteenth Amendment should give women, as citizens, the right to vote. She voted in an election in Rochester, New York, and was fined. Hoping to push the case to the Supreme Court, Anthony refused to pay the fine. The case, however, was dropped in order to avoid this test of law. In the Anthony reading "Constitutional Argument," she argues her right to vote as a citizen under the terms guaranteed by the Fourteenth Amendment. This excerpt is from a speech Anthony gave in 1873.

In 1923 the Equal Rights Amendment (ERA) was introduced into Congress to counter the inadequacies of the Fourteenth Amendment concerning women and citizenship. The ERA affirms that both women and men hold equally all of the rights guaranteed by the U.S. Constitution. It would provide a remedy for gender discrimination for both women and men and, at the constitutional level, provide equal legal status to women for the first time in our country's history. It was rewritten in the 1940s to read: "Equality of rights under the law shall not be denied or abridged by the United States or by any state on account of sex"; and it eventually passed Congress (almost 50 years later) in 1972. Unfortunately, it failed to be ratified by the states and suffered a serious defeat in 1982. The most important effect of the ERA would have been to clarify the status of gender discrimination for the courts, whose decisions still show confusion about how to deal with such claims. For the first time, "sex" would have been a suspect classification like race. It would require the same high level of "strict scrutiny" and have to meet the same high level of justification—a "necessary" relation to a "compelling" state interest—as the classification of race.

Although survey after survey showed overwhelming public support for the ERA among women and men, it was officially defeated on June 30, 1982, when it failed to be ratified by the states. It fell three states short of the 38 states needed for ratification. Although the ERA continues to be introduced into each session of Congress, passage of the amendment has yet to regain the momentum it did during the 1970s (even though in 1988 a Harris poll showed 78 percent approval). In order for the ERA to be fully amended, two-thirds of each house in Congress must pass it first, followed by its ratification by 38 states. As opposition to the ERA grew, some states retracted their prior ratification, and others, such as Illinois, changed laws in order to make ratification more difficult. Indiana became the 35th and last state to ratify the ERA in 1977, and the Republican Party removed ERA support from its platform. Many years later, ratification efforts continue, with women and men in many of the unratified states working under the "three-state strategy." This strategy argues that because there was no actual time limit for ratification in the original ERA, the amendment remains only three states short of official ratification. A bill in the 108th Congress of 2003–2004 stipulated that the House of Representatives shall take any necessary action to verify ratification of the ERA when an additional three states ratify. In addition, 19 states have state ERAs or equal rights guarantees in their constitutions. Many groups are working together toward the legislation of the Equal Rights Amendment at all levels. These groups include the League of Women Voters U.S., American Association of University Women, Business & Professional Women/USA, National Organization for Women, National Women's Political Caucus, ERA Campaign, and the Equal Rights Amendment Organization.

Opponents of the ERA have mistakenly claimed the amendment to be anti-family, reporting that it would deny a woman's right to be supported by her husband and encourage women to desert motherhood. There was also worry that it would legislate abortion and gay and lesbian rights as well as send women into combat. In addition, anti-ERA sentiments were voiced by business interests (such as members of the insurance industry) that profited from gender discrimination. The media sensationalized the issue and did not accurately report about what the ERA would and would not do, and conservative political organizations spent a lot of money and many hours organizing against it.

Most feminist leaders today agree that women would be better off if the ERA had been ratified in 1977. They would have received better opportunities for equality and would have been supported by stronger laws fighting gender discrimination in employment, education, and other areas of society. Some people feel that we no longer need a constitutional amendment because there have been piecemeal federal and state laws to protect against gender discrimination. However, as we have seen, federal laws are not as safe as they have been and can be repealed by a simple majority. Similarly, courts change policy as the makeup of the courts changes. A constitutional amendment requires three-quarters of the legislature to vote to repeal it. Although many people assume the continuity of women's rights, the U.S. Supreme Court is central in maintaining or potentially overturning several taken-for-granted rights. These rights include reproductive privacy, affirmative action, protection against gender-based discrimination, family and medical leave, and quality health care services.

Reprinted with permission from Nicole Hollander.

An illustration of how the government has handled women and citizenship concerns the treatment of women who have married non-U.S. citizens. Prior to the mid-1920s, non-native-born women who married U.S. citizens automatically became American, and native-born women who married non-U.S. citizens automatically lost their citizenship and were expected to reside in their husband's country. They also lost their right to vote, once women had been given the vote in 1920. When laws were passed to retain women's citizenship in the mid-1920s, still only men were able to pass on citizenship to their children. Laws equalizing citizenship on these issues were eventually passed in the mid-1930s.

In addition to rights, citizenship also entails such obligations as taxation, jury duty, and military service. Although women have shared taxation with men, in the past they have been prevented from service and/or exempted from jury duty because of their role as mothers and housewives. It was not until the 1970s that the Supreme Court declared that juries had to be representative of the community. Even then juries were often racially biased such that it was not unusual for an African American to face a White jury. A 1986 Supreme Court ruling stated that juries could not be constituted on the basis of race, and a 1994 ruling declared that gender too could

LEARNING ACTIVITY   **The League of Women Voters**

The League of Women Voters was founded by Carrie Chapman Catt in 1920 during the convention of the National American Woman Suffrage Association, just 6 months before the Nineteenth Amendment was ratified. In its early years, the league advocated for collective bargaining, child labor laws, minimum wage, compulsory education, and equal opportunity for women in government and industry. Today the league is still involved in advocacy for justice, working on such issues as Medicare reform, campaign finance reform, and environmental preservation, as well as continuing the work begun over 80 years ago to encourage women to use their political voices. To learn more about the League of Women Voters or to join the league, visit their Web site at *www.lwv.org*.

ACTIVIST PROFILE **Wilma Mankiller**

With her election as chief of the Cherokee Nation, Wilma Mankiller took both a step forward and a step backward. Although Mankiller was the first woman to serve as chief of a major Native American tribe in modern times, her election recalled the importance women had among the Cherokee before colonization by Europeans. Precontact Cherokee society was matrifocal and matrilineal. Women owned the property and maintained the home and were intimately involved in tribal governance.

Mankiller first became committed to involvement in Native American rights in 1969 when Native activists, including some of her own siblings, occupied Alcatraz island in San Francisco Bay. The 19-month occupation became a turning point in Mankiller's life. She became director of the Native American Youth Center in Oakland, California, and in 1973 she watched as her brother joined other Native American activists as they held off FBI agents for 72 days at Wounded Knee, South Dakota.

Following a divorce, Mankiller returned to her family's land in Oklahoma and began to work for the Cherokee Nation; as an economic stimulus coordinator, she had the task of encouraging Cherokee people to train in environmental health and science and then return to their communities to put their knowledge to use. In 1981 she became director of the Cherokee Nation Community Development Department, and her work was so successful that she attracted the attention of Chief Ross Swimmer, who asked her to run as his deputy chief in 1983.

Despite sexist rhetoric and verbal threats from opponents, Swimmer and Mankiller won. In 1985 Swimmer was named head of the Bureau of Indian Affairs by President

Ronald Reagan, and Mankiller became chief of the Cherokee Nation. In 1987 Mankiller ran on her own and was elected chief in her own right. That year, *Ms.* magazine named her Woman of the Year. She was re-elected in 1991, winning by 83 percent of the vote. During her tenure as chief, Mankiller focused on addressing high unemployment and low education rates among Cherokee people, improving community health care, implementing housing initiatives and child and youth projects, and developing the economy of northeastern Oklahoma. She created the Institute for Cherokee Literacy, emphasizing the need for Cherokee people to retain their traditions. She did not run for re-election in 1995. In 1998 President Bill Clinton awarded her the Presidential Medal of Freedom.

not be used as a basis for jury competence. The obligation for military service, which many women have wanted to share with men, is outlined in more detail later in the chapter. Of course, women have served in auxiliary roles as nurses, transport drivers, and dispatchers for many years and are now able to participate in combat positions within some divisions of the armed services.

Although women tend to be as involved as men in electoral politics (and sometimes even more involved) in terms of voting, showing support, and volunteering for campaigns, there are markedly fewer women involved in official political positions associated with campaigns. Women still constitute a relatively small number of candidates for local, state, and national offices, and their presence is greater at the local rather than national levels. As political offices get more visible, higher level, better paid, and more authoritative or powerful, there are fewer women in these positions. Several explanations may explain this gap. Although some suggest that women are just not interested and that they lack the credentials, the main reasons are conflict between family and work roles, lack of political financing, and discrimination and sexist attitudes toward women in politics.

The 109th Congress of 2004–2005 included 68 women (45 Democrats and 23 Republicans), or 15.5 percent in the House of Representatives; 14 women (9 Democrats and 5 Republicans), or 14 percent in the Senate; and 82 women total (54 Democrats and 28 Republicans), or 15 percent overall in Congress. Of these 82 women in Congress, 22, or 27 percent, are women of color. These figures, although much improved compared to pre-1990s statistics, are still alarming; they illustrate male and White domination in society and challenge the extent to which women and people of color are represented. However, remember that females do not necessarily represent women's interests, just as people of color do not necessarily support issues that improve the status of non-White groups. Many feminists vote for men in political office over opposing women candidates because they understand that being a female does not necessarily mean that her politics, or those of the party she represents, are pro-women. In terms of the gender gap in voting, on the average women tend to lean toward the Democratic Party more than men do and are more likely to be concerned about such issues as education, welfare, health care, and the environment. During the 2004 presidential election, however, the gender gap declined, although 51 percent of women voted for John Kerry and

Where Women Rule: A Sample of Female Representatives in National Legislatures Worldwide

Simple statistics merely hint at complex stories. Rwandan genocide has increased the number of female representatives but so, it appears, has Scandinavian social democracy. It may be no surprise that Saudi Arabia trails the pack, but how do you explain the Islamic Republic of Pakistan beating out the United States? Note that in no country's national legislature have female reps been able to crack the 50% mark.

Nation	Women/Total Seats	%Female	Nation	Women/Total Seats	%Female
Rwanda	39/80	48.8	Greece	42/300	14.0
Sweden	158/349	45.3	Ireland	22/166	13.3
Denmark	68/179	38.0	Chile	15/120	12.5
Finland	75/200	37.5	France	70/594	11.8
Netherlands	55/150	36.7	Lesotho	14/120	11.7
Norway	60/165	36.4	Italy	71/618	11.5
Cuba	219/609	36.0	Zimbabwe	15/150	10.0
Spain	126/350	36.0	Cambodia	12/123	9.8
Argentina	87/256	34.0	Hungary	38/386	9.8
South Africa	131/400	32.8	Russian Federation	44/450	9.8
Germany	194/603	32.2			
Iceland	19/63	30.2	Brazil	44/513	8.6
Mozambique	75/250	30.0	Serbia & Montenegro	10/126	7.9
New Zealand	34/120	28.3			
Vietnam	136/498	27.3	Uzbekistan	18/250	7.2
Australia	38/150	25.3	Japan	34/480	7.1
Switzerland	50/200	25.0	Nigeria	24/359	6.7
Uganda	75/304	24.7	Iran	13/290	4.5
Pakistan	74/342	21.6	Turkey	24/550	4.4
Canada	62/301	20.6	Haiti	3/83	3.6
China	604/2985	20.2	Egypt	11/454	2.4
North Korea	138/687	20.1	Bangladesh	6/300	2.0
United Kingdom	118/659	17.9	Niger	1/83	1.2
			Kuwait	0/65	0.0
Israel	18/120	15.0	Micronesia	0/14	0.0
USA	62/435	14.3	Saudi Arabia	0/120	0.0

Source: Adapted from the Dutch-based politics and culture magazine *Ode*. www.odemagazine.com. Based on statistics at *www.thewhitehouseproject.org*.

58 percent of men voted for George W. Bush. While there are exceptions, men are more likely as a group to vote for a strong defense, anti-welfare, and anti–affirmative action policies: the stance of the Republican party. This does not of course imply that all men are Republican, only that as a group, they are more likely to favor the issues put forward by this political party.

HISTORICAL MOMENT   **Shirley Chisholm for President**

Shirley Chisholm was born to a mother from Barbados and a father from British Guiana. She grew up in Barbados and Brooklyn and graduated with honors from Brooklyn College with a major in sociology. Following graduation, she worked at the Mt. Calvary Childcare Center in Harlem and became active in local politics. She completed a master's in education at Columbia University in 1952 and then managed daycare centers.

Chisholm ran for a state assembly seat in 1964 and won, serving in the New York General Assembly until 1968. While in the New York legislature, she focused on issues of education and daycare. In 1968 she ran for and won a seat in the U.S. Congress representing New York's Twelfth Congressional District, becoming the first Black woman in the House of Representatives. Chisholm quickly distinguished herself as an outspoken advocate for the poor and for women's and civil rights and against the war in Vietnam.

During a speech on equal rights for women before the House of Representatives in 1969, Chisholm pointed out, "More than half of the population of the United States is female. But women occupy only 2 percent of the managerial positions. They have not even reached the level of tokenism yet. No women sit on the AFL-CIO council or Supreme Court. There have been only two women who have held Cabinet rank, and at present there are none. Only two women now hold ambassadorial rank in

(continued)

the diplomatic corps. In Congress, we are down to 1 senator and 10 representatives. Considering that there are about 3½ million more women in the United States than men, this situation is outrageous."

In January 1972, Chisholm announced her candidacy for the Democratic nomination for the presidency: "I stand before you today as a candidate for the Democratic nomination for the Presidency of the United States. I am not the candidate of Black America, although I am Black and proud. I am not the candidate of the women's movement of this country, although I am a woman, and I am equally proud of that. I am not the candidate of any political bosses or special interests. I am the candidate of the people."

Chisholm became the first woman considered for the presidential nomination. Although she was defeated, she did garner more than 150 votes from the delegates to the Democratic National Convention in Miami. She continued to serve in Congress until 1982. She wrote two books: *Unbossed and Unbought* and *The Good Fight*. She died January 1, 2005 at the age of 80.

WOMEN AND THE LAW

The United States inherited British common law that utilized the doctrine of *femme couverte* (also known as *feme covert*), or covered women: Husband and wife were one person under law, and she was his sexual property. As a result, married women could not seek employment without the husband's consent, keep their own wages, own property, sue, exercise control over their children, and control their reproductive lives. As already discussed in Chapter 10, because husbands and wives were "one" in marriage, wives were sexual property of husbands, and rape within marriage was legally condoned. It was legally impossible to charge a husband with raping his wife because it would imply that the husband was raping himself. Although the Married Women's Property Act of 1848 allowed women to own and inherit property, the other constraints on their lives remained intact through the twentieth century. Even with the passage of these property acts, however, the law allowed the husband to control community property (jointly owned legally by husband and wife) until the 1970s.

Prior to the 1960s most states decriminalized violence in the family and operated marital rape exemption laws. It was not until the 1980s and 1990s that women had legal protections against violence; these protections include legislation such as the rape shield laws, mandatory arrest procedures in cases of domestic violence, public notification programs about convicted sex offenders in communities, the creation of protective or temporary restraining orders, state rape reform laws, and the 1994 Violence Against Women Act. Also prior to the 1960s, women's reproductive lives were a function of state control because the state had criminalized access to contraceptive information and procedures. As discussed in Chapter 6, before the passage of *Griswold v. Connecticut* in 1965, women had no legal right to contraceptives, and before the early 1970s with the passage of state abortion rulings and *Roe v. Wade*,

NO GIRLS

"Ub, oh, Regina has her lawyer with her . . ."

they had no legal right to an abortion. The issue of reproductive rights is still controversial, and the legal arena is the site for many of these battles today, especially in the area of parental notification and consent.

In terms of work and employment, *Muller v. Oregon* in 1908 reaffirmed the state's justification for limiting women's employment. This legislation approved Oregon's right to prevent women from working in factories or similar facilities for more than 10 hours a day based on the state's interest in protecting the reproductive functions of women. It was considered important for the "well-being of the race" that women's

Women in Elective Office

Visit the site of the Center for American Women in Politics at *www.rci.rutgers. edu/~cawp*. Follow the link to "Facts and Findings" and select "Women in Statewide Elective Office" from the pull-down menu to discover which women currently hold elective office in the United States. Next use the pull-down menu to discover who are the women of color currently in elective office. What elective positions do women in your state hold?

IDEAS FOR ACTIVISM

- Visit the home page for Women Leaders Online at *www.wlo.org.* Women Leaders Online (WLO) is the first and largest women's activist group on the Internet. WLO provides action alerts to make people aware of issues that need activism. The organization also promotes voter education and facilities e-mail access to your U.S. senators and representatives.
- For more information about political issues of concern to women, visit the home page of the Feminist Majority Foundation at *www.feminist.org.* Follow the link to "Take Action" for ideas about what you can do to make a difference.

ability to contract freely be limited. As discussed in Chapter 8, by the 1960s various civil rights legislation was passed including the Equal Pay Act and Title VII, preventing employers from discriminating against women and people of color in employment. Affirmative action legislation of the 1970s and sexual harassment legislation of the 1980s further attempted to dismantle gender- and race-based inequities in the labor force. Challenges remain in this area, however, as systems of inequality still shape labor force experiences.

The state also affects women through the institution of marriage. Women had access to divorce in the nineteenth century, although divorce was much more difficult to obtain. In addition, divorce carried a considerable stigma, especially to the divorced wife. Prior to the advent of no-fault divorce in the 1970s (divorce on demand by either or both parties), partners had to sue for divorce. Grounds to sue were based on a spouse's violation of the marriage contract such as by cruelty, abandonment, or adultery, and the courts needed to prove that someone had committed a crime. This procedure was difficult and expensive for women; it also tended to involve a double standard of behavior based on gender. Nonetheless, because this procedure allowed wives to show that husbands were "guilty," wives might receive relatively generous compensation. With the advent of no-fault divorce, this has changed because no one is charged with blame.

Likewise, *alimony,* the payment that women have traditionally received as compensation for their unpaid roles as wives and mothers, has been reduced or eliminated through various legislation since 1970. Although eliminating alimony indicates a more gender-neutral situation where women are not simply viewed as dependent wives and mothers and may even have higher earnings than the husband, it has caused problems. This is because despite the gender-neutral language and intentions, society is stratified along gender, and women still tend to be financially subordinate to men. Although financial loss after divorce is significant for both men and women, women continue to bear the brunt of a breakup financially. This is because women tend to have lower salaries and therefore have less to live on, and also because women are more likely to have custody of children and endure more financial costs associated with single parenting. Financial hardship is often exacerbated by court-mandated child support that does not get paid to women. Some states have enforced legislation to track errant child-support monies and enforce payment.

Affirmative Action: Myth Versus Reality

MYTH: Women don't need affirmative action any more.

REALITY: Though women have made gains in the last 30 years, they remain severely underrepresented in most nontraditional professional occupations as well as blue-collar trades. The U.S. Department of Labor's Glass Ceiling Commission Report (1995) states that although White men are only 43 percent of the Fortune 2000 workforce, they hold 95 percent of the senior management jobs.

MYTH: Under affirmative action, minorities and women receive preferences.

REALITY: Affirmative action does not require preferences, nor do women and minorities assume that they will be given preference. Race, gender, and national origin are factors that can be considered when hiring or accepting qualified applicants, which is similar to the preferences given to veterans in hiring and to children of alumni in college admissions.

MYTH: Affirmative action is really quotas.

REALITY: Affirmative action provides women and minorities with full educational and workplace opportunities. Race, national origin, and gender are among several factors to be considered, but relevant and valid job or educational qualifications are not to be compromised. Further, the Supreme Court has made clear that affirmative action or programs that claim to be affirmative action are illegal if (1) an unqualified person receives benefits over a qualified one; (2) numerical goals are so strict that the plan lacks reasonable flexibility; (3) the numerical goals bear no relationship to the available pool of qualified candidates and could therefore become quotas; (4) the plan is not fixed in length; or (5) innocent bystanders are impermissibly harmed.

MYTH: Affirmative action leads to reverse discrimination.

REALITY: Evidence demonstrates that reverse discrimination is rare. For example, of the 91,000 employment discrimination cases before the Equal Employment Opportunities Commission, approximately 3 percent are reverse discrimination cases. Further, a study conducted by Rutgers University and commissioned by the U.S. Department of Labor (1995) found that reverse discrimination is not a significant problem in employment and that a "high proportion" of claims brought by White men are "without merit."

MYTH: Affirmative action programs that aid the economically disadvantaged—needs-based programs—are enough to address discrimination.

REALITY: Women and minorities face discrimination as they climb the corporate ladder and bump up against the glass ceiling.

MYTH: Unqualified individuals are being hired and promoted for the sake of diversity/affirmative action.

REALITY: Only affirmative action plans that do not compromise valid job or educational qualifications are lawful. Plans must be flexible, realistic, reviewable, and fair. The Supreme Court has found that there are at least two permissible bases for voluntary affirmative action by employers under Title VII: (1) to remedy a clear and convincing history of past discrimination by the employer or union, and (2) to cure a manifest imbalance in the employer's workforce.

MYTH: Affirmative action does not have a place in government contracts.

(continued)

REALITY: Congress has created federal procurement programs to counter the effects of discrimination that have raised artificial barriers to the formation, development, and utilization of businesses owned by disadvantaged individuals, including women and minorities. Only qualified businesses can participate in these procurement programs. These programs are still needed because although minorities own almost 9 percent of all businesses and women own 34 percent of all businesses, together minorities and women receive only about 8.8 percent of the over $200 billion in federal contract awards.

MYTH: Title VII alone is sufficient to address discrimination.

REALITY: Affirmative action means taking positive, proactive, and preemptive steps to root out discrimination, rather than waiting for after-the-fact litigation. Title VII addresses discrimination, but it does so only after an instance of discrimination has been claimed. Affirmative action policies are a means to end discrimination in a far less costly and disruptive way than protracted litigation.

MYTH: Underrepresentation of minorities and women in the corporate world (or other high-paying jobs) is not due to discrimination.

REALITY: Although discrimination is not the sole reason for the lack of women and minorities in the corporate world, we must still deal with past and present discrimination. A study of the 1982 Standard MBA graduating class found that in 1992, 16 percent of the men held CEO titles compared to 2 percent of the women. Twenty-three percent of men become corporate vice presidents, but only 10 percent of the women, whereas 15 percent of men served as directors, compared to 8 percent of the women.

MYTH: The so-called earnings gap between men and women has closed significantly in recent years; therefore, affirmative action is no longer needed to achieve pay equity.

REALITY: In 1993, the total amount of wages women lost due to pay inequity was nearly $100 billion. The average woman loses approximately $420,000 over a lifetime due to unequal pay practices. Working women still earn just 76 cents for every dollar men earn. Much of this wage gap is due to the fact that women are still segregated into traditionally female-dominated jobs where wages are low. Further, the pay gap exists even within the same occupation. In 86 occupations tracked by the Bureau of Labor Statistics, women earn 20 to 35 percent less than men.

MYTH: Most analyses that point to wage differentials between men and women do not take into account differences in hours worked and years of uninterrupted work experience between the sexes. Female earnings are depressed because women work, on average, fewer hours per week than men and have more interruptions over their working lives than do men.

REALITY: The wage inequities most often cited are based on Department of Labor and Census Bureau data on year-round, full-time workers who have a permanent attachment to the workforce. These data do not compare full-time male workers to part-time female workers, nor do they compare permanent workers to part-time and contingent workers.

Source: www.civilrights.org/aa/mythreal.html.

PUBLIC POLICY

State policies determine people's rights and privileges, and, as a result, the state has the power to exclude groups, discriminate against groups, and create policies in favor of groups. By maintaining inequality, the state reflects the interests of the dominant groups in society and supports policies that work in their interests and reinforce their power. Native Americans, for example, have suffered because of state policies that required forced relocation, and African Americans have been harmed by Jim Crow laws that helped enforce segregation in the South and prevented African Americans from voting. There were miscegenation laws in the United States that prevented interracial marriage and aimed to maintain racial purity and superiority, and many states instigated laws that prevented African Americans from residing in certain communities and/or being in a town after sundown. Some of these laws were still on the books into the late twentieth century.

An example of how policy reinforces systems of inequality is seen in lesbian and gay plaintiffs who are in the court system for child custody, contract, or property disputes. It is also evident in current discussions concerning gay marriage and civil unions. Homophobia in the system tends to work against gays and lesbians. As discussed in Chapter 7, the Defense of Marriage Act (DOMA), which allows states not to recognize gay unions performed in other states, prevents lesbians and gay men from enjoying the privilege of state recognition of marriage, although currently there are several states that recognize these unions.

Welfare policy is especially illustrative of the ways the state is a conduit for the perpetuation of systems of inequality. Poverty in the United States is powerfully structured by racial and gender inequities, and patterns of income and wealth are strongly skewed along these lines. Ideologies (recall from Chapter 2 that these are sets of beliefs that support institutions in society) about who is deserving of wealth rely on the individualistic notion that success is a result of hard work and ambition; thus, anyone who works hard and pushes him- or herself will succeed economically. The corollary of this, of course, is that the fault associated with lack of economic success rests with the individual. This was referred to in Chapter 2 as the bootstrap myth. This myth avoids looking at structural aspects of the labor force and social systems that perpetuate classism and instead focuses on the individual. It helps explain the stigma associated with welfare in the United States and the many stereotypes associated with women on welfare—that they are lazy, cheat the system, and have babies to increase their welfare check. Women on welfare often face a triple whammy: they are women facing lower-paid work, they are mothers and have domestic responsibilities and childcare expenses, and they are single with only one paycheck. Indeed, if women earned as much as comparable men, then single women generally would see a rise in their incomes and a substantial drop in poverty rates. If we applied this comparable situation to single mothers, poverty rates would be cut almost in half, from 25 percent to 13 percent. Having a job does not necessarily lift women out of poverty. Having a job does not also guarantee sufficient retirement income, as the contemporary debate on Social Security reveals. Women will be disproportionately affected by Social Security reforms, especially any possible privatization.

In 1996 the passing of the Personal Responsibility and Work Opportunity Rec-onciliation Act (PRWORA) terminated the major source of welfare, Aid to Families with Dependent Children (AFDC), and replaced it with Temporary Assistance to Needy Families (TANF). Critics of this and other policies of the 1990s have argued that not only have such policies failed to make low-income families self-sufficient, but they have kept wages low and undermined women's independence. The Welfare Reform Bill of 2002 raises the number of hours mothers receiving welfare have to work outside the home, study, or be involved in training, from 30 to 40 hours at the same time that daycare in most states is totally inadequate. President George W. Bush has also attempted to provide incentives for women to marry as a strategy for reduc-ing welfare costs. Communities of color experience some of the most devastating consequences of poverty, and welfare "reform" has increased the vulnerability of individuals (especially single mothers and children) in these communities. Sharon Hays writes of the inadequacies of welfare reform in "Flat Broke with Children" and focuses on the cultural logic of personal responsibility.

A most obvious example of policies working to favor dominant groups is the practice often called "wealthfare," "welfare for the rich," or "aid to dependent cor-porations" (a play on words regarding AFDC) by some scholars. These policies reflect the ties political leaders have to the economic system and the ways the government subsidizes corporations and reduces taxes and other payments to the state for some corporations and businesses. Wealthfare involves five major types: direct grants; allowing publicly funded research and development to be used free by private for-profit corporations; discounted fees for public resources (such as grazing fees on public land); tax breaks for the wealthy; and corporate tax reductions and loopholes. It has been estimated that more than $200 billion in corporate welfare could be saved over the next 5 years if policies reining in these favors were instigated. Neither Republican nor Democratic lawmakers want to do this because they fear losing donations to their respective parties.

THE CRIMINAL JUSTICE SYSTEM

The law can be defined as formal aspects of social control that determine what is permissible and what is forbidden in a society. The courts are created to maintain the law through adjudicating conflicts that may be unlawful and deciding punish-ments for people who have broken the law. The role of the police is to enforce these laws and keep public order. Prisons are responsible for punishing those who have broken the law and protecting society from people who have committed crimes. All these fit together to maintain the control of the state.

Although women are especially likely to be victims of certain crimes, such as rape and battering, they constitute a small proportion of people arrested for crimes (about 20 percent) and a smaller number of those who are sent to prison (about 7 percent of prisoners are female). Women of color are overrepresented as prison inmates. These figures are related to gendered forms of behavior that encourage more males into violence and risk-related activities as well as the perception by crim-inal justice officials that women (especially White women) are less dangerous than men. Among men, poor men and men of color are more likely to be considered a

Women in Prison

- In 2003, 101,179 women were in prison.
- The number of women prisoners increased 3.6 percent in 2003 (men increased by 2.0 percent).
- By the end of 2003, women accounted for 6.9 percent of all prisoners, up from 6.1 percent in 1995.
- Since 1995, the number of women prisoners has grown 48 percent.
- The largest number of women prisoners were held in Texas (13,487), followed by the federal system (11,635) and California (10,656). Together these three jurisdictions accounted for over a third of women prisoners.
- Mississippi, Oklahoma, and Louisiana had the highest incarceration rates for women. Rhode Island, Massachusetts, Maine, and New Hampshire had the lowest.
- White women in prison numbered 39,107, Black women 35,050, and Latinas 16,172.
- Black women are twice as likely as Latinas and nearly five times more likely than White women to be in prison.

Source: Bureau of Justice Statistics Bulletin, "Prisoners in 2003," November 2004.

danger to society and tend to receive the longest sentences. The highest levels of incarceration are among young African American males. Robin Templeton writes about this incarceration, its consequences for communities, and the need to address the structural, socioeconomic causes of violence. She is active in a grassroots anti-incarceration movement to educate about and change criminal justice policy.

Nonetheless, the rate of crime committed by women has increased in recent years with the largest increase being drug-related criminal behavior. The Bureau of Justice Statistics reports that just under a half of all women (and a tenth of all men) in correctional facilities indicated physical and/or sexual abuse before their current sentence. A large number of these incidents occurred before the age of 18 years. Most of the homicides enacted by women involve male victims, and they are most likely to have taken place in the home, often in self-defense. Women are more likely to be first-time offenders than men, are less likely to use firearms, and are more likely to use kitchen knives and other household implements. This evidence again suggests that much female homicide is done in self-defense. Although prior to the 1980s women who killed in self-defense almost always lost their plea, today juries are more understanding of the experiences of battered women. Even so, it is still very difficult for women to convince a jury that they were being abused, and there are many women in prison suffering very long sentences for these acts. Defendants must meet two criteria for claiming justifiable homicide as self-defense that include reasonable fear or perception of danger such that killing was the only course of action to protect the defendant's life and the confrontation of the defendant with deadly force by the assailant. In addition, among men and women who kill in self-defense during a rape where the assailant is a man, men who kill are more likely to be acquitted than women who kill. Likewise, the crimes of passion that men commit on discovering an adulterous wife are viewed more sympathetically than when women kill adulterous men.

Another example of the double standard concerning women as victims is U.S. asylum law that provides protection for immigrants fleeing their country if they are being persecuted because of race, religion, nationality, political opinion, or membership in a social group. Although there have been important advancements in asylum law that have protected women fleeing abusive husbands and gays and lesbians who fear persecution in their country, protection for battered women under these circumstances is still difficult to obtain. Finally, all marginalized people (women and men) are at risk of being victimized by hate crimes: a constant problem in contemporary U.S. society.

THE MILITARY

The military, a branch of government that is constituted to defend against foreign and domestic conflict, is a central component of the state and political system. As mentioned in Chapter 2, the military has strong ties to the economic system through a military-industrial complex that supports industries that manufacture weapons. Military presence overseas, as well as wars fought in the United States, tend to be related to U.S. economic interests like the need for oil or control of other resources, including the need for political "stability" in nations to maintain global corporate endeavors. The Pentagon has connections to other branches of the state, especially the government and its representatives. The military is a very male-dominated arena, not only in terms of actual personnel who serve but in terms of the ways it is founded upon so-called masculine cultural traits like violence, aggression, hierarchy, competition, and conflict. The military uses misogynistic and homophobic attitudes to enforce highly masculine codes of behavior. Carol Burke addresses this transmission of military culture in the reading "Gender, Folklore, and Changing Military Culture."

Throughout most of history, women were not allowed to serve in the military except in such auxiliary forces as nursing. It was not until World War II that women who served in any military capacity were given formal status and not until 1976 that women were allowed into the military academies. In terms of race, the armed forces were officially segregated until 1948. Currently the percentage of military personnel who are people of color increased from 28 percent in 1995 to 38 percent in 2000. In 2003, 21 percent of military personnel were African American, compared to their distribution of 12 percent in the general population. These figures are disproportionate compared to the general population and reflect the lack of opportunities for people of color in the civilian realm. Despite their relative high numbers of service, people of color are less likely than Whites proportionately to be found in leadership positions. This is true for women of all races as well.

In 1981 the Supreme Court reaffirmed that it is constitutional to require registering men but not women for the draft. Men at this point are subject to conscription if a draft is in process and women are not, although women are allowed to serve if they wish. The rationale for the 1981 decision centered on the fact that women were not allowed in combat positions, although it also involved the notion that

Women in the Military

Women have served in the U.S. armed forces since 1901, when the Army Nurse Corps was established. Currently, 350,000 women serve in the U.S. military, almost 15 percent of active duty personnel. Milestones affecting women:

1967   Military abolishes 2 percent cap on women serving in the armed forces.

1973   Draft ends. Armed forces seek more women.

1976   Women admitted to service academies.

1978   Women allowed permanent assignment to Navy support ships.

1981   U.S. Supreme Court rules that excluding women from the draft is constitutional.

1991   About 41,000 women are sent to the Gulf War. Five die from hostile fire.

1993   Defense Secretary Les Aspin orders combat aviation and combat surface ships opened to women.

1994   Rule changes open more than 80,000 Army and Marine positions to women. Combat assignments to infantry, armor, artillery, and special operations remain off-limits.

PERCENTAGE OF WOMEN IN MILITARY BRANCHES

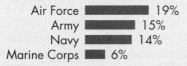

Air Force   19%
Army   15%
Navy   14%
Marine Corps   6%

PERCENTAGE OF MILITARY POSITIONS OPEN TO WOMEN

Air Force   99%
Navy   91%
Army   70%
Marine Corps   62%

NUMBER OF WOMEN WHO SERVED IN PREVIOUS CONFLICTS

World War I	33,000	Persian Gulf	41,000
World War II	400,000	Somalia	1,000
Korean War	120,000	Haiti	1,200
Vietnam	7,000	Bosnia	13,935
Grenada	170	Kosovo	5,660
Panama	770		

Source: Defense Department, Women's Research and Education Institute. By Suzy Parker, USA TODAY.

women have responsibilities in the home and family. After women's service in the Gulf War in 1991, the pressure was on for President Clinton in 1993 to order a repeal of the ban on women in combat positions, and now most Navy and Air Force positions are open to women. The Army and Marines still prevent women from combat positions in field artillery, armor, infantry, submarines, and special units, although they are allowed service as pilots, supply officers, drivers, fuel handlers, interpreters, checkpoint workers, medics, and so on. In addition, as their service in the Iraq War has shown, although women are assigned to rear units, they are often temporarily assigned to combat units. Overall, 2005 figures from the Pentagon show that women make up 15 percent of the U.S. armed forces (see the box on p. 633 for percentages of women in various military branches), approximately 45 percent of whom are women of color. Like men of color, women of color are also overrepresented in the armed forces. Despite current legislation attempting to limit their role in direct combat, in 2005 approximately 22,000 women made up 13 percent of military personnel serving in Iraq. About 45 percent of these women serving in Iraq are mothers and almost 50 percent are women of color.

In recent years the treatment of women in the military has received considerable public attention, at the same time that sexualized violence and harassment of women has been recognized as a widespread problem within the U.S. armed services. Take, for example, the story of Shannon Faulkner, who attempted to attend the all-male military academy the Citadel. Even though a court demanded the Citadel accept women, it still is a very inhospitable place for women cadets. Similarly, in 1991 the Tailhook scandal revealed that in this gathering of high-ranking Navy flying personnel, considerable sexual harassment had been an ongoing practice. The report from the Defense Department described men wearing t-shirts with inscriptions like "Women Are Property" as well as engaging in rowdy and misogynous behavior. A 1997 Army report found widespread harassment aimed at women personnel. Sexual assault reports involving members of the military rose to 1,700 in 2004, up from the previous two years, according to Pentagon statistics. Of these cases, 75 percent included a service member as a victim and 77 percent as an alleged offender. The Pentagon reports that in the combat operations of Afghanistan and Iraq through February 2004, 112 incidents of rape, assault, and other forms of sexual misconduct were reported. Pressed by anti-violence and women's advocacy groups, the Pentagon established a task force in 2004 to study the problems of sexualized violence in the military. Carol Burke discusses these issues in her article on military culture.

Finally, the military has a long history of homophobia that has included the execution, persecution, and dismissal of gay soldiers. Although polls consistently show strong support for removing the current anti-gay ban (in a 2003 Gallup poll, 79 percent polled were in favor and that included 91 percent of 18- to 29-year-olds and 68 percent of those over 65 years old), arguments in favor of such prejudice mirror those proposing racial segregation in earlier times. These include: The morale and fighting spirit of military personnel will drop if openly gay and lesbian personnel are present, and gays and lesbians pose a national security threat. Through the 1980s, more than 15,000 military personnel were discharged because of homosexuality. By the mid-1990s President Clinton had created the "don't ask, don't tell" policy. It was supposed to be a compromise, although it has few supporters.

Women in Black: For Justice, Against War

Perhaps you've seen them—a small group of women dressed in black standing silently on a street corner or in some other public place and perhaps on your campus. They are Women in Black, part of a global network of women advocating for peace and opposing injustice, war, militarism, and other forms of violence. Women in Black began in Israel in 1988, as Israeli women stood in weekly vigils to protest the Israeli occupation of the West Bank. They did not chant or march. Rather, they stood at a busy intersection with a simple sign that read "Stop the Occupation." Bypassers shouted at them, calling them "whores" and "traitors." They did not shout back but maintained a silent dignity. Eventually, Women in Black vigils were organized around the world to support the women in Israel. As war came to Croatia and Bosnia in 1992, Women in Black groups began to oppose the violence there. And so the movement has continued to spread as women around the world have responded to war. In both the Gulf War and the wars in Afghanistan and Iraq, women across the globe and in the United States have stood in protest. Any group of women anywhere can hold a Women in Black vigil against any form of violence, militarism, or war. Women in Black also engage in nonviolent and nonaggressive action—blocking roads or entering military bases. To find out if there is already a vigil in your area or to learn how to start your own vigil, visit *www.womeninblack.org*.

Discharges are still allowed under the policy, and, as one study reports, dismissals increased after the initiation of the policy. In addition, lesbians were disproportionately discharged. In this way, the government policy on lesbians and gays in the military illustrates how the state has differential effects on some groups compared to others.

The state is a very powerful institution that has enormous effects upon women's everyday lives. It is important to understand how gender, race, and class mold and shape government, law, and policy, and how these institutions reflect and promote the needs of some groups over others.

Constitutional Argument

Susan B. Anthony (1898)

Friends and Fellow-Citizens:—I stand before you under indictment for the alleged crime of having voted at the last presidential election, without having a lawful right to vote. It shall be my work this evening to prove to you that in thus doing, I not only committed no crime, but instead simply exercised my citizen's right, guaranteed to me and all United States citizens by the National Constitution beyond the power of any State to deny.

Our democratic-republican government is based on the idea of the natural right of every individual member thereof to a voice and a vote in making and executing the laws. We assert the province of government to be to secure the people in the enjoyment of their inalienable rights. We throw to the winds the old dogma that government can give rights. No one denies that before governments were organized each individual possessed the right to protect his own life, liberty and property. When 100 or 1,000,000 people enter into a free government, they do not barter away their natural rights; they simply pledge themselves to protect each other in the enjoyment of them through prescribed judicial and legislative tribunals. They agree to abandon the methods of brute force in the adjustment of their differences and adopt those of civilization. Nor can you find a word in any of the grand documents left us by the fathers which assumes for government the power to create or to confer rights. The Declaration of Independence, the United States Constitution, the constitutions of the several States and the organic laws of the Territories, all alike propose to *protect* the people in the exercise of their God-given rights. Not one of them pretends to bestow rights.

All men are created equal, and endowed by the Creator with certain inalienable rights. Among these are life, liberty and the pursuit of happiness. To secure these, governments are instituted among men, deriving their just powers from the consent of the governed.

Here is no shadow of government authority over rights, or exclusion of any class from their full and equal enjoyment. Here is pronounced the right of all men, and "consequently," as the Quaker preacher said, "of all women," to a voice in the government. And here, in this first paragraph of the Declaration, is the assertion of the natural right of all to the ballot; for how can "the consent of the governed" be given, if the right to vote be denied? Again:

> Whenever any form of government becomes destructive of these ends, it is the right of the people to alter or abolish it, and to institute a new government, laying its foundations on such principles, and organizing its powers in such form, as to them shall seem most likely to effect their safety and happiness.

Surely the right of the whole people to vote is here clearly implied; for however destructive to their happiness this government might become, a disfranchised class could neither alter nor abolish it, nor institute a new one, except by the old brute force method of insurrection and rebellion. One-half of the people of this nation today are utterly powerless to blot from the statute books an unjust law, or to write there a new and a just one. The women, dissatisfied as they are with this form of government, that enforces taxation without representation—that compels them to obey laws to which they never have given their consent—that imprisons and hangs them without a trial by a jury of their peers—that robs them, in marriage, of the custody of their own persons, wages and children—are this half of the people who are left wholly at the mercy of the other half, in direct violation of the spirit and letter of the declarations of the framers of this government, every one of which was based on the immutable principle of equal rights to all. By these declarations, kings, popes, priests, aristocrats, all were alike dethroned and placed on a common level, politically, with the lowliest born subject or serf. By them, too, men, as such, were deprived of their divine right to rule and placed on a political level with women. By the practice of these declarations all class and caste distinctions would be abolished, and slave, serf, plebeian, wife, woman, all alike rise from their subject position to the broader platform of equality.

The preamble of the Federal Constitution says:

We, the people of the United States, in order to form a more perfect union, establish justice, insure domestic tranquillity, provide for the common defence, promote the general welfare and secure the blessings of liberty to ourselves and our posterity, do ordain and establish this Constitution for the United States of America.

It was we, the people, not we, the white male citizens, not we, the male citizens; but we, the whole people, who formed this Union. We formed it not to give the blessings of liberty but to secure them; not to the half of ourselves and the half of our posterity, but to the whole people—women as well as men. It is downright mockery to talk to women of their enjoyment of the blessings of liberty while they are denied the only means of securing them provided by this democratic-republican government—the ballot. . . .

R E A D I N G **89**

Unequal
A Global Perspective on Women Under the Law

Jessica Neuwirth

Around the world, real discrimination against women persists—much of it in blatant, tolerated, *legal* form. Why? It makes no sense. The right to equality has been affirmed repeatedly, in international law, national constitutions and various treaties. Name them: the Universal Declaration of Human Rights, the International Covenant on Civil and Political Rights, the Convention on the Elimination of All Forms of Discrimination Against Women (CEDAW)—all provide for equality before the law and equal protection. The Beijing Platform for Action, adopted at the 1995 United Nations Fourth World Conference on

Women, states the need to "ensure equality and nondiscrimination under the law and in practice" and to "revoke any remaining laws that discriminate on the basis of sex."

It sounds good. But the reality on the ground, in cities and villages, homes and schools, and even in the courts, is quite different. Many discriminatory laws still relate to family law, limiting a woman's right to marry, divorce, and remarry, and allowing for such marital practices as polygamy. Mali, Sudan, and Yemen are among countries with laws still mandating "wife obedience" in marital relations. Sudan's 1991 Muslim Personal Law Act provides that a husband's rights include being "taken care of and amicably obeyed" by his wife. Yemen's 1992 Personal Status Act even enumerates the elements of wife obedience, including requirements that a wife "must permit him [her husband] to have licit intercourse with her," that she "must obey his orders," and that "she must not leave the conjugal home without his permission."

But if you think blatant legal discrimination is a problem only in Muslim societies and/or developing countries, think again. Many nations, including the United States, explicitly discriminate on the basis of sex in the transmission of citizenship: to children, depending on the sex of the parent, and/or through marriage, depending on the sex of the spouse. The U.S. law—which gives children born abroad and out of wedlock differing rights to citizenship, depending on whether their mothers or fathers are U.S. citizens—was upheld by the Supreme Court in 2001: Children of U.S. mothers have a lifetime right to citizenship, while children of U.S. fathers (including all those GIs stationed overseas) must take legal steps, before turning 18, to claim citizenship.

In its 5–4 decision, the Court held that the law was justified on the basis of two governmental interests: "assuring a biological parent-child relationship exists" and a "determination to ensure that the child and the citizen parent have some demonstrated opportunity or potential to develop . . . a relationship that . . . consists of the real, everyday ties that provide a connection between child and citizen parent, and, in turn, the United States." The majority opinion, authored by Justice Anthony M. Kennedy, did not address the fact that such a relationship was arbitrarily required by law for U.S. citizen fathers but not U.S. citizen mothers. In the dissent, Justice Sandra Day O'Connor noted, "Indeed, the majority's discussion may itself simply reflect the stereotype of male irresponsibility that is no more a basis for the validity of the classification than are stereotypes about the 'traditional' behavior patterns of women."

Other "personal status" laws that discriminate on the basis of sex range from the denial of women's right to vote in Kuwait to the prohibition against women driving in Saudi Arabia. Inheritance and property laws are also key areas where discrimination exists. Lesotho's laws provide that "no immovable property shall be registered in the name of a woman married in community of property." Chile's Civil Code mandates that "the marital partnership is to be headed by the husband, who shall administer the spouses' joint property as well as the property owned by his wife." Until 2002, the law in Nepal was that daughters had the right to a share of family property only if they were at least 35 years old and unmarried; after years of effort, the Nepali Women's Movement succeeded in amending the law—but just in part: Now, daughters are born with the same right to family property as are sons, but the law requires women to *return* any such property upon marriage.

In many countries, criminal offenses—their definitions as well as rules governing admissible evidence—are explicitly sex-discriminatory. In Pakistan, for example, written legal documents concerning financial obligations must be attested to by two men, or by one man and two women. In rape cases there, four Muslim adult males must testify to witnessing the rape; there is no provision for testimony from female witnesses. Marital rape is explicitly excluded from rape laws in many nations—for example, India, Malaysia, and Tonga. Ethiopia, Lebanon, Guatemala, and Uruguay exempt men from penalty for rape—if they subsequently marry their victims. Northern Nigeria's penal code notes that assault is not an offense if inflicted "by a husband for the purpose of correcting his wife" so long as it "does not amount to the infliction of grievous hurt." And in cases of so-called honor killings, men who murder their wives are exempt from punishment by law in Syria, Morocco, and Haiti. In Jordan, a campaign against "honor" killings did change the law—but only to make it gender neutral, exempting any spouse from punishment for an "honor" killing. Since virtually all such killings are perpetrated by men, this amendment removes the appearance of sex discrimination, not the discrimination itself.

Laws that explicitly discriminate are only the tip of the iceberg. The denial of equal opportunity in education and employment, exclusion from political representation, deprivation of sexual and reproductive rights, plus the use of social forces and physical violence to intimidate and subordinate women—all these are violations of the right to equality. In many countries, abortion is a criminal offense that burdens women with medical consequences, often fatal, of unsafely terminating a pregnancy. In some countries—the Philippines, for example—prostitution is a criminal offense for the prostituted female but not for the male customer. In virtually all countries, there are laws, policies, and practices that, though not explicitly discriminatory, in practice deny women equality. This in itself is illegal. Whenever laws perpetuate women's inequality—even when their language appears gender neutral—they constitute discrimination in violation of international norms.

In June 2000, a Special Session of the U.N. General Assembly reviewed implementation of the Beijing Platform, five years after its adoption. An Outcome Document was adopted, outlining achievements, obstacles, and further actions to be taken by governments and by the U.N. to implement the Platform. Paragraph 21 cites gender discrimination as one such obstacle to implementation of the Platform, noting that discriminatory legislation persists. It notes, too, that new laws discriminating against women have been introduced (in Nigeria, for example). The Document also provides that countries should review legislation "striving to remove discriminatory provisions as soon as possible, preferably by 2005." The preliminary draft had noted 2005 as an unequivocal target date for the elimination of discriminatory laws; the final document reflects a compromise, with the target date stated as a preference. Elimination of such laws doesn't require financial expenditure. It requires political will, in the form of a legislative act. This political will is obviously absent; the very notion of setting a target date five years into the future—merely to remove explicitly discriminatory legal provisions—was hotly contested at the General Assembly Special Session.

Still, there has been progress. A number of countries have repealed discriminatory laws since the adoption of the 1995 Beijing Platform for Action. Venezuela adopted a new constitution that removed discriminatory citizenship provisions. Mexico rescinded a law that required a woman to wait 300 days from the dissolution of marriage before remarrying. Turkey rescinded a law that designated the husband as the head of a marital union, responsible for all family savings. Papua New Guinea removed the exemption of marital rape from its definition of rape, and Costa Rica removed the exemption from punishment for rapists who subsequently married their victims. Switzerland amended a law that had barred women in the military from using arms other than for self-defense, thus opening all military functions/responsibilities to women. In 2001 (after threat of financial sanctions from the European Commisson), France rescinded a law prohibiting women from night employment in industrial "workplaces of any nature, be they public or private, civil or religious, even if such establishments are for the purpose of professional education or charitable work."

Laws are changing. But the pace of change is lethargic, while the need for change is urgent. The substantial gap between the rhetoric and the reality of sex-equality rights indicates the lack of meaningful commitment to applicable treaty obligations and commitments governments have made. Public pressure can play a role in helping to overcome such lethargy. The diplomatic community can feel shame under pressure, and that itself is a powerful technique too rarely used by governments, themselves fearful of the same spotlight. NGOs, of course, continually work to shatter the silence. But until governments match their interest in setting standards with an interest in implementing the standards they set, the integrity of the legal process will remain a question. That there are any laws explicitly discriminating against women is unacceptable, and must be universally seen and acknowledged as such—even in the diplomatic corridors of the United Nations.

Flat Broke with Children

Sharon Hays

Most welfare mothers have not been activists for the rights of the poor. Some have joined or established poverty advocacy groups to publicly protest the Personal Responsibility Act. Others have individually lodged their complaints against changes in the system. But the majority of welfare mothers, like the majority of Americans, have expressed their support for the "end to welfare as we know it."[1]

Poor mothers' support for welfare reform is the single most striking indication that welfare mothers are not the social "outsiders" portrayed in the Personal Responsibility Act. Most welfare mothers share the core values of most Americans. They share a concern with contemporary problems in work and family life and a commitment to finding solutions—including the overhaul of the welfare system. The trouble is, welfare reform was founded on the assumption that welfare mothers do not share American values and are, in fact, personally responsible for *undermining* our nation's moral principles. The policies and procedures instituted by welfare reform have thus been aimed at "fixing" these women.

This paradoxical state of affairs raises questions of just who has the right to fix whom, and what, exactly, is broken and in need of repair. Still, the problems in work and family life that informed welfare reform are real problems that have impacted us all. Similarly, the broader moral principles implied in the cultural logic of reform—principles of independence, productivity, citizenship, strong families, community spirit, and obligations to others—are worthy and widely shared. Yet from the start, welfare reform was also plagued by cultural distortions, exclusionary stereotypes, and a narrowly drawn and internally inconsistent vision of what counts as the proper commitment to work, family, and nation. And the policies instituted by welfare reform have left the nation's poorest mothers in a position in which no matter how committed they are to the work ethic and family values, under current conditions, the majority will remain unable to achieve either the model of the happily married homemaker or the model of the successful supermom, just as the majority will remain unable to lift their families out of poverty.

The inadequacies of welfare reform clearly follow from structured inequalities in American society. But the inadequacies of welfare reform also follow from a serious problem in the cultural logic of personal responsibility itself.

The notion of personal responsibility denies the embeddedness of all individuals in the wider society and their reliance on it. It is an image of unfettered individualism—of every man, woman, and child as an island unto themselves. This logic most obviously neglects the "dependency" of children and the fact that no parent is "unfettered." It also neglects the importance, the reality, and the necessity of wider social ties and connections. It makes invisible, in other words, our interdependence.

It is this failure to take account of the full measure of our interdependence that allows for the construction of "us-versus-them" scenarios that not only demonize welfare recipients but also call into question the values and behaviors of all of us who find ourselves unable to mimic the mythological model of perfected self-reliance: seamlessly juggling our multiple commitments without ever needing to depend on our friends, our families, our neighbors, or the nation to support us. This individualistic logic similarly undergirds our privatization of the work of caring for others, leaving it hidden, undervalued, and inadequately supported. And this logic upholds the privatization of the labor market, leaving it insufficiently regulated by the public and allowing competitive, profit-seeking employers to ignore the existence of children, circumvent the minimum standards for sustenance, and exploit the most vulnerable among us.

All this explains why, in the long run, the Personal Responsibility Act will not be a law we can proudly hail as a national "success." Women, children, nonwhites, and the poor will be hardest hit. But the consequences of reform will leave nearly all of us losers, in economic, political, and moral terms. To make sense of this and to examine how the road to hell can, in fact, be paved with good intentions (or at least a mix of good intentions, harsh realities, and incomplete moral reasoning), let me begin again, with the principles and problems that initially prompted this massive change in law.

SHARED VALUES, SYMBOLIC BOUNDARIES, AND THE POLITICS OF EXCLUSION

In responding to welfare reform, the welfare mothers I met often offered a perfect mirror of the complex mix of higher values, genuine concerns, exclusionary judgments, and cultural distortions that informed the Personal Responsibility Act. One mother, Denise, captured nearly all these elements in her response, offering the full range of the more prominent patterns I encountered. A black woman with two daughters, at the time I met her Denise was recently employed at Mailboxes-R-Us for $6.50 an hour and was making ends meet with the help of welfare reform's (time-limited) income supplement, transportation vouchers, and childcare subsidy. This is what she had to say when I asked her for her overall assessment of reform:

> When I was younger, years ago, anybody could get on welfare. And I think that's what's good about welfare reform. People have to show some sort of

initiative. Before, the welfare office didn't pressure you to find a job, but now they do. And I think that's a good system. They've really helped me out a lot.

> Plus, I think people are sick of having to pay their tax money. They say, "Look, I am out here working, and I don't make that much money, and I have kids of my own. I'm tired of having to take care of your babies." People are getting upset and it's rightly so. I think it's rightly so.

> And lots of people abuse the system. You see it every day. A lot of people that you run into and a lot of people that live in your neighborhood—I mean a lot of people do hair and get paid in cash. And I hear about these people who had children just to get a welfare check, just because they didn't want to go out and work. I've seen women that's on welfare, they're looking good and their children look poorly. I see that happening.

> Some of them are lazy and don't want to work. I think that some just want to stay home with their kids. But then they should have thought about that before they had the children.

At this point in her argument, Denise had hit upon nearly all the concerns of hardworking Americans who conscientiously pay their taxes, raise their children, and struggle to make it all work. She had also hit upon nearly all the well-worn stereotypes of poor mothers—implicitly labeling them as welfare cheats, lazy couch potatoes, promiscuous breeders, and lousy parents. But Denise wasn't finished.

> I think some people on welfare are being greedy—taking away from people that are homeless, people that really need the help. I mean there are truly people out there *living* at the Salvation Army. I hear tell that there are people who can't get in those shelters because they're so full. And I think that's the sad part about it. Those women that don't really need welfare shouldn't be taking money away from the homeless.

> But there are gonna be problems. Like, there are women that want to go out there and get a job, but who's gonna watch their kids? And there are people who will still need that little extra help to pay the bills. So that's a glitch in the system.

And some of these women are already pregnant, and they're already poor, and they really do need the help. I think that we have to weigh things and maybe investigate a bit more. There are a lot of people that are disabled and need welfare; there are women who have been abused. Some of those people that are in a lot of trouble, you know, their kids are gonna be the ones you see on TV, shooting up the schools and everything.[2]

I know a lot of people say that this welfare reform is a good thing—and it is really gonna help a lot of people. But in the end things are probably gonna get worse. There's gonna be more crime 'cause people can't get on welfare and they're not gonna have any money and they're gonna go out and rob people, and kill people. And it happens, it happens. So that's a problem with the system.

If Denise had been responding to a national survey, "Do you approve of welfare reform?" her answer would simply be coded as a "yes." Yet you can't help noticing that she has a number of mixed feelings on this question.

This same sort of ambivalence is evident in Americans' response to welfare reform. Although most are positive about reform, the majority of Americans also say that they are "very" concerned about poverty. Most additionally believe that the national standards for poverty are set too low, stating that a family of four with an income of less than $20,000 is, in fact, "poor," even if the federal government does not label them as such. More significantly, a majority of Americans are in favor of further aid to the poor—including the expansion of job opportunities, tax credits, medical coverage, subsidies for childcare and housing, and the provision of better schools. Still, Americans worry about the government's ability to appropriately and effectively provide that aid, and many don't want to have to pay higher taxes to subsidize the poor.[3]

Denise is also much like most Americans in that the central moral categories she uses to frame her response are work and family values, independence and commitment to others, self-sufficiency and concern for the common good. Women should take the "initiative," they should work, they should not rely on the help of others, they should support their own children, they should think twice before they give birth to children they cannot afford to raise. At the same time, people should not be "greedy," they should care for those who are more vulnerable than themselves, and they should consider the impact of their actions on the nation as a whole. All this makes perfect sense, and all this resonates perfectly with our nation's values. The trouble is that managing these commitments is hard enough if you have a spouse, a house in the suburbs, two cars in the garage, good health insurance, reliable childcare, a willingness to make compromises, a great deal of determination, empathy, and energy, and a household income of $60,000. The more items on this list that you lack, the tougher it becomes to live up to this demanding system of values. Denise, like most Americans, implicitly understands these "glitches." Yet her reasoning becomes a bit cloudy at this point—in large measure, I would argue, because of the loophole provided by the final significant element in her response to welfare reform.

It is hard to miss that Denise's support for the Personal Responsibility Act is predicated on the construction of a moral distinction between herself and all those "other" bad welfare mothers who fail to live up to social standards. Denise is making use of what Michèle Lamont has called "symbolic boundaries" to develop an implicit hierarchy of social worth. Like most people who use this strategy, she is not simply engaging in a mean-spirited attack on others or a self-interested attempt to highlight her own virtues. These symbolic boundaries also allow her to positively affirm shared values and specify the proper way to live one's life.[4]

Yet, given that many observers consider Denise herself a member of the deviant group she describes, the fact that she and other welfare mothers persist in this technique is curious. It testifies not just to the power and ubiquity of boundary making as a social strategy, it also speaks to the power and ubiquity of the demonization of poor single mothers. When welfare mothers distinguish themselves from those other "bad" women, they are calling on widely disseminated negative images of welfare mothers. These images seem to match all those strangers, those loud neighbors, those people who appear to spend their lives hanging out on street corners. The lives of the women they actually know, on the other hand, seem much more complex, their actions more understandable, their futures more redeemable.

The demonization of welfare mothers and the dichotomy between "us" and "them" can thus provide a dividing line that allows Denise and other Americans to say, if some welfare mothers can't make it, it's not because the problems they encounter in trying to manage work and family and still keep their heads above water are that bad or that widespread; it's because they didn't try hard enough or weren't good enough. Symbolic boundaries thus become *exclusionary* boundaries—simultaneously offering a means to affirm shared values and a means to think of "outsiders" in terms of individual blame. The obvious problem, in Denise's case, is that her own logic might ultimately leave her as one of the "accused." In broader terms, this exclusionary process means that all those Americans who are suffering from childcare woes, second shifts, inadequate health insurance, precarious jobs, unmanageable debt, and unstable communities are left to feel that their problems are *personal* problems for which no public solutions can be found.

READING THE GOOD NEWS

In the months and years following welfare reform, newspaper headlines offered a seemingly unequivocal vision of success: "10,000 Welfare Recipients Hired by Federal Agencies." "Number on Welfare Dips Below 10 Million." "White House Releases Glowing Data on Welfare." "Businesses Find Success in Welfare-to-Work Program." "The Welfare Alarm That Didn't Go Off." "Most Get Work after Welfare."[5] The message was clearly upbeat, congratulatory. It seemed that one could almost hear the clucking sounds emanating from Capitol Hill.

Yet the newspapers also followed a second story, one more cautious and disturbing: "Most Dropped from Welfare Don't Get Jobs." "New York City Admits Turning away Poor." "Penalties Pushing Many Off Welfare." "Mothers Pressed into Battle for Child Support." "As Welfare Rolls Shrink, Load on Relatives Grows." "Welfare Policies Alter the Face of Food Lines."[6] The bigger picture, the one that could put a damper on all the celebrations, was carried in the stories behind these headlines. But overall, this reality seemed drowned out by the first story, the good news.

Given the inadequacies of the Personal Responsibility Act—the relentless bureaucracy, the sanctions, the unpaid work placements, the grossly insufficient childcare subsidies, the policies that operate at cross-purposes, and the genuine hardship suffered by current and former welfare recipients—why has welfare reform been deemed such a success? Part of the reason, as I've argued, is that the cultural message of reform has always been more important than its practical efficacy. A simpler answer is that the success of welfare reform has been measured by the decline of the welfare rolls. The trimming of the rolls from 12.2 million recipients at the start of reform to 5.3 million in 2001 is read as a sign that all those former welfare recipients are going to work, getting married, or otherwise taking care of themselves in the same (mysterious) way the poor have always taken care of themselves. But what, exactly, is behind the decline of the welfare rolls?

Financial success is clearly not the central reason that so many have left welfare. Although the booming economy of the 1990s had a crucial impact on welfare mothers' ability to get off the rolls and find some kind of work, even in that prosperous decade, the majority of former welfare recipients were not faring well. Between 1996 and 2000, the number of families living in desperate (welfare-level) poverty declined by only 15 percent, yet the number of welfare recipients declined by over half.[7] Although all the answers are not yet in, from the work of policy institutes, scholars, journalists, and my own research, I can piece together the following portrait. In the context of a highly favorable economy, the welfare rolls were cut in half for four central reasons:

1. More welfare clients were getting jobs more quickly than they did under the old system.
2. More poor families were being discouraged from using welfare than was true under AFDC.
3. More were leaving welfare faster and returning more slowly than they did in the past.
4. More welfare mothers were being sanctioned or otherwise punished off the welfare rolls.

The best news in all this is the number of welfare mothers who have found jobs. Nationwide, as I've noted, researchers estimate that approximately 60 percent of all the adults who left welfare since reform were working, at least part of the time, in 2002. This reality not only offered good news to the proponents of reform; it also offered, for a time at least, a real sense of hope to many welfare mothers. On the other hand, only half of the former welfare recipients who found work were actually making sufficient money to raise their families out of poverty. Only one-third were able to remain employed continuously for a full year. A good number would thus end up, at one time or another, among the 40 percent of former welfare recipients who had neither work nor welfare. Some of those would go back to the welfare office again and start the process anew: policy analysts suggest that over one-third of those who left since reform had already returned to welfare at least once by 2002. In any case, even among those who were employed during that prosperous decade, according to federal statistics their earnings averaged only $598 a month for the support of themselves and their children. Other researchers have estimated average hourly wages at $7.00 an hour and average annual earnings at between $8,000 and $10,800.[8]

. . .

The second group contributing to the decline of the welfare rolls is even less upbeat. This is the relatively invisible group of discouraged welfare clients—those poor mothers who have left or avoided welfare rather than face the increased stigma and the demanding "rigmarole" of rules and regulations that came with reform. This includes, first, all those mothers and children who never show up on any paperwork but have nonetheless been deeply affected by the law. These are the mothers who went to Sunbelt City's "diversionary workshop" and just headed back home without ever filling out an application. These are all the potential applicants in New York City and elsewhere who, by state rules, were not allowed to apply until they had completed their job search, many of whom simply never went back to the welfare office. These are also all those very poor families who have heard the stories on the streets and on the news and are now more reluctant to go to the welfare office than they were in the past. Finally, this group includes all the welfare clients who have filled out the forms, begun their job search, started the workshops, or taken a workfare placement, but then just stopped showing up—depressed, ill, angry, without childcare, without hope, unable or unwilling to meet the new standards. Some proportion of these women will eventually find jobs, and if they made it through the application process and if researchers are able to track them, they will be counted in the first category of "successes," working somewhere, for some period of time, for that $598 a month, no benefits.[9] For those who go long stretches without work or welfare, it is difficult to determine precisely how they and their children will survive (although I will speculate on their fate in a moment).

Once it becomes clear that welfare reform has resulted in both encouragement and discouragement, the third reason behind the decline of the rolls can be surmised. The Personal Responsibility Act has effectively transformed the process of "cycling." As I've noted, long before reform, most welfare clients cycled on and off the welfare rolls, moving between jobs and welfare. Now that welfare reform has instituted the "carrots" of supportive services and the "sticks" of time limits, sanctions, and work rules, the process of cycling has been altered—speeded up at the exiting end and slowed down at the return end. That is, poor mothers are now getting jobs or getting off welfare faster than they would have in the past, and they are also entering or returning to the welfare office more slowly and reluctantly. Given that welfare rolls are counted from moment to moment, on paper this speed up/slow down appears as an absolute decline in the welfare rolls.[10] It says nothing, however, about the health and well-being of poor mothers and their kids.

Finally, about one-quarter of welfare recipients are now sanctioned or denied benefits for failure to comply with welfare rules. . . . In one careful study of three major U.S. cities, 17 percent of clients had their benefits stopped or reduced as a result of sanctions or procedural penalties. In Wisconsin, the most carefully analyzed welfare program in the nation, 31 percent of the caseload was sanctioned in 1999, 21 percent in 2000. (Of those Wisconsin clients who had the wherewithal to appeal their cases, 70 percent of appeals were resolved in favor of clients, suggesting that many of these penalties were unfounded or improperly administered). . . .

These sanctioning practices, along with discouragement, faster cycling, and below-poverty wages explain why the number of welfare-eligible families who actually receive welfare benefits has fallen at a much faster pace than the rate of dire poverty. It is clear, in other words, that a substantial portion of desperately poor mothers and children are being punished, worn down, or frightened off the welfare rolls.

Putting it all together, in the context of a booming economy *more than two-thirds of the mothers and children who left welfare have either disappeared or are working for wages that do not meet federal standards for poverty.* At best, only 30 percent of the decline of the welfare rolls represents a "successful" escape from poverty—and many of those successes are only temporary, and many would have occurred with or without reform. The state of Wisconsin, marked as the most outstanding welfare program in the nation, matches these proportions precisely.[11]

In the meantime, there are still millions of poor women and children on welfare and hundreds of thousands coming in anew—or coming back again, unable to find or keep work or to establish some other means of survival under the terms of welfare reform. All of them are desperately poor.

. . .

Looking on the brighter side, welfare reform, and the money that came with it—the income supplements, childcare subsidies, bus vouchers, work clothing, and for the lucky ones, the new eyeglasses, the help in buying used cars or making a down payment on an apartment—has been truly helpful, improving the lives of many poor mothers and children, at least for a time. Further, in some cases reform has meant that mothers are getting *better* jobs than they would have in the past, thanks to the education and mentoring offered by some state welfare programs. As many as 10 to 15 percent of welfare mothers are in a better position now than they would have been had this law not been passed. Perhaps equally important, though harder to quantify, is the positive sense of hope and social inclusion that many recipients experienced (in the short term at least) as a result of the supportive side of welfare reform.

The number of families that have been genuinely helped by reform is neither insignificant nor superfluous. At a practical as well as moral level, the services and income supports offered by the Personal Responsibility Act have clearly been positive. Yet in the long run and in the aggregate, poor mothers and children are worse off now than they were prior to reform. Among those who are working and still poor, among those without work or welfare, and among those who are still facing constant and intense pressure to find work and figure out some way to care for their children, we can only guess what impact this law will have on their ability to retain hope over the long term. Even the U.S. Census Bureau (not anyone's idea of a bleeding heart organization) has found itself answering the question "Is work better than welfare?" in the negative, at least for those without substantial prior education and work experience.[12] With a slower economy and increasing numbers of poor families due to hit their time limits in coming years, there are reasons to expect that conditions will become increasingly difficult.

NOTES

1. See Abramovitz (1999) for welfare mothers' activism; see Public Agenda (2001), Wertheimer et al. (2001), Draut (2001), and Seccombe et al. (1999) for welfare mothers' opinions regarding welfare.
2. Denise is referring to then-prominent news stories on the Columbine school shooting and the other school shootings that followed.
3. See National Public Radio et al. (2001).
4. On symbolic boundaries, see Lamont (1992, 2000). For a connected, yet distinct, treatment of "moral boundaries," see Tronto (1993). For an analysis of the construction of welfare mothers as the "other" in the division between "us" and "them," see Gans (1995), Handler and Hasenfeld (1997).
5. In order, these newspaper articles are Pear (1999A), Pear (1998), Pear (1999B), Havemann and Vobejda (1998), Goldberg (1999).
6. In order, these newspaper articles are Hernandez (1998), Swarns (1999), Associated Press (1999), DeParle (1999A), Rivera (1997), Revkin (1999).
7. Dalaker (2000), Lamison-White (1997), Pear (2002).
8. See U.S. Department of Health and Human Services (1999A), Holzer and Stoll (2001), Acs and Loprest (2001), Moffit (2002).
9. Over 30 states nationwide either use diversionary programs or require prospective clients to complete specified work requirements *before* they may apply for benefits (Moffit 2002). See also Loprest (1999), Swarns (1999), and National Campaign for Jobs and Income Support (2001A, 2001B).
10. As noted, prior to reform, the process of cycling meant that the majority of welfare clients never stayed on welfare for longer than two years, though many would eventually return (e.g., Bane and Ellwood 1994; Harris 1993, 1996). There is no irrefutable statistical evidence to confirm or disconfirm my point regarding the speed up/slow down process caused by reform, though virtually all the larger trends suggest this reality, as did my experience in the welfare office.
11. See Wisconsin Joint Legislative Audit Committee (2001).
12. See Bauman (2000); Edin and Lein (1997) were the first to clearly demonstrate this point. Of course, the proponents of welfare reform disagree with this assessment. For a reasonable, careful, and well-informed positive assessment of reform, see Moffit (2002).

REFERENCES

Abramovitz, Mirni. 1999. "Toward a Framework for Understanding Activism Among Poor and Working-Class Women in Twentieth-Century America," pp. 214–248 in *Whose Welfare?* edited by Gwendolyn Mink. Ithaca, NY: Cornell University Press.

Acs, Gregory, and Pamela Loprest. 2002. *Initial Synthesis Report of the Findings from ASPE's "Leavers" Grants.* Washington, DC: Urban Institute.

Associated Press. 1999. "Penalties Pushing Many Off Welfare." *Poughkeepsie Journal,* March 29:A2.

Bane, Mary Jo, and David T. Ellwood. 1994. *Welfare Realities: From Rhetoric to Reform.* Cambridge, MA: Harvard University Press.

Bauman, Kurt J. 2000. *The Effect of Work and Welfare on Living Conditions in Single Parent Households.* U.S. Bureau of the Census, Population Division, Working Paper Series No. 46 (August). Washington, DC: U.S. Government Printing Office.

Dalaker, Joseph. 2001. *Poverty in the United States.* U.S. Census Bureau, Current Population Reports, Series P60-214. Washington, DC: U.S. Government Printing Office.

DeParle, Jason. 1999A. "As Welfare Rolls Shrink, Load on Relatives Grows." *New York Times,* February 21:A1.

Edin, Kathryn, and Laura Lein. 1997. *Making Ends Meet: How Single Mothers Survive Welfare and Low-Wage Work.* New York: Russell Sage Foundation.

Gans, Herbert J. 1995. *The War Against the Poor: The Underclass and Antipoverty Policy.* New York: Basic Books.

Goldberg, Carey. 1999. "Most Get Work After Welfare, Studies Suggest," *New York Times,* April 17:A1.

Handler, Joel F., and Yeheskel Hasenfeld. 1997. *We the Poor People: Work, Poverty, and Welfare.* New Haven, CT: Yale University Press.

Harris, Kathleen Mullan. 1993. "Work and Welfare Among Single Mothers in Poverty," *American Journal of Sociology* 99 (September): 317–352.

Harris, Kathleen Mullan. 1996. "Life after Welfare: Women, Work, and Repeat: Dependency." *American Sociological Review* 61 (June): 407–426.

Havemann, Judith, and Barbara Vobejda. 1998. "The Welfare Alarm that Didn't Go Off." *Washington Post,* October 1:A1.

Hernandez, Raymond. 1998. "Most Dropped from Welfare Don't Get Jobs." *New York Times,* March 23:A1.

Holzer, Harry J., and Michael A. Stoll. 2001. *Meeting the Demand: Hiring Patterns of Welfare Recipients in Four Metropolitan Areas*. Washington, DC: Brookings Institution.

Lamison-White, Leatha. 1997. *Poverty in the United States: 1996*. U.S. Bureau of the Census, Current Population Reports, Series P60-19B. Washington, DC: U.S. Government Printing Office.

Lamont, Michèle. 1992. *Money, Morals, and Manners*. Chicago: University of Chicago Press.

Lamont, Michèle. 2000. *The Dignity of Working Men: Morality and the Boundaries of Race, Class, and Immigration*. New York: Russell Sage Foundation.

Loprest, Pamela. 1999. *Families Who Left Welfare: Who Are They and How Are They Doing?* Washington, DC: Urban Institute.

Moffitt, Robert A. 2002. *From Welfare to Work: What the Evidence Shows*. Welfare Reform and Beyond: Policy Brief #13. Washington, DC: Brookings Institution.

National Campaign for Jobs and Income Support. 2001A. *A Recession Like No Other: New Analysis Finds Safety Net in Tatters as Economic Slump Deepens*. Washington, DC: National Campaign for Jobs and Income Support.

National Campaign for Jobs and Income Support. 2001B. *Leaving Welfare, Left Behind: Employment Status, Income, and Well-Being of Former TANF Recipients*. Washington, DC: National Campaign for Jobs and Income Support.

National Public Radio, Kaiser Family Foundation, and Kennedy School of Government. 2001. *Poverty in America*. Washington, DC: National Public Radio.

Pear, Robert. 1998. "Number on Welfare Dips Below 10 Million." *New York Times*, January 21:A12.

Pear, Robert. 1999A. "White House Releases Glowing Data on Welfare." *New York Times*, August 1:A12.

Pear, Robert. 1999B. "10,000 Welfare Recipients Hired by Federal Agencies." *New York Times*, March 1:A12.

Pear, Robert. 2002. "Governors Want Congress to Ease Welfare's Work Rule." *New York Times*, February 24.

Public Agenda. 2001. "Welfare: Public Opinion." http://www.publicagenda.org/issues.

Revkin, Andrew C. 1999. "Welfare Policies Alter the Face of Food Lines." *New York Times*, February 26:A1.

Rivera, Carla. 1997. "Mothers Pressed into Battle for Child Support." *Los Angeles Times*, March 24:A1.

Seccombe, Karen, Kimberly Battle Walters, and Delores James. 1999. "Welfare Mothers" Welcome Reform, Urge Compassion." *Family Relations* 48: 197–206.

Swarns, Rachel L. 1999. "New York City Admits Turning Away Poor." *New York Times*, January 22: B3.

Tronto, Joan C. 1993 [1994]. *Moral Boundaries: A Political Argument for an Ethic of Care*. New York: Routledge.

U.S. Department of Health and Human Services. 1999A. *Characteristics and Financial Circumstances of TANF Recipients*. Washington, DC: U.S. Government Printing Office.

Wertheimer, Richard, Melissa Long, and Sharon Vandivere. 2001. *Welfare Recipients' Attitudes Toward Welfare, Nonmarital Childbearing, and Work: Implications for Reform?* Series B, No. B-37. Washington, DC: Urban Institute.

Wisconsin Joint Legislative Audit Committee. 2001. *An Evaluation: Wisconsin Works (W-2) Program, Department of Workforce Development*. Madison, WI: Legislative Audit Bureau.

She Who Believes in Freedom
Young Women Defy the Prison Industrial Complex

Robin Templeton

In 2001 the prison population in the United States exceeded 2 million people, most of them illiterate, most under- or unemployed, most in jail for non-violent crimes, and a vast majority people of color. The gargantuan total of 6.5 million people in the United States are under some form of correctional supervision.[1]

Twenty-three-year-old Alicia Yang is trying to lower those numbers by dedicating her life to fighting the prison industrial complex. She says, "I know we need to build a fierce, strategic movement to deal with the prison crisis, but I also know we need to take care of people, to reach into people's hearts. We need to heal communities. Ultimately, we need to create a society that's based on redemption, a society that would refuse to allow 2 million people, most of them poor, to be locked up in cages."

Yang's cousin became one of the numbers when he got a life sentence in a California penitentiary. Like many young women who share her opposition to mass incarceration, Yang is driven by more than political analysis. She says she was reborn as an anti-incarceration activist because her cousin's imprisonment is like having part of her soul locked away. Then, shifting in her seat, she raises her voice and ebulliently describes visiting her cousin behind bars and getting to know some of the men with whom he's jailed: "They showed me the resiliency of the human spirit and allowed me—for the first time in my life—to really taste freedom."

How does freedom taste? "It's not like a flavor but a focus," Yang explains. "I examined my own life and started taking freedom very seriously. This fight against the prison industrial complex is a freedom struggle. Because prisons destroy and enslave life, the focus of our work against prisons has to be restoring life, liberating life."

Like slavery, that other "peculiar institution," prisons decimate life by stealing people from their communities, forcing families apart, and converting human beings into disposable parts that generate immense profit for private interests. The punishment sector has been one of the fastest-growing and most lucrative industries in the United States. Most prisoners do some form of work under repressive conditions and earn pennies per hour. Prisoners provide a pool of cheap labor that can be infinitely filled and exponentially enlarged. Eighteen private prison companies do business in the United States—Corrections Corporation of America and Wackenhut are the largest, operating eighty-one and fifty-two prisons respectively—and hundreds more corporations contract with publicly "owned" prisons to sell goods and services, usually at inflated, "captive market" prices. All the while, the institution perpetuates its legitimacy by criminalizing and bestializing the very lives it controls.

Yang's prison visits became for her an experience of restoring dignity and resurrecting hope in the face of a machine that dehumanizes life at a scale that is nearly—considering that African-American men have a greater than one in four chance of being incarcerated—genocidal. Visits with her cousin led Yang to teach in a prison-based adult education program. Subsequently, she started organizing on police and prison-related issues with an organization in Oakland called Asian American Youth Promoting Advocacy and Leadership. She explains, "We'd present workshops breaking down the prison industrial complex—using all the economic arguments about how much it costs to lock someone up and the terrible statistics about how many people of color are behind bars. But more and more, I just wanted to talk to people in my community about healing. I really wanted to stop and say: 'We won't be whole until we bring our sisters and brothers home from prison; until we learn to trust and forgive each other.'"

SISTERS AT THE CENTER OF THE PRISON CRISIS

In the tenacity of her convictions as well as in her vacillation on what is to be done about the prison industrial complex, Alicia Yang is not alone. A new generation of young people is at the forefront of grassroots organizing against mass incarceration in the United States. They are demanding accountability from law enforcement and corrections agencies that are rife with abuse. And they are organizing toward investing prison funds in rebuilding eviscerated social programs, especially schools, instead.

According to data compiled by the Prison Activist Resource Center, over the past twenty years, at the local, state, and federal levels, spending on incarceration has increased 571 percent while spending on K–12 education has risen only 33 percent. The number of prison guards has increased 250 percent while the number of K–12 teachers has dropped by 8 percent. And over the past two decades, while the number of students graduating from high school has dropped by 2.7 percent, the number of people filling the nation's prisons and jails has increased by over 400 percent.[2]

Because the vast majority of these prisoners are incarcerated for nonviolent offenses, young antiprison activists say that prisons should not be a default public works program. People living in poverty and facing structural racism should have their basic human needs met, should have access to good schools and jobs, and should get treatment, not punishment, if they develop an addiction. But while the activists' goal is to create a society in which the prison industrial complex is unnecessary, they know that violent crime is a pernicious reality and that members of their communities need to be protected from it. In response to critics who say that violent criminals must be kept off the street, activists who want to shut down the prison industrial complex say that the priority should be changing the socioeconomic conditions which create violence. When asked about the child murderers, rapists, and serial killers, these activists do not readily contend that these few members of the population should not be kept away from the public. But, they underscore, people convicted of violent offenses are only a small fraction of those in prison and are illegitimately used to justify the buildup of a massive industry. And, they remind their critics, one of the most violent demographic groups in the United States is white men in their thirties, a segment of the population grossly underrepresented in the prison system.

Today women in general and young women in particular are the fastest-growing segments of the prison population in the United States. The prison crisis is for young women of color and poor women a double-edged sword: They have to take care of families, pick up the broken pieces, and earn income when men are removed from their communities. And they are increasingly entangled in the criminal justice system themselves. Dozens of criminal justice organizers have told me that the harder the system clamps down on young women, the harder they fight back. By founding grassroots organizations or taking control of preexisting ones in their communities, advocating that social services meet their and their children's needs so that they do not end up in the criminal justice system, and creating new forms of cultural expression that challenge criminalization, young women are disproportionately assuming leadership in the nascent movement against the prison industrial complex.

Largely as a result of their foremothers' work, young women are redefining grassroots leadership by ensuring that everyone is given credit for her work behind the scenes, building organizations from the bottom up, and constantly cultivating new leadership. But the scale of the prison crisis is also drawing on and pulling out something deeper. Young women are determined to fight prisons but also—at the risk of sounding biologically deterministic—to nurture human beings.

. . .

MEET THE INCARCERATION GENERATION

Third wave feminists are the daughters of the "baby boomer" women's libbers of the 1960s and '70s. Those of us in the "third wave" are now in our twenties and thirties. The spike in prison construction in the United States began in our formative years, exactly coinciding with our maturation. The number of prison inmates in the United States quadrupled from 1980 to 2000, from 500,000 to 2 million.[3] During this time the U.S. population grew only 20 percent. California particularly dramatizes the prison boom of the last two decades of the twentieth century. In 1980 the state had twelve prisons. By 1998 it was home to thirty-three prisons but had constructed only one new state university.[4] In other words, young women have grown up with the biggest, most catastrophic prison boom in world history. Young women of color and low-income young women bring to the antiprison movement knowledge that they must respond not only to the social and economic conditions of those whose lives are torn apart by the powers that punish but also to their personal and spiritual needs.

America imprisons more human beings per capita than any country on the planet, with the exception of Rwanda. It costs about $41 billion a year for the United States to warehouse its 2 million prisoners.[5] Even adjusting for inflation, overall criminal justice spending has nearly doubled since the mid-1980s. And relative to population growth, per capita prison spending increased 69 percent, from $217 to $366, from 1983 to 1995.[6] These increases are irrational because exorbitant prison spending is throwing money at a problem that does not exist. The last time crime rates increased in the United States

was between 1965 and 1973. Since then general crime trends have been stable or declined. From 1991 to 1998, violent crime in the United States fell by 25 percent.[7]

Most of these tough-on-crime dollars are spent incapacitating people for nonviolent offenses. Over the past twenty years, the growth of the nonviolent prison population has far outpaced the incarceration rate for violent offenders: 77 percent of those entering prisons and jails are sentenced for nonviolent offenses. From 1980 to 1997, the number of prisoners charged with violent offenses doubled while the number of nonviolent prisoners tripled, and the number of people convicted for drug offenses increased elevenfold. These numbers are steeper still for women. Eighty-five percent of women are imprisoned for nonviolent offenses.[8]

The drive to lock up nonviolent prisoners is all the more pernicious given that prisons constitute one of the United States' most well-endowed public works programs. The prison industrial complex—fueled by the War on Crime and the War on Drugs much as the Cold War drove its military predecessor—delivers big profits to private prison contractors and service providers, economic development for depressed rural areas, and jobs to blue-collar workers facing a deindustrialized economy. Working people from urban areas are increasingly removed from their communities to work in far-flung rural communities. The runaway growth of the U.S. prison system also corresponds—not coincidentally—with the structural decimation of public policy responses to poverty and other social problems.

The California Bay Area youth organizer Raquel Laviña offers this economic analysis: "For young women of color and poor women, it's not only that we're getting harassed by police and more and more often going to prison, but that the community is a different place when so many people get taken away. There are so many young women without their babies' fathers because over half of the men in their community are either dead or in jail. Women of color feel a responsibility for the men in our community. We have to hold the liberation of men and women at the same time."

Laviña explains that the prison industrial complex is a primary point of struggle for her generation and for those coming up after her: "It's a symbol of the freedom we don't have. There are so many things impacting young people of color and poor youth—poverty, homelessness, substandard education. But the police coming at you and taking people away from your community is immediate and direct. The others are more slow-burn ways of killing you. You know the police aren't there to protect you but the business across the street."

WOMEN AND GIRLS ON LOCKDOWN

Hermon Getachew, twenty-one-year-old director of the organization Sister Outsider in the Brownsville and East Flatbush neighborhoods of Brooklyn, knows that many young women are motivated by their own experiences to organize for a just criminal justice system. "I've had a lot of encounters with the police," Getachew says. "It really hits home, the women you see in jail—they're just there on bench warrants, drug charges, and for self-defense. Girls end up in the system when they're just trying to support themselves. It just boils down to money. I know women who have to support themselves and their families at the age of fourteen, and no one is trying to give those women, especially those from immigrant communities, a job."

While prison spending siphons employment and education resources out of needy communities, "prisons do not disappear problems, they disappear human beings," charges the lifelong antiprison activist Angela Y. Davis.[9] Increasingly, prisons are disappearing "problematic" women. According to the National Council on Crime and Delinquency, twenty-five years ago women were virtually invisible in the criminal justice system. Today more than 140,000 women are in U.S. prisons and jails, nearly triple the number in 1985. The number of women imprisoned in California alone is nearly twice that of women incarcerated nationwide thirty years ago. African-American women, the fastest-growing segment of the U.S. prison population, are incarcerated at a rate eight times that of white women. Latina women are incarcerated at four times the rate of white women.

Seventy percent of women in prison have been convicted of nonviolent offenses, and 80 percent of adult women prisoners have children—most are single mothers of children under eighteen. Half of all women imprisoned in the United States are African-American. As a result of War on Drugs legislation like mandatory minimums, women are twice as likely as men to be incarcerated for drug-related offenses. Men, however, are more likely than women to receive drug treatment.[10]

From 1930 to 1950, a total of five women's prisons were built in the United States. During the 1980s alone, thirty-four were constructed. According to a recent Amnesty International report: "Even this could not keep pace with the swelling numbers of women in prison. Women's prisons are understaffed, overcrowded, lack recreation facilities, serve poor quality food, suffer chronic shortages of family planning counselors and services, obstetrics and gynecological specialists, drug treatment and childcare facilities, and transportation funds for family visits—which are necessary due to the remote locations of the women's prisons. A 2000 study by the General Accounting Office, commissioned by the Washington, D.C., congressional delegate Eleanor Holmes Norton, found that women in prison are more likely to suffer from HIV infection and mental illness than are incarcerated men.[11]

Like adult women, girls have become increasingly caught up in the criminal justice system in recent decades. Between 1993 and 1997, in almost every offense category, increases in arrests were greater—or decreases in arrests were smaller—for girls than for boys. Research on girls in detention consistently shows that girls rarely pose a threat to others' safety but that they are at the highest risk levels for becoming substance addicted and sexually active, and for failing out of school. "Tragically," says a report by the National Council on Crime and Delinquency, "these problems are almost always correlated with histories of violent victimization, poverty, and deeply fragmented families and public service systems."[12] According to the American Bar Association, between 1988 and 1997 delinquency cases involving girls jumped 83 percent. The spike was not in response to increased crime or violence by girls but rather "re-labeling of family conflicts as violent offenses, gender bias in the processing of minor offenses, changes in police practice . . . and a lack of services aimed at helping troubled girls."[13]

Further, the criminalization of poor people is a double-edged swipe at women, who are disproportionately poor. Two-thirds of adults living in poverty in the United States are women, and the poverty rate for children in female-headed households is over 50 percent. In fact, the wage gap between male and female workers is declining only because the real earnings of low-income men are falling. A female worker still earns seventy-two cents to a man's dollar.[14]

Suemyra Shah, a nineteen-year-old board member of the National Coalition to Abolish the Death Penalty, speaks to the prison system's dual attack on poor young women. "Young women are especially affected because we've always been the keepers of the family. Women have always played a central role, not only in leading political struggles but also in centering and preserving life. And it's escalating now, with the [criminal justice] system taking so many young people away from the community."

. . .

IN OUR HANDS

In response to the punitive zeal fueling the prison industrial complex, the leadership of the up-and-coming antiprison movement—with young women at the forefront—is decidedly interested in redemption. The inclusive style of leadership that young women bring to this seedling movement is rooted in a strong belief in community, passed down, perhaps, by grandmothers raising many of the 1.5 million children otherwise rendered parentless by prisons in this country. It is a method of leadership as

determined to tackle adversaries as it is to build hope by reclaiming human beings from a system that irredeemably labels them "criminal." The processes of hope, restoration, and bringing people back into their communities are personal. But they are also political acts because they reverse the cultural and socioeconomic process of criminalization that vilifies people who are desperate for resources and isolated from others. This is not to say that "criminalized" people do not perform criminal acts. But young women who critique the criminal justice system are saying—at their peers' parole hearings, when they talk to the media, in hip-hop lyrics, and in conversation over the dinner table—that criminal mistakes should not define the sum total of one's humanity.

. . .

Maintaining a relationship with a loved one or family member behind bars begins at the level of individual experience but extends into the realm of collective accountability. "You have no idea what it's like to love someone who is being tortured inside a prison. You never get used to living with so much horror," says asha bandele, an editor at *Essence* magazine and author of *The Prisoner's Wife.* bandele describes how this experience stretches into the domain of collective responsibility: "Whenever I hear of police and prison abuses, it doesn't matter if I know the person or not because it could always be happening to anyone I love.

"I've often wondered," bandele says, "out of all the social justice work that could be my calling, why this work? Why immerse myself in a world where I know that someone I love may be kept from me and the rest of the community forever? I'm finally coming to understand that I do this work because I want to be free."

The work that young women are doing embodies an emphasis on freedom, liberation, and humanity. Recently the Center for Young Women's Development in San Francisco spearheaded a dialogue with young women in juvenile hall about what issues they felt were most pressing. As Lateefah Simon puts it, "We thought it was important to do something in the system where we usually have no power, and could show youth in the hall that things could indeed be changed." Working with the young women in the hall, the center was able to uncover harassment of queer women. Simon notes that, "even though none of our leadership was out and queer, we took on this issue because it came up so much as an issue that was important to the girls in the hall. We are developing their voices and their vision. Recognizing and supporting the fullness of everyone's humanity is embedded in the culture of the organization."

The center organized a group of legal experts to help draft a model policy for the city of San Francisco to address the concerns of queer youth in juvenile detention. As a result of the group's advocacy, and after a long struggle, the mayoral commission on juvenile justice and probation recently adopted the policy the center created—the first of its kind in the nation. The policy stipulates that juvenile hall staff be trained to work with queer youth and that monitoring and oversight be implemented to ensure that the concerns and complaints of queer youth are heard and tended to. Additionally, two center staffers (fifteen and seventeen years old, both former sex workers) were part of a mayoral committee to research and make recommendations to the city council on practical alternatives to incarceration for young women who have been arrested for prostitution. Formerly incarcerated girls (sixteen to nineteen years old) also developed workshops on "how to stay out of the system," which they present as an ongoing program in San Francisco's juvenile hall—a precedent for the facility.

Recognizing the power of the collective efforts of young women, Simon notes, "Our power comes from the truth we speak. We are the first youth who have been through the system to serve on the juvenile probation commission. We told the commission real stories about real youth who have been in the hall. We could tell them which correction officers had been abusive, and we gave them testimony of the girls we work with. This issue is not sexy and it's not easy, but it's proof that we're really going to be doing this work on the inside for the long haul."

NOTES

1. Jerome Miller, "American Gulag," *YES! Magazine* 15 (February 2000), http://www.futurenet.org/15prisons/miller.htm.

2. Prison Activist Resource Center, "Education vs. Incarceration: A Stacked Deck," http://www.prisonactivist.org/factsheets/ed-vs-inc.pdf.

3. Fox Butterfield, "Study Finds Big Increase in Black Men as Inmates Since 1980," *New York Times,* 28 August 2002, late ed., A1.

4. "Class Dismissed: Higher Education vs. Corrections During the Wilson Years," Press Release, Center for Juvenile and Criminal Justice (2002), http://www.cjcj.org/pubs/classdis/classdis.html.

5. Alan Elsner, "U.S. Prison Population Social Costs Mount," Reuters, 23 January 2001.

6. Tracy L. Huling, "Prisons as a Growth Industry in Rural America: An Exploratory Discussion of the Effects on Young African American Men in the Inner Cities," paper presented at Consultation of the U.S. Commission on Civil Rights, April 15, 1999; also in "The Crisis of the Young African Male in the Inner Cities," U.S. Commission on Civil Rights, Washington, D.C., July 2000.

7. Elsner, "U.S. Prison Population Social Costs Mount."

8. John Irwin and Jason Ziedenberg, "America's One Million Nonviolent Prisoners," Press Release, Justice Policy Institute (March 1999).

9. Angela Y. Davis, "Masked Racism: Reflections on the Prison Industrial Complex," *Colorlines* 1, no. 2 (Fall 1998), 12.

10. Mandatory minimum laws remove judges' discretion to determine sentences according to the crime committed and according to its context. For example, a drug addict who is charged with drug possession may be best served by an effective treatment program; however, as a result of mandatory minimum laws, the judge is forced to sentence the addict to twenty years of hard time. Mandatory minimum sentences mostly and most unfairly apply to drug offenses. Organizations like Families Against Mandatory Minimums point out that both drug addicts and the partners of drug dealers—mostly women—are caught in the net of mandatory minimums.

11. Arthur Santana, "Female Prison Ranks Double; Citing Study, Norton Plans to Improve Conditions, *Washington Post,* 1 February 2000, A08.

12. Ibid.

13. Karen Gullo, "Report Decries Jailing Girls," *Chicago Tribune,* 16 May 2001, 8.

14. Real earnings are the real value of a dollar earned. Low-income male workers may make more in dollars today than they did ten years ago, but the value of that money is falling. This explains why a factory worker in 1965 might have been able to buy a new car or a house, but his twenty-first-century equivalent is taking the bus and renting. Women made so much less than men in 1965 that their wages have risen relative to low-income men's but only because they were starting at such a deficit; the wage floor was very low. David Moberg, "Bridging the Gap: Why Women Still Don't Get Equal Pay," *In These Times*, 8 January 2001, 24.

R E A D I N G **92**

Gender, Folklore, and Changing Military Culture

Carol Burke

Culture is simply a way of life informed by those who came before us, by how we grow up, and by the beliefs we hold; it is manifest in the rituals we observe, the jokes we tell, the slang we use, the clothes we wear, the food we eat, the work we do, and the ways we interact with those who share our workplace. Members of the military, whether on duty or off, combatants or noncombatants, active-duty or retired, share an identity fashioned by an always distinctive, frequently compelling, and occasionally bizarre military culture. Military culture embraces not only the official traditions of military life (formal dress parades, heroes' welcomes, Blue Angel flyovers, military dress, deference to rank) but also their unofficial, ostensibly transgressive counterparts: parodies, pranks, fake commendations, the hazing of new recruits, the drinking games that inevitably follow a formal "dining in" (that is, a dinner for visiting officers and other dignitaries). The relationship between official culture and its parody is intimate, a secret sharing. At the end of Airborne training, for example, a soldier chooses a military mentor or relative to fasten his wings, a small metal pin, onto his uniform. Back in the barracks, another ceremony follows the official one. Here fellow soldiers award the same wings a second time: one by one the soldier's buddies step up and punch the wings, its pins exposed, directly into the proud pincushion's flesh. Only then, when pricked by his peers, has the soldier earned his "blood wings."

On the rare occasions that the military brass has admitted to such rituals, it has either dismissed them as adolescent high jinks or selectively defended them as essential to the formation of unit cohesion. Yet what might have been tolerated as a harmless prank or promoted as a useful way to maintain morale in the armed forces of a former day takes on a sinister cast in a professional military committed by statute and policy to the inclusion of women. I say sinister, not immoral or criminal, because I do not claim that women are more moral or more civilized than men. On the contrary, the folklore of the military, the prospect of absorbing the traditions and living the life of a disciplined and close-knit unit, is what attracts most women to the armed services. Indeed, many of them have been raised in military families. It is because women share the aspirations of men for full membership in the corps but are excluded from the initiatory warrior rituals for no reason other than their gender that the unavowed collaboration between official and unofficial practices is sinister—or, to put it more academically, that the American military culture is fundamentally and dangerously cultic. Although unofficial military traditions have a rich history in the all-male military institution, which has been convinced that it cannot make soldiers and officers without first making men, the same traditions have now become potent antagonists of the reforms necessary to create a gender-blind professional military in a digital era. Today, muscle-bound macho nostalgia is more likely to thwart than to impel the successful execution of the military's mission.

To grasp how military culture is transmitted from one generation of recruits to the next, we need only to look at boot camp. Boot camp transforms recruits from jocks and nerds, boys from the 'hood and women from the suburbs, into knockoffs of model soldiers by stripping them of their clothes, shaving off their hair, forbidding them their accustomed freedoms, and instilling military discipline in them as second nature. Drill instructors, the engineers of their transformation, control every minute of the recruits' days: they deprive them of sleep, tax them physically, infantilize them, and, if the recruits are male, feminize them through the kind of humiliation designed to impress on them that to be degraded is to be female ("Come on, ladies").

Under this perversely scripted scenario there can be no parity between the experiences of men and women in basic training. We can corroborate that claim by reconstructing the subterranean history of the marching chant: the "jodie" in the Army and the Marine Corps, the "cadence call" in the Navy. Such chants celebrate the need to repudiate the pleasures associated with a recruit's civilian past and to embrace a martial future (or, more literally, to leave your girl and love your rifle).

Cindy, Cindy, Cindy Lou
Love my rifle more than you.

You used to be my beauty queen,
Now I love my M-16.

Used to go to the county fair,
Now I don't take you anywhere.

Send me off to Vietnam
Goin' to get me some Viet Cong.

With my knife or with my gun
Either way it's just as fun.

The history of such marching chants snakes through military culture from its elusive roots in American popular song during World War II, to the incorporation of the African American work-song tradition after the Korean War, when more and more African Americans filled the ranks of drill instructors, to the macabre turn of the outlawed genre in the Vietnam and post-Vietnam years with choruses of "Napalm sticks to kids; napalm sticks to ribs."

If the marching chant keeps the beat of boot camp days, the climactic rite of passage celebrates its culmination. As in primitive societies the world over, the rite of passage dramatically enacts the transformation from boyhood to manhood, the induction of the initiate into full membership in the cult. Veteran sailors ("shellbacks") crossing the equator summon King Neptune from his royal depths to initiate the "polliwogs"—those making their maiden crossing of the equator (especially fresh officers)—through a series of humiliating rituals. Such "crossing-the-line ceremonies," performed on board ships since the 1600s, ritualistically subvert military hierarchy by installing a new command for at least a day: the costumed sailor as King Neptune, his cross-dressing buddy as his queen, and their royal baby (generally the fattest sailor on board, dressed in a diaper). The scantily clad initiate must run through a gauntlet of wet towels and paddles, worm his way through the "whale's asshole," a long tube filled with the leavings of the previous day's meals, consume foul-tasting libations, and endure total-immersion baptism in a vat of putrid-smelling liquid. In some ceremonies the polliwog is required to lick lard from the belly of the royal baby, in others to simulate oral sex by sucking on a section of rubber hose extending from the groin of King Neptune. The equator is not the only line that is crossed.

Stories of less elaborate yet thematically similar rituals that celebrate the ways in which a crusty chief petty officer teaches arrogant, inexperienced officers a lesson circulate widely among enlisted troops. The fool's errand is a typical one. The young ensign is sent to deliver a flask of "primary water" from one part of a submarine to another. Routinely, anyone transporting any substance that might be radioactive must be scanned immediately after he completes the task to insure that he is not contaminated. When the ensign reports, the sailor passes a wand over his body while concealing in the palm of his hand a small amount of the substance that will activate the alarm. First the sailor passes the wand over the front of the ensign. He proceeds down the back of his neck and his back. When the wand gets near his anus, the alarm sounds.

Before their elective summer cruise aboard a submarine, midshipmen at the Naval Academy frighten and amuse each other with such stories. They tell of experienced sailors eager to put green midshipmen in their places, humiliating them by taping two of them in a 69 position. Such pranks and rituals and the legends they spawn articulate in erotic overtones the struggle between rank and experience.

. . . Ritual orders soldiers' lives. From the cut of their hair to the crease in their shirts to the edge dressing on their shoes, soldiers prepare themselves for work. Simple acts are freighted with significance; done well, they identify the individual as one who successfully conforms to the norm, an idealized version of the anonymous disciplined soldier who grasps and is held by his place in the chain of command. Such precisely regulated behavior prescribes conformity for the service member's family as well. Reports of misbehavior at the base school often make their way back to a superior; "If an officer can't control his family," the adage goes, "how can he control his men?" The higher the rank of a male officer is, the more extensive the social obligations demanded of his wife are; yet the husbands of female officers rarely fill an analogous supporting role.

The ritual life extends to the battlefield as well. Before going into battle, warriors of all cultures perform rituals (maybe only as simple as a prayer or a cheer). In Vietnam, one unit filled a porcelain toilet bowl with beer, or liquor when they had it,

and one by one the soldiers dipped out a libation before heading out of camp. Troops decorated helmets with political, religious, and personal slogans, carried tokens as good luck charms, fashioned in-country patches, and painted planes and helicopters as ferocious animals or friendly mascots, or, like their World War II predecessors, adorned them with long-legged, large-breasted women.

In wartime, the soldier or sailor whose service is drawing to a close is a subject of envy and uneasiness. To mark this transitional status, members of all branches of the military exchange short-timer calendars, either a patriotic or a bawdy image intricately divided into 365 shapes which the short-timer progressively colors, one each day until he returns home and the calendar is completely filled in. Short-timer sayings ("He's so short he could jump off a dime"; "He's so short he could wipe an ant's ass") and superstitions about the inadvisability of fighting alongside someone who has less than a month to serve proliferate during times of war.

An even more pervasive aspect of military culture is the demotic idiom of soldiers and sailors. Military folk speech is replete with acronyms: *snafu* may be the best known, but perhaps more useful in the end is *fng*, "fuckin' new guy." Military speech is seasoned with terms of praise and blame that sanction certain kinds of behavior; for instance, *to bilge* is to tell on a fellow midshipman. Its enormous lexicon of slang is both reliably conventional and unstintingly prolific. Like other groups of workers, military units invent their own language. The richly metaphorical speech that colors military life permits soldiers and sailors to converse on two levels at once, to affect compliance with authority while safely ridiculing a superior, complaining about a dreaded task, and distinguishing themselves as insiders who have mastered a lingo impenetrable to outsiders.

Whether they are from the same branch of the service, the same subspecialty, or the same company, members of the armed services recycle the repertoire of their immediate predecessors and invent new slang to fit their circumstances. In the same way, they pass along legends glorious and inglorious from soldier to soldier, unit to unit, and war to war: stories of bullets deflected by Bibles, dog tags, and amulets and tales of battlefield ghosts and crazed combat soldiers. These legends deal in the marvelous and the uncanny. The tellers claim authenticity for the events they narrate and demand credence from their audience. Stories of preternatural visitations, undeserved luck, and unforeseen misfortune are located in historical (as opposed to mythic) time and involve strange events that occurred to someone just like them, just over the horizon of this hill, this battle, this war.

Every war produces its share of angel helper stories. In the typical tale, an older soldier helps a struggling younger soldier, one too tired or too wounded to keep up with his retreating buddies. When he wakes the next morning, eager to thank his rescuer, the young soldier finds that the one who helped him back to friendly lines never existed or died in combat months or years before. Phantom soldiers fight in every war. The spirits of downed pilots repeat their distress calls on the anniversary of their death. In one Vietnam account, a soldier fights valorously until the day when he sees himself in VC clothing, stalking through the bushes. Such radical ambivalence marks the end of his tour of duty.

Some legends actually make their way into civilian discourse. The Vietnam War, more than any other, produced a constellation of lore associated with the return home. An account often told to sum up what happened to the returning vet, whose sacrifices went unacknowledged and whose heroism was unhailed by an American population fed up with the war, is the spat-upon story. The war-weary soldier walks across the tarmac from his plane, but instead of hearing the cheers and bands that welcomed his predecessors, he walks through a jeering crowd, one of whom spits on him. Although the account defies reality—how many troop transport planes flew into commercial airports?—it is always told seriously. This story epitomized for many the terrible irony of the war. But such a story predates Vietnam. It was told about Korean War vets,

whose pain and hardship seemed to many in the States to have been for naught. The story penetrated popular culture as well. In the fifties film *Shock Corridor*, a journalist going undercover in an insane asylum tells a first-person version of this story in order to bolster his disguise as a shell-shocked Korean vet.

Stories of unappreciative civilians spitting on veterans, of soldiers returning home from Vietnam early only to be shot by their fathers, who suspect they are intruders, of extraordinary draft evasion attempts that failed, even of crazed combat soldiers fashioning necklaces from the ears of the enemy: these stories and many more constitute the legendary repertoire of Vietnam.

Just as the telling of legends serves both a psychological and a social purpose within the folk group, so the makeshift rituals devised by military personnel to cope with extraordinary circumstances of deprivation have similar purposes. The experiences of female prisoners who endured harrowing internment in Japanese prison camps in the Philippines during World War II are a case in point. Sixty-eight nurses imprisoned on Bataan and Corregidor fashioned greeting cards on scraps of paper to commemorate significant occasions in their lives. They made dolls from bits of discarded fabric. They outfitted one doll in a perfect nurse's uniform, down to the details of kit and toothbrush; the doll was the only nurse who maintained regulation uniform during the women's long internment. These nurses and their male counterparts demonstrated astonishing resourcefulness in preserving an identity—a visible, distinctively military identity—apart from the one prescribed by their harsh captors. They buried jokes about their overseers in camp plays. They drew humorous caricatures depicting obese Japanese soldiers and emaciated GIs. They kept diaries in tiny script on scraps of paper and secreted them, despite the risk of certain beating or even death if they were discovered. Faced with virtual extinction at the hands of real enemies, the men and women who lived in prison camps were able to rely on their military training and culture not just to survive but to create viable communities.

One sector of the military that comes with its own set of traditions is the service academy. Anxious that more and more members of the middle class would invade its officer corps, French noblemen invented the service academy in the eighteenth century. To reserve the top positions in the military for their sons, they constructed an institution designed not only to provide a general education in academic subjects but to train its members in new military techniques. England was not long in following the French example. Contemporary service academies in democratic countries like America, Canada, and Australia were modeled on the British public school.

In every military academy from Sandhurst to West Point, from Annapolis to Kingston in Canada, the first year (or a portion of it) marks a period of transition from childhood to manhood, from civilian status to membership in the corps. Upperclassmen debase their juniors in painful but traditional ways. Rarely do upperclassmen invent new forms of humiliation; the most brutal merely increase the frequency of their aggression. Both through "plebe indoctrination" at the U.S. Naval Academy and through ritual abuse (called "bastardization") at the Australian Defense Force Academy, three fourths of the student body assumes the role of master and one fourth reluctantly plays the part of slave. Ceremonies confirm the end of this period and mark the exchange of probationary status for membership.

The history of service academies is punctuated by thorough reviews of such indoctrination systems, usually initiated after charges of hazing have made their way into the press. In Australia, official inquiries have addressed scandal about every seven years. Recent scandals in the United States have afflicted more than service academies; they have exposed misogynistic practices that were previously excused as military culture ("high jinks" or "letting off steam"). At its annual gathering of pilots, the now infamous Tailhook Convention, partygoers sported "He-Man Woman Hater Club" T-shirts and "rhino headgear" in honor of the rhino wall "trophy," equipped with protruding penis, from which women were urged to "suck down the booze." Pilots went "ballwalking" and "mooning" through the hospitality suites of the Las Vegas Hilton. Some women—compliant participants and prostitutes—exposed their breasts to aviators, who zapped them with squadron logos; even unwilling female officers and civilians could not escape the assaults of drunken officers, who propelled them down a two-hundred-man gauntlet.

Since the Tailhook investigation, which produced few culprits and no convictions, two Marines and a sailor have been convicted of brutally raping a twelve-year-old schoolgirl in Okinawa, and midshipmen at the Naval Academy have been accused of rape and pedophilia. These scandals, coupled with harsh criticisms of proposed reforms that were said to threaten "emasculation" of the nation's warriors by conservatives like James Webb, a former secretary of the Navy, roiled the waters of Admiral Jeremy Boorda's command. Boorda's subsequent suicide played in the press as another sensational episode in the Navy's alarming fall from its former prestige as the "gentleman's service."

If Tailhook exposed the excesses of officer culture by a group of drunken, cocksure aviators and the leadership's inability to discipline its own, Aberdeen raised questions about the sober and sinister application of discipline against women. At the Tailhook Convention, male officers assaulted female officers and civilian women in the urine- and beer-soaked hallways. At Aberdeen Proving Ground, drill instructors coerced or sexually assaulted women under their command. Whereas the naval scandal laid bare the arrogance of naval command, Aberdeen raised questions about the absolute nature of the privileged relationship between the all-powerful drill instructor and the powerless recruit. The potential for abuse by drill instructors has always existed; the zeal to erase a civilian identity and to inscribe a military one has resulted in injury and even death in training. With more women in training, with the great differential in power between trainers and trainees, and with the lack of mediation or effective oversight, abuse can assume a sexist form. Conventionally, male initiation in warrior cultures begins with infantilization and feminization and proceeds to practices designed to rid the adolescent of all traces of the female. To the extent that the military brass have permitted training to operate as a male rite of passage, they have furthered a culture hostile to women.

The Aberdeen scandal has not only invited censure by critics who claim that the Army has not gone far enough in insuring female recruits fair and professional treatment; it has also fired up the reactionaries, who blame neither the system nor the perpetrators but the women themselves. Calling for separate but equal training programs, these people maintain that it is "natural" or "inevitable" for such situations to occur when men and women are placed in close quarters to undergo an experience as intense as basic training. This rationale fails to take into account that the problem is not the amorous relations of peers but sexual relations that, because of the extraordinary difference in power, can never be purely consensual.

Very few critics and commentators would argue that there is not or should be no military culture. It is important, however, to understand the extent to which the military's culture has come to be at odds with its mission. Why should women and homosexuals take the place of the vanquished enemy? Why are rampant misogyny and homophobia countenanced throughout the armed services? Why does the military respond to the accident of gender or sexual preference with more intensity than it responds to the accident of skin color or social class?

The answer cannot be that the military is a reflection of society: it is not and never has been. In some cases the institution has been more socially progressive than the civilian world. Whatever the quarrels that members of both political parties have had with the military since the McCarthy era, they have generally agreed that the armed services should be an arena where merit will rule. With his decision to racially integrate the military, so the story goes, Harry Truman opened the doors of the nation's greatest meritocracy to a large group of disenfranchised

African Americans, who found in the military the opportunity for advancement that was closed to them in society at large. Progress has not been continuous, and its effects have not been uniform. Some African Americans, most notably General Colin Powell, have moved into the military's highest offices, yet integration of the military is still far from complete. Although African Americans account for 22 percent of enlisted forces, they constitute only 8.5 percent of officers (U.S. Department of Defense [DOD], Defense Equal Opportunity Management Institute [DEOMI], 1998). Such residual effects of racism have not, however, been justified as necessary to the preservation of the military's cultural identity.

If culture is the defense, then an investigation of culture may hold the answer to the systematic prejudice toward women and gays, who are treated as if they are a race or a class in an organization where the markers of race and class are otherwise rigorously suppressed. Although the answer is complex, a suggestion of its major coordinates may be in order here. First, the treatment of women and homosexuals is not symmetrical (women who are homosexual lose their status as women). A professional military is no longer a civilian army. I suspect that the rise of the militia movement is an aftereffect of the abolition of the draft, with fantasy taking the place of experience; militiamen are antiprofessionals with guns. Professional military culture defines itself against nonprofessionals. It is not the failure of women to meet standards that excludes them from certain places and positions in the military, but the failure of the military to *apply* standards, as if the definition of the specific skills and abilities needed for each specialty would open the way for women to qualify for billets in the infantry and the cavalry and to serve aboard submarines.

In considering the cultural aspects of the military, we must distinguish them from cultic aspects as they have been practiced in the last half-century. Military culture is made, not born; it has a history; its future should be directed toward serving democratically approved ends. . . .

The Postwar Moment
Lessons from Bosnia Herzegovina

Cynthia Cockburn

A postwar moment is one of promise—but too often of missed opportunities. So long as there is war or threat of war, heavy militarization and pre-occupation with security strategies can be justified. Every kind of progressive social or economic policy and development in that society may be held hostage. Not now—later!

A postwar moment is the time when policy can diversify again. There may be policy moves on several fronts at once, demobilization, the reconstructions of the economy, the shift from emergency services to social rehabilitation, the reconstruction of state, political structures, and law in a new constitution. But will these changes bring a democratic, inclusive, and equal society necessary for postwar healing, social justice, and substantive peace? This depends on many factors, but one that is crucial and often overlooked is whether the transition includes the questioning and transformation of gender power relations.

In October 2000, the UN Security Council adopted its Resolution 1325. It called on all actors involved in conflict and post-conflict conditions to incorporate a gender perspective in their work. What is more, it called on the UN to recognize gender issues in its own field based operations and to expand women's role, especially among military observers, civilian police, human rights and humanitarian personnel. It committed the Security Council to work in consultation with local and international women's organizations for these purposes. The resolution had identified, as many women knew, that international peacekeepers have very often neglected women's needs and strengths. What is more, the peacekeepers had played into the militaristic cultures found in war zones and in some cases even contributed to the exploitation and abuse of local women and girls.

This new gender thinking in the UN, its peacekeeping operations and postwar interventions, is solidly based on our bad experiences, the effects of mistakes made in past interventions. Bosnia Herzegovina is one such experience. I would like to illustrate this theme of postwar moments, gender issues, and the effectiveness of this new thinking in postwar reconstruction by highlighting what went wrong in Bosnia, some of the effects and attempts at correction. I will be drawing on work that is gathered in my publication: *The Postwar Moment: Militaries, Masculinities and International Peacekeeping.*

Why are women likely to have a particular agenda for the postwar moment? What's the essence of women's take on a peace process? Why is it that from where men stand it often looks as though using a gun may be the best way to solve a problem, while women don't agree? It's not because women have some natural inborn affinity for peace. It's women's experience of life. It's that the system we live in puts women in a particular relation to society.

Three ideologies tend to be very influential in societies that have been at war. They're the "brother" ideologies of militarism, nationalism, and patriarchy. The inequalities and distortions of gender in a patriarchal society, that masculinity and men are ascribed higher values than femininity and women, are part and parcel of the power relations of militarism and nationalism. If women are given importance in these cultural constructs, it is as wives and mothers, not for their value as human beings themselves. Women's independence and autonomy, their choices, and their self respect do not flourish in militarized, nationalistic, or patriarchal societies.

The General Framework Agreement for Peace (GFAP) in Bosnia and Herzegovina was negotiated in the U.S. air force base in Dayton, Ohio, and signed in Paris in 1995. It brought to an end four years of death and destruction, confirmed the ceasefire, provided for the withdrawal of foreign combatants, and established a zone of separation between warring factions. But Dayton wasn't just an agreement between the war makers to end the fighting. It actually introduced a whole new constitution for the country and a system of electoral politics. It provided for the conversion from a communist country to a market economy, and the groundwork for a whole new society. This in fact is what a peace agreement can be about and that is why it is important to look ahead to the changes that are possible. International bodies were given an almost colonial role, actually running a protectorate, in the shade of which, the native Bosnian political system and civil society were supposed to grow to maturity. It should have been obvious at the signing that responsibilities were being placed on the international community to observe human rights and democracy in its own operation—and that included gender equity. Christine Chinkin and Kate Paradine have written that the Accords presented the west with "an opportunity to structure a model for women's empowerment that could benefit women elsewhere, including Western Europe." But the Agreement failed to "re-imagine gender relations and to provide a contemporary model of citizenship and democracy for women."

When Madeleine Rees, head of the Sarajevo mission of the UN High Commissioner for Human Rights, arrived several years into the peace operation, she was shocked to find a total absence of women and of gender awareness in the Dayton peace process or in subsequent international interventions. There were strong reasons to have expected something different. Why?

First, the war in Bosnia had been a highly gendered affair. The war was specifically aimed at uprooting a large number of civilians. The aggressors, by destroying houses, gardens, farms,

and local economies, wanted to make it unthinkable for their targets to ever return home. This war against the domestic environment was against everything women represented or held dear. A high proportion of those who experienced first expulsion and flight, then dislocation, were women and children.

After the end of war, two thirds of the population and the vast majority of household heads were now women. Meanwhile, the health and welfare services needed to support women in this responsibility had totally collapsed. And yet, it was the women who persistently started and ran the small local humanitarian and advocacy agencies both during and after the war. They were, in fact, laying the foundations of a postwar civil society.

But power in Bosnia, as in other postwar societies, was a highly masculine affair. The towns and cantons were governed by nonrepresentative bureaucracies, often consisting of family relatives, mafias, local elites, and heads of armed factions such as the military, militia, or secret police. Often the purpose of war is not to win but to prolong the opportunities for profiteering. Power is maintained through various levels and applications of violence. After all, genocide, mass displacement, rape, enforced prostitution, and custodial violence were not incidental to the Bosnian conflict—they were its very goals. The tools for success had been designed with minute attention to gender—the gender of the victim, of the perpetrators, of gender values in the society and its cultures. So, should not some, if not all of the 50,000 personnel deployed in the 1996 Bosnian peace operations, have been at least curious about the gender issues?

A second reason to expect better of the Dayton operation was that gender awareness had already entered into the intergovernmental policy process worldwide. There was no excuse this time for neglecting gender and women's rights in the shaping of the peace agreement. In fact, Rees says that this was more than a lost opportunity. The omission was frankly appalling.

But where was civil society, as a whole, in all this? The first thrust of the international community was to set up new formal structures for political representation and decision making. But only after the popular vote failed to move forward did the effort turn to fostering civil society—including NGOs. Yet again women's NGOs were not seen as significant. When finally things began to shift, it was women, in fact essentially three women, Madeleine Rees, Heike Alefson (Council of Europe Office), and Elizabeth Rasmussen (head of the Democratization Branch of the Organization for Security and Cooperation in Europe), who initiated the change. They formed a Gender Coordinating Group [GCG] to initiate awareness and action on gender in international agencies.

While not totally successful, this group was able to have influence on many issues. They were too late to get women a voice in the drafting of the new law on domestic violence, but they were in time to have an input to the drafting of employment laws. Senior international representatives initially intended to cut maternity rights and benefits to a level below that given in the former Yugoslavia. The GCG and local NGOs worked together to prevent this further reduction of support.

The lack of a clear gender policy has serious effects. For example, the trafficking of women, a new form of sexual slavery, is rapidly becoming big business worldwide. Soon it will reach the proportions of the drug trade. Traffickers thrive in conditions of war and poverty. In a border town in Bosnia there is a lorry park they call Arizona market. Traders bring commodities that they buy cheap in Serbia and sell dear across the Dayton line. One commodity is women. They come from Moldova and Romania, often as young as 14. They may be told that they will be a waitress or a dancer in "the West." They have no passport, no papers, can't speak the language, and may not even know which country they are in. It is estimated that 30% of the clients and 80% of the traders' revenue come from the international community. Brothels and bars cluster around the bases of the international peacekeeping military. This should have been of great concern to UN officials; it certainly concerned the local Bosnian NGOs. Yet women who exposed the problem or the profiteers were sidelined. One woman in the International Police Training Force who blew the whistle was fired, and not even the GCG could prevent it. She later brought and won a wrongful dismissal case.

There are two main lessons that can be learned from the Bosnian experience. First, it is absolutely vital that a gender analysis from the very outset is placed at the heart of peacekeeping operations or postwar reconstruction. It should be mainstreamed so that everyone, not just women, not just gender focal points, but everyone thinks about the gender realities of the war and of peace. Second, local women's NGOs must be consulted, befriended, made partners with the international community, and have equal rights in the process.

Peace can not be done without the input of grassroots organizations that represent different subsets of the people affected by the conflict. Trade Unions, youth groups, and environmental lobbies are a few, for instance. If total inclusion of civil society in a peace process is necessary, how can it be made legitimate? Most importantly, what about women and women's organizations in this postwar moment? Can they rightfully demand a space and a voice to express their gender specific experiences or issues? Might not women raise issues such as violence, gun ownership, the right for conscientious objection, or better political representation? Women can't be expected to contribute or make very refined arguments if they are allowed only to shout from the sidelines and demonstrate from the streets. We need to monitor for signs that civil society is being placed center stage, where it can make a positive, detailed input into a future political structure and society. Mechanisms such as citizen forums, funding budgets for interventions, or a commission of inquiry come to mind.

One could also ask of the peace process, whether the international representatives and negotiators meet the test of gender inclusion. How familiar are they with CEDAW (Convention on Equality and Elimination of Discrimination) or Resolution 1325? How many of these international organizations are headed by women, how many hold responsible positions, and how real is the "gender mainstreaming" in their own operations?

Resolution 1325 did not come from out of the blue. It followed from a long sequence of UN developments in women and gender starting with the Decade of Women in 1975. So, what has followed in the period since the adoption of Resolution 1325? Dyan Mazurana points to the creation of "gender affairs" offices as part of the UN peacekeeping operations in Kosovo and in East Timor. There were plans for a similar office in the democratic Republic of Congo. The Report of the Panel on United Nations Peace Operations recommended the establishment of a gender unit in the UN Department of Peacekeeping

Operations (DPKO). It argued for a fair distribution of women and men in peacekeeping posts. Unfortunately, it did not get implemented. In the spring of 2001, the DPKO quietly dropped the proposal for a budget request and no gender unit has been formed.

As Dyan puts it: "local, governmental, and international women's advocates and organizations need to be at the forefront of monitoring and evaluating the developments in each and every peace process to see that they happen." It is quite clear from the experience of women in Bosnia that resolutions are not enough. Each and every time we must anticipate the opportunities of the postwar moment and work together to realize them as best we can.

DISCUSSION QUESTIONS FOR CHAPTER 11

1. What are some of the ways the state maintains social inequality? Have you experienced discrimination by the state in any way?

2. How does the early American assumption that citizens were White men perpetuate contemporary social inequities?

3. Do you believe that full equality can be achieved under our present system of democracy and capitalism? Why or why not?

4. What myths that maintain inequity do you see operating in the state, the law, and social policies?

5. What changes do you believe should be made in order to create a more just state?

SUGGESTIONS FOR FURTHER READING

Arneil, Barbara. *Politics and Feminism: An Introduction.* Malden, MA: Blackwell, 1999.

Baer, Judith A. *Our Lives Before the Law: Constructing a Feminist Jurisprudence.* Princeton, NJ: Princeton University Press, 1999.

Enloe, Cynthia. *Maneuvers: The International Politics of Militarizing Women's Lives.* Berkeley: University of California Press, 2000.

Forrell, Caroline, and Donna Matthews. *A Law of Her Own: The Reasonable Woman as a Measure of Man.* New York: New York University Press, 2000.

Katzenstein, Mary Fainsod, and Judith Reppy, eds. *Beyond Zero Tolerance: Discrimination in Military Culture.* Lanham, MD: Rowman and Littlefield, 1999.

LaDuke, Winona. *The Winona LaDuke Reader: A Collection of Essential Writings.* Stillwats, MN: Voyageur, 2002.

Ricciutelli, Luciana, Angela Miles, and Margaret McFadden, eds. *Feminist Politics, Activism and Vision: Local and Global Challenges.* London: Zed Books, 2005.

Woods, Harriet. *Stepping Up to Power: The Political Journey of American Women.* Boulder, CO: Westview, 2000.

CHAPTER 12

Religion and Spirituality in Women's Lives

Religion is a complex and complicating feature of many women's lives. Although many women feel empowered by religion because it offers them a place of belonging, comfort, acceptance, and encouragement, others feel oppressed by religion because it excludes and sometimes denigrates women. In this way, as this chapter will explore, religion remains a significant personal and political force in women's lives. Many of the social and cultural battles raging in American society are cast in religious terms—abortion, gay marriage, sex education, racial violence, domestic violence, to name a few—and many women organize their lives around their religious convictions.

The Southern Baptist controversy illustrates the experiences of many women in religious traditions. Throughout the 1980s and early 1990s, Southern Baptists, the nation's largest Protestant denomination with more than 14 million members, were embroiled in a controversy between fundamentalist and moderate leaders. The Baptist battles began over the issue of inerrancy (the notion that the Bible is without error in history, science, or doctrine) but quickly expanded to include, and then emphasize, social issues such as abortion, homosexuality, and the role of women in the home and church. As the fundamentalists grew in political power, they led the Southern Baptist Convention to pass resolutions excluding women from pastoral leadership in the churches and encouraging wives to submit to their husbands. Fundamentalist victory, however, did not come without a long, bitter conflict in which many women, particularly women in ministry, left the denomination. Other women decided to stay and focus their efforts on the autonomous local churches that carried on in the Baptist tradition of dissent, unbound by convention resolutions. Many women became involved in alternative Baptist organizations that grew out of the controversy and promised women more visibility, opportunity, and support as seminary professors and denominational leaders. The women who found positions as seminary professors often faced resistance from students and misunderstanding from colleagues. Numbers of women became associate pastors in moderate Baptist churches, but very few were offered senior pastor positions. Women in the pews heard the rhetoric of equality, but it came from the lips of the men who held the top positions in the churches and newly formed Baptist organizations.

The willingness of so many moderate Southern Baptist women to stay in Baptist churches despite the anti-woman actions of the Southern Baptist Convention indicates the powerful pull of religion. Even women who strongly opposed the policy of the Southern Baptist Convention often became active participants in other Christian denominations: few left Christianity entirely. This simultaneous push and pull of religion, as exemplified by the experience of Southern Baptist women, merits careful feminist analysis. As both a force that can oppress and empower, religion has a dramatic potential to work politically—either to continue women's oppression or to support women's liberation. Understanding this complex dynamic involves a close reading of the discourse of religion.

RELIGION AS OPPRESSIVE TO WOMEN

Southern Baptists are not alone in Christianity, nor is Christianity alone in world religions, in functioning as an oppressive force to women. This section discusses four ways that religion as belief and institutional practice has helped subordinate women. First, central to religion's oppressive function is the notion of a divinely ordained order of creation in many religions in which woman is deemed inferior. This notion is often supported by creation myths that embed woman's inferior status in the religious community's narrative of identity; these are the stories a religious community tells about itself in order to make itself known to both members and the outside community. For example, a common interpretation of the second Hebrew myth of creation (although feminist biblical scholars take issue with this interpretation) is that Eve is created after Adam because she is to serve him and be his inferior. Later in the Christian testament, one writer argues that woman's secondary status is a result of Eve's role as temptress in the fall of humanity. As Elizabeth Cady Stanton pointed out in her "Introduction to *The Woman's Bible*" over a hundred years ago, the Bible has most often been used to maintain the oppression of women by excluding them from particular roles in church, family, and society.

Second, women's lower status is further maintained by excluding women from sacred rituals. Women have not been allowed to celebrate the Eucharist, pray in public, dance sacred dances, hear confession, make sacrifices, baptize, enter the holy of holies, read sacred scriptures aloud in public, preach, or teach men. One argument for the exclusion of women from priesthood has been that the priest stands as a representative of God, and a woman cannot represent God because she is female. The underlying assumption is that men are more Godlike than women. When worshippers see only men as representatives of God, it reinforces the notion that men are more Godlike, and women's exclusion continues.

Third, religions maintain women's oppression very directly through church laws that require wives to submit to their husbands, that regulate women's sexuality, and that create highly defined gender roles for women and men. For example, these laws may keep women in abusive relationships or prevent them from having access to birth control and/or abortion. Women may be told by church authorities that their role in the home is to be the support person for the husband and to submit to his divinely ordained authority in the home. Then, when abuse occurs, a woman may be told that she is to continue to submit because that is her role and that God will change her

IDEAS FOR ACTIVISM

- Invite a group of women pastors, ministers, priests, and rabbis to participate in a panel discussion of women in ministry.
- Organize a women's spirituality group.
- Organize an educational event to explore women in the world's religions. If possible, invite practitioners of various faiths to speak about women in their religious tradition.
- Investigate the official stance of your own religious tradition on women's roles and women's issues. Where there is room for improvement, write religious leaders to express your opinion.
- Organize an event to commemorate the women who died in the "burning times."

LEARNING ACTIVITY **That Old-Time TV Religion**

Watch several episodes of religious programming on television, such as the *700 Club* and two or three televised worship services. Who are the key personalities? What is their message? In the worship services, who is speaking? Who is singing? Who is leading? What messages about gender are conveyed, not only in the words themselves but also in the roles played by different people? What messages about race, class, sexual identity, and/or ability are conveyed? Do you think these shows are helpful to people? Why or why not? Are they helpful to women? Who do you think benefits from these shows? Are there ways in which these shows reinforce the subordination of women and other nondominant groups? Keep a log of your observations to share with your classmates.

husband because of her obedience to God's commandments. The husband's abusive behavior then becomes the wife's responsibility because his changing is contingent upon her submission. This situation is exacerbated by a prohibition on divorce in some denominations, preventing women from permanently leaving abusive marriages.

Finally, historically and currently, religions also exercise power over women through church and state sanctioned control. During its early years, Christianity taught a spiritual unity that integrated the oppressiveness of Roman laws and gave women some status in the church (although women's place was still subordinate and Jesus' teachings about equality did not manifest in the teachings and practices of the church). Some women found solace in devotional life of the convent where they could live a religious life as well as hold leadership positions and avoid the constraints of traditional femininity that included marriage and childbearing. In the "burning times" (between the eleventh and fourteenth centuries), millions of women in Europe were murdered as witches. For many of these women, "witchcraft" was simply the practice of traditional healing and spirituality and the refusal to profess Christianity.

For other women, the charge of witchcraft had nothing to do with religious practices and everything to do with accusations rooted in jealousy, greed, and fear of female sexuality. But in the frenzy of the times, defending oneself against an accusation of witchcraft was practically impossible, and an accusation alone generally meant death.

Other examples include the ways Christian imperialism has proved destructive for women and men of color and reinforced racism and ethnocentrism. The genocide of Native Americans was conducted with the underlying belief that it was the God-given destiny of Europeans to conquer the native peoples of the Americas. Without understanding African cultures, Christian missionaries insisted indigenous African peoples adopt Western ways. The legacy of Christian racism continued in the American South, where many Christians defended slavery based on their reading of scripture. Following reconstruction, hate groups such as the Ku Klux Klan arose, calling for the continued dominance of the White, anglo, Christian race. This continues today with the messages of such groups as the Christian Identity Movement and the Aryan Nation (as well as the Klan). In Germany, thousands of Christians joined in Hitler's plan to build a master race and contributed directly to the genocide of 6 million Jews. In the 1950s and 1960s, while many Christians worked tirelessly for the civil rights movement and African American churches in particular became sites of resistance to racism, many others defended segregation and participated in acts of racial hatred. Only in 2000 did Bob Jones University, a fundamentalist institution of higher education in South Carolina, repeal its rule against interracial dating. Despite the many advances in the twentieth century, the twenty-first century began with the continuing problems of racism and intolerance by many who profess Christianity. It continues with an association between the executive branch of government and policies providing a conduit for structured inequalities.

In India, many Hindu women are raised to see self-immolation as a high form of religious commitment. *Sati,* the act by which a wife throws herself on the burning pyre with her dead husband, was considered a great act of honor by the codifiers of Hindu law and became glorified in Hindu legends told to little girls. In the nineteenth century, the British who occupied and colonized India outlawed sati. Nonetheless, as recently as 1987, 18-year-old Roop Kanwar was burned alive on her husband's funeral pyre. Karen McCarthy Brown relates the story of Roop Kanwar to fundamentalism in her essay titled "Fundamentalism and the Control of Women."

Currently the Religious Right, a political movement of religious ultraconservatives in the United States that has received support from the political establishment, is attempting to exert control over women by influencing the U.S. legal system. Faith-based initiatives that provide government funds to religious institutions tend to blur the line between church and state, and often serve to reduce women's choice and autonomy. Religious influence on social policy has managed to chip away at abortion rights by convincing lawmakers to pass various restrictions on abortion, and attention has also been focused on limiting the gains made by the gay and lesbian rights movement. A particularly telling example of the power of the Religious Right to influence American politics came in the Defense of Marriage Act (DOMA), mentioned in Chapters 7 and 11, that allows states not to recognize gay unions performed in other states. At the time the law passed, no state even allowed gay marriage. DOMA was a significant departure from precedent in which every state recognized the legal contracts entered into by other states.

The Muslim practice of wearing the veil (*hijab*) presents an especially complex example of the simultaneously oppressive and empowering role of religion in women's lives. From a Western perspective, the practice of veiling is often viewed as absolutely oppressing. Although many Muslim women criticize this as coercion, they also see choosing to wear the veil as an empowering practice of ethnic and cultural identity in the face of Western influence. Muslim women often explain that they feel safer when veiled in public. The veil indicates that a woman is devout and virtuous, and therefore Muslim men will not objectify and sexualize a veiled woman. In fact, very often these women express sympathy for North American women, who must constantly fear sexual assault in public places. The veil, they claim, protects them and therefore allows them the freedom to move about publicly without fear, and, in some cases, it allows them to claim their identity and take a stand against the hegemonic forces of Western imperialism. As the reading by Asra Q. Nomani explains, there is a movement to address the ways rights granted by Islam to women have been denied in contemporary manifestations of the Muslim faith.

RELIGION AS EMPOWERING TO WOMEN

Despite religion's long history of oppressing women, women have also experienced profound support, encouragement, and satisfaction in religion. This section focuses on those aspects of empowerment. First, for many women religion provides an environment in which they experience real community with other women. Women in traditional marriages who work in the home may find their only real social outlet in the church. Here they build connections with other women and participate in personally meaningful experiences in a community context.

Second, religion may provide women with opportunities for building and exercising leadership skills within religious organizations. Particularly for women in traditional families, this allows them to develop skills they might not learn otherwise. For example, although Southern Baptists have generally excluded women from pastoral leadership in the churches, the Woman's Missionary Union (WMU), auxiliary to the Southern Baptist Convention, has provided thousands of women with the opportunity to become lay leaders in their churches, as well as in associational, state, and national WMU organizations. WMU is a missions education organization for women. In local church WMU organizations, women plan, budget, and implement programs for education and action. WMU curriculum materials teach young girls that they can do anything God calls them to do. The subversive power of this message is clear in talking to Southern Baptist women in ministry. Many of them report first experiencing their call to ministry in a WMU organization. Similarly, Catholic women have been empowered through convent experiences, in which they exercise leadership and enjoy community with other women.

Third, leadership within the church or religious organization may facilitate women's power within their local or regional communities as well as encourage their participation in various forms of social activism. For example, in Santeria, a Caribbean religion, women who are healers, or *santeras*, have great personal power and hold immense social power in their communities. These women willingly enter into altered states of consciousness and allow the spirits to use them to bring about

HISTORICAL MOMENT   **Becoming a Bishop**

Until 1984, no Black woman had been elected bishop of a major religious denomination in the United States, but in that year, the Western Jurisdictional Conference of the United Methodist Church elected Leontine Kelly its first African American woman bishop and only the Church's second female bishop.

Both Kelly's father and brother were Methodist ministers. Kelly married and had three children but divorced in the early 1950s. She remarried a Methodist minister in 1956 and returned to college to earn a bachelor's degree and become a social studies teacher. Kelly was drawn to preaching and became a certified lay preacher. When her husband died in 1969, she accepted the church's invitation for her to become pastor. She earned a master of divinity (MDiv) from Wesley Theological Seminary in 1976 and became an ordained minister in the Methodist Church. From 1977 to 1983 she was pastor of Asbury–Church Hill United Methodist Church in Richmond, Virginia, and then became assistant general secretary of evangelism for the United Methodist General Board of Discipleship.

Kelly's nomination to the post of bishop by a group of California clergywomen was not without controversy. Some thought her unfit for the position because she was a Black woman. Others opposed her nomination because she was divorced. Nonetheless, she was elected and then named bishop for the San Francisco Bay area, making her the chief administrator and spiritual leader for more than 100,000 United Methodists in Northern California and Nevada. She remained at that post for 4 years until her retirement in 1988.

In the fall of 2000, the United Methodist Church elected three African American women as bishops, the first since Leontine Kelly: Violet Fisher, Linda Lee, and Beverly Shamana. Kelly commented, "I will always be the first African American woman bishop of the United Methodist Church, but praise God I am no longer the only."

healing. When a person visits a *santera,* the *santera* sees all the spirits with that person, and the *santera* is often able to reveal to the person what she or he needs to do. This ability puts the *santera* in an extremely powerful position, especially when the person consulting her is a politician or government official, as is often the case. Furthermore, as Caribbean women visit *santeras,* they see women who wield power in their culture and who can act as role models for them.

Another example of the role of religion in encouraging social activism is that of Jesse Daniel Ames, who helped organize the antilynching movement in the early part of the twentieth century. She worked through women's missions organizations in Methodist and Baptist churches in the South. Black churches were at the heart of the 1950s and 1960s civil rights movement in which many early leaders of second wave feminism had their first experiences of political organizing. A key component of Judaism is social justice, and Jewish women have long been actively involved in anti-Semitic, anti-racist, anti-sexist, and anti-heterosexist work. Ernestine Louise Rose, who fought for women's rights and against slavery during the 1840s and 1850s, challenged New York state lawmakers in 1854 to allow women to retain their own property and

Women of Faith

Interview three women who actively participate in a religious community. Ask about their experiences as women in their faith. Use the following questions or develop your own interview protocol.

- What is your religious community's stance on women's roles in home, society, and the religious community itself?
- What roles do women fulfill in your religious community?
- In what activities do you participate in your religious community?
- In what ways has your religious community been empowering for you as a woman? Has your religious community ever been oppressive to you as a woman?
- What do you gain by your participation in your religious community?
- How might your religious community better serve women?

Gather the data obtained by several other students in your class and examine your findings. Do you see any common themes arising from your interviews? What do your data suggest about these women's experiences in their faith communities? Can you make any generalizations from the data about how women experience religion as both empowering and oppressive?

ACTIVIST PROFILE **Nannie Helen Burroughs**

Nannie Helen Burroughs was only 21 years old when she delivered her stirring speech, "How the Sisters Are Hindered from Helping," at the 1900 National Baptist Convention in Richmond, Virginia. This speech proved to be instrumental in the formation of the Women's Convention Auxiliary to the National Baptist Convention, the largest African American women's organization in the country at that time. The Women's Convention promptly elected Burroughs its corresponding secretary and continued to re-elect her every year from 1900 to 1948. In 1948 she became the convention's president and served in that role until her death in 1961.

Burroughs was also a tireless activist—challenging lynching and segregation, denouncing employment discrimination, opposing European colonization of Africa, and promoting women's suffrage. After the Nineteenth Amendment was passed, she founded the National League of Republican Colored Women and worked to encourage African American women to become politically involved. She also established the Women's Industrial Club, which offered short-term housing to African American women and taught them basic domestic skills. The club also offered moderately priced lunches for downtown office workers. During the Depression, Burroughs formed Cooperative Industrial, Inc., which provided free facilities for a medical clinic, hair salon, and variety store.

One of Burroughs's driving passions was the education of African American women. In 1909, with the support of the National Baptist Convention, she opened the National Trade and Professional School for Women and Girls in Washington, D.C., and served as the institution's president. The school emphasized a close connection between education and religion. Its curriculum focused on the development of practical and professional skills and included a program in Black history in which every student was required to take a course. Burroughs's motto for the school was "We specialize in the wholly impossible." In 1964 the school was renamed the Nannie Burroughs School. In 1975 Mayor Walter E. Washington proclaimed May 10 Nannie Helen Burroughs Day in the District of Columbia in recognition of Burroughs's courage in advocating for education for African American women despite societal norms.

have equal guardianship of children with their husbands. When male politicians urged women to postpone their quest for suffrage and focus on the rights of former slaves, Rose declared, "Emancipation from every kind of bondage is my principle." She also spoke out against anti-Semitism and set the tone for twentieth-century Jewish feminists' critique of Judaism's traditional attitudes toward women.

Finally, for many women, religion provides a place in which they find a sense of worth as a valued person. The poem "God Says Yes to Me" by Kaylin Haught illustrates an accepting, loving God that has the potential to empower women. In the early twenty-first century, many women participate in revivals of ancient woman-centered religions and have become empowered through the revaluing of

LEARNING ACTIVITY **How Well Do You Know the Goddess?**

Match the Goddess to her name.

_____ 1. Odudua

_____ 2. Coatlicue

_____ 3. Izanami-no-kami

_____ 4. Demeter

_____ 5. Tho-og

_____ 6. Kali

_____ 7. Astarte

_____ 8. Kokyan Wuhti

_____ 9. Freyja

_____ 10. Haumea

_____ 11. Po Ino Nogar

_____ 12. Hathor

_____ 13. Anu

_____ 14. Asherah

_____ 15. Artemis Ephesus

a. Egyptian mother Goddess and Goddess of the underworld, the queen of heaven and mother of light.

b. "Queen of Heaven." Assyrian creator of life, mother and guardian. Goddess of fertility, love, sexuality, and justice.

c. Celtic creator of life. Mother Goddess of the earth and moon. The mother of all heroes or deities.

d. Scandinavian creator of life. Leader of the Valkyries.

e. "Great, Invincible, and Magnificent Founder and Savior, Commander and Guide, Legislator and Queen." Creator and mother Goddess of Anatolia.

f. The mother of Hawaii. Mother and guardian, mother of Pele and the Hawaiian people.

g. Creator of life who brings fertility and love. Goddess of the Yoruba people of Nigeria.

h. Tibetan primordial being. The eternal mother who is self-formed. She is the preexisting space.

i. "The Great Mother Goddess." Mesopotamian Goddess of justice, earth, nature, and goodness.

j. Hindu Goddess. She who gives life and also destroys it. The symbol of eternal time.

k. "Spider Grandmother." Hopi creator of life. Benificent deity who created humans, plants, and animals.

l. "Serpent Skirt." Mother Goddess of all Aztec deities of Mexico, the ruler of life and death.

m. Greek mother and guardian. One of the twelve great Greek Olympian deities. She has power over the productivity of the earth and the social order of humans.

n. "Female-Who-Invites." Japanese creator of life, earth and nature, heaven and hell.

o. "Great One." Vietnamese creator of life. World fertility Goddess who brings rice to the people and protects the fields and harvests.

Answers: 1. g 2. l 3. n 4. m 5. h 6. j 7. b 8. k 9. d 10. f 11. o 12. a 13. c 14. i 15. e

Source: Martha Ann and Dorothy Myers Imel, *Goddesses in World Mythology: A Biographical Dictionary* (New York: Oxford University Press, 1993).

the feminine implicit in this spirituality. Wicca, or witchcraft, is a Goddess- and nature-oriented religion whose origins pre-date both Judaism and Christianity. Current Wiccan practice involves the celebration of the feminine, connection with nature, and the practice of healing. As Starhawk suggests in "Witchcraft and Women's Culture," witchcraft encourages women to be strong, confident, and independent and to love the Goddess, the earth, and other human beings. This notion of witchcraft is very different from the cultural norms associated with witches that are propagated at Halloween.

WOMEN AND GOD-LANGUAGE

Many theorists contend that one of the most powerful influences in molding gender and maintaining gender oppression is language. The language religions use to talk about God is especially powerful in shaping the ways we think about men and women. Any language we use to talk about God is of necessity metaphorical. We create images that can only partially represent the full reality of the concept of God. Unfortunately, those images sometimes become understood in literal rather than metaphorical ways. So, instead of thinking of God *as* Father, we may come to think God *is* Father. Throughout Jewish and Christian history, the preponderance of images for God have been masculine—Father, King, Lord, Judge, Master—and the effect has been that many people image God as male even though, intellectually, they might know this is not true. God is often imagined as White too.

In ancient times, the image of the Great Mother Goddess was primary in many cultures, but as war-centered patriarchal cultures developed, the life-giving Goddess had to be defeated by the warring God. In ancient Babylonian mythology, Tiamat was the Great Mother, but she was eventually slaughtered by her son Marduk, the God of war. Yahweh, the God of the ancient Israelites, was originally a consort of the Canaanite Mother Goddess, but, as the Israelites moved toward a patriarchal monotheism (belief in just one God), Yahweh became prominent as the Great Father God, and worship of the Goddess was harshly condemned by Yahweh's priests. The prominence of a single masculine image of deity then became reflected in the exclusion of women from the priesthood and eventually from the concept of Israel itself.

In response to the hegemony of masculine images of God, feminist theologians have constructed alternative feminine images of deity. Some theologians, such as Virginia Mollenkott, have returned to the Jewish and Christian testaments to point out the existence of feminine images within scripture. Other theologians, such as Sallie McFague, have challenged people to develop new models of God such as God as mother, God as lover, and God as companion. And yet other women have returned to the ancient images of the Goddess herself. In "Grandmother of the Sun: The Power of Woman in Native America," Paula Gunn Allen explains Native American feminine images of deity.

The political nature of the decision to challenge normative God-language does not go unnoticed by traditionalists wishing to cling to male images. The Southern Baptist Convention issued a statement declaring that God is not *like* a father, but God *is* Father. And a group of mainline churchwomen created a furor within their denominations when at a conference they chose to call God "Sophia," a biblical, but feminine, name for deity.

LEARNING ACTIVITY   **Exploring New Metaphors for Deity**

Metaphors are images drawn from familiar human experiences, used in fresh ways to help explore realities that are not easily accessible in our everyday experience. All language about deity is metaphorical because no one image or analogy can capture the essence of deity. Throughout the history of Jewish and Christian faiths, in particular, deity has been variously imaged as Father, Shepherd, King, Lord, and Master. Originally, these metaphors helped many people explore and grapple with different aspects of the nature of deity. Many contemporary theologians, however, suggest the need for new metaphors for deity, shocking metaphors that will cause people to think about deity in new ways. Theologian Sallie McFague contends, "The best metaphors give both a shock and a shock of recognition." In good metaphors, we see something about reality, and we see it in new ways.

What are some of the metaphors for deity with which you are familiar? In what ways have those metaphors been helpful? In what ways are those metaphors limiting? What do you perceive as the consequences of taking these metaphors literally? Are there some metaphors you think have outlived their usefulness?

Following are a number of new metaphors for deity that are being utilized in current theological discussion. What do you think of these metaphors? In what new ways do they cause you to think about deity? What new ideas about deity do they suggest to you? In what ways do they call you to reappraise images of deity?

- God as mother
- God as lover
- God as companion
- God as gambler
- The earth and God's body

Can you think of any shocking new metaphors that help you think about deity in original ways?"

REINTERPRETING AND RECONSTRUCTING TRADITIONS

For those feminist women who have chosen to remain in religious traditions, the task of reworking oppressive elements has been great. Theology itself has been constructed with male experience as normative and has not taken into account the experiences of both men and women. Since the 1960s, feminist theologians have undertaken the task of rethinking traditional theological notions from the perspective of women's experiences. For example, the traditional notion of sin expressed in the story of the Fall in Genesis is that of pride and the centrality of the self. Redemption in the Christian testament then involves the restoration of what man lacks—sacrificial love. Yet the normative experience for women is not pride and self-centeredness, given that women are generally socialized to be self-negating for the sake of their families, and, in fact, encouraging women to be self-sacrificing as a form of redemption simply exacerbates women's situation. Feminist theology, as Alicia Ostriker suggests in her poem "Everywoman Her Own Theology," brings women's experiences to the center and reconstructs theological concepts in keeping with those experiences.

Because of the predominance of Christianity in the United States, the Bible and its various interpretations play a large role in shaping women's lives. Given this importance, feminist re-examinations of religion are on a continuum from reinterpretation to reconstruction. *Reinterpretation* involves recognizing the passages that are particularly problematic for women and highlighting and reintegrating the passages that extol equality between women and men. Proponents of such reinterpretation include Christian feminists who maintain a positive view of scripture as they continue to accept scripture as an authority in their lives. The goal of *reconstruction,* however, is to move beyond reinterpretation and recognize the patriarchal underpinnings of various interpretations and the ways they have been used to oppress women.

As an example of a reconstructionist account, Christian testament scholar Elisabeth Schüssler Fiorenza encourages readers of scripture to look for the presence of women in the margins and around the edges of the text. She calls for biblical readers to re-create the narratives of women that were left out of but hinted at in the text. In a similar fashion, the reading "Standing Again at Sinai" by Jewish feminist scholar Judith Plaskow calls for a reconceptualization of notions of God, Torah, and Israel that are inclusive of women. Other reconstructions of scripture include "womanist" biblical interpretations of women of color that analyze the Bible in light of both sexism and racism. In these accounts the Bible itself is subject to scrutiny in terms of its expressions of justice and injustice. Readers of the Bible with this perspective focus on the moral and ethical imperatives of justice contained therein and with an eye toward struggle for liberation for women of color.

Women have begun to challenge and reconstruct religious traditions as well as scripture. For example, Jewish women have developed feminist haggadahs, texts containing the ritual for celebrating the Passover seder. These feminist haggadahs commemorate the women of the Exodus, the liberation of the Israelites from slavery in Egypt. In one haggadah, the four sons of the traditional ceremony become four daughters, and the lives of the women celebrating Passover are inserted in the ceremony to create a living history and a new story.

Perhaps one of the most contentious reconstructions of religious traditions is the ordination of women. Although feminist church historians have recovered a long tradition of women as rabbis, priests, pastors, bishops, and evangelists, most Christian denominations did not ordain women until the latter part of the twentieth century. Many still do not. One exception to this is the Quakers, who have a long and unique history of women's equality in the congregation. Although Quakers do not ordain anyone, some groups of Quakers do record ministers, and women have always been among the recorded. In silent Quaker meetings, women as well as men are assumed to be able to receive and speak a word from God. Beginning in the 1960s, many mainline Protestant churches began to ordain women ministers, although men still make up the larger percentage of senior pastors in almost every denomination. Roman Catholics still prohibit women from becoming priests, although there is a growing movement within Catholicism, particularly American Catholicism, to change this policy. Several churches, such as the United Church of Christ, the Unitarian Universalist Association, and the Episcopalians, ordain openly gay and lesbian clergy.

"... and so, then I said, 'You think that just because I'm a woman I can't preach, just because I'm a woman I can't hold office in the convention, just because I'm a woman I can't do evangelism, just because I'm a woman I can't teach theology!' And he said, 'Yes.'"

Reprinted with permission from Norma Young.

CREATING NEW SPIRITUAL TRADITIONS

Although some feminists believe in the reinterpretation and reconstruction of scriptures and choose to work within existing denominations, others prefer to create their own empowering religious texts and organizations. For some, traditional religious scriptures are so essentially androcentric that they can only reproduce patriarchal social relations. They see no possibility of liberation for women in scripture because even reconstruction of biblical texts cannot change the patriarchal core of, for example, the Bible. Rather, these reconstructions simply perpetuate the patriarchal order. Feminist philosopher Mary Daly argues that patriarchal language is not accidental or incidental to the Bible but is an essential element of it, rendering the Bible useless in the liberation of women. These women look beyond traditional scripture for their spiritual insights and understandings. Wiccan groups, discussed above, fall into this category too.

In this way, although many women have expressed their spirituality within formal religious traditions, many others have created forms of spiritual expression outside churches, synagogues, and mosques. Women's spirituality is an empowering force that has taken such various forms as meditation, poetry, art, prayer, ritual, and social action. Spirituality enables women to experience connection with creation, with other human beings, and with the divine within themselves.

For many feminists, spirituality is a central force in their politics. The awareness of the interconnectedness of all things motivates feminist action toward justice and peace and encourages women to work together across differences. Nature-based spiritualities affirm the connections among all living things and seek to protect the natural environment on which we all depend. Feminist spirituality values and affirms the diversity that makes up the unity of creation, and it challenges women to restructure the systems of power that create and maintain injustice. The reading "Religion and Feminism's Fourth Wave" by Pythia Peay demonstrates this commitment to change. It discusses an ecumenical group: a gathering of women across many different religious faiths who share a desire for spiritually informed activism. As Marge Piercy writes:

> Praise our choices, sisters, for each doorway
> open to us was taken by squads of fighting
> women who paid years of trouble and struggle,
> who paid their wombs, their sleep, their lives
> that we might walk through these gates upright.
> Doorways are sacred to women for we
> are the doorways of life and we must choose
> what comes in and what goes out. Freedom
> is our real abundance.*

---

* "The Sabbath of Mutual Respect," *The Moon Is Always Female* (New York: Knopf, 1980).

Introduction to *The Woman's Bible*

Elizabeth Cady Stanton (1895)

From the inauguration of the movement for woman's emancipation the Bible has been used to hold [woman] in the "divinely ordained sphere," prescribed in the Old and New Testaments.

The canon and civil law; church and state; priests and legislators; all political parties and religious denominations have alike taught that woman was made after man, of man, and for man, an inferior being, subject to man. Creeds, codes, Scriptures and statutes, are all based on this idea. The fashions, forms, ceremonies and customs of society, church ordinances and discipline all grow out of this idea.

. . .

The Bible teaches that woman brought sin and death into the world, that she precipitated the fall of the race, that she was arraigned before the judgment seat of Heaven, tried, condemned and sentenced. Marriage for her was to be a condition of bondage, maternity a period of suffering and anguish, and in silence and subjection, she was to play the role of a dependent on man's bounty for all her material wants, and for all the information she might desire on the vital questions of the hour, she was commanded to ask her husband at home. Here is the Bible position of woman briefly summed up.

. . .

These familiar texts are quoted by clergymen in their pulpits, by statesmen in the halls of legislation, by lawyers in the courts, and are echoed by the press of all civilized nations, and accepted by woman herself as "The Word of God." So perverted is the religious element in her nature, that with faith and works she is the chief support of the church and clergy; the very powers that make

her emancipation impossible. When, in the early part of the Nineteenth Century, women began to protest against their civil and political degradation, they were referred to the Bible for an answer. When they protested against their unequal position in the church, they were referred to the Bible for an answer.

This led to a general and critical study of the Scriptures. Some, having made a fetish of these books and believing them to be the veritable "Word of God," with liberal translations, interpretations, allegories and symbols, glossed over the most objectionable features of the various books and clung to them as divinely inspired. Others, seeing the family resemblance between the Mosaic code, the canon law, and the old English common law, came to the conclusion that all alike emanated from the same source; wholly human in their origin and inspired by the natural love of domination in the historians. Others, bewildered with their doubts and fears, came to no conclusion. While their clergymen told them on the one hand that they owed all the blessings and freedom they enjoyed to the Bible, on the other, they said it clearly marked out their circumscribed sphere of action: that the demands for political and civil rights were irreligious, dangerous to the stability of the home, the state and the church. Clerical appeals were circulated from time to time conjuring members of their churches to take no part in the anti-slavery or woman suffrage movements, as they were infidel in their tendencies, undermining the very foundations of society. No wonder the majority of women stood still, and with bowed heads, accepted the situation.

God Says Yes to Me

Kaylin Haught

I asked God if it was okay to be melodramatic
and she said yes
I asked her if it was okay to be short
and she said it sure is
I asked her if I could wear nail polish
or not wear nail polish
and she said honey
she calls me that sometimes
she said you can do just exactly

what you want to
Thanks God I said
And is it even okay if I don't paragraph
my letters
Sweetcakes God said
who knows where she picked that up
what I'm telling you is
Yes Yes Yes

Fundamentalism and the Control of Women

Karen McCarthy Brown

Religious fundamentalism is very difficult to define; yet many of us—scholars and journalists in particular—think we know it when we see it. For those attuned to gender as a category of analysis, a stab of recognition is often occasioned by the presence of high degrees of religiously sanctioned control of women. In conservative religious movements around the world, women are veiled or otherwise covered; confined to the home or in some other way strictly limited in their access to the public sphere; prohibited from testifying in a court of law, owning property, or initiating divorce; and they are very often denied the authority to make their own reproductive choices.

I propose to take up the thread of the control of women and follow it into the center of the maze of contemporary fundamentalism. Yet I will not argue, as might be expected, that the need to control women is the main motivation for the rise of fundamentalism, but rather that aggravation of this age-old, widespread need is an inevitable side effect of a type of stress peculiar to our age.

I will suggest that the varieties of fundamentalism found throughout the world today are extreme responses to the failed promise of Enlightenment rationalism. Fundamentalism, in my view, is the religion of the stressed and the disoriented, of those for whom the world is overwhelming. More to the point, it is the religion of those at once seduced and betrayed by the promise that we human beings can comprehend and control our world. Bitterly disappointed by the politics of rationalized bureaucracies, the limitations of science, and the perversions of industrialization, fundamentalists seek to reject the modern world, while nevertheless holding onto its habits of mind: clarity, certitude, and control. Given these habits, fundamentalists necessarily operate with a limited view of human activity (including religious activity), one confined largely to consciousness and choice. They deny the power of those parts of the human psyche that are inaccessible to consciousness yet play a central role in orienting us in the world. Most of all they seek to control the fearsome, mute power of the flesh. This characteristic ensures that fundamentalism will always involve the control of women, for women generally carry the greater burden of human fleshliness.

This essay is an exploratory one. Its topic is huge and it ranges widely, crossing over into several academic disciplines other than my own. Occasionally I am forced to paint with a broad stroke and a quick hand. Writing that is preliminary and suggestive can be risky, but the connections I see between religious fundamentalism and other, larger aspects of our contemporary world seem compelling enough to lead me to take that risk. My argument begins close to home, in the United States, with Christian anti-abortion activism.

THE ANTI-ABORTION MOVEMENT IN THE UNITED STATES

The "pro-life movement" emerged in the 1970s as a new type of religio-political organization. It was a bottom-up movement that used sophisticated, top-down technology. In the early stages of the movement, the organizing work was done around kitchen tables. But the envelopes stuffed at those tables were sent to addresses on computer-generated mailing lists, the product of advanced market-research techniques. This blend of grass-roots organization and advanced technology quickly brought a minority movement[1] to a position of significant political power. The combination of traditional and modern methods also reveals an ambivalence toward the ways of the modern world

that I will later argue is characteristic of fundamentalist movements.

Many observers have noted an inconsistency in the pro-life position. The very groups who launch an emotional defense of the fetus's right to life are curiously indifferent to children outside the womb. As a rule, pro-lifers do not support social programs focused on issues such as child abuse, day care, foster care, or juvenile drug use. They oppose welfare programs in general and have taken no leadership in educational reform beyond concern with sex education, public school prayer, and the theory of evolution. Furthermore, their so-called pro-life argument is deeply compromised by staunch support for increased military spending and for the death penalty. It seems clear that the pro-life position is not a consistent theological or philosophical stance. A quite different kind of consistency emerges from the full range of this group's social policy positions. Their overriding concern is that of maintaining strong and clear social boundaries—boundaries between nation-states, between law-abiding citizens and criminals, between the righteous and the sinful, between life and death, and not coincidentally, between men and women. This is a group centrally concerned with social order and social control.

Beyond the trigger of the 1973 Supreme Court decision in *Roe v. Wade,* stresses with a broader historical range have contributed to a focus on boundary maintenance in the anti-abortion movement. The upheavals of the 1960s created the immediate historical context of the anti-abortion movement of the 1970s. Student activists of the 1960s questioned the authority of parents, educators, and politicians. Black activists challenged the cherished American myths of equal opportunity and equal protection under the law. And the Vietnam War not only raised questions about U.S. military prowess but also planted doubts about the moral valence of the international presence and policy of the United States. These are very specific reasons why Americans in the 1970s might have felt that the social and moral orders were becoming dangerously befuddled.

. . .

A WORLD SUDDENLY TOO BIG

From the mid-nineteenth century into the early decades of the twentieth, the writings of travelers, missionaries, and, eventually, anthropologists were popular bedside reading materials in the United States. Americans were fascinated by exotic "others." They were concerned about their own place in this expanding, newly complex world. Most of these books did more than titillate. With their implicit or explicit social Darwinism, they also carried deeply comforting messages of progress and of Western superiority. Such messages, coming from many sources, infused an air of optimism into an otherwise disorienting age. During the same general time span, the seeds of American fundamentalism were sown and came to fruition.

Some of the social forces that shaped this period—expanding knowledge of and contact with the larger world, and increased communication—had emerged over a relatively long period of time. Others, such as the burgeoning of cities, the dramatic increase in immigrant populations, and a series of shifts in women's roles, had occurred more recently.[2] All of these forces came together in the second half of the nineteenth century to contribute to a general sense of vertigo; the world was becoming too big, too complicated, and too chaotic to comprehend. Most important, each individual's own place in it was uncertain. Religion, given its basic orientational role in human life, emerged as a natural arena for dealing with the resulting stress.

From that period until this in the United States, conservative Christians have come under a double attack. On one level, they have had to deal with the general stress of the times; and on the other, with the direct challenge of Enlightenment rationalism in the form of biblical higher criticism and evolutionary theory. The reaction of some groups of Christians has been ironic: they have responded to the threat by mimicking Enlightenment rationalism. The religion-versus-science debate pits against one another groups who share a common intellectual style: each claims to possess the truth. Believers, like rationalists, stress consciousness, clarity, and control.[3] Morality is codified; sacred narratives are taken literally and sometimes attempts are made to support them with "scientific evidence"; all sorts of truths are listed and enumerated; scripture becomes inerrant. Furthermore, conscious consent to membership in the community of belief, on the model of "making a decision for Christ," becomes increasingly important.

These are the religious groups we call fundamentalists. Their central aim is to make of their religion an Archimedean point in the midst of a changing world. But to do so, they must limit their religion's responsiveness to its social environment; and as a result they are left with little flexibility to respond to the complexity of their own feelings or to the challenge of a changing world. Sometimes they fall into aggressively defending brittle truths. This is what makes fundamentalism in the contemporary world problematic and, in some cases, dangerous.

. . .

FUNDAMENTALISM CROSS-CULTURALLY

Up to this point, I have been concerned with Christian fundamentalism in the United States, but in the process I have focused on dimensions of the story that serve, without denying the significance of local variations, to characterize fundamentalism around the globe. Religious fundamentalism is born in times and places where, for a variety of reasons, the world suddenly seems too complex to comprehend; and one's place in it, too precarious to provide genuine security.

One example is modern India, where the cult that developed around the recent immolation of a young woman on her husband's funeral pyre has been described as an instance of fundamentalism. John Hawley demonstrates that the background for the *sati* of Roop Kanwar was emerging Hindu nationalism in India augmented by a multitude of local destabilizing forces in Deorala, the site of the immolation. Furthermore, as Hawley and other authors have pointed out, Deorala is not a truly deprived area, and its residents are not traditionalists out of contact with the larger realities of modern India. I would therefore suggest, along with Hawley, that fundamentalism is not primarily a religion of the marginalized, as some have argued. Its more salient feature is that it develops among people caught off balance. Hence, fundamentalist groups often arise in situations where social, cultural, and economic power is up for grabs; many, like these groups now being referred to as Hindu fundamentalists, arise in postcolonial situations. Far from being essentially marginal to the societies in which they exist, fundamentalists are often directly involved in the political and economic issues of their time and place. And they often have a significant, if precarious, stake in them.

For the Rajputs in Deorala, traditional sources of pride and authority are being challenged by increasing contact with the cities of Jaipur and Delhi, and through them, all of India. These Rajputs are experiencing the disorientation of having to depend on economic and political systems beyond their control. Marwari merchants and industrialists, financial backers of the cult of the goddess Sati, are destabilized in another way. As their economic role expands throughout India, they risk their livelihood in a wider, less familiar, and less predictable world than the one in which earlier generations operated. The Marwari focus on the district around Jhunjhunu with its important Sati shrine gives them their emotionally saturated Archimedean point. The case of the Marwari businessmen suggests, even more directly than does that of the Rajputs, that fundamentalism is not a religion of the marginalized, but of the disoriented.

In the contemporary Indian context, rallying around the *sati* of Roop Kanwar (like anti-abortion activity in the United States) reasserts social control and demonstrates moral worth. It strengthens gender boundaries and provides an example of undiluted, innocent virtue that vicariously underwrites the virtue of Rajputs and Marwaris in general. Furthermore, as in the United States, insecurity about social control and moral rectitude is displaced onto the body of a woman. But in the *sati* ritual described by Hawley, the drive to kill the devouring, fleshly goddess and to enshrine the pure, spiritual one is much more painfully literal.

Both men and women attended the *sati* of Roop Kanwar, and both men and women subsequently revere her. At first glance this may seem difficult to understand, but the complicity of Indian women in the practice of *sati* has to be considered on more than one level. At the deepest level its explanation lies in the fear of women's will and women's flesh that men and women share, and in the relief that both feel when these forces are kept in check. But on another level there are explanations of a much more practical nature. Most Indian women's economic security heavily depends on marriage. A woman doing homage at a Sati shrine thus signals to her husband and to the world at large, as well as to herself, that she intends to be good and to do good, according to her society's standards. Thus she chooses to ignore any anger or fear she might feel about the practice, in the name of living a secure and ordered life. It is a herculean task for women to try to define the meaning and worth of their lives in terms different from those that prevail in their community. So some security can always be found in surrendering to, and even helping to strengthen, the accepted gender norms.

. . .

THE FAILED PROMISE OF ENLIGHTENMENT RATIONALISM

Modern communications, transnational economic pressures, and wars waged from the opposite side of the globe have brought many populations intimate knowledge of the vastness and complexity of their worlds. In the late twentieth century, the others in relation to whom we must define ourselves are more available to our experience and imagination than ever before; yet few if any of us have a satisfactory model for understanding ourselves within this complex, stressful world.

We all live in and are defined by a world too big and unstable for intellect or belief to comprehend, and we all react to intimations—as well as a few pieces of hard evidence[4]—of the failed promise of the Enlightenment. Academics, politicians, and ordinary folk the world over are immersed in this challenge and most commonly react to it (as fundamentalists do) by assuming that, with sufficient effort, the chaos can be first comprehended and then managed. In this way fundamentalists are simply extreme versions of the rest of us.

An emphasis on the control of women is characteristic of fundamentalism, but there is some of it everywhere in the world. The anti-abortion movement in the United States arises out of a much broader context in which, among other signals of misogyny, public power and authority have been denied to women for centuries. And the Sati cult could not have become an issue in Indian nationalism if in general Indian women were not seen as sources of pollution as well as of blessing—as a result of which they have been subject to a variety of social controls through the ages. When the mind and the spirit are cut off from the body, women become magnets for the fear raised by everything in life that seems out of control. The degree to which control is exercised over women is therefore a key to the profundity of stresses felt by most persons and groups. Fundamentalism is a product of extreme social stress.

Religion, whose primary function is to provide a comprehensible model of the world and to locate the individual safely and meaningfully within it, is an obvious place for this type of stress to express itself and seek redress. But as long as religions deal with this stress by positing a world that can be directly known, and in which it is possible to determine one's own fate, they only reinforce the controlling tendencies of enlightenment rationalism and do nothing to move us beyond it to whatever comes next. We should be suspicious of any religion that claims too much certainty or draws the social boundaries too firmly. In this period marked by the gradual breakdown of Enlightenment rationalism and Euro-American hegemony in the world, something more is necessary. We need help in accepting ourselves as organic creatures enmeshed in our world rather than continuing to posture as cerebral masters granted dominion over it. This requires that we learn to trust the wisdom of our mute flesh and accept the limitations inherent in our humanity. If we could do this, it would radically diminish our scapegoating of women and all the other "others" who provide a convenient screen on which to project fears.

The resurgence of religion that we are experiencing at the turn of this millennium should not be viewed in an entirely negative light. If any system of orientation in the world can help us now, it seems likely to be a religious one. There is no small comfort in knowing that, as the grand ambitions spawned by the Enlightenment falter in the present age, what is likely to emerge is not what several generations of social scientists predicted. It is not civilization marching toward increasing secularization and rationalization. What is slowly being revealed is the hubris of reason's pretense in trying to take over religion's role.

NOTES

1. From the beginning of the anti-abortion movement to the present, opinion polls have consistently shown that the majority of people in the United States favor a woman's right to have an abortion.
2. Betty A. DeBerg, *Ungodly Women: Gender and the First Wave of American Fundamentalism* (Minneapolis: Fortress Press, 1990), has an excellent discussion of the general changes—and particularly the changes in women's roles—attendant to the formation of fundamentalism in the United States. . . .
3. Often the only kind of control that fundamentalists can exercise over a chaotic and threatening world rests in their claim to have a privileged understanding of the deeper meaning of the chaos. Fundamentalists who engage in "end-time" thinking thus sometimes find themselves in the position of welcoming the signs of modern social decay because these signal the approach of the time when God will call home the chosen few.
4. The growing ecological crisis is one of the most tangible pieces of this evidence; it also reinforces the point that reason alone is an insufficient problem-solving tool, because we are incapable of holding in consciousness the full range of the interconnectedness of things.

Grandmother of the Sun
The Power of Woman in Native America

Paula Gunn Allen

There is a spirit that pervades everything, that is capable of powerful song and radiant movement, and that moves in and out of the mind. The colors of this spirit are multitudinous, a flowing, pulsing rainbow. Old Spider Woman is one name for this quintessential spirit, and Serpent Woman is another. Corn Woman is one aspect of her, and Earth Woman is another, and what they together have made is called Creation, Earth, creatures, plants, and light.

At the center of all is Woman, and no thing is sacred (cooked, ripe, as the Keres Indians of Laguna Pueblo say it) without her blessing, her thinking.

> ... In the beginning Tse che nako, Thought Woman finished everything, thoughts, and the names of all things. She finished also all the languages. And then our mothers, Uretsete and Naotsete said they would make names and they would make thoughts. Thus they said: Thus they did.[1]

This spirit, this power of intelligence, has many names and many emblems. She appears on the plains, in the forests, in the great canyons, on the mesas, beneath the seas. To her we owe our very breath, and to her our prayers are sent blown on pollen, on corn meal, planted into the earth on feather-sticks, spit onto the water, burned and sent to her on the wind. Her variety and multiplicity testify to her complexity: she is the true Creatrix for she is thought itself, from which all else is born. She is the necessary precondition for material creation, and she, like all of her creation, is fundamentally female—potential and primary.

She is also the spirit that informs right balance, right harmony, and these in turn order all relationships in conformity with her law.

To assign to this great being the position of "fertility goddess" is exceedingly demeaning: it trivializes the tribes and it trivializes the power of woman. Woman bears, that is true. She also destroys. That is true. She also wars and hexes and mends and breaks. She creates the power of the seeds, and she plants them. As Anthony Purley, a Laguna writer, has translated a Keres ceremonial prayer, "She is mother of us all, after Her, mother earth follows, in fertility, in holding, and taking again us back to her breast."[2]

The Hopi account of their genatrix, Hard Beings Woman, gives the most articulate rendering of the difference between simple fertility cultism and the creative prowess of the Creatrix. Hard Beings Woman (Huruing Wuhti) is of the earth. But she lives in the worlds above where she "owns" (empowers) the moon and stars. Hard Beings Woman has solidity and hardness as her major aspects. She, like Thought Woman, does not give birth to creation or to human beings but breathes life into male and female effigies that become the parents of the Hopi—in this way she "creates" them. The male is Muingwu, the god of crops, and his sister-consort is Sand Altar Woman who is also known as Childbirth Water Woman. In Sand Altar Woman the mystical relationship between water, worship, and woman is established; she is also said to be the mother of the katsinas, those powerful messengers who relate the spirit world to the world of humankind and vice versa.[3]

Like Thought Woman, Hard Beings Woman lived in the beginning on an island which was the only land there was. In this regard she resembles a number of Spirit Woman Beings; the Spirit genatrix of the Iroquois, Sky Woman, also lived on an island in the void which only later became the earth. On this island, Hard Beings Woman is identified with or, as they say, "owns" all hard substances—moon, stars, beads, coral, shell, and so forth. She is a sea goddess as well, the single inhabitant of the earth, that island that floats alone in the waters of space. From this meeting of woman and water, earth and her creatures were born.[4] . . .

Contemporary Indian tales suggest that the creatures are born from the mating of sky father and earth mother, but that seems to be a recent interpolation of the original sacred texts. The revision may have occurred since the Christianizing influence on even the arcane traditions, or it may have predated Christianity. But the older, more secret texts suggest that it is a revision. It may be that the revision appears only in popular versions of the old mythic cycles on which ceremony and ritual are based; this would accord with the penchant in the old oral tradition for shaping tales to reflect present social realities, making the rearing and education of children possible even within the divergent worlds of the United States of America and the tribes.

According to the older texts (which are sacred, that is, power-engendering), Thought Woman is not a passive personage: her potentiality is dynamic and unimaginably powerful. She brought corn and agriculture, potting, weaving, social systems, religion, ceremony, ritual, building, memory, intuition, and their expressions in language, creativity, dance, human-to-animal relations, and she gave these offerings power and authority and blessed the people with the ability to provide for themselves and their progeny.

Thought Woman is not limited to a female role in the total theology of the Keres people. Since she is the supreme Spirit, she is both Mother and Father to all people and to all creatures. She is the only creator of thought, and thought precedes creation.[5]

Central to Keres theology is the basic idea of the Creatrix as She Who Thinks rather than She Who Bears, of woman as creation thinker and female thought as origin of material and nonmaterial reality. In this epistemology, the perception of female power as confined to maternity is a limit on the power inherent in femininity. But "she is the supreme Spirit, . . . both Mother and Father to all people and to all creatures."[6] . . .

In Keres theology the creation does not take place through copulation. In the beginning existed Thought Woman and her dormant sisters, and Thought Woman thinks creation and sings her two sisters into life. After they are vital she instructs them to sing over the items in their baskets (medicine bundles) in such a way that those items will have life. After that crucial task is accomplished, the creatures thus vitalized take on the power to regenerate themselves—that is, they can reproduce others of their kind. But they are not in and of themselves self-sufficient; they depend for their being on the medicine power of the three great Witch creatrixes, Thought Woman, Uretsete, and Naotsete. The sisters are not related by virtue of having parents in common; that is, they are not alive because anyone bore them. Thought Woman turns up, so to speak, first as Creatrix and then as a personage who is acting out someone else's "dream." But there is no time when she did not exist. She has two bundles in her power, and these bundles contain Uretsete and Naotsete, who are not viewed as her daughters but as her sisters, her coequals who possess the medicine power to vitalize the creatures that will inhabit the earth. They also have the power to create the firmament, the skies, the galaxies, and the seas, which they do through the use of ritual magic.

. . .

THE HEART OF POWER

. . .

Pre-Conquest American Indian women valued their role as vitalizers. Through their own bodies they could bring vital beings into the world—a miraculous power whose potency does not diminish with industrial sophistication or time.

They were mothers, and that word did not imply slaves, drudges, drones who are required to live only for others rather than for themselves as it does so tragically for many modern women. The ancient ones were empowered by their certain knowledge that the power to make life is the source of all power and that no other power can gainsay it. Nor is that power simply of biology, as modernists tendentiously believe. When Thought Woman brought to life the twin sisters, she did not give birth to them in the biological sense. She sang over the medicine bundles that contained their potentials. With her singing and shaking she infused them with vitality. She gathered the power that she controlled and focused it on those bundles, and thus they were "born." Similarly, when the sister goddesses Naotsete and Uretsete wished to bring forth some plant or creature, they reached into the basket (bundle) that Thought Woman had given them, took out the effigy of the creature, and thought it into life. Usually they then instructed it in its proper role. They also meted out consequences to creatures (this included plants, spirits, and katsinas) who disobeyed them.

The water of life, menstrual or postpartum blood, was held sacred. Sacred often means taboo; that is, what is empowered in a ritual sense is not to be touched or approached by any who are weaker than the power itself, lest they suffer negative consequences from contact. The blood of woman was in and of itself infused with the power of Supreme Mind, and so women were held in awe and respect. The term *sacred,* which is connected with power, is similar in meaning to the term *sacrifice,* which means "to make sacred." What is made sacred is empowered. Thus, in the old way, sacrificing meant empowering, which is exactly what it still means to American Indians who adhere to traditional practice. Blood was and is used in sacrifice because it possesses the power to make something else powerful or, conversely, to weaken or kill it.

Pre-contact American Indian women valued their role as vitalizers because they understood that bearing, like bleeding, was a transformative ritual act. Through their own bodies they could bring vital beings into the world—a miraculous power unrivaled by mere shamanic displays. They were mothers, and that word implied the highest degree of status in ritual cultures. The status of mother was so high, in fact, that in some cultures Mother or its analogue, Matron, was the highest office to which a man or woman could aspire.

The old ones were empowered by their certain knowledge that the power to make life is the source and model for all ritual magic and that no other power can gainsay it. Nor is that power really biological at base; it is the power of ritual magic, the power of Thought, of Mind, that gives rise to biological organisms as it gives rise to social organizations, material culture, and transformations of all kinds—including hunting, war, healing, spirit communication, rain-making, and all the rest. . . .

A strong attitude integrally connects the power of Original Thinking or Creation Thinking to the power of mothering. That power is not so much the power to give birth, as we have noted, but the power to make, to create, to transform. Ritual means transforming something from one state or condition to another, and that ability is inherent in the action of mothering. It is the ability that is sought and treasured by adepts, and it is the ability that male seekers devote years of study and discipline to acquire. Without it, no practice of the sacred is possible, at least not within the Great Mother societies.

And as the cultures that are woman-centered and Mother-ritual based are also cultures that value peacefulness, harmony, cooperation, health, and general prosperity, they are systems of thought and practice that would bear deeper study in our troubled, conflict-ridden time.

NOTES

1. Anthony Purley, "Keres Pueblo Concepts of Deity," *American Indian Culture and Research Journal* 1 (Fall 1974): 29. The passage cited is Purley's literal translation from the Keres Indian language of a portion of the Thought Woman story. Purley is a native-speaker Laguna Pueblo Keres.
2. Ibid., 30–31.

3. Hamilton A. Tyler, *Pueblo Gods and Myths*, Civilization of the American Indian Series (Norman, OK: University of Oklahoma Press, 1964), 37. Evidently, Huruing Wuhti has other transformative abilities as well. Under pressure from patriarchal politics, she can change her gender, her name, and even her spiritual nature.

4. Ibid., 93.

5. Purley, "Keres Pueblo Concepts," 31.

6. Ibid.

R E A D I N G **98**

The Islamic Bill of Rights for Women in Mosques

Asra Q. Nomani

1. Women have an Islamic right to enter a mosque.
2. Women have an Islamic right to enter through the main door.
3. Women have an Islamic right to visual and auditory access to the *musalla* (main sanctuary).
4. Women have an Islamic right to pray in the musalla without being separated by a barrier, including in the front and in mixed-gender congregational lines.
5. Women have an Islamic right to address any and all members of the congregation.
6. Women have an Islamic right to hold leadership positions, including positions as prayer leaders and as members of the board of directors and management committees.
7. Women have an Islamic right to be full participants in all congregational activities.
8. Women have an Islamic right to lead and participate in meetings, study sessions, and other community activities without being separated by a barrier.
9. Women have an Islamic right to be greeted and addressed cordially.
10. Women have an Islamic right to respectful treatment and exemption from gossip and slander.

THE CONVENTION

CHICAGO—. . . I was committed to being honest about who I am. Most women, although not all, wore the hijab in Chicago. Even women who didn't ordinarily cover their hair did for the convention so that they wouldn't be the subject of gossip. I cover my hair only in the mosque, and I wasn't going to do it now just for public appearance.

After all of the other panelists had spoken—most with PowerPoint presentations—I took the podium. I gazed softly at the audience and thanked the Islamic Society of North America. I explained that the presentation was the result of almost two years of work inspired by the transformative experience of praying together with my family in Mecca on the holy pilgrimage of the hajj in February 2003. I had made that journey with the help of the Islamic Society of North America, and I thanked the society for that experience and the opportunity to speak at the convention. My points were simple. "Islam is at a crossroads much like the place where the prophet Muhammad found himself when he was on the cusp of a new dawn with his migration to Medina from Mecca. Medina became 'the City of Illumination' because of the wisdom with which the prophet nurtured his ummah. In much the same way, the Muslim world has the opportunity to rise to a place of deep and sincere enlightenment, inspired by the greatest teachings of Islam. It is our choice which path we take. It is our mandate to take action to ensure that we define our communities as tolerant, inclusive, and compassionate places that value and inspire all within our fold."

The problem was clear. "There are many model mosques that affirm women's rights. Yet women are systematically denied rights that Islam granted them in the seventh century in mosques throughout America. Islam grants all people inalienable rights to respect, dignity, participation, leadership, voice, knowledge, and worship. These rights must be granted to women, as well as men, in the mosques and Islamic centers that are a part of our Muslim communities. Islamic teaching seeks expressions of modesty between men and women. But many mosques in America and beyond have gone well beyond that principle by defining themselves with cultural traditions that perpetuate a system of separate accommodations that provides women with wholly unequal services for prayer and education. And yet, excluding women ignores the rights the prophet Muhammad gave them in the seventh century when he created a Muslim ummah in Medina and represents innovations that emerged after the prophet died."

I gave evidence of the rights denied in mosques throughout America and laid out the Islamic arguments that had empowered me to take action in my mosque in Morgantown. "It is

time for our communities to embody the essential principles of equity, tolerance, and inclusion within Islam," I said. "And it is incumbent upon each of us as Muslims to stand up for those principles."

I told them what I had come to realize in the two years since January 2001 when the Dalai Lama had set me on my path toward Mecca. Terrorists transformed our world into a more dangerous place when they attacked the World Trade Center and the Pentagon on September 11, 2001. Before we knew it, a minority of Islamic fundamentalists who preached hatred of the West were defining Islam in the world. Alas, moderates, including myself, have been a "silent majority," remaining largely quiet. A combination of fear, shame, and apathy has contributed to a culture of silence among even those of us who are discontented with the status quo in Muslim society. Moderate Muslims have a great responsibility to define Islam and their communities in the world. For me, this effort started at home when I walked up to the front door of my mosque for the first time on the eve of Ramadan 2003. It is time, I said, for us to reclaim the rights Islam granted to women in the seventh century. Toward that end, I humbly introduced my poster with the Islamic Bill of Rights for Women in Mosques.

The rights are simple: the right to enter a mosque; the right to use the main door; the right to have visual and auditory access to the *musalla* (the main sanctuary); the right to pray in the main sanctuary without being separated by a barrier; the right to address any and all members of the congregation; the right to hold leadership positions, including positions on the board of directors; the right to be greeted and addressed cordially; and the right to receive respectful treatment and to be exempt from gossip and slander.

After reading the rights, I told the audience, "Ultimately, it is incumbent upon Islamic organizations, community leaders, academics, and mosques to respond to this call for improved rights for women in mosques by endorsing and promoting a campaign, modeling it after their very successful educational and legal campaigns to protect the civil liberties of Muslim men and women in other areas. To do so would honor not only Muslim women but also Islam. The journey is never complete, and a long road remains in front of us, but we have as inspiration a time in the seventh century when a new day lay ahead of a caravan trader who had as much to fear as we do today but nonetheless transcended his doubts and fears to create an ummah to which we all belong today. Allow us all to rise to our highest potential."

With a deep breath, I sat down, not knowing what to expect next.

Although there were four other speakers, a torrent of questions came at me when members of the audience stood at the microphone.

There were three hecklers. One admonished me for not saying the code phrase "Peace be upon him" after the name of the prophet. Another part of our inside language is "Sall-Allahu aleyhi wa sallam" (May the peace and blessings of Allah be upon him, abbreviated as SAW), said after any mention of the prophet or an angel. "The Clans" in the Qur'an (33:56) says, "The Prophet is blessed by God and His angels. Bless him then, you that are true believers, and greet him with a worthy salutation."

At the dais, the director of the Long Island mosque, Faroque Khan, a physician originally from India, had just spoken about the powerful interfaith work his mosque had done after 9/11 by opening its doors, and he defended me from his seat. "She is a brave daughter of Islam. Do not criticize her for such little things." The critics were undeterred. A young man stood up and identified himself as a member of the Muslim Students' Association. "Where is your proof?" he demanded angrily, shaking his head, his beard a blur in front of me. I pointed to the seventy-four footnotes in the reprint of the article my father and I wrote for the *Journal of Islamic Law and Society*. "The Sunnah of the prophet will never change," he said, shaking his head fiercely again. I stared at his eyes, so wide and menacing. *I will never forget those eyes,* I told myself, not realizing how useful that observation would become when I confronted the young man's rage again, days later.

At that moment, though, I didn't know I'd ever cross paths with him again, and I actually felt sorry for him that he felt so threatened by the simple bill of rights. I wanted to scream: these rights *are* the Sunnah of the prophet. I knew what lay beneath his anger. Some men don't want to relinquish the power and control it has taken them centuries to accumulate. Some men think it is their God-given right to express this power and control over women. But the prophet gave women rights that men deny them today, and it is our Islamic duty to reclaim those rights so that we can be stronger citizens of the world.

A twenty-four-year-old African American woman from Boston, Nakia Jackson, stood up. The women in her mosque prayed in a urine-stained, rat-infested room that doubled as a storage closet. And they accepted the status quo. "I feel so alone. What advice do you have for someone like me?" she asked, her voice trembling.

"You are not alone," I told her. "So often I have stood physically alone in my mosque in Morgantown. But I have felt the spiritual press of so many kindred spirits who stand with me. I am with you. You are not alone."

Afterward, I was mobbed. I hugged so many women, young and old, that I lost count. And I received the encouragement of so many men, young and old, that my faith was renewed. "We did it!" I told my parents when I called home later.

THE PROFESSOR

LOS ANGELES—"The professor would like to invite you, your mother, and Shibli to visit him at his home," said Naheed Fakoor, an Afghan American woman who was the assistant extraordinaire to UCLA law professor Khalid Abou El Fadl. She mentioned delicately that he rarely invited anyone to his home. I understood the power of this invitation. In my estimation, we were getting an audience with the pope of tolerant Islam.

A year earlier I had not even known that this professor existed. It had taken me months to memorize all the syllables of his name and the order in which they are said. More often than not,

I referred to him as "Abou Khalid ... oh, you know, the UCLA professor of law." My kindred spirits within the Muslim world knew of whom I spoke. When I told Dr. Alan Godlas, the Islamic studies professor at the University of Georgia, that I was going to be meeting "the Professor," as Naheed allowed me to call him, Dr. Godlas got excited. "He is the best hope for Islam in America," he said. Not only could the Professor speak to disenfranchised Muslims like me, but he had the grounding in Islamic jurisprudence and original texts to be able to communicate with the mainstream puritanical set who were in positions of authority in our communities. His students and friends had created a Web site for him called scholarofthehouse.org, inspired by an award he received by that name when he was a student at Yale University. They called him "the most important and influential Islamic thinker in the modern age."

...

What separated Khalid Abou El Fadl from many intellectuals was his training in Egypt and Kuwait in Islamic jurisprudence: he was a high-ranking sheikh. I didn't know about him until a friend sent me a copy of a book he had written, *The Place of Tolerance in Islam*. My mother read it first. When she was finished, she closed its cover with a sigh of relief. "Since my childhood days," she said, "I was told that only Muslims would go to heaven and no others. I would ask, 'Why?' We were born Muslim by accident. Why should others be denied heaven because they were born Christian, Jew, Buddhist, or Hindu? Nobody would answer me. They would tell me not to ask such stupid questions. For the first time, someone has answered my question and confirmed my belief that this assumption is wrong and that, in fact, the doors of heaven are open to all good people." She paused. "Khalid Abou El Fadl is a great man," my mother said. "He is the first person who helped me understand and *believe* in Islam." When I had called him to seek his guidance on the trial that I faced, I told him my mother's story. "Al-hamdulillah," he said, simply. Praise be to Allah.

It was enough to speak to him by phone. It was an honor to be beckoned for an audience. My response surprised even me. After all, I had met with senators, celebrities, and heads of state. What was a *professor*? But I knew I had to make this trip. I just didn't know why.

In Los Angeles I framed the Islamic Bill of Rights for Women in Mosques for the Professor and wrote below it two words: "In Gratitude." ... I brought a copy of *Time* magazine with an essay in which I'd written about the struggle for the soul of Islam and an article in which the Professor argued against the theological logic that al-Qaeda leaders such as Abu Mousab al-Zarqawi use to sanction the beheading of prisoners. Since Danny's beheading, militants from Iraq to Saudi Arabia had turned to this execution-style brutality to kill hostages. The Professor told *Time,* "Al-Zarqawi searches for the trash that everyone threw out centuries ago and declares the trash to be Islam." His words resonated with me on so many levels, including in the battle to win rights for women in our Muslim world. Having some idea that the meeting would certainly be meaningful, but not knowing quite how, I departed for his home with curious anticipation.

After winding slowly through rush-hour traffic, we arrived at the Professor's house at the corner of a street in a Los Angeles suburb. It was surrounded by a security fence, a reminder of the danger in which he lived. He had taken on Wahhabi ideology with frontal attacks on their theology as flawed and un-Islamic. Even Muslim American organizations lashed out at him when he penned an op-ed for the *Los Angeles Times* after 9/11, criticizing Muslim leaders for not condemning the attacks.

The Professor's assistant, Naheed, warmly beckoned us through the gate. His wife, a gentle and beautiful woman by the appropriate name of Grace, welcomed us at the door with a smile and embrace. The door opened into rooms that swept into each other. The walls were lined from floor to ceiling with one thing: books. The books in some sets were lined up next to each other so that their bindings spelled words in Arabic. ...

The Professor emerged in a flowing black cape, under which an embroidered collar peeked out from the traditional Arab gown he was wearing.

What struck me immediately was his physical vulnerability. He leaned on a cane and walked smoothly but slowly with small steps, extending his hand toward me gently. This in itself was significant. Saudi scholars had ruled that a man shaking hands with a woman was "evil" and *haram,* or unlawful. I took his hand gently. "Thank you for the honor of this invitation to visit you," I said. Not close enough to extend her hand to the Professor, my mother raised her cupped right hand to her forehead in a high-browed Indian Muslim gesture of respect between men and women. "Adhab," she said, in an Urdu greeting.

The Professor immediately lent me his support in the trial that my mosque had started against me. He reveled in the spirit of the Islamic Bill of Rights for Women in Mosques. "This is good," he said. And he cheered the writing that I was doing.

When it was time for prayer, the Professor did another remarkable thing. He prayed with his son on his left side and his wife on his right side. Naheed, my mother, and I lined up behind them. He needed help going into prostration and then standing up again, but his spatial arrangement was more than just practical. He believed in the intrinsic right of women to stand on a par with men.

In prayer at the Professor's house, I felt free for the first time in so long. Even though I was physically behind the Professor, I did not feel disrespected. Many Muslim men say they are expressing respect for women in their desire to protect them through segregation. But I knew the Professor didn't want to silence me. We sat around a circular dining table until late into the night, and he honored me when he revealed that he had read my first book and supported my voice. "It is a great victory that you are writing. You can only testify to the truth that you know," he said. "And you are doing that." He spoke with candor, even using the word *sucks,* and he lamented that Muslim leaders ran their communities as if they were playing Monopoly, collecting properties and building symbolic hotels of power.

The next night we returned, and my mother, Naheed, the Professor's wife, and I prayed in the same row as the Professor and his son. When we broke from prayer, the Professor led us through a tour of his library. To call it a library is an understatement. His books filled every wall in his room. ("Does he sell them?" my mother asked afterward, perplexed about why he collected so many books. "Mom!" I admonished her, but privately I could understand her curiosity.) He pored through Arabic texts to show me the works of the two thousand women jurists Islam has had since its inception in the seventh century. A year earlier I couldn't even name the century in which Islam was born. Now I knew the number of women jurists we've had. I was both amazed and astonished. On these shelves was the secret history of feminine power that centuries of male domination had erased. He pulled down a book published by a *madhab,* or school of jurisprudence, that had been destroyed. Both the school and its prayer had been led by a woman, he told me. "What?" I exclaimed. "A woman?"

"Yes, a woman."

I was surprised to see a familiar book on his shelves—my first book, *Tantrika.* And it was the hardcover edition with the image of a woman's bare torso on the front. Some Muslims had protested the cover when editor Ahmed Nassef put it on the Muslim WakeUp! Web site. I had put a yellow Post-it over the torso when I took the book to the Islamic Society of North America convention. But here it was, uncensored, beside the works of the great Muslim jurists. And to my shock, the Professor asked me to autograph the book. So many men—and even some women—within my religion had discounted me and discredited me because I wrote truthfully about the most intimate challenges in my life. But the Professor did not make me feel ashamed. Instead, he affirmed me.

I handed the book back to him with an inscription that couldn't capture the gift he had given me with the respect he had shown for my intellect, voice, and being. As he stood, he lost his balance and his cane slipped from his grip. My heart fell as I witnessed the physical vulnerability that accompanied the Professor's spiritual fortitude. Grace moved swiftly to help him regain his balance. Without pause, he looked me in the eye and took my hand, gently, in parting.

"Asra, do not let anyone deter you. Continue to be courageous," he said clearly. "You are on the right path."

"Thank you, Professor," I said quietly. Touched by his words and his sincere gestures of kindness and respect toward my family and me, my heart wept. He recognized that I had struggled hard to resolve the dissonance between the intimate areas of my life and my religion. So often we live with guilt about our sexual lives. But I had found a peace with the decisions I'd made about my

body, and I had claimed the worthiness of my spirit. I could embrace Islam.

Religion isn't meant to destroy people. The Professor recognized that I had struggled to answer the question of who I am and where my faith rests in my identity as a Muslim woman. I knew he was not speaking just to me but to all people—women and men, girls and boys—who choose the path of honesty, justice, tolerance, and compassion. This has been my struggle, but it is the struggle of all people as well. . . .

R E A D I N G **99**

Standing Again at Sinai

Judith Plaskow

EXPLORING THE TERRAIN OF SILENCE

. . . The central Jewish categories of Torah, Israel, and God are all constructed from male perspectives. Torah is revelation as men perceived it, the story of Israel told from their standpoint, the law unfolded according to their needs. Israel is the male collectivity, the children of a Jacob who had a daughter, but whose sons became the twelve tribes. God is named in the male image, a father and warrior much like his male offspring, who confirms and sanctifies the silence of his daughters. Exploring these categories, we explore the parameters of women's silence.

In Torah, Jewish teaching, women are not absent, but they are cast in stories told by men. As characters in narrative, women may be vividly characterized, as objects of legislation, singled out for attention. But women's presence in Torah does not negate their silence, for women do not decide the questions with which Jewish sources deal. When the law treats of women, it is often because their "abnormality" demands it. If women are central to plot, the plots are not

about them. Women's interests and intentions must be unearthed from texts with other purposes, for both law and narrative serve to obscure them.

The most striking examples of women's silence come from texts in which women are most central, for there the normative character of maleness is especially jarring. In the family narratives of Genesis, for example, women figure prominently. The matriarchs of Genesis are all strong women. As independent personalities, fiercely concerned for their children, they often seem to have an intuitive knowledge of God's plans for their sons. Indeed, it appears from the stories of Sarah and Rebekah that they understand God better than their husbands. God defends Sarah when she casts out Hagar, telling Abraham to obey his wife (Gen. 21:12). Rebekah, knowing it is God's intent, helps deceive Isaac into accepting Jacob as his heir (Gen. 25:23; 27:5–17). Yet despite their intuitions, and despite their wiliness and resourcefulness, it is not the women who receive the covenant or who pass on its lineage. The establishment of patrilineal descent and the patriarchal family takes precedence over the matriarch's stories. Their relationship to God, in some way presupposed by the text, remains an undigested element in the narrative. What was the full theophany to Rebekah, and how is it related to the covenant with Isaac? The writer does not tell us; it is not sufficiently important. And so the covenant remains the covenant with Isaac, while Rebekah's experience floats at the margin of the story.

The establishment of patrilineal descent and patriarchal control, a subtext in Genesis, is an important theme in the legislation associated with Sinai. Here again, women figure prominently, but only as objects of male concerns. The laws pertaining to women place them firmly under the control of first fathers, then husbands, so that men can have male heirs they know are theirs. Legislation concerning adultery (Deut. 22:22, also Num. 5:11–31) and virginity (Deut. 22:13–21) speaks of women, but only to control female sexuality to male advantage. The *crime* of adultery is sleeping with another man's wife, and a man can bring his wife to trial even on suspicion of adultery, a right that is not reciprocal. Sleeping with a betrothed virgin constitutes adultery. A man who sleeps with a virgin who is not betrothed must simply marry her. A girl whose lack of virginity shames her father on her wedding night can be stoned to death for harlotry. A virgin who is raped must marry her assailant. The subject of these laws is women, but the interest behind them is the purity of the male line.

The process of projecting and defining women as objects of male concerns is expressed most fully not in the Bible, however, but in the Mishnah, an important second-century legal code. Part of the Mishnah's Order of Women (one of its six divisions) develops laws discussed in the Torah concerning certain problematic aspects of female sexuality. The subject of the division is the transfer of women—the regulation of women who are in states of transition, whose uncertain status threatens the stasis of the community. The woman who is about to enter into a marriage or who has just left one requires close attention. The law must regularize her irregularity, facilitate her transition to the normal state of wife and motherhood, at which point she no longer poses a problem. . . .

Thus Torah—"Jewish" sources, "Jewish" teaching—puts itself forward as *Jewish* teaching but speaks in the voice of only half the Jewish people. This scandal is compounded by another: The omission is neither mourned nor regretted; it is not even noticed. True, the rabbis were aware of the harshness of certain laws pertaining to women and sought to mitigate their effects. They tried to find ways to force a recalcitrant husband to divorce his wife, for example. But the framework that necessitated such mitigations went unquestioned. Women's Otherness was left intact. The Jewish passion for justice did not extend to Jewish women. As Cynthia Ozick puts it, one great "Thou shalt not"—"Thou shalt not lessen the humanity of women"—is missing from the Torah.

For this great omission, there is no historical redress. Indeed, where one might expect redress, the problem is compounded. The prophets, those great champions of justice, couch their pleas for justice in the language of patriarchal marriage. Israel in her youth is a devoted bride, subordinate and obedient to her husband/God (for example, Jer. 2:2). Idolatrous Israel is a harlot and adulteress, a faithless woman whoring after false gods (for example, Hos. 2,3). Transferring the hierarchy of male and female to God and his people, the prophets enshrine in metaphor the legal subordination of women. Those who might have named and challenged women's marginalization thus ignore and extend it.

The prophetic metaphors mark an end and a beginning. They confront us with the injustice of Torah; they link that injustice to other central Jewish ideas. If exploring Torah means exploring a terrain of women's silence, this is no less true of the categories of Israel or God.

Israel, the bride, the harlot, the people that is female (that is, subordinate) in relation to God is nonetheless male in communal self-perception. The covenant community is the community of the circumcised (Gen. 17:10), the community defined as male heads of household. Women are named through a filter of male experience: that is the essence of their silence. But women's experiences are not recorded or taken seriously because women are not perceived as normative

Jews. They are part of but do not define the community of Israel.

The same evidence that speaks to women's silence in the tradition, to the partiality of Torah, also reflects an understanding of Israel as a community of males. In the narratives of Genesis, for example, the covenant moves from father to son, from Abraham to Isaac to Jacob to Joseph. The matriarchs' relation to their husbands' God is sometimes assumed, sometimes passed over, but the women do not constitute the covenant people. Women's relation to the community is also ambiguous and unclear in biblical legislation. The law is couched in male grammatical forms, and its content too presupposes a male nation. "You shall not covet your neighbor's wife" (Ex. 20:17). Probably we cannot deduce from this verse that women are free to covet! Yet the injunction assumes that women's obedience is owed to fathers and husbands, who are the primary group addressed.

The silence of women goes deeper, however, than who defines Torah or Israel. It also finds its way into language about God. Our language about divinity is first of all male language; it is selective and partial. The God who supposedly transcends sexuality, who is presumably one and whole, comes to us through language that is incomplete and narrow. The images we use to describe God, the qualities we attribute to God, draw on male pronouns and experience and convey a sense of power and authority that is clearly male. The God at the surface of Jewish consciousness is a God with a voice of thunder, a God who as lord and king rules his people and leads them into battle, a God who forgives like a father when we turn to him. The female images that exist in the Bible and (particularly the mystical) tradition form an underground stream that occasionally reminds us of the inadequacy of our imagery without transforming its overwhelmingly male nature.

This male imagery is comforting and familiar—comforting because familiar—but it is an integral part of a system that consigns women to the margins. Since the experience of God cannot be directly conveyed in language, imagery for God is a vehicle that suggests what is actually impossible to describe. Religious experiences are expressed in a vocabulary drawn from the significant and valuable in a particular culture. To speak of God is to speak of what we most value. In attributing certain qualities to God, we both attempt to point to God and offer God's qualities to be emulated and admired. To say that God is just, for example, is to say both that God acts justly and that God demands justice. Justice belongs to God but is also ours to pursue. Similarly with maleness, to image God as male is to value the quality and those who have it. It is to define God in the image of the normative community and to bless men—but not women—with a central attribute of God.

But our images of God are not simply male images; they are images of a certain kind. The prophetic metaphors for the relation between God and Israel are metaphors borrowed from the patriarchal family—images of dominance softened by affection. God as husband and father of Israel demands obedience and monogamous love. He repays faithfulness with mercy and loving-kindness, but punishes waywardness, just as the wayward daughter can be stoned at her father's door (Deut. 22:21). When these family images are combined with political images of king and warrior, they reinforce a particular model of power and dominance. God is the power over us, the One out there over against us, the sovereign warrior with righteousness on his side. Family and political models of dominance and submission are recapitulated and rendered plausible by the dominance and submission of God and Israel. The silence and submission of women becomes part of a greater pattern that makes it appear fitting and right.

. . .

Clearly, the implications of Jewish feminism reach beyond the goal of equality to transform the bases of Jewish life. Feminism demands a new understanding of Torah, Israel, and God. It demands an understanding of Torah that begins by acknowledging the injustice of Torah and then goes on to create a Torah that is whole. The silence of women reverberates through the tradition, distorting the shape of narrative and skewing the content of the law. Only the deliberate recovery of women's hidden voices, the unearthing and invention of women's Torah, can give us Jewish teachings that are the product of the whole Jewish people and that reflect more fully its experiences of God.

Feminism demands an understanding of Israel that includes the whole of Israel and thus allows women to speak and name our experience for ourselves. It demands we replace a normative male voice with a chorus of divergent voices, describing Jewish reality in different accents and tones. Feminism impels us to rethink issues of community and diversity, to explore the ways in which one people can acknowledge and celebrate the varied experiences of its members. What would it mean for women *as women* to be equal participants in the Jewish community? How can we talk about difference without creating Others?

Feminism demands new ways of talking about God that reflect and grow out of the redefinition of Jewish humanity. The exclusively male naming of God supported and was rendered meaningful by a cultural and religious situation that is passing away. The emergence of women allows and necessitates that the long-suppressed femaleness of God be recovered and explored and reintegrated into the Godhead. But feminism presses us beyond the issue of gender to examine the nature of the God with male names. How can we move beyond images of domination to a God present *in* community rather than over it? How can we forge a God-language that expresses women's experience?

R E A D I N G   **100**

Everywoman Her Own Theology

Alicia Ostriker

I am nailing them up to the cathedral door
Like Martin Luther. Actually, no,
I don't want to resemble that *Schmutzkopf*
(See Erik Erikson and N. O. Brown
On the Reformer's anal aberrations,
Not to mention his hatred of Jews and peasants),
So I am thumbtacking these ninety-five
Theses to the bulletin board in my kitchen.

My proposals, or should I say requirements,
Include at least one image of a god,
Virile, beard optional, one of a goddess,
Nubile, breast size approximating mine,
One divine baby, one lion, one lamb,
All nude as figs, all dancing wildly,
All shining. Reproducible
In marble, metal, in fact any material.

Ethically, I am looking for
An absolute endorsement of loving-kindness.
No loopholes except maybe mosquitoes.

Virtue and sin will henceforth be discouraged,
Along with suffering and martyrdom.
There will be no concept of infidels;
Consequently the faithful must entertain
Themselves some other way than killing infidels.

And so forth and so on. I understand
This piece of paper is going to be
Spattered with wine one night at a party
And covered over with newer pieces of paper.
That is how it goes with bulletin boards.
Nevertheless it will be there.
Like an invitation, like a chalk pentangle,
It will emanate certain occult vibrations.

If something sacred wants to swoop from the
    universe
Through a ceiling, and materialize,
Folding its silver wings,
In a kitchen, and bump its chest against mine,
My paper will tell this being where to find me.

Witchcraft and Women's Culture

Starhawk

From earliest times, women have been witches, *wicce,* "wise ones"—priestesses, diviners, mid-wives, poets, healers, and singers of songs of power. Woman-centered culture, based on the worship of the Great Goddess, underlies the beginnings of all civilization. Mother Goddess was carved on the walls of paleolithic caves, and painted in the shrines of the earliest cities, those of the Anatolian plateau. For her were raised the giant stone circles, the henges of the British Isles, the dolmens and cromlechs of the later Celtic countries, and for her the great passage graves of Ireland were dug. In her honor, sacred dancers leaped the bulls in Crete and composed lyric hymns within the colleges of the holy isles of the Mediterranean. Her mysteries were celebrated in secret rites at Eleusis, and her initiates included some of the finest minds of Greece. Her priestesses discovered and tested the healing herbs and learned the secrets of the human mind and body that allowed them to ease the pain of childbirth, to heal wounds and cure diseases, and to explore the realm of dreams and the unconscious. Their knowledge of nature enabled them to tame sheep and cattle, to breed wheat and corn from grasses and weeds, to forge ceramics from mud and metal from rock, and to track the movements of moon, stars, and sun.

Witchcraft, "the craft of the wise," is the last remnant in the west of the time of women's strength and power. Through the dark ages of persecution, the covens of Europe preserved what is left of the mythology, rituals, and knowledge of the ancient matricentric (mother-centered) times. The great centers of worship in Anatolia, Malta, Iberia, Brittany, and Sumeria are now only silent stones and works of art we can but dimly understand. Of the mysteries of Eleusis, we have literary hints; the poems of Sappho survive only in fragments. The great collections of early literature and science were destroyed by patriarchal forces—the library of Alexandria burnt by Caesar, Charlemagne's collection of lore burnt by his son Louis "the Pious," who was offended at its "paganism." But the craft remains, in spite of all efforts to stamp it out, as a living tradition of Goddess-centered worship that traces its roots back to the time before the triumph of patriarchy.

The old religion of witchcraft before the advent of Christianity was an earth-centered, nature-oriented worship that venerated the Goddess, the source of life, as well as her son-lover-consort, who was seen as the Horned God of the hunt and animal life. Earth, air, water, fire, streams, seas, wells, beasts, trees, grain, the planets, sun, and most of all, the moon, were seen as aspects of deity. On the great seasonal festivals—the solstices and equinoxes, and the eves of May, August, November, and February—all the countryside would gather to light huge bonfires, feast, dance, sing, and perform the rituals that assured abundance throughout the year.

When Christianity first began to spread, the country people held to the old ways, and for hundreds of years the two faiths coexisted quite peacefully. Many people followed both religions, and country priests in the twelfth and thirteenth centuries were frequently upbraided by church authorities for dressing in skins and leading the dance at the pagan festivals.

But in the thirteenth and fourteenth centuries, the church began persecution of witches, as well as Jews and "heretical" thinkers. Pope Innocent the VIII, with his Bull of 1484, intensified a campaign of torture and death that would take the lives of an estimated 9 million people, perhaps 80 percent of whom were women.

The vast majority of victims were not coven members or even necessarily witches. They were old widows whose property was coveted by someone else, young children with "witch blood," midwives who furnished the major competition to the male-dominated medical profession, freethinkers who asked the wrong questions.

An enormous campaign of propaganda accompanied the witch trials as well. Witches were said to have sold their souls to the devil, to practice obscene and disgusting rites, to blight crops and murder children. In many areas, the witches did worship a Horned God as the spirit of the hunt, of animal life and vitality, a concept far from the power of evil that was the Christian devil. Witches were free and open about sexuality—but their rites were "obscene" only to those who viewed the human body itself as filthy and evil. Questioning or disbelieving any of the slander was itself considered proof of witchcraft or heresy, and the falsehoods that for hundreds of years could not be openly challenged had their effect. Even today, the word *witch* is often automatically associated with "evil."

With the age of reason in the eighteenth century, belief in witches, as in all things psychic and supernatural, began to fade. The craft as a religion was forgotten; all that remained were the wild stories of broomstick flights, magic potions, and the summoning of spectral beings.

Memory of the true craft faded everywhere except within the hidden covens. With it went the memory of women's heritage and history, of our ancient roles as leaders, teachers, healers, seers. Lost, also, was the conception of the Great Spirit, as manifest in nature, in life, in woman. Mother Goddess slept, leaving the world to the less than gentle rule of the God-Father.

The Goddess has at last stirred from sleep, and women are reawakening to our ancient power. The feminist movement, which began as a political, economic, and social struggle, is opening to a spiritual dimension. In the process, many women are discovering the old religion, reclaiming the word *witch* and, with it, some of our lost culture.

Witchcraft, today, is a kaleidoscope of diverse traditions, rituals, theologies, and structures. But underneath the varying forms is a basic orientation common to all the craft. The outer forms of religion—the particular words said, the signs made, the names used—are less important to us than the inner forms, which cannot be defined or described but must be felt and intuited.

The craft is earth religion, and our basic orientation is to the earth, to life, to nature. There is no dichotomy between spirit and flesh, no split between Godhead and the world. The Goddess is manifest in the world; she brings life into being, *is* nature, *is* flesh. Union is not sought outside the world in some heavenly sphere or through dissolution of the self into the void beyond the senses. Spiritual union is found in life, within nature, passion, sensuality—through being fully human, fully one's self.

Our great symbol for the Goddess is the moon, whose three aspects reflect the three stages in women's lives and whose cycles of waxing and waning coincide with women's menstrual cycles. As the new moon or crescent, she is the Maiden, the Virgin—not chaste, but belonging to herself alone, not bound to any man. She is the wild child, lady of the woods, the huntress, free and untamed—Artemis, Kore, Aradia, Nimue. White is her color. As the full moon, she is the mature woman, the sexual being, the mother and nurturer, giver of life, fertility, grain, offspring, potency, joy—Tana, Demeter, Diana, Ceres, Mari. Her colors are the red of blood and the green of growth. As waning or dark moon, she is the old woman, past menopause, the hag or crone that is ripe with wisdom, patroness of secrets, prophecy, divination, inspiration, power—Hecate, Ceridwen, Kali, Anna. Her color is the black of night.

The Goddess is also earth—Mother Earth, who sustains all growing things, who is the body, our bones and cells. She is air—the winds that move in the trees and over the waves, breath. She is the fire of the hearth, of the blazing bonfire and the fuming volcano; the power of transformation and change. And she is water—the sea, original source of life; the rivers, streams, lakes and wells;

the blood that flows in the rivers of our veins. She is mare, cow, cat, owl, crane, flower, tree, apple, seed, lion, sow, stone, woman. She is found in the world around us, in the cycles and seasons of nature, and in mind, body, spirit, and emotions within each of us. Thou art Goddess. I am Goddess. All that lives (and all that is, lives), all that serves life, is Goddess.

Because witches are oriented to earth and to life, we value spiritual qualities that I feel are especially important to women, who have for so long been conditioned to be passive, submissive and weak. The craft values independence, personal strength, *self*—not petty selfishness but that deep core of strength within that makes us each a unique child of the Goddess. The craft has no dogma to stifle thought, no set of doctrines that have to be believed. Where authority exists, within covens, it is always coupled with the freedom every covener has, to leave at any time. When self is valued—in ourselves—we can see that self is everywhere.

Passion and emotion—that give depth and color and meaning to human life—are also valued.

Witches strive to be in touch with feelings, even if they are sometimes painful, because the joy and pleasure and ecstasy available to a fully alive person make it worth occasional suffering. So-called negative emotion—anger—is valued as well, as a sign that something is wrong and that action needs to be taken. Witches prefer to handle anger by taking action and making changes rather than by detaching ourselves from our feelings in order to reach some nebulous, "higher" state.

Most of all, the craft values love. The Goddess' only law is "Love unto all beings." But the love we value is not the airy flower power of the hippies or the formless, abstracted *agape* of the early Christians. It is passionate, sensual, personal love, *eros*, falling in love, mother-child love, the love of one unique human being for other individuals, with all their personal traits and idiosyncrasies. Love is not something that can be radiated out in solitary meditation—it manifests itself in relationships and interactions with other people. It is often said "You cannot be a witch alone"—because to be a witch is to be a lover, a lover of the Goddess, and a lover of other human beings.

R E A D I N G **102**

Religion and Feminism's Fourth Wave

Pythia Peay

On September 11, 2001, California psychotherapist Kathlyn Schaaf was overwhelmed by a powerful thought. Watching the violent images on television, she suddenly felt the time had come to "gather the women." She wasn't alone. Schaaf and 11 others who shared her response soon created Gather the Women, a Web site and communications hub that 5,000 women have used to chronicle their local events in support of world peace. As women assembled near the pyramids in Egypt and held potluck dinners in Alaska, staged candlelight vigils and other rituals in countries around the world, it confirmed Schaaf's gut instinct that an untapped reserve of energy "lies like oil beneath the common ground the women share."

Since then, the group has organized a series of congresses to connect women's groups. Their work is one example of a new kind feminism, slowly growing for a decade and now bursting out everywhere. At its heart lies a new kind of political activism that's guided and sustained by spirituality. Some are calling it the long-awaited "fourth wave" of feminism—a fusion of spirituality and social justice reminiscent of the American civil rights movement and Gandhi's call for nonviolent change.

This phenomenon is most visible in the popular conferences organized by women spiritual and religious leaders. Just as important are those meeting privately to meditate and pray, to study the world, and to support each other in social action. These gatherings share a commitment to a universal spirituality that affirms women's bonds across ethnic and religious boundaries. They're also exploring a new feminine paradigm of power that's based on tolerance, mutuality, and reverence for nature—values they now see as crucial to curing the global pathologies of poverty and war.

Previous advances in American feminism have rarely happened smoothly; the gains of one generation have often both shaped and conflicted with the ambitions of the next. First-wave feminists fought for women's suffrage. Led in the 1970s by icons like Gloria Steinem and Betty Friedan, a second wave pushed for economic and legal gains. Their ideals would eventually clash with the spirited individualism of third-wave feminists, women in their 20s and 30s who still advocate for women's rights while embracing a "girlie culture" that celebrates sex, men, gay culture, and clothes.

But as never before, today's conservative political environment has united women across the feminist spectrum. The result differs from earlier forms of feminism in several ways. For one, it espouses a new activism based not in anger, but in joy. It also tends to be focused outward, beyond the individual to wider issues, often global in scope. In the words of author Carol Lee Flinders, "Feminism catches fire when it draws on its inherent spirituality," which means something else can happen as well. "When you get Jewish, Catholic, Buddhist, Hindu, and Sufi women all practicing their faith in the same room," she recently said, "another religion emerges, which is feminine spirituality."

Though Flinders and other writers have been calling on women to reconnect with the sacred for years, many agree that the tipping point was 9/11. Before then, a women's spirituality conference called Sacred Circles, held biannually at Washington National Cathedral in the nation's capital, had focused on *personal* spirituality. More recently, however, program director Grace Ogden said she felt compelled to use the gatherings to address religious violence. "There was this sense of something gone terribly wrong," she said, "of communities splitting apart and a growing suspicion of people of Arab descent or other traditions." Her planning committee has since become more interfaith than in the past. Recent Sacred Circles conferences have stressed the role of compassion and tolerance in addressing political, economic, and religious differences.

Appalled by the lack of women in positions of religious authority on 9/11, Dena Merriam, a New York arts writer and public relations executive, joined others trying to form an international network of women religious leaders from the major faiths. In October 2002, they launched the Global Peace Initiative of Women Religious and Spiritual Leaders in Geneva, Switzerland. Associated with the United Nations, the initiative wants to get religious leaders more involved in U.N. peace-building plans. Specific programs aim to help young women of different faiths to communicate in places like Jerusalem that have been torn by conflict.

Merriam, the group's convener, said that one of women's strengths in peace work stems from their greatest weakness—their long exile from authority inside mainstream institutions. "Suddenly women are beginning to realize that their outsider status is an asset," she said, leaving them free to act directly, outside institutional lines. Many women are following the fate of U.N. Resolution 1325, which, if passed, will mandate that women be involved in all peace negotiations.

Feminism's new direction was perhaps most striking at the Women & Power conference sponsored by the Omega Institute and V-Day in New York City last September. The 3,000 participants heard celebrity feminists like Jane Fonda, Sally Field, and Gloria Steinem herself note the shift. Playwright Eve Ensler, founder of V-Day, a movement to stop global violence against women and girls, addressed the need to change the face of power. Today, she said, our power is seen in terms of "country over country, tribe against tribe." The new paradigm, however, has to be about power "in the service of"—collaboration, not conquest.

The free flow of creative expression at these assemblies marks a radical departure from the church coffees of our mothers' era. Participants often join together in fashioning new rites and rituals from ancient traditions, shaping forms at once old and new. Organizers at the Women & Power conference draped one room in carpets and labeled it the Red Tent area, evoking the Jewish ritual popularized by the book of that name. Elizabeth Lesser, a co-founder of the Omega Institute, said the room was like "an ancient gathering place where women were laughing, crying, brushing each other's hair, praying, and meditating. It seemed to satisfy women's deepest longings and was spiritual in a very feminine way."

At gatherings big and small, many are realizing that putting themselves in the service of the world is feminism's next step. At a time when the United States is viewed with increasing distrust by other countries, feminism's shift toward cultivating a spiritually informed activism may help to repair our diplomatic ties. No less important is the depth that comes from quiet reflection closer to home. As Carol Lee Flinders notes, a "serious spiritual life with a strong inward dimension" is crucial in itself, releasing the energy that can turn visionary feminist theory into action.

Meanwhile, as feminism allows more women to reach positions of power in American culture, increasing numbers have discovered that material success does not satisfy their hunger for meaning and connection. Women are becoming increasingly clear and vocal about the need to integrate an emerging set of feminine-based values into the culture. As the Democratic Party searches for a guiding set of values, it might consider turning to the women's spirituality movement for inspiration.

DISCUSSION QUESTIONS FOR CHAPTER 12

1. Why do you think the control of women is a central component in many religions?

2. How do you think religion has been both empowering and oppressive for women?

3. How do you think the availability of a greater variety of images of God might impact religion and religion's influence on social life?

4. How might women work toward reform from within religious traditions? Why might some women feel the need to abandon religious traditions completely?

5. How have negative stereotypes of witchcraft served to perpetuate the oppression of women? Why do you think practices of women's spirituality were (and still are) perceived as such a threat?

6. How do nondominant religious traditions challenge the influence of hegemonic Christianity in U.S. society?

SUGGESTIONS FOR FURTHER READING

Armstrong, Karen. *The Spiral Staircase: My Climb Out of Darkness*. New York: Anchor, 2005.

Barazangi, Nimat Hafez. *Woman's Identity and the Qur'an: A New Reading*. Gainesville: University Press of Florida, 2004.

Cochran, Pamela. *Evangelical Feminism: A History.* New York: New York University Press, 2004.

Higginbotham, Joyce, and River Higginbotham. *Paganism: An Introduction to Earth-Centered Religions.* St. Paul, MN: Llewellyn Publications, 2002.

Mitchem, Stephanie. *Introducing Womanist Theology.* Maryknoll, NY: Orbis, 2002.

Plaskow, Judith, and Donna Berman, eds. *The Coming of Lilith: Essays on Feminism, Judaism, and Sexual Ethics, 1972–2003.* Boston: Beacon Press, 2005.

CHAPTER 13

Activism, Change, and Feminist Futures

THE PROMISE OF FEMINIST EDUCATION

In Chapter 1 we discussed the objectives of women's studies as a discipline. These objectives include, first, an understanding of the social construction of gender and the intersection of gender with other systems of inequality in women's lives; second, a familiarity with women's status, contributions, and individual and collective actions for change; and third, an awareness of ways to improve women's status. A fourth objective of women's studies is that you will start thinking about patterns of privilege and discrimination in your own life and understand your position vis-à-vis systems of inequality. We hope you will learn to think critically about how societal institutions affect individual lives—especially your own. We hope you will gain new insights and confidence and that new knowledge will empower you.

Feminist educators attempt to give students more inclusive and socially just forms of knowledge and to support teachers using their power in nonexploitive ways. Women's studies usually involve nonhierarchical, egalitarian classrooms where teachers respect students and hope to learn from them as well as teach them. The focus is on the importance of the student voice and experience and encouraging both personal and social change. Most women's studies classes, however, are within colleges that do not necessarily share the same goals and objectives. Many feminist educators operate within the social and economic constraints of educational institutions that view "counter-hegemonic" education—that is, education that challenges the status quo—as problematic and/or subversive. Despite these constraints, feminist education, with its progressive and transformative possibilities, is an important feature on most campuses.

For many students, and perhaps for you too, the term *feminism* is still problematic. Many people object to the political biases associated with feminist education and believe knowledge should be objective and devoid of political values. It is important to emphasize that all knowledge is associated with power, as knowledge arises from communities with certain positions, resources, and understandings of the world. This means that all knowledge (and not just feminist knowledge) is ideological in that it is in some way associated with history and politics. To declare objectivity or value-neutrality is to mask the workings of power within knowledge. Although feminist education is more explicit than other forms of knowledge in speaking of its relationship to power in society, this does not mean it is more biased or ideological than other forms of knowledge. As civil rights activists declared, "If you're not part of the solution, then you're part of the problem." In other words, whether you are part of the problem or part of the solution (however you define problem and solution), you are equally political.

Many people support the justice-based goals of feminism but do not identify with the label. The reading by Lisa Marie Hogeland titled "Fear of Feminism: Why Young Women Get the Willies" addresses this issue. She also looks in depth at continuing resistance to feminism as politics and as a way of life. She makes the important distinction between *gender consciousness* and *feminist consciousness,* explains why one does not necessarily imply the other, and discusses the fear of reprisals and consequences associated with a feminist consciousness.

ACTIVISM

We live in a complex time. White women have made significant progress over the past decades and have begun the twenty-first century integrated into most societal institutions. Although the progress of women of color lags behind the gains made by White women, they too are beginning to be heard. Yet, the big picture is far from rosy, as society has not been transformed in its core values as feminists throughout the last century would have liked. An equitable sharing of power and resources in terms of gender, race, class, and other differences has not been actualized. In addition, as women receive more public power, they are encouraged to internalize more private constraints concerning the body and sexuality.

These times at the turn of the century have been touted as prosperous even while the gap between the rich and the poor in the United States is the largest among industrialized nations and is increasing. The median salary for CEOs at the top 100 U.S. corporations is $33.4 million/year compared to the average salary of the U.S. worker at $16.23/hour. Despite the widespread belief that the U.S. remains a more mobile society (that means people can move out of poverty or move into more wealth), economists say that in recent decades the typical child starting out in poverty in the United States has a worse chance at prosperity than one in continental Europe or Canada. The U.S. and Britain stand out as the least mobile among postindustrial societies. In 2003 it was estimated that the top 1 percent of people in the U.S. own 40 percent of the country's wealth. U.S. Census data for 2002 show 25 percent of children under 6 years old live in poverty and one in five children goes to bed hungry. Economists and sociologists emphasize that personal debt is a major problem in the United States with personal debt currently at about 120 percent of personal income. Despite this, U.S. workers tend to work about 9 weeks more a year than their European counterparts. Violence is increasing in our society in all walks of life; women, people of color, and gays and lesbians are frequently the target of hate and hostility; and the balance of power in the world seems fragile and in the hands of relatively few (often egocentric, delusional) men. Wars surround us. The picture is one of great optimism and yet simultaneous despair.

In the reading "Taking the High Road," Suzanne Pharr writes that violence, bigotry, and hatred are related in important ways to the alienation and disconnection felt by some people in contemporary society. She encourages us to address the rage, cynicism, and mean-spiritedness of this historical moment and come up with a transformational politics that encourages a consciousness shift and extends generosity and compassion toward others. In other words, any movement for justice-based equalities must have a strong moral foundation based on love, human dignity, and community.

As Audre Lorde, one of the most eloquent writers of the feminist second wave, once declared, "Silence will not protect you." Lorde wrote about the need to be part of social change efforts, and she encouraged us to speak out and address the problems in our lives and communities. And, as the reading by Michael Kimmel, "Real Men Join the Movement," implies, speaking out and addressing inequities involves learning how to be an ally to people who are different from you and who do not enjoy the privileges you enjoy. Kimmel emphasizes the necessity of men joining with women to make this world better for everyone. In this sense, coalitions are a central aspect of social change efforts.

In the past four decades there has been significant resistance to the status quo, or established power, in U.S. society, despite enormous backlash from the conservative right and other groups that seeks to maintain this power. Response to this backlash is the focus of the reading by Ruth Rosen, "Epilogue: Beyond Backlash." The strength of justice-based resistance has been its multi-issue and multistrategic approach. *Multistrategic* means relying on working coalitions that mobilize around certain shared issues and involve different strategies toward a shared goal. *Multi-issue* means organizing on many fronts over a variety of different issues that include political, legal, and judicial changes, educational reform, welfare rights, elimination of violence, workplace reform, and reproductive issues. The reading "Reflections of a Human Rights Educator" by Dazón Dixon Diallo focuses on activism by "Sisterlove," a group that educates on the intersections of HIV/AIDS, sexism, racism, and human rights. The human rights framework encourages coalitions to apply human rights standards associated with justice and human dignity to address individual and community problems.

As discussed in Chapter 1, some liberal or moderate activists have worked within the system and advocated change from within. Their approach locates the source of inequality in barriers to inclusion and advancement and has worked to change women's working lives through comparable worth, sexual harassment policy, and parenting leaves. Legal attacks on abortion rights have been deflected by the work of liberal feminists working within the courts, and affirmative action and other civil rights legislation have similarly been the focus of scholars, activists, and politicians working in the public sphere. These organizations tend to be hierarchical with a centralized governing structure (president, advisory board, officers, and so forth) and local chapters around the country. Other strategies for change take a radical approach (for example, radical or cultural feminism) and attempt to *transform* the system rather than to adapt the existing system. Together these various strategies work to advocate justice-based forms of equality. Contemporary feminism (both

Size Does Matter and Nine Other Tips for Effective Protest

- *Size does matter.* The most memorable protests—and the ones the media tends to cover—are the big ones: Think of the 1968 March on Washington and the Million Man March in 1995. The best way to put masses of people on the streets? Forge coalitions in order to broaden your base of potential protesters.
- *Get organized.* A large crowd is not, ipso facto, an effective performance. In November 1997, the Disney/Haiti Justice Campaign pulled together a sizable number of protesters outside the Disney Store in Times Square to denounce the company's Haitian sweatshops, but organizers failed to start a picket line or lead energetic chants. Many in the crowd simply milled around with their hands in their pockets or sipping coffee.
- *Location, location, location.* Many large, well-organized protests happen outside corporate headquarters or foreign consulates. Unfortunately, those tend to be on side streets with little pedestrian traffic and no adjoining public spaces. Simply relocating the event to a busy nearby corner can increase the audience tenfold.
- *Distinguish yourself.* In December 1997, the East Timor Action Network marched up Madison Avenue to the Indonesian Consulate to protest the occupation of East Timor. Only a few carried signs; the rest were indistinguishable from other pedestrians on the crowded street. Solution? Form a picket line or sit down en masse on the busy sidewalk.
- *Get the crowd involved.* Successful protests encourage audience participation—appearing exclusive is a sure way to alienate onlookers from your cause. At a 1997 World AIDS Day vigil in New York, for example, organizers handed out chalk to passersby and asked them to write on a nearby fountain the names of loved ones who had died of AIDS.
- *Put it down on paper.* A simple, clearly written leaflet that explains who is protesting, why, and how to get involved is crucial. Sure, it may end up in the nearest trash can, but some people will read it, and a few might show up at the next event.
- *Manage the media.* Of course, the biggest prize for any protest is media coverage. Inform local newspapers and TV and radio stations (not just "progressive" media) a few days in advance.
- *Above all, be spectacular.* Eye-catching costumes, a sea of candles in a dark plaza, limp bodies being carried from a street to a police van—these telegenic images make for good press. At an August 1997 march prompted by the police beating of Haitian immigrant Abner Louima, many waved toilet plungers—the tool with which Louima was allegedly beaten and sodomized—transforming an ordinary object into an unforgettable symbol of violent racism.
- *Meteorology matters.* A wet and cold protester is usually a demoralized one. Plan for foul weather by establishing an alternative day; if timing is critical, find a nearby indoor or protected space to which protesters can retreat. To be sure, there are exceptions: A dedicated group braving the elements can convey a profound sense of commitment to a cause—assuming, of course, that someone's watching.
- *Use protest to beget protest.* Any single march or demonstration should be one link in a larger chain. Most political movements, after all, must endure for years

(continued)

to attain their goals. So think about the morning after: How can the momentum generated (if any) be maintained? How soon is too soon for the next protest? What worked, what didn't? Protests should be carefully crafted performances designed to be unforgettable and moving for audiences and participants alike. Only meaningful and memorable protests can effectively challenge people to think differently and motivate still further protest in the days and years ahead.

Source: Jeff Goodwin, *Mother Jones*, March/April 1990.

self-identified third wave activism and others) uses both liberal and radical strategies to address problems and promote change.

Although differences in strategy are sometimes a source of divisiveness among activists and feminists, they are also a source of strength in being able to work on multiple issues from multiple approaches. Indeed, any given issue lends itself to both reformist and radical approaches. Lesbian and gay rights, for example, is something that can be tackled in the courts and in the voting booths as organizations work toward legislation to create domestic partner legislation or community civil protections. At the same time, consciousness-raising activities and grassroots demonstrations, such as candlelight vigils for victims of hate crimes and Queer Pride parades, work on the local level. Together, different strategies improve the quality of life.

One important aspect to consider is that simply increasing women's participation and leadership does not necessarily imply a more egalitarian or feminist future. As you know, there are White women and women and men of color who are opposed to strategies for improving the general well-being of disenfranchised peoples. Changing the personnel—replacing men with women, for example—does not necessarily secure a different kind of future. Although in practice liberal feminism is more sophisticated than, for example, simply considering female candidates merely because they are women, it has been criticized for promoting women into positions of power and authority irrespective of their stance on the social relations of gender, race, class, and other differences.

Contemporary U.S. feminism is concerned with issues that are increasingly global; inevitable in the context of a global economy and militarism worldwide.

LEARNING ACTIVITY **Feminist.com**

Visit the Web site of feminist.com at *www.feminist.com* and follow the link to the activism page. There you'll find links to action alerts and legislative updates for a number of feminist organizations, including the National Organization for Women (NOW), Sisterhood Is Global, Women Organizing for Change, and Planned Parenthood. Follow these links to learn what actions you can take. The Web site also offers links to government resources and voter education and other activist resources.

IDEAS FOR ACTIVISM

- Organize an activism awareness educational event on your campus. Invite local activists to speak about their activism. Provide opportunities for students to volunteer for a wide variety of projects in your area.
- Find out about your school's recycling program. If there's not one in place, advocate with administrators to begin one. If one is in place, try to find ways to help it function more effectively and to encourage more participation in recycling. If recycling services are not provided in your local community, advocate with city and county officials to begin providing these services.
- Find out what the major environmental issues are in your state and what legislative steps need to be taken to address these concerns. Then organize a letter-writing campaign to encourage legislators to enact laws protecting the environment.
- Identify a major polluter in your community and organize a nonviolent protest outside that business demanding environmental reforms.
- Sponsor a workshop on conflict management and nonviolence for campus and community members.

These concerns have resulted in the sponsorship of numerous international conferences and have promoted education about women's issues all over the world. And, as communication technologies have advanced, the difficulties of global organization have lessened. International feminist groups have worked against militarism, global capitalism, and racism, as well as supporting issues identified by indigenous women around the world. This activism culminated in 1995 with the United Nations Fourth World Conference on Women held in Beijing, China (the first conference was held in Mexico City in 1975, the second in Copenhagen in 1980, and the third in Nairobi in 1985). More than 30,000 women attended the Beijing conference and helped create the internationally endorsed Platform for Action. This platform is a call for concrete action involving human rights of women and girls as part of universal human rights, the eradication of poverty of women, the removal of obstacles to women's full participation in public life and decision making, the elimination of all forms of violence against women, the assurance of women's access to educational and health services, and actions to promote women's economic autonomy. The text of the Platform for Action also discussed in the reading by Ruth Rosen. Since the Beijing conference in 1995, conventions under the leadership of the Commission on the Status of Women have been held in 2000 and 2005 to re-formalize the platform in light of global changes since the conference. Activism continues for U.S. ratification of the convention on the Elimination of All Forms of Discrimination Against Women (CEDAW), adopted in 1979 by the United Nations General Assembly. As an international bill of rights for women, it defies discrimination and sets up national agenda for change. As already mentioned, the United States has not ratified CEDAW in part because it fears treaty provisions would supercede U.S. laws and sovereignty.

UN Millennium Development Goals

1. Eradicate extreme poverty and hunger
   - Reduce by half the proportion of people living on less than a dollar a day
   - Reduce by half the proportion of people who suffer from hunger

2. Achieve universal primary education
   - Ensure that all boys and girls complete a full course of primary schooling

3. Promote gender equality and empower women
   - Eliminate gender disparity in primary and secondary education preferably by 2005, and at all levels by 2015

4. Reduce child mortality
   - Reduce by two thirds the mortality rate among children under five

5. Improve maternal health
   - Reduce by three quarters the maternal mortality ratio

6. Combat HIV/AIDS, malaria, and other diseases
   - Halt and begin to reverse the spread of HIV/AIDS
   - Halt and begin to reverse the incidence of malaria and other major diseases

7. Ensure environmental sustainability
   - Integrate the principles of sustainable development into country policies and programmes; reverse loss of environmental resources
   - Reduce by half the proportion of people without sustainable access to safe drinking water
   - Achieve significant improvement in lives of at least 100 million slum dwellers, by 2020

8. Develop a global partnership for development
   - Develop further an open trading and financial system that is rule-based, predictable and non-discriminatory. Includes a commitment to good governance, development and poverty reduction—nationally and internationally
   - Address the least developed countries' special needs. This includes tariff- and quota-free access for their exports; enhanced debt relief for heavily indebted poor countries; cancellation of official bilateral debt; and more generous official development assistance for countries committed to poverty reduction
   - Address the special needs of landlocked and small island developing States
   - Deal comprehensively with developing countries' debt problems through national and international measures to make debt sustainable in the long term
   - In cooperation with the developing countries, develop decent and productive work for youth
   - In cooperation with pharmaceutical companies, provide access to affordable essential drugs in developing countries
   - In cooperation with the private sector, make available the benefits of new technologies—especially information and communications technologies

By the year 2015 all 189 United Nations Member States have pledged to meet the above goals.

Source: http://www.un.org/millenniumgoals/index.html.

ACTIVIST PROFILE **Haunani-Kay Trask**

Haunani-Kay Trask is one of the world's foremost Hawaiian Studies scholars and a successful activist for indigenous rights. Trask was the first full-time director of the Center for Hawaiian Studies at the University of Hawai'i-Manoa and a founding member of Ka Lāhui Hawai'i, Hawai'i's largest sovereignty organization.

Hawai'i was independently ruled by a unified monarchy first organized under Kamehameha I in 1810 and recognized by the world community of nations as an independent nation. In 1893 the U.S. minister assigned to Hawai'i conspired with non-Hawai'ian residents to overthrow the government, and, while President Grover Cleveland acknowledged the wrong done and called for restoration of the monarchy, the U.S. government annexed Hawai'i in 1898. Native Hawai'ians have been fighting for sovereignty since then. In 1993, President Bill Clinton signed an apology resolution of Native Hawai'ians on the 100th anniversary of the overthrow of the monarchy.

The calls for Hawai'ian independence continue, and Haunani-Kay Trask provides a respected voice in the sovereignty movement. She is the author of *From a Native Daughter: Colonialism & Sovereignty in Hawai'i* and *Eros and Power: The Promise of Feminist Theory* and two volumes of poetry, *Light in the Crevice Never Seen* and *Night Is a Sharkskin Drum*. She also wrote and co-produced a film, *Act of War: The Overthrow of the Hawaiian Nation,* and she has co-anchored a weekly television show that highlights Hawai'ian cultural and political issues. She has been a Fellow at the Pacific Basin Research Center at Harvard University, a National Endowment for the Arts Writer-in-Residence at Santa Fe, New Mexico, a Rockefeller Resident Fellow at the University of Colorado at Boulder, and an American Council of Learned Societies Research Fellow.

FUTURE VISIONS

How might the future look? How will our knowledge of gender, race, and class-based inequalities be used? Does our future hold the promise of prosperity and peace or economic unrest and increased militarization? Will technology save us or quicken our destruction? Will feminist values be a part of future social transformation as envisioned in the reading by Baumgardner and Richards? Future visions are metaphors for the present; we anticipate the future in light of how we make sense of the present and have come to understand the past. This approach encourages us to look at the present mindfully, so that we are aware of its politics, and creatively, so that we can see the possibility for change. In her playful poem "Warning," Jenny Joseph looks to the future to offer some guidance in the present.

There are some social trends that have implications for the future. Given the higher fertility rates among the non-White population as well as immigration figures, Whites will eventually become a relatively smaller percentage of the population until they are no longer a majority in the United States. Latinas/os are the largest growing group, estimated to increase from the current 12.5 percent of the U.S. population to represent 18 percent by 2025. In addition, the rise in births between 1946 and 1960 (the baby boomer cohort) and the decline through the 1970s will mean a large percentage of the population will be over 65 years old within the next couple of decades. 2005 Census reports suggest that by 2030 there will be about 70 million older persons (65 years and older), more than twice their number in 2000 and reaching approximately 20 percent of the population. Currently, persons 65 years and older represent about 13 percent of the population. And, although some people have always lived to be 80, 90, and 100 years old, this number will grow in response to better nutrition and health care among certain segments of the population. As the baby boomers age, they will create stress on medical and social systems. They might also influence family systems as several generations of aged family members could require care at the same time. This is complicated by the fact that families are becoming smaller, and divorce and remarriage rates will probably continue at current rates. Ties between stepfamilies and other nonfamilial ties are most likely going to become more important in terms of care and support.

In our society, where the profit motive runs much of our everyday lives, where citizens have lost respect for political and governmental institutions, and where people are working longer hours and becoming more disconnected from families and communities, the issue of integrity is something to consider. The definition of integrity is two part: one, a moral positioning about the distinction between right and wrong, and two, a consistent stance on this morality such that we act out what we believe and attempt to live our ideals. "Do as I say and not as I do" is an example of the very opposite of integrity. What might it mean to live with feminist-inspired integrity as well as envision a future where feminist integrity is central? We'll discuss seven implications here.

First, it is important to set feminist priorities and keep them. In a society where sound bytes and multiple, fragmented pieces of information vie to be legitimate sources of knowledge, we must recognize that some things are more important than others. Priorities are essential. Postmodernism might have deconstructed notions of

Principles of Environmental Justice

1. Environmental justice affirms the sacredness of Mother Earth, ecological unity and the interdependence of all species, and the right to be free from ecological destruction.
2. Environmental justice demands that public policy be based on mutual respect and justice for all peoples, free from any form of discrimination or bias.
3. Environmental justice mandates the right to ethical, balanced, and responsible uses of land and renewable resources in the interest of a sustainable planet for humans and other living things.
4. Environmental justice calls for universal protection from nuclear testing, extraction, production and disposal of toxic/hazardous wastes and poisons that threaten the fundamental right to clean air, land, water, and food.
5. Environmental justice affirms the fundamental right to political, economic, cultural, and environmental self-determination of all peoples.
6. Environmental justice demands the cessation of the production of all toxins, hazardous wastes, and radioactive materials, and that all past and current producers be held strictly accountable to the people for detoxification and containment at the point of production.
7. Environmental justice demands the right to participate as equal partners at every level of decision making, including needs assessment, planning, implementation, enforcement, and evaluation.
8. Environmental justice affirms the right of all workers to a safe and healthy work environment, without being forced to choose between an unsafe livelihood and unemployment. It also affirms the right of those who work at home to be free from environmental hazards.
9. Environmental justice protects the right of victims of environmental injustice to receive full compensation and reparations for damages as well as quality health care.
10. Environmental justice considers governmental acts of environmental injustice a violation of international law, the Universal Declaration on Human Rights, and the United Nations Convention on Genocide.
11. Environmental justice must recognize a special legal and natural relationship of Native Peoples to the U.S. government through treaties, agreements, compacts, and covenants affirming sovereignty and self-determination.
12. Environmental justice affirms the need for urban and rural ecological policies to clean up and rebuild our cities and rural areas in balance with nature, honoring the cultural integrity of all our communities, and providing fair access for all to the full range of resources.
13. Environmental justice calls for the strict enforcement of principles of informed consent and a halt to the testing of experimental reproductive and medical procedures and vaccinations on people of color.
14. Environmental justice opposes the destructive operations of multinational corporations.
15. Environmental justice opposes military occupation; repression and exploitation of lands, peoples and cultures, and other life forms.

(continued)

16. Environmental justice calls for the education of present and future generations that emphasizes social and environmental issues, based on our experience and an appreciation of our diverse cultural perspectives.

17. Environmental justice requires that we, as individuals, make personal and consumer choices to consume as little of Mother Earth's resources and to produce as little waste as possible; and make the conscious decision to challenge and reprioritize our lifestyles to ensure the health of the natural world for present and future generations.

Source: People of Color Environmental Leadership Summit, 1991. *www.umich.edu/~jrazer/nre/whatis.html.*

truth to the point where some argue that there is no such thing as the truth; yet, some things are truer than others. Figure out your truths and priorities based upon your own values, politics, and/or religion.

Second, it is important that we live and envision a society that balances personal freedom and identity with public and collective responsibility. Suzanne Pharr writes about this in "Taking the High Road" when she says that transformational politics call for living with communal values by which we learn how to honor the needs of the individual as well as the group. The United States is a culture that values individualism very highly and often forgets that although the Constitution says you have the right to do something, I also have the right to criticize you for it. Similarly, we must question the limitations associated with certain rights. Is your right still a right if it violates my rights or hurts a community? And, just because the Constitution says

Women Working for Peace

The International Peace Bureau (IPB) is the world's oldest and most comprehensive international peace federation. Founded in 1892, the organization won the Nobel Peace Prize in 1910. Its role is to support peace and disarmament initiatives. Current priorities include the abolition of nuclear weapons, conflict prevention and resolution, human rights, and women and peace. To learn more about the IPB, visit the Web site at *www.ipb.org.*

The Women's International League for Peace and Freedom (WILPF), founded in 1915 to protest the war in Europe, suggests ways to end war and to prevent war in the future; as well, it seeks to educate and mobilize women for action. The goals of the WILPF are political solutions to international conflicts, disarmament, promotion of women to full and equal participation in all society's activities, economic and social justice within and among states, elimination of racism and all forms of discrimination and exploitation, respect of fundamental human rights, and the right to development in a sustainable environment. For more information, including action alerts and readings, visit the WILPF homepage at *www.wilpf.org.*

Female Nobel Peace Laureates

Twelve women have been honored with the Nobel Peace Prize for their work for justice:

Baroness Bertha Von Suttner (1905) Austrian honored for her writing and work opposing war.

Jane Addams (1931) International President, Women's International League for Peace and Freedom.

Emily Greene Balch (1946) Honored for her pacifism and work for peace through a variety of organizations.

Betty Williams and Mairead Corrigan (1976) Founders of the Northern Ireland Peace Movement to bring together Protestants and Catholics to work for peace together.

Mother Teresa (1979) Honored for her "work in bringing help to suffering humanity" and her respect for individual human dignity.

Alva Myrdal (1982) Honored with Alfonso Garcia Robles for their work with the United Nations on disarmament.

Aung San Suu Kyi (1991) Burmese activist honored for nonviolent work for human rights in working for independence in Myanmar.

Rigoberta Menchú Tum (1992) Honored for her work for "ethno-cultural reconciliation based on respect for the rights of indigenous peoples."

Jody Williams (1997) Honored for her work with the International Campaign to Ban Landmines.

Shirin Ebadi (2003) Honored for her efforts to promote democracy and human rights.

Wangari Maathai (2004) Honored for her contribution to sustainable development, democracy, and peace.

Source: http://womenshistory.about.com/education/womenshistory/msubnobelpeace.htm.

something is your right, that does not necessarily make that act a moral choice. Although the Constitution exists to protect choices and rights, it does not tell us which choices and rights are best.

Third, recognize that corporate capitalism does not function in everybody's interests. In this sense, *economic* democracy must not be confused with *political* democracy. Many of us have learned that capitalist societies are synonymous with democracies and that other economic systems are somehow undemocratic in principle. We live in a society that attempts a political democracy at the same time that economic democracy, or financial equity for all peoples, is limited. Unfortunately, capitalism has had deleterious effects on both physical and human environments, and consumerism has changed families and communities by encouraging people to accumulate material possessions beyond their immediate needs. Perhaps a motto for the future might be "pack lightly."

© Copyright Judy Horacek from UNREQUITED LOVE, 1994. www.horacek.com.au. Reprinted with permission.

Fourth, a present and future with a core value of feminist integrity is one that understands the limitations of technology as well as its liberating aspects. The future vision must be one of sustainability: finding ways to live in the present so that we do not eliminate options for the future. It is important to balance economic, environmental, and community needs in ways that do not jeopardize sustainability. This means being in control of technology so that it is used ethically and productively: an issue that is related to the previous point about capitalist expansion. Corporations have invested heavily in new technologies that do not always work for the collective good.

Fifth, feminist integrity requires advocating a sustainable physical environment. There is only one world and we share it; there is an interdependence of all species. Given this, it makes no sense to destroy our home through such behaviors as global climate change, environmental pollution, and species eradication. Sustainable environmental practices start with addressing issues associated with capitalist global

expansion and technological development, as discussed previously. Also associated is the need for environmental justice because the poor and communities of color have suffered disproportionately in terms of environmental pollution and degradation. Environmental justice calls for protection from nuclear testing, extraction, production, and disposal of toxic and hazardous wastes and poisons that threaten the fundamental right to clean air, land, water, and food. It also demands that workers have the right to safe and healthy work environments without being forced to choose between unsafe livelihood and unemployment.

Sixth, a peaceful and sustainable future is one that respects human dignity, celebrates difference and diversity, and yet recognizes that diversity does not necessarily imply equality. It is not enough to be tolerant of the differences among us, although that would be a good start; it is necessary to recognize everyone's right to a piece of the pie and work toward equality of outcome and not just equality of access. We believe we must create social movements that derive from an ethic of caring, empathy, and compassion.

Seventh and finally, we believe it is important to have a sense of humor and to take the time to play and celebrate. As socialist labor reformer Emma Goldman once said, "If I can't dance, I don't want to be part of your revolution."

A justice-based politics of integrity embraces equality for all peoples. It is an ethic that has the potential to help create a peaceful and sustainable future, improving the quality of our lives and the future of our planet. An ethic that respects and values all forms of life and seeks ways to distribute resources equitably is one that moves away from dominance and uses peaceful solutions to environmental, societal, and global problems. As a blueprint for the future, a focus on justice and equality has much to offer. As Ruth Rosen writes in the reading "Epilogue: Beyond Backlash," in her reference to the movement for women's human rights, the struggle has begun and there is no end in sight!

Fear of Feminism
Why Young Women Get the Willies

Lisa Marie Hogeland

I began thinking about young women's fear of feminism, as I always do in the fall, while I prepared to begin another year of teaching courses in English and women's studies. I was further prodded when former students of mine, now graduate students elsewhere and teaching for the first time, phoned in to complain about their young women students' resistance to feminism. It occurred to me that my response—"Of course young women are afraid of feminism"—was not especially helpful. This essay is an attempt to trace out what that "of course" really means; much of it is based on my experience with college students, but many of the observations apply to other young women as well.

Some people may argue that young women have far less to lose by becoming feminists than do older women: they have a smaller stake in the system and fewer ties to it. At the same time, though, young women today have been profoundly affected by the demonization of feminism during the 12 years of Reagan and Bush—the time when they formed their understanding of political possibility and public life. Older women may see the backlash as temporary and changeable; younger women may see it as how things are. The economic situation for college students worsened over those 12 years as well, with less student aid available, so that young women may experience their situation as extremely precarious—too precarious to risk feminism.

My young women students often interpret critiques of marriage—a staple of feminist analysis for centuries—as evidence of their authors' dysfunctional families. This demonstrates another reality they have grown up with: the increased tendency to pathologize any kind of oppositional politics. Twelve years of the rhetoric of "special interests versus family values" have created a climate in which passionate political commitments seem crazy. In this climate, the logical reasons why all women fear feminism take on particular meaning and importance for young women.

To understand what women fear when they fear feminism—and what they don't—it is helpful to draw a distinction between gender consciousness and feminist consciousness. One measure of feminism's success over the past three decades is that women's gender consciousness—our self-awareness as women—is extremely high. Gender consciousness takes two forms: awareness of women's vulnerability and celebration of women's difference. Fear of crime is at an all-time high in the United States; one of the driving forces behind this fear may well be women's sense of special vulnerability to the epidemic of men's violence. Feminists have fostered this awareness of violence against women, and it is to our credit that we have made our analysis so powerful; at the same time, however, we must attend to ways this awareness can be deployed for nonfeminist and even antifeminist purposes, and most especially to ways it can be used to serve a racist agenda. Feminists have also fostered an awareness of women's difference from men and made it possible for women (including nonfeminists) to have an appreciation of things pertaining to women— perhaps most visibly the kinds of "women's culture" commodified in the mass media (soap operas and romance, self-help books, talk shows, and the like). Our public culture in the U.S. presents myriad opportunities for women to take pleasure in being women—most often, however, that pleasure is used as an advertising or marketing strategy.

Gender consciousness is a necessary precondition for feminist consciousness, but they are not the same. The difference lies in the link between gender and politics. Feminism politicizes gender consciousness, inserts it into a systematic analysis of histories and structures of domination and privilege. Feminism asks questions—difficult and complicated questions, often with contradictory and confusing answers—about how gender consciousness can be used both for and against women, how vulnerability and difference help and hinder women's self-determination and freedom. Fear of feminism, then, is not a fear of gender, but rather a fear of politics. Fear of politics can be understood as a fear of living in consequences, a fear of reprisals.

The fear of political reprisals is very realistic. There are powerful interests opposed to feminism—let's be clear about that. It is not in the interests of white supremacy that white women insist on abortion rights, that women of color insist on an end to involuntary sterilization, that all women insist on reproductive self-determination. It is not in the interests of capitalism that women demand economic rights or comparable worth. It is not in the interests of many individual men or many institutions that women demand a nonexploitative sexual autonomy—the right to say and mean both no and yes on our own terms. What would our mass culture look like if it didn't sell women's bodies—even aside from pornography? It is not in the interests of heterosexist patriarchy that women challenge our understandings of events headlined MAN KILLED FAMILY BECAUSE HE LOVED THEM, that women challenge the notion of men's violence against women and children as deriving from "love" rather than power. It is not in the interests of any of the systems of domination in which we are enmeshed that we see how these systems work—that we understand men's violence, male domination, race and class supremacy, as systems of permission for both individual and institutional exercises of power, rather than merely as individual pathologies. It is not in the interests of white supremacist capitalist patriarchy that women ally across differences.

Allying across differences is difficult work, and is often thwarted by homophobia—by fears both of lesbians and of being named a lesbian by association. Feminism requires that we confront that homophobia constantly. I want to suggest another and perhaps more subtle and insidious way that fear of feminism is shaped by the institution of heterosexuality. Think about the lives of young women—think about your own. What are the arenas for selfhood for young women in this culture? How do they discover and construct their identities? What teaches them who they are, who they want to be, who they might be? Our culture allows women so little scope for development, for exploration, for testing the boundaries of what they can do and who they can be, that romantic and sexual relationships become the primary, too often the only, arena for selfhood.

Young women who have not yet begun careers or community involvements too often have no public life, and the smallness of private life, of romance as an arena for selfhood, is particularly acute for them. Intimate relationships become the testing ground for identity, a reality that has enormously damaging consequences for teenage girls in particular (the pressures both toward and on sex and romance, together with the culturally induced destruction of girls' self-esteem at puberty, have everything to do with teenage pregnancy). The feminist insistence that the personal is political may seem to threaten rather than empower a girl's fragile, emergent self as she develops into a sexual and relational being.

Young women may believe that a feminist identity puts them out of the pool for many men, limits the options of who they might become with a partner, how they might decide to live. They may not be wrong either: how many young men feminists or feminist sympathizers do you know? A politics that may require making demands on a partner, or that may motivate particular choices in partners, can appear to foreclose rather than to open up options for identity, especially for women who haven't yet discovered that all relationships require negotiation and struggle. When you live on Noah's ark, anything that might make it more difficult to find a partner can seem to threaten your very survival. To make our case, feminists have to combat not just homophobia, but also the rule of the couple, the politics of Noah's ark in the age of "family values." This does not mean that heterosexual feminist women must give up their intimate relationships, but it does mean that feminists must continually analyze those pressures, be clear about how they operate in our lives, and try to find ways around and through them for ourselves, each other, and other women.

For women who are survivors of men's violence—perhaps most notably for incest and rape survivors—the shift feminism enables, from individual pathology to systematic analysis, is empowering rather than threatening. For women who have not experienced men's violence in these ways, the shift to a systematic analysis requires them to ally themselves with survivors—itself a recognition that *it could happen to me*. Young women who have not been victims of men's violence hate being asked to identify with it; they see the threat to their emergent sense of autonomy and freedom not in the fact of men's violence, but in feminist analyses that make them identify with it. This can also be true for older women, but it may be lessened by the simple statistics of women's life experience: the longer you live, the more likely you are to have experienced men's violence or to know women who are survivors of it, and thus to have a sense of the range and scope of that violence.

My women students, feminist and nonfeminist alike, are perfectly aware of the risks of going unescorted to the library at night. At the same time, they are appalled by my suggesting that such gender-based restrictions on their access to university facilities deny them an equal education. It's not that men's violence isn't real to them—but that they are unwilling to trace out its consequences and to understand its complexities. College women, however precarious their economic situation, and even despite the extent of sexual harassment and date rape on campuses all over the country, still insist on believing that women's equality has been achieved. And, in fact,

to the extent that colleges and universities are doing their jobs—giving women students something like an equal education—young women may experience relatively little overt or firsthand discrimination. Sexism may come to seem more the exception than the rule in some academic settings—and thus more attributable to individual sickness than to systems of domination.

Women of all ages fear the existential situation of feminism, what we learned from Simone de Beauvoir, what we learned from radical feminists in the 1970s, what we learned from feminist women of color in the 1980s: feminism has consequences. Once you have your "click!" moment, the world shifts, and it shifts in some terrifying ways. Not just heterosexism drives this fear of political commitment—it's not just fear of limiting one's partner-pool. It's also about limiting oneself—about the fear of commitment to something larger than the self that asks us to examine the consequences of our actions. Women fear anger, and change, and challenge—who doesn't? Women fear taking a public stand, entering public discourse, demanding—and perhaps getting—attention. And for what? To be called a "feminazi"? To be denounced as traitors to women's "essential nature"?

The challenge to the public-private division that feminism represents is profoundly threatening to young women who just want to be left alone, to all women who believe they can hide from feminist issues by not being feminists. The central feminist tenet that the personal is political is profoundly threatening to young women who don't want to be called to account. It is far easier to rest in silence, as if silence were neutrality, and as if neutrality were safety. Neither wholly cynical nor wholly apathetic, women who fear feminism fear living in consequences. Think harder, act more carefully; feminism requires that you enter a world supersaturated with meaning, with implications. And for privileged women in particular, the notion that one's own privilege comes at someone else's expense—that my privilege *is* your oppression—is profoundly threatening.

Fear of feminism is also fear of complexity, fear of thinking, fear of ideas—we live, after all, in a profoundly anti-intellectual culture. Feminism is one of the few movements in the U.S. that produce nonacademic intellectuals—readers, writers, thinkers, and theorists outside the academy, who combine and refine their knowledge with their practice. What other movement is housed so substantially in bookstores? All radical movements for change struggle against the anti-intellectualism of U.S. culture, the same anti-intellectualism, fatalism, and disengagement that make even voting too much work for most U.S. citizens. Feminism is work—intellectual work as surely as it is activist work—and it can be very easy for women who have been feminists for a long time to forget how hard-won their insights are, how much reading and talking and thinking and work produced them. In this political climate, such insights may be even more hard-won.

Feminism requires an expansion of the self—an expansion of empathy, interest, intelligence, and responsibility across differences, histories, cultures, ethnicities, sexual identities, othernesses. The differences between women, as Audre Lorde pointed out over and over again, are our most precious resources in thinking and acting toward change. Fear of difference is itself a fear of consequences: it is less other women's difference that we fear than our own implication in the hierarchy of differences, our own accountability to other women's oppression. It is easier to rest in gender consciousness, in one's own difference, than to undertake the personal and political analysis required to trace out one's own position in multiple and overlapping systems of domination.

Women have real reasons to fear feminism, and we do young women no service if we suggest to them that feminism itself is safe. It is not. To stand opposed to your culture, to be critical of institutions, behaviors, discourses—when it is so clearly *not* in your immediate interest to do so—asks a lot of a young person, of any person. At its best, the feminist challenging of individualism, of narrow notions of freedom, is transformative, exhilarating, empowering. When we do our best work in selling feminism to the unconverted, we make clear not only its necessity, but also its pleasures: the joys of intellectual and political work, the moral power of living in consequences, the surprises of coalition, the rewards of doing what is difficult. Feminism offers an arena for selfhood beyond personal relationships but not disconnected from them. It offers—and requires—courage, intelligence, boldness, sensitivity, relationality, complexity, a sense of purpose, and, lest we forget, a sense of humor as well. Of course young women are afraid of feminism—shouldn't they be?

R E A D I N G **104**

Real Men Join the Movement

Michael Kimmel

Cory Shere didn't go to Duke University to become a profeminist man. He was going to be a doctor, covering his bets with a double major in engineering and premed. But his experiences with both organic chemistry and feminist women conspired to lead this affable and earnest 20-year-old Detroit native in a different direction. Now in his junior year, he still has a double major—women's studies and psychology. And he works with a group of men to raise awareness about sexual assault and date rape.

Eric Freedman wasn't profeminist either, when he arrived at Swarthmore College three years ago. A 20-year-old junior literature major from Syracuse,

New York, he became involved in a campus antiracism project and began to see the connections among different struggles for equality. At an antiracism workshop he helped organize, he suddenly found himself speaking about male privilege as well as white privilege. This fall, he's starting a men's group to focus on race and gender issues.

Who are these guys? And what are they doing in the women's movement?

They are among a growing number of profeminist men around the country. These aren't the angry divorcés who whine about how men are the new victims of reverse discrimination, nor are they the weekend warriors trooping off to a mythopoetic retreat. They're neither Promise Keepers nor Million Man Marchers vowing to be responsible domestic patriarchs on a nineteenth-century model.

You might think of profeminist men as the "other" men's movement, but I prefer to consider it the "real" men's movement, because by actively supporting women's equality on the job or on the streets and by quietly changing their lives to create that equality at home, profeminist men are also transforming the definition of masculinity. Perhaps this is the movement about which Gloria Steinem rhapsodized when she wrote how women "want a men's movement. We are literally dying for it."

Profeminist men staff the centers where convicted batterers get counseling, organize therapy for rapists and sex offenders in prison, do the workshops on preventing sexual harassment in the workplace or on confronting the impact of pornography in men's lives. On campus, they're organizing men's events during Take Back the Night marches; presenting programs on sexual assault to fraternities, dorms, and athletic teams; taking courses on masculinity; and founding campus groups with acronyms like MAC (Men Acting for Change), MOST (Men Opposed to Sexist Tradition), MASH (Men Against Sexual Harassment), MASA (Men Against Sexual Assault), and, my current favorite, MARS (Men Against Rape and Sexism). Maybe John Gray was right after all—real men *are* from Mars!

FEMINISM AND MEN'S LIVES

I first met Cory, Eric, and about a dozen other young profeminist men in April at the Young Feminist Summit, organized by NOW, in Washington, D.C. They were pretty easy to spot among the nearly one thousand young women from colleges all over the country. As we talked during an impromptu workshop, I heard them describe both the exhilaration and isolation of becoming part of the struggle for women's equality, the frustrations of dealing with other men, the active suspicions and passive indifference of other students.

It felt painfully familiar. I've spent nearly two decades in feminist politics, first as an activist in antirape and antibattery groups, and later helping to organize the National Organization for Men Against Sexism (NOMAS), a network of profeminist men and women around the country. More recently, I've tried to apply the insights of academic feminist theory to men's lives, developing courses on men, debating with Robert Bly and his followers, and writing a history of the idea of manhood in the United States.

Of course, men like Cory and Eric are a distinct minority on campus. They compete with the angry voice of backlash, those shrill interruptions that scream "Don't blame me, I never raped anyone! Leave me alone!" They compete with that now familiar men-as-victims whine. Men, we hear, are terrified of going to work or on a date, lest they be falsely accused of sexual harassment or date rape; they're unable to support their scheming careerist wives, yet are vilified as bad fathers if they don't provide enough child support to keep their ex-wives in Gucci and Donna Karan after the divorce.

In the public imagination, profeminist men also compete with the mythopoetic vision of the men's movement as a kind of summer-camp retreat, and the earnest evangelical Promise Keepers with their men-only sports-themed rallies, and the Million Man March's solemn yet celebratory atonement. All offer men solace and soul-work, and promise to heal men's pain and enable them to become more nurturing and loving.

All noble goals, to be sure. But to profeminist men, you don't build responsibility and democracy by exclusion—of women, or of gays and lesbians.

And profeminist men compete with the most deafening sound coming from the mouths of American men when the subject is feminism: silence. Most men, on campus and off, exude an aura of studied indifference to feminism. Like the irreverent second child at the Passover seder, they ask, "What has this to do with me?"

A lot. Sure, feminism is the struggle of more than one-half of the population for equal rights. But it's also about rethinking identities, our relationships, the meanings of our lives. For men, feminism is not only about what we *can't* do—like commit violence, harassment, or rape—or *shouldn't* do, like leave all the child care and housework to our wives. It's also about what we *can* do, what we *should* do, and even what we *want* to do—like be a better father, friend, or partner. "Most men know that it is to all of our advantage—women and men alike—for women to be equal," noted NOW President Patricia Ireland, in her Summit keynote address. Far from being only about the loss of power, feminism will also enable men to live the lives we say we want to live.

This isn't the gender cavalry, arriving in the nick of time to save the damsels from distress. "Thanks for bringing this sexism stuff to our attention, ladies," one might imagine them saying. "We'll take it from here." And it's true that some men declare themselves feminists just a bit too effortlessly, especially if they think it's going to help them get a date. (A friend calls it "premature self-congratulation," and it's just as likely to leave women feeling shortchanged.)

In part, this explains why I call them "profeminist men" and not "feminist men" or "male feminists." As an idea, it seems to me, feminism involves an empirical observation—that women are not equal—and the moral position that declares they should be. Of course, men may share this empirical observation and take this moral stance. And to that extent men support feminism as an ideal. But feminism as an identity also involves the felt experience of that inequality. And this men do not have, because men are privileged by sexism. To be sure, men may be oppressed—by race, class, ethnicity, sexuality, age, physical ability—but men are not oppressed *as men*. Since only women have that felt experience of oppression about gender, it seems sensible to make a distinction in how we identify ourselves. Men can support feminism and can call ourselves "antisexist" or "profeminist." I've chosen profeminist because, like feminism, it stresses the positive and forward-looking.

In a sense, I think of profeminist men as the Gentlemen's Auxiliary of Feminism. This honorable position acknowledges that we play a part in this social transformation, but not the most significant part. It's the task of the Gentlemen's Auxiliary to make feminism comprehensible to men, not as a loss of power—which has thus far failed to "trickle down" to most individual men anyway—but as a challenge to the false sense of entitlement we have to that power in the first place. Profeminism is about supporting both women's equality and other men's efforts to live more ethically consistent and more emotionally resonant lives.

. . .

The routes taken by today's profeminist men are as varied as the men themselves. But most do seem to have some personal experience that made gender inequality more concrete. For some, it involved their mother. (Remember President Clinton describing how he developed his commitment to women's equality when he tried to stop his stepfather from hitting his mother? Of course, one wishes that commitment had facilitated more supportive policy initiatives.) Max Sadler, a 17-year-old senior at Trinity High School in New York City, watched his professional mother hit her head on the glass ceiling at her high-powered corporate job—a job she eventually quit to join a company with more women in high-level positions. Max shared her frustration and also felt ashamed at the casual attitudes of her male colleagues.

Shehzad Nadeem, a 19-year-old student at James Madison University in Virginia, remembered the way his older sister described her experiences.

"I could barely believe the stories she told me, yet something deep inside told me that they were not only true, but common. I realized that we men are actively or passively complicit in women's oppression, and that we have to take an active role in challenging other men." Shehzad joined MOST (Men Opposed to Sexist Tradition), which has presented workshops on violence and sexual assault at Madison dorms.

. . .

Or perhaps it was having a feminist girlfriend, or even just having women friends, that brought these issues to the fore for men. "I grew up with female friends who were as ambitious, smart, achieving, and confident as I thought I was—on a good day," recalls Jason Schultz, a founder of MAC at Duke, who now organizes men's programs to combat campus sexual assault. "When I got to college, these same women began calling themselves feminists. When I heard men call women 'dumb chicks' I knew something was wrong."

. . .

THE PROFEMINIST "CLICK!"

But there has to be more than the presence of feminist role models, challenges from girlfriends, brilliant assignments, or challenging support from professors. After all, we all have women in our lives, and virtually all of those women have had some traumatic encounter with sexism. There has to be something else.

Feminists call it the "click!"—that moment when they realize that their pain, fears, confusion, and anger are not theirs alone, but are shared with other women. Do profeminist men have "clicks!"? Yes, but they don't typically come from righteous indignation or fear, but rather from guilt and shame, a gnawing sense of implication in something larger and more pervasive than individual intention. It's that awful moment when you hear women complain about "men" in general and realize, even just a little bit, that you are what they're talking about. (Much of men's reactive defensiveness seems to be a hedge against these feelings of shame.)

Suddenly, it's not those "bad" men "out there" who are the problem—it's all men. Call it the Pogo revelation: "We have met the enemy, and he is us."

That's certainly the way it felt for Jeff Wolf (not his real name). A sexually naive college sophomore, he found himself growing closer and closer to a woman friend, Annie, during a study date. They talked long into the night and eventually kissed. One thing began to lead to another, and both seemed eager and pleased to be with the other. Just before penetration, though, Jeff felt Annie go limp. "Her eyes glazed over, and she went kind of numb," he recalled, still wincing at the memory.

This is the moment that many a college guy dreams of—her apparent surrender to his desire, even if it was induced by roofies or alcohol. It's a moment when men often space out, preferring to navigate the actual encounter on automatic pilot, fearing that emotional connection will lead to an early climax.

As Annie slipped into this mental coma, though, Jeff stayed alert, as engaged emotionally as he was physically. "What had been so arousing was the way we had been connecting intellectually and emotionally," he said. After some patient prodding, she finally confessed that she'd been raped as a high school sophomore, and ever since, had used this self-protective strategy to get through a sexual encounter without reliving her adolescent trauma. Jeff, it seemed, was the first guy who noticed.

. . .

Others say their "click!" experience happened later in life. In the 1970s, psychologist David Greene was deeply involved in political activism, when he and his wife had a baby. "Not that much changed for me; I still went around doing my thing, but now there was a baby in it." On the other hand, his wife's life was totally transformed by the realities of round-the-clock child care. She'd become a mother. "After several weeks of this, she sat me down and confronted me," he recalls. "The bankruptcy of my politics quickly became clear to me. I was an oppressor, an abuser of privilege—I'd become the enemy I thought I was fighting against." The couple meticulously divided housework and child care, and David learned that revolutions are fought out in people's kitchens as well as in the jungles of Southeast Asia. Terry Kupers, a 54-year-old psychiatrist, and author of *Revisioning Men's Lives,* remembers his first wife initiating some serious talks about the "unstated assumptions we were making about housework, cooking, and whose time was more valuable." Not only did Kupers realize that his wife was right, "but I also realized I liked things better the new way."

. . .

PROFEMINISM TODAY—AND TOMORROW

And just as sisterhood is global, so too are profeminist men active around the world. Men from nearly 50 countries—from Mexico to Japan—regularly contribute to a newsletter of international profeminist scholars and activists, according to its editor, Oystein Holter, a Norwegian researcher. Scandinavian men are working to implement a gender equity mandated by law. Liisa Husu, a senior advisor to Finland's gender equity commission, has developed a parliamentary subcommittee of concerned men. (When I met with them last fall, we spent our day discussing our mutual activities, after which they whisked me off to an all-male sauna resort on the shore of an icy Baltic Sea for a bit of male-bonding as a follow-up to all that equity work.) Scandinavian men routinely take parental leave; in fact, in Sweden and Norway they've introduced "Daddy days," an additional month of paid paternity leave for the men to have some time with their newborns after the mothers have returned to work. About half of Swedish men take paternal leave, according to fatherhood expert Lars Jalmert at the University of Stockholm.

The world's most successful profeminist organization must be Canada's White Ribbon Campaign. Begun in 1991 to coincide with the second anniversary of the Montreal Massacre—when a young man killed 14 women engineering students

at the University of Montreal on December 6, 1989—its goal was to publicly and visibly declare opposition to men's violence against women by encouraging men to wear a white ribbon as a public pledge. "Within days, hundreds of thousands of men and boys across Canada wore a ribbon," noted Michael Kaufman, one of the campaign's founders. "It exceeded our wildest expectations—even the prime minister wore a ribbon." This year, WRC events are also planned for Norway, Australia, and several U.S. colleges; in Canada, events include an Alberta hockey team planning a skating competition to raise money for a local women's shelter. WRC organizers have also developed curricula for secondary schools to raise the issue for boys.

But just as surely, some of the most important and effective profeminist men's activities are taking place in American homes every day, as men increasingly share housework and child care, reorganize their schedules to be more responsive to the needs of their families, and even downsize their ambitions to develop a family strategy that does not revolve exclusively around *his* career path. "Housework remains the last frontier" for men to tame, argues sociologist Kathleen Gerson in her book *No Man's Land.* . . .

But the payoff is significant. If power were a scarce commodity or a zero-sum game, we might think that women's increased power would mean a decrease in men's. And since most men don't feel very powerful anyway, the possibilities of further loss are rather unappealing. But for most men, all the power in the world does not seem to have trickled down to enable individual men to live the lives we say we want to live—lives of intimacy, integrity, and individual expression. By demanding the redistribution of power along more equitable lines, feminism also seeks a dramatic shift in our social priorities, our choices about how we live, and what we consider important. Feminism is also a blueprint for men about how to become the men we want to be, and profeminist men believe that men will live happier, healthier, and more emotionally enriched lives by supporting women's equality.

Part of profeminist men's politics is to visibly and vocally support women's equality, and part of it is to quietly and laboriously struggle to implement that public stance into our own lives. And part of it must be to learn to confront and challenge other men, with care and commitment. "This cause is not altogether and exclusively woman's cause," wrote Frederick Douglass in 1848. "It is the cause of human brotherhood as well as human sisterhood, and both must rise and fall together."

R E A D I N G   **105**

Reflections of a Human Rights Educator

Dazón Dixon Diallo

In my early days as an activist, I spent a lot of my time examining the problems in the world, and dreaming of ways to eradicate the pain and suffering of life on Earth. So many forces work against the elimination of oppression, and so few choices exist for those of us who want a safer, saner, and more peaceful planet. Thus, I chose to be a fighter, although my weapons were (and are) education, organizing, and mobilizing. But still, I had to fight. The fight was against the marginalization of women of color in the feminist health movement. The fight was against a new disease with deadly consequences, and a strange penchant for already reviled and disrespected "minorities." The fight was, and still is, against the fear and hatred of difference and change. I had to fight against something, because I believed it was the only way to contribute to the social change that we all so desperately need.

As a woman of African descent born in the southern United States, I am among the masses of people who experience some form of oppression on a daily basis. I am from and in the grassroots, where change is essential for moving beyond survival to thriving. Whether the issue is HIV, sexual violence, gender discrimination, poverty, or lack of access, my own experience is inextricably intertwined with the struggle of millions of other souls throughout the world. Some of my struggle has resulted in the creation and development of an HIV/AIDS program for African-American women called SisterLove Women's AIDS project.

When we formed SisterLove in 1989, we were on the cutting edge of the HIV/AIDS tide that was sweeping through the lives and families of women in our communities. We thought, then, that if we provided enough education, intervention, and support services to women at greatest risk for HIV, and for those living with HIV or AIDS, maybe the disease wouldn't hit our communities as hard as it was hitting gay men all over the United States. By 1992, when we became incorporated, we had heard lots of women's stories of pain, fear, rejection, and immobilization. And it became clear that HIV needed to be articulated and addressed in the context of women's lives.

We had been dealing with women's lives in the context of HIV, and it was a flawed strategy. Holistically speaking, we were indirectly responding to a myriad of issues—substance abuse, violence, poverty, misogyny, internalized oppression, family neglect/abandonment. . . the list could go on and on—that were layered inside the iceberg, of which HIV was only the tip. We knew that HIV was the connecting point for a lot of these experiences, but getting folks, especially the mainstream feminist groups and the growing numbers of AIDS activists, to see the direct connection was difficult and as labor intensive as helping folks understand HIV and its risks. We didn't have the tools or the language to pull these issues together.

In 1996, Loretta J. Ross founded the National Center for Human Rights Education (NCHRE), the first human rights education organization in the United States that focuses primarily on domestic human rights violations including civil, political, economic, social, cultural, developmental, environmental, and sexual rights. NCHRE's mission is to build a human rights movement in the United States by training community leaders and student activists to apply human rights standards to issues of injustice. Ms. Ross introduced these concepts to SisterLove staff and volunteers, and we found the framework within which the HIV/AIDS work we were already doing could be buoyed, strengthened, and articulated in a manner through which the humanity of those living with HIV/AIDS and those at risk could be defended, protected, respected, and valued.

SisterLove's introduction to human rights education was a revelation of sorts. What a simple notion: that if all of us working on social justice issues could define those issues and combat human suffering through a common framework, then we may just effect the change that is needed. As we began to use the human rights education approach, it became even clearer that a perverse reality prevails in the simplicity of this notion and the complexity of its meaning.

I recently illustrated this "simplicity in complexity" when I gave a presentation titled "HIV/AIDS, Gender, and Human Rights: Women and Girls at the Apex and the Intersection." I used a visual that looked more like a simple infant's crib mobile than a complex diagram. Yet, the simplicity of the child's mobile perfectly conveyed the complexity of the categories of issues and populations most affected by those issues. HIV is the apex of the experience, and the axis upon which the issues turn in people's lives. The issues are the hanging baubles that keep spinning in motion, while those who experience the pain from these issues are lying or sitting in the center looking up at all this action, just out of their reach.

Working at the intersection of HIV/AIDS, gender, and human rights is a challenging exercise in

working on complex issues for the sake of simplifying the work of social change. When I consider the litany of issues that impede the health and development of women at risk and women living with HIV or AIDS, I often feel overwhelmed by the interconnectedness of the layers of possible responses and necessary actions that must take place. Simultaneously, I feel empowered by the simple notion that many of these issues could be eliminated, prevented, or abolished if human dignity was valued. This is not yet the situation in the United States.

While SisterLove formed initially to answer the needs of people with information about the impact and risks of HIV/AIDS, we quickly moved to include women's reproductive and sexual health and rights on our agenda. As we began to articulate HIV/AIDS issues in the context of the human rights framework, we were faced with the reality that human rights education was actually a more critical need than building an advocacy movement around HIV/AIDS in communities of color, because at that time more than 92 percent of the U.S. population had never heard of the UN Declaration of Human Rights (UNDHR).

Today's fight against HIV/AIDS requires not only continued medical research, education for prevention, and compassion for all individuals without imposing gender-based boundaries on who they love. The fight *also* requires us to examine our attitudes and beliefs about poverty and classism, racism, sexism, homophobia, and human rights. In addition to "finding a cure," our aptitude for halting the spread of HIV/AIDS rests upon our ability to convince those who have generally been unseen and unheard to fight for everyone's right to health information, ethical treatment, and responsive health care. Yet, it is impossible to expect people to fight for rights they do not know they have.

With so few human rights treaties ratified by the United States, and with nearly no existing legal recourse for retribution or compensation for victims of human rights violations, it is strategically important to focus on the moral imperative of creating a human rights culture in the United States. In a woman-only context, women coming into SisterLove are taught how to think about their rights. SisterLove focuses on learning and sharing black and African feminist theory because the "inclusion" of voices of color and their networks in the white-dominated mainstream human rights movements ignores the potential of the community of color to mobilize its own population and develop its own organization models. SisterLove recognizes the need to look outside the U.S. model of women's sexuality, which is based on white men's desire, to the international community to find models more suited to the experience of African-American women. In this way, HIV/AIDS was the centerpiece that helped define the myriad of interlocking reproductive health issues affecting Black women and other women of color—women marginalized by the broader society and even more so by the women's movement and its proponents.

SisterLove began to use the language of human rights in all of our programs and components, such as the Healthy Love Workshop and the Love-House, a transitional housing program for HIV+ women and their children. The Healthy Love Workshop is an interactive group-level intervention that addresses HIV and reproductive health information while providing women with practical tools and applications to negotiate safer sex or abstinence, to use condoms and other latex barriers in their sexual activity, and to understand the social and political context in which individual and community change must take place in order to stem the spread of HIV and the impact of AIDS. We incorporate the human rights education paradigm so that women can envision their participation in HIV prevention as an opportunity to affect social change in their own households as well as in the streets of their communities.

We use a similar strategy for the HIV+ residents in the LoveHouse, who learn how to incorporate their understanding of rights and entitlement to human dignity into their understanding of how the Social Security System works, how funding reaches (or doesn't!) their communities to provide the necessary services and support programs, and how to access the information and care they need for themselves and their families. This work develops grassroots leadership with a deep understanding of the bridges connecting what happens in the lives of women in the United States to what happens for women living in other communities in the world similar to our own.

Nowadays, as I continue this work, I spend a lot of time thinking of the world that I want to live in, and the things we need in order to live without pain and suffering. Learning how to use the human rights education framework shifted my paradigm of thinking about how I may affect change and build a just and peaceful existence for all of humanity and life on Earth. As my mother still says, "Education never stops, so you never stop educating." Human rights education provides the opportunity to mobilize groups by bridging isolated issues and individual lived experiences with the language and understanding of basic protections of the things all human beings need to live in dignity and have quality lives. Using the human rights framework has taught me that it is much more productive to strategize around that which you are fighting for, rather than what you are fighting against. Those of us who wear the idealist's "rose colored glasses" know that *"change gonna come"* because of the positive and productive energies of the young and the old, the black and the white, the homosexual and the heterosexual, the advantaged and the disadvantaged. This energy, which we call love, is what moves us at SisterLove to continue our work. The power of love knows no bounds.

Taking the High Road

Suzanne Pharr

In the mid-1990s, we are seeing a rapid rise of mean-spiritedness, fed by radio and television, the rhetoric of cynical politicians, and the embittered disillusionment of people whose hopes and dreams have been destroyed and whose lives feel threatened. It is a mean-spiritedness that seems to feed upon itself, seeking everywhere someone to blame, someone who is the cause of this pain, this disappointment, this failure to succeed. The airwaves are filled with rancor and anger, cynicism and accusation. Recently, I have been asking people to describe the mood of the country. They respond, "depressed, angry, overwhelmed, feeling isolated and cut off, mistrustful, mean, hurt, fearful." To succeed, our organizing must address these feelings.

As progressive and moderate voices are excluded or silenced or mimic this rage and cynicism, I worry about our better selves diminishing from lack of nurturance and support. I think of our better selves as that place where compassion, sympathy, empathy, tolerance, inclusiveness, and generosity reside.

All of our strategies for social change will mean very little if we do not have access to that place inside us where generosity, for example, lives. Much of our work has to be focused on nurturing the life of the spirit, on keeping the door to our better selves as wide open as possible.

Cultural work offers one of our best means of nurturing the individual spirit and our sense of connection to others. It is through the creation of art and culture that the spirit is fed and kept alive and our common humanity is expressed and exposed.

Yet in much of our social change work, we incorporate art and culture only as "add-ons"—the concert after a conference, the song or poem at the beginning of the meeting. We rarely see cultural organizing as social change work. One reason is that we are often stuck in the same old methods of organizing and do not question how people learn, what moves us to change. Another reason is that we can sometimes become too focused on a single goal or issue and do not consider the wholeness of ourselves and our constituency. In building a movement, eating and singing together may be as important as handing out leaflets. Being able to involve our families with us in our work may be as important as recruiting new members. The basis for successful organizing work is people who are connected, not separated, people who feel whole, not fragmented.

Storytelling is one of the strongest cultural expressions; it helps us feel whole and connected. Nothing is more critical than storytelling to defining our humanity. When telling our stories, we assert both our individuality and our connection to others, and we make others aware of our identity and history. What better way to counter gross stereotyping, demonizing, and dehumanization than by presenting a multiplicity of voices and experiences, each individualized, each unique, and each connected to a common history?

In the early days of the women's antiviolence movement, women met in groups to tell the story of the violence that had occurred in their lives. For many, it was the first time they had told anyone what happened—the rape, incest, battering, torture—and telling the story to others brought them out of isolation and gave them connection to a group. But what followed next was the foundation for a women's antiviolence movement: after women heard each others stories, they came to recognize the great similarities among them. Through discussing these commonalities, they created an analysis of the relationship between the perpetrator of violence and its target, and they recognized that though the victim is frequently blamed for the violence, the fault lies with the perpetrator and the society that accepts the violence. Those desiring to end violence against themselves and other women then moved to take action: creating safe homes and battered women's shelters, hotlines and support groups, working with police, changing laws, confronting batterers and rapists, providing political education and changing public policy.

For whatever reasons, progressive people have not always talked a great deal about the strong moral convictions underlying why we do this work of social justice: *it is because we believe every person counts, has human dignity, and deserves respect, equality, and justice.* This morality is the basis for our vision, and all our work flows from this basic belief.

We are living in a time in which people are crying out for something to believe in, for a moral sense, for purpose, for answers that will bring some calm to the chaos they feel in their lives. I believe it is our moral imperative to help each other make connections, to show how everyone is interrelated and belongs in community. It is at our peril if we do work that increases alienation and robs meaning from life. Today's expressions of violence, hatred, and bigotry are directly related to the level of alienation and disconnection felt by people. For our very survival, we must develop a sense of common humanity.

It may be that our most important political work is figuring out how to make the full human connection, how to engage our hearts as well as our minds, how to heal the injuries we have suffered, how to do organizing that transforms people as well as institutions.

We have to think about our vision of change.

I am not arguing that we should give up direct action, civil disobedience, issue campaigns,

political education, confrontation, membership and voter drives, et cetera. We need to do these things and much more. I am suggesting that we rethink the meaning of social change and learn how to include the long-term work of transforming people as we work for social justice. We must redefine "winning." Our social change has to be more than amassing resources and shifting power from the hands of one group to another. We must seek a true shift in consciousness, one that forges vision, goals, and strategies from belief, not just from expediency, and allows us to become a strong political force.

The definition of transformational politics is fairly simple: it is political work that changes the hearts and minds of people; supports personal and group growth in ways that create healthy, whole people, organizations, and communities; and is based on a vision of a society where people—across lines of race, gender, class, and sexuality—are supported by institutions and communities to live their best lives.

It calls for living with communal values. We face a daunting challenge here because our culture glorifies individualism. Creating community requires seeing the whole, not just the parts, and understanding how they interrelate. However, the difficult part is learning how to honor the needs of the individual as well as those of the group, without denying the importance of either. It requires a balance between identity and freedom on the one hand and the collective good and public responsibility on the other. It requires ritual and celebration and collective ways to grieve and show anger; it requires a commitment to resolve conflict.

Building connection and relationship demands that we give it time, not just in meetings but in informal opportunities surrounding meetings, structured and unstructured. Our communities are where our moral values are expressed. It is here that we are called upon to share our connection to others, our interdependence, our deepest belief in what it means to be part of the human condition, where people's lives touch one another, for good or for bad. It is here where the rhetoric of belief is forced into the reality of living. It is from this collection of people, holding within it smaller units called families, that we build and live democracy—or, without care and nurturance, where we detach from one another and destroy our hope for survival.

It is one thing for us to talk about liberation politics; it is of course another to live it. We lack political integrity when we demand liberation for one cause or one group of people and act out oppression or exploitation toward others. In our social change organizations in particular we can find ourselves in this dangerous position: where we are demanding, for example, liberation from sexism but within the organization we act out racism, economic injustice, and homophobia. Each is reflected in who is allowed to lead, who makes the highest and lowest salaries, who is allowed to participate in the major decision-making, who decides how resources are used. If the organization does not have a vision and a strategy that also include the elimination of racism, sexism, economic injustice, and homophobia (as well as oppressions relating to age, physical ability, et cetera), then internal conflict is inevitable.

. . .

I believe that all oppressions in this country turn on an economic wheel; they all, in the long run, serve to consolidate and keep wealth in the hands of the few, with the many fighting over crumbs. Without work against economic injustice, against the dehumanizing excesses of capitalism, there can be no deep and lasting work on oppression. The theocratic Right has been successful in driving wedges between oppressed groups because there is little common understanding of the linkages common to all oppressions. Progressives have contributed to these divisions because, generally, we have dealt only with single pieces of the fabric of injustice. Often we have no knowledge of a shared history. We stand ready to be divided. Our challenge is to learn how to use the experiences of our many identities to forge an inclusive social change politics. The question that faces us is how to do multi-issue coalition-building from an identity base. The hope for a multiracial, multi-issue movement rests in large part on the answer to this question.

If women are treated as people undeserving of equality within civil rights organizations, or lesbians and gay men are, how can those organizations demand equality? If women of color and poor women are marginalized in women's rights organizations, how can those organizations argue that women as a class should be moved into full participation in the mainstream? If lesbian and gay organizations are not feminist and antiracist in all their practices, what hope is there for the elimination of homophobia and heterosexism in a racist, sexist society? It is an issue of integrity.

When we grasp the value and interconnectedness of our liberation issues, then we will at last be able to make true coalition and begin building a common agenda that eliminates oppression and brings forth a vision of diversity that shares both power and resources.

Epilogue
Beyond Backlash

Ruth Rosen

"If you're on the right track, you can expect some pretty savage criticism," veteran feminist Phyllis Chesler warned young women at the close of the twentieth century. "Trust it. Revel in it. It is the truest measure of your success." Words of wisdom from one of the pioneer activists who understood the meaning of a fierce backlash.

No movement could have challenged so many ideas and customs without threatening vast numbers of women and men. Some activists viewed the backlash as either a political conspiracy or a media plot hatched to discredit feminists. But the backlash, in fact, reflected a society deeply divided and disturbed by rapid changes in men's and women's lives, at home and at work.

Abortion genuinely polarized American women. Working women, as sociologist Kristin Luker discovered, tended to support abortion rights, while homemakers, who depended on a breadwinner's income, were more likely to regard children as a means of keeping husbands yoked to their families and so opposed it. The backlash, which had grown alongside the women's movement, gained strength in 1973 after the Supreme Court, in its *Roe v. Wade* decision, made abortion legal. The Catholic Church—and later the evangelical Christian Right—quickly mobilized to reverse that decision. By 1977, Congress had passed the Hyde Amendment, which banned the use of taxpayers' money to fund abortions for poor women. By 1980, the New Right had successfully turned abortion into a litmus test for political candidates, Cabinet officials, and Supreme Court justices. By 1989, the Supreme Court's *William L. Webster v. Reproductive Health Services* decision began the process of chipping away at women's right to abortion.

A long, drawn-out struggle over the Equal Rights Amendment also helped consolidate opposition to the women's movement. Passed quickly by Congress in a burst of optimism in 1972, the ERA needed to be ratified by thirty-eight state legislatures in order to become a part of the Constitution. Within a year, the ERA received swift ratification or support from thirty states, but then it stalled, and in 1978, proponents extracted a reluctant extension from Congress. By 1982, the ERA, unable to gain more state ratifications, had been buried, a victim of the rising symbolic politics of a triumphant political movement of the Right.

The ten-year battle over the ERA and the escalating struggle over abortion helped mobilize conservative women. Ironically, women of the Right learned from the women's movement, even if in opposition to it. In a kind of mirror-image politicking, they began to form their own all-female organizations, including Happiness of Motherhood Eternal (HOME), Women Who Want to Be Women (WWWW), American Women Against the Ratification of the ERA (AWARE), Females Opposed to Equality (FOE), and the Eagle Forum. Soon, they engaged in their own kinds of local and national consciousness-raising activities. Their tactics, like those of the women's movement, included polite protest and lobbying in Washington, as well as more militant rallies and protests. But unlike the women's movement, the fringes engaged in actual terrorism at abortion clinics.

The political struggle also catapulted several conservative women to national prominence. Among them was Phyllis Schlafly, a shrewd attorney who nonetheless—like Betty Friedan almost two decades earlier—described herself as "just a housewife," and founded Stop ERA, which she credited with defeating the ERA. An influential if little-known member of the conservative Right, Schlafly had written a book, *The Power of the Positive Woman* (1977), which attacked feminists for their negative assessments of women's condition in the United States. Schlafly also blamed "limousine liberals," "the cosmopolitan elite," and "chic fellow travelers" for living in a rarefied world that cared little about the traditional family and its values. Schlafly used her antifeminism as a vehicle for reinventing herself as a national celebrity. Thanks to the media, her name soon became a household word.

The growing engagement of women in the religious and secular New Right legitimated an increasing fusillade of attacks on feminism by right-wing male religious and political leaders. In *The New Right: We're Ready to Lead*, Richard Viguerie, one of those leaders, announced that the New Right had to fight "anti-family organizations like the National Organization for Women and to resist laws like the Equal Rights Amendment that attack families and individuals." Schlafly, Viguerie, and other leaders of the New Right blamed the hedonistic values of American culture on feminists. For them, an independent woman was by definition a selfish, self-absorbed creature who threatened the nation's "traditional values."

Support for the growing backlash came from many directions, including many women who were not members of any New Right organization. Some of those disgruntled women now felt overwhelmed by the double responsibilities they bore at home and at work; they blamed feminism for their plight. The media took its cue from such women. A new formulaic narrative appeared in the print media, that of the repentant career woman who finally realizes that feminism had very nearly ruined her life. Editors began to dispatch reporters in search of professional women who had quit their high-status jobs and returned home with great sighs of relief to care for their husbands and children.

Like the "first woman" stories of the 1970s, these cautionary tales of the 1980s obscured the actual lives of the vast majority of women in the labor force, for whom there was no choice but to get up every morning and go to work. Most working mothers labored at low-paid jobs, and husbands generally avoided even a reasonable share of the housework from their now-employed spouses. So women daily returned home to what sociologist Arlie Hochschild dubbed the "second shift." Even successful professional women were discovering that they, too, had no choice but to enter careers on men's terms. Their new employers expected them to be available "25 hours a day, seven days a week" and their husbands, too, expected the same services they would have received from an unemployed wife. To secure promotions, career women—but not men—felt compelled to choose whether to dedicate their prime child-bearing years to their careers and remain childless, or to face the daunting prospect of trying to do it all.

Despite the difficulties women and men experienced as they tried to adjust to this newly configured home life, it's important to recognize that the women's movement did not invariably pit men against women. This was not a battle between the sexes; it was part of the highly gendered and racialized cultural wars that polarized Americans in the wake of the 1960s. Men and women fought *together* on both sides of the divide, for this was a struggle between social and cultural ideals.

. . .

Feminist responses to the backlash began to appear in literature as well. During the heady years of the 1970s, feminist utopian novels had become the *genre du jour*. Some of the most prominent novels—Marge Piercy's *Woman on the Edge of Time* or Ursula Le Guinn's *The Left Hand of Darkness*—had played with gender and sexual identity and optimistically imagined new ways of achieving gender equality. In the wake of the backlash, the Canadian novelist Margaret Atwood published a bleak dystopian novel, *The Handmaid's Tale* (1986), which quickly became a bestseller. This chilling novel took the destructive potential of the religious backlash seriously and offered a scary answer to the question: "What if the religious Right actually gained political power?"

Despite the sense of gloom and defeat that many feminists experienced at the time, American women were, in fact, increasingly embracing the goals of the women's movement. Reasons were not hard to fathom. Growing numbers of women were falling into poverty. Diana Pearce's 1978 phrase "the feminization of poverty" caught a startling and unexpected reality of American life. Divorce rates, which had doubled since 1965, had created a new cohort of women who joined the poor when their marriages ended. By 1984, working women began to outnumber women who worked at home and the glamorization of the superwoman and her career choice had eroded the prestige of homemaking. The growing tendency of middle-class women to postpone marriage and motherhood, combined with an increase in single mothers and divorced mothers, created a critical mass of women who now wondered how they were going to support themselves and their children. Polls steadily revealed what the much-publicized backlash obscured, that a majority of women now looked favorably upon the goals of the women's movement.

Women's attitudes had, in fact, changed rapidly. In a 1970 Virginia Slims opinion poll, 53 percent of women cited being a wife and mother as "one of the best parts of being a woman." By 1983, that figure had dropped to 26 percent. In 1970, very few women expressed concern over discrimination. By 1983, one-third of women agreed that "male chauvinism, discrimination, and sexual stereotypes ranked as their biggest problem"; while 80 percent agreed that "to get ahead a woman has to be better at what she does than a man." Nor did women still believe they lived privileged lives, as they had in 1975, when one-third of Americans viewed men's lives as far more difficult. By 1990, nearly half of all adults assumed that men had the easier life.

At the height of the backlash, in short, more American women, not fewer, grasped the importance of the goals of the women's movement. In 1986, a Gallup poll asked women, "Do you consider yourself a feminist?" At a time when identifying yourself as a feminist felt like a risky admission, 56 percent of American women were willing to do so (at least privately to Gallup's pollsters). Women of all classes were also becoming aware of the ways in which gender shaped their lives. Sixty-seven percent of all women, including those who earned under $12,500 *and* those who made more than $50,000, favored a strong women's movement. Pollsters consistently found that more African-American women approved of the goals of the women's movement than did white women. A 1989 poll found that 51 percent of all men, 64 percent of white women, 72 percent of Hispanic women, and 85 percent of African-American women agreed with the statement "The United States continues to need a strong women's movement to push for changes that benefit women."

In 1989, *Time* magazine ushered in a new decade with yet one more pronouncement of the death of feminism. Its cover story, "Women Face the '90s," bore the subtitle "During the '80s, they tried to have it all. Now they've just plain had it. Is there a future for feminism?" But, inside, the reader discovered quite a different story. Feminism was endangered, *Time* magazine suggested, not because it had failed, but precisely because it had been so successful. "In many ways," the article declared,

> feminism is a victim of its own resounding achievements. Its triumphs—in getting women into the workplace, in elevating their status in society and in shattering "the feminine mystique" that defined female success only in terms of being a wife and a mother—have rendered it obsolete, at least in its original form and rhetoric.

The growth of gender consciousness had, in fact, altered society and culture in countless ways. In August 1980, a *New York Times* editorial declared that the women's movement, once viewed as a group of "extremists and troublemakers," had turned into an "effective political force." The editorial concluded that "the battle for women's rights is no longer lonely or peripheral. It has moved where it belongs—to the center of

American politics." In 1984, commenting on legislation that would grant child support for all families and give wives access to their husbands' pensions, the *Times* editorialized that "'Women's Issues' have already become everyone's." And so they had. Perhaps the important legacy was precisely that "women's issues" had entered mainstream national politics, where they had changed the terms of political debate.

Everyday life had changed in small but significant ways. Strangers addressed a woman as Ms.; meteorologists named hurricanes after *both* men and women; schoolchildren learned about sexism before they became teenagers; language became more gender-neutral; popular culture saturated society with comedies, thrillers, and mysteries that turned on changing gender roles; and two decades after the movement's first years, the number of women politicians doubled. Even more significantly, millions of women had entered jobs that had once been reserved for men.

Although women had not gained the power to change institutions in fundamental ways, they had joined men in colleges and universities in unprecedented numbers. In the 1950s, women had constituted only 20 percent of college undergraduates, and their two most common aspirations, according to polls of the time, were to become the wife of a prominent man and the mother of several accomplished children. By 1990, women constituted 54 percent of undergraduates and they wanted to do anything and everything. Women had also joined men in both blue-collar and professional jobs in startling numbers. In 1960, 35 percent of women had worked outside the home; by 1990, that figure had jumped to 58 percent. During the same period, the number of female lawyers and judges leaped from 7,500 to 108,200; and female doctors from 15,672 to 174,000.

The cumulative impact of decades of revelations, education, debates, scandals, controversies, and high-profile trials raised women's gender consciousness, which in turn eventually showed up in a long-awaited political "gender gap." In 1871, Susan B. Anthony had prematurely predicted that once women got the right to vote, they would vote as a bloc. A gender gap did not appear until 1980,

when more men than women voted for Ronald Reagan, whose opposition to the Equal Rights Amendment and abortion may have moved some women into the Democratic column. More important was Reagan's pledge to dismantle the welfare state, which nudged even more women toward the Democrats, the party more likely (theoretically) to preserve the safety net. Eventually, the gender gap would cause at least a temporary realignment of national politics. In 1996, 16 percent more women than men voted for Bill Clinton for president. Some political analysts now believed that women were voting their interests as workers, family caregivers, or as single or divorced mothers.

Gender gap or not, the rightward tilt of American politics led to the demonization of poor women and their children. As some middle-class women captured meaningful and well-paid work, ever more women slid into poverty and homelessness, which, on balance, the women's movement did too little, too late, to change. On the other hand, the lives of many ordinary working women, who had not become impoverished, improved in dramatic ways. In 1992, a *Newsweek* article described how twenty years of the women's movement had changed Appleton, Wisconsin (the hometown of Joseph McCarthy and the John Birch Society). Women, the magazine reported, had taken on significant roles in local politics. In addition, the article observed,

> There are women cops and women firefighters, and there are women in managerial jobs in local business and government. There is firm community consensus, and generous funding with local tax dollars, for Harbor House, a shelter for battered women. And there is an active effort, in the Appleton public schools, to eliminate the invidious stereotyping that keeps young women in the velvet straitjacket of traditional gender roles.

GLOBAL FEMINISM

As ideas from the Western women's movement traveled across the Atlantic, American feminists learned more than they taught. On October 25,

1985, President Vigdis Finnbogadottir of Iceland joined tens of thousands of women who had walked off the job in a twenty-four-hour protest against male privilege on the island. She also refused to sign a bill that would have ordered striking flight attendants back to work. Iceland's telephone system collapsed, travel came to a halt, and groups of men crowded into hotels for the breakfast their wives refused to cook for them.

As feminism began spreading beyond industrialized nations, American feminists also encountered new definitions of "women's issues." Sometimes "freedom" meant better access to fuel and water, toppling a ruthless dictator, or ending a genocidal civil war. The gradual emergence of global women's networks made such encounters and confrontations inevitable.

Many of these networks grew out of the United Nation's 1975 International Women's Year. At the first World Conference on Women in Mexico, delegates urged the UN to proclaim the years between 1975 and 1985 "The Decade for Women." At each subsequent UN conference, there were two parallel meetings—one for delegates who represented their governments and another for women who participated in the nongovernmental organization (NGO) meetings. The numbers of NGO participants mushroomed. Six thousand women participated in the second conference, held in 1980 at Copenhagen; fourteen thousand attended the third in 1985 in Nairobi; and a startling thirty thousand arrived in Huairou, China, for the fourth in 1995.

What President Kennedy's Commission on the Status of Women had done for American women activists, the UN's World Conferences now did at a global level. Proximity bred intimacy and spread knowledge. The thousands of women rubbing shoulders or debating in Mexico, Denmark, Kenya, or China were learning from and teaching each other about their lives. Aside from their differences, they were also discovering the ubiquity of certain kinds of shared oppression—violence and poverty that had once seemed local, rather than global. And, in the process, they were nurturing and legitimating a global feminism, which was quite literally being born at UN conferences as they watched.

That didn't mean that women everywhere interpreted the information newly available to them in the same way. From the start, the NGO forum meetings witnessed serious clashes between "First" and "Third" World women, and between women whose nations were at war. Over time, the atmosphere began to improve. Western feminists began to *listen,* rather than *lecture,* and women from developing countries, who had formerly viewed Western concerns over clitoridectomies, dowry deaths, wife-beatings, and arranged marriages as so many instances of cultural imperialism—the urge of developed countries to impose their values and customs on underdeveloped nations—began the painful process of redefining their own customs as crimes.

Here was the essence of global feminism—addressing the world's problems *as if women mattered.* Human rights organizations, for instance, had traditionally focused exclusively on state-sanctioned violence against political activists. But most women encountered violence not in prison or at protests, but in their homes and communities. Viewed as customs rather than crimes, wife-beating, rape, genital excision, dowry deaths, and arranged marriages had never been certified as violations of women's human rights.

At a 1993 UN World Conference on Human Rights in Vienna, women from all over the globe movingly testified to the various forms of violence that had devastated their lives. Feminists successfully made their case; the conference passed a resolution that recognized violence against women and girls as a violation of their human rights. One immediate consequence of this historic redefinition of human rights was that Western nations could now grant *political* asylum to women fleeing certain violence or death from husbands or other relatives.

Two years later, at a 1995 UN Conference on Development and Population in Cairo, feminists criticized accepted development policies that promoted massive industrial or hydroelectric projects as *the* way to improve the standard of living of developing nations. Such projects, they argued, irreversibly damaged the human and natural ecology, provided work for indigenous men, but not for women, and undermined women's traditional economic role and social authority. Instead, they advocated small-scale cottage industries, through which women could earn money for their education. They also attacked those population experts who took it, as an article of faith, that population growth automatically declined when industrial development lifted people out of poverty. Citing the failure of such policies, feminists countered that educating women and giving them control over their reproductive decisions was a far more effective way of controlling population growth. As one reporter wrote, "The deceptively simple idea of a woman making a decision about her future is one of the cornerstones of the emerging debate on global population policy."

The "Platform for Action," the document that emerged from the Beijing conference in 1995, asked the nations of the world to see social and economic development through the eyes of women. Although the "Platform" recognized the differences that separated women, it also emphasized the universal poverty and violence that crippled the lives of so many of the world's women. In addition to affirming women's rights as human rights, the conference also declared three preconditions for women's advancement; equality, development, and peace. To many participants, the event seemed like a miracle, a moment existing out of time, when the world's women imagined a different kind of future, even if they had little power to implement it.

By publicizing even more gender consciousness, the 1995 Fourth World Conference on Women probably encouraged greater numbers of the world's women to challenge traditional forms of patriarchal authority. In the years following the conference, feminist activists and scholars began the process of redefining rape (when it occurred during a military conflict) as a war crime, publicizing the particular plight of refugees (most of whom were women), and rethinking the role women might play in reconstructing societies ravaged by war.

At the same time, women in both developed and developing nations began debating the impact of feminism itself on global culture and economics. Was feminism yoked only to concepts of individual rights? Was it simply an inevitable by-product of Western consumer capitalism, whose effects would rupture the ties that bound families and communities together—and to the land? Or could feminism help protect the rights of women as they left family and land behind and entered the global wage economy? Could women's rights, redefined as human rights, provide a powerful new stance from which to oppose totalitarian societies of both the Right and the Left? Many theories proliferated, heated debates took place, but the answers—even many of the questions—lay in the future.

There is no end to this story. Over a hundred years ago, the suffragist Matilda Gage turned her gaze toward the future. The work of her generation of activists, she wrote, was not for them alone,

> nor alone for the present generation, but for all women of all time. The hopes of posterity were in their hands, and they were determined to place on record for the daughters of 1976, the fact that their mothers of 1876 had thus asserted their equality of rights, and thus impeached the government of today for its injustice towards women.

Nearly a century later, veteran feminist Robin Morgan, along with thousands of other twentieth-century "daughters," took up the unfinished agenda left by the suffrage movement. Morgan, too, realized that she struggled for future daughters and worried that her generation might squander precious opportunities.

> I fear for the women's movement falling into precisely the same trap as did our foremothers, the suffragists: creating a bourgeois feminist movement that never quite dared enough, never questioned enough, never really reached out beyond its own class and race.

As women in developing countries become educated and enter the marketplace as wage-earners, they will invariably intensify existing cultural conflicts between religious and secular groups, and between those sectors of society living under preindustrial conditions and those who connect through cyberspace in a postmodern global society. Like small brushfires, these cultural wars may circle the globe, igniting a wild and frightening firestorm. Inevitably, some women will feel defeated as they encounter wave after wave of backlash. But in the darkness of their despair, they should remember that resistance is not a sign of defeat, but rather evidence that women are challenging a worldview that now belongs to an earlier era of human history.

Each generation of women activists leaves an unfinished agenda for the next generation. First Wave suffragists fought for women's citizenship, created international organizations, dedicated to universal disarmament, but left many customs and beliefs unchallenged. Second Wave feminists questioned nearly everything, transformed much of American culture, expanded the idea of democracy by insisting that equality had to include the realities of its women citizens, and catapulted women's issues onto a global stage. Their greatest accomplishment was to change the terms of debate, so that women mattered. But they left much unfinished as well. They were unable to change most institutions, to gain greater economic justice for poor women, or to convince society that child care is the responsibility of the whole society. As a result, American women won the right to "have it all," but only if they "did it all."

It is for a new generation to identify what they need in order to achieve greater equality. It may even be their solemn duty. In the words of nineteenth-century suffragist Abigail Scott Duniway:

> The young women of today, free to study, to speak, to write, to choose their occupation, should remember that every inch of this freedom was bought for them at a great price. It is for them to show their gratitude by helping onward the reforms of their own times, by spreading the light of freedom and truth still wider. The debt that each generation owes to the past it must pay to the future.

The struggle for women's human rights has just begun. As each generation shares its secrets, women learn to see the world through their own eyes and discover, much to their surprise, that they are not the first and that they are not alone. The poet Muriel Rukeyser once asked, "What would happen if one woman told the truth about her life?" Her answer: "The world would split open." And so it has. A revolution is under way, and there is no end in sight.

R E A D I N G **108**

Warning

Jenny Joseph

When I am an old woman I shall wear purple
With a red hat which doesn't go, and doesn't suit me.
And I shall spend my pension on brandy and summer gloves
And satin sandals, and say we've no money for butter.
I shall sit down on the pavement when I'm tired

And gobble up samples in shops and press alarm bells

And run my stick along the public railings
And make up for the sobriety of my youth.
I shall go out in my slippers in the rain
And pick the flowers in other people's gardens
And learn to spit.

You can wear terrible shirts and grow more fat
And eat three pounds of sausages at a go
Or only bread and pickle for a week
And hoard pens and pencils and beermats and
   things in boxes.

But now we must have clothes that keep us dry
And pay our rent and not swear in the street

And set a good example for the children.
We must have friends to dinner and read the
   papers.
But maybe I ought to practise a little now?
So people who know me are not too shocked or
   surprised
When suddenly I am old, and start to wear purple.

R E A D I N G   **109**

A Day with Feminism

Jennifer Baumgardner and Amy Richards

Women and men are paid equal wages for work of comparable value, as is every race and ethnic group, co-parenting is a given, men lengthen their lives by crying and otherwise expressing emotion, and women say "I'm sorry" only when they truly should be. To the extent that we can imagine this even now, this is the equality feminists have been working for since that day in Seneca Falls in 1848. With each generation, the picture will get bigger and at the same time more finely detailed.

When Elizabeth Cady Stanton and her crew wrote the Declaration of Sentiments, they knew that this nation's Declaration of Independence would have no justice or power unless it included the female half of the country. For these women, equality was being full citizens who were able to own and inherit property, just as men were, to have the right to their own children, and the ability to vote. In 1923, Alice Paul had the vision to write the Equal Rights Amendment so that laws could not be made based on sex, any more than they could be made based on race, religion, or national origin. By the 1970s, Betty Friedan, Audre Lorde, Gloria Steinem, and Shirley Chisholm could imagine women's equality in the paid workforce, a new vision of family and sexuality, and legislative bodies that truly reflected the country.

They could not have foreseen a twenty-three-year-old White House intern who owned her own libido and sexual prowess the way Monica Lewinsky did. (They certainly wouldn't have imagined that a woman with that much access to power would just want to blow it.)

Now, at the beginning of a new millennium, we have witnessed a woman running for President who has a chance of winning, a first lady who translates that unparalleled Washington experience into her own high-flying political ambitions, easily reversible male birth control, gay parenting, a women's soccer team that surpasses the popular appeal of men's, and parental leave for both parents. And we can imagine more: federally subsidized child-care centers for every child and legalized gay marriage in all fifty states. A number of leaps are still needed to bring us to a day of equality, but at least we can begin to picture what such a future might hold.

Whether children are born to a single mother, a single father, two mothers, two fathers, or a mother and a father, a family is defined by love, commitment, and support. A child who has two parents is just as likely to have a hyphenated last name, or choose a whole new name, as she or he is to have a father's or birth mother's name. Carrying on a lineage is an individual choice, not the province of the father or the state.

Men work in child-care centers and are paid at least as well as plumbers, sanitation workers, or firefighters. When kids sit down to their breakfast Wheaties, they are as likely to confront a tennis star like Venus Williams as a golf pro like Tiger Woods. On TV, the male and female newscasters are about the same age and, whether black or white, are as likely to report foreign policy as sports. In general, people on camera come in all shapes and sizes. If you are watching drama, women are just as likely to be the rescuers as the rescued, and men are just as likely to ask for help as to give it. Women are as valued for their sense of humor as men are for their sex appeal. On Monday-night television, women's soccer or basketball is just as popular as men's basketball or football. Barbie no longer has feet too tiny to stand on or finds math hard; nor do girls. G. I. Joe, now a member of a peacekeeping force, likes to shop at the mall. In grade school, boys and girls decorate their bedrooms with posters of female athletes.

By the time girls hit junior high, they have already had the opportunity to play sports, from soccer to Little League, hockey to wrestling, and they share gymnastics and ballet classes with boys. Boys think ballet and gymnastics are cool. Kids hit puberty fully aware of how their bodies work: erections, nocturnal emissions, periods, cramps, masturbation, body hair—the works. These topics still cause giggling, curiosity, and excitement, but paralyzing shame and utter ignorance are things of the past. In fact, sweet-sixteen birthdays have given way to coming-of-age rituals for both genders, and don't assume that the birthday kid has never been kissed. Around the time that girls and boys are learning how to drive, both have mastered manual stimulation for their own sexual pleasure.

In high school, many varsity teams have coed cheerleaders, athletes all, but mostly cheering is left to the fans. Differences in girls' and boys' academic performance are as indistinguishable as differences in their athletic performance though they are very different as unique individuals.

Some girls ask other girls to the prom, some boys ask boys, and that is as okay as going as a mixed couple. Some go alone or not at all, and that's okay, too. Athletic scholarships have no more prestige or funding than arts scholarships.

Students take field trips to local museums where women are the creators of the art as often as they are its subjects. In preparation for this trip, students study art history from Artemisia Gentileschi to Mark Rothko, from Ndebele wall paintings to Yayoi Kusama. The museums themselves were designed by architects who may have been among the 11 percent of architects who were female in the 1990s. Military school is open to everyone and teaches peacekeeping as much as defense. Women's colleges no longer exist, because women no longer need a compensatory environment, and women's history, African-American history, and all those remedial areas have become people's and world history.

Women achieved parity long ago, so the idea of bean counting is irrelevant. At Harvard, 75 percent of the tenured professors are women, and at nearby Boston College, 30 percent of the tenured faculty is female. History courses cover the relevance of a movement that ended sexual violence against women. Though there is still a throwback incident now and then, men are even more outraged by it than women are. Once a year, there is a party in the quad to commemorate what was once called Take Back the Night.

Women walking through a park at night can feel just as safe as they do during the day, when kids play while white male nannies watch over them, right along with women and men of every group. In fact, it's as common to see a white man taking care of a black or a brown baby as it is to see a woman of color taking care of a white baby.

Sex is separate from procreation. Because there is now a national system of health insurance, birth control and abortions are covered right along with births, and the Hyde Amendment's ban of federal funding for abortions is regarded as a shameful moment in history, much like the time of Jim Crow laws. A judicial decision known as *Doe v. Hyde* effectively affirmed a woman's right to bodily integrity, and went way past the right to privacy guaranteed by *Roe v. Wade*. Abortion isn't morally contested territory because citizens don't interfere with one another's life choices, and women have the right to determine when and whether to have no children, a single child, or five children.

Environmentally sound menstrual products are government-subsidized and cost the same as a month's worth of shaving supplies. After all, women's childbearing capacity is a national asset, and young, sexually active men often opt for freezing their sperm or undergoing a simple vasectomy to control their paternity. Many men choose vasectomies, given that it's the least dangerous and most foolproof form of birth control—as well as the easiest to reverse. Men are screened for chlamydia, human papilloma virus, herpes, and other sexually transmitted diseases during their annual trip to the andrologist. Doctors learn how to detect and treat all of the above, in both men and women. Although the old number of three million or so new cases of STDs each year has dropped to half that amount, STDs are still as common (and about as shameful) as the common cold—and are finally acknowledged as such.

The Equal Rights Amendment has put females in the U.S. Constitution. There are many women of all races in fields or institutions formerly considered to be the province of men, from the Virginia Military Institute and the Citadel to fire departments and airline cockpits. Women are not only free to be as exceptional as men but also as mediocre. Men are as critiqued or praised as women are. Women's salaries have jumped up 26 to 40 percent from pre-equality days to match men's. There are no economic divisions based on race, and the salary categories have been equalized. This categorization is the result of legislation that requires the private sector—even companies that employ fewer than 50 people—to report employees' wages. Many older women are averaging half a million dollars in back pay as a result of the years in which they were unjustly underpaid. Women and men in the NBA make an average of $100,000 per year. Haircuts, dry cleaning, and clothes for women cost the same as they do for men.

The media are accountable to their constituency. Magazines cover stories about congressional hearings on how to help transition men on welfare back into the workforce. Many of these men are single fathers—by choice. Welfare is viewed as a subsidy, just as corporate tax breaks used to be, and receiving government assistance to help rear one's own child is as destigmatized as it is to be paid to rear a foster child. Howard Stern, who gave up his declining radio show to become a stay-at-home granddad, has been replaced on radio by Janeane Garofalo, who no longer jokes primarily about her "back fat" and other perceived imperfections. (Primary caregiving has humanized Stern so that people no longer have to fear for his influence on his offspring.) Leading ladies and leading men are all around the same age. There is always fanfare around *Time* magazine's Person of the Year and *Sports Illustrated*'s coed swimsuit issue. *Rolling Stone* covers female pop stars and music groups in equal numbers with male stars, and women are often photographed for the cover *with* their shirts on. Classic-rock stations play Janis Joplin as often as they play Led Zeppelin.

Women who choose to have babies give birth in a birthing center with a midwife, a hospital with a doctor, or at home with a medicine woman. Paid child-care leave is for four months, and it is required of both parents (if there is more than one). Child rearing is subsidized by a trust not unlike Social Security, a concept pioneered by the welfare-rights activist Theresa Funiciello and based on Gloria Steinem's earlier mandate that every child have a minimum income. The attributed economic value of housework is figured into the gross national product (which increases the United States' GNP by almost 30 percent), and primary caregivers are paid. Whether you work in or out of the home, you are taxed only on your income; married couples and people in domestic partnerships are taxed as individuals, too. When women retire, they get as much Social Security as men do, and all people receive a base amount on which they can live.

The amount of philanthropic dollars going to programs that address or specifically include women and girls is now pushing 60 percent, to make up for all the time it was about 5 percent.[1] More important, these female-centered programs no longer have to provide basic services, because the government does that. [2] All school meals, vaccinations, public libraries, and museums are government-funded and thus available to everybody. Taxpayers have made their wishes clear because more than 90 percent of the electorate actually votes.

"Postmenopausal zest" is as well documented and as anticipated as puberty. Women in their fifties—free from pregnancy, menstruation, and birth control—are regarded as sexpots and envied for their wild and free libidos. "Wine and women," as the saying goes, "get better with age."

Every man and woman remembers exactly where they were the moment they heard that the Equal Rights Amendment passed. The President addressed the nation on the night of that victory and said, "Americans didn't know what we were missing before today . . . until we could truly say

that all people are created equal." The first man stood at her side with a tear running down his face.

The social-justice movement, formerly known as feminism, is now just *life*.

NOTES

1. In 1997, according to research undertaken by Women and Philanthropy, only 5.7 percent of philanthropic dollars went to programs specifically benefiting women and girls.
2. At present, some of life's basic necessities are either not available to those who need them or must be paid for with private funding. For example, between 21 and 23 percent of U.S. adults are functionally illiterate, according to the Literacy Volunteers of America. Yet this organization, the largest literacy-training initiative in America, does not get a dime from the government and is funded almost exclusively by individual donors and corporations.

DISCUSSION QUESTIONS FOR CHAPTER 13

1. How has your experience in a feminist classroom had on impact on you?

2. What do you consider important factors for building a "beloved community"?

3. How do you envision a just future? How do you think we can get there?

4. What does integrity mean to you? How does integrity affect your work for justice?

5. What impact might a "transformational politics" have on our society?

6. Why are peace and the environment important women's issues?

7. What will you take away from this class to help you make your way in the world?

SUGGESTIONS FOR FURTHER READING

Braithwaite, Ann, Susan Heald, Susanne Luhmann, and Sharon Rosenberg. *Troubling Women's Studies: Pasts, Presents, and Possibilities*. Toronto: Sumach Press, 2005.

Clare, Eli, and Suzanne Pharr. *Exile and Pride*. Boston: South End, 1999.

Eisenstein, Zillah. *Against Empire: Feminisms, Racism, and "the" West*. London: Zed Books, 2004.

Kennedy, Elizabeth Lapovsky, and Agatha Beins. *Women's Studies for the Future*. Piscataway, NJ: Rutgers University Press, 2005.

Mellor, Mary. *Feminism & Ecology*. New York: New York University Press, 1998.

Naples, Nancy A. *Community Activism and Feminist Politics: Organizing Across Race, Class, and Gender.* New York: Routledge, 1997.

———. *Grassroots Warriors: Activist Mothering, Community Work, and the War on Poverty.* New York: Routledge, 1998.

Ryan, M. J., ed. *The Fabric of the Future: Women Visionaries of Today Illuminate the Path to Tomorrow.* Berkeley: Conari, 2000.

Schrepfer, Susan R. *Nature's Altars: Mountains, Gender, and American Environmentalism.* Lawrence: University Press of Kansas, 2005.

Shiva, Vandana. *Earth Democracy: Justice, Sustainability, and Peace.* Boston: South End, 2005.

Credits

Index